WHERE THE BIRDS ARE

A Guide to All 50 States and Canada

John Oliver Jones

WILLIAM MORROW AND COMPANY, INC.
NEW YORK

To my wife, Whitney, my family, friends, and associates — for their support, comments, and suggestions.

To the tens of thousands of amateurs and professionals for their work improving and protecting wildlife habitat, identifying, observing, recording, and reporting birding information at home and afield — without their dedication this book would not have been possible.

The information provided and described in this guide has been obtained from the most reliable sources available. The author and publisher have made every effort to assure the information is accurate and current at the time of publication, and do not assume any liability for errors, omissions, or the correctness of contents or procedures described herein.

Copyright © 1990 by John Oliver Jones

State Maps and Canada Map copyright © 1990 by John Oliver Jones

Maps of The Nature Conservancy preserves in California, published in *California Wild Lands* by Dwight Holing, copyright © 1988 by The Nature Conservancy, and used by permission of the California Field Office.

Maps of The Nature Conservancy preserves in Wisconsin, published in *The Places We Save*, copyright © 1988 by the Wisconsin Chapter of The Nature Conservancy, and used by permission of the Wisconsin Chapter.

The ABA code is reprinted from "How to See 703 Birds in 1983" by Benton Basham, copyright © 1983 by the American Birding Association, Inc., and used by permission.

Library of Congress Cataloging-in-Publication Data

Jones, John Oliver.
   Where The Birds Are / by John Oliver Jones
     p. cm.
   ISBN 0-688-05178-2 (pbk.)
    1. Birds--United States--Handbooks, manuals, etc. 2. Birds--Canada--Handbooks, manuals, etc. 3. Birds--United States--Societies, etc.--Directories. 4 Birds--Canada--Societies, etc.--Directories. I. Title
                    89-49399
                      CIP

Printed in the United States of America
First Edition
1 2 3 4 5 6 7 8 9 10
BOOK DESIGN BY JOHN OLIVER JONES

TABLE OF CONTENTS

ACCESS IS THE KEY TO SUCCESSFUL BIRDING

My objective in *Where The Birds Are* is to give you access to birds and to people who observe and monitor their behavior as a vocation or hobby. This guide was my shortcut to successful birding and it can be yours as well.

The ten most important questions about birds and birding are answered. Those answers, organized for easy access, will help you find lots of birds, elusive birds, and the best birding information sources in the least amount of time.

THE DIFFERENCE BETWEEN *WHERE THE BIRDS ARE* & FIELD GUIDES TO BIRDS

Field guides to bird identification show you the birds, including their appearance variations, habitat preferences, and behavior. *Where The Birds Are* takes you to the places where those birds may be found as accurately as currently available data allow, and tells you when you are most likely to find them.

Each field guide covers hundreds of species, with a thousand or more illustrations to show plumage variations that occur between birds of different age or sex. All birders, especially beginners, experience frustration when they see a new bird and search for its picture among the thousands in their field guide. One of the major causes of this frustration is not knowing which species you might encounter.

Where The Birds Are tells you where and when many birds and specific birds may be found by indicating the seasons and places those birds have been recorded by professional wildlife biologists and experienced amateurs. It gives you access to important birding information sources, people who know about local migration patterns, recent sightings of unusual, rare, or elusive birds, and access to local field trips and nature tours.

SUCCESSFUL BIRDING IS REWARDING & VERY IMPORTANT FOR BEGINNING BIRDERS

Now you can select locations where one or more species you want to observe have been recorded. You can study them in your field guide before you go afield and increase your odds of finding and identifying those birds.

There is nothing more rewarding to a beginning birder than early success or, for an experienced birder, adding one of those hard-to-find species to a life list.

THE WORLD OF BIRDS & BIRDING IS AT YOUR FINGERTIPS

To help you find specific information efficiently I've arranged *Where The Birds Are* in three sections: Chapters on each of the 50 states and Canada with maps (pages 25-202), the Bird Chart (pages 203-383), and the Field Guide Index (pages 384-392).

The appendices (pages 393-398) include a Rare & Limited Species Supplement to the Bird Chart, Study Ideas, and Project and Field Trip Worksheets.

THE TEN IMPORTANT QUESTIONS & THEIR ANSWERS

1. Where are the best places to find lots of birds or specific birds?
A. **At locations described in the state chapters and included in the Bird Chart pages.**

2. When are the best seasons or times to go?
A. **Check the Bird List Summaries and bird lists in the Bird Chart.**

3. What birds nest or visit there and when?
A. **Species are noted in the state chapters and detailed in the Bird Chart.**

4. Which pages in your Field Guide show the birds you expect to see there?
A. **The Field Guide Index, where the bird species appear in the same order as in the Bird Chart pages, tells you.**

5. How do you get there?
A. **The maps and directions in the state chapters show you how.**

6. Is other recreation permitted?
A. **Sure, check the descriptive details in the state chapters.**

7. How do you compare birding opportunities at one location with another?
A. **By comparing Bird List Summaries and the abundance codes for specific species in the Bird Chart.**

8. What are the best sources for bird sighting information and activities like field trips?
A. **The birding hotlines, bird clubs, and the many local and regional offices listed in the state chapters.**

9. Where are they and how do you reach them for current information?
A. **They are symbolized in the special state maps and their name/city addresses are provided in the state chapters. When possible, listings for information sources include the street address and/or phone number.**

10. Who are the experts, the bird and wildlife managers and professional ornithologists?
A. **Read about them in the Birding Information Sources described on pages 11-21 of this guide.**

ANOTHER PURPOSE, ANOTHER BENEFIT

I had another, less obvious purpose in writing this book. I hope a new interest in birds and birding will become important to you, whether for a few years or a lifetime. The great mobility of birds makes them special. They are messengers that carry news about the condition of our environment close to home and far away - mirrors reflecting the health of planet earth.

If *Where The Birds Are* stimulates you and your family as much as it did my own, perhaps you will one day become one of the volunteers who help in monitoring, counting, and reporting the species you observe. Birding is fun, successful birding even more fun. Counting and monitoring birds provides a different challenge and satisfaction, and contributes to our knowledge of the natural world we share. You too can make a difference in the world of birds and birding!

If you haven't already done so, turn to the chapter on your home state and take a moment to scan the pages and maps. They tell you where the birds are and, perhaps even more important, who the birding information sources are and how to reach them.

A BIRD'S-EYE VIEW
OF THE WORLD
OF BIRDS & BIRDING

The state maps have distinctive red symbols to show birding locations and information sources. They provide a bird's-eye view of the world of birds and birding in each state. The symbols correspond to those alongside the name of each birding area or information source.

The symbols with red outlines and numbers are office or information source locations. Birding locations are solid red symbols with the number in white. You can see the geographic relationship of the birding areas and information sources to cities, major roads, waterways, and most importantly, to one another.

MAP DETAIL

The symbols show approximate office, bird club, or birding area location. When local maps are included in the text they give you most of the details on routes in the vicinity of a refuge, preserve, sanctuary, or reserve.

States publish official highway maps and revise them on a regular basis. The maps are free on request from the state tourist division and other state agencies. Official state highway maps contain more detail than my special maps, the local maps, or a road atlas.

Some birding area and information source locations in this guide do not appear on, or are not indexed in, your road atlas. An official highway map is larger with more cities and towns in the index. It provides a full perspective and will help you determine the best routes to an area.

National Forest Service maps show most forest roads, campgrounds, office locations, and recreation areas. Although the federal agency offices in this guide have various types of area maps available, the most detailed federal maps are prepared by the U.S. Geological Survey. There are 57,000 7.5-minute quadrangle maps available that show elevation, habitat, and road detail in color. Each map represents 31,360 to 44,800 acres. You may request an index and ordering information for these quadrangle maps by calling 1-800-USA-MAPS.

BIRDING HOTLINES

Most birding hotlines, also known as Rare Bird Alerts, provide a recorded message and are usually updated weekly or more often. They are maintained by volunteer birders and financially supported by the National Audubon Society, its local chapters, or other state or local birding clubs.

Hotlines are a source of specific bird sighting information, bird club activity, and field trip information. They tell you where and when bird species have recently been observed locally, helping you to zero in on specific birds the same way this guide does. These rare bird alerts are a source of current information - another access route to birds.

New hotlines are created every year and occasionally older ones may change their phone number. Updates are published on a monthly basis in the American Birding

Association's newsletter, "Wingtips." If a hotline number is no longer in service, contact one of the other birding information sources in this guide.

LOCAL BIRDING GROUPS

Local birding groups are usually the best sources for information about local birding activities because they sponsor those activities. Most local Audubon Chapters and other bird and nature clubs do not have a permanent office. Their members serve as officers or committee chair-persons for varying time periods, usually a year or two. Most groups publish a newsletter for members.

To reach a birding group president or field trip coordinator, check with any state, or federal agency office, or local chamber of commerce, regarding how to reach an active Chapter or nature club member. Libraries are a good information source if they usually receive complimentary copies of local birding group newsletters. Local universities and natural history museums are also generally aware of the clubs in their vicinity.

OTHER STATE CHAPTER HEADINGS

The headings in this guide include SPECIAL BIRDING AREAS, NATIONAL AUDUBON SOCIETY, THE NATURE CONSERVANCY, U.S. FISH & WILDLIFE SERVICE, NATIONAL PARK SERVICE, NATIONAL FOREST SERVICE, BUREAU (of) LAND MANAGEMENT, and STATE AGENCIES.

Birding areas and office locations appear under these headings. The birding areas are described in some detail. The name, location, state map symbol and number, and telephone number is provided for National Forest Supervisor and selected Ranger District offices, Bureau of Land Management State and District offices, and the state wildlife agency offices. State tourist agency information is also included under the STATE AGENCIES headings.

ABBREVIATIONS

There are a few listing procedures I have followed. To save space, I have used abbreviations in the directions and text. Some examples are: Rt. for route; Hwy. for highway; mi. for miles; Orn. for Ornithological; Soc. for Society.

BIRDING AREA DESCRIPTIONS

Most descriptions of birding locations include a map of the area, travel directions, habitat details, area birding highlights, literature available, recreation opportunities, and the best seasons to visit. If no phone number is given, either there is no phone or the staff is not large enough to handle phone inquiries in addition to assigned conservation tasks.

Habitat includes area size and elevation figures, in addition to details about the terrain. The capsule view gives you enough information to enable you to know what questions to ask, such as necessary clothing and equipment, possible weather extremes, and how much time to allow for your visit.

Birding highlights note selected migrant, nesting, and year-round resident species, and their relative abundance during certain times of the year. The bird names for sub-species or races are enclosed in quotation marks. "Great" or "Cackling" Canada Geese, "California" Least Tern, and "Black" Brant are examples.

Area descriptive literature and permitted recreation opportunities are listed. Most literature is available on request at no charge and many locations can provide detailed refuge, sanctuary, or preserve recreation related maps. The literature typically contains a great deal more habitat, wildlife, historical, and management data than could be included in the space available in this guide.

Fishing, hunting, and certain other activities may be allowed at certain times of the year. Always ask about the seasonal nature of a recreational activity, any laws or limits that may apply, and about special rules, regulations, and maps that show check station and blind locations.

FREE LITERATURE

How much free literature is available from all the offices listed in this guide? Between 1 and 100 pages each depending on who manages an area and the funds they have available for that material. The National Parks typically have the most literature and the smaller preserves and sanctuaries the least. Altogether there are between 5,000 and 10,000 pages of free literature available describing the managed areas and the wildlife and recreation opportunities noted in this guide.

TAKE ADVANTAGE OF BIRDING OPPORTUNITIES AS YOU TRAVEL

According to the American Travel Council, 35 percent of us make travel and recreation decisions en route to, or after we arrive at, our destination. The maps and directions to local areas covered in this guide help you find birding areas. The ability to take advantage of unexpected birding opportunities is fun and rewarding, especially when you find birds you have not seen before.

BIRD CHECKLISTS

National Wildlife Refuges, National Parks, The Nature Conservancy Preserves, and Audubon Sanctuaries are often the best places to observe birds. Their habitat management practices are designed to attract birds, both migrants and year-round residents. A record of bird sightings is usually available in a bird checklist. Some lists also include other wildlife reported in that location.

THE BIRD LIST SUMMARY & BIRD CHART TELL YOU THE BIRDING POTENTIAL

Did you notice the Bird List Summaries as you scanned those chapter pages? The season abbreviations are spring (s), summer (S), fall (F), and winter (W). The five relative bird abundance codes used in a Summary (A, C, U, O, and R) are explained in detail in the Bird Chart Introduction on page 203. Not all bird lists (checklists) use these five codes; some use only three or four.

Seasonal abundance totals give you a perspective on birding potential at a refuge, sanctuary, or preserve. Seasonal totals for abundant and common birds are in red to show where and when you might see the largest variety of birds. The summary lists endangered and rare/limited species, and total numbers of species seen and nesting. Each summary refers you to the Bird Chart pages where the complete bird list may be studied.

The Bird Chart column format and the Rare & Limited Species Supplement consolidate 210 bird lists and sighting information on 643 different species found across the United States. This format allows easy study and comparison of information on nesting and abundance. The species are organized in American Ornithologists' Union (A.O.U.) Checklist, 6th edition, order. You can also determine from the chart which birds are not likely to be seen.

MY BIRD LIST CRITERIA

How do you evaluate a bird list? Bird checklists vary in appearance, species listing order, and approach to abundance information. There are no universal standards, so I established my own criteria to determine which checklists to include in the Bird Chart pages.

All the lists used in the Bird Chart contain seasonal abundance information, and most of them have nesting data. Each list is from an area managed by one or more full-time wildlife professionals to benefit birds and their habitat. You can talk to these people about migrants, year-round residents, and other wildlife.

OTHER TYPES OF BIRD LISTS

Bird checklists may present recorded sighting information in different ways. Lists that do not meet my criteria are noted in the state chapters. Some lack seasonal data, while others may emphasize habitat details or monthly abundance in graphic form. The Bitterroot National Forest in Idaho and Montana, over 1.6 million acres, has a sixteen-page forest bird list with ten bird habitat abbreviations, four abundance and four status codes. This type of list is useful for experienced birders who are familiar with various types of habitat.

Hundreds of bird and other species lists are available from state, federal, and private agencies and organizations. Some are simply lists of common and scientific species names. Others are designed for use as checklists.

FIELD GUIDE INDEX & SIGHTING LOG - CHECKLIST

The Field Guide Index (pages 384-392) is a multi-purpose reference tool. Page or plate numbers give you quick reference to bird illustrations and habitat details in each of the major field guides. These nine guides include Peterson's new Western Guide and the revised Golden and National Geographic bird guides (see Bibliography, page 399).

The Sighting Log - Checklist provides space to record your past and future bird sightings. Use it to note species you have identified. Keep a log of your birding success as you see new birds. There is even space to record sighting dates for both sexes and young birds.

THE ABA CODES ADD AN EXTRA CHALLENGE

The American Birding Association (ABA) Code is part of the Field Guide Index. The code ranks each bird from one to five. Low numbers (1 and 2) are easier to find, while the 3, 4, and 5 codes indicate less numerous and progressively more difficult to find species. The codes were developed by Benton Basham, a well-known birder, and are based on the strategy he used to find 703 species in one year, 1983.

When I see and identify a bird, knowing the species has a 3 or 4 code adds to my feeling of accomplishment. My excitement at seeing my first Great Gray Owl on a fencepost in my backyard was even greater when I found that it had an ABA code of 3. I think the ABA codes will add to your enjoyment and sense of accomplishment too!

APPENDIX - THE RARE & LIMITED SPECIES SUPPLEMENT

This Bird Chart supplement (pages 393-394) lists 63 species and notes the birding locations where they may be found. The supplement accommodates the ABA Code, nesting and seasonal abundance details, the Sighting Log - Checklist, and Field Guide Index information. Most species in the supplement are rare birds or difficult to find, have a very restricted range, or have been seen at only one or two locations covered in the Bird Chart.

APPENDIX - STUDY IDEAS & WORKSHEETS

The Study Ideas section suggests how this guide may be used by those new to birding, or by teachers in natural history workshops, as part of a lesson plan or incorporated in class projects. These ideas may be adopted by parents who wish to encourage or include their children as they add to their own knowledge about birds.

Study ideas include determining field trip birding objectives, research and study of supporting information as an aid in achieving those objectives, contact and interaction with professional conservationists to secure current information, and final field trip planning and study. After the trip, reviewing and reporting on results (preparing workbook pages or diary, and the Sighting Log - Checklist record) are important.

Project and Field Trip Worksheets are included to aid in bird study and field trip planning. They may be copied for personal and classroom use.

WHERE THE BIRDS ARE UNLOCKS THE WORLD OF BIRDS AND BIRDING

Now you have a feel for the contents of *Where The Birds Are*. You have seen how easy it is to find places where and times when lots of different birds may be found. You know where to reach professionals who manage bird habitats in North America, those people who have current information about birds and birding.

Most of us do not have time to commit our bird field guide to memory or participate in field trips on weekend mornings when most local trips take place. Field trips often conflict with our lifestyle - that Girl Scout outing, Little League game, 4H project, shopping, work responsibility, weekend fishing trip, or other family or recreation interests.

Where The Birds Are provides a shortcut to successful birding, places the access information you need at your fingertips, and opens the door to birding within the context of your lifestyle.

For the first time since Roger Tory Peterson created the earliest practical field guide 55 years ago, there is a practical, economical guide to locating those birds.

There are many organizations and government agencies that exist for the purpose of promoting habitat preservation, conservation education, and the scientific study of birds. Their activities help sustain and improve the world of birds and birding for all of us. The brief overview that follows includes those groups that are the most useful for the beginning and traveling birders.

Our primary source of information when we study birds are field guides to bird identification, which are referred to in the Field Guide Index.

WHY EACH FIELD GUIDE HAS A DIFFERENT APPROACH

Differences of opinion on bird and wildlife management practices and analysis of research data are common. The mobile nature of birds, our changing environment, and a rapid increase in the accumulation of scientific data are a few of the reasons why information on birds is constantly increasing. Experts do agree that bird information is only as good as the data from which it is derived, and the care and expertise of those who analyze and organize it into a useful form.

Field guides reflect the data available to the authors at the time of publication or revision, as well as their personal bird identification concepts. Consequently guides vary in sequence, species names, bird family affiliations, number of species covered, and range that is shown on the maps.

SHOULD YOU HAVE MORE THAN ONE FIELD GUIDE?

Many birders have several field guides, both for the above reasons and because bird species photos and illustrations differ in each guide. A species may be easier to recognize from a different photo angle or by the illustration of a less obvious field mark.

Identification of unfamiliar species may be easier in one particular field guide because of the illustration or description. Another field guide may be easier to carry or use in the field. Here are a few examples:

The first Lewis' Woodpecker that I ever saw had a plumage about midway between immature and adult. When compared to the illustrations in my four guides the bird was much lighter green on its back and outer wings. A bright flash of pinkish-red on the underparts caught my eye as it flew away. I analyzed descriptions from several guides to make positive identification.

The illustrations of Clark's Nutcrackers in my guides show the bird with a short- to medium-length bill. The first one I identified had a relatively longer bill than the birds pictured in my guides, and was using it vigorously on the pine cones in a pine tree.

RANGE IS NOT ALWAYS WHERE THE BIRDS ARE

Range maps do not always show where the birds are. The small range maps in bird field guides are based on an analysis of thousands of bird sighting reports that represent countless hours of study, analysis, illustration, and revision by experienced people. The range map shading may indicate a small range for one species while another has a range representing millions of acres across many states.

In the Bird Chart pages in this book, a bird listed as abundant or common may be more than a thousand miles outside the range indicated on the map in your field guide. That fact exemplifies the mobile nature of birds and the difficulty in securing, or mapping bird sighting information from every square mile in North America on a range map.

Range maps represent information on probable bird location in a general sense. They have been an indispensable tool to birders for years. *Where The Birds Are* is specific about bird location and helps you to zero in on the species where and when they are most likely to be seen, whether they are within or outside the ranges shown in your field guide.

Most bird checklists have space on the back for you to note species you observe that are not listed. Visitors are encouraged to inform the refuge, sanctuary, or preserve office about these unlisted species, and if identification is confirmed, the data is added to accumulated sighting and survey records. Your notes then become a part of the information used in future checklist and range map revisions - a contribution to our collective knowledge of the natural world.

BIRD BANDING, ANOTHER VITAL INFORMATION SOURCE

One of the most popular and widespread sources of information about birds is acquired through banding. Qualified individuals, both professional ornithologists and experienced amateurs, are licensed by the U.S. Fish & Wildlife Service to trap birds and place a metal band just above the toes. Each band has its own unique number that enables the researcher to recognize the individual bird when it is recaptured.

Some ornithologists use additional markers to enable them to identify the bird from a distance rather than having to trap the bird each time to read the number on the metal band. These markers include colored plastic neck bands and nasal discs used on various waterfowl, dyes used on shorebirds and Snow Geese, and colored plastic leg bands used on terns and passerines, among other birds.

Only licensed individuals may trap and band birds. Anyone, even the most novice birder, can see a color-marked bird in the field, or find a dead one, and report it to the Bird Banding Laboratory, Carefully note the color bands or other markings, including any numbers you can detect, and describe them in a letter that includes the date and location of your observation.

If you find a dead bird that is banded, remove the band if possible and send it with your letter describing when, where, and if readily apparent, how the bird died. If you cannot remove the band, copy its unique number carefully and double-check to avoid any errors. Send your reports to: Bird Banding Laboratory, Office of Migratory Bird Management, Laurel, MD 20708.

The Bird Banding Laboratory will tell you when, where, and by whom the bird was banded, and will notify the bander with the information that you have provided. This partnership between professional ornithologists and amateur birders has provided valuable data for research on migration times, routes, and destinations, local movements, population changes, longevity, and behavior.

WHO ARE THE BIRDING AUTHORITIES, AMATEURS & EXPERTS?

The birding authorities and experts are ornithologists (scientists who study birds), as well as people specializing in other biological sciences such as botanists, zoologists, and ecologists, government agency and private conservation group wildlife scientists and managers, university professors, museum curators, and amateur birders. They may belong to one or more of the professional organizations: The American Ornithologists' Union (A.O.U.), the Association of Field Ornithologists, the Cooper Ornithological Society, and the Wilson Ornithological Society are the best known professional groups in American ornithology.

State and federal agencies and most of their local offices covered in this guide have staff biologists or other wildlife professionals including ornithologists. Many government personnel and professional organization members are members of the National Audubon Society, a state Audubon Alliance organization, The Nature Conservancy, or other national or local conservation group, nature club, or birding organization.

One influential national organization is the American Birding Association, Inc. (ABA), a not-for-profit group of dedicated birders. ABA objectives are to educate the public, promote birding and the study of wild birds, and to contribute to the development of improved methods of bird population study. New members are always welcome.

Experts in every agency and organization rely on help from the thousands of amateurs who love birds and other wildlife. These dedicated men and women volunteer countless hours observing and reporting on bird activity and make an important contribution to the research of agency officials, scientists, and university ornithologists. Amateurs also volunteer to staff public information desks, improve habitat, build bird houses, and raise money for habitat and wildlife protection every day. Many are experts in their own right but, regardless of their training or expertise, all play a vital supporting role in the world of birds and birding.

CONSERVATION GROUP & AGENCY PROFILES

Bird information and local birding activity involves federal, state, and private agencies and organizations with common interests and often overlapping jurisdictions. Three conservation groups, the National Audubon Society together with the other members of the Audubon Alliance, The Nature Conservancy, and Ducks Unlimited, are the most active in preservation of birds and their habitat.

Hundreds of other conservation groups and government agencies place at least some emphasis on birds. The largest are the National Wildlife Federation, U.S. Fish & Wildlife Service, National Park Service, National Forest Service, Bureau of Land Management (BLM), the state wildlife agencies, and the Canadian Wildlife Service. One new organization, the Western Hemisphere Shorebird Reserve Network, is also described in this guide.

NATIONAL AUDUBON SOCIETY

The National Audubon Society (NAS) has been a major force supporting bird education, preservation, and birding as a hobby in North America since 1940. Today they are involved in many environmental issues at the national and local level. Habitat preservation and birding continue to be emphasized by the National Audubon Society and approximately 500 local Audubon Chapters.

The Society operates seven Wildlife Education Centers and manages over 70 Wildlife Sanctuaries in 21 states. The Education Centers and the nine Sanctuaries open to the public (in 13 states) are numbered and described in the state chapters. The Sanctuary bird lists that meet my criteria are included in the Bird Chart.

Facilities, viewing opportunities, and guided activity possibilities vary from one location to another. The Centers often have more programs for children and adults than the Sanctuaries do. In some cases National Audubon Society members are admitted to a sanctuary or education center at no charge. Admission fees help defray a portion of operation and maintenance of these locations.

THE AUDUBON ALLIANCE

The Audubon Alliance includes ten independent state and regional Audubon Societies. They were established between 1896 and 1914 to formulate and promote early environmental legislation, specifically the protection of seriously declining wild bird and wildlife populations at state and federal levels. Members of the Alliance continue to be active locally and nationally in wildlife research, conservation, environmental legislative issues, and regularly schedules recreational birding activities for members and others interested in wildlife conservation.

The Audubon Naturalist Society of the Central Atlantic States (ANS) operates a 40-acre wooded wildlife sanctuary in Chevy Chase, MD, where natural history study programs for adults and youth and college-level field ecology courses are offered (Co-sponsored by the U.S. Department of Agriculture Graduate School). ANS supports regional programs of habitat preservation including studies of water quality in the Potomac River and Chesapeake Bay.

The Connecticut Audubon Society, headquartered in Fairfield, has established fourteen wildlife sanctuaries in the state to protect habitat for herons, waterbirds, and gulls, with a focus on the federally endangered Least and Roseate terns and Piping Plovers. Other Society activities include youth education at two nature centers, and conservation legislation at the state level.

The Florida Audubon Society, in Maitland, is active in education and provides films and television programs on Florida's delicate ecosystem to towns throughout the state. At the legislative level, planning and management of the state's rapid growth and the acquisition and protection of wildlife habitat are Society priorities.

The Illinois Audubon Society, in Wayne, concentrate on maintaining the large Bald Eagle population, as well as other habitat protection projects, including wetlands and wildlands along the Illinois and Mississippi Rivers, closed canopy forest areas, and restoration of tall-grass prairie areas in the state.

The Maine Audubon Society, in Falmouth, organized a statewide annual Common Loon census and a "Loon Festival." They successfully encouraged amendment to the state's endangered species law protecting habitat for threatened wildlife.

The Audubon Society of New Hampshire biologists and volunteers study habitat needs, carry out wildlife surveys and prepare management plans to protect wildlife. Headquartered in Concord, the Society provides natural history education at schools and day camps and offers adult courses and field trips to increase public awareness of the environment.

The Massachusetts Audubon Society (MAS) was founded in 1896 by women concerned that the fashion tastes of high society Bostonians were endangering the Snowy Egrets in the Everglades. The activities of MAS, now located in Lincoln, focus on public education about birds and their protection, and other environmental concerns, include pollution, energy conservation, and endangered species preservation.

The New Jersey Audubon Society (NJAS), in Franklin Lakes, operates Cape May Bird Observatory and has played a major part in safeguarding many natural areas. Their "Operation Flightpath" and "World Series of Birding" programs serve to draw attention to the area's strategic location in the western hemisphere as a major migration route for birds, provide research opportunities and data, and educate the public on habitat and wildlife preservation.

The New York Audubon Society, in Latham, directs a "Nestbox Network" project has resulted in the placing and monitoring the use of over 10,000 nestboxes for Bluebirds and other species that nest in the state. Other activities include the "NY Loon Conservation Project" in the Adirondacks and off the Long Island coast, and the "International Bird Feeding Survey" which encourages backyard bird feeding during the winter.

The Audubon Society of Rhode Island (ASRI), in Smithfield, emphasizes public education and the monitoring of pollution, development, and wildlife management issues. ASRI manages over 5,000 acres of wildlife refuge habitat, and is involved in joint habitat programs with others including The Nature Conservancy, the RI Dept. of Environmental Management, and the U.S. Fish and Wildlife Service.

LOCAL NATURE CLUBS, AUDUBON CHAPTERS, & HOW TO CONTACT THEM

Nature Clubs and Audubon Chapters in the U.S. have a rotating group of volunteer officers. Few have a permanent office address. The National Audubon Society and the Audubon Alliance do not publish a Chapter directory for this reason. The National Audubon Society furnished an up-to-date computer printout of their Chapters for use in this guide. Audubon Chapter, Audubon Alliance offices, and other nature club names, cities and state map symbol numbers appear under the LOCAL BIRDING GROUPS heading.

Audubon Chapter and nature club officers and members know about local wildlife sanctuaries, preserves, reserves, other good local birding areas, and species migration patterns. They often aid Federal, state, and private organizations by helping with official bird counts and reporting bird sightings on a regular basis. These groups may offer a local bird checklist, manage a local preserve, and most have a monthly meeting, publish a newsletter, and sponsor field trips. Potential new members are always welcome.

If you are new to birding and wish to learn more about the fascinating subject of birds, contact a Chapter or nature club near where you live or plan to visit. Ask personnel at the local Wildlife Refuge, National Forest, National Wildlife Refuge, or state wildlife agency office about how to contact an active member or current Chapter or club president.

THE NATURE CONSERVANCY

The mission of The Nature Conservancy (TNC) is to find, protect, and maintain the best examples of natural communities, ecosystems, and endangered species in the natural world. They work with educational institutions and public and private conservation agencies to identify and protect ecologically significant lands and waters, and wildlife. Their focus includes birds as part of their overall interest in conservation of all life forms.

The Nature Conservancy and its members have acquired over 4 million acres in the western hemisphere. Their goal is to protect 9 million acres by the year 2000, including 200 significant preserve sites in Central and South America.

FIELD OFFICES, CHAPTERS, & PRESERVES

There are 54 TNC Field and Chapter offices and staff size varies with each location. The majority of more than 1,100 preserves owned and managed by TNC are closed to visitors in order to allow undisturbed scientific field study and protect sensitive and rare species.

The Directors of Stewardship at TNC Field Offices and Chapters have identified and provided information on 291 preserves, many listed for the first time in this guide. Some of these preserves have been transferred to other public and private conservation organizations. If there is a bird checklist that meets my criteria, it has been included in the Bird Chart.

Most preserves do not have full-time managers and recreation is limited to passive nature study during daylight hours. Managed preserves usually have more recreational opportunities and information about wildlife species and birds.

TNC preserves are often sensitive to human activity and visitor facilities may be limited. Rules for visitors are more restrictive than those for most National Wildlife Refuges. Permission to visit may be required and foot traffic restricted to marked trails. Some TNC preserve descriptions note single file hiking is discouraged. The admonishment to "leave only footprints and take only memories" is the best advice to follow when visiting these typically unmanned areas.

Contact the local Field or Chapter office about membership, visiting or guided tour availability, birding possibilities, and other information that is not included in the preserve descriptions. TNC offices may have a small staff active in the field. In those cases an address is given for your inquiry instead of a phone contact.

DUCKS UNLIMITED

Ducks Unlimited (DU) is dedicated to perpetuating waterfowl on the North American continent and western hemisphere. It is a nonprofit, nonpolitical organization whose members raise money for preservation and enhancement of wetlands in North America. Over 100 DU Regional Directors and State Committee Chairmen work with federal, state, and private groups, and with local DU Chapter Committees to identify, protect, and fund wetland purchase and preservation activities. Fellowship and common interests in waterfowl and wildlife are shared at fund raising dinners and auctions of more than 4,000 local committees.

Primary breeding grounds in Canada produce the majority of our waterfowl. Nesting, resting, and wintering areas in the U.S and nesting and wintering areas of Mexico are all of concern to Ducks Unlimited. Many of the birding areas covered in this guide have been added to, improved, or established as a result of DU interest.

NATIONAL WILDLIFE FEDERATION

The National Wildlife Federation (NWF) is dedicated to encouraging an awareness among people of the world of the need for wise use and proper management of those resources of the Earth upon which our lives depend: the soil, air, water, forests, minerals, plant life, and wildlife.

The NWF maintains a comprehensive conservation education program, publishes numerous periodicals and educational materials, sponsors outdoor education programs, and actively supports conservation legislation at national and state levels.

NATIONAL WILDLIFE FEDERATION AFFILIATES & LOCAL CHAPTERS

There are NWF-affiliated wildlife organizations in every state, Puerto Rico, and the Virgin Islands. The affiliates are primarily devoted to the wise use, conservation, aesthetic appreciation, and restoration of wildlife and other natural resources, and are supported by a network of local chapters.

Local chapter members include conservationists, nature-lovers, rod and gun enthusiasts, farmers, and people who share a sense of basic responsibility for the preservation of natural resources and wildlife of the county, state, and nation.

FEDERAL & STATE AGENCIES

Government agencies play an important role in the world of birds, birding, and outdoor recreation. Many of the staff wildlife biologists conduct research that focuses on birds and their habitats. The size of these agencies is huge and as a result management is decentralized. One consequence is that office names and locations are not commonly known.

Agency personnel are often active birders and may belong to a local Audubon or NWF chapter, or some other conservation organization or nature club. Therefore, one or more people in an agency office are likely to be familiar with local conservation group chapters and their interests and activities.

U.S. FISH & WILDLIFE SERVICE

The U.S. Fish & Wildlife Service (USFWS) operates under the U.S. Department of the Interior. It is the lead Federal agency in conservation of migratory birds, endangered species, certain mammals, and sports fishes.

The USFWS administers over 90 million acres of wildlife habitat. Every National Wildlife Refuge (NWR) where visitors are permitted, or where you may view birds from outside the refuge (such as an island refuge), is described in the relevant state chapter in this guide. The USFWS Regional Offices are also listed.

USFWS NATIONAL WILDLIFE REFUGES

Refuge descriptions in the state chapters contain details about office locations and management structure. On-site refuge management and staff personnel are the best source for current birding information. Part or all of a refuge may be closed to visitors to protect a rare species, habitat, or during nesting periods. Always call the office to ask about visiting policy and conditions before traveling any distance to visit a refuge. In Alaska, with some exceptions, refuges are legally open to certain compatible public uses without permission.

When you contact a refuge office a staff member will be glad to help you. They can usually tell you about the arrival or departure of bird species and unusual recent sightings - or will note places on their refuge tour maps where you have the best chance of observing specific birds. At any small or remote refuge the staff may be in the field and the office closed temporarily during business hours.

NWR staff and volunteer personnel play an active role locally in natural history education. They conduct workshops for elementary and secondary teachers and guide refuge tours for students.

NATIONAL PARK SERVICE

The National Park Service (NPS) administers 341 locations, comprising 79 million acres in 49 states and the District of Columbia, under the U.S. Department of the Interior. Each is briefly described in their "The National Parks: Index 1987," which is available from the Superintendent of Documents, U.S. Government Printing Office, Washington, DC 20402.

Among those 341 National Park Service sites are 49 National Parks, 14 National Seashores or Lakeshores, and 12 National Preserves. The Everglades site in Florida is an example of a National Park. Point Reyes National Seashore in California is of special interest because over 430 bird species have been recorded there. There are 23 NPS location classifications including an International Historic Site and the White House in Washington. Fifty-one park locations are described in this guide, selected as the most accessible and rewarding for birders.

When you contact a NPS location be sure to request the brochure with a park road map. The maps are excellent and the brochures list the various phone numbers you can call for specific visitor activity schedules, guided tour reservations, permits, and other information. Rangers lead guided tours at many of the Park Service locations, especially during peak visiting times.

National Park Service locations often have more visitors than other wildlife areas. An off-season visit may be worth considering if you want to avoid crowds. The National Park Service provides many services to visitors through concessionaires and cooperating associations. For example, The Yellowstone Institute offered 68 field courses from June through mid-September 1989. The courses are sponsored by the Yellowstone Association for Natural Science, History & Education in cooperation with the Park Service.

Note: Cooperating associations are local or regional nonprofit groups who provide money and volunteer services for selected Federal facilities around the country. Their members voluntarily staff visitor centers, work in the field to improve facilities and habitat, contribute funds, and sell merchandise to raise funds for improvements.

NATIONAL FOREST SERVICE

The National Forest Service (NFS) operates under the U.S. Department of Agriculture and administers more than 191 million acres comprising our National Forests, Recreation, and Grassland Areas. They cooperate with other federal, state, and private organizations in wildlife, fish, and habitat management and conduct research in these fields.

Among the 154 Forest, Grassland, and Ranger District Offices listed or numbered in the applicable state chapters, one is within a day's drive from wherever you live in the lower 48 states. The 9 Regional Forest Service Offices are also listed. When you contact a Region or Supervisor office for maps or literature, they may direct you to a Ranger District for local information.

The staff at Forest Service offices are glad to tell you which campgrounds are open or not crowded, what roads are closed, and will show you how to reach them on their excellent maps, which are available for $1 or $2 each. They also know whether a bird checklist is available and can discuss noteworthy birding areas.

EYES ON WILDLIFE PROGRAM

Be sure to ask about the new National Forest Service "Eyes On Wildlife Program." The purpose of the program is to direct people to quality improved or unimproved wildlife viewing areas, places where you are most likely to see birds and other wildlife, even whales. There may not be any signs or brochures available. You could find yourself in a boggy area observing beavers at work, or perched on a rock high above the Pacific savoring a view of bird or other wildlife activity.

BUREAU OF LAND MANAGEMENT

The Bureau of Land Management (BLM) operates under the Department of the Interior and administers public lands, primarily the more open grass and desert areas in the western United States, under multiple-use principles. These include outdoor recreation, fish and wildlife production, livestock grazing, timber, industrial development, watershed protection, and on-shore mineral production.

There are 12 BLM State and 59 District Offices responsible for 337 million acres, about 43 percent of our federal land. The land area managed by the BLM is more than twice the size of Texas. There are 170 Resource Area Offices that work under the Districts. When you contact a State or District BLM Office they may refer you to a Resource Area Office for specific and current local information.

The BLM publishes hundreds of special land area maps that vary in size, coverage, and content. You may purchase them at BLM offices or by mail. BLM land is scattered, divided into large and small parcels, and may be under lease. Maps are an important reference resource for visitors.

BLM office personnel are knowledgeable about land access, birding, wildlife species, and recreation. At local offices brochures and maps of individual recreation areas, trails, and campgrounds are available. Be sure to inquire about a local bird checklist and birding opportunities.

STATE WILDLIFE AGENCIES

State wildlife management agencies are placing a greater emphasis on nonconsumptive wildlife recreation such as birding. Tourism departments emphasize travel opportunities and typically focus on wildlife recreation opportunities at state parks and forests which may also be managed by the state wildlife management agency.

WILDLIFE, GAME & HERITAGE AREAS

State resources and wildlife management responsibilities include thousands of other land areas beside their 30 million acres of parks and forests. Wildlife

Management, Game Management, and Heritage Areas account for almost 23 million acres. Minnesota has over 900 areas and at least seven states have more than 100. With some exceptions they are open to all users - the birder, hiker, nature photographer, hunter, fisherman, and outdoor enthusiast.

State wildlife agency headquarters and regional or district offices have current information on wildlife areas, recreation opportunities, and license and user fees. They are likely to know about scheduled local conservation group activities like birding field trips, Audubon, The Nature Conservancy, Ducks Unlimited, and National Wildlife Federation Chapter activities.

Regulations, highway and wildlife area maps, books, literature, and bird lists are available through state wildlife offices. A few state agencies manage especially noteworthy areas. Examples are noted in the Florida, Kansas, Michigan, New Jersey, and New York chapters.

STATE TOURIST DEPARTMENTS

Many state tourist departments have a free 800 phone number to accommodate callers from out of state. Free tourist literature and official state highway maps can be obtained by a phone call. They can often fill your request for wildlife-related literature published by their state wildlife agency. Some of the 800 phone numbers are answered by independent literature distribution center personnel. They may refer you to non-toll-free phone numbers for answers to specific questions about travel or outdoor recreation.

CANADIAN WILDLIFE SERVICE

The Canadian Wildlife Service (CWS) is part of the Federal Department of the Environment. The CWS works closely with the U.S. Fish & Wildlife Service in monitoring and protecting migratory birds. Visitor policy is changing to accommodate a growing interest in nonconsumptive wildlife recreation.
For detailed information on the three principal types of protected areas in Canada, contact any CWS Regional Office. Each of the location types is described in the Canada chapter (pages 197-202), along with details on birding hotlines, local birding groups, and province and territory agencies.

This is the first guide book to list all the Canadian areas. Listings include area name, size in acres, Province or Territory, and Canadian Wildlife Service Regional Office contacts. An asterisk * by an area name indicates a brochure or bird list is available from the office.

A two-page map of Canada has numbered symbols in red that show the approximate location of each listed area. Some areas in Canada are inaccessible except by chartered aircraft, or may require a special government permit, especially above the 60th parallel (above 60°N in northern latitudes).

WESTERN HEMISPHERE SHOREBIRD RESERVE NETWORK (WHSRN)

Shorebirds are hemispheric globetrotters and WHSRN is a voluntary collaboration of government and private organizations committed to shorebird conservation. WHSRN gives international recognition to important shorebird habitats, and promotes cooperative management and protection of reserve sites in the western hemisphere as part of an international reserve network. The WHSRN is supported by grants from philanthropic organizations and is staffed by National Audubon Society and Manomet Bird Observatory personnel.

Launched in 1985 on the basis of research by the Academy of Natural Sciences, the Canadian Wildlife Service, and the Manomet Bird Observatory, the reserve network unites wildlife agencies, private conservation groups, and other organizations in an international effort to solve conservation challenges faced by migratory shorebirds and their habitats.

WHSRN reserves are established at locations that support either more than 250,000 shorebirds over the year or in excess of 30 percent of any single shorebird species. The reserve system in the U.S. includes San Francisco Bay in California, the Stillwater Wildlife Management Area in Nevada, Great Salt Lake in Utah, Cheyenne Bottoms in south-west Kansas, and the beaches of Delaware Bay in Delaware and New Jersey.

In Canada the designated WHSRN site meeting these criteria is the Bay of Fundy, including Shepody Bay in New Brunswick and Minas Basin in Nova Scotia. These six western hemisphere locations are indicated on the applicable state and Canada maps and described in the relevant chapters.

FOR BEGINNING & DISCOURAGED BIRDERS

Most beginning birders are overwhelmed by the vast content of field guides. My son was. We went through his accumulation of books (he is a confirmed bibliophile) and found three field guides and two other books on birds. All were gifts from relatives and had never been read or used.

Many people have purchased field guides but never learned to use them. Birding is not made easier by the fact that the objects of study have an annoying habit of flying away before a birder can figure out what they are.

Who are these people? They are housewives, engineers, salesmen, secretaries, auto mechanics, nurses, retirees, parents, and young people from every walk of life. They do not go on field trips with experienced birders because they do not know about those trips, they cannot participate at the scheduled times, or they are embarrassed by their lack of knowledge or the difficulty they have trying to use their field guide effectively.

Most people feel embarrassed in any environment where they lack knowledge. The world of birds and birding is no different. But consider the next few facts and you should relax about your lack of birding knowledge and overcome any feelings of embarrassment you may have had in the past.

Ornithology is the branch of zoology concerned with birds. But birds and birding knowledge involves many other disciplines. From a scientific standpoint, conservation and wildlife (preserving natural resources), ecology (bird and habitat relationships), biology (life processes), and taxonomy (bird classification) are all included in the study of birds, or ornithology.

Most experts in the world of birds and birding specialize in one or several areas. That's why most birding field guides represent the combined effort of at least several individuals, experts on one or several families of birds, or a particular aspect of field guide preparation.

LEARN ABOUT BIRDS ONE BIRD AT A TIME

How did they learn so much about birds and become specialists? One bird at a time! The same way you will learn. The more they learned about birds the more confident they became - just as you will! Successful use of your bird guide is easier when you go where the birds are. Studying selected species and their photos or illustrations in your field guide before you go afield also helps.

WHAT YOU
DO NOT HAVE TO DO
TO BE
A SUCCESSFUL BIRDER

You do not have to be a naturalist or scientist. You do not need a mentor at your side coaching and advising you. You do not have to be an adult or a retired senior citizen. You do not have to learn scientific names for the birds. You do not have to participate in formally scheduled field trips. You do not have to change your lifestyle.

WHAT YOU
DO HAVE TO DO

You do have to read. You do have to be patient. You do have to study the bird illustrations and written material. You do have to combine those elements sometimes to make a positive species identification. You should keep a record of the birds you have identified so that you remember them and readily recognize them in the future.

SUCCESSFUL BIRDING

As a beginning birder consider starting with duck identification. During most seasons the bird lists in the Bird Chart pages show a dozen or more duck species present. Ducks are larger than most other bird species and therefore usually easier to locate and observe.

Like other bird family groups, the species, age, and gender differences result in distinctive feeding behaviors, habitats, and field marks. Swans, geese, and ducks frequent the same lake, marsh and wetland, and seashore areas.

The basic knowledge you acquire in learning to identify ducks can be applied to identifying other birds. The small variations you encounter among some species will help you sharpen your visual skills and pick up on the behavioral differences explained in your field guide.

**USE THE
BIRD CHART PAGES**

It is easy to practice your duck ID skills on other birds while afield. Just check a few other abundant and common birds noted in the same area bird list in the Bird Chart and study them in your field guide before your trip.

**CONTACTING
THE INFORMATION
SOURCES**

Weekend travelers should note that some government offices, visitor centers, and The Nature Conservancy offices are open only during regular business hours Monday through Friday. There are exceptions. National Park Service and selected National Wildlife Refuge visitor centers, Audubon Centers, and managed TNC preserves are open on weekends.

Bird availability and habitat conditions are unpredictable. But you can compensate for these intangibles when you know where to get the most current bird and birding-related data. Personal contact with people in wildlife management is the solution. The sources mentioned in this book are always glad to answer any questions, no matter how elementary. After all, they are in the business, whether amateur or professional, of increasing public awareness of our environment and its well-being.

It is always a good idea to call ahead for current local information. Agency or organization policy on responding to your request for literature varies. Some state tourist agencies say to allow six weeks. Your request may be received at a busy time and their response would be delayed.

I have rarely had to wait a full week for information I've requested by phone and recommend using the phone rather than mail. Don't forget to ask if a bird checklist is available and about birding areas.

**THE NATURE
CONSERVANCY
PRESERVES**

The amount of information available about birds and birding at The Nature Conservancy preserves in this guide varies. TNC preserves with limited access and literature availability are included because of their birding potential and the TNC policy of continuous accumulation of information about those areas. The Nature Conservancy have an ongoing program of adding to their computerized inventory of habitat and wildlife information database. It is the most comprehensive private database of environmental information in the world.

BIRDING HOTSPOTS

Certain areas are widely recognized by experienced birders as offering special birding opportunities. Large flocks or many species may be present during spring and fall migrations at some locations. Others feature unusual species that may be rare or endangered, have a narrow range, or can be seen only a few weeks or months a year. These hotspots include:

On the Atlantic Coast, the Bay of Fundy in Canada, Cape May in New Jersey, both sides of Delaware Bay, and the Everglades and Key West in southern Florida; along the Pacific Coast or slightly inland, the southern California desert area, San Francisco Bay and Point Reyes National Seashore, and Adak Island in Alaska; both sides of the Mississippi River, and the Rio Grande in Arizona, New Mexico, and western Texas; and areas on the Gulf of Mexico coast, particularly in Alabama, Mississippi, and Texas.

VIEWING EQUIPMENT

In binoculars and spotting scopes there is a relationship between magnification (power) and the potential for distortion through the lens. A higher lens power will bring the bird closer but there is more chance for distortion, usually caused by movement like breathing and heart action on binoculars, or heat rising on scopes. Lens quality generally relates to clarity of the image through the full viewing area provided by the lens.

The way to know the power best for you is to borrow binoculars of different powers and try them in the field. How much potential there is for distortion depends on your body position (physical stress), the weather, and time of day. Zoom binoculars and spotting or telescopes, with a tripod or window mount, can add to your viewing opportunities. Spotting or telescopes with a 45° ocular may be more comfortable to use.

THE REST OF THE STORY

The story on birding, wildlife, and habitat management is really a story without an end — because the environment and information about it are always changing. The weather, population growth, urbanization, our continuing study of wildlife and the relationship between life forms all contribute to our knowledge and understanding of the natural world.

With this constant flux and the thousands of official and independent information sources it is difficult to know all the birding opportunities and species data available to us. *Where The Birds Are* helps to bridge this information gap. It lists more than 2,200 information sources and birding locations. The Bird Chart presents 46,808 species sighting records containing nearly 165,000 specific nesting and abundance codes.

When you use this guide to increase your own knowledge of birds and the interdependence of all life forms, or help others to develop an interest in the natural world, you contribute to the "body of common knowledge" necessary for the protection of the environment and another chapter in the rest of the story — improving and enriching our quality of life.

BIRDING HOTLINE
Statewide   205-987-2730

LOCAL BIRDING GROUPS
Map/Chapter/City
① Mobile Bay Audubon/Mobile
② Tennessee Valley Audubon
     /Meridianville
③ The Shoals Audubon/Florence
④ Tuscaloosa Audubon/Tuscaloosa
⑤ Mobile Bird Club/Mobile

NATIONAL AUDUBON SOCIETY

Dauphin Island Bird Sanctuary ❶
Donald Bland - Warden
PO Box 189
Dauphin Island, AL   205-861-2882

Take I-10 west from Mobile to Rt. 193,
turn south and continue for 30 miles.
Dauphin Island is on the west side of the
entrance to Mobile Bay.

This 164-acre sanctuary is a major resting
and feeding site for migrating songbirds.
Dauphin Island is the first land many
birds encounter in the spring after their
northern flight across the Gulf of Mexico.
Camping and other facilities are available
adjacent to this walk-in sanctuary.

U.S. FISH & WILDLIFE SERVICE
NATIONAL WILDLIFE REFUGES

Bon Secour ❶   (office at refuge)
PO Box 1650
Gulf Shores, AL 36542   205-968-8623

Bird List AL-1 Bon Secour Summary
289 birds listed, 126 nesting birds
Bird Chart pages 204-221

Totals by Season		s	S	F	W
Abundant	A	35	11	39	27
Common	C	94	32	1	58
Uncommon	U	1	72	93	69
Occasional	O	35	44	25	23
Rare	R	12	7	13	23

Endangered Species: Brown Pelican,
Wood Stork, Bald Eagle, Peregrine
Falcon, Piping Plover, Least Tern

Bon Secour is located 50 miles west of
Pensacola, Florida, and 50 miles southeast
of Mobile. The refuge has five units.

Four of these units can be reached from
Hwy. 180: Sand Bayou Unit adjacent to
Oyster Bay; Little Point Clear Unit on the
Mobile Bay side of the point; Fort
Morgan Unit at the end of the peninsula;
and Perdue Unit at the west end of Little
Lagoon and surrounding Gator Lake.

Take Hwy. 180 west from Gulf Shores for
approximately 5.5 miles to the visitor
center, located at the northwest end of the
Perdue Unit.

The fifth unit, Little Dauphin Island, is on
the west side of the entrance to Mobile
Bay and is reached via I-10 and then
Hwy. 193 going south from Mobile. It is
adjacent to Dauphin Island.

Habitat: 4,000 acres of dunes, pine-oak
woodlands, undisturbed barrier beaches,
coastal marsh, and open waters. Located
along the Mississippi Flyway, Bon
Secour's varied habitat is used by millions
of spring and fall migrants.

Most migratory songbirds arrive in mid-
March. Ospreys arrive in mid-April.
Wading birds, including Great Blue

Herons and Cattle Egrets, nest during May
and June. The fall migration begins in
August and peaks around mid-October.

In addition to migrants, Brown Pelicans
and a wide variety of wading birds and
shorebirds can be seen year-round.

Refuge brochure, fishing, hiking, boating.
Spring, Fall

Choctaw ❷   (office in town)
Box 808
2704 Westside College Ave.
Jackson, AL 36545   205-246-3583

Bird List AL-2 Choctaw Summary
139 birds listed, 67 nesting birds
Bird Chart pages 204-221

Totals by Season		s	S	F	W
Abundant	A	1	0	2	4
Common	C	13	21	14	16
Uncommon	U	29	27	26	23
Occasional	O	60	35	56	49
Rare	R	8	5	15	13

Endangered Species: Wood Stork, Bald
Eagle

Take Hwy. 69 north from Jackson to Coffeeville. At Coffeeville take Hwy. 84 west for 10 miles (across Tombigbee River). Watch for refuge signs on Hwy. 84. Turn right on Co. Rd. 21 for 4.5 miles to Barrytown. Turn right at Barrytown on Co. Rd. 25 to Womack Hill and bear right on dirt road to refuge.

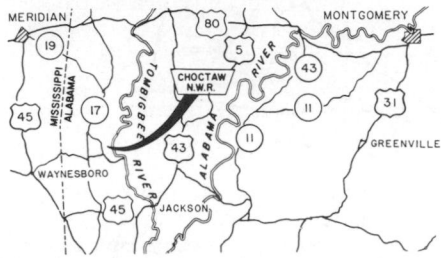

Habitat: 4,218 acres. The refuge consists of southern Alabama river-bottom land, with mixed hardwoods, spruce pine, and loblolly pine on the higher ground. Sweet gum and oak are the dominant hardwoods.

Nesting wading birds include Little Blue Herons and Cattle Egrets. Great Egrets and Great Blue Herons are permanent residents. The winter bird populations are primarily waterfowl with Mallards and Wood Ducks in the greatest numbers.

Area brochure, fishing, hunting, boating.
Fall, Winter

Eufaula 🖪 (office at refuge)
Route 2, Box 97-B
Eufaula, AL 36027   205-687-4065

Bird List AL-3 Eufaula Summary
243 birds listed, no nesting data
Bird Chart pages 204-221

Totals by Season		s	S	F	W
Abundant	A	4	7	21	28
Common	C	74	54	49	50
Uncommon	U	76	40	62	44
Occasional	O	46	26	46	26
Rare	R	21	24	27	22

Endangered Species: Brown Pelican, Wood Stork, Bald Eagle, Peregrine Falcon, Piping Plover, Least Tern

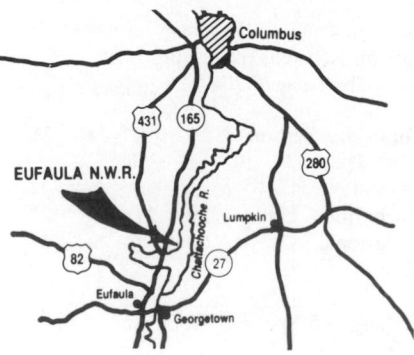

Refuge headquarters is located near the center of the refuge. Take U.S. Hwy. 431 north out of Eufaula 4.5 miles, and turn right onto Old State Hwy. 165. Drive 2.5 miles to the refuge office.

Habitat: 11,160 acres on the upper reaches of the Walter F. George Reservoir. Forty percent of the refuge is water. The remainder includes large tracts of land planted in winter grains, pine and hardwood forests, uplands, and marsh.

Egrets, herons, shorebirds, gulls, and terns, as well as the occasional alligator, feed and breed in the wetland areas. Upland areas are used for food and shelter by Bobwhites, Common Ground-Doves, and a variety of songbirds.

Area brochure, fishing, hunting, boating, auto tour, observation tower, photo blind, hiking. Lake Point Resort State Park, located adjacent to the refuge, offers a variety of facilities including a marina, golf course, swimming area, lodge, cabins, camping, and picnicking.
Spring, Fall, Winter

Wheeler 🖪 (office at refuge)
PO Box 1643
Decatur, AL 35602   205-353-7243
Entry Fee

The Wheeler office also administers the Blowing Wind Cave, Fern Cave, and Watercress Darter units.

Bird List AL-4 Wheeler Summary
271 birds listed, 87 nesting birds
Bird Chart pages 204-221

Totals by Season		s	S	F	W
Abundant	A	6	1	19	11
Common	C	9	68	21	69
Uncommon	U	93	44	77	36
Occasional	O	19	10	22	9
Rare	R	23	20	19	21

Endangered Species: Wood Stork, Bald Eagle, Peregrine Falcon, Piping Plover, Least Tern.

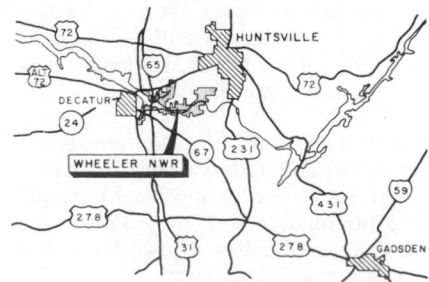

The refuge is located in the Tennessee River Valley just east of Decatur. The entrance is on the north side of Hwy. 67

about 1.5 miles east of its junction with U.S. Hwy. 31 and 2.5 miles west of its junction with I-65.

Habitat: 34,500 acres of deep river channels, creeks, tupelo swamps, open backwater embayments, hardwoods, pine uplands and agricultural fields.

Waterfowl peak in winter with over 50,000 ducks and 30,000 Canada Geese. The Blue-winged Teal migration reaches its peak during April as flocks of warblers and other small migrants pass through.

The August migration begins with Purple Martins congregating for their southward move. Most of the small bird migrants arrive and depart during October and November. Bald and Golden eagles may be seen in December.

Area brochure, hunting, fishing, mammals, amphibians and reptiles lists.
Spring, Fall, Winter

NATIONAL FOREST SERVICE
Map/Forests/City

△	Supervisor /Montgomery	205-832-4470
△2	Bankhead /Double Springs	205-489-5111
△3	Conecugh/Andalusia	205-222-2555
△4	Talladega/same	205-362-2909
△5	Tuskegee/same	205-727-2652

STATE AGENCIES

Game & Fish Division
Dept. of Conservation
& Natural Resources
64 North Union St.
Montgomery, AL   205-261-3469

Map/District/City

①	Tanner/Tanner	205-353-2634
②	Jacksonville /Jacksonville	205-435-5422
③	Tuscaloosa/Tuscaloosa	205-339-5716
④	Montgomery /Montgomery	205-261-3623
⑤	Forkland/Forkland	205-289-5631
⑥	Andalusia/Andalusia	205-222-5415
⑦	Jackson/Jackson	205-246-2165

Bureau of Tourism & Travel
532 South Perry St.   205-261-4169
Montgomery, AL 36104   800-252-2262

BIRDING HOTLINE
Statewide (Anchorage)   907-248-2473

LOCAL BIRDING GROUPS
Map/Chapter/City
- ① Anchorage Audubon/Anchorage
- ② Arctic Audubon/Fairbanks
- ③ Juneau Audubon/Juneau
- ④ Kenai Audubon/Kenai
- ⑤ Kodiak Audubon/Kodiak
- ⑥ Fairbanks Bird Club/Fairbanks

THE NATURE CONSERVANCY
Alaska Field Office
601 West Fifth Ave., Suite 550
Anchorage, AK 99501   907-276-3133

JOINT FEDERAL/STATE INFO CENTERS
There are three "Public Lands" Information Centers in Alaska. Their personnel can answer questions, provide literature, or direct you to the correct agency personnel for these seven state and federal agencies: The Alaska Div. of Tourism, Alaska Dept. of Natural Resources, Alaska Dept. of Fish & Game, Bureau of Land Management, National Park Service, U.S. Fish & Wildlife Service, and U.S. Geological Survey.

A new center is planned for Ketchican, Alaska, and tentatively scheduled to open in 1991. Winter hours are 10am to 5pm Tuesday through Saturday. Summer hours are usually 9am to 7pm seven days a week.

Alaska Public Land Information Center
605 West 4th Avenue
Anchorage, AK 99501   907-271-2737
The number for
deaf access (TTY) is   907-271-2738

Alaska Public Land Information Center
250 Cushman Street
Fairbanks, AK 99701   907-451-7352

Alaska Public Land Information Center
PO Box 359
Tok, AK 99780   907-883-5667

U.S. FISH & WILDLIFE SERVICE NATIONAL WILDLIFE REFUGES
U.S Fish & Wildlife Service Region 7
1011 East Tudor Road
Anchorage, AK 99503   907-786-3538

Alaska Overview
Alaska's refuges range in size from the 320,893-acre Izembek Refuge, to the 19.6-million-acre Yukon Delta. Nearly all of Alaska can be described as untouched wilderness. Only the Kenai and Tetlin refuges have normal road access. A boat or plane is required to visit their interior regions, and to reach any of the other refuges in Alaska.

The climate, short growing season, and general ecological conditions are harsh. The concentrations of fishes, birds, and mammals that visitors often read about are typically seasonal phenomena taking place only during migration, breeding, or spawning. Birding and recreation opportunities vary on each refuge and by season.

Be prepared for inclement weather and cool temperatures in the summer. Mosquitoes are most abundant after snow and ice ponds melt; they decrease in numbers from mid-summer through fall, to be replaced by gnats and noseeums. Insect repellent, headnet, and a screened tent are essential to avoid discomfort. Always take along adequate supplies for an unexpected overnight or extended visit to wait out bad weather, especially if dependant on a bush plane or boat for egress.

Caution: Always check with refuge personnel to determine access, which activities are allowed, and current visitor regulations.

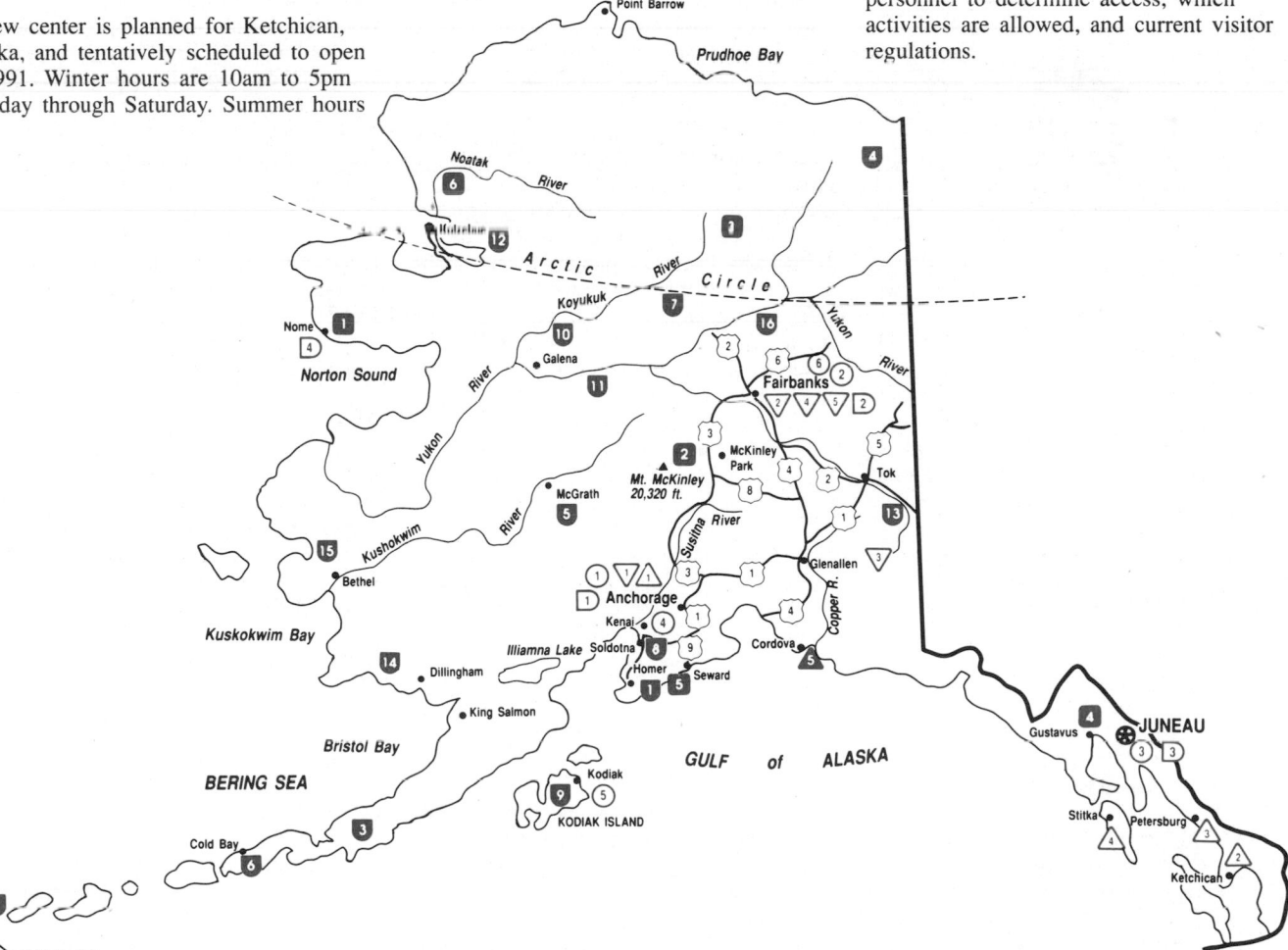

Safety tips: Become familiar with safety procedures and survival equipment. Know where emergency equipment is located on bush aircraft. Leave a travel plan describing your trip with a friend and notify them when you return. Boil all water before drinking and other uses, because Giardiasis a water-borne disease, is common in Alaska.

Maintain a safe distance from bears and moose, particularly when they have young offspring. Avoid using well-worn bear trails. Talk loudly or use noisemakers when hiking. Do not store food near your sleeping site and avoid camping near a food source, such as a salmon stream or berry patch.

When you contact any of the Alaska refuges be sure to request copies of the full color 17" by 24" brochure and map titled, "National Wildlife Refuges of Alaska", and "Summary of Regulations on Alaska Refuges". Both are available at no charge.

The small map shown below provides a perspective of the size of the state of Alaska against a background of the lower 48 states.

Alaska Maritime 1   (office in town)
202 West Pioneer Ave.
Homer, AK 99603   907-235-6546

Alaska Maritime includes the following units: Alaska Peninsula, Aleutian Islands, Bering Sea, Chukchi, and Gulf of Alaska. It stretches from the Aleutians in the west to Foster Island by the Canadian border in the east. The Aleutian Islands unit is listed and described separately.

Habitat: 3,557,032 acres on more than 2,400 islands, headlands, rocks, islets, spires, and reefs of the southern Alaskan coast, primarily in the Aleutians, include tundra, rain forest, cliffs, volcanoes, beaches, lakes, and streams. Over half of the refuge, 2.64 million acres, is designated as wilderness.

From 15 to 30 million marine birds use the refuge, nesting on rock ledges, boulder rubble, pinnacles, or in crevices or burrows. The specific nesting preference of each species permits them to nest in large colonies on small islands.

Area brochure. Boating, fishing, hunting, camping, and picnicking.
June through August best time depending on the Alaska Maritime unit.

Aleutian Islands Unit 2
Alaska Maritime
Naval Air Station Adak (Island)
PO Box 5251
FPO Seattle, WA   907-592-2406

Two bird lists are available. An Aleutian Islands bird checklist contains details on 127 species and subspecies, and lists 59 casual or accidental birds. The Adak Island checklist charts bird abundance by month and includes habitat codes. Thirty-four species are noted as "Asiatic" in origin. The Adak Island list was adapted to the Bird Chart format.

Bird List AK-1 Adak Island Summary
79 birds listed, 30 nesting birds
Bird Chart pages 204-221

Totals by Season		s	S	F	W
Common	C	20	15	16	18
Uncommon	U	17	18	13	12
Rare	R	29	20	31	22

Endangered Species: Bald Eagle, Peregrine Falcon
Rare/Limited Species: Least Auklet, Whooper Swan, Common Pochard, Tufted Duck, Far Eastern Curlew

The Aleutian Islands Unit consists of a chain of 200 steppingstone islands reaching out from the Alaska mainland for 1,000 miles into the Bering Sea toward Kamchatka Peninsula of the Soviet Union. The nearly 80 named islands in the refuge, including Adak Island, are in three groups from west to east: the Fox, Andreanof, and Near Islands.

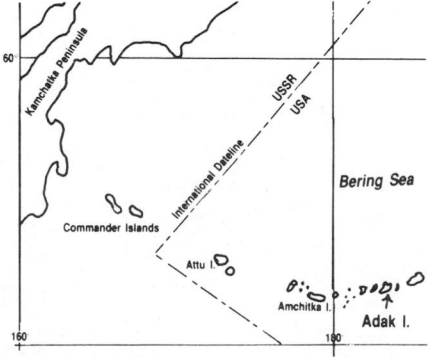

Habitat: A submarine mountain range with many active volcanoes runs under the Bering Sea between Alaska and Siberia. Many of the islands in this unit are the emergent peaks of that range. Larger islands show their geological heritage with lakes, streams, boulder beaches, rocky

cliffs, and reefs. Some of the islands have large areas covered by abandoned military installations.

The Aleutian Islands are best known for their many seabird colonies, some of which harbor thousands or even millions of birds. Among the nesting species are Northern Fulmars, both Red-legged and Black-legged kittiwakes, Arctic and Aleutian terns, Glaucous-winged Gulls, Fork-tailed and Leach's storm-petrels, and 12 species of alcids.

Waterfowl are found in large numbers around the islands. Breeding species include the Northern Pintail, Greater Scaup, Red-breasted Merganser, Common Eider, and "Common" Teal, the Eurasian subspecies of the Green-winged Teal. The "Aleutian" Canada Goose now nests only on Buldir Island, although this subspecies used to live on all of the Andreanof Island's as well.

Large rafts of wintering waterfowl are primarily composed of Oldsquaws, King Eiders, and Harlequin Ducks. Half of the world's Emperor Geese also winter on the Aleutian Islands.

Black Oystercatchers, Rock Sandpipers, and Red-necked Phalaropes nest on the islands throughout the refuge. Rock Ptarmigans are also common across most of the Aleutian Islands, while Willow Ptarmigans are common residents on Unimak.

Bald Eagles and "Peale's" Peregrine Falcons are the most common raptors. Gyrfalcons and Rough-legged Hawks also breed on the islands, but the Gyrfalcons are more commonly seen during the winter.

"Gray-crowned" Rosy Finches, Savannah, Fox, and Song sparrows, Lapland Longspurs, and Snow Buntings are the most abundant of the few North American passerines occurring in the Aleutians, which are better known for the Asiatic vagrants that can often be seen. These include Oriental Cuckoo, Eye-browed Thrush, Arctic Warbler, Siberian Rubythroat, Gray-spotted Flycatcher, White, Gray, and Yellow wagtails, and Brambling and Rustic buntings. Whooper Swan, Falcated Teal, Steller's Sea Eagle, Wood Sandpiper, Black-tailed Godwit, and Slaty-backed and Black-headed gulls have also been noted.

Area brochure, mammals list, hiking, camping, picnicking, hunting, fishing, trapping, cross-country skiing, and beachcombing. Some islands have restricted access in order to protect

wildlife.
Spring, Fall, Winter

Alaska Peninsula 3 & Becharof NWRs
PO Box 277
King Salmon, AK 99613   907-246-3339

The Alaska Peninsula and Becharof refuges provide habitat for 222 species of wildlife: 146 birds, 35 fishes, and 41 mammals. A list is available. Both refuges are located on the peninsula.

Habitat: 3,500,000 acres with an additional 1,200,000 in the Becharof Refuge. The refuge is on the south side of the Alaska Peninsula, overshadowed by the Aleutian Range. The peninsula has 14 volcanoes, nine of them active, that form part of the "Ring of Fire" around the Pacific Ocean. Towering mountains, broad valleys, fjords, tundra, glacial lakes, steep cliffs, and sweeping beaches offer a variety of birding opportunities.

About one-third of the Becharof Refuge is nationally designated wilderness, including Paule Bay. The bay is host to two large colonies of seabirds, and is part of the 400,000 acres of the Becharof Refuge that have been designated as a wilderness area.

Alaska Peninsula/Becharof brochure, boating, hunting, fishing (the world's record grayling was caught on the Peninsula Refuge), camping, picnicking.
Spring, Summer

Arctic 4   (office in town)
Federal Bldg. & Courthouse, Room 226
101 12th Avenue
Fairbanks, AK 99701   907-456-0250

This is the most northern of the wildlife refuges, located in the northeastern corner of Alaska adjacent to the Canadian border.

Habitat: 19,049,236 acres of undisturbed arctic habitat that is biologically self-sufficient. The Brooks Range, which forms part of the Continental Divide, has deep valleys which extend up to its glaciated peaks. The treeless tundra covers the plain that descends from the northern slope to the Arctic Ocean. A gravel reef lies between the shoreline and the Arctic ice pack. On the south slopes of the range the valleys are characterized by many lakes, sloughs, and wetlands. The vegetation ranges from stunted white spruce and balsam poplar in upland muskeg to denser, taller forests in the south.

A variety of birds are dependent on the refuge both for nesting and migration staging grounds. Golden Eagles, Rough-legged Hawks, Gyrfalcons, and Peregrine Falcons all build their nests on the cliffs. Various shorebirds, waterfowl, and loons nest around the tundra wetlands during June and July, and are preyed on by jaegers. Snowy Owls find their rodent prey, primarily lemmings, on the tundra.

In July and August thousands of waterfowl, particularly Oldsquaws and Snow Geese, gather at lagoons and estuaries. They follow various flyways south into Asia, Africa, and the South Pacific as well as North and South America. The only birds found on the north slope during the winter are ptarmigans, Snowy Owls, Common Ravens, Gyrfalcons, and American Dipper.

The only means of access to the refuge is by air. Commercial air service is available from Fairbanks to Fort Yukon, Arctic Village, and Kaktovik, which are the usual visitor jump-off points. There are no marked trails.

Area brochure. Boating, camping, hunting, fishing, river-running.
Summer, Fall

Innoko 5   (office in town)
PO Box 69
McGrath, AK 99627   907-524-3251

Innoko lies approximately 300 miles northwest of Anchorage in the central Yukon River Valley. The upper unit of this two-unit refuge lies between the Yukon River on the north and west, and the Kaiyuh Mountains on the east and south. The lower unit, which includes the middle portion of the Innoko River and its drainage, lies between the Yukon River on the west and the Kuskokwim Mountains on the east.

Habitat: 3,850,000 acres.
Upper unit - Most of the unit consists of black spruce muskeg, bogs, marshes, and wet meadows. Forests of white spruce, birch, aspen, and cottonwood grow near the Yukon River with stands of willow and alder in the wetter areas.

Lower unit - About half of the unit consists of black spruce muskeg, wet meadow, sedge or horsetail marshes, and numerous lakes and ponds. The other half has hills covered primarily with spruce and birch. White spruce, paper birch, and aspen grow on permafrost-free slopes. Stunted black spruce forests, with an understory of lichens, mosses, and shrubs, grow in the poorly-drained areas and on the northern slopes. A mixture of white spruce, paper birch, cottonwood, and aspen grows with willows and alders on the banks of the Yukon River.

The wetlands are used by more than 100,000 breeding waterfowl and shorebirds. Among the more numerous species are Greater White-fronted and "Lesser" Canada geese, Northern Pintails, American Wigeons, Northern Shovelers, scaups, scoters, Red-necked Grebes, Lesser Yellowlegs, and Hudsonian Godwits.

Area brochure. A 134-species bird list with species abundance and residency status is available on request. Camping or backpacking is strictly primitive; there are no facilities. Hunting, trapping. Access in summer is by float-plane and in the winter by ski-equipped airplane. McGrath is the most common access point.
Summer, Fall

Izembek 6   (office in town)
PO Box 127
Cold Bay, AK 99571   907-523-2445

Izembek is one of six locations designated as Ramsar Sites in the U.S.A. The refuge faces north, and is at the end of the Alaska Peninsula. Cold Bay is less than a mile from the refuge.

Habitat: 320,893 acres and approximately 38 miles in length, varying in width from 3 to 25 miles, with 500 square miles of land and 149 square miles of tidal waters. The refuge has U-shaped valleys, glaciers, snowfields, thermal springs, smoking volcanoes, and a number of lakes and rivers. The 5- by 30-mile Izembek Lagoon has one of the world's largest eelgrass beds, and provides food and shelter for many species.

The maritime climate is characterized by frequent storms with persistent clouds, high winds, and low temperatures. Average annual precipitation is 34 inches, and temperatures generally vary between 0° and 65° F. Fall is the wettest season and spring the driest.

Izembek was created primarily to serve the "Black" Brants that stage their fall migration at the lagoon. Approximately 200,000 "Black" Brants, nearly all of the North American population, arrive at Izembek Lagoon each fall from their nesting areas on the Yukon-Kuskokwim Delta and the Arctic coast and leave in early November.

The lagoon also feeds and rests most of the North American Emperor Goose population during the fall, as well as tens of thousands of "Taverner's" Canada and occasional "Cackling" Canada Geese. Spectacular concentrations of ducks and shorebirds join the geese in the fall. Northern Pintails, Mallards, Oldsquaws, Harlequin Ducks, and Rock Sandpipers are among the most common species, while Steller's Eiders are the most abundant duck wintering in the area.

Area brochure. A 142-species bird list with abundance and residency status is available. Foot trails, boating, hunting, fishing, camping, picnicking.
Spring, Summer, Fall, Winter

Kanuti 7   (office in town)
Federal Bldg. & Courthouse
Room 226
101 12th Avenue
Fairbanks, AK 99701   907-456-0329

Bird List AK-2 Kanuti Summary
153 birds listed, 144 nesting birds
Bird Chart pages 204-221

Totals by Season		s	S	F	W
Common	C	85	77	78	14
Uncommon	U	40	43	47	8
Rare	R	25	26	23	10

Endangered Species: Bald Eagle, Peregrine Falcon
Rare/Limited Species: Siberian Tit, Northern Wheatear

Located 150 miles northwest of Fairbanks straddling the Arctic Circle.

Habitat: 1,430,000 acres. The Kanuti Flats are an interior basin of rolling plains between the Kanuti and Koyukuk rivers, interspersed with thousands of lakes, ponds, streams, and marshes.

The waterfowl nesting on the wetlands number in the hundreds of thousands, and include "Greater" White-fronted and Canada geese. Various shorebirds also breed on the wetlands, while Wilson's Warblers, Boreal Chickadees, Common and Hoary redpolls, Great Horned Owls, and both eagles live in the uplands.

Boating, hunting, fishing, camping, picnicking.
Summer

Kenai 8   (office at refuge)
PO Box 2139
Soldotna, AK 99669   907-262-7021

Bird List AK-3 Kenai Summary
145 birds listed, 100 nesting birds
Bird Chart pages 204-221

Totals by Season		s	S	F	W
Abundant	A	6	10	3	0
Common	C	50	41	41	9
Uncommon	U	52	44	54	11
Rare	R	34	30	39	18

Endangered Species: Bald Eagle, Peregrine Falcon

Kenai may be reached by car and is located 110 highway miles (20 air miles) southwest of Anchorage on Hwy. 1. To reach the headquarters from the entrance, continue south through Soldotna and turn left after crossing the Kenai River Bridge, then follow signs to the headquarters.

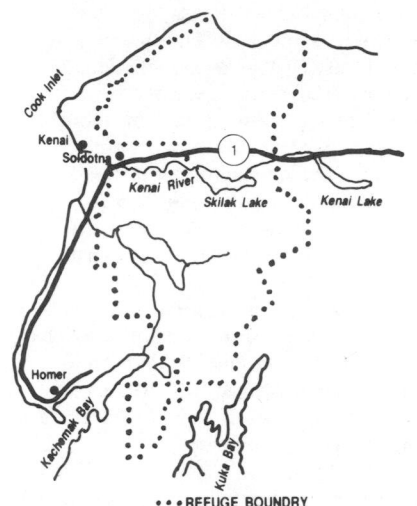

•••REFUGE BOUNDRY

Habitat: 1,970,000 acres on the western slopes of the Kenai Mountains and in the forested lowlands that border Cook Inlet. The lowlands have spruce and birch forests intermingled with hundreds of lakes. The Kenai Mountains, with their glaciers, rise to more than 6,000 feet. The range of different habitats, from mountain and tundra to wetland and forest, provides a sample of Alaska's variety.

Birds readily recognized on migration or over-wintering in the south may look quite different on northern nesting grounds. Certain birds may be found in unexpected surroundings, such as some sandpipers and other shorebirds, which nest in Alaska's mountains. All three ptarmigan species can also be found breeding on high slopes.

The proximity of Siberia allows birders to see rare species that can be seen in North America only in Alaska. There may be the opportunity to add Asiatic species to a life list.

Many species of waterfowl use the Chickaloon Flats as a stopover point during spring and fall migration. Trumpeter Swans nest by isolated lakes. The refuge also provides nesting habitat for marsh and water birds, passerines, hawks, and owls.

Area brochure, canoe and hiking trail brochures, aircraft regulations with map. Boating, hunting, fishing, trapping, camping, scenic drive.
Spring, Summer, Fall

Kodiak 9   (office in town)
1390 Buskin River Road
Kodiak, AK 99613   907-487-2600

Bird List AK-4 Kodiak Summary
162 birds listed, 94 nesting birds
Bird Chart pages 204-221

Totals by Season		s	S	F	W
Abundant	A	19	16	13	9
Common	C	65	55	58	38
Uncommon	U	38	39	44	27
Rare	R	29	24	37	33

Endangered Species: Bald Eagle, Peregrine Falcon
Rare/Limited Species: Black-footed Albatross, Laysan Albatross, Mottled Petrel, Parakeet Auklet

Located 30 miles south off the coast of the mainland. Kodiak is the largest island in the Gulf of Alaska. Access is by air or boat.

Habitat: 1,865,000 acres on the southwestern two-thirds of Kodiak, and parts of Uganik and Afognak islands. Most of the refuge is close to one of the many water sources, including seven major watersheds, 11 large lakes, shallow marshes, bogs, salt flats, and the oceans tidal zones. Fireweed, salmonberry, blueberry, and rose bushes interspersed with thickets of willow, alder, and elderberry cover the islands interiors.

Kodiak is a major wintering area for over a million seabirds. More than 200 pairs of Bald Eagles nest on Kodiak's cliffs and trees, and are year-round residents.

The lowlands provide food and nesting grounds for a variety of shorebirds. Thousands of seabirds nest on the shores, including Arctic and Aleutian terns, Harlequin Ducks, Black Scoters, and both goldeneyes.

Rock Sandpipers and Black Turnstones reside on the beaches. Shoreline rocks and cliffs are home to Black-legged Kittiwakes, Horned and Tufted puffins, Black Oystercatchers, Common Murres, and Black and Pigeon Guillemots.

Other common island birds include Northwestern Crows, Black-billed Magpies, Common Ravens, Glaucous-winged Gulls, Fox, Golden-crowned, and Savannah sparrows, Wilson's Warblers, Golden-crowned Kinglets, Winter Wrens, Pine Siskins, American Pipits, Rock and Willow ptarmigans, and Lapland Longspurs.

Area brochure, recreation cabin guide, visitors guide, sport-fishing guide. Plant,

fish, and marine mammals lists and bear brochures. Boating, hiking, hunting, fishing, camping, picnicking.
Spring, Summer, Fall

Koyukuk ⑩   (office in town)
PO Box 287
Galena, AK 99741   907-656-1231

Located 320 miles northwest of Fairbanks in west-central Alaska, just north of the confluence of the Koyukuk and Yukon rivers.

Habitat: 3,550,000 acres of the Koyukuk River floodplain, hills with boreal forests, and Nogahabara Dunes, a 10,000-acre active dune field. Fourteen rivers, hundreds of streams, and over 15,000 lakes also irrigate the basin. Lowland forests are gradually replaced with tundra vegetation at about 3,000 feet of elevation.

About 75,000 Canada and Greater White-fronted geese and 250,000 ducks, primarily Northern Pintails, American Wigeons, scaups, and scoters, are fledged each year. Approximately 150 Trumpeter Swans breed at this refuge, which is at the northwestern limit of the species. Migrating geese gather in large flocks on the sandbars of the Yukon River in the spring and fall.

Area brochure, boating, fishing, hunting, camping, picnicking.
Summer

Nowitna ⑪   (office in town)
PO Box 287
Galena, AK 99741   907-656-1231

Located 150 miles west of Fairbanks in the central Yukon Valley.

Habitat: 1,560,000 acres which range from flat lowlands with wetlands to rolling hills with alpine tundra. The forests are primarily white and black spruce, but also include balsam poplar, paper and other birches, alders, and willows. The Nowitna River, a nationally designated wild river, flows through the refuge.

A variety of waterfowl species can be seen. Trumpeter Swans nest on the refuge and Canada and Greater White-fronted geese are present. American Wigeons, Mallards, Northern Pintails, Northern Shovelers, Green-winged Teals, Common Goldeneyes, and Greater and Lesser scaups are the most common breeding ducks, although Buffleheads, Common and Red-breasted mergansers, Canvasbacks, Barrow's Goldeneyes, and all three scoters are also present in smaller numbers.

Pacific and Common loons breed in large numbers. Sandhill Cranes are present. Spotted Sandpipers, Lesser Yellowlegs, Semipalmated Plovers, and Common Snipe are among the more common shorebirds. The Mew Gull, common across Eurasia and the Pacific northwest, breeds at this refuge with Herring and Bonaparte's gulls. Arctic Terns nest on sandbars of the Nowitna River.

Several birds of prey inhabit the refuge including the Bald Eagle, Northern Harrier, and Rough-legged and Red-tailed hawks. The Red-tailed is the most common and may occur in a light or dark (Harlan's) phase. Five species of owls occur at the refuge, including the Northern Hawk and Boreal owls.

Belted Kingfishers and Bank Swallows nest in river banks. Cliff, Tree, and Violet-green swallows are also present. The most common woodpeckers are Downy, Hairy, Northern Three-toed, and Black-backed, as well as the Northern Flicker. Ruffed and Spruce grouse and Willow and Rock ptarmigans represent the grouse family. Common Ravens and Gray Jays remain on the refuge throughout the winter.

Among the many passerines breeding at the refuge, American Robins, Swainson's and Gray-cheeked thrushes, Wilson's and Yellow warblers, Northern Waterthrushes, and American Tree, White-crowned, and Savannah sparrows are the most abundant.

Area brochure, hunting, fishing, river floating, boating, trapping, hiking, camping.
Visit in late May or early June to avoid the worst of the mosquitos. July generally has the best weather but insect populations peak at that time.

Selawik ⑫   (office in town)
PO Box 270
Kotzebue, AK 99752   907-442-3799

Located 360 miles northwest of Fairbanks on the Arctic Circle.

Habitat: 2,150,000 acres of estuaries, lakes, river deltas, and tundra slopes are dominated by the extensive system of tundra wetlands between the Waring Mountains and Selawik Hills.

A large number of migratory waterbirds return from North and South America, Asia, Africa, and Australia, including hundreds of thousands of ducks, to breed and rest at Selawik.

Area brochure, various species lists. A 185-species bird list with abundance and

residency status is available. Boating, hunting, fishing, river rafting, hiking, camping, trapping.
Summer

Tetlin ⑬   (office in town)
PO Box 155
Tok, AK 99780   907-883-5312

Bird List AK-5 Tetlin Summary
171 birds listed, 122 nesting birds
Bird Chart pages 204-221

Totals by Season		s	S	F	W
Common	C	46	40	16	5
Uncommon	U	74	69	66	15
Occasional	O	22	28	31	12
Rare	R	28	24	12	7

Endangered Species: Bald Eagle, Peregrine Falcon
Rare/Limited Species: Siberian Tit, Northern Wheatear, Yellow Wagtail

The northeast boundary of the refuge parallels the Alaska Highway beginning 25 miles southeast of Tok.

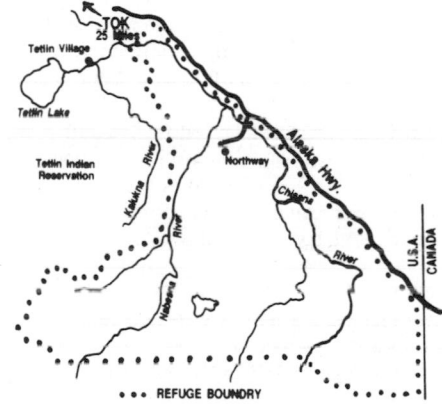

Habitat: 700,000 acres of the Upper Tanana River Basin. Most of the refuge is an undulating plain interspersed with hills and mountains, forests, ponds, lakes, and extensive marshes. The Chisana and Nabesna rivers are prominent and join to form the Tanana River. Although the most extensive habitat is black spruce forest, other woodlands include mixed riparian-coniferous, deciduous, and riparian forests.

Tetlin is important both to breeding species and to those migrating from northern breeding grounds to their wintering range. Some of the species that breed in the area are Sandhill Cranes, Trumpeter Swans, Canada Geese, American Wigeons, Green-winged and Blue-winged teals, Mallards, Northern Pintails, Northern Shovelers, and Greater and Lesser scaups.

Bald Eagles, Red-tailed Hawks, Northern

Harriers, Pacific Loons, and Lesser Golden-Plovers are among the many birds that migrate through Tetlin with passerines during spring and fall.

During spring migration Ruby-crowned Kinglets and Blackpoll and Wilson's warblers may be seen in the lowland forests.

Area brochure, hunting, fishing, hiking, boating, trapping, river rafting.
Spring, Summer, Fall

Togiak 🄄   (office in town)
PO Box 270
Dillingham, AK 99576   907-842-1063

Bird List AK-6 Togiak Summary
185 birds listed, 114 nesting birds
Bird Chart pages 204-221

Totals by Season		s	S	F	W
Common	C	83	73	74	11
Uncommon	U	40	43	48	15
Rare	R	54	56	41	8

Endangered Species: Bald Eagle, Peregrine Falcon
Rare/Limited Species: Garganey, Mottled Petrel, Spectacled Eider, Common Ringed Plover, Bristle-thighed Curlew, Long-toed Stint, Red-legged Kittiwake, Parakeet Auklet, Least Auklet, Yellow Wagtail, McKay's Bunting, Common Rosefinch

Togiak is located between Kuskokwim and Bristol bays in southwestern Alaska.

Habitat: 4,105,000 acres. The northern 2.3 million acres, which are designated wilderness, include wetlands, open water, meadows, tundra, mountains, and forests. The coastline ranges from cliffs and offshore pinnacles to sandy beaches. Some geological features on the refuge were caused by glaciers, such as the deep lakes in the Wood River Mountains and Togiak Valley, a two-mile-long "tuya" formed by lava erupting under a glacier.

Waterfowl and shorebirds return from wintering areas in Siberia, Japan, Mexico, South America, New Zealand, and the South Pacific to rest or breed at Togiak. More than a million seabirds inhabit the offshore waters and cliffs near Capes Newenham and Pierce during the summer.

Waterfowl are attracted to eelgrass beds and aquatic invertebrates in Chagvan and Nanvak bays and the berries on nearby uplands. Common, King, and Steller's eiders, Northern Pintails, Greater Scaups, "Black" Brants, and Emperor, Greater White-fronted, and Canada geese are the most common species.

Millions of seabirds, including Horned Puffins, murres, cormorants, and gulls, rest on the coastal headlands.

The interior portions of the refuge host Bald Eagles and Northern Goshawks, both year-round residents, Rough-legged Hawks, Gyrfalcons, Peregrine Falcons, Ospreys, and Short-eared and Snowy owls.

Area brochure, river map and brochure. Boating, hunting, fishing, hiking, rafting, river running.
Summer

Yukon Delta 🄅
PO Box 346
Bethel, AK 99559   907-543-3151

A 208-species bird list is available on request. It contains species residency status, and documentation on unusual bird sightings.

Habitat: 19,624,458 acres of the 26-million-acre delta of the Yukon and Kuskokwim rivers. Nunivak Island and 50 associated islands totaling 1,700 square miles, extending 20 miles into the Bering Sea southwest of the delta, are also included.

The many habitats found in the delta region include tundra marshes, alpine fell-fields, uplands with peaks 2,000 to 4,000 feet high, volcanic cones, spruce, birch, and poplar forests, and coastal plain, with numerous lakes, streams, sloughs, and bays. Cliffs, dunes, sandy and rocky beaches, and saltwater lagoons characterize the islands' coastlines.

The delta habitat is used by more than 100 million shorebirds and water birds of over 50 different species during their breeding and migration seasons. The nesting waterfowl include three-quarters of the Emperor Geese in the world, a large proportion of the "Black" Brant population, and most of the "Cackling" Canada Goose and "Pacific" Greater White-fronted Goose. Ducks outnumber geese by a factor of three to one, and the most numerous species are Greater Scaup, Oldsquaw, and Northern Pintail. Spectacled and Common eiders breed in smaller numbers. Loons, grebes, gulls, jaegers, plovers, sandpipers, Common Snipes, and Sandhill Cranes also nest on the delta's coastal plain.

Bristle-thighed Curlews breed in the uplands north of the delta, known as the Andreafsky Wilderness, as do various Asian species such as the Northern Wheatear. The Kisaralik River canyon in the Kilbuck Mountains hosts ten raptor species, including Golden Eagles and

Gyrfalcons.
The island cliffs support large seabird colonies. Kittiwakes and murres are the most common nesters, and puffins, auklets, guillemots, and cormorants breed in smaller numbers. Aleutian Terns can be found at the lagoons, eiders and Harlequin Ducks molt in the sheltered bays, and Rosy Finches find their food along the beaches.

Area brochure. Boating, hiking, hunting, fishing, camping, picnicking.
Spring, Summer, Fall

Yukon Flats 🄆
Federal Bldg. & Courthouse
Room 226
101 12th Avenue
Fairbanks, AK 99701   907-456-0440

The refuge, which lies along the Arctic Circle, extends 220 miles from east to west, and provides a prime example of ecological gradations over its 120 miles from north to south.

Habitat: 8,630,000 acres of wetland basin between the Brooks Range to the north and the White Mountains on the south. The Yukon River winds 300 miles through the wetland, which also has 40,000 lakes, ten major streams, and innumerable ponds and sloughs that irrigate the marshes, meadows, and muskeg. White spruce, paper birch, and aspen extend from the hillsides down into the flats.

More than 100 species have been seen on the flats. Millions of waterfowl from Africa, Asia, and North and South America arrive in May to nest at the refuge. The most numerous species are Northern Pintail, American Wigeon, scaups, and scoters. Mallards, Northern Shovelers, Green-winged Teals, Canvasbacks, and Canada and Greater White-fronted geese nest in smaller numbers. Sandhill Cranes, Common, Red-throated, and Pacific loons, and various grebes are common, and an occasional Trumpeter Swan may also be seen. A few species of hawks, owls, grouse, and woodpeckers, as well as Gray Jays and Common Ravens, are year-round residents.

Area brochure, hunting, fishing, hiking, camping, river floating. The area is remote and isolated. Variable weather and water levels can combine to make a visit dangerous for those not prepared and equipped.
Spring, Summer, Fall

NATIONAL PARK SERVICE
National Park Service Alaska Region
2525 Gambell Street
Anchorage, AK 99503   907-261-2690

Note: The Alaska Overview, Cautions, and Safety tips regarding the National Wildlife Refuges also apply when visiting National Parks and Preserves. Most Federal and state lands are only accessible by plane, boat, or overland (no roads). Over 90 percent of the areas described in this chapter are part of the national wilderness preservation system.

Bering Land Bridge ❶
National Preserve
PO Box 220
Nome, AK 99762   907-443-2522

2,784,960 acres on the Seward Peninsula in northwestern Alaska, this preserve has ash explosion craters and lava flow areas that are rare in the Arctic. Some 112 migratory birds have been recorded at the preserve and a few nest here in large numbers.

Preserve brochure, fishing, river floating, boating, and canoeing. No federal facilities.

Denali National Park ❷
& Preserve   907-683-2294
PO Box 9
Denali National Park, AK 99755

The 4,716,726-acre Denali contains Mt. McKinley, North America's highest mountain at 20,320 feet. Caribous, Dall sheep, moose, grizzly bears, timber wolves, and 157 species of birds may be seen.

A 12-page newspaper "Denali Alpenglow" describes the range of recreation opportunities in the park.

Gates of the Arctic ❸
National Park & Preserve
201 First Ave., PO Box 74680
Fairbanks, AK 99707   907-456-0281

With 7,523,888 acres, this is one of the largest parks in the world and lies north of the Arctic Circle. It includes a portion of the Central Brooks Range, which is the northernmost extension of the Rocky Mountains.

Color brochure with park map. No federal facilities.

Glacier Bay National Park ❹
& Preserve
Bartlett Cove
Gustavus, AK 99826   907-697-2230

3,225,284 acres of great tidewater glaciers and a dramatic range of plant communities, including rocky terrain covered by ice less than 200 years ago and a lush temperate rain forest, are home to a large variety of wildlife, including eagles.

Color brochure with park map.

Kenai Fjords National Park ❺
PO Box 1727
Seward, AK 99664   907-224-3874

The park entrance of 670,000-acre Kenai Fjords is located within 10 miles of Seward. This park includes one of the four major ice caps in the U.S., the 300-square-mile Harding Ice Field, and coastal fjords.

A rich, varied rain forest and adjoining marine waters are home to tens of thousands of breeding birds as well as a multitude of sea lions, sea otters, and seals. Seabirds, including Horned and Tufted Puffins, Common Murres, Black-legged Kittiwakes, and other gulls, breed on the steep cliffs and spend the winter months near the rocky shores.

Color brochure with park map. Limited federal facilities.

Noatak National Preserve ❻
PO Box 287
Kotzebue, AK 99752   907-442-3890

The 6,574,481-acre Noatak River basin is the largest mountain-ringed river basin in the nation that is still virtually unaffected by man. The 65-mile-long Grand Canyon of Noatak is a transition zone and migratory route for plants and animals between subarctic and arctic environments. The flora diversity is the greatest in the northern latitudes.

Preserve brochure. No federal facilities.

NATIONAL FOREST SERVICE
National Forest Service Alaska Region
Federal Bldg., PO Box 21628
Juneau, AK 99802   907-586-8863

Map/Forest/City
⚠	Chugach/Anchorage	907-271-2500
⚠	Tongass/Ketchikan	907-225-3101
⚠	Tongass/Petersburg	907-772-3841
⚠	Tongass/Sitka	907-747-6671

Copper River Delta
c/o Chugach National Forest
201 E. 9th Avenue, Suite 206
Anchorage, AK 99501   907-271-2500

The Copper River Delta, which is a proposed Western Hemisphere Shorebird Reserve Network site in the Chugach National Forest, is considered the most important shorebird staging area in the western hemisphere during May. Around 20 million shorebirds, primarily Dunlins and Western Sandpipers, feed at the delta after their long northward migration before dispersing to their breeding grounds.

BUREAU LAND MANAGEMENT
BLM State Office
222 West 7th Avenue #13
Anchorage, AK 99513   907-271-5555

Map/District/City
▽	Anchorage/same	907-267-1246
▽	Arctic/Fairbanks	907-356-5130
▽	Glenallen/same	907-267-1369
▽	Kobuk/Fairbanks	907-356-5384
▽	Steese-White Mountain /Fairbanks	907-356-5367

STATE AGENCIES

Alaska Department of
Wildlife Conservation
1255 West 8th Street
PO Box 3-2000
Juneau, AK 99802   907-465-4190

Map/Region/City
1	So. Central/Anchorage	907-267-2193
2	Interior/Fairbanks	907-456-5156
3	South East/Juneau	907-465-4265
4	Arctic/Nome	907-443-2825

Alaska Division of Tourism
PO Box E-001
Juneau, AK 99811   907-465-2010

BIRDING HOTLINES
Phoenix   602-832-8745
Tucson   602-798-1005

LOCAL BIRDING GROUPS
Map/Chapter/City
① Huachuca Audubon/Sierra Vista
② Maricopa Audubon/Phoenix
③ Northern Arizona Audubon/Sedona
④ Prescott Audubon/Prescott
⑤ Tucson Audubon/Tucson
⑥ White Mountain Aud./Show Low
⑦ Yuma Audubon/Yuma
⑧ Southwest Hawk Watch/Tucson

THE NATURE CONSERVANCY
Arizona Field Office ⬦FO
300 E. University Blvd., Suite 230
Tucson, AZ 85705   602-622-3861

Hassayampa River ⬦1
(office at visitor center)
PO Box 1162
Wickenburg, AZ 85358   602-684-2772
Suggested non-member visitor donation.

Bird List AZ-1 Hassayampa Summary
227 birds listed, 79 nesting birds
Bird Chart pages 204-221

Totals by Season		s	S	F	W
Abundant	A	2	1	3	4
Common	C	55	43	41	38
Uncommon	U	8	32	11	61
Occasional	O	20	17	34	18
Rare	R	34	4	28	16

Endangered Species: Bald Eagle
Rare/Limited Species: Bridled Titmouse

Approximately 50 miles northwest of Phoenix and 3 miles southeast of Wickenburg. Entrance on west side of road along Rte. 60/89/93 at milepost 114. Wooden preserve sign spans entrance road and split-rail fence lines the driveway.

Habitat: 333-acre desert including a 5-mile stretch of the river and one of the best remaining stands of cottonwood-willow riparian woodlands in Arizona, a 3-acre palm-fringed lake, and a spring-fed marsh. Over 230 bird species have been recorded here, including the Bridled Titmouse, a Mexican species found in a few areas of Arizona and New Mexico.

Self-guided tours and scheduled guided activities and birdwalks (reservations advised). Closed Mondays and Tuesdays. Bookstore and visitor center in old adobe residence, which is a State Historic Landmark.

Tour map, calendar of events.
Spring, Fall

Mile Hi/Ramsey Canyon ⬦2
(office at preserve)
RR #1, Box 84
Hereford, AZ 85615   602-378-2785
Suggested non-member visitor donation.

Located 87 miles southeast of Tucson, 10 miles south of Sierra Vista. From I-10 take Rte. 90 south and stay on the bypass around Sierra Vista. At the intersection with Rte. 92, continue south for 6 miles to Ramsey Canyon Road and turn west for 4 miles to Mile Hi. The last half-mile is a narrow dirt road that crosses a creek and is not suitable for trailers or motorhomes.

Habitat: 300 acres at 5,525 to 6,300 feet, bounded on three sides by the Coronado National Forest. The environment here is cool and moist due to a stream that flows throughout the year, and the canyon's high walls and east-west orientation.

The preserve is noted for its 14 species of hummingbirds seen between April and October. More than 150 species have been seen at Ramsey Canyon, including Sulphur-bellied Flycatcher, Painted Redstart, and Elegant Trogon, species normally occurring in Mexico.

Six housekeeping cabins for rent are booked two years in advance during the hummingbird season. Only 14 cars, in addition to cabin resident vehicles, can be accommodated at one time. Be sure to phone in advance for reservations as visitor carrying capacity is limited.

Preserve brochure and reservation form, book store and visitor center. Bird list, guided tours, and other activities available.
Spring, Summer

Muleshoe Ranch ⬦3   (office at ranch)
RR #1, Box 1542
Willcox, AZ 85643   602-384-2626

About 110 miles from Tucson and 30 miles northwest of Willcox. Take the first exit ramp (#336) west of Willcox which

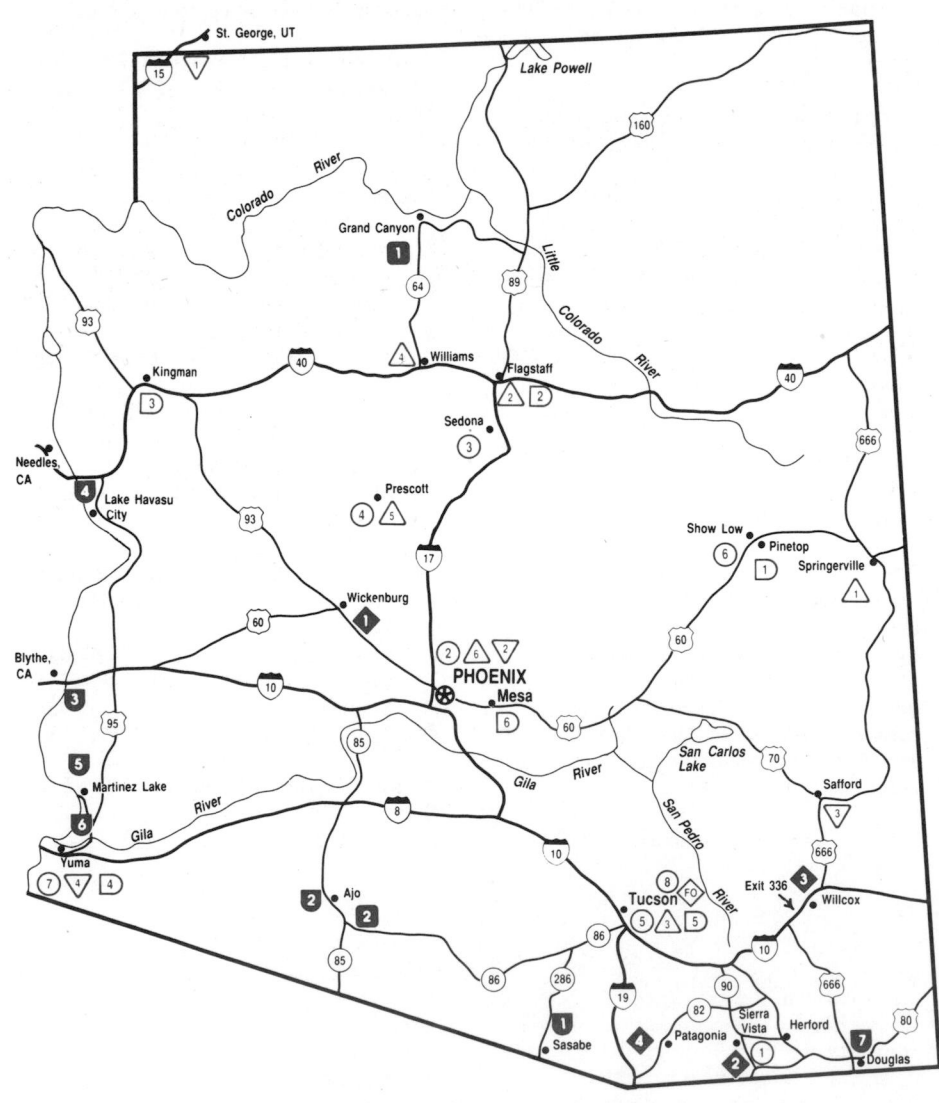

crosses over I-10 immediately. Turn right and continue along the frontage road which turns north. At intersection with Taylor and Airport roads (first stop sign), turn left (west) on Airport. Drive about 15 miles on this gravel road to a "Y" junction just beyond a set of mailboxes, and bear right at the junction. Continue approximately 14 miles to the Muleshoe parking area, which is across the wash from headquarters. There are several washes to cross but a regular car can make the trip unless it has rained; then the last 15 miles are impassable even with four-wheel drive. Call ahead about road conditions before visiting this preserve.

Habitat: 54,660 acres at 3,300 to 7,660 feet on a desert mountaintop. The vegetation ranges from Sonoran desert scrub to ponderosa pine and Arizona cypress forest on the mountains. A mosaic of land owned and cooperatively managed with the U.S. Forest Service and Bureau of Land Management.

Each spring Common Black-Hawks, Gray and Zone-tailed hawks, and hundreds of songbirds return to nest in the lush riparian woodlands. Over 150 bird species occur here regularly.

Area leaflet, bird list, picnicking, camping. Spring, Fall

Patagonia-Sonoita Creek Sanctuary ◆
PO Box 815
Patagonia, AZ 85624   602-394-2400

Located about 62 miles south of Tucson. In Patagonia turn west off Rte. 82 onto 4th Ave., then turn left on Pennsylvania Ave. Continue across Sonoita Creek until you reach the parking area at the main gate.

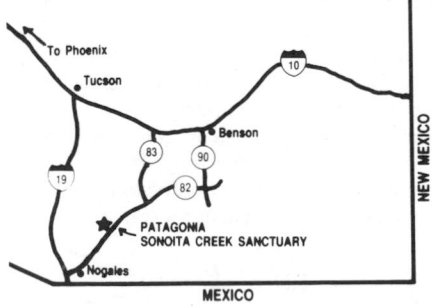

Habitat: 309 acres of flood plain at 4,000-foot elevation and between the Santa Rita and Patagonia mountains. The creek flows year-round, nourishing the cottonwoods and willows that line its banks.

The sanctuary was acquired with the assistance of the Tucson Audubon Society. Over 275 bird species have been sighted

here, many of which range principally in Mexico. Birds of note are the Gray Hawk, Northern Beardless-Tyrannulet, Rose-throated Becard, and Vermilion Flycatcher.

The sanctuary is noted for the wide variety of warblers that are seen during spring and fall migrations, as well as the 22 species of flycatchers. The elusive Montezuma Quail can be seen occasionally in the highland scrub and open woodlands by the patient birder.

Sanctuary brochure, bird list available. Spring

U.S. FISH & WILDLIFE SERVICE NATIONAL WILDLIFE REFUGES

Buenos Aires 🔳   (office at refuge)
PO Box 109
Sasabe, AZ 85633   602-823-4251

Buenos Aires is one of the more remote refuges in the United States. From Tucson, take Hwy. 86 southwest for 16 miles to junction with Hwy. 286. Turn left and take Hwy. 286 south for about 41 miles to refuge entrance. Then take refuge road 2.5 miles to headquarters. Hwy. 286 continues for 6.5 miles, ending at Sasabe on the Mexican border. The refuge is about one hour from Tucson.

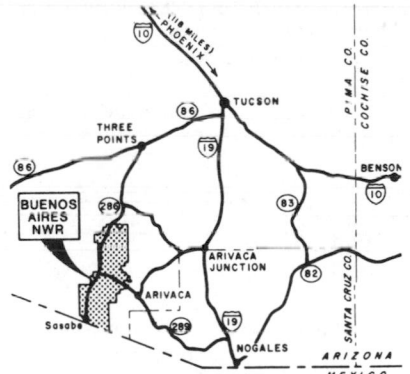

Habitat: About 112,500 acres that are primarily rolling desert with large mesquite grassland. A large basin running north-south is surrounded by mountain ranges. There are 125 lakes, ponds, and marsh (cienga) areas. Lake Aguirre is the largest body of water and covers 125 acres when full.

Buenos Aires is the only refuge where it is possible to see four species of quails, Montezuma, Scaled, and Gambel's quails and "Masked" Bobwhite, in one location. The "Masked" Bobwhite is an endangered subspecies of the Northern Bobwhite. It was extinct in the United States for 90 years and has recently been reintroduced from Mexico to this refuge.

The bird population increases during

migration in April and May and as ducks and shorebirds begin nesting. Other species of interest include the Northern Beardless-Tyrannulet, Rose-throated Becard, and Hooded Oriole.

A large number of waterfowl winter at the refuge and, because of its location, Mexican species seldom seen in the U.S. are potential visitors.

No brochure. A bird checklist is available but does not have seasonal abundance information. Camping, hunting, auto tour road. RV park in Arivaca 5 miles from refuge.
Spring, Summer, Fall, Winter

Cabeza Prieta 🔳   (office in town)
1611 North 2nd Ave.
Ajo, AZ 85321   602-387-6483

Bird List AZ-2 Cabeza Summary
149 birds listed, 42 nesting birds
Bird Chart pages 204-221

Totals by Season		s	S	F	W
Common	C	43	16	39	26
Uncommon	U	29	17	26	19
Occasional	O	18	10	34	15
Rare	R	29	5	27	13

Caution: No one may enter the refuge without obtaining a valid Refuge Entry Permit and signing a Military Hold Harmless Agreement. Permits are available at the refuge office in Ajo.

Most of the refuge is within the boundaries of the Barry M. Goldwater Air Force Range. When the air-to-air range airspace above the refuge is used to practice aerial gunnery on towed targets, all public entry to the refuge under the air-to-air range is prohibited. The refuge is located directly west of Ajo. Caution: The refuge includes some of the most arid desert in North America. Roads are rough, requiring 4WD and high ground clearance.

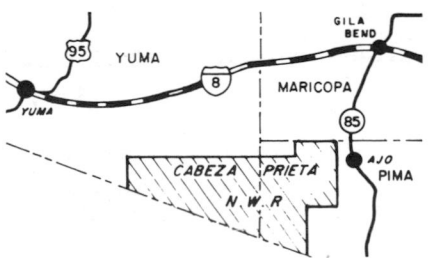

Habitat: 860,000 acres in southwestern Arizona, the refuge shares a 56-mile international border with Sonora, Mexico. Rugged mountains and broad valleys dotted with sand dunes and lava flows. Although most of the refuge's numerous mountains rise less than 3,000 feet above the valleys, they are extremely rugged.

The best birding can be found in the vegetation along the washes, particularly in areas where there is a permanent source of water. The best of these areas occur in the northeast section of the refuge, near Ajo.

Most of the birds on the refuge are migratory. Numerous warblers, swallows, and flycatchers, including Say's Phoebes, are seen during migration periods. Other species such as Turkey Vulture, American Kestrel, and Gambel's Quails are commonly seen year-round.

Refuge brochure, amphibian and reptile list, camping, hunting. No potable water. Some birds begin spring migration in late February and fall migrations may start in late July.
Spring, Winter

Cibola ❸ (office at refuge)
PO Box AP
Blythe, CA 92226   602-857-3253

Bird List AZ-3 Cibola Summary
182 birds listed, 47 nesting birds
Bird Chart pages 204-221

Totals by Season		s	S	F	W
Abundant	A	3	4	4	3
Common	C	77	39	84	53
Uncommon	U	48	25	43	30
Occasional	O	34	22	41	31
Rare	R	3	5	0	13

Endangered Species: Wood Stork

Located along the lower Colorado River 20 miles south of Blythe, California. Approximately two-thirds of the refuge is in Arizona and one-third in California.

Office is in the northeast corner of the refuge. Access is south from Palo Verde on Hwy. 78 for approximately 16 miles to the refuge entry sign. Follow the signs to refuge headquarters.

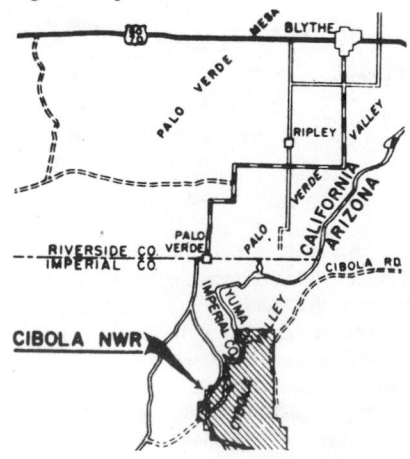

Habitat: 16,627 acres in a 12-mile-long refuge. The main portion of the refuge is alluvial river bottom with dense growths of salt cedar, mesquite, and arrowweed. The Colorado River flows through the refuge in both a dredged channel and a portion of its original channel. The refuge includes 2,000 acres of farmland and 785 acres of desert foothills and ridges. Present wetlands include the 600-acre Cibola Lake, approximately 10 miles of Colorado River backwaters, seasonally flooded croplands, the Hart Mine Marsh.

Although there are birds to be observed year-round, the greatest variety of species may be seen during the spring and fall migrations.

Nesting birds include the Great Egret, Great Blue Heron, Black-crowned Night-Heron, Least Bittern, Clapper Rail, and White-winged Dove. The endangered "Yuma" Clapper Rail is found in suitable marshes throughout the refuge. Upland species include Gambel's Quail and Greater Roadrunner.

The refuge is noted for its summer population of egrets, herons, doves, and the Phainopepla, and its winter populations of Canada Geese, "Greater" Sandhill Cranes, the largest of the three subspecies, and many ducks, primarily Northern Pintail, American Wigeon, and Green-winged Teal.

Refuge brochure, auto tour route, hunting, fishing.
November to late January

Havasu ❹ (office in town)
1406 Bailey St., Box A
Needles, CA 92362   619-326-3853

Bird List AZ-4 Havasu Summary
248 birds listed, 80 nesting birds
Bird Chart pages 204-221

Totals by Season		s	S	F	W
Abundant	A	4	3	8	8
Common	C	82	62	89	56
Uncommon	U	62	37	58	39
Occasional	O	34	24	38	29
Rare	R	32	17	38	38

Endangered Species: Wood Stork, Bald Eagle, Peregrine Falcon

Havasu refuge headquarters is in Needles, Ca. The refuge extends along the Colorado River in three units located between Needles, CA, and Lake Havasu City, AZ. These are the Topock Marsh, Topock Gorge, and Bill Williams units. A refuge "Public Use Regulations" brochure with local maps shows refuge access points in Arizona and California.

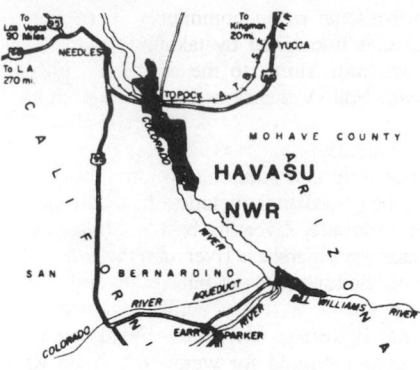

Habitat: 44,746 acres with 300 miles of shoreline along the Colorado River and its backwaters, sloughs, swamps, and delta. The wide washes and rocky ridges of the adjacent desert extend to the river banks.

Because of its southerly location, the refuge is a wintering area and stopover point for migrating birds. Five species of wrens breed at the refuge, including Cactus, Canyon, and Rock wrens.

This is a heavily used refuge with water-oriented activities attracting many visitors. There are special regulations regarding use of the Colorado River and float trips through Topock Gorge.

Refuge brochure with unit maps and regulations, mammals list, hunting, fishing, boating, camping.
Winter

Imperial Valley ❺ (office at refuge)
Red Cloud Mine Rd.
PO Box 72217
Martinez Lake, AZ 85365   602-783-3371

Bird List AZ-5 Imperial Summary
223 birds listed, 67 nesting birds
Bird Chart pages 204-221

Totals by Season		s	S	F	W
Abundant	A	6	6	7	7
Common	C	62	34	63	43
Uncommon	U	59	32	51	34
Occasional	O	52	43	65	52
Rare	R	13	14	20	19

Endangered Species: Wood Stork, Bald Eagle, Peregrine Falcon

The refuge headquarters is located 3 miles

north of the resort community of Martinez Lake. It is reached by taking Hwy. 95 north from Yuma, to the Martinez Lake Road. Follow the signs to the office.

Habitat: 25,765 acres. The refuge is 30 miles long and straddles the California-Arizona border. It includes a stretch of the Colorado River, its backwater lakes, ponds and marshes, river bottomland, and lower Sonoran Desert habitat.

Imperial Refuge is important as a wintering ground for western "Great Basin" Canada Geese and many species of ducks. Among the nesters are Great Blue and Green-backed herons, Great Egrets, both bitterns, White-winged Doves, and the "Yuma" Clapper Rail, an endangered subspecies.

Area brochure, mammals list, hunting, fishing, boating, hiking. Lookout points and observation tower.
Spring, Fall

Kofa ⑥   (office in town)
356 West First Street
PO Box 6290
Yuma, AZ 85366   602-783-7861

Bird List AZ-6 Kofa Summary
156 birds listed, 25 nesting birds
Bird Chart pages 204-221

Totals by Season		s	S	F	W
Common	C	45	26	35	19
Uncommon	U	17	15	24	16
Occasional	O	36	24	47	30
Rare	R	12	10	29	19

Endangered Species: Brown Pelican, Peregrine Falcon

There are two entrances to the refuge. From Yuma, take Hwy. 95 north to milepost 77 for the first entrance, or 12 miles further for the other entrance. Most refuge roads are not maintained and many are passable only by 4WD.

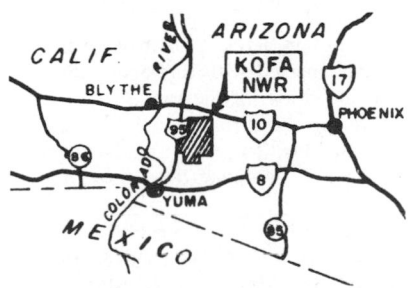

Habitat: 660,000 acres of desert habitat that includes broad, gently sloping foothills as well as sharp, needle-point peaks. Ranges contain natural potholes and man-made waterholes that hold run-off water.

Although the refuge was established for the protection and management of desert bighorn sheep that live in the Kofa and Castle Dome Mountains, the small, widely scattered water holes have attracted a surprising number of birds. The breeding species include Golden Eagle, Costa's Hummingbird, and Verdin.

Caution: No drinking water. Be aware of desert travel hazards, and cautious around the many shafts, tunnels, and open pits remaining from past mining activity.

Area leaflet with map, mammal list, foot trails, picnicking, camping, hunting.
November to April

San Bernardino ⑦   (office in town)
Route 1, Box 228R
Douglas, AZ 85607   602-364-2104

Note: To visit the refuge, call or write for a special use permit.

Headquarters is located in the Forest Service building on St. Rte. 80 in Douglas. Entrance to the refuge is currently through the Johnson Historical Museum Property. At the present time there is no manager at San Bernardino NWR. The refuge is scheduled to open in 1990.

Habitat: 2,309 acres at 3,720 to 3,920 feet elevation. The eastern and western uplands drop abruptly to flat bottomlands that run north-south. Part of the Yaqui River headwaters flow through the valley toward western Chihuahua and eastern Sonora, Mexico.

The uplands consist of 900 acres of Chihuahuan desert scrub and 577 acres of desert grassland. Bottomlands include 508 acres of mesquite bosque, 254 acres of fallow fields, and 70 acres of riparian forest, riparian scrub, marshlands, and aquatic habitats.

This refuge will be of particular interest to birders because of its proximity to Mexico. The water resources attract species rarely found in the United States.

Bird list.
Spring, Fall

NATIONAL PARK SERVICE

Grand Canyon National Park ❶
PO Box 129
Grand Canyon, AZ 86023   602-638-7888

1,218,375 acres, including 177.7 miles of the Colorado River, the Grand Canyon, and parts of Glen Canyon and the Lake Mead National Recreation Area.
A free newspaper "The Guide" contains current information about recreation opportunities here.

Organ Pipe Cactus ❷
National Monument
Route 1, Box 100
Ajo, AZ 85321   602-387-6849

On 330,688 acres of Sonoran Desert, plants and animals found nowhere else in the United States are protected.
Brochure with map, bird list available.

NATIONAL FOREST SERVICE
Map/Forest/City

△	Apache-Sitgreaves/	
	Springerville	602-333-4301
△2	Coconino/Flagstaff	602-527-7400
△3	Coronado/Tucson	602-629-6483
△4	Kaibab/Williams	602-635-2681
△5	Prescott/Prescott	602-445-1762
△6	Tonto/Phoenix	602-225-5200

BUREAU LAND MANAGEMENT
BLM State Office
3707 North 7th St., PO Box 16563
Phoenix, AZ 85011   602-241-5504

Map/District/City

▽	Arizona Strip/	
	St. George, UT	801-673-3545
▽2	Phoenix/Phoenix	602-863-4464
▽3	Safford/Safford	602-428-4040
▽4	Yuma/Yuma	602-726-6300

STATE AGENCIES

Arizona Game & Fish Comm. HQ
2222 W. Greenway Road
Phoenix, AZ 85023   602-942-3000

Map/Region/City

①	Pinetop/Pinetop	602-367-4281
②	Flagstaff/Flagstaff	602-774-5045
③	Kingman/Kingman	602-753-3300
④	Yuma/Yuma	602-344-3436
⑤	Tucson/Tucson	602-628-5376
⑥	Mesa/Mesa	602-981-9400

Arizona Office of Tourism
1480 E. Bethany Home Rd., #180
Phoenix, AZ 85014   602-542-8687

BIRDING HOTLINE

Statewide   501-753-5853

LOCAL BIRDING GROUPS
Map/Chapter/City
1. Aud. Soc. of Central Arkansas /Little Rock
2. Dogwood Trails Audubon/Ft. Smith
3. Garland County Aud./Hot Springs
4. Greers Ferry Aud./Heber Springs
5. Little Red River Aud./Fairfield Bay
6. Mena Nature Club/Mena
7. Northwest Arkansas Audubon /Fayetteville
8. Ozark Audubon/Mountain Home
9. Petit Jean Audubon/Conway
10. Three Rivers Audubon/Pine Bluff

THE NATURE CONSERVANCY

Arkansas Field Office FO
300 Spring Bldg., Suite 717
Little Rock, AR 72201   501-372-2750

Note: Information on the Cossatot, Moro Bottoms, Railroad Prairie, and Warren Prairie preserves is also available from the Arkansas Natural Heritage Commission office at 225 East Markham St., Little Rock, AR 72201. Phone 501-371-1706

Cossatot River State Park I and Natural Area
Contact Stan Speight,
Resident Park Ranger
Route 1, Box 170-A
Wickes, AR 71973   501-385-2201

4,300 acres. Map available, hiking trails under construction, campground and comfort stations planned. Picnicking, canoeing, fishing.
Spring, Fall, Winter

Note: Land acquired in cooperation with the Arkansas State Park Department and Arkansas Heritage Commission. The Conservancy is transferring ownership to the state in several installments.

Electric Island ②
118 acres - Contact Field Office

Electric Island in Lake Hamilton is close to Hot Springs and accessible only by boat. Interpretive trail under construction. Picnicking, fishing, boating and water skiing.
Spring, Summer, Fall, Winter

Moro Bottoms ③
173 acres - Contact Field Office

Co-owned and managed by The Nature Conservancy and Arkansas Natural Heritage Commission. Hiking trails under construction. Self-guided walking trail. Map available. Picnicking.
Fall

Railroad Prairie ④ State Natural Area
256 acres - Contact Field Office

Acquired cooperatively with Arkansas Natural Heritage Commission which now owns and manages the area. Map available, brochure planned, picnicking.
Spring, Fall

Warren Prairie ⑤
304 acres - Contact Field Office

Map and plant list available, picnicking.
Spring, Fall

U.S. FISH & WILDLIFE SERVICE NATIONAL WILDLIFE REFUGES

Northeast Arkansas RC Refuge Complex
PO Box 279
Turrell, AR 72384   501-343-2595

A refuge administrative office and information resource for Big Lake, Cache River, and Wapanocca NWR's. The office is located at the Wapanocca refuge.

Big Lake   (office at refuge)
PO Box 67
Manila, AR 72442   501-564-2429

See Bird List AR-3 Wapanocca Summary page 40 and Bird Chart pages 204-221

Refuge office is located 2 miles east of Manila or 18 miles west of Blytheville on St. Hwy. 18. The refuge extends from St. Hwy. 18 north 10.5 miles to the Missouri state line.

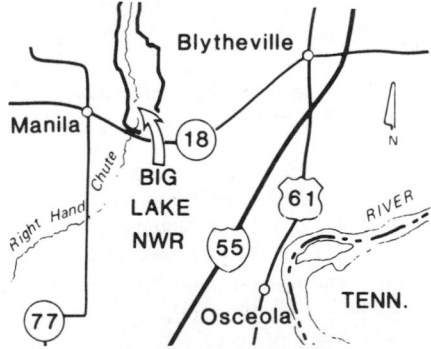

Habitat: 11,038 acres. Primarily open water interspersed with timbered swampland. Most of the refuge is under water during the spring floods of March, April, and May. Towering stands of pure virgin cypress dominate the landscape.

November to March are the best months for waterfowl, hawks, and eagles, while March through May are good for sandpipers, Yellow-billed Cuckoos, and migrating warblers. Indigo Buntings, "Bullock's" Northern Orioles, and Barred Owls are among the breeding species.

Big Lake, in the path of the Mississippi

Flyway, attracts over 100,000 migratory waterfowl each year and Mallards account for 90 percent of them. Wood Ducks and Hooded Mergansers are among the few ducks that are year-round residents.

There has been a recent increase in diving ducks, primarily Canvasbacks and Ruddy Ducks, and Bald Eagles.

Area brochure, foot trail, auto tour route, interpretive displays, hunting, fishing, boating (no motors).
Spring, Summer, Fall, Winter

Cache River ② (office at Turrell)
c/o Northeast Arkansas Refuge Complex
PO Box 279
Turrell, AR 72384 501-343-2595

See Bird List AR-3 Wapanocca Summary page 40 and Bird Chart pages 204-221

A part of the Northeast Arkansas Refuge Complex, Cache River NWR contains numerous tracts of land along the river and Bayou DeView in the counties of Jackson, Woodruff, Prairie, and Monroe.

Access to many tracts is through private lands and all refuge visitors should obtain permission to cross private land to reach refuge lands.

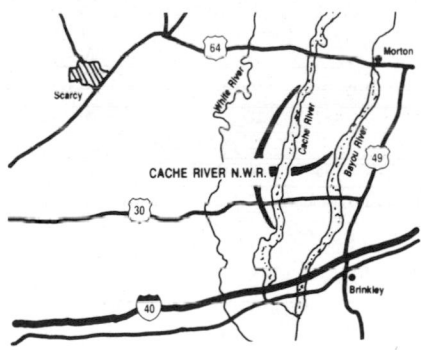

Habitat: The primary objectives of the refuge are to provide habitat for migratory waterfowl and preserve some of the few remaining tracts of bottomland and hardwoods in the middle and lower Cache River Basin.

No public-use facilities, but the public may observe and photograph wildlife throughout the year. Parts of the refuge area are closed to public use from November through February.

Fishing, hunting.
Spring, Summer, Fall, Winter

Felsenthal ③ (office at refuge)
PO Box 1157
Crossett, AR 71635 501-364-3167
Also headquarters for Overflow NWR.

Bird List AR-1 Felsenthal Summary
211 birds listed, 96 nesting birds
Bird Chart pages 204-221

Totals by Season		s	S	F	W
Abundant	A	15	11	11	12
Common	C	74	53	69	50
Uncommon	U	65	32	65	34
Occasional	O	32	17	37	19
Rare	R	15	7	10	9

Endangered Species: Wood Stork, Bald Eagle, Peregrine Falcon, Least Tern, Red-cockaded Woodpecker

Major road access to Felsenthal is via U.S. Hwy. 82, which runs east/west roughly bisecting the refuge between Strong and Crossett. Refuge headquarters is located approximately 5 miles west of Crossett on the highway.

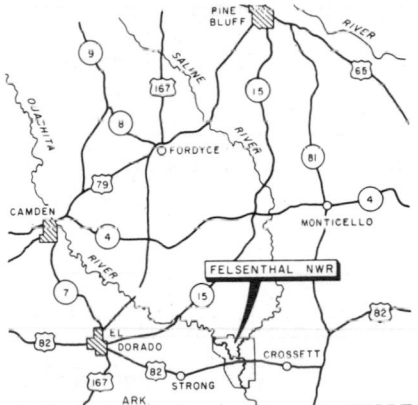

Habitat: 64,755 acres at 50 to 70 feet elevation, with about 50,000 acres of bottomland hardwood forests. A variety of water bodies ranging from the Ouachita and Saline Rivers to creeks, sloughs, oxbow lakes are used by Wood Ducks and overwintering waterfowl.

High water levels on the Ouachita River in the fall flood the bottomland and hardwood forests, thereby attracting large flocks of waterfowl. The Bald Eagle is an occasional winter visitor usually present from November to February. Wood Storks are abundant during the summer and fall, while the Red-cockaded Woodpecker is a year-round resident.

Area brochure, fishing, hunting, camping, boating, wildlife observation.
Fall, Winter

Holla Bend ④ (office in town)
115 S. Denver St.
PO Box 1043
Russellville, AR 72801 501-968-2800
Entry Fee

Bird List AR-2 Holla Bend Summary
206 birds listed, no nesting data
Bird Chart pages 204-221

Totals by Season		s	S	F	W
Abundant	A	12	9	12	12
Common	C	69	48	58	38
Uncommon	U	35	21	37	21
Occasional	O	51	18	50	29
Rare	R	11	6	17	4

Endangered Species: Wood Stork, Bald Eagle, Peregrine Falcon, Least Tern

From Russellville take St. Hwy. 7 south, crossing the Arkansas River at Dardanelle. Continue on Hwy. 7 for 3 miles to junction with St. Hwy. 154. Turn left on 154 for about 2 miles to the refuge gate.

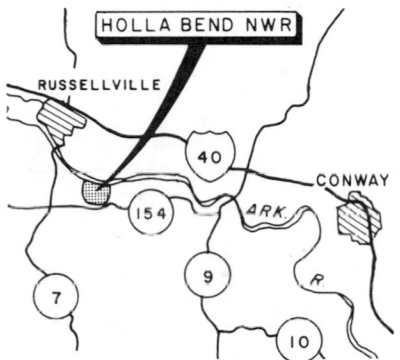

Habitat: 6,368 acres. When the Arkansas River channel was straightened for navigation, an island between old and new channels was created, which is the refuge area. There is water in the old channel and several shallow water impoundments. Much of the area is in cropland to provide feeding and resting areas for migrating and wintering waterfowl.

The refuge is in the transition area of eastern and western birds. Greater Roadrunners reside in limited numbers and the Scissor-tailed Flycatcher is common from spring through fall. Bald Eagles frequent the refuge from November to March. An occasional Golden Eagle may be observed.

Pools and mudflats attract a variety of egrets, herons, and shorebirds in season. In winter the refuge may host upwards of 10,000 Canada Geese, the largest wintering population of this species in Arkansas.

Alligators were reintroduced and a small population survives in the refuge lakes and larger permanent ponds.

Area brochure, mammal list, observation tower and wildlife trail, 8-mile auto tour, fishing, archery hunting.
Spring, Summer, Fall, Winter

Overflow ⑤ (office at Felsenthal refuge)
c/o Felsenthal NWR
P.O. Box 1157
Crossett, AR 71635 501-364-3167

See Bird List AR-1 Felsenthal Summary page 39 and Bird Chart pages 204-221

From Wilmot take St. Rd. 52 west to the refuge boundary. The road ends just inside the refuge. From Crossett, take U.S. 82 east 8 miles to junction with St. Rd. 81. Take St. Rd. 81 south approximately 6 miles to junction with St. Rd. 52, then turn left (east) on St. Rd. 52 to the refuge boundary.

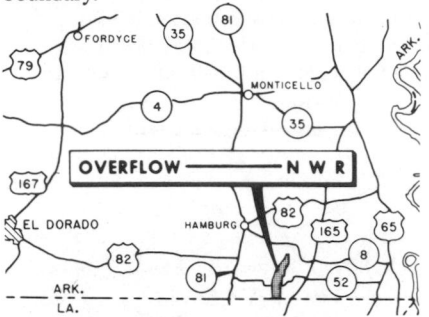

Habitat: 10,000 acres of bottomland hardwood forests, sloughs, creeks, bayous and open fields.

Wood Ducks, Mallards, and other waterfowl populations depend on bottomland habitat such as that of Overflow Refuge.

Area brochure, hunting.
Fall, Winter

Wapanocca 6   (office at refuge)
PO Box 279
Turrell, AR 72384   501-343-2595

Bird List AR-3 Wapanocca Summary
227 birds listed, 68 nesting birds
Bird Chart pages 204-221

Totals by Season		s	S	F	W
Abundant	A	8	4	7	8
Common	C	97	52	83	45
Uncommon	U	51	27	64	25
Occasional	O	27	14	27	16
Rare	R	33	9	34	19

Endangered Species: Wood Stork, Bald Eagle, Peregrine Falcon, Least Tern

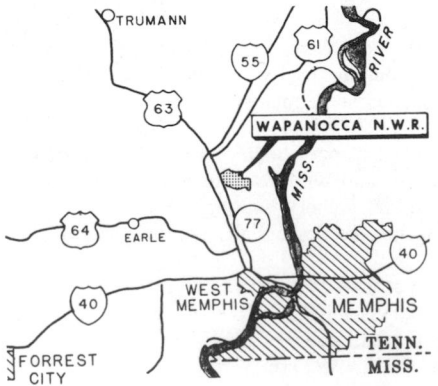

Take Turrell-Twist exit from I-55 about 16 miles north of West Memphis, at Hwy. 42. Go east on Hwy. 42 for 2 miles (crossing Hwy. 77). The refuge office (Northwest Arkansas Refuge Complex) is past the railroad overpass and on the right.

Habitat: 5,485 acres. The heart of the refuge is 600-acre Wapanocca Lake, a shallow old oxbow of the Mississippi River. Surrounding the lake is 1,200 acres of cypress and willow swamp. The rest of the refuge is equally divided between remnants of bottomland hardwood forests, and croplands of the refuge's farm unit.

January brings peak numbers of Canada Geese and large numbers of various ducks. Bald Eagles roost in cypress trees. In February Red-tailed Hawks are common. American Kestrels and Northern Harriers may be seen. The warbler migration begins in March. Prothonotary Warblers nest in swamp areas and Mississippi Kites fly over from fields during May. In August numerous swallows pursue their insect prey over the lake and the warbler fall migration begins.

Auto trail, boat trail, observation platform, fishing, hunting. Public boat ramp located 2 miles south of the refuge headquarters.
Spring, Summer, Fall, Winter

White River 7   (office in town)
704 Jefferson St., PO Box 308
DeWitt, AR 72042   501-946-1468

Bird List AR-4 White River Summary
231 birds listed, 86 nesting birds
Bird Chart pages 204-221

Totals by Season		s	S	F	W
Abundant	A	8	1	6	10
Common	C	68	42	53	38
Uncommon	U	72	48	67	35
Occasional	O	50	20	45	21
Rare	R	23	15	18	21

Endangered Species: Wood Stork, Bald Eagle, Peregrine Falcon, Least Tern

Open to the general public from March 1 through October 31.

Access is by way of Hwys. 1, 17, and 44. Check with refuge personnel prior to visit because of weather, road conditions, and often extended periods of high water.

Habitat: 113,380 acres at 150-foot elevation include 101,000 acres of bottomland hardwood forest, 11,180 acres of lakes, streams, and impoundments, and 1,200 acres of farmland and recreational areas. Most of the area is subject to flooding several months of each year.

Located on the White River a few miles above its confluence with the Mississippi River, the refuge ranges from 3 to 10 miles wide and extends along the White River for approximately 65 miles. Wildlife habitat is dominated by 13 different forest types containing 31 major tree species.

Thousands of ducks and geese winter in the area and Wood Ducks occur year-round. Large numbers of Bald Eagles are present during the winter.

Sizable populations of birds such as Downy, Pileated, and Red-headed woodpeckers, Blue Jay, Tufted Titmouse, Northern Cardinal, and Rufous-sided Towhee are permanent residents. Many others use this refuge during their spring migration, including warblers and shorebirds. Yellow-crowned Night-Herons, Least Bittern, and King Rail are less common breeders.

Area brochure, amphibians and reptiles list, hunting, fishing, camping, boating, boat ramps, hiking, auto trail route, wildlife observation points.
Spring, Summer, Fall (to October 31st)

NATIONAL FOREST SERVICE
Map/Forest/City

△1	Ouachita/Hot Springs	501-321-5202
△2	Ozark-St. Francis /Russellville	501-968-2354
△3	St. Francis/Marianna	501-295-5278

STATE AGENCIES

Arkansas Game & Fish Commission
Information Department
2 Natural Resources Drive
Little Rock, AR 72205   501-223-6351

In Arkansas there are no district or regional agency offices. Agency personnel are assigned to and reside in each county. Information department specialists can answer your questions or refer you to other agencies or private groups.

Department of Parks & Tourism
#1 Capitol Mall
Little Rock, AR 72201   800-482-8999
from out of state   800-643-8383

LOCAL BIRDING GROUPS
Map/Chapter/City

1. Altacal Audubon/Chico
2. Buena Vista Audubon/Vista
3. Central Sierra Audubon/Columbia
4. Coachella Valley Audubon
   /Rancho Mirage
5. Conejo Valley Aud./Thousand Oaks
6. Eagle Lake Audubon/Susanville
7. Eastern Sierra Audubon/Bishop
8. El Dorado Audubon/Long Beach
9. Fresno Audubon/Fresno
10. Golden Gate Audubon/Berkeley
11. Kern Audubon/Bakersfield
12. Kern River Valley Audubon
    /Wofford Hts.
13. La Purisima Audubon/Lompoc
14. Laguna Hills Audubon/Laguna Hills
15. Lake Almanor Audubon
    /Lake Almanor Peninsula
16. Lake Tahoe Audubon/S. Lake Tahoe
17. Los Angeles Audubon/Los Angeles
18. Los Padres Audubon/Santa Monica
19. Madrone Audubon/Santa Rosa
20. Marble Mountain Aud./Greenview
21. Marin Audubon/Mill Valley
22. Mendocino Audubon/Little River
23. Monterey Peninsula Audubon/Carmel
24. Morro Coast Audubon/Morro Bay
25. Mt. Diablo Audubon/Walnut Creek
26. Mt. Shasta Area Aud./Mt. Shasta
27. Napa-Solano Audubon/Vallejo
28. North Cuesta Audubon/Atascadero
29. Ohlone Audubon/Hayward
30. Palomar Audubon/Escondido

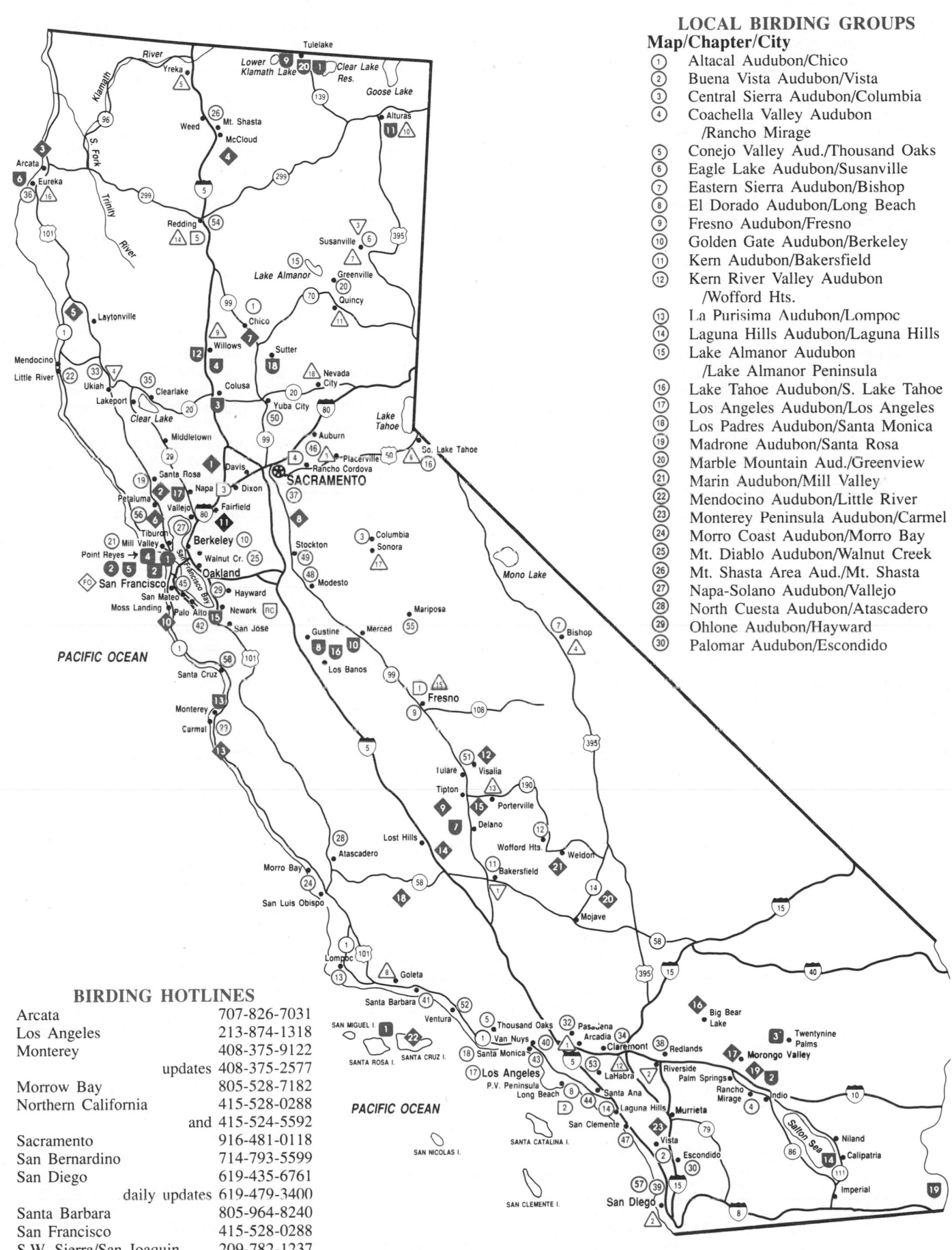

BIRDING HOTLINES

Arcata	707-826-7031
Los Angeles	213-874-1318
Monterey	408-375-9122
updates	408-375-2577
Morrow Bay	805-528-7182
Northern California	415-528-0288
and	415-524-5592
Sacramento	916-481-0118
San Bernardino	714-793-5599
San Diego	619-435-6761
daily updates	619-479-3400
Santa Barbara	805-964-8240
San Francisco	415-528-0288
S.W. Sierra/San Joaquin	209-782-1237

Map/Chapter/City

NATIONAL AUDUBON SOCIETY

Richardson Bay Audubon ❶
Sanctuary & Education Center

376 Greenwood Beach Road
Tiburon, CA 94920   415-388-2524
Entrance fee
Open Wednesday–Sunday, 9a.m. to 5p.m.

Bird List CA-1 Richardson Summary
171 birds listed, no nesting data
Bird Chart pages 204-221

Totals by Season		s	S	F	W
Abundant	A	5	4	6	18
Common	C	68	46	77	61
Uncommon	U	44	21	36	27
Rare	R	22	20	27	27

Endangered Species: Brown Pelican

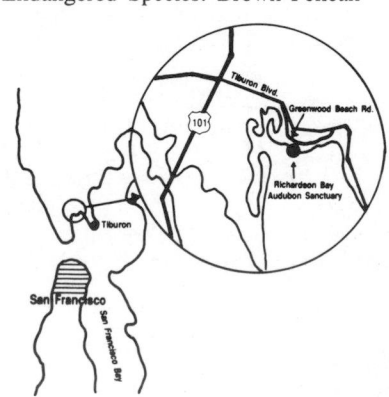

Take Rt. 101 north from San Francisco to Tiburon Blvd. Turn east and continue to Greenwood Beach Road, turning right to the Sanctuary and Center.

Habitat: 900 acres of tidal bay lands and 11 land acres, which include a freshwater pond, grasslands, and coastal scrub.

Richardson Bay supports large numbers of wintering and migrating shorebirds and waterfowl. Spring and summer months are less active but support nesting landbirds. The sanctuary regularly produces unusual species during spring and fall migrations.

The Book Nest at the Center is one of the most extensive natural history bookstores. Children's programs, guided and self-led natural history field trips. Area brochure, walking trail, boating (May–September), fishing. The Richardson Bay bird checklist charts abundance detail by month and was edited for use in the Bird Chart.

Winter is the best time.

SPECIAL BIRDING AREA

San Francisco Bay WHSRN ❷

c/o Point Reyes Bird Observatory
4990 State Route One
Stinson Beach, CA 94970   415-868-1221

San Francisco Bay was included as part of the network in 1990. The 1988 shorebird counts indicated that 800,000 shorebirds visited in spring and 400,000 during the fall migration.

The Point Reyes Bird Observatory has a banding station at the end of Mesa Road in Bolinas. The public is welcome at the station or at the office at Stinson Beach.

THE NATURE CONSERVANCY

California Field Office
785 Market Street
San Francisco, CA 94103   415-777-0487

A new directory to the California Preserves by Dwight Holing, titled *California Wild Lands*, is available from the field office for $9.95. It contains detailed descriptions, the historical background, and larger access maps for all 23 preserves, and includes a 15-page species list.

North

Boggs Lake ❶

Located north of Nampa near Cobb and between Middletown and Kelseyville.

From Cobb, north of Napa, take Bottle Rock Road northeast for 6.5 miles. Watch carefully on right for Harrington Flat

Road. Turn right and go 1 mile. Lake is on left. Park on left shoulder at preserve entrance. Contact the Conservancy office in San Francisco for details on April through June tours.

Habitat: This 141-acre preserve lies 8 miles southwest of Clear Lake. Boggs Lake is a vernal pool, part of a million-year-old lava flow near the base of Mt. Hannah on the eastern flank of the Mayacamas Mountains. In late spring and early summer as seasonal runoff recedes, blooming wildflowers form concentric rings of color around the shrinking pool.

A total of 142 birds have been identified at Boggs Lake. Brown Creepers, Violet-green Swallows, and Purple Martins nest in the mixed forest. Pileated, Downy, and Hairy woodpeckers tap trees for insects. Western Bluebirds hover over the open meadow, and Common Poorwills occasionally nest in its dry rocky edges. Various migrating warblers forage at the preserve.

Common Ravens and Turkey Vultures feed on carrion and dead carp. Great Blue Herons catch frogs and other amphibians along the shore. Green-backed Herons and Wilson's Phalaropes feed at Boggs Lake during migration.

Willow Flycatchers pursue their prey in the manzanita growing along the banks. Olive-sided Flycatchers may be heard singing higher in the trees.

The open water of the preserve attracts waterfowl in winter, including Mallards, Wood Ducks, and Hooded Mergansers. American Coots and Red-winged Blackbirds frequent the tules. Ospreys and Bald Eagles arrive in winter.

Fairfield Osborn ❷

6543 Lichau Road
Penngrove, CA 94951   707-795-5069

Take Hwy. 101 north through Petaluma to the Cotati exit (Sonoma State exit). Follow Cotati Road east to Petaluma Hill

Road. Turn right and go about 0.5 mile to Roberts Road. Turn left onto Roberts, then right onto Lichau Road. When almost to the end of Lichau Road, stop at parking area by mailbox 6543.

Habitat: 210 acres covered with oaks, evergreens, and patches of chaparral and grassland. A perennial stream and its four tributaries run through the preserve, and riparian communities thrive along their banks. Nearly 300 vascular plants grow in the wide variety of habitats.

Soras and Virginia Rails hide in the nettle, sedge, and rushes on the marshes. They may respond to clapping hands with a call that sounds like a cross between a laugh and a slurping pig. In their search for sap and insects attracted by the sap, Red-breasted Sapsuckers have punctured their regular rows of holes in the trunks of an old willow planted at the end of the marsh. Red-winged Blackbirds and Black Phoebes roost at Cattail Pond, and Wood Ducks and Mallards can be seen paddling and feeding on plants and insect larvae.

The oak wildlands at Fairfield Osborn are a rewarding birding spot. In late spring flocks of Pine Siskins pass through on their northward migration. The well-camouflaged Brown Creeper spirals its way up trunks, probing the bark with its curved bill for insect prey. Plain Titmice, Chestnut-backed Chickadees, and Bushtits fly through the forest in flocks, while Steller's and Scrub jays can be heard scolding. Western Screech-Owls and Great Horned Owls are best observed where the trail emerges from the riparian forest, roosting during the day and flying out at night to hunt their rodent prey. Cooper's, Red-tailed, and Sharp-shinned hawks, Golden Eagles, and Turkey Vultures ride the thermals.

Maps, brochures on request. Open daylight hours on weekends only.
Year-round wildflower display.
Spring and Fall for bird migration.

Lanphere-Christensen Dunes
6800 Lanphere Road
Arcata, CA 95521   707-822-6378

Contact Preserve office for use permit and about Saturday tours (September–June). The preserve stretches between the mouth of the Mad River and Humboldt Bay on the edge of California's rain-soaked northern coast.

Habitat: 338 acres of narrow sand spit abutting a spruce and pine forest.

Over 200 species of birds have been identified at the preserve, including 15 species of raptors which roost in the forest.

McCloud River
Preserve Manager
PO Box 409
McCloud, CA 96057   916-926-4366

Take St. Hwy. 89 east from I-5 to McCloud. Turn right at Shell station onto Squaw Valley Road and follow signs to AhDiNa campground. One mile past the campground the road dead-ends at the preserve trailhead. Park and walk 0.5 mile to the preserve headquarters.

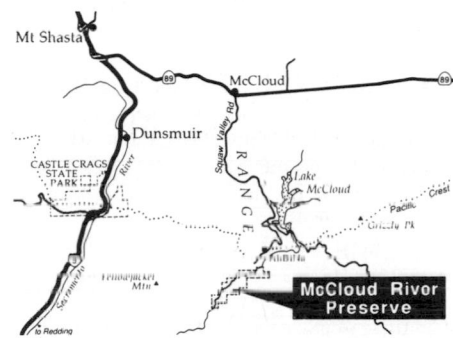

Habitat: 2,330 acres of rough river canyon have a unique microclimate closely resembling the high country. A mixed evergreen forest with undergrowth and a variety of wildflowers.

Preserve HQ, self-guided nature trail, 5 miles of hiking trails. Trout fishing (catch and release only) is limited to 10 anglers at any one time. Contact Field Office in San Francisco or the preserve manager for fishing permit.
Spring, Summer, Fall

Northern California Coast Range
42101 Wilderness Lodge Road
Branscomb, CA 95417   707-984-6653

From St. Hwy. 101, turn west at Laytonville onto Branscomb Road and drive 16.3 miles (past Branscomb). Turn north (right) on Wilderness Lodge Road for 3 miles to preserve headquarters at end of road.

Habitat: 7,520 acres of a complex natural community including douglas firs and coastal redwoods.

The Range supports a large variety of birds. The vibrant Lazuli Bunting passes through on its spring migration. Black Phoebes build their nests of mud and straw in the rafters of abandoned homesteads. Turkey Vultures and Common Ravens may be observed riding the updrafts over the meadows as they look for carrion.

In the forest birders can find Black-headed Grosbeaks, Solitary Vireos, Chestnut-backed Chickadees, Orange-crowned and Wilson's warblers, and other birds.

Year-round wildlife sightings.
Spring and Fall best due to migration.

Ring Mountain
3152 Paradise Drive, #101
Tiburon, CA, 94920   415-435-6465

Located 15 miles north of downtown San Francisco. Take Hwy. 101 north to the Paradise Drive exit in Corte Madera (do not go to the town of Tiburon). Follow Paradise Drive east for 1.7 miles. Just after Westward Drive is a fire road with a gate and sign on the right. Park off the pavement on the shoulder and walk to the hiking trail.

Habitat: 377 acres including the 602-foot-high summit. The greenish soil, which is a product of decaying serpentine, is low in nutrients and high in magnesium and heavy metals.

Plants such as Tiburon mariposa lily and serpentine reedgrass that have survived in serpentine soil have become so specialized that they cannot thrive in more fertile soils. The geology is the most unusual in the bay area, and some of the rocks are unique in composition and texture. The trail to the summit also passes through areas of sandstone soil supporting native grasses and trees, where birds and other animals take shelter. Ring Mountain is a popular spot with hikers, wildflower and wildlife enthusiasts, and geologists.

Open during daylight hours all year. No permission required to visit. March–June for wildflowers.

Vina Plains   916-891-8462
Located 13 miles north of Chico near Vina and Woodson Bridge St. Rec. Area.

The preserve borders Hwy. 99, 13 miles north of Chico. The entry gate is on the east side of the highway, approximately 0.3 mile north of Singer Creek and opposite Haille Road.

Habitat: 1,950 acres of dry grassland or vernal pools and rich grassland depending on the season.

Tiny invertebrates in the vernal pools provide food for migratory waterfowl and shorebirds. Waders including Great Egrets, Great Blue Herons, Greater Yellowlegs, Black-necked Stilts, and Killdeer. Waterfowl such as Tundra Swans, Snow and Canada geese, American Wigeons, Mallards, and Northern Pintails feed from the surface.

Rodents attract a number of ranging predators, including Northern Harriers, Red-tailed Hawks, and Prairie Falcons. Bald Eagles who winter at nearby lakes and rivers fly over Vina Plains on occasion. The most common birds are field feeders, such as Horned Lark, Western Meadowlark, Savannah Sparrow, and Brewer's Blackbird.

Contact the Management Docent Chair/Tour Coordinator about tours on Saturdays and Sundays during March through mid-May or until the ponds have dried. Group tours may be arranged at other times.

Central

Cosumnes River ⑧
Preserve Manager
6500 Desmond Road
Galt, CA 95632   916-684-2816

Take Twin Cities Road exit off I-5 (from the south, 26 miles north of Stockton; from the north 22 miles south of Sacramento). Follow Twin Cities Road east to Franklin Blvd. Turn right onto Franklin Blvd. and proceed south 1.5 miles to the nature trail entrance.

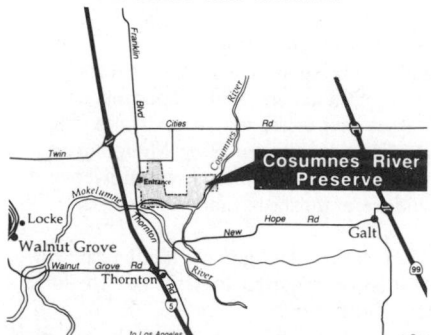

Habitat: 1,100 acres include 700 acres of valley oak, one of the largest oaks. The Cosumnes River which is the largest undammed river in the Central Valley, overflows its banks periodically during winter rains. The seasonal freshwater marshes formed by the floodwaters attract a large number of migratory waterfowl.

The "Greater" and "Lesser" races of the Sandhill Crane migrate through the area, and hundreds winter at Cosumnes River. The Swainson's Hawk, an endangered species in California, is among the more than 200 species of birds that have been seen.

Self-guided nature trail. Contact the Preserve Manager for information.
Spring, Summer, Fall, Winter

Creighton Ranch ⑨
Preserve Manager, PO Box 3840
Visalia, CA 93278   209-627-4328
Please call ahead before visits from October 1 to January 31.

From Los Angeles, travel north on Hwy. 99 to Ave. 144 at Tipton. Take Ave. 144 west (also called Hwy. 190) about 10 miles to the preserve entrance, located on the north side of the road where it crosses Lakeland Canal.
From San Francisco go south on I-5, turn east onto Hwy. 152, to Hwy. 99. Take Hwy. 99 south to Hwy. 43 at Selma. Continue south past Hanford and Corcoran to Ave. 144 (Hwy. 190) and turn east, continuing 2 miles to the preserve gate.

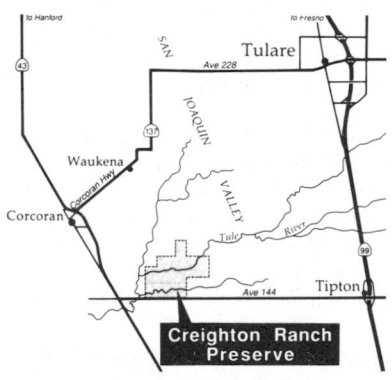

Habitat: 3,280 acres of a diverse range of vegetation types, including eight endangered plant communities, support the richest fauna in the San Joaquin Valley. More than 220 species of birds have been sighted, including Horned Grebe, Bald Eagle, Sage Thrasher, Black-throated Blue Warbler, and Lark Bunting.

The interpretive center near the preserve entry has brochures, maps, and displays that explain the principal natural features of the area. Picnic tables, restrooms.
Spring, Fall, Winter

Elkhorn Slough ⑩
Elkhorn Slough Foundation
PO Box 267
Moss Landing, CA 95039   408-728-2822

The Reserve is managed by the California Dept. of Fish & Game under an agreement with the Division of Marine

and Estuarine Management and the National Oceanic and Atmospheric Administration. Elkhorn Slough interpretive guides staff the Reserve Visitor Center.

Elkhorn Slough is about a two and a half hour drive from San Francisco. Take Hwy. 1 south, turn left on Dolan Road near Moss Landing, and go 3.5 miles to Elkhorn Road. Turn left and go another 2.5 miles to the National Estuarine Reserve Visitor Center on the left-hand side of the road. The Center is open 9a.m. to 5p.m. Thursday through Sunday.

Habitat: 388-acre coastal wetland adjacent to the 1,300-acre Elkhorn Slough National Estuarine Research Reserve. Three rare communities are represented: northern eusaline lagoon, northern coastal salt-marsh, and coastal freshwater marsh.

Wintering shorebirds, including Willets, American Avocets, Marbled Godwits, and dowitchers, number in the tens of thousands and can be found feeding in the mudflats with various herons. Northern Pintails, teals, and Northern Shovelers are among the many flocks of waterfowl that stop at Elkhorn Slough during their spring and fall migrations. Western Grebes are a common winter resident, arriving in the fall and leaving in spring. The endangered Brown Pelican roosts by the salt ponds during the summer in the largest population north of Point Conception. Another endangered species, the Peregrine Falcon, has been seen seasonally, hunting over the slough. The oaks are a good spot to see various resident and migrating perching birds such as Plain Titmice, Northern Flickers, and Downy Woodpeckers.

Hiking trails. Naturalist on hand at the visitor center to answer questions.
Fall, Winter

Jepson Prairie ⑪
Institute of Ecology
University of California
Davis, CA 95616   916-752-6580

Visitation by docent-led tours only. Contact the Institute for reservations or access permission. Tours are held on weekends 10a.m. to noon from mid-February to the end of flowering season, usually mid-May.

A one and a half hour drive east from San Francisco via I-80, near Fairfield.

Habitat: 1,566 acres of original prairie and vernal pools, including Olcott Pool, one of the world's largest.

The prairie supports rodents and the Red-tailed and other hawks who feed on them, while Olcott Pool is home to waterfowl and shorebirds breeding on its shores. A wooded trail is a good spot to see Loggerhead Shrikes, jays, flycatchers, and roosting Great Horned Owls.

Kaweah Oaks ⬧12
Preserve Manager
PO Box 3840
Visalia, CA 93278   209-627-4328

Kaweah Oak Preserve is located 7 miles east of Visalia on the north side of Hwy. 198. Turn north on Road 182 and drive 0.5 mile to the preserve gate.

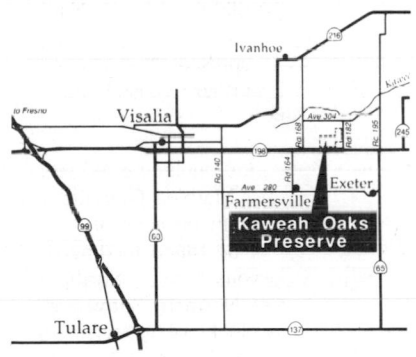

Habitat: 324 acres, about 45 percent of which is wooded. The remainder is divided between stream bed, open field, and meadow. Several ponds and an oxbow called Turtle Pond are nesting sites for Great Blue Herons, Mallards and, in very wet years, Wood Ducks.

On the self-guided nature trails keep a lookout on tree trunks for various breeding woodpeckers, including Northern Flickers, Downy, Nuttall's, and Acorn woodpeckers, and Red-breasted Sapsuckers.

Other nesters at the preserve include the House Wren, Tree Swallow, Ash-throated Flycatcher, Plain Titmouse, Black-headed and Blue grosbeaks, Lazuli Bunting, and "Bullock's" Northern Oriole.

In spring and fall the area is a birder's paradise as Solitary and Warbling vireos,

Orange-crowned, Yellow-rumped, and Black-throated Gray warblers sing and flit through the branches. A large nest in an old western sycamore is home to a pair of Red-tailed Hawks.

Information kiosk, picnic tables, and drinking fountain.
Spring

Landels-Hill Big Creek ⬧13
South of Carmel and north of Big Sur

Access by Conservancy field trips only. For information contact the Field Office in San Francisco. About 45 miles south of Carmel and 15 miles north of Big Sur. All but 40 acres transferred to the University of California's Natural Land Preserve.

Habitat: Cone Peak, which climbs 5,155 feet in three miles, has the most abrupt rise in the Lower 48. The extreme climate differences between the summit and sea level create a series of narrow habitat zones that include 23 different plant communities.

The four-mile loop trail climbs more than one thousand feet up Cone Peak, and the sample of various habitats is well worth the somewhat strenuous hike. The trail passes Big Creek and its tributaries, which drain Cone Peak, and goes through redwoods, hardwood forests, scrub, and grassland. At least 125 bird species have been identified at the preserve. Down by the ocean 38 species of shorebirds and seabirds, including the endangered Brown Pelican, can be seen. From January through April migrating Orcas and Gray Whales are visible from the shore.

Paine Wildflower ⬧14
Preserve Manager
PO Box 3840
Visalia, CA 93278   209-627-4328

For information contact the Preserve Manager.

Take I-5 to Hwy. 46 near Lost Hills. Head east on Hwy. 46 for 4.3 miles to its junction with Corcoran Road. Turn left, and drive 2.2 miles to a poor-quality dirt road that leads off to the right. This road junction is at the southwest corner of the original 40-acre preserve.

Habitat: A 600-acre remnant of alkali playa habitat, composed of mounds of light and sandy loam deposited by the wind, low hummocks, and slight depressions. The depressions fill up when it rains, forming shallow vernal pools that evaporate quickly and leave cracked mud.

Large numbers of ducks, geese, and shorebirds are attracted to the vernal pools. Late April and early May are the best times to see songbirds as they pass through on spring migration.

The alkali-tolerant flora supports a wide variety of animals, including several rare or endangered species, and attracts a number of different birds of prey. Together with the Kern National Wildlife Refuge just five miles north, the preserve helps to protect a staircase of habitats from lowland saltbush at Paine to freshwater marsh.

Spring, Winter

Pixley Vernal Pools ⬧15
Preserve Manager
PO Box 3840
Visalia, CA 93278   209-627-4328

Between Tipton and Pixley on Hwy. 99 take Ave. 120 east for 5 miles to Road 160. Turn south, continue for 1.8 miles, and watch for preserve on left.

Habitat: 40 fenced acres of 25 to 75 vernal pools (depending on the rainfall) surrounded by miles of farmland.

Depending on rainfall spring is the best time to visit. Ducks and shorebirds feed and rest at the pools during migration. Red-tailed Hawks and Black-shouldered Kites soar over the grassland in search of prey.

Spring

South

Big Bear Valley ⬧16
Friends of Big Bear Valley Volunteers
PO Box 1418
Sugarloaf, CA 92386   714-866-4190

About 2 hours east of Los Angeles. Take Hwy. 38 or Hwy. 18 from Los Angeles through the city of Big Bear Lake. Then take North Shore Drive (Hwy. 18) east until it begins to loop around Baldwin Lake. Parking is available in the gated area in front of "Horse House" shack on the left (north) side of the highway for group tours. You can turn left onto Holcomb Valley Road (paved and marked) and proceed about 0.5 mile to a dirt parking area on the left at the end of the barbed wire fence at the Pacific Crest Trail crossing.

Habitat: 562 acres, in 15 parcels. Surviving pebble plains and vernal meadows in the Big Bear Valley support the highest concentration of unique plant species in the continental United States.

Unusual birds congregate at the preserve, and at least nine species of sparrows, including the Nevada race of the Sage Sparrow, nest here. In spring grassland species such as Western Meadowlarks and Killdeer can be found. Summer is a good time to watch for Williamson's and Red-breasted sapsuckers, Olive-sided Flycatchers, and Hermit Thrushes. Soras and Virginia Rails live in the vegetation at the lake's edge, with Great Blue Herons and Black-crowned Night-Herons feeding nearby. Thousands of Eared Grebe chicks hitch rides on their parents' backs, a behavior that is unique to the grebe family.

In the fall up to 3,000 Turkey Vultures pass overhead, and between 70,000 and 80,000 migrating waterfowl alight in Big Bear and Baldwin lakes. Large flocks of American White Pelicans, and various raptors, including Ospreys, Swainson's and Ferruginous hawks, and Black-shouldered Kites pass through on migration. In winter the largest number of Bald Eagles anywhere in southern California is seen, as 25 to 30 perch along the lake shores.

The hike along the Pacific Crest Trail to the east offers spectacular vistas over Baldwin Lake and the San Bernardino Mountains to the south, and the Mojave Desert to the north. Bald Eagle tours are by reservation during January and February. There are regularly scheduled wildflower walks from late spring through early summer.

The Friends work in concert with the Conservancy and the U.S. Forest Service to preserve habitat in the valley.

Spring, Summer, Fall, Winter

Big Morongo ⑰

Preserve Manager
PO Box 780
Morongo Valley, CA 92256 619-363-7190

From Los Angeles head east on I-10 for 95 miles to Hwy. 62. Turn north on Hwy.

62, continue for 10.5 miles, turn right on East Drive (first road after the Morongo Preserve sign) and left into the preserve at the first hard-surface road. Trails begin at the parking lot kiosk. They enter the riparian forest and extend the six-mile length of the canyon. The parking lot is open from 7:30 a.m. to sunset daily.

Habitat: 3,920 acres (80 under Conservancy ownership, 140 leased from San Bernardino County, and about 3,700 under cooperative management with the Bureau of Land Management). The preserve is in the ecotonal area between the Mojave and Colorado deserts, and the coast. This unusual blend of environments allows flora and fauna from all three habitats to coexist. The coastal Nuttall's Woodpecker and desert-dwelling Ladder-backed Woodpecker both nest at the preserve.

The Big Morongo is one of the best birding locations in the state. The 72 breeding species include the Yellow-breasted Chat and Indigo Bunting. Roger Tory Peterson included this preserve in his list of places to visit in California during his North America record-tying "Big Day" in 1983. This stop netted him, among others, "Least" Bell's Vireo, Vermilion and Dusky flycatchers, and Black-chinned Sparrow.

Among the unusual migrants are Black-throated Blue and Tennessee warblers, Red-eyed Vireo, American Redstart, and Ovenbird. This is one of the few areas west of the Mississippi that is visited by birders searching for rare eastern migrants.

Interpretive displays, restrooms, nature trails ranging from short, level loops to long, hilly canyon hikes, picnic tables, drinking fountain.
Birding is good year-round.

Carrizo Plain ⑱

Preserve Manager
PO Box 15810   805-546-8378
San Luis Obispo, CA 93401

From Hwy. 99, take Hwy. 119 west. At Taft, head south on Hwy. 33 through Maricopa (to either Elkhorn Road or continue farther) to Soda Lake Road at Reyes Station. Head north to Soda Lake. From Hwy. 101, take Hwy. 58 east through Santa Margarita to California Valley. Turn right on Co. Road (Soda Lake Road) and head south to Soda Lake.

Habitat: 180,000 (proposed) acres, the largest remaining example of San Joaquin Valley habitat. An 8-mile-wide by 50-mile-long expanse of arid scrub and grassland surrounded by two mountain

ranges, the Caliente and Temblor. The 3,000-acre Soda Lake is the largest remaining natural alkaline wetland in central and southern California.

State and federal agencies, The Nature Conservancy, and private owners are working together to protect this unusual area. Pronghorn antelope and two herds of thule elk have been introduced by the California Department of Fish and Game to replace the huge herds of the last century.

It is a critical wintering habitat for Sandhill Cranes, which start arriving in October with a peak of 4,000 to 6,000 present in January. Waterfowl include American Wigeons, Canvasbacks, Eared and Pied-billed grebes, Tundra Swans, Greater White-fronted Geese, and Wilson's Phalaropes. The raptors that hunt over Carrizo Plain include Bald Eagles, Northern Harriers, and Short-eared Owls.

Late winter to early spring are the best birding times because Soda Lake is usually filled with water. A self-guided nature trail along the western edge of the lake provides the best example of all four of Carrizo's habitats.

Spring, Winter

Coachella Valley ⑲

Preserve Manager
PO Box 188
Thousand Palms, CA 92276 619-323-1234

Open every day from sunrise to sunset. Individuals and groups are welcome. For information contact preserve manager. This refuge is jointly administered with the USFWS. On-site management is by The Nature Conservancy.

The preserve is roughly 10 miles east of Palm Springs. From I-10 exit onto Ramon Road, drive east to Thousand Palms Cyn Road. Turn left (north), drive 2 miles to the preserve's entrance on left (look for red wagon wheels). Park in designated parking area and walk 100 yards to the Visitor Center in the Palm House.

Habitat: 13,000 acres of desert and one of

the largest groves of native fan palms in the entire southwest. Surrounded by vegetation typical of the Colorado Desert, the jungle-like oasis of palms, willows, cottonwoods, and mesquite thrives as a result of a natural underground dam made by earthquake faults, which brings water to the surface. The remainder of the preserve ranges from desert washes to sand dunes and mesas in a unique blow-sand ecosystem.

The Coachella Valley Preserve and Thousand Palms Oasis are havens for a great variety of birds. The lush vegetation, tall trees, and open water attract everything from Black-chinned Hummingbirds to Great Blue Herons. Phainopepla, Hooded Oriole, Cactus Wren, Black Phoebe, Verdin, and Gambel's Quail are among the 25 species that nest at the oasis.

The best way to explore the preserve is to take the self-guided interpretive trail, an easy, mile-long loop that begins at Palm House. Watch for birds in the trees and bushes.
Spring, fall, and winter are the best times to visit, as summer temperatures may exceed 120 °F.

Desert Tortoise ⑳
Desert Tortoise Preserve Committee Inc.
PO Box 453
Ridgecrest, CA 93555
or
Bureau of Land Management (BLM)
Ridgecrest Resource Area
122 East Dolphin Avenue
Ridgecrest, CA 93555   619-375-7125

From Los Angeles, travel northwest on I-5 to its intersection with Hwy. 14. Head east then north on Hwy. 14 through the town of Mojave. At California City Blvd., turn right and travel through California City to Randsburg-Mojave Road. The preserve entrance road is on the left side of the road 5.5 miles from the city.

Habitat: 39 square miles proposed (about 25,000 acres). Elevations range from 1,920 to 3,100 feet. Primarily shrub-covered flats and low, rolling hills crossed by dry washes and wash stringers that sometimes carry flash floods during the rainy season. There are about 3 square miles of steep, rocky canyons.

This is a cooperative preservation effort of the Desert Tortoise Preserve Committee, the State Wildlife Conservation Board, the Bureau of Land Management, and The Nature Conservancy. At the interpretive center a kiosk illustrates natural history displays and trail loop brochures for connecting trails that start there.

Four distinct plant communities, creosote bush scrub, joshua tree woodland, saltbrush scrub, and canyon, support a wide variety of birds. Le Conte's Thrashers, Ash-throated Flycatchers, Say's Phoebes, Horned Larks, Loggerhead Shrikes, and Cactus Wrens can be found in the bush. Turkey Vultures, Red-tailed Hawks, and Golden Eagles search for their prey from the open sky. Greater Roadrunners, Gambel's Quails, and Chukars remain on the ground, rarely flying except in short, quick bursts.

Spring

Kern River ㉑
Preserve Manager
PO Box 1662
Weldon, CA 93283   619-378-2531

From Bakersfield, go east 57 miles on Hwy. 178 through Kern River Canyon and Lake Isabella areas. Exactly 1.1 miles past the Kernville Airport turnoff, turn left onto the preserve.

From Mojave take Hwy. 14 north about 43 miles to Hwy. 178. Go west on Hwy. 178 for about 30 miles, over Walker Pass and through Canebreak and Onyx to Weldon. Preserve entrance is on right, 1 mile beyond Weldon.

Habitat: 1,127 acres at 2,600-foot elevation. The south fork of the Kern River flows through the preserve. Three ecological provinces, the Central Valley, Sierra Nevada, and Mojave Desert, overlap here and account for an unusual mix of wildlife.

A unique reforestation program is underway to enhance habitat for the Yellow-billed Cuckoos that nest here. The preserve has the largest population of Willow Flycatchers in the state. Other species of note are Yellow-headed and Tricolored blackbirds, Black-headed and Evening grosbeaks, Lawrence's Goldfinch, and White-throated Swift.

Wood Ducks nest by the river's backwaters and California Towhees feed on wild currants along its banks. A number of birds can be found at the ponds, including Black-crowned Night-Herons fishing at the edge, and Blue-winged Teals, Mallards, and Northern Pintails.

Spring, early Summer

Santa Cruz Island ㉒
The Nature Conservancy
Preserve Headquarters and Exhibit
213 Stearns Wharf
Santa Barbara, CA 93101   805-962-9111

Exhibit open 10a.m. to 4p.m. daily (no charge). From Hwy. 101, take the Harbor exit. Follow Cabrillo Blvd. to Stearns Wharf at the foot of State Street. Parking is available in the city lot on Cabrillo Blvd. or on the wharf. The wharf is crowded on summer weekends.

Access to Santa Cruz Island is by either Conservancy-sponsored charter boat or private boat. The Conservancy offers day trips to the island from April through November. Private yachts require a landing permit in advance (no permits available on the island). Information about trips and private charter service to the island is available at the Preserve Headquarters.

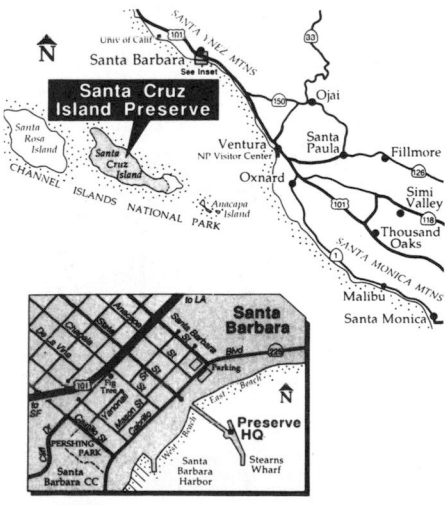

Habitat: 62,000 acres located 23 miles off the coast across the Santa Barbara Channel. Flat expanses, both in the island's central valley and the marine terraces ringing the island's peaks are punctuated by several over 2,000 feet. Pelican Bay, the destination of most field trips, is one of the most diverse areas of the island. During the boat trip, seabirds and marine mammals are usually abundant. Hiking on the island is over rough terrain and you must be in good physical condition to enjoy all that this preserve has to offer.

Birds are the island's most common vertebrates and 217 species have been seen here, including Grasshopper Sparrows, Horned Larks, and Western Meadowlarks in the grasslands, and Rufous-sided Towhees beneath the chaparral. Endemic Orange-crowned Warblers whinny overhead. Both towhee and warbler have larger body parts here, especially bills and feet, than mainland birds of these two species.

The Santa Cruz Island Scrub Jay, a subspecies found nowhere else in the world, is 25 percent larger and a much deeper blue than its mainland counterpart.

Spring, Fall

Santa Rosa Plateau
Preserve Manager
22115 Tenaja Road
Murrieta, CA 92362   714-677-6951

About 40 miles south of Riverside. Take the Clinton Keith Road exit from I-15 near Murrieta. Drive south 5 miles to where Clinton Keith Road ends at Tenaja Road and the preserve entrance (locked gate).

Self-guided tours available on a drop-in basis. Guided tours led by a trained docent are available for schools and other groups by reservation. Contact the preserve manager for information.

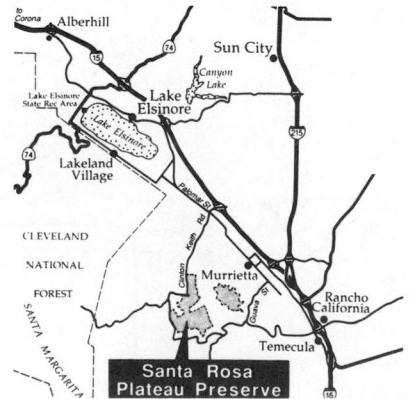

Habitat: 3,100 acres, ranging up to 2,200 feet. The plateau lies at the southern end of the Santa Ana Mountains, and is capped by several crumbling mesas. From

December through May rainwater collects in the 13 vernal pools. The Mesa de Colorado Pool, at more than 30 acres, is one of the largest in California. Several creeks which flow through the preserve dry up in summer, but deep holes in the stream beds contain water year-round.

The riparian growth provides shelter for many nesting species. In winter the pools provide food for ducks, geese, grebes, gulls, Greater Yellowlegs, Whimbrels, Least Sandpipers, and Long-billed Dowitchers.

A number of woodpeckers live on the preserve, including Acorn, Lewis', Nuttall's and Downy woodpeckers, Yellow-bellied and Red-breasted sapsuckers, and Northern Flickers. Three nest boxes are used by Western Bluebirds.

Black-shouldered Kites and Red-shouldered Hawks soar over the field. Black Phoebes, Lesser Goldfinches, and Red-winged Blackbirds nest in the willows by the creeks. An abundance of waterfowl, including Green-winged and Cinnamon teals, Mallards, Northern Pintails, Northern Shovelers, and Ring-necked Ducks use the vernal pools regularly during the wet season.

Two miles down the road from the parking area is the preserve headquarters, an old adobe that dates back to the 1800's. Pick up brochures and maps to the two self-guided trails here.

Spring, Fall

U.S. FISH & WILDLIFE SERVICE NATIONAL WILDLIFE REFUGES

Clear Lake ❶
c/o Klamath Basin Refuges
Route 1, Box 7
Tulelake, CA 96134   916-667-2231

See Bird List CA-3 Lo. Klamath Summary page 50 and Bird Chart pages 222-239

One of the three Klamath Basin National Wildlife Refuges located in California (three others are in Oregon); see Klamath Basin Refuges, page 50, for directions to the administrative headquarters. Clear Lake is closed to the public from spring through fall to protect nesting birds. (Check at the office about access.)

To reach Clear Lake NWR, take Hwy. 139 south from Tulelake for 15 miles to the junction with Clear Lake Reservoir Road, turn east and continue for approximately 10 miles.

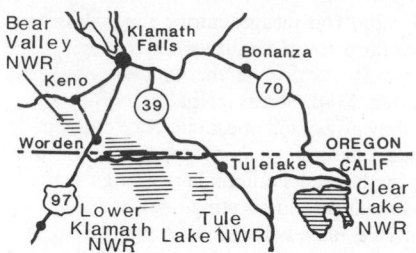

Habitat: 33,440 acres at 4,100 feet elevation. 13,440 upland acres covered with bunchgrass, low sagebrush, and juniper surround 20,000 acres of water.

Various colonial waterbirds such as pelicans and cormorants nest on small islands in Clear Lake.

Area brochure, mammals list, hunting. November through March

Coachella Valley ❷
c/o Salton Sea NWR
PO Box 120
Calipatria, CA 92233   619-348-5278

This refuge is jointly administered with The Nature Conservancy, and is fully described on pages 46–47 under TNC Preserve 19. The refuge administrative headquarters is at Salton Sea NWR four miles south of Niland. See the Salton Sea listing for directions to that office.

Spring, fall and winter are best times to visit, as summer temperatures may exceed 120 °F.

Colusa ❸
c/o Sacramento Valley NWR
Route 1, Box 311
Willows, CA 95988   916-934-2801

The administrative office is at the Sacramento Valley NWR. See that listing for directions to the office.

See Bird List CA-6 Sacramento Summary page 51 and Bird Chart pages 222-239

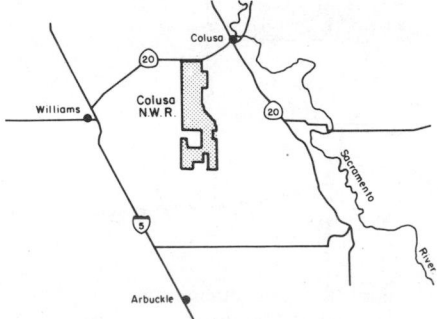

Colusa is one of four refuges in the Sacramento Valley Refuges complex located from 50 to 90 miles north of Sacramento. From I-99 turn east onto

Hwy. 20. The refuge entrance is located 0.5 mile west of Colusa.

Habitat: 4,042 acres at sea level. Permanent ponds, seasonal marsh, uplands, riparian habitat, and rice and other croplands produce abundant waterfowl foods and provide resting areas on relatively little acreage. Water grass or wild millet and associated wetland plants and barley provide additional food.

Northern Pintails, Mallards, American Wigeons, Northern Shovelers, Green-winged Teals, plus Snow, Ross', Greater White-fronted, and "Cackling" Canada geese are the most common waterfowl during the fall and winter. Ducks begin to arrive in August and are joined by geese in September and October. Their numbers may exceed 2 million by December when the wetland areas to the north are frozen.

Hunting, fishing, wildlife observation, auto tour route. Area brochure, mammals list. Fall and Winter are best.

Delevan 4

c/o Sacramento NWR
Route 1, Box 311
Willows, CA 95988   916-934-2801

The administrative office is at the Sacramento Valley NWR. See that listing for directions to the office.

See Bird List CA-6 Sacramento Summary page 51 and Bird Chart pages 222-239

Delevan is one of four refuges in the Sacramento Valley Refuges complex located from 50 to 90 miles north of Sacramento. The entrance is at the southeast corner of the refuge. Take U.S. Hwy. 99 south from Willows for 10 miles, then go 4 miles east on Maxwell Road.

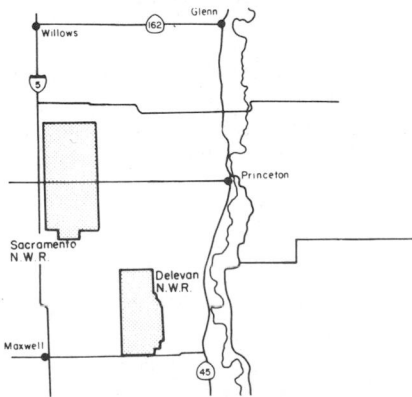

Habitat: 5,633 acres of permanent ponds, seasonal marsh, uplands, riparian, and croplands. Marsh and rice culture, wild millet and associated wetland food plants,

and barley attract waterfowl and other birds.

The bird life is usually the same as at Colusa, a sister refuge and part of the Sacramento NWR group.

Hunting, fishing, wildlife observation. Area brochure, mammals list. Fall and Winter are best.

Farallon 5

c/o San Francisco Bay NWR
PO Box 524
Newark, CA 94560   415-792-0222

The refuge headquarters and visitor center are at the San Francisco Bay NWR. Check that listing for details.

Bird List CA-2 Farallon Summary
246 birds listed, 16 nesting birds
Bird Chart pages 222-239

Totals by Season		s	S	F	W
Abundant	A	11	10	12	6
Common	C	9	3	17	10
Uncommon	U	22	1	33	14
Occasional	O	62	15	3	21
Rare	R	73	36	64	25

Endangered Species: Brown Pelican, Peregrine Falcon
Rare/Limited Species: Black-footed Albatross, Buller's Shearwater, Ashy Storm-Petrel, South Polar Skua, Xantus's Murrelet, Tropical Kingbird

Habitat: 211 acres of the rocky Farallon Islands 30 miles west of San Francisco. Although the refuge is closed to the public, wildlife can be observed and photographed from boats.

Brown Pelican, Brandt's Cormorant, Common Murre, Western Gull, Ashy Storm-Petrel, and Cassin's Auklet are among the species breeding in the largest seabird colony south of Alaska.

Summer.

Humboldt Bay 6

(near Eureka)
c/o San Francisco Bay NWR
PO Box 524
Newark, CA 94560

The refuge headquarters and visitor center are at the San Francisco Bay NWR, almost 300 miles south of Eureka. Humboldt Bay NWR is a "walk-in" refuge located west of and adjacent to Eureka, extending along the bay and west of Hwy. 101. Access is from the highway.

Habitat: 2,085 acres. Most of the refuge is water, but there are 399 acres of estuarine

habitat, 151 acres are grassland, and 11 acres of sand.

Brown Pelicans and Peregrine Falcons are both uncommon visitors to Humboldt Bay. Other species of particular interest are the "Black" Brant, Northern Pintail, Common Loon, Tundra Swan, and Snowy Plover.

Environmental education, wildlife observation, hunting, fishing. Spring, Winter

Kern 7   (office at refuge)

PO Box 670
Delano, CA 93216   805-725-2767

Bird List CA-4 Kern Summary
199 birds listed, 57 nesting birds
Bird Chart pages 222-239

Totals by Season		s	S	F	W
Abundant	A	22	14	25	23
Common	C	45	31	36	36
Uncommon	U	50	18	49	27
Occasional	O	49	33	50	42
Rare	R	15	11	18	18

Endangered Species: Bald Eagle, Peregrine Falcon
Rare/Limited Species: California Thrasher

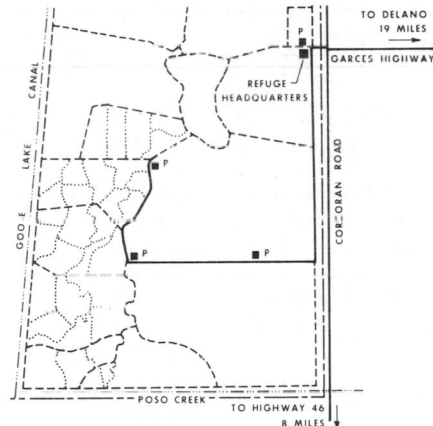

Entrance is 19 miles west of Delano on Garces Highway, at the junction with Corcoran Road.

Habitat: 10,618 acres at 300 feet of elevation. Over 1,200 acres are cultivated for waterfowl feed, 2,000 acres are flooded from October through March and managed as a marsh, 2,260 acres support native plants and endangered animals, and 5,000 are undeveloped.

From October through March a variety of species, including large numbers of waterfowl and shorebirds, are present. Waterfowl populations reach a peak in January and February. In rare wet years Killdeer, American Avocets, and Black-necked Stilts nest in great numbers. The summer months are extremely dusty, hot, and dry. Refuge ponds are generally dry from May through August.

Area brochure, mammals list, hunting, wildlife observation and photography. No formal nature trails exist, but visitors may walk on the minor roads and dikes to view wildlife.
October through March are best.

Kesterson 8

PO Box 2176
Los Banos, CA 93635   209-826-3508

The San Luis NWR office administers this refuge. See that listing for office access details.

See Bird List CA-9 San Luis Summary page 52 and Bird Chart pages 222-239

Located 4 miles east of Gustine on Hwy. 140. Parking lot at entrance. Foot traffic only.

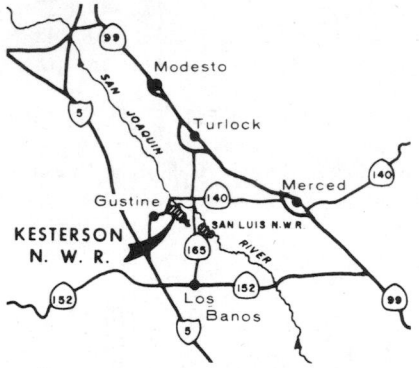

Habitat: 5,900 acres at 70-foot elevation. A historic flood plain of the San Joaquin River, the flat grasslands are often disrupted by narrow meandering channels of former streams. The area also has native marshes and vernal pools.

Visiting bird species including eagles, falcons, Red-tailed Hawks, and other raptors. Geese, ducks, cranes, and other waterbirds and upland species can be found here. Black-crowned Night-Herons nest within several dense cattail stands.

Area brochure, hunting.
Spring, Summer, Winter

Klamath Basin Refuges

c/o Tule Lake NWR   (office at refuge)
Route 1, Box 74
Tulelake, CA 96134   916-667-2231

This is the office for and location of the Tule Lake NWR and the office and information source for the six refuges in the Klamath Basin complex, Clear Lake, Lower Klamath, and Tule Lake in California, and Bear Valley, Klamath Forest, and Upper Klamath in Oregon. See the individual refuge listings in the respective states for specific information and highlights.

See Bird List CA-3 description and the Lo. Klamath Summary (this page), and Bird Chart pages 222-239.

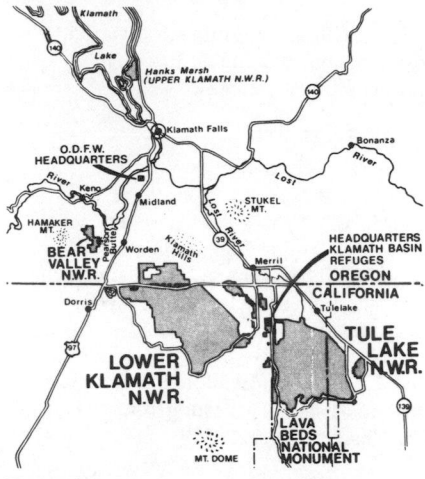

From Tulelake, go 5 miles west on the East-West Road, then south (left) about 0.1 mile on Hill Road to the Klamath Basin administrative office.

Habitat: 151,375 acres in six refuges, ranging from marshes and open water to meadows, coniferous forests, croplands, sagebrush and juniper uplands, cliffs, and rocky slopes.

The six Klamath refuges support a wonderful diversity and abundance of resident and migratory wildlife. A total of 411 species of wildlife have been observed, including 254 species of birds recorded on or near the six refuges.

Numerous waterfowl and marsh birds breed at the refuges, including grebes, pelicans, cormorants, herons and egrets, shorebirds, gulls and terns.

Large populations of waterfowl and raptors overwinter at the refuges. Lower Klamath and Tule Lake support one of the largest wintering concentrations of Bald Eagles in the contiguous U.S.

Area brochure, mammals list, hunting, some fishing. Upper Klamath and Tule Lake have canoe trails.
Best birding times are March and early November.

Lower Klamath 9

(refuge is in California & Oregon)
c/o Klamath Basin Refuges
Route 1, Box 74
Tulelake, CA 96134   916-667-2231

The Lower Klamath map is included with the Klamath Basin Refuges description. From Tulelake, take Hwy. 139 northwest 4 miles to Hwy. 161, then turn west for approximately 9 miles to refuge entrance and beginning of the refuge auto tour route.

The Bird List CA-3 and the Lo. Klamath Summary combines three California Klamath Basin refuges, Tule Lake, Lower Klamath, and Clear Lake (the locations where species covered are more likely to be seen). The CA-3 list was developed from local seasonal abundance data in the Klamath Basin Wildlife List that contains refuge codes indicating the birds most likely to be seen at each refuge.

Bird List CA-3 Lo. Klamath Summary
212 birds listed, 141 nesting birds
Bird Chart pages 222-239

Totals by Season		s	S	F	W
Abundant	A	17	12	20	3
Common	C	71	58	62	35
Uncommon	U	78	66	83	49
Rare	R	42	36	39	44

Endangered Species: Bald Eagle, Peregrine Falcon

Habitat: 47,600 acres at 4,100 feet of elevation. The mix of shallow marshes, open water, grassy uplands, and croplands was the first waterfowl refuge in the United States, created in 1908 by President Theodore Roosevelt.

Lower Klamath, along with Tule Lake Refuge, is noted for its wintering Bald Eagles. They begin arriving in November and hundreds are typically present in January and February.

Area brochure, auto tour route, hunting. Wildlife list includes birds, mammals, amphibians, reptiles, and fishes.
Spring, Summer, Fall, Winter

Merced 10

c/o San Luis NWR Complex
340 "I" Street
PO Box 2176
Los Banos, CA 93635   209-826-3508

See Bird List CA-9 San Luis Summary page 52 and Bird Chart pages 222-239

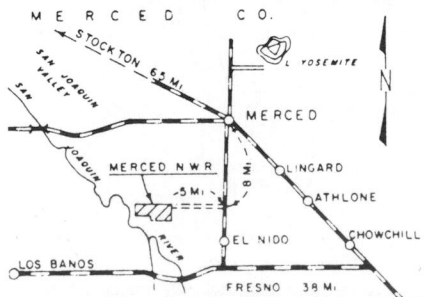

Take Hwy. 59 for 8 miles south from

Merced, then go west 8 miles on Sandy Mush Road to the refuge entrance.

Habitat: 2,561 acres. Half are wooded uplands and, of the other half, about 600 acres are croplands and 700 are marshes that are flooded from late October through April.

The flooded marshes provide food and rest for thousands of migrating and wintering birds. Duck populations are highest in December, while geese are more numerous in January. Merced is the best part of the San Luis Refuge Complex for seeing the small Ross' Goose as well as the Sandhill Cranes. Over 200 species of birds frequent the refuge, including eagles, other raptors, and various waterbirds.

Area brochure, hunting. Refuge visitors are restricted to the auto tour route roadway.
Spring, Summer

Modoc 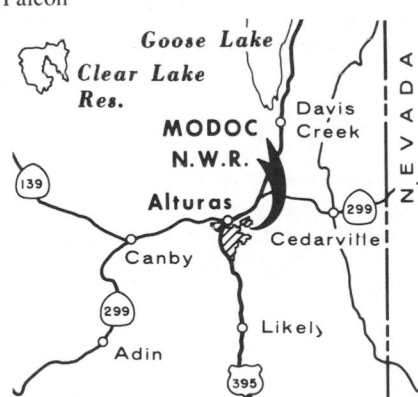   (office at refuge)
PO Box 1610
Alturas, CA 96101   916-233-3572

Bird List CA-5 Modoc Summary
214 birds listed, 74 nesting birds
Bird Chart pages 222-239

Totals by Season		s	S	F	W
Abundant	A	14	18	13	3
Common	C	52	38	47	18
Uncommon	U	52	26	50	20
Occasional	O	61	47	58	32
Rare	R	22	27	15	26

Endangered Species: Bald Eagle, Peregrine Falcon

Located 3 miles southeast of Alturas on Hwy. 395. Take Main St. south out of Alturas to Co. Road No. 56. Turn left for 0.5 mile to Co. Road No. 115. Turn south and go 1 mile to refuge headquarters road. Turn left and follow this road to the office.

Habitat: 6,283 acres at 4,365 feet of elevation and surrounding the confluence

of the north and south forks of the Pit River. Freshwater lakes and ponds, farmland, irrigated meadows, sagebrush upland, and riparian corridors.

Waterfowl and Sandhill Cranes are most numerous during the spring and fall, when the breeding populations are augmented by flocks migrating to nesting grounds farther north. Up to 700 Tundra Swans pass through, while Canada Geese, Cinnamon Teals, Gadwalls, American Wigeons, Northern Pintails, Redheads, and Ruddy Ducks remain to breed.

Various shorebirds, including Black-necked Stilts, Willets, American Avocets, and Killdeers also nest at the refuge. The varied habitat provides food and roosting sites for species that breed in other areas, such as the American White Pelican.

Area brochure, hunting, fishing in Doris Reservoir. The refuge bird checklist contains five special habitat codes.
Spring, Summer, Fall

Sacramento 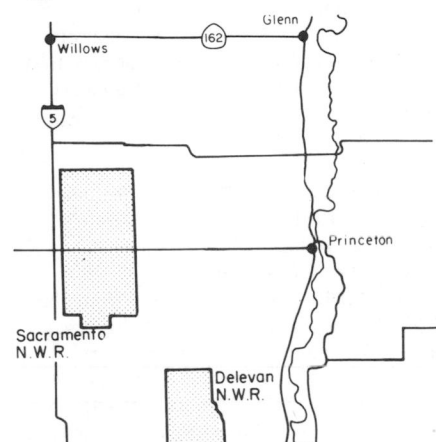   (office at Refuge)
Sacramento Valley Refuges Office
Route 1, Box 311
Willows, CA 95988   916-934-2801

The Sacramento Valley administration office and information resource serves Sacramento and three other refuges: Colusa, Delevan, and Sutter.

Bird List CA-6 Sacramento Summary
212 birds listed, 88 nesting birds
Bird Chart pages 222-239

Totals by Season		s	S	F	W
Abundant	A	5	1	11	9
Common	C	52	35	40	42
Uncommon	U	52	49	50	52
Rare	R	89	72	83	57

Endangered Species: Bald Eagle, Peregrine Falcon
Rare/Limited Species: Yellow-billed Magpie

Willows is 1 mile east of I-5 and about 90 miles north of Sacramento. Exit off I-5 east toward Willows and turn south (right) into Old Hwy. 99 (not shown on most road maps). The refuge entrance and administrative office is 6 miles south of Willows, east off the highway, and 1.5 miles north of Norman-Princeton Road.

Habitat: 10,776 acres of permanent ponds, seasonal marsh, uplands, riparian habitat, and food production lands. Intensely managed marsh and rice culture produce abundant resting areas and waterfowl foods.

Northern Pintails, Mallards, American Wigeons, Northern Shovelers, Green-winged Teals, and Snow, Ross', Greater White-fronted, and "Cackling" Canada geese are most commonly seen during the fall and winter.

The first ducks arrive in August and are joined by geese in September and October. When wetlands farther north freeze up during the winter, the flocks at Sacramento may exceed 2 million.

The refuge's wildlife list features birds, and includes reptiles, amphibians, fishes, and mammals. Area brochure, hunting, fishing, walking trail, auto tour route, group programs.
Spring, Fall, Winter

Salinas River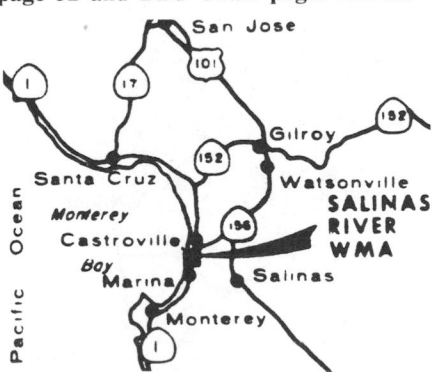
c/o San Francisco Bay NWR
PO Box 524
Newark, CA 94560   415-792-0222

The refuge headquarters and visitor center are at the San Francisco Bay NWR.

See Bird List CA-8 S.F. Bay Summary page 52 and Bird Chart pages 222-239

Salinas River Refuge is located 11 miles north of Monterey, where the river empties into Monterey Bay. Take the Del Monte Blvd. exit from Hwy. 1 and drive 0.75 mile west to the parking lot at the end of the unpaved road.

Habitat: 518 acres, 137 of grasslands, 78

salt marsh, 32 sand dunes, 130 ocean, 22 beach, 45 lagoon, and 74 river.

The estuary attracts various waterbirds. The endangered Brown Pelican rests and feeds in its waters, which also support waders, waterfowl, gulls, and terns. Peregrine Falcons may be seen pursuing their prey. The endangered Smith's blue butterfly feeds and lays its eggs in wild buckwheat growing in the dunes.

Area brochure, hunting, fishing, hiking. Spring, Fall, Winter

Salton Sea 14   (office at refuge)
PO Box 120
Calipatria, CA 92233   619-348-5278

Administrative office and an information resource for Tijuana Slough NWR.

Bird List CA-7 Salton Sea Summary
278 birds listed, 70 nesting birds
Bird Chart pages 222-239

Totals by Season		s	S	F	W
Common	C	72	35	73	62
Uncommon	U	60	34	60	48
Occasional	O	47	44	58	55
Rare	R	42	31	50	42

Endangered Species: Brown Pelican, Wood Stork, Bald Eagle, Peregrine Falcon, Least Tern
Rare/Limited Species: Blue-footed Booby, Yellow-footed Gull

Take Hwy. 111 south from Niland, turn west (left) onto Sinclair Road, and continue west for 6 miles to refuge headquarters.

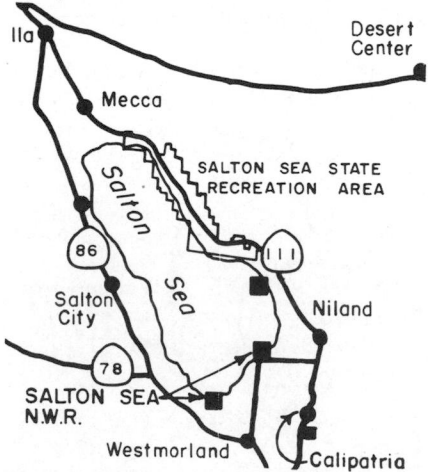

Habitat: 35,000 acres, with 2,200 acres of marsh and cropland. The remainder of the refuge, created in 1930, is now submerged under the 380-square-mile Salton Sea, which is more than 200 feet below sea level.

The Salton Sea refuge holds the

distinction of having the most diverse array of bird species found on any of the National Wildlife Refuges. Over 370 species have been recorded here and in the adjacent Imperial Valley.

Among the thousands of wintering birds, Canada, Snow, and Ross' geese, Northern Pintail, White-faced Ibis, Eared Grebe, Black-necked Stilt, and American Avocet are some of the more common species.

The "Yuma" Clapper Rail has a small breeding population. Both pelicans may be seen most of the year.

Wildlife list features birds, and includes mammals, reptiles, amphibians, and fishes. Area brochure. Hunting, boating, fishing, hiking on designated trails.
November to May are best.

San Francisco Bay 15
San Francisco Bay Refuge Complex
PO Box 524
Newark, CA 94560   415-792-0222
Recorded Information   415-792-3178

San Francisco Bay Refuge Complex is the administrative office and information resource for San Francisco Bay NWR and six other refuges: Antioch Dunes, Castle Rock, Farallon, Humboldt Bay, Salinas River, and San Pablo Bay.

Bird List CA-8 SF Bay Summary
227 birds listed, 83 nesting birds
Bird Chart pages 222-239

Totals by Season		s	S	F	W
Abundant	A	16	7	26	28
Common	C	61	48	50	48
Uncommon	U	67	55	64	48
Occasional	O	25	19	39	31
Rare	R	41	32	34	41

Endangered Species: Brown Pelican, Bald Eagle, Peregrine Falcon, Least Tern

The San Francisco Refuge Complex headquarters and visitor center is located in the Dumbarton Bridge Toll Plaza just off Marshlands Road. The Dumbarton Bridge road is Hwy. 84 with access from Hwy. 101 and Bayshore Freeway near Palo Alto, or Hwy. I-880/Hwy.17 (Nimitz Freeway) near Newark.

Note: The San Francisco Bay Refuge Complex Environmental Education Center (EEC) is located in the marshes at Alvisco, on the southern tip of San Francisco Bay, about 15 miles from the complex administrative office. To reach the EEC facility, continue south on I-880/Hwy. 17 past Hwy. 84 toward San Jose to Hwy. 237. Turn west (right) onto Hwy. 237, then turn north (right) onto

Zanker Road. Continue past the San Jose/Santa Clara Water Pollution Control Plant and over the railroad track to the EEC entrance road on the right.

Habitat: 23,000 acres of mud flats, salt marshes, salt ponds, and open water around the head of San Francisco Bay from Coyote Hills Slough (east side) to Bair Island and Steinberger Slough (west side).

The 1,600 square miles of estuary in San Francisco Bay make it the largest on the Pacific Flyway. Used by more than 800,000 waterbirds at a time, it provides food and rest for millions of birds during spring and fall migration peaks, including half of the west coast Canvasback population. Among the 250 species that can be seen on the refuge each year is the endangered "Yuma" Clapper Rail.

Area brochure, mammals list. Hunting, fishing, boats, hiking, picnicking. Spring, Fall, Winter

San Luis 16   (office in town)
San Luis Refuge Complex
1340 "I" Street
PO Box 2176
Los Banos, CA 93635   209-826-3508

A refuge, information resource, and refuge administrative office for San Luis, Kesterson, and Merced NWR's. Also known as the Central San Joaquin Valley Refuge Complex.

Bird List CA-9 San Luis Summary
202 birds listed, 70 nesting birds
Bird Chart pages 222-239

Totals by Season		s	S	F	W
Abundant	A	10	4	13	20
Common	C	50	31	40	33
Uncommon	U	58	36	41	42
Occasional	O	39	16	43	22
Rare	R	28	16	25	33

Endangered Species: Bald Eagle, Peregrine Falcon

Rare/Limited Species: Yellow-billed Magpie, California Thrasher

Located approximately 10 miles north of Los Banos. From Los Banos, take St. Hwy. 165 (North Mercy Springs Road) north 8 miles, then turn right onto Wolfsen Road and travel northeast 2 miles to the refuge.

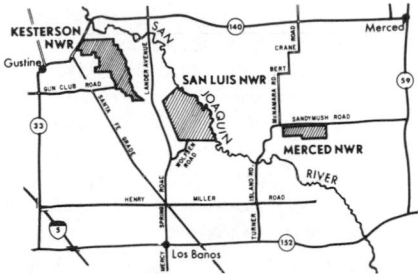

Habitat: 7,430 acres, including 2,240 acres of shallow marsh-like ponds, wooded sloughs, and grasslands. A small tract is farmed to produce additional food for wildlife. Canals and dikes ensure wetlands year-round.

Travel is restricted to the Main Tour Drive and the Thule Elk Drive. Green-winged Teals, Gadwalls, Northern Shovelers, and Cinnamon Teals are abundant and easily seen from the road. Snow and Canada geese are present in large concentrations, and Sandhill Cranes are abundant during fall and winter.

March is the best month for general sightseeing. Wildflowers are most abundant during April. Most birds nest during April, May, and June. San Luis, with its wooded sloughs, offers a variety of passerines and raptors, including breeding Black-shouldered Kites.

Area brochure, mammals list, hunting, fishing. The San Luis bird checklist indicates species more apt to be seen at San Luis, Kesterson, or Merced. Spring, Summer, Fall, Winter

San Pablo Bay 🔟

c/o San Francisco Bay NWR
PO Box 524
Newark, CA 94560

415-792-0222
The refuge headquarters and visitor center are at the San Francisco Bay NWR.

See Bird List CA-8 SF Bay Summary page 52 and Bird Chart pages 222-239

Take Hwy. 37 west from Vallejo about 10 miles. Just before crossing Tolay Creek (and reaching the junction of Hwy. 37 with Hwy. 121), turn left (south) onto a road which runs parallel to the creek along a levee. Continue for 2.75 miles to

Lower Tubbs Island and a parking area and refuge trailhead.

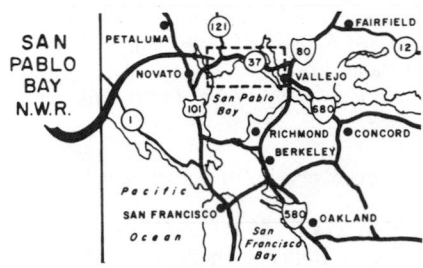

Habitat: 11,697 acres. Most of the refuge consists of marshes and open water accessible only by boat.

The endangered Brown Pelican can be found during summer and fall and the "Yuma" Clapper Rail breeds at the refuge. San Pablo Bay harbors the largest Canvasback and scaup populations on the west coast.

Environmental education, wildlife interpretation, wildlife/wildlands observation, hunting, fishing. Spring, Fall, Winter

Sutter 🔟

(southwest of Yuba City)
c/o Sacramento NWR
Route 1, Box 311
Willows, CA 95988   916-934-2801

Contact the Sacramento Valley Refuges administrative office about refuge conditions.

See Bird List CA-6 Sacramento Summary page 51 and Bird Chart pages 222-239

From Yuba City go west on Hwy. 20 for 2.5 miles and turn south onto George Washington Blvd. Go 5 miles to Oswald Road and turn west. Continue about 4 miles to where Oswald Road ends, at Schlag Road. Turn north, go 0.5 miles to Hughes Road and turn left. A parking area is located about 1 mile west.

Habitat: 2,591 acres at sea level. Permanent ponds, seasonal marsh, uplands, riparian habitat, and food production lands. Marsh and rice culture produce abundant preferred waterfowl foods and resting areas.

Northern Pintails, Mallards, American Wigeons, Northern Shovelers, Green-winged Teals and Snow, Ross', Greater White-fronted, and "Cackling" Canada geese are most commonly seen during the fall and winter. Ducks begin arriving in August and are joined by geese in September and October.

Hunting, fishing, wildlife observation. Fall, Winter

Tijuana Slough 🔟

c/o Salton Sea NWR
PO Box 120
Calipatria, CA 92233   619-348-5278

The refuge headquarters is at the Salton Sea NWR, southeast of Palm Springs.

Contact the U.S. Fish and Wildlife Service office at Imperial Beach City Hall, 825 Imperial Beach Blvd., Imperial Beach (619-575-1290), for local information.

Tijuana Slough is located west and south adjacent to Imperial Beach. Access via Imperial Beach Boulevard or Fifth St. It is now part of the Tijuana River National Estuarine Research Reserve. The refuge is located at the north end of the research reserve.

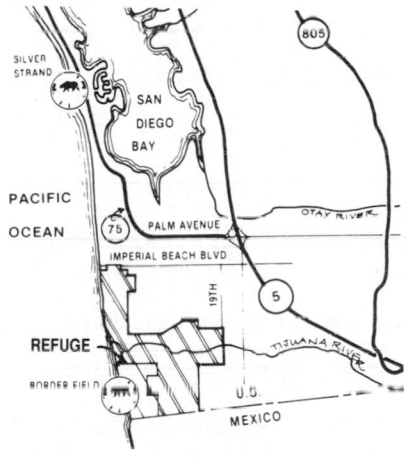

Habitat: 2,513 acres at the mouth of the Tijuana River, including sand dunes, mud flats and tidal sloughs, low, middle, and high marsh, uplands, and the river bed. 350 species have been recorded in the area, 302 of which have been seen within the reserve.

The reserve is a prime wintering spot for shorebirds, waterfowl, and raptors, including Golden Eagles, Red-tailed Hawks, Ospreys, Peregrine Falcons, American Kestrels, Black-shouldered Kites, and Northern Harriers.

The endangered "Light-footed" Clapper Rail and "California" Least Tern breed within the reserve. Visitors include the Brown Pelican and endangered "Belding's" Savannah Sparrow.

Foot trails, horseback riding, photography, surf fishing, nature study, picnicking. Spring, Fall, Winter

Tule Lake 🔟   (office at refuge)
c/o Klamath Basin Refuges
Route 1, Box 74
Tulelake, CA 96134   916-667-2231

**See Bird List CA-3 Lo. Klamath
Summary page 50 and Bird Chart
pages 222-239**

Tule Lake is one of the Klamath Basin
Refuges whose headquarters office is
located at the Tule Lake refuge on Hill
Road, six miles west of the town of
Tulelake.

Habitat: 38,908 acres of mostly open
water and croplands, at 4,100 feet of
elevation. Approximately 16,400 acres are
farmed to provide food for migrating and
wintering waterfowl.

Tule Lake and Lower Klamath are noted
for their wintering eagles. Eagles begin
arriving in November and hundreds are
usually present in January and February.

A self-guided auto tour route of Tule
Lake NWR begins at the headquarters
building, located at the northwest corner
of the refuge. A self-guided canoe trail is
open from July through September.

Area brochure, wildlife list, canoe trail
brochure, bicycling, hunting.
Spring, Summer, Fall, Winter

NATIONAL PARK SERVICE

Channel Islands National Park 🔟
1901 Spinnaker Drive
Ventura, CA 93001   805-644-8262

249,353 acres encompassing five islands
off southern California: Anacapa, San
Miguel, Santa Barbara, Santa Cruz, and
Santa Rosa. Nesting seabirds, sea lion
rookeries, and unique plants characterize
the area. Anacapa, Santa Barbara, and
Santa Cruz are administered by the

National Park Service.

A large portion of Santa Cruz is also
administered by The Nature Conservancy.
A permit is required to visit San Miguel
and Santa Rosa. San Miguel is run jointly
by the U.S. Navy and National Park
Service.

Park brochure with map, camping leaflet.

Golden Gate 🔟
National Recreation Area
Fort Mason, Building 201
San Francisco, CA 94123   415-556-0560

73,116 acres along the shoreline areas of
San Francisco, Marin, and San Mateo
counties include ocean beaches, redwood
forest, lagoons, and marshes.

Recreation area brochure with map. A
quarterly newspaper "Park Events" is
available.

Joshua Tree 🔟
National Monument   619-367-7511
74485 National Monument Drive
Twentynine Palms, CA 92277

559,954 acres of desert habitat include a
representative stand of Joshua trees and a
great variety of other plants. Greater
Roadrunners and Burrowing Owls pursue
their reptile and rodent prey across the
desert.

Monument brochure with map.

Point Reyes National Seashore 🔟
Point Reyes, CA 94956   415-663-8522

This 71,045-acre peninsula just north of
San Francisco is noted for long beaches
backed by tall cliffs, lagoons and
estuaries, forested ridges, and offshore
bird and sea lion colonies.

At the Point Reyes National Seashore
almost 430 species have been recorded.
Climate and habitat diversity here have
resulted in the greatest avian diversity of
any U.S. park, and more recorded birds
than 40 of the 50 states.

Seashore brochure with map, high/low tide
table, bird list available, birdwatching
leaflet, separate leaflets cover
campgrounds, fishing, etc.

NATIONAL FOREST SERVICE
NFS Pacific Southwest Region
630 Sansome St.
San Francisco, CA 94111   415-556-0122

Map/Forest/City

🔺	Angeles/Arcadia	818-574-5200
🔺	Cleveland/San Diego	619-557-5050
🔺	Eldorado/Placerville	916-622-5061
🔺	Inyo/Bishop	619-873-5841
🔺	Klamath/Yreka	916-842-6131
🔺	Lake Tahoe Basin Management Unit
	/South Lake Tahoe	916-573-2600
🔺	Lassen/Susanville	916-257-2151
🔺	Los Padres/Goleta	805-683-6711
🔺	Mendocino/Willows	916-934-3316
🔺	Modoc/Alturas	916-233-5811
🔺	Plumas/Quincy	916-283-2050
🔺	San Bernardino
	/San Bernardino	714-383-5588
🔺	Sequoia/Porterville	209-784-1500
🔺	Shasta Trinity/Redding	916-246-5222
🔺	Sierra/Fresno	209-487-5155
🔺	Six Rivers/Eureka	707-442-1721
🔺	Stanislaus/Sonora	209-586-3234
🔺	Tahoe/Nevada City	916-265-4531

BUREAU LAND MANAGEMENT
BLM State Office
Federal Bldg.
2008 E. Cottage Way, E-2841
Sacramento, CA 95825   916-978-4746

Map/District/City

🔻	Bakersfield/Bakersfield	805-861-4191
🔻	Ca. Desert/Riverside	714-351-6394
🔻	Susanville/Susanville	916-257-5381
🔻	Ukiah/Ukiah	707-462-3873

STATE AGENCIES

California Dept. of Fish & Game
1416 Ninth Street
Box 944209
Sacramento, CA 94244   916-445-3531

Map/Region/City

①	Fresno/Fresno	209-222-3761
②	Long Beach
	/Long Beach	213-590-5126
③	Napa/Napa	707-944-2011
④	Rancho Cordova
	/Rancho Cordova	916-355-0922
⑤	Redding/Redding	916-225-2362

California Office of Tourism
PO Box 9278
Van Nuys, CA 91409   800-862-2543
From out-of-state call same number.

BIRDING HOTLINE
Statewide   303-423-5582

LOCAL BIRDING GROUPS
Map/Chapter/City
1. Aiken Audubon/Colorado Springs
2. Arkansas Valley Audubon/Pueblo
3. Aud. Soc. of W. CO/Grand Junction
4. Boulder Audubon/Boulder
5. Denver Audubon/Denver
6. Evergreen Naturalists Aud. Soc. /Evergreen
7. Fort Collins Audubon/Fort Collins
8. Greeley Audubon/Greeley
9. Heart of the Rockies Aud./Salida
10. Rabbit Ears Aud./Steamboat Springs
11. Roaring Fork Aud./Glenwood Spgs.
12. San Juan Audubon/Durango
13. San Luis Valley Audubon/Alamosa
14. Boulder Bird Club/Boulder
15. Denver Field Orn./Denver
16. Durango Bird Club/Durango

THE NATURE CONSERVANCY
Colorado Field Office
1244 Pine Street
Boulder, CO 80302   303-444-2950

Phantom Canyon ◆
1,600 acres - Contact Field Office
Visits to this new preserve near Livermore are by reservation only. Facilities and literature are being developed.

Bird List CO-1 Phantom Summary
171 birds listed, 36 nesting birds
Bird Chart pages 222-239

Totals by Season		s	S	F	W
Abundant	A	12	8	5	1
Common	C	20	19	11	6
Uncommon	U	73	60	44	24
Rare	R	24	28	17	12

Endangered Species: Bald Eagle, Peregrine Falcon

U.S. FISH & WILDLIFE SERVICE NATIONAL WILDLIFE REFUGES
U.S. Fish & Wildlife Service Region 6
Box 25486
Denver Federal Center
Denver, CO 80225   303-236-7920

Alamosa ❶   (office at refuge)
PO Box 1148
Alamosa, CO 81101   719-589-4021

Bird List CO-2 Alamosa Summary
183 birds listed, 70 nesting birds
Bird Chart pages 222-239

Totals by Season		s	S	F	W
Abundant	A	13	16	10	4
Common	C	45	42	38	12
Uncommon	U	28	27	29	6
Occasional	O	45	33	38	9
Rare	R	29	23	25	23

Endangered Species: Peregrine Falcon, Whooping Crane, Least Tern

Also administrative headquarters for the Alamosa/Monte Vista Refuge Complex. Take Hwy. 160 east from Alamosa for 4 miles to El Rancho Lane. Turn south and go 2 miles to the refuge.

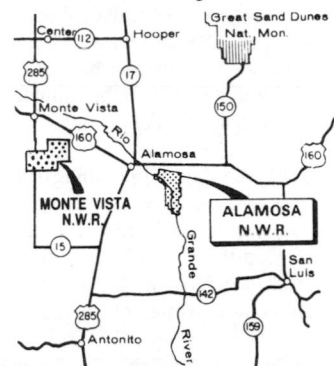

Habitat: 11,168 acres of riverbottom wetland at an elevation of 7,500 to 7,800 feet. The Rio Grande, which borders the refuge on the west, extends many sloughs and oxbows into the refuge. The river is bordered by cottonwood and other riparian habitat. The San Luis valley has an arid climate, although its groundwater is fed by many mountain streams.

Numerous waterfowl species can be found on Alamosa's waterways, but Mallards, and Blue-winged and Cinnamon teals are the most common. Various wading species breed here, such as the American Avocet, Killdeer, Common Snipe, Wilson's Phalarope, Black-crowned Night-Heron, and Snowy Egret. The riparian habitat attracts many of the valley's passerines. Raptors that use the refuge include breeding Swainson's Hawks and Northern Harriers and wintering Rough-legged Hawks and Prairie Falcons.

Two trails follow the river for birders interested in hiking. Birding is permitted on a walk-in basis from a bluff overlook.

Area brochure, mammals list, hunting. Spring, Fall

Arapaho ❷   (office at refuge)
PO Box 457
Walden, CO 80480   303-723-8202

Arapaho refuge also manages the Hutton Lake and Pathfinder NWR's in Wyoming.

Bird List CO-3 Arapaho Summary
150 birds listed, 69 nesting birds
Bird Chart pages 222-239

Totals by Season		s	S	F	W
Abundant	A	0	5	3	1
Common	C	25	38	26	4
Uncommon	U	32	32	34	9
Occasional	O	42	34	45	11
Rare	R	26	23	31	6

Endangered Species: Bald Eagle, Peregrine Falcon

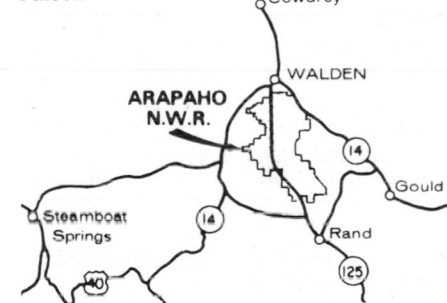

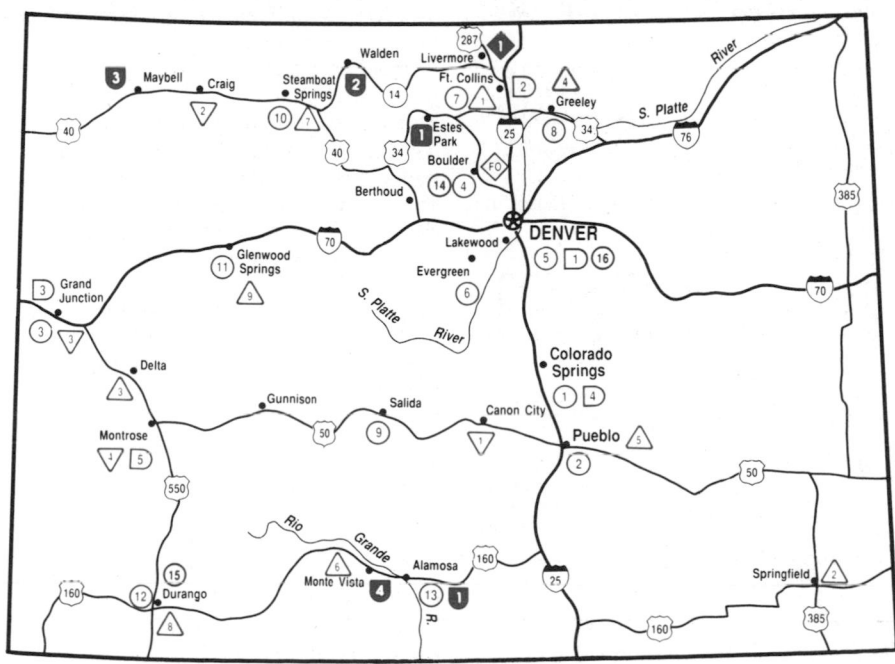

Take Hwy. 125 from Walden 7 miles south. Turn east (left) onto the gravel County Road 32 at the refuge sign, and proceed less than 1 mile.

Habitat: 18,253 acres located in a glacial basin in the mountains of north central Colorado. The floodplain, cut by many streams, is primarily irrigated meadow. Sagebrush grasslands cover the rises.

Waterfowl start to arrive in April after the ice melts, and peak at more than 5,000 ducks in late May. Mallards, Gadwalls, and American Wigeons are the most numerous species of the 14 that remain to breed at Arapaho. A variety of marsh birds and shorebirds use the wetlands, including breeding Soras, Virginia Rails, and Wilson's Phalaropes, and migrating Long-billed Dowitchers.

Eared Grebes, Swainson's Hawks, Sage Grouse, and Burrowing Owls are among the less common breeding species. Golden Eagles may be seen throughout the year riding the thermals. Two subspecies of Rosy Finch, "Black" and "Brown-capped," can be seen on the higher rises.

Wildlife list including mammals, fishes, amphibians, and reptiles. Area brochure, auto tour, trails, hunting, fishing. Spring, Fall

Browns Park ❸ (office at refuge)
1318 Highway 318
Maybell, CO 81640　　　303-365-3613

Bird List CO-4 Abundance Summary
181 birds listed, 78 nesting birds
Bird Chart pages 222-239

Totals by Season		s	S	F	W
Abundant	A	5	4	1	2
Common	C	69	59	66	9
Uncommon	U	29	20	25	14
Occasional	O	46	35	35	15
Rare	R	15	9	10	7

Endangered Species: Bald Eagle, Peregrine Falcon

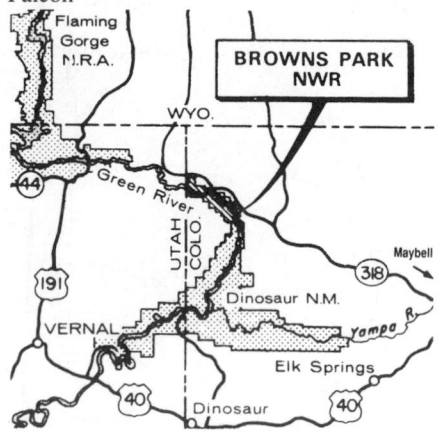

Take Hwy. 318 from its junction with U.S. 40, just outside Maybell, 50 miles west to the refuge. Watch for the headquarters sign. Headquarters is just off Hwy. 318 at northern end of the refuge.

Habitat: The refuge lies on the Green River in the far northwestern corner of Colorado at 5,300–6,000 feet of elevation. Water is pumped to maintain about 6,000 acres of developed waterfowl habitat in the semiarid climate, where the annual rainfall is less than 10 inches.

A large variety of ducks, including Ruddy Ducks, Redheads, all three teals, and Canvasbacks, breed at the refuge. Sage Grouse and Gambel's Quails also nest at Brown's Park, where Bald and Golden eagles are common winter residents.

Area brochure, auto tour route, hunting, boating, fishing, camping, picnicking. Spring, Fall

Monte Vista ❹ (office at Alamosa)
c/o Alamosa NWR
PO Box 1148
Alamosa, CO 81101　　　719-589-4021

See Bird List CO-2 Alamosa Summary page 55 and Bird Chart pages 222-239

Take Hwy. 15 south from Monte Vista for 6 miles to refuge entrance on left (see Alamosa map on page 49).

Habitat: 14,189 acres at 7,500 to 7,800 feet. Numerous dikes and ponds in an arid valley fed by mountain streams.

Pintails and Mallards are the most common of the 10,000 ducks that winter on Monte Vista's ponds. Spring migration in March and April swells the population to more than 20,000 birds.

Monte Vista is a major crane resting and feeding area during the spring and fall migrations. Whooping Cranes are often seen in the foster care of "Greater" Sandhill Cranes, a program to increase the numbers of the endangered species.

The Avocet Trail, a 6-mile auto tour route, is a self-guiding loop open from sunrise to sunset during winter, spring, and summer.

Area brochure, auto tour, hunting, mammals list. Spring, Fall

NATIONAL PARK SERVICE

Rocky Mountain ❶
National Park　　　(east) 303-586-2371
Estes Park, CO 80517 (west) 303-627-3471

265,200 acres of mountain peaks, accessible by Trail Ridge Road, which crosses the Continental Divide. Peaks towering more than 14,000 feet shadow wildlife and wildflowers in these 414 square miles of the Rockies' Front Range. General information and campgrounds leaflets, bird list.

NATIONAL FOREST SERVICE
NFS Rocky Mountain Region
11177 West 8th Ave.
PO Box 25127
Lakewood, CO 80225　　　303-236-9431

Map/Forest/City
△ Arapaho & Roosevelt Forests
　/Ft.Collins　　　303-224-1277
△ Comanche Grassland (Carrizo Unit)
　/Springfield　　　719-523-6591
△ Grand Mesa-Uncompahgre
　& Gunnison Forests
　/Delta　　　303-874-7691
△ Pawnee Grasslands
　/Greeley　　　303-353-5004
△ Pike & San Isabel
　Forests/Pueblo　　　719-545-8737
△ Rio Grande
　/Monte Vista　　　719-852-5941
△ Routt/Steamboat Spgs.　303-879-1722
△ San Juan/Durango　　303-247-4874
△ White River
　/Glenwood Springs　　303-945-2521

BUREAU LAND MANAGEMENT
BLM State Office
2850 Youngfield St.
Lakewood, CO 80215　　　303-236-1700

Map/District/City
▽ Canon City
　/Cannon City　　　719-275-0631
▽ Craig/Craig　　　303-824-8261
▽ Grand Junction
　/Grand Junction　　　303-243-6552
▽ Montrose/Montrose　　303-249-7791

STATE AGENCIES

Colorado Division of Wildlife
6060 Broadway
Denver, CO 80216　　　303-297-1802

Map/Region/City
　Central/Denver　　　303-291-7230
　Northeast/Ft. Collins　303-484-2836
　Northwest/Gr. Junction 303-248-7175
　Southeast
　/Colorado Springs　　303-473-2945
　Southwest/Montrose　303-249-3431

Colorado Tourism Board
5500 S. Syracuse
Suite 267
Englewood, CO 80111　　　800-433-2656

BIRDING HOTLINE

Statewide   203-254-3665

LOCAL BIRDING GROUPS

Map/Chapter/City

1. Aretas A. Saunders Aud./Stratford
2. Darien Audubon/Darien
3. Greenwich Audubon/Old Greenwich
4. Housatonic Audubon/Sharon
5. Lillinonah Audubon/Southbury
6. Litchfield Hills Aud./Litchfield
7. Mattabeseck Audubon/Middletown
8. Menunkatuck Audubon/Guilford
9. Naugatuck Valley Audubon/Derby
10. New Cannan Audubon/New Cannan
11. Northeast CT Audubon/Storrs
12. Pequot Audubon/Mystic
13. Potapaug Audubon/Old Lyme
14. Quinnipiac Valley Audubon
     /Wallingford
15. Saugatuck Vallcy Aud./Westport
16. CT Audubon Society/Fairfield
17. New Haven Bird Club/New Haven
18. Natchaug Orn. Soc./Mansfield
19. Western CT Bird Club/Southbury
20. Waterbury Naturalist Club/Waterbury

NATIONAL AUDUBON SOCIETY

Audubon Center in Greenwich ❶ & Fairchild Wildflower Garden

613 Riversville Road
Greenwich, CT 06831   203-869-5272
Entrance fee for non-Audubon members

This quiet, 407-acre sanctuary includes two tracts of land, the Audubon Center in Greenwich and the Audubon Fairchild Garden. More than 160 species of birds have been recorded here. The Center is open from 9 a.m. to 5 p.m., Tuesday through Sunday and closed Monday and holiday weekends. Fairchild Garden is open daily from dawn to dusk.

The Audubon Center in Greenwich is located at the corner of Riversville Road and John Street and consists of 280 acres of open woodlands, meadows, ponds, and streams. A variety of resident winter birds can be observed at close range at the Center's feeding station during the cold months of the year. Other birding opportunities include nature trails, a model backyard wildlife habitat, vantage points including bird blinds on Mead Lake, and the Quaker Ridge Hawk Watch Site.

The 127-acre Audubon Fairchild Garden is located on North Porchuck Road one mile from the Audubon Center. Most of the ferns and flowering plants of Connecticut can be seen in the Fairchild Garden.

Sanctuary/Education Center brochure with travel directions from Connecticut, New York, and the North, by car or bus (the Merritt Parkway is restricted to cars). Bird list available.
Spring, Summer, Fall, Winter

Northeast Audubon Center ❷

Route 4, Box 171
Sharon, CT 06069   203-364-0520
Entrance fee for non-Audubon members

One half of this scenic 684-acre tract is designated as a natural area, which is off limits to visitors. The other half, containing nearly 11 miles of foot trails, is maintained for environmental education.

The center is located in the northwest corner of Connecticut, about 2 miles southeast of Sharon on St. Rte. 4.

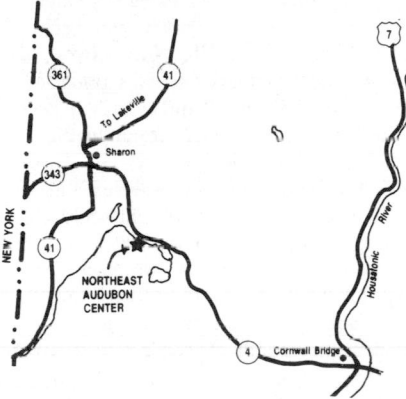

A two-day "Annual Audubon Festival" is held here in late July or early August. A daily admission fee for the festival covers adult and children's programs, exhibits, and tours.

Center and Education Program brochures, trail map, bird list.
Spring, Summer, Fall, Winter

THE NATURE CONSERVANCY

Connecticut Chapter Field Office
55 High Street
Middletown, CT 06457   203-344-0716

A free preserve brochure entitled "Saving Land for Future Generations" is available from the Field Office. It lists the preserves noted here, provides specific directions to each, and explains Connecticut Chapter activity and the Connecticut River Protection Program. These preserves are worth visiting at any season except as noted.

Helen G. Altschul Preserve ◆

A mature oak forest and forested wetland of 164 acres near Stamford featuring a 1.5-mile walking trail. The east branch of the Mianus River flows through the preserve.
Summer, Fall, Winter

Harry E. Barnes Memorial ◆ Preserve & Nature Center

Red maple swamp, oak and hickory forest, glacial features, and hiking trails compliment the museum and Nature Center on this 154-acre preserve near Bristol.

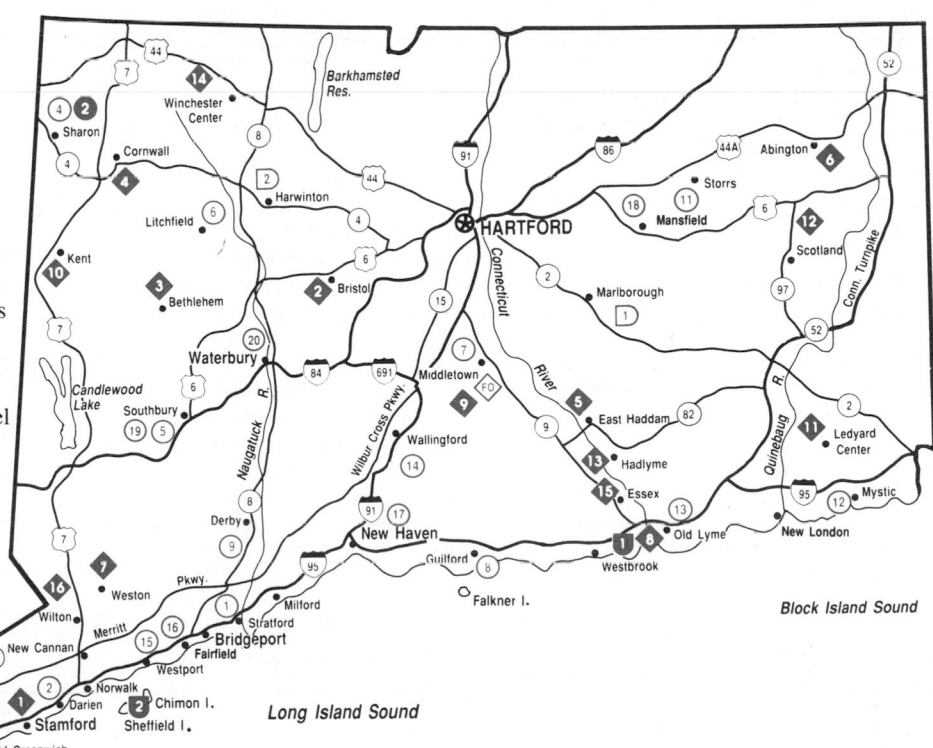

Bellamy Preserve
Open and wooded areas include walking trails through the 90 acres of remnant orchards and former red pine plantations on the north side of Bethlehem, at the foot of Long Meadow Pond.

Cathedral Pines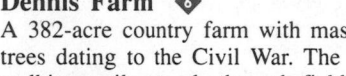
The 42-acre preserve of 200-foot white pines near Cornwall can be sampled on the mile-long Mohawk Trail, or toured more extensively on an all-day hike.

Chapman Pond
A secluded 326-acre area including Chapman Pond, a freshwater tidal pond off the Connecticut River and near East Haddam. Access by canoe only, which is easier during periods of high tide.

Dennis Farm
A 382-acre country farm with massive trees dating to the Civil War. The 2-mile walking trail extends through fields and woodlands near Abington.

Devil's Den
c/o Lucius Pond Ordway
Devil's Den Preserve
PO Box 1162
Weston, CT 06883   203-226-4991

An available brochure includes visitor regulations and a fold-out map of hiking and cross-country trails at this 1,540-acre preserve. Habitat varies from wetland, stream, and pond, to mature forest, and rocky knolls.

Griswold Point
A 22-acre, mile-long barrier beach, near Old Lyme, at the mouth of the Connecticut River with access by canoe. A summer warden closes the area during the endangered Piping Plover's and Least Tern's nesting season.
Spring, Summer (except as noted), Fall, Winter

Higby Mountain
A basalt trap rock ridge and hiking trail are features of this 159-acre area near Middletown. Blue blazes marking the Mattabesset Trail begin just uphill from the parking area.

Iron Mountain Reservation
A 1.5-mile trail leads hikers through deciduous and hardwood forests, rock outcrops, and dry oak woods to the summit of Ore Hill. This 276-acre preserve is near Kent.

Poquetanuct Cove
Near Ledyard Center, this 234-acre preserve features a looped hiking trail through a mature hemlock forest along the cove. It is home to Great Horned Owls,

Ospreys, and Red-shouldered Hawks.

Rock Springs Wildlife Refuge
Glacial features, a bubbling spring, and trails to an overlook with an excellent view and along sparkling Little River are attractions at this 444-acre refuge near Scotland. Many species are present, including Northern Bobwhites, Ruffed Grouse, and American Woodcocks.

Selden Creek
A superb 55-acre freshwater marsh near Hadlyme that is home to many rare plants and wildlife.
Access by canoe only.

Silas Hall Pond Preserve
A 94-acre preserve with unspoiled bog, pond, steep forested slopes, beaver dams, and hiking trail near Winchester Center.

Turtle Creek Wildlife Sanctuary
This 93-acre sanctuary includes pond and marsh, mountain laurel thickets, and beech groves under dense hemlock along the Connecticut River near Essex. The Turtle Creek brochure notes bird species with season and residency status, mammals, ferns, trees, and flowering plants.

A variety of ducks, wading birds, and other marsh birds can be seen in the marsh at the mouth of Turtle Creek. Birds migrating along the Connecticut River Valley stop at this sanctuary, providing particularly good birding during spring and fall.

Two miles of nature trails offer an excellent learning experience for children.

Weir Preserve
Weir Preserve of The Nature Conservancy
PO Box 7033
Wilton, CT 06897

A 98-acre preserve with swamp, open fields, forests, and a waterfall. Mountain laurel, red trillium, columbine, and lady's slipper provide a spectacular show of color during summer.

Wood Ducks and Mallards nest in the swamp areas of the preserve, while Pileated Woodpeckers, Ruffed Grouse, and Great Horned Owls live in the forest. Eastern Bluebirds, White-breasted Nuthatches, Black-capped Chickadees, and Blue-winged Warblers are more often noted.

An excellent 26-page Weir Preserve Trail Guide is available that describes 11 points of interest along the well-marked trail.

U.S. FISH & WILDLIFE SERVICE NATIONAL WILDLIFE REFUGES

The Salt Meadow and Stewart B. McKinney in Connecticut are two of six refuges in the Ninigret Refuge Complex. The Ninigret headquarters and four other refuges are in Rhode Island.

Salt Meadow
c/o Ninigret Refuge Complex
Shoreline Plaza, Route 1A
PO Box 307
Charlestown, RI 02813   401-364-9124

Bird List CT-1 Salt Meadow Summary
255 birds listed, 66 nesting birds
Bird Chart pages 222-239
Note: The bird list and summary represents species found at Salt Meadow and Stewart B. McKinney NWR's.

Seasonal Abundance	s	S	F	W
Abundant	A	4	3	7	4
Common	C	59	46	81	26
Uncommon	U	70	47	60	42
Occasional	O	57	48	50	42
Rare	R	42	20	44	27

Endangered Species: Bald Eagle, Peregrine Falcon, Piping Plover, Roseate Tern, Least Tern

Salt Meadow is located south of I-95 and north of the Boston Post Road (Rte. 1) between Westbrook and Clinton. Take exit 64 from I-95 south onto Old Clinton Road and follow it southeast to the refuge entrance on the right.

Habitat: 183 acres of tidal salt marsh, shrubland, woodland, and open field.

The refuge is an important nesting, resting, feeding, and wintering area for migratory birds, including waterfowl, shorebirds, wading birds, and songbirds.

Three-mile foot trail, nature observation.
Spring, Summer, Fall

Stewart B. McKinney
c/o Ninigret Refuge Complex
Shoreline Plaza, Route 1A
PO Box 307
Charlestown, RI 02813   401-364-9124

The Stewart B. McKinney refuge consists of four separate land units totaling 130 acres. The Milford Point Unit is on the mainland. Three other units, Sheffield, Chimon, and Falkner Islands in Long Island Sound are close to the Connecticut coast and accessible only by boat.

Milford Point

Take exit 34 from I-95 to Rte. 1, turn left (east) and continue to next traffic light. Turn right onto Lansdale Ave. and proceed to Milford Point Road. Turn right and go about 5 miles on Milford Point Road to Seaview Ave. Turn right, go to the end of the road (0.3 miles) and "Smith-Hubbell (Audubon) Wildlife Sanctuary" sign and turn right into parking lot. Milford Point access is via the shoreline below mean high water.

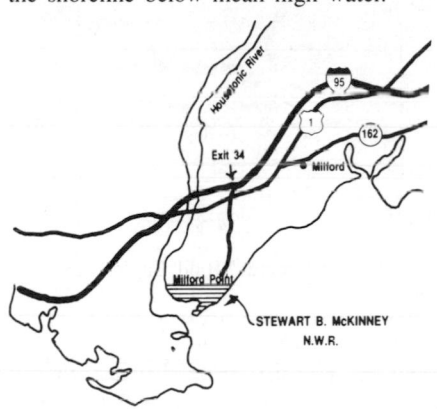

Habitat: This 6-acre barrier peninsula is comprised primarily of dredge fill and sandy beaches and dunes. The unit shelters the salt marshes of the adjacent 865-acre Wheeler State Wildlife Management Area.

Milford Point is open from September 1 to March 31. The refuge is one of the few nesting areas for two endangered species, the Least Tern and the Piping Plover, and closes during the summer.

Sheffield Island

Accessible only by boat, 1.5 miles south of Norwalk.

Habitat: 52 acres include woodland, shrubland, sandy beach and rocky shore.

The diverse habitats supports a variety of nesting and migratory species, including Ospreys and various herons.

The refuge is open year-around, although there are no trails or facilities and a portion of the island is privately owned.

Chimon Island

This 68-acre tract of sandy and rocky shores, woodland, and shrubland is 1 mile east of Sheffield Is.

Chimon Island is the site of one of the largest wading bird colonies in the Northeast. More than 125 species of birds utilize the island during various seasons.

The unit is open September 1 to March 31. A 3-acre beach, operated by the Town of Norwalk during the summer season, is open all year from dawn to dusk. No trails or other facilities are available.

Falkner Island

A 4.5-acre island located 3 miles south of Guilford. Open from September 1 to March 31.

Habitat: Comprised chiefly of shrubland and rocky shore. It is closed to visitors during the summer because it supports significant populations of the Common Tern and the endangered Roseate Tern. No trails or other facilities are available. Hiking.

STATE AGENCIES

Dept. of Environmental Protection Wildlife Bureau HQ
State Office Bldg.
165 Capitol Ave.
Hartford, CT 06106   203-566-4683

Map/District/City
1 Eastern/Marlborough   203-295-9523
2 Western/Harwinton   203-485-0226

Connecticut Tourism Division
210 Washington St.
Hartford, CT 06106   800-282-6863
from out-of-state, Maine
through Virginia call   800-243-1685

BIRDING HOTLINE
Statewide   215-567-2473

LOCAL BIRDING GROUPS
Map/Chapter/City
① Delaware Audubon/Wilmington
② Delmarva Orn. Soc./Greenville
③ Delaware Nature Soc./Hockessin

SPECIAL BIRDING AREA

Delaware Bay Reserve ①
c/o Western Hemisphere Shorebird
Rreservr Network (WHSRN)
801 Pennsylvania Avenue SE
Suite 301
Washington, DC 20003   202-547-9009

State, federal, and private areas in
Delaware and New Jersey, along both
shores of Delaware Bay, host 80 percent
of the Red Knots migrating along the
Atlantic coast. More than one million Red
Knots and other shorebirds pause here in
May to feed and rest before continuing on
to their Arctic and Hudson Bay nesting
grounds.

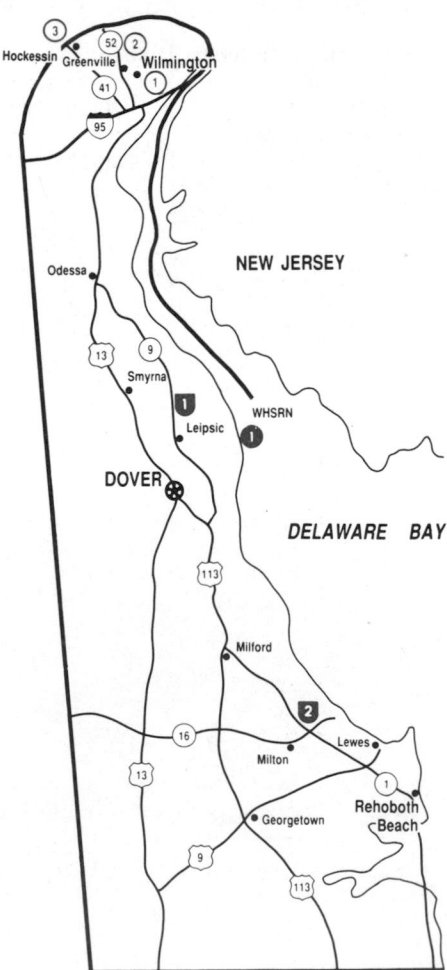

U.S. FISH & WILDLIFE SERVICE NATIONAL WILDLIFE REFUGES

Bombay Hook ①   (office at refuge)
Route 1, Box 147
Smyrna, DE 19977   302-653-9345
Entry Fee

Bird List DE-1 Bombay Hook Summary
261 birds listed, 100 nesting birds
Bird Chart pages 222-239
Note: Most of the species in Bird List
DE-1 may be observed at the Prime Hook
refuge 30 miles south of Bombay Hook.

Totals by Season		s	S	F	W
Abundant	A	17	15	31	9
Common	C	2	69	94	45
Uncommon	U	33	32	32	24
Occasional	O	72	57	75	46
Rare	R	21	25	24	37

Endangered Species: Bald Eagle, Peregrine
Falcon, Least Tern

From Leipsic take St. Rte. 9 north for 2
miles, then turn east for 2.5 miles on
Whitehall Neck Road to refuge
headquarters.

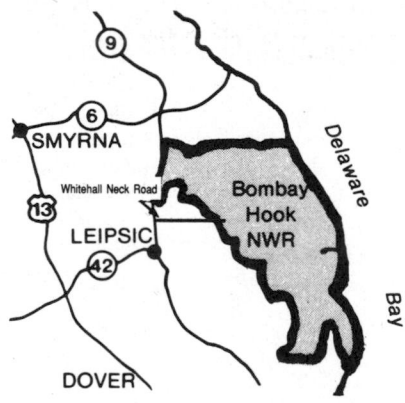

Habitat: 15,122 acres extending for 8
miles along the western shore of the
Delaware Bay. About 80 percent of this
refuge is tidal salt marsh. There are 1,100
acres of impounded freshwater pools,
1,030 acres of timbered swamps, and
about 1,000 acres of agricultural land.

Waterfowl populations reach their peak in
October and November, when over
100,000 ducks and geese utilize the
refuge. Another peak occurs in March, as
the waterfowl return to northern breeding
grounds.

Early shorebird migrants arrive in April,
and are at their highest concentrations
during May and August when they return
from their breeding grounds in the north.
Wading birds and songbirds are most
abundant during May, August, and
September. Herons, egrets, and Glossy
Ibises reach their peak numbers during the

summer months.
Area brochure, bird, mammal, reptile, and
amphibian lists, fishing, crabbing, hunting,
hiking, auto tour route, 3 observation
towers.
Spring, Fall, Winter

Prime Hook ②   (Office at refuge)
Route 1, Box 195
Milton, DE 19968   302-684-8419

The refuge is located 12 miles southeast
of Milford and 10 miles northwest of
Lewes. Take Rte. 1 southeast from
Milford to Rte. 16. Turn east on Rte. 16
(Broadhill Beach Road) for 1 mile and
turn left onto the refuge road. Drive 1.6
miles to the office.

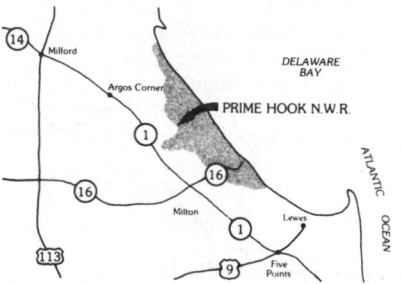

Habitat: 8,817 acres on the west shore of
Delaware Bay, with 6,867 acres of
freshwater and tidal marshes, and water.
There are also 850 acres of timber and
brush and 1,100 acres of grasslands and
croplands.

Prime Hook is a major stopover point for
thousands of migrating waterfowl during
spring and fall. Canada and Snow geese,
and American Black and Wood ducks are
among the most common species. The
shorebird and warbler migrations peak in
May. The marshes also provide nesting
habitat for various waterfowl and other
water birds.

Hunting, fishing, canoeing, boating,
hiking, wildlife observation.
Spring, Fall, Winter

STATE AGENCIES

Division of Fish & Wildlife
Dept. of Natural Resources &
Environmental Control
Richardson & Robbins Bldg.
89 Kings Highway
PO Box 1401
Dover, DE 19903   302-736-4580

Delaware Tourism
Townsend Bldg.
Dover, DE 19901   800-282-8667
from out-of-state   800-441-8846

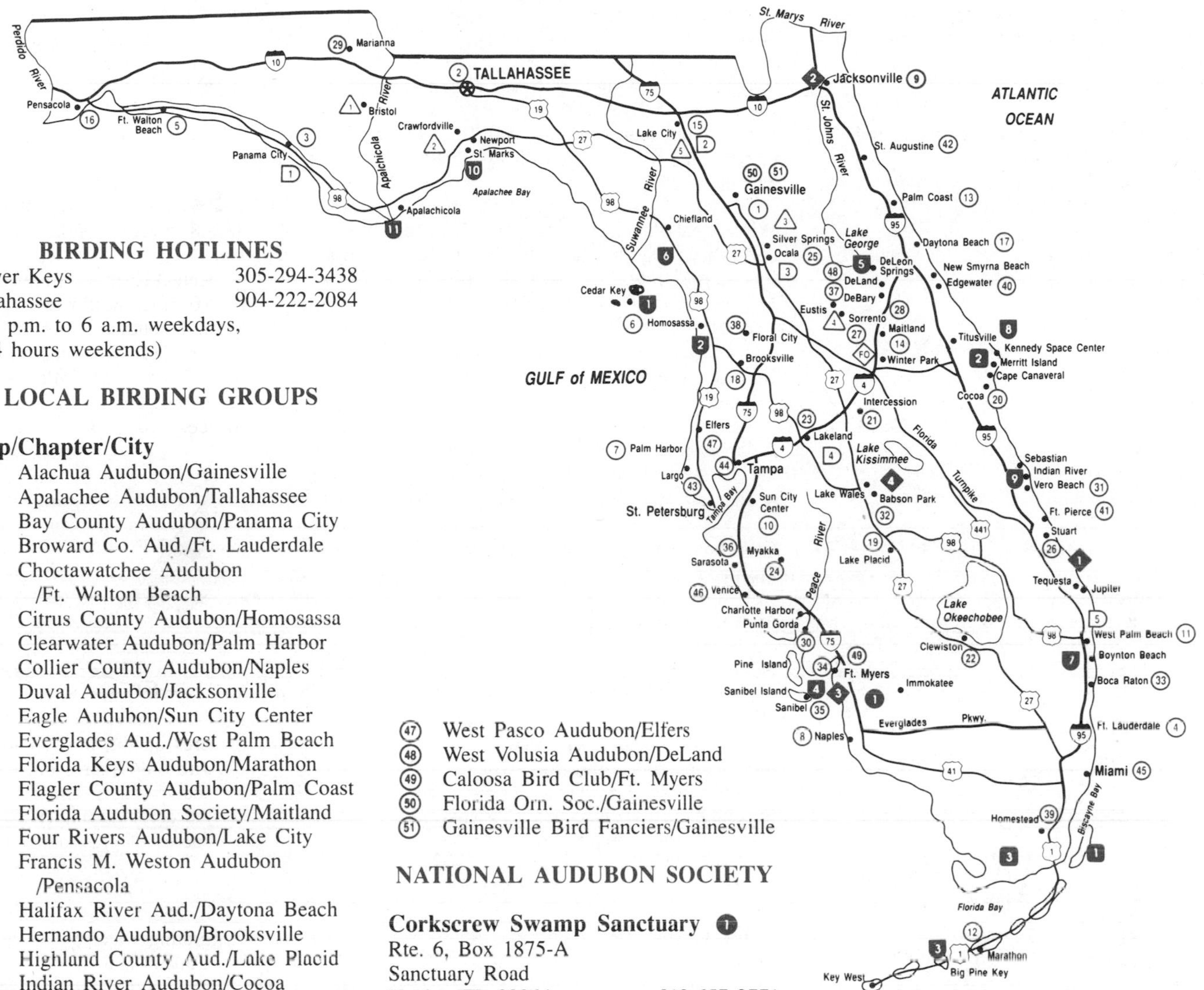

BIRDING HOTLINES

Lower Keys	305-294-3438
Tallahassee	904-222-2084

(6 p.m. to 6 a.m. weekdays,
24 hours weekends)

LOCAL BIRDING GROUPS

Map/Chapter/City

1. Alachua Audubon/Gainesville
2. Apalachee Audubon/Tallahassee
3. Bay County Audubon/Panama City
4. Broward Co. Aud./Ft. Lauderdale
5. Choctawatchee Audubon /Ft. Walton Beach
6. Citrus County Audubon/Homosassa
7. Clearwater Audubon/Palm Harbor
8. Collier County Audubon/Naples
9. Duval Audubon/Jacksonville
10. Eagle Audubon/Sun City Center
11. Everglades Aud./West Palm Beach
12. Florida Keys Audubon/Marathon
13. Flagler County Audubon/Palm Coast
14. Florida Audubon Society/Maitland
15. Four Rivers Audubon/Lake City
16. Francis M. Weston Audubon /Pensacola
17. Halifax River Aud./Daytona Beach
18. Hernando Audubon/Brooksville
19. Highland County Aud./Lake Placid
20. Indian River Audubon/Cocoa
21. Kissimmee Valley Audubon /Intercession
22. Lake Okeechobee Aud./Clewiston
23. Lake Region Audubon/Lakeland
24. Manatee County Audubon/Myanka
25. Marion Audubon/Ocala
26. Martin County Audubon/Stuart
27. Oklawaha Valley Audubon/Sorrento
28. Orange Audubon/Maitland
29. Panhandle Audubon/Marianna
30. Peace River Audubon/Punta Gorda
31. Pelican Island Audubon/Vero Beach
32. Ridge Audubon/Babson Park
33. Royal Palm Audubon/Boca Raton
34. S.W. Florida Audubon/Ft. Myers
35. Sanibel-Captiva Audubon/Sanibel
36. Sarasota Audubon/Sarasota
37. Seminole Audubon/DeBary
38. Singing Forest Audubon/Floral City
39. South Dade Audubon/Homestead
40. S.E. Volusia Audubon/Edgewater
41. St. Lucie Audubon/Ft. Pierce
42. St. Johns Co. Aud./St. Augustine
43. St. Petersburg Audubon/Largo
44. Tampa Audubon/Tampa
45. Tropical Audubon/Miami
46. Venice Area Audubon/Venice
47. West Pasco Audubon/Elfers
48. West Volusia Audubon/DeLand
49. Caloosa Bird Club/Ft. Myers
50. Florida Orn. Soc./Gainesville
51. Gainesville Bird Fanciers/Gainesville

NATIONAL AUDUBON SOCIETY

Corkscrew Swamp Sanctuary ❶

Rte. 6, Box 1875-A
Sanctuary Road
Naples, FL 33964   813-657-3771
Visitor Fee

Bird List FL-1 Corkscrew Summary

188 birds listed, 76 nesting birds
Bird Chart pages 222-239

Totals by Season		s	S	F	W
Common	C	66	40	61	64
Uncommon	U	67	26	70	69
Rare	R	44	14	44	53

Endangered Species: Wood Stork, Bald Eagle, Peregrine Falcon

The entrance to Corkscrew Swamp is located on Sanctuary Road, 1.5 miles from Co. Road 846. The intersection of Sanctuary Road and Co. Road 846 is 14 miles west of Immokatee, 21 miles east of Route 41, and 15 miles east of exit 17 on I-75.

Habitat: 11,000-acre remnant wilderness area containing one of the largest remaining virgin stands of bald cypress trees. Some trees exceed 120 feet in height and 25 feet in circumference, and have been core-dated at over 700 years old. Understory is a tangle of vines, air plants, shrubs, and aquatic plants.

The unusual nesting season, December through April, coincides with the dry season when water levels are low and therefore food is more accessible. During the wet, humid summer with water levels up to 4.5 feet higher, the subtropical vegetation grows quickly. Corkscrew is one of the few locations where the American Swallow-tailed Kite is a common breeding species.

Visitor's center, 2-mile boardwalk trail, picnic tables, wheelchairs available. Naturalist guided group tours may be arranged by advanced request.

Area brochure, self-guided tour book, abundant wildlife.
Spring, Winter

THE NATURE CONSERVANCY

Florida Field Office
1353 Palmetto Ave.
Winter Park, FL 32789   407-628-5887

Blowing Rocks ❶

Resident Manager
PO Box 3795
Tequesta, FL 33469   407-575-2297

Located on Jupiter Island below the Hobe Sound National Wildlife Refuge and adjacent Jonathan Dickinson State Park. From U.S. Hwy. 1 take St. Rte. 707 east to the island.

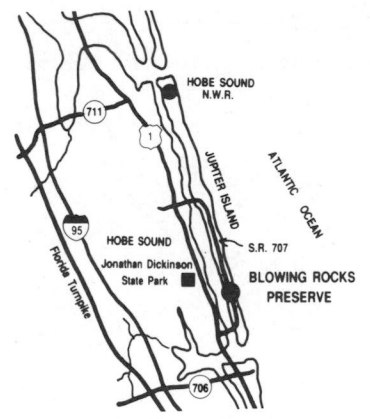

Habitat: 113 acres include the largest Anastasia limestone outcropping on the east coast, as well as shifting ocean front dune, coastal strand, interior mangrove wetlands, and tropical coastal hammock.

The endangered Brown Pelican can be seen flying in tight flocks or diving for its prey, while Great Blue Herons and other waders study the shallow waters on the coast in search of fish.

Area brochure with map, nature trails. Fishing, swimming.
Spring, Summer, Fall, Winter

The Hon. Theodore Roosevelt ❷

Contact field office for visiting details. Preserve is under lease to Jacksonville University for educational, scientific, and passive recreational use.

Habitat: 640 acres of maritime hammock

forest, dune scrub, and fresh and salt water marshes.

The hardwood hammock forest, which is the primary habitat at this preserve, is home to birds such as the Wild Turkey and Painted Bunting, as well as armadillos and opossum.

White-eyed Vireos, Rufous-sided Towhees, and other passerines are attracted to the low, dense growth of the dune scrub in the northeast section of the preserve. Large rookeries of Great Blue Herons, Great Egrets, and Black-crowned Night-Herons are located in the low-lying freshwater marshes.

A large variety of marsh birds, including the endangered Wood Stork, are attracted to the salt water marshes and tidal creeks.

Area brochure with map, nature trails.
Spring, Fall, Winter

Matanzas Pass ❸

c/o Manager
PO Box 2692
Ft. Myers, FL 33932

Contact the manager for access information concerning this 42-acre preserve on Estero Island near Ft. Myers Beach. A boardwalk extends through a hammock and mangrove forest to the bay.

Winter

Tiger Creek ❹

c/o Central Florida Land Steward
225 E. Stuart Ave.
Lake Wales, FL 33853   813-676-0521

About 10 miles east of Lake Wales, just west of Lake Weohyakapka. Preserve foot trails can be reached from U.S. 27 by taking Hwy. 60 east to Lake Walk-in-the-Water Road. Go 3.5 miles south on this road and turn west on Wakeford Road which dead ends at the preserve entrance. Contact Bok Tower Gardens, which shares in the management of Tiger Creek, at 813-676-1408 before visiting.

Habitat: 4,400 acres of hardwood swamps and hammocks, sand pine, and oak scrub on the edge of Florida's highest land mass, Lake Wales Ridge.

Some of the rarest flora and fauna in Florida may be found at Tiger Creek, including the Florida sand skink, scrub lizard, pygmy fringe tree, bonamia and the threatened "Florida" Scrub Jay.

Area brochure with map. Hiking trails.
Spring, Fall, Winter

U.S. FISH & WILDLIFE SERVICE NATIONAL WILDLIFE REFUGES

Cedar Keys ❶

c/o Lower Suwannee NWR
Rt. 1, Box 1193-C   904-493-0238
Chiefland, FL 32626

Bird List FL-2 Cedar Keys Summary
237 birds listed, 82 nesting birds
Bird Chart pages 222-239

Totals by Season		s	S	F	W
Abundant	A	14	12	11	16
Common	C	7	76	12	7
Uncommon	U	50	24	48	47
Occasional	O	24	11	24	13
Rare	R	10	3	12	8

Endangered Species: Brown Pelican, Wood Stork, Bald Eagle, Peregrine Falcon, Piping Plover, Least Tern, Red-cockaded Woodpecker

Refuge headquarters is located at the Lower Suwannee Refuge. Take Hwy. 347 southwest from Chiefland. Go about 15 miles to the refuge headquarters road, turn right and follow signs to the office.

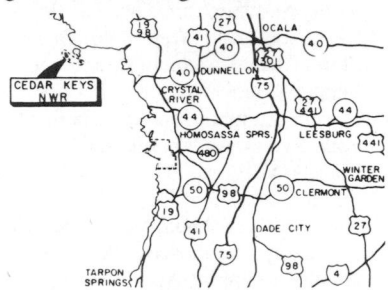

Habitat: The islands, located in the Gulf of Mexico and ranging in size from 6 to 165 acres, are surrounded by shallow sand and mud flats, which make them relatively inaccessible except by boat at high tide. Only the beaches are open to the public.

With a recorded peak of over 200,000 nesting birds in a single year and an average of approximately 50,000, Cedar Keys ranks as one of the largest nesting areas in Florida. The more abundant nesting species include the White Ibis, Double-crested Cormorant, Great Blue and Tricolored herons, and Snowy Egrets. The Brown Pelican colony is the most northern one of any significance. Other common nesters include the Common Ground-Dove and Gray Kingbird.

Area brochure, shell collecting, picnicking, beachcombing.
Public use season is July through December.

Chassahowitzka ❷

Rt. 2, Box 44   (office near refuge)
Homosassa, FL 32646   904-382-2201

Bird List FL-3 Chassahow. Summary
234 birds listed, 78 nesting birds
Bird Chart pages 222-239

Totals by Season		s	S	F	W
Abundant	A	22	12	18	24
Common	C	82	55	86	82
Uncommon	U	56	32	52	53
Occasional	O	24	6	23	13
Rare	R	17	8	18	13

Endangered Species: Brown Pelican, Peregrine Falcon, Wood Stork, Bald Eagle, Piping Plover, Least Tern
Rare/Limited Species: Budgerigar

The refuge headquarters are located on the west side of U.S. Hwy. 19, 4 miles south of Homosassa Springs. This is also headquarters for Egmont Key, Passage Key, and Pinellas NWR's, small islands in Tampa Bay; and for Crystal Key NWR, an island located in Kings Bay.

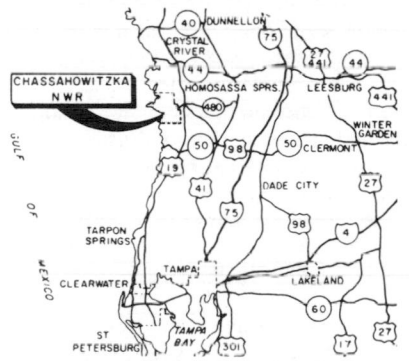

Habitat: 30,500 acres on the Gulf Coast of saltwater bays, estuaries, and brackish marshes, with a fringe of hardwood swamps along the eastern boundary and the Homosassa River along much of the northern edge.

Chassahowitzka is a prime wintering area for both pelicans and 19 species of waterfowl, including Green-winged and Blue-winged teals, American Black Ducks, Mallards, Northern Pintails, American Wigeons, and Hooded and Red-breasted mergansers. The outer keys have large colonies of Double-crested Cormorants, as well as Great Blue, Little Blue, and Green-backed herons and Black-crowned and Yellow-crowned night-herons.

A variety of migratory warblers stop to rest and feed at the refuge en route to and from their wintering grounds in Central and South America.

Area brochure, fishing, hunting, 0.5-mile nature trail. With the exception of the headquarters area, the refuge is accessible by boat only.
Late Spring, Winter.

Florida Keys Refuges ❸
PO Box 510   (office on Big Pine Key)
Big Pine Key, FL 33043   305-872-2239

Bird List FL-4 Florida Keys Summary
217 birds listed, 53 nesting birds
Bird Chart pages 222-239

Totals by Season		s	S	F	W
Abundant	A	10	9	10	11
Common	C	37	17	42	34
Uncommon	U	53	21	60	51
Occasional	O	34	27	37	28
Rare	R	32	14	45	37

Endangered Species: Brown Pelican, Bald Eagle, Peregrine Falcon, Piping Plover, Roseate Tern, Least Tern
Rare/Limited Species: Brown Noddy

Three refuges, National Key Deer, Great White Heron, and Key West, are made up of scattered islands within sight of one another, stretching for approximately 60 miles from the vicinity of East Bahia Honda Key on the east to Marquesas Keys on the west.

Except for a portion of Key Deer Refuge on Big Pine and Little Torch Keys, all of the refuge islands are accessible only by boat.

Headquarters for the three refuges is on Big Pine Key approximately 110 miles southwest of Miami. Take the Overseas Highway (Hwy. 1) from the mainland toward Key West. Approximately 0.5 mile past milepost 31, take the Hwy. 940 exit north onto Key Deer Blvd. Go about 2 miles, turn west on Watson Blvd. and continue to the refuge headquarters.

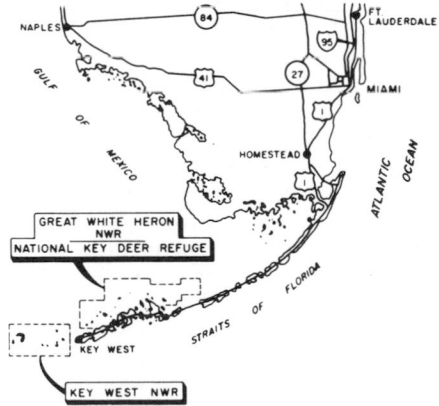

National Key Deer Refuge
Habitat: A variety of tropical and subtropical vegetation on the higher interiors of the keys is ringed by red and black mangroves. The substrate of oolitic limestone holds rainwater for extended periods. Slash pine and silver and thatch palms grow on the larger keys.

The bird life includes the "Great White"

morph of the Great Blue Heron, White-crowned Pigeon, Gray Kingbird, and Black-whiskered Vireo.

Great White Heron Refuge
Habitat: 6,781 acres of low keys covered with mangroves, stretching 40 miles from east to west. Partly overlaps the Key Deer refuge.

The refuge gives permanent protection to the "Great White" Heron. In addition, the refuge protects other rare birds, including the White-crowned Pigeon and Roseate Spoonbill.

Key West Refuge
Habitat: 2,019 acres, including all keys within 25 miles west of Key West except for Ballast Key.

Terns, Magnificent Frigatebirds, Roseate Spoonbills, White-crowned Pigeons, and "Great White" Herons are among the many species that spend part or all of the year on these keys.

Area brochure, mammals, reptiles and amphibians list, hiking.
Spring, Fall, Winter.

J.N. "Ding" Darling ❹
1 Wildlife Drive   (office at refuge)
Sanibel, FL 33957   813-472-1100
Entry fee

The bird species list, which shows abundance by month, was adapted for use in this book with the permission of the Sanibel-Captiva Audubon Society, J.N. "Ding" Darling Wildlife Society, and Sanibel-Captiva Conservation Foundation.

Bird List FL-5 "D" Darling Summary
245 birds listed, 63 nesting birds
Bird Chart pages 222-239

Totals by Season		s	S	F	W
Abundant	A	32	25	24	33
Common	C	6	56	1	86
Occasional	O	38	15	35	25
Rare	R	65	44	69	56

Endangered Species: Brown Pelican, Wood Stork, Bald Eagle, Peregrine Falcon, Piping Plover, Roseate Tern, Least Tern
Rare/Limited Species: Ringed Turtle Dove, Canary-winged Parakeet

J.N. "Ding" Darling Refuge is located on Sanibel Island southwest of Fort Myers. Take Hwy. 867 (Summerlin Road) southwest from Fort Myers about 13 miles to Punta Rassa. This road becomes a causeway (toll road) to Sanibel Island. On the island, take Periwinkle Way 2.5 miles to Tarpon Bay Road, turn right 0.25 mile to Sanibel-Captiva Road, turn left and go 2 miles to a refuge headquarters sign on the right side of the road.

This is also the administrative office for the following J.N. "Ding" Darling satellite refuges: Pine Island (297 acres on 7 islands), Matlacha Pass (160 acres on 5 islands), and Caloosahatchee and Island Bay (20 acres on 5 islands). All are mangrove islands in Pine Island Sound and Charlotte Harbor. Check at the refuge visitor center for details.

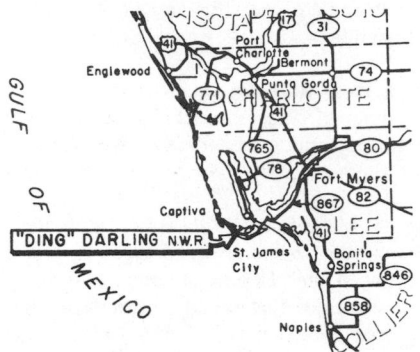

Habitat: Sanibel Island is a 5,014-acre, 12-mile long subtropical barrier island composed of sand, shell, and silt in dry ridges and wet sloughs. The island is fringed with mangrove trees, shallow bays, and white sandy beaches.

Favorite birding sites include the causeway islands, Gulf beaches, lighthouse area, Bailey Tract, Gasparilla Trail, Blind Pass, Tarpon Bay, Sanibel-Captiva Conservation Foundation, and the offshore islands.

Migrating passerines such as Painted Buntings and Hooded Warblers are common from March through May. Black-throated Blue Warblers are more commonly seen in the fall.

The refuge provides breeding habitat for Yellow-crowned Night-Herons, Great Blue and Little Blue herons, and Mottled Ducks.

During the winter various waterfowl can be seen, including Blue-winged Teal, Northern Pintails, and Red-breasted Mergansers.

Area brochure, wildlife drive, nature trails, canoe trails, fishing, wildlife exhibits, interpretative programs.
Spring, Fall

Lake Woodruff 5
Grand Avenue   (office in town)
PO Box 488
De Leon Springs, FL 32028 904-985-4673

Bird List FL-6 L. Woodruff Summary
211 birds listed, 67 nesting birds
Bird Chart pages 222-239

Totals by Season		s	S	F	W
Abundant	A	1	0	2	6
Common	C	43	32	42	39
Uncommon	U	48	27	51	42
Occasional	O	68	26	73	47
Rare	R	24	20	23	28

Endangered Species: Wood Stork, Bald Eagle, Peregrine Falcon, Least Tern

Turn west off U.S. Hwy. 17 in De Leon Springs (7 miles north of Deland), go 1 block to Grand Avenue and turn south. Go approximately 1 mile to the office.

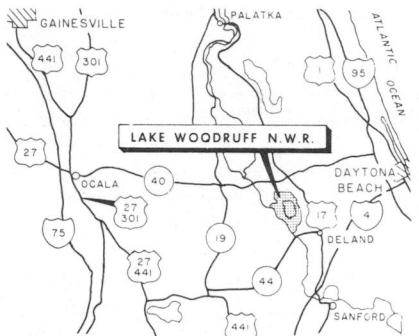

Habitat: Comprising 18,400 acres, the majority of the refuge is freshwater marshes, streams, and lakes. One-fourth is timbered swamps bordering the waterways and lakes. About 1,000 acres consist of pine flatwoods and scrub oak-pine.

Much of the refuge is accessible only by boat, and most birders use the man-made dikes for access and viewing.

A variety of waterbirds use the refuge, including Fulvous Whistling-Ducks, Limpkins, and the endangered Wood Stork. Wood Ducks and Mallards breed at Woodruff, while 16 other duck species winter on the refuge's extensive waterways. Blue-winged Teals, the first ducks to migrate through, arrive in September, and the waterfowl migration is well underway by November.

Wood Ducks and passerines begin to nest in March and April, while young Bald Eagles are ready to fledge. Gallinules and rails, which nest later in the season, can be seen with their young in July and August. American Swallow-tailed Kites may be seen hawking for insects. Hundreds of vultures can be seen roosting on Tick Island during October, and a variety of warblers are migrating through.

Area brochure, hunting, fishing, guided tours (by reservation). Mammals, amphibians, reptiles, fishes lists.
Winter

Lower Suwannee 6
Rt. 1, Box 1193C   (office at refuge)
Chiefland, FL 32626   904-493-0238

Note: For important Lower Suwannee information see the Cedar Keys Map, the Bird List FL-2 Cedar Keys Summary on page 62, and Bird Chart pages 222-239.

Take Hwy. 347 southeast from Chiefland and go about 15 miles to the refuge headquarters road and signs, turning right to the headquarters. This office also manages the Cedar Keys NWR.

Habitat: 40,000 acres along either side of the Suwannee River. The refuge also fronts on the Gulf of Mexico. Habitats include tidal or estuarine marshes, floodplain bottomland, hardwood forests interlaced with cypress-lined creeks, sloughs, wooded swamps, and upland sand oak communities.

Thousands of shorebirds and diving ducks, such as Redheads and Buffleheads, flock to the salt marshes and tidal flats. Other waterfowl, including Blue-winged and Green-winged teals, Wood Ducks, and Hooded and Common mergansers, winter on the inland wetlands. Raptors that breed on the refuge include Ospreys, American Swallow-tailed Kites, and the endangered "Southern" Bald Eagle.

White Ibises, various species of herons, and Wood Storks can be seen from early spring through mid-November. Ospreys and Bald Eagles are frequently seen fishing during late spring as their young demand more food.

Area brochure, hunting, fishing, hiking, 0.8-mile trail, boating.
Spring, Winter

Loxahatchee 7
Rt. 1, Box 278   (office at refuge)
Boynton Beach, FL 33437   407-734-8303
Entry Fee

Bird List FL-7 Loxahatchee Summary
216 birds listed, 62 nesting birds
Bird Chart pages 222-239

Totals by Season		s	S	F	W
Abundant	A	49	22	56	48
Common	C	51	34	51	35
Uncommon	U	65	32	66	50
Occasional	O	16	11	16	14
Rare	R	16	5	19	33

Endangered Species: Wood Stork, Bald Eagle, Peregrine Falcon, Least Tern
Rare/Limited Species: Caribbean Coot

In Boynton Beach, take Boynton Beach Blvd. west to Route 441 (dead end) and turn south (left). Go 2 miles to the refuge HQ and visitor center on your right.

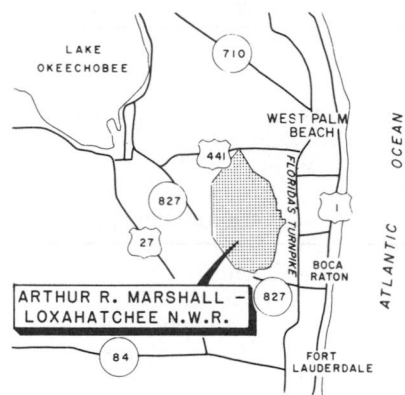

Habitat: 145,635 acres of Everglades habitat include tree islands interspersed with stands of sawgrass, wet prairies, and sloughs.

Loxahatchee is one of the few refuges where the Smooth-billed Ani is a common year-round resident. Various owls, woodpeckers, and songbirds are also visible from the Cypress Swamp boardwalk.

Area brochure, canoe trail, nature trail, fishing, hunting, airboat rides available.
Spring, Summer, Fall, Winter

Merritt Island 🔳
PO Box 6504 (office at refuge)
Titusville, FL 32782 407-867-0667

Bird List FL-8 Merritt Is. Summary
268 birds listed, 88 nesting birds
Bird Chart pages 240-257

Totals by Season		s	S	F	W
Common	C	72	47	89	88
Uncommon	U	45	22	37	28
Occasional	O	73	39	76	48
Rare	R	46	30	53	53

Endangered Species: Brown Pelican, Wood Stork, Bald Eagle, Peregrine Falcon, Piping Plover, Roseate Tern, Least Tern

Merritt Island extends for 25 miles along Florida's east coast midway between Jacksonville and West Palm Beach. The refuge, adjacent to and partially overlapping Canaveral National Seashore and NASA's Kennedy Space Center, is accessible from New Smyrna Beach (northern access point) and, via Hwy. 406, from Titusville (south end of the refuge). The refuge office also manages the Pelican Island NWR (see Pelican Island description).

From I-95 in Titusville, take Hwy. 406 east approximately 6 miles to junction

with Hwy. 402, turn right and go about 2.75 miles to the refuge office. From Daytona Beach, take FL A1A south 18.5 miles to the visitor center at the south end of the refuge. The center is closed Sundays from April to October and on all Federal holidays. Portions of the refuge may be closed because of NASA's launch activities.

Habitat: 140,393 acres ranging from fresh-water impoundments and vast salt-water estuaries to brackish marshes. The marshes give way to hardwood hammocks and pine flatwoods and there are 2,500 acres of citrus groves.

The diverse landscape provides habitat for many birds. Open waters are wintering areas for 50,000 to 70,000 ducks of 23 species and over 100,000 American Coots. The refuge also provides a year-round home to Great Blue and Green-backed herons, Cattle Egrets, Wood Storks, Anhingas, Brown Pelicans, and other species.

Shallow water grasslands harbor shorebirds, wading birds, and raptors. The hammocks attract Pileated Woodpeckers and migrating warblers.

Area brochure, auto tour routes, hiking trails, boating, canoe trail, fishing, hunting.
Spring, Fall, Winter

Pelican Island 🔳
c/o Merritt Island NWR
PO Box 6504
Titusville, FL 32782 407-867-0667

Pelican Island was established in 1903 as the nation's first national wildlife refuge. Public use of the island itself be held to a minimum to avoid disturbance to nesting birds. There are opportunities to view and photograph nesting activities from a reasonable distance offshore.

Refuge headquarters is at the Merritt Island Refuge (see Merritt Island map). Pelican Island is located in Indian River County on Florida's east coast about 45 miles south of Cape Kennedy. The refuge is near the town of Sebastian and extends for several miles along the east side of the Indian River. Inquire in Sebastian for local directions. Primary access is by boat.

Habitat: 4,359 acres, mostly bottomlands and mangrove islands. The refuge and surrounding shallow water provide year-round habitat for many nesting birds.

This island, best known for its Brown Pelican rookery, also supports large colonies of other species. Cattle and Great egrets, White Ibises, Tricolored Herons, Anhingas, and Double-crested Cormorants all nest on Pelican Island.

Area brochure.
Spring, Summer, Fall, Winter

St. Marks 🔟 (office at refuge)
PO Box 68
St. Marks, FL 32355 904-925-6121
Entry Fee

Bird List FL-9 St. Marks Summary
275 birds listed, 98 nesting birds
Bird Chart pages 240-257

Totals by Season		s	S	F	W
Abundant	A	17	12	23	21
Common	C	87	52	73	57
Uncommon	U	75	55	87	64
Occasional	O	23	14	29	14
Rare	R	50	37	49	39

Endangered Species: Brown Pelican, Wood Stork, Bald Eagle, Peregrine Falcon, Piping Plover, Least Tern, Red-cockaded Woodpecker
Rare/Limited Species: Budgerigar

From Newport take Hwy. 98 east for 1 mile to the junction with Hwy. 59. Turn right on Hwy. 59 and go for 3 miles to refuge headquarters.

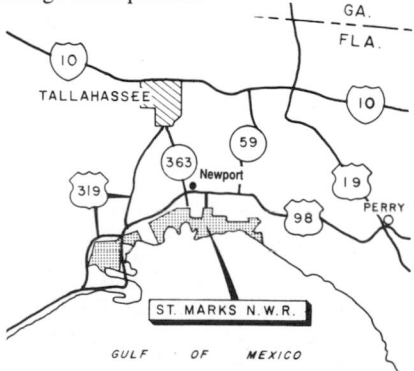

Habitat: 65,000 land acres and 32,000 acres in Apalachee Bay include natural salt marshes, tidal flats, freshwater impoundments, hardwood swamps, and pine woods.

Shorebirds are most common during late spring and early fall. The refuge provides extensive wintering habitat for waterfowl.

Endangered birds such as the Bald Eagle, Least Tern, and Red-cockaded Woodpecker nest on the refuge. Bald Eagles are seen primarily during winter, while Ospreys are most common in spring and summer.

Area brochure, interpretive hiking trail, hunting, fishing, boating, crabbing. Reptile, mammal and amphibian lists. Spring, Fall

St. Vincent ⓤ
PO Box 447   (office in town)
Apalachicola, FL 32320   904-653-8808

Bird List FL-10 St. Vincent Summary
183 birds listed, no nesting data
Bird Chart pages 240-257

Totals by Season		s	S	F	W
Abundant	A	26	16	28	23
Common	C	93	47	77	71
Uncommon	U	24	25	40	26
Occasional	O	17	18	15	14
Rare	R	7	5	8	11

Endangered Species: Brown Pelican, Wood Stork, Bald Eagle, Peregrine Falcon, Piping Plover, Least Tern

St. Vincent Refuge headquarters is on Hwy. 98 West in Apalachicola. This refuge is an undeveloped barrier island approximately 9 miles offshore from Apalachicola. Refuge access is by boat only.

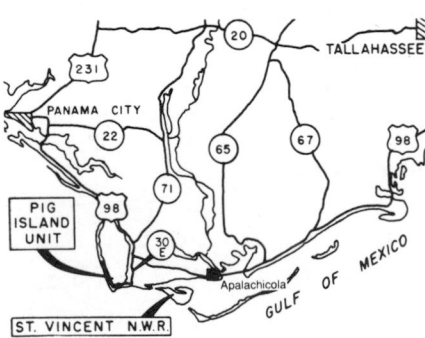

Habitat: 12,358-acre, triangular island 9 miles long, 4 miles wide at the east end, and gradually tapering to a narrow western point. The terrain includes rolling sand dunes, scrub oak, live oak ridges, pine flatwoods, cabbage palm, magnolia hammocks, tidal marsh, and freshwater lakes and swamps.

In the spring, Ospreys nest in dead snags

around freshwater lakes and Wood Ducks use nest boxes. Young Bald Eagles start to fledge. Wood Storks are most commonly seen during the spring and summer.

As the shorebird and passerine migrations are concluding in the fall, the wintering waterfowl begin to arrive. Peregrine Falcons pass through, and Bald Eagles and Great Horned Owls begin to nest during the winter.

Area brochure, boating, fishing, hunting, limited camping, hiking.
Spring, Fall, Winter

NATIONAL PARK SERVICE

Biscayne National Park ①
PO Box 1369
Homestead, FL 33090   305-867-0634

Bird List FL-11 Biscayne Summary
178 birds listed, 23 nesting birds
Bird Chart pages 240-257

Totals by Season		s	S	F	W
Abundant	A	4	2	4	4
Common	C	55	34	57	50
Uncommon	U	37	15	40	37
Occasional	O	30	30	32	32
Rare	R	12	7	13	31

Endangered Species: Brown Pelican, Wood Stork, Bald Eagle, Peregrine Falcon, Piping Plover, Least Tern Rare/Limited Species: Greater Flamingo, La Sagra's Flycatcher, Bahama Mockingbird

Habitat: 173,039 acres, primarily reef and water. A north-south chain of 44 keys or islands total 4,373 land acres. Biscayne Bay is on the west and the Atlantic Ocean on the east side of the chain, where Magnificent Frigatebirds are commonly seen.

Park brochure with map, glass-bottom boat trips.

Canaveral National Seashore ②
PO Box 6447
Titusville, FL 32782   305-867-0634

Canaveral National Seashore is adjacent to and partially overlaps the Merritt Island National Wildlife Refuge.

See Bird List FL-8 Merritt Is. Summary on page 65 and Bird Chart pages 240-257.

Habitat: 57,627 acres along 25 miles of undeveloped barrier islands preserve the natural beach, dune, marsh, and lagoon habitats for a variety of wildlife, including

many species of birds. The Kennedy Space Center occupies the southern end of the island and temporary seashore closures are possible due to launch-related activities.

Seashore/Refuge brochure with map, activity schedule, common bird and various other leaflets.

Everglades National Park ③
PO Box 279
Homestead, FL 33030   305-247-6211

Bird List FL-12 Abundance Summary
251 birds listed, 84 nesting birds
Bird Chart pages 240-257

Totals by Season		s	S	F	W
Common	C	22	60	18	5
Uncommon	U	73	39	72	50
Rare	R	36	25	40	57

Endangered Species: Brown Pelican, Wood Stork, Bald Eagle, Peregrine Falcon, Piping Plover, Roseate Tern, Least Tern

At 1,398,938 acres, the Everglades is the largest remaining subtropical wilderness in the contiguous United States. Its extensive fresh and saltwater areas, open prairies, mangrove estuaries, and pine forests are home to an abundant wildlife that includes birds confined to a narrow range, such as the American Swallow-tailed Kite, Roseate Spoonbill, and Limpkin. The park has been designated as a Ramsar Site.

Park brochure with map, quarterly "Visitors Guide", boat tours available.

Gulf Islands National Seashore ④
1801 Gulf Breeze Parkway
Gulf Breeze, FL 32561   904-934-2600

Gulf Islands National Seashore is located in two states, Florida and Mississippi. See the Mississippi chapter pages 109–110 for the Bird List MS-4 Gulf Is. Summary, and related Bird Chart pages 276-293 for species details.

Habitat: 65,816 acres, including 9,366 land acres. In Florida, the National Seashore includes beaches on the offshore islands and the mainland, the Naval Live Oak Reservation, historic ruins, and military forts on the mainland.

Masked and Brown boobies and Magnificent Frigatebirds are uncommon visitors during the summer.

Seashore brochure with map, 8-page newspaper "The Gulf Islands Barnacle", leaflets on camping, wildlife, and other activities.

NATIONAL FOREST SERVICE

National Forests in Florida (Supervisor)
City Center Building
227 No. Bronough St.
Suite 4061
Tallahassee, FL 32301   904-681-7265

Map/Forest-Ranger District/City

△ Apalachicola-same
     /Bristol   904-643-2283
△ Apalachicola-Wakulla
     /Crawfordville   904-681-7598
△ Ocala-Lake George
     /Silver Springs   904-625-2520
△ Ocala-Seminole/Eustis   904-357-6172
△ Osceola-same
     /Lake City   904-752-2577

STATE AGENCIES

Dept. of Natural Resources

Bureau of Land & Aquatic
Resource Management
Majority Stoneman Douglas Bldg.
3900 Commonwealth Blvd.
Tallahassee, FL 32399

Write for an "Aquatic Preserves" brochure. The brochure names and locates forty state managed aquatic preserves. All but three are situated along the Florida coastline.

Game & Freshwater Fish Comm.

Farris Bryant Building
Tallahassee, FL 32301   904-488-1960

Map/Region/City

[1] Northwest
     /Panama City   800-342-1676
[2] Northeast/Lake City   800-342-8501
[3] Central/Ocala   800-342-9620
[4] South/Lakeland   800-282-8002
[5] Everglades
     /West Palm Beach   800-432-2046

Florida Division of Tourism

505 Collins Building
Tallahassee, FL 32301   904-487-1462
from out-of-state call   800-635-7820

BIRDING HOTLINE
Statewide   912-987-1052

LOCAL BIRDING GROUPS
Map/Chapter/City
1. Albany Audubon/Albany
2. Atlanta Audubon/Atlanta
3. Augusta Audubon/Augusta
4. Coastal Ga. Aud./St. Simons Is.
5. Columbus Audubon/Hamilton
6. Ocmulgee Audubon/Macon
7. Ogeechee Audubon/Savannah
8. Briar Creek Bird Study Group /Sylvania
9. Chattahoochee Valley Natural History Club/Columbus
10. Okefenokee Bird Club/Waycross
11. The Withlacoochee Watchers /Valdosta

THE NATURE CONSERVANCY
Georgia Field Office
4725 Peachtree Corners Circle
Suite 395
Norcross, GA 30092   404-263-9225

Contact this office (north of Atlanta) about field trips to the preserves and other areas.

Heggies Rock
100 acres near Appling, north of Augusta - Contact Field Office for access details and directions.

Habitat: Primarily exposed granite flatrock which attracts large numbers of migrants.
Spring, Fall

Marshall Forest
220 acres northwest of Rome - Contact Field Office for details and area map.

Drive north through Rome on U.S. 411. Pass the Floyd County Hospital and turn left on Horseleg Road. The preserve lies on both sides of the road after you cross the creek. Trail entrances and a small parking lot are on the right side of the road.

Habitat: 220-acre forest is a unique mixture of northern trees such as red and chestnut oaks, and trees typical of southern coastal plains, especially the longleaf pine. The self-guiding trail passes more than 300 species of wildflowers and other plants.

Innovative braille trail for the visually impaired.
Spring

U.S. FISH & WILDLIFE SERVICE NATIONAL WILDLIFE REFUGES
U.S. Fish & Wildlife Service Region 4
Richard B. Russell Federal Bldg.
75 Spring St., SW
Atlanta, GA 30303   404-331-0833

Savannah Coastal Refuges
Refuge Complex Office
Federal Court Building
125 Bull Street   (office in town)
PO Box 8487
Savannah, GA 31412   912-944-4415

This is the headquarters for a seven-refuge complex. The refuges total over 53,339 acres and span a 100-mile stretch of coastline extending from Pinckney Island Refuge near Hilton Head, South Carolina, to Wolf Island Refuge near Darien, Georgia. The Savannah, Wassaw Island, Tybee Island, Harris Neck, and Blackbeard Island refuges are situated between them.

Inquire about area and auto tour brochures and the Savannah Coastal Refuges bird checklist, which covers 299 species. The list contains an individual refuge code, abundance, and occurrence detail. Wildlife viewing is good throughout the year.

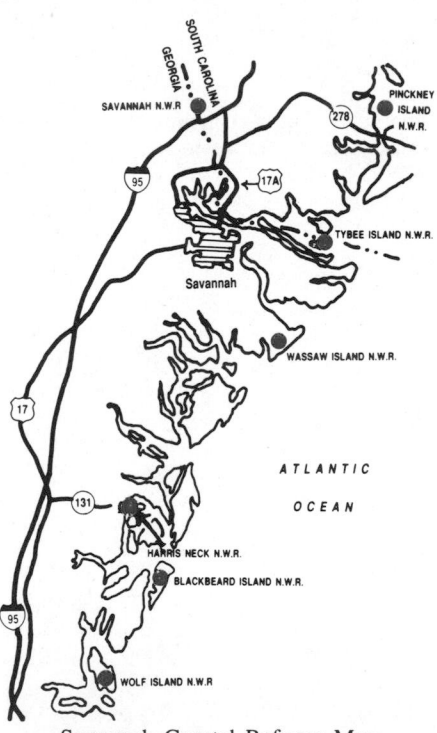

Savannah Coastal Refuges Map

January: Waterfowl are wintering in large numbers on all coastal refuges, particularly Savannah NWR.
February–March: While wintering waterfowl leave, Wood Ducks start to nest. Migratory songbirds start to arrive from their wintering grounds in Central and South America.
April: The beaches of Wassaw and Blackbeard are primary staging areas for resting and feeding shorebirds. Breeding songbirds arrive in large numbers. The songbirds that have wintered at Savannah leave for their breeding grounds in the

north. This is an excellent month for birding at all of the Coastal refuges.
May: Birding continues to be good as spring migration draws to a close and nesting egrets and herons can be observed in their rookeries.
June: Great Egrets, Tricolored Herons, and Anhingas nest in their largest numbers at the Harris Neck rookeries.
July: Breeding songbirds such as the Painted Bunting are best viewed at Harris Neck, while Purple Gallinules can be easily found at Savannah NWR. Beach nesters, including Black Skimmers, Laughing Gulls, Wilson's Plovers, and Least Terns, breed on Blackbeard and Wassaw Island.
August: The fall waterfowl migration begins with the arrival of the first Blue-winged Teals. The Savannah and Harris Neck refuges are particularly good spots to see large flocks of White Ibises.
September: As migrant songbirds and shorebirds arrive, warblers are common in the refuge's woodlands, and large concentrations of Dunlin, Black-bellied Plovers, and dowitchers rest and feed at Wassaw, Blackbeard, and Harris Neck.
October: As the fall waterfowl migration continues, various dabbling and diving ducks feed in the waters of the Savannah NWR. Northern Harriers can be found on freshwater and saltwater marshlands throughout the complex. Shorebird and songbird migrations continue, although many of Harris Neck's breeding songbirds may be found well into October.
November: The wintering waterfowl population peaks, and a large variety of wintering visitors, including wrens and sparrows, can be found.
December: Harris Neck and Savannah refuges are the best spots for looking at the large waterfowl concentrations, while loons and scaups can be found in large numbers off Blackbeard and Wassaw.

Blackbeard Island ❶

Blackbeard Island is a barrier island off the coast from an area called Shellman's Bluff on the Julienton River. It is accessible only by boat. Arrangements for trips to the refuge can be made at Shellman's Bluff. From Savannah, take U.S. 17 south for approximately 51 miles to Shellman's Bluff Road, which terminates at the town on the Julienton River.

Habitat: 5,618 acres consist of long, low, parallel ridges which are forested with live oaks and slash pine, as well as fresh water pools and marshlands. 3,000 acres have been designated National Wilderness.

Spring and fall migrations bring many songbirds to the forested areas, while large flocks of shorebirds feed on the beaches.

Fishing, archery hunting, hiking.

Harris Neck ❷

From Savannah, take I-95 south to exit 12, travel south on U.S. 17 for about 1 mile, then east on St. Rte. 131 for 7 miles to the refuge entrance gate.

Habitat: 2,765 acres of saltwater marsh, grassland, mixed deciduous woods, and cropland.

The swamps support large rookeries of herons and egrets. During the winter Mallards, Gadwalls, Green-winged Teals, and other ducks gather in large rafts on the marshlands and freshwater pools.

Auto access, hiking, fishing, hunting.

Pinckney Island ❸

Take U.S. 278 east from Hardeeville, South Carolina, for 18 miles to the refuge entrance. The entrance is also 0.5 miles west of Hilton Head Island.

Habitat: The 4,053-acre refuge includes Pinckney, Corn, Big and Little Harry, and Buzzard islands, and numerous small hammocks. Nearly 67 percent of the refuge consists of salt marsh and tidal creeks. Pinckney Island, the only island open for public use, consists of salt marsh, forests, brushland, fallow fields, and freshwater ponds.

The variety of habitats provide food and shelter to many species, and make Pinckney Island a popular spot year-round for wildlife study and photography.

Refuge brochure, hiking, bicycling.

Savannah ❹

From Port Wentworth take U.S. 17 for 4 miles north to refuge entrance (take I-95 exit 19 to reach U.S. 17 North). From Hardeeville, South Carolina, take U.S. 17 south for 8 miles.

Habitat: 25,608 acres. Consists of freshwater marshes, tidal rivers and creeks, and river bottom hardwood swamp. The refuge includes 3,000 acres of freshwater impoundments that were formerly rice fields, and are now managed for migratory waterfowl.

The mild winters attract a large variety of birds from October through April, including sparrows, wrens, and the waterfowl whose population is greatest between November and February.

Fishing, hunting, walking trails, auto tour route.

Tybee Island ❺

Located in the mouth of the Savannah River, the refuge is opposite Fort Pulaski National Monument on the shore, which is 12 miles from Savannah on U.S. 80. Heavy boat traffic in the treacherous currents in the river make navigation to Tybee Island hazardous.

Habitat: 100 acres, much of which is covered with sand dredged from the Savannah River by the Army Corps of Engineers. Other parts of the island are covered with eastern red cedar, wax myrtle, and groundsel, or bordered by salt marsh.

Many migratory species, as well as the endangered Brown Pelican, rest and feed on the shore at low tide.

Wassaw Island ❻

A barrier Island in Chatham County off the coast southeast of Savannah, Wassaw can be reached only by boat, which can be arranged with a local marina.

Habitat: 10,070 acres include beaches, woodlands of primarily live oak and slash pine, and vast salt marshes.

Egrets and herons nest in large rookeries on Wassaw Island, where a number of wading birds can be seen during the summer. It is also home to various endangered and threatened species such as the southern race of the Bald Eagle, the Brown Pelican, and loggerhead sea turtles which come ashore at night to lay their eggs.

Beachcombing, hiking, hunting.
Spring, Fall

Wolf Island ❼

A barrier island in McIntosh County off the Georgia coast from Darian, Wolf Island can only be reached by boat, available from local marinas.

Habitat: 5,126 acres that also include Egg and Little Egg islands. Over 75% of the refuge is saltwater marsh.

Recreational use is generally permitted only on the beach because of the densely vegetated interior. Birding is most rewarding at low tide during the spring and fall migrations, when shorebirds can be seen resting and feeding.

Spring, Fall

Okefenokee ❽ (visitor center at refuge)
Rt. 2, Box 338
Folkston, GA 31537   912-496-3331
Entry Fee

Bird List GA-1 Okefenokee Summary
209 birds listed, 77 nesting birds
Bird Chart pages 240-257

Totals by Season		s	S	F	W
Abundant	A	1	1	4	2
Common	C	75	48	73	59
Uncommon	U	53	24	54	29
Occasional	O	34	12	31	32
Rare	R	45	17	43	26

Endangered Species: Wood Stork, Bald Eagle, Peregrine Falcon, Red-cockaded Woodpecker

Okefenokee NWR extends 38 miles from north to south and 25 miles from east to west. There are three entrances.
East Entrance: Take St. Hwy. 121/23 for 8 miles southeast from Folkston, and then go 3 miles west from the main entrance sign. North Entrance: From Waycross, take Hwy 1 & 23 10 miles southeast then turn right on Hwy. 177 and go 10 miles to the entrance.
West Entrance: From Fargo, take Hwy 177 northeast 17 miles to the entrance.

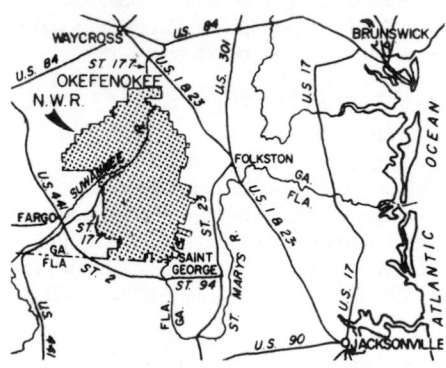

Habitat: 396,000 acres including 353,981 acres of National Wilderness. A huge, shallow, peat-filled depression of flooded and semi-flooded forests and prairies. Most of the swamp is covered with cypress, black gum, and bay forests. About 15 percent is flooded or semi-flooded prairie and another 6 percent are islands. The prairies are dotted with little lakes and ponds and various-sized clumps of trees and shrubs, locally called "houses." The peripheral upland and the islands within the swamp are forested with pine interspersed with hardwood hammocks. This refuge has been designated as a Ramsar Site.

January: Waterfowl and large numbers of "Greater" Sandhill Cranes present.
March: Northern Parula and Eastern Kingbirds arrive. Nesting dances by "Florida" Sandhill Cranes. Ducks, Tree Swallows, American Robins, Eastern Phoebes, Cedar Waxwings, and "Greater" Sandhill Cranes depart on migration.
April: Wading bird rookeries are active

and Sandhill Crane and Osprey chicks are hatching. Prothonotary Warblers are common.
May: The endangered Red-cockaded Woodpeckers are nesting.
July: Young herons, egrets, and ibises now fully fledged. Wood Storks feed on flooded prairies. Red-headed Woodpeckers and Pine Warblers are present, although difficult to see in the pine forest uplands.
September: Fall migration begins as many warblers move through area.
November: Robins and migrating "Greater" Sandhill Cranes arrive. Migratory waterfowl numbers increase.

Area brochure, boat trail, bicycle trail, interpretive trail, auto tour route, picnicking, boating, fishing, hunting, hiking, camping. Services and tours are available from concessionaires.
Spring, Fall, Winter

Piedmont 9 (office at refuge)
Rt. 1, Box 670
Round Oak, GA 31038   912-986-5441

Bird List GA-2 Piedmont Summary
192 birds listed, 78 nesting birds
Bird Chart pages 240-257

Totals by Season		s	S	F	W
Common	C	54	40	52	40
Uncommon	U	46	29	46	26
Occasional	O	45	22	43	30
Rare	R	24	16	18	13

Endangered Species: Bald Eagle, Red-cockaded Woodpecker

From Round Oak take the paved road 3 miles west to the refuge office.
Alternate route: Take I-75 to exit 61 (Tift College), in Forsyth, then take Juliette Road east 18 miles to the refuge office.

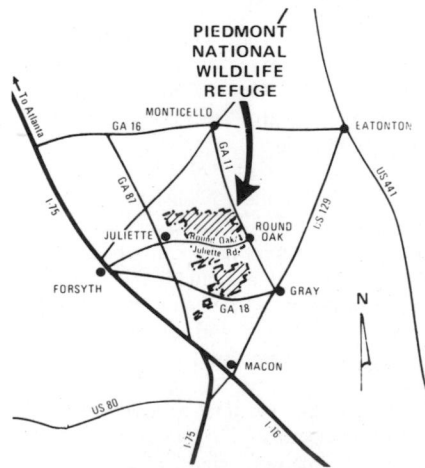

Habitat: 35,000 acres of rehabilitated farm land. Loblolly pine dominate on sites with poorer soils. Stands of hardwoods grow in some small sheltered upland valleys and border creek bottoms. In the bottoms, the

major trees are sweetgum, and water and willow oaks. Upland hardwood sites dominated by oaks and hickories. Refuge wetlands include beaver ponds, 11 man-made ponds, and miles of streams.

Some of the most common species are Wood Duck, Red-tailed Hawk, Chimney Swift, Pileated Woodpecker, Eastern Kingbird, Brown Thrasher, Northern Bobwhite, Eastern Bluebird, and Brown-headed Nuthatch.

Area brochure, six-mile auto tour route, hunting, fishing, two walking trails. Spring and early Summer best.

NATIONAL PARK SERVICE

Cumberland Island 1
National Seashore
PO Box 806
St. Mary's, GA 31558   912-882-4336

36,415 acres of unspoiled beaches and dunes, marshes, and freshwater lakes. Accessible by tour boat only, Cumberland Island has hosted more than 300 resident and migratory species.

Seashore brochure with map, bird list, information leaflets.

NATIONAL FOREST SERVICE
National Forest Service Southern Region
1720 Peachtree Road NW
Atlanta, GA 30367   404-347-4191

Map/Forest/City
△1	Chattahoochee /Gainesville	404-536-0541
△2	Oconee/Monticello	404-468-2244

STATE AGENCIES

Game & Fish Division
Department of Natural Resources
2258 Northlake Parkway
Tucker, GA 30084   404-656-3510

Map/City
1	Atlanta	404-656-3522
2	Armuchee	404-295-6041
3	Gainesville	404-532-5303
4	Thomson	404-595-4211
5	Fort Valley	912-825-6354
6	Albany	912-439-4254
7	Fitzgerald	912-423-2988
8	Sapelo Island	912-485-2251
9	Social Circle	404-557-2532

Dept. of Industry Trade & Tourism
230 Peachtree St., NW
PO Box 1776
Atlanta, GA 30301   404-656-3590

LOCAL BIRDING GROUP

Map/Chapter/City

① Hawaii Audubon/Honolulu

Note: When birding in Hawaii you may want to borrow or purchase a field guide covering local and/or Pacific birds to aid you in field identification. *A Field Guide to the Birds of Hawaii and the Tropical Pacific* by Pratt, Bruner, and Barrett and illustrated by Pratt, published in 1987 by Princeton University Press of Princeton, New Jersey, is a excellent reference.

THE NATURE CONSERVANCY

Hawaii Field Office ⟨FO⟩
1116 Smith St., Suite 201
Honolulu, HI 96817   808-537-4508

Week-long natural history group tours are available through the Field Trip Coordinator at this office.

Kamakou ◆

PO Box 40
Kualapuu
Molokai, HI 96757   808-567-6680

Access possible by 45-minute drive in a four-wheel-drive vehicle but roads are often impassable. No four-wheel-drives are available for rent on Molokai Island, but TNC runs guided tours that leave from the airport.

Habitat: A 2,744-acre forest that ranges from 2,000 to 4,000 feet in elevation, and from dry forests and shrubs at lower elevations to rain forest near the summit. Of more than 250 species of plants that grow at Kamakou, 219 are found only in Hawaii. The rain forest supplies 60% of the water used on Molokai, which has lost most of its original forest.

Kamakou is one of the most magnificent rain forests in the world. Countless native insects provide food for many of the birds living in the forest, including two rare and endemic species, the Molokai Thrush, Olomao (a subspecies of the Hawaiian Thrush), and Molokai Creeper, Kakawahie, last observed in 1962. The Apapane, a crimson honeycreeper, feeds on the nectar of the ohia, while the green Common Amakihi, with its short, curved bill, can be found throughout the Kamakou forest. The Pueo, an endemic subspecies of the Short-eared Owl, flies over the forest in its hunting forays.

Area brochure, picnicking, guided tours, day hiking.
Spring, Summer, Fall, Winter

Waikamoi ◆❷

PO Box 1716/Makawao
Maui, HI 96768   808-572-7849

Guided tours only. Drive to Haleakala National Park via Hwy. 37, 377, and 378. No food or gas is available. Access is limited for public safety.

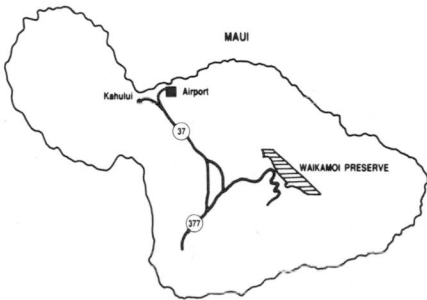

Habitat: 5,230 acres at 3,800 to 7,500 feet in elevation, ranging from subalpine scrub at the summit to rain forest at lower elevations. The rain forest flora, including the koa and ohia plants, and the many insects support the unique bird life of Hawaii's forests in a complex ecosystem.

Waikamoi is the only preserve where the endangered Maui Parrotbill, the Akohekohe or Crested Honeykeeper, and the yellow-green Maui Creeper can be found. More common species include Iiwi, a scarlet honeycreeper with a large curved bill, the green Common Amakihi, and the crimson Apapane.

The endangered Uau, or Dark-rumped Petrel, can be found breeding on the subalpine slopes of Haleakala, where another endangered species, the Nene, or Hawaiian Goose, was recently reintroduced.

Public hikes usually begin from Hosmer Grove campground just outside the preserve. Conservancy hikes are scheduled on the second Sunday of each month. Make reservations to visit this preserve with the Preserve Manager. Parties may be accommodated at other times by contacting the manager well in advance.

In addition, the National Park Service conducts hikes at Waikamoi Preserve on Monday and Friday mornings at 9 a.m. Contact Haleakala National Park for details and reservations: PO Box 369, Makawao, HI 96768, phone 808-572-9306

Area brochure, picnicking, guided tours only.
All seasons are good for visits.

U.S. FISH & WILDLIFE SERVICE NATIONAL WILDLIFE REFUGES

Hawaii and Pacific Islands ⟨RC⟩ Refuge Complex

300 Ala Moana Blvd.
PO Box 50167
Honolulu, HI 96850   808-541-1201

The refuges of the Hawaii and Pacific Islands National Wildlife Refuges Complex are described in categories: the

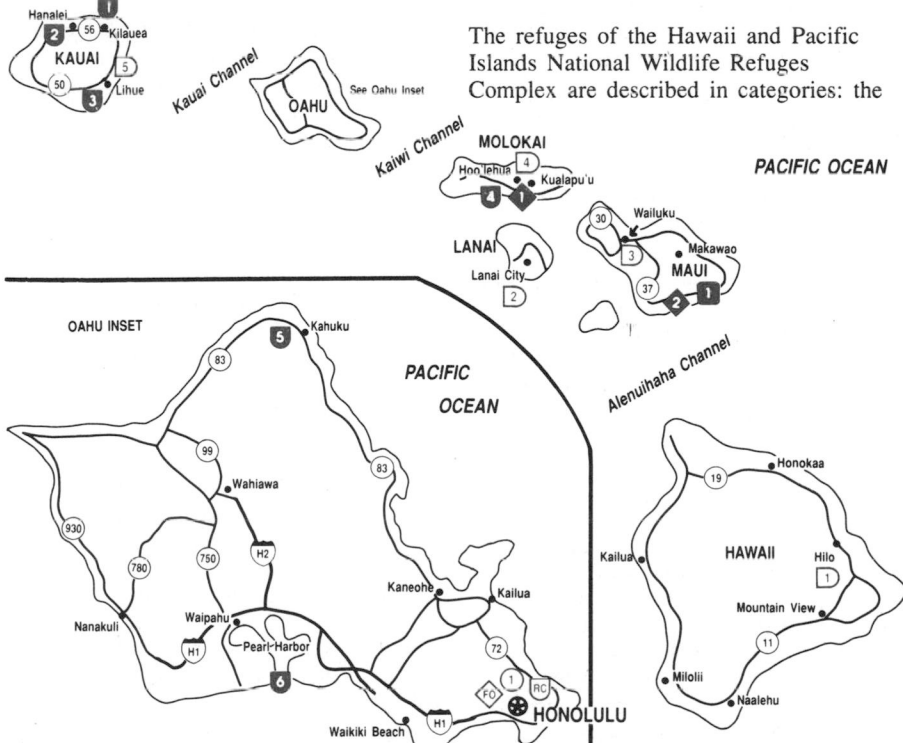

main refuge, open to the public year-round, the Wetland Refuges, and the Remote Island Refuges.

Kilauea Point ❶
PO Box 87
Kilauea, Kauai, HI 96754   808-828-1413
Entry Fee

Note: Kilauea Point is the only Hawaiian refuge that is open to the public on a regular basis, Monday through Friday from 10 a.m. to 2 p.m.

Located 1 mile north on a paved road from Kilauea and Kuhio Hwy., on the north coast of the island of Kauai.

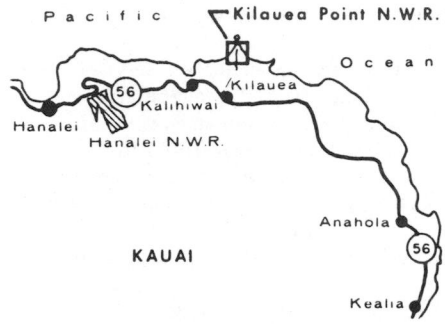

Large colonies of Wedge-tailed Shearwaters and Red-footed Boobies nest at Kilauea Point. Other seabird species, such as the Laysan Albatross, the Great Frigatebird, and the Red-tailed Tropicbird, may also be seen.

Visitor center, foot trails.
Spring, Summer, Fall, Winter

Wetland Refuges

Some wetland refuges may be visited by special permit or have exterior observation points. These refuges are home for four endangered waterbirds: the Hawaiian Duck or Koloa, the Hawaiian races of the Common Moorhen and the American Coot or Alas Keo Keo, and the Hawaiian Stilt, a subspecies of the Black-necked Stilt. These species do not migrate to the mainland and are only found on the main Hawaiian Islands.

Over two dozen species of ducks and geese, mainly Northern Pintails and Northern Shovelers, occasionally migrate from Canada, Alaska, or Asia, between April and September. Shorebirds, including the Pacific race of the Lesser Golden-Plover, Wandering Tattler, Ruddy Turnstone, and Sanderling, migrate from the mainland every year. Black-crowned Night-Herons are common residents.

Hanalei ❷
Kauai Island—917 acres. Closed to the

public. The state highway north of the refuge features an interpretive overlook and viewing opportunity.

Huleia ❸
Kauai Island—240 acres along the Huleia River. Viewing possible from the Menehune overlook along the road.

Kakahaia ❹
Molokai Island—An inland freshwater fish pond near the south coast provides habitat for stilts and coots. A small county beach is located across the coast highway and is open to the public.

James Campbell ❺
Oahu Island—A 142-acre habitat-restoration project. Open on certain weekends and by special permit.

Pearl Harbor ❻
Oahu Island—40 acres. Open by special permit only.

Remote Island Refuges

Public access is restricted because of the slow recovery of these vulnerable areas when disturbed. Management activity is limited to controlling predators, exotic plants, or other factors adversely affecting the habitat or resident wildlife.

The remote islands have over 14 million seabirds of 18 species, with Sooty Terns the most abundant nesters. Albatrosses, shearwaters, petrels, tropicbirds, boobies, frigatebirds, and noddies are also common.

Hawaiian Islands NWR—1,800 acres of emergent rocky islands, sandy islets, and over 250,000 acres of submerged land including the major atoll lagoons between Nihoa Island and Pearl and Hermes reefs in the northwestern portion of the Hawaiian Archipelago.

The terrestrial habitat of the Hawaiian Islands NWR is shared by endemic land birds on the small islands of Nihoa and Laysan. The Nihoa and Laysan finches are representatives of the unique Hawaiian Honeycreeper subfamily that includes several other species in the main Hawaiian Islands. The "Nihoa" Millerbird is an endemic representative of the Old World Warbler subfamily. It was extirpated on Laysan and now is confined to 168-acre Nihoa Island. The Laysan Duck has made a significant comeback, although it is still endangered.

Johnston Atoll NWR—Four islands located 825 miles southwest of Honolulu. 12 species of breeding seabirds.

Jarvis Island NWR—1,300 miles south of

Honolulu. This 1,100-acre island is surrounded by 36,419 acres of submerged lands. Eight species of migratory seabirds nest on the island.

Baker Island NWR—A 340-acre island supporting four migratory seabird species and located 1,600 miles from Honolulu.

Howland Island NWR—200 miles from Baker Island. Includes 400 acres of emergent land supporting eight species of migratory seabirds.

Rose Atoll NWR—The eastern-most emergent land in the Samoan Archipelago. Two small islets of less than 20 acres, protected by a square reef, provide cover and nest sites for 12 species of migratory seabirds. At a latitude of 14.5° south, it is the southernmost refuge in the National Wildlife Refuge system.

NATIONAL PARK SERVICE

Haleakala National Park ❶
PO Box 369
Makawao, HI 96768   808-572-9306

28,655 acres preserve the outstanding Haleakala Crater and protect the fragile ecosystem of Kipahulu Valley and Oheo Gulch and the many rare and endangered species. The National Park Service also conducts hikes on Monday and Friday mornings at 9 a.m. at The Nature Conservancy Waikamoi Preserve located north of and adjacent to Haleakala National Park.

Park brochure with map. Leaflets describe individual Hawaiian bird species, nature trail, camping, hiking, crater cabins, and other activities.

STATE AGENCIES

Division of Forestry & Wildlife
Dept. of Land & Natural Resources
Kalanimoku Bldg.
1151 Punchbowl Street
Honolulu, HI 96813   808-548-2861

Map/Island/City
①	Hawaii/Hilo	808-961-7221
②	Lanai/Lanai City	808-565-6688
③	Maui/Wailuku	808-244-4352
④	Molokai/Hoolehua	808-553-5415
⑤	Kauai/Lihue	808-245-4444

Hawaii Visitors Bureau
2270 Kalakaua Blvd.
PO Box 8527
Honolulu, HI 96815   808-923-1811

BIRDING HOTLINE
Southeast Idaho   208-236-3337

LOCAL BIRDING GROUPS
Map/Chapter/City
1. Golden Eagle Audubon/Boise
2. Northern Idaho Audubon
   /Bonners Ferry
3. Palouse Audubon/Moscow
4. Portneuf Valley Audubon/Pocatello
5. Prairie Falcon Audubon/Buhl
6. Snake River Audubon/Idaho Falls
7. Idaho Ornithological Council
   /Pocatello

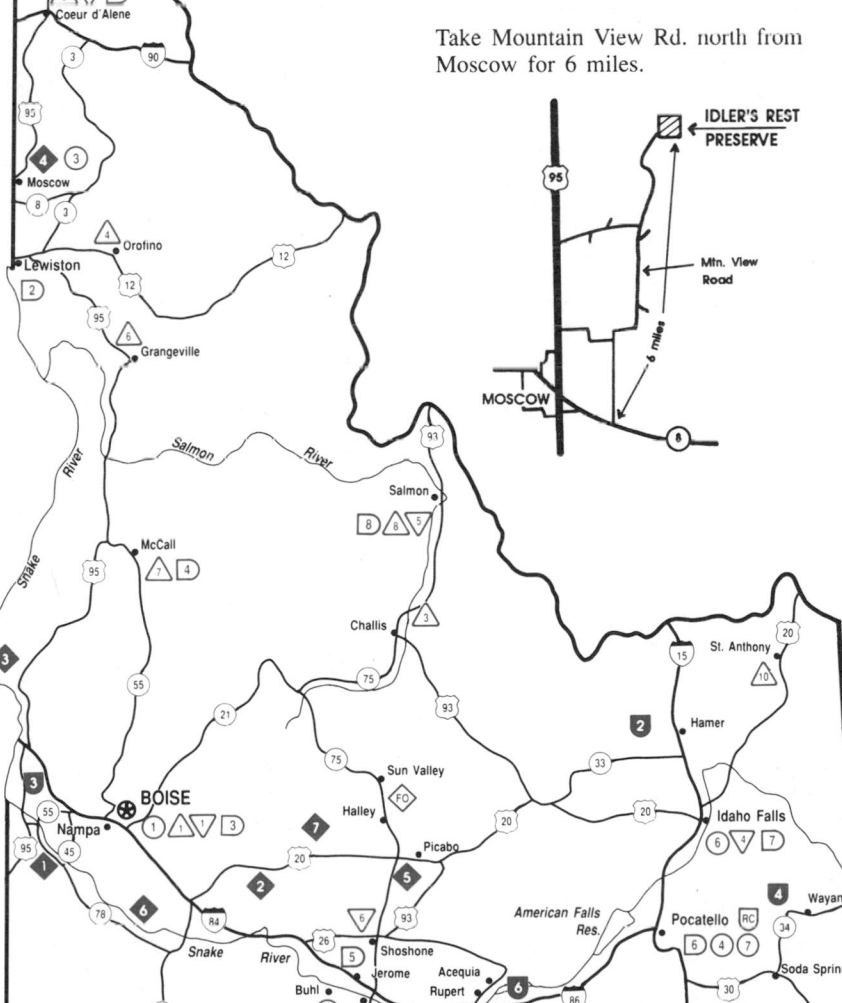

THE NATURE CONSERVANCY
Idaho Field Office ◇FO (office in Halley)
PO Box 64
Sun Valley, ID 83353   208-726-3007

Dautrich Memorial Desert ◆1
885 acres—Contact Field Office
Spring, Winter

Hill City Marsh ◆2
3,000 acres—Contact Dale Turnipseed,
Idaho Fish & Game, at the Jerome Idaho
office.
Spring, Winter

Hixson-Sharptail ◆3
4,200 acres—Contact Field Office
Map, bird list.
Spring

Idlers Rest ◆4   (office at college)
Idlers Rest Custodian
c/o U. of Idaho College of Forestry
Dept. of Wildland Rec. Mgt.
Moscow, ID 83843   208-885-7911

Take Mountain View Rd. north from
Moscow for 6 miles.

Habitat: 33 acres nestled against Moscow
Mountain. The 0.5-mile "highland" trail
takes visitors through a western red cedar
grove and three other vegetative zones.
Woodpeckers and Great Horned Owls may
be seen along the trail.

Area brochure, trail guide. Walking only.
Spring, Winter

Silver Creek ◆5   (office at preserve)
Lou & Cindy Lunte—Managers
PO Box 624
Picabo, ID 83353

About 3 miles west of Picabo and south
off Rte. 20. A 35-minute drive from Sun
Valley.

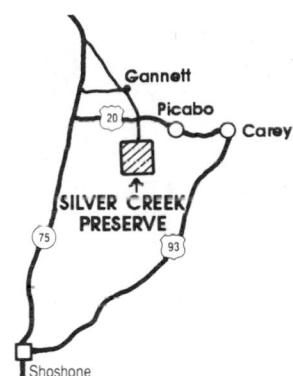

Habitat: 2,800 acres of a unique desert
community, including one of the richest
birds-of-prey habitats in the Rocky
Mountain Region. The headwaters of
Silver Creek are from crystal-clear
springs. Agriculture, ranching, and
wildlife.

Area brochure, bird list.
Summer, Fall

Snake River Birds of Prey ◆6
Natural Area
The Idaho Field Office has details on its
380-acre portion of the natural area. A
brochure and bird list is available from
the BLM District Office in Boise.

Spring, Fall, Winter

Stopp-Soldier Creek ◆7
120 acres—Contact Field Office
Bird list.
Spring, Fall

U.S. FISH & WILDLIFE SERVICE
NATIONAL WILDLIFE REFUGES

Bear Lake ▮1   (office in town)
370 Webster St.
PO Box 9
Montpelier, ID 83254   208-847-1757

Bird List ID-1 Bear Lake Summary
151 birds listed, 60 nesting birds
Bird Chart pages 240-257

Totals by Season		s	S	F	W
Abundant	A	2	12	3	0
Common	C	38	25	17	1
Uncommon	U	34	22	33	12
Occasional	O	42	26	44	12
Rare	R	20	6	19	21

Endangered species: Bald Eagle, Peregrine Falcon, Whooping Crane

Take Hwy. 89 south from Montpelier for 6 miles to St. Charles, then east on causeway along north shore of Bear Lake.

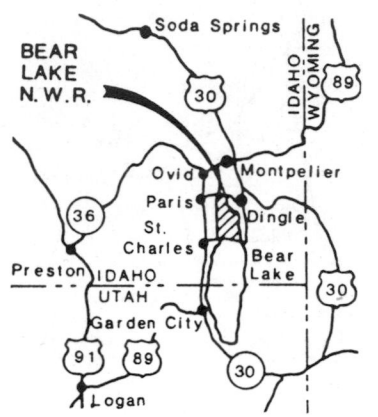

Habitat: 17,597 acres of marsh, open water, and grassland at an elevation of 5,925 feet.

April through June are the best months for Redheads, Canvasbacks, White-faced Ibises, and western Canada Geese. The Gadwalls molt during August.

The few winter birds include Common Goldeneyes, Rough-legged Hawks, Golden Eagles, Gray Partridges, Rosy Finches, and an occasional Bald Eagle.

Area brochure, fishing, hunting.
Spring, Fall

Camas ❷ (office at refuge)
2150 East 250 North
Hamer, ID 83425 208-662-5423

Bird List ID-2 Camas Summary
176 birds listed, 80 nesting birds
Bird Chart pages 240-257

Totals by Season		s	S	F	W
Abundant	A	9	17	9	1
Common	C	41	50	34	8
Uncommon	U	38	35	36	10
Occasional	O	17	16	23	15
Rare	R	21	33	22	20

Endangered species: Bald Eagle, Peregrine Falcon

Turn east off I-15 at Hamer. Go north on Frontage Road 3 miles. Cross freeway to the west at sign pointing to refuge headquarters. Inquire about access to the Snake River Sector of the refuge.

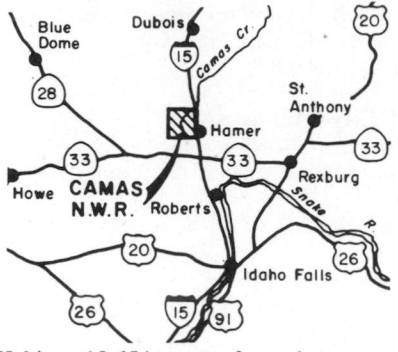

Habitat: 10,654 acres of marshes, meadows, and uplands at 4,800 feet.

Great, Snowy, and Cattle egrets, Black-crowned Night-Herons, and White-faced Ibises nest in colonies. Among the many spring migrants are grebes, American White Pelicans, Sandhill Cranes, Willets, American Avocets, Long-billed Curlews, and Black-necked Stilts.

Camas provides excellent resting and feeding habitat for migratory birds and nesting habitat for waterfowl including Mallards, Redheads, Northern Pintails, Northern Shovelers, Lesser Scaup, Gadwalls, American Wigeons, Blue-winged and Cinnamon teals, and Canada Geese. In summer an occasional Peregrine Falcon may be observed and Bald Eagles are present in spring and winter.

Area brochure, mammals list, hunting.
Spring, Fall

Deer Flat ❸ (office at refuge)
PO Box 448
Nampa, ID 83651 208-467-9278

Bird List ID-3 Deer Flat Summary
191 birds listed, 86 nesting birds
Bird Chart pages 240-257

Totals by Season		s	S	F	W
Abundant	A	15	18	18	7
Common	C	35	34	31	20
Uncommon	U	32	32	43	19
Occasional	O	50	42	42	28
Rare	R	21	26	21	18

Endangered species: Bald Eagle, Peregrine Falcon
Rare/Limited Species: Black-vented Oriole

Take Orchard Ave. 4 miles west from Nampa, then south on Lake Road 0.5 mile to dam embankment. Go west (right) across embankment to end of road and refuge office. Includes Lake Lowell and Snake River Sectors.

Habitat: 11,586 acres of marsh, islands, sagebrush flats, and riparian woodlands at 2,530 feet.

Of special interest are the shorebirds in late summer and fall. There is a wintering Bald Eagle population and a large number of Mallards in November and December. The islands host nesting Canada Geese, gulls, and wading birds.

Area brochure, mammals list. Fishing, hunting, boating, picnicking, swimming. Bird list contains habitat codes.
Spring, Fall, Winter

Grays Lake ❹ (office at refuge)
74 Grays Lake Road
Wayan, ID 83285 208-574-2755

Bird List ID-4 Grays Lake Summary
173 birds listed, 111 nesting birds
Bird Chart pages 240-257

Totals by Season		s	S	F	W
Abundant	A	10	7	6	0
Common	C	43	46	29	5
Uncommon	U	46	59	48	11
Occasional	O	51	25	46	22
Rare	R	19	11	8	9

Endangered species: Bald Eagle, Whooping Crane

From Soda Springs, turn north onto Rte. 34. Turn at refuge sign 1 mile west of Wayan. Access limited and personnel not always at office.

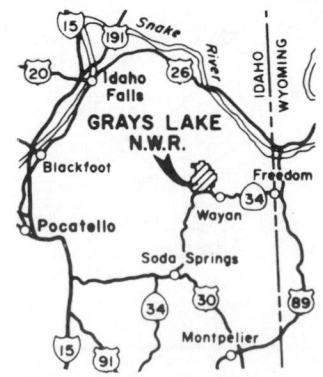

Habitat: 17,385 acres of high-mountain marsh at 6,385 feet of elevation, at the foot of Caribou Mountain.

Grays Lake hosts a breeding population of more than 200 pairs of "Greater" Sandhill Cranes. In September and October, more than 3,000 cranes gather from other colonies as well before they migrate to their wintering grounds in Mexico. In 1975 a Sandhill-Whooping Crane cross-fostering project was begun. May, June, and September are best for viewing aquatic birds including Whooping Cranes.

Area brochure, mammals list, hunting.
Spring, Summer

Kootenai 5   (office at refuge)
HCR60, Box 283
Bonners Ferry, ID 83805   208-267-3888

Bird List ID-5 Kootenai Summary
218 birds listed, 100 nesting birds
Bird Chart pages 240-257

Totals by Season		s	S	F	W
Abundant	A	14	15	11	4
Common	C	52	49	25	6
Uncommon	U	54	33	59	20
Occasional	O	36	38	55	28
Rare	R	34	40	40	20

Endangered species: Bald Eagle, Peregrine Falcon

Take the dike road west from Bonners Ferry along the south shore of Kootenai River for 5 miles to the refuge. Continue another 1.5 miles to refuge office located on West Road. Watch for logging trucks.

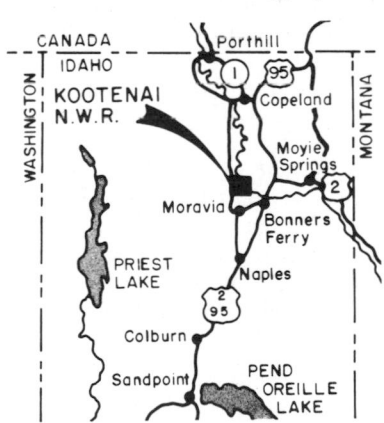

Habitat: 2,746 acres of ponds at 1,750 feet. Grassland, cultivated cropland, shrubs, and a timbered west ridge.

In February the Tundra Swans arrive for the spring and Barrow's Goldeneyes begin courtship displays. In March, Canada Geese begin nesting, American Robins and Mountain Bluebirds appear. In April, Calliope and Black-chinned hummingbirds

arrive as the Ruffed Grouse are drumming and Common Snipe are winnowing. In the fall the Bald Eagles and Rough-legged Hawks arrive. Duck populations, mostly Mallards, peak in November.

Area brochure, wildlife list including birds, fish, amphibians, reptiles, and mammals. Foot trails, auto tour, fishing, hunting, ice skating. Check with office about handicapped access.
Spring, Fall

Minidoka 6   (office at refuge)
Route 4, Box 290
Rupert, ID 83350   208-436-3589

Bird List ID-6 Minidoka Summary
199 birds listed, 82 nesting birds
Bird Chart pages 240-257

Totals by Season		s	S	F	W
Abundant	A	3	8	14	0
Common	C	51	48	27	14
Uncommon	U	47	34	43	21
Occasional	O	67	43	50	38
Rare	R	18	14	11	5

Endangered species: Bald Eagle, Peregrine Falcon

Take St. Hwy. 24 from Rupert for 6 miles northeast to Acequia. Continue on Hwy. 24 for 1 mile and turn east (right) on Co. Hwy. 400, at the refuge sign and go for 6 miles. The refuge office is at Lake Walcott. The Snake River flows through the refuge.

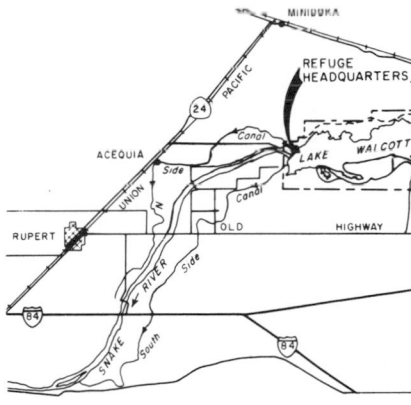

Habitat: 25,630 acres, including 11,000 backwater acres of Bureau of Reclamation (Minidoka Dam/Lake Walcott). Aquatic vegetation and uplands, which include sagebrush and grassland, and range at 4,280 feet.

Redheads, Lesser Scaups, Ruddy Ducks, and Canvasbacks are common breeders, but migrate farther south for the winter. American White Pelicans, Double-crested Cormorants, and various terns are also present during spring and summer. Golden

and Bald eagles are frequently seen in winter and spring.

Area brochure, mammals list, boating, fishing, hunting. Bureau of Reclamation facilities are nearby.
Spring, Fall

Southeast Idaho Refuge Complex [RC]
1246 Yellowstone Ave.   A-4
Pocatello, ID 83201   208-237-6616

A refuge administrative office and information resource for Bear Lake, Camas, Grays Lake, and Minidoka.

NATIONAL FOREST SERVICE

Map/Forest/City
1 Boise/Boise	208-334-1516
2 Caribou/Malad City	208-236-6700
3 Challis/Challis	208-879-2285
4 Clearwater/Orofino	208-476-4541
5 Idaho Panhandle /Coeur d'Alene	208-765-7223
6 Nez Perce /Grangeville	208-983-1950
7 Payette/McCall	208-634-8151
8 Salmon/Salmon	208-549-2420
9 Sawtooth /Twin Falls	208-737-3200
10 Targhee/St.Anthony	208-624-3151

BUREAU LAND MANAGEMENT
BLM State Office
3380 Americana Terrace
Boise, ID 83706   208-334-1771

Map/District/City
1 Boise/Boise	208-334-1582
2 Burley/Burley	208-678-5514
3 Coeur d'Alene/same	208-765-1511
4 Idaho Falls/Idaho Falls	208-529-1020
5 Salmon/Salmon	208-756-5401
6 Shoshone/Shoshone	208-886-2206

STATE AGENCIES

Idaho Dept. of Fish & Game HQ
600 South Walnut
Box 25
Boise, ID 83707   208-334-3700

Map/Region/City
1 Coeur d'Alene/same	208-765-3111
2 Lewiston/Lewiston	208-743-6502
3 Boise/Garden City	208-334-3725
4 & Boise/McCall	208-634-8139
5 Jerome/Jerome	208-324-4350
6 Pocatello/Pocatello	208-232-4703
7 Idaho Falls/Idaho Falls	208-522-7783
8 & Idaho Falls/Salmon	208-756-2271

Department of Commerce
Tourist Information   208-334-2470
Statehouse, Room 108
Boise, ID 83720
from out-of-state call   800-635-7820

BIRDING HOTLINES

Central Illinois 217-785-1083
Chicago 708-671-1522

LOCAL BIRDING GROUPS
Map/Chapter/City

① Champaign County Audubon/Urbana
② Chicago Audubon/Chicago
③ Decatur Audubon/Decatur
④ Du Page Audubon/Wheaton
⑤ John Wesley Powell Aud./Normal
⑥ Kankakee Area Aud./Bourbonnais
⑦ Kishwaukee Audubon/DeKalb
⑧ Lake County Aud./Libertyville
⑨ Mussleman Audubon/Quincy
⑩ N.W. Illinois Audubon/Freeport
⑪ Peoria Audubon/Peoria
⑫ Prairie Woods Audubon
　/Arlington Heights
⑬ Round River Audubon/Belleville

⑭ Sinnissippi Audubon/Rockford
⑮ Thorn Creek Audubon/Park Forest
⑯ Vermilion County Audubon/Danville
⑰ Chicago Orn. Society/Chicago
⑱ Evanston-North Shore Bird Club
　/Evanston
⑲ Illinois Audubon Society/Wayne
⑳ Knox County Bird Club/Knoxville
㉑ Peoria Academy of Science/Peoria
㉒ No. Central IL Orn. Soc./Rockford

THE NATURE CONSERVANCY

Illinois Field Office
79 West Monroe St., Suite 708
Chicago, IL 60603

Cedar Glen Eagle Roost ◆

Resident Manager
PO Box 150
Warsaw, IL 62379

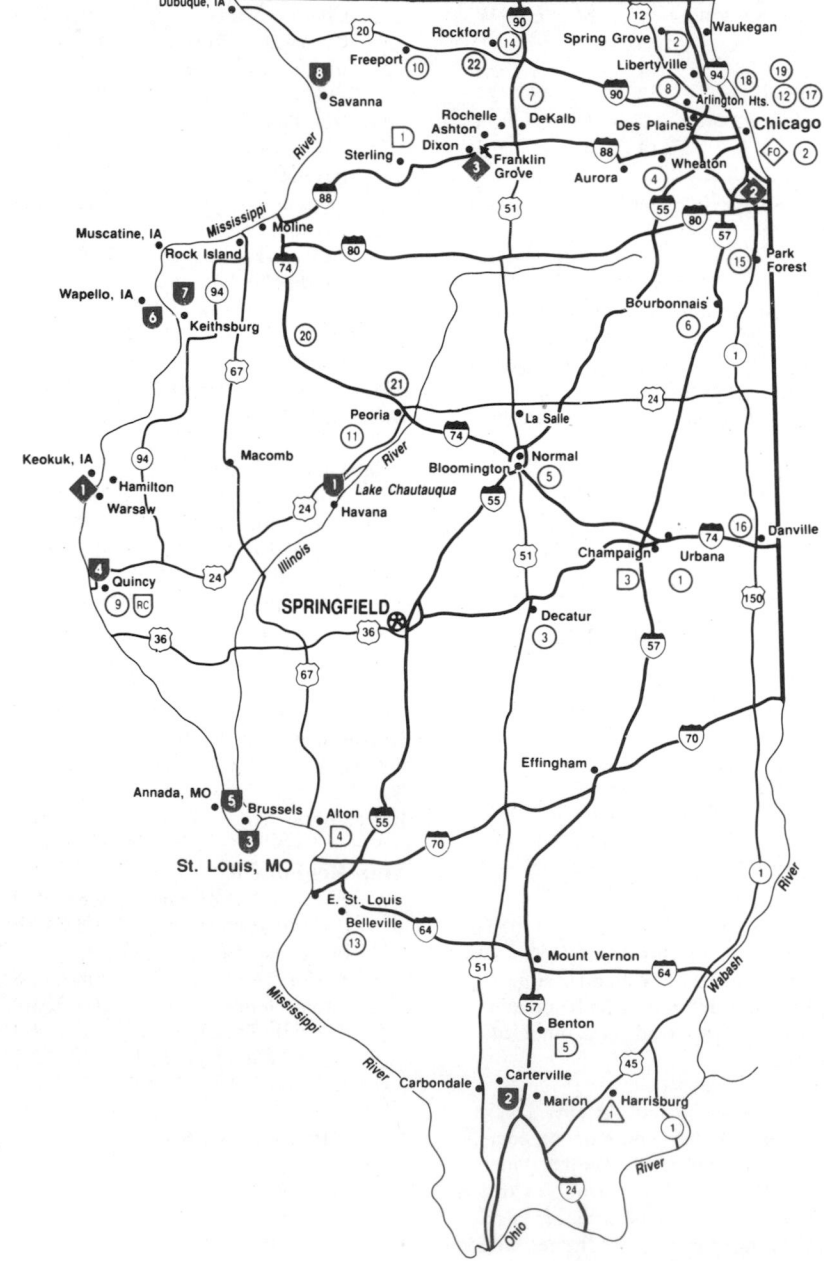

Kibbe Station is located about 45 miles west of Macomb, south of Hamilton near Warsaw. Take Hwy. 136 west from Macomb 41 miles to Hamilton, then go southwest on the Great River Road about 4 miles to the preserve. The station is managed by Western Illinois University. Cedar Glen Eagle Roost is just across the Mississippi River from the mouth of the Des Moines River.

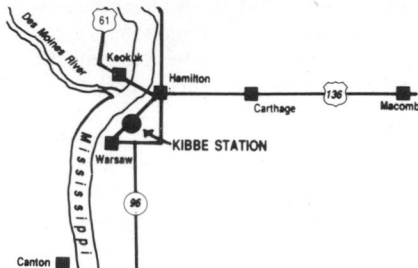

Habitat: 790 acres along the Mississippi River include a restored prairie community, islands in the Mississippi, and roosting sites along the river for Bald Eagles.

In addition to the eagles, migratory waterfowl, Wild Turkeys, and Pileated Woodpeckers may be seen at Cedar Glen.

Many activities are scheduled by the Keokuk Tourism office. January is the best time for eagle watching. Contact the Field Office, the Kibbe Life Sciences Station resident manager, or the Keokuk (Iowa) Tourism office for details.
Hiking trails, cross-country skiing, picnicking.
Late Fall, Winter

Markham Prairie ◆

Contact Field Office for details.
Managed by Northeastern IL University.
Non-resident manager usually on site.

About 20 miles from the Chicago loop. Take the Dan Ryan Exp. (I-94) south to I-57. Go south on I-57 and exit east on 159th St. Continue east to Whipple St. just east of Kedzie (a McDonalds is on the corner). Turn left (north) on Whipple St. and go to its end, at the entrance to the preserve. The gate appears to be locked but it is not.

Habitat: 300 acres at the south end of Lake Michigan at elevations of 605 to 615 feet, composed of native grassland and wetland. This preserve is the largest remaining high-quality tall-grass prairie in Illinois and has been dedicated by the National Park Service as a National Natural Landmark.

The wetland and prairie support more than 350 species of insects, 13 reptiles and amphibians, 12 mammals, and 21 breeding birds. Bird sightings include the Black-billed Cuckoo, Eastern Kingbird, Carolina Wren, Yellow-breasted Chat, and American Redstart.

Species list, area leaflet. Remain on walking trails when visiting.
Spring, Summer, early Fall

Nachusa Grasslands

Contact Field Office for a preserve brochure with detailed local map. The preserve is managed by Western Illinois University and a non-resident manager is often present. Nachusa Grasslands is located just north of Franklin Grove and west of Rochelle between Ashton and Dixon. A preserve sign and the entrance is on Lowden Road.

Habitat: 600 acres of prairie hillside merging into oak savannah. The rolling topography also includes sandstone outcroppings, streams with thickets, and marshes.

Careful observation generally reveals Grasshopper and Henslow's sparrows, Upland Sandpipers, Red-eyed and Bell's vireos, and Dickcissels in the varied habitats.

Occasional guided tours, area brochure, written directions (a must). Hiking trails, picnic.
Late Spring, Summer, Fall

U.S. FISH & WILDLIFE SERVICE NATIONAL WILDLIFE REFUGES

Chautauqua   (office at refuge)
Route 2
Havana, IL 62644   309-535-2290

Bird List IL-1 Chautauqua Summary
254 birds listed, 71 nesting birds
Bird Chart pages 240-257

Totals by Season		s	S	F	W
Abundant	A	17	14	23	7
Common	C	94	53	84	22
Uncommon	U	57	23	67	17
Occasional	O	28	38	36	37
Rare	R	52	41	43	16

Endangered Species: Bald Eagle, Peregrine Falcon, Piping Plover, Least Tern

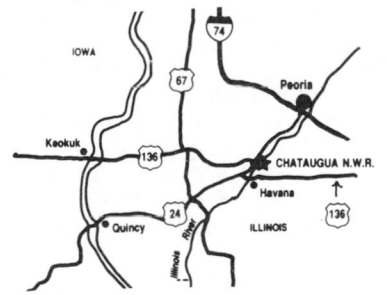

From Havana take the Manito Road north for approximately 10 miles to the refuge entrance sign. Turn left and follow signs to the office.

Habitat: 4,400 acres of Illinois River floodplain dominated by 3,500-acre Lake Chautauqua. The Illinois River forms the western border of the refuge, and its riparian habitat includes mixed bottomland hardwood forests, willow swamps, and sedge marshes. Shallow floodplain lakes abut the refuge on the north and south. A sandy bluff rises 70 feet above the east side of the lake. The succession of plant communities that follow the bluff down to the floodplain demonstrate the varying requirements of the different plants. An upland hardwood complex, dominated by oaks and hickories, florishes at the top of the bluff. In the decent to the floodplain cottonwoods and red and silver maples grade into sycamore, ash, and finally black willows. Large seepage springs keep portions of the eastern shoreline free from ice even in the coldest weather.

Common summer residents on the refuge include Great Blue and Green-backed herons, Black-crowned Night-Herons, and Great Egrets.

Other water birds and shorebirds are common during migration. Concentrations of these birds along the lake and mudflats are spectacular in August and early September.

Some of the greatest gatherings of ducks and geese along the Illinois River can be observed during fall and winter at Chautauqua. The average peak during early winter normally exceeds 100,000 ducks and up to 40,000 Canada and Snow geese. Mallards comprise the majority of the ducks with smaller numbers of Wood Ducks, Northern Pintails, American Wigeons, Black Ducks, Blue-winged and Green-winged teals, Lesser Scaups, Northern Shovelers, Redheads, Common Goldeneyes, and mergansers.

Bald Eagles winter along the river. They usually arrive in October and remain until the ice melts in the spring.

Area brochure, fishing, hunting, nut, berry and mushroom picking, boat access, interpretive foot trail.
Fall and Winter best.

Crab Orchard   (office at refuge)
PO Box J
Carterville, IL 62918   618-997-3344
Entry fee

Bird List IL-2 Crab Orchard Summary
245 birds listed, 103 nesting birds
Bird Chart pages 240-257

Totals by Season		s	S	F	W
Abundant	A	1	1	4	3
Common	C	6	76	90	59
Uncommon	U	82	25	60	27
Occasional	O	26	21	53	14
Rare	R	22	15	14	15

Endangered Species: Bald Eagle, Least Tern

The refuge is located between Carbondale and Marion. From I-57 in Marion, take the New Rte. 13 exit west for about 1.75 miles, turn left on Rte. 148 and go 1 mile to the refuge office.

Habitat: 43,000 acres include a 4,000-acre wilderness, about 5,000 acres of agricultural fields, 2,700 acres of livestock pasture, 12 natural areas, and 3 lakes. The refuge is divided into 2 units.

Primarily a waterfowl refuge, Crab Orchard is centered around providing a winter feeding and resting area for Canada Geese. During the fall and winter, many species of ducks visit the refuge and Bald Eagles may often be seen.

Area brochure, nature trail, picnic tables, boat ramp, boat dock, hunting, fishing, observation tower, hiking, camping.
Spring, Fall

Mark Twain Refuge Complex
Great River Plaza   (office in town)
311 N. 5th Street, Suite 100
Quincy, IL 62301   217-224-8580

This office manages the three district offices responsible for local area and refuge management in the nine divisions within the refuge complex. The districts are Brussels (Illinois), Annada (Missouri), and Wapello (Iowa). The refuge areas total about 23,500 acres along approximately 250 miles of the Mississippi and Illinois rivers.

The Mark Twain bird checklist combines

sighting information for the nine refuge areas but distinguishes with special codes four general areas: Gardner Division and Brussels District, both in Illinois, and the Annada and Wapello Districts in Missouri and Iowa respectively. The Mark Twain checklist is split into four separate lists in the bird chart.

The three district offices of the refuge complex and the nine refuge divisions are all noted in this chapter. Appropriate Bird List Summary data, district office, and division information is provided for the Wapello and Annada Districts, and their Illinois divisions. The other divisions are described in the Iowa and Missouri chapters.

The Mark Twain Refuge Complex map is followed by refuge details organized according to the Mark Twain management structure.

Brussels District ③ (office near town)
Mark Twain NWR
Box 107
Brussels, IL 62013   618-883-2524

Bird List IL-3 Brussels Summary
229 birds listed, 87 nesting birds
Bird Chart pages 240-257

Totals by Season		s	S	F	W
Abundant	A	4	3	7	3
Common	C	94	66	84	39
Uncommon	U	75	44	60	22
Occasional	O	24	14	25	25
Rare	R	14	6	14	7

Endangered Species: Bald Eagle, Peregrine Falcon, Least Tern

The Brussels District Office is located just off Co. Road 754, approximately 4 miles southeast of Brussels and about 30 miles northwest of St. Louis, Missouri.
The Brussels District includes three divisions, Calhoun, Gilbert Lake, and Batchtown. These refuge areas are open annually from December 15 to October 15. The district office is open all year.

Habitat: The Calhoun and Gilbert Lake areas are typical river bottomland habitat composed of backwater sloughs and lakes bordered by hardwood timber and farm fields, and frequently inundated by floodwaters.
The Calhoun Division contains 4,500 acres on the Illinois River in Calhoun County. The Gilbert Lake Division is 656 acres on the Illinois River in Jersey County. Both areas are located northeast of Brussels.

Heavy migrations of warblers, shorebirds, and waterfowl attract birders from March through May. The first waterfowl and other waterbirds return from the north in late summer, and their numbers increase throughout the early fall. Large flights of migrating hawks follow the Mississippi Flyway. Bald Eagles arrive later in the fall, and their population peaks in late December and January.

Habitat: Batchtown contains 2,249 acres, including lakes, backwater sloughs, woodlands, agricultural fields, and "moist soil units" on which the water levels are raised or lowered to promote growth. The Batchtown Division is north of Brussels and located on the Mississippi River.

The fall migrations of waterfowl and Bald Eagles are the primary attractions. Thousands of ducks and geese and numerous Bald Eagles migrate through the area during fall and winter, pausing on the refuge's fields and waterways for food and shelter.

Division brochures, fishing boat ramp, nut, berry, and mushroom picking.
Spring, Fall

Gardner Division ④
This division is part of the Annada District (office in Annada, MO, note Illinois map on page 76). Gardner Division is located in Illinois just 12 miles north of Quincy (center of the refuge complex map on this page). Visitor information is available at the Mark Twain Refuge Complex office in Quincy.

Bird List IL-4 Gardner Summary
219 birds listed, 86 nesting birds
Bird Chart pages 240-257

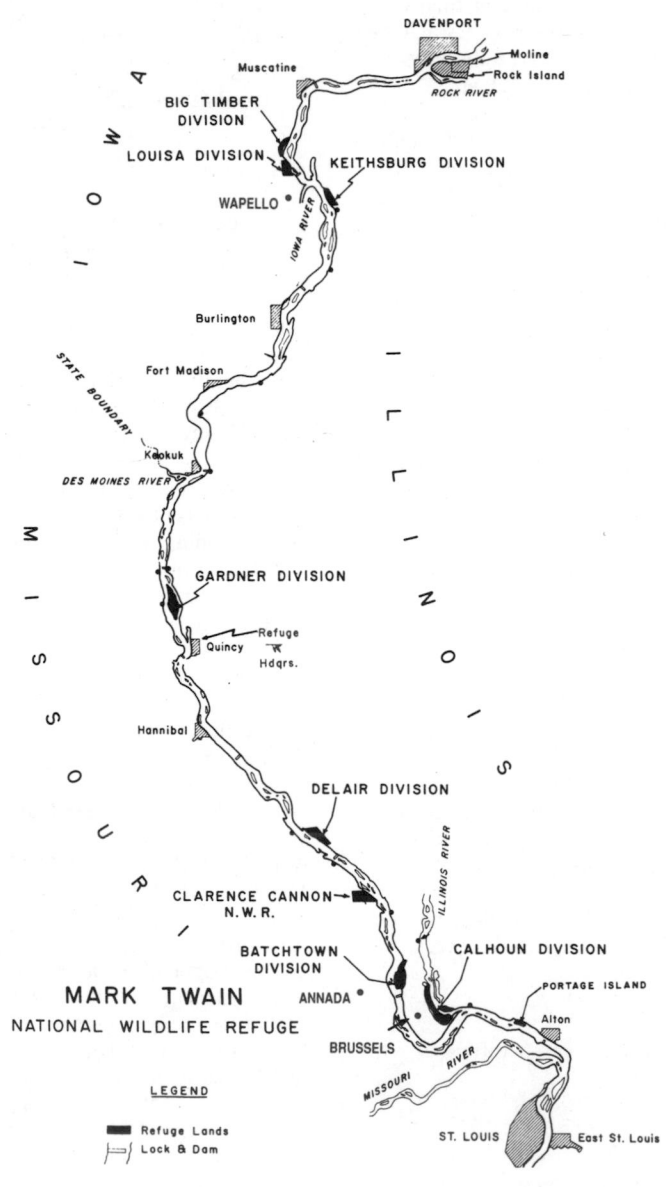

MARK TWAIN
NATIONAL WILDLIFE REFUGE

LEGEND
■ Refuge Lands
Lock & Dam

Totals by Season		s	S	F	W
Abundant	A	4	3	7	3
Common	C	93	65	83	38
Uncommon	U	75	44	60	22
Occasional	O	24	14	25	25
Rare	R	9	6	6	6

Endangered Species: Bald Eagle, Peregrine Falcon, Least Tern

Habitat: A series of 32 islands in the Mississippi River accessible only by boat, this 4,831-acre division is mostly old-growth maple, cottonwood, and mixed hardwood forest. About 750 acres are farmed to provide feed for waterfowl and other wildlife.

In early spring, American Woodcocks may be seen performing their spectacular courtship flights.

Area brochure, boating, hiking, fishing, hunting, nut, berry, and mushroom picking.
Spring, Fall

Annada District 5
(office in Missouri)
This district manages three divisions. The Delair Division in Illinois is closed to the public. In addition to the Gardner Division, the Annada District is responsible for the Clarence Cannon NWR located in Missouri.

Annada District details in the Missouri chapter include the Bird List MO-1 Annada Summary.

Wapello District 6
c/o Louisa Division   (office on refuge)
R.R. 1, Box 75
Wapello, IA 52653   319-523-6982

The Wapello District has three divisions, the Keithsburg Division in Illinois, and the Louisa and Big Timber divisions in Iowa (described in the Iowa chapter).

District headquarters is located on the Louisa Division Refuge in Iowa. Wapallo District details in the Iowa chapter include the Bird List IA-2 Wapallo Summary.

Keithsburg Division 7
Located approximately one mile north of Keithsburg in Mercer County, Illinois (see Mark Twain NWR map on page 78). Keithsburg is open from January through mid-September.

Habitat: 1,400 acres. Primarily bottomland timber interspersed with shallow sloughs and marshes adjacent to the Mississippi River just south of the Louisa Division.

During the fall migration concentrations of more than 50,000 ducks have been common at Keithsburg. The waterfowl, Bald Eagles, shorebirds, and wading birds found here enjoy the same habitats at Louisa. Major waterfowl species include Mallard, Wood Duck, American Wigeon, and Green-winged and Blue-winged teals.

Area brochure, boat ramp, fishing, hunting, berry, nut, and mushroom picking.
Spring, early September

Upper Mississippi River 8
National Wildlife & Fish Refuge
c/o Savanna District   (office in town)
US Post Office Building
PO Box 250
Savanna, IL 61074   815-273-2732

The refuge encompasses 195,000 acres of wooded islands, marshes and water-bodies extending 284 miles from Wabasha, Minnesota, south to Rock Island, Illinois.

Refuge headquarters is in Winona, Minnesota (Winona District). The Minnesota chapter includes a full description of this refuge, the bird life,

and habitat. See the Wisconsin (La Crosse District) and Iowa (McGregor District) chapters for the Upper Mississippi River Wildlife & Fish Refuge office contacts and refuge Bird List Summary data.

Detailed refuge "pool maps" are available by pool number, which correspond to the river dam and lock system in the four refuge districts. A Location Map (below) indicates all of these maps. Pool maps 12, 13, and 14 cover the Savanna District.

Area brochure, pool maps, mammals list, reptiles and amphibians list. Boating, back country use, hunting, fishing, camping, picnicking, swimming.
Spring, Summer, Fall

NATIONAL FOREST SERVICE
Shawnee National Forest Supervisor △
901 South Commercial Street
Harrisburg, IL 62946   618-253-7114

STATE AGENCIES

Division of Wildlife Resources
Lincoln Tower Plaza
524 South Second Street
Springfield, IL 62706   217-782-6384

Department of Conservation
Chicago Office
100 West Randolph, Suite 4-300
Chicago, IL 60601   312-814-2070

Map/Region/City
1	Region #1/Sterling	815-625-2968
2	Region #2 /Spring Grove	815-675-2385
3	Region #3/Champaign	217-333-5773
4	Region #4/Alton	618-462-1181
5	Region #5/Benton	618-435-8138

Illinois Office of Tourism
620 E. Adams St., 3rd Floor
Springfield, IL 62701   217-785-1032
toll free   800-223-0121

**Upper Mississippi River
National Wildlife & Fish Refuge
POOL MAP LOCATOR**
(office locations in red)

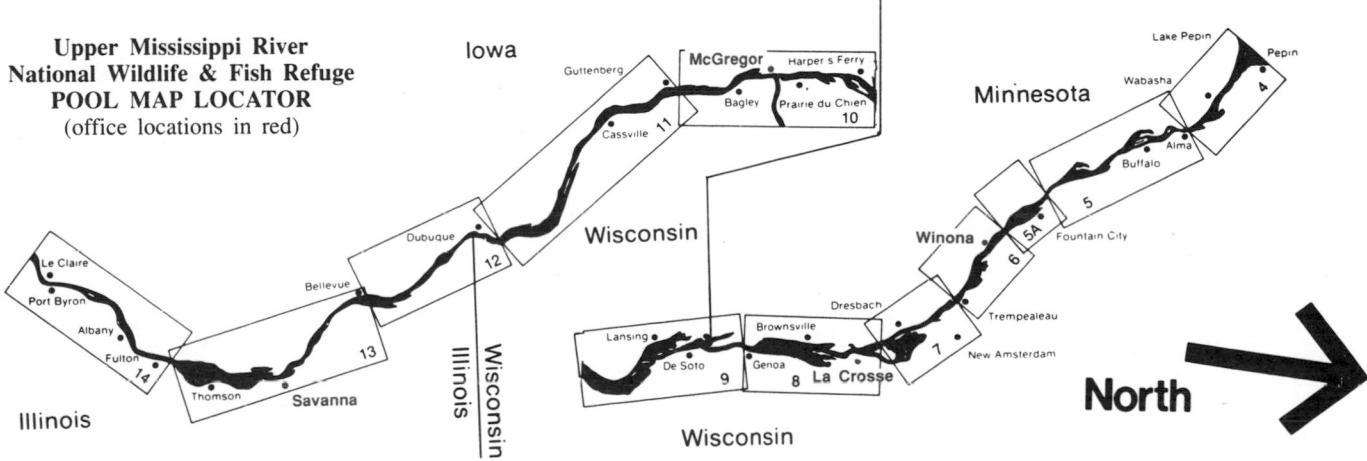

BIRDING HOTLINE
Statewide   317-259-0911

LOCAL BIRDING GROUPS
Map/Chapter/City
1. Amos W. Butler Aud./Indianapolis
2. Dunes Calumet Audubon/Hobart
3. East Central Indiana Aud./Albany
4. Evansville Audubon/Evansville
5. Illiana Cypress Audubon/Vincennes
6. Knob & Valley Aud./Indianapolis
7. Potawatomi Audubon/LaPorte
8. Sassafras Audubon/Bloomington
9. South Bend Audubon/South Bend
10. Stockbridge Audubon/Ft. Wayne
11. Sycamore Audubon/W. Lafayette
12. Tippecanoe Audubon/Warsaw
13. Wabash Valley Aud./Terre Haute
14. Whitewater Valley Aud./Richmond
15. Northwestern Indiana Bird Club
    /Chesterton

THE NATURE CONSERVANCY
Indiana Field Office
4200 N. Michigan Rd.
Indianapolis, IN 46208   317-923-7547

A complete description of the following 22 preserves, which includes driving directions and a local map, is available from the Field Office. Preserves are managed by TNC or local or state agencies as noted. There is no on-site management.

Anderson Falls Preserve
44 acres near Petersville in Bartholomew County

Anderson Falls are 14 feet high and over 100 feet wide. The ravines are characterized by a mature beech-maple forest, while white oak, hickory, and buckeye trees are most common on the ridges. The preserve, with its developed trails, is managed by Bartholomew County Park and Recreation Board.

Berns-Meyer Woods Preserve
20 acres near Pulaski in Pulaski County

An old-growth forest in a flat region of Indiana with various soil types and a slight range in elevation. Lower, wetter parts of this small preserve feature red maple, basswood, cottonwood, and tulip trees, while red and white oak, sugar maple, and shagbark hickory grow in the drier areas. There are marked trails with points of special interest labelled. Managed by the Indiana Dept. of Natural Resources, Div. of Nature Preserves.

Chapman Lake Wetlands Preserve
150 acres near Warsaw in Kosciusko County

Many species of shorebirds and songbirds are attracted to the large cattail-bullrush community that is interspersed with patches of marl beach prairie. The Chapman Lake Conservation Club assists the Indiana Dept. of Natural Resources, Div. of Nature Preserves with management of the preserve. Only passive recreation, such as hiking, birding, and photography, is permitted. No trails have been developed.

Crooked Lake Preserve
100 acres near Churubusco in Whitley County

The preserve is located along 3,500 feet on the east side of Crooked Lake. This glacial, spring-fed lake is one of the cleanest and, with a depth of 105 feet, one of the deepest in Indiana. The wooded bluff overlooks a two-acre island provides habitat for birds and other animals. A self-guiding trail brochure is available from the Indiana Dept. of Natural Resources, Div. of Nature Preserves, which manages the preserve.

Deep River Preserve
39 acres near Gary in Lake County

This area is an oasis of wildness in heavily populated Lake County. Deep River provides examples of several ecosystems, including an oak-hickory forest on the slopes and uplands and bottomland woods in the floodplain. The river and its spring-fed tributary sustain plant and wildlife species that are dependent on flowing waters and a moist habitat. Trails are developed and the area is managed by the Lake County Parks and Recreation Dept.

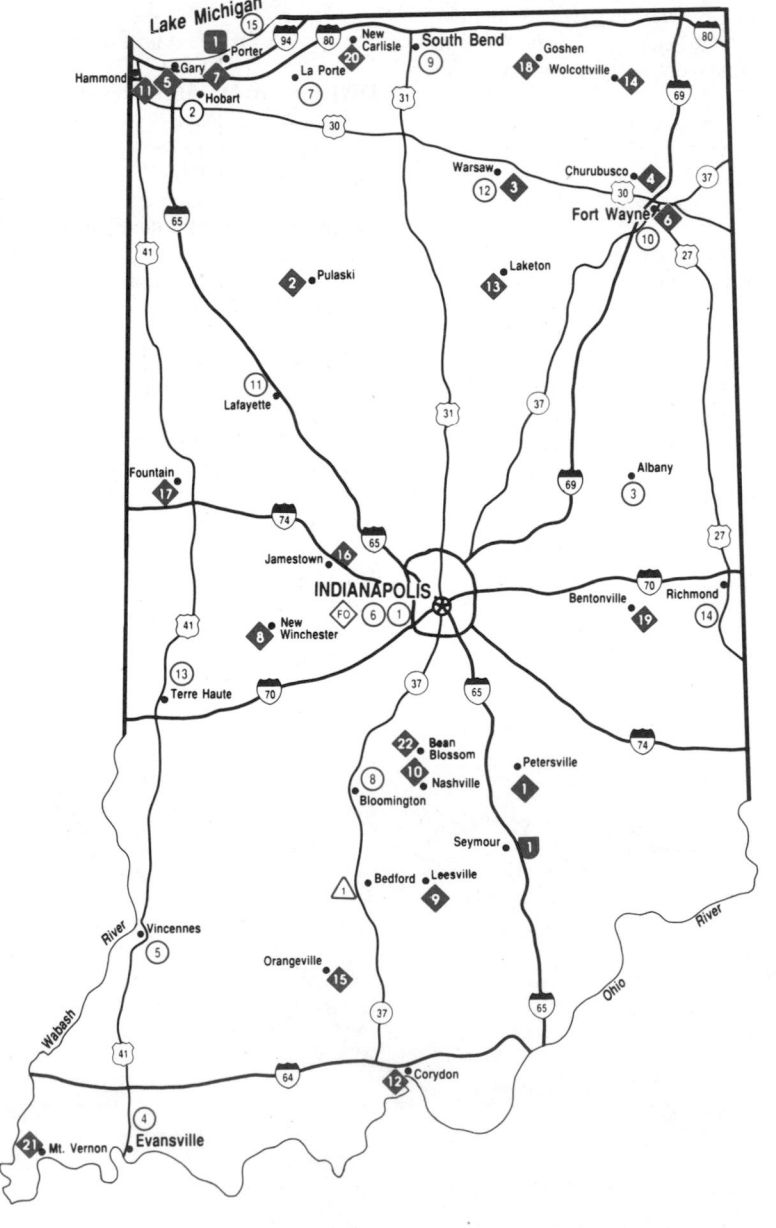

Fox Island ⬥⑥
602 acres near Fort Wayne in Allen County

The preserve, which includes the largest expanse of contiguous woodland in the county, is managed by the Allen County Parks and Recreation Board. The marshes, seasonal ponds, quaking bogs, dune and wetland forests, pine plantation, and old fields provide a large range of habitats for the numerous and varied wildlife.

The existing trails focus on the wetlands, geology, trees, and shrubs. The "Foxwood Trail" is specially designed for anyone unable to hike the main trails, including young, old, handicapped, and sight-impaired. Field study programs have been prepared for schools and other interested groups.

Gibson Woods Preserve ⬥⑦
129 acres near South Gary in Lake County

This preserve protects some of the last remaining ridge and swale topography once found in abundance on the southern shores of Lake Michigan. The large, unbroken dune ridges are second only to those of the Indiana Dunes National Lakeshore. In the complex of plant communities a variety of rare flora can be found, including speckled alder, paper birch, golden sedge, and large yellow lady slipper. Red-shouldered Hawks, American Bitterns, and Blue-winged Teals may be seen, as well as Franklin's ground squirrels, Blanding's turtles, and Karner blue butterflies.

The Gibson Woods Environmental Awareness Center serves as an outdoor education facility. Three trails range from .5 to 2 miles in length, with boardwalks over the wet swale areas. Self-guiding brochure is available for one trail. Managed by the Lake County Parks and Recreation Dept.

The Oscar & Ruth Hall ⬥⑧
Woods Preserve
94 acres near New Winchester in Putnam County

Hall Woods contains some of the best white oak-dominated woods remaining in Indiana. Intermittent streams flow into Big Walnut Creek through deep ravines which cut the otherwise level hilltops. Trails have not been developed. Managed by the Indiana Dept. of Natural Resources, Div. of Nature Preserves.

Hemlock Bluff Preserve ⬥⑨
45 acres near Leesville in Jackson County

The shale overhangs along Guthrie Creek and the steep 175-foot slope characterize Hemlock Bluff. The hemlock community is a glacial remnant, which depends on the cool, moist conditions of the northwest-facing escarpment to withstand intrusions by the beaches, maples, and oaks growing on top of the bluff.

Educational and recreational opportunities include hiking on a well-developed trail and observation of a variety of ferns, wildflowers, birds, and other animals that frequent the area. The preserve is managed by the Indiana Dept. of Natural Resources, Div. of Nature Preserves.

Hitz-Rhodehamel ⬥⑩
Woods Preserve
271 acres near Nashville in Brown County

A large, high-quality forest covers the varied topography, including ridge tops, ravines, and uplands. The chestnut-oak woods growing on dry slopes have an open understory featuring blueberry, huckleberry, diverse mosses and lichens, and the rare whorled pogonia. This preserve, which is managed by The Nature Conservancy, has walking trails.

Hoosier Prairie Preserve ⬥⑪
439 acres near Hammond in Lake County

Indiana's largest high-quality prairie is situated only minutes from the industrialized Calumet region. The ecological diversity, among the greatest in the state, includes over 350 vascular plants. Prescribed burns conducted during each spring or early fall maintain the sun-dependent prairie by preventing invasion of woody plants. The nature trail and preserve are managed by the Indiana Dept. of Natural Resources, Div. of Nature Preserves.

Indian Creek Woods ⬥⑫
116 acres near Corydon in Harrison County

The woods abut the 150-acre Hayswood Nature Preserve along 1.5 miles of Indian Creek. Located on a steep, wooded, 170-foot bluff, it provides a view up to the 360-foot Pilot Knob in the Hayswood preserve. Indian Creek Woods provide excellent examples of rock outcroppings and the dynamics of forest ecology. Several trails through Hayswood Nature Preserve include one for handicapped people. The preserve is managed by Harrison County Parks and Recreation.

Laketon Bog Preserve ⬥⑬
32 acres near Laketon in Wabash County

Located between Eel River and a bluff, the bog is a peat-filled hollow that retains its moisture with seepage from the bottom of the bluff. The Laketon Bog has an abundance of spring wildflowers and several rare plants, including yellow and showy lady slippers. A boardwalk leads to the floodplain forest through the bog. The preserve is managed by Indiana Dept. of Natural Resources, Div. of Nature Preserves.

Olin Lake Preserve ⬥⑭
304 acres near Wolcottville in LaGrange County

Olin Lake, the largest in Indiana without any development on its shoreline, resembles pristine lakes in the northern wilderness. Marl, a white, calcareous compound that precipitated out of the water, covers the lake bottom and inhibits the growth of aquatic vegetation. Olin Lake Preserve is managed by the Indiana Dept. of Natural Resources, Div. of Nature Preserves.

Orangeville Rise Preserve ⬥⑮
3 acres near Orangeville in Orange County

A 100-foot-wide tributary of Lost River reemerges at Orangeville Rise, flowing south through a channel. The rare blind cavefish inhabits the subterranean streams that feed the tributary. This National Natural Landmark is managed by The Nature Conservancy.

Pine Hills Preserve ⬥⑯
470 acres west of Jamestown in Montgomery County

Groves of evergreens and various hardwoods cover the rugged hills, gorges, and sandstone bluffs. The varied terrain, cut by five miles of clear streams, also supports many wildflowers, ferns, rare plants, and animals.

Pine Hills was the first project of The Nature Conservancy in Indiana and became the state's first nature preserve. It is managed by the Indiana Dept. of Natural Resources, Div. of Nature Preserves.

Portland Arch Preserve ⬥⑰
265 acres near Fountain in Fountain County

Portland Arch is particularly well known for its geological features and botanical diversity. The arch itself was created by a tributary of Bear Creek eroding a tunnel through a massive sandstone formation. The north trail goes from an upland oak-hickory forest, through a ravine and the arch, to Bear Creek Canyon. The south trail crosses old fields and steep forested ridges. Birds in the tops of the bottomland beech-maple woods can be seen at eye-level from the cliffs. Portland Arch is managed by the Indiana Dept. of Natural Resources, Div. of Nature Preserves.

Shoup-Parsons [18] Swamp Woods Preserve
17 acres in Goshen, Elkhart County

A diverse plant life is supported by the varying water conditions, including flood plain, uplands, marsh, and swamp. The preserve is well known as an excellent birding area. It is managed by Goshen Parks and Recreation Dept.

Shrader-Weaver [19] Woods Preserve
108 acres near Bentonville in Fayette County

This National Natural Landmark contains an old-growth forest, an old field, and a pioneer home built in 1830 from the clay and limestone present on the property. The old field illustrates succession as woody species invade and the field reverts to forest. Wildflowers cover the old-growth forest floor in spring. There are two self-guiding trails, one through the upland forest, and the other through the old field and lowland forest. The preserve is managed by the Indiana Dept. of Natural Resources, Div. of Nature Preserves.

Spicer Lake Preserve [20]
149 acres near New Carlisle in St. Joseph County

Spicer Lake, formed by a melting block of ice left behind by the last glacier, is an excellent example of lake succession. Peat builds up as the surrounding vegetation dies and supplies more "soil" that is used by the encroaching plants. This process has reduced Spicer Lake to 3.5 acres of open water. A boardwalk trail, with access for the handicapped, extends to the lake edge. It is managed by St. Joseph County Dept. of Parks and Recreation.

Twin Swamps Preserve [21]
520 acres near Mt. Vernon in Posey County

Twin Swamps is named for its bald cypress and overcup oak sloughs. The impressive size and quality of the two swamps is demonstrated along the boardwalk and foot trails, which make this one of the state's most accessible

preserves. Twin Swamps is managed by the Indiana Dept. of Natural Resources, Div. of Nature Preserves.

Whip-poor-will [22] Woods Preserve
560 acres near Bean Blossom in Brown County

The rolling hills, deep ravines, and intermittent streams support a variety of plant communities, including dry, dry-mesic, and mesic upland and ravine forests. The preserve is particularly noted for its fine chestnut-oak forest. No trails have been developed on this preserve, which is managed by The Nature Conservancy and the Indiana Dept. of Natural Resources, Div. of Nature Preserves.

U.S. FISH & WILDLIFE SERVICE NATIONAL WILDLIFE REFUGES

Muscatatuck [1]   (Office at refuge)
R.R. 7, Box 189A
Seymour, IN 47274   812-522-4352
Entry fee

Bird List IN-1 Muscatatuck Summary
228 birds listed, 109 nesting birds
Bird Chart pages 240-257

Totals By Season		s	S	F	W
Abundant	A	10	9	9	7
Common	C	55	47	52	37
Uncommon	U	3	54	88	34
Occasional	O	38	28	34	32
Rare	R	2	3	6	3

Endangered Species: Bald Eagle

From the I-65 exit in Seymour, take Rt. 50 east for 3 miles to the refuge entrance. Follow signs to the office.

Habitat: 7,700 acres include 1,300 acres

of permanent or seasonal lakes and marshes, 1,000 acres of grasslands or crop fields, 2,400 acres of old farm fields reverting to forest, and 3,000 acres of forest. The Muscatatuck River forms the southern boundary.

The objectives of the refuge are to provide habitat for migratory waterfowl and endangered species as well as nesting areas for Wood Ducks.

Wood Ducks, Great Blue Herons, and Canada Geese are common nesting species and may be seen throughout the summer. The greatest number of waterfowl visit the refuge during the spring and fall. Fall migration may also include a few transient flocks of Sandhill Cranes, some Ospreys, and an occasional Bald Eagle, in addition to the more common Northern Harrier.

Refuge brochure, fishing, hunting, hiking, mushroom and berry picking.
Spring and fall best.

NATIONAL PARK SERVICE

Indiana Dunes [1] National Lakeshore
1100 N. Mineral Springs Road
Porter, IN 46304   219-926-7561

12,857 acres of dunes rise 180 feet above Lake Michigan's southern shore. Other natural features include beaches, bogs, marshes, swamps, and prairie remnants. The Paul H. Douglas Center for Environmental Education is located at the Lakeshore.
Brochure with map.

Wayne-Hoosier Nat'l. Forests Supt. △
811 Constitution Ave.
Bedford, IN 47421   812-275-5987

STATE AGENCIES

Division of Fish & Wildlife
Department of Natural Resources
607 State Office Bldg.
Indianapolis, IN 46204   317-232-4080

Fish & Wildlife headquarters is the best source for statewide information and literature on non-consumptive wildlife programs.

Tourism Development Office
Department of Commerce
One N. Capitol
Indianapolis, IN 46204   317-232-8860
from out-of-state call   800-292-6337

BIRDING HOTLINE

Statewide	319-338-9881
Sioux City	712-262-5958

LOCAL BIRDING GROUPS
Map/Chapter/City

① Big Bluestem Audubon/Ames
② Cedar Rapids Aud./Cedar Rapids
③ Dubuque Audubon/Dubuque
④ Grinnell Audubon/Grinnell
⑤ Iowa River Valley Greenbelt
   Audubon/Eldora
⑥ Loess Hills Audubon/Sioux City
⑦ N. Iowa Prairie Lakes Audubon
   /Spirit Lake
⑧ Prairie Rapids Audubon/Waterloo
⑨ Rolling Hills Audubon/Indianola
⑩ Southeast Iowa Audubon/Fairfield
⑪ Upper Iowa Audubon/Decorah
⑫ Ottumwa Bird Club/Ottumwa

THE NATURE CONSERVANCY

Iowa Field Office ◈
431 East Locust, Suite 200
Des Moines, IA 50309   515-244-5044

The preserves are worth visiting year-round except as noted. There are no regularly scheduled guided tours of preserves, but tours are conducted from time to time. Day hiking and cross-country skiing are permitted at all locations.

Ames High Prairie Preserve ◆
22 acres near Ames
Spring, Summer, Fall

Behrens Pond & Woodland ◆
30 acres near Cedar Rapids
Spring, Fall

Berry Woods ◆
42 acres near Indianola

Brayton-Horsley Prairie ◆
55 acres near Sumner
Species list available.
Spring, Summer, Fall

Cedar Hills Sand Prairie ◆
91 acres near Cedar Falls
Species list available.

Crossman Prairie ◆
10 acres near Riceville
Species list available.
Spring, Summer, Fall

The Diggings ◆
7 acres near Ft. Dodge
Area brochure and trail map available.

Five Ridge Preserve ◆
790 acres near Sioux City
Area brochure, bird list available.

Freda Haffner Preserve ◆
110 acres near Milford
Bird list available.

Greiner Family Preserve ◆
84 acres near Muscatine
Species list available.
Spring, Fall, Winter

Hanging Bog ◆
16 acres near Cedar Rapids

Hoffman Prairie ◆
36 acres near Mason City
Species list available.
Spring, Summer, Fall

Lock & Dam #14 Eagle Area ◆
8 acres near Bettendorf
Bald Eagle count map available.

Retz Memorial Forest ◆
49 acres near Elkader

Savage Memorial Woods ◆
12 acres near Mount Pleasant

Silver Lake Fen ◆
5 acres near Lake Park
Species list available.
Spring, Summer, Fall

Sioux City Prairie ◆
157 acres near Sioux City
Bird list available.

Steele Prairie ◆
200 acres near Cherokee
Species list available.

Williams Prairie ◆
21 acres near Iowa City
Species list available.

U.S. FISH & WILDLIFE SERVICE NATIONAL WILDLIFE REFUGES

Desoto ◼   (office at refuge)
Route 1, Box 114
Missouri Valley, IA 51555   712-642-4121

Bird List IA-1 Desoto Summary
240 birds listed, 81 nesting birds
Bird Chart pages 240-257

Totals by Season		s	S	F	W
Abundant	A	6	7	5	6
Common	C	66	40	49	19
Uncommon	U	63	38	52	22
Occasional	O	48	18	44	15
Rare	R	38	18	17	26

Endangered Species: Bald Eagle, Peregrine Falcon, Piping Plover, Least Tern

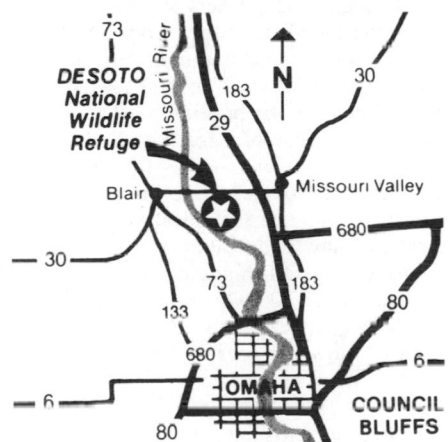

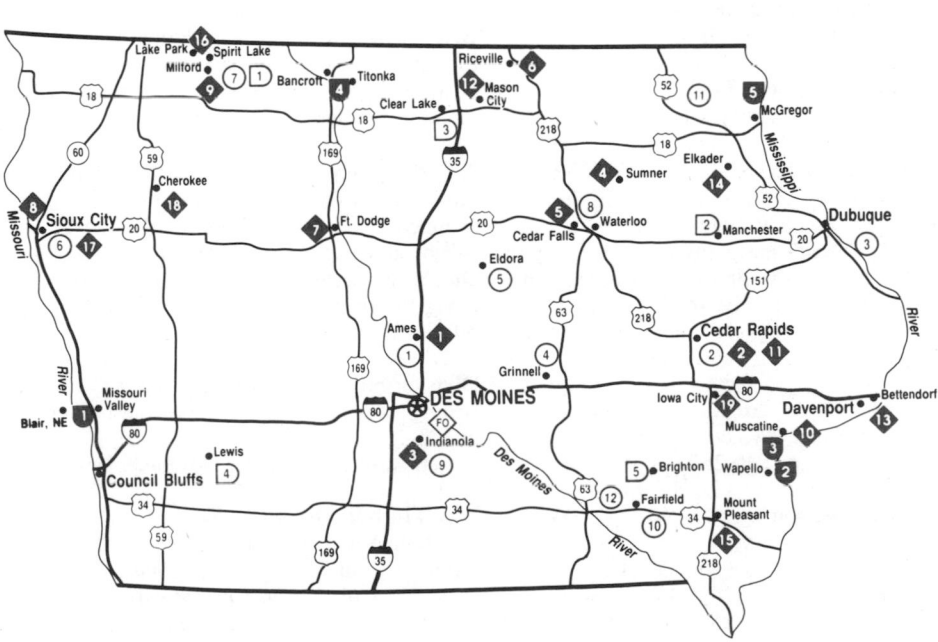

From Blair, Nebraska, take U.S. Hwy. 30 east for 5 miles. From I-29, take the Missouri Valley exit (#75) and go 5 miles west on U.S. Hwy. 30.

Habitat: 7,823 acres include a 750-acre oxbow, Desoto Lake, small ponds and cattail marshes, a stretch of the Missouri River, and grasslands, croplands, rose hedges, and mature woodlands. The refuge, which lies in the fertile Missouri River Valley, extends into Nebraska.

An assortment of warblers, gulls, shorebirds and other bird life can be observed on the refuge during the spring and fall migrations. Ducks and geese congregate on the lakes and in fields during March and early April.

In summer, the woods, fields of native prairie grasses, and rose hedges attract a variety of songbirds, as well as Ring-necked Pheasants and Northern Bobwhites. Red-headed Woodpeckers are common along the woodland edge. Wood Ducks may be seen in ponds throughout the refuge. Steep banks at several locations along Desoto Lake provide burrowing sites for colonies of Bank Swallows.

October and November are the peak waterfowl months. In typical years 200,000 Snow and "Blue" geese use the refuge during fall migration. Peak populations of 125,000 or more ducks, mostly Mallards, are also common. Bald Eagles follow the geese into the area and many remain until March.

Area brochure, fishing, boating, hunting, hiking, picnicking, auto tour route, visitor center, mushroom gathering.
Spring, Fall

Wapello District 2
c/o Louisa Division   (office on refuge)
R.R. 1, Box 75
Wapello, IA 52653   319-523-6982

The Mark Twain Refuge Complex Wapello District has 3 divisions, the Big Timber and Louisa divisions in Iowa, and the Keithsburg division in Illinois (see Illinois chapter page 78 for refuge complex map).

Bird List IA-2 Wapello Summary
219 birds listed, 84 nesting birds
Bird Chart pages 240-257

Totals by Season		s	S	F	W
Abundant	A	4	3	7	3
Common	C	93	65	83	37
Uncommon	U	74	43	59	22
Occasional	O	25	15	26	26
Rare	R	9	6	6	6

Endangered Species: Bald Eagle, Peregrine Falcon, Least Tern

The Louisa NWR is home to the Wapello District headquarters. From Wapello take the Louisa Co. Road X-61 (the Great River Road) east for 6 miles, turn left, and follow signs to refuge headquarters.

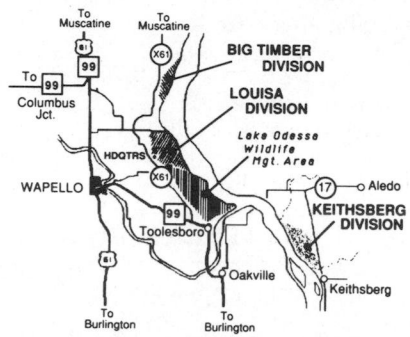

Louisa Habitat: 3,338 acres in the Mississippi River floodplain. Much of the area is now in "moist soil units," which are drained in the summer to promote natural plant growth and re-flooded in the fall to provide wildlife feed. On higher ground, farming provides corn, winter wheat, milo, buckwheat, and Japanese millet for wildfowl food.

Migrating waterfowl are attracted to this combination of water and natural seed source. More than 100.000 ducks and 6,000 geese are common during migration as they stop to rest and feed at the refuge, which is located along the Mississippi Flyway. Mallards, Northern Pintails, Gadwalls, American Black Ducks, teals, and Canada and Snow geese visit Louisa.

Bald Eagles are often seen during migration and over 50 have been observed at the refuge as they feed on fish and sick or injured waterfowl.

A wide variety of shorebirds and wading birds feed at the refuge during the summer. Hundreds of Wood Ducks can be found during all but the coldest months. During spring they nest in hollow trees along the river bluffs and throughout the refuge.

Division brochures, foot trail, boating, fishing, hunting, berry, nut, and mushroom picking.
March-April and October-November best.

Big Timber Division 3
The refuge is located approximately 10 miles south of Muscatine on Louisa Co. Road X-61 (the Great River Road). A boat for access to the backwater sloughs and marshes or the islands is a must.

Habitat: 3,376 acres. Known locally as The Breaks, the area includes backwater sloughs and bottomland timber, and the islands of Ramsey, Turkey Towhead, Turkey, and Otter. The refuge is located in Mississippi River navigation pool 17.

Various waterfowl, including Mallards, Northern Pintails, American Wigeons, Northern Shovelers, Lesser Scaups, and teals, find food and rest during their spring migration north in March and April.

The warbler migration peaks during mid-May. The Pileated Woodpecker, which nests at Big Timber, is among the commonly seen woodpeckers. Barred and Great Horned owls are also a common reward for the careful observer.

Large numbers of herons and egrets feed in refuge wetlands throughout the summer.

The fall migration of raptors peaks during late October. Ospreys may be seen in September and October, while Bald Eagle concentrations peak early in December and again during February.

Area brochure, boat ramp, fishing, hunting, berry, nut, and mushroom picking.
October-November and March-April are best times.

Union Slough 4   (office at refuge)
Route 1, Box 52
Titonka, IA 50480   515-928-2523

Bird List IA-3 Union Slgh Summary
217 birds listed, 96 nesting birds
Bird Chart pages 240-257

Totals by Season		s	S	F	W
Abundant	A	8	4	14	1
Common	C	83	71	83	17
Uncommon	U	49	48	49	14
Occasional	O	28	13	17	12
Rare	R	18	13	18	9

Endangered Species: Bald Eagle, Peregrine Falcon, Least Tern

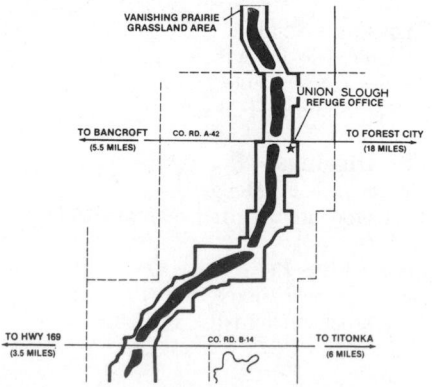

From Bancroft, take city road A-42 east 6 miles to the refuge and office.

Habitat: 2,845 acres extending for 8 miles along Union Slough and Buffalo Creek (Kossuth County) in north central Iowa. There are 1,100 acres of marsh in six separate units. The remaining acres include farm crops and native grasses.

Ducks are the most plentiful waterfowl using the refuge in spring and fall, although Canada and Greater White-fronted geese also use the refuge during migration. Some Mallards, Blue-winged Teals, Wood and Ruddy ducks, and occasionally other species nest. A few Tundra Swans usually stop each year and populations of Ring-necked Pheasants and Gray Partridges breed in the grasslands.

American White Pelicans, Great Blue Herons, Double-crested Cormorants, Black-crowned Night-Herons, and Soras are common residents from spring to fall. A variety of shorebirds are also common during this period, as well as Ring-billed and Franklin's gulls, and Common and Forster's terns. Black Terns nest at the refuge.

The winter months bring several species of hawks and owls to the refuge along with Horned Larks and Snow Buntings. Some Mallards over-winter on the marsh.

Area brochure, fishing, nature trails, picnicking.

Spring, Fall

Upper Mississippi River [5] Wildlife & Fish Refuge
McGregor District
Hwy. 18
PO Box 460
McGregor, IA 52157   319-873-3423

From McGregor, take Hwy. 18 north 0.5 miles to the district office.

The refuge encompasses 195,000 acres of wooded islands, marshes and water-bodies extending 284 miles from Wabasha, Minnesota, to Rock Island, Illinois.

Refuge headquarters is in Winona, Minnesota (Winona District). See the Minnesota chapter for a complete description of the refuge, bird life, and habitat. See the Illinois (Savanna District) and Wisconsin (La Crosse District) chapters for the Upper Mississippi River Wildlife & Fish Refuge office contacts and the La Crosse Bird List Summary.

Detailed refuge "pool maps" are available by pool number, which correspond to the river dam and lock system in the four refuge districts. A Location Map (below) indicates all of these maps. Pool maps 9, 10, 11, 12, 13, and 14 cover the McGregor District.

Bird List IA-4 McGregor Summary
265 birds listed, 127 nesting birds
Bird Chart pages 258-275

Totals by Season		s	S	F	W
Abundant	A	28	24	24	4
Common	C	99	63	84	18
Uncommon	U	89	62	97	27
Occasional	O	13	11	16	18
Rare	R	27	18	15	34

Endangered Species: Bald Eagle, Peregrine Falcon

Area brochure, pool maps, mammals, reptiles, and amphibians lists, boating, back country use, hunting, fishing, camping, picnicking, swimming.
Spring, Summer, Fall

STATE AGENCIES

Iowa Conservation Commission
Wallace State Office Bldg.
Des Moines, IA 50319   515-281-8174

Map/Region/City
[1]	Northwest/Spirit Lake	712-336-1840
[2]	Northeast/Manchester	319-927-3276
[3]	North Central /Clear Lake	515-357-3517
[4]	Southwest/Lewis	712-769-2587
[5]	Southeast/Brighton	319-694-2430

Iowa Visitors & Tourism Div.
Development Commission
600 E. Court Ave.   515-281-3401
Des Moines, IA 50309   800-345-4692

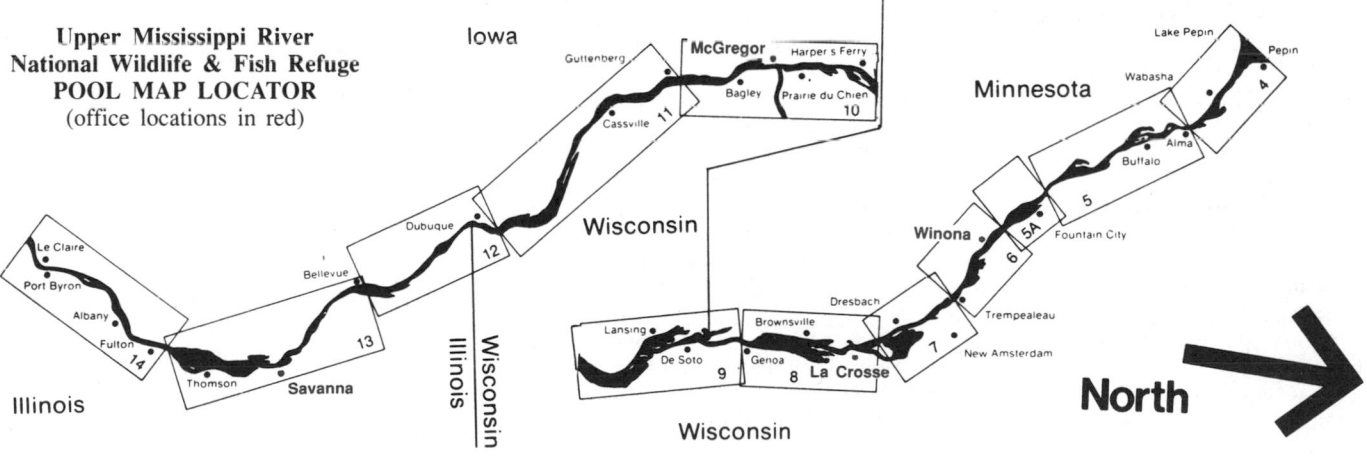

Upper Mississippi River National Wildlife & Fish Refuge POOL MAP LOCATOR (office locations in red)

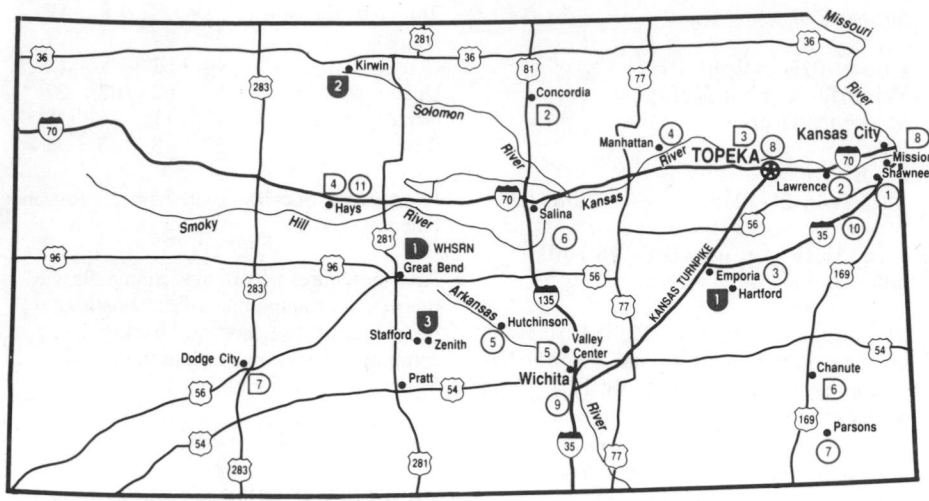

LOCAL BIRDING GROUPS
Map/Chapter/City

1. Burroughs Audubon of KC /Shawnee Mission
2. Jayhawk Audubon/Lawrence
3. Kanza Audubon/Emporia
4. Northern Flint Hills Aud./Manhattan
5. Sandhills Audubon/Hutchinson
6. Smoky Hills Audubon/Salina
7. Southeast Kansas Audubon/Parsons
8. Topeka Audubon/Topeka
9. Wichita Audubon/Wichita
10. Baldwin Bird Club/Baldwin City
11. Ellis County Bird Club/Hays

U.S. FISH & WILDLIFE SERVICE NATIONAL WILDLIFE REFUGES

Flint Hills 🚩   (office at refuge)
PO Box 128
Hartford, KS 66854   316-392-5553

Bird List KS-1 Flint Hills Summary
285 birds listed, 88 nesting birds
Bird Chart pages 258-275

Seasonal Abundance	s	S	F	W
Abundant	A	42	22	36	19
Common	C	81	40	78	19
Uncommon	U	75	29	72	33
Occasional	O	39	27	40	17
Rare	R	26	35	29	32

Endangered Species: Bald Eagle, Peregrine Falcon, Piping Plover, Least Tern

From Emporia take Hwy. 50 east (I-35). Exit onto Hwy. 130 south. Go south for 8 miles to Hartford High School. Turn right, go 3 blocks, turn right again, and go 1 block to the refuge office.

Habitat: 18,500 acres of native grassland, hardwood forest, shallow marshes, flooded sloughs, and croplands in the Neosho River Valley. The refuge is located at the upstream end of John Redmond Reservoir.

Thousands of migratory waterfowl feed and rest during spring and fall migrations.

Numerous shorebirds arrive in the spring along with eight species of bitterns and herons, three of which nest at the refuge. Greater Prairie Chickens and Scissor-tailed Flycatchers, rare or absent at most other locations, are both common and nest at Flint Hills. April and May are the best months for observing passerines.

Redheads, Canvasbacks, and American White Pelicans migrate through the area in October. The waterfowl migration peak occurs in November.

In late fall and early winter, Golden and Bald eagles arrive at the refuge. The winter population of Bald Eagles may reach 120 in number.

Area brochure, boating, picnicking, camping, fishing, hunting, interpretive trail, wild food gathering.
Spring, Fall

Kirwin 2   (office at refuge)
Route 1, Box 103
Kirwin, KS 67644   913-543-6673

Bird List KS-2 Kirwin Summary
191 birds listed, 46 nesting birds
Bird Chart pages 258-275

Seasonal Abundance	s	S	F	W
Abundant	A	9	5	8	1
Common	C	51	33	53	19
Uncommon	U	28	18	29	13
Occasional	O	65	56	65	23
Rare	R	18	18	20	18

Endangered Species: Bald Eagle, Peregrine Falcon, Whooping Crane, Piping Plover, Least Tern

From Kirwin, take Hwy. 9 west for 4 miles, turn left, and go 1 mile south to the refuge office.

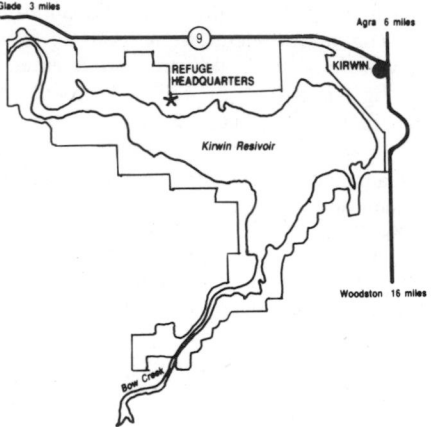

Habitat: 10,778 acres in the narrow North Fork of the Solomon River Valley around Kirwin Reservoir. Includes 5,378 acres of water at conservation pool level, 3,500 acres of grassland, and 1,900 acres of cropland. This refuge of broken and rolling hills forms part of the transition zone between the tall-grass prairies of the east and short-grass plains of the west.

The first spring migrants to arrive are Northern Pintails, Northern Shovelers, Gadwalls, Green-winged and Blue-winged teals, and various shorebirds. Nesting waterbirds include Canada Geese, Mallards, Great Blue Herons, and Double-crested Cormorants.

Among the upland game species are Ring-necked Pheasant, Northern Bobwhite, Greater Prairie Chicken, and "Rio Grande" Wild Turkey.

In late September, American White Pelicans and winter gulls are among the first fall migrants to arrive. Late arrivals include Greater White-fronted Geese, Cinnamon Teals, American Wigeons, and other dabbling ducks.

Northern Harriers, Red-tailed and Swainson's hawks, and American Kestrels are common at Kirwin. A small number of Peregrine Falcons are also present. Golden and Bald eagles arrive in late fall or early winter.

Area brochure, fishing, hunting, camping, picnicking, scenic drive, nature trails, biking, water skiing, mammals list.
Spring, Fall

Quivira 3   (office at refuge)
Route 3, Box 48A
Stafford, KS 67578   316-486-2393

Bird List KS-3 Quivira Summary
252 birds listed, 88 nesting birds
Bird Chart pages 258-275

Seasonal Abundance	s	S	F	W
Abundant	A	33	11	36	10
Common	C	79	55	74	29
Uncommon	U	62	56	62	25
Occasional	O	43	34	39	29
Rare	R	23	20	23	23

Endangered Species: Bald Eagle, Peregrine Falcon, Whooping Crane, Piping Plover, Least Tern

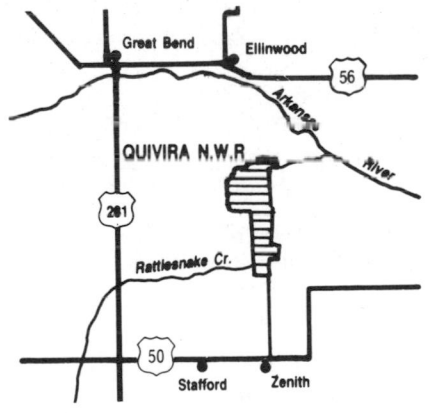

Take Hwy. 50 east for 6 miles from Stafford to Zenith (grain elevator). Turn left onto the Zenith blacktop road and go about 8 miles north to the office.

Habitat: 21,820 acres include the Big Salt Marsh and Little Salt Marsh, ancient basins with a history of waterfowl use. A 15-mile canal system and 25 miles of dikes provide nearly 5,000 acres of managed wetlands and marshes that include 30 water units ranging in size from 10 to 1,500 acres. The 362-acre Santana Natural Area preserves an example of the original prairie and includes 15 acres of century-old cottonwoods.

During the spring and fall migrations the refuge is a staging area for 500,000 birds from both eastern and western North America. American White Pelicans, Sandhill Cranes, and a variety of shorebirds are abundant visitors, while the Whooping Crane may be seen occasionally.

Snowy Plovers and American Avocets are common nesters, while the Black-necked Stilt and White-faced Ibis have started to nest here in recent years.

Five species of hawks, Northern Harrier, Mississippi Kite, and Cooper's, Swainson's, and Red-tailed hawks, are common breeders at the refuge. American Kestrels are frequently seen during migration, and Red-tailed and Cooper's hawks and Northern Harriers remain throughout the year. Large numbers of Bald Eagles, accompanied by a few Golden Eagles, are present from November until March.

Area brochure, hunting, fishing.
Spring, Fall

STATE AGENCIES

Kansas Dept. of Wildlife & Parks
Headquarters Office
Route 2, Box 54A
Pratt, KS 67124   316-672-5911

Cheyenne Bottoms 1
Wildlife Area & WHSRN
One of 71 state-managed wildlife areas totaling 243,000 acres. Cheyenne Bottoms Wildlife Area contains 13,416 acres and is located 5 miles north and 5 miles east of Great Bend. Check with the Southwest Regional Office of the Dept. of Wildlife & Parks, in Dodge City, for access details.

A state wildlife area dedicated in 1989 as part of the Western Hemisphere Shorebird Reserve Network, Cheyenne Bottoms is one of the most important inland staging sites for migratory shorebirds in the western hemisphere.

A booklet titled "A Hunting Guide to Kansas" describes wildlife areas by region, gives the area size in acres and the approximate location, and includes selected local maps. It is available from any agency office.

Map/Region or District/City
1	North Central /Concordia	913-243-3857
2	Northeast/Topeka	913-273-6740
3	Northwest/Hays	913-628-8614
4	South Central /Valley Center	316-755-2711
5	Southeast/Chanute	316-431-0380
6	Southwest/Dodge City	316-227-8609
7	KC District /Shawnee Mission	913-722-6024

Kansas Travel & Tourism Division
400 W. 8th, 5th Floor
Topeka, KS 66603   913-296-2009
in state   800-252-6727

LOCAL BIRDING GROUPS
Map/Chapter/City

1. Buckley Hills Audubon/Versailles
2. Daviess County Audubon/Owensboro
3. Frankfort Audubon/Frankfort
4. Henderson Audubon/Henderson
5. Jackson Purchase Audubon/Paducah
6. Lincoln Trail Audubon/Cecilia
7. Little River Audubon/Hopkinsville
8. Louisville Audubon/Louisville
9. S. Central Ky. Aud./Bowling Green
10. Tradewater River Audubon /Madisonville
11. Beckham Bird Club/Louisville
12. Kentucky Orn. Soc./Louisville

NATIONAL AUDUBON SOCIETY

Clyde E. Buckley ①
Wildlife Sanctuary
1305 Germany Road
Frankfort, KY 40601   606-873-5711

From Frankfort, take Rte. 60 southeast towards Versailles. Pass I-64, and turn right onto Rte. 1681, and follow to the end (bottom of hill). Turn left and go to Midville School's ballpark. Turn right at the ballpark and go 1 mile to Germany Road. Turn right and proceed 1.2 miles to the sanctuary on the left.

Habitat: 275 acres of wooded hill country on the bluffs of the Kentucky River, with open fields, creeks, and streams.

A wide variety of birds and wildlife frequents the area. Herons, Mallards, American Black and Wood ducks, Belted Kingfishers, raptors, and various warblers and other songbirds are seasonally plentiful.

The three color-coded hiking trails, which range from .25 to 3 miles long, offer much to the quiet observer. The Marion E. Lindsey Bird Blind has one-way windows where you can observe feeding station activity. Visitor facilities include a display barn where literature is available. The Emma E. Buckley Center features exhibits, lecture area, and a gift shop.

Contact the manager about special programs available by reservation. The sanctuary is closed to visitors on Monday and Tuesday. Museum open Saturday and Sunday. Sanctuary brochure with map, trails map, bird list.
Spring, Summer, Fall, Winter

Jefferson County ②
Memorial Forest
c/o Metro Parks Office
1297 Trevilian Way
Louisville, KY 40201   502-459-0440

The Jefferson County Memorial Forest (dedicated as an Audubon Sanctuary) is contiguous with Forest View and Tom Wallace parks.

The forest is located southeast of Louisville, just outside the outer loop (I-265) around the city. From I-65 south, take the outer loop west for 2 miles to National Turnpike. Turn left onto the turnpike, travel south to Fairdale Road, and turn right. Follow Fairdale Road 1 mile to Fairdale and Holsclaw Hill Road. For the Forest Ranger Station and the Tom Wallace Park, turn right and make a left onto Mitchell Hill Road, which comes up immediately, and continue to the station and park. For Forest View Park, turn left on Holsclaw Hill Road and continue about a 1 mile to the park entrance on your left.

Habitat: 4,355 acres including 2,462-acre Jefferson County Memorial Park, 566-acre Forest View Park, and 327-acre Tom Wallace Park.

Park and sanctuary brochures, area maps, hiking trails. One trail is paved to accommodate handicapped people. Camping, picnicking, bicycling, fishing.
Spring, Summer, Fall, Winter

THE NATURE CONSERVANCY
Kentucky Chapter Office ⬦
324 West Main Street
Frankfort, KY 40601   502-875-3529

A brochure describing TNC preserves in Kentucky will be available soon. For information about visiting these locations, as well as maps, specific directions, and guided hikes, contact the Field Office. There are trail signs at each preserve.

The best birding seasons at these preserves are spring and fall.

Bad Branch ①
604 acres near Whitesburg

Boone County Cliffs ②
74 acres near Burlington

Brigadoon ③
195 acres near Glasgow

Lilley Cornett Woods ④
554 acres near Cumberland

Guides must accompany hikers on the trails. Two-mile Shop Hollow Trail, which has many wildflowers in May, and Big Everidge Trail, a strenuous trail, are two- and four-hour tours respectively. The estimated 700 breeding pairs of birds here include Red-shouldered and Broad-winged hawks and Barred Owls. Many of the breeding songbirds are warblers.

Mantle Rock ⑤
191 acres near Joy

Metropolis Lake ⑥
123 acres near Paducah

Pilot Knob ⑦
320 acres near Stanton

NATIONAL FOREST SERVICE
Daniel Boone National Forest Sup. △
100 Vaught Road
Winchester, KY 40391   606-745-3100

STATE AGENCIES

Kentucky Dept. of
Fish & Wildlife Resources
#1 Game Farm Road
Frankfort, KY 40601   502-564-4336

KY Dept. of Travel Development
Capital Plaza Tower   502-564-4930
Frankfort, KY 40601   800-225-8747

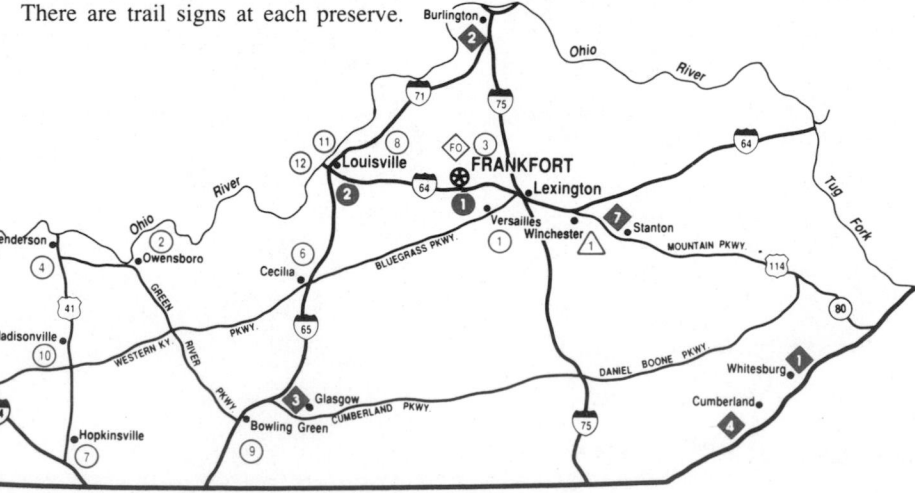

BIRDING HOTLINES
Baton Rouge   504-293-2576
New Orleans   504-246-2473

LOCAL BIRDING GROUPS
Map/Chapter/City
1. Baton Rouge Audubon/Baton Rouge
2. Natchitoches Audubon/Natchitoches
3. Orleans Audubon/New Orleans
4. Ouiska Chitto Audubon/Kinder
5. Crescent Bird Club/New Orleans
6. Terrebonne Bird Club/Houma

THE NATURE CONSERVANCY
Louisiana Field Office (FO)
PO Box 4125
Baton Rouge, LA 70812   504-338-1040

Spring and fall are the best visiting times for these preserves in Louisiana. Contact the Field Office for visitor information and regulations.

Charter Oak Nature Preserve 1
Approximately 5 miles north of Hickory, just off Hwy. 41. This 120-acre habitat is a prime example of bay swamp. Picnicking.

Lake Cocodrie 2
West from Hwy. 167 toward Glenmora and 1 mile east along the lakeshore from Johnson's Landing lies a 160-acre preserve along Lake Cocodrie. Fishing, hiking, picnicking, non-motorized boat use.

Schoolhouse Springs Nature Preserve 3
Just north of Eros and off Hwy. 144 in Jackson Parish. This 30-acre preserve includes a spring-fed stream harboring rare and endangered aquatic fauna.

Tunica Hills 4
North of Baton Rogue in West Feliciana Parish and 1 mile past Polly Creek on Old Tunica Trace. A 430-acre preserve. Picnicking, hiking, horseback riding.

White Kitchens Nature Preserve 5
On the north side of the intersection of Hwys. 90 and 190 in St. Francis Parish near Slidell. A 550-acre cypress-tupelo swamp and freshwater marsh.

The highlights at White Kitchens are a large waterbird rookery and a Bald Eagle nest. Some volunteer on-site management. Canoeing, fishing, picnicking.

U.S. FISH & WILDLIFE SERVICE NATIONAL WILDLIFE REFUGES

Bogue Chitto 1   (office in town)
1010 Gause Blvd., Bldg. 936
Slidell, LA 83254   504-646-7554

This refuge office also manages Delta NWR and Breton Islands (accessible by boat).

Bird List LA-1 Bogue Chitto Summary
157 birds listed, no nesting data
Bird Chart pages 258-275

Totals by Season		s	S	F	W
Abundant	A	21	17	20	16
Common	C	66	47	66	37
Uncommon	U	55	18	56	25
Occasional	O	0	0	0	2
Rare	R	6	2	6	1

Endangered Species: Bald Eagle, Peregrine Falcon, Bachman's Warbler

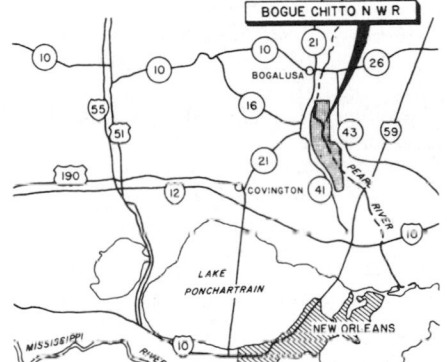

The refuge is located about 30 miles northwest of New Orleans, along the Louisiana-Mississippi line. Take I-10 east from New Orleans past Slidell to Hwy. 41 exit. Go north on Hwy. 41 (which parallels the refuge on the right) to where it joins Hwy. 21 at Bush, and continue on Hwy. 21 to the end of the refuge. Most access is by boat or canoe.

Habitat: 26,000 acres of mixed bottomland hardwoods and cypress-tupelo brakes. Floodplain of Pearl and Bogue Chitto rivers with a continuing habitat acquisition program underway. Both rivers flow through the refuge and join near Bush. The refuge is 15 miles long, from 2 to 7 miles wide, and is 30 to 40 feet above sea level.

A superior recreation area with 150 bird species. During spring and early summer American Swallow-tailed and Mississippi kites soar over the refuge. Egrets, herons, and Wild Turkeys raise their young and look for food on the sandbars along streams. During the fall and winter, large concentrations of waterfowl such as Wood Ducks, Mallards, Hooded Mergansers, and Ring-necked Ducks gather by the rivers. A variety of warblers feed in the woods

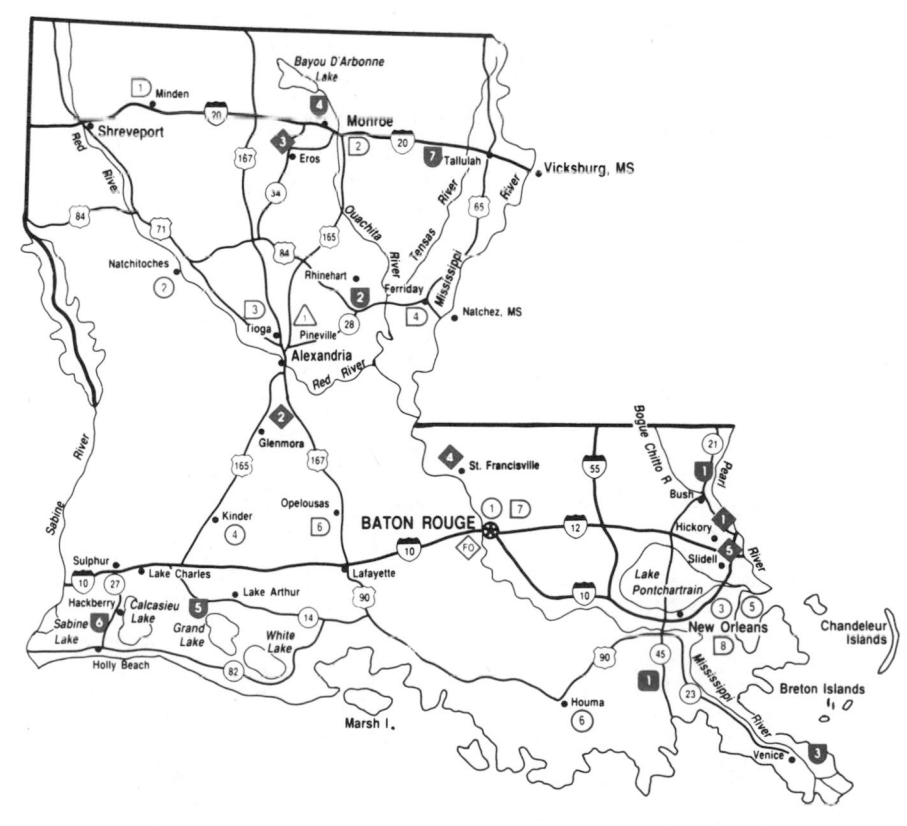

and brakes as they pass in their southbound migration.

Area brochure, boating, canoe trail, camping, fishing, hunting.
Spring, Fall

Catahoula 2 (office at refuge)
PO Drawer 2
Rhinehart, LA 71363 318-992-5261

Bird List LA-2 Catahoula Summary
155 birds listed, 35 nesting birds
Bird Chart pages 258-275

Totals by Season		s	S	F	W
Abundant	A	9	10	11	9
Common	C	57	42	52	40
Uncommon	U	35	29	32	26
Occasional	O	31	22	26	18
Rare	R	6	7	6	6

Endangered Species: Bald Eagle, Piping Plover, Wood Stork

Take Hwy. 28 east from Alexandria for 32 miles to Hwy. 84. Turn north on Hwy. 84 for about 0.5 miles, then left (at the refuge sign) and continue about 0.5 miles on a dirt road to the refuge headquarters.

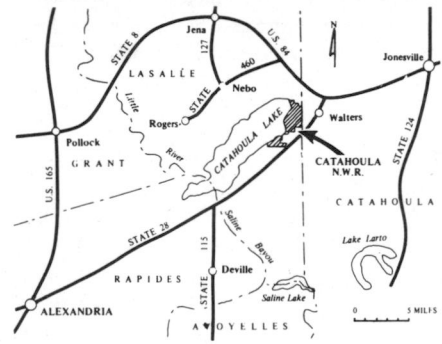

Habitat: 5,308 acres nestled along the southeast side of Catahoula Lake are one of the most important natural waterfowl wintering areas in North America. Low-lying bottomlands supporting dense stands of swamp privet and water elm, interspersed with scattered cypress and water locust.

Chufa, a sedge, is one of the principal waterfowl foods here. The natural production of chufa in the lake is dependent on proper water level fluctuations. A large water control structure on the lake is operated by refuge personnel under the provisions of an agreement between the U.S. Fish and Wildlife Service, the Army Corps of Engineers, and the Louisiana Dept. of Wildlife and Fisheries.

In spring the songbirds appear, many traveling north to their summer breeding grounds. In summer the impoundment is drained to stimulate growth of waterfowl foods. Hundreds of herons, egrets, and ibises invade the shallow waters to feed.

When temperatures cool in the fall Northern Pintails, Blue-winged and Green-winged teals, Ring-necked Ducks, and Mallards concentrate, peaking in late November or early December. Occasionally a Bald Eagle visits and decides to spend the winter.

Area brochure, 9-mile auto tour, self-guided wildlife trail, hiking, camping, hunting, fishing. Good year-round.

Delta (also Breton Islands) 3
c/o Bogue Chitto NWR
1010 Gause Blvd., Bldg. 936
Slidell, LA 70458 504-646-7554

The refuge office is in Slidell, north of New Orleans.

Bird List LA-3 Delta Summary
236 birds listed, no nesting data
Bird Chart pages 258-275

Totals by Season		s	S	F	W
Abundant	A	32	16	25	28
Common	C	21	40	80	49
Uncommon	U	37	27	38	37
Occasional	O	19	15	15	10
Rare	R	8	12	7	19

Endangered Species: Bald Eagle, Peregrine Falcon, Piping Plover, Wood Stork, Least Tern

Take Hwy. 23 south from New Orleans for about 38 miles to Venice. The refuge is close to the mainland at the mouth of the Mississippi River, and access is by boat.

The Breton Islands NWR is northeast of Delta NWR in the Gulf of Mexico from 10 to 35 miles offshore. The Chandeleur and other island groups are included in this offshore refuge area.

Habitat: 48,800 acres of the Mississippi

River delta, composed of marshes, shallow ponds, channels, and bayous. The only dry ground is on banks of the channels.

Breton habitat consists of low, sandy beaches on the Gulf side and, on the Sound side, ponds, inlets, and saltwater marshes.

Delta and Breton provide shelter, feeding, and nesting sites for many bird species. Among them are Snow Geese and up to 18 species of ducks. The Sound is wintering habitat for up to 20,000 Redheads. In some years 200,000 ducks and 50,000 geese winter at Delta. The most common island nesters are Caspian, Forster's, Royal, and Sandwich terns, Laughing Gulls, and Black Skimmers.

During the summer, various wading birds and shorebirds search for fish and other foods in the ponds and channels. Circling flocks of Magnificent Frigatebirds signal the approach of an offshore storm. The Brown Pelican (Louisiana's state bird), an endangered species, is on the increase at Delta.

Among the common mammals that live in this delta ecosystem are white-tailed deer, rabbits, minks, raccoons, and opossums.

Combined area brochure for Delta, Breton, and the other islands, hunting, fishing, boating (a must).
Birding and recreation year-round.

D'Arbonne & Upper Ouachita 4
Federal Bldg., Room #312
201 Jackson Street
PO Box 3065
Monroe, LA 71201 208-574-2755

D'Arbonne NWR is about 10 miles northwest of Monroe, bordered by the west side of Hwy. 143. For access to the east side of the refuge, turn left from Hwy. 143 onto Hollins Bluff Road or any of the parking areas on the west side of this highway. There is also north access on Deep Well Road and west access using Parish Road 5558 or Saline Creek Road.

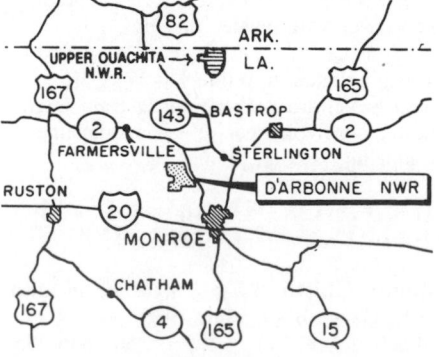

Upper Ouachita NWR borders the west

bank of the Ouachita River and extends to the Arkansas state line. Take Hwy. 143 north to Parish Road 2204 and turn east. Where Parish Road 2204 ends in the refuge, turn left (north) to the refuge subheadquarters.

Habitat: D'Arbonne, with 17,421 acres, includes segments of Bayou D'Arbonne and its floodplain, some of the surrounding pine and hardwood uplands, permanent open water, and grass/shrub habitats. The Upper Ouachita has 20,900 acres of bottomland.

Bird species occurring at both refuges are essentially the same, although abundance of given species may vary due to differences in habitat. Annual flooding can affect bird abundance at both areas.

During March the Wood Ducks are nesting, while Prothonotary Warblers flit along the waterways and White-eyed Vireos can be found in the uplands. The Blue-winged Teal population peaks in April, and American White Pelicans are occasionally noted.

Combined area brochure and wildlife events calendar. Auto tour (D'Arbonne), hunting, fishing, boating, back country use. The available refuge bird list contains abundance detail by month.
Spring, Summer, Fall, Winter.

Lacassine 5   (office at refuge)
Route 1, Box 186
Lake Arthur, LA 70549   318-774-5923

Bird List LA-4 Lacassine Summary
229 birds listed, 50 nesting birds
Bird Chart pages 258-275

Totals by Season		s	S	F	W
Abundant	A	25	17	31	18
Common	C	60	30	41	39
Uncommon	U	55	32	55	31
Occasional	O	56	32	58	42
Rare	R	15	8	17	20

Endangered Species: Bald Eagle, Peregrine Falcon, Wood Stork, Least Tern

Open to visitors from March 1 until October 15. For those willing to make the effort, excellent opportunities exist for wildlife observation, nature study, and birding. Most of the refuge is only accessible by boat.

The refuge office is on the Mermentau River, 12 miles downriver from the town of Lake Arthur. Take Hwy. 14 west from Lake Arthur for 7 miles, then 5 miles south on Hwy. 3056 (Lowry Road).

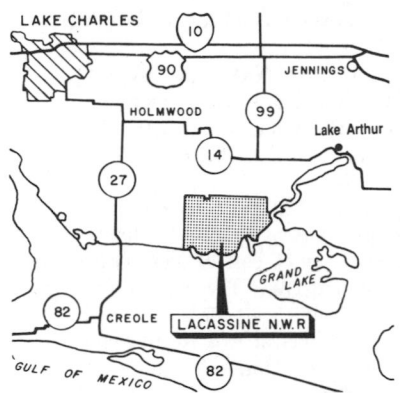

Habitat: 31,776 acres of southern Louisiana marshlands include 16,000-acre Lacassine Pool, created by enclosing a marsh with a low levee. Primarily freshwater marsh and dense emergent vegetative growths of maidencane and bull tongue, with few natural ridges or spoil banks. 3,300 acres south of the pipeline canal and west of Bayou Misere have been designated as wilderness area.

Lacassine supports large concentrations of wintering waterfowl. The Greater White-fronted Goose population is the largest in the Mississippi Flyway, while the Fulvous Whistling-Duck population is one of the largest in the U.S.A. Other common waterfowl include Northern Pintails, Blue-winged and Green-winged teals, Ring-necked Ducks, Gadwalls, and American Wigeons. Nesters include Wood and Mottled ducks.

The marshlands are also home to a variety of other water birds, and gained notoriety for the first colony of Cattle Egrets found breeding outside Florida. Roseate Spoonbills, White and White-faced ibises, Great and Snowy egrets, Black-crowned Night-Herons, and Great Blue, Tricolored and Little Blue herons can be seen nesting, as well as Olivaceous Cormorants, Anhingas, and Purple Gallinules.

Area brochure, boating, fishing, hunting.
Spring, Summer

Sabine 6   (office at refuge)
3000 Main Street
Hwy. 27 South
Hackberry, LA 70645   318-762-3816

Bird List LA-5 Sabine Summary
253 birds listed, 39 nesting birds
Bird Chart pages 258-275

Totals by Season		s	S	F	W
Abundant	A	12	7	12	18
Common	C	68	28	59	44
Uncommon	U	76	22	74	48
Occasional	O	42	12	51	25
Rare	R	30	9	31	27

Endangered Species: Bald Eagle, Peregrine Falcon, Wood Stork, Least Tern

Located in southwestern Louisiana and about 30 miles south of Sulphur on Hwy. 27. Turn onto Hwy. 27, either south off I-10 at Sulphur, or north (about 10 miles) off Hwy. 82 at Holly Beach. The only road through the refuge is Hwy. 27, which passes the headquarters. The refuge is in two sections separated by Calcasieu Lake.

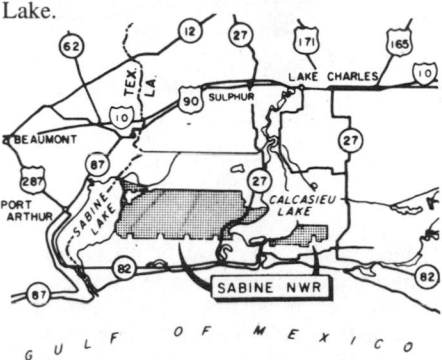

Habitat: 142,000 acres and a wide variety of habitats, including three fresh water impoundments, numerous ridges, bayous, man-made canals and levees, ponds, lakes, and wooded islands.

The winter months can be most rewarding for the birder interested in waterfowl, when many species of ducks use the refuge. Large flocks of Snow Geese may be seen from the road. Migration periods are particularly rewarding for the transient shorebirds that show up and the rare passerines brought in by cold fronts in the early spring.

A supplemental bird list covering birds seen off the refuge in Cameron Parish is available at the refuge office. Area brochure, auto tour, foot trails, boating, fishing, hunting.
Good for year-round recreation.

Tensas River 7   (office at refuge)
Route 2, Box 295
Tallulah, LA 71282   318-574-2664

Bird List LA-6 Tensas River Summary
219 birds listed, no nesting data
Bird Chart pages 258-275

Totals by Season		s	S	F	W
Abundant	A	24	17	22	17
Common	C	68	34	64	27
Uncommon	U	72	31	71	44
Rare	R	46	24	42	29

Endangered Species: Bald Eagle, Peregrine Falcon, Wood Stork

From I-20 at the Tallulah exit (17 miles west of Vicksburg, Mississippi) take Hwy. 65 north briefly to Hwy. 80. Turn left (west) onto Hwy. 80 and continue about 10 miles to Parish Road, turning left (south) toward I-20. The road becomes gravel at the I-20 underpass and parallels the Tensas River and ends at the refuge headquarters.

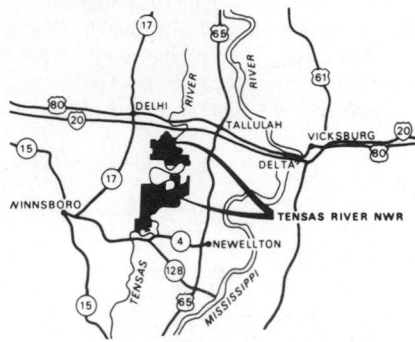

Habitat: 4,000 acres, part of the largest bottomland hardwood area remaining in the Mississippi delta. A great variety of trees and shrubs, vines, and other plants provide food and shelter for a diversity of wildlife.

The Barred Owl and Pileated Woodpecker are common. Seasonal visitors include various species of migratory ducks. Songbirds arrive in spring.

One of the last verified sightings of North America's largest woodpecker, the Ivory-billed Woodpecker, occurred here in the early 1940's. Most ornithologists believe that the North American race of this species is now extinct.

Area brochure, foot trails, fishing, hunting.
Spring, Summer, Fall, Winter

NATIONAL PARK SERVICE

Jean Lafitte National 1
Historical Park & Preserve
423 Canal Street, Room 210
New Orleans, LA 70130   504-589-3882

20,000 acres in three separate units comprise this park: The Chalmette Unit is located 7 miles east of New Orleans on St. Bernard Hwy. The French Quarter Unit includes a visitor center in the French Market at 916 North Peters St. The Barataria Unit is 15 miles south of New Orleans.

Bird List LA-7 Jean Lafitte Summary
198 birds listed, 56 nesting birds
Bird Chart pages 258-275
Note: The bird list is based on sighting information from the Barataria Unit.

Totals by Season		s	S	F	W
Abundant	A	12	9	16	16
Common	C	88	42	87	52
Uncommon	U	59	17	73	40
Rare	R	6	5	6	20

Endangered Species: Bald Eagle, Peregrine Falcon

To reach the Barataria Unit, take LA 45 south from the West Bank Expwy. located just south of New Orleans and the Mississippi River. Continue on LA 45 past the junction of LA 3134, Ames Blvd., and the park entry sign, to the visitor center on the right. About 20 minutes from downtown New Orleans.

The best birding trails at this park are the Palmetto, Bayou Coquille, Ring Levee, and Big Woods. Each one varies in habitat and birding opportunities depending on the season.

The Bayou Coquille Trail yields various passerines and wading birds, as well as hawks and owls flying over the marsh. The Ring Levee is known for its breeding birds, including Prothonotary and Hooded warblers, Northern Parulas, Pileated Woodpeckers, and Acadian Flycatchers.

NATIONAL FOREST SERVICE
Kisatchie National Forest Sup. ⚠
2500 Shreveport Hwy.
PO Box 5500
Pineville, LA 71360   318-473-7160

STATE AGENCIES

Department of Wildlife & Fisheries
PO Box 15570
Baton Rouge, LA 70895   504-765-2934

Map/District/City
1	Minden/Minden	318-371-3050
2	Monroe/Monroe	318-343-4044
3	Tioga/Tioga	318-487-5885
4	Ferriday/Ferriday	318-757-4571
5	Lake Charles/same	318-491-2575
6	Opelousas/Opelousas	318-948-0255
7	Baton Rouge /Baton Rouge	504-765-2934
8	New Orleans /New Orleans	504-568-5612

Louisiana Office of Tourism
PO Box 44291
Baton Rouge, LA 70804   504-342-8119
from out-of-state call   800-334-8626

BIRDING HOTLINE
Statewide   207-781-2332

LOCAL BIRDING GROUPS
Map/Chapter/City
1. Merrymeeting Audubon/Bath
2. Mid Coast Audubon/Rockland
3. Northeast Audubon/Presque Isle
4. Proust Neck Audubon/Proust Neck
5. Western Maine Audubon/Farmington
6. York County Audubon/Eliatbunk
7. Augusta Nature Club/Augusta
8. Bangor Nature Club/Bangor
9. Maine Audubon Society/Falmouth
10. Stanton Nature Club/Auburn

NATIONAL AUDUBON SOCIETY

Borestone Mountain Audubon ①
Wildlife Sanctuary
Jack Dunstan - Warden
PO Box 112
Monson, ME 04464
May through October   207-997-3607
November through April   207 997 3558
Entry fee

Borestone Mountain Sanctuary lies at the southern edge of Maine's Great North Woods, 10 miles north of Monson. It is bordered on one side by the Appalachian Trail. Take Rtes. 6 and 15 north from Guilford. Turn right on Elliotsville Road, just past Monson, and continue across Big Wilson Bridge and the Canadian Pacific Railroad tracks to the gate house and parking lot on left.

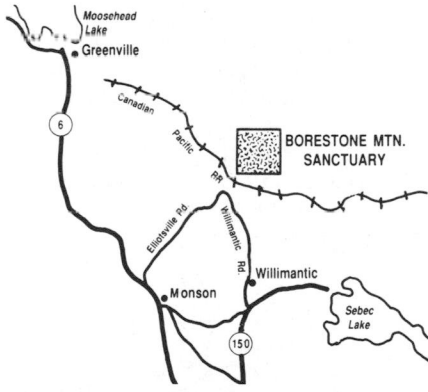

The trail offers a pleasant climb of about 3 miles to the summit and a spectacular view of the surrounding area.

Gatehouse and information center opens at 8 a.m. every day from June 1 to October 31. Trail closes at dusk.

Uncut for a century, Borestown's forest is mixed hardwoods and softwoods beginning with beech and birch and changing to spruce and fir just below the summit. A staffed visitor center is halfway up at Sunrise Pond where wildlife, natural history exhibits, and historical artifacts are

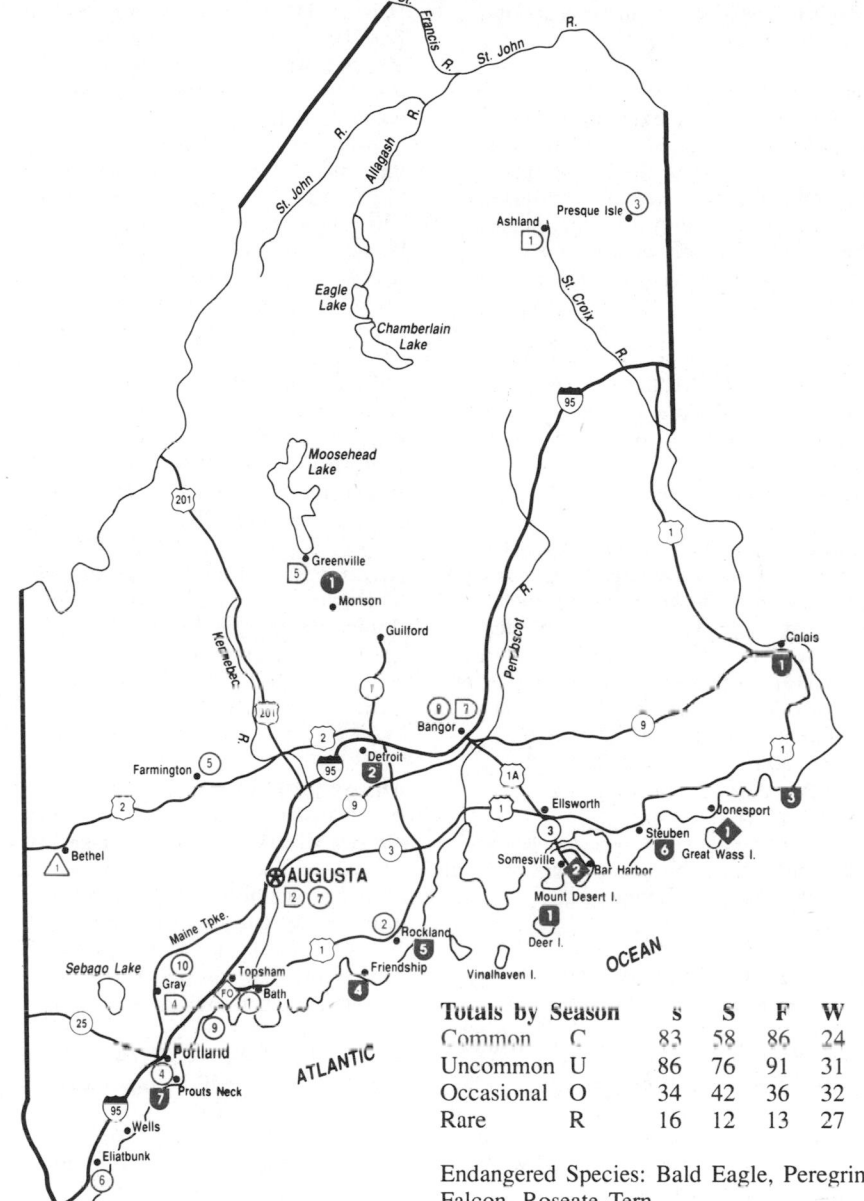

on display.

Self-guided trail booklet, wildflower and bird species lists, picnicking.
Summer, Fall

THE NATURE CONSERVANCY
Maine Field Office ⟨FO⟩
122 Main Street
PO Box 338
Topsham, ME 04086   207-729-5181

Great Wass Island ◆
Local volunteer stewardship committee and seasonal caretaker. Day use only.
Contact the Maine Field Office for details.

Bird List ME-1 Great Wass Summary
229 birds listed, 66 nesting birds
Bird Chart pages 258-275

Totals by Season		s	S	F	W
Common	C	83	58	86	24
Uncommon	U	86	76	91	31
Occasional	O	34	42	36	32
Rare	R	16	12	13	27

Endangered Species: Bald Eagle, Peregrine Falcon, Roseate Tern

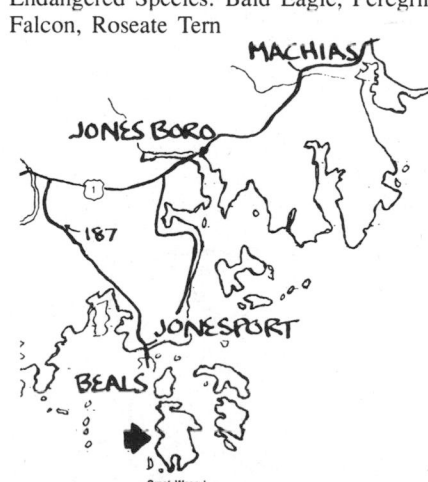

From Rte. 1 take Rte. 187 to Jonesport, crossing bridge over Moosabech Beach to Beals. Go through Beals to Great Wass Island. Follow the road which turns to dirt, to Black Duck Cove about 3 miles

from Beals. There is a marked parking area on the left.

Habitat: 1,543 acres relatively untouched by human presence. Exposed granite bedrock cliffs at the southern end of the island. The waters of the Bay of Fundy and Gulf of Maine meet here to mix and produce a cool humid oceanic climate. The island's interior supports one of Maine's largest stands of jack pine, with their stunted, twisted, almost bonsai-like form.

Two trails, Little Cape Point Trail (2 miles) and Mud Hole Trail (1.5 miles), lead to the ocean. By following the shore from one trail to the other, the total distance covered is 5 miles.

Wildlife is plentiful on Great Wass Island. Osprey nest and Bald Eagles regularly feed and roost on the preserve. Boreal bogs and spruce forests sustain nesting Palm Warblers, Lincoln Sparrows, Boreal Chickadees, and Spruce Grouse. Offshore, Common Eiders assemble in large rafts, and Great Blue Herons and shorebirds may be seen on the tidal flats and marshes.

Come prepared for any type of weather and wear rugged shoes. Area brochure and map, picnicking, swimming.
Summer, Fall

Indian Point Blagden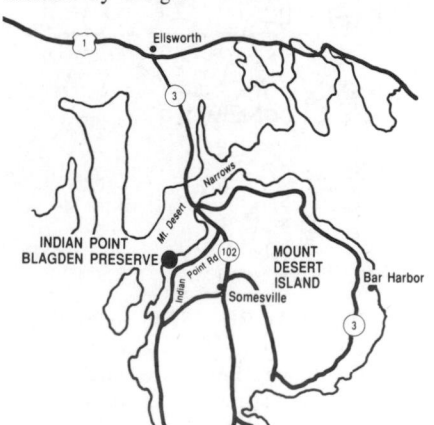

Stanwood & Ethleen Hamblen - Caretakers
Indian Point
Mount Desert, ME 04660　207-288-4838

Take Rte. 3 south from Ellsworth, across the Trenton bridge onto Mount Desert Island (8.5 miles). Bear right at first fork in the road (0.5 mile), taking Rte. 102/198 toward Somesville. After 1.8 miles, take a right on the Indian Point Road, continue for 1.7 miles, and bear right at the first fork. The entrance to the preserve is about 200 yards further on the right, and is marked by a sign.

Habitat: 110 acres on the western side of Bar Harbor. Most of the preserve is forested, with tall red spruce, white cedar, and balsam fir. The woods are generally mature and there are also major blowdown areas, the largest of which is more than 10 acres. Yellow and white birch, red oak, and red maple are more common along the forest edge and in the blowdown areas. More than 8 acres of tamarac are in the wetter area near the center of the preserve. A small freshwater pond lies just off the entrance road.

This range of habitat types supports abundant wildlife; the birds are numerous, and include both wood and shore species. Ruby-crowned Kinglets and Ospreys are among the 144 species noted in the preserve bird checklist.

Area brochure with maps, visitor center, hiking trails, swimming, cross-country skiing.
Spring, Summer, Fall

U.S. FISH & WILDLIFE SERVICE NATIONAL WILDLIFE REFUGES

Moosehorn

(Headquarters on refuge at Baring Unit)
Calais, ME 04619　　207-454-3521

Also the administrative office for Petit Manan, Seal Island (closed to the public), Bois Bubert Island, Franklin Island, Cross Island, and Carlton Pond Waterfowl Production Area (WPA).

Bird List ME-2 Moosehorn Summary
216 birds listed, 140 nesting birds
Bird Chart pages 258-275

Totals by Season		s	S	F	W
Abundant	A	12	13	11	3
Common	C	82	72	78	16
Uncommon	U	46	51	49	21
Occasional	O	42	25	37	20
Rare	R	17	18	12	18

Endangered Species: Bald Eagle, Peregrine Falcon

Office is located south of Calais. Take U.S. Rte. 1 south of Calais toward Baring, to the Charlotte Road junction, turn left and follow Charlotte Road south to the refuge headquarters sign.

Habitat: Baring Unit - 16,065 acres, marked by glaciers, hills, outcrops, valleys, streams, lakes, bogs, and marshes. The forest is composed of aspen, maple, birch, spruce, and white pine. Edmunds Unit - 6,600 acres with several miles of rocky shoreline, where the daily tide fluctuation is 24 feet. Approximately 2,780 acres of the Edmunds Unit and 4,680 acres of the Baring Unit have been designated wilderness.

Moosehorn is the only refuge where the American Woodcock is intensively studied and managed. It is managed chiefly to increase habitat for the woodcock and waterfowl. The spectacular spring courtship flights of the male woodcock may be observed at dawn and dusk. More than 3,000 woodcocks are present on the refuge in spring and fall migrations, while the average summer population is 1,800.

The many lakes and flowages also support a variety of breeding and migrating waterfowl and wetland species, including the Canada Goose, American Black, Wood and Ring-necked ducks, and loons.

Area brochure, hiking, cross-country skiing, snowmobiling, fishing.
Spring, Fall

Carlton Pond WPA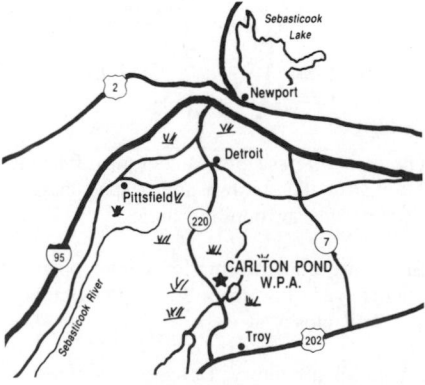

c/o Moosehorn NWR
Calais, ME 04619　　207-454-3521

From Detroit, take Hwy. 220 southeast for approximately 15 miles. The management area is east of the highway where it crosses Carlton Stream.

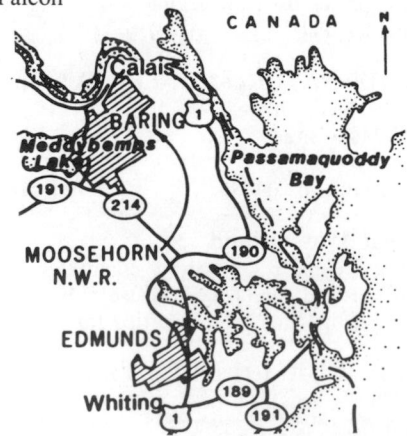

Habitat: 1,069 acres at 200 to 300 feet elevation. Open water, both deep and shallow freshwater marshes, and upland forest.

Carlton Pond is one of three known areas in the state that has an active Black Tern colony. Common waterfowl species found in the area include Mallards, Wood, American Black, and Ring-necked ducks, Hooded Mergansers, and Blue-winged and Green-winged teals. Great Blue Herons, American Bitterns, Tree Swallows, Marsh Wrens, Northern Harriers, and Ospreys have also been sighted.

Cross Island ③
c/o Moosehorn NWR
Calais, ME 04619   207-454-3521

See Petit Manan Bird List Summary, and Bird Chart pages 258-275

Habitat: Six islands form this complex: Cross Island, 1,306 acres; Scotch Island, 10 acres; Inner Double Head Shot Island, 8 acres; Outer Double Head Shot Island, 14 acres, Mink Island, 11 acres; and Old Man Island, 6 acres. Rocks and rocky cliffs, some over 100 feet high, cobble beaches, and salt marshes dominate the shoreline.

Colonial seabirds that nest on these islands include Black Guillemots, Razorbills, Great Black-backed and Herring gulls, and Double-crested Cormorants. Various raptors that breed on the islands include Bald Eagles and Ospreys.

Public use of the islands is limited because of the distance from the mainland. Access by boat only.
Spring, Summer, Fall

Franklin Island ④
c/o Moosehorn NWR
Calais, ME 04619   207-454-3521

See Petit Manan Bird List Summary, and Bird Chart pages 258-275

Habitat: 12-acre island off Friendship, dominated by spruce trees and raspberry thickets.

Fox Island hosts one of the largest Common Eider colonies in the state. Also nesting on the island are Ospreys, Leach's Storm-Petrels, and Black-crowned Night-Herons.

Closed to public access from April 1 to July 31 to protect the seabird colonies.
Fall

Seal Island ⑤
c/o Moosehorn NWR
Calais, ME 04619   207-454-3521

See Petit Manan Bird List Summary, and Bird Chart pages 258-275

Landing on the island is not permitted.

Habitat: 65 acres of grass and granite on a treeless island 25 miles off Rockland.

Contains some of the best colonial seabird nesting habitat on the coast of Maine. Seal Island is the site of a puffin and tern colony restoration project cosponsored by the National Audubon Society, Canadian Wildlife Service, and U.S. Fish and Wildlife Service. Other nesting birds include Leach's Storm-Petrels, Common Eiders, and gulls.

Petit Manan ⑥
c/o Moosehorn NWR
Calais, ME 04619   207-454-3521

Bird List ME-3 Petit Manan Summary
252 birds listed, 98 nesting birds
Bird Chart pages 258-275

Totals by Season		s	S	F	W
Abundant	A	4	3	8	2
Common	C	60	52	58	15
Uncommon	U	74	65	76	18
Occasional	O	41	29	34	12
Rare	R	28	19	25	5

Endangered Species: Bald Eagle, Peregrine Falcon, Piping Plover, Roseate Tern

From Steuben, take Rte. 1 east about 3 miles, turn right on Pigeon Hill Road, and go approximately 10 miles to parking lot at end of the road where there is an information display.

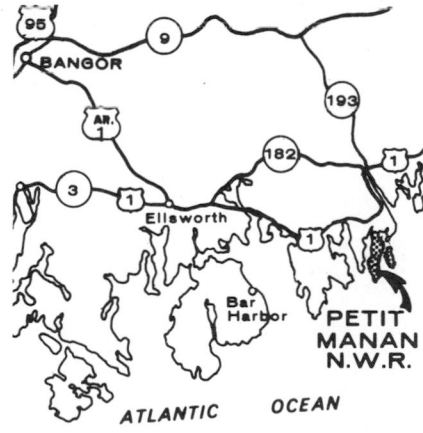

Habitat: 3,135-acre complex consisting of 1,991 acres on Petit Manan Peninsula, a rugged area with spruce forests, jackpine stands, blueberry barrens, raised heath peatlands, and fresh and saltwater marshes; 1,130 acres on Bois Bubert Island, similar in character to Petit Manan Peninsula; 9 acres on Petit Manan Island, a treeless island off the Peninsula; and 5 acres on Nash Island, a rocky, treeless island.

Petit Manan Peninsula and Bois Bubert Island are important stopover points for migratory birds and a noted area for seabirds such as the Roseate Tern, shorebirds, songbirds, waterfowl, and raptors, including the Bald Eagle and Peregrine Falcon.

Petit Manan Island is the site of a successful tern colony restoration project by the USFWS, and now has one of the largest tern and Laughing Gull colonies in the Gulf of Maine. Nash Island is also used by various nesting colonial seabirds. Access is restricted from April through July to protect these colonies; contact refuge manager before attempting to visit any of the islands.

Area brochure, limited hiking, cross-country skiing, clamming in some areas.
Spring, Summer

Rachel Carson ⑦
RR 2, Box 751
Route 9 East
Wells, ME 04090   207-646-9226

Bird List ME-4 R. Carson Summary
247 birds listed, 86 nesting birds
Bird Chart pages 258-275

Totals by Season		s	S	F	W
Abundant	A	6	3	4	1
Common	C	58	53	59	25
Uncommon	U	85	61	81	24
Occasional	O	55	46	56	34
Rare	R	13	14	20	13

Endangered Species: Bald Eagle, Peregrine Falcon, Piping Plover, Roseate Tern, Least Tern

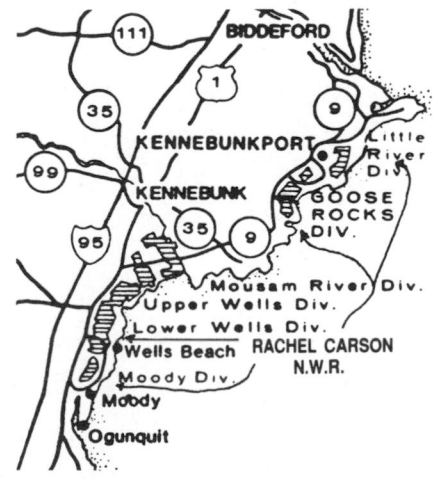

Headquarters located at Upper Wells Division. The nine divisions are, from north to south: Spurwink River, Goosefare

Brook, Little River, Goose Rocks, Mousam River, Upper Wells, Lower Wells, Moody, and Brave Boat Harbor.

From Wells, take Hwy. 1 for 1.75 miles north to refuge headquarters sign.

Habitat: 3,000 acres in 9 parcels that dot the coast from Portland to Kittery. The wetland water quality is protected by vegetation at the edge, which serves as a natural filter. Each division has a tidal river, surrounding marsh and upland.

Southern coastal Maine is a migration and staging route for much of the North American shorebird population. Thousands of shorebirds feed along coastal beaches and mud flats as they migrate south. The most abundant species in the late summer and fall are the Semipalmated Plover, Black-bellied Plover, Ruddy Turnstone, Dunlin, Least Sandpiper, Whimbrel, Lesser and Greater yellowlegs, and Short-billed Dowitcher.

Raptors in the areas include Sharp-shinned, Red-tailed, and Broad-winged hawks, Northern Harrier, American Kestrel, and Great Horned and Barred owls.

The region is the primary wintering area for American Black Ducks. Other abundant species include Canada Goose, Mallard, Bufflehead, Red-breasted Merganser, and Common Goldeneye.

Area brochure, hiking, picnicking, hunting. Spring, Summer, Fall

NATIONAL PARK SERVICE

Acadia National Park ❶
PO Box 177
Bar Harbor, ME 04609   207-288-3338

41,365 acres of the rugged coastal area of Mount Desert Island (which has the highest elevation on the eastern seaboard), Schoodic Peninsula on the mainland, and the cliffs of Isle au Haut. Park brochure with map, information leaflet, bird list with seasonal abundance chart.

NATIONAL FOREST SERVICE

White Mountain National Forest
PO Box 638
Laconia, NH 03247   603-524-6450

Map/Ranger District/City
⚠ Evans Notch/Bethel   207-824-2134

STATE AGENCIES

Maine Dept. of Inland Fisheries & Wildlife
284 State Street
Augusta, ME 04333   207-289-2536

Map/Region (city)
1	Ashland	207-435-3231
2	Augusta	207-289-2175
3	Bangor	207-947-5211
4	Gray	207-657-2345
5	Greenville	207-695-3756

Maine Publicity Bureau
State Development Office
State House Station #59
August, ME 04333   207-289-2423

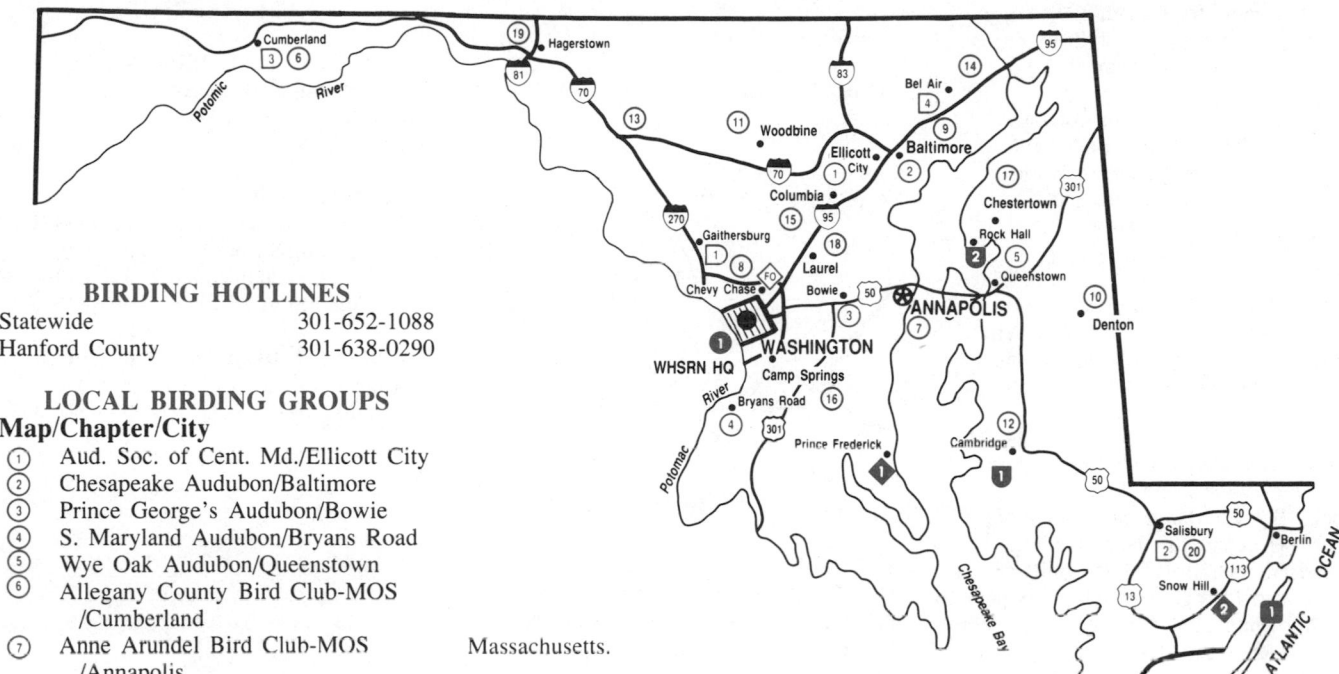

BIRDING HOTLINES

Statewide	301-652-1088
Hanford County	301-638-0290

LOCAL BIRDING GROUPS
Map/Chapter/City

① Aud. Soc. of Cent. Md./Ellicott City
② Chesapeake Audubon/Baltimore
③ Prince George's Audubon/Bowie
④ S. Maryland Audubon/Bryans Road
⑤ Wye Oak Audubon/Queenstown
⑥ Allegany County Bird Club-MOS /Cumberland
⑦ Anne Arundel Bird Club-MOS /Annapolis
⑧ Audubon Naturalist Soc. of Central Atlantic States/Chevy Chase
⑨ Baltimore Chapter-MOS/Baltimore
⑩ Caroline County Bird Club-MOS /Denton
⑪ Carroll County Bird Club-MOS /Woodbine
⑫ Dorchester Heritage Bird Club /Cambridge
⑬ Frederick County Bird Club-MOS /Frederick
⑭ Harford County Chapter-MOS /Churchville
⑮ Howard County Chapter-MOS /Columbia
⑯ Jug Bay Bird Club-MOS /Camp Springs
⑰ Kent County Chapter-MOS /Chestertown
⑱ Patuxent Bird Club-MOS/Laurel
⑲ Washington County Orn. Society /Hagerstown
⑳ Wicomico Bird Club-MOS /Salisbury

Western Hemisphere Shorebird ❶ Reserve Network (WHSRN)
Suite 301
801 Pennsylvania Avenue, SW
Washington, DC 20003   202-547-9009

This is the central office for the designation and development of important shorebird reserve sites in North, Central, and South America. The five dedicated reserves in the United States are noted in the California, Delaware, Kansas, Nevada, New Jersey, and Utah chapters.

The WHSRN staff and their activities are funded by the National Audubon Society and the Manomet Bird Observatory in Massachusetts.

THE NATURE CONSERVANCY
Maryland Field Office ⬥
Chevy Chase Metro Bldg.
2 Wisconsin Circle, Suite 410
Chevy Chase, MD 20815

Battle Creek Cypress Swamp ◆
Sanctuary Manager
c/o Courthouse
Prince Frederick, MD 20678 301-535-5327

A 100-acre preserve near Prince Frederick. Boardwalk trail winds one-quarter mile through the swamp. Nature center, preserve brochure with map, hiking, picnicking, self-guiding walking tour.
Spring, Fall

Nassawango Creek ◆
(Bald Cypress Swamp Preserve)
c/o Furnacetown Foundation
PO Box 207
Snow Hill, MD 21863   301-632-2032
Entry fee

A 2,700-acre preserve near Snow Hill and adjacent to historic Furnace Town Village. A boardwalk trail through cypress swamp is a self-guiding tour route.
Hiking, picnicking.
Spring, Fall

U.S. FISH & WILDLIFE SERVICE NATIONAL WILDLIFE REFUGES

Blackwater ❶   (office at refuge)
Route 1, Box 121
Cambridge, MD 21613   301-228-2677

Bird List MD-1 Blackwater Summary
252 birds listed, 99 nesting birds
Bird Chart pages 258-275

Totals by Season		s	S	F	W
Abundant	A	16	10	19	11
Common	C	72	52	70	30
Uncommon	U	86	51	81	55
Occasional	O	34	27	44	32
Rare	R	18	13	21	27

Endangered Species: Bald Eagle, Peregrine Falcon, Least Tern

Located 12 miles southwest of Cambridge. Take St. Hwy. 335 south to the refuge entrance sign, turn left on the refuge road, and drive 0.75 mile to the visitor center. The headquarters is 1 mile farther east.

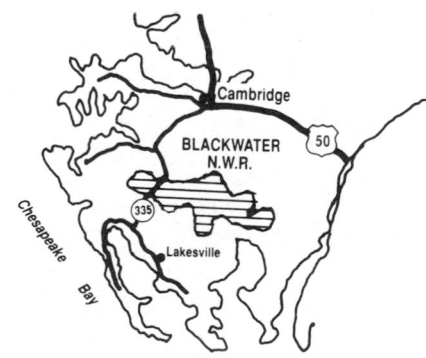

Habitat: 16,698 acres. Mostly composed of rich tidal marsh characterized by fluctuating water levels and variable salinity. Other habitat types include freshwater ponds, mixed woodlands, and a small amount of cropland.

Originally established as a duck preserve, Blackwater has become one of the chief wintering areas for Canada Geese using the Atlantic Flyway. The fall migration reaches its peak in November.

The refuge is also a haven for three endangered bird species. Bald Eagles are a common year-round resident, while migrating Peregrine Falcon and Least Terns are seen occasionally.

Other resident birds include Great Blue Herons, Rufous-sided Towhees, Brown-headed Nuthatches, Ospreys, Northern Bobwhites, American Woodcocks, and various woodpeckers.

Seasonal highlights: In February the first northward migrants, including Killdeer, American Robins, and Eastern Bluebirds, appear. During March most migratory waterfowl depart for their breeding grounds in the north. Marsh birds return by mid-April. Migratory songbirds peak in late April and early May, with warblers the most abundant. Osprey chicks hatch in early June, and the eaglets fledge.

Shorebird and wading bird numbers increase in August as their fall migration begins. The Bald Eagles begin to disperse. In September Ospreys begin to leave the marsh as the vanguard of the migrating waterfowl arrives. The last migratory songbirds to leave are the blackbirds, which depart in October and November. Waterfowl numbers increase, peaking in late October and declining by end of December. Tundra Swans arrive in early November. Bald Eagle numbers increase with arrival of migrants from the north.

Area brochure, wildlife drive, observation tower, interpretive trails, bicycle route, fishing, boating.
Mid-October to mid-March is best.

Eastern Neck [2]   (office at refuge)
Route 2, Box 225
Rock Hall, MD 21661   301-639-7056

Bird List MD-2 East. Neck Summary
243 birds listed, 106 nesting birds
Bird Chart pages 258-275

Totals by Season		s	S	F	W
Abundant	A	17	9	20	11
Common	C	81	51	88	42
Uncommon	U	79	51	77	43
Occasional	O	17	9	18	14
Rare	R	34	24	38	38

Endangered Species: Bald Eagle, Peregrine Falcon, Least Tern

Eastern Neck is located on an island at the mouth of the Chester River on the eastern side of the Chesapeake Bay in Kent Co. From Rock Hall, take St. Hwy.

445 south for 5.5 miles to where it crosses the Eastern Neck Narrows. Continue south on refuge road for 2.5 miles, following the signs to the headquarters.

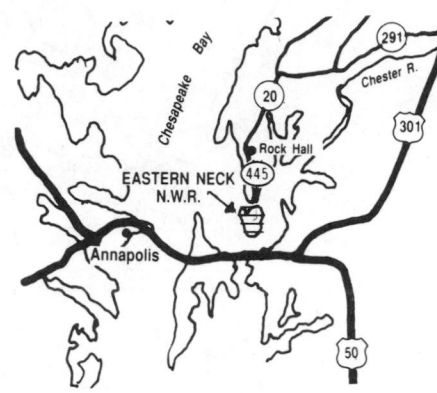

Habitat: 2,285 acres of shoal waters, sand beaches, marshes, swamps, open fields, hedgerows, and woodlands.

Both diving and puddle ducks use the area and swans concentrate around the island by the thousands. Northern Bobwhites, Mourning Doves, Bald Eagles, and Ospreys nest on the island. Various woodpeckers and many songbirds can be seen in the timbered areas and hedgerows. Shorebirds, wading and marsh birds frequent the shores and marshes all year.

Waterfowl numbers peak in November. Tundra Swans, Canada Geese, Buffleheads, American Wigeons, Northern Pintails, Mallards, American Black Ducks, Canvasbacks, and scaups are the most common species. Sea ducks, such as Oldsquaws and White-winged Scoters, are also present. Most waterfowl leave by early April.

Area brochure, wildlife trails, boardwalk, observation tower, hunting.
Spring, Fall

NATIONAL PARK SERVICE

Assateague Is. National Seashore [1]
Route 2, Box 294
Berlin, MD 21811   301-641-1441

39,630 acres on a 37-mile-long barrier island with its sandy beach, migratory waterfowl, and wild ponies, includes the 9,021-acre Chincoteague National Wildlife Refuge in Virginia, administered by the U.S. Fish & Wildlife Service. See the Chincoteague NWR description in the Virginia chapter for birding details.

Seashore brochure with map, blue crab and wild ponies leaflets, mammals, reptiles, and amphibians lists.

STATE AGENCIES

Forest, Park & Wildlife Service
Dept. of Natural Resources
Tawes State Office Bldg.
Annapolis, MD 21401   301-269-3195

Map/Region/City
[1]	Southern/Gaithersburg	301-258-0817
[2]	Eastern/Salisbury	301-749-2461
[3]	Western/Cumberland	301-879-4500
[4]	Central/Bel Air	301-836-4550

Maryland Tourist Development
45 Calvert Street
Annapolis, MD 21401   800-543-1036

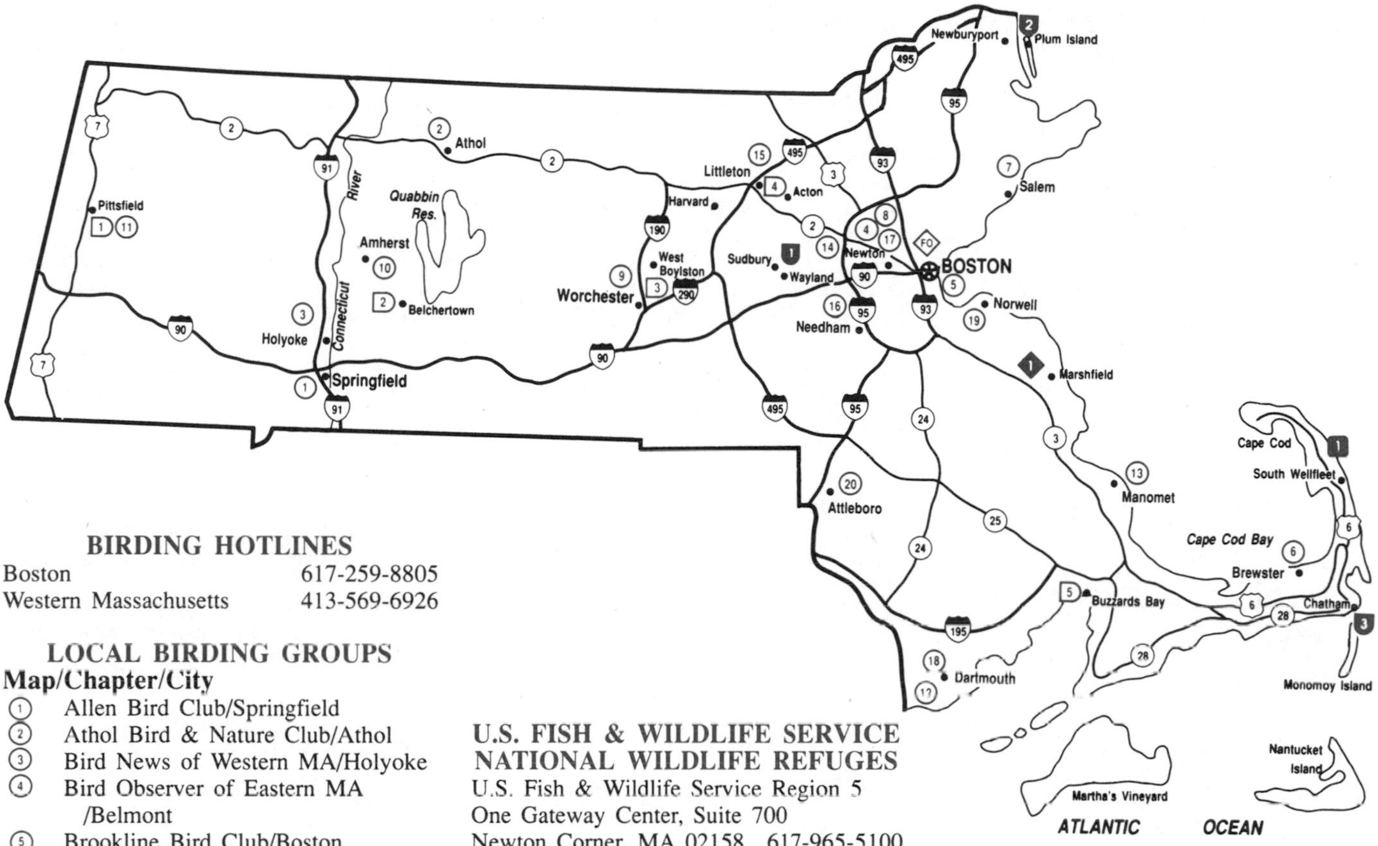

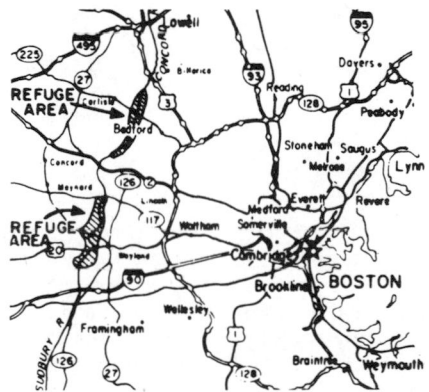

BIRDING HOTLINES
Boston   617-259-8805
Western Massachusetts   413-569-6926

LOCAL BIRDING GROUPS
Map/Chapter/City
1. Allen Bird Club/Springfield
2. Athol Bird & Nature Club/Athol
3. Bird News of Western MA/Holyoke
4. Bird Observer of Eastern MA /Belmont
5. Brookline Bird Club/Boston
6. Cape Cod Bird Club/Brewster
7. Essex County Orn. Club/Salem
8. Felix Cutler Bird Club of Lexington /Lexington
9. Forbush Bird Club/Worcester
10. Hampshire Bird Club/Amherst
11. Hoffman Bird Club/Pittsfield
12. Lloyd Center for Environmental Studies/South Dartmouth
13. Manomet Bird Observatory /Manomet
14. MA Audubon Society/Lincoln
15. Nashoba Valley Bird Club/Littleton
16. Needham Bird Club/Needham
17. Nuttall Bird Club/Cambridge
18. Paskamansett Bird Club/Dartmouth
19. South Shore Bird Club/Norwell
20. Stony Brook Bird Club/Attleboro

THE NATURE CONSERVANCY
Massachusetts Field Office
294 Washington Street, Room 740
Boston, MA 02108   617-423-2545

Black Pond
Managed by MA Audubon
Southeast Regional Center
2000 Main Street
Marshfield, MA 02050   617-837-9400

94 acres of swamp, forest, meadow, and quaking sphagnum bog near Norwell. Open to passive recreational use. A "Discovery Information Guide," and information about the preserve are available from the Center.

U.S. FISH & WILDLIFE SERVICE NATIONAL WILDLIFE REFUGES
U.S. Fish & Wildlife Service Region 5
One Gateway Center, Suite 700
Newton Corner, MA 02158   617-965-5100

Great Meadows   (office at refuge)
Weir Hill Road
Sudbury, MA 01776   617-443-4661

Bird List MA-1 Gr. Meadows Summary
226 birds listed, 85 nesting birds
Bird Chart pages 258-275

Totals by Season		s	S	F	W
Abundant	A	7	3	16	2
Common	C	48	38	33	13
Uncommon	U	61	42	54	17
Occasional	O	41	29	56	25
Rare	R	48	29	44	38

Endangered Species: Bald Eagle, Peregrine Falcon

Headquarters is located at Weir Hill. From Wayland, take Rte. 27 north for 1.7 miles.

Turn right onto Water Row Road, go 1.2 miles to its end, and turn right onto Lincoln Road. Travel 0.5 mile, then turn left onto Weir Hill Road.

Habitat: 3,000 acres located within a heavily populated urban area close to Boston. The refuge consists of open water, marshes, and upland areas stretching along the Sudbury and Concord rivers in the towns of Sudbury, Wayland, Lincoln, Concord, Bedford, Carlisle, and Billerica.

Each spring and fall wading birds, Canada Geese, American Black Ducks, Blue-winged and Green-winged teals, Mallards, and other waterfowl converge on the refuge's impoundments to rest, feed, and nest. Wood Duck nest boxes are located throughout the refuge.

Area brochure, hiking trails, snowshoeing, cross-country skiing, observation tower, photo blinds, canoeing, boating, fishing. Spring, Fall

Parker River   (office at refuge)
Northern Boulevard
Plum Island
Newburyport, MA 01950   617-465-5753

Bird List MA-2 Parker R. Summary
303 birds listed, 72 nesting birds
Bird Chart pages 258-275

Totals by Season		s	S	F	W
Abundant	A	15	12	16	3
Common	C	57	40	46	17
Uncommon	U	89	53	2	36
Occasional	O	77	0	86	51
Rare	R	41	17	33	22

Endangered Species: Bald Eagle, Peregrine Falcon, Piping Plover, Roseate Tern, Least Tern

Headquarters is at the northern tip of Plum Island, 32 miles northeast of Boston. This is also the administrative office for Monomoy NWR. Take the Rte. 113, exit off I-95 east to Hwy. 1-A and go left. Continue to signs indicating the refuge and Plum Island. The only entry to the refuge is through the main gate.

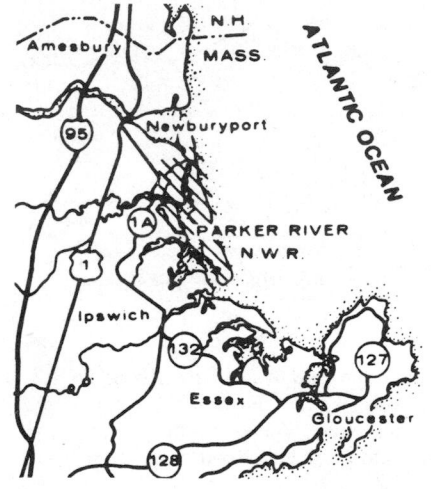

Habitat: 4,662 acres of salt and freshwater marshes, beaches, and dunes. Includes the southern two thirds of Plum Island and is one of the few natural barrier beach-dune-saltmarsh complexes remaining on the northeast coast.

The extensive salt marshes serve as an important feeding and resting area for migratory birds.

Seasonal highlights: In spring, northbound migrations of waterfowl, raptors, early shorebirds, and wading birds begin. During summer, Snowy Egrets may be seen. Large flocks of shorebirds and swallows start their migration in late August. Waterfowl migration gets underway in September and October. In November, migrating Canada and Snow geese arrive. American Black Duck numbers peak, and sea ducks swim in large rafts offshore. Snow Buntings, Horned Larks, and Lapland Longspurs feed in large flocks. Snowy Owls, Rough-legged Hawks, and Northern Harriers are among the raptors frequently seen during winter months.

Area brochure, beachcombing, trail hiking, surf-fishing, plum and cranberry picking. March through early June and August through October are best.

Monomoy 3
c/o Parker River NWR
Northern Boulevard, Plum Island
Newburyport, MA 01950   617-465-5753

Open Memorial Day to Labor Day
Seasonal office at Monomoy 617-945-0594

Bird List MA-3 Monomoy Summary
285 birds listed, 50 nesting birds
Bird Chart pages 258-275

Totals by Season		s	S	F	W
Abundant	A	11	5	14	6
Common	C	54	40	81	19
Uncommon	U	25	21	15	7
Occasional	O	58	35	84	40
Rare	R	80	40	60	24

Endangered Species: Bald Eagle, Peregrine Falcon, Piping Plover, Roseate Tern, Least Tern
Rare/Limited Species: Tufted Duck, Eurasian Curlew

Refuge headquarters is located next to the Chatham Weather Station on Morris Island in Chatham, MA. On Cape Cod, take U.S. Rte. 6 east to St. Rte. 137, then south to St. Rte. 28, and east through Chatham to Chatham Light. Turn left at the lighthouse, then take the first right. Refuge headquarters is on left side of road. The refuge is located at the "elbow" of Cape Cod and most of it is accessible only by boat.

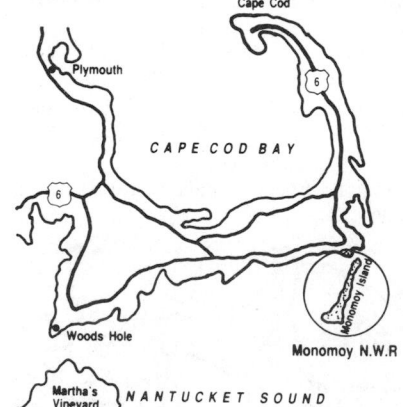

Habitat: 2,097 acres of sand dunes, freshwater ponds, and salt and freshwater marshes, encompassing all of Monomoy Island and a portion of Morris Island. Monomoy is best known for its shorebird migrations. Adults can be seen in their fresh breeding plumage during the spring, and their population peaks in May. When they begin their southward migration in July, the shorebirds are in their drabber

winter plumage. The Willet is one of the few shorebirds that breed on the islands. Seabirds nesting in the colony include Herring and Great Black-backed gulls, the largest concentration in Massachusetts of Laughing Gulls, and Roseate and Least terns.

During the fall and winter, thousands of waterfowl can be seen offshore, including eiders, scoters, Brants, and Red-breasted Mergansers.

Area pamphlet, beachcombing, hiking, fishing.
Summer

NATIONAL PARK SERVICE

Cape Cod National Seashore 1
South Wellfleet, MA 02663   508-349-3785

43,526 acres of ocean beaches, dunes, woodlands, freshwater ponds, and marshes make up this park on outer Cape Cod.

Park brochure with map, bicycle trails guide, and lists of self-guiding nature trails, birds, and monthly ranger-guided activities.

STATE AGENCIES

Div. of Fisheries & Wildlife
Leverett Saltonstall Building
Government Center
100 Cambridge Street
Boston, MA 02202   617-727-3151

Map/District/City
1	Western/Pittsfield	413-447-9789
2	Connecticut Valley /Belchertown	413-323-7632
3	Central/West Boylston	617-835-3607
4	Northeast/Action	617-263-4347
5	Southeast /Buzzards Bay	617-759-3406

Massachusetts Div. of Tourism
100 Cambridge Street
13th Floor
Boston, MA 02202   617-727-3201

BIRDING HOTLINES
Southeastern Michigan   313-278-4288
Statewide   616-471-4919

LOCAL BIRDING GROUPS
Map/Chapter/City
①   Aud. Soc. of Kalamazoo/Kalamazoo
②   Detroit Audubon/Royal Oak
③   Michigan Audubon/Lansing

The Michigan Audubon Society has 42 local chapters across the state. Call the central office in Lansing for information.

THE NATURE CONSERVANCY
Michigan Field Office   ◇
2840 E. Grand River, Suite 5
East Lansing, MI 48823   517-332-1741

These preserves are open to the public for passive recreation. Direct ownership of some properties has been transferred to other institutions or agencies. A directory covering 29 current TNC projects in Michigan is available from the Field Office for $5. Updates and revisions to the directory are provided free.

Colonial Point Forest Preserve ❶
258 acres in Cheboygan County adjacent to Burt Lake. Also known as "Hartwick Pines of Hardwoods," this forest preserve attracts Red-eyed Vireos, Black-throated Green Warblers, and Ovenbirds during the summer months.

Dickinson Island ❷
7.25 acres which are part of a state-owned 1,500-acre unit on Dickinson Island in the St. Clair River delta. The preserve, which includes lake plain, wet prairie, and oak openings, attracts waterfowl during migration periods. There is a rookery for Great Blue Herons and Great Egrets.

Erie Marsh Preserve ❸
2,168 acres in Monroe County. Closed to the public in October and November. The marsh attracts both migrating and nesting shorebirds, waterfowl, and a variety of other birds. The preserve is also a prime hawk-watching area during migration.

Grand Mere State Park ❹
650 acres, which are part of a 1,184-acre unit near Stevensville on Lake Michigan, include three small lakes, woodlands, dunelands, bogs, and swamps. White-eyed Vireos and Canada Warblers nest here.

Grass River Natural Area ❺
A 1,050-acre natural area with conifer swamps, marsh, and other wetland habitats west of Mancelona. There is an interpretive building and boardwalk. Hiking trails begin at the parking lot. A naturalist leads guided tours during the summer months; for tour reservations call 616-533-8709.

Harbor Island ❻
695 acres and the largest island in Potaganissing Bay, near the eastern tip of the Upper Peninsula and located 2.5 miles north of Drummond Island. An interior forest is surrounded by marshey shoreline. Access is by boat. Harbor Island is a unit of the Seney National Wildlife Refuge.

Nordhouse Dunes ❼
598 acres which are part of a 3,360-acre unit of the Nordhouse Dunes/Ludington State Park complex. The complex extends

for 12 miles along Lake Michigan near

Ludington. Ten miles of marked trails in what may be the largest windblown dune area on a freshwater lake in the U.S.

Skegemog Swamp Wildlife Area ❽
2,700 acres of marshes, coniferous swamps, fens, and bogs, west of Rapid City. Common Loons and Bald Eagles have been observed. A boardwalk leads through a portion of the swamp.

Walkinshaw Wetlands ❾
1,031-acre marsh and wetland habitat with several creeks. Over 200 Sandhill Cranes may be seen in late September or early October as they feed during their migration. Northern Harriers, shorebirds, and waterfowl have also been observed.

U.S. FISH & WILDLIFE SERVICE NATIONAL WILDLIFE REFUGES

Seney 🔲   (office at refuge)
Seney, MI 49883   906-586-9851

Bird List MI-1 Seney Summary
206 birds listed, 135 nesting birds
Bird Chart pages 258-275

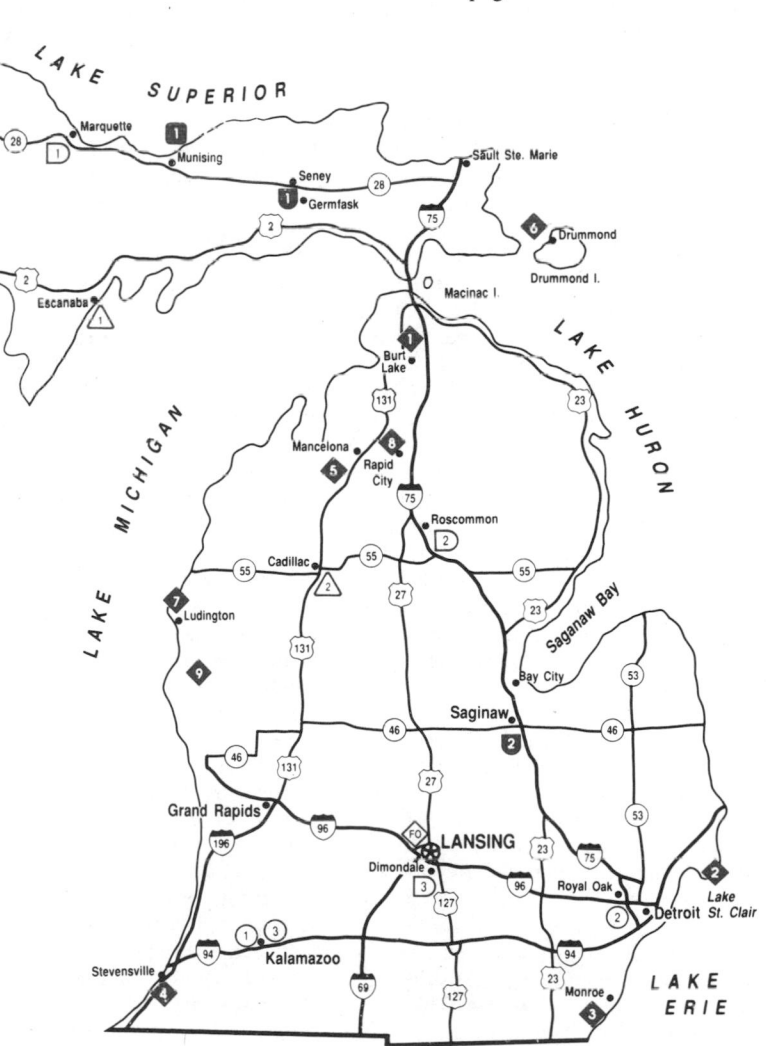

Totals by Season		s	S	F	W
Abundant	A	14	13	13	2
Common	C	83	68	78	14
Uncommon	U	48	44	51	7
Occasional	O	39	27	37	14
Rare	R	16	31	19	7

Endangered Species: Bald Eagle, Peregrine Falcon

Refuge headquarters is located on Hwy. M-77 approximately 3 miles north of Germfask. Also administers Harbor Island and Huron Island NWRs. The latter is a Wilderness Area with access by permit only.

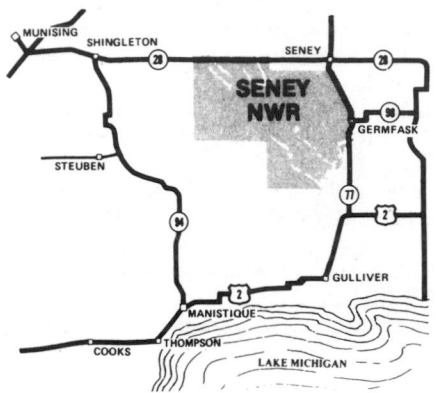

Habitat: 95,455 acres, of which 25,150 acres is designated wilderness. Includes 7,000 acres of open water in 21 major pools. The refuge is in the Great Manistique Swamp, which is characterized by open marshes and immense areas of rushes and sedges. Scattered in the marshes are shallow pools of clear, cold water and sandy knolls and ridges that support stands of mature red pine. Much of the area is reclaimed farm land.

A nesting population of Canada Geese has been established and is easily seen in the spring. Ducks that nest in the area include Mallards, American Black, Wood, and Ring-necked ducks, Common Goldeneyes, Green-winged and Blue-winged teals, and Hooded and Common mergansers. Peak populations of waterfowl are present during the spring and fall migrations. Sandhill Cranes can be observed prior to fall migration.

Other nesting species include Common Yellowthroat, Canada, Pine, Chestnut-sided, Black-and-white, Yellow, Nashville, and Magnolia warblers, Hermit and Swainson's thrushes, American Bittern, Killdeer, Cedar Waxwing, and Red-eyed Vireo.

Various other birds are present but are more difficult to see, including Ruffed, Spruce, and Sharp-tailed grouse, Yellow Rails, and American Woodcocks.

Raptors include Bald Eagle, Northern Harrier, and Great Horned Owl.

Area brochure, visitor center, auto tour route, nature trail, picnicking, fishing, hunting, canoeing, berry-picking, cross-country skiing, snowshoeing.
Summer

Shiawassee 🄁
6975 Mower Road
Route 1
Saginaw, MI 48601   517-777-5930

Located 6 miles south of Saginaw on Hwy. 13. Turn onto Curtis Road, and continue for 0.75 mile to headquarters.

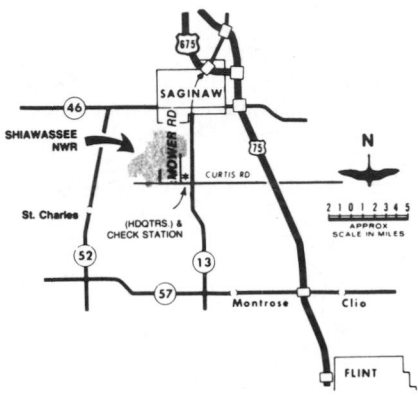

Habitat: 9,000 acres of shallow marshes, agricultural lands, bottomland hardwoods, and grasses, as well as a series of controlled pools, wetlands, and croplands. The six waterways that cross the refuge join to form the Saginaw River.

The refuge protects a traditional resting place for thousands of migratory waterfowl. Tundra Swans stop at the refuge from mid-March to mid-April on their northward migration, in addition to Canada Geese and various ducks. Mallards and American Black Ducks are the most common species, but American Wigeons, Northern Pintails, Wood Ducks, and teals are also present.

Great Blue and Green-backed herons nest in the area. Red-tailed and Rough-legged hawks, Northern Harriers, and American Kestrels hunt over the marshes throughout the summer.

Spotted, Solitary, and Semipalmated sandpipers and Greater and Lesser yellowlegs can be seen along the shoreline. Hairy and Downy woodpeckers find plenty of old trees in the wooded areas and visitors may spot White-breasted Nuthatches, Brown Creepers, Gray Catbirds, Brown Thrashers, Cedar Waxwings, and Red-eyed and Warbling vireos.

Area brochure, nature trail, fishing, limited hunting.
Spring, Fall

NATIONAL PARK SERVICE

Pictured Rocks 🄁
National Lakeshore
PO Box 40
Munising, MI 49862   906-387-3700

72,898 acres of multicolored sandstone cliffs, broad beaches, sand bars, dunes, waterfalls, inland lakes, ponds, marshes, and wood and coniferous forests provide habitat for numerous birds and animals at this scenic area on Lake Superior.

Lakeshore brochure with map, free quarterly "Lakeshore Observer" newspaper, leaflets on hiking, backcountry camping, lakeshore geology, a 211-species bird checklist, wildflower and other species lists.

NATIONAL FOREST SERVICE

Map/Forest/City
🄁	Hiawatha/Escanaba	906-786-4062
🄂	Huron-Manistee	
	/Cadillac	616-775-2421
🄃	Ottawa/Ironwood	906-932-1330

STATE AGENCIES

Wildlife Division
Michigan Dept. of Natural Resources
PO Box 30028
Lansing, MI 48909   517-373-1263

The Michigan Nongame Wildlife Fund publishes "Birdwatching At Its Best," a fold-out, 17" by 22" color brochure. It describes 13 good birding areas in the state and is available at no charge.

Map/Region/City
🄁	Region 1/Marquette	906-226-7505
🄂	Region 2/Roscommon	517-275-5151
🄃	Region 3/Dimondale	517-322-1300

There are 14 Wildlife Districts working under the three regional offices in Michigan.

Michigan Travel Bureau
Michigan Department of Commerce
PO Box 30226
Lansing, MI 48909   800-543-2937

BIRDING HOTLINES

Duluth   218-525-5952
Statewide   612-544-5016

LOCAL BIRDING GROUPS
Map/Chapter/City
① Agassiz Audubon/Warren
② Albert Lea Audubon/Alden
③ Audubon Chapter of Minneapolis
   /Robbinsdale
④ Austin Audubon/Austin
⑤ Central Mn. Audubon/St. Cloud
⑥ Duluth Audubon/Duluth
⑦ Lake Superior Audubon
   /Grand Marais
⑧ MN River Valley Aud./Bloomington
⑨ Mississippi Headwaters Audubon
   /Bemidji
⑩ St. Paul Audubon/St. Paul
⑪ Upper Hiawatha Valley Audubon
   /Goodhue
⑫ White Pine Audubon/Finlayson
⑬ Wild River Audubon/Chisago City
⑭ Wilderness Heritage Aud./Gr. Rapids
⑮ Zumbo Valley Audubon/Rochester
⑯ Bee-Nay She Council/Brainerd
⑰ Cottonwood County Bird Club
   /Mountain Lake
⑱ Hiawatha Valley Bird Club
   /Winona
⑲ Minnesota Orn. Society
   /Minneapolis

NATIONAL AUDUBON SOCIETY

Northwoods Audubon Center ❶
Route 1, Box 288
Sandstone, MN 55072   612-245-2648

535 acres at 1,100 feet of elevation in
east-central Minnesota. The Center is
operated by the Minnesota Audubon
chapters and has been open on a
reservation-only basis. Trails and literature
are being developed for public use in
1990. There is a fee for the guided tours.

Day hiking, picnicking, canoeing as part
of guided programs, cross-country skiing.

THE NATURE CONSERVANCY
Minnesota Field Office ◇FO◇
1313 Fifth Street, S.E.
Minneapolis, MN 55414   612-379-2134

Area maps and lists of birds and plants
are available for all preserves. Best
visiting time is summer except as noted.
None of the sites have visitor facilities
beyond a registration box with a map.
Most do not have trails. A "Preserve
Guide" (maps and preserve descriptions) is
available from the Field Office.

Agassiz Dunes ◆❶
435 acres near Fertile in Polk and
Norman Counties containing a large dune
field.

Black Dog Fen ◆❷
100 acres near Burnsville, in Dakota
County, protect two endangered plant
communities, calcareous fen and mesic
black soil prairies.

Blue Devil Valley ◆❸
29 acres near Granite Falls in Yellow
Medicine County. Basalt outcroppings are
surrounded by dry prairie.

Bluestem Prairie ◆❹
2,458 acres adjacent Buffalo River State
Park and 4 miles southeast of Glyndon, in
Clay County, support Greater Prairie
Chickens and other grassland species. The
TNC Western Preserve Office is located
at this preserve.

Chippewa Prairie ◆❺
943-acre prairie, north of Milan in
Chippewa and Swift counties and adjacent
to the Lac Qui Parle Wildlife
Management Area.

Clinton Prairie ◆❻
160 acres, 6 miles west of Clinton in Big
Stone County, of black soil prairie.

Cold Springs ◆❼
61 acres near Cold Springs, in Stearns
County, along the Sauk River by Hwy.
23. This is a heron nesting site from mid-
April through July. Entrance to the herony
is restricted during this period but there is
a vantage point from Observation Hill, a
ridge that overlooks the river on the south
side of Hwy. 23.

Egret Island ◆❽
34 acres in Pelican Lake near Ashby, in
Grant County. From April through July
the island is off limits. Egret Island has
the largest concentration of colonial
nesting birds in Minnesota. Black-crowned
Night-Herons, Great Blue Herons, Great
Egrets, and Double-crested Cormorants,
which may be seen in the thousands, are
among the 38 species seen on the island.

Felton Prairie Complex ◆❾
A 6,000-acre complex of quality prairie
which includes public and private land in
Felton Township, Clay County. Blazing
Star Prairie is a 160-acre part of the
complex where Sprague's Pipits, Baird's
Sparrows, and Chestnut-collared Longspurs
have been observed.

Foxhome & ◆❿
Kettledrummer Prairies
240-acre Foxhome and 200-acre

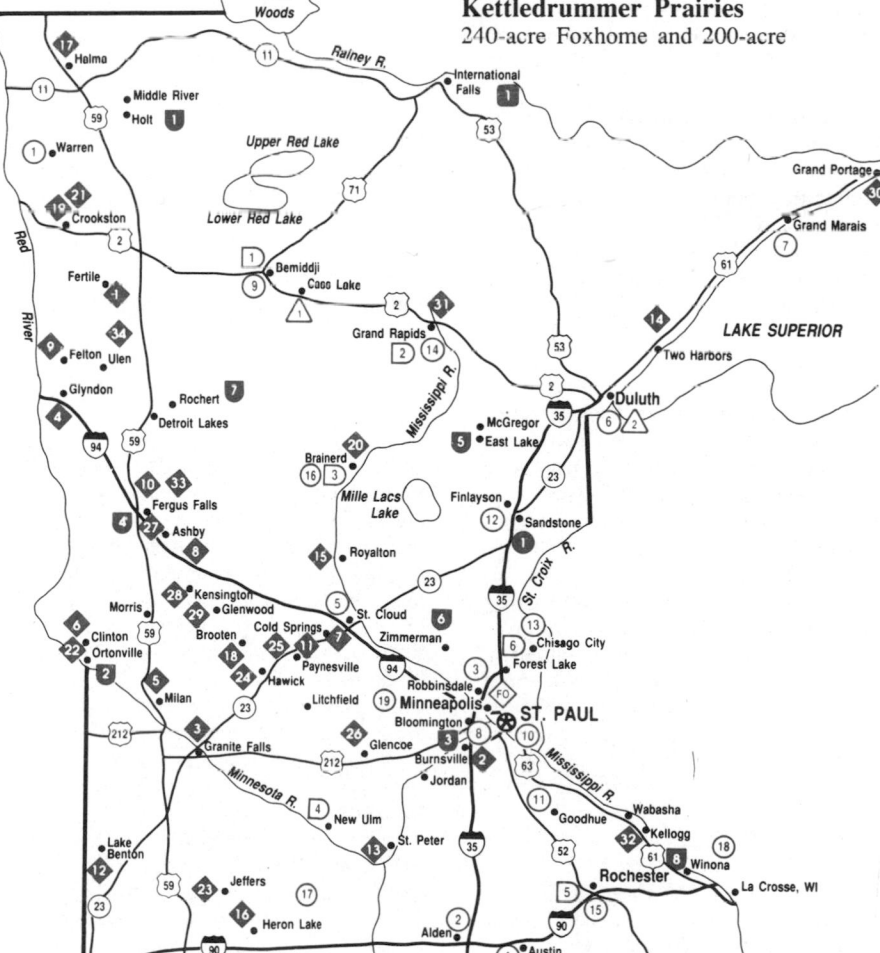

Kettledrummer are near each other and close to Fergus in Wilkin County. The low, moist areas are favored habitat for Greater Prairie Chickens. During March and April the birds may be observed on the booming grounds. Observe from a distance to avoid disturbing or flushing the birds.

Helen Allison Savanna ⑪
57 acres about 3.5 miles north of Paynesville in Anoka County. This grassland attracts Upland Sandpipers and Marbled Godwits.

Hole-In-The-Mountain Prairie ⑫
299 acres south of Lake Benton in Lincoln County on the edge of the Bemis Moraine. The area is noted for rare Dakota, ottoe, and pawnee skipper butterfly populations.

Kasota Prairie ⑬
38 acres 3.5 miles southwest of St. Peter in LeSuere County. A profusion of wildflowers may be seen from April to October.

Langley River ⑭
80 acres about 20 miles north of Two Harbors, an abandoned logging camp in Lake County where almost every species of butterfly known in Minnesota may be observed.

MacDougall Homestead ⑮
255 acres 2 miles west of Royalton, in Morrison County, with three vegetative communities: prairie, and coniferous and deciduous forests. Visitors are asked to stay out of the heron rookery from April through July. Over 57 species of birds have been observed at the Homestead.

North Heron Lake ⑯
52 acres in Jackson County, 5 miles from Heron Lake, with a major lake attracting Forster's Terns, American White Pelicans, American Avocets, Black-crowned Night-Herons, and other waterbirds. The preserve is closed in October.

Norway Dunes ⑰
320 acres near Halma in Kittson County. This preserve provides an example of presettlement vegetation types, oak sand savanna, dry-mesic prairie grasses, shrub swamp, and marsh.

Ordway Prairie ⑱
582 acres of rolling hills with numerous wet depressions near Brooten in Pope County.

Pankratz Memorial Prairie ⑲
320 acres near Crookston in Polk County. Greater Prairie Chickens and Marbled Godwits have been observed on the mesic

and wet blacksoil prairie.

Paul Bunyan Savanna ⑳
160 acres near Brainerd in Crow Wing County, this jack pine savannah is managed in cooperation with the adjacent Paul Bunyan Arboretum.

Pembina Trail ㉑
2,044 acres near Crookston, in Polk County. The mesic blacksoil prairie, which is mixed with sedge meadows, marsh, and shrub swamps, supports Sandhill Cranes, Yellow Rails, Wilson's Phalaropes, and Short-eared Owls.

Plover Prairie ㉒
435 acres near Ortonville, in Lac Qui Parle County. Its varied habitat, which includes wetlands, marshes, and sedge meadows, supports breeding populations of Upland Sandpiper, Marbled Godwit, and many species of waterfowl.

Red Rock Prairie ㉓
26 acres near Jeffers in Cottonwood County. A red quartzite ridge runs through the prairie.

Regal Meadow ㉔
145 acres near Harwickin, in Kandiyohi County, of marsh and wet mesic prairie. Permission to visit must be obtained in advance from the Field Office.

Roscoe Prairie ㉕
57 acres, about 3.5 miles northeast of Paynesville, in Stearns County. Upland Sandpipers and Marbled Godwits have been observed on this prairie.

Schaefer Prairie ㉖
160 acres of blacksoil prairie and pothole marshes, 7 miles west of Glencoe in McLeod County, support 245 native plant species.

Seven Sisters Prairie ㉗
148 acres near Ashby in Otter Trail County include seven rounded knolls on a hill 200 feet above the north shore of Lake Christiana. The preserve has a number of western plants not normally found in Minnesota.

Staffanson Prairie ㉘
95 acres near Kensington, in Douglas County, with 60 acres of quality prairie around an open pothole which is surrounded by wetland vegetation.

Strandness Prairie ㉙
40 acres near Glenwood, in Pope County. Prairie and wetlands provide cover for nesting Mallards, Pintails, Blue-winged Teals, Gadwalls, Ring-necked Ducks, Lesser Scaups, and other birds.

Susie Island ㉚
132 acres in Lake Superior and about 4.5 miles east from Grand Portage in Cook County. Accessible only by boat and with no landing facilities. Extreme caution advised. Check the weather before boating. Adjacent islands are part of the Grand Portage Indian Reservation and permission is required to land on them.

Wabu Woods ㉛
104 acres in two tracts near Grand Rapids and adjacent Deer Lake, in Itasca County. A bog, hardwoods, and old-growth cedars provide diversity.

Weaver Dunes ㉜
492 acres near Kellogg, in Wabashu County, and part of the largest sand dune area in southeast Minnesota along the Mississippi River. Peregrine Falcons were released at this site from 1982 to 1986. The wildflower display is best seen during the spring.

Western Prairie North ㉝
476 acres near Fergus Falls, in Wilkin County. This mesic and wet tallgrass prairie is the center of the Greater Prairie Chicken range in Minnesota. The habitat also supports Marbled Godwits and Upland Sandpipers.

Zimmerman Prairie ㉞
80 acres 5.5 miles located northeast of Ulen in Becker County, and situated in the bed of a small glacial lake. This habitat also supports Marbled Godwits, Greater Prairie Chickens, and Upland Sandpipers.

U.S. FISH & WILDLIFE SERVICE NATIONAL WILDLIFE REFUGES
U.S. Fish & Wildlife Service Region 3
Federal Building
Fort Snelling
Twin Cities, MN 55111   612-725-3507

Agassiz ❶ (office on refuge)
Middle River, MN 56737   218-449-4115

Bird List MN-1 Agassiz Summary
248 birds listed, 132 nesting birds
Bird Chart pages 276-293

Totals by Season		s	S	F	W
Abundant	A	8	8	9	0
Common	C	78	65	60	8
Uncommon	U	81	54	78	10
Occasional	O	39	23	41	10
Rare	R	29	38	18	7

Endangered Species: Bald Eagle, Peregrine Falcon, Piping Plover

From Holt, take Co. Road 7 east for 11 miles to the refuge headquarters.

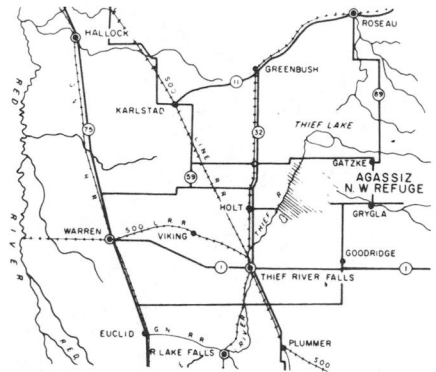

Habitat: 61,000 acres. The terrain is flat with an average of only 1 foot change in elevation per mile. Open water and freshwater marshes occupy 36,000 acres. On the higher ground, there are extensive areas of willows, open grasslands and scattered stands of hardwoods. Two spruce-tamarack bogs, with associated bog lakes, are in a 4,000-acre area managed as a wilderness.

The primary management objective of the refuge is to provide habitat for duck production. The restored shallow water marshes attract 17 species of breeding ducks each year. There is also an established flock of "Giant" Canada Geese that nest on the refuge.

In April and May songbirds pass through on migration. There is a breeding colony of Franklin's Gulls, and five species of grebes, Red-necked, Horned, Eared, Western, and Pied-billed, nest here. Great Blue and Green-backed herons, Black-crowned Night-Herons, Great Egrets, and Least and American bitterns also nest.

Tundra Swans and American White Pelicans migrate through in spring and fall.

Area brochure, mammals list, observation tower, observation deck, auto tour route. Spring and Fall best.

Big Stone ❷ (office in town)
25 NW 2nd Street
Ortonville, MN 56278   612-839-3700

Bird List MN-2 Big Stone Summary
237 birds listed, 107 nesting birds
Bird Chart pages 276-293

Totals by Season		s	S	F	W
Abundant	A	5	5	9	0
Common	C	96	68	80	15
Uncommon	U	63	39	59	11
Occasional	O	44	28	40	29
Rare	R	17	15	16	32

Endangered Species: Bald Eagle, Peregrine Falcon

The refuge is located 2 miles southeast of Ortonville on Hwy. 7.

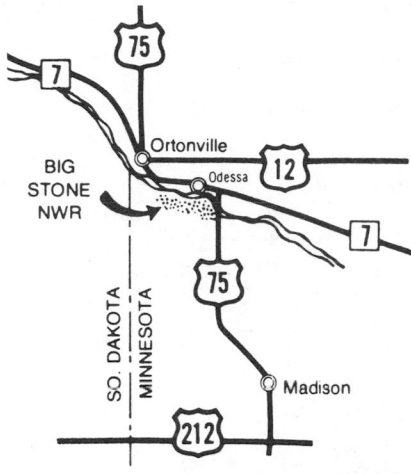

Habitat: 10,795 acres. About 4,250 acres consist of marsh and open water created by a 3-mile dam across the Minnesota River Valley. Approximately 850 acres are low woodlands, 1,700 acres are native prairie, 100 acres are granite rock outcrops, and 4,000 acres are croplands.

The greatest numbers of waterfowl are present during early April and mid-October.

A rookery of Double-crested Cormorants, Great Blue Herons, Great Egrets, and Black-crowned Night-Herons is located on the refuge. Western, Eared, and Pied-billed grebes use the area to rear their young. The flooded woodlands provide nesting sites for Wood Ducks and Hooded Mergansers.

The Northern Flicker, and Red-headed, Red-bellied, Hairy, and Downy woodpeckers nest, and the Pileated Woodpecker is an occasional visitor.

In the woodlands Indigo Bunting, Dickcissel, American Goldfinch, and Savannah, Grasshopper, Vesper, Chipping, Clay-colored, and Song sparrows nest. Nesting warblers include the Yellow Warbler and Common Yellowthroat. Black-and-white and Nashville warblers are common visitors among the many passerines that take shelter and feed in the low-lying woodlands.

Area brochure, auto tour route, foot trail, canoe trail, mammals list, fishing, hunting, cross-country skiing, snowshoeing. Spring and Fall best.

Minnesota Valley ❸ (office in town)
4101 E. 80th Street
Bloomington, MN 55420   612-854-5900

Bird List MN-3 MN Valley Summary
241 birds listed, no nesting data
Bird Chart pages 276-293

Totals by Season		s	S	F	W
Abundant	A	27	21	26	8
Common	C	11	59	8	11
Uncommon	U	62	30	58	28
Occasional	O	6	3	8	6
Rare	R	25	22	28	8

Endangered Species: Bald Eagle, Peregrine Falcon, Piping Plover

The refuge is an urban green belt along a 34-mile stretch of the Minnesota River from Fort Snelling to Jordan. It is comprised of 7 management units, 4 of which have trails and interpretive facilities. Acquisition of refuge lands is not complete. Presently much of the land is in private ownership. Refuge brochure map shows the primary access points.

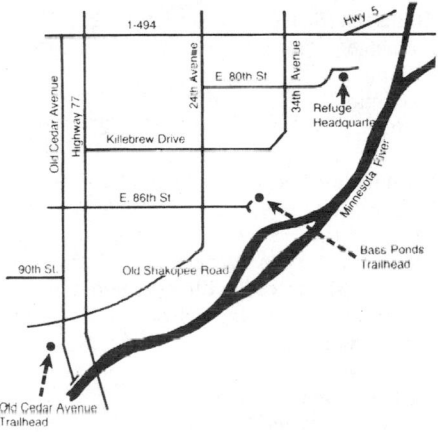

Habitat: Long Meadow Lake unit: 2,200 acres of marshes, hardwood-forested bluffs, and bottomlands.
Black Dog Lake unit: 1,306 acres of land and water.
Bloomington Ferry unit: 380 acres of floodplain forests and wetlands.
Wilkie-Rice Lake unit: contains exceptional wetlands.
Upgrala unit: 2,400 acres of lake, marsh, fields and forested riverbanks.
Chaska Lake unit: 580 acres of marsh-edged lake surrounded by farmland and floodplain forest.
Louisville Swamp: 2,400 acre mix of marsh, bottomland hardwoods, and oak savannah.

Migrants include ducks, geese, American White Pelicans, Tundra Swans, and Bald Eagles. Warblers are attracted to the shrubby understory and are abundant during spring and fall. Red-tailed, Sharp-shinned, Broad-winged, and Rough-legged hawks and Northern Harriers are common migrants through the Minnesota Valley.

Herons, egrets, and Wood Ducks nest in the floodplain forests. Woodlands on the bluffs contain Great Horned Owls, Northern Orioles, and Blue Jays. A notable year-round resident is the Pileated Woodpecker. Ground-nesting sparrows can be found in the grassy openings.

Area brochure, hiking, bicycling, observation blinds, horseback riding trails, fishing, fruit, berry ,and mushroom picking, hunting, cross-country skiing, snowshoeing, snowmobiling. Spring, Summer, Fall

Minnesota Wetlands Complex 4
Waterfowl Production Areas (WPAs)
Route 1, Box 76
Fergus Falls, MN 56537　　218-739-2291

Bird List MN-4 MN WPAs Summary
243 birds listed, 124 nesting birds
Bird Chart pages 276-293

Totals by Season		s	S	F	W
Abundant	A	19	12	21	3
Common	C	26	91	17	15
Uncommon	U	63	27	73	24
Rare	R	24	23	25	25

Endangered Species: Bald Eagle, Piping Plover

There are 4 WPA management districts in western Minnesota, with the main office in Fergus Falls at East Highway 210. The other 3 are:

Detroit Lakes District
Route 3, Box 47D
Detroit Lakes, MN 56501　218-847-4431

Morris District
Route 1, Box 208
Mill Dam Road
Morris, MN 56267　　　612-589-1001

Litchfield District
305 North Sibley
Litchfield, MN 55355　　612-693-2849

The bird list was compiled for the 125,000 acres scattered throughout a 28-county area in western Minnesota. There are approximately 700 WPAs ranging in size from 30 to 2,000 acres, with an average size of 200 acres.

WPAs have a variety of wetlands, prairie, forest, and upland habitat combinations. Most areas are open throughout the year.

Maps showing the location of the WPAs are available at the district offices.
Summer

Rice Lake　5　　　(office on refuge)
Route 2, Box 67
McGregor, MN 55760　　218-768-2402

From McGregor, take Hwy. 65 south for 5 miles, turn right at East Lake, and go 2 miles west on gravel road to the office.

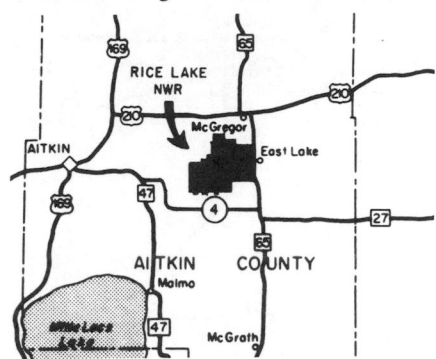

Habitat: 18,056 acres, dominated by 4,500-acre Rice Lake, which is noted for its extensive wild rice beds. Also contains open water and heavily forested uplands with scattered grasslands, small lakes, and croplands. The refuge is located in the transition zone between the coniferous forests of northern Minnesota and the hardwood forests of the southern part of the state.

The refuge is an important resting and feeding area for ducks, especially Ring-necked Ducks, Lesser Scaups, and Mallards. Many species of waterfowl nest on the refuge, including an established Canada Goose flock. Nearly two dozen species of hawks and owls may be seen at the area, and Bald Eagles are often seen during migrations.

Area brochure, bird list, mammals list, walking trail, fishing, hunting, picnicking. Spring and Fall best.

Sherburne　6　　　(office on refuge)
Route 2
Zimmerman, MN 55398　　612-389-3323

Bird List MN-5 Sherburne Summary
213 birds listed, 113 nesting birds
Bird Chart pages 276-293

Totals by Season		s	S	F	W
Abundant	A	9	7	7	1
Common	C	74	51	55	12
Uncommon	U	68	50	55	14
Rare	R	32	29	24	27

Endangered Species: Bald Eagle, Peregrine Falcon

From Zimmerman, go 4.5 miles north on Hwy. 169 to the refuge sign. Turn west, and go 5 miles to the refuge.

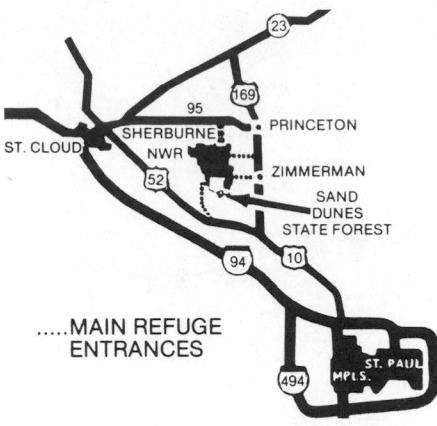

.....MAIN REFUGE ENTRANCES

Habitat: 30,665 acres encompass much of the St. Francis River Valley. Over 20 impoundments and natural lakes, wetlands with cattails and marsh grasses, which give way in dryer areas to prairie vegetation with oak savannas, scattered dense woodlands, and cropland.

The refuge is both a stopover point for migrating waterfowl and a prime nesting area. Most waterfowl species that commonly migrate along the Mississippi Flyway stop to rest and feed. Canada Geese, Mallards, Green-winged and Blue-winged teals, Northern Shovelers, Redheads, Canvasbacks, Wood and Ring-necked ducks, and Hooded Mergansers all nest on the refuge. Common Loons and Red-necked and Pied-billed grebes also nest at Sherburne.

Sandhill Cranes migrate through Sherburne and Great Blue and Green-backed herons are common nesters. Nine species of hawks have been sighted at the area, including nesting species such as Northern Harriers, and Cooper's and Red-shouldered hawks.

Breeding woodpeckers include the Red-headed, Hairy and Downy woodpeckers, Northern Flicker, and Yellow-bellied Sapsucker.

Area brochure, auto tour route, hunting, fishing, canoeing, hiking, cross-country skiing, snowshoeing. Spring, Summer, Fall

Tamarac　7　　　(office on refuge)
HC10, Box 145
Rochert, MN 56578　　　218-847-2641

Bird List MN-6 Tamarac Summary
245 birds listed, 109 nesting birds
Bird Chart pages 276-293

Totals by Season		s	S	F	W
Abundant	A	13	6	13	0
Common	C	88	68	85	11
Uncommon	U	85	64	85	19
Rare	R	54	32	55	18

Endangered Species: Bald Eagle, Peregrine Falcon

From Detroit Lakes, take Hwy. 34 east for 8 miles, turn north on Co. Road 29, and go 10 miles to the refuge.

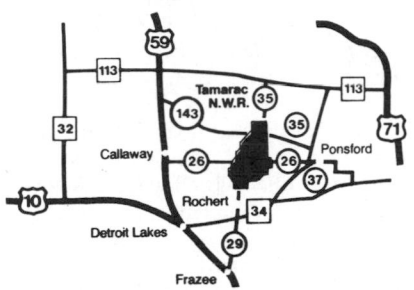

Habitat: 43,000 acres, including nearly 18,000 acres of various types of wetlands such as shallow lakes, swamps, bogs, and potholes. Uplands include second-growth aspen, hardwood forests along with white pine and tamarac, croplands, and some grasslands.

Thousands of migrating ducks and geese can be seen at Tamarac. While Canvasbacks and Northern Shovelers continue on to breeding grounds farther north, Redheads, Green-winged and Blue-winged teals, American Wigeons, Lesser Scaups, Mallards, Wood and Ring-necked Ducks, Common Goldeneyes, and a small flock of Canada Geese nest at the refuge.

Bald Eagles nest on the refuge and in the fall Golden Eagles stop on their way south. Great Blue Herons, Ospreys, Pileated Woodpeckers, Turkey Vultures, and Common Loons also may be seen on the refuge.

Area brochure, auto tour route, hunting, fishing, boating, hiking trail, picnicking, cross-country ski trail.
Spring, Fall

Upper Miss. River 🔳 (office in town)
Wildlife & Fish Refuge HQ
Exchange Bldg., Room 100   507-454-7351
or
Winona District office, Room 101
51 East Fourth Street
Winona, MN, 55987   507-452-4232

The refuge encompasses 195,000 acres of wooded islands, marshes, and water bodies extending 284 miles from Wabasha south to Rock Island, Illinois.

There are four Upper Mississippi River Refuge district offices. The Winona District is in Minnesota. Three others, La Crosse in Wisconsin, McGregor in Iowa, and Savanna in Illinois, are briefly described in the appropriate state chapter.

A Bird List Summary for Upper Mississippi River National Wildlife & Fish Refuge is in the Iowa chapter (Bird List IA-4 McGregor), and Wisconsin chapter (Bird List WI-4 La Crosse).

Twelve refuge "pool maps" for segments of the Upper Mississippi River Wildlife & Fish Refuge are available. The locations covered by the maps are illustrated in the Illinois and Iowa chapters on page 79 and 85 respectively. The map numbers (4 & 5, 5A & 6, 7, 8, 9, 10, 11, 12, 13, and 14) relate to the river dam and lock system in the four refuge districts. These are large, detailed maps and include important information about the pool covered.

Habitat: River bottoms forming the refuge are from 2 to 5 miles wide and contain differing life zones and climactic conditions. Eleven dams and locks within the refuge boundaries form a series of pools that vary from 10 to 30 miles long. The dams have raised water levels, creating a maze of channels, sloughs, marshlands, and open lakes over the bottomlands. Excellent stands of aquatic plants have developed, creating habitat for waterfowl and other wildlife.

The Mississippi Flyway is one of the four major migration routes in North America. Thousands of Tundra Swans rest during their spring migration, while Canvasbacks use the refuge pools primarily during the fall. Up to 75% of the Canvasbacks in North America may be seen on pools 7 and 8 below Winona. Other ducks seen include Lesser Scaups, Redheads, Buffleheads, Ruddy and Ring-necked ducks, American Wigeons, Gadwalls, and teals. Thousands of Wood Ducks feed in the sloughs, nesting in hollow trees on islands and bluffs.

Large rookeries of Great Blue Herons and various egrets can be found in the remote areas of the refuge. Herons, egrets, bitterns, and rails all feed in the bottomlands of the refuge.

Warblers, vireos, thrushes, and sparrows flit and feed by the hundreds in spring and fall. Pileated Woodpeckers and Whip-poor-wills can be found in more remote woods. Bald Eagles are winter visitors, gathering below the dams or near tributary mouths.

Area brochure, pool maps (#'s 4 & 5, 5A & 6, Winona District), mammals, reptiles, and amphibians lists. Boating, back-country use, hunting, fishing, camping, picnicking, swimming.
Spring, Summer, Fall

NATIONAL PARK SERVICE

Voyagers National Park 🔳
PO Box 50   218-283-9821
International Falls, MN 56649

281,059 acres include 83,789 acres of various waterways. The interconnected northern lakes, dotted with islands and surrounded by forests, were once the route of French-Canadian fur-traders.

Park brochure with map, 12-page "Rendezvous" newspaper, leaflet covering naturalist-guided activities.

NATIONAL FOREST SERVICE
Map/Forest/City
⚠ Chippewa/Cass Lake   218-335-2226
⚠ Superior/Duluth   218-720-5324

STATE AGENCIES

MN Dept. of Natural Resources
Section of Wildlife
500 Layafette Road
St. Paul, MN 55155   612-296-3344

A "Guide to Minnesota Prairies" is available through the Minnesota Dept. of Natural Resources, Natural Heritage Program. Nine of the TNC Preserves noted in this chapter are among those covered in the guide.

Map/Region/City
1️⃣ Region 1/Bemidji   218-755-3958
2️⃣ Region 2
    /Grand Rapids   218-327-4413
3️⃣ Region 1/Brainard   218-828-2615
4️⃣ Region 2/New Ulm   507-354-2196
5️⃣ Region 1/Rochester   507-285-7435
6️⃣ Region 2/Forest Lake 612-296-5800

MN Office of Tourism
Dept. of Trade & Economic Development
375 Jackson Street, Room 250
St. Paul, MN 55101   800-652-9747
from out-of-state call   800-328-1461

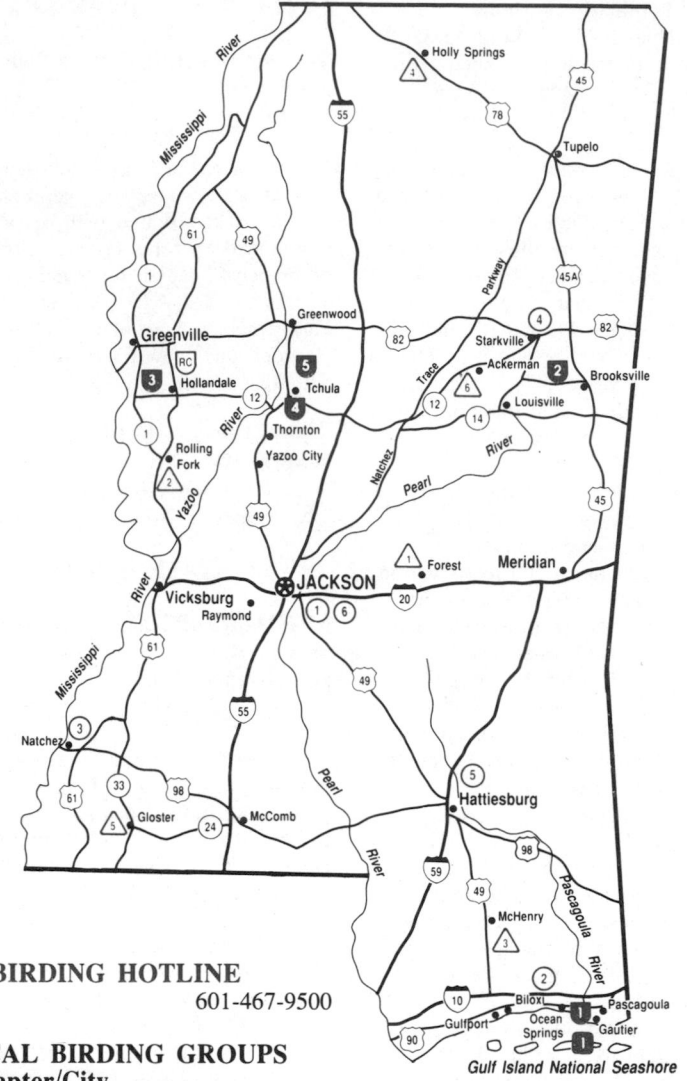

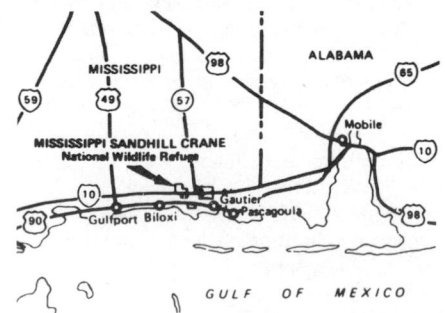

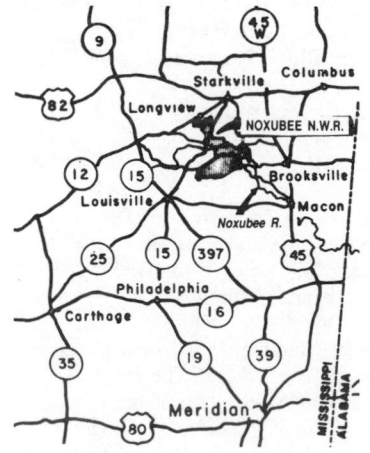

18,000 acres. Planted pine, crop units, meandering creeks, and semi-open wet savanna habitat. Savannas are meadows established in acidic, water-logged soil, unfit for most land use. Due to past commercial and agricultural development, habitat restoration is required, and is underway to provide protection and management of the small remaining crane population.

Bird life is moderately abundant and most diverse during spring and fall migration. Wading birds often visit Bayou Castelle near the refuge headquarters and in other open-water areas. Northern Harriers and Red-tailed Hawks can be seen hunting over the savannas in winter. Warblers and other songbirds frequent roadside trees and shrubby vegetation throughout the area.

Area brochure, foot trails, visitor center. Spring, Summer, Fall, Winter

Noxubee ②   (office at refuge)
Route 1, Box 142
Brooksville, MS 39739   601-323-5548

Bird List MS-2 Noxubee Summary
240 birds listed, no nesting data
Bird Chart pages 276-293

Totals by Season		s	S	F	W
Abundant	A	4	6	6	10
Common	C	69	52	65	49
Uncommon	U	78	40	88	38
Occasional	O	14	5	16	9
Rare	R	23	25	31	37

Endangered Species: Wood Stork, Bald Eagle, Piping Plover, Red-cockaded Woodpecker

About midway between Louisville and Starkville off Hwy. 25, and about 150 miles northeast of Jackson. Take Hwy. 25 and turn east on Louisville Road to the refuge office.

Habitat: 46,278 acres of woodland interspersed with fields, lakes, and

BIRDING HOTLINE
Coast   601-467-9500

LOCAL BIRDING GROUPS
Map/Chapter/City
① Jackson Audubon/Jackson
② Mississippi Coast Audubon/Biloxi
③ Natchez Area Audubon/Natchez
④ Oktibbeha Audubon/Starkville
⑤ Pine Woods Audubon/Hattiesburg
⑥ Mississippi Orn. Soc./Jackson

U.S. FISH & WILDLIFE SERVICE NATIONAL WILDLIFE REFUGES

Mississippi Sandhill Crane ①
7200 Crane Lane   (office at refuge)
Gautier, MS 39553   601-497-6322

Bird List MS-1 Sandhill Summary
158 birds listed, 62 nesting birds
Bird Chart pages 276-293

Totals by Season		s	S	F	W
Abundant	A	8	8	8	16
Common	C	47	36	43	35
Uncommon	U	66	35	59	48
Occasional	O	18	15	17	11
Rare	R	8	1	5	6

Take exit 61 from I-10 onto Gautier-Vancleave Road and go north 0.7 mile to

Crane Lane. Turn right (east) to the refuge office and visitor center.

The Gautier, Ocean Springs, and Fontainebleau refuge units all lie within the limited nesting range of the federally endangered "Mississippi" Sandhill Crane, a subspecies of the more abundant Sandhill Crane.

Habitat: Three separate land units totaling

streams. Pines are predominant along the high ridges, bottomland hardwoods in the river and creek bottoms, and cypress-gum in the lower, seasonally flooded areas.

In spring swallows, warblers, egrets, and herons appear. In the fall and winter months waterfowl congregate by the thousands, and Bald Eagles may be present. Some species, such as the endangered Red-cockaded Woodpecker and the Wild Turkey, are year-round residents.

Area brochure, visitor center, foot trails, fishing, hunting.
Spring, Summer, Fall, Winter

Yazoo Refuge ③ RC
& Refuge Complex (office at refuge)
Route 1, Box 286
Hallandale, MS 38748   601-839-2638

The Hillside, Morgan Brake, Matthew Brake, and Panther Swamp NWRs are managed from the Yazoo Refuge Complex office. Bird list MS-3 is a combined list for all five refuges.

Bird List MS-3 Yazoo Summary
233 birds listed, 75 nesting birds
Bird Chart pages 276-293

Totals by Season		s	S	F	W
Common	C	50	47	47	48
Uncommon	U	90	39	85	50
Occasional	O	47	21	52	39
Rare	R	9	3	14	7

Endangered Species: Wood Stork, Bald Eagle, Least Tern

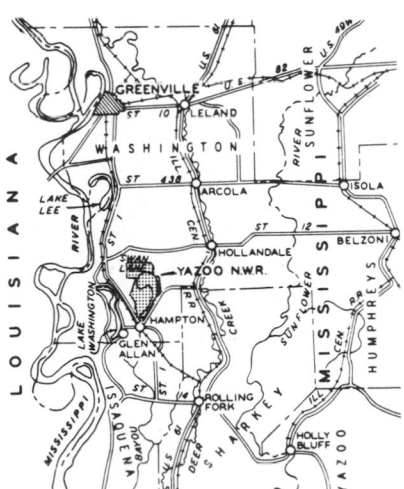

The Yazoo refuge and RC office is between Greenville and Vicksburg, close to the Mississippi River. It may be reached from the east via U.S. Hwy. 61 and St. Hwy. 436, and from the west via St. Hwy. 1. Roadside markers are located on both state highways with directional arrows to headquarters.

Visitors are always welcome, but roads are often impassible during the winter months for all but 4-wheel drive vehicles.

Habitat: 12,470 acres of fields managed for waterfowl and mixed woodlands of cypress, sweet gum, oaks, cottonwoods, pecans, and other trees, amidst impoundments, natural lakes, and bayous.

The first ducks arrive in early fall, and the rapidly growing flocks of waterfowl feed on the various grains that are grown for that purpose. Among the 180 species recorded at Yazoo Refuge alone are five resident species of woodpeckers, several herons and egrets, and the Northern Bobwhite.

Area brochure, auto tour, foot trails, hunting. Bird checklist contains codes for each of the five refuges.
Spring, Fall, Winter

Hillside ④
c/o Yazoo Refuge Complex
Route 1, Box 286
Hallandale, MS 38748   601-839-2638

See Bird List MS-3 and Yazoo Summary.

Take Hwy. 49 East from Yazoo City about 10 miles toward Thornton. Follow the signs to the refuge entrance east of Thornton. The highway borders the refuge boundary on the west from Techeva Creek at the Holmes/Yazoo County line to the Hillside Floodway levee just north of Parker Bayou.

Habitat: 15,383 acres of bottomland habitat. Hardwoods grow in the drier areas, bald cypress and tupelo in the wetter regions, and bottombush, water elm, swamp privet, and willow in the more shallow depressions. The refuge serves as a silt collection sump in the Mississippi-Yazoo River.

Mallards are the dominant waterfowl species in winter, with American Wigeons,

Northern Pintails, Green-winged Teals, and Wood Ducks also common. Many species of shorebirds and other migratory and resident birds can be found.

Area brochure, boating, fishing, hunting.
Spring, Summer, Fall, Winter

Morgan Brake ⑤
c/o Yazoo Refuge Complex
Route 1, Box 286
Hallandale, MS 38748   601-839-2638

See Bird List MS-3 and Yazoo Summary.

A Yazoo refuge satellite located in the Yazoo River Basin of the Mississippi Delta between the loessal hills and U.S. Hwy. 49 East, 14 miles south of Greenwood and 3 miles north of Tochula in Holmes County. The highway both borders and runs through the refuge.

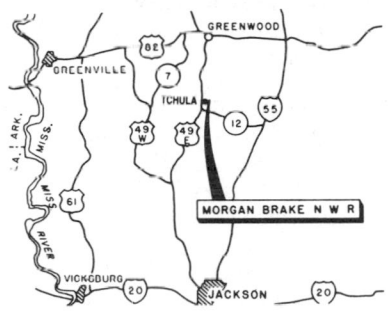

Habitat: 1,330 acres of bottomland hardwood forests with habitat similar to that at Hillside Refuge.

Area brochure, boating, fishing, hunting. A trail system consists of five roads which have been closed to visitors for several years during wet periods.
Spring, Summer, Fall, Winter

NATIONAL PARK SERVICE

Gulf Islands National Seashore ①
3500 Park Road
Ocean Springs, MS 39564   904-932-5302

Bird List MS-4 Gulf Is. Summary
280 birds listed, no nesting data
Bird Chart pages 276-293

Note: This list represents sighting records from the Florida and Mississippi units of Gulf Islands National Seashore.

Totals by Season		s	S	F	W
Common	C	72	54	63	63
Uncommon	U	83	43	85	37
Occasional	O	48	31	53	43
Rare	R	52	26	47	55

Endangered Species: Brown Pelican, Wood Stork, Bald Eagle, Peregrine

Falcon, Piping Plover, Least Tern, Red-cockaded Woodpecker

73,958 acres, including 10,078 land and beach acres. Wildlife sanctuaries on the offshore island unit of the Mississippi portion of this National Seashore are accessible only by boat. On the mainland are an urban park with a nature trail, a picnic area, and a campground at Ocean Springs.

National Seashore brochure with map, 8-page newspaper "The Gulf Islands Barnacle," leaflets on wilderness camping, wildlife viewing and other activities.

NATIONAL FOREST SERVICE
National Forests in Mississippi
Supervisor Office
100 W. Capitol Street
Jackson, MS 39269   601-965-4391

Map/Forest-District/City
△	Bienville-same/Forest	601-469-3811
△	Delta-same	
	/Rolling Fork	601-873-6256
△	De Soto-Biloxi	
	/McHenry	601-928-5291
△	Holly Springs-same	
	/Holly Springs	601-252-2633
△	Homochitto-same	
	/Gloster	601-225-4281
△	Tombigbee-same	
	/Ackerman	601-285-3264

BUREAU LAND MANAGEMENT
BLM Jackson District Office
300 Woodrow Wilson Drive
Suite 326
Jackson, MS 39213   601-965-4405

One of two BLM district offices for the Eastern States. The headquarters office is in Virginia.

STATE AGENCIES

Dept. of Wildlife Conservation
PO Box 451
Jackson, MS 39205   601-961-5300

Mississippi does not have district or regional wildlife conservation offices. Call the above phone number for general information. For specific local information they will refer you to a county conservation officer if necessary (there are 82 counties in Mississippi).

Mississippi Tourism Division
PO Box 22825
Jackson, MS 39205   601-359-3414
Nationwide (outside MS)   800-647-2290

BIRDING HOTLINES
Kansas City   816-795-8177
Statewide   314-445-9115

LOCAL BIRDING GROUPS
Map/Chapter/City
1. Burroughs Audubon/Kansas City
2. Chariton Audubon/Kirkville
3. Columbia Audubon/Columbia
4. East Ozarks Aud./Farmington
5. Four Seasons Aud./Cape Girardeau
6. Grand Gulf Audubon/Tecumseh
7. Greater Ozarks Audubon/Springfield
8. Midland Empire Audubon/Agency
9. Mosage Audubon/Otterville
10. Ozark Gateway Audubon/Webb City
11. Ozark Rivers Audubon/Rolla
12. River Bluffs Audubon/Jefferson City
13. Scenic Rivers Audubon/Poplar Bluff
14. St. Louis Audubon/Florissant
15. Webster Groves Nature Society /St. Louis

THE NATURE CONSERVANCY
Missouri Field Office (FO)
2800 S. Brentwood Blvd.
Saint Louis, MO 63144   314-968-1105

Contact Field Office for preserve details and visitor regulations.

Bennett Spring Savanna 1
160 acres near Long Lane and about 4 to 5 miles south of Bennett Spring State Park on Co. Hwy. 00.

Cook Meadows 2
280 acres near Golden City. From Golden City, go north on Hwy. 160 for 1.7 miles, turn left on Co. Hwy. U, and continue for 1 mile to next road. Turn left, and go 0.5 mile to preserve sign.
Day hiking.

Jamerson C. McCormack 3
Loess Mounds
158 acres near Mound City. Take Co. Hwy. E south of Mound City to Hwy. 159 and turn right. Continue for 1 mile to parking lot and preserve sign on left.
Day hiking, special viewing areas.

Lichen Glade 4
40 acres, approximately 5 miles west of Osceola on Co. Hwy. B.
Day hiking, wildflower areas.

Marmaton River Bottoms 5
Wet Prairie
540 acres near Nevada. Take U.S. Hwy. 71 for 2.5 miles north from Nevada to Co. Road H and turn left. Continue west across Marmaton River for 1.2 miles, and turn left on County Road. Go 1 mile south, turn left (east) for .25 mile along the north section line of section 19 to the northwest corner of the preserve.
Day hiking.

Monegaw Prairie 6
270 acres, approximately 3 miles west of Eldorado Springs on Hwy. 54.
Day hiking.

Shut-In Mountain Fen Preserve 7
540 acres near Eminence. Go east 6 miles from Eminence on Hwy. 106 to its intersection with Co. Hwy. H. Turn right and continue south on Co. Hwy. H for 2 to 3 miles to Shut-In Meadows Road, and turn east for a mile. Park along the road. Day hiking. Wildflower viewing areas (3 fens).

Victor Glade 8
47 acres approximately 2.5-3 miles south of Hillsboro on Victoria Hillsboro Road.
Day hiking, wildflowers.

Zahorsky Woods 9
56 acres northwest of the Steelville City limits on Hwy. 19.
Day hiking, wildflowers.

U.S. FISH & WILDLIFE SERVICE NATIONAL WILDLIFE REFUGES

Annada District 1   (office at refuge)
Clarence Cannon NWR
PO Box 88
Annada, MO 63330   316-847-2333

This district, part of the Mark Twain National Wildlife Refuge headquartered in Illinois, manages three divisions. These are the Clarence Cannon NWR, and the Gardner and Delair Divisions in Illinois.

Bird List MO-1 Annada Summary
222 birds listed, 84 nesting birds
Bird Chart pages 276-293

Totals by Season		s	S	F	W
Abundant	A	4	3	7	3
Common	C	93	65	83	37
Uncommon	U	74	43	59	22
Occasional	O	24	13	24	25
Rare	R	11	7	8	6

Endangered Species: Bald Eagle, Peregrine Falcon, Least Tern

The Annada District Office is on the Clarence Cannon Refuge, which is situated along the west bank of the Mississippi River, 1 mile east of Hwy. 79 and the town of Annada.

Habitat: 3,774 acres of forests, grasslands,

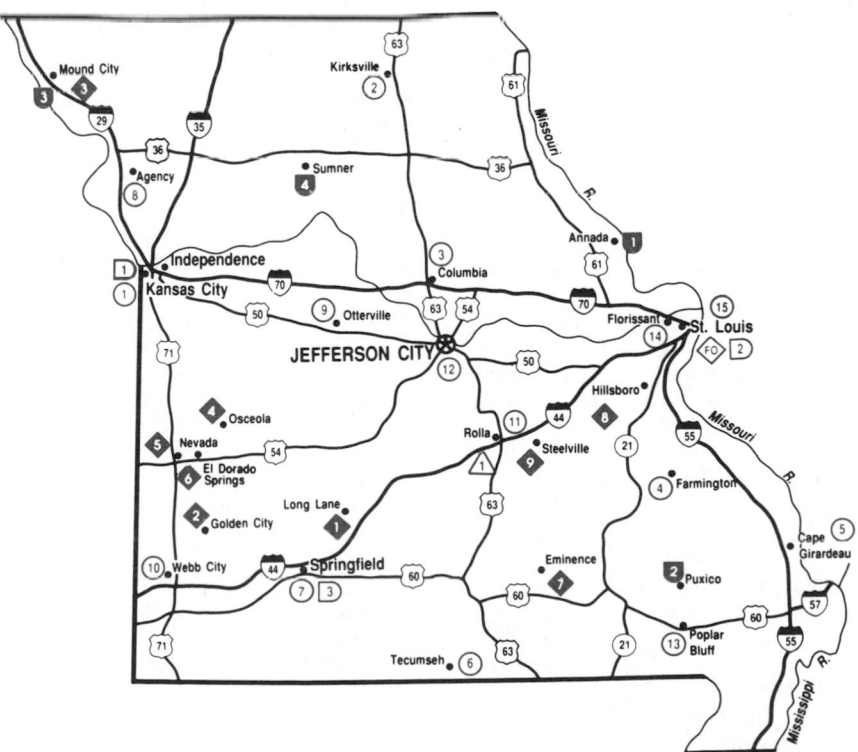

agricultural fields, and permanent and seasonally flooded impoundments in the Mississippi River floodplain.

The refuge wetlands support large populations of a variety of waterbirds. Thousands of waterfowl can be seen during spring and fall as they follow the Mississippi Flyway to and from their breeding grounds in the north. Wood Ducks remain through all but the coldest months, and nest in boxes and trees during early spring. The shorebird migration peaks at the beginning of May. Various wading birds, including bitterns, herons, egrets, and rails, feed in the wetlands during the summer. The warbler migration peaks early in May. Bald Eagles are attracted to the refuge in the fall when they feed on sick or injured waterfowl.

Area brochure, berry, nut, and mushroom picking.
Spring, Fall

Mingo ❷ (office at refuge)
Route 1, Box 103
Puxico, MO 63960   314-222-3589
Entry fee

Bird List MO-2 Mingo Summary
245 birds listed, 108 nesting birds
Bird Chart pages 276-293

Totals by Season		s	S	F	W
Abundant	A	11	8	10	11
Common	C	88	62	56	35
Uncommon	U	84	41	75	35
Rare	R	47	28	42	38

Endangered Species: Bald Eagle, Peregrine Falcon

From Puxico, go 1.5 miles north on Hwy. 51 to the headquarters and visitor center.

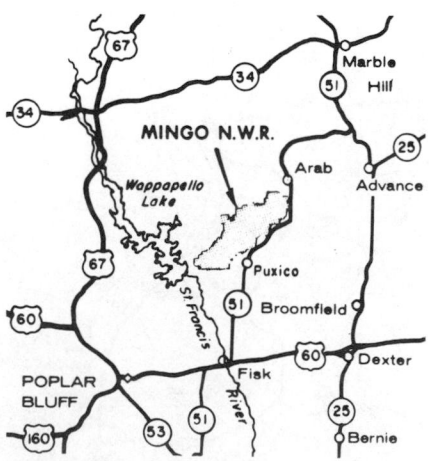

Habitat: 21,676 acres. Refuge lands lie in an ancient channel of the Mississippi River. Approximately 16,000 acres are bottomlands swamp with limestone bluffs

and steep hills on the east and west sides. Much of the area is timbered, with oak the dominant species. There are 700 acres of cropland, while acres of pastures and abandoned fields from pre-refuge farming attempts are in various successional stages of returning to natural habitats.

Ducks number in the hundreds of thousands during spring and fall migrations. Mallards, Northern Pintails, Green-winged Teals, American Wigeons, Gadwalls, and Northern Shovelers are the most common species. Many overwinter in the area and some remain to nest.

Other species that nest on the refuge include Chimney Swift, Ruby-throated Hummingbird, Belted Kingfisher, Eastern Wood-Pewee, and Olive-sided and Acadian flycatchers.

Red-headed, Red-bellied, and Downy woodpeckers are common and nest in the area. Pileated and Hairy woodpeckers may be seen occasionally and have been known to nest at Mingo.

A wide variety of warblers have been seen during the spring and fall migrations with the Nashville, Yellow-rumped, Black-throated Green, Prothonotary, and Kentucky warblers and Northern Parula common to the area.

Area brochure, fishing, limited hunting, canoeing, hiking, picnicking, nature trail, observation blind, observation towers, auto tour route, bicycling, horseback riding, berry and nut picking.
Spring, Summer, Fall

Squaw Creek ❸ (office at refuge)
PO Box 101
Mound City, MO 64470   816-442-3187

Bird List MO-3 Squaw Cr. Summary
268 birds listed, 104 nesting birds
Bird Chart pages 276-293

Totals by Season		s	S	F	W
Abundant	A	11	2	13	4
Common	C	79	52	58	21
Uncommon	U	84	58	79	23
Occasional	O	53	34	56	26
Rare	R	26	33	37	36

Endangered Species: Bald Eagle, Peregrine Falcon, Piping Plover, Least Tern

From Mound City, take I-29 south 4.5 miles to Hwy. 159 (exit 79), then go west on Hwy. 159 to the refuge entrance and headquarters.

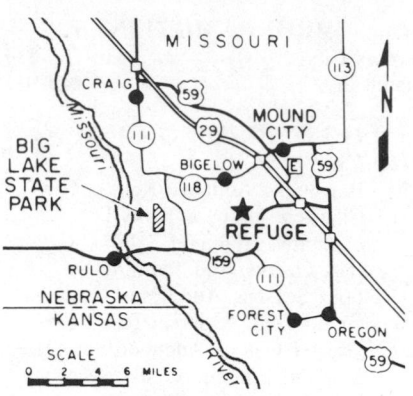

Habitat: 6,919 acres are predominantly marsh with some upland prairie, farmland, and timber.

Various migratory birds stop to rest and feed at the refuge during spring and fall. The spring migration of waterfowl moves through the refuge from February through April and large concentrations of geese and ducks can be found in most years. The fall waterfowl migration begins in October and continues through December. The Snow Goose population may approach 200,000, while 250,000 or more ducks are common.

Passerines move through in April and May, including the warblers, which peak during the first two weeks in May.

Shorebirds can be found on the mudflats from mid-August through mid-September. Up to 300 Bald Eagles, one of the largest concentrations in the U.S.A., can be seen from mid-November until the first of the year.

Area brochure, hiking, auto tour route, observation towers.
Spring, Fall

Swan Lake ❹ (office at refuge)
PO Box 68
Sumner, MO 64681   816-856-3323

Bird List MO-4 Swan Lake Summary
233 birds listed, 85 nesting birds
Bird Chart pages 276-293

Totals by Season		s	S	F	W
Abundant	A	7	2	10	1
Common	C	96	57	76	27
Uncommon	U	82	50	88	27
Occasional	O	28	28	26	16
Rare	R	16	16	20	16

Endangered Species: Bald Eagle, Peregrine Falcon, Piping Plover, Least Tern

From Sumner, go 1 mile south on Swan Lake Drive to the main refuge entrance. The refuge is closed October 16 through February except for special permit hunting.

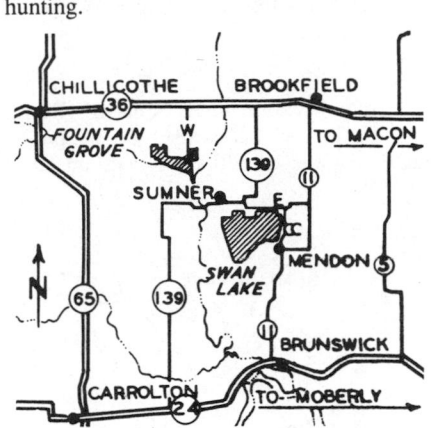

Habitat: 10,670 acres. Approximately half the acreage is covered by shallow lakes, 2,000 acres are cultivated for wildlife, and about 3,500 acres are managed for wild plants for waterfowl. Along Yellow Creek, which forms the southern boundary, there are 1,000 acres of bottomland hardwoods

and oxbow lakes.

The refuge is the primary wintering area for the eastern prairie populations of Canada Geese, whose numbers exceed 100,000 each year.

Bald Eagles arrive shortly after the waterfowl. The area is also on the migration route of large numbers of hawks, with Red-tailed and Broad-winged hawks the most common. Northern Harriers and American Kestrel are also seen in the spring and fall.

Breeding species common from spring through fall include the Belted Kingfisher, Northern Flicker, Red-bellied, Red-headed, and Downy woodpeckers, Eastern Kingbird, Eastern Phoebe, Eastern Wood-Pewee, Tufted Titmouse, House Wren, Brown Thrasher, and Wood Thrush.

Area brochure, auto tour route, hunting,

fishing, hiking, photo blind, observation tower.
Spring, Fall

NATIONAL FOREST SERVICE
Mark Twain National Forest Sup. ⚠
401 Fairgrounds Road
Rolla, MO 65401   314-364-4621

STATE AGENCIES

Missouri Dept. of Conservation
PO Box 180
Jefferson City, MO 65102   314-751-4115

Map/Office-City
1 Kansas City   816-356-2280
2 St. Louis   314-726-6800
3 Springfield   417-864-8224

Missouri Div. of Tourism
Truman State Office Bldg.
PO Box 1055
Jefferson City, MO 65102   314-751-4133

BIRDING HOTLINES

Statewide (Missoula)   406-721-2935
To Report   406-728-1296

LOCAL BIRDING GROUPS
Map/Chapter/City

① Bitterroot Audubon/Hamilton
② Five Valleys Audubon/Missoula
③ Flathead Audubon/Bigfork
④ Last Chance Audubon/Helena
⑤ Pintlar Audubon/Anaconda
⑥ Rosebud Audubon/Miles City
⑦ Sacajawea Audubon/Bozeman
⑧ Upper Missouri Breaks Audubon
    /Great Falls
⑨ Yellowstone Valley Aud./Billings

THE NATURE CONSERVANCY

Montana Field Office ◇
Last Chance Gulch and 6th, PO Box 258
Helena, MT 59624   406-443-0303

Pine Butte Preserve ◆ (office at ranch)

Pine Butte Guest Ranch
HC58 Box 34C
Choteau, MT 59422   406-466-2377

Call for specific directions. Entry prohibited without permission from the preserve manager. Northwest of Choteau, off Hwy. 89.

Habitat: 20,000 acres ranging from 4,500 to 8,580 feet in elevation. Lush wetlands, rolling prairies, alpine meadows, and mature forests display a diverse flora and support the abundant wildlife, including the threatened grizzly bear. Abuts Bob Marshall Wilderness and located along the east front of the Rocky Mountains, 60 miles southeast of Glacier National Park.

At least 130 species of birds nest on the preserve or pass through on migration. During spring migration warblers, Long-billed Curlews, raptors, and songbirds of every description can be observed.

Egg Mountain, a new part of the preserve, is one of the most important "dinosaur digs" in the world. The first discoveries of baby dinosaurs in nests were made at this location.

Picnicking allowed. Ranch accommodates up to 20 guests.
Spring, Summer, Fall

U.S. FISH & WILDLIFE SERVICE NATIONAL WILDLIFE REFUGES

Benton Lake ▯   (office at refuge)

PO Box 450
Black Eagle MT 59414   406-727-7400
Entry fee

Bird List MT-1 Benton Lake Summary
167 birds listed, 59 nesting birds
Bird Chart pages 276-293

Totals by Season		s	S	F	W
Abundant	A	14	13	14	1
Common	C	19	22	21	1
Uncommon	U	42	25	39	5
Occasional	O	58	35	58	7
Rare	R	19	8	18	5

Endangered Species: Bald Eagle, Peregrine Falcon

Refuge is 14 miles north of Great Falls. Take Hwy. 87 north to St. Rte. 225. Bear left onto St. Rte. 225 (called Bootlegger Trail), continue to refuge entrance on left.

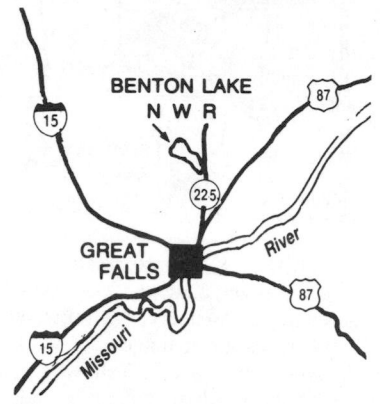

Habitat: 12,383-acre marsh and wetland at 4,150 feet. Over 600 upland acres are planted with small grains to supplement the natural foods. Lake and Muddy Creeks are the main water sources. Outside the refuge an additional 8,000 acres, including 17 Waterfowl Production Areas (WPA's), are administered by the refuge.

The most numerous nesters are Gadwall, Northern Shoveler, Lesser Scaup, Blue-winged Teal, and Canada Goose. Other breeding species include Franklin's Gull, Eared Grebe, and American Coot.

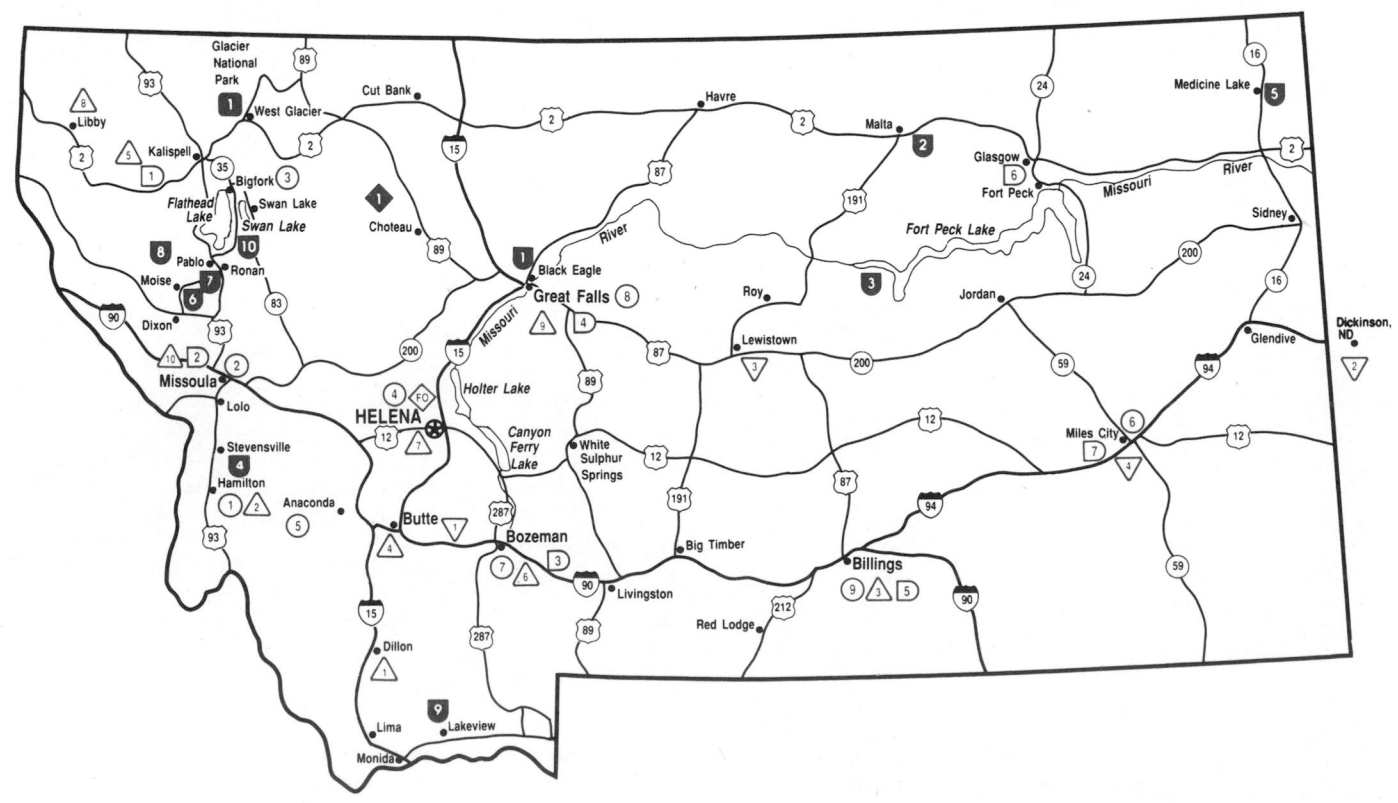

The rolling grassland hosts Horned Lark, Lark Bunting, McCowan's and Chestnut-collared longspurs, and various sparrows. Beginning in early fall hundreds of Swainson's Hawks and Northern Harriers wheel over the refuge.

Area and hunting brochures available, auto tour. A well-known birding spot and state wildlife management area called Freezeout Lake is close by, near Choteau.
Spring, Fall

Bowdoin (office at refuge)
PO Box J
Malta, MT 59538   406-654-2863

Other locations under Bowdoin management: Black Coulee, Creedman Coulee, Hewitt Lake, and Lake Thibadeau. Inquire at refuge office about access to these locations and road conditions.

Bird List MT-2 Bowdoin Summary
206 birds listed, 102 nesting birds
Bird Chart pages 276-293

Totals by Season		s	S	F	W
Abundant	A	31	28	28	4
Common	C	67	48	59	6
Uncommon	U	42	42	35	7
Occasional	O	25	24	22	4
Rare	R	20	22	16	2

Endangered Species: Bald Eagle, Peregrine Falcon, Piping Plover

Take old U.S. Hwy. 2 east from Malta for 7 miles. Refuge sign and office is on right (south) off highway.

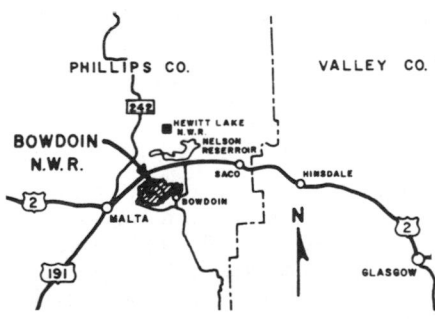

Habitat: 15,437 acres at 4,500 feet with 8,000 acres of marsh and water interspersed with grassy uplands.

Massive flocks of waterfowl are present during late spring and fall. American White Pelicans and California and Ring-billed gulls are among the birds that nest on the islands.

Franklin's Gulls and Black-crowned Night-Herons, young and adult American Coots, Eared Grebes, Soras, and American Bitterns abound. Ring-necked Pheasants,

and Sharp-tailed Grouse are among the few year-round residents.
Area brochure, hunting.
Spring, Fall

Charles M. Russell (CMR) 🟦
PO Box 110   (office in town)
Lewistown, MT 59457   406-538-8706

Bird List MT-3 CM Russell Summary
252 birds listed, 98 nesting birds
Bird Chart pages 276-293

Totals by Season		s	S	F	W
Abundant	A	8	24	7	4
Common	C	7	70	94	16
Uncommon	U	36	39	41	12
Occasional	O	32	21	23	21
Rare	R	40	10	26	8

Endangered Species: Bald Eagle, Peregrine Falcon, Piping Plover
Rare/Limited Species: Ivory Gull

Lewistown is at the junction of Hwys. 191 and 87. One of the access points to the western part of the refuge is via Hwy. 191 north for 67 miles and past the Sand Creek Wildlife Station at Roy.

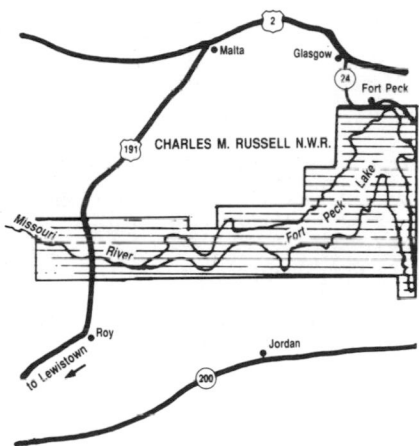

Habitat: CMR is over 100 miles long and contains 1,094,301 acres on both sides of Fort Peck Lake and the Missouri River. Average elevation is 3,600 feet. Gently rolling grasslands slope abruptly to river.

Western Meadowlarks, Vesper Sparrows, Upland Sandpipers, Long-billed Curlews, and Mourning Doves are among the species that breed on the refuge. Mid-April through June is best for birding.

Area brochures, auto tour route, species lists, boating, fishing, hunting, camping, swimming.
Spring, Summer, Fall

Inquire at any of the following CMR offices about local access, conditions, and recreation facilities.

Fort Peck Wildlife Station
PO Box 166
Fort Peck, MT 59223   406-526-3464

Jordan Wildlife Station
PO Box 63
Jordan, MT 59337   406-557-6145

Sand Creek Wildlife Station
PO Box 89
Roy, MT 59471   406-464-5181

Lee Metcalf 🟦   (office in town)
West Third Street, PO Box 257
Stevensville, MT 59870   406-777-5552

Bird List MT-4 Lee Metcalf Summary
206 birds listed, 98 nesting birds
Bird Chart pages 276-293

Totals by Season		s	S	F	W
Abundant	A	12	10	9	2
Common	C	46	36	31	13
Uncommon	U	56	53	55	35
Occasional	O	47	38	38	19
Rare	R	27	10	13	19

Endangered Species: Bald Eagle, Peregrine Falcon

From Hwy. 93 at the Stevensville junction caution light, turn east and continue 2 miles to Stevensville. Signs direct you to the refuge and office as you enter town.

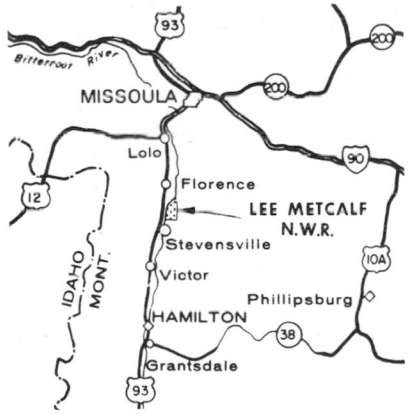

Habitat: 2,700 acres of central valley riverbottom land bordering the Bitterroot River, between the Bitterroot and Sapphire Mountains. Elevation is 3,400 feet.

This is one of the few locations in the U.S.A. where Canada Geese nest in trees. The geese arrive early and use old Osprey nests, dead trees, or platforms, adding their own feathers. The Ospreys often try to drive the geese from these nesting sites during spring and early summer.

Tundra Swans visit briefly in spring. Bald Eagles are common in winter. Northern Harriers and Red-tailed Hawks, and American Kestrels are common in all other seasons.

Area brochure, auto tour, foot trails, hunting, fishing, picnicking. Privately owned Teller Wildlife Refuge close by. Spring, Summer, Fall

Medicine Lake 5 (office at refuge)
HC51, Box 2
Medicine Lake, MT 59247   406-789-2305

Other locations under Medicine Lake management include Lamesteer NWR and 40 wetland management areas containing 9,000 acres in three counties. Inquire at refuge office about access and conditions.

Bird List MT-5 Medicine L. Summary
219 birds listed, 96 nesting birds
Bird Chart pages 276-293

Totals by Season		s	S	F	W
Abundant	A	27	28	16	1
Common	C	42	36	40	5
Uncommon	U	50	30	54	9
Occasional	O	55	30	63	11
Rare	R	27	17	18	6

Endangered Species: Bald Eagle, Peregrine Falcon, Whooping Crane, Piping Plover

Take Hwy. 16 south from town, 1 mile to refuge entrance. Turn left (east) to office.

Habitat: 31,457 acres in two units at 4,700 feet. North unit has 8,700-acre Medicine Lake and 8 other lakes. South unit has 1,280-acre Homestead Lake and adjacent uplands.

Medicine Lake is the site of one of the largest American White Pelican rookeries. During the summer they soar over the refuge. Grebes, Ring-billed and California gulls, Double-crested Cormorants, and Great Blue Herons nest. A quarter of a million waterfowl stopover during spring and fall migrations. The endangered Whooping Crane may visit in spring and fall and thousands of Sandhill Cranes are present in late October.

The prairie grassland is the summer home to Burrowing and Short-eared owls, Lark

Buntings, Baird's and Le Conte's sparrows, Chestnut-collared and McCown's longspurs, and an occasional Sprague's Pipit. In early spring Sharp-tailed Grouse begin their courtship rituals on numerous dancing grounds.

Area, auto tour, and fishing brochures, guide to the waterfowl production areas, hunting, fishing, picnicking.
Spring, Summer, Fall

National Bison Range 6
(office and museum on refuge)
Moise, MT 59824   406-644-2211

Caution - stay in vehicle if bison or other game animals are close.

Ninepipe & Pablo NWR's are managed from the National Bison Range office.

Bird List MT-6 Bison Range Summary
188 birds listed, 79 nesting birds
Bird Chart pages 276-293

Totals by Season		s	S	F	W
Abundant	A	12	14	11	3
Common	C	59	49	45	18
Uncommon	U	30	29	34	18
Occasional	O	45	42	31	21
Rare	R	20	22	18	2

Endangered Species: Bald Eagle, Peregrine Falcon

Take Hwy. 93 (also marked St. Rte. 200) north 37 miles from Missoula. Go left on St. Rte. 200 toward Dixon for 5.7 miles, then north on St. Rte. 212 for 4.7 miles to the refuge entrance on the right.

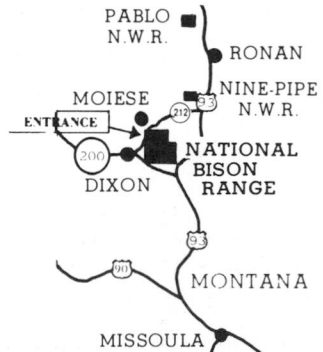

Habitat: Nearly 19,000 acres at an average elevation of 4,500 feet. Grassland and park-like patches of timber with steep hills and narrow canyons Located at the south end of Flathead Valley with Mission Wilderness to the east.

Ring-necked Pheasants, Blue Grouse, and Gray Partridges may be found in the uplands. The Western Tanager and Lazuli Bunting are common nesting species. Teals and other waterfowl feed on

Mission Creek in fall and winter. Golden Eagles are common throughout the year.

Area brochure, mammals list, Big Game Count, Bison Museum, fishing, two-hour auto tour, foot trails, picnic area. Handicapped facility.
Spring, Summer, Fall

Ninepipe 7
c/o National Bison Range
Moise, MT 59827   406-644-2211

Bird List MT-7 Ninepipe Summary
188 birds listed, 74 nesting birds
Bird Chart pages 276-293
(List is for Ninepipe and Pablo NWRs)

Totals by Season		s	S	F	W
Abundant	A	5	4	9	1
Common	C	40	35	27	5
Uncommon	U	51	38	42	21
Occasional	O	61	64	62	28
Rare	R	4	10	5	2

Endangered Species: Bald Eagle, Peregrine Falcon, Least Tern

Ninepipe is located on Hwy. 93 about 5 miles south of Ronan.

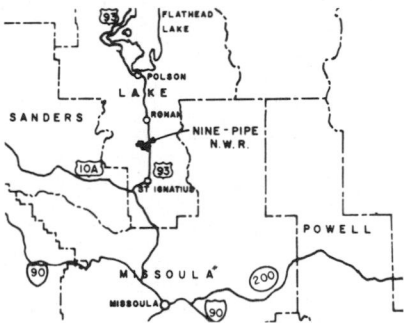

Habitat: 2,000 acres of water, marsh, and upland grasses at 4,400 feet of elevation.

Late March to early May and October through November are best for waterfowl migration. The most numerous nesters are Canada Geese, Mallards, and Redheads. Less common species are Northern Pintail, American Wigeon, Ruddy Duck, Gadwall, Common Merganser, and American Coot.

One area brochure for Ninepipe & Pablo NWR's, fishing.
Spring, Summer, Fall.

Note: These are Tribal Lands operated by the U.S. Fish & Wildlife Service under agreement with Confederated Salish & Kootenai Tribes and Bureau of Indian Affairs Flathead Irrigation Project.

Pablo 8
c/o National Bison Range
Moise, MT 59824   406-644-2211

See Bird List MT-7 Ninepipe Summary on page 116.

Located 15 miles northwest of the Ninepipe NWR. Take Hwy. 93 north from Ronan 5 miles to Pablo. Follow signs west to refuge.

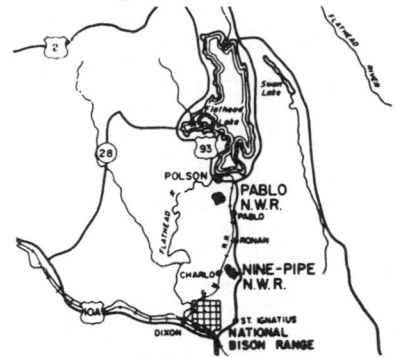

Habitat: 2,500 acres of water, marsh, and upland grasses at 4,600 feet.

See Nincpipc/Pablo NWR brochurc.
Spring, Summer, Fall

Red Rock Lakes 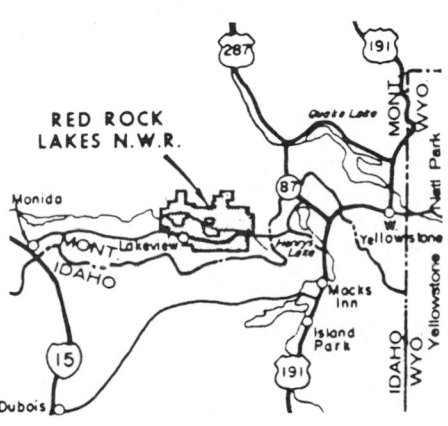(office at Lakeview)
Monida Star Route, Box 15
Lima, MT 59739   406-276-3347

Bird List MT-8 Red Rock Summary
203 birds listed, 152 nesting birds
Bird Chart pages 294-311

Totals by Season		s	S	F	W
Abundant	A	7	6	8	1
Common	C	86	91	62	16
Uncommon	U	45	48	53	14
Occasional	O	41	43	32	21
Rare	R	2	2	2	0

Endangered Species: Bald Eagle, Peregrine Falcon

From I-15 at Monida drive east 28 miles on dirt road to refuge office at Lakeview. Road generally open from May to November. Phone ahead or inquire locally about road conditions.

Habitat: 40,300 acres at 6,100 feet elevation include 14,000 acres of lakes and flat marshland which merges into the foothills of the Gravelly Range to the north.

"Greater" Sandhill Cranes as well as 18 species of waterfowl including Barrow's Goldeneye raise their young here.

Great Blue Herons, Willets, American Avocets, Long-billed Curlews, and Black Terns nest on the refuge. The timbered slopes and aspen stands attract Blue and Ruffed grouse, raptors, and many songbirds. Brewer's Sparrows are common in the sagebrush during spring and summer.

Area brochure, recreation guide, Trumpeter Swan brochure and species list. Fishing, hunting, picnicking, camping.
Spring, Summer, Fall

Swan River 🔟   (office in town)
c/o Northwest Montana WMD
700 Creston Hatchery Road
Kalispell, MT 59739   406-755-7870

Bird List MT-9 Swan River Summary
170 birds listcd, 78 ncsting birds
Bird Chart pages 294-311

Totals by Season		s	S	F	W
Common	C	44	54	24	10
Uncommon	U	60	59	60	25
Occasional	O	52	27	29	23
Rare	R	7	5	3	7

Endangered Species: Bald Eagle

Refuge is located 38 miles southeast of Kalispell on the west side of St. Rte. 83 and at the south end of Swan Lake.

Habitat: 1,568-acre marsh at 3,000 feet elevation. A canoe trip through the refuge on the Swan River is excellent for birding throughout the spring, summer, and fall.

Bald Eagles, Great Blue Herons, Black Terns, and various waterfowl, raptors, and songbirds all nest at Swan River. Canada Geese, Tundra Swans, Mallards, and Barrow's and Common Goldeneyes winter in the open waters, canals, and creeks.

Fishing, boating.
Spring, Summer, Fall

NATIONAL PARK SERVICE

Glacier National Park 🔟
West Glacier, MT 59936   406-888-5441

Bird List MT-10 Glacier Summary
223 birds listed, 124 nesting birds
Bird Chart pages 294-311

Totals by Season		s	S	F	W
Abundant	A	10	10	8	4
Common	C	95	92	61	28
Uncommon	U	54	46	53	21
Rare	R	44	35	25	26

Endangered Species: Bale Eagle, Peregrine Falcon

1,013,572 acres. Dramatic peaks range above 10,000 feet and the park includes glaciers, lakes and streams, and a wide variety of wildflowers and wildlife. The breeding species includes six species of owls and eight woodpeckers.
Park brochure with map, mammals checklist. A park newspaper describes seasonal activities. Going-To-The-Sun Highway through the park is usually open June to late October.

NATIONAL FOREST SERVICE
National Forest Service Northern Region
200 East Broadway, PO Box 7669
Missoula, MT 59801   406-329-3511

Map/Forest/City

⚠	Beaverhead/Dillon	406-683-3900
⚠	Bitterroot/Hamilton	406-363-3131
⚠	Custer/Billings	406-657-6361
⚠	Deerlodge/Butte	406-496-3400
⚠	Flathead/Kalispell	406-755-5401
⚠	Gallatin/Bozeman	406-587-8702
⚠	Helena/Helena	406-449-5201
⚠	Kootenai/Libby	406-293-6211
⚠	Lewis & Clark	
	/Great Falls	406-727-0901
⚠	Lolo/Missoula	406-329-3750

BUREAU LAND MANAGEMENT
BLM State Office
222 N. 32nd Street, PO Box 36800
Billings, MT 59107   406-657-6561

Map/District/City

▽	Butte/Butte	406-494-5059
▽	Dickson/Dickson, ND	701-225-9148
▽	Lewistown/Lewistown	406-538-7461
▽	Miles City/Miles City	406-232-4331

STATE AGENCIES

Dept. of Fish, Wildlife & Parks
1420 E. Sixth Street
Helena, MT 59620   406-444-2535

Map/Region/City

1	Kalispell/Kalispell	406-752-5501
2	Missoula/Missoula	406-542-5500
3	Bozeman/Bozeman	406-586-5419
4	Great Falls/Great Falls	406-454-3441
5	Billings/Billings	406-252-4654
6	Glasgow/Glasgow	406-228-9347
7	Miles City/Miles City	406-232-4365

Tourist Information   406-444-2654
1424 9th Ave.   out-of-state 800-541-1447
Helena, MT 59620

BIRDING HOTLINE

5p.m.–8a.m.   402-453-0724

LOCAL BIRDING GROUPS
Map/Chapter/City

① Audubon Soc. of Omaha/Omaha
② Big Bend Audubon/Kearney
③ Grand Island Audubon/Grand Island
④ N.E. Nebraska Audubon/Wayne
⑤ Omaha Audubon/Omaha
⑥ Prairie Audubon/Hastings
⑦ Wachiska Audubon/Lincoln
⑧ Wildcat Audubon/Gering
⑨ Audubon Naturalists' Club/Lincoln
⑩ Nebraska Orn. Union/Lincoln
⑪ Tout Bird Club/North Platte

THE NATURE CONSERVANCY

Nebraska Field Office ⬖
LeDioyt Landmark
1001 Farnam-on-the-Mall
Omaha, NE 68102

Niobrara Valley ◆
Niobrara Valley Preserve Manager
Route 1
Johnstown, NE 69214   402-722-4440

From Valentine, take Hwy. 12 east to Norden. Take the gravel road south 8 miles from Norden toward Johnstown. Cross the Niobrara River Bridge and go .25 miles where there is a mailbox at the preserve headquarters driveway.

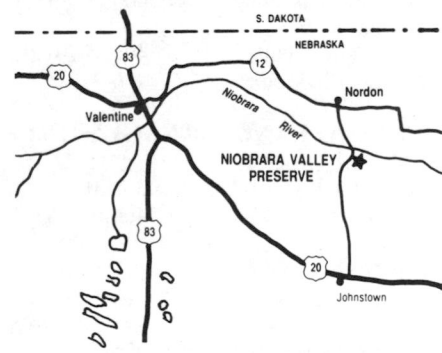

Habitat: 51,000 acres where the northern boreal, eastern deciduous, and Rocky

Mountain pine forests meet the prairies. This ia a resting site for migrating Bald Eagles and Whooping Cranes. Mule deer, antelope, pronghorn sheep, and Wild Turkey, are among the species that live in the Niobrara Valley.

SPECIAL BIRDING AREA

The Platte River between Grand Island and Lexington, and from North Platte to Sutherland.

Hundreds of thousands of Sandhill Cranes stage in mid-to-late March along an 80-mile stretch of the Platte River between Grand Island and Lexington, and a 20-mile stretch between North Platte and Sutherland. The city of Grand Island celebrates "Wings Over The Platte" each year with the cooperation of the USFWS and the Nebraska Game & Parks Commission. There are daily educational programs and bus tours to view the cranes along the river during the peak of their stopover.

U.S. FISH & WILDLIFE SERVICE NATIONAL WILDLIFE REFUGES

Crescent Lake ⓤ
HC 68, Box 21
Ellsworth, NE 69340   308-762-4893

Bird List NE-1 Crescent L. Summary
233 birds listed, 83 nesting birds
Bird Chart pages 294-311

Totals by Season		s	S	F	W
Abundant	A	14	10	10	1
Common	C	52	39	46	5
Uncommon	U	59	45	55	6
Occasional	O	50	51	44	37
Rare	R	49	29	51	8

Endangered Species: Bald Eagle, Peregrine Falcon

The refuge and office are reached by taking the dirt road leading north from

Oshkosh, the last place where food and lodging are available. Few sandhill roads are surfaced and, while travel with almost any vehicle is possible over the better roads, the side trails are most safely traveled with high 4-wheel-drive trucks.

Habitat: 45,818 acres of hilly native grassland, freshwater marshes and lakes, a few tree groves, and brush. Located in the 12-million-acre Nebraska Sandhills.

The Sharp-tailed Grouse do their courtship dance in mid-April, as American White Pelicans, Wilson's Phalaropes, and other marsh and water birds arrive, followed shortly thereafter by the warblers. The peak spring songbird migration occurs during mid-May. Many species of waterfowl use the refuge during migration, primarily Canada and Snow geese, Mallards, Northern Pintails, Gadwalls, Northern Shovelers, Canvasbacks, Redheads, Common Goldeneyes, American Wigeons, mergansers, and scaups. During the nesting season Mallards, Blue-winged Teals, and Ruddy Ducks predominate. Eared Grebes may be seen on their floating nests on Smith and Deer lakes during the early summer, while Double-crested Cormorants nest on Goose Lake.

Ring-necked Pheasants and Long-billed Curlews are common on the uplands. Upland Sandpipers are often seen on fence posts. Great Horned and Burrowing owls, Golden and Bald eagles are also present.

Many small passerines are attracted to the groves that have been planted on the refuge. Some of the more common birds are Eastern and Western kingbirds, Blue Jay, Brown Thrasher, Mountain and Eastern bluebirds, Yellow-rumped Warbler, American Redstart, Rufous-sided Towhee, and White-crowned Sparrow. Both meadowlarks can be seen in late April or early May.

Teals begin to arrive in August. The peak of the fall waterfowl migration occurs in November. Golden Eagles and Northern Harriers are among the hawks present

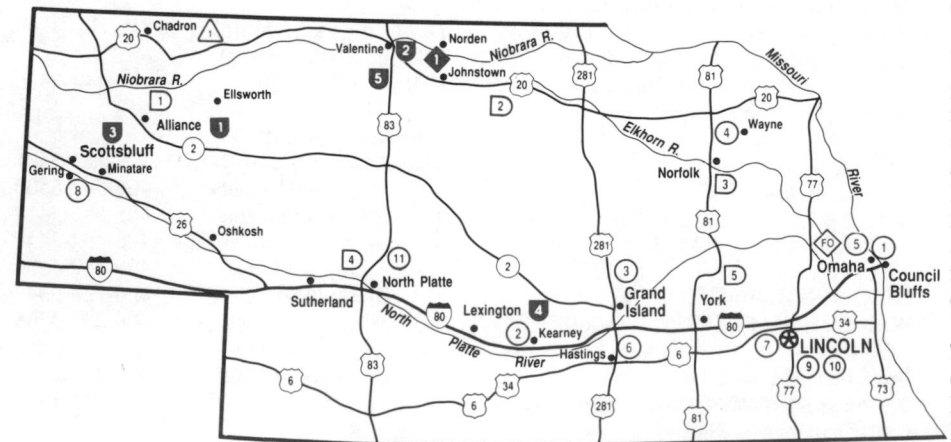

during the winter.

Area brochure, 1.5-mile nature trail, auto tour route, photo blind, fishing, hunting. Spring and Fall best.

Fort Niobrara ❷
Hidden Timber Route
HC 14, Box 67
Valentine, NE 69201   402-376-3789

This is the office for the Fort Niobrara/Valentine Refuge Complex. Valentine NWR is listed separately.

Bird List NE-2 Ft. Niobrara Summary
201 birds listed, 76 nesting birds
Bird Chart pages 294-311

Totals by Season		s	S	F	W
Abundant	A	9	8	8	2
Common	C	62	57	59	12
Uncommon	U	78	53	78	21
Occasional	O	26	22	28	5
Rare	R	14	7	12	3

Endangered Species: Bald Eagle, Peregrine Falcon, Piping Plover

Take Hwy. 12 east of Valentine for approximately 5 miles to the refuge entrance sign. A visitor center is located on the refuge. Headquarters is 1 mile past the entrance on Hwy. 12.

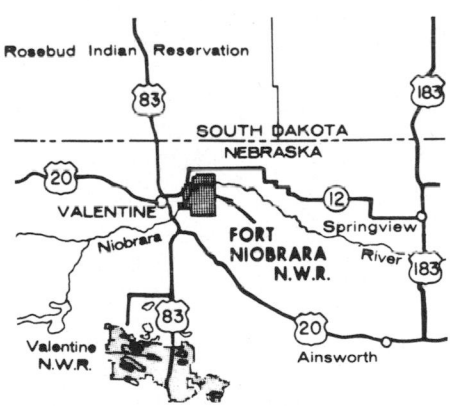

Habitat: 19,122 acres along the Niobrara River Canyon. Approximately two-thirds of the refuge, including lands south and east of the Niobrara River, are sandhills prairie. Mixed hardwoods line the river throughout the length of the refuge.

The refuge is managed primarily for buffalos, elks, and Texas longhorns.

The grasslands provide nesting habitat for many species. Sharp-tailed Grouse and Greater Prairie Chickens gather in the spring for elaborate courtship displays. During the summer, Horned Larks, Upland Sandpipers, Long-billed Curlews, and a variety of sparrows and buntings can be

found.

Other passerines depend on the riparian woodlands for food, shelter, and nesting habitat, while waterbirds flock to the sandbars during the spring and fall migrations.

Bald and Golden eagles are frequently seen during the winter months.

Area brochure, auto tour route, hiking, canoeing, picnicking.
Spring, Summer, Fall

North Platte ❸
c/o Crescent Lake NWR
HC 68, Box 21
Ellsworth, NE 69340   308-762-4893

To reach North Platte NWR from Minatare, take the county road straight north for about 6 miles to the lower end of the refuge. From Scottsbluff, take Hwy. 71 north for approximately 3 miles and then go east on the county road for 5 miles.

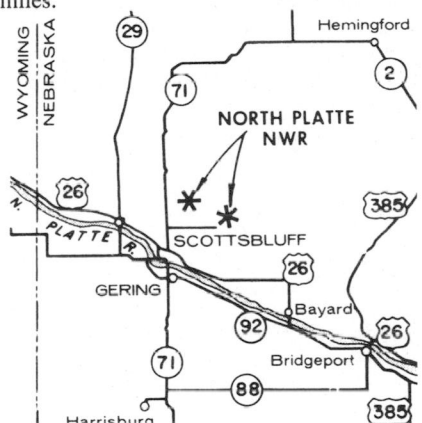

Habitat: 5,047 acres. The North Platte NWR is superimposed over four irrigation reservoirs: Lake Minatare, Lake Winters Creek, Little Lake Alice, and Lake Alice.

Large numbers of waterfowl utilize the refuge during migration, along with various shorebirds and songbirds. Wintering populations vary widely depending on the availability of open water.

Area brochure, hiking, bicycling, horseback riding, picnicking, fishing, canoeing and rowboating. Closed to provide sanctuary to waterfowl from October 1 to January 15. Public use of the refuge when it is open is often heavy. Spring and September best.

Rainwater Basin WMD ❹
U.S. Fish & Wildlife Service
PO Box 1786
Kearney, NE 68847   308-236-5015

Bird List NE-3 Rainwater Summary
256 birds listed, 102 nesting birds
Bird Chart pages 294-311

Totals by Season		s	S	F	W
Abundant	A	28	9	24	6
Common	C	1	58	98	22
Uncommon	U	67	35	61	27
Occasional	O	25	15	18	22
Rare	R	22	9	10	10

Endangered Species: Bald Eagle, Peregrine Falcon, Whooping Crane, Least Tern

The Rainwater Basin area of south central Nebraska encompasses approximately 4,200 square miles and lies within the counties of Gosper, Phelps, Kearney, Harlan, Franklin, Adams, Hamilton, Clay, Polk, Butler, York, Seward, Fillmore, Saline, Nuckolls, and Thayer.

Habitat: Agricultural fields, irregularly distributed grasslands, freshwater wetlands, and riparian habitats along drainages and creek bottoms on flat or somewhat rolling loess plains.

The USFWS manages 40 Waterfowl Production Areas and a 16,000-acre refuge for the abundant waterfowl that use the Rainwater Basin during their spring and fall migrations. Late March and early April generally show the highest concentrations of ducks and geese.

A map showing the 40 production areas is available from the WMD office. Their bird checklist includes a list of best birding locations in all counties within the wetlands management area.
Spring, Fall

Valentine ❺
c/o Hidden Timber Route
HC 14, Box 67
Valentine, NE 69201   402-376-3789

Bird List NE-4 Valentine Summary
233 birds listed, 95 nesting birds
Bird Chart pages 294-311

Totals by Season		s	S	F	W
Abundant	A	12	11	11	3
Common	C	55	53	55	5
Uncommon	U	32	14	30	12
Occasional	O	66	41	69	23
Rare	R	57	24	57	15

Endangered Species: Bald Eagle, Peregrine Falcon, Whooping Crane, Piping Plover, Least Tern

Take Hwy. 83 south from Valentine for 14 miles and turn west on St. Spur 16B to a refuge sub-office. Hwy. 83 crosses the refuge south of its intersection with St. Spur 16B.

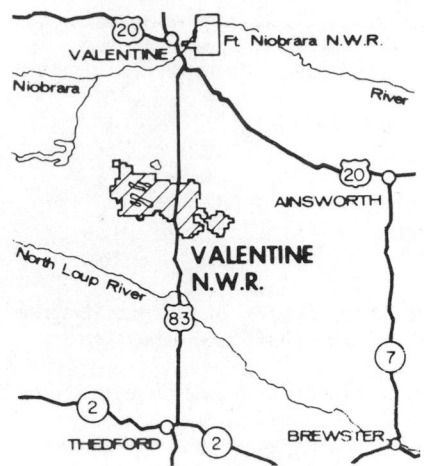

Habitat: 71,516 acres, of which approximately 48,000 are grassy sandhills, 12,000 are meadows, and 11,516 are covered by 36 natural lakes and numerous potholes. Located along an ecological transition zone, where species of eastern and western North America intermingle.

Valentine's central location draws a large variety of species from east and west to its fields and waters, including Eastern and Western meadowlarks, which are both common breeders.

The most abundant nesting waterfowl are Blue-winged Teals, Mallards, Northern Pintails, Gadwalls, Redheads, Ruddy Ducks, and Northern Shovelers. The rare Trumpeter Swan has successfully bred on the lakeshores. Other waterfowl, including Green-winged Teals and Lesser Scaups, are common migrants whose numbers peak in May and again in late October or early November.

Long-billed Curlews and breeding Upland Sandpipers can be found in the hills and seen on fence posts. Shorebirds, which are early fall migrants, are most abundant in September. The male Wilson's Phalarope, like all phalaropes, incubates the eggs and watches the young while his more colorful mate does the courting.

Greater Prairie Chickens and Sharp-tailed Grouse gather on dancing grounds. Sandhill Cranes fly through the refuge in large numbers during the spring and fall. Bald and Golden eagles are chased into the area by cold weather and winter storms but fly back to their northern breeding grounds in May after the spring thaw.

Area brochure, photo blind, hiking, fishing, hunting.
Spring, Fall

NATIONAL FOREST SERVICE
Nebraska National Forest Supervisor △
270 Pine Street
Chadron, NE 69337   308-432-3367

STATE AGENCIES

Nebraska Game & Parks Comm.
2200 N. 33rd Street
PO Box 30370
Lincoln, NE 68503   402-464-0641

Map/District
①	Alliance	308-762-5605
②	Bassett	402-684-3511
③	Norfolk	402-371-4950
④	North Platte	308-532-6225
⑤	York	402-362-5707

Nebraska Div. of Travel & Tourism
Lincoln, NE 68509   800-742-7595
from out-of-state call   800-228-4307

LOCAL BIRDING GROUPS
Map/Chapter/City
① Lahontan Audubon/Reno
② Red Rock Audubon/Las Vegas

U.S. FISH & WILDLIFE SERVICE NATIONAL WILDLIFE REFUGES

Desert NWR & Refuge Group ❶
1500 N. Decatur Blvd.   (office in town)
Las Vegas, NV 89108   702-646-3401

The Desert NWR & Refuge Group office manages three other refuge areas: Amargosa Pupfish Station, Ash Meadows, and Moapa Valley. They also jointly manage Pahranagat NWR. Inquire at Las Vegas office for visitor details and any refuge permits required.

Bird List NV-1 Desert Summary
243 birds listed, 118 nesting birds
Bird Chart pages 294-311

Totals by Season		s	S	F	W
Common	C	49	54	46	33
Uncommon	U	64	38	64	22
Occasional	O	86	47	82	44
Rare	R	26	22	26	20

Endangered Species: Bald Eagle, Peregrine Falcon
Rare/Limited Species: Grace's Warbler

From I-15 take U.S. 95 west to Decatur Blvd. exit. Turn north to refuge office on right.

For refuge access, take U.S. 95 northwest for 22 miles. A sign on the east side of U.S. 95 marks the 4-mile gravel road to Corn Creek Field Station (a refuge sub-office).

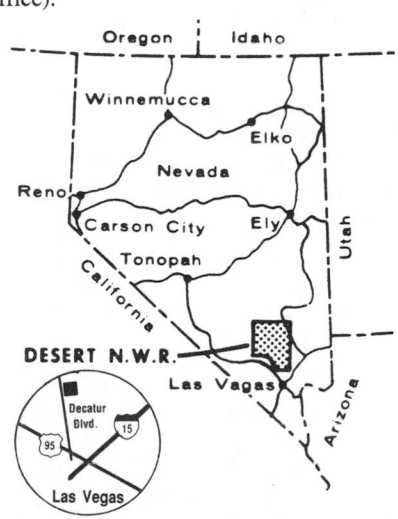

Habitat: Over 1.5 million acres of Mojave Desert, ranging from 2,500 to nearly 10,000 feet in elevation, demonstrate five different life zones: creosote brush and salt brush, yucca and Joshua tree, pinyon

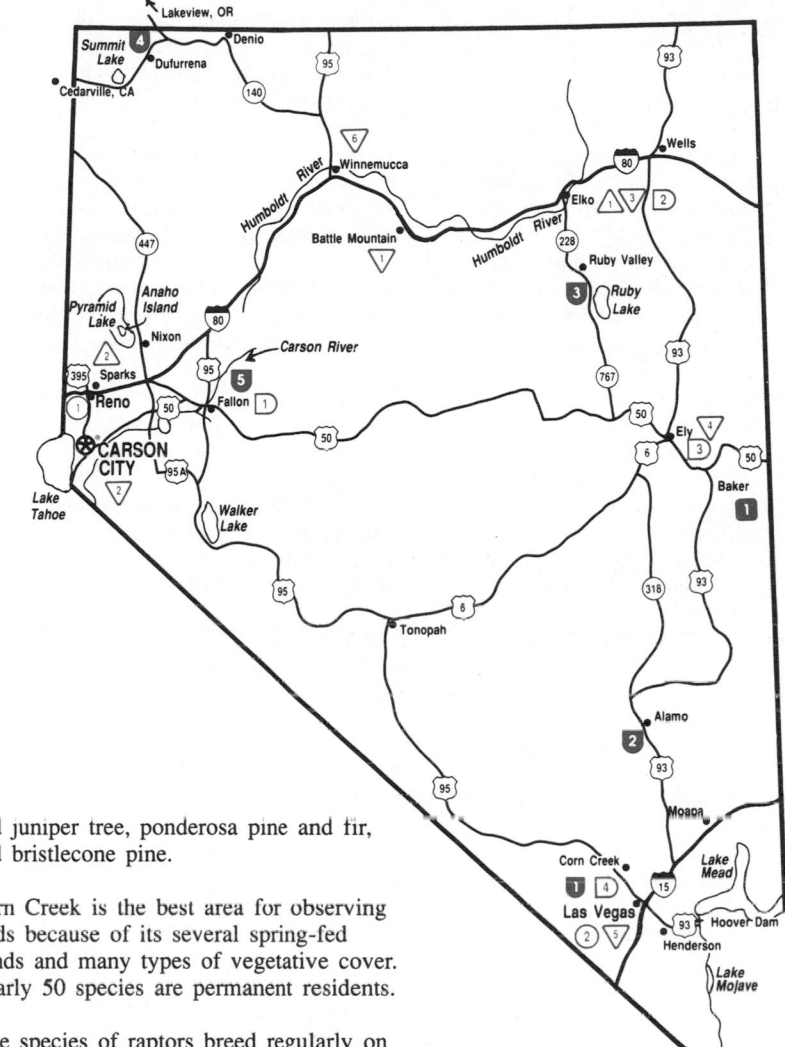

and juniper tree, ponderosa pine and fir, and bristlecone pine.

Corn Creek is the best area for observing birds because of its several spring-fed ponds and many types of vegetative cover. Nearly 50 species are permanent residents.

Five species of raptors breed regularly on the refuge. Cooper's and Sharp-shinned hawks are numerous in the wooded regions while Red-tailed Hawks fly over the open country in search of prey. Golden Eagles and Swainson's hawks also nest at the Desert NWR, although they are most commonly seen during the spring migration.

Area brochure, mammals, amphibians, and reptiles lists, camping, picnicking, trails. Spring, Fall

Pahranagat ❷   (office at refuge)
Highway 93, PO Box 445
Alamo, NV 89001   702-725-3417

Bird List NV-2 Pahranagat Summary
186 birds listed, 42 nesting birds
Bird Chart pages 294-311

Totals by Season		s	S	F	W
Common	C	49	36	49	24
Uncommon	U	60	22	60	23
Occasional	O	65	27	63	40
Rare	R	7	3	5	6

Endangered Species: Bald Eagle, Peregrine Falcon

From I-15 northeast of Las Vegas take U.S. Hwy. 93 north to refuge on west side of highway (94 miles from Las Vegas and 4 miles south of Alamo).

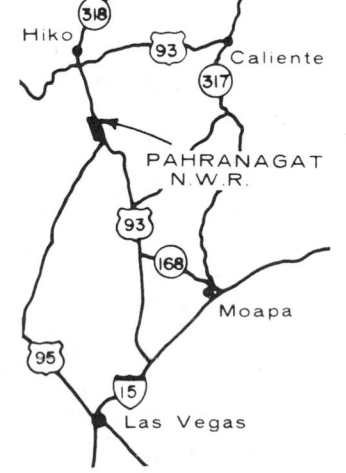

Habitat: 5,380 acres of marsh, open water, native grass meadow, and cultivated croplands at 4,900 feet. Includes North

Marsh, Upper Lake, Middle Pond, and Lower Lake.

Pahranagat's meadows and waters attract the largest concentrations of waterfowl and shorebirds during spring and fall migrations. Green-winged and Cinnamon teals and Mallards are common breeders, while Blue-winged teals, Canvasbacks, and Redheads stopover on their migrations. Great Blue Herons and egrets are found along the shore. Red-tailed Hawks nest at Pahranagat, while Northern Harriers breed elsewhere but can be found at the refuge throughout the year.

Warblers, orioles, finches, and sparrows inhabit the cottonwoods bordering North Marsh and Upper Lake. The cultivated and open fields attract Western Meadowlarks, Killdeer, and Yellow-headed Blackbirds. The upland desert provides habitat for Gambel's Quails, Greater Roadrunners, and a variety of sparrows.

Area brochure, fishing, hunting, camping, picnicking. Non-motorized or electric-motor boating permitted, but no boat ramp available.
Spring, Fall, Winter

Ruby Lake 3 (office at refuge)
Ruby Valley, NV 89833   702-779-2237

Bird List NV-3 Ruby Lake Summary
206 birds listed, 136 nesting birds
Bird Chart pages 294-311

Totals by Season		s	S	F	W
Abundant	A	11	15	15	0
Common	C	65	62	54	25
Uncommon	U	58	63	70	24
Occasional	O	36	23	29	19
Rare	R	16	12	16	11

Endangered Species: Bald Eagle, Peregrine Falcon

About 63 miles southeast of Elko. Office is on west side of St. Rte. 767 at refuge entrance.

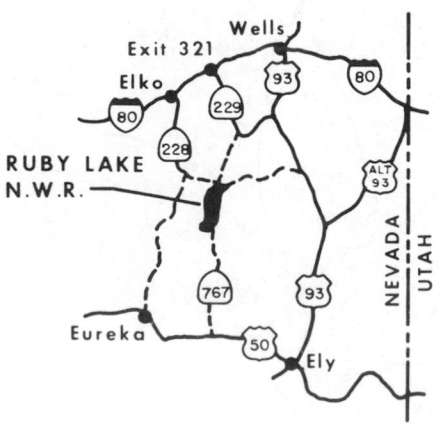

Habitat: 37,632 acres, at an elevation of 5,100 feet, of marsh, lake, and sagebrush along the eastern flank of the Ruby Mountains.

Several pairs of Trumpeter Swans nest each year at Ruby Lake, which is also an important nesting site for Redheads and Canvasbacks. Other breeding waterbirds at Ruby Lake include American Coots, grebes, Sandhill Cranes, Great Blue Herons, Black-crowned Night-Herons, White-faced Ibises, and Snowy Egrets.

Peregrine Falcons, Bald and Golden eagles, and other raptors, are present at various times.

Area, hunting, and fishing brochures, boating. A BLM campground is adjacent to the refuge.
Spring, Summer, Fall

Sheldon 4 (office in town)
U.S. Post Office Building
Room 308
Lakeview, OR 97630   503-947-3315

This refuge is part of Sheldon/Hart Mountain refuge complex, which has its main office in Oregon.

Bird List NV-4 Sheldon Summary
179 birds listed, 86 nesting birds
Bird Chart pages 294-311

Totals by Season		s	S	F	W
Abundant	A	1	8	1	0
Common	C	30	36	33	8
Uncommon	U	75	35	60	15
Occasional	O	54	51	50	35
Rare	R	8	4	8	0

Endangered Species: Bald Eagle, Peregrine Falcon

The refuge is located in Nevada, about 45 miles northeast of Cedarville, California, and 75 miles southeast of Lakeview, Oregon. Hwy. 140 bisects the refuge. Some refuge personnel are stationed at Dufurrena, a refuge subheadquarters on Hwy. 140, about 30 miles west of Denio.

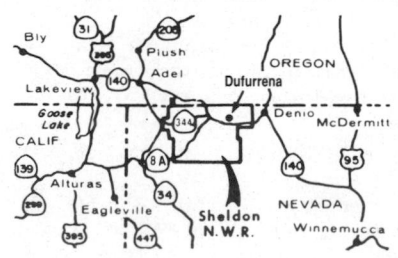

Habitat: 575,000 acres ranging from 4,500 to 7,600 feet in elevation. High semi-

desert with large tablelands and rolling hills, interrupted by narrow valleys and canyons, occasional reservoirs, and creeks.

Mountain mahogany and bitterbush in the mountains. Sagebrush, alkaline lakes, marshes, grassy spring-fed meadows, greasewood flats, juniper-covered uplands, and aspen stands in secluded canyons.

The bird migrations are heavy in spring and fall. Numerous passerines and raptors remain at Sheldon throughout the summer, attracted by the cliffs and riparian areas. The birding is best from May to October.

Area brochure and map, wildlife list, fishing, hunting, camping, picnicking.
Spring, Summer, Fall

Stillwater 5
(office at Municipal Airport)
1510 Rio Vista Road, Box 1236
Fallon, NV 89406   702-423-5128

The Stillwater NWR office manages Fallon and Anaho Island NWRs.

Note: Stillwater NWR is part of the Western Hemisphere Shorebird Reserve Network and has been identified as having in excess of 300,000 shorebirds.

Bird List NV-5 Stillwater Summary
152 birds listed, 72 nesting birds
Bird Chart pages 294-311

Totals by Season		s	S	F	W
Abundant	A	15	18	19	4
Common	C	37	29	28	17
Uncommon	U	43	29	41	28
Occasional	O	37	27	31	33
Rare	R	16	11	17	17

Endangered Species: Bald Eagle

From Fallon go about 5 miles east on U.S. Hwy. 50. Turn left (east) on Stillwater Road where U.S. Hwy. 50 turns south, and continue for 13 miles to the refuge.

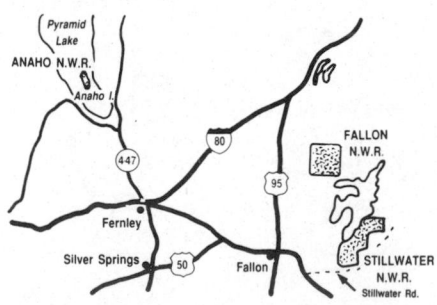

Habitat: 163,000 acres including 24,203-acre Stillwater Wildlife Management Area, 17,902-acre Fallon, and 248-acre Anaho Island NWR. Marsh, ponds, lakes, and dry alkaline desert at an elevation of 6,000 feet.

In years of sufficient water, the wintering waterfowl population peaks at 200,000 ducks, 6,000 geese, and 8,000 Tundra Swans. Common breeding ducks include Cinnamon Teals, Redheads, Gadwalls, Ruddy Ducks, Northern Shovelers, Mallards, and Northern Pintails.

Black-necked Stilts, Snowy Plovers, Long-billed Curlews, and Wilson's Phalaropes are common nesting shorebirds that remain at Stillwater from early spring through late fall.

Anaho Island, one of the few nesting sites of American White Pelicans in western North America, has a colony of up to 9,500 pelicans. Caspian Terns also nest on the island. Therefore, boating is restricted and boats are not allowed within 500 feet of the island, which is off-limits.

Stillwater and Anaho NWR brochures, species lists, boating, fishing, hunting, camping, picnicking, swimming. Spring, Summer, Fall

NATIONAL PARK SERVICE

Great Basin National Park ❶
Baker, NV 89311   702-234-7331

77,109 acres of habitats ranging from Sonoran sagebrush to Arctic alpine tundra. A remnant icefield on 13,063-foot Wheeler Peak with the southernmost glacier in the U.S., 75-foot limestone Lexington Arch, and the tunnels and galleries of Lehman Caves are major geological features of the park. The "Black" Rosy Finch can be found around the icefield on the mountain, above the ancient bristlecone pine forest.

The "Bristlecone", a free 8-page park newspaper, park brochure with map, Lehman Caves guide, leaflets on campgrounds and recreation opportunities, species checklists.

NATIONAL FOREST SERVICE
Map/Forest/City

△	Humboldt/Elko	702-738-5171
△	Toiyabe/Sparks	702-784-5331

BUREAU LAND MANAGEMENT
BLM State Office
Federal Building
850 Harvard Way
PO Box 12000
Reno, NV 89520   702-784-5311

Map/District/City

▽	Battle Mountain/same	702-635-5181
▽	Carson City/same	702-882-1631
▽	Elko/same	702-738-4071
▽	Ely/same	702-289-1865
▽	Las Vegas/same	702-388-6403
▽	Winnemucca/same	702-623-3676

STATE AGENCIES

Nevada Department of Wildlife
PO Box 10678
Reno, NV 89520   702-789-0500

Map/Region/City

①	Fallon/Fallon	702-423-3171
②	Elko/Elko	702-738-5332
③	& Ely/Ely	702-289-3281
④	Las Vegas/Las Vegas	702-385-0285

Nevada Commission on Tourism
600 East Williams, Suite 207
Carson City, NV 89710   702-885-4322
from out-of-state call   800-638-2328

BIRDING HOTLINE
Statewide   603-224-9900
Monday through Friday, 5p.m.–9a.m.;
weekends, 24 hours

LOCAL BIRDING GROUPS
Map/Chapter/City
① Beaver Brook Assoc./Hollis
② New Hampshire Audubon Society
   (NHAS)/Concord

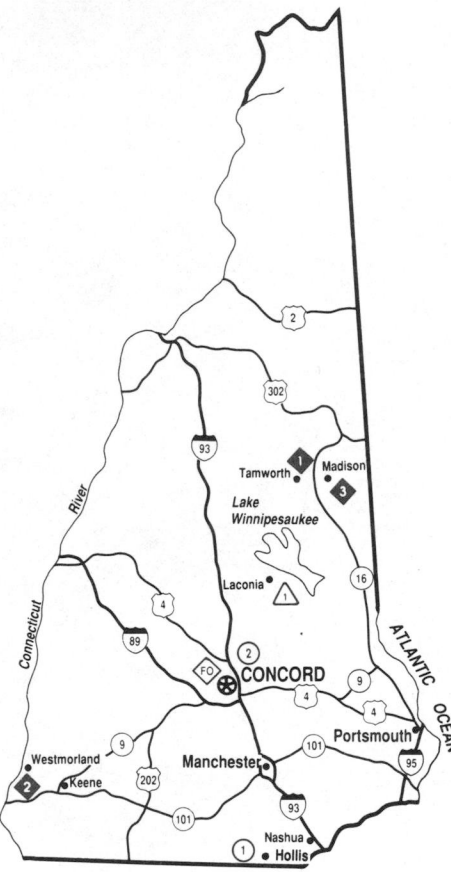

Ten local chapters of NHAS exist across
the state. Call the central office in
Concord for information.

THE NATURE CONSERVANCY
New Hampshire Field Office ㉖
5 South State Street, Suite 1A
Concord, NH 03301   603-224-5853

The following areas are open to year-
round passive recreation. A map of each
location, a brochure about the Bolles
Reserve, and visitor regulations are
available from the Field Office. Day
hiking, picnicking, and cross-country
skiing are permitted.

Frank Bolles Nature Reserve ❶
247 acres near Tamworth in Carroll
County at the foot of Mount Chocorua
and on the shore of Chocorua Lake.

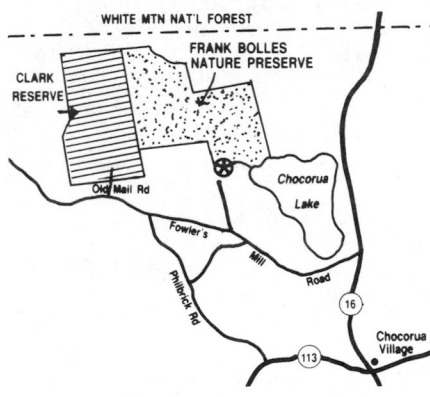

There are wooded swamps, forests, and
clearings. Heron Pond is an 8-acre
kettlehole, where the water level varies
from the local water tables.

The adjacent 268-acre Clark Reserve is
owned by the Chocorua Lake
Conservation Foundation. The two
reserves protect a total 515 acres.

Warwick Preserve ❷
40 acres in Cheshire County near
Westmoreland and on the edge of
Butterfield Hill.

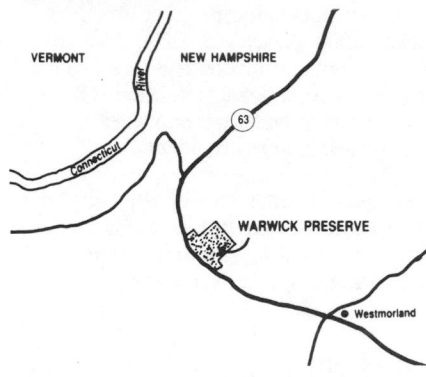

This rugged area includes a series of cliffs
and outcrops, with a ravine. The area is
rich in many wildflower species
uncommon in New Hampshire and also
has a mixed forest. The rock outcrops
offer views of the Connecticut River
Valley and Partridge Brook watershed.

West Branch Pine Barrens ❸
303 acres near Madison of a flatland area
with streams flowing through. Canoeing is
allowed adjacent to the preserve on Silver
Lake.

NATIONAL FOREST SERVICE
White Mountain National Forest △
PO Box 638
Laconia, NH 03247   603-524-6450

STATE AGENCIES

New Hampshire Fish & Game
2 Hazen Drive
Concord, NH 03301   603-271-3211

Vacation Travel Promotion Office
6 Loudon Road
Concord, NH 03301   603-271-2666

BIRDING HOTLINES
Cape May Bird Observatory 609-884-2626
Statewide   201-766-2661

LOCAL BIRDING GROUPS
Map/Chapter/City
1. Atlantic Audubon/Absecon
2. Bergen County Aud./W. Caldwell
3. Highlands Audubon/Oak Ridge
4. Jersey Shore Audubon
   /Point Pleasant Beach
5. Monmouth County Aud./Red Bank
6. Morris Highlands Audubon/Denville
7. New Jersey Audubon Society
   (NJAS)/Franklin Lakes
8. Cape May Bird Observatory
   /Cape May
9. Echo Lake Naturalists' Club
   /Mountainside
10. Fike Nature Association/Wyckoff
11. Gloucester Co. Nature Club/Mantua
12. Montclair Bird Club
    /Upper Montclair
13. Ocean Nature and Conservation Soc.
    /Toms River
14. Summit Nature Club/Lebanon
15. Sussex County Bird Club/Newton
16. Trenton Naturalist Club/Trenton
17. Urner Ornithological Club/Newark
18. Vineland Nature Club/Vineland
19. Washington Crossing Audubon
    /Pennington
20. Watchung Nature Club/Fanwood

SPECIAL BIRDING AREAS

Delaware Bay Reserve ①
c/o Western Hemisphere Shorebird
Reserve Network (WHSRN)
801 Pennsylvania Avenue, SE, Suite 301
Washington, DC 20003   202-547-9009

State, federal, and private areas in New
Jersey and Delaware, along both shores of
Delaware Bay, host 80 percent of the Red
Knots on the East Coast. More than 1
million shorebirds pause during May to
feed and rest before continuing on to their
Arctic and Hudson Bay nesting grounds.

Cape May Bird Observatory ②
707 East Lake Drive   (CMBO office)
c/o New Jersey Audubon Society
PO Box 3
Cape May Point, NJ 08212 609-884-2736

Bird List NJ-1 Cape May Summary
327 birds listed, no nesting data
Bird Chart pages 294-311

Totals by Season		s	S	F	W
Abundant	A	21	8	28	9
Common	C	31	84	42	44
Uncommon	U	75	54	74	64
Occasional	O	50	47	47	58
Rare	R	30	31	23	37

Endangered Species: Brown Pelican, Bald

Eagle, Peregrine Falcon, Piping Plover,
Roseate Tern, Least Tern

Cape May is best known for its rare
migrants and annual hawk flights. CMBO
ornithologists conduct an annual hawk
watch from August 15 to November 30 at
Cape May Point State Park. The 40,000–
90,000 migrating birds of prey include the
highest counts of Merlins and Peregrine

Falcons in North America.

The Cape May Migratory Bird Refuge is
located to the east of Cape May Point.
Note the William D. & Vane C. Blair –
Cape May Migratory Bird Refuge
description and area map on page 126.

CMBO, the information clearinghouse for
birders visiting Cape May, conducts

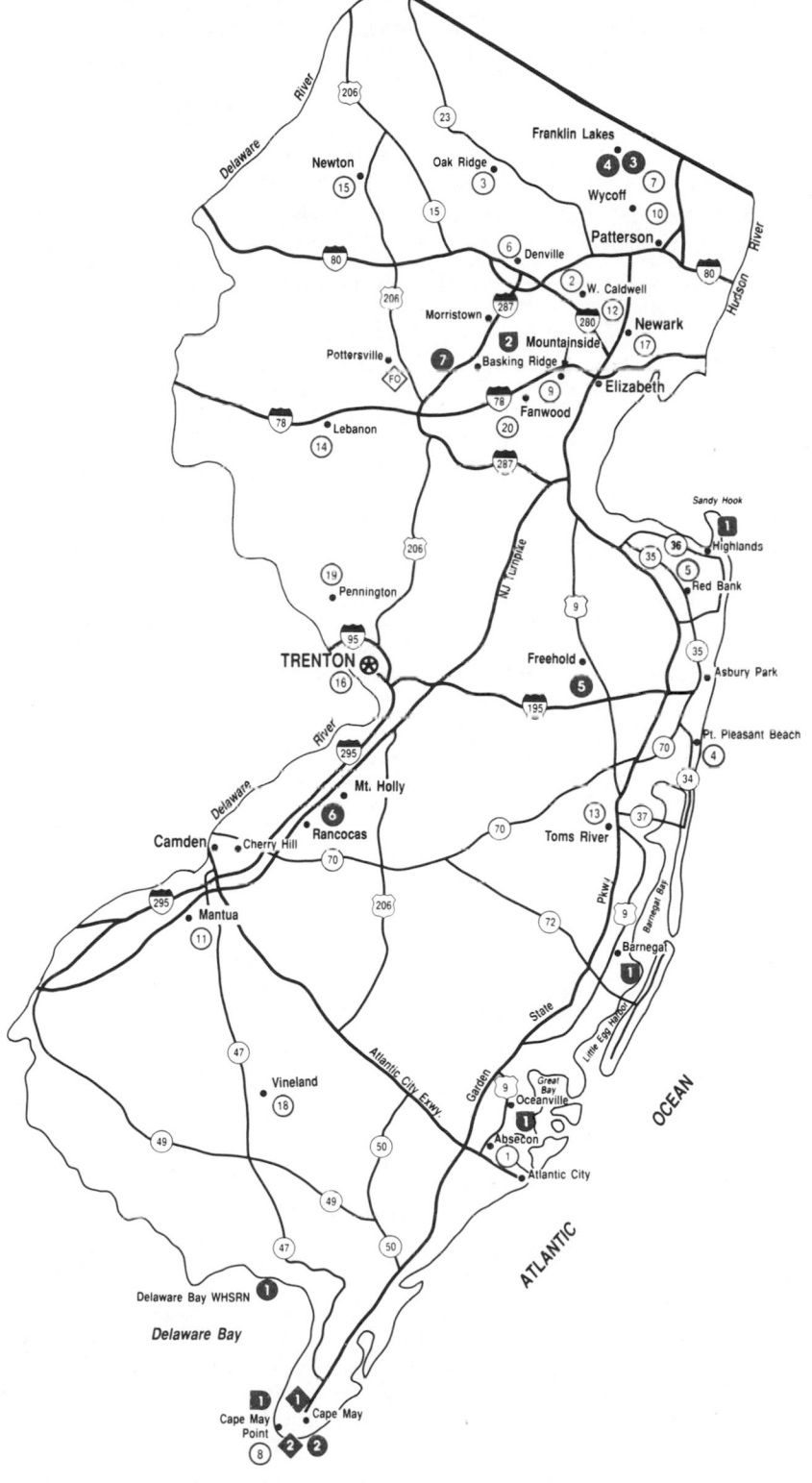

ornithological research, educational programs, field trips, hawk-banding demonstrations during September and October, and workshops throughout the year.
Area maps and checklists.

Lorrimer Nature Center ❸

c/o New Jersey Audubon Society
790 Ewing Avenue
Franklin Lakes, NJ 07417   201-891-2185

From Rte. 208 take Ewing Ave. exit south and go 1 mile. Entrance and sign are on the right.

Habitat: 14.75 acres of upland habitat, primarily wooded, plus visitor center. The spring and fall migration periods are most productive, with peak concentrations in May, September, and October.

Weekly birding field trips and programs.
Spring, Fall

Montclair Hawk Watch ❹

c/o New Jersey Audubon Society
PO Box 125
Franklin Lakes, NJ 07417   201-891-1211

From the Garden State Parkway, take exit 151 (Watchung Ave.). Drive west 2.1 miles and turn right onto Upper Mountain Road. Continue north .7 mile, turn left onto Bradford Ave., then right after .1 mile onto Edgecliff. The parking lot is .3 mile down the road on the right. Backtrack 100 yards to trail on right leading to stairway.

One of North America's premier hawk-watching junctions, where continuous observations have been conducted by the members of the Montclair Bird Club since 1957. Fall migration is best from September through November, while the spring highlights occur during April and May. Peak flights of Broad-winged Hawks may be seen during mid-September. The average fall total is 20,000–25,000 hawks of 16 species, including Bald Eagle and Peregrine Falcon.

Owl Haven Nature Center ❺

Englishtown-Freehold Road
Mt. Holly, NJ 08060   201-780-7007

From the Rte. 9 traffic circle in Freehold, go north 1 mile to Rte. 522 exit (Jughandle). Turn right onto Englishtown-Freehold Road (Rte. 522) and go 1 mile. Entrance and sign are on right.

The Nature Center, located on Monmouth Battlefield State Park, is operated by New Jersey Audubon. Regular birding trips and programs are scheduled.

Rancocas Nature Center ❻

Rancocas Mt. Holly Road
Mt. Holly, NJ 08060   609-261-2495

Operated by New Jersey Audubon and located in Rancocas State Park.
From Rte. 295 take exit 45A (Rancocas Road). Go 1.8 miles to the entrance and sign on the right.

The proximity of the nature center to the Delaware River produces a bountiful spring migration, including 24 species of warblers during April and May.

Regular birding field trips and programs.

Scherman Hoffman Sanctuary ❼

11 Hardscrabble Road
Bernardsville, NJ 07924   201-766-5787

A sanctuary and nature center operated by New Jersey Audubon Society.

From Rte. 287 South, take the Bernardsville exit (N. Maple Avenue exit heading north). Cross Rte. 202 onto Child's Road and turn right after .1 mile onto Hardscrabble Road. Go 1 mile and turn right up the drive at the sign.

Habitat: 263 acres with an extensive trail system through mature hardwood forests and managed fields.

A total of 195 species of birds have been recorded at this sanctuary, which is best known for its spring migrations and its 60 nesting species.

Regular programs, bird identification courses, and field trips are offered. Hours 9a.m.–5p.m. Tuesday–Saturday; noon–5p.m. Sunday. Lower parking area and trails open from dawn to dusk every day.
Spring, Summer

THE NATURE CONSERVANCY

New Jersey Field Office   ⒡⒪
17 Fairmount Road
PO Box 181
Pottersville, NJ 07979   201-439-3007

A special New Jersey Preserve Guide is available for $4 from the Field Office. It provides details on 18 TNC preserve projects in New Jersey.

Bennett Bogs Preserve ❶

c/o New Jersey Field Office
Jointly acquired and managed with NJAS.

From Cape May take Broadway north across Cape May Canal where Broadway becomes Seashore Road. Continue 2 miles and turn left on Tabernacle Road. Go to stop sign, turn left on Shunpike Road, and park in the parking lot.

Habitat: 24 acres of swamp and vernal ponds surrounded with woodlands. Very delicate habitat where visiting is encouraged only in late summer and fall.

Birding, nature study, and wildflowers. Stay on the preserve path at all times. Preserve brochure, guided tours.
Fall

Wm. D. & Vane C. Blair ❷
Cape May Migratory Bird Refuge

c/o New Jersey Field Office or
TNC Cape May Preserve Committee
PO Box 86
Cape May, NJ 08204

Well known as one of the best birding areas in North America, the refuge has one of the densest concentrations of migrating hawks.

See Bird List NJ-1 Cape May Summary and Bird Chart pages 294-311

Go south on Garden State Pkwy. to the end where it joins Lafayette St. in Cape May. Bear right onto West Perry St. and go south to Sunset Blvd. Turn west and continue for 1 mile. The parking area and refuge are on the left past Bayshore Road.

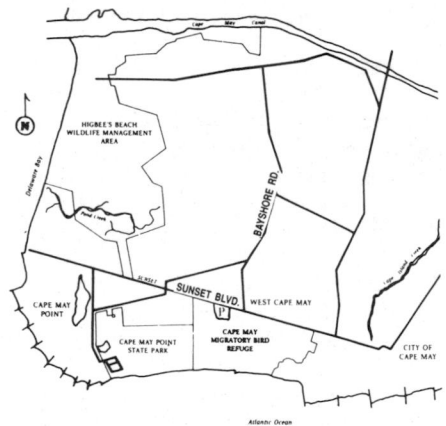

Habitat: 187-acre coastal area and a former town site now reclaimed by nature.

The refuge is open from dawn to dusk every day. Walking trails, fishing.
Spring, Summer, Fall, Winter.

U.S. FISH & WILDLIFE SERVICE NATIONAL WILDLIFE REFUGES

Edwin B. Forsythe Ⓤ (office at refuge)
Great Creek Road
Box 72
Oceanville, NJ 08231   609-652-1665

Bird List NJ-2 Forsythe Summary
289 birds listed, 109 nesting birds
Bird Chart pages 294-311

Totals by Season		s	S	F	W
Abundant	A	10	8	10	4
Common	C	55	31	53	12
Uncommon	U	81	54	84	40
Occasional	O	77	73	81	63
Rare	R	41	28	43	48

Endangered Species: Brown Pelican, Bald Eagle, Peregrine Falcon, Piping Plover, Roseate Tern, Least Tern

The Edwin B. Forsythe NWR has been designated as a Ramsar Site. There are two refuge divisions. The Brigantine Division office is less than 1 mile east of Oceanville on U.S. 9. The Barnegat Division office is located in Barnegat, west of U.S. 9.

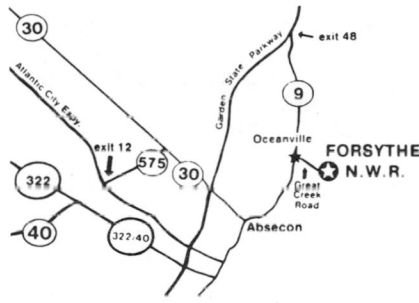

Habitat: Two divisions totalling over 34,000 acres of coastal salt meadows, upland fields, woodlands, and open bays and channels.

The northbound waterfowl migration reaches its peak in late March and early April. The area is a traditional migration and wintering area for American Black Ducks. Canada Geese, Gadwalls, Northern Shovelers, and Ruddy Ducks nest. The Cross Dike area is closed to the public to protect the Peregrine Falcons that use a nesting tower year-round.

Shorebird and wading bird numbers increase between late April and the end of May. Egrets and herons are plentiful. Glossy Ibis numbers peak during the last week in April. Warblers can best be seen on bright, warm days during the first week in May. Ruddy Turnstones migrate through in May and June.

Shorebirds and warblers return in August and wading birds begin to gather. In September ducks start to arrive and the teal migration is underway. Terns and skimmers prepare to leave for their wintering grounds in South America.

The concentrations of ducks reach a peak in the first week in November as the Snow Geese begin arriving. Peak Snow Goose numbers occur from mid-November to mid-December. Bald Eagles start to arrive in December. During January and

February thaws Rough-legged Hawks, Short-eared Owls, and Eastern Bluebirds can be observed.

Area brochure, hunting, fishing, crabbing. Brigantine Division—8-mile auto tour route, 2 interpretive trails.
Barnegat Division has no public use facilities.
Spring, Fall

Great Swamp 2   (office at refuge)
Pleasant Plains Road
RD 1, Box 544
Basking Ridge, NJ 07920   201-647-222

Bird List NJ-3 Great Swamp Summary
222 birds listed, 97 nesting birds
Bird Chart pages 294-311

Totals by Season		s	S	F	W
Abundant	A	24	23	21	10
Common	C	68	52	73	15
Uncommon	U	46	25	38	23
Occasional	O	51	35	42	39
Rare	R	14	11	17	27

Endangered Species: Bald Eagle, Peregrine Falcon

From the Morristown area take I-287 south to exit 26 (North Maple Ave.), turn left on Madisonville Road and then right on Pleasant Plains Road. Follow Pleasant Plains Road to the refuge headquarters.

Habitat: 6,818 acres of marsh and water, hardwood swamp, upland timber, and pasture and agricultural fields. The forests are characterized by plants of both northern and southern botanical zones, including many large, old oak and beech trees, and stands of mountain laurel. The eastern half of the refuge has been designated a Wilderness Area.

Canada Geese can commonly be seen along with Mallards and American Black Ducks. Red-tailed Hawks are common in fall and winter while American Kestrels hunt over the swamp all year. Great Horned and Barred owls nest in the area.

Red-bellied, Downy, and Hairy woodpeckers are year-round residents.

Common flycatchers include Willow and Great Crested flycatchers, Eastern Kingbird, and Eastern Phoebe. Black-capped Chickadee, Tufted Titmouse, and White-breasted Nuthatch are abundant year-round. White-eyed, Red-eyed, and Yellow-throated vireos are common except in the winter. During migrations Blue-winged, Chestnut-sided, Black-throated Blue, Blackpoll, and Black-and-white warblers are frequently seen. The colorful Scarlet Tanagers, Northern Cardinals, and Rose-breasted Grosbeaks are common.

Area brochure, mammals, reptiles, amphibians, fishes, and wildflower lists, observation center, boardwalk trails, photo blinds, limited hunting.
Spring, Fall

NATIONAL PARK SERVICE

Gateway Natl. Recreation Area 1
Sandy Hook Unit
PO Box 437
Highlands, NJ 07732   201-872-0115

The Sandy Hook Unit features beaches, plant and animal life, and historic structures, including Sandy Hook Lighthouse (1764), thought to be the oldest operational light in the U.S.

Recreation Area brochure with map.

STATE AGENCIES

NJ Div. of Fish, Game & Wildlife
CN 400
Trenton, NJ 08625
General Information   609-292-2965
Nongame Species   609-292-9400

Higbee Beach 1
Wildlife Management Area
Cape May, NJ

Higbee Beach is one of the best and possibly the least disturbed birding areas around Cape May. Note the local Cape May map on page 126. From Sunset Blvd. in Cape May take Bayshore Road north for 1.8 miles and turn west at the second paved road (does not show on map) to where it dead ends. An unimproved road leads west through the woods to the beach.

In September and October one of the best early morning vantage points is on the high dunes located inland from Higbee Beach, where birds can be seen headed north in a continuous stream.

NJ Division of Travel & Tourism
One W. State Street, CN826
Trenton, NJ 08625   505-827-0291
from out-of-state call   800-537-7397

BIRDING HOTLINE
Statewide   505-662-2101

LOCAL BIRDING GROUPS
Map/Chapter/City
1. Central NM Audubon/Albuquerque
2. Gallup Area Audubon/Gallup
3. Mesilla Valley Audubon/Las Cruces
4. Sangre De Cristo Audubon/Santa Fe
5. Southeastern Audubon/Roswell
6. Southwestern Audubon/Silver City
7. Four Corners Bird Club/Farmington
8. Otero County Bird Club/Alamogordo

NATIONAL AUDUBON SOCIETY

Randall Davey Audubon Center ●
End of Upper Canyon Road
PO Box 9314
Santa Fe, NM 87504   505-983-4609
Entrance fee for non-members

Bird List NM-1 Rand. Davey Summary
132 birds listed, no nesting data
Bird Chart pages 294-311

Totals by Season		s	S	F	W
Common	C	13	20	16	13
Uncommon	U	39	20	37	13
Occasional	O	51	31	44	13
Rare	R	11	11	9	6

Rare/Limited Species: Grace's Warbler

Located on Upper Canyon Road 3 miles
east from Santa Fe's Plaza.

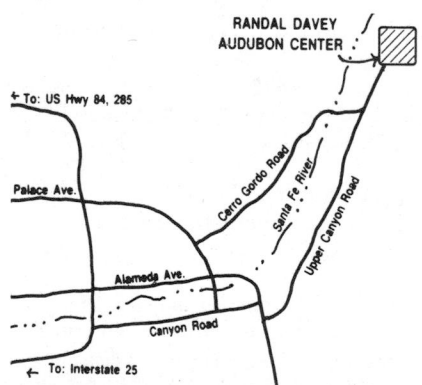

RANDAL DAVEY AUDUBON CENTER

To: US Hwy 84, 285
Palace Ave.
Cerro Gordo Road
Santa Fe River
Alameda Ave.
Upper Canyon Road
Canyon Road
To: Interstate 25

Habitat: 135 acres at the entrance to Santa
Fe Canyon. The sanctuary has woodlands
of pine and pinyon/juniper with a large
meadow, and borders the Santa Fe
National Forest.

The center offers a full range of programs
and self-guiding nature trails. Hours are
9a.m.–5p.m. daily. Guided tours are
offered on weekends during the summer.
Two or three birding float trips on the
Rio Chama and Rio Grande are available
in May and June.

Center brochure, trail guide, outdoor
science field studies brochure.
Spring, Summer, Fall

THE NATURE CONSERVANCY
New Mexico Field Office ⒡ⓞ
107 Cieniga Street
Santa Fe, NM 87501   505-988-3867

Corrales Bosque ●
440 acres of broadleaf deciduous forest, in
Corrales north of Albuquerque and along
the Rio Grande.

Over 250 species have been observed in
Corrales Bosque. Breeding birds include
Wood Ducks, Red-headed Woodpeckers,
Willow Flycatchers, Yellow Warblers, and
Eastern Kingbirds.

Preserve leaflet with map, hiking trails,
picnicking, swimming, non-motorized
boating.
Spring, Fall

Rattlesnake Springs ❷
13.5 acres of riparian desert oasis at the
base of Guadalupe Mountain, 26 miles
from Carlsbad and adjacent to a section of
Carlsbad Caverns National Park.

More than 250 species of birds have been
recorded in the area. Bell's Vireos,
Painted Buntings, Vermilion Flycatchers,
and Marsh Wrens can often be found.

This oasis provides habitat for the only
Orchard Orioles and Eastern Bluebirds
known to breed in New Mexico. Other
vagrants from the east have been noted
occasionally at Rattlesnake Springs.

Preserve leaflet, picnicking, hiking (do not
walk in or through the marshland; stay on
the edge).
Spring, Fall

U.S. FISH & WILDLIFE SERVICE
NATIONAL WILDLIFE REFUGES
U.S. Fish & Wildlife Service Region 2
PO Box 1306
Albuquerque, NM 87103   505-766-2321

Bitter Lake ❶   (office at refuge)
PO Box 7
Roswell, NM 88201   505-622-6755

Bird List NM-2 Bitter Lake Summary
283 birds listed, no nesting data
Bird Chart pages 294-311

Totals by Season		s	S	F	W
Abundant	A	9	4	8	10
Common	C	59	37	52	25
Uncommon	U	57	32	51	41
Occasional	O	65	39	64	48
Rare	R	64	38	47	42

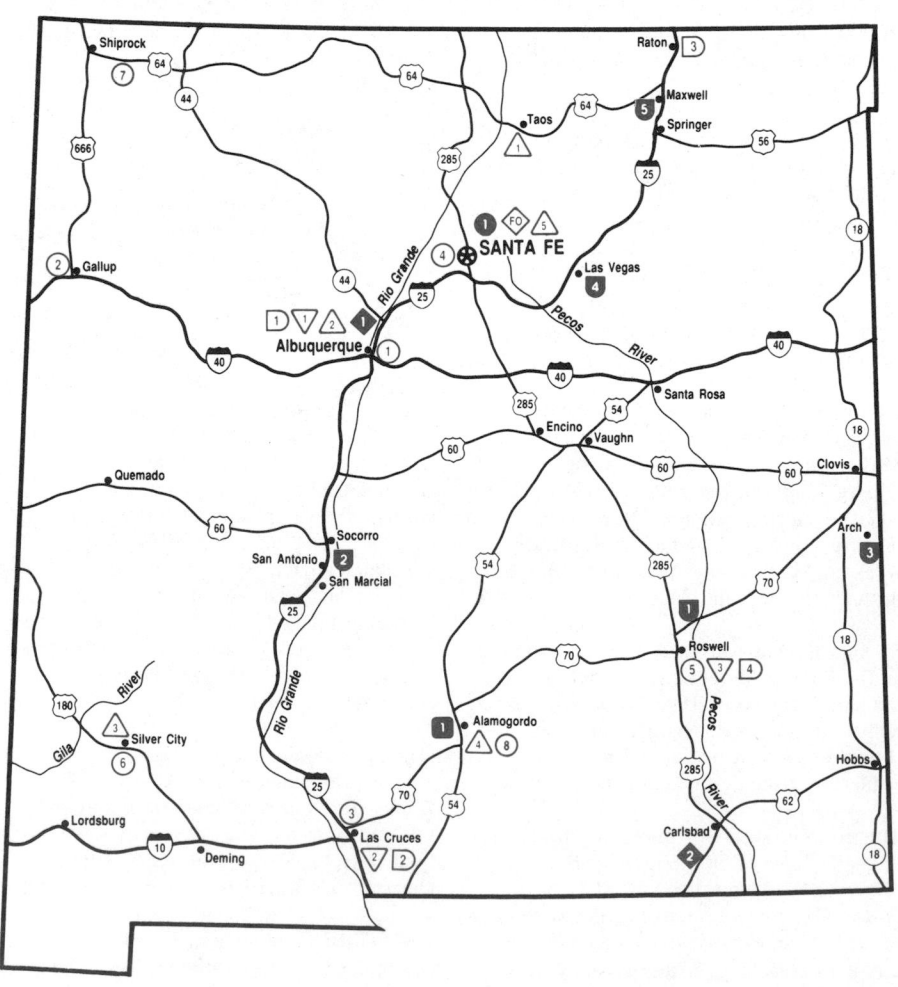

Endangered Species: Bald Eagle, Peregrine Falcon, Least Tern
Rare/Limited Species: Gray-breasted Jay

From Roswell take Hwy. 285 north for approximately 2 miles, turn right on Old Roswell-Clovis Hwy. (at a small refuge direction sign) for approximately 3 miles to the refuge road and sign. Follow road 5 miles to the office.

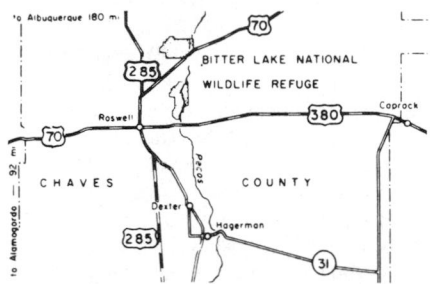

Habitat: 23,310 acres in two units. The northern tract, 9,620 acres of brushy sand dunes, grasslands, and alkali flats, is the Salt Creek Wilderness. The southern tract, with 13,690 acres, includes the 700-acre Lake St. Francis and the Bitter Lake Research Natural Area. The Pecos River flows through the eastern edge of the refuge and the bottomland is covered by salt cedar. Several hundred acres are farm land while the remainder of the southern tract is a shrub-grassland community with saltbush, mesquite, and alkali sacaton, with manmade lakes and many natural sinkholes.

The spring shorebird migration peaks in late April. Among the species seen are Wilson's Phalaropes, American Avocets, Black-necked Stilts, Long-billed Dowitchers, and Least Sandpipers. In May Least Terns arrive and begin to breed, while the population of migrating Black Terns peaks in May and August. During June and July Gadwalls, Green-winged and Blue-winged teals, Snowy Egrets, Snowy Plovers, Killdeers, and Greater Roadrunners raise their broods. White-faces Ibises begin to appear in August with the first of the fall shorebird migrants.

September brings American White Pelicans and the beginning of the fall waterfowl migration, including American Wigeons and Northern Pintails. Redheads, Common Goldeneyes, and Ruddy and Ring-necked ducks follow later in the month. White-faced Ibis, heron, and bittern populations peak around mid-month.

"Lesser" Sandhill Cranes arrive in October, and their numbers are greatest in November. Most of this subspecies winter in western Texas and southeastern New Mexico, and Bitter Lake is a major roosting site. Snow Geese, begin to appear along with Ross' Geese and reach their peak numbers in December. Other waterfowl that are most numerous from November to January are Buffleheads, Ruddy Ducks, Gadwalls, Northern Pintails, Northern Shovelers, and mergansers.

Area brochure, auto tour route, observation platform, hunting, fishing. Fall, Winter

Bosque del Apache ❷
PO Box 1246   (office at refuge)
Socorro, NM 87801   505-835-1828

Bird List NM-3 B. dl Apache Summary
252 birds listed, 95 nesting birds
Bird Chart pages 294-311

Totals by Season	s	S	F	W
Abundant A	12	13	20	17
Common C	71	32	56	38
Uncommon U	67	56	82	43
Occasional O	55	42	54	48
Rare R	20	9	17	11

Endangered Species: Bald Eagle, Peregrine Falcon, Whooping Crane
Rare/Limited Species: Montezuma Quail

Located 93 miles south of Albuquerque along the Rio Grande in the desert of southcentral New Mexico. From the north, take I-25 (St. Hwy. 85) south to the San Antonio exit and go 8 miles south on St. Hwy. 1. From the south, take the San Marcial exit and go 10.5 miles north on St. Hwy. 1 (St. Hwy. 1 runs parallel to and lies east of I-25/St. Hwy. 85).

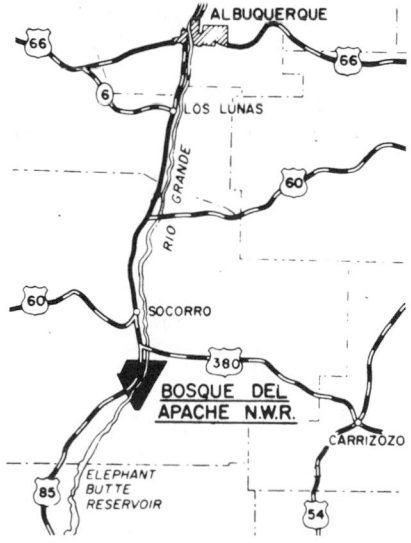

Habitat: 57,191 acres, including 30,287 acres of wilderness. The Rio Grande flows through the middle of the refuge. Temporary marsh areas and ponds are flooded during the winter and drained during the summer, when 1,400 acres of crops are grown for wildlife food.

The shorebird migration includes American Avocets, Black-necked Stilts, and phalaropes. Cactus Wrens, Scrub Jays, Western and Ash-throated flycatchers, Western Bluebirds, Black-headed and Blue grosbeaks, and Black Phoebes visit seasonally. Permanent residents include Greater Roadrunners, Gambel's Quails, Canyon and Rock wrens, and Say's Phoebes.

Bosque del Apache is a wintering area for over 30,000 Snow Geese, 12,000 Sandhill Cranes, 20,000 ducks, and the endangered Whooping Crane.

Area brochure, auto tour route, visitor information center, 2 walking trails, observation tower, hunting, fishing. Winter

Grulla ❸   (office in Texas)
c/o Muleshoe NWR
PO Box 549
Muleshoe, TX 79347   806-946-3341

Bird List NM-4 Grulla Summary
88 birds listed, 21 nesting birds
Bird Chart pages 294-311

Totals by Season	s	S	F	W
Abundant A	5	5	5	4
Common C	41	22	45	27
Uncommon U	26	14	21	12
Occasional O	7	17	10	10
Rare R	3	9	4	8

Endangered Species: Bald Eagle

Located near Arch, New Mexico, and managed from Muleshoe NWR in Texas. The entrance to Grulla is to the right off Hwy. 88, a few miles east of Arch. The east end of Grulla is open to the public and there is a visitor parking lot.

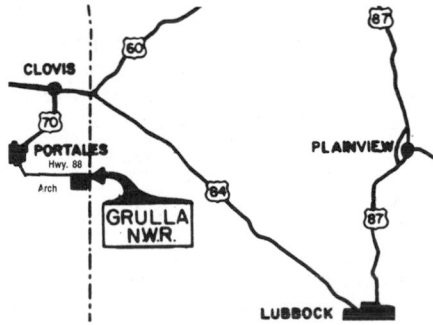

Habitat: 3,236 acres of which 67 percent is Salt Lake and the rest is grassland.

Shorebird and waterfowl abundance depends on the water level in Salt Lake. Up to 85,000 Sandhill Cranes may be present in December.

Area brochure.
Fall, Winter

Las Vegas ⚃   (office at refuge)
Route 1, Box 399
Las Vegas, NM 87701   505-425-3581

Bird List NM-5 Las Vegas Summary
238 birds listed, 76 nesting birds
Bird Chart pages 294-311

Totals by Season		s	S	F	W
Abundant	A	2	0	7	8
Common	C	73	61	62	25
Uncommon	U	85	79	81	41
Occasional	O	43	46	41	43
Rare	R	7	4	9	14

Endangered Species: Bald Eagle, Peregrine
Falcon, Whooping Crane

Located southeast of Las Vegas off I-25.
From Las Vegas, go 2 miles east on St.
Hwy. 104, turn south on St. Hwy. 281,
and go about 4 miles to the headquarters.

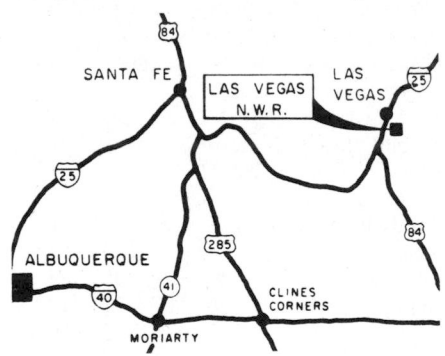

Habitat: 8,750 acres of marsh and streams,
timbered canyons, native grassland, and
agricultural fields.

The refuge is situated on the Great Plains
where the prairie meets the Rocky
Mountains. Birds common to both the
eastern and western United States visit
and live on the refuge.

The rare Prairie Falcon nests on the
refuge and the endangered Peregrine
Falcon, and Golden and Bald eagles visit
in the winter. American Kestrels are
permanent residents and Northern Harriers,
Sharp-shinned, Red-tailed, Swainson's,
Cooper's, Rough-legged, and Ferruginous
hawks are seasonal visitors.

In an arid region such as the Las Vegas
refuge, overall bird populations depend on
the amount of water available. Migrating
birds generally will bypass the refuge in a
dry year, but when water is adequate
waterfowl and shorebirds stop over.
Canada, Snow, and Greater White-fronted
geese, Mallards, Gadwalls, Northern
Pintails, and Blue-winged Teals are
common. Grebes, Long-billed Curlews,

Wilson's Phalaropes, and American
Avocets migrate through.

Area brochure, nature trail, hunting,
fishing.
Fall, Winter

Maxwell ⚄   (office at refuge)
PO Box 276
Maxwell, NM 87728   505-375-2331

Bird List NM-6 Maxwell Summary
185 birds listed, 47 nesting birds
Bird Chart pages 294-311

Totals by Season		s	S	F	W
Abundant	A	3	13	17	1
Common	C	43	37	42	14
Uncommon	U	23	25	25	22
Occasional	O	53	43	52	24
Rare	R	19	14	16	7

Endangered Species: Bald Eagle, Peregrine
Falcon

From Raton, take I-25 south about 30
miles to the Maxwell exit. From Maxwell,
go 0.75 miles north on Old U.S. 85, turn
west on St. Hwy. 505 for 2 miles, turn
north at the refuge sign, and go about 2
miles to the headquarters.

Habitat: 3,300 acres at 6,000 feet.
Includes 3 lakes, and extensive cropland
which is farmed to furnish feed for
migratory birds.

The lakes and cropland attract large
numbers of waterfowl during spring and
fall migrations, as well as a variety of
nesting species. Mallards, Northern
Pintails, and Cinnamon, Blue-winged, and
Green-winged teals all breed on the
refuge. Gadwalls, American Wigeons,
Northern Shovelers, Redheads, Ruddy
Ducks, Canvasbacks, Buffleheads, and
Common Mergansers are among the
migratory species. Great Blue Herons,
American Avocets, and other species of
wading birds and shorebirds also stop to
feed at Maxwell during spring and fall.

"Mountain" Burrowing Owls, Lewis'

Woodpeckers, Say's Phoebes, Rock
Wrens, and Scaled Quails nest.

Area brochure, fishing, hiking by permit.
Spring, Fall

NATIONAL PARK SERVICE

White Sands National Monument ❶
PO Box 458
Alamogordo, NM 88310   505-437-1058

143,732 acres, including 230 square miles
of gypsum dunes rising 60 feet high. The
park and its inhabitants demonstrate the
adaptations necessary for animals and
plants to survive in its harsh environment.
Plants extend their root systems to remain
on top of the constantly shifting dunes.
Small animals, protected from predators
by blending in with their environment,
show a much paler coloration than
populations living on darker substrates.

Monument brochure with map, bird
checklist, "Hours & Activities" brochure.

NATIONAL FOREST SERVICE
NFS Southwestern Region
Federal Bldg.
517 Gold Avenue, SW
Albuquerque, NM 87102   505-842-3292

Map/Forest/City
△	Carson/Taos	505-758-6200
△	Cibola/Albuquerque	505-275-5207
△	Gila/Silver City	505-388-8201
△	Lincoln/Alamogordo	505-437-6030
△	Santa Fe/Santa Fe	505-988-6940

BUREAU LAND MANAGEMENT
BLM State Office
J.P. Montoya Federal Bldg.
South Federal Place, PO Box 1449
Santa Fe, NM 87504   505-988-6316

Map/District/City
▽	Albuquerque/same	505-761-4504
▽	Las Cruces/Las Cruces	505-525-8228
▽	Roswell/Roswell	505-622-9042
▽	Tulsa/Tulsa, OK	918-581-6480

STATE AGENCIES

New Mexico Dept. of Game & Fish
Villagra Bldg., State Capitol
Santa Fe, NM 87503   505-827-7911

Map/Area/City
①	Northwest/Albuquerque	505-841-8881
②	Southwest/Las Cruces	505-524-6090
③	Northeast/Raton	505-445-2311
④	Southeast/Roswell	505-624-6135

New Mexico Tourism & Travel
1100 St. Francis Drive
Santa Fe, NM 87503   505-827-0291
from out-of-state call   800-545-2040

BIRDING HOTLINES

Albany	518-439-8080
Buffalo	716-896-1271
New York	212-832-6523
Rochester	716-461-9593

LOCAL BIRDING GROUPS

Map/Chapter/City

① Bedford Audubon/Mt. Kisco
② Bradley Audubon/Jackson Heights
③ Buffalo Audubon/Buffalo
④ Canada Valley Audubon/Herkimer
⑤ Capital Region Audubon/Delmar
⑥ Central Westchester Aud.
/White Plains
⑦ Delaware Otsego Audubon/Oneonta
⑧ Four Harbors Audubon/East Setauket
⑨ Genesee West Audubon/North Chili
⑩ Great South Bay Audubon/Bayport
⑪ High Peaks Audubon/Ticonderoga
⑫ Hudson-Mohawk Bird Club/Albany
⑬ Hudson Valley Audubon
/Hastings-on-Hudson
⑭ Huntington Audubon/Huntington
⑮ Jamestown Audubon/Jamestown
⑯ John Burroughs Nat. Hist. Soc.
/New Paltz
⑰ The Linnaean Society of NY
/New York
⑱ Lyman Langdon Audubon
/Port Washington

⑲ Mohawk Valley Audubon
/Palatine Bridge
⑳ Moriches Bay Audubon/Moriches
㉑ New York City Audubon/New York
㉒ North Fork Audubon/Middletown
㉓ No. Adirondack Aud./Plattsburgh
㉔ Old Erie Audubon/Rome
㉕ Onondaga Audubon/Syracuse
㉖ Orange County Aud./Middletown
㉗ Owasco Valley Audubon/Auburn
㉘ Putnam Highlands Aud./Montrose
㉙ Rockland Audubon/New City
㉚ Saw Mill River Audubon/Chappaqua
㉛ Scarsdale Audubon/Scarsdale
㉜ S.E. Iowa Audubon/Jackson Hts.
㉝ South Shore Audubon/Freeport
㉞ Southern Adirondack Audubon
/Glens Falls

㉟ St. Lawrence Adirondack Audubon
/Canton
㊱ Sullivan County Audubon/Monticello
㊲ Yonkers Audubon/Yonkers
㊳ Allegany County Bird Club/Belmont
㊴ Baldwin Bird Club/Seaford
㊵ Brooklyn Bird Club/Brooklyn
㊶ Burroughs-Audubon Nature Club
/Rochester
㊷ Cattaragus Co. Bird Club/Olean
㊸ Cayuga Bird Club/Ithaca
㊹ Chemango Bird Club/Hamilton
㊺ Cornell Laboratory of Orn./Ithaca
㊻ Cortland Co. Bird Club/Cortland
㊼ Alan Devoe Bird Club/Chatham
㊽ Federation of New York State Bird
Clubs/Syracuse

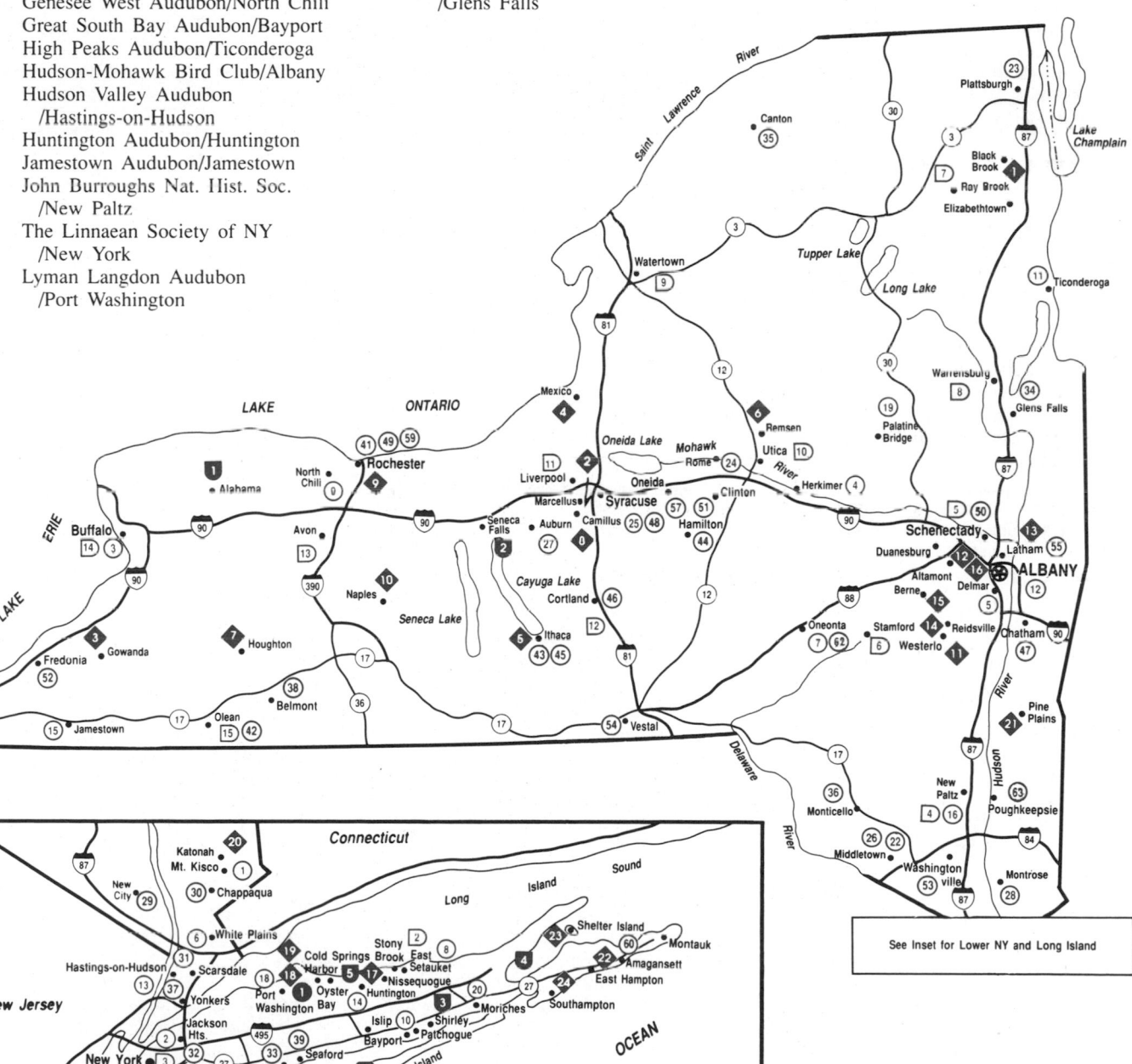

See Inset for Lower NY and Long Island

Lower NY and Long Island Inset

Map/Chapter/City

④⑨ Genesee Orn. Society/Rochester
⑤⓪ Hudson-Mohawk Bird Club
/Schenectady
⑤① Kirkland Bird Club/Clinton
⑤② Lake Erie Bird Club/Fredonia
⑤③ Edgar A. Mears Bird Club/
Washingtonville
⑤④ Naturalists' Club of Broome County
/Vestal
⑤⑤ New York Audubon Society/Latham
⑤⑥ North County Bird Club/Flushing
⑤⑦ Oneida Bird Club/Oneida
⑤⑧ Queens County Bird Club/Flushing
⑤⑨ Rochester Birding Assoc./Rochester
⑥⓪ South Fork Natural History Soc.
/Amagansett
⑥① Staten Island Inst. of Arts &
Sciences: Sect. of Natl. History
/Staten Island
⑥② Tioga Bird Club/Oneonta
⑥③ Ralph T. Waterman Bird Club
/Poughkeepsie

NATIONAL AUDUBON SOCIETY

Theodore Roosevelt ❶
Memorial Bird Sanctuary

Theodore Roosevelt Sanctuary Inc.
134 Cove Road
Oyster Bay, NY 11771   516-922-3200

Take Long Island Expwy. (I-495) to exit
41 north, then take Rte. 106 into the
village of Oyster Bay. Turn right on East
Main St. and go 1.5 miles to the TR
Sanctuary sign on the left. Parking lot is
on the right.

Follow signs as you walk past the Young
Memorial Cemetery entrance (where
Theodore Roosevelt is buried) to the
sanctuary entrance at back gate.

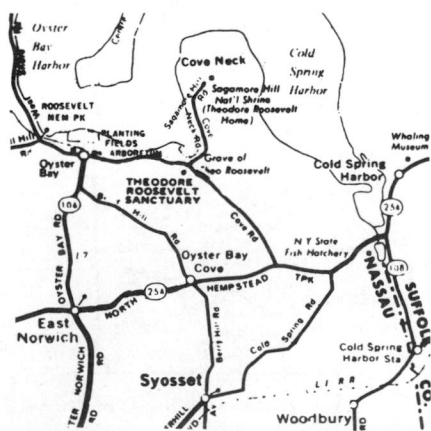

Visitors Center, Ornithological Library
and specimen collection, Wildlife Care
Facilities, Trailside Shop, Nature Trails,
Ethel Roosevelt Derby bird observatory
room, Theodore Roosevelt Bird
Observatory, educational programs,
workshops and excursions.

This 12-acre sanctuary environment offers
membership, fellowship, and experience to
beginning and advanced birders. Bird list,
brochures, guided and self-guiding tours.

THE NATURE CONSERVANCY

New York Field Office
1736 Western Avenue
Albany, NY 12203   518-869-6959

The 24 TNC Preserves listed below are
described under the TNC chapter office
that has management responsibility.

Adirondack Nature Conservancy

PO Box 188
Albany, NY 12932   518-873-2610

Silver Lake Camp Preserve ❶

63 acres near Black Brook. Contact
Adirondack Conservancy in Elizabethtown
for a map and descriptive brochure.
Hiking trails, boardwalk. Spring is best
for wildflowers.

Central & Western NY Chapters

315 Alexander Street
Rochester, NY 14604   716-546-8030

Baltimore Woods ❷

Centers for Nature Education
PO Box 133
Marcellus, NY 13108   315-673-1350

160 acres about 10 miles southwest of
Syracuse. Brochure, local area map,
picnicking, 4 miles of self-guiding
walking trails, cross-country skiing.
Resident manager, small visitor center,
nature education programs.
Spring, Summer, Fall, Winter

Deer Lick ❸

400 acres near Gowanda and Lake Erie.
Four self-guiding trails of 1.1 to 3.3 miles
in length. Drinking water at Mellissa's
Spring on the White and the Yellow
trails. Adjacent to New York State's Zoar
Valley Multiple Use Area.
Spring, Summer, Fall

Derby Hill Bird Observatory ❹

Onondaga Audubon Society
Sage Creek Road
Mexico, NY 13114   315-963-8291

This 60-acre area was transferred to, and
is managed by, the Onondaga Audubon
Society. Between March and May as
many as 66,000 raptors, plus millions of
blackbirds and other species, pass over
Derby Hill on their northward migration.

Area brochure, area map listing peak
raptor periods, picnicking, primitive
camping during the hawk watch period.
Spring, Summer

Eldridge Wilderness ❺

This 87-acre wilderness close to Ithaca is
located atop South Hill and from 650 to
1,000 feet above the town. The trail has
inner and outer loops. The outer loop
circles the wilderness perimeter while the
shorter inner loop crosses the forest. Over
138 species of birds, 75 wildflowers, and
50 trees may be seen.

The trail is often wet and hikers may
want to wear boots when visiting.
Brochure and map available.
Spring, Summer, Fall.

Lake Julia ❻

846 acres near Remsen with 10 different
types of habitat. Permission to visit from
the Chapter or Field Office is required.
The Gibson Nature Trail runs parallel to
Lake Julia and is easy to hike or cross-
county ski.
Summer, Fall

Moss Lake ❼

81-acre preserve near Houghton, including
Moss Lake, a 15-acre bog lake in a kettle
hole surrounded by glacial debris. The
lake and surrounding woods have attracted
a wide variety of birds. Horned and Pied-
billed Grebes, Canvasbacks and Redheads,
Ospreys, Yellow-bellied Flycatchers,
Swainson's Thrushes, and 17 species of
warblers are among the 75 species that
have been recorded at this preserve.

Trails around the lake and through the
woods. Descriptive leaflet, picnic tables.
Summer, Fall

Noyes ❽

c/o Richard Roberts
117 North Way
Camillus, NY 13031   315-963-8291

This 90-acre preserve now owned by the
Onondaga Audubon Society borders Lake
Ontario for three-fourths of a mile. Birds
and wildflowers are seasonally abundant.
A large Bank Swallow colony occupies
the cliffs above the shore of the lake.
Northern Saw-Whet Owls migrate through
the area. A bird-banding program has
documented one Veery returning to the
same location at Noyes for eight
consecutive springs.

Three miles of color-marked trails are
suitable for hiking or cross-country skiing.
Spring

Thousand Acre Swamp ❾

296 acres east of Rochester and part of an
800-acre swamp. A number of deer
inhabit the swamp and red and gray foxes,
coyotes, Red-tailed Hawks, and Green-
backed Herons have been observed.

A 670-foot boardwalk crosses a portion of the swamp, and there are marked trails for hiking.
Spring, Summer, Fall.

West Hill 🔟
313 acres north of Naples in Ontario County with magnificent views, especially during the fall. The high hills overlook Bristol Hills, Canandaigua Lake, the Conklin Gorge, and the High Tor Game Management Area. Eighteen of the 115 species of birds recorded at West Hill nest there among 350 species of plants.

Nature trails.
Summer, Fall

Eastern New York Chapter
1736 Western Avenue
Albany, NY 12203   518-869-0453

Preserve brochures or descriptive leaflets and local maps are available from the Eastern New York Chapter for the following preserves. They are all worth visiting year-round except as noted. All have nature trails. Bird lists are available for Bear Swamp and Limestone Rise preserves.

Bear Swamp 🔟
310 acres located in the town of Westerlo. This wooded swamp preserve is a registered National Natural Landmark. White-breasted Nuthatches, Great Crested Flycatchers, Chestnut-sided Warblers, Hermit Thrushes, Yellow Warblers, and Red-eyed Vireos nest at Bear Swamp.

Two loop trails, .75 mile and 2 miles, and a short trail, called Little Bear.

Christman Sanctuary 🔟
97 acres southeast of Duanesburg. The more difficult trail has steep dropoffs to the Bozenkill River.

Stewart Preserve 🔟
123 acres east of Albany with two trails that have moderate climbs and wet sections. Be careful of poison ivy.

Hannacroix Ravine 🔟
323 acres close to Reidsville with Hannacroix Creek flowing through the preserve. Waterfalls and gorge near the trailhead at Cass Hill Road. This isolated preserve should be used with extreme caution in winter.

Kenrose Sanctuary 🔟
360 acres west of Albany near Berne. Past agricultural use and timber harvesting are evident but some of the old trees are still here, including one large red oak estimated at 175 to 225 years old.

The 1.7 mile Orange Trail has some steep climbs and takes about 2 hours to complete. Be cautious and on the lookout for woodchuck holes in the trail.

Limestone Rise 🔟
62 acres near Altamont and west of Albany that feature a 1.3-mile trail of moderate difficulty. Over 50 bird species have been recorded here, including Turkey Vultures, Northern Flickers, Eastern Wood Pewees, Ruby-crowned Kinglets, Scarlet Tanagers, Purple Finches, and Rufous-sided Towhees.

Long Island Chapter
250 Lawrence Hill Road   516-367-3225
Cold Springs Harbor, NY 11724

Call the office for directions to these preserves. They are open for passive recreation and each offers self-guided nature trails.

David Weld Sanctuary 🔟
114 acres near Nissequogue. Sanctuary brochure, local map, and species list available. Hiking, cross-country skiing.

Hope Goddard Iselin Preserve 🔟
20 acres near Cold Spring Harbor. Preserve brochure, map, species list.

Uplands Farm 🔟
95 acres in Cold Spring Harbor at the site of the Long Island Chapter Office. Brochure, map, species list.

Lower Hudson Chapter
223 Katonah Ave., 2nd floor
Katonah, NY 10536   914-232-9431

A. W. Butler 🔟
Memorial Sanctuary
A 358-acre sanctuary near Mount Kisco and Byram Lake Reservoir. Thousands of migrating hawks are observed in the fall from the hawk watch platform. Of the 140 species noted, 50 nest at the sanctuary.

Self-guiding trail guide to the three trails. Sanctuary brochure and map.
Spring, Fall

Thompson Pond Preserve 🔟
466 acres including 100-acre Thompson Pond, located just south of Pine Plains. Red-tailed Hawks soar here in spring and summer. Canada Geese, ducks, Pileated Woodpeckers, Turkey Vultures, and Ospreys have been observed.

Local area map, hiking trail, canoeing, fishing.
Spring, Fall

South Fork/Shelter Island Chapter
PO Box JJJJ
East Hampton, NY 11937   516-324-1330

Call the office for directions to these preserves. Preserve brochures, maps, and species lists are available. There are self-guiding walking trails and all three locations are suitable for year-round visits.

Accabonac Harbor 🔟
This 90-acre tidal marsh is near East Hampton.

Mashomack Preserve 🔟
Preserve Director
PO Box 410
Shelter Island, NY 11964   516-749-1001

2,040 acres about 90 miles from New York City on eastern Long Island. From North Haven via East Hampton on the South Fork, or Greenport on the North Fork, take a ferry to Shelter Island. Take Rte. 114 to the preserve. It is located on the east side of Rte. 114 near the southern ferry landing.

Preserve brochure, trail guide, visitor center.
Spring, Summer, Fall, Winter

Wolf Swamp 🔟
26-acre Wolf Swamp is near Southampton.

U.S. FISH & WILDLIFE SERVICE NATIONAL WILDLIFE REFUGES

Iroquois 🔟
PO Box 517
Alabama, NY 14003   716-948-5445

Bird List NY-1 Iroquois Summary
223 birds listed, 106 nesting birds
Bird Chart pages 312-329

Totals by Season		s	S	F	W
Abundant	A	3	1	1	0
Common	C	68	54	59	9
Uncommon	U	70	39	57	20
Occasional	O	46	40	40	29
Rare	R	23	18	23	20

Endangered Species: Bald Eagle, Peregrine Falcon

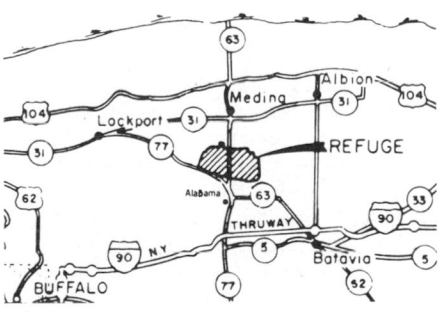

From Alabama, take Hwy. 63 north to
Casey Road. Turn left at the refuge sign
to the headquarters.

Habitat: 10,818 acres of marshlands,
wooded swamp, wet meadows, pasture,
and cropland.

In May some of the more common
warbler migrants are the Bay-breasted,
Blackpoll, Black-and-white, Cerulean,
Chestnut-sided, Magnolia, Wilson's, and
Yellow warblers.

Canada Geese usually arrive in early
March and their flocks increase to peak
levels during the first half of April. The
11 species of waterfowl that remain to
nest on the refuge include Wood Ducks,
Mallards, Blue-winged Teals, and Hooded
Mergansers.

Breeding raptors include Great Horned
and Barred owls, and Red-tailed and Red-
shouldered hawks. Eastern Screech-Owls
and American Kestrels also nest when
they can find suitable cavities.

The fall migration begins between mid-
September and the first week of October.
A few Ospreys and Bald and Golden
eagles may also migrate through.

Area brochure, hunting, fishing, hiking
trails, cross-country skiing, snowshoeing,
photo blinds, canoeing by permit, visitor
center.
Spring, Fall

Montezuma ❷
3395 Route 5/20 East
Seneca Falls, NY 13148   315-568-5987
Entry fee

Bird List NY-2 Montezuma Summary
244 birds listed, 114 nesting birds
Bird Chart pages 312-329

Totals by Season		s	S	F	W
Abundant	A	7	3	8	0
Common	C	98	75	95	14
Uncommon	U	3	3	3	3
Occasional	O	79	65	75	38
Rare	R	35	22	25	11

Endangered Species: Bald Eagle, Peregrine
Falcon

From Rochester, take NY St. Thruway
(I-90) west to exit 41, turn right onto
Rte. 414, and continue to first stop light.
Turn left onto Rte. 318, continue to Rte.
5/20, and turn left. Refuge is about 1
mile. From Syracuse, take I-90 east to
exit 40, turn right onto Rte. 34, and
follow to Auburn. Turn right on Rte. 20
(which becomes Rte. 5 as well). The
refuge is 10 miles west of Auburn.

Habitat: 6,432 acres include 3,500 acres
of diked pools, wetlands, grassland, and
forest.

From late February through April, Canada
and Snow geese and various ducks,
including scaups, Common Goldeneyes,
and Common Mergansers, migrate
through. The shorebird migration takes
place from May to mid-June. The peak of
the warbler migration is in mid-May.

The young of Canada Geese and several
duck species start to hatch in early May.
Great Blue Herons nest in trees whose
roots are submerged in Tschache Pool.
Black-crowned Night-Herons may also be
seen.

The fall migration begins in mid-August.
Sandpipers can be seen on mudflats, while
herons and egrets use the shallow water
areas. Canada Geese and ducks begin
moving through in mid-September, with
goose and duck numbers reaching a peak
in mid-November.

Area brochure, visitor center, hunting,
auto tour route, hiking trail, observation
tower.
Spring, Summer, Fall

The Long Island ⓡⓒ
National Wildlife Refuge Complex

The refuge complex is comprised of eight
separate units, with administrative
headquarters at the Wertheim refuge.
Three units, Wertheim, Target Rock, and
Morton, are open to the public. The others
are closed and access is by special permit
only.

Many bird species are common to all the
refuges although individual refuges may
have habitat more suitable for a particular
species. Large numbers of warblers
migrate through the refuges in both spring
and fall.

The Long Island area provides habitat for
wintering waterfowl and great rafts of
ducks are often seen from the shore of
Huntington Bay. Mallards, American
Black Ducks, and Canada Geese can be
seen on brackish ponds near the beaches.
Greater Scaups and Common Goldeneyes
frequent tidal areas all winter.

Wertheim ❸   (office on refuge)
(Long Island Refuge Complex)
PO Box 21
Shirley, NY 11967   516-286-0485

Bird List NY-3 Wertheim Summary
231 birds listed, 87 nesting birds
Bird Chart pages 312-329

Totals by Season		s	S	F	W
Abundant	A	9	9	9	7
Common	C	56	50	58	29
Uncommon	U	74	52	80	37
Occasional	O	28	14	30	27
Rare	R	21	17	21	31

Endangered Species: Bald Eagle, Peregrine
Falcon, Least Tern

On Long Island, take Hwy. 27A east to
Smith Road, turn right, and go to sign
indicating refuge headquarters.

Habitat: 2,400 acres of land and water on
the south shore of Long Island. Oak-pine
forests, ponds, rivers, bays, and fresh,
brackish, and saltwater marshes. The
Carmans River enters from the north,
meanders through the refuge, and empties
into Bellport Bay. Yaphank Creek, Little
Neck Run, and Big Fish Creek join the
Carmans River within the refuge
boundaries.

The refuge is an important wintering area
for American Black Ducks and an
occasional Bald Eagle.

Area brochure, nature trail (accessible
only by boat), fishing, crabbing.
Spring, Fall

Morton ❹
c/o Wertheim NWR
PO Box 21
Shirley, NY 11967   516-286-0485

229 birds listed, 66 nesting birds
Bird Chart pages 312-329

Totals by Season		s	S	F	W
Abundant	A	1	1	1	1
Common	C	33	24	27	11
Uncommon	U	42	91	45	79
Occasional	O	7	2	7	3
Rare	R	21	13	24	25

Endangered Species: Bald Eagle, Peregrine Falcon, Piping Plover, Roseate Tern, Least Tern

Habitat: 187 acres of beaches, woodlands, and fields. Jessups Neck, a peninsula which forms the northern two-thirds of Morton, has wooded bluffs bordered by sandy, rocky, and gravelly beaches. The southern third of the refuge has a combination of woodland, brush, and open fields.

Portions of the refuge are closed in late spring and summer to protect the endangered Piping Plovers and Least Terns, which nest on the beach.

Area brochure, hiking, visitor center.
Spring, Fall

Target Rock 5
c/o Wertheim NWR
PO Box 21
Shirley, NY 11967   516-286-0485

Bird List NY-5 Target Rock Summary
198 birds listed, 47 nesting birds
Bird Chart pages 312-329

Totals by Season		s	S	F	W
Abundant	A	5	5	6	3
Common	C	31	24	26	21
Uncommon	U	43	29	45	22
Occasional	O	38	17	33	13
Rare	R	55	25	58	30

Endangered Species: Bald Eagle, Peregrine Falcon, Piping Plover, Least Tern

From Huntington, take Rte. 25A west to West Neck Road and turn right. Follow West Neck Road, which becomes Lloyd Harbor Road and ends at the refuge.

Habitat: 80 acres along the shore of Huntington Bay with a small brackish pond near the shore, hardwood forests,

and old formal gardens.

Target Rock is known for the large concentration of warblers during the May migration. Mallards and American Black Ducks nest and may be seen around the pond. Northern Bobwhites, Ring-necked Pheasants, and Mourning Doves are year-round residents.

Area pamphlet, walking trails, photo blind.
Spring, Fall

NATIONAL PARK SERVICE

Fire Island National Seashore 1
120 Laurel Street
Patchogue, NY 11772   516-289-4810

This 19,578-acre barrier island off the south shore of Long Island offers excellent birding opportunities. The Seashore is noted for its large hawk migration during the fall.

Seashore brochure with map, ferry schedule, various leaflets on facilities, services, recreation opportunities. Bird list with 16 habitat codes, other species lists.

Gateway 2
National Recreation Area
Floyd Bennett Field, Bldg. 69
Brooklyn, NY 11234   212-630-0126

26,310 acres that include beaches, marshes, islands, and adjacent waters in the New York harbor area. This park offers a wide range of birding and other recreational opportunities. Gateway includes four units. Sandy Hook in New Jersey, Jamaica Bay, Breezy Point, and Staten Island in New York.

Over 300 species have been observed at Jamaica Bay in Queens, including many unusual shorebirds seen at East Pond during spring and fall migrations. Piping Plovers breed along the beach at Breezy Point.

Recreation Area brochure, bird list for Jamaica Bay, list of fish species.

STATE AGENCIES

Jones Beach State Park 1
Box 1000
Wantagh, NY 11793   516-785-1600

Bird List NY-6 Jones Beach Summary
290 birds listed, 76 nesting birds
Bird Chart pages 312-329

Totals by Season		s	S	F	W
Abundant	A	44	31	51	22
Common	C	46	30	75	29
Uncommon	U	74	33	66	28
Occasional	O	28	9	33	17
Rare	R	39	22	36	44

Endangered Species: Brown Pelican, Bald Eagle, Peregrine Falcon, Piping Plover, Roseate Tern, Least Tern

Located on the south side of Long Island, east of the town of Lido Beach, and west of Fire Island National Seashore. From the Northern State Pkwy. take either Meadowbrook State Pkwy. or Wantagh Pkwy. south to Jones Beach State Park.

Habitat: Over 2,400 acres along the south shore of Long Island.

Bureau of Wildlife
New York State Department
of Environmental Conservation
50 Wolf Road
Albany, NY 12233   518-474-2121

Map/Region/City
2	Region 1/Stony Brook	516-751-7900
3	Region 2	
	/New York City	212-488-2755
4	Region 3/New Platz	914-255-5453
5	Region 4/Schenectady	518-382-0680
6	Sub-Office/Stamford	607-652-7364
7	Region 5/Ray Brook	518-891-1370
8	Sub-Office	
	/Warrensburg	518-623-3671
9	Region 6/Watertown	315-782-0100
10	Sub-Office/Utica	315-793-2554
11	Region 7/Liverpool	315-428-4497
12	Sub-Office/Cortland	607-753-3095
13	Region 8/Avon	716-226-2466
14	Region 9/Buffalo	716-874-4600
15	Sub-Office/Olean	716-372-0645

NY Division of Tourism
Dept. of Commerce
Albany, NY 12245   518-474-4116
from out-of-state call   800-225-5697

BIRDING HOTLINE
Statewide 704-332-2473

LOCAL BIRDING GROUPS
Map/Chapter/City
① Elisha Mitchell Audubon/Asheville
② Forsyth County Aud./Winston-Salem
③ Gaston Audubon/Gastonia
④ Grandfather Mtn. Audubon /Blowing Rock
⑤ Mecklenburg Audubon/Charlotte
⑥ New Hope Audubon/Chapel Hill
⑦ Outer Banks Audubon/Kitty Hawk
⑧ T. Gilbert Pearson Aud./Greensboro
⑨ Wake Audubon/Raleigh
⑩ Wayne Audubon/Goldsboro
⑪ Carolina Bird Club/Tyron
⑫ Chapel Hill Bird Club/Chapel Hill
⑬ North Carolina Maritime Museum /Beaufort
⑭ Tyron Bird & Nature Club/Tyron

THE NATURE CONSERVANCY
North Carolina Field Office
Carr Mill, Suite 223
Carrboro, NC 27510 919-967-7007

The Field Trip Coordinator for this office plans from 65 to 70 field trips from April through October. Each trip includes one or more preserves and only guided field trip visits are permitted.

Contact the TNC Coordinator about current trip schedules and participation. A Preserve Directory is available and includes a detailed description of each preserve.

Bat Cave ●
93 acres in Henderson County. The preserve supports 46 species of birds, including Cerulean and Swainson's warblers. The cave network used to serve as bat hibernation habitat. Human activity and vandalism caused the bats to abandon the caves. Therefore, caving is now limited to scientific research by special permit.

Big Yellow Mountain ②
426 acres in the Blue Ridge Mountains just west of Minneapolis. Jointly managed with the Southern Appalachian Highlands Conservancy (Kingsport, TN).

Bluff Mountain ③
758 acres, 4 miles west of Jefferson. Wildflowers abundant from April through October. Broad-winged Hawks and Black and Turkey vultures ride the thermals rising from the bluff.

Camassia Slopes ④
176 acres along the north bank of the Roanoke River in Northampton County near Rehoboth. Over 60 bird species, including Wild Turkeys, are known to breed in the vicinity. Another 40 species use the area during migration.

Carolina Bays ⑤
403 acres include nine bays in three contiguous counties near Red Springs.

Green Swamp ⑥
15,722 acres, 5 miles north of Supply. The endangered Red-cockaded Woodpecker nests in old-growth pines.

Lanier Quarry Savanna ⑦
55 acres southeast of Maple Hill. Maintained as breeding habitat for the Henslow's Sparrow, a species of special concern in North Carolina, and the threatened Bachman's Sparrow.

Nags Head Woods ⑧
680 acres on a barrier island off the coast near Kitty Hawk. Dunes, dense forest, and freshwater ponds. Visitor Center and trail system.

U.S. FISH & WILDLIFE SERVICE NATIONAL WILDLIFE REFUGES

Alligator River ❶
PO Box 1969
Manteo, NC 27954 919-473-1131

About 250 miles of old logging roads traverse the area. They are open to public use and four-wheel-drive vehicles are recommended. Some parts of the refuge are closed to boats and motorized vehicles while others are closed during parts of the year.

Habitat: 141,200 acres on the mainland part of coastal North Carolina include unique pocosin habitat, as well as fresh and brackish marshes, hardwood and pine forests, and cypress hardwood and white cedar swamps.

Alligator River is used as a stopover point by many of the birds migrating along the Atlantic Flyway. A program is underway to reestablish the red wolf, which was declared extinct in the wild in 1980.

Area brochure, refuge map, red wolf brochure, hunting, fishing. No public use facilities.
Spring, Summer, Fall, Winter

Cedar Island ❷ (office on refuge)
Lola Road
Cedar Island, NC 28520 919-225-2511

Headquarters is approximately 40 miles northeast of Beaufort. Take Hwy. 70 to St. Rte. 12 and turn left. Continue to the fork and bear right onto Lola Road to the refuge headquarters.

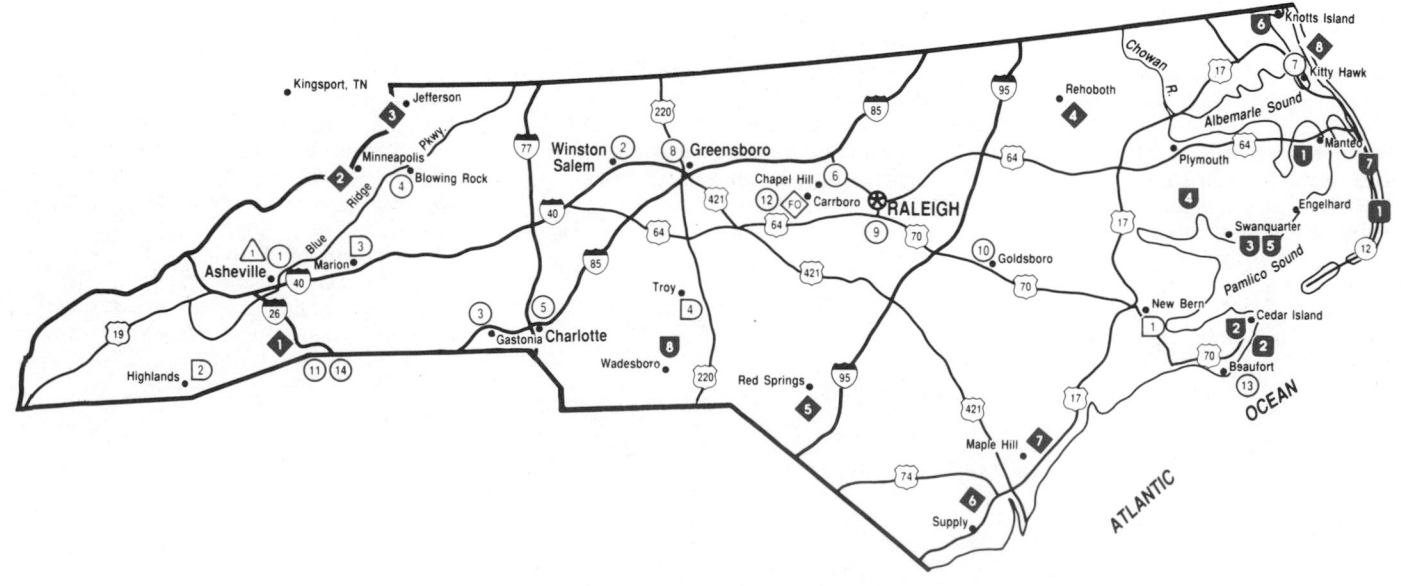

Habitat: 12,525 acres, of which 80 percent is irregularly flooded saltmarsh, including black needle-rush, cordgrass, saltgrass, and switchgrass. 2,450 acres of woodland are dominated by loblolly, longleaf, and pone pine, with live oak in upland areas. 75 acres have been cleared for administrative purposes.

Thousands of gulls and terns nest on the most remote sandy beaches. Black Skimmers use their long lower bill to skim the surface of the bays. American Oystercatchers and dowitchers forage along the shoreline, while egrets, herons, bitterns, and rails feed and nest in the salt marshes. Songbirds are abundant during the spring and fall migrations.

Raptors commonly found inhabiting marshes and wooded uplands include Great Horned Owls, Red-tailed Hawks, and Northern Harriers. Ospreys nest near the open water.

In the fall and winter, large rafts of Redheads form on the open bay and creek areas. Other species of diving ducks that may be seen include Buffleheads, scaups, and Red-breasted Mergansers.

Area brochure, auto tour routes, hunting.
Spring, Summer, Fall, Winter

Mattamuskeet ❸ (office at refuge)
Route 1, Box N-2
Swanquarter, NC 27885   919-926-4021

Note: bird list combines sighting records for Mattamuskeet and Swanquarter refuges.

Bird List NC-1 Matta/Swan Summary
225 birds listed, 58 nesting birds
Bird Chart pages 312-329

Totals by Season		s	S	F	W
Abundant	A	5	4	6	13
Common	C	56	45	55	63
Uncommon	U	44	32	49	31
Occasional	O	25	16	20	24
Rare	R	9	10	15	17

Endangered Species: Brown Pelican, Bald Eagle, Peregrine Falcon, Least Tern

The headquarters entrance road is located off Rte. 94, 1.5 miles north of U.S. Hwy. 264 between Swanquarter and Engelhard. Mattamuskeet NWR is also the administrative office for Cedar Island, Pungo, and Swanquarter NWRs, which are listed and described separately.

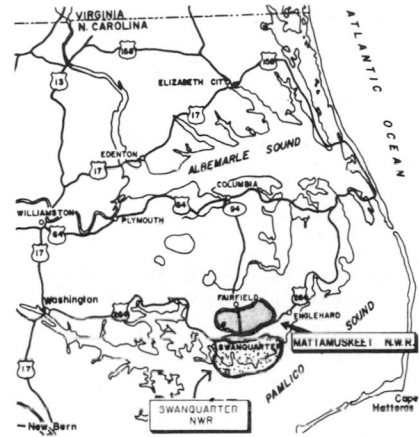

Habitat: 50,000 acres include the 40,000-acre Lake Mattamuskeet, the largest natural lake in North Carolina. The lake is 18 miles long, 5 to 6 miles wide, and averages 2 feet in depth. The habitats that surround the lake include 400 acres of agricultural fields, 1,000 acres of pine woodlands, and 2,000 acres of mixed hardwoods bordering the refuge in narrow strips.

Mattamuskeet's lake and fields attract large flocks of migrating and wintering waterfowl that have followed the Atlantic Flyway. Thousands of Canada Geese and small flocks of "Lesser" Snow Geese are joined by Tundra Swans and 22 species of ducks.

Bald Eagles are seen occasionally, while Ospreys and Sharp-shinned Hawks are common nesters. Red-bellied and Pileated woodpeckers are common all year.

Other year-round residents include Great Horned and Barred owls, Eastern Screech-Owls, Belted Kingfishers, Eastern Meadowlarks, Brown-headed Nuthatches, and Northern Bobwhites.

Area brochure, fishing, hunting.
Spring, Summer, Fall, Winter

Pungo ❹
c/o Mattamuskeet NWR
Route 1, Box N-2
Swanquarter, NC 27885   919-926-4021

Bird List NC-2 Pungo Summary
206 birds listed, no nesting data
Bird Chart pages 312-329

Totals by Season		s	S	F	W
Abundant	A	9	9	12	13
Common	C	23	20	26	20
Uncommon	U	64	48	48	47
Occasional	O	33	26	46	38
Rare	R	18	9	17	21

Endangered Species: Bald Eagle, Peregrine Falcon
Rare/Limited Species: Barnacle Goose

To reach the refuge from Plymouth, take Hwys. 32/45/99 south, continuing on Hwy. 45 for 17 miles.

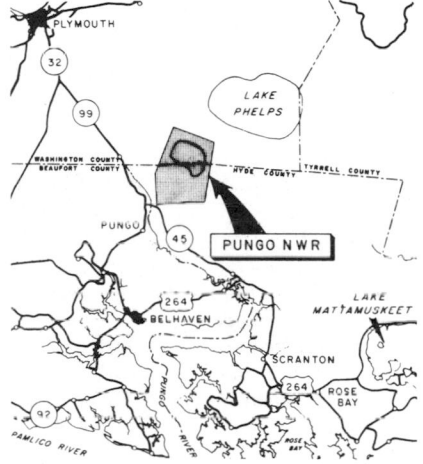

Habitat: 12,350 acres of water, marsh, brush, and croplands. Includes 2,300-acre Pungo Lake, numerous canals, and over 1,300 acres of cropland.

The refuge is a wintering ground for large numbers of waterfowl, which may be observed from October through March. Thousands of Canada and Snow geese, Tundra Swans, Mallards, Northern Pintails, American Black Ducks, American Wigeons, and teals can often be seen during the winter months. A few Mallards, and American Black and Wood ducks breed at the refuge as well.

During spring and fall migration, songbirds can be seen in thickets along refuge trails, roads, and waterways. Herons, egrets, and shorebirds are frequently observed around Pungo Lake and the refuge waterways.

Area brochure, auto tour route, observation tower, hunting.
Spring, Summer, Fall, Winter

Swanquarter ❺
c/o Mattamuskeet NWR
Route 1, Box N-2
Swanquarter, NC 27885   919-926-4021

See Bird List NC-3 Matta/Swan and Bird Chart pages 312-329

Bell Island Recreation Area is the only public area on Swanquarter Refuge. The area may be reached by a 2-mile access road off U.S. Hwy. 264 just west of Swanquarter. The remainder of the refuge is inaccessible except by boat.

Habitat: 15,500 acres bordering Pamlico Sound include 12,730 of marsh and 2,770 of woodlands. 11,130 acres of the marsh are low, flat salt-marsh islands interspersed with potholes, creeks, and tidal drains. In some higher areas, saltwater intrusion has transformed 1,600 acres of forest land into a marsh dominated by sawgrass and sedges. The woodlands are located mainly on Bell Island and in the Juniper Bay area. About 8,800 acres of the refuge are designated wilderness.

Swanquarter's woodlands and marshes are used by a variety of nesting and migrating birds, including shorebirds, wading birds, raptors, and passerines. Laughing, Bonaparte's, Herring, and Ring-billed gulls are year-round residents, while a variety of terns may be seen occasionally. Several raptors can be observed regularly, including Northern Harriers, Ospreys, and Red-shouldered and Red-tailed hawks.

The bays and creeks attract large flocks of Canvasbacks, Lesser Scaups, Buffleheads, Ruddy Ducks, and Canada Geese, during the winter, as well as a number of Tundra Swans. American Wigeons, Mallards, and American Black Ducks can be found on the potholes around the saltmarsh islands.

Area brochure, hunting, fishing from pier. Spring, Summer, Fall, Winter

Mackay Island 6 (office on refuge)
PO Box 31
Knotts Island, NC 27950   919-429-3100

Bird List NC-3 Mackay Summary
174 birds listed, 52 nesting birds
Bird Chart pages 312-329

Totals by Season		s	S	F	W
Abundant	A	1	0	5	4
Common	C	46	36	47	40
Uncommon	U	24	19	25	19
Occasional	O	41	25	32	23
Rare	R	17	24	25	24

Endangered Species: Bald Eagle, Peregrine Falcon, Least Tern, Red-cockaded Woodpecker

Headquarters is located on Mackay Island Road just west of the junction with Knotts Island Road, at the edge of the town of Knotts Island.

Habitat: 7,055 acres, including 842 in Virginia, of marsh, water, and some uplands and woodlands.

During the spring and summer, the woodlands contain a variety of songbirds including Carolina Wrens and Prairie and Prothonotary warblers. Thousands of ducks, geese, and swans flock to the refuge's marshes during the winter.

The Knotts Island Causeway (St. Rte. 615), which crosses the refuge, offers good viewing points for most of the waterfowl and marsh birds occurring in the Back Bay/Currituck Sound area.

Area pamphlet, hunting, fishing, hiking. Spring, Summer, Fall, Winter

Pea Island 7 (office at refuge)
PO Box 1969
Manteo, NC 27954   919-987-2394

Bird List NC-4 Pea Island Summary
276 birds listed, 71 nesting birds
Bird Chart pages 312-329

Totals by Season		s	S	F	W
Abundant	A	2	12	3	0
Common	C	38	25	17	1
Uncommon	U	34	22	33	12
Occasional	O	42	26	44	12
Rare	R	20	6	19	21

Endangered Species: Brown Pelican, Bald Eagle, Peregrine Falcon, Piping Plover, Roseate Tern, Least Tern
Rare/Limited Species: Barnacle Goose

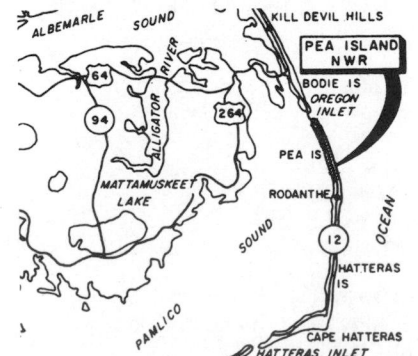

The office is located 6.5 miles south of Oregon Inlet on St. Hwy. 12.

Habitat: 31,615 acres, of which 5,915 are coastal barrier island and 25,700 are Proclamation Boundary Waters in Pamlico Sound. Pea and Hatteras islands extend more than 12 miles along North Carolina's Outer Banks, and include various dikes, ponds, and wildfowl croplands.

A large variety of waterbirds nest on the refuge. Sandwich, Gull-billed, Royal, and the endangered Least terns are among the most common of the breeding terns. Willets, Black Skimmers, American Oystercatchers, and the endangered Piping Plover also nest in the dunes and on the beaches. Colonies of Tricolored and Little Blue herons, as well as other herons and egrets, can be seen in the impoundments and marshy areas on the Pemlico Sound. Brown Pelicans may also be found feeding in the impoundments during summer and fall, although they do not breed at Pea Island. Peregrine Falcons migrate along the shore, and are most common during the fall. The waterfowl diversity is the greatest during October and November, although the numbers of Snow and Canada geese, Tundra Swans, and 25 species of ducks peak during January.

Insects are abundant from May through September, so insect repellent and appropriate protective clothing is recommended.

Area brochure, amphibian, reptiles, and mammals lists, surf fishing, crabbing. Spring, Summer, Fall, Winter

Pee Dee 8 (office on refuge)
Route 1, Box 92
Wadesboro, N.C. 28170   704-694-4424

Bird List NC-5 Pee Dee Summary
171 birds listed, no nesting data
Bird Chart pages 312-329

Totals by Season		s	S	F	W
Abundant	A	11	9	13	11
Common	C	90	70	90	62
Uncommon	U	13	6	7	5
Occasional	O	23	19	21	18
Rare	R	6	5	7	14

Endangered Species: Wood Stork, Bald Eagle, Peregrine Falcon, Red-cockaded Woodpecker

From Wadesboro, take U.S. Hwy. 52 north for 6 miles to the office.

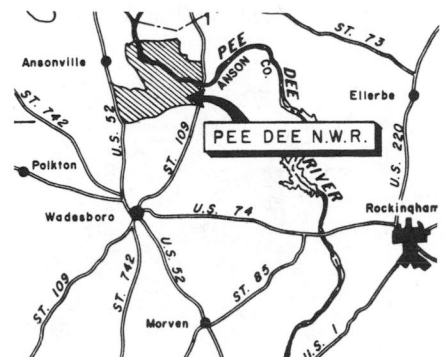

Habitat: 8,443 acres on the bank of the Pee Dee River include 6,300 acres of woodlands, of which 4,900 acres of hardwoods and 1,400 are pine. The remainder of the refuge is composed of croplands and wetlands, including lakes and streams in addition to the Pee Dee River.

Waterfowl populations peak during January and February. Wood Ducks lay their eggs in March and April, and the young have left the nest boxes by June. Blue-winged Teals are present in varying numbers throughout the year, while Green winged Teals arrive in the fall and depart in the spring. Waterfowl numbers increase in October as Canada Geese begin to arrive for the winter, and peak in November. Most of the refuge is closed during December to provide extra sanctuary for the waterfowl.

Bald and Golden eagles may be seen occasionally during January and February. The raptors that winter at Pee Dee start to appear in October. Northern Harriers arrive in greater numbers during November, when an occasional Osprey or Bald Eagle may fly through.

American Woodcocks begin their courtship activities in late February, while resident passerines start to nest in March or April.

Area brochure, mammals, amphibians, and reptiles lists, young people's wildlife checklist, hunting, fishing, observation blinds, interpretive trail, photo blind.
Spring, Summer, Fall, Winter

NATIONAL PARK SERVICE

Cape Hatteras National Seashore ⬛
Route 1, Box 675
Manteo, NC 27954   919-473-2111

Bird List NC-6 C. Hatteras Summary
246 birds listed, no nesting data
Bird Chart pages 312-329

Totals by Season		s	S	F	W
Abundant	A	15	3	17	13
Common	C	60	32	58	31
Uncommon	U	80	42	83	43
Occasional	O	36	19	42	50
Rare	R	24	14	22	23

Endangered Species: Brown Pelican, Bald Eagle, Peregrine Falcon, Piping Plover, Roseate Tern, Least Tern

30,319 acres, including 26,326 land acres. Beaches, migratory waterfowl, fishing, and points of historical interest such as the Cape Hatteras Lighthouse overlooking the "graveyard of the Atlantic," are features of the first National Seashore.

Seashore brochure with map, Beach Trail Guide, various leaflets about species and recreation opportunities. Newspaper "In The Park" is seasonal and has 16 pages of visitor information.
Spring, Fall

Cape Lookout National Seashore ⬛
415 Front Street
PO Box 690
Beaufort, NC 28516   919-728-2121

Bird List NC-7 C. Lookout Summary
260 birds listed, no nesting data
Bird Chart pages 312-329

Totals by Season		s	S	F	W
Common	C	51	42	81	51
Uncommon	U	4	68	1	58
Rare	R	41	26	38	27

Endangered Species: Brown Pelican, Bald Eagle, Peregrine Falcon, Piping Plover, Least Tern

28,414 acres, including 8,741 land acres. This series of undeveloped barrier islands and surrounding waters extend 55 miles along the lower Outer Banks, embracing beaches, dunes, historic Portsmouth Village, and Cape Lookout Lighthouse.

Seashore brochure with map, Lighthouse brochure, camping guide, various leaflets about fishing and other recreation opportunities.

NATIONAL FOREST SERVICE
North Carolina
National Forests Supervisor ⚠
100 Otis Street
PO Box 2750
Asheville, NC 28802   704-257-4200

Map/Forest-Ranger District/City
①	Croatan-Croatan /New Bern	919-638-5628
②	Nantahala-Highlands /Highlands	704-526-3765
③	Pisgah-Grandfather /Marion	704-652-2144
④	Uwharrie-Uwharrie /Troy	919-576-6391

STATE AGENCIES

NC Wildlife Resources Commission
Archdale Bldg.
512 N. Salisbury Street
Raleigh, NC 27611   208-334-3700

NC Division of Travel & Tourism
430 N. Salisbury Street
Raleigh, NC 27611   800-847-4862

LOCAL BIRDING GROUPS
Map/Chapter/City
1. Elkhorn Audubon/Bismark
2. Fargo-Moorhead Audubon/Fargo
3. Grand Forks Audubon/Grand Forks
4. Sheyenne Audubon/Valley City
5. ND Natural Science Soc./Jamestown

THE NATURE CONSERVANCY

Cross Ranch Nature Preserve ◆
Preserve Manager
Hensler, ND 58547   701-794-8741

From Washburn take Hwy. 200 west for 3 miles to Hensler. Turn right onto Rte. 1806, travel south 5 miles, and turn east at the Cross Ranch sign. Drive east for 4.5 miles to another preserve sign and turn north for 1.5 miles to the office.

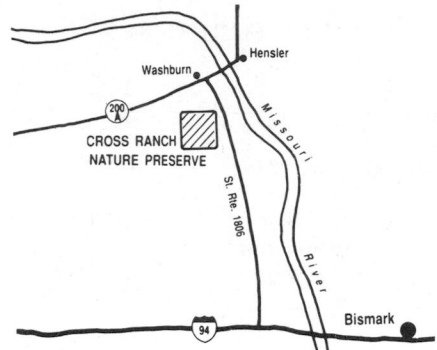

Habitat: Over 6,000 acres include mixed grass prairie, upland woody draws, and prairie potholes.

The preserve has both ecological and historical value. Among the abundant wildlife are eastern and western songbirds, eagles, hawks, owls, and turkeys. Over 100 archeological sites have been found, with some dating to 6000 B.C.

Pamphlet, self-guiding prairie nature trail brochure, bird and mammals lists. Passive recreation includes day hiking, cross-country skiing. No public facilities but the adjacent Cross Ranch State Park has facilities.
Open year-round.

John E. Williams Memorial ◆ Nature Preserve
(see Cross Ranch Nature Preserve)

Limited access. Located 6 miles northeast of Turtle Lake. For maps and use information contact the Cross Ranch preserve manager.

During May, June, and July, the breeding population of the endangered Piping Plover is one of the largest in the world. Fall and spring draw a variety of shorebirds and waterfowl by the thousands.

U.S. FISH & WILDLIFE SERVICE NATIONAL WILDLIFE REFUGES

Arrowwood ❶
Rural Route 1, Box 65
Pingree, ND 58476   701-285-3341

Bird List ND-1 Arrowwood Summary
246 birds listed, 105 nesting birds
Bird Chart pages 312-329

Totals by Season		s	S	F	W
Common	C	64	53	59	7
Uncommon	U	10	54	4	18
Rare	R	59	27	52	12

Endangered Species: Bald Eagle, Peregrine Falcon, Piping Plover

From the refuge sign just north of Edmunds on Rtes. 281/52, go east on the gravel road for 6 miles. Then turn north for 1 mile to the headquarters.

Habitat: 15,935 acres of prairie upland along each side of a chain of four lakes. Wooded coulees lead back from the lakes.

Sharp-tailed Grouse have a number of established leks where they display in the spring. Gray Partridges, Ring-necked Pheasants, and Greater Prairie Chickens also nest. The grasslands provide nesting sites for Marbled Godwits and numerous upland songbirds, among them the Baird's Sparrow.

There are major migrations of waterfowl and shorebirds in spring and fall. Canada Geese and more than a dozen species of ducks nest on the refuge, including large numbers of Blue-winged Teals, Northern Shovelers, American Wigeons, and Northern Pintails. Five species of grebes, Pied-billed, Horned, Red-necked, Eared, and Western, also nest along the lakes. Purple Martins and Tree, Northern Rough-winged, Bank, Cliff, and Barn swallows also nest.

Area brochure, auto tour route, limited hunting, fishing, hiking, picnicking, cross-country skiing, snowshoeing.
Spring, Summer, Fall

Audubon ❷   (office at refuge)
Rural Route 1
Coleharbor, ND 58531   701-442-5474

Bird List ND-2 Audubon Summary
205 birds listed, 85 nesting birds
Bird Chart pages 312-329

Totals by Season		s	S	F	W
Abundant	A	26	24	21	2
Common	C	52	37	40	4
Uncommon	U	42	26	56	7
Occasional	O	60	33	64	14
Rare	R	24	25	20	18

Endangered Species: Bald Eagle, Peregrine Falcon, Whooping Crane, Piping Plover, Least Tern

U.S. Hwy. 83, the main road between Bismark and Minot, passes the west edge of the refuge approximately 4 miles north

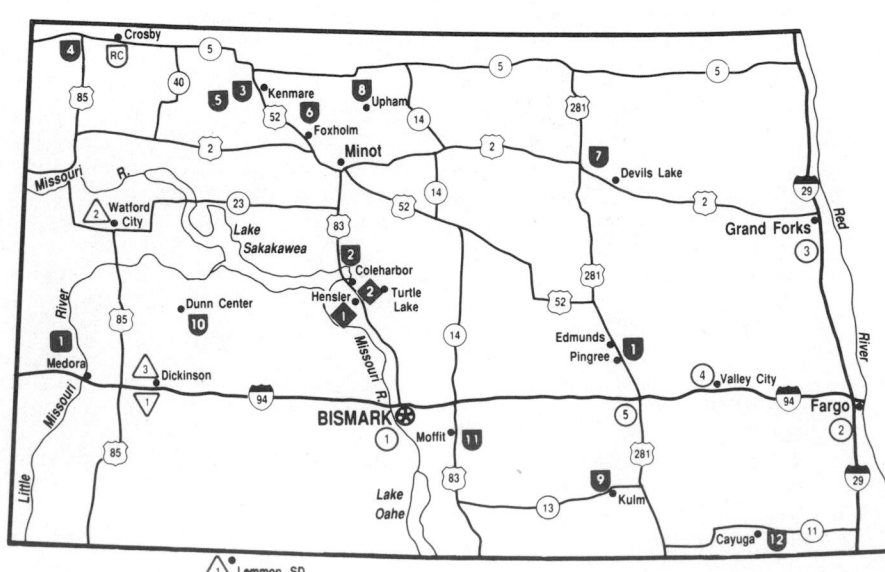

of Coleharbor. Refuge headquarters is 0.75 mile east of Hwy. 83 and 0.5 mile south of the sub-impoundment embankment. Turn right onto the embankment road and follow signs to headquarters and for the auto tour route.

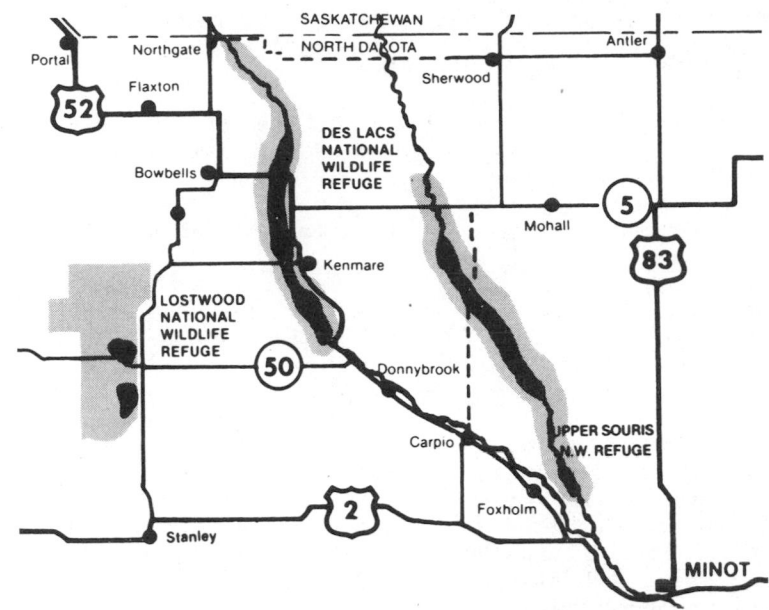

Habitat: 14,735 acres on the south side of Lake Audubon, a sub-impoundment of Lake Sakakawea. Part of the Audubon Wildlife Management Area, which includes an 11,200-acre state-managed area adjacent to the refuge. This is an area of prairies, wetlands, reclaimed farmlands, tree plantings, and more than 140 islands.

Migratory birds, including ducks, geese, and shorebirds, visit the refuge during the spring and fall migrations. During the summer flocks of American White Pelicans and Double-crested Cormorants can be seen on the lake. Shorebirds such as American Avocets, Marbled Godwits, and Willets nest on the islands. On the prairies Burrowing Owls, Upland Sandpipers, Killdeers, Sharp-tailed Grouse, Bobolinks, and Western Meadowlarks can be found.

Area brochure, auto tour route, ice fishing, limited deer hunting.
Spring, Fall

Des Lacs 🛈 🆁🅲   (office at refuge)
Des Lacs Refuge Complex
PO Box 578
Crosby, ND 58730   701-965-6488

The Complex includes Des Lacs, the Crosby Wetland Management District, and Lake Zahl and Lostwood refuges. Bird List ND-3 Souris Loop covers all of these areas and the Upper Souris Refuge.

Bird List ND-3 Souris Loop Summary
266 birds listed, 147 nesting birds
Bird Chart pages 312-329

Totals by Season		s	S	F	W
Abundant	A	21	8	28	1
Common	C	71	61	66	7
Uncommon	U	64	39	61	6
Occasional	O	48	46	50	16
Rare	R	43	24	39	22

Endangered Species: Bald Eagle, Peregrine Falcon, Whooping Crane, Piping Plover

From Kenmare, go 0.5 mile west on Ward Co. Road No. 1 to the headquarters.

Habitat: 18,800 acres along the Des Lacs River extending from the Canadian border to 8 miles south of Kenmare. The river valley contains marshes and three natural lakes.

The marshes attract many species of ducks as well as Western Grebes, which perform their unique courtship displays in the spring. Sharp-tailed Grouse have a number of active leks on the refuge. American White Pelicans fish for their small prey in the lakes and marshes during the summer, although they do not breed at the refuge. LeConte's Sparrows can be found in the tall vegetation in the wetter areas, while Sprague's Pipits, Baird's Sparrows, and Chestnut-collared Longspurs are common in the uplands.

In the fall, the waterways of the refuge are a major stopover point for thousands of ducks and shorebirds, as well as "Lesser" Snow Geese and Tundra Swans.

Area brochure, auto tour route, picnicking, photo blind, limited hunting, boating, cross-country skiing, snowshoeing.
Spring, Summer, Fall

Crosby WMD & Lake Zahl 🛈
Crosby, ND 58730   701-965-6488

Crosby Wetland Management District is located in Divide, Burke, and Williams counties in northwestern North Dakota. Lake Zahl is located in northern Williams County.

Habitat: The wetland management district encompasses 3,219-acre Lake Zahl and more than 17,000 acres of croplands farmed exclusively for waterfowl, in addition to 66,000 acres of wetlands under easement contracts. The district represents three geological formations: a drift plain with large, shallow potholes in Northern Burke and northeastern Divide counties; the Altamont Moraine, which crosses the district from northwest to southeast; and the Coteau Slope, which slopes gradually down toward the Missouri River and includes the Lake Zahl refuge.

Lake Zahl, managed primarily for the breeding waterfowl, also hosts thousands of migrating geese, ducks, and other water birds. The most numerous ducks are Mallards, Gadwalls, and Blue-winged Teals, while "Giant" Canada Geese now breed throughout the Wetland Management District. Other common breeders of the wetlands are Black-crowned Night-Herons, American Coots, and five species of grebes. American Avocets, Marbled Godwits, Willets, and Upland Sandpipers are among the shorebirds that nest at the refuge and may be seen in the prairie wetlands.

Red-tailed and Swainson's hawks, Northern Harriers, and Burrowing, Great Horned, and Short-eared owls are among the raptors that breed in the district. Golden and Bald eagles migrate through during spring and fall, and some stay in the area if the winter is mild.

Area brochure, archery hunting at Lake Zahl.
Spring, Summer, Fall

Lostwood 5   (office at refuge)
Rural Route 2
Kenmare, ND 58746   701-848-2722

Part of the Des Lacs Refuge Complex (see local map on page 141). From Kenmare, go 12 miles west on Ward Co. Road No. 2, turn south on Hwy. 8, and go 4 miles to the headquarters.

Habitat: 26,747 acres, including a 5,577-acre wilderness area. A remnant of the original prairie wetlands, it includes grasslands, brushfields, and brushy coulees with some aspen groves.

Waterfowl and other waterbirds are the highlights on this refuge. Blue-winged Teals, Mallards, Gadwalls, and American Wigeons are observed in significant numbers. "Giant" Canada Geese also nest on the refuge. Virginia Rails, Marbled Godwits, and American Avocets wade in the wetlands. LeConte's and Baird's sparrows and Sprague's Pipits forage in the grasslands. In the early spring, Sharp-tailed Grouse perform their courtship displays on numerous dancing grounds.

Area brochure, hiking trails, cross-country skiing, snowshoeing.
Spring, Summer, Fall

Upper Souris 6   (office at refuge)
Rural Route 1
Foxholm, ND 58738   701-468-5467

Part of the Des Lacs Refuge Complex (see local map on page 141). From Foxholm, take Co. Road 11 north for 7 miles to the refuge. The headquarters are located near the Lake Darling Dam.

Habitat: 32,000 acres extending for nearly 30 miles along both sides of the Souris River in northwestern North Dakota include grasslands, marshes, and water impoundments. Lake Darling, at 10,000 acres, is the largest impoundment.

Waterfowl numbering up to 100,000 can be seen during spring and fall migrations. Tundra Swans, Northern Pintails, Canvasbacks, Redheads, Buffleheads, and other waterfowl either nest or use the refuge during migration. Up to five species of grebes can be found during the summer. A colony of Double-crested Cormorants and Great Blue Herons is located near the Grano Recreation Area. American White Pelicans also use the refuge for feeding and resting. Birders will also be able to find Baird's, LeConte's, and Sharp-tailed sparrows and Sprague's Pipits.

Area brochure, mammals and grasses lists, auto tour route, canoe and walking trails,

hunting, fishing, berry-picking, photo blinds, picnic tables.
Spring, Fall

Devils Lake 7   (office in town)
Wetland Management District
218 SW 4th Street
PO Box 908
Devils Lake, ND 58301   701-662-8611

The district is a blend of "fee" and "easement" areas totaling 221,989 acres and includes 11,194-acre Lake Alice Refuge and Sullys Hill National Game Preserve (NGP) with 1,674 acres. It also includes 27-acre Stump Lake, Kellys Slough, Lake Ardoch with 3,966 acres, and 9 other easement refuges totaling 15,891 acres. There are 187 waterfowl production areas comprising 40,113 acres, and 2,521 waterfowl production easements total 149,124 wetland acres.

Lake Alice is located northwest of Devils Lake. Take Hwy. 2 northwest for approximately 16 miles, then go north on county road for approximately 4 miles to refuge. Check at Devils Lake office for current information.

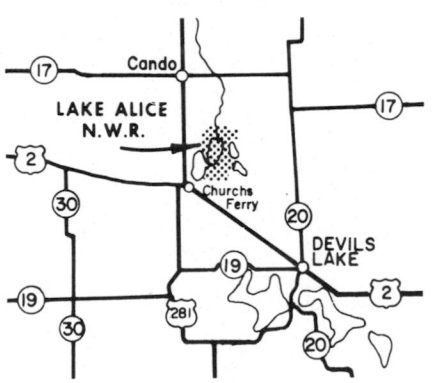

Sullys Hill NGP is located approximately 10 miles southwest of Devils Lake adjacent to Hwy. 57.

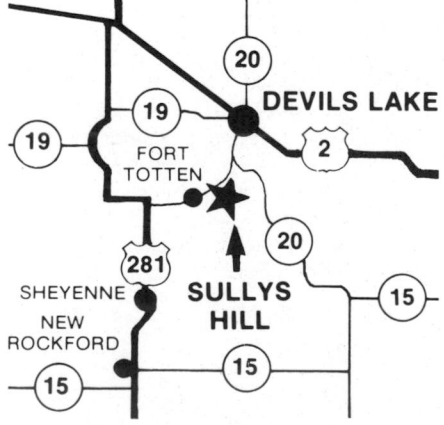

Habitat: 221,989 acres of lakes, marsh, and wooded hills in 8 counties in northeastern North Dakota.

The preserve's wooded hills are attractive to birds not normally seen in the open areas of the state. In addition, a wide variety of waterfowl, shorebirds, and marsh birds may be found around Sweetwater Lake, along the shore of Devils Lake, and in the marsh of Fort Totten Bay. Birding is best from late April to early June and from late August to mid-October.

The area (Sullys Hill) bird list has 267 species but does not include seasonal abundance data. Area brochures, auto tour route, maps, foot trails, picnicking, hunting.
Spring, Fall

J Clark Salyer 8   (office at refuge)
Wetland Management District
Box 66
Upham, ND 58789   701-768-2548

From Upham, go 3 miles north on St. Hwy. 14 to refuge sign and the headquarters.

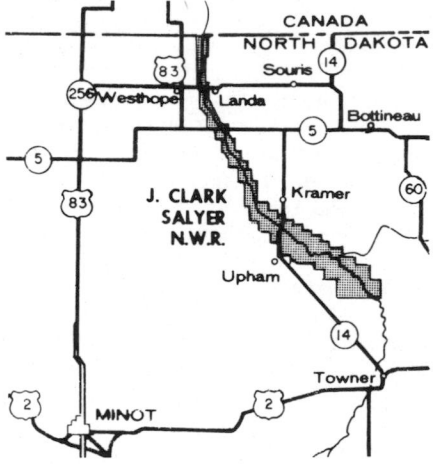

Habitat: 58,700 acres. Much of the original marsh has been restored along the lower reaches of the Souris River. Low dikes created pools along the 75 miles of river within the refuge boundary, which contains 50 natural and man-made islands, about 36,000 acres of grasslands interspersed with thick woodlands and dense brush, and 3,500 of cropland.

Salyer is an important feeding and resting area for hundreds of thousands of waterfowl that migrate through on the Central Flyway. The refuge also has been developed into an important breeding ground for ducks.

The refuge is in the geographical zone that separates eastern and western species and hosts birds from both areas. The bird list has 250 species. More than 125 species nest at Salyer, including the American White Pelican, Sandhill Crane,

Lark Bunting, longspurs, and Baird's and LeConte's sparrows. A Double-crested Cormorant colony is located in the southern portion of the refuge and there are rookeries of Great Blue Herons and Black-crowned Night-Herons.

Sharp-tailed and Ruffed grouse, Ring-necked Pheasants, Gray Partridges, and Wild Turkeys live in the uplands.

Area brochure, 2 auto tour routes, canoe trail, observation towers, hunting, fishing, ice fishing, picnicking.
Spring, Summer, Fall

Kulm ❾ (office in town)
Wetland Management District
1st Street SW, PO Box E
Kulm, ND 58456 701-647-2866

Kulm WMD protects the prairie pothole region of south-central North Dakota through its management of 42,000 acres of waterfowl production areas, 97,000 acres of wetlands under easement and three private refuges that include upland grasslands.

Temporary wetlands provide food and nesting territories for ducks and, when the wetland dries out in the fall, cover for upland game birds. More permanent wetlands provide habitat for migrating birds, including waterfowl.

Because of the size of the WMD, there is not a bird list specific to the area. A statewide list is available with 351 species, of which 207 nest, 95 are migrants, and 49 occur only occasionally or accidentally.

Area brochure, hunting, trapping, hiking.
Spring, Summer, Fall

Lake Ilo ❿ (office at refuge)
Box 127
Dunn Center, ND 58626 701-548-4467

Bird List ND-4 Lake Ilo Summary
205 birds listed, 83 nesting birds
Bird Chart pages 312-329

Totals by Season		s	S	F	W
Abundant	A	25	24	20	2
Common	C	54	38	41	4
Uncommon	U	41	25	56	7
Occasional	O	60	33	64	14
Rare	R	24	25	20	18

Endangered Species: Bald Eagle, Peregrine Falcon, Whooping Crane, Piping Plover, Least Tern

From Dunn Center, go 1 mile east on Hwy. 200 to the lake.

Habitat: 4,043 acres that include 1,250-acre Lake Ilo. There are 1,200 acres of open grasslands, with the remaining area reclaimed farmland, food plots, and tree plantings.

The marshes, sloughs, and small ponds found on the refuge attract large numbers of marsh, wading, and shorebirds. American Bitterns, Great Blue Herons, and Eared, Pied-billed, and Western grebes have all been known to nest on the refuge. Populations of these birds are greatest during fall migrations. The main nesting ducks include Mallards, Northern Pintails, Gadwalls, Blue-winged Teals, Northern Shovelers, and Lesser Scaups.

The transitional zone of vegetation near the water's edge provides some of the best birding. The riparian community of cottonwoods, honeysuckle, caragana, and numerous forbs attract the largest variety of songbirds to be found on the refuge. Upland game birds that live in the farmland, food plots, and treed areas include Ring-necked Pheasants, Sharp-tailed Grouse, and Gray Partridges.

Spring, Fall

Long Lake ⓫ (office at refuge)
Rural Route 1
Moffit, ND 58560 701-387-4397

Bird List ND-5 Long Lake Summary
203 birds listed, 78 nesting birds
Bird Chart pages 312-329

Totals by Season		s	S	F	W
Abundant	A	6	4	9	1
Common	C	61	44	57	4
Uncommon	U	45	42	42	7
Occasional	O	22	16	17	7
Rare	R	53	18	33	9

Endangered Species: Bald Eagle, Peregrine Falcon, Whooping Crane, Piping Plover, Least Tern

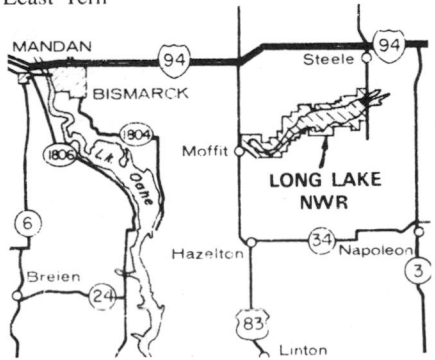

From Moffit, take Hwy. 83 south 1 mile and then go 3 miles east on the county road to the office. Long Lake NWR is also administrative headquarters for a small satellite unit, Slade NWR, and

waterfowl production areas in 3 counties. Habitat: 22,300 acres. Long Lake is approximately 16,000 acres, and the remaining 6,300 acres consists of rolling prairie, with small areas planted with trees and shrubs and approximately 500 acres of cultivated uplands. The refuge ranges from less than 0.5 mile to 2 miles in width and is approximately 18 miles long.

Northern Pintails and Mallards usually lead the northward flight of waterfowl, beginning late in March. Other puddle ducks and water and marsh birds follow shortly, with peak flights of waterfowl occurring near mid-April. The most common nesting ducks are the Northern Pintail, Blue-winged Teal, Gadwall, Mallard, Northern Shoveler, and Lesser Scaup. A small number of "Greater" Canada Geese nest on the refuge.

The endangered Piping Plover nests at the refuge, as well as the Upland Sandpiper. Spotted Sandpipers, Willets, Marbled Godwits, American Avocets, and Wilson's Phalaropes usually nest on lowlands adjacent to dikes and marsh areas. Gray Partridges and Sharp-tailed Grouse breed in the grassy uplands. Endangered Whooping Cranes occasionally rest at the refuge.

Area brochure, fishing, boating (no motors), picnic area.
Spring, Fall

Tewaukon ⓬ (office at refuge)
Rural Route 1
Cayuga, ND 58013 701-724-3598

Bird List ND-6 Tewaukon Summary
236 birds listed, 98 nesting birds
Bird Chart pages 312-329

Totals by Season		s	S	F	W
Abundant	A	14	13	15	0
Common	C	74	51	57	8
Uncommon	U	57	41	47	6
Occasional	O	63	32	58	14
Rare	R	21	17	31	25

Endangered Species: Bald Eagle, Peregrine Falcon, Least Tern

From Cayuga, take Co. Road 12 south for 5.5 miles to the refuge.

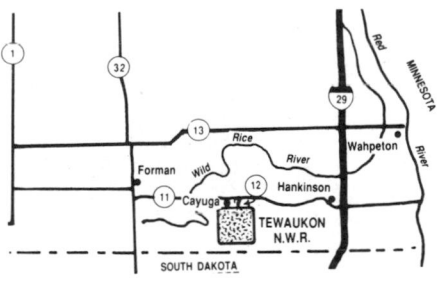

Habitat: 8,438 acres located on both sides of the Wild Rice River. Also includes 9 large impoundments totalling 2,100 acres, 31 ponds of 5 to 20 acres each, and 100 potholes. Many miles of trees and shrubs have been planted for shelter and there are about 900 acres of cropland. The refuge headquarters also manages 11,893 acres of waterfowl production areas and 32,000 acres of waterfowl production easement in 3 counties.

The Western Grebe performs its courtship dance during the spring, when courting behavior of many duck species and Canada Geese can also be observed. Both American and Least bitterns and Green-backed Herons also nest here.

Birds from both the Central and Mississippi flyways use the refuge and WMDs. Late summer and fall feature a buildup of cormorants, American White Pelicans, and Great Egrets. Large numbers of Franklin's and Ring-billed gulls roost on Lake Tewaukon in September. From mid-October to freeze-up, large numbers of waterfowl move through the refuge with thousands of Snow and Canada geese, Mallards, Lesser Scaups, and Tundra Swans.

Area brochure, fishing, picnicking, hiking. Spring, Fall

NATIONAL PARK SERVICE

Theodore Roosevelt ❶
National Park
PO Box 7
Medora, ND 58645   701-623-4466

Bird List ND-7 Roosevelt Summary
170 birds listed, 58 nesting birds
Bird Chart pages 312-329

Totals by Season		s	S	F	W
Common	C	58	53	48	10
Uncommon	U	38	25	36	7
Occasional	O	26	27	18	38
Rare	R	11	14	5	4

Endangered Species: Bald Eagle, Peregrine Falcon, Whooping Crane

70,416 acres include badlands along the Little Missouri River and part of the Theodore Roosevelt Elkhorn Ranch. Park brochure with map, various species lists, recreation activity leaflets.
Spring, Summer, Fall.

NATIONAL FOREST SERVICE

Custer National Forest Supervisor
2602 First Avenue North
PO Box 2556
Billings, MT 59103   406-657-6361

The supervisor's office for the National Grasslands in North Dakota is in Montana.

Map/Grassland-Ranger District/City
△ Cedar River NG-Grand River
  /Lemmon, SD   605-374-3592
⚠ Little Missouri NG-McKenzie
  /Watford City, ND   701-842-2393
⚠ Little Missouri NG-Medora
  /Dickinson, ND   701-225-5151

BUREAU LAND MANAGEMENT

BLM District Office ▽
2933 Third Avenue West
Dickinson, ND 58601   701-225-9148

This is the only BLM office in North Dakota and reports to the Billings Montana BLM State Office.

STATE AGENCIES

North Dakota Game & Fish Dept.
100 North Bismark Expressway
Bismark, ND 58501   701-221-6300

North Dakota Tourism Division
Liberty Memorial Bldg.
State Capitol Grounds
Bismark, ND 50505   800-472-2100
from out-of-state call   800-437-2077

BIRDING HOTLINES

Cincinnati	513-521-2847
Cleveland	216-289-2473
Columbus	614-221-9736
Blendon Woods Metro Park	614-895-6222
Southwestern Ohio	513-277-6446
Toledo	419-877-5003
Youngstown	216-742-6661

LOCAL BIRDING GROUPS
Map/Chapter/City

1. Appalachian Front Aud./Hillsboro
2. Audubon Soc. of Greater Cleveland /Cleveland
3. Audubon Soc. of Ohio/Cincinnati
4. Black River Audubon/Elyria
5. Black Swamp Audubon/Defiance
6. Blackbrook Audubon/Painesville
7. Canton Audubon/Canton
8. Clark County Audubon/Springfield
9. Cleveland Audubon/Euclid
10. Columbus Audubon/Columbus
11. Dayton Audubon/Dayton
12. Firelands Audubon/Huron
13. Greater Akron Audubon/Akron
14. Hocking Valley Audubon/Athens
15. Licking County Audubon/Lancaster
16. Maumee Valley Audubon/Toledo
17. Mohican Audubon/Mansfield
18. Oxford Audubon/Oxford
19. R.B. Hayes Audubon/Freemont
20. Tri-Moraine Audubon/Lima
21. Western Cuyahoga Audubon/Parma
22. Youngstown Audubon/Youngstown
23. Burroughs Nature Club of Marion /Marion
24. Burroughs Nature Club of Willoughby/Willoughby
25. Cincinnati Bird Club/Cincinnati
26. Grant M. Cook Bird Club /Youngstown
27. Kirtland Bird Club/Cleveland
28. Salem Bird Study Club/Salem
29. Shawnee Nature Club/Friendship
30. Wayne Nature Club/Wooster
31. Wheaton Club/Columbus

NATIONAL AUDUBON SOCIETY

Allwood Audubon Center ❶
& Farm
1000 Allwood Road
Dayton, OH 45414   513-890-7360
Entrance fee for non-members

This 200-acre wildlife sanctuary is located north of I-70 and west of the airport access road. The entrance is on Allwood Road, east and then south of its intersection with U.S. Rte. 40. Open to visitors 9a.m–5p.m. Monday–Saturday, and from 1p.m.–5p.m. on Sunday. It is closed on some holidays.

Habitat: Native woods, prairies, marshes, meadows, and a working farm sustain a variety of flora and fauna.

The sanctuary management offers varied programs for the general public on weekends, warden-led guided and self-guided walks, seasonal events like woodcock watches, bird walks, exhibits, and nature courses. Special educational programs for school children and adult education workshops are available.

Sanctuary brochure with map, visitor center, 5 miles of hiking trails, auto tour route, cross-country skiing.
Spring, Summer, Fall, Winter

THE NATURE CONSERVANCY
Ohio Field Office ⓕⓞ
1504 West 1st Avenue
Columbus, OH 43212   614-486-6789

Contact the Field Office for literature and information about activities and preserve visits.

A 60-page "Guide to the Ohio Preserves of the Nature Conservancy" is available for $5 from the Field Office. It includes local area maps and detailed descriptions of 20 TNC preserves and notes 72 of the TNC projects in Ohio.

Four TNC preserves open to the public are briefly described here. A bird list is available for three of these preserves (all but Browns Lake Bog). A preserve manager oversees Buzzardroost Neck and Lynx Prairie, and may be reached through the Field Office. A visit to any of these preserves is rewarding throughout the year.

Browns Lake Bog ❶
80 acres, at an elevation of 940 to 980 feet, near Shreve. Special viewing area from the boardwalk. Day hiking.

Buzzardroost Rock ❷
526 acres, at an elevation of 800 to 1,000 feet, near Lynx, on the edge of the Appalachia Preserve System. Viewing platform on top of Buzzardroost. Day

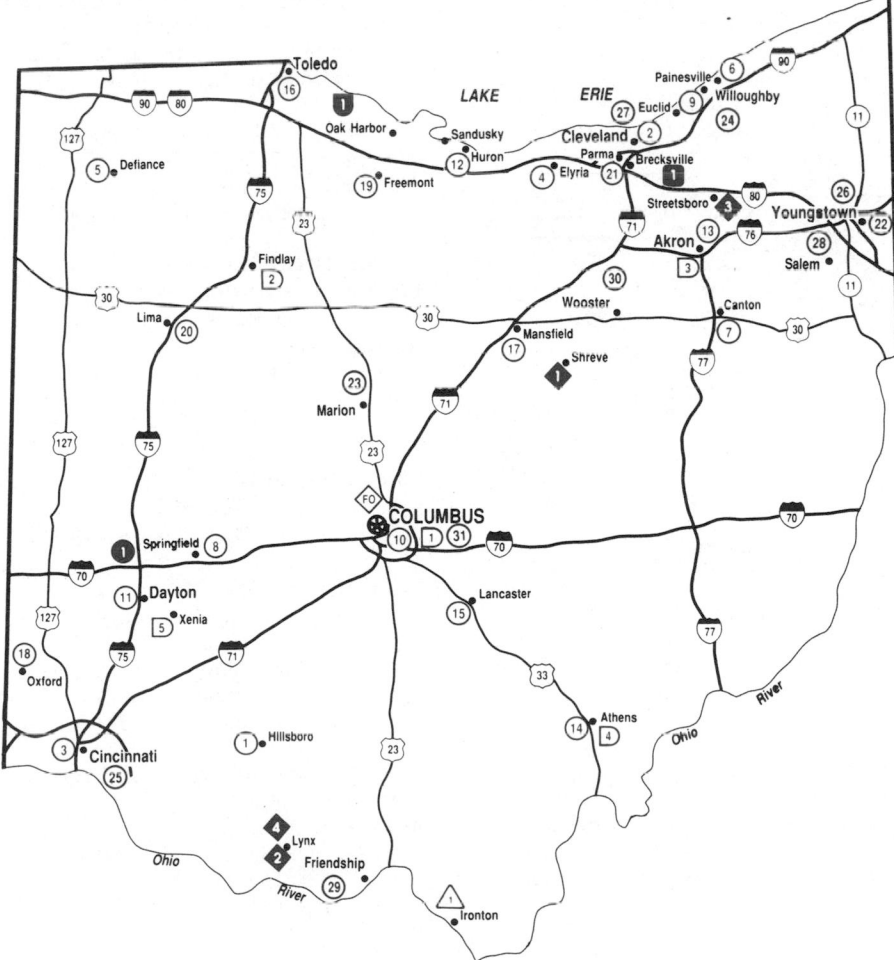

hiking, species list.

J. Arthur Herrick Fen ❸

126 acres, at an elevation of 1,030 to 1,080 feet, near Streetsboro. Boardwalk, day hiking.

Lynx Prairie ❹

200 acres, at an elevation of 760 to 860 feet, near Lynx, on the edge of the Appalachia Preserve System. Species list, day hiking.

U.S. FISH & WILDLIFE SERVICE NATIONAL WILDLIFE REFUGE

Ottawa ❶   (office at refuge)

1400 W. State Route 2
Oak Harbor, OH 43449   419-898-0014

Bird List OH-1 Ottawa Summary
271 birds listed, 124 nesting birds
Bird Chart pages 312-329

Totals by Season		s	S	F	W
Abundant	A	29	20	26	7
Common	C	16	48	10	20
Uncommon	U	43	52	53	33
Occasional	O	30	26	34	20
Rare	R	42	29	39	47

Endangered Species: Bald Eagle, Peregrine Falcon, Piping Plover

Refuge headquarters is located on St. Rte. 2 about 15 miles east of Toledo and north of the village of Oak Harbor.

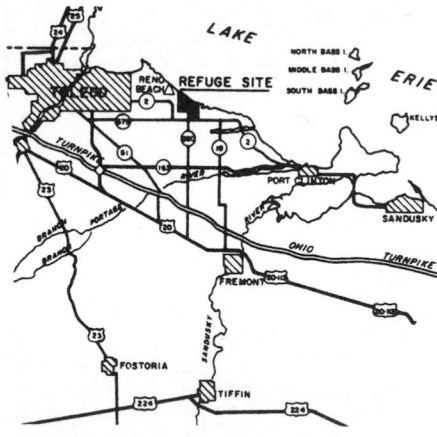

Habitat: 5,794 acres that are the last remainder of a 300,000-acre swamp that extended from Sandusky, Ohio to Detroit, Michigan. Includes some uplands and woodlands.

Ottawa is a major stopover point for migrating waterfowl such as Trumpeter Swans and Canvasbacks. A large variety of waterfowl remains to breed on the swamps, including Mallards, American

Black and Wood ducks, Blue-winged Teals, and American Wigeons. The refuge is also an excellent spot for migrating Cape May, Black-throated Blue, Black-and-white, Tennessee, Nashville, and Blackburnian warblers during spring and fall. Yellow and Chestnut-sided warblers nest at Ottawa.

Great Egrets, Black-crowned Night-Herons and Great Blue Herons, feed on the marsh. Killdeer and yellowlegs can be seen near the marshes. In the surrounding wooded or upland areas Barn Swallows, American Goldfinches, Indigo Buntings, Northern Cardinals, Brown Thrashers, and American Woodcocks can be seen.

Area brochure, walking trail, photo blinds, limited fishing and hunting, cross-country skiing.
Spring, Fall

NATIONAL PARK SERVICE

Cuyahoga Valley National ❶ Recreation Area

15610 Vaughn Road
Brecksville, OH 44141   216-526-5256

32,460 acres linking the urban centers of Cleveland and Akron, preserving the rural character of the Cuyahoga River Valley and such historic resources as the century-old Ohio and Erie canal system.

Recreation area brochure with map, bird checklist with season and habitat codes. The checklist covers 231 species, of which 109 are coded as noteworthy.

NATIONAL FOREST SERVICE

Ironton Ranger District ⚠
Wayne Hoosier National Forest
(Indiana & Ohio)
Ironton, OH 45638   614-532-3223

STATE AGENCIES

Ohio Division of Wildlife

Fountain Square, Bldg. C-4
Columbus, OH 43224   614-265-6305

Map/District/City

①	Dist. One/Columbus	614-481-6300
②	Dist. Two/Findlay	419-424-5000
③	Dist. Three/Akron	216-644-2293
④	Dist. Four/Athens	614-594-2211
⑤	Dist. Five/Xenia	513-372-9261

Ohio Division of Travel & Tourism

State Office Tower
30 E. Broad Street
Columbus, OH 43216   800-282-5393

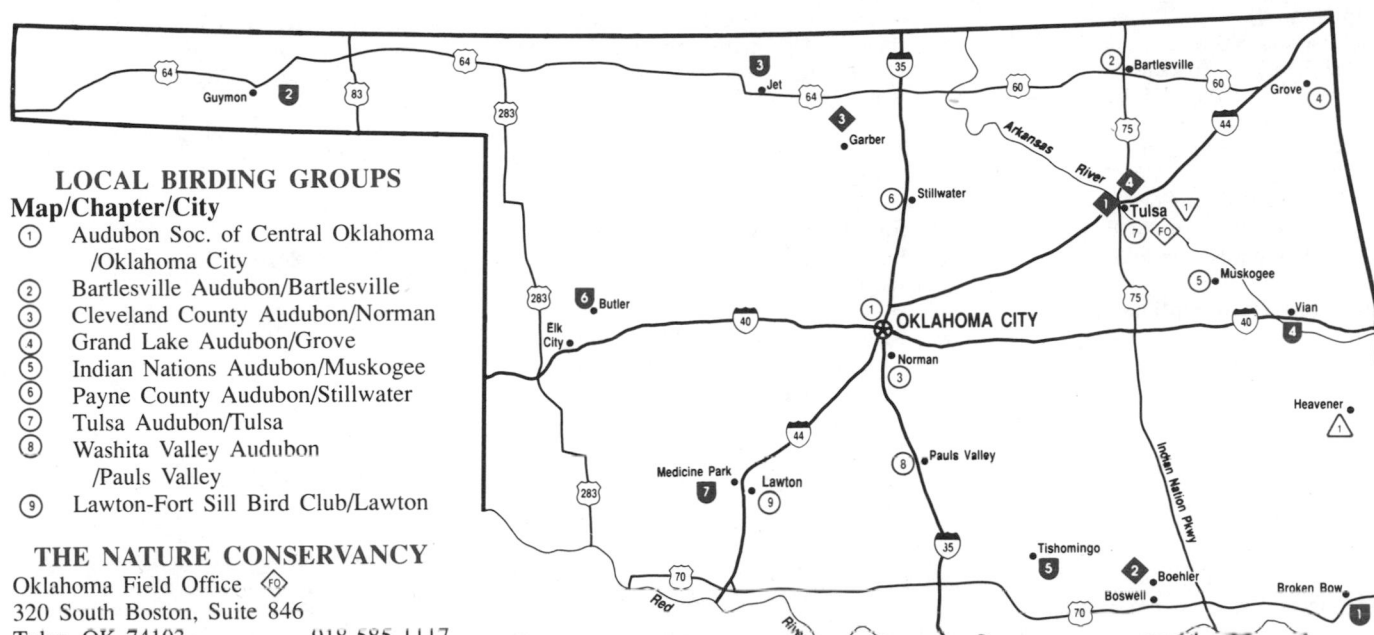

LOCAL BIRDING GROUPS
Map/Chapter/City

1. Audubon Soc. of Central Oklahoma /Oklahoma City
2. Bartlesville Audubon/Bartlesville
3. Cleveland County Audubon/Norman
4. Grand Lake Audubon/Grove
5. Indian Nations Audubon/Muskogee
6. Payne County Audubon/Stillwater
7. Tulsa Audubon/Tulsa
8. Washita Valley Audubon /Pauls Valley
9. Lawton-Fort Sill Bird Club/Lawton

THE NATURE CONSERVANCY

Oklahoma Field Office
320 South Boston, Suite 846
Tulsa, OK 74103   918-585-1117

Contact the Field Office for information, maps, and visitor regulations.

Arkansas River Least Tern ◆

Oxley Nature Center
5701 E. 36th Street
North Tulsa, OK 74115

Owned by the city of Tulsa and assorted private owners.

Exit I-44 on the east bank of the Arkansas River onto Riverside Dr. north to Oxley Nature Center on 36th St.

Habitat: 1,400 acres at 600 feet of elevation along 5 miles of the Arkansas River and within the city limits of Tulsa.

The endangered Least Tern nests from May until August. Access to nesting areas are prohibited during the breeding season, but several points in the Park offer excellent vistas for observation. During spring and fall migrating shorebirds congregate in the area. In winter months the "Southern" Bald Eagle and an occasional Peregrine Falcon may be seen.

Picnicking, bicycling, hiking, fishing, non-motorized boating, cross-country skiing.
Spring, Summer

Boehler Seeps & Sandhills ◆

77 acres, at 550 feet, of upland sandhill woodland and a hillside seep, or bog, near Boehler.

From Boswell go 1 mile west on Hwy. 70 to blacktop road. Turn north and continue for 10 miles to Boehler. Drive 0.25 mile west from Boehler to the preserve, in the very SE corner of Atoka County.

Picnicking, day hiking, wildflowers.
Spring, Summer

E.C. Springer Prairie ◆

40 acres, at 1,100 feet, near Garber. Area is fenced and locked. Big bluestem and switchgrass prairie.

Located in NE Garfield County not far from Enid. Go 10.5 miles north of Garber on Hwy. 74. Preserve is located 0.25 mile east of Hwy. 74 (walking access only).

Picnicking, day hiking, wildflowers.
Spring, Summer

Redbud Valley ◆

82 acres, at 650 feet, of grassy upland and forested ravines along the south side of Bird Creek.

Take I-44 east from Tulsa to 161st E. Ave. exit (at large truck stop). Go north about 4 miles to preserve parking lot on west side of road.

A large variety of birds and other wildlife find food and rest among the unique plants of Redbud Valley, particularly during fall migration.

Area brochure with trail map, picnicking, day hiking, cross-country skiing.
Spring, Summer, Fall

U.S. FISH & WILDLIFE SERVICE NATIONAL WILDLIFE REFUGES

Little River ◆

635 South Park Street
PO Box 340
Broken Bow, OK 74728   405-584-6211

From Broken Bow take Hwy. 70 for 4.5 miles (south) to refuge boundary. The refuge extends east and west from the highway along Little River.

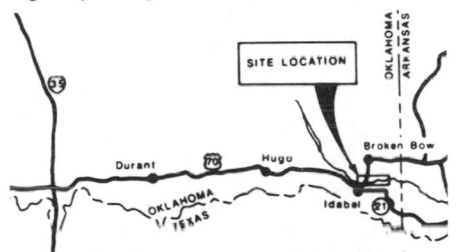

Habitat: 15,000 acres in the floodplain along the north side of Little River. Most of the refuge is forested with bottomland species such as willow oak, sweetgum, cypress, white oak, and holly. Some areas on higher ground support loblolly pine, hickory, and walnut. Old oxbows and sloughs are interspersed through the low wet areas. The refuge contains most of the remaining bottomland hardwood habitat in southeastern Oklahoma.

More than 225 species of birds have been recorded on the refuge. Waterfowl, primarily Mallards, Wood Ducks, American Wigeons, Green-winged Teals, and Gadwalls may be observed in the seasonally flooded bottomland. There are several rookeries used by a variety of herons and egrets. Many other migrating birds nest on the refuge, including Red-shouldered and Red-tailed hawks, Mississippi Kites, Turkey Vultures, and Pileated Woodpeckers.

Area brochure, hiking, hunting, fishing.
Spring, Fall, Winter

Optima ❷

c/o Washita NWR
Rural Route 1, Box 68
Butler, OK 73625   405-626-4794

Headquarters is located at the Washita NWR north of Elk City. This refuge, operated through a Cooperative Agreement with the Army Corps of Engineers, is part of the Optima Reservoir Project.

Bird List OK-1 Optima Summary

246 birds listed, 106 nesting birds
Bird Chart pages 330-347

Totals by Season		s	S	F	W
Abundant	A	3	5	3	1
Common	C	62	36	60	20
Uncommon	U	1	0	2	0
Occasional	O	27	57	24	55
Rare	R	50	47	49	42

Endangered Species: Bald Eagle, Least Tern

Optima is 15 miles east of Guymon on Hwy. 3, which crosses the refuge.

Habitat: 4,333 acres located on the Coldwater Creek arm of Optima Reservoir. 1,600 acres are flooded when the reservoir is raised to conservation pool level. A total of 540 acres, in four parcels, are dominated by eastern cottonwood trees, and grasslands dominate the remainder of the refuge. Almost 50 percent of the prairie vegetation is sandsage-bluestem and another 30 percent is covered with grama-buffalo grass.

Scissor-tailed Flycatchers, Eastern and Western kingbirds, Northern "Bullock's" Orioles, and Red-headed Woodpeckers are the more conspicuous landbirds during the spring and summer.

A variety of raptors may be seen throughout the year. Turkey Vultures, Mississippi Kites, Northern Harriers, Swainson's and Red-tailed hawks, American Kestrels, and an occasional Prairie Falcon and Golden Eagle nest. Other raptors seen during migration and winter including Bald Eagles, Ferruginous Hawks, and Merlins.

All waterfowl species that migrate along the Central Flyway stop at the refuge. A wide variety of other waterbirds are also found at Optima, including the Western Grebe, Least Tern, Snowy Plover, and Sandhill Crane.

Area brochure, fishing, hunting, hiking.
Spring, Fall, Winter

Salt Plains ❸   (office at refuge)

Route 1, Box 76
Jet, OK 73749   405-626-4794

Bird List OK-2 Salt Plains Summary

243 birds listed, 98 nesting birds
Bird Chart pages 330-347

Totals by Season		s	S	F	W
Abundant	A	27	3	26	9
Common	C	94	67	84	34
Uncommon	U	38	25	40	22
Occasional	O	35	31	31	30
Rare	R	44	21	38	36

Endangered Species: Bald Eagle, Peregrine Falcon, Whooping Crane, Piping Plover, Least Tern

From Jet, take St. Hwy. 38 north for 13.8 miles to the headquarters.

Habitat: 32,000 acres, 12,000 acres that are salt flats, 10,000 acres of impoundments, and 10,000 acres upland. The uplands, predominantly native grasslands with a substantial acreage of invading brush and forest, include 1,300 acres of crop fields. A system of small freshwater ponds and marshes has been constructed.

In the spring and fall, large flocks of ducks and geese migrating along the Central Flyway stop at Salt Plains. The Canada Goose is the most common, but Greater White-fronted and Snow geese are also numerous during the winter. Northern Pintails and Green-winged Teals are among the most abundant ducks.

Many other waterbirds use the refuge. The most numerous breeder is the Franklin's Gull. Among the shorebirds commonly seen are American Avocets, Long-billed Dowitchers, and Hudsonian and Marbled godwits. Larger birds include American White Pelicans, herons, and Sandhill Cranes.

The Mississippi Kite is a common nester.

Northern Bobwhites and Ring-necked Pheasants nest in large numbers. Wild Turkeys are seen during spring and fall.

Area brochure, nature trail, fishing, boating, camping, picnicking, swimming, water skiing, observation tower.
Spring, Fall

Sequoyah ❹   (office at refuge)

Route 1, Box 18A
Vian, OK 74962   918-773-5251

Bird List OK-3 Sequoia Summary

250 birds listed, 96 nesting birds
Bird Chart pages 330-347

Totals by Season		s	S	F	W
Abundant	A	5	13	13	14
Common	C	73	45	58	43
Uncommon	U	53	31	62	29
Occasional	O	63	25	49	18
Rare	R	31	13	34	29

Endangered Species: Bald Eagle, Peregrine Falcon, Piping Plover, Least Tern

Take the Vian exit off of I-40 and go 3 miles south to the refuge headquarters.

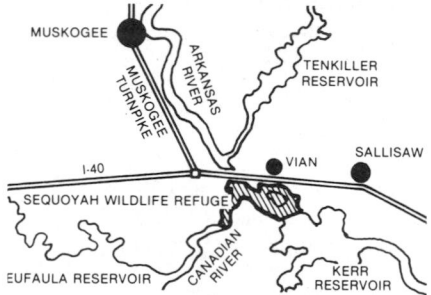

Habitat: 20,800 acres at the junction of the Canadian and Arkansas rivers. Half the area is water. The remainder is steep shoreline or bottomland next to Kerr Reservoir, with numerous ponds and sloughs, cottonwood and willow trees, and some croplands.

Waterfowl are abundant during spring, fall, and winter. The refuge hosts the largest concentration of Snow Geese in the state. Upland songbirds and hawks, and Northern Bobwhites are commonly seen.

Area brochure, auto tour route, photo blind, observation tower, hiking trail, fishing, hunting, boating.
Spring, Fall, Winter

Tishomingo ❺   (office at refuge)

Route 1, Box 151
Tishomingo, OK 73460   405-371-2402

Bird List OK-4 Tishomingo Summary

243 birds listed, 81 nesting birds
Bird Chart pages 330-347

Totals by Season		s	S	F	W
Abundant	A	23	16	24	18
Common	C	90	42	70	47
Occasional	O	77	65	98	51
Rare	R	24	34	24	20

Endangered Species: Wood Stork, Bald Eagle, Peregrine Falcon, Piping Plover, Least Tern
Rare/Limited Species: Barnacle Goose

The refuge office is 3.5 miles southeast of Tishomingo. A sign on Hwy. 78 (Main Street) in town indicates the correct road.

Habitat: 16,464 acres include the 4,500-acre Cumberland Pool of Lake Texoma. Seasonally flooded flats and willow shallows at the pool's edge provide excellent wildlife habitat. Upland areas include grassland, wild plum thickets, and oak-hickory-elm woodlands. The 900 acres of croplands provide forage for waterfowl.

Migrating American White Pelicans, grebes, ducks, herons, sandpipers, gulls, and numerous upland birds can be seen on the refuge. The Scissor-tailed Flycatcher, Painted Bunting, and Lark Sparrow are among the most common and conspicuous nesting landbirds.

Summer birds include wading and woodland birds. The southward migration of shorebirds, herons, cormorants, and Franklin's Gulls begins in August.

Waterfowl start to arrive in September, reaching their peak between November and February. The geese are predominantly Canadas, but also include Greater White-fronted and Snow geese. Mallards, Green-winged Teals, and other dabblers are the most common ducks. During that time 50 to 90 Bald Eagles may also be present.

Area brochure, nature trail, observation tower, hunting, fishing, boating.
Spring, Summer, Fall, Winter

Washita 🔢   (office at refuge)
Route 1, Box 68
Butler, OK 73625   405-664-2205

Bird List OK-5 Washita Summary
220 birds listed, 67 nesting birds
Bird Chart pages 330-347

Totals by Season		s	S	F	W
Abundant	A	6	9	8	9
Common	C	52	36	46	31
Uncommon	U	55	32	51	30
Occasional	O	67	41	75	34
Rare	R	29	12	29	16

Endangered Species: Bald Eagle, Peregrine Falcon, Whooping Crane, Least Tern

Take Hwy. 66 east from Elk City for 3 miles, turn north onto Hwy. 34, and drive toward Hammond to Hwy. 33. Turn east, go 7 miles, then north for 1 mile and west for 0.5 mile to the refuge headquarters. Much of Wachita is closed October 15–March 15 to provide a waterfowl sanctuary.

Habitat: 8,200 acres on the upper reaches of Foss Reservoir. Open waters, shallow marshes, and 2,000 acres of planted crops. Fields of native and introduced grasses in the uplands. Brushy draws, bottomlands, and wooded creek and river banks are scattered throughout.

Both eastern and western birds use this mixed grass prairie. The refuge is heavily used by waterfowl and Sandhill Cranes while a large variety of water and marsh birds use the refuge in lesser numbers.

Area brochure, mammals list, fishing, hunting, boating, hiking.
Spring, Fall

Wichita Mountains 🔢 (office at refuge)
Route 1, Box 68
Butler, OK 73625   405-664-2205

Bird List OK-6 Wichita Mts. Summary
212 birds listed, 61 nesting birds
Bird Chart pages 330-347

Totals by Season		s	S	F	W
Common	C	50	34	46	40
Uncommon	U	66	31	55	32
Occasional	O	25	19	29	21
Rare	R	45	34	36	23

Endangered Species: Bald Eagle

At the Medicine Park/Hwy. 49 exit off I-44, take Hwy. 49 west for 9 miles to the refuge boundary. Continue on Hwy. 49 for about 15 miles to the office near the west end.

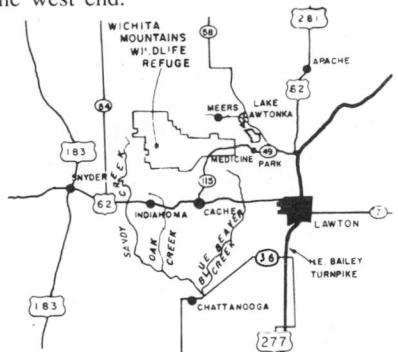

Habitat: 59,020 acres of which 22,400 acres is open to public use. The higher portions of the Wichita Mountains are interspersed with valleys, parks, and over 100 lakes and ponds. The wooded slopes and stream banks are predominantly oak with some juniper and other species.

Managed primarily for big game animals, its varied habitat attracts a wide range of birds. This mid-continent location is a crossroads for eastern and western species, both resident and migrant.

Area brochure, visitor center, camping, hiking, fishing, boating (limited), swimming, trail system, picnicking.
Spring, Fall

NATIONAL FOREST SERVICE
Choctaw Ranger District △
Ouachita National Forest
(Arkansas & Oklahoma)
PO Box B
Heavener, OK 74937   918-653-2991

BUREAU LAND MANAGEMENT
BLM State Office
J.P. Montoya Federal Bldg.
South Federal Place, PO Box 1449
Santa Fe, NM 87504-1449   505-988-6316

Map/District/City
▽   Tulsa/Tulsa   918-581-6480

STATE AGENCIES

OK Dept. of Wildlife Conservation
Game Division Nongame Program
1801 N. Lincoln
PO Box 53465
Oklahoma City, OK 73152   405-521-3855

OK Tourism & Recreation Dept.
500 Will Rogers Bldg.
Oklahoma City, OK 73105   405-521-2409

BIRDING HOTLINES

Statewide 503-292-0661
Southern Oregon 503-826-7011
10p.m. to 6a.m. weekdays only

LOCAL BIRDING GROUPS
Map/Chapter/City

① Audubon Soc. of Corvallis/Corvallis
② Cape Arago Audubon/North Bend
③ Central Oregon Audubon/Bend
④ Kalmiopsis Audubon/Wedderburn
⑤ Klamath Basin Aud./Klamath Falls
⑥ Lane County Audubon/Eugene
⑦ Portland Audubon/Portland
⑧ Rogue Valley Audubon/Jacksonville
⑨ Salem Audubon/Salem
⑩ Siskiyou Audubon/Grants Pass
⑪ Umpqua Audubon/Roseburg
⑫ Grande Ronde Birding Club
   /La Grande
⑬ Oregon Field Ornithologists/Eugene
⑭ South Willamette Ornithological
   Club/Eugene

THE NATURE CONSERVANCY

Oregon Field Office ⬦
1205 NW 25th Avenue
Portland, OR 97210 503-228-9561

Cascade Head Natural Area ◆

300 acres near Otis—contact Field Office for directions and permission to visit. Guided tours may be arranged for groups of 20 or more.

High cliffs ascend from the sea and give way to coastal prairie and forests of spruce and hemlock. Part of this sanctuary is closed to the public and hikers should stay on the trails to protect the habitat.

U.S. FISH & WILDLIFE SERVICE NATIONAL WILDLIFE REFUGES

U.S. Fish & Wildlife Service Region 1
Lloyd 500 Building, Suite 1692
500 NE Nultnomah Street
Portland, OR 97232 503-231-6214

Klamath Basin Refuges RC

c/o Tule Lake Refuge (office at refuge)
Route 1, Box 74
Tulelake, CA 96134 916-667-2231

See California chapter for directions to the office at Tule Lake. This is the office and information center for the six refuges in the Klamath complex, which consists of Bear Valley, Klamath Forest, and Upper Klamath, all located in the upper Klamath valley area in Oregon, and Clear Lake, Lower Klamath, and Tule Lake refuges located in California.

Bear Valley ▮

(Klamath Basin)
near Worden, OR

The Bird List OR-1 and the Up. Klamath Summary combine the three Klamath Basin refuges in Oregon, Bear Valley, Klamath Forest, and Upper Klamath. The OR-1 list was developed from local seasonal abundance data in the Klamath Basin Wildlife List, which contains refuge codes indicating the birds most likely to be seen at each refuge.

Bird List OR-1 Up. Klamath Summary
222 birds listed, 160 nesting birds
Bird Chart pages 330-347

Totals by Season		s	S	F	W
Abundant	A	16	12	18	3
Common	C	66	58	60	36
Uncommon	U	89	77	87	52
Rare	R	46	38	43	52

Endangered Species: Bald Eagle, Peregrine Falcon
Rare/Limited Species: White-headed Woodpecker

Bear Valley NWR is located about 1.75 miles west of Worden, via country road.

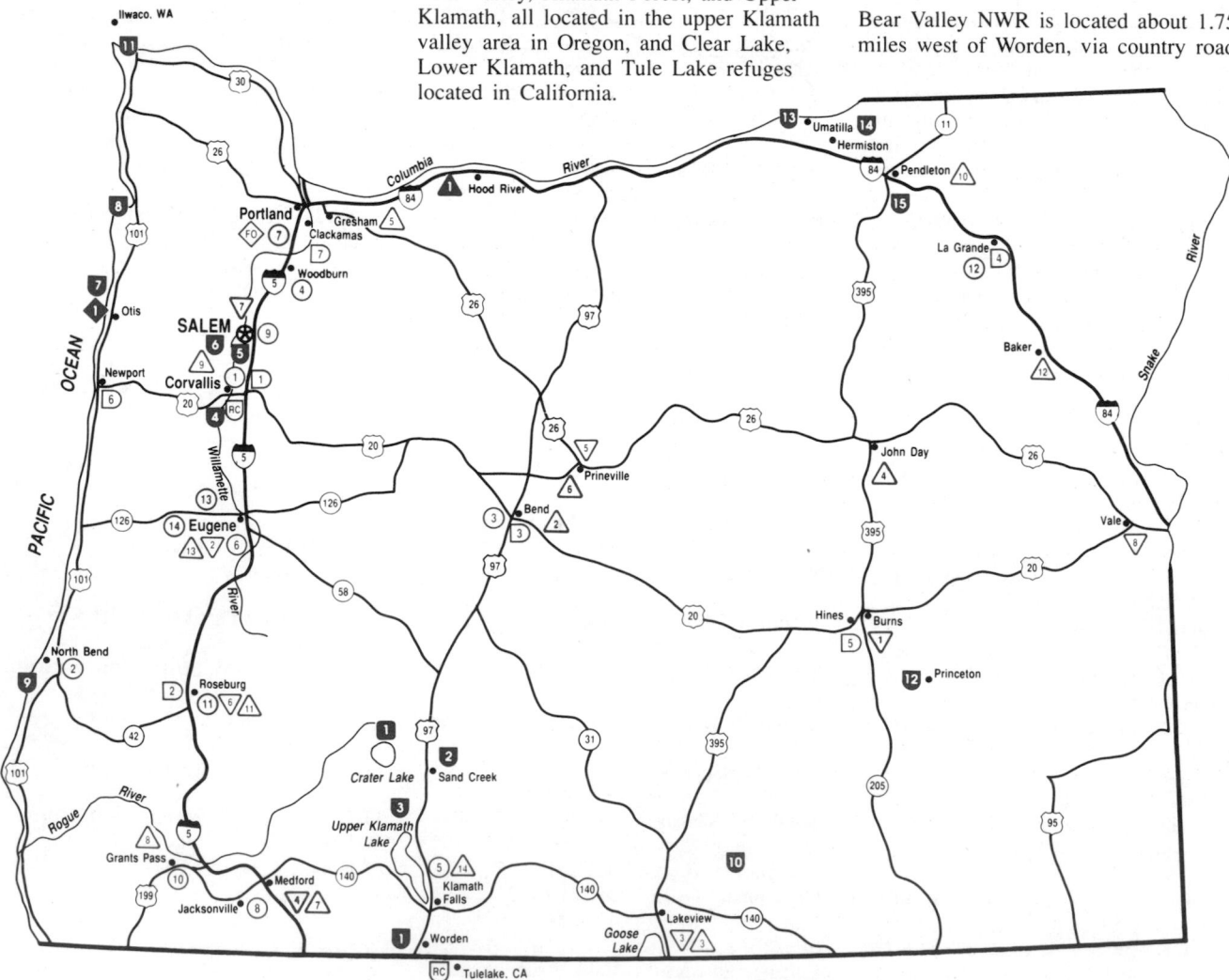

This local area map shows Bear Valley, the other two Klamath Basin refuges in southern Oregon, and the Klamath Basin refuges in northern California.

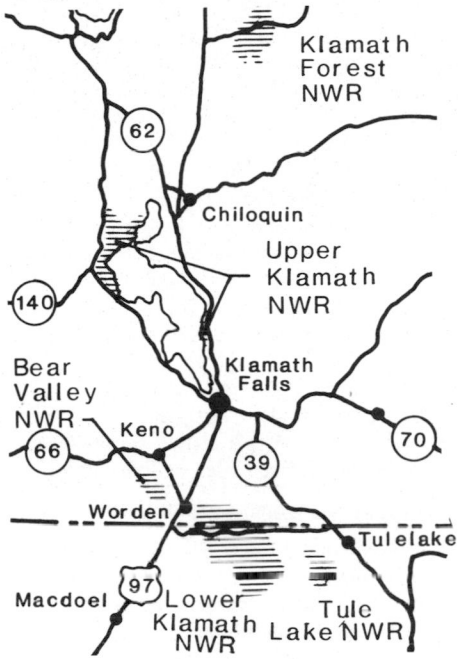

Habitat: 4,120 acres in Bear Valley with large stands of old growth timber.

The refuge is one of five Bald Eagle roosts in the Klamath Basin. In recent years nearly 300 eagles have used the roost in one night. Eagles are easy to see from the vicinity of Worden, just off Hwy. 97, when they fly in and out of the roost area.

Public access to this refuge is restricted in order to protect the sensitive wintering habitat for the eagles. Bear Valley is closed to all access from November 1 through March 30.

Area brochure, Klamath Basin Wildlife List with refuge codes for birds at each refuge, as well as lists of amphibians, mammals, reptiles, and fishes.
Winter best (from the road as noted)

Klamath Forest ❷
Near Sand Creek, OR

Klamath Forest refuge is located east of the small town of Sand Creek. From Hwy. 97 at Sand Creek take the Silver Lake Hwy. east for about 6 miles.

Habitat: 16,377 acres. A large natural marsh makes up the majority of the refuge. Meadows around the marsh give way to pine forests.

The meadows attract feeding Sandhill Cranes, shorebirds, waterfowl, and raptors hunting for their prey. The pine forest

supports a diversity of species not found on most of the other Basin refuges.

The Klamath Basin refuges attract the majority of migrating Pacific Flyway waterfowl and support peak fall concentrations of nearly one million birds.

In April and May, waterfowl and shorebirds stop in the basin on their way north. The refuge marshes are among the most prolific waterfowl and marsh bird production areas in the northwest. August and September are good months to view a variety of water birds such as pelicans, cormorants, egrets, herons, gulls, terns, and grebes. Waterfowl migration begins with the arrival of Pintails and Greater White-fronted Geese. Peak numbers are usually present early in November.

Area brochure, limited fishing.
Spring, Fall

Upper Klamath ❸
Northwest of Klamath Falls, OR

Take Hwy. 140 west from Klamath Falls for approximately 32 miles to its junction with West Side Road which runs north. The refuge lies just east of West Side Road and extends for several miles along it. Access to the refuge is at Rocky Point Resort.

Habitat: 14,376 acres consisting entirely of marsh and open water. Accessible only by boat.

The marsh provides nesting habitat for waterfowl and colonial birds such as pelicans, egrets, and herons. Red-necked Grebes, Least Bitterns, Wood Ducks, Bald Eagles, and Ospreys also nest at the refuge. Some of the marsh areas are closed to public access from spring through fall to protect these nesting activities.

Area brochure, canoe trail, fishing.
Spring, Fall

Willamette Valley Refuges
(Western Oregon Refuge Complex)

The three Willamette Valley National Wildlife Refuges, William L. Finley, Ankeny, and Baskett Slough, were established primarily as wintering areas for "dusky" Canada Geese. All are shown on the local area map in the next column. Finley NWR has the most diverse habitat.

William L. Finley ❹ ℞
Western Oregon Refuge Complex
26208 Finley Refuge Road
Corvallis, OR 97333   503-757-7236

The refuge complex office is located on the Finley refuge and serves as the headquarters for the three Willamette Valley refuges and four other refuges located along the Oregon coast. Wildlife, habitat, and weather conditions may result in temporary closure of portions of these refuges, especially between October and May. Check with the office for current information about visiting.

Note: The Willamette Valley Refuges bird list contains species and abundance codes for each of the valley refuges noted above. The list has been split into three lists for easy reference to birds most likely to be seen at each refuge.

Bird List OR-2 W.L. Finley Summary
193 birds listed, 93 nesting birds
Bird Chart pages 330-347

Totals by Season		s	S	F	W
Abundant	A	14	6	9	11
Common	C	53	47	38	36
Uncommon	U	60	45	53	43
Occasional	O	22	25	38	19
Rare	R	36	32	34	33

Endangered Species: Bald Eagle, Peregrine Falcon

To reach Finley and the refuge complex office from Corvallis, take Rte. 99W south for 8.5 miles to the refuge sign. Turn west and go 2 miles on a gravel road to headquarters.

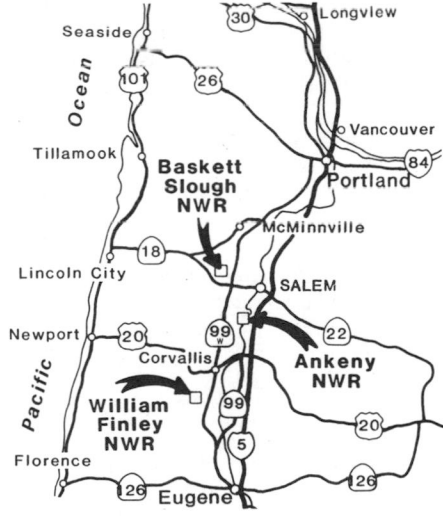

Habitat: 5,325 acres, ranging from marshes and meadows, pastures, and cultivated fields to Oregon ash thickets, second-growth Douglas fir, and oak and maple woodlands.

Nearly all species of birds found in the Willamette Valley are attracted to Finley. An interpretive trail called Woodpecker Loop passes through a range of habitats. Six species of woodpeckers breed at the refuge, and five of them may be observed along the trail: the Acorn, Hairy, and Pileated woodpeckers, Northern Flicker, and Red-breasted Sapsucker.

Refuge and self-guided trail brochures, "Oregon's Coastal Wildlife Refuges" brochure, visitor center, foot trails, hiking, fishing.
Spring, Fall, Winter

Ankeny 5
c/o William L. Finley RC
26208 Finley Refuge Road
Corvallis, OR 97333   503-757-7236

Bird List OR-3 Ankeny Summary
162 birds listed, 84 nesting birds
Bird Chart pages 330-347

Totals by Season		s	S	F	W
Abundant	A	14	6	9	11
Common	C	53	47	38	36
Uncommon	U	52	38	49	38
Occasional	O	19	24	35	18
Rare	R	20	24	20	20

Endangered Species: Bald Eagle, Peregrine Falcon

Located 12 miles south of Salem, west of I-5. Take the Talbot exit and proceed north on Jorgenson Road to Wintel Road and turn left (west) to the refuge. Contact the office for current conditions and access information.

Habitat: 2,796 acres of Willamette Valley croplands, the Sidney Irrigation Ditch, and numerous hedgerows, thickets of Oregon ash, and isolated Douglas firs.

A large variety of waterfowl breed at Ankeny or spend the fall and winter months feeding in the Willamette Valley. Mallards, Northern Pintails, and Green-winged Teals are the most commonly seen ducks, and Trumpeter Swans are a common winter visitor.

Hunting.
Spring, Fall, Winter

Baskett Slough 6
c/o William L. Finley RC
26208 Finley Refuge Road
Corvallis, OR 97333   503-757-7236

Bird List OR-4 Baskett Sl. Summary
171 birds listed, 86 nesting birds
Bird Chart pages 330-347

Totals by Season		s	S	F	W
Abundant	A	14	6	9	11
Common	C	53	45	38	36
Uncommon	U	51	39	50	39
Occasional	O	18	23	33	19
Rare	R	29	27	25	28

Endangered Species: Bald Eagle, Peregrine Falcon

Take St. Hwy. 22 west from Salem for 12 miles (1.5 miles west of Hwy. 99W). Turn north to the refuge at the sign. Contact the office for current conditions and access information.

Habitat: 2,492 acres, including upland areas, an ancient lakebed, and irrigated hillsides. The refuge includes Morgan Lake, which provides excellent habitat for marsh and water birds.

In the spring, Mallards and Cinnamon Teals nest on marsh shores, while Wood Ducks and Hooded Mergansers nest in hollow trees in the surrounding woodlands. Great Blue Herons and Killdeers are common along the lakeshore throughout the year.

California Quails, Ring-necked Pheasants, and Ruffed Grouse breed in the uplands. Species inhabiting the oak, and thickets, and grassy hillsides include Scrub and Steller's jays, Red-breasted and White-breasted nuthatches, Rufous-sided Towhee, Bewick's Wren, Black-capped Chickadee, and American Goldfinch. Birds found in the Douglas fir stands and old logged-over sites where maple and dogwoods have taken over include Chestnut-backed Chickadee, Brown Creeper, Bushtit, Dark-eyed Junco, and Great Horned Owl.

During the fall Tundra Swans and Greater White-fronted, Snow, Emperor, and Canada geese are among the waterfowl that migrate through.

Area brochure, walking trails, hunting.
Spring, Fall, Winter

Oregon's Coastal Wildlife Refuges
(Western Oregon Refuge Complex)

Certain public uses are permitted. Inquire at the headquarters of the Western Oregon Refuge Complex in Corvallis at the W. L. Finley NWR.

Hundreds of thousands of seabirds representing more than a dozen species nest on the isolated coastal islands and headlands of the Oregon coast. All public entry on Oregon's off-shore rocks, islands, and reefs is prohibited.

Each seabird species uses a specific nest type and site. The species include Western Gull, Fork-tailed and Leach's storm-petrels, Cassin's and Rhinoceros auklets, Tufted Puffin, Common Murre, Brandt's and Pelagic cormorants, Pigeon Guillemot, and Black Oystercatcher.

Three Arch Rocks 7
This group of rocks has long been the site of Oregon's largest seabird colony. About 75,000 Common Murres nest on almost every available ledge. Tufted Puffins and storm-petrels nest in burrows, while Pigeon Guillemots, cormorants, and gulls nest on the cliffs and the level areas of these rocks.

Cape Meares 8
Most of the refuge's 138 acres are covered by an old-growth forest of Sitka spruce and western hemlock. Vertical sea cliffs, which drop several hundred feet, provide nesting habitat for Tufted Puffins, Pelagic Cormorants, and Pigeon Guillemots.

Hiking is permitted along the section of the Oregon Coast Trail that passes through this forest to Cape Meares State Park.

Oregon Islands
Approximately 1,400 islands rocks and reefs along the length of the Oregon coastline. Puffins, auklets, guillemots, murres, gulls, cormorants, and storm-petrels nest on the islands.

Bandon Marsh 9
289 acres of salt marsh, at the mouth of the Coquille River, that are an important area for migrating shorebird and wintering waterfowl.

Hart Mountain 10
National Antelope Refuge
PO Box 111   (office at refuge)
Lakeview, OR 97630   503-947-3315

Bird List OR-5 Hart Mt. Summary
236 birds listed, 137 nesting birds
Bird Chart pages 330-347

Totals by Season		s	S	F	W
Abundant	A	20	15	27	0
Common	C	79	78	83	20
Uncommon	U	60	38	54	19
Occasional	O	48	31	51	48
Rare	R	17	17	12	7

Endangered Species: Bald Eagle, Peregrine Falcon

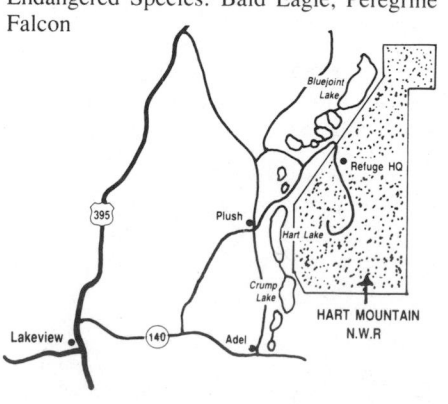

Hart Mountain is located 65 miles northeast of Lakeview. It can be reached by county roads from U.S. Hwy. 395 and Oregon Hwy. 140. Check local maps for the best routes to this remote refuge.

Habitat: Characterized by 275,000 acres Hart Mountain, is a massive fault block ridge rising 8,065 feet above sea level. The steep west side rises abruptly 3,600 feet from the floor of Warner Valley in a series of rugged cliffs, steep slopes, and knifelike ridges. The face of Hart Mountain is cut by several deep gorges. Hart, Potter, and DeGarmo Canyons, the most rugged, extend from the valley floor to the top of the main ridge. The east side of the mountain descends in a series of hills and low ridges to the sagebrush-grass ranges. Hart Mountain is well watered by many springs and creeks.

Warner Valley supports large flocks of migrating waterfowl and other water birds during spring and fall. Breeding species are found in the meadows and around the lakes, as well as in spring-fed riparian areas and the vast sagebrush and grassland habitat.

Throughout the warmer months, a wide variety of birds of prey and smaller birds are present, attracted to the numerous rugged cliffs adjoining isolated spring-fed riparian areas and the vast sagebrush and grassland portions of the refuge.

Area brochure, hunting, fishing, camping, hiking, backpacking (by permit).
Mid-May through October best.

Lewis and Clark ⑪
c/o Willapa NWR
HC 01, Box 910
Ilwaco, WA 98624   206-484-3482

The administrative office is at Willapa NWR, on Hwy. 101 about 11 miles east of Ilwaco, WA (see Willapa, page 188).

Lewis and Clark NWR is a chain of estuary islands that begin just above Tongue Point and follow the Oregon shore

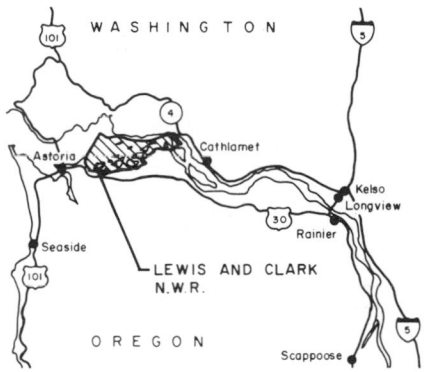

of the main channel of the Columbia River upriver to Tenasillahe Island. Accessible only by boat.

Habitat: 35,000 acres of river, islands, bars, mud flats and tidal marshes, and some upland.

The estuary is both a stopping area for migrating waterfowl and a wintering area. The most common species are Tundra Swans, Canada Geese, Mallards, Northern Pintails, American Wigeons, Canvasbacks, and Lesser Scaups.

Great Blue Herons, gulls, and shorebirds wade the extensive sandbars and mud flats. Grebes and cormorants dive the deeper water of the channels. The willow, cottonwood, and spruce trees of vegetated islands provide nesting sites and lookout perches for numerous songbirds, hawks, and Bald Eagles.

Area brochure, bird list, hunting, fishing, boating.
Spring, Fall, Winter

Malheur ⑫   (office at refuge)
PO Box 245
Princeton, OR 97721   503-493-2612

Bird List OR-6 Malheur Summary
249 birds listed, 131 nesting birds
Bird Chart pages 330-347

Totals by Season		s	S	F	W
Abundant	A	9	7	11	0
Common	C	66	51	59	11
Uncommon	U	80	56	86	37
Occasional	O	34	28	38	40
Rare	R	48	46	44	48

Endangered Species: Bald Eagle, Peregrine Falcon

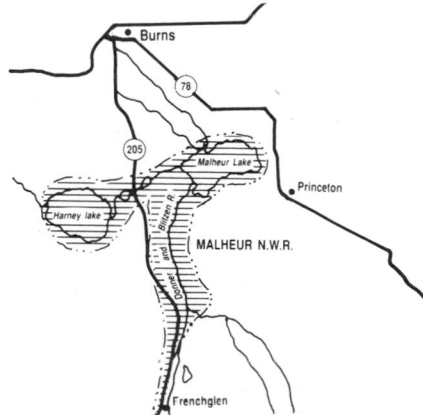

Refuge headquarters is on the south shore of Malheur Lake, 40 miles south of Burns. From Burns, drive east on St. Hwy. 78 for 2 miles, turn south on St. Hwy. 205 for 25 miles, then go east on the county road toward Princeton for 9 miles. The last six miles of the road to

the headquarters are gravel surfaced. The refuge may also be reached from the east by leaving St. Hwy. 78 at Princeton and driving west on the gravel-surfaced county road for 15 miles.

Habitat: 185,000 acres at 4,100 feet of elevation, with Malheur, Harney, and Mud lakes, many ponds in the Blitzen Valley, alkali flats, rimrocks, and sagebrush-covered hills. The area is surrounded with desert and the habitat is dependent on water from the Silvies and Blitzen rivers.

Malheur is a major nesting and stopover area for migratory birds. Large flocks of Canada, Snow, and Greater White-fronted geese, "Lesser" Sandhill Cranes, and Tundra Swans begin to arrive in February, and their populations peak in late March. The passerine migration peaks in mid-May. The refuge headquarters, P Ranch, and Page Springs are the best areas to observe the songbird migration.

Great Horned Owls and Golden Eagles begin nesting in late February, and Canada Geese, Trumpeter Swans, and "Greater" Sandhill Cranes in April.

Shorebirds congregate on exposed mud flats and alkali playas in preparation for their fall migration. The peak of the southbound songbird migration occurs in August. "Greater" Sandhill Cranes stage at Malheur gathering in large flocks before migrating to California. The fall waterfowl migration peaks in October when Snow Geese, Tundra Swans, and Canvasbacks arrive. The wintering population of Rough-legged Hawks arrives during October. Eagles prey upon flocks of waterfowl in the Blitzen Valley during December and January.

Malheur NWR is remote. Freezing temperatures are common from September through May. Drought periods typically last 1–3 months. Be prepared for temperature extremes and to travel long distances over gravel roads. Carry drinking water and mosquito repellent if you visit in the summer.

Area brochure, auto tour route, mammals list, foot trails, boating, fishing, hunting.
Spring, Fall

Umatilla ⑬   (office in town)
Post Office Building
6th and I Streets
PO Box 239
Umatilla, OR 97882   503-922-3232

Umatilla NWR includes five separate units along 18 miles of the Columbia River in Oregon and Washington. The Boardman and McCormack units are in Oregon, and

the Paterson, Ridge, and Whitcomb units in Washington. The Ridge and Whitcomb units include the Blalock, Telegraph, Straight Six, Sand Dune, and Long Walk islands in the Columbia River.
Unit maps, recreation opportunities, and refuge access points are described in detail in the refuge literature.

The Umatilla office also supervises four other refuges. Cold Springs and McKay Creek NWRs in Oregon are described in this chapter, and McNary and Toppenish NWRs in Washington are described in the Washington chapter.

Bird List OR-7 Umatilla Summary
185 birds listed, 69 nesting birds
Bird Chart pages 330-347

Totals by Season		s	S	F	W
Abundant	A	6	6	4	3
Common	C	48	43	36	24
Uncommon	U	41	35	35	26
Occasional	O	39	31	38	28
Rare	R	18	11	12	10

Endangered Species: Bald Eagle

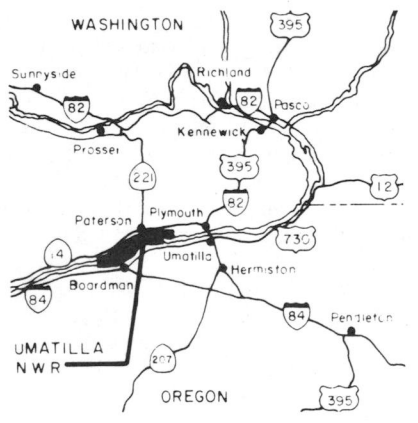

Habitat: 29,370 acres include 16,500 acres of water, 1,100 acres of crops, 700 acres of marsh, and 11,070 acres of cheatgrass-sagebrush desert.

Nearly all species of waterfowl common to the west may be seen at the refuge during the spring. Other species inhabit the refuge's prairie and desert lands. Long-billed Curlews nest and raise their young on grassy prairies. Burrowing Owls nest in abandoned badger dens.

The fall waterfowl migration attracts Bald Eagles and other raptors to the refuge. Horned Larks and a large number of other small birds winter in the area.

Area brochures, fishing, hunting, boating. Some of the islands in the Columbia River are closed to visitors from October 1 to June 30.
Spring, Fall, Winter

Cold Springs 🎏

c/o Umatilla NWR
6th and I Streets
PO Box 239
Umatilla, OR 97882   503-922-3232

Cold Springs NWR is located east of Hermiston. From Hermiston, take East Highland Ave. east for 6.5 miles. Turn left on the Stanfield Loop Road and go 0.5 miles to the refuge entrance and information kiosk.

Habitat: 3,117 acres. When Cold Springs Reservoir is full, 1,550 acres of water, and 1,567 acres of upland. At minimum pool, the reservoir covers approximately 200 acres. Stands of cottonwood, willow, and Russian olive are interspersed with bitterbush, big sagebrush, and other upland desert vegetation. Thick underbrush surrounds the reservoir.

The southeastern portion of the refuge attracts tens of thousands of songbirds to the food and shelter during the fall and winter. Large numbers of waterfowl can be seen as they spend part of the day resting on the refuge. The waterfowl feed away from the refuge and it is not uncommon to see large flights of ducks and geese, primarily Mallards and Canada Geese, arriving or departing. American Wigeons, Green-winged Teals, and Northern Pintails are also present. Bald Eagles may be seen on the northwestern portion of the refuge in the winter.

Mallards, teals, Wood Ducks, and many songbirds are year-round residents, and remain on the refuge to nest and rear their young.
Area brochure, fishing, limited boating, hiking.
Fall, Winter

McKay Creek 🎏

c/o Umatilla NWR
6th and I Streets
PO Box 239
Umatilla, OR 97882   503-922-3232

McKay Creek NWR is located south of Pendleton. Take Hwy. 395 south for 8 miles to the refuge entrance sign.

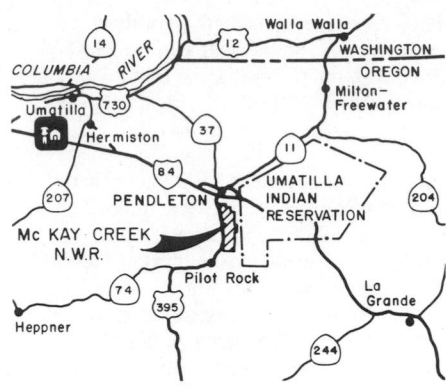

Habitat: 1,837 acres with 1,300 acres of open water at full pool and 537 acres of upland cooperatively managed by the Bureau of Reclamation and USFWS. An average of 250 acres of pool remain in August and the exposed mudflats produce an abundance of vegetation.

During the spring and summer several species of waterbirds, including Least and Western sandpipers, Killdeers, California and Ring-billed gulls, Great Blue Herons, and Black-crowned Night-Herons frequent the refuge. A large variety of passerines are attracted to the thick underbrush and wooded areas surrounding the reservoir.

Golden and Bald eagles frequent the refuge. The abundant small mammals support many other raptors, including American Kestrels, Northern Harriers, and Red-tailed and Swainson's hawks. Mallards and Canada Geese are the most common waterfowl wintering at the refuge, but American Wigeons, Green-winged Teals, and Northern Pintails are also present.

The refuge is close from the first Monday after state waterfowl season, typically between the end of December and mid-January, through the last day of February.

Area brochure, fishing, hunting, hiking.
Spring, Fall

NATIONAL PARK SERVICE

Crater Lake National Park 🎏

PO Box 7
Crater Lake, OR 97604   503-594-2211

183,224 acres including Crater Lake, known worldwide for its deep blue color. The lake lies within the caldera of Mt. Mazama, a volcano of the Cascade Range that erupted about 6,800 years ago. The caldera formed by the collapse of Mt. Mazama was gradually filled by annual rain and melting snow. Its depth of 1,932 feet makes it the deepest lake in the United States.

Park brochure with map, 8-page
newspaper "Crater Lake Reflections"
providing current visitor information,
species leaflets, bird checklist.

NATIONAL FOREST SERVICE
NFS Pacific Northwest Region
319 SW Pine Street
PO Box 3623
Portland, OR 97208   503-221-2877

. **Columbia River Gorge** ▲
National Scenic Area
Waucoma Center, Suite 200
902 Wasco Avenue
Hood River, OR 97031   503-386-2333

Map/Forest/City
△2 Deschutes/Bend   503-388-2175
△3 Fremont/Lakeview   503-947-2151
△4 Malheur/John Day   503-575-1731
△5 Mount Hood/Gresham   503-666-0700
△6 Ochoco/Prineville   503-447-6247
△7 Rogue River/Medford   503-776-3600

△8 Siskiyou/Grants Pass 503-479-5301
△9 Siuslaw/Corvallis   503-757-4480
△10 Umatilla/Pendleton   503-276-3811
△11 Umpqua/Roseburg   503-672-6601
△12 Wallowa-Whitman
     /Baker   503-523-6391
△13 Willamette/Eugene   503-687-6521
△14 Winema/Klamath Falls 503-883-6714

BUREAU LAND MANAGEMENT
BLM State Office
825 NE Multnomah Street
PO Box 2965
Portland, OR 97208   503-231-6277

Map/District/City
▽ Burns/Burns   503-573-5241
▽ Eugene/Eugene   503-683-6600
▽ Lakeview/Lakeview   503-947-2177
▽ Medford/Medford   503-776-4173
▽ Prineville/Prineville 503-447-4115
▽ Roseburg/Roseburg   503-672-4491
▽ Salem/Salem   503-399-5646
▽ Vale/Vale   503-473-3144

STATE AGENCIES

Oregon Dept. of Fish & Wildlife
506 SW Mill Street
PO Box 3503
Portland, OR 97208   503-229-5403

Map/Region/City
1 Northwest #1
   /Corvallis   503-757-4186
2 Southwest #2
   /Roseburg   503-440-3353
3 Central #3/Bend   503-388-6363
4 Northeast #4
   /La Grande   503-963-2138
5 Southeast #5/Hines   503-573-6582
6 Marine #6/Newport   503-867-4741
7 Columbia #7
   /Clackamas   503-657-2000

Oregon Tourism Division
595 Cottage Street, NE
Salem, OR 97310   800-543-8888
from out-of-state   800-547-7842

BIRDING HOTLINES

Philadelphia   215-567-2473
                      and 301-652-1088
Western Pennsylvania 412-963-0560
Wilkes-Barre   717-825-2473

LOCAL BIRDING GROUPS
Map/Chapter/City

① Allegheny Plateau Audubon
   /Johnstown
② Applachian Audubon/Birdsboro
③ Aud. Soc. of Western PA/Pittsburgh
④ Batramian Audubon/Slippery Rock
⑤ Bucks County Audubon/New Hope
⑥ Conococheague Aud./Chambersburg
⑦ Gifford Pinchot Audubon/Milford
⑧ Greater Wyoming Valley Audubon
   /Dallas
⑨ Juniata Valley Audubon/Altoona
⑩ Lehigh Valley Audubon/Emmaus
⑪ Lycoming Audubon/Williamsport
⑫ Northeastern PA Audubon/Hawley
⑬ Pocono Mtn. Audubon/Baronsville
⑭ Presque Isle Audubon/Erie
⑮ Quittapahills Audubon/Palmyra
⑯ Seneca Rocks Audubon/Cranberry
⑰ Seven Mountains/Lewisburg
⑱ South Mountain Audubon/Gettysburg
⑲ Summit Nature Club/Camp Hill
⑳ Tiadaghton Audubon/Wellsboro
㉑ Valley Forge Audubon/Paoli
㉒ Wapiti Audubon/DuBois
㉓ Wyncote Audubon/Ft. Washington
㉔ York Audubon/York
㉕ Baird Ornithological Club/Reading
㉖ Delaware Valley Ornithological Club
   /Philadelphia

㉗ Harrisburg Natural History Society
   /Harrisburg
㉘ Hawk Mountain Sanctuary Assoc.
   /Kempton
㉙ Lancaster Co. Bird Club/Lancaster
㉚ Moravian College Conservation
   Assoc./Bethlehem
㉛ State College Bird Club
   /State College
㉜ Todd Bird Club/Indiana
㉝ West Branch Bird Club/Lock Haven
㉞ West Chester Bird Club
   /West Chester
㉟ Westmoreland County Bird Club
   /Greensburg

NATIONAL AUDUBON SOCIETY

Crosswicks Wildlife Sanctuary ❶
Wyncote Audubon Society
c/o Briar Bush Nature Center
1212 Edge Hill Road
Abington, PA 19001   215-572-1175

Located in Abington Township. Taking Meetinghouse Road, turn right onto Delene Road and continue to its intersection with Crosswicks Road. Turn left to the sanctuary entrance.

No on-site manager. Contact Wyncote Audubon Society or Briar Bush Nature Center for current information on seasonal birding and wildlife viewing opportunities. Four trails (marked blue, green, red and yellow) in this 10-acre, walk-in sanctuary are maintained by the Wyncote Audubon Society.

Area brochure, maps, hiking, cross-country skiing.
Spring, Summer, Fall, Winter

THE NATURE CONSERVANCY
Pennsylvania Field Office ⬦
1218 Chestnut Street, Suite 807
Philadelphia, PA 19107   215-925-1065

Contact the Field Office for preserve and visiting details, and the Pennsylvania Preserve Guide.

Bristol Marsh ❶
Near Bristol—Contact Field Office

From northern Philadelphia take Franklin Ave. (U.S. Hwy. 13) north beyond city limits (Franklin Ave. becomes Bristol Pike). Continue on Bristol Pike for several miles to junction with New Rogers Road (Hwy. 413) and Pond St. Follow Pond St. to Mill St. and turn right to the Delaware River. Turn right from Mill St. into the large Borough parking lot. Bristol Marsh is at the south end of the lot.

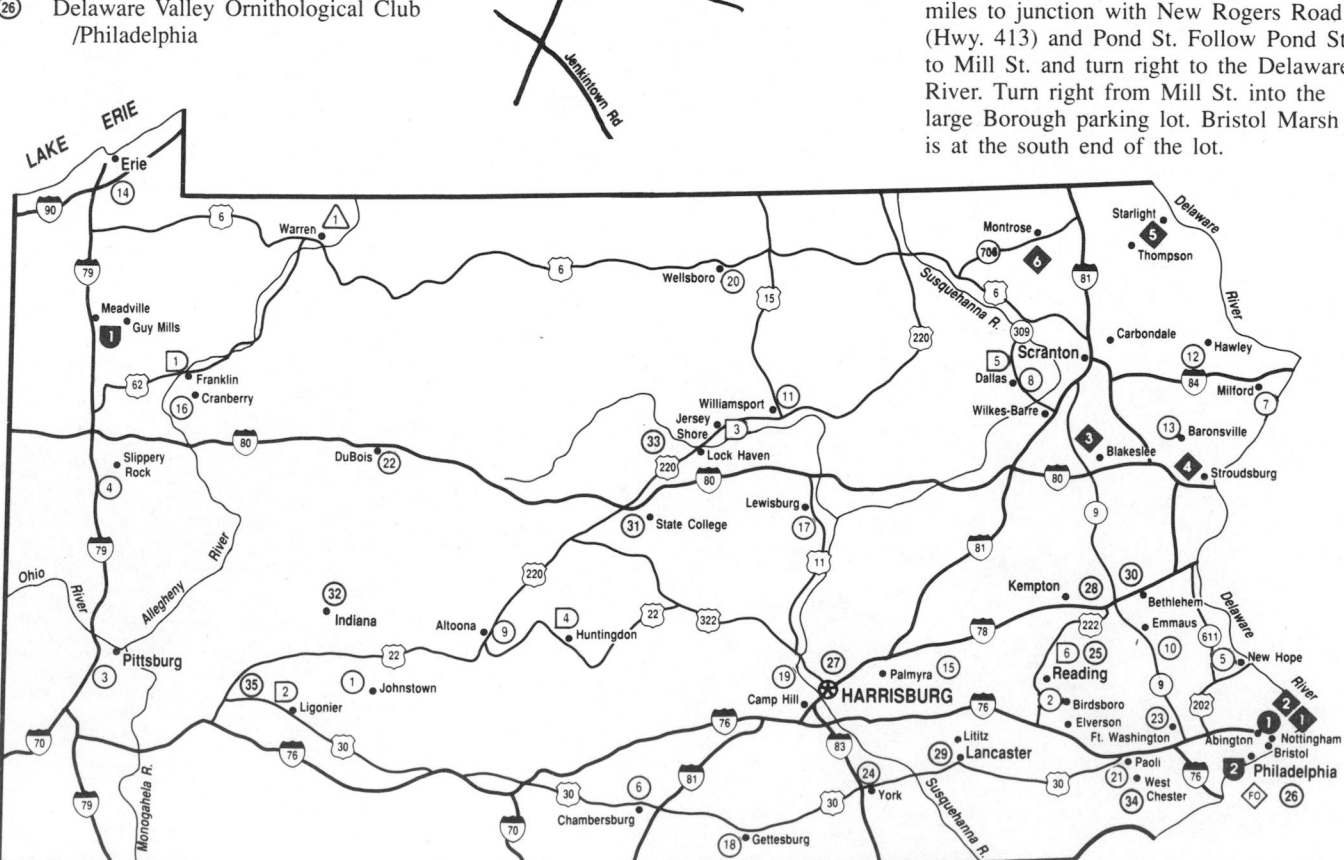

Habitat: 20.5-acre freshwater tidal marsh and home to six rare plant species.

The marsh provides food and haven for a variety of migratory waterbirds and other wildlife, including Spotted Sandpipers, Mallards, and Canada Geese.

Viewing platforms and a nature trail are under development. Area brochure has map.
Spring, Summer, Fall

Goat Hill Serpentine Barrens ❷
Near Nottingham—Contact Field Office

From U.S. Hwy. 1 headed south take St. Hwy. 272 (Nottingham exit) north for 1 mile and turn left onto Lees Bridge Road. Go 3 miles, turn left on Red Pump Road, and go 0.7 mile to the powerline, to the well-marked parking lot. The best access to this preserve is via the cleared trail beneath the powerline.

Habitat: 803 acres of eastern serpentine barrens ranging in elevation from 180 to 450 feet. One of the best remaining examples of this unusual ecosystem, Goat Hill's dry barrens, on an enormous outcropping of green serpentine rock, support a unique assemblage of plants and animals which have evolved to thrive in the infertile terrain. Octoraro Creek, designated a state scenic river, winds through the preserve.

The barrens, with their brilliant mats of moss-pink and other wildflowers, are of special interest to birders. Among the birds that nest here are the declining Whip-poor-will, Barred Owl, and at least 17 species of warblers.

TNC Preserve Guide includes map.
Spring, Summer, Fall, Winter

Long Pond ❸
Near Blakeslee—Contact Field Office about public use and scheduled tours.

Habitat: 10,000 acres planned ranging in elevation from 1,820 to 1,970 feet.

Long Pond is surrounded by 15,000 acres of the most diverse ensemble of boreal wetlands and mesic scrub oak/pitch pine barrens in Pennsylvania. Throughout the area there are small vernal ponds with a multitude of rare plants, isolated bogs, and huge wetland forests of balsam fir, tamarack, and red spruce.

The sounds of migrating waterfowl may be heard in the emergent and open-water areas in the fall.

TNC Preserve Guide includes map,

canoeing.
Spring, Summer, Fall, Winter

Tannersville Cranberry Bog ❹
(Stuart M. Steni Memorial Preserve)
Naturalist (Preserve Manager)
Monroe County Conservation District
RD 2, Box 2335-A
Stroudsburg, PA 18360   717-992-7334

From Stroudsburg take I-80 west to exit 45. After the ramp follow St. Hwy. 175 north to St. Hwy. 611. Go south on St. Hwy. 611 for 1.1 miles. In Tannersville turn left onto Cherry Lane Road and after 2 miles turn right onto Bog Road. Go several hundred yards to a small parking area on left. Park and follow foot trails.

Habitat: A 719-acre boreal bog, which is the descendant of a glacial lake, at elevations ranging from 910 to 950 feet with an average of 915 feet.

Nearly 40 feet of peat have accumulated on the floor of the ancient lake. Grasses, sedges, and other plants flourished around the edges of the bog and altered the habitat. After thousands of years of succession, a boreal forest of black spruce and tamarack grew up. The boardwalk at Tannersville Cranberry Bog crosses these many successional stages.

Many mammals and migratory birds find refuge in the range of habitats. This wetland has been designated a National Natural Landmark.

The bog is open to the public, but bog vegetation is very fragile. The bog and boardwalk are accessible by guided tour only. Other parts of the preserve (including wetlands, stream, and forest) are accessible on self-guiding trails.

TNC Preserve Guide includes map.
Spring, Summer, Fall, Winter

Thompson Wetlands ❺
Contact Field Office about public use policy and scheduled tours,
or:
Patricia H. Christian
Box 24
Starlight, PA 18461   717-278-1174

From Scranton, take I-81 north to exit 27. Continue north on U.S. Hwy. 6 through Carbondale. Turn left onto St. Hwy. 171 and go for about 20 miles to Thompson. The preserve is located 1 mile north of town on the east side of St. Hwy. 171.

Habitat: 453 acres, with elevations of 1,680 to 1,720 feet. Mature eastern hemlock swamp forest, with areas of hardwood forest, wet meadows, old fields,

and exotic pine plantations.

The large variety of flora include more than 375 species of vascular plants and 14 different kinds of sphagnum moss. The preserve includes Plew's Swamp and Weir's Pond. American Black Ducks still nest here and Barred Owls breed in the surrounding woods.

To protect the fragile wetland area visitors must remain on the roadway trail unless accompanying a guided tour. Contact Ms. Christian about regular or special tours.

TNC Preserve Guide includes map.
Spring, Summer, Fall, Winter

Woodbourne Forest ❻
& Wildlife Sanctuary
Resident Naturalist
RD 6, Box 6294
Montrose, PA 18801   717-278-3384

Woodbourne Forest Preserve is located on St. Hwy. 29, 5.3 miles south of the traffic light in downtown Montrose. The parking lot is marked with a sign. Follow the trail through the field and into the forest.

Habitat: 648 acres, ranging in elevation from 1,300 to 1,650 feet, contain the largest virgin woods remaining in PA. A 200-acre hemlock/northern hardwood forest dates back to the 17th century. Moist hillsides and stream banks support a diversity of ferns and clubmoss.

Cooper's Hawks are among the many breeding birds. The self-guided nature tour is open from dawn to dusk and, with permission of the resident naturalist, other areas of the preserve may also be toured. Scientists, students, and groups larger than eight persons should contact the resident naturalist.

TNC Preserve Guide includes map. Tour map, bird and other wildlife lists.
Spring, Summer, Fall, Winter

U.S. FISH & WILDLIFE SERVICE NATIONAL WILDLIFE REFUGES

Erie ❶
RD 1, Wood Duck Lane
Guy Mills, PA 16327   814-789-3585

(office at refuge)

Bird List PA-1 Erie Summary
236 birds listed, 112 nesting birds
Bird Chart pages 330-347

Totals by Season		s	S	F	W
Abundant	A	16	18	19	5
Common	C	63	48	65	15
Uncommon	U	60	35	55	17
Occasional	O	35	14	34	19
Rare	R	39	30	44	41

Endangered Species: Bald Eagle, Peregrine Falcon

Refuge headquarters is located 0.7 mile east of Guys Mills or 10 miles east of Meadville. From Hwy. 77 turn right (east) into Hwy. 198 and then south onto refuge road.

Erie has two separate land divisions, both of which lie approximately 1,340 feet above sea level. Sugar Lake Division is 10 miles east of Meadville on the outskirts of Guys Mills. Seneca Division is approximately 10 miles north of Sugar Lake Division, or 4 miles southeast of Cambridge Springs along the east side of Hwy. 408.

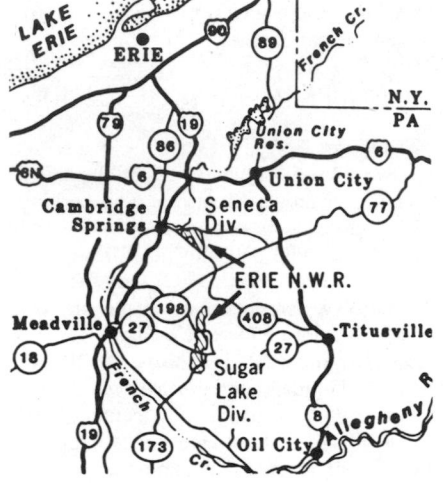

Habitat: Sugar Lake Division—5,137 acres in a narrow valley, which includes Woodcock and Lake creeks. Beaver ponds, pools, and marshlands along the creeks are bounded by forested slopes, croplands, grasslands, and wet meadows.

Seneca Division—3,227 acres in a forested valley where Muddy and Dead creeks provide most of the wetland habitat.

Peak waterfowl migrations occur in March to early April and from September to November. Easily seen are Canada Geese, Wood Ducks, Mallards, Blue-winged Teal, and Hooded Mergansers. Less numerous migrants include Green-winged Teals, American Wigeons, Buffleheads, and Ring-necked and American Black ducks.

There are more Wood Ducks nesting on the refuge than any other duck. In the spring goslings and their parents also can be seen.

During spring and summer nesting songbirds are abundant. The Henslow's Sparrow, a rare bird in most areas of the United States, nests at Erie.

Common Snipes and other shorebirds can be seen in small groups feeding on mudflats during the summer and fall.

Three species of owls, Eastern Screech-Owls and Great Horned and Barred owls, breed at the refuge as well as being permanent residents.

Bald Eagles and Ospreys visit the refuge in search of food. Red-tailed Hawks and American Kestrels are common raptors that also nest at Erie.

Area brochure, hunting, fishing, hiking, environmental education, observation blind.
Spring, Summer, Fall

Tinicum National Environmental ❷ Center & Refuge
(visitor center at refuge)
Suite 104, Scott Plaza 2
Philadelphia, PA 19113   215-521-0662

Bird List PA-2 Tinicum Summary
273 birds listed, 85 nesting birds
Bird Chart pages 330-347

Totals by Season		s	S	F	W
Abundant	A	15	13	16	2
Common	C	90	37	91	35
Occasional	O	76	49	78	43
Rare	R	75	67	79	79

Endangered Species: Bald Eagle, Peregrine Falcon, Piping Plover, Least Tern

The main entrance of the Tinicum National Environmental Center (visitor center) is at 86th Street and Lindbergh Boulevard in southwest Philadelphia. The Environmental Center is open daily from 8:30 a.m.–4 p.m. There is a parking area in Delaware County, just north of I-95 on Rte. 420, for access to hiking trails and fishing.

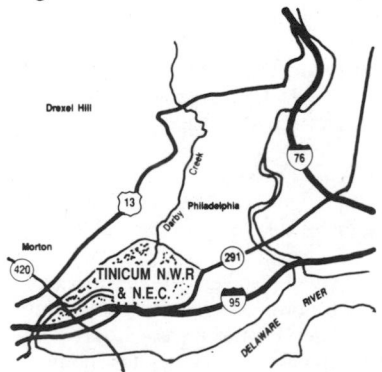

Habitat: The refuge contains 1,200 acres. Most of the land is former tidal wetland altered by diking, dredging, or filling. The highly disturbed condition of this area presents a unique opportunity to restore former wetlands and preserve the

remaining ones.

During mid-March to May the northbound waterfowl migration is in full swing. In April hawks, herons, egrets, and sparrows pass through. The apex of the warbler migration occurs during the first two weeks of May and northbound sandpipers pass through. Peak populations of herons and egrets occur during August and September. From September to mid-October gulls, terns, and warblers migrate south.

The southbound waterfowl, hawk, and sparrow migrations take place from mid-October to mid-November. Red-tailed Hawks, Northern Harriers, and Short-eared Owls are common from mid-November through March.

The foot trails, wildlife observation platform, and boardwalk provide an opportunity to see and study wildlife within metropolitan Philadelphia and the adjoining Delaware County.

Area brochure, fishing, bicycling, photography. Scheduled nature exploration walks.
Spring, Summer, Fall, Winter

NATIONAL FOREST SERVICE
Allegheny National Forest Supervisor △
Spiridon Bldg.
222 Liberty Street
PO Box 847
Warren, PA 16365   814-723-5150

STATE AGENCIES

Pennsylvania Game Commission
8000 Derry Street
PO Box 1567
Harrisburg, PA 17120   717-787-3633

Note: The Fish and Game Commissions are separate in Pennsylvania and have different offices.

Map/Region/City
1	Northwest/Franklin	814-432-3187
2	Southwest/Ligonier	412-238-9523
3	Northcentral /Jersey Shore	717-398-4744
4	Southcentral /Huntingdon	814-643-1831
5	Northeast/Dallas	717-675-1143
6	Southeast/Reading	215-926-3136

Department of Commerce
Tourist Information
433 Forum Bldg.
Harrisburg, PA 17120   800-847-4872

BIRDING HOTLINES
Statewide   401-231-5728
To report   401-231-6444

LOCAL BIRDING GROUP
Map/Chapter/City
① Audubon Society of Rhode Island
  (ASRI)/Smithfield
② Rhode Island Ornithological Club
  /Smithfield

THE NATURE CONSERVANCY
Rhode Island Field Office ⓕⓞ
240 Hope Street
Providence, RI 02906   401-331-7110

Lewis-Dickens Farm & ◆
Rodman's Hollow Preserve
Block Island, RI

The island is accessible via ferry boat
from New London, CT, Port of Galilee or
Providence/Newport, RI. Contact Field
Office for permission to visit the preserve
during spring and summer months, for
specific directions, and about guided
walks held throughout the summer.

Walks are sponsored by the Rhode
Island Department of Environmental
Management, 22 Hayes Street, Providence,
RI 02908. The "Block Island Times,"
available on the island, publishes a
schedule of the guided walks.

Block Island owes its reputation as an
excellent birding spot to its position along
the Atlantic Flyway. It serves as an
important stopover point and a haven for
passerines that have been blown to sea by
strong northwest winds. The preserve area
supports the greatest concentration of rare
birds, plants, and invertebrates on the
island.

Habitat: Over 400 acres in two adjacent
sections at the southwest corner of Block
Island. The rolling coastal meadows at the
Lewis-Dickens Farm are host to ground-
nesting birds. The shrubby growth of
Rodman's Hollow provides extensive
feeding grounds for Northern Harriers.

U.S. FISH & WILDLIFE SERVICE NATIONAL WILDLIFE REFUGES

Ninigret, Sachuest Point, Trustom Pond,
and Block Island in Rhode Island are four
of six refuges in the Ninigret Refuge
Complex. The two other refuges are
located in Connecticut.

Ninigret NWRs ⓤ   (office in town)
Refuge Complex Office & Refuge
Shoreline Plaza, Route 1A
PO Box 307
Charlestown, RI 02813   401-364-9124

Bird List RI-1 R.I. NWR's Summary
289 birds listed, 69 nesting birds
Bird Chart pages 330-347

Totals by Season		s	S	F	W
Abundant	A	5	3	8	4
Common	C	63	48	86	28
Uncommon	U	73	49	63	44
Occasional	O	64	50	57	47
Rare	R	53	29	58	34

Endangered Species: Bald Eagle, Peregrine
Falcon, Piping Plover, Roseate Tern, Least
Tern

About 40 miles south of Providence. From
Hwy. 1, take the Green Hill Beach exit
onto Rte. 1A. Travel 1 mile to the plaza
entrance on your right and the Refuge
Complex Office.

There are two entrances to Ninigret
Refuge where the visitor may park and
continue by foot on the trails. The east
entrance, which is closer to Ninigret Pond,
is located approximately 5 miles south of
the office and is reached through Ninigret
Park off Rte. 1A. The west refuge
entrance is off Hwy. 1.

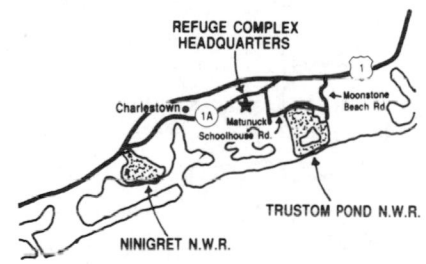

Habitat: 400 acres include grassland,
forest, shrubland, wooded swamps,
freshwater ponds, and a short stretch of
barrier beach along 1,700-acre Ninigret
Pond, Rhode Island's largest coastal pond.

Ninigret Pond and the refuge provide food
and habitat for a large variety of nesting
and migrating birds. Breeding passerines
such as White-eyed Vireos and Wood
Thrushes sing in defense of their
territories and in search of a mate.
American Woodcocks perform their
courtship flights at dusk, and Ospreys
return to reclaim their nests.

Large rafts of American Black Ducks,
mergansers, and other waterfowl spend the
fall and winter on Ninigret Pond. The
hawk migration reaches its peak from
mid-September through the first part of
October.

Area brochure, two mile-long footpaths,
observation platforms, fishing.
Spring, Summer, Fall, Winter

Trustom Pond ②
c/o Ninigret Refuge Complex Office
Shoreline Plaza, Route 1A
PO Box 307
Charlestown, RI 02813   401-364-9124

Located about 40 miles south of
Providence. From U.S. Hwy. 1 take the
Moonstone Beach exit. Follow Moonstone
Beach Road south for 1 mile, then turn
right onto Matunuck Schoolhouse Road.
Continue 0.7 mile to the refuge entrance
on your left.

Habitat: Over 640 acres include open
fields, shrublands, woodlands, freshwater
ponds and swamps, and 160-acre Trustom
Pond, Rhode Island's only coastal pond
free from shoreline development. A barrier
beach forms the refuge's southern
boundary along Block Island Sound.

The barrier beach is one of the few
nesting sites on the east coast for two
federally endangered species, the Least
Tern and the Piping Plover. The beach is
closed during their April–August nesting
season.

Ospreys return in late March. American
Woodcocks perform their evening
courtship flights. Prairie Warblers,
Bobolinks, and other songbirds can be
heard as they defend territories and attract
mates.

The southbound shorebird migration
begins in late July and peaks in August.
The fall hawk migration is at its best
between mid-September and early October.

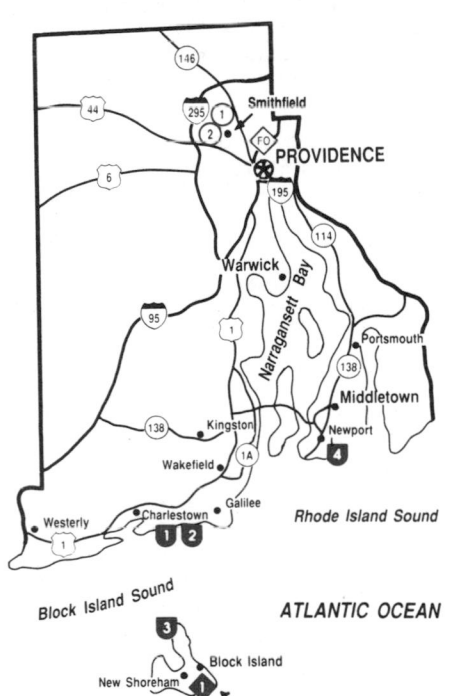

Ruddy Ducks, scaups, and other waterfowl form large rafts on Trustom Pond throughout the fall.

During winter Short-eared Owls are present in the fields and Great Horned Owls brood their eggs and chicks.

Foot trails, fishing.
Spring, Fall

Block Island 🖪
c/o Ninigret Refuge Complex Office
Shoreline Plaza, Route 1A
PO Box 307
Charlestown, RI 02813   401-364-9124

The refuge is located at the northern tip of Block Island, approximately 12 miles off the Rhode Island coast. Regular ferry service is available from New London, CT, and the Port of Galilee or Providence/Newport, RI. Air service is available from the State Airport in Westerly. On the island travel north on Corn Neck Road to its end. A sandy path leads west to the refuge entrance.

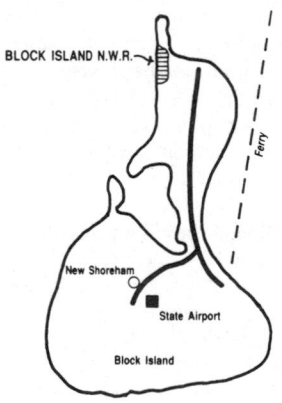

Habitat: 46 acres of sandy beaches and rolling dunes. Much of the property adjacent to the refuge, including 105-acre Sachem Pond, is managed by the Town of New Shoreham on the island as a conservation unit. The island's open habitats and low-growing vegetation afford excellent birding opportunities.

The refuge serves as a stopover for many species of songbirds, shorebirds, raptors, and waterfowl during the spring and fall migrations. The diversity is particularly high during the fall, when migrants flying over the ocean from Nova Scotia and other northern areas join the birds that have been swept east from their normal route.

Various loons, grebes, and waterfowl swim in large rafts offshore and Snow Buntings flock around the shore and in the dunes in the winter.

Surf fishing, hiking.
Spring, Fall

Sachuest Point 🖪
c/o Ninigret Refuge Complex Office
Shoreline Plaza, Route 1A
PO Box 307
Charlestown, RI 02813   401-364-9124

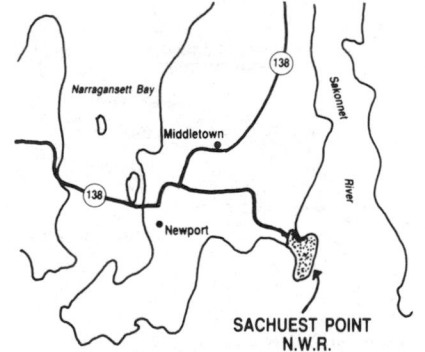

Located east of Newport in Middletown. From Rte. 138, go east on Miantonomi Ave. 0.6 mile then continue east onto Green End Ave. for 1.2 miles. Turn right (south) onto Paradise Ave., travel 1.3 miles, and turn left onto Hanging Rock Road. Continue 0.3 mile and bear right onto Sachuest Point Road. Follow it to the refuge entrance.

Habitat: 242 acres include salt and freshwater marshes, shrubland, grassland, and sandy beaches and dunes.

In the spring Common Terns arrive to nest in large colonies on the offshore islands while Common Yellowthroats, American Goldfinches, and other passerines begin their breeding season.

Tree Swallows congregate in large flocks during late August and early September. The hawk migration is best from mid-September through early October. Harlequin Ducks, eiders, scoters, and other waterfowl arrive and remain throughout the winter.

In the winter, various birds of prey, including Snowy and Short-eared owls and Rough-legged Hawks, are often present. Purple Sandpipers and Sanderlings winter along the rocky shore.

Area brochure. A 3-mile trail system winds through the upland areas and along the shore. Observation platforms afford panoramic views of refuge lands and the ocean. A visitor center features exhibits and audio-visual programs.
Spring, Fall

STATE AGENCIES

Division of Fish & Game
Department of Environmental Management
Government Center
Tower Hill Road
Wakefield, RI 02879   401-789-3094

Rhode Island Tourism Division
7 Jackson Walkway
Providence, RI 02903   401-277-2601

BIRDING HOTLINE
Statewide   704-332-2473

LOCAL BIRDING GROUPS
Map/Chapter/City
1. Charleston Nat. Hist. Soc./Charleston
2. Columbia Audubon/Columbia
3. Greenville Audubon/Greenville
4. Hilton Head Is. Audubon
   /Hilton Head Isle
5. Long Cane Audubon/Greenwood
6. Piedmont Audubon/Spartanburg
7. Waccamaw Audubon/Myrtle Beach
   Carolina Bird Club/Tyron, NC
   (see (11) on NC map)

NATIONAL AUDUBON SOCIETY

Francis Beidler Forest ❶
Route 1, Box 600
Harleyville, SC 29448   803-462-2150
Entry fee

The sanctuary is open to visitors from 9a.m.–5p.m. Tuesday–Sunday and closed during holidays. The visitor center staff offers a slide program and can answer questions about the area.

From Charleston, take I-26 west to exit 187, and then St. Hwy. 27 south to U.S Hwy. 78. Turn right, and continue west to the fork. Bear right onto U.S. Hwy. 178, then turn north onto St. Rt. 28 and follow the Beidler Forest signs from there to the sanctuary. The sanctuary is 40 miles northwest of Charleston.

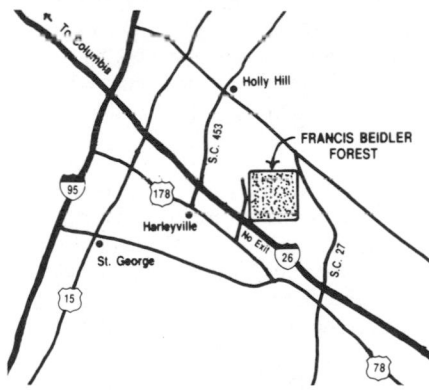

Habitat: 5,800 acres of southern forest and swamp with seasonal variations in water level. The bald cypress and tupelo gum trees, some over 600 years old, are one of the oldest virgin stands in the world.

During April and May the staff canoes into the swamp once a week to conduct a breeding bird survey on a designated 20-acre plot. Past surveys rank the virgin forest nesting density among the top four in the country.

On Saturdays and Sundays in April and May, and on Thursdays during the rest of the year (conditions permitting), the sanctuary naturalists lead inexpensive half-day canoe trips. Reservations are required as most trips are booked up to three months in advance.

Area brochure, 26-page self-guided tour booklet to 1.5 mile boardwalk, bird list, picnicking, guided canoe trips, handicapped access to visitor center.
Spring, Summer, Fall, Winter

THE NATURE CONSERVANCY
South Carolina Field Office ◇
PO Box 5475
Columbia, SC 29250   803-254-9049

Flat Creek Nature Area ❶
& 40-Acre Rock Preserve
598 acres near Taxahaw. A National Natural Landmark with red cedar woodlands, a beaver pond, and 40-Acre Rock which in reality is a 14-acre flat rock, one of the largest in the Piedmont Area.

Preserve, local map, and self-guiding trail brochure is available from the Field Office. The larger part of the preserve is managed by the Nongame & Heritage Trust Program of the South Carolina Wildlife & Marine Resources Department in Columbia.

Hiking, picnicking. Area brochure $1.
Spring

Peachtree Rock ❷
306 acres near Edmund

An interpretive trail guide is available that describes an unusual series of formations that originated 50 million years ago, and which are accompanied by a waterfall, sandstone outcrops, and uncommon flora.

Area map, hiking, picnicking. Brochure $1.
Spring, Fall

Washo Reserve ❸
1040 acres near McClellanville, including a 200-year-old freshwater cypress lake and a cypress-gum swamp. The reserve has one of the oldest heron and egret rookeries in continuous use in North America.

As many as 50 pairs of Ospreys nest at the reserve, making it of special interest to birders. More than 200 other species of birds frequent the area in and around Washo.

A self-guiding nature trail has 19 numbered stations along the 3-mile route, a leisurely 2-hour walk. The boardwalk and waterfowl blinds provide viewing opportunities along the trail and five stations offer good birding opportunities.

Area map, hiking, picnicking, reserve guide to nature trail $2.
Spring, Summer

U.S. FISH & WILDLIFE SERVICE NATIONAL WILDLIFE REFUGES

Cape Romain ❶   (office at refuge)
390 Bull Island Road
Awendaw, SC 29429   803-928-3368

Bird List SC-1 Cape Romain Summary
279 birds listed, 111 nesting birds
Bird Chart pages 330-347

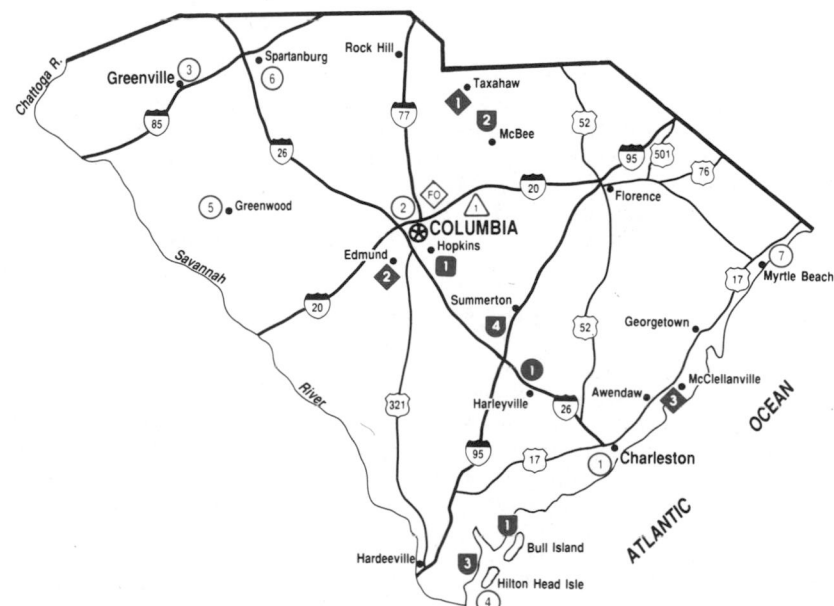

Totals by Season		s	S	F	W
Abundant	A	14	10	16	24
Common	C	96	71	95	74
Uncommon	U	44	30	50	46
Occasional	O	60	31	53	30
Rare	R	35	18	35	39

Endangered Species: Brown Pelican, Wood Stork, Bald Eagle, Peregrine Falcon, Piping Plover, Least Tern, Red-cockaded Woodpecker

Cape Romain stretches for 22 miles along the coast of South Carolina. From Charleston take Hwy. 17 north for 22 miles to the Hwy. 432 exit. Just off the exit, turn right on Seewee Road and go 3 miles to the refuge sign. Turn left to the visitors center. The visitors center area is the only part of the refuge accessible by automobile. Bull Island lies nearly 3 miles off the mainland and is accessible only by boat.

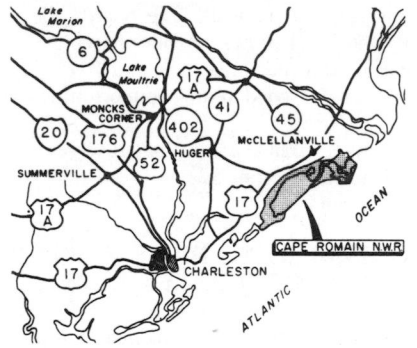

Habitat: 34,000 acres, including the 5,000-acre Bull Island. Shallow bays, marsh, woodland, and open water. Bull Island has a live oak, magnolia, pine, and palmetto forest and several shallow fresh and brackish water ponds.

Spring is the best time of the year to look for birds at the refuge. Painted Buntings and other songbirds and warblers are present in the greatest numbers during March and April. Shorebirds also return. The summer is hot and humid. Two endangered birds, Brown Pelicans and Least Terns, breed at the refuge, and Wood Storks and Red-cockaded Woodpeckers may also be found.

The passerine migration peaks in October when Yellow Warblers and other songbirds may be seen. Waterfowl begin to arrive in September, and their numbers peak in November and early December. During this time most of the Atlantic Coast's American Oystercatcher population is on the refuge. Peregrine Falcons fly through during the fall. American Swallow-tailed Kites and Pileated Woodpeckers are regular winter residents.

Area brochure, mammals, amphibians, and reptiles lists, boat launch, hiking, fishing, hunting. Interpretive trails on Bull Island.
Spring, Summer, Fall, Winter

Carolina Sandhills ❷ (office at refuge)
Route 2, Box 330
McBee, SC 29101   803-335-8401

Bird List SC-2 Sandhills Summary
191 birds listed, 80 nesting birds
Bird Chart pages 330-347

Totals by Season		s	S	F	W
Abundant	A	5	4	5	5
Common	C	73	62	72	53
Uncommon	U	22	14	23	20
Occasional	O	33	19	25	18
Rare	R	25	10	37	30

Endangered Species: Bald Eagle, Red-cockaded Woodpecker

From McBee, take U.S. Hwy. 1 and go 4 miles northeast to the refuge headquarters.

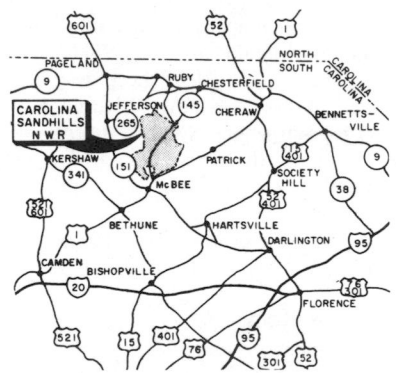

Habitat: 46,000 acres, primarily longleaf pine and scrub oak forests, with 1,200 acres of open fields and 30 man-made lakes. Located along the fall line separating the Piedmont Plateau from the Atlantic Coastal Plain, its soils are mainly rolling beds of deep sand. Numerous creeks flow into Black Creek on the east or Lynches River on the west. The riparian vegetation primarily consists of bottomland species and dense stands of evergreen shrubs.

The Red-cockaded Woodpecker, an endangered species, is common throughout the year, and its breeding population is one of the largest. Wood Ducks and a small flock of Canada Geese nest here in spring and summer. Wintering waterfowl start to appear in late September and remain through April, scattered over the many lakes and ponds. Northern Pintails, Green-winged Teals, American Wigeons, and American Black and Ring-necked ducks are the most common species, although Blue-winged Teals and Hooded Mergansers may also be present.

Common raptors include Red-tailed Hawks, American Kestrels, and both Turkey and Black vultures. Bald Eagles may be seen on rare occasions throughout the year. Wild Turkeys have been restocked on the refuge and Northern Bobwhites are abundant.

Area brochure, auto tour route, boat access, wildlife foot trail, observation blind, observation tower, fishing, hunting.
Spring, Summer, Fall, Winter

Pinckney Island ❸
c/o Savannah Coastal Refuges Complex

Take U.S. Hwy. 278 east from Hardeeville for 18 miles to the refuge entrance. The entrance is also 0.5 miles west of Hilton Head Island.

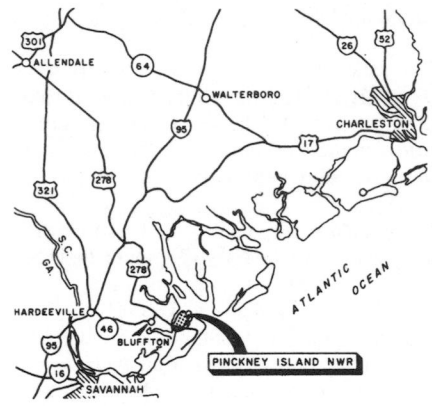

Pinckney Island Refuge is part of the Savannah Coastal Refuges Complex and is fully described in the Georgia chapter. Pinckney Island is also indicated on the Savannah Coastal Refuges Complex Map on page 68.

The 4,053-acre refuge includes Pinckney, Corn, Big and Little Harry, Buzzard islands and numerous small hammocks. Nearly 67 percent of the refuge consists of salt marsh and tidal creeks. Pinckney Island is the only island open for public use.

Area brochure, foot trails, hunting.
Spring, Summer, Fall, Winter

Santee ❹   (office at refuge)
Route 2, Box 66
Summerton, SC 29148   803-478-2217

The refuge is divided into four management units extending along the north shore of Lake Marion. The refuge office and visitors center is on the Bluff unit west of Hwy. 301. The Dingle Pond, Pine Island, and Cuddo units lie east of the highway. Take Hwy. 301 south of Summerton for 7 miles to refuge sign, turn right, and follow signs to the office.

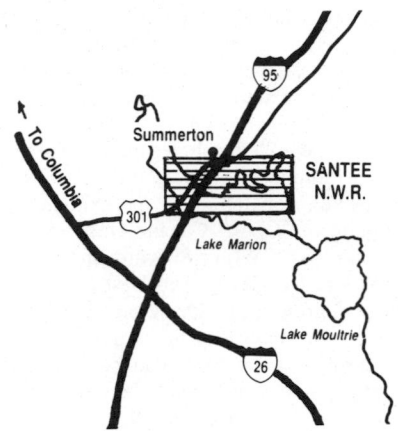

Habitat: 15,095 acres along 18 miles of the northern shore of Santee Cooper's Lake Marion, including mixed hardwoods, pine plantations, croplands and old fields, marshes, ponds, impoundments, and open water.

Wood Ducks, Purple Martins, and Eastern Bluebirds begin looking over the nesting boxes in February. Raptors are plentiful during March. Indigo Buntings, Blue Grosbeaks, orioles, tanagers, and vireos, return during April as the warbler migration approaches its peak. The migration continues through May as nesting activities begin.

Shorebirds returning from their nesting grounds can be seen on the pond and lake edges during July and August. Warblers begin to migrate south in August and the songbird migration peaks in September. Terns leave for wintering grounds along the coast of South America as American Kestrels, Blue-winged Teals, and various gulls are the vanguard of the winter residents. Double-crested cormorants, White-throated and Song sparrows, and various raptors and waterfowl begin to arrive in numbers during October. Bald Eagles may be seen near waterfowl concentrations in November because the old or injured birds are easy prey for the eagles. Large flocks of waterfowl are present in December, and their population peaks during January. Tundra Swans may be seen occasionally during the winter months.

Area brochure, bird list, boat ramp, nature trail, observation tower, mammals, amphibians, and reptiles lists, hunting, fishing. Insect repellent needed during summer.
Spring, Summer, Fall, Winter

NATIONAL PARK SERVICE

Congaree Swamp 🔳
National Monument
200 Caroline Sims Road
Hopkins, SC 29061   · 803-776-4396

The 15,138-acre Congaree Swamp contains a significant tract of southern bottomland hardwood forest and many other plant and animal species associated with alluvial floodplains. Several national and state record trees are located within the park.

Monument brochure with map, trail map, species lists available.

NATIONAL FOREST SERVICE
Francis Marion-Sumter   △
National Forests Supervisor
1835 Assembly Street
PO Box 2227
Columbia, SC 29202   803-765-5222

STATE AGENCIES

SC Wildlife & Marine
Resources Dept.
Div. of Wildlife & Freshwater Fisheries
Robert C. Dennis Building
PO Box 167
Columbia, SC 29202   803-758-0001

SC Division of Tourism
1205 Pendleton Street
PO Box 71
Columbia, SC 29202   803-734-0237

LOCAL BIRDING GROUPS
Map/Chapter/City
① Lakota Audubon/Brookings
② Missouri Breaks Audubon/Pierre
③ Aberdeen Bird & Wildflower Club
    /Aberdeen
④ South Dakota Ornithologists' Union
    /Aberdeen

THE NATURE CONSERVANCY

Samuel H. Ordway Jr. ❶
Memorial Prairie Preserve
HCR 1, Box 16
Leola, SD 57456   605-439-3475

This 7,800-acre preserve is located
northwest of Aberdeen near Leola.
Contact the preserve manager for
directions.

A nature trails guide book is available.
The three trails offer hikes of 0.75, 1, and
3.4 miles. The numbered stops along the
trails are keyed to descriptions and
explanations in the guide book.

Thousands of waterfowl, including
Mallards, Gadwalls, Northern Pintails, and
Northern Shovelers, nest by the preserve's
400 potholes. Ferruginous Hawks build
their stick nests on the hillcrests.
Wildflowers are lush on the hillsides
during spring and summer.

Area brochure, walking trails, camping
facilities are nearby at Leola and Eureka.
Spring, Summer, Fall

U.S. FISH & WILDLIFE SERVICE
NATIONAL WILDLIFE REFUGES

Lacreek ❶   (office at refuge)
HWC 3, Box 14
Martin, SD 57551   605-685-6508

Bird List SD-1 Lacreek Summary
213 birds listed, 93 nesting birds
Bird Chart pages 330-347

Totals by Season		s	S	F	W
Abundant	A	23	18	12	4
Common	C	54	35	41	10
Uncommon	U	63	50	53	26
Occasional	O	64	48	48	35

Endangered Species: Bald Eagle, Peregrine
Falcon, Whooping Crane

The refuge headquarters is located 13
miles southeast of Martin. Turn right from
Hwy. 18 onto the refuge road.

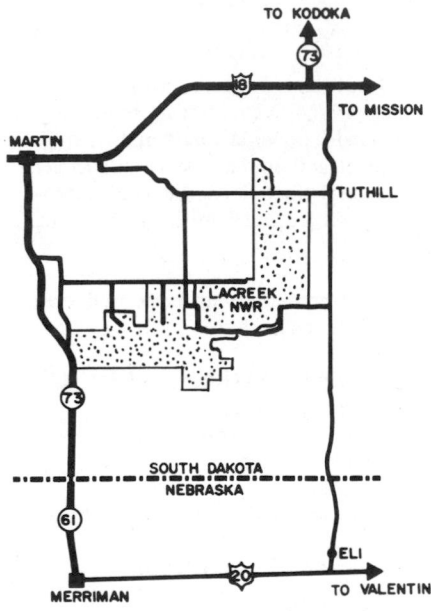

Habitat: 16,410 acres at 3,300 feet of
elevation, including sub-irrigated
meadows, shortgrass prairie uplands, 5,000
acres of dike-impounded fresh water
marshes, and native sandhills. The refuge

lies in the shallow Lake Creek Valley on
the northern edge of the Nebraska
Sandhills, in the transition region between
eastern and western flora and fauna.

The Trumpeter Swan breeds at Lacreek,
and is common throughout the year. There
is a nesting population of approximately
200 pairs of "Giant" Canada Geese as
well. American White Pelicans and
Double-crested Cormorants nest in a large
colony. During early spring and late
summer concentrations of migrating
shorebirds and songbirds can be seen. The
waterfowl population peaks between late
October and the middle of November.

Brochure, auto tour, permission required
to use trails, fishing, hunting.

The 360-acre Little White River
Recreation Area is located just north of
the refuge. The area offers camping,
picnicking, boating, swimming, fishing,
hunting.
Spring and Fall best

Lake Andes ❷   (office in town)
Rural Route 1, Box 77
Lake Andes, SD 57356   605-487-7603

Bird List SD-2 Lake Andes Summary
214 birds listed, 85 nesting birds
Bird Chart pages 330-347

Totals by Season		s	S	F	W
Abundant	A	9	9	10	5
Common	C	64	45	40	12
Uncommon	U	50	34	42	7
Occasional	O	68	56	74	20
Rare	R	13	13	6	16

Endangered Species: Bald Eagle, Peregrine
Falcon, Piping Plover, Least Tern

The headquarters is located in the town of
Lake Andes. The lake and refuge begin
just east of town.

Habitat: The Lake Andes Refuge is
divided into three units. The Lake Andes
unit consists of 4,700 acres of open water
interspersed with marsh vegetation. The
Owens Bay unit is an 832-acre refuge
with a 240-acre marsh surrounded by

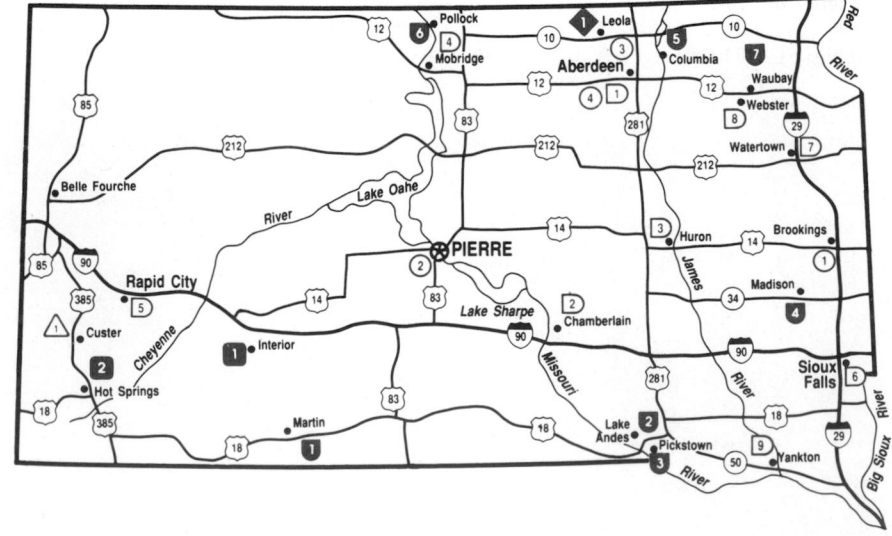

approximately 592 acres of native grass cover. The Youngstrom Unit provides 320 acres of additional marsh habitat at the north end of Lake Andes. The Lake Andes office also manages the Karl E. Mundt NWR.

Within the 20-county Lake Andes Waterfowl Management District over 20,000 acres of waterfowl habitat are managed. Perpetual easements protect another 83,000 wetland acres from drainage.

Nearly any species of bird indigenous to the prairie pothole country may be observed at the refuge. The best opportunities for birding are between early April and mid-October, with Spring and fall migrations offering the greatest diversity.

Area brochure, foot trails, boating, fishing, picnicking, hunting.
Spring, Summer, Fall

Karl E. Mundt ③
c/o Lake Andes NWR
Rural Route 1, Box 77
Lake Andes, SD 57356   605-487-7603

Public use of the Karl E. Mundt NWR is prohibited to protect the Bald Eagles. The refuge was established as the first Federal eagle sanctuary. An excellent eagle observation point is located close to the refuge on Army Corps of Engineers property directly below the Ft. Randall Dam near Pickstown.

Habitat: Missouri River bottomland.

Area brochure.
Spring, Fall

Madison WMD ④
PO Box 48
Madison, SD 57042   605-256-2974

The Madison Wetland Management District includes 250 areas managed for waterfowl production in nine counties. These areas range from 40 to 400 acres.

Sand Lake ⑤   (office at refuge)
Rural Route 1, Box 253
Columbia, SD 57433   605-885-6320

Bird List SD-3 Sand Lake Summary
239 birds listed, 111 nesting birds
Bird Chart pages 330-347

Totals by Season		s	S	F	W
Abundant	A	13	10	14	0
Common	C	78	63	46	10
Uncommon	U	83	53	70	16
Occasional	O	42	28	39	20
Rare	R	11	11	12	21

Endangered Species: Bald Eagle, Peregrine Falcon, Piping Plover, Least Tern

Located 27 miles north and east of Aberdeen. From Aberdeen, take U.S. Hwy. 12 east to Co. Rd. 16 (Bath Corner, 7 miles east of Aberdeen). Drive 20 miles north, through Columbia, to the refuge entrance.

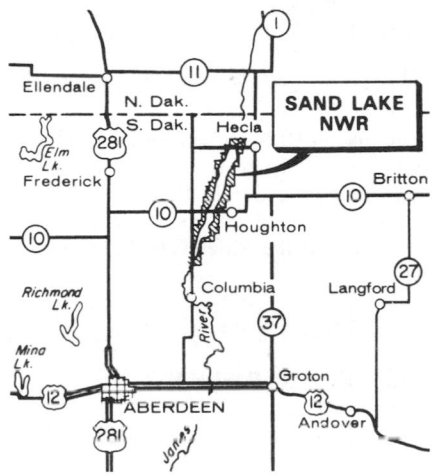

Habitat: 21,451 acres at 1,300 feet of elevation include a portion of the James River, and Mud and Sand lakes, which cover over half the refuge. Woodlands, grasslands, and croplands make up the remainder.

Hundreds of thousands of Snow Geese and other migratory waterfowl rest and feed on Sand Lake during the spring and fall migrations. From May to September a wide variety of birds feed and nest in this prairie marsh ecosystem.

Area brochure, 15-mile auto tour route, hiking, bicycling, picnicking, fishing, hunting, 100-foot high observation tower.
Spring, Summer, Fall

Pocasse ⑥
c/o Sand Lake NWR
Rural Route 1, Box 253
Columbia, SD 57433   605-885-6320

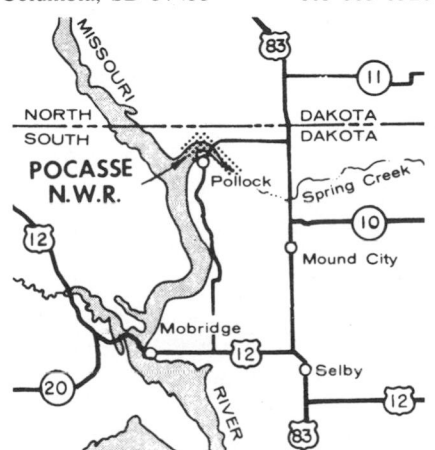

Pocasse NWR is located in north-central South Dakota near Pollock on Lake Pocasse. There is no office at the refuge. Pocasse is a sub-impoundment of the Oahe Reservoir.

Habitat: 2,585 acres, of which 1,545 acres are marsh and 1,040 acres are uplands. The Missouri River forms the western boundary of the refuge, and Spring Creek flows through the refuge from the south.

The refuge provides habitat for waterfowl and is a migratory resting area for Sandhill Cranes, geese, ducks, and other birds. Bald Eagles, Whooping Cranes, and Peregrine Falcons occasionally use the refuge during migration.

Fishing, swimming, boating, camping, picnicking, hunting.
Spring, Fall

Waubay ⑦
Rural Route 1, Box 79
Waubay, SD 57273   605-947-4521

Bird List SD-4 Waubay Summary
244 birds listed, 109 nesting birds
Bird Chart pages 348-365

Totals by Season		s	S	F	W
Abundant	A	11	5	14	0
Common	C	95	68	92	7
Uncommon	U	44	40	45	4
Occasional	O	51	32	46	26
Rare	R	31	29	26	20

Endangered Species: Bald Eagle, Peregrine Falcon, Piping Plover

Located north of Waubay via Rte. 1, which leads to the refuge road and headquarters building.

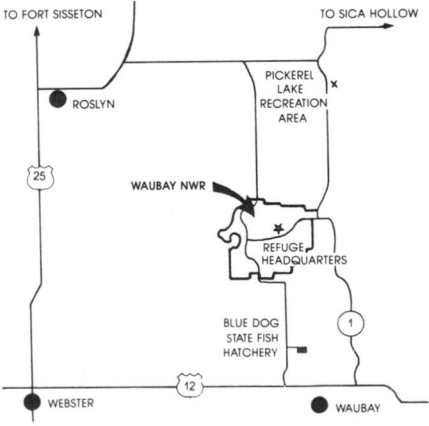

Habitat: 4,650 acres of lakes, marshlands, grasslands, and woodlands in the prairie pothole region.

Both eastern and western bird species can be found. During March to April and

October to November peak waterfowl numbers occur. Migrations of warblers and shorebirds occur in May and September.

Waubay is one of the southernmost nesting locations of the Red-necked Grebe. Double-crested Cormorants nest on nearby islands. American White Pelicans, bitterns, Upland Sandpipers, Wilson's Phalaropes, Franklin's Gulls, and 16 species of waterfowl are among the large variety of breeding species. Eastern Bluebirds use the nest boxes that are provided for them.

Area brochure, loop trails, wildlife observation tower, picnic area, cross-country ski trail, hunting.
Spring, Summer, Fall

NATIONAL PARK SERVICE

Badlands National Park ❶
PO Box 6
Interior, SD 57750   605-433-5361

243,302 acres with 64,250-acre wilderness area. Carved by erosion, this scenic landscape contains fossils of animals that lived 37 million years ago. Prairie grasslands support bison, antelope, deer, and bighorn sheep.

Park brochure with map, programs leaflet, mammals checklist and notes.

Wind Cave National Park ❷
Hot Springs, SD 57747   605-745-4600

28,292 acres of the Black Hills include limestone caverns decorated with beautiful honeycomb-shaped boxwork and calcite crystal formations. Herds of elk, mule

deer, antelope, and bison can be seen, as well as prairie dog towns.

Park brochure with map, wildlife leaflet and checklist, park information leaflet.

NATIONAL FOREST SERVICE
Black Hills National Forest Supervisor △
Highway 385 North
Route 2, PO Box 200
Custer, SD 57730   605-673-2251

BUREAU LAND MANAGEMENT

There are no BLM district offices in South Dakota. There is a South Dakota Resource Area office in Belle Fourche (phone 605-892-2526), under the supervision of the Miles City Montana district office.

STATE AGENCIES

Game, Fish & Parks HQ
445 East Capitol
Pierre, SD 57501   605-773-3485

Map/Region/City
①	Aberdeen/Aberdeen	605-622-2391
②	Chamberlain	
	/Chamberlain	605-734-5622
③	Huron/Huron	605-353-7145
④	Mobridge/Mobridge	605-845-7814
⑤	Rapid City/Rapid City	605-394-2391
⑥	Sioux Falls	
	/Sioux Falls	605-339-6621
⑦	Watertown/Watertown	605-886-4769
⑧	Webster/Webster	605-345-3381
⑨	Yankton/Yankton	605-668-3436

South Dakota Tourism
Capitol Lake Plaza
Pierre, SD 57501   1-800-952-2217
from out-of-state call   1-800-843-1930

BIRDING HOTLINE

Statewide   615-356-7636

LOCAL BIRDING GROUPS

Map/Chapter/City

1. Cherokee Audubon/Madisonville
2. Cumberland-Harpeth Aud./Nashville
3. Emma Bell Miles Aud./Chattanooga
4. Greater Knoxville Aud./Knoxville
5. Memphis Audubon/Memphis
6. Warioto Audubon/Clarksville
7. Watauga Audubon/Kingsport
8. Tennessee Ornithological Society (TOS)/Chattanooga
9. Buffalo River Chapter - TOS /Lawrenceburg
10. Chattanooga Bird Club - TOS /Chattanooga
11. Columbia Chapter - TOS/Columbia
12. Cumberland County - TOS /Crossville
13. Greenville Chapter - TOS/Greenville
14. Lee R. Herndon Chapter - TOS /Elizabethton
15. Highland Rim Chapter - TOS /Manchester
16. Jackson Chapter - TOS/Jackson
17. Knoxville Chapter - TOS/Knoxville
18. Memphis Chapter - TOS/Memphis
19. Murfreesboro Chapter - TOS /Murfreesboro
20. Nashville Chapter - TOS/Nashville
21. John W. Sellars Chapter - TOS /Lebanon

THE NATURE CONSERVANCY

Tennessee Field Office
226 Capitol Boulevard Bldg.
PO Box 3017
Nashville, TN 37219   615-242-1787

Species lists are available from the Field Office for these preserves.

Barnett's Woods ◆

40 acres near Woodlawn featuring rare plant species and wildflower areas. From Clarksville, take Rte. 79 (Dover Hwy.) west toward Ft. Campbell for 12.5 miles. Go south on Coopers Creek Road for 1.4 miles. The Barnett house and preserve are on the left. Small dirt road leads to the preserve.

Picnicking, day hiking.
Summer, Fall

Hubbard's Cave ◆

Caving experience is essential, and permission from the Field Office is required for all visitors. The 50-acre preserve near McMinnville in Warren County has Tennessee's largest population of the endangered gray bat. The endangered Indiana bat also uses the preserve.

Day hiking, picnicking, wildflower areas.
Summer

Sneed Road Cedar Glade ◆

A 1-acre preserve near Nashville in an open prairie-like cedar glen with rare plant species. From Nashville, take Hillsboro Road to its junction with U.S. 431 and Sneed Road. The preserve is located on the north side of Sneed Road about .7 miles to the west of the junction.

Picnicking.
Spring, Summer

Wash Morgan Hollow ◆

A 77-acre sheltered ravine known locally for its bird habitat and rich floral diversity. Located near Cookeville. Take Hwy. 135 north for 10 miles to Dodson Branch. Go right on Steep Rock Road, take the left fork onto Spring Creek Road, and go 1 mile. Wash Morgan is the hollow on the left.

Picnicking, day hiking.
Spring

U.S. FISH & WILDLIFE SERVICE NATIONAL WILDLIFE REFUGES

Cross Creeks ◉ (office at refuge)

Route 1, Box 229
Dover, TN 37058   615-232-7477

Bird List TN-1 Cross Creeks Summary
244 birds listed, 90 nesting birds
Bird Chart pages 348-365

Totals by Season		s	S	F	W
Abundant	A	0	0	3	7
Common	C	85	62	71	42
Uncommon	U	82	33	71	35
Occasional	O	34	16	42	13
Rare	R	26	23	39	19

Endangered Species: Wood Stork, Bald Eagle, Peregrine Falcon, Least Tern

From Dover, go east for 2.2 miles on St. Hwy. 49, then turn north on a county road for 1.3 miles to the headquarters.

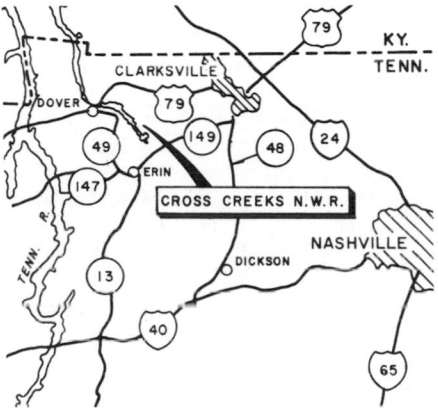

Habitat: 8,862 acres extending 11 miles along Lake Barkley on the Cumberland River. One-fourth of the reserve is covered by deciduous woodlands, and the remainder evenly divided between agricultural fields and open water.

The Bald Eagle returned in 1983 after a 22-year absence. The few breeding pairs are augmented during the winter months, when up to 11 individuals may be seen. Red-tailed and Red-shouldered hawks are common throughout the year.

Northern Flickers, and Red-bellied, Downy, and Hairy woodpeckers are common. An occasional Yellow-bellied Sapsucker, or Pileated or Red-headed woodpecker may be seen. Passerines are particularly common during migration periods, when a large variety of warblers and sparrows stop for rest and food.

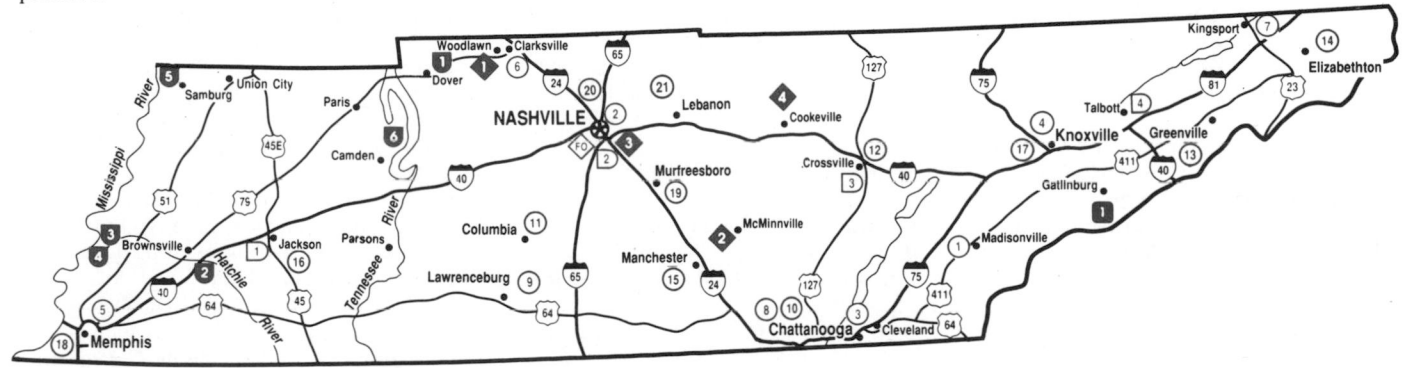

The refuge provides wintering habitat for large numbers of waterfowl, including Canada Geese and 17 species of ducks.

Area brochure, visitor center, auto tour route, foot trail, bicycling, fishing, hunting.
Spring, Summer, Fall, Winter

Hatchie ❷

Highway 76 and I-40
PO Box 187
Brownsville, TN 38012   901-772-0501

Bird List TN-2 Hatchie Summary
211 birds listed, 87 nesting birds
Bird Chart pages 348-365

Totals by Season		s	S	F	W
Abundant	A	1	11	4	5
Common	C	15	56	9	50
Uncommon	U	55	29	54	30
Occasional	O	14	15	14	6
Rare	R	17	19	21	14

Endangered Species: Wood Stork, Bald Eagle

Refuge office is south of I-40 on Hwy. 76 between Memphis and Jackson (near Brownsville). To reach the refuge from the west take exit 52 from I-40 and go east 1.5 miles to Hwy. 76 and the refuge sign. From the east take exit 56 and go south on Hwy. 76 to the refuge sign.

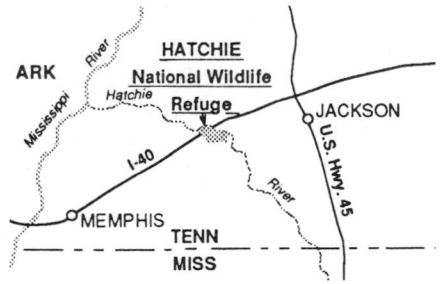

Habitat: 11,556 acres along the Hatchie River include over 9,400 acres of bottomland forests crossed by meandering creeks. There are a number of oxbow lakes and some uplands.

Large numbers of waterfowl utilize the refuge at various times of the year. Wood Ducks and Hooded Mergansers are the most common year-round residents.

During the spring and summer the woods are filled with songbirds, including Acadian Flycatchers, Northern Parulas, and Yellow-throated, Cerulean, Kentucky, and Hooded warblers. Migrants such as Rose-breasted Grosbeaks, and Vesper and White-crowned sparrows are common during spring and fall. Barred and Great Horned owls, as well as Eastern Screech-Owls, breed in the bottomland forests.

Area brochure, hiking, limited hunting, fishing, boating.
Spring, Summer, Fall, Winter

Chickasaw ❸

c/o Hatchie NWR
PO Box 187
Brownsville, TN 38012   901-772-0501

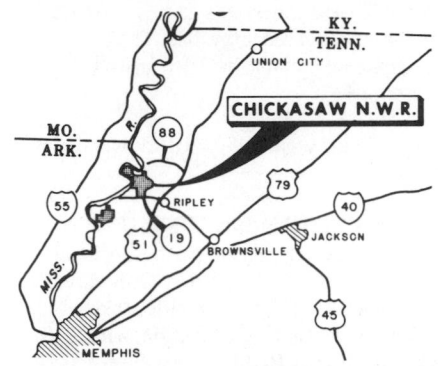

Habitat: A 20,940-acre refuge located on the Mississippi River just west of Ripley. Bottomland area with sloughs and ponds.

For information on access and current conditions contact the Hatchie refuge office. There is a brochure available on hunting and fishing.
Spring, Summer, Winter

Lower Hatchie ❹

c/o Hatchie NWR
PO Box 187
Brownsville, TN 38012   901-772-0501

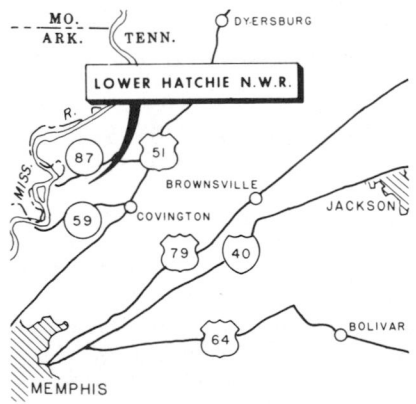

A 4,138-acre refuge located on the Mississippi River near Covington. There is a boat ramp at Champion Lake on the refuge. For information on access and current conditions contact the Hatchie refuge office. A hunting and fishing brochure is available.
Spring, Summer, Fall, Winter

Reelfoot & Lake Isom ❺

Route 2, Highway 157
Union City, TN 38261   901-538-2481

Bird List TN-3 Lake Isom Summary
238 birds listed, 100 nesting birds
Bird Chart pages 348-365

Totals by Season		s	S	F	W
Abundant	A	4	2	9	9
Common	C	15	70	11	57
Uncommon	U	71	36	69	29
Occasional	O	24	19	23	11
Rare	R	15	4	17	25

Endangered Species: Wood Stork, Bald Eagle, Peregrine Falcon, Least Tern

Headquarters is on Hwy. 157, a few miles south of the Kentucky-Tennessee state line, or 6 miles north of Samburg.

Reelfoot refuge is located on and around the upper portion of Reelfoot Lake. Access is via Hwy. 157 on the east side and Hwy. 78 on the west side. Lake Isom refuge is located 5 miles south of Reelfoot Lake. Access is via Hwy. 22.

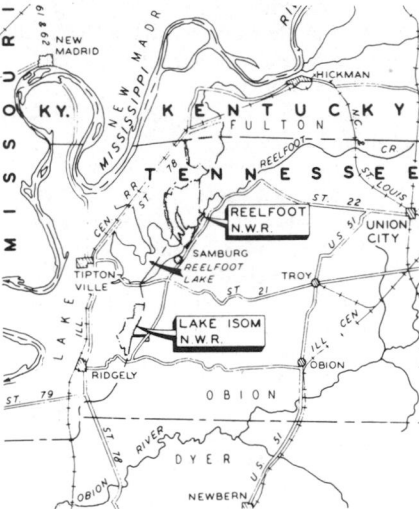

Habitat: Reelfoot has 10,428 acres, and Lake Isom, 1,846 acres. Reelfoot Lake, which was formed by a series of severe earthquakes during the winter of 1811-12, is located on the Mississippi River floodplain. Stands of bald cypress surround the lakes. The swamp forests bordering the lakes are almost impenetrable. Thick mats of aquatic vegetation grow on the lake surfaces, and vast stretches of head-high grasses extend into much of the shallow water.

In the spring, large numbers of Northern Shovelers and Blue-winged Teals arrive during their northbound migration in March, and nesting Ospreys return. Shorebirds and ducks are abundant in April. Spring migration peaks in May, with a variety of passerines and waterbirds moving through. Great Blue Herons, Great Egrets, and Yellow-crowned Night-Herons may be observed fishing during June. Large numbers of Gadwall and American Wigeons begin to arrive in October. Waterfowl and songbird observation is good on Grassy Island during November. Migrating waterfowl and Bald Eagles arrive in September. Their numbers build throughout the fall and winter, when they are best seen on the Long Point Unit, and reach their peak in January. Their populations fall off in February as Bald Eagles leave the refuge to start their nests.

Area brochure, auto tour route, foot trail, boardwalk, observation tower, hunting, fishing, boating, boat ramp.
Spring, Summer, Fall, Winter

Tennessee ⑥   (office in town)
101 W. Blythe Street
PO Box 849
Paris, TN 38242   901-642-2091

Bird List TN-4 Tennessee Summary
255 birds listed, 87 nesting birds
Bird Chart pages 348-365

Totals by Season		s	S	F	W
Abundant	A	13	4	13	10
Common	C	2	63	0	49
Uncommon	U	61	27	61	31
Occasional	O	24	21	29	15
Rare	R	14	9	16	13

Endangered Species: Bald Eagle, Peregrine Falcon, Least Tern

The refuge is in 3 separate units along 80 miles of the Tennessee River. Access to all units is via all-weather roads from main highways. Watch for direction signs.

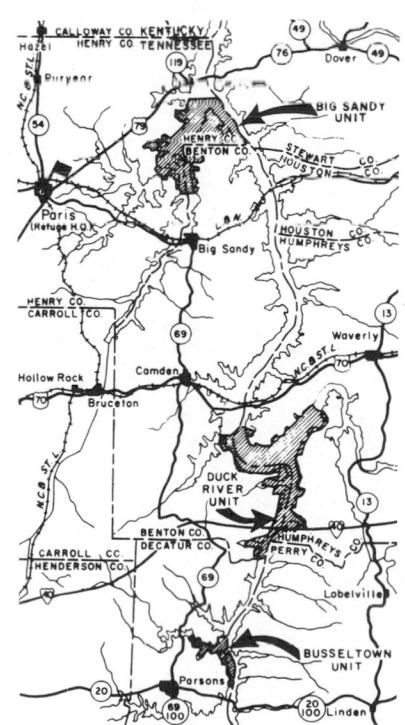

Big Sandy, the northern-most unit, is located east of Hwy. 79, 8 to 12 miles northeast of Paris. The Duck River Unit is southeast of Camden. Hwy. 69 touches

one corner of the unit on the east shore of Kentucky Lake, and I-40 crosses the south end of the unit. The Busseltown unit is located northeast of Parsons in the right angle formed by Hwy. 69 and Hwy. 20. Maps showing the most logical route to an area are available from the refuge office.

Habitat: 51,358 acres superimposed on Tennessee Valley Authority lands and waters along Kentucky Lake. Big Sandy unit has 21,348 acres, Duck River unit has 26,738 acres, and Busseltown unit has 3,272 acres. The three units include 27,358 acres of water, 19,000 acres of woodland, and 5,000 acres of farmland.

Great Blue Herons begin nesting at Grassy Lake rookery in March, and their young hatch in June. Waterfowl leave the refuge in large numbers during the spring and an occasional Common Loon may be seen migrating through. Wild Turkeys perform their courtship in April. Ospreys stop over during migration. Wood Ducks begin nesting in May when warblers and other songbirds are migrating through.

Shorebirds are abundant and varied, and can best be seen at Pace Point or Duck River bottoms in August, when Cattle Egrets can be seen in open areas. Flocks of Blue-winged Teals come in before mid-month and a few Canada Geese and other ducks begin to arrive by the end of the month. The passerine concentration peaks during October and Bald Eagles begin arriving in the area. Mallards, American Black Ducks, and American Wigeons arrive in large numbers during November. Red-tailed Hawks are at their fall migration peak and a few Golden Eagles move into the area. Populations of various waterbirds grow during December and peak during January, when Bald Eagles are most numerous. Herring and Ring-billed gulls begin to gather and stage in February and the waterfowl begin leaving.

Area brochure, auto tour route, foot trail, fishing, hunting, boating, mammals list.
Spring, Summer, Fall, Winter

NATIONAL PARK SERVICE

Great Smoky Mountains ❶
National Park
Gatlinburg, TN 37738   615-436-1200

520,269 acres are among the best examples of temperate deciduous forest. The loftiest range east of the Black Hills of South Dakota, and one of the oldest uplands on earth. A coniferous forest grows along the 6,000-foot-high peaks of the Great Smoky Mountains, which have a diversified and luxuriant plant life, often

of extraordinary size, and extensive coniferous and deciduous forests. Ruffed Grouse and Common Ravens are among the species that can be seen in this park.

Park brochure with map, free 12-page newspaper "Smokies Guide", mammals list, bird checklist with season and habitat codes.

NATIONAL FOREST SERVICE
Cherokee National Forest Supervisor △
2800 North Ocoee Street NW
PO Box 2010
Cleveland, TN 37320   615-476-9700

STATE AGENCIES

Tennessee Wildlife Resource Agency
Ellington Agricultural Center
PO Box 40747
Nashville, TN 37204   615-360-0500

Map/Region/City
① Region 1/Jackson   901-423-5725
② Region 2/Nashville   615-360-0622
③ Region 3/Crossville   615-484-9571
④ Region 4/Talbott   615-587-4670

Dept. of Tourist Development
320 Sixth Avenue North
PO Box 23170
Nashville, TN 37202   615-741-2158

BIRDING HOTLINES
Statewide (Lone Star RBA)

In Houston	713-747-8826
In Texas	800-828-2473
Austin	512-451-3308
North Central Area	817-237-3209

Lower Texas

Rio Grand Valley (Weslaco, TX)	512-565-6773
San Antonio	512-733-8306
Sinton	512-364-3634
Upper Texas Coast (Houston)	713-821-2846

LOCAL BIRDING GROUPS
Map/Chapter/City

1. Bastrop County Aud./Cedar Creek
2. Bexar Audubon/San Antonio
3. Big County Aud./Abilene
4. Central Texas Audubon /Waco
5. Coastal Bend Audubon /Corpus Christi
6. Dallas County Audubon /Dallas
7. El Paso Trans-Pecos Aud. /El Paso
8. Fort Worth Audubon /Fort Worth
9. Frontiera Audubon /McAllen
10. Houston Audubon/Houston
11. Huntsville Audubon /Huntsville
12. Llano Estacado Audubon /Lubbock
13. Prairie & Timbers Audubon /McKinney

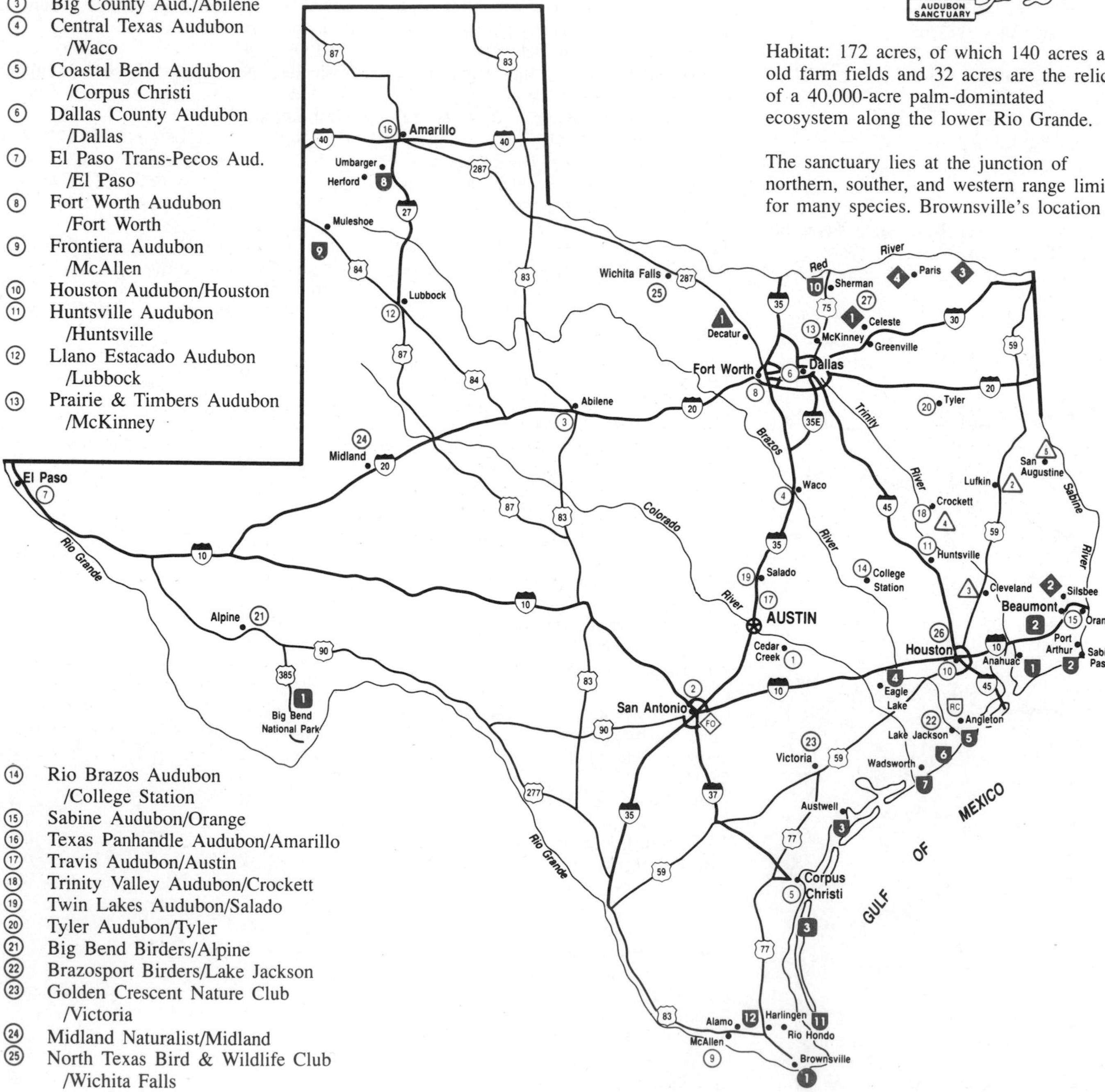

14. Rio Brazos Audubon /College Station
15. Sabine Audubon/Orange
16. Texas Panhandle Audubon/Amarillo
17. Travis Audubon/Austin
18. Trinity Valley Audubon/Crockett
19. Twin Lakes Audubon/Salado
20. Tyler Audubon/Tyler
21. Big Bend Birders/Alpine
22. Brazosport Birders/Lake Jackson
23. Golden Crescent Nature Club /Victoria
24. Midland Naturalist/Midland
25. North Texas Bird & Wildlife Club /Wichita Falls

26. Texas Ornithological Society /Houston
27. Texoma Outdoor Club/Sherman

NATIONAL AUDUBON SOCIETY

Sabal Palm Grove ❶
Rose Farmer—Manager
PO Box 5052
Brownsville, TX 78523   512-541-8034
Entry fee

Visitor hours are 8a.m.–5p.m. Thursday through Monday, from November through April. Visits may be arranged at other times through the sanctuary manager.

Sabal Palm Grove is southeast of Brownsville. Take Southmost Road (FM 1419) from town for about 6 miles to the sanctuary entrance on the right.

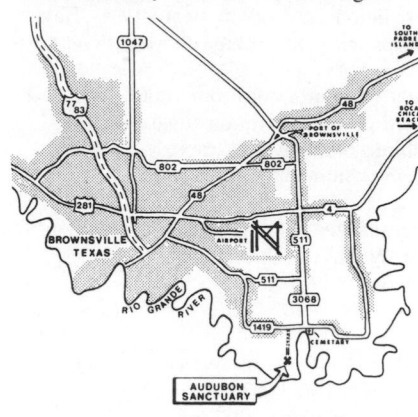

Habitat: 172 acres, of which 140 acres are old farm fields and 32 acres are the relict of a 40,000-acre palm-domintated ecosystem along the lower Rio Grande.

The sanctuary lies at the junction of northern, souther, and western range limits for many species. Brownsville's location at the southern tip of Texas makes it a prime spot to see species that rarely venture north of the Mexican border.

The Plain Chachalaca, Green Jay, Buff-bellied Hummingbird, White-tipped Dove, Black-bellied Whistling Duck, Pauraque, Least Grebe, Groove-billed Ani, Altamira Oriole, Great Kiskadee, and Olive Sparrow all spend part of the year at or near Sabal Palm Grove. The bird checklist enumerates 276 species seen at or near the sanctuary.

Sanctuary brochure, visitor center, hiking trails, bird list.
Early Spring, Winter

THE NATURE CONSERVANCY
Texas Field Office
PO Box 1440
San Antonio, TX 78295   512-224-8774

Contact the Field Office for access details and visitor regulations.

Clymer Meadow

From Dallas take I-30 about 50 miles east to Greenville. Turn north onto Hwy. 69 and continue about 11 miles to Celeste. Turn left and take FM 1562 west about 2.5 miles. Turn right onto dirt road just before the large, green, cylindrical tank. Proceed 0.8 miles and turn left onto property (look for the Conservancy sign).

Habitat: 283 acres are the largest and best example of Blackland Prairie remaining in Texas, possibly in North America. Clymer Meadow's various forbs and native grasses attract a variety of species, both migratory and sedentary.

Area brochure with local map available, picnicking, hiking.
Spring, Summer, Fall, Winter

Roy E. Larsen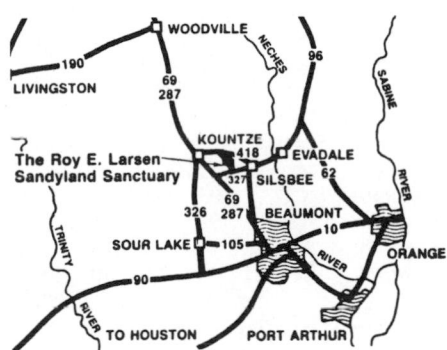
Sandylands Sanctuary
Ike McWhorter—Manager
PO Box 909
Silsbee, TX 77656   409-385-4135

From Beaumont take Hwy. 96 north to Silsbee. Turn left and go west on Hwy. 327. Nature trail and preserve office are on left side of Hwy. 327 just before Village Creek.

Habitat: 2,275 acres of forest and wetland communities in the Big Thicket region of Texas. Arid, sandy lands support the greatest variety of wildflowers in the Thicket, but are otherwise sparsely vegetated. Ponds that have formed in the low areas are surrounded by baygall communities with lush wetland vegetation. Rare orchids and carnivorous plants grow among acid-loving ferns and sphagnum moss.

An 8-mile canoe trail and the Sandylands Nature trail provide access to the diverse ecosystem. Contact the Manager about the availability of guided tours.
Area brochure map has canoe trail detail. Picnicking, hiking, swimming, non-motorized boating. Day use only.
Spring, Fall, Winter

Lennox Woods Preserve

Habitat: 159 acres, with an old growth timber area, dry upland, and flat bottomland along Pecan Bayou. The Texas Forest Service, which dates old trees, has recorded a loblolly pine on Lennox dating back to 1848, and a post oak dating back to 1694. Lennox Woods is believed to be typical of undisturbed floodplains as they once occurred throughout this part of Texas.

Area brochure, hiking. Beware of poisonous snakes in warm weather.
Spring, Summer, Fall, Winter

Tridens Prairie

Tridens Prairie is located at the southwest corner of U.S. 82 and FM 38, 6 miles west of Paris Texas in Lamar County.

Habitat: A 97-acre remnant of Blackland Prairie, which once covered most of northeast Texas.

During the third weekend in May there is an Annual Wildflower Day at Tridens Prairie. Most of the grasses blossom in the fall.

Area brochure, hiking.
Spring, Summer, Fall

U.S. FISH & WILDLIFE SERVICE NATIONAL WILDLIFE REFUGES

Anahuac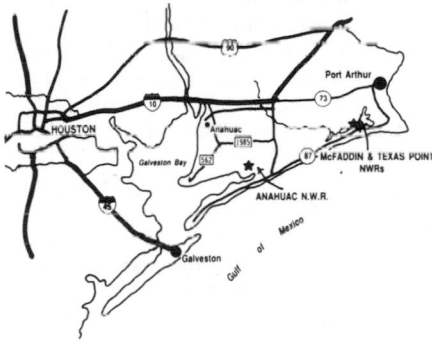
Trinity Street and Washington Avenue
PO Box 278
Anahuac, TX 77514   409-267-3337

Bird List TX-1 Anahuac Summary
252 birds listed, 40 nesting birds
Bird Chart pages 348-365

Totals by Season		s	S	F	W
Abundant	A	25	9	28	18
Common	C	75	30	72	41
Uncommon	U	55	18	58	36
Occasional	O	32	7	29	29
Rare	R	9	8	21	14

Endangered Species: Wood Stork, Bald Eagle, Peregrine Falcon, Piping Plover, Least Tern

The office is located near the County Courthouse. To reach the refuge from the office in Anahuac, take Belton Lane 2.5 miles east and then turn right onto Hwy. 562. Go 6.5 miles south, turn left on St. Road 1985 and go 4.5 miles to refuge sign. Turn right on gravel road and go 3 miles to the visitor information booth at the refuge entrance.

Habitat: 24,356 acres of coastal marsh and wet prairie at the upper end of East Galveston Bay.

During the spring migration Shoveler Pond and Teal Slough can be productive for warblers and other passerines as well as the ducks for which they are named. The refuge is a prime nesting area for the Mottled Duck, a year-round resident. Clapper and King rails are also present throughout the year, while Great Blue, Tricolored, and Green-backed herons, Great and Snowy egrets, and White and White-faced ibises leave the refuge during the winter.

Between October and March, up to 20 species of ducks and 4 of geese may be found on the refuge. Canada, Greater White-fronted, and Snow geese are abundant in the winter and on rare occasions the Ross's Goose also can be seen. Mallards, Gadwalls, Northern Pintails, Green-winged Teals, and Northern Shovelers are the most abundant ducks during the winter.

Area brochure, hunting, fishing, hiking trails. Watch out for alligators, poisonous

snakes, and fire ants, and come prepared for mosquitoes.
Spring, Winter

McFaddin & Texas Point ❷
c/o Anahuac NWR
PO Box 278
Anahuac, TX 77514   409-267-3337
or
McFaddin Field Office
PO Box J
Sabine Pass, TX 77655   409-971-2909

These refuges are close together (see Anahuac map, page 171) and located along Hwy. 87, about 15 miles south of Port Arthur. Access is from Hwy. 87.

Habitat: 50,654 acres of marshland in two refuges on the upper Texas coast.

These marshlands are important wintering areas for migratory waterfowl. Large concentrations of Snow, Greater White-fronted, and Canada geese use the marsh from October through March. Wintering duck populations may reach 100,000 with 23 species represented. The Mottled Duck nests on the marsh and is the only resident waterfowl species. The "Southern" Bald Eagle and "Arctic" Peregrine Falcon may on rare occasions be seen during the peak spring and fall migration periods.

Shorebird numbers during migration and wading bird numbers throughout most of the year can be impressive. Migrating warblers and other small birds also stop to rest and feed at the marshes in large numbers.

Area brochure, waterfowl hunting, fishing, crabbing, camping, picnicking, beachcombing.
Spring, Winter

Aransas ❸   (office at refuge)
PO Box 100
Austwell, TX 77950   512-286-3559

Bird List TX-2 Aransas Summary
268 birds listed, no nesting data
Bird Chart pages 348-365

Totals by Season		s	S	F	W
Common	C	92	33	74	69
Uncommon	U	5	43	0	59
Rare	R	55	37	45	37

Endangered Species: Brown Pelican, Wood Stork, Peregrine Falcon, Whooping Crane, Piping Plover, Least Tern

From Austwell, go south on FM 774 for 0.5 mile, Turn left on FM 2040, and go 6.5 miles to refuge entrance.

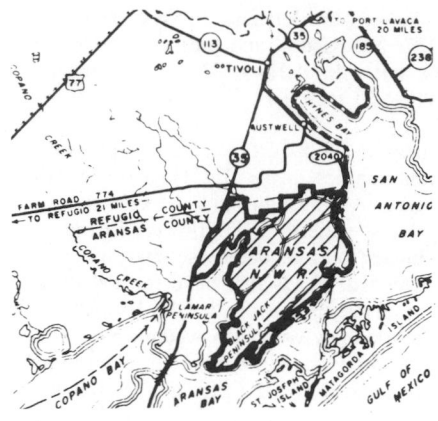

Habitat: 54,829 acres of wooded sand dunes, brushland, oak mottes, bluestem meadows, and cordgrass prairies with long, narrow freshwater ponds, all ringed by tidal marshes.

The refuge was established in 1937 to provide protection for Whooping Cranes on their wintering grounds along the Gulf of Mexico. Up to 150 birds in two wild populations overwinter at Aransas. They leave on their northward migration in April.

Hundreds of Painted and Indigo buntings, flycatchers, warblers, and tanagers move through the refuge in the spring. This part of the Texas coast is the lower end of a migration funnel through which thousands of birds fly to and from Central and South America. There is a lull in bird sightings during the summer as various residents retire to the brush and offshore islands to nest. The migrants start to return in August, and the mild winters and abundant food supplies attract both Brown and American White pelicans, egrets, Roseate Spoonbills, ducks, and geese.

Area brochure, mammals, amphibians, and reptiles lists, hunting, fishing, 6 walking trails, observation tower, wildlife interpretive center.
Spring, Fall, Winter

Attwater Prairie Chicken ❹
PO Box 518   (office at refuge)
Eagle Lake, TX 77434   409-234-5940

The Attwater Prairie Chicken bird list is being revised. An up-to-date list will be available in late 1990 or 1991.

From Eagle Lake, take FM 3013 7 miles northeast to the refuge entrance. Headquarters is 2 miles west of the entrance on FM 3013.

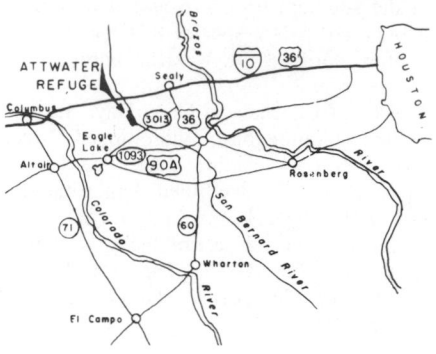

Habitat: 8,000 acres of native prairies, croplands, marshes, ponds, and woodlands.

The refuge was established to preserve and restore critical habitat for the endangered "Attwater's" race of the Greater Prairie Chicken. The estimated entire population in 1989 was 432 birds in 8 counties. Human visitation is closely controlled during the prairie chickens' booming season, February through April, because the birds are easily disturbed.

Black-shouldered Kite, Crested Caracara, Prairie Falcon, Roseate Spoonbill, both whistling ducks, Sprague's Pipit, and LeConte's and Harris' sparrows are among the more noteworthy species that are seen each year.

Area brochure, auto tour route, walking trails, observation blinds by reservation February 1–April 30 during the booming season. The Pipit Trail is open from sunrise to sunset May 1–January 31 and 10a.m.–4p.m. February 1–April 30.
Spring, Fall, Winter

Brazoria Refuge ❺
1216 North Velasco
PO Drawer 1088
Angleton, TX 77515   409-849-7771

The Brazoria Refuge Complex includes the Brazoria, San Bernard, and Big Boggy refuges. The Brazoria refuge is closed except during the first weekend of most months. Be sure to call ahead and confirm access times before visiting.

Bird List TX-3 Brazoria Summary
272 birds listed, 71 nesting birds
Bird Chart pages 348-365

Totals by Season		s	S	F	W
Abundant	A	5	5	6	9
Common	C	93	57	80	72
Uncommon	U	99	41	92	57
Occasional	O	17	5	17	12
Rare	R	41	24	40	36

Endangered Species: Brown Pelican, Wood Stork, Bald Eagle, Peregrine Falcon, Whooping Crane, Piping Plover,

Least Tern

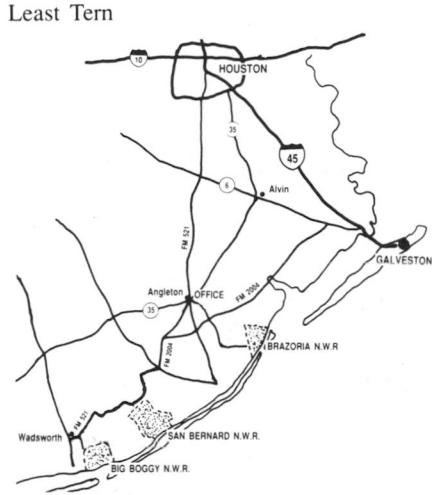

To reach the Brazoria refuge from the office at the intersection of Hwy. 35 and FM 523 in the Palms Shopping Center in Angleton, take FM 523 southeast for 9.5 miles to Co. Road 227, turn left, and go 1.7 miles to refuge gate on the right.

Habitat: 10,407 acres, at 3 feet below to 6 feet above sea level, include saline and non-saline marshes and prairies, salt/mud flats, and an irregular freshwater stream.

Birders often identify more than 200 species of birds on and around the refuge during the Audubon Society's annual Christmas Bird Count.

The Texas Gulf coast is the major wintering area for most of the Central Flyway waterfowl. The area is the primary wintering grounds of "Lesser" Snow Geese and for smaller populations of Canada and Greater White-fronted geese. Goose populations reach a peak during December and January. Northern Pintails, Mallards, Green-winged and Blue-winged teals, Gadwalls, Mottled Ducks, and American Wigeons also winter on the refuge.

Wading birds and shorebirds, such as herons, ibises, Roseate Spoonbills, American Avocets, Black-necked Stilts, Common Moorhens, Common Snipes, and six other species of sandpipers can be seen almost anytime of the year. Various species of uncommon marsh and water birds, such as Yellow Rails, Reddish Egrets, American Bitterns, and Wood Storks, can occasionally be observed.

Flocks of wintering Sandhill Cranes depend on the upper prairies. The Peregrine Falcon is an uncommon visitor through the fall, winter, and spring.

Area brochure, hunting, fishing.
Spring, Fall, Winter

San Bernard ⑥
c/o Brazoria RC (see page 172)

From Hwy. 35 just west of Angleton, go 7 miles south on new Hwy. 288 to Lake Jackson. Turn right on FM 2004, go 7 miles to its end at the intersection of Hwy. 36 and FM 2611, and head south on FM 2611 for 4 miles. Turn left on FM 2918, go 1 mile to Co. Road 306, turn right, and go 1 mile to San Bernard headquarters on left.

Habitat: 24,455 acres at elevations ranging from 3 feet below to 9 feet above mean sea level of flat coastal prairie and salt marsh with numerous swales and potholes, several saltwater lakes, one intermittent stream, and a small grove of trees in the northwest corner.

The upland prairies support populations of quails, doves, hawks, owls, vultures, and kites. Eagles, Ospreys, and Crested Caracaras are seen occasionally.

From October through March, Northern Pintails, Mallards, Green-winged and Blue-winged teals, Gadwalls, Mottled Ducks, and American Wigeons can be seen. The area is in the major wintering grounds of "Lesser" Snow Geese which, with Canada and Greater White-fronted geese, reach peak numbers during December and January.

Area brochure, fishing, oystering and crabbing, hunting.
Spring, Fall, Winter

Big Boggy ⑦
c/o Brazoria RC (see page 172)

From Hwy. 60 in Wadsworth, go east on FM 521 for 2.9 miles, turn right on Chinquapin Road, and go 7 miles to refuge on the right.

This is a new refuge. Check with the refuge complex office for current information.

Buffalo Lake ⑧   (office at refuge)
PO Box 228
Umbarger, TX 79091   806-499-3382
Entry fee

This refuge office is responsible for Grulla NWR in New Mexico (see page 129). Muleshoe NWR (description following) is also a sub-refuge.

Bird List TX-4 Buffalo L. Summary
246 birds listed, 42 nesting birds
Bird Chart pages 348-365

Totals by Season		s	S	F	W
Abundant	A	6	8	7	11
Common	C	22	20	12	9
Uncommon	U	40	26	33	17
Occasional	O	71	40	68	26
Rare	R	63	33	59	32

Endangered Species: Bald Eagle, Peregrine Falcon, Roseate Tern, Least Tern

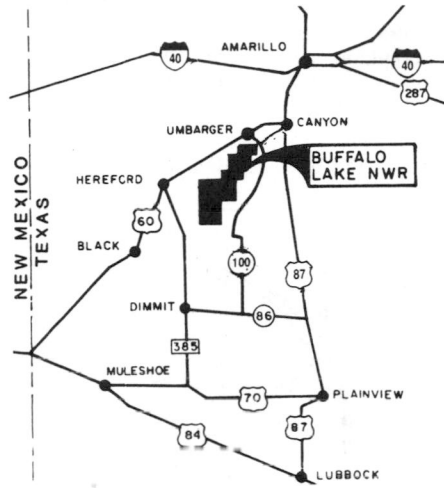

From Hereford, take U.S. 60 northeast to the small community of Umbarger, turn south on Hwy. 168, and go 1.5 miles to the refuge entrance on the right.

Habitat: 7,664 acres includes 4,400 acres of short-grass prairie, 1,964 acres of water, 300 acres of marsh, and 1,000 acres croplands.

The refuge is noted as a wintering and resting place for waterfowl. Bird numbers depend on there being adequate water in Buffalo Lake. When there is water, thousands of ducks and geese can be seen during the fall and winter.

Bald Eagles and Peregrine Falcons occasionally visit. Swainson's and Red-tailed hawks are more common and Coopers, Rough-legged, and Sharp-shinned hawks and Northern Harriers are regular visitors.

Northern Bobwhites are commonly seen and there are occasional sightings of Scaled Quails and growing numbers of Ring-necked Pheasants. Semipalmated Plovers and Killdeers are common in the spring and are joined by the Snowy Plover during the summer. Greater Yellowlegs, Baird's Sandpipers, and Wilson's Phalaropes are also common in the summer. Western and Eastern kingbirds and Scissor-tailed Flycatchers are abundant at the refuge.

Area brochure, auto tour route, picnicking, camping, walking trails, observation deck.
Spring, Winter

Muleshoe 9   (office at refuge)
PO Box 549
Muleshoe, TX 79347   806-946-3341

Bird List TX-5 Muleshoe Summary
243 birds listed, 59 nesting birds
Bird Chart pages 348-365

Totals by Season		s	S	F	W
Abundant	A	18	10	20	14
Common	C	60	31	62	35
Uncommon	U	48	27	48	27
Occasional	O	30	29	32	22
Rare	R	41	32	52	44

Endangered Species: Bald Eagle, Peregrine
Falcon, Least Tern

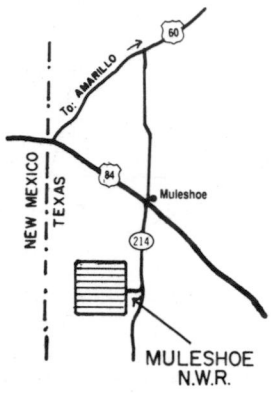

From Muleshoe, go 20 miles south on
Hwy. 214 to refuge sign, turn right, and
go 2.25 miles on gravel road to the
office.

Habitat: 5,809 acres of short-grass
rangelands with scattered mesquite. Three
sink-type lakes have no outlets and
depend entirely on runoff for water
supply. When full they provide 600 acres
of water. There are two caliche
outcroppings near the northern and
western boundaries and prominent draws
lead to the lakes.

The refuge hosts the largest wintering
concentration of Sandhill Cranes in North
America. The cranes reach peak numbers
between late December and mid-February,
when over 100,000 are present.

Large numbers of waterfowl, primarily
ducks with a few geese, are also present
when the water level is sufficient. The
Northern Pintail is the most common
species, followed by American Wigeon,
Mallard, Green-winged Teal, and Ruddy
Duck.

Greater Roadrunner, Scaled Quail,
Common Nighthawk, Horned Lark, Cactus
Wren, Curved-billed Thrasher, and Lark
Sparrow are among the most common and
noteworthy species breeding on the refuge.

Area brochure, camping, picnicking.
Fall, Winter

Hagerman 10   (office at refuge)
Route 3, Box 123
Sherman, TX 75090   214-786-2826

Bird List TX-6 Hagerman Summary
272 birds listed, 86 nesting birds
Bird Chart pages 348-365

Totals by Season		s	S	F	W
Abundant	A	11	6	15	12
Common	C	52	33	52	34
Uncommon	U	71	39	74	42
Occasional	O	85	40	68	34
Rare	R	31	35	38	29

Endangered Species: Wood Stork, Bald
Eagle, Peregrine Falcon, Piping Plover,
Least Tern

From Sherman, go west on Rte. 82 to FM
1417, turn right, and go 5.5 miles to the
refuge sign. Turn left and continue 6
miles west to the office.

Habitat: 11,320 acres lying on the Big
Mineral Arm of Lake Texoma, on the
Red River between Oklahoma and Texas.
Includes 3,000 acres of marsh and water
and 8,000 acres of upland and farmland.

During the spring, fall, and winter the
refuge marshes are in constant use by
migrating and wintering waterfowl.
Canada Geese are the most numerous but
there are also Greater White-fronted and
Snow geese and occasional Ross' Geese.

Diving ducks, such as Redheads,
Canvasbacks, scaups, and Ring-necked
Ducks, move through in the spring and
fall, with a few staying through the
winter. Migrating Northern Shovelers and
Blue-winged Teals move in each spring
when the Mallards, Northern Pintails,
Green-winged Teals, and other ducks that
have overwintered move out.

The upland habitat provides a home for
many songbirds, as well as Northern
Bobwhite and Greater Roadrunner.

Area brochure, auto tour route, nature
trail, observation tower, picnicking,
fishing, boating.
Spring, Fall, Winter

Laguna Atascosa 11   (office at refuge)
PO Box 450
Rio Hondo, TX 78583   512-748-3607
Entry fee

Bird List TX-7 L. Atascosa Summary
329 birds listed, 90 nesting birds
Bird Chart pages 348-365

Totals by Season		s	S	F	W
Abundant	A	20	12	22	17
Common	C	67	32	73	50
Uncommon	U	29	46	91	76
Occasional	O	44	37	56	50
Rare	R	33	24	33	54

Endangered Species: Brown Pelican,
Wood Stork, Bald Eagle, Peregrine
Falcon, Piping Plover, Least Tern
Rare/Limited Species: Aplomado Falcon,
Red-billed Pigeon, Ringed Kingfisher,
Northern Beardless-Tyrannulet, Mexican
Crow, Varied Bunting, White-collared
Seedeater, Botteri's Sparrow, Altamira
Oriole, Audubon's Oriole

From Harlingen, take FM 106 east for 25
miles to the refuge sign.

Habitat: 45,187 acres on the lower Gulf
Coast include salt and freshwater marshes,
coastal prairie, savannah, and thorn brush.

This is the southernmost waterfowl refuge
in the United States. Waterfowl winter in
large numbers at Laguna Atascosa, and up
to 80 percent of the Redhead population
may be present. There is a heron rookery
north of the refuge, but the birds feed and
rest on the refuge area. Commonly seen
are the Tricolored and Great Blue heron,
and Great, Snowy, and Reddish egrets.

The songbird migration occurs in late
April and early May. Summer is the best
time to see the more exotic Mexican
species. Fall and winter are best for
migratory waterfowl and Sandhill Cranes.

Area brochure, 2 auto tour routes, 3
walking trails, picnicking.

Santa Ana 12   (office at refuge)
Route 2, Box 202A
Alamo, TX 78516   512-787-3079

Bird List TX-8 Santa Ana Summary
334 birds listed, 87 nesting birds
Bird Chart pages 348-365

Totals by Season		s	S	F	W
Abundant	A	5	5	6	7
Common	C	56	28	47	34
Uncommon	U	70	28	72	54
Occasional	O	94	29	2	76
Rare	R	69	31	73	87

Endangered Species: Wood Stork, Peregrine Falcon, Piping Plover, Least Tern

Rare/Limited Species: Hook-billed Kite, Northern Jacana, Red-billed Pigeon, Ferruginous Pygmy-Owl, Ringed Kingfisher, Northern Beardless-Tyrannulet, Rose-throated Becard, Cave Swallow, Mexican Crow, Clay-colored Robin, Varied Bunting, White-collared Seedeater, Altamira Oriole, Audubon's Oriole

From Alamo, which is 8 miles east of McAllen on Hwy. 83, take FM 907 south to the end of the road and turn left at the refuge sign.

Habitat: 2,000 acres of thorn forest.

The Central and Mississippi flyways converge just north of the lower Rio Grande Valley and funnel large numbers of migrating birds into this area.

Species rarely seen elsewhere in the U.S. include Least Grebe, Olivaceous Cormorant, Black-bellied Whistling Duck, Masked Duck, Hook-billed and Black-shouldered kites, Common Black-Hawk, Harris', Gray, White-tailed, and Zone-tailed hawks, Crested Caracara, Plain Chachalaca, Northern Jacana, Red-billed Pigeon, Inca Dove, Ruddy Ground-doves, Green Parakeet, Red-crowned, Red-lored, and Yellow-headed parrots, Groove-bill Ani, Ferruginous Pygmy-owl, Elf Owl, Pauraque, Green Violet-ear, Buff-bellied Hummingbird, Ringed Kingfisher, Northern Beardless-Tyrannulet, Brown-crested Flycatcher, Great Kiskadee, Couch's Kingbird, Rose-throated Becard, Green and Brown jays, Mexican Crow, Clay-colored and Rufous-backed robins, Aztec Thrush, Long-billed Thrasher, Tropical Parula, Gray-crowned Yellowthroat, Golden-crowned Warbler, Crimson-collared Grosbeak, Blue Bunting, Olive Sparrow, and White-collared Seedeater.

The refuge drive is open from 9a.m. to 4:30 p.m. seasonally but is closed to private vehicles during the peak visiting times when the refuge Interpretive Tram is in operation. The tram schedule varies during the operation period which begins on November 25th and ends April 24th.

Area brochure, visitor center, auto tour route, numerous walking trails, photo blind. The fee for tram rides is $2 for adults and $1 for children.
Spring, Fall, Winter

NATIONAL PARK SERVICE

Big Bend National Park ❶
Big Bend National Park, TX 79834
915-477-2251

735,416 acres of mountains and desert within the great bend of the Rio Grande. Park brochure with map, free "El Paisano" park newspaper with recreation details, leaflets on birds, wildflowers, trails, bicycling, reptiles, the Rio Grande, hiking, and backpacking, ranger lead activities, etc. Bird and other species checklists are available.

Big Thicket National Preserve ❷
3785 Milam
Beaumont, TX 77701   409-839-2689

Bird List TX-9 Big Thicket Summary
178 birds listed, 97 nesting birds
Bird Chart pages 348-365

Totals by Season		s	S	F	W
Abundant	A	19	17	16	11
Common	C	43	38	34	35
Uncommon	U	35	28	32	28
Occasional	O	28	14	18	22
Rare	R	15	6	6	17

Endangered Species: Wood Stork, Bald Eagle, Red-cockaded Woodpecker

85,733 acres, including Appalachian, coastal marsh, and arid southwest communities. A great number of plant and animal species coexist in this "biological crossroads of North America." Study, research, and birding opportunities are excellent.

Preserve brochure with map, campsite directory, leaflets on hiking trails, scheduled activities, and wildlife species.

Padre Island National Seashore ❸
9405 S. Padre Island Drive
Corpus Christi, TX 78418   512-937-2621

Bird List TX-10 Padre Is. Summary
304 birds listed, 25 nesting birds
Bird Chart pages 348-365

Totals by Season		s	S	F	W
Common	C	88	18	80	62
Uncommon	U	92	41	92	59
Rare	R	60	44	56	79

Endangered Species: Brown Pelican, Bald Eagle, Peregrine Falcon, Piping Plover, Least Tern

130,696 acres of barrier island stretching along the Gulf Coast for 80.5 miles and noted for its wide sandy beaches, excellent fishing, and abundant bird and marine life. Seashore brochure with map, species checklists, various recreation guides.

NATIONAL FOREST SERVICE
National Forests in Texas Supervisor
Homer Garrison Federal Bldg.
701 North First Street
Lufkin, TX 75901   409-639-8501

Caddo-LBJ National Grasslands ⚠
Farm Road 730 South
PO Box 507
Decatur, TX 76234   817-627-5475

Map/Forest-Ranger Dist./City
⚠	Angelina-same/Lufkin	409-634-7709
⚠	Sam Houston-San Jacinto /Cleveland	713-592-6462
⚠	Davy Crockett-Natches /Crockett	409-544-2046
⚠	Sabine-Tenaha /San Augustine	409-275-2632

STATE AGENCIES

Texas Parks & Wildlife Dept.
4200 Smith School Road
Austin, TX 78744   512-479-4800
in Texas call   800-792-1111

There are 28 Parks & Wildlife regional and field offices located throughout Texas. The current address, city, and phone number for each office appears on the back cover of the "Texas Hunting Guide" published annually in July.

Tourism Division
Texas Dept. of Commerce
PO Box 12008
Austin, TX 78711   512-462-9191
from out-of-state call   800-888-8839

BIRDING HOTLINE
Statewide   801-530-1299

LOCAL BIRDING GROUPS
Map/Chapter/City
① Bridgerland Audubon/Logan
② Kolob-Virgin River Aud./Cedar City
③ Mt. Timpanoggo Audubon/Payson
④ Utah Audubon/Salt Lake City
⑤ Wasatch Audubon/Ogden

SPECIAL BIRDING AREA

Great Salt Lake ❶
c/o Western Hemisphere
Shorebird Reserve Network
801 Pennsylvania Avenue, SE, Suite 301
Washington, DC 20003

In order to meet WHSRN criteria an area must support more than 250,000 shorebirds over the course of a year, or 30% of a flyway population of any shorebird species.

THE NATURE CONSERVANCY
Great Basin Field Office
PO Box 11486, Pioneer Station
Salt Lake City, UT 84102   801-531-0999

No TNC preserves are open to the public at the time of publication. However, the Lytle Ranch Preserve, which was acquired by TNC and transferred to Brigham Young University, is open.

Lytle Ranch Preserve ◆
Preserve Manager
PO Box 398
Santa Clara, UT 84765
or call:
Dr. Stanley Welsh   801-378-2289
Dr. Andrew Barnum   801-673-4811

Contact Manager, or Dr. Welsh or Dr. Barnum for visitor regulations and large party reservations.

Take I-15 from Las Vegas, NV, to Littlefield, AZ, exit. Take old Hwy. 91

north for about 18 miles to Castile Cliff (ruins). Turn left over cattle guard onto dirt road with BLM sign for Lytle Ranch. Go 8 miles to Lytle Ranch fork (marked) and bear right. Continue for 3 miles (road winds downward into a wash). Before crossing the wash, head north by corrals and catchpens for 0.5 miles to Preserve Manager's residence and parking.

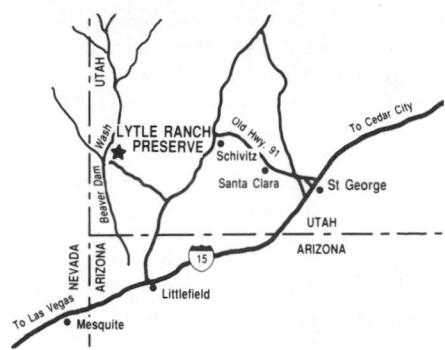

Habitat: 462 acres in the Mojave Desert. The climate is hot and arid with possible temperature and weather extremes in both summer and winter. Do not disturb biological experiments.

The Lytle Ranch preserve attracts species that have not been recorded anywhere else in Utah. Due to the climatic extremes of the Mojave Desert, the preserve is used primarily by seasonal migrants, including Phainopepla, Vermilion Flycatcher, Hooded Oriole, and White-winged Dove.

Day hiking (bring your own water and be prepared for rugged desert climate; nearest phone is 30 miles south at Littlefield). Spring, Summer, Fall, Winter

U.S. FISH & WILDLIFE SERVICE NATIONAL WILDLIFE REFUGES

Fish Springs ▮ (office at the refuge)
PO Box 568
Dugway, UT 84022   801-522-5353

Bird List UT-1 Fish Springs Summary
157 birds listed, 54 nesting birds
Bird Chart pages 348-365

Totals by Season		s	S	F	W
Abundant	A	23	24	18	10
Common	C	20	11	14	13
Uncommon	U	20	28	14	13
Occasional	O	33	27	23	19
Rare	R	17	12	16	8

Endangered Species: Bald Eagle, Peregrine Falcon

Fish Springs is located on the south edge of the Great Salt Lake Desert, 104 miles southwest of Tooele and 78 miles northwest of Delta. It is extremely isolated and can be reached only by gravel roads across uninhabited desert. Local inquiry into road conditions is advised.

No food or lodging is available in the Fish Springs area, and the nearest gas station is 40 miles away.

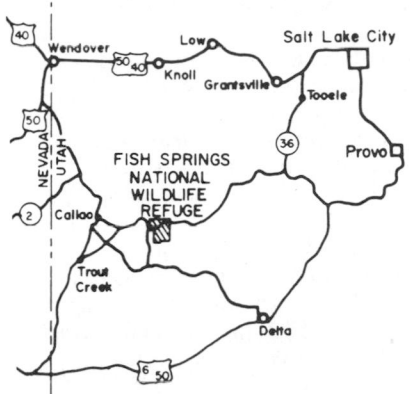

Habitat: 18,000 acres include a 10,000-acre spring-fed marsh developed to increase waterfowl use. The springs rise from a fault zone along the east edge of the Fish Springs Range and provide sufficient water for 9 large impoundments and adjacent marshland.

Various waterfowl species use the refuge, including Tundra and Trumpeter swans during the winter. Canada Geese, Mallards, Cinnamon Teals, Northern Pintails, Gadwalls, Redheads, Canvasbacks, and Ruddy Ducks all breed at Fish Springs, as well as Great Blue Herons, Snowy Egrets, and Black-crowned Night-Herons, which nest in large rookeries on the refuge.

There are fewer numbers of birds in the spring and summer but a greater variety of species. American Avocets, Black-necked Stilts, Eared Grebes, and various waterfowl, marsh birds, shorebirds, and passerines are among the birds that are commonly seen.

Area brochure, hiking, picnicking, hunting, BLM campground near the refuge.
Spring, Fall

Bear River ❷
Migratory Bird Refuge
Box 459
Brigham City, UT 84302   801-744-2201

Note: The Bear River refuge is CLOSED due to serious flooding and flood damage in 1984. The refuge personnel hope to be able to re-open the refuge in the mid-90's.

Ouray ❸   (office in town)
1680 W. Highway 40, Room 1220
Vernal, UT 84078   801-789-0351

Bird List UT-2 Ouray Summary
202 birds listed, 78 nesting birds
Bird Chart pages 348-365

Totals by Season		s	S	F	W
Abundant	A	0	0	2	0
Common	C	62	74	50	14
Uncommon	U	60	33	69	13
Occasional	O	14	10	19	9
Rare	R	49	23	42	15

Endangered Species: Bald Eagle, Peregrine Falcon, Whooping Crane

From Vernal, take Rtes. 40/149 west for 15 miles. Turn south on Rte. 88 at the refuge sign and continue 13 miles to the refuge entrance.

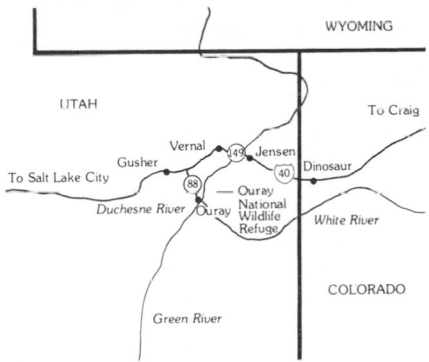

Habitat: 11,482 acres illustrating the successive zones between marsh and riparian habitat and dry uplands. The Green, Duchesne, and White rivers flow through the refuge, and the Green River floods the marshes. Cottonwoods and dense brush line the riverbottoms, while greasewood brush surrounds the marshes. Successive zones include salt and alkali sacaton grass, curly-grass on the alluvial fans, and steep, eroding clay bluffs topped by green needle grass, Indian ricegrass, cactus, and desert shrubs.

The refuge was created to provide habitat for the 12 species of ducks that breed on its floodplain, including Cinnamon Teals, Redheads, and Common Mergansers. Northern Pintails, Mallards, and Canada Geese are the only waterfowl that commonly overwinter at Ouray. The spring migration begins in early March, and duck populations peak in April. Fall migration, which starts in August, peaks in October. Sandhill Cranes, accompanied by the rare Whooping Crane, may be seen on their northward migration during

March and April.

Golden Eagles breed at the refuge, and are common throughout the year. Bald Eagles, Northern Harriers, and Red-tailed and Rough-legged hawks are commonly seen during the winter.

Area brochure, auto tour route, fishing, hunting.
Spring, Fall

NATIONAL FOREST SERVICE
NFS Intermountain Region
Federal Bldg.
324 25th Street
Ogden, UT 84401   801-625-5354

Map/Forest/City
△1	Ashley/Vernal	801-789-1181
△2	Dixie/Cedar City	801-586-2421
△3	Fishlake/Ritchfield	801-896-4491
△4	Nanti-LaSal/Price	801-637-2817
△5	Unita/Provo	801-377-5780
△6	Wasatch-Cache /Salt Lake City	801-524-5030

BUREAU LAND MANAGEMENT
BLM State Office
324 South State Street
Salt Lake City, UT 84111   801-524-3146

Map/District/City
▽1	Cedar City/Cedar City	801-586-2401
▽2	Moab/Moab	801-259-6111
▽3	Richfield/Richfield	801-896-8221
▽4	Salt Lake City /Salt Lake City	801-524-5348
▽5	Vernal/Vernal	801-789-1362

STATE AGENCIES

Utah Division of Wildlife Resources
1596 West North Temple Street
Salt Lake City, UT 84116   801-533-9333

Map/Resource Office (City)
1	Cedar City	801-586-2455
2	Ogden	801-479-5143
3	Price	801-637-3310
4	Springville	801-489-5678
5	Vernal	801-789-3103

Division of Travel Development
Community & Economic
Development Department
Council Hall/Capitol Hill
Salt Lake City, UT 84114   801-538-1030

BIRDING HOTLINE

Statewide   802-457-2779
Monday through Saturday, 5p.m.–8a.m.,
and all day Sundays.

LOCAL BIRDING GROUPS
Map/Chapter/City
1. Ascutney Mtn. Audubon/Springfield
2. Central Vermont Aud./Montpelier
3. Green Mountain Aud./Burlington
4. Mad River Valley Audubon/Warren
5. Northeast Kingdom Audubon
   /St. Johnsbury
6. Otter Creek Audubon/Middlebury
7. Rutland County Aud./Wallingford
8. Southeastern VT Audubon
   /West Brattleboro
9. Taconic Tri-State Audubon/Pownal
10. Vermont Institute of Natural Science
    /Woodstock

THE NATURE CONSERVANCY

Vermont Field Office   FO
27 State Street
Montpelier, VT 05602   802-229-4425

A Vermont Project Directory describing
69 projects totalling over 60,000 acres is
available.

The following preserves are open for
passive recreational use, including birding.

Amity Pond Natural Area   1

183 acres located .5 mile east of Bernard
Village between Skyline Drive and Broad
Brook Road. This is a state-designated
Natural Area.

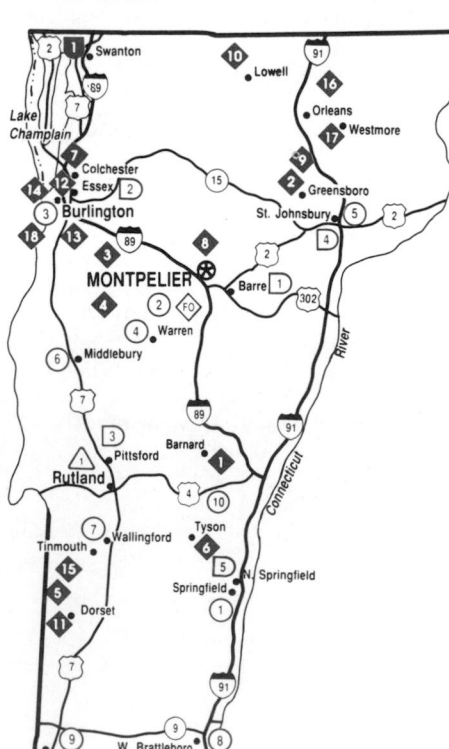

Barr Hill Preserve   2

256 acres near Greensboro. Sterling
Nature Trail runs through the preserve. A
self-guiding Trail Guide is available at the
preserve or from the Field Office.

Burt Forest   3

10,853 acres in three units. The preserve
area is in Mt. Mansfield, Putnam, and
Camel's Hump State Forests. Managed by
the Vermont Dept. of Forests, Parks, &
Recreation (phone 802-244-8711).

Camel's Hump Lots   4

315 acres on Long Trail at 1,500 feet of
elevation and north of Camel's Hump
summit. Managed as part of the Camel's
Hump State Forest.

Dorset Bat Cave   5

150 acres near the summit of Mt. Aeolus
at 2,400 feet of elevation. No visitors are
allowed from September through May to
protect the hibernating bats.

Echo Lake   6

295 acres with 1,500 feet along the shore
of Echo Lake, now managed as a state
park. A wooded area has a deer yard.
Located .5 mile from Tyson Village.

Ethan Allen Farms   7

293 acres that were once Ethan Allen's
home farm, about 4 miles north of
Burlington near North Street. Nature trail
borders the Winooski River. Picnic shelter
and canoe access along the river.

Hunger Mountain   8

610 acres with a popular hiking trail,
jointly owned and managed with the
Central Vermont Audubon Society. A
small parking area is off Middlesex Road
#41, accessible off Rte. 12 north of
Montpelier.

Long Pond   9

72 acres and one of the few undeveloped
lakes in Vermont. Canoe access to Long
Pond is from Town Hwy. 65.

Long Trail   10

Two parcels of 117 and 1,946 acres,
managed by the Green Mountain Club,
and protecting parts of Long Trail from
just south of Canada to Lovell.

Prentiss Pond   11

10 acres, with 6 consisting of swamp and
woodland, located .5 mile west of Dorset.
Managed by the Dorset Sportsman Club
(802-867-4420). A fishing derby for local
children is held each summer.

Shelburne Bay   12

93 acres and 1,600 feet on the bank of
the White River, near the Sharon-Pomfret

town line. A spring seep supports several
rare plants.

Shelburne Pond   13

533 unspoiled acres near Burlington
include bogs, swamps, and marshland
areas. It is a joint project of the
Conservancy and University of Vermont.
Abundant wildlife and fishing access.

Sloop Island   14

Less than an acre, the island's rocky
substrate supports a cover of elm,
basswood, and shrubs. Sloop Island is
north of the Charlotte-Essex ferry
crossing, and reachable only by boat.

Tinmouth Channel   15

1,100 acres of wetland surrounding
Tinmouth Channel where the fishing,
canoeing, and birding are good. Stream
currents are strong here.

Willoughby Falls   16

2.5-acre Willoughby Falls is noted for the
rainbow trout migration. During April
the trout swim up the falls to Lake
Willoughby where they spawn. Located
about .5 mile east of Orleans Village.

Willoughby Lake   17

12 acres with 1,200 feet of lakeshore and
woodland are managed by the town of
Westmore as a town beach.

Winooski River Delta   18

58 acres of sandy delta at the junction of
Winooski River and Lake Champlain in
Colchester. A good spot for birding,
fishing, and picnicking.

U.S. FISH & WILDLIFE SERVICE NATIONAL WILDLIFE REFUGES

Missisquoi   1   (office at refuge)
RFD 2
Swanton, VT 05488   802-868-4781

Bird List VT-1 Missisquoi Summary
197 birds listed, 83 nesting birds
Bird Chart pages 348-365

Totals by Season		s	S	F	W
Abundant	A	6	5	4	1
Common	C	54	59	36	11
Uncommon	U	22	17	13	7
Occasional	O	73	53	93	16
Rare	R	21	26	23	11

Endangered Species: Bald Eagle, Peregrine
Falcon

Take Hwy. 78 for 2 miles northwest from
Swanton to the headquarters. The refuge
is located on the eastern shore of Lake
Champlain near the Canadian border. It is
about 50 miles north of Burlington.

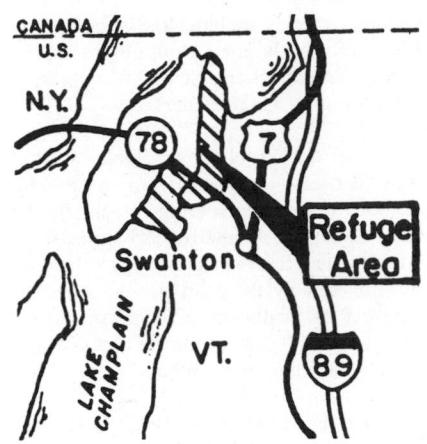

Habitat: 5,651 acres of marsh, open water, and wooded swamp dominated by silver maple, with narrow bands of croplands on the ridges. The refuge, which occupies much of the Missisquoi River delta, is crossed by numerous channels and the remnants of old water courses.

The delta attracts large flocks of a variety of waterfowl. Populations peak during April, September, and October. Only six species commonly remain to breed. The most abundant species are American Black Ducks, Mallards, Wood Ducks, and Common Goldeneyes.

In addition to ducks, the rich habitat attracts a large variety of other breeding birds. Great Blue Herons, American Bitterns, and Common Moorhens are among the nesting waterbirds, while the resident raptors include Northern Harriers, Red-tailed Hawks, and Great Horned and Barred owls.

Area brochure, mammals list, fishing, hunting, hiking, 1.5-mile interpretive trail. Spring, Summer, Fall

NATIONAL FOREST SERVICE

Green Mtn. & Finger Lakes NFS △
Federal Bldg.
151 West Street
PO Box 519
Rutland, VT 05701   802-733-0300

STATE AGENCIES

Fish & Wildlife Department

Agency of Environmental Conservation
Montpelier, VT 05602   802-828-3371

Map/District & City

1	Barre/same	802-828-2454
2	Essex/same	802-879-6563
3	Pittsford/same	802-483-2300
4	St. Johnsbury/same	802-748-8787
5	Springfield /N. Springfield	802-886-2215

Vermont Travel Division

Agency of Development
& Community Affairs
134 State Street
Montpelier, VT 05602   802-828-3236

BIRDING HOTLINES

Statewide   301-652-1088
         and 804-929-1736

LOCAL BIRDING GROUPS
Map/Chapter/City

① Cape Henry Audubon/Portsmouth
② Colonial Audubon/Hampton
③ Fairfax Audubon/Arlington
④ Northern Neck of Virginia Audubon
     /Kilmarnock
⑤ N. Shenandoah Valley Aud./Boyce
⑥ Rappahannock Aud./Fredericksburg
⑦ Richmond Audubon/Richmond
⑧ Virginia Beach Aud./Virginia Beach
⑨ Virginia Soc. of Ornithology (VS0)
     /Annandale
⑩ Augusta Bird Club - VSO/Staunton
⑪ Bristol Bird Club - VSO/Bristol
⑫ Charlottesville-Albermarle Bird Club
     - VSO/Charlottesville
⑬ Clinch Mountain Bird Club - VSO
     /Nickelsville
⑭ Clinch Valley Bird Club - VSO
     /Tazewell
⑮ Cumberland Bird Club - VSO/Wise
⑯ Eastern Shore Bird Club - VSO
     /Accomac
⑰ Foothills Bird Club - VSO
     /Martinsville
⑱ Hampton Roads Bird Club - VSO
     /Hampton
⑲ Lynchburg Bird Club - VSO
     /Lynchburg
⑳ Marion Bird Club - VSO/Marion
㉑ Monticello Bird Club - VSO
     /Charlottesville
㉒ Montpelier Naturalists - VSO
     /Orange
㉓ New River Valley Bird Club - VSO
     /Blacksburg
㉔ Northern Virginia Chapter - VSO
     /Arlington
㉕ Roanoke Valley Bird Club - VSO
     /Roanoke
㉖ Rockbridge Bird Club - VSO
     /Lexington
㉗ Rockingham Bird Club - VSO
     /Harrisonburg
㉘ Margaret H. Watson Bird Club
     - VSO/Darlington Heights
㉙ Westmoreland Bird Club - VSO
     /Montross
㉚ Williamsburg Bird Club - VSO
     /Williamsburg

THE NATURE CONSERVANCY
Virginia Field Office   Ⓕ⓪
1110 Rose Hill Drive, Suite 200
Charlottesville, VA 22901

A new Guide to Conservancy Preserves in Virginia is available from this office for $5.50. It features an overview of TNC activity and projects in Virginia. There are descriptions of 20 preserves including those open to the public.

Falls Ridge ◆❶
Bill Bradley - Preserve Manager
Route 2, Box 289
Christianburg, VA 24073

Habitat: 655 acres are part of a steep rugged ridge that rises from the valley of the north fork of the Roanoke River. Common Ravens, Great Horned Owls, Red-tailed and Red-shouldered hawks, Pileated Woodpeckers, and wildcats have been seen at the preserve.

Area map and brochure available. Five fire roads for walking. Contact manager for details and permission to visit.
Spring, Summer, Fall

Fraser ◆❷
Preserve Managers
Joe Keiger
2126 North Rolfe Street
Arlington, VA 22209   703-538-4952
or
David Askkegaard
6111 North 35th Street
Arlington, VA 22209   703-538-6994

Habitat: 220 acres of marsh, springs, streams, ponds, rocky cliffs, and various stages of old field succession from open meadow to mature hardwoods. The Potomac River forms the northern boundary of the property.

The 110 species of birds that have been observed include the Bald Eagle. The 39 breeding species include Red-shouldered Hawks, Ruby-throated Hummingbirds, Downy Woodpeckers, Scarlet Tanagers, and Blue-gray Gnatcatchers.

Area map and brochure available. Walking paths lead east and west from the parking lot, both ultimately veering toward the Potomac River. A total of 2.5 miles of trails in the preserve connect to other paths owned by the Northern Virginia Region Park Authority. Contact manager for details and permission before visiting.
Spring, Summer, Fall, Winter

U.S. FISH & WILDLIFE SERVICE NATIONAL WILDLIFE REFUGES

Back Bay ❶
4005 Sandpiper Road
PO Box 6286
Virginia Beach, VA 23456   804-721-2412
Entry fee

Bird List VA-1 Back Bay Summary
286 birds listed, 91 nesting birds
Bird Chart pages 348-365

Totals by Season		s	S	F	W
Abundant	A	17	10	18	13
Common	C	67	50	71	40
Uncommon	U	1	67	94	64
Occasional	O	49	31	46	34
Rare	R	36	24	41	43

Endangered Species: Brown Pelican, Bald Eagle, Peregrine Falcon, Piping Plover, Roseate Tern, Least Tern

The refuge is located on the Atlantic coast in the southeastern corner of Virginia, directly south of the city of Virginia Beach. Access is off Rte. 60. False Cape State Park shares a common boundary with the refuge on the south.

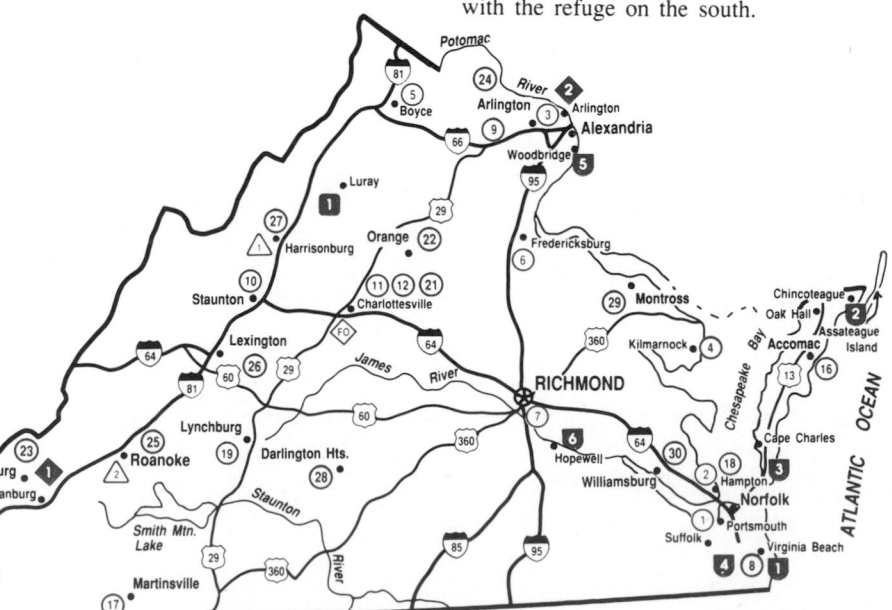

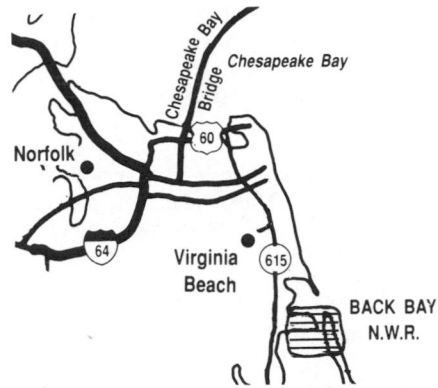

Habitat: 4,600 acres of beach dunes, woodlands, and marsh typical of the barrier islands along the Atlantic Coast. The marsh consists primarily of numerous islands in Back Bay. An additional 4,600 acres of the bay are designated for the protection of migrating species.

Most of the waterfowl migrate north by the end of March. Songbird and shorebird migrations begin in April and peak in May, as many begin to nest by the end of the month. Ospreys arrive at the refuge.

Shorebirds and waterfowl begin to arrive in September on their southward migration as the swallows and songbirds depart. Concentrations of raptors migrating south generally move through the area near the end of the month. In October waterfowl numbers continue to build and most other species have left by the end of the month. Waterfowl populations peak during November and December. During January and February cold weather may cause the bay to freeze, forcing thousands of birds south.

Area brochure, hiking, biking, fishing, nature trails.
Spring, Fall, Winter

Chincoteague **2**   (office at refuge)
PO Box 62
Chincoteague, VA 23336   804-336-6122

Bird List VA-2 Chincoteague Summary
295 birds listed, 99 nesting birds
Bird Chart pages 348-365

Totals by Season		s	S	F	W
Abundant	A	19	16	21	7
Common	C	82	69	0	49
Uncommon	U	56	31	53	41
Occasional	O	40	28	38	40
Rare	R	57	44	55	32

Endangered Species: Brown Pelican, Bald Eagle, Peregrine Falcon, Piping Plover, Roseate Tern, Least Tern

From Oak Hall, take Hwy. 175 east for 11 miles to the refuge. Follow the signs to the refuge visitor center. The refuge is located at the south end of Assateague Island off the coast of Virginia.

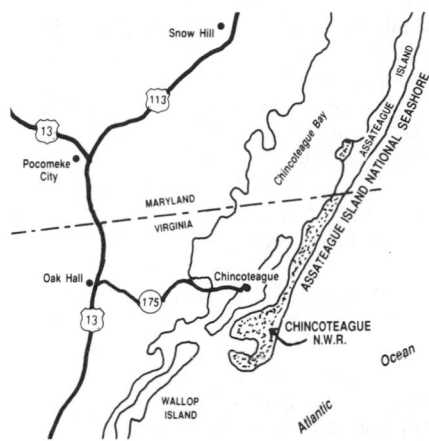

Habitat: A typical barrier island, with wide beaches, grassbound dunes, and extensive salt marshes bordering on Chincoteague Bay. Pine and oak woodlands with ponds and potholes are scattered near the southern end of the island. Several man-made freshwater impoundments attract waterfowl.

Birders consider Chincoteague Refuge to be one of the finest places in the East to add sightings to their life lists. Shorebirds are among the most numerous because they use the island and its marshes as a last staging area before crossing thousands of miles of open ocean to their wintering ground in South America. Thousands of ducks and geese, such as Brants, winter on the refuge. Herons and egrets nest in large rookeries on the refuge, and can usually be found on the impoundments from mid-spring to late fall.

Assateague Island National Seashore is also the located on Assateague Island. It is described in the Maryland chapter.

Area brochure, boating, hiking, biking, surf fishing, clamming, crabbing, shell collecting. Wildlife and boat tours are available from a concessionaire.
Spring, Summer, Fall, Winter

Eastern Shore of Virginia **3**
RFD 1 Box 122B
Cape Charles, VA   804-331-2760

Bird List VA-3 E. Shore VA Summary
281 birds listed, no nesting data
Bird Chart pages 348-365

Totals by Season		s	S	F	W
Abundant	A	5	5	27	7
Common	C	48	33	86	41
Uncommon	U	31	69	6	78
Occasional	O	47	36	35	36
Rare	R	3	3	14	23

Endangered Species: Brown Pelican, Bald Eagle, Peregrine Falcon, Piping Plover, Least Tern

The Eastern Shore of Virginia Refuge was established in 1984. It is located east of the northern toll plaza of the Chesapeake Bay Bridge Tunnel at the tip of the Delmarva Peninsula. Traveling south on Rte. 13, make a left turn onto Rte. 600 (just before reaching the bridge tunnel toll plaza), continue for 0.5 mile to an intersection, and make a right turn onto the refuge.

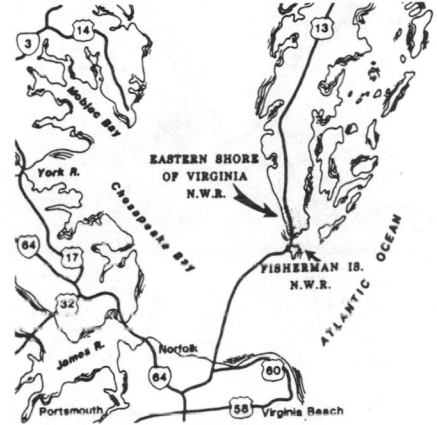

Habitat: 1,850 acres on the east side of Chesapeake Bay include a mix of loblolly pine/holly forest, scrub thickets, open fields, tidal salt marsh, and barrier islands. A number of structures on the refuge remain from its days as a military base.

The refuge is a major stop for land birds during their fall migration because of its strategic location along the Atlantic Flyway. Raptors and songbirds are particularly abundant.

The combination of mild winters and diverse habitats make the refuge a prime wintering area as well. The area has one of the highest Christmas Bird Counts (more than 150 species) north of Florida. The refuge is managed with special emphasis on the American Black Duck, Snow Goose, Brant, American Woodcock, Osprey, and a variety of colonial waterbirds.

Nature trail.
Spring, Fall, Winter

Great Dismal Swamp **4**
PO Box 349   (office at refuge)
Suffolk, VA 23434   804-986-3705

Bird List VA-4
Dismal Swamp Summary
207 birds listed, 96 nesting birds
Bird Chart pages 366-383

Totals by Season		s	S	F	W
Abundant	A	3	3	0	0
Common	C	51	45	43	33
Uncommon	U	61	45	63	38
Occasional	O	53	13	51	32
Rare	R	25	15	34	19

Endangered Species: Bald Eagle

From Suffolk, take Rte. 13 south to Rte. 32, continue south on Rte. 32 for 4.5 miles, and follow signs to refuge headquarters.

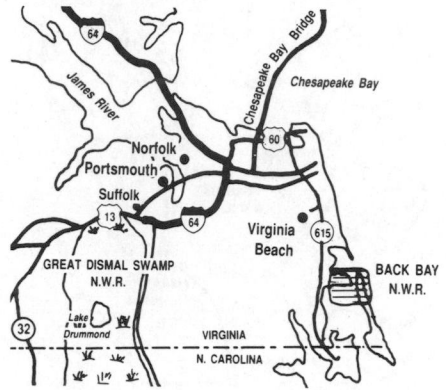

Habitat: 106,000 acres of forested wetland include 3,100-acre Lake Drummond. The wetland, greatly altered by drainage and repeated logging, demonstrates five major forest types, pine, Atlantic white cedar, maple-blackgum, tupelo-bald cypress, and sweetgum-oak-popular, and three non-forested types, remnant marsh, sphagnum bog, and evergreen shrub. The swamp is usually dry, and the danger of fire is high from June to October.

The greatest diversity of bird species occurs during spring migration. Migrating songbirds peak in early May. A total of 34 species of warblers have been noted at the refuge. The Swainson's Warbler is more common in the Great Dismal Swamp than in other coastal locations.

During the winter Red-tailed and Red-shouldered hawks begin to court. Great Horned Owls are incubating their eggs in late January and February. Other common nesting species include the Barred Owl, Pileated Woodpecker, and Prothonotary Warbler.

Area brochure, mammals, reptiles, and amphibians lists, boardwalk trail, hiking, biking, fishing, boating, hunting.
Spring (April–June best)

Mason Neck 5   (office in town)
14416 Jefferson Davis Highway
Suite 20A
Woodbridge, VA 22191   703-690-1297

Bird List VA-5 Mason Neck Summary
212 birds listed, 104 nesting birds
Bird Chart pages 366-383

Totals by Season		s	S	F	W
Abundant	A	19	13	23	16
Common	C	52	40	52	27
Uncommon	U	84	43	80	34
Occasional	O	37	28	40	32
Rare	R	9	4	6	12

Endangered Species: Bald Eagle, Peregrine Falcon, Least Tern

Mason Neck is located 18 miles south of Washington, DC on a peninsula in the Potomac River known as Mason Neck. From Alexandria, take Hwy. 1 south to the Hwy. 601 (Belmont Road) exit and turn left. Turn left again onto Hwy. 242 (Gunston Road) and follow it to the parking lot on the east side of the refuge.

Habitat: 2,277 acres include approximately 2,000 acres of mature hardwood forest, the largest freshwater marsh in northern Virginia, a number of tributary creeks, and nearly six miles of shoreline on the Potomac River.

Mason Neck, the first refuge established for the endangered Bald Eagle, supports both a breeding population and an additional influx during winter. The wintering population arrives during October. The resident birds rebuild their nests and, in February, lay two eggs that will hatch in April.

Waves of migrating songbirds may be seen in the woods during April and May. Over 300 pairs of Great Blue Herons nest on the refuge in one of the largest rookeries in Virginia. Nest boxes are provided for Wood Ducks, Eastern Screech-Owls, and Eastern Bluebirds.

Waterfowl flock to the Potomac River and Great Marsh during the fall and winter. The Potomac is often the only body of water in the area that does not freeze up during the winter, and therefore attracts a variety of diving and sea ducks, including Hooded Mergansers, Oldsquaws, and Buffleheads.

Area brochure, 3-mile Woodmarsh Trail, 0.75-mile Great Marsh Trail, interpretive hikes and programs, photography blind (permits required).
Spring, Fall.

Presquile 6   (office at refuge)
PO Box 620
Hopewell, VA 23860   804-458-7541

Access to Presquile is through privately owned property, and landowner permission is required. Transportation for groups can be arranged to and from the refuge on a ferry owned and operated by the government. Contact the refuge manager in advance on Monday, Wednesday, or Friday.

Bird List VA-6 Presquile Summary
198 birds listed, no nesting data
Bird Chart pages 366-383

Totals by Season		s	S	F	W
Abundant	A	18	18	23	15
Common	C	85	69	77	47
Uncommon	U	53	24	57	27
Occasional	O	27	15	24	9
Rare	R	11	9	13	18

Endangered Species: Bald Eagle, Peregrine Falcon, Least Tern

Located on a man-made island in the James River near the town of Hopewell. From Richmond, take I-95 south. Turn east on Hwy. 10 and continue to Hwy. 827. Turn left, following Hwy. 827 to the ferry landing.

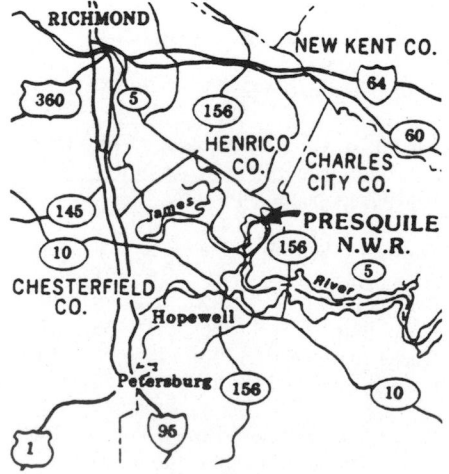

Habitat: 1,329-acre island in the James River that includes 800 acres of tidal swamp, 250 acres tidal marsh, and 275

acres agricultural land. A colony of Bank Swallows, nesting in the steep clay banks adjacent to the navigational channel, is the only colony known in a radius of 100 miles.

Wood Ducks and an occasional pair of American Black Ducks nest in the swamp and marsh. There are concentrations of waterfowl in the winter, primarily Canada and Snow geese and puddle ducks. Several species of diving ducks use the refuge in small numbers. Among the raptors, Red-shouldered and Red-tailed hawks are common year-round. An occasional Bald Eagle may be seen.

Area pamphlet, nature trail, picnic area, hunting.
Spring, Summer, Fall, Winter

NATIONAL PARK SERVICE

Shenandoah National Park ◧
Route 4, Box 348
Luray, VA 22835   703 999 2266

Bird List VA-7 Shenandoah Summary
203 birds listed, no nesting data
Bird Chart pages 366-383

Totals by Season		s	S	F	W
Abundant	A	16	12	12	4
Common	C	62	44	68	20
Uncommon	U	57	40	55	34
Occasional	O	50	25	48	21

Endangered Species: Bald Eagle, Peregrine Falcon

195,346 acres of hardwood forests along the crest of the Blue Ridge Mountains.

Skyline Drive winds through forests and provides vistas of the historic Shenandoah Valley and the Piedmont. Common Ravens, Eastern Meadowlarks, Veerys, Wild Turkeys, Barred Owls, and American Woodcocks are common, and 35 species of warblers have been identified.
Park brochure with map, free "Shenandoah Overlook" seasonal newspaper covering park activities and visitor opportunities.

NATIONAL FOREST SERVICE

Map/Forest/City
△	George Washington /Harrisonburg	703-433-2491
△	Jefferson/Roanoke	703-982-6270

BUREAU LAND MANAGEMENT
BLM Eastern States Office
350 South Pickett Street
Alexandria, VA 22304   703-274-1369

STATE AGENCIES

Dept. of Game & Inland Fisheries
4101 West Broad Street
PO Box 11104
Richmond, VA 23230   804-257-1000

Division of Tourism
Dept. of Economic Development
Ninth Street Office Bldg.
Richmond, VA 23219   804-786-4484

BIRDING HOTLINE
Statewide   206-526-8266

LOCAL BIRDING GROUPS
Map/Chapter/City
① Admiralty Audubon/Pt. Townsend
② Black Hills Audubon/Olympia
③ Blue Mountain Aud./Walla Walla
④ E. Lake Washington Aud./Bellevue
⑤ Kitsap Audubon/Poulsbo
⑥ Kittitas Audubon/Ellensburg
⑦ Lower Columbia Basin Audubon
   /Richland
⑧ North Cascades Aud./Bellingham
⑨ North Central WA Aud./Wenatchee
⑩ Olympic Peninsula Audubon/Sequim
⑪ Pilchuck Audubon/Everett
⑫ Rainier Audubon/Auburn
⑬ San Juan Islands Audubon/Lopez
⑭ Seattle Audubon/Seattle
⑮ Skagit Audubon/Sedro Woolley
⑯ Spokane Audubon/Spokane
⑰ Tacoma Audubon/Tacoma
⑱ Vancouver Audubon/Vancouver
⑲ Whidbey Audubon/Oak Harbor
⑳ Willapa Hills Audubon/Longview
㉑ Yakima Audubon/Yakima
㉒ Canyon Birders/Clarkston
㉓ Grays Harbor Bird Club/Aberdeen

THE NATURE CONSERVANCY
Washington Field Office ◇FO
1601 Second Avenue, Suite 910
Seattle, WA 98101   206-728-9696

Yellow Island   ◆
11 acres located near Deer Harbor.
Nestled among the San Juan Islands
between mainland Washington and
Victoria, BC, and 20 minutes by boat
from Friday Harbor. There is a resident
manager. Island visits are allowed between
sunrise and sunset. Please stay on the
marked trails.

Bald Eagles are attracted to the tall trees,
while Harlequin Ducks forage in the
intertidal zone.

Area brochure, boating, trails.
Spring, Summer

U.S. FISH & WILDLIFE SERVICE
NATIONAL WILDLIFE REFUGES

Columbia ⓤ   (office in town)
44 South 8th Avenue
PO Drawer F
Othello WA, 99344   509-488-2668

Bird List WA-1 Columbia Summary
197 birds listed, 87 nesting birds
Bird Chart pages 366-383

Totals by Season		s	S	F	W
Abundant	A	8	5	6	2
Common	C	35	23	22	22
Uncommon	U	54	46	55	28
Occasional	O	53	51	71	21
Rare	R	25	13	12	11

Endangered Species: Bald Eagle, Peregrine
Falcon

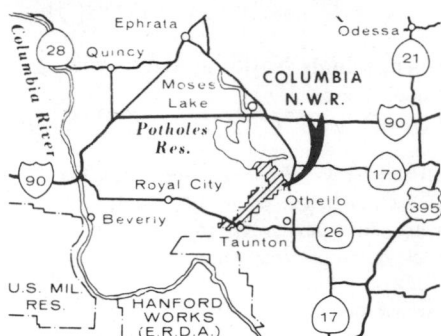

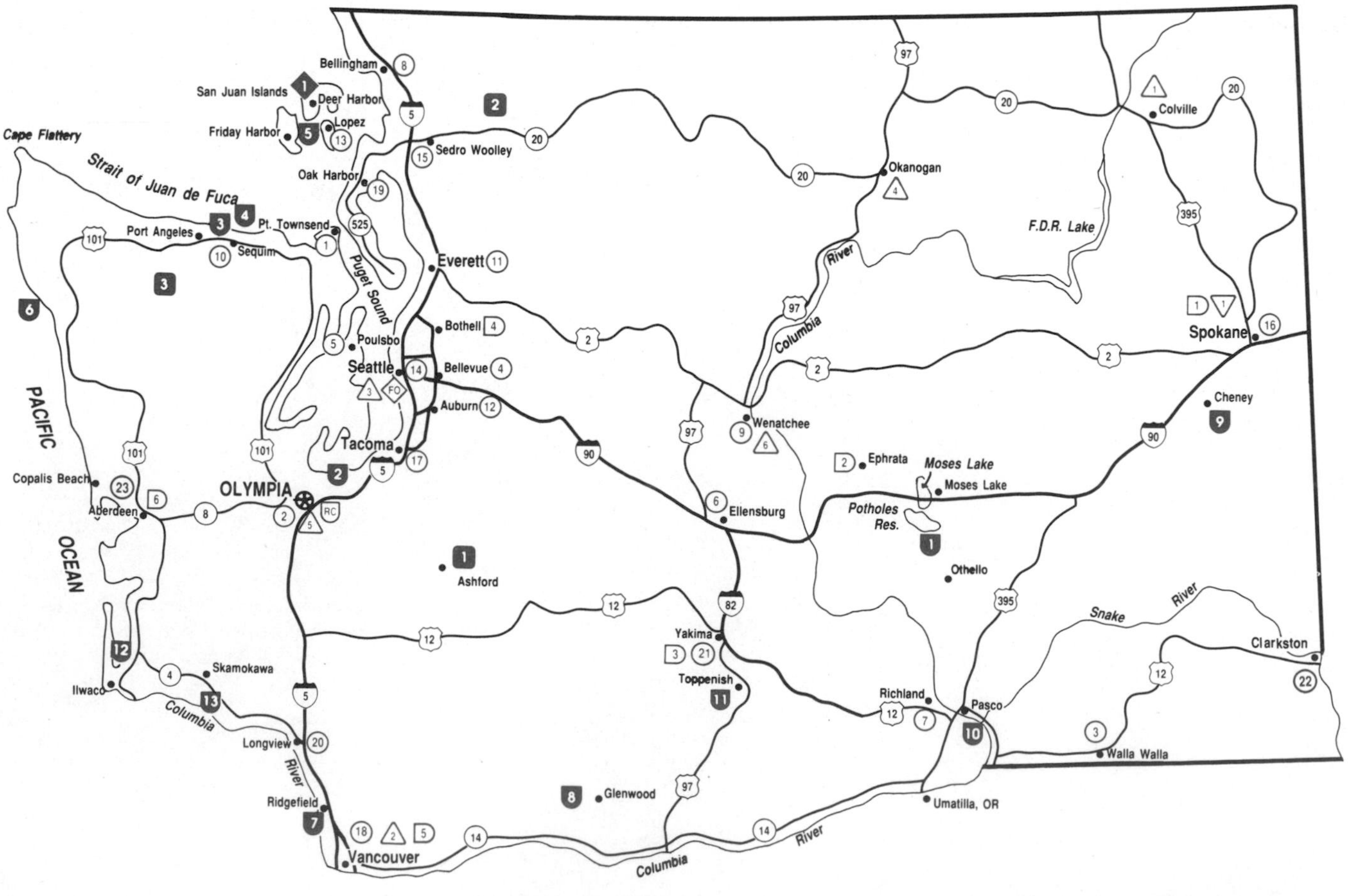

From Othello, take Broadway Ave. north to McMannaman Road, turn left, and go 6 miles west. From Moses Lake, take Hwy. 17 south to the O'Sullivan Dam Road, turn right, and go 6 miles west.

Habitat: 23,100 acres of rugged cliffs, canyons, arid sagebrush grasslands, and lakes, sloughs, marshes, and other wetlands. Seepage from the Columbia Basin Irrigation Project has created over 50 lakes, sloughs with accompanying wet meadows and marshes, and 15 miles of streams and canals.

Waterfowl use the lakes, sloughs and marshes. Mallards, Blue-winged and Cinnamon teals, Redheads, and Ruddy Ducks are the most common ducks during warm weather, and nest on the refuge. American Coots are also abundant.

The ledges, cracks, and holes in the numerous basalt cliffs provide nest sites for Red-tailed Hawks, American Kestrels, Great Horned and Common Barn owls and a few Common Ravens. The cliffs are also used by large colonies of Cliff Swallows. Great Blue Herons are frequently seen at the tops of cliffs and rock outcrops near water.

Area brochure, mammals, reptiles, and amphibians lists, hunting, fishing, hiking. During the spring and summer the entire refuge is open to the public. The areas of waterfowl concentrations are closed to public entry during fall and winter.
Spring, Summer, Fall

Puget Sound and Coastal Washington Refuge Complex

There are two migratory bird refuges and five seabird refuges in the complex. The Nisqually and Dungeness refuges are open to visitors. The seabird refuges are closed to public use, but birds may be observed from a distance.

Nisqually 2 RC
Nisqually Refuge Complex Office
100 Brown Farm Road
Olympia, WA 98506   206-753-9467

The refuge complex includes the Nisqually and Dungeness refuges.

Bird List WA-2 Nisqually Summary
176 birds listed, 87 nesting birds
Bird Chart pages 366-383

Totals by Season		s	S	F	W
Abundant	A	7	5	11	8
Common	C	69	54	69	53
Uncommon	U	59	39	61	46
Rare	R	16	21	15	17

Endangered Species: Bald Eagle, Peregrine Falcon

The office for the refuge complex is just off I-5 at exit 114, and approximately 7 miles east of Olympia. Follow signs to the headquarters.

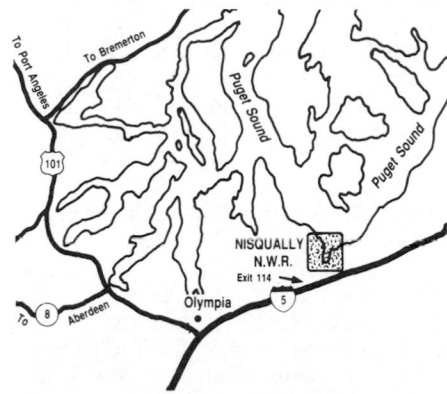

Habitat: 1,796 acres on the delta where the Nisqually River flows into Puget Sound. The 10 different habitat types range from salt marshes, mudflats, and estuaries to freshwater marshes, grasslands, and forests. A 5-mile-long dike separates saltwater and freshwater habitats. Outside the dike salt marshes and open mudflats are washed by Puget Sound's tides. Inside the dike, freshwater marshes are surrounded by cattails, sedges, and open grasslands.

Shorebirds, gulls, and herons feed on the sea side of the dike. Resting and wintering waterfowl can be found on the freshwater marshes and grasslands. Hawks and owls feed on the mice and voles in the grasslands. Marsh Wrens and Soras inhabit the cattails and sedges.

Bewick's Wrens, Pileated Woodpeckers, and Great Horned Owls live in the woodland area along the Nisqually River. Evening and Black-headed grosbeaks, Cedar Waxwings, and finches are found along McAllister Creek.

Area brochure, land and marine mammals, fishes, amphibians, and reptiles lists, boating, fishing, clamming, foot trails.
Spring, Fall, Winter

Dungeness 3
c/o Nisqually NWR
100 Brown Farm Road
Olympia, WA 98506   206-753-9467

Bird List WA-3 Dungeness Summary
232 birds listed, 91 nesting birds
Bird Chart pages 366-383

Totals by Season		s	S	F	W
Abundant	A	2	3	5	7
Common	C	75	70	69	61
Uncommon	U	77	55	85	37
Occasional	O	14	9	13	9
Rare	R	38	26	48	33

Endangered Species: Bald Eagle, Peregrine Falcon

To reach the refuge from Port Angeles, take Hwy. 101 east for approximately 11 miles. Turn left on Kitchen Road and go 3 miles north to the Dungeness Recreation Area. Access to the refuge is by foot or horseback.

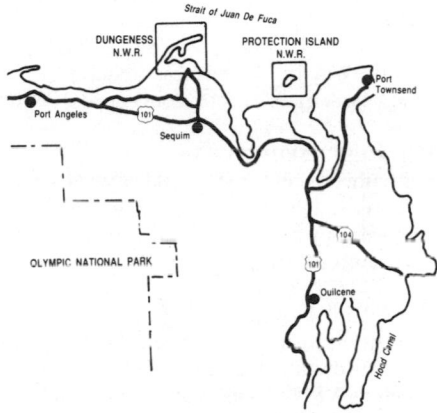

Habitat: 756 acres. Dungeness Spit stretches for 5.5 miles into the Strait of Juan de Fuca. Formed by eroding soil, wind, and water currents, it breaks the rough sea waves to form a quiet bay, sand and gravel beaches, and tideflats. There is some upland and wooded area.

Shorebirds and waterfowl feed and nest along the beaches. Some of the "Black" Brant that wintered in the area will also remain to nest. Phalaropes, turnstones, and sandpipers may be seen searching for food along the water's edge. Cormorants, Great Blue Herons, and Red-tailed Hawks may also be seen during the summer, when Chestnut-backed Chickadees and many warblers utilize the uplands.

In the fall thousands of scaups, scoters, Mallards, Dunlins, and plovers may be seen. "Black" Brants, which depend on eelgrass for food, are present throughout the winter months. Also common during the winter are Bald Eagles, Canada Geese, Harlequin Ducks, Surf and White-winged scoters, gulls, guillemots, grebes, cormorants, and goldeneyes.

Area brochure, hiking, boating, fishing, clamming, horseback riding, land and marine mammals, amphibians, and reptiles lists.
Spring, Fall, Winter

Seabird Refuges & Special Note!
The next three refuges are closed to the public. Stay at least 200 yards offshore to avoid disturbing breeding seabirds.

Protection Island 4
Located at the mouth of Discovery Bay off Washington's Olympic Peninsula.

Protection Island alone harbors 72 percent of Puget Sound's seabirds. Its high, grassy slopes are used by burrow-nesting species, including 17,000 pairs of Rhinoceros Auklets. Pigeon Guillemots, Pelagic Cormorants, Tufted Puffins, Black Oystercatchers, and over 4,000 pairs of Glaucous-winged Gulls also nest on the island.

At John Wayne Marina near Sequim, panels explain the Protection Island NWR.

San Juan Islands 5
Eighty-three reefs, rocks, and islands in the San Juan Islands of northern Puget Sound are in the refuge. The islands have also been designated as wilderness.

All of Turn Island and five acres on Matia Island are managed as Marine State Parks. Information on the San Juan Islands NWR is located at marinas and resorts throughout the San Juan Islands. The remainder of Matia Island except the designated Wilderness Trail is closed to the public.

Seabirds, including Pigeon Guillemots, cormorants, and gulls, nest on the islands that have high cliffs and grassy slopes.

Washington Islands 6
There are 870 islands, rocks, and reefs that comprise the Washington Islands refuges. They extend for more than 100 miles along Washington's coast, from Cape Flattery to Copalis Beach. Copalis, Flattery Rocks, and Quillayute Needles are among the refuges. They all provide vital sanctuary for the 14 species of seabirds that nest and raise their young in the islands.

Rhinoceros Auklets, Tufted Puffins, Cassin's Auklets, and Leach's and Fork-tailed storm-petrels nest in burrows. Other seabirds such as Common Murres, Brandt's, Pelagic, and Double-crested cormorants, and gulls build nests on the high, open ledges. During migration more than one million seabirds may be present at one time.

Information about the wildlife of Washington Islands is available at Lake Ozette, Rialto, Second, and Ruby beaches, and Kalaloch along the Washington coast.

Ridgefield 7 (office in town)
301 North Third Street
PO Box 457
Ridgefield, WA 98642   206-887-4106

Bird List WA-4 Ridgefield Summary
181 birds listed, 80 nesting birds
Bird Chart pages 366-383

Totals by Season		s	S	F	W
Common	C	51	32	35	39
Uncommon	U	46	42	44	24
Occasional	O	50	45	57	52
Rare	R	19	17	14	22

Endangered Species: Bald Eagle, Peregrine Falcon

One entrance to the refuge is approximately 1 mile north of the headquarters on Third Street. The other entrance is approximately 0.75 mile south of Ridgefield on South 9th Street.

Habitat: 4,615 acres of marshes, grasslands, and woodlands in three units along the Columbia River. The Carty unit includes Columbia River floodplain and basalt outcroppings, wooded with ash, oak, and Douglas fir. The Roth unit is flatter and forested with cottonwood, ash, and willow and includes floodplain. The River "S" unit and Bachelor Island are protected from flooding by dikes. Crops and grasslands are cultivated for waterfowl food.

A variety of migrating songbirds rest and feed on the refuge during spring and fall. Some waterfowl, including Mallards and Cinnamon Teals, as well as various shorebirds and passerines, remain to nest. Up to 200,000 waterfowl overwinter between Portland, Oregon, and the mouth of the Columbia River. Among them are three subspecies of Canada Geese, "Dusky," "Cackler," and "Taverner's," Tundra Swans, Northern Shovelers, American Wigeons, Green-winged Teals, and Northern Pintails. Mallards, Cinnamon Teals, Great Blue Herons, and Red-tailed Hawks are permanent residents.

Roth unit, Bachelor Island, and a portion of River "S" unit are closed from October 1 to April 15.

Area brochure, mammals, reptiles, and amphibians lists, hunting, fishing, hiking, boating.
Spring, Fall, Winter

Conboy Lake 8 (office at refuge)
Box 5
Glenwood, WA 98619   509-364-3410

From Trout Lake, take the Glenwood Road (a local county road) east toward Glenwood for about 10 miles to refuge sign. Turn right and go about 1 mile to the headquarters.

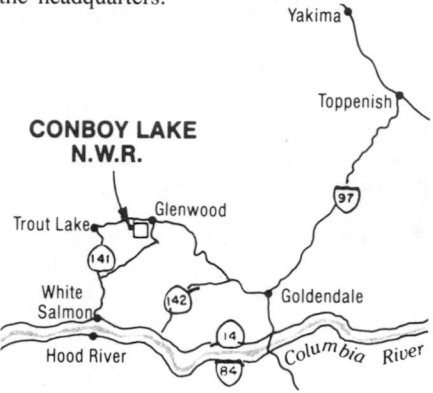

Habitat: 5,500 acres include portions of seasonal Conboy Lake marshlands and pine-forested uplands. The lake is full early in the year due to spring runoff and the rains of the previous fall. By the end of the summer only the deepest parts hold water.

This refuge is known primarily for its migrating waterfowl and Sandhill Cranes. Swans, geese, and ducks converge on the lake in February and March to feed before moving on to their breeding grounds farther north. Fall migration brings flocks of ducks and geese to the reduced lake for brief stops.

A few ducks and geese nest. Other nesting species such as Common Snipes, Sandhill Cranes, and various songbirds arrive in early summer.

Area brochure, hiking, hunting, fishing.
Spring, Fall, Winter

Turnbull 9 (office at refuge)
Route 3, Box 385
Cheney, WA 99004   509-235-4723

Bird List WA-5 Turnbull Summary
202 birds listed, 108 nesting birds
Bird Chart pages 366-383

Totals by Season		s	S	F	W
Abundant	A	12	28	12	3
Common	C	49	31	48	9
Uncommon	U	52	45	56	20
Occasional	O	47	30	45	37
Rare	R	22	33	24	19

Endangered Species: Brown Pelican, Bald Eagle, Peregrine Falcon

From Cheney, take the Cheney-Plaza Road south for approximately 4 miles, turn left at the refuge sign, and go 2 miles east to headquarters.

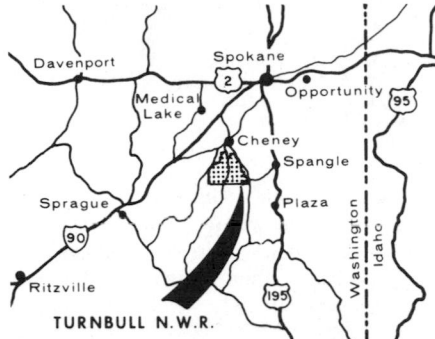

TURNBULL N.W.R.

Habitat: 17,280 acres of rugged scabrock, pine, aspen, and grasslands interspersed with 20 small lakes and over 100 ponds.

Sizable numbers of ducks, geese, swans, and other waterbirds nest and raise young at Turnbull. Many of the lakes are managed primarily for diving ducks such as Redheads, Canvasbacks, and Lesser Scaups. Canada Geese use the area for nesting and as a stopover point during migration. Spring and fall present the greatest variety of birds, and late spring is the best time to observe nesting activities and young birds.

Area brochure, auto tour route, hiking. Unpredictable weather and bad roads may limit access. Spring and fall migrations present the most spectacular show of birds.
Spring, Summer, Fall

Umatilla
Post Office Building
6th and I Streets
PO Box 239
Umatilla, OR 97882   503-922-3232

See pages 153 and 154, in the Oregon chapter, for a full description of Umatilla, the headquarters for the McNary and Toppenish refuges.

McNary 10
c/o Umatilla NWR
Sub-office located on the refuge.

McNary has three divisions, McNary, Strawberry Island, and Hanford Islands.

Bird List WA-6 McNary Summary
159 birds listed, 57 nesting birds
Bird Chart pages 366-383

Totals by Season		s	S	F	W
Abundant	A	11	5	13	8
Common	C	42	48	37	29
Uncommon	U	34	30	37	17
Occasional	O	32	20	27	26
Rare	R	14	10	18	19

Endangered Species: Bald Eagle

McNary is located in the Lower Columbia Basin, 6 miles southeast of Pasco, adjacent to the confluence of the Snake and Columbia rivers. From Pasco, take Hwy. 395 south for approximately 2 miles to the refuge entrance sign.

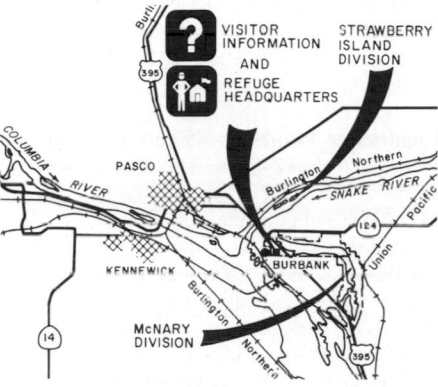

Habitat: 3,366 acres, including Strawberry Island in the Snake River, and the six Hanford Islands, located upstream in the Columbia River north of Richland.

McNary supports breeding populations of 14 species of ducks. Diving ducks include Redheads, Canvasbacks, and Lesser Scaups, while Mallards, Northern Pintails, American Wigeons, Gadwalls, Northern Shovelers, and all three teals are among the dabbling ducks that nest at the refuge. Mallards and Northern Pintails, the earliest nesters, lay their eggs in April and early May. Gadwalls and teals, among the latest when they lay their eggs in late May or June, still have young broods in July.

Various other waterbirds also breed at the refuge. The most common shorebirds are the American Avocet, Long-billed Curlew, Killdeer, and Wilson's Phalarope. Colonial species such as Forster's Terns and Ring-billed and California gulls nest on the river islands. Songbirds can be found at the west end of Burbank Slough and the interpretive trail, where they find food and protection from predators. Northern Harriers are common throughout the year. Sharp-shinned, Cooper's, and Red-tailed hawks are seen less often.

Area brochure, fishing, hunting, interpretive trail. The Hanford Islands Division is closed from July 1 to January 1.
Spring, Summer, Fall

Toppenish 11
c/o Umatilla NWR
Sub-office located on the refuge.

The three units of the Toppenish refuge are all located on the Yakima Indian Reservation.

Bird List WA-7 Toppenish Summary
206 birds listed, 108 nesting birds
Bird Chart pages 366-383

Totals by Season		s	S	F	W
Abundant	A	12	7	7	5
Common	C	61	45	46	21
Uncommon	U	60	40	54	35
Occasional	O	32	27	39	25
Rare	R	17	15	41	22

Endangered Species: Bald Eagle, Peregrine Falcon

For the Lower Toppenish unit, take Hwy. 97 south from Toppenish for about 5 miles to the refuge sign.
For the Upper Toppenish unit, take Hwy. 97 south 1.5 miles to Yost Road. Turn right and go west about 11 miles to the refuge sign.
For the Status unit, take Hwy. 22 southeast from Toppenish for about 12 miles to refuge sign.

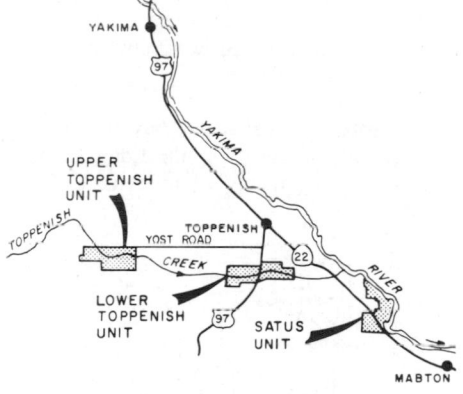

Habitat: 1,762 acres include brushy creek bottoms, wet meadows, croplands, and sagebrush uplands.

Waterbirds, such as Mallards, Northern Shovelers, and Wood Ducks, and many songbirds nest during early spring and summer. An estimated 1,500 ducks are fledged each year. A breeding colony of Bobolinks nests between Yost Road and Toppenish Creek. Lewis' Woodpeckers breed in abundance. Near the end of the summer, shorebirds pass through on their southward migration.

Waterfowl populations build in September and reach a peak in early November. Mallards, Northern Pintails, and Canada Geese are the most numerous species. The area is noted for the large numbers of

Bald Eagles, Prairie Falcons, and other raptors present during the winter. Marsh birds, including herons, egrets, gulls, and terns, are present during the fall.

Adjacent shrubsteppe, a vanishing habitat in Washington, is home to some species becoming rare in the state such as Sage Thrasher, Long-billed Curlew, and Sage Sparrow.

Area brochure, visitor center, foot trails, hunting.
Spring, Fall

Willapa ⑫
Highway 101
Ilwaco, WA 98624　　　　　206-484-3482

Administrative headquarters for the Julia Butler Hansen Refuge for White-tailed Deer in Washington and the Lewis & Clark NWR in Oregon.

Bird List WA-8 Willapa Summary
235 birds listed, 88 nesting birds
Bird Chart pages 366-383

Totals by Season		s	S	F	W
Abundant	A	10	3	10	18
Common	C	78	48	78	67
Uncommon	U	88	76	89	59
Rare	R	35	34	28	26

Endangered Species: Brown Pelican, Bald Eagle, Peregrine Falcon

Headquarters is located on Hwy. 101 on the mainland southeast of the Long Island unit and approximately 11 miles east of Ilwaco.

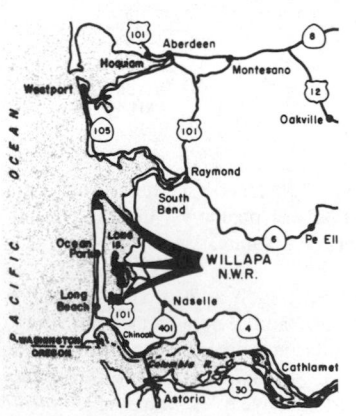

Habitat: 11,500 acres of uplands and tidelands around Willapa Bay in 5 units, Leadbetter Point, Lewis, Long Island, Porter Point, and Riekkola.

The greatest diversity of birds is present during the winter. Large flocks of Canada Geese, "Black" Brants, American Wigeons, Canvasbacks, Buffleheads, scaups, and scoters share the bay with loons, grebes, mergansers, and cormorants. Dunlins, plovers and sandpipers line the tideflats.

Spring and fall migrations bring large concentrations of waterfowl and shorebirds to the refuge. Shorebirds and seabirds often number in the hundreds of thousands as they stop to feed and rest during their migrations. In spring and summer, nesting species include grouse, Bald Eagles, herons, woodpeckers, and shorebirds.

Willapa Bay—Vast beds of eelgrass at the lower levels of the intertidal zone are a staple food for "Black" Brants. Thousands of bay and sea ducks, loons, grebes, and cormorants find food and protection on the bay.

Leadbetter Point—1,435-acre reach of salt marsh, sand dunes, and spruce-pine wood lots located on the northern tip of Long Beach Peninsula. Tens of thousands of shorebirds feed and rest on the beaches, bay tidal flats, and salt marshes during spring and fall migration peaks. During the nesting season a portion of Leadbetter Point is closed to protect the nesting area of the Snowy Plover.

Long Island—5,000-acre wooded island of dense, rain-drenched coastal forest surrounded by tidal marshes and extensive mudflats located in the southeast corner of the bay. Birdlife ranges from waterfowl to tiny insectivorous hole-nesters.

Lewis—Freshwater marshes at the south end of the bay provide waterfowl with resting and wintering habitat. A small flock of Trumpeter Swans frequently spends the winter.

Riekkola—Grasslands established on diked tidelands at the south end of the bay provide feeding areas for migrating Canada Geese, ducks, and shorebirds.

Area brochure, Leadbetter Point unit and Long Island unit brochures, hiking, boating, clamming, crabbing, fishing, hunting.
Spring, Fall, Winter

Julia Butler Hansen Refuge ⑬
for Columbian White-tailed Deer
c/o Willapa NWR
HC 01, Box 910
Ilwaco, WA 98624　　　　　206-484-3482

The refuge office is approximately 4 miles southeast of Skamokawa on Hwy. 4. The mainland unit of the refuge begins just south and east of Skamokawa with Hwy. 4 skirting the edge of the refuge for several miles. The Tenasillahe Island unit is offshore in the Columbia River.

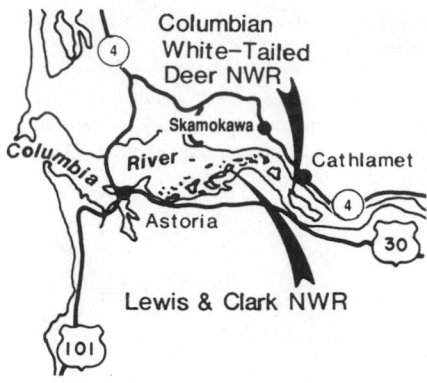

Habitat: 4,400 acres. Grasslands interspersed with willows, red alder, and sitka spruce woodland in one mainland and three island units along the Columbia River bottomland.

In the spring Wilson's Warblers, Bewick's Wrens, American Goldfinches, Golden-crowned Sparrows, and a variety of thrushes are common.

Red-tailed Hawks feed on the rodents in the open areas and Bald Eagles use refuge trees as perches. Refuge sloughs and shorelines attract shorebirds and waterbirds such as Great Blue Herons, Common Snipe, sandpipers, and grebes.

Migrant waterfowl pass through the refuge in the fall. The most common species are American Wigeons, and "Dusky" and "Lesser" Canada Geese. Tundra Swans, Canada Geese, and ducks, which spend the winter on the lower Columbia River, feed on the short grass and crops left in the refuge fields.

Area brochure, hiking, boating, fishing, hunting, camping.
Spring, Fall, Winter

NATIONAL PARK SERVICE

Mount Rainier National Park ❶
Tahoma Woods, Star Route
Ashford, WA 98304　　　　　206-569-2211

Bird List WA-9 Mt. Rainier Summary
122 birds listed, 92 nesting birds
Bird Chart pages 366-383

Totals by Season		s	S	F	W
Abundant	A	2	2	2	1
Common	C	29	29	29	7
Uncommon	U	35	38	41	12
Occasional	O	16	18	20	6
Rare	R	18	20	22	7

Endangered Species: Bald Eagle, Peregrine Falcon

235,404 acres include the largest single-peak glacial system in the United States radiating from the summit and slopes of an ancient volcano, with dense forests and subalpine flowered meadows below.

Park brochure with map, species lists, camping, backcountry trip planning guide, activity leaflets for fishing and boating, horseback riding, climbing, hiking. Summer, Fall

North Cascades National Park **2**
2105 Highway 20
Sedro Woolley, WA 98284

504,780 acres of high, jagged peaks intercept moisture-laden winds, producing glaciers, icefalls, waterfalls, and other water phenomena in this wild alpine region. Lush forests and meadows, plant and animal communities thrive in the valleys.

Park brochure with map, trails and recreation areas map.
Summer, Fall

Olympic National Park **3**
600 East Park Avenue
Port Angeles, WA 98362   206-452-4501

914,818 acres contain a mountain wilderness with the best remnant of Pacific Northwest rain forest of Sitka spruce, active glaciers, rare Roosevelt elk, and 57 miles of wild ocean shore. Mt. Olympus reaches 8,000 feet above sea level. The shores support breeding colonies of a variety of alcids, including Common Murres, Pigeon Guillemots, Marbled Murrelets, Rhinoceros Auklets, and Tufted Puffins.

Park brochure and map, leaflets on camping and other activities. Bird list with graphic seasonal abundance chart, mammals and record trees lists.
Spring, Summer, Fall

NATIONAL FOREST SERVICE
Map/Forest/City

△	Colville/Colville	509-684-3711
△	Gifford-Pinchot /Vancouver	206-696-7500
△	Mt. Blaks-Snoqualmie /Seattle	206-442-5400
△	Okanogan/Okanogan	509-442-2704
△	Olympic/Olympia	206-753-9534
△	Wenatchee/Wenatchee	509-662-4335

BUREAU LAND MANAGEMENT
BLM State Office
825 NE Multnomah Street
PO Box 2965
Portland, OR 97208   503-231-6277

Map/District/City
▽ Spokane/Spokane, WA 509-456-2570

STATE AGENCIES

Washington Dept. of Wildlife
600 North Capitol Way
Olympia, WA 98504   206-753-5700

Map/Region/City

1	Region 1/Spokane	509-456-4082
2	Region 2/Ephrata	509-754-4624
3	Region 3/Yakima	509-575-2740
4	Region 4/Bothell	206-775-1311
5	Region 5/Vancouver	206-696-6211
6	Region 6/Aberdeen	206-533-9335

Tourism Development Division
Department of Economic Development
101 General Administration Bldg.
Olympia, WA 98504   206-586-2102
for literature call   800-544-1800

LOCAL BIRDING GROUPS
Map/Chapter/City
1. George M. Sutton Audubon/Bethany
2. Huntington Tri-State Audubon /Huntington
3. Mountaineer Audubon/Morgantown
4. Patomac Valley Aud./Charlestown
5. Brooks Bird Club (BBC)/Wheeling

THE NATURE CONSERVANCY
West Virginia Field Office ◁FO▷
922 Quarrier Street, Suite 414
PO Box 3754
Charleston, WV 25337   304-345-4350

Brush Creek ◆1
Near Athens—Contact Field Office

From Athens exit off I-77, turn east
toward Athens, then immediately left (north) on Co. Rte. 14, which parallels the interstate. Go about 2.5 miles and take an oblique turn to the right (easy to miss), and go down the hill. Park at bridge. Follow the trail downstream to the falls, and beyond to the preserve.

Habitat: 123 acres with the tracks of an old railway providing a trail throughout the preserve, past 40-foot Bush Creek Falls just outside the boundary, and down to the Bluestone River. Bush Creek cuts a 400-foot-deep canyon as it flows toward the river. Spring is a particularly good season to visit both for the blooming wildflowers and migrating warblers.

Area brochure and map available, picnicking, nature trails.
April–June, October, and Winter are best.

Cranesville Swamp ◆2
Near Cranesville and about 9 miles north of Terra Alta—Contact Field Office

From Friendsville, MD, exit off Rte. 48, take Rte. 42 north paralleling Rte. 48 to church at top of hill. Turn left and cross over Rte. 48. Follow this road about 3–4 miles, turn left onto White Rock Road, and go 8–10 miles (almost to Cranesville Swamp). At one point the road makes a wide 90-degree turn to the right and is marked Cranesville Road. After a long, steep decent into a wide valley, make a right turn just past the Lake Ford Church. Bear right at the next fork, about 0.5 mile, and watch for the preserve sign.

Habitat: 350 acres at an elevation of 2,500 feet and surrounded by hills, some as high as 2,900 feet. The relict colony of plants and animals has been preserved by the altitude since the last ice age.

Area brochure and map available, picnicking, nature trails.
May, June, October, and Winter are best.

NATIONAL FOREST SERVICE
Monongahela NF Supervisor △
USDA Bldg.
200 Sycamore Street
Elkins, WV 26241   304-636-1800

STATE AGENCIES

Dept. of Natural Resources
Wildlife Division
Charleston, WV 25305   304-348-2771

Map/District/City
1. Fairmont/Fairmont   304-366-5880
2. Romney/Romney   304-822-3551
3. French Creek /French Creek   304-924-6211
4. St. Albans/St. Albans   304-755-9141
5. Parkersburg /Parkersburg   304-420-4550

Tourist Information
Department of Commerce
2101 Washington Street, East
Charleston, WV 25305   800-225-5982
from out-of-state call same number

BIRDING HOTLINES

Madison   608-255-2476
    except 9a.m.–3p.m. weekdays
Statewide   414-352-3857

LOCAL BIRDING GROUPS
Map/Chapter/City
① Aldo Leopold Aud./Stevens Point
② Burnett County Audubon/Danbury
③ Chequamegon Audubon/Ashland
④ Fond Du Lac County Audubon
    /Fond Du Lac
⑤ Fox River Valley Aud./Appleton
⑥ Hunt Hill Audubon/Sarona
⑦ Kettle Moraine Audubon/West Bend
⑧ Lakeland Audubon/Elkhorn

⑨ Madison Audubon/Madison
⑩ Milwaukee Audubon/So. Milwaukee
⑪ Northeastern WI Aud./Green Bay
⑫ Sand County Audubon/Oxford
⑬ Sheboygan County Aud./Sheboygan
⑭ Winnebago Audubon/Oshkosh
⑮ Wisconsin Metro Aud./New Berlin
⑯ Chequamegon Bay Birders/Ashland
⑰ Chippewa Wildlife Society
    /Chippewa Falls
⑱ Green Bay Bird Club/Green Bay
⑲ O.J. Gromme Bird Club
    /Fond du Lac
⑳ Benjamin F. Goss Bird Club
    /Waukesha
㉑ Ned Hollister Bird Club/Beloit
㉒ Hoy Nature Club/Racine
㉓ Oshkosh Bird Club/Oshkosh

㉔ Plymouth Bird & Nature Club
    /Plymouth
㉕ Whitnall Park Natural History Soc.
    /Franklin
㉖ Wisconsin Society for Ornithology
    /Stevens Point

NATIONAL AUDUBON SOCIETY

Schlitz Audubon Center ❶
1111 East Brown Deer Road
Milwaukee, WI 53217   414-352-2880
Entry fee

Bird List WI-1 Schlitz Summary
233 birds listed, no nesting data
Bird Chart pages 366-383

Totals by Season		s	S	F	W
Abundant	A	16	5	8	1
Common	C	58	23	41	8
Uncommon	U	53	25	58	17
Occasional	O	36	27	37	16
Rare	R	57	41	57	35

Endangered Species: Bald Eagle, Peregrine Falcon

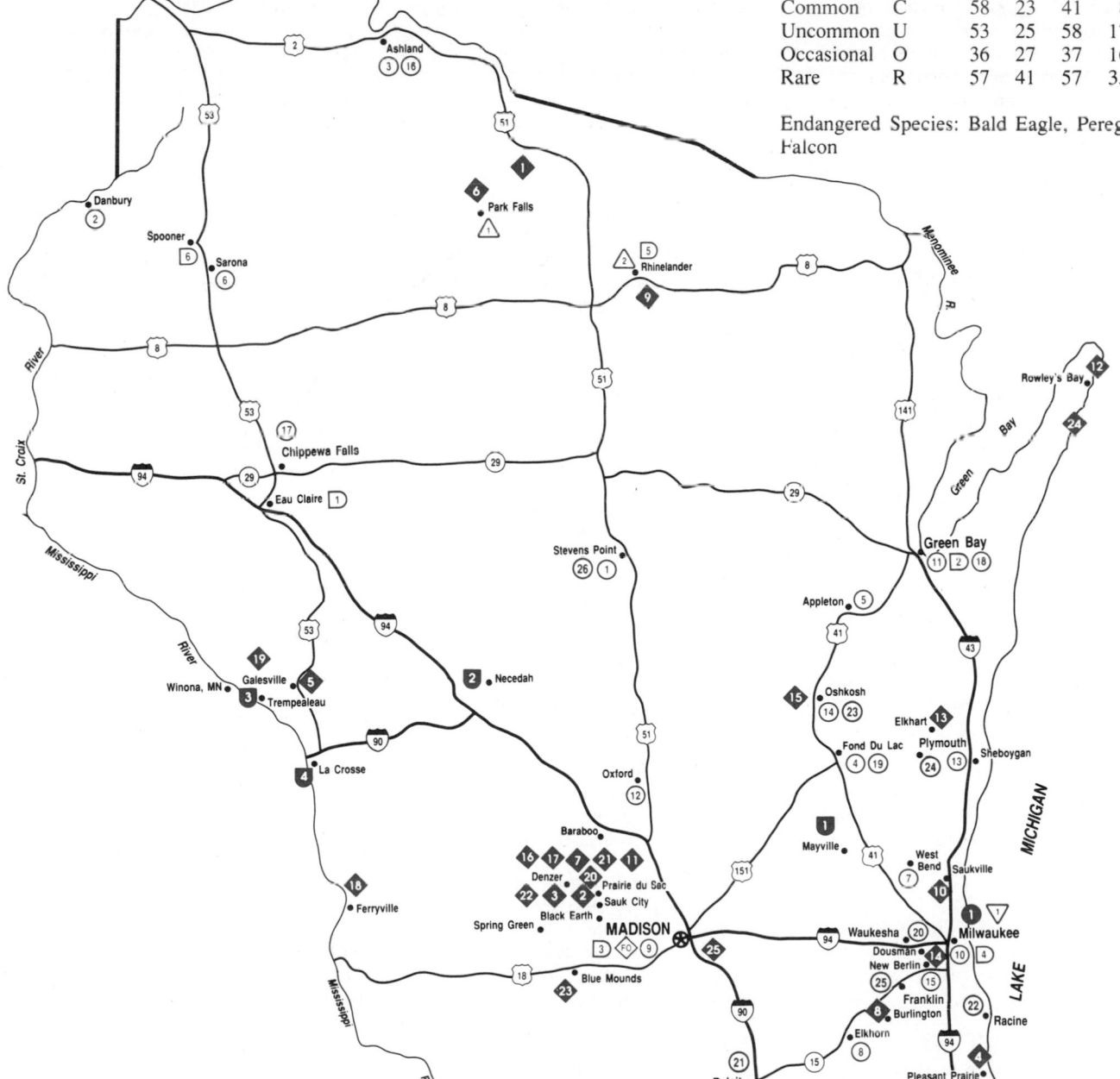

The entrance to the Schlitz Audubon Center is on East Brown Deer Road, east off of North Lake Dr. (St. Rte. 32, which parallels Lake Michigan). The Center is open 9a.m.–5p.m. Tuesday through Sunday.

Habitat: 225 acres on the shore of Lake Michigan with a diversity of habitats and wildlife. The 6 miles of trails have 35 numbered observation points, an observation tower, interpretive building with classrooms, auditorium, library, natural history book store, and gift shop.

Sanctuary brochure, self-guiding numbered trail guide, cross-country skiing.
Spring, Fall

THE NATURE CONSERVANCY

Wisconsin Field Office ◆
PO Box 1642
Madison, WI 53701   608-251-8140

An 88-page illustrated directory of the Wisconsin preserves is available from the Field Office for $14.95 plus $2 shipping and handling. Titled *The Places We Save*, the guide gives an overview of TNC activity, descriptive details on 42 preserves, with detailed maps, visitor regulations, and directions. Preserves open to visitors are briefly described below.

Bass Lake ◆
710 acres in Iron County near the Lac Du Flambeau Indian Reservation. A walking trail leads to Bass Lake on the preserve.

Baxter's Hollow ◆
/R.D. & Linda Peters
2,900 acres in Sauk County between Sauk City and Baraboo. More than 134 bird species have been recorded at Baxter's Hollow, which is an important nesting area for forest-dwelling birds.

Black Earth Rettenmund Prairie ◆
17 acres in Dane County west of Black Earth. The Prairie has been dedicated as a State Natural Area.

Chiwaukee Prairie ◆
165 acres in the town of Pleasant Prairie in southeast Kenosha County. Upland

Sandpipers, King Rails, Marsh Wrens, and Eastern Meadowlarks are among the 76 species recorded on the prairie.

Decorah Mounds ◆
40 acres located 2 miles east of Galesville in Trempealeau County. Among the species recorded are Turkey Vultures, Rose-breasted Grosbeaks, Red-bellied Woodpeckers, and Indigo Buntings.

Flambeau River ◆
1,060 acres above Park Falls and owned by the Wisconsin Dept. of Natural Resources. This State Natural Area provides important nesting and feeding habitat for Bald Eagles and Osprey. Cooper's and Red-tailed hawks nest in the woods along the river.

Hemlock Draw ◆
533 acres in the Baraboo Hills section of Sauk County. Over 60 species of breeding birds have been recorded, including Barred Owls, Ruffed Grouse, Wood Thrushes, and various warblers and woodpeckers.

Hoganson ◆
219 acres 2 miles northwest of Burlington and part of the Honey Creek wetland. The preserve is a nesting site for Sandhill Cranes. Other species noted include Wood Ducks, Great Blue Herons, and Barn Swallows.

Holmboe Conifer Forest ◆
32 acres near Rhinelander on the south bank of Pelican River. Designated a Wildlife Sanctuary and State Natural Area. Green-backed Heron, Spotted Sandpiper, Eastern Wood-Pewee, Purple Martin, Red-eyed Vireo, Veery, and Hermit Thrush are among the species that have been observed.

Kurtz Woods ◆
31 acres near Saukville which are designated as a State Natural Area. There are 82 species of trees and spring ephemerals, including thick stands of sugar maple and American beech.

Leopold Memorial Woods ◆
83 acres northeast of Sauk City. The dense hemlock and maple woods attract Acadian Flycatchers.

Mink River Estuary ◆
796 acres on the east shore of the peninsula at Rowley's Bay and near Newport State Park. Over 250 species have been recorded at this sanctuary for nesting and migrating birds.

Muehl Springs ◆
75 acres north of Elkhart. Canoe access to the preserve on Muehl's Creek at

Hwy. 67. Wood Ducks, white-tailed deer, and beavers have been observed.

Nelson Oak Woods ◆
115 acres south of Dousman. The oak woods attract a variety of forest dwelling birds.

Omro Prairie ◆
5 acres west of Oshkosh. The preserve is a unique natural resource where more than 62 species of prairie plants grow along the old railroad right-of-way.

Pan Hollow ◆
65 acres in two tracts, Butler Woods and Gerald Scott Memorial Woods, north of Denzer. Steep cliffs and woodlands slope to an intermittent stream bottom.

Pine Hollow ◆
144 acres, much of it forested, north of Denzer, designated a State Natural Area.

Rush Creek Bluffs ◆
1,143 acres on the bank of the Mississippi River northwest of Ferryville. Owned by the Wisconsin Dept. of Natural Resources, dedicated as a State Natural Area. Red-shouldered Hawks nest on the preserve.

Sacia Memorial Ridge ◆
29 acres northwest of Galesville. Along the ridge two knolls offer spectacular views to the west. The oak forest and dry prairie support American Woodcocks, Rose-breasted Grosbeaks, Ruffed Grouse, and many other species.

Schluckebier Sand Prairie ◆
23 acres west of Prairie du Sac where two tracts are divided by the county road. A naturally restored prairie habitat and wooded border where Indigo Buntings, Dickcissels, Bobolinks, and Cedar Waxwings have been seen.

South Bluff Oak Forest ◆
100 acres north of Sauk City with woods, meadows, sloping rock ridges, and bush cover. The breeding birds include American Redstart, Hooded, Mourning, and Chestnut-sided warblers, and Broad-winged Hawks.

Spring Green ◆
260 acres north of Spring Green not far from the Wisconsin River. A thick oak forest, rock ridges, and sandy areas provide habitat diversity.

Thousand's Rock Point Prairies ◆
8 acres southwest of Blue Mounds in two land parcels. They provide habitat for more than 25 nesting birds including Grasshopper, Vesper, Henslow's, Savannah, Song, and Field sparrows.

Toft Point ㉔

633 acres designated a State Natural Area and National Natural Landmark, owned by the University of Wisconsin-Green Bay. Located in Door County along Lake Michigan, the forest at Toft Point is home to Red-breasted Nuthatches, Winter Wrens, Olive-sided Flycatchers, and other species.

Waubesa Wetlands ㉕

193 acres of low marshy grass and wetlands southeast of Madison. The preserve is a nesting area for Sandhill Cranes, Great Blue Herons, American Bitterns, and American Coots. Blue-gray Gnatcatchers, Common Yellowthroats, and Common Grackles may be seen.

U.S. FISH & WILDLIFE SERVICE NATIONAL WILDLIFE REFUGES

Horicon ❶

Route 2
Mayville, WI 53050   414-387-2658

Bird List WI-2 Horicon Summary
216 birds listed, 112 nesting birds
Bird Chart pages 366-383

Totals by Season		s	S	F	W
Abundant	A	10	8	10	2
Common	C	85	62	82	14
Uncommon	U	5	53	6	23
Rare	R	11	7	12	4

Endangered Species: Bald Eagle

From Madison, take Hwy. 151 north. Go about 4 miles east on Rte. 49, turn right on Co. Road Z, and continue about 3 miles to the entrance sign. Follow signs to the headquarters.

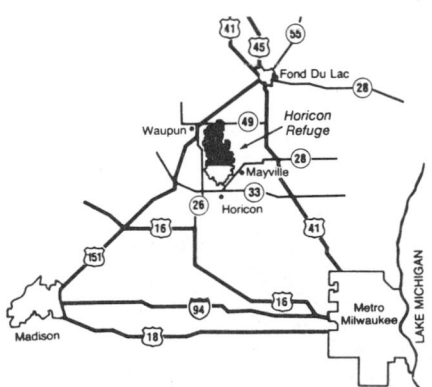

Habitat: 20,900 acres, of which 15,400 acres are wetland with predominantly cattail marsh and some shallow open water, 5,000 acres rare upland grasslands, and 500 acres rare woodland. The marsh is fed by the Rock River, intermittent streams, and groundwater springs. The refuge is part of the 31,000-acre Horicon Marsh, the largest freshwater cattail marsh

in the United States.

The marsh is used during spring and fall migrations by 21 species of waterfowl, of which 14 remain to breed. It is a major staging area for migrating Canada Geese and there is also a large resident flock. Flocks of Mallards, Blue-winged and Green-winged teals, American Wigeons, Ruddy Ducks, Northern Shovelers, Lesser Scaups, Gadwalls, and Northern Pintails also pass through on migration.

Pied-billed Grebes, American Bitterns, Cattle Egrets, Black Terns, Soras, and Virginia Rails are among the 112 species that breed on the marsh.

Area brochure, hiking, hunting, fishing, cross-country skiing, snowshoeing.
Spring, Summer, Fall

Necedah ❷

Star Route West, Box 386
Necedah, WI 54646   608-565-2551

Bird List WI-3 Necedah Summary
224 birds listed, 103 nesting birds
Bird Chart pages 366-383

Totals by Season		s	S	F	W
Abundant	A	12	8	14	4
Common	C	74	58	63	11
Uncommon	U	72	38	64	8
Occasional	O	26	16	29	14
Rare	R	28	24	29	20

Endangered Species: Bald Eagle, Peregrine Falcon

From the town of Necedah, take Hwy. 21 west onto the refuge. Follow the signs for about 4 miles to the headquarters.

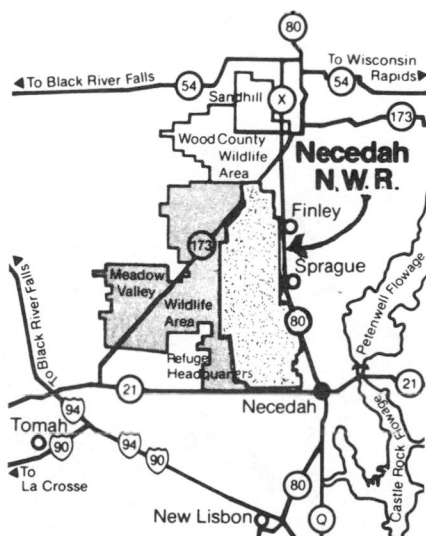

Habitat: 44,000 acres characterized by numerous ponds and marshy areas separated by sandy ridges and islands. A

network of old drainage ditches maintains water levels in man-made impoundments. Primary vegetation is jack pine-scrub oak mixtures on the uplands and aspen and scrub willow in the lowlands.

The spring and fall waterfowl migrations are the most interesting aspects of birding at Necedah, which is host to the greatest number of birds in late April. Tundra Swans may also be seen in the spring.

Some of the largest concentrations of the "Greater" Sandhill Crane occur on the refuge during spring and fall migration. Several pair nest on the refuge and their spring courtship dance may be observed.

Other spring courtship activities include the drumming of Ruffed Grouse and the American Woodcock's high flights at dawn and dusk. Wild Turkeys may occasionally be seen strutting for a flock of hens.

Bald Eagles gather on the refuge in the fall and overwinter with the Rough-legged Hawks.

Area brochure, auto tour route, hiking, photo blinds, cross-country skiing, limited hunting and fishing, berry picking.
Spring, Fall

Trempealeau ❸   (office at refuge)

Route 1, Box 326
Trempealeau, WI 54661   608-539-2311

Note: Access has been restricted due to bridge reconstruction on the main refuge access road. Contact the refuge office for permission to visit, and directions to an alternate access route, before visiting the refuge.

From Winona, MN, cross the Mississippi River on MN St. Hwy. 43, turn right (southeast) on WI Hwy. 35/54, and go approximately 8 miles to refuge sign. Turn right and go about 1 mile to visitor contact station.

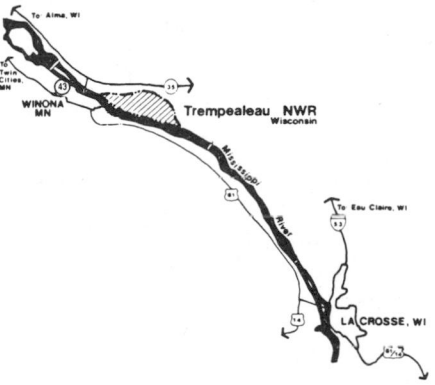

Habitat: 5,617 acres of the Mississippi

River floodplain. Approximately 80 percent of the refuge is composed of wetlands, and the remainder is scattered bottomlands, hardwoods, and a central upland area. The river valley is 3 to 6 miles in width and bordered by tall forested bluffs.

The floodplain supports thousands of birds ranging from waterfowl to warblers during migration periods. Other birds, including ducks, bitterns, Black Terns, and Double-crested Cormorants, remain to breed. Wading birds such as herons and egrets may be seen feeding in the shallow waters during the summer. The shrub edge that marks the border between two stages of plant succession, prairie and forest, attracts a large variety of passerines. The adjacent floodplain forest attracts Red-shouldered Hawks, Barred Owls, and their rodent prey.

Area brochure, auto tour route, nature trail, hunting, fishing, snowshoeing, cross-country skiing, mushroom, nut, and berry picking.
Spring, Fall

Upper Mississippi River Wildlife & Fish Refuge

La Crosse District   (office in town)
Post Office Bldg., Room 208
PO Box 415
La Crosse, WI 54601   608-784-3910

The refuge encompasses 195,000 acres of wooded islands, marshes, and water bodies extending 284 miles from Wabasha, Minnesota, to Rock Island, Illinois.

Refuge headquarters is in Winona, Minnesota (Winona District). See the Minnesota chapter for a complete description of the refuge, bird life, and habitat. See the Iowa and Illinois chapters for information on the McGregor and Savanna refuge districts.

Bird List WI-4 LaCrosse Summary
265 birds listed, 126 nesting birds
Bird Chart pages 366-383

Totals by Season		s	S	F	W
Abundant	A	28	24	24	4
Common	C	99	63	84	18
Uncommon	U	89	62	97	27
Occasional	O	13	11	16	18
Rare	R	27	18	15	34

Endangered Species: Bald Eagle, Peregrine Falcon

Habitat: The La Crosse district encompasses the eastern portions of pools 4, 5, 5A, 6, 7, 8, 9, 10, 11, and 12 on the Mississippi River (see Pool Map Locator below). They extend from Pepin (north of La Crosse) to the Illinois border adjacent to Dubuque, IA. Canvasbacks can be found in large flocks during fall migration. Pools 7 and 8 near La Crosse may harbor up to 75% of the continental population of this species.

Area brochure, pool maps, mammals, reptiles, and amphibians lists. Boating, back country use, hunting, fishing, camping, picnicking, swimming.
Spring, Summer, Fall

NATIONAL FOREST SERVICE

National Forest Service Eastern Region
310 West Wisconsin Avenue, Room 500
Milwaukee, WI 53203   414-291-3693

Map/Forest/City

1. Chequamegon
   /Park Falls   715-762-2461
2. Nicolet/Rhinelander 715-362-3415

BUREAU LAND MANAGEMENT

BLM Milwaukee District Office
PO Box 631
Milwaukee, WI 53201   414-291-4400

One of two district offices for the eastern states. The headquarters office is in Virginia.

STATE AGENCIES

Bureau of Wildlife Management
Department of Natural Resources
PO Box 7956
Madison, WI 53707   608-267-7472

Map/District/City

1. West Central
   /Eau Claire   715-836-2821
2. Lake Michigan
   /Green Bay   414-497-4040
3. Southern/Madison   608-266-2626
4. Southeast/Milwaukee 414-562-9500
5. North Central
   /Rhinelander   715-362-7616
6. Northwest/Spooner   715-635-2101

Department of Natural Resources Natural Areas

101 S. Webster Street
Madison, WI 53702   608-266-2277

Contact the department for current information and literature on State Natural Areas. Some of the areas are described in *The Places We Save*, published by the Wisconsin Field Office of The Nature Conservancy.

Wisconsin Division of Tourism

PO Box 7970
Madison, WI 53707   608-266-2161
from out-of-state call   800-432-8747

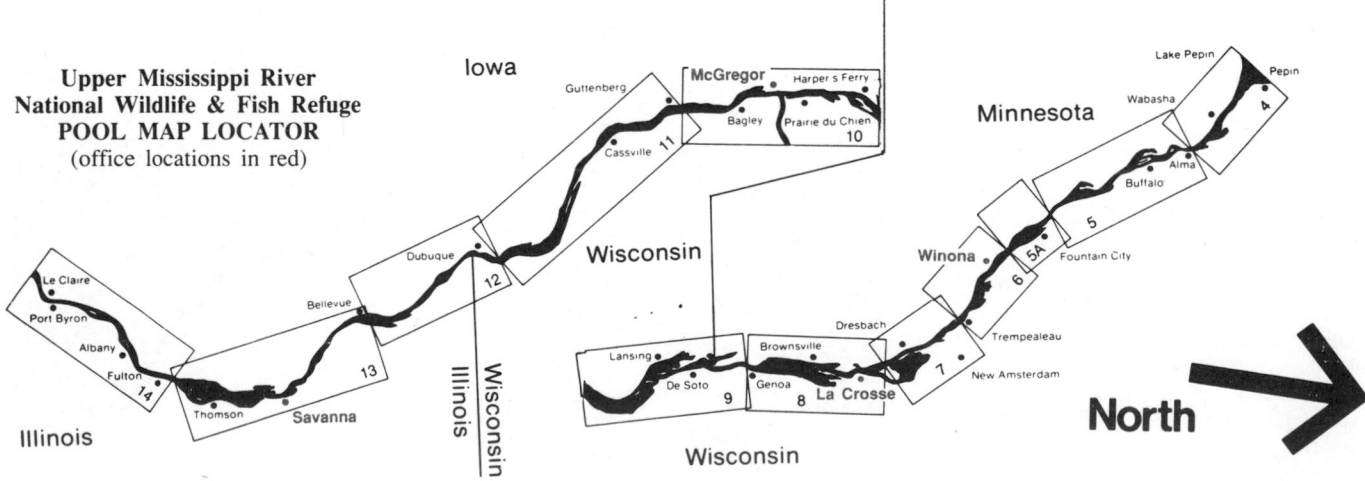

Upper Mississippi River National Wildlife & Fish Refuge POOL MAP LOCATOR
(office locations in red)

BIRDING HOTLINE
Statewide 307-265-2473

LOCAL BIRDING GROUPS
Map/Chapter/City
1. Alpine Audubon/Laramie
2. Bighorn Audubon/Sheridan
3. Cheyenne High Plains Audubon /Cheyenne
4. Fremont County Audubon/Lander
5. Murie Audubon/Casper
6. Jackson Hole Bird Club/Jackson

U.S. FISH & WILDLIFE SERVICE NATIONAL WILDLIFE REFUGES

Hutton Lake 1
c/o Arapaho NWR
PO Box 457
Walden, CO 80480   303-723-8202

Bird List WY-1 Hutton L. Summary
153 birds listed, 61 nesting birds
Bird Chart pages 366-383

Totals by Season		s	S	F	W
Abundant	A	12	11	7	1
Common	C	40	44	38	3
Uncommon	U	54	35	48	6
Occasional	O	14	14	25	7
Rare	R	8	5	10	6

Endangered Species: Bald Eagle, Peregrine Falcon

To reach Hutton Lake from Laramie, take St. Hwy. 230 south for 12 miles to Co. Road 37 (just before mile marker 13). Turn left on Co. Road 37 and go 7 miles east to the junction with Co. Road 34. Turn left and go approximately 3.5 miles northeast to the refuge entrance on the left.

Habitat: 2,000 acres containing 5 small lakes arranged in a half-moon shape in which a variety of aquatic plants provide food for waterbirds. A lush meadow is located in the western and northern parts of the refuge. The remainder is a native grassland interspersed with a greasewood-dominated alkali flat.

The refuge, established as a resting and breeding ground for migratory birds, is one of the chain of sanctuaries along the Central Flyway migration route. The most common birds are dabbling ducks, and 13 duck species breed at Hutton Lake.

Area pamphlet, mammals and reptiles lists.
Spring, Fall

National Elk Refuge 2
PO Box C   (office at refuge)
Jackson, WY, 83001   307-733-9212

Bird List WY-2 Jackson H. Summary
Jackson Hole Bird List
219 birds listed, 125 nesting birds
Bird Chart pages 366-383

Totals by Season		s	S	F	W
Abundant	A	9	8	5	0
Common	C	76	72	77	23
Occasional	O	90	82	86	41
Rare	R	27	34	36	21

Endangered Species: Bald Eagle, Peregrine Falcon, Whooping Crane

Headquarters is located on Broadway St. 1 mile east from the Jackson town square. The refuge lies just northeast of the town of Jackson and directly south of Grand Teton National Park.

Habitat: 25,000 acres of grassland meadows and swamps along the valley floor, timbered areas along the Gros Ventre River, and sagebrush and rock outcroppings along the foothills. The grasslands are managed by extensive irrigation and prescribed burning.

The varied habitat attracts a large number of different species. Marsh Wrens, Yellow-headed Blackbirds, and Common Yellowthroats feed and nest by the edges of the marsh. Sandhill Cranes and Long-billed Curlews haunt the meadows and open marshes. Trumpeter Swans nest at the Flat Creek Marsh, along Hwy. 26. Canada Geese, Mallards, Barrow's Goldeneyes, and Common Mergansers are among the most common waterfowl breeding at the refuge, while Green-winged and Blue-winged teals, Gadwalls, American Wigeons, and Buffleheads are more numerous during spring and fall migrations.

Common Ravens, Black-billed Magpies, and Bald Eagles are common winter visitors. Other raptors include American Kestrels, Ospreys, Northern Harriers, and Red-tailed, Swainson's, and Rough-Legged hawks.

Area brochure, hunting, fishing, limited hiking, mammals list.
Spring, Summer, Fall

Pathfinder 3
c/o Arapaho NWR
PO Box 457
Walden, CO 80480   303-723-8202

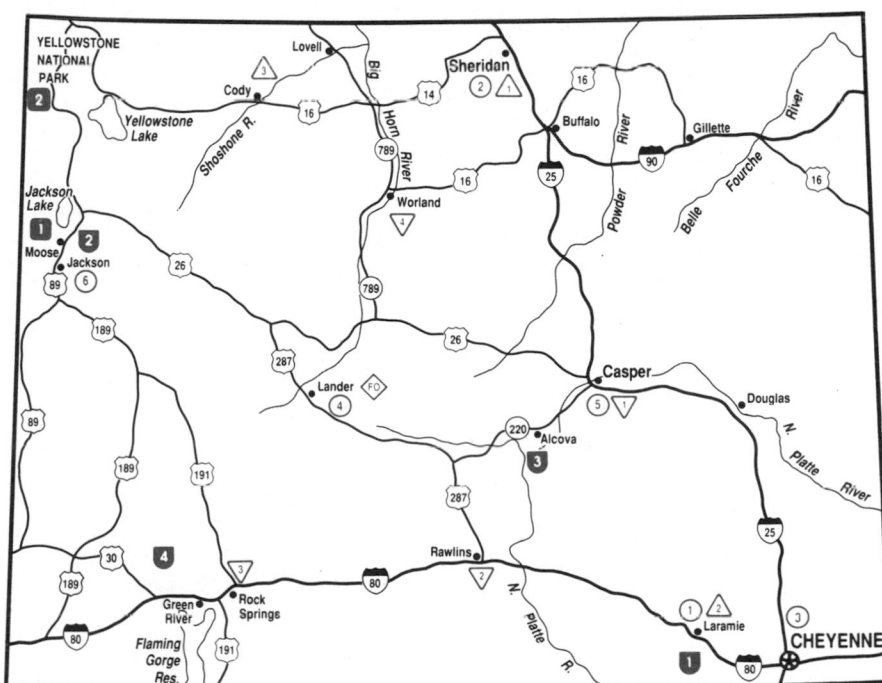

The refuge is located 50 miles southwest of Casper and 20 miles from the town of Alcova. The four refuge units are on or adjacent to Pathfinder Reservoir. St. Hwy. 220 passes by the northwest corner of the refuge. Acquire local maps for access roads and inquire locally for road conditions.

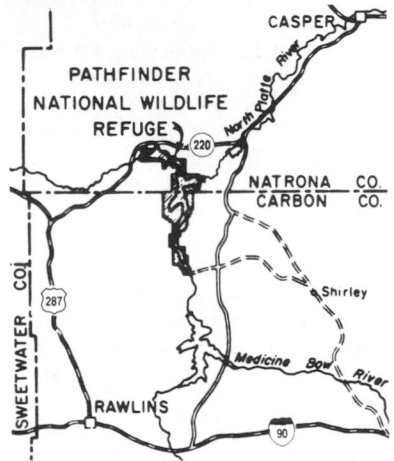

Habitat: 16,807 acres typical of much of the semi-desert lands of Wyoming. The reservoir, whose depth fluctuates as much as 50 feet, provides more water than other similar areas. The largest unit of the refuge includes all of the Sweetwater arm of the reservoir. The three small units are at Goose Bay, DeWeese Creek, and at the junction of Sage Creek and the North Platte River.

A large variety of waterfowl and other waterbirds migrate through Pathfinder in large numbers, while other species remain to breed. Nesting birds, although they are common in late spring and early summer, are not easily seen as they care for their eggs and young, and many are cryptically colored.

Area pamphlet, reptiles and mammals lists, fishing, hunting.
Spring, Fall

Seedskadee 4   (office at refuge)
PO Box 700
Green River, WY 83001   307-875-2187

Bird List WY-3 Seedskadee Summary
224 birds listed, 120 nesting birds
Bird Chart pages 366-383

Totals by Season		s	S	F	W
Abundant	A	4	9	2	3
Common	C	60	44	57	20
Uncommon	U	65	54	66	19
Occasional	O	64	62	52	14
Rare	R	12	11	13	16

Endangered Species: Bald Eagle, Peregrine Falcon

Refuge headquarters is located 37 miles north of the town of Green River. Drive west from Green River on I-80 to the La Barge Road, St. Hwy. 372, exit. Take St. Hwy. 372 north 28 miles to the headquarters turnoff. (Except for the main entrance road and the headquarters area tour route, all access roads are unimproved. 4-wheel-drive recommended.)

Habitat: 13,816 acres lying in the heart of the Great Basin country at 6,300 feet in elevation. Vegetation is typical of high plains desert with sagebrush covered benchlands and few trees. The grass-covered river bottoms have stands of cottonwood, willow, and other brush.

The area is a historical breeding ground for many waterfowl species including Canada Geese, Mallards, teals, Northern Pintails, and Gadwalls. There is a large nesting population of various raptors, including Golden Eagles. Sandhill Cranes and shorebirds are abundant. Great Blue Herons nest in five rookeries on the refuge. Sage Grouse are common throughout the year, and in summer their flocks can be seen near the river.

Area brochure, auto tour routes, fishing, hunting, boating (limited), hiking. Nearest services at La Barge or Green River.
Spring, Fall

NATIONAL PARK SERVICE

Grand Teton National Park 1
PO Drawer 170
Moose, WY 83012   307-733-2880

310,521 acres of sagebrush, alpine forests, marshes, meadows, and peaks. The park supports a herd of more than 3,000 elk during the summer.

This series of blue-gray peaks, which rises more than a mile above the sagebrush flats, was once a noted landmark for Indians and "mountain men." The park includes part of Jackson Hole, the winter feeding ground of the largest American elk herd.

Park brochure with map, park newspaper "Teewinot," covers current information and regulations. Bird-finding guide, species lists, and activity leaflets.
Summer

Yellowstone National Park 2
PO Box 168   307-344-7381
Yellowstone National Park, WY 82190

Bird List WY-4 Yellowstone Summary
209 birds listed, 160 nesting birds
Bird Chart pages 366-383

Totals by Season		s	S	F	W
Abundant	A	5	4	3	0
Common	C	57	53	49	15
Occasional	O	59	57	62	22
Rare	R	72	62	61	32

Endangered Species: Bald Eagle, Peregrine Falcon

2,219,784 acres include Old Faithful and some 10,000 other geysers and hot springs, making this the earth's most distinctive geyser area. Lakes, waterfalls, high mountain meadows, and part of the Grand Canyon also characterize Yellowstone.

Park brochures and map, climate summary, free seasonal newspaper, "Yellowstone Today", wildlife checklist.
Summer

NATIONAL FOREST SERVICE
Map/Forest/City

⚠ Bighorn/Sheridan	307-672-0751
⚠ Medicine Bow/Laramie	307-745-8971
⚠ Shoshone/Cody	307-527-6241

BUREAU LAND MANAGEMENT
BLM State Office
2515 Warren Avenue
PO Box 1828
Cheyenne, WY 82003   307-772-2111

Map/District/City

▽ Casper/Casper	307-261-5101
▽ Rawlins/Rawlins	307-324-7171
▽ Rock Springs /Rock Springs	307-382-5350
▽ Worland/Worland	307-347-9871

STATE AGENCIES

Wyoming Game & Fish Department
Information Section
Cheyenne, WY 82002   307-777-7735

Wyoming Travel Commission
I-25 at College Drive
Cheyenne, WY 82002   307-777-7777
from out-of-state call   800-225-5996

PRIVATE BIRDING GROUPS

Birding "hotlines", birding organizations and clubs are noted for each province and territory. There are more than one hundred local birding groups in Canada. Club leadership and locations change every year or two.

To contact local chapters of these groups about planned local birding activities, inquire at the listed office, or check with federal, provincial, or local wildlife or tourist agency offices about the existence of a local birding group and how to reach a chapter officer.

CANADIAN WILDLIFE SERVICE (CWS)

The responsibilities of the Canadian Wildlife Service are to monitor and protect wildlife, improve wildlife habitat, and accommodate a growing interest in nonconsumptive wildlife recreation. Their work is supported by private wildlife groups, such as Ducks Unlimited and Wildlife Habitat Canada.

There are three types of wildlife areas administered by the Canadian Wildlife Service: National Wildlife Areas, Migratory Bird Sanctuaries, and Ramsar Sites. These areas are listed under the Province or Territory where they are located. The map number and the size in acres of each area is also listed. If publications about visiting restrictions or wildlife populations are available, an asterisk * appears after the area name.

A land ownership code abbreviation is noted after the names of Migratory Bird Sanctuaries and Ramsar sites. The abbreviations are Federal (F), Provincial (P), or Private (Pr).

National Wildlife Areas (NWA) — The Canadian Wildlife Service manages forty-five National Wildlife Areas, all of which are Federally owned lands. The purpose is to enhance wildlife habitat and minimize the impact of human visitation and recreation activities. Access may be restricted due to the sensitivity of an area or the population it supports.

Migratory Bird Sanctuaries (MBS) — Migratory bird conservation is the primary purpose on the ninety-nine Migratory Bird Sanctuaries. A permit issued by the Canadian Wildlife Service must be obtained before entering any Sanctuary north of 60°N latitude. The timing, location, and intensity of any proposed visit or activity are subject to restrictions in order to minimize impacts on the birds

and habitats. As a matter of policy, CWS consults with the nearest community before issuing a Sanctuary Visitor Permit. Forty-five days should be allowed for permit consultation.

Ramsar Sites (RS) — Ramsar is a town in Iran where a conference was held in 1971 to draft a Convention on Wetlands of International Importance Especially as Waterfowl Habitat. Seventeen countries and several international organizations participated at the invitation of the Iranian government. One major objective was to "stem the progressive encroachment on and loss of wetlands now and in the future". The Ramsar Convention took effect in 1975 after ratification by 7 of the countries.

The intention of the founding countries was to draw international attention to threats of serious damage to wetlands that are recognized to be of international importance. Ramsar Site designation is a means of ensuring that the potential hazards of proposed development are thoroughly examined, and that all possible remedies or measures meant to reduce the impacts are fully explored, properly designed, and put in place before any change in status occurs.

Canada has the longest coastline of any country in the world and about 14% (385 million acres) of Canada's total area of 9,976,000 square kilometers are wetlands. The majority of those lands are north of 60°N. There are currently 30 Ramsar Sites in Canada. They may be part or all of a National Park (NP), National Wildlife Area, or Migratory Bird Sanctuary. Thirteen are separate areas, and seventeen overlap other jurisdictions. A site may be under combined Federal-Provincial ownership.

Listing Details — The numbered symbols on the map of Canada correspond to the numbers and land area names that follow. To the right of an area name, the size in acres is given. In Canada the typical unit of measurement used for land areas is the hectare. A hectare is equivalent to 2.5 acres in the United States.

PROVINCE & TERRITORY AGENCIES

Province and territory tourism and wildlife management agencies are excellent information resources. They offer free highway maps, tour guide books, species lists, commercial literature, and fishing and hunting regulations. Local office and information center locations within each province are available on request.

ALBERTA

Birding Hotline

Calgary   403-237-8821

Local Birding Group

Federation of Alberta Naturalists
PO Box 1472
Edmonton, Alberta, Canada T5J 2N5

CWS - Western & Northern Region

Environment Canada - CWS 403-468-8075
Twin Atria Bldg., 2nd Floor
4999 98 Avenue
Edmonton, Alberta, Canada T6B 2X3

(Region includes Alberta, Manitoba, Saskatchewan, and the Northwest Territories)

National Wildlife Areas

1 Blue Quills *		242
2 Meanook		529
3 Spiers Lake		158

Migratory Bird Sanctuaries

4 Inglewood (Pr)		636
5 Red Deer (Pr)		517
6 Richardson Lake (P)		50,505
7 Saskatoon Lake (P)		4,534

Ramsar Sites

8 Whooping Crane Summer Range (F)		6,718,804
9 Peace-Athabaska Delta (F) (NP)		1,277,746
10 Hay-Zama Lakes (P)		198,840
11 Beaverhill Lake (P)		71,781

Fish & Wildlife Division 403-442-2605
Dept. of Energy & Natural Resources
Main Floor, North Tower
Petroleum Plaza
9945 - 108 Street
Edmonton, Alberta, Canada T5K 2C9

Travel Alberta   in Alberta 800-222-6501
Dept. E   from the U.S. 403-427-4321
PO Box 2500   in Edmonton 427-4321
Edmonton, Alberta, Canada T5J 2Z4

BRITISH COLUMBIA

Birding Hotlines

Vancouver   604-876-9690
Victoria   604-592-3381

Local Birding Group

Federation of British Columbia Naturalists
1200 Hornby St.   604-687-3333
Vancouver, BC, Canada V6Z 2E6

CWS - Pacific & Yukon Region

Environment Canada - CWS 604-946-8546
5421 Robertson Road
Delta, British Columbia Canada V4K 3Y3

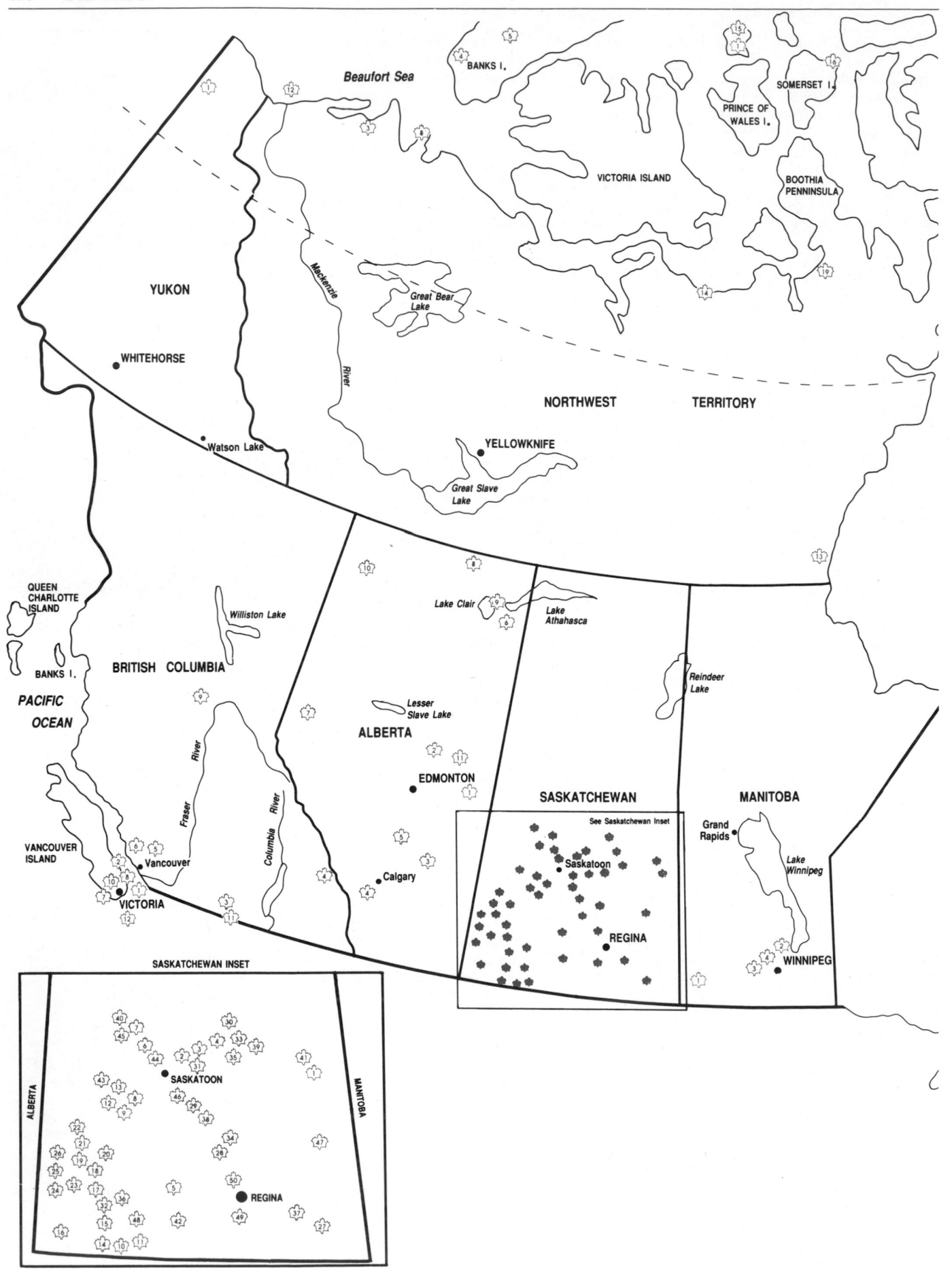

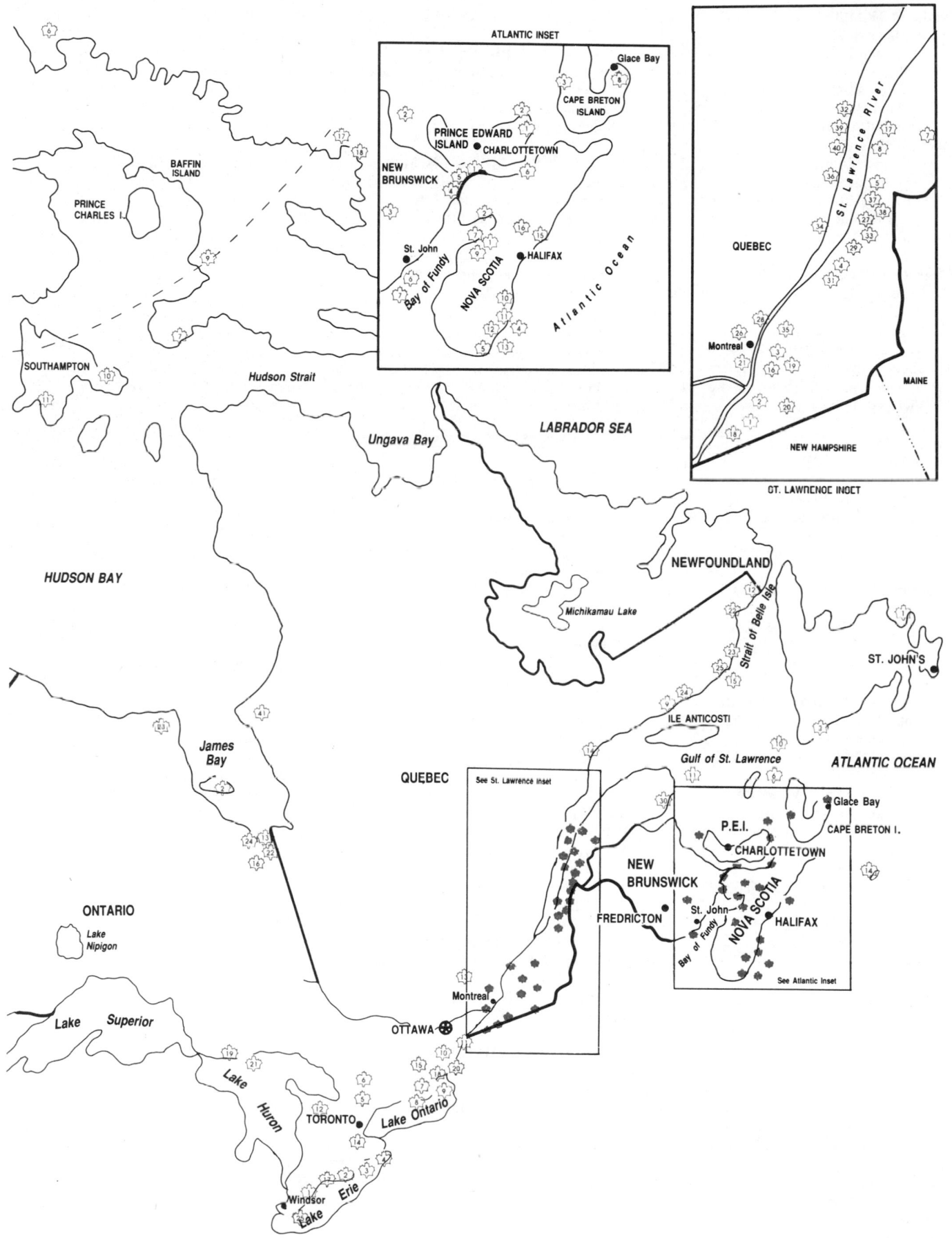

National Wildlife Areas

1	Alasken (RS)	739
2	Qualicum (three units)	208
	Nanoose Bay Unit	
	Rosewall Creek Unit	
	Marshall-Stevenson Unit	
3	Vaseux-Bighorn	1,957
4	Columbia (four units)	
	Wilmer Unit	1,166
	Spillimacheen Unit	509
	Brisco Unit	373
	Harrowgate Unit	425
5	Widgeon Valley	309

Migratory Bird Sanctuaries

6	Christie Islet (Pr)	not available
7	Esquimalt Lagoon (F,P,Pr)	517
8	George C. Reifel (F,Pr)	2,585
9	Nechako River (P,Pr)	716
10	Shoal Harbour (P)	597
11	Vaseux Lake (P)	1,114
12	Victoria Harbour (P)	6,761

Ramsar Site

Alasken (see NWA # 1)

Fish & Wildlife Branch　604-387-9737
Ministry of Environment & Parks
780 Blanshard Street
Victoria, BC, Canada V8V 1X5

Tourism British Columbia　604-387-1642
1117 Wharf Street
Victoria, BC, Canada V8W 2Z2

MANITOBA

Local Birding Group

Manitoba Naturalists Society　204-943-9029
302-128 James Ave.
Winnipeg, Manitoba, Canada R3B 0N8

CWS - Western
& Northern Region

Environment Canada - CWS　403-468-8075
Twin Atria Bldg., 2nd Floor
4999 98 Avenue
Edmonton, Alberta, Canada T6B 2X3

National Wildlife Areas

1	Pope	77
2	Rockwood	79

Ramsar Sites

3	Delta Marsh (P)	91,466
4	Oak-Hammock Marsh	
	Wildlife Area	not available

Department of Natural Resources
Box 24
1495 St. James Street　204-945-6784
Winnipeg, Manitoba, Canada R3H 0W9

Travel Manitoba
Business Development & Tourism
Winnipeg, Manitoba　204-945-3777
Canada R3C 3H8　800-665-0040

NEW BRUNSWICK

Local Birding Group

New Brunswick Federation of Naturalists
c/o New Brunswick Museum
277 Douglas Ave.
Saint John, NB, Canada E2K 1E5

CWS - Atlantic Region

Environment Canada - CWS　506-536-3025
31 West Main Street, Box 1590
Sackville, NB, Canada E0A 3C0

(Region includes New Brunswick,
Newfoundland and Labrador, Nova Scotia,
and Prince Edward Island)

National Wildlife Areas

1	Cape Jourimain *	1,455
2	Portage Island	1,085
3	Portobello Creek	4,863
4	Shepody * (three units) (RS)	2,419
	Germantown Marsh Unit	
	Mary's Point Unit (RS)	
	New Horton Unit	
5	Tintamarre * (three units)	4,917
	Jolicure Unit	
	Hog Lake Unit	
	Towers Goose Unit	

Migratory Bird Sanctuaries

6	Grand Manan (P,Pr)	994
7	Machias Seal Island (F)	40

Ramsar Site

Shepody Bay/Mary's Point
(see NWA #4)

Fish & Wildlife Branch　506-453-2345
Dept. of Natural Resources
349 King Street
Fredericton, NB, Canada E3B 5H1

Tourism New Brunswick
PO Box 12345　from NB 800-442-4442
Fredericton, NB, Canada E3B 5C3
from Canada & USA　800-561-0123

NEWFOUNDLAND & LABRADOR

Local Birding Group

Newfoundland Natural History Society
PO Box 1013
St. John's, Newfoundland
Canada A1C 5M3

CWS - Atlantic Region

Environment Canada - CWS　506-536-3025
31 West Main Street, Box 1590
Sackville, NB, Canada E0A 3C0

Migratory Bird Sanctuary

1	Terra Nova	3,460

Ramsar Site

2	Grand Codroy Estuary (P)	3,679

Wildlife Division
Newfoundland & Labrador　709-737-2630
Information & Education Branch
Building T-851, Pleasantville
PO Box 4750
St. John's, Newfoundland
Canada A1C 5T7

Dept. of Development & Tourism
(Newfoundland & Labrador)
PO Box 2016　709-576-2830
St. John's, Newfoundland　800-563-6353
Canada A1C 5R8

NOVA SCOTIA

Birding Hotline

Provincewide　602-852-2428

Local Birding Group

Nova Scotia Bird Society
Nova Scotia Museum
1747 Summer Street
Halifax, Nova Scotia, Canada B3H 3A6

CWS - Atlantic Region

Environment Canada - CWS　506-536-3025
31 West Main Street
Box 1590
Sackville, NB, Canada E0A 3C0

National Wildlife Areas

1	Boot Island	133
2	Chiqnecto * (two units) (RS)	2,520
	Amherst Point Sanctuary Unit	
	John Lusby Marsh Unit	
3	Sea Wolf Island	133
4	Port Joli/Port Hebert	126/104
5	Sand Pond	1,287
6	Wallace Bay *	1,446

Migratory Bird Sanctuaries

7	Amherst Point * (F,Pr)	1,710
8	Big Grace Bay Lake (P,Pr)	954
9	Kentville (F,Pr)	795
10	Port Joli (F,Pr)	1,114
11	Port Hebert (Pr)	1,392
12	Haley Lake	398
13	Sable River (Pr)	1,034
14	Sable Island (F)	9,345

Ramsar Sites

Chiqnecto (see NWA #2)
15	Musquodoboit Harbour Outlet	
	Estuary (P)	7,655
16	Southern Bight-Minas	
	Basin (F,Pr)	106,578

Dept. of Lands & Forests　902-424-5935
PO Box 698
Halifax, NS, Canada B3J 2T9

Nova Scotia Tourism　902-424-5000
5151 Terminal Road, 3rd Floor
PO Box 456
Halifax, NS, Canada B3J 2R5

ONTARIO

Birding Hotlines

Hamilton	416-648-9537
Long Point BO	519-586-3959
Ottawa	613-596-4888
Windsor (Detroit)	313-278-4288
Windsor (Point Pelee)	519-252-2473

Local Birding Group

Federation of Ontario Naturalists
355 Lesmill Road   416-444-8419
Don Mills, Ontario
Canada M3B 2W8

CWS - Ontario Region

Environment Canada - CWS 519-681-0486
152 Newbold Court
London, Ontario, Canada N6E 1Z7

National Wildlife Areas

2	St. Clair * (RS)	598
	Big Creek (two units)	2,026
	Big Creek Unit	
3	Hahn Marsh Unit	
4	Long Point * (RS)	8,031
5	Mohawk Island	5
6	Wye Marsh	116
7	Eleanor Island	2
8	Wellers Bay	101
9	Scotch Bonnet Island	2
10	Prince Edward Point	1,384
	Mississippi Lake	581

Migratory Bird Sanctuaries

11	Eleanor Island (F) (see NWA #6)	
12	Beckett Creek (P,Pr)	398
13	Chantry Island (F)	239
14	Southern James Bay (P)	100,573
15	Fielding (Pr)	5,170
16	Guelph (Pr)	2,466
17	Mississippi Lake (F,P,Pr)	1,710
18	Moose River (P)	5,766
19	Pinafore Park (Pr)	1,591
20	Rideau (F,Pr)	3,181
21	St. Joseph's Island (F,P)	3,738
22	Upper Canada (P)	10,578
23	Young Lake (Pr)	2,107
	Hanna Bay (F,P)	118,509

Ramsar Sites

	St. Clair * (see NWA #1)	
	Long Point * (see NWA #3)	
24	Southern James Bay (see MBS #13)	
	Polar Bear	
25	Provincial Park (P)	9,578,918
	Point Pelee National Park (F)	6,204

Wildlife Branch   416-965-4251

Ministry of Natural Resources
Queen's Park
Toronto, Ontario, Canada M7A 1W3

Ontario Travel

77 Bloor Street West
Toronto, Ontario
Canada M7A 2R9
all North America call   800-268-3735

PRINCE EDWARD ISLAND

Local Birding Group

Natural History Society of P.E.I.
PO Box 2346
Charlottetown, PEI, Canada C1A 1R4

CWS - Atlantic Region

Environment Canada - CWS 506-536-3025
31 West Main Street, Box 1590
Sackville, NB, Canada E0A 3C0

Migratory Bird Sanctuary

1	Black Pond (P,Pr)	517

Ramsar Site

2	Malpeque Bay (F,P,Pr)	97,193

Fish & Wildlife Division   902-892-0311

Dept. of Community & Cultural Affairs
PO Box 2000, 3 Queen Street
Charlottetown, PEI, Canada C1A 7N8

Prince Edward Island Tourism

PO Box 2000
Charlottetown, PEI
Canada C1A 7N8   902-892-7411

QUEBEC

Birding Hotline

Eastern Quebec (in French) 819-778-0737

Local Birding Group

The Province of Quebec
Society for the Protection
of Birds, Inc.   514-937-0224
4832 de Maisonnevue Bl. W.
Montreal, Quebec, Canada H3Z 1M5

CWS - Quebec Region

Environment Canada - CWS 418-527-9104
1130 de Galilee
Quebec, Quebec, Canada G1P 4B7

National Wildlife Areas

1	Lac Saint-François (RS)	3,299
2	Îles de la Paix	299
3	Îles de Contrecoeur	561
4	Cap Tourmente (RS)	5,510
5	La Baie de l'Isle-Verte (RS)	1,055
6	Pointe de l'Est	1,690
7	Pointe-au-Père	49
8	Îles de l'Estuarie (eight islands)	890

Migratory Bird Sanctuaries

9	Betchouane (Pr)	1,829
10	Bird Rocks (P)	2,386
11	Bonaventure Is. and Percé Rock (P)	5,329
12	Brador Bay (P)	1,988
13	Carillon Island (Pr)	1,989
14	Corossol Island (P)	1,869
15	Île à la Brume (P)	17,697
16	Île aux Herons (P)	2,386
17	Île aux Basques (Pr)	3,977
18	Îles de la Paix (F)	4,375
19	Mont Saint-Hilaire (Pr)	3,778
20	Philipsburg (Pr)	2,187
21	Senneville (Pr)	1,193
22	Saint-Augustin (P)	21,992
23	Îles Sainte-Marie (P)	17,896
24	Watshishou (Pr)	44,540
25	Baie des Loups (P)	15,907
26	Couvee Islands (F)	60
27	Toris-Saumons (P)	875
28	Île Saint-Ours (F)	1,193
29	Montmagny (P)	636
30	Saint-Omer (P)	239
31	Saint-Vallier (P)	1,591
32	L'Isle-Verte (F)	1,193
33	L'Islet (P)	239
34	Cap Saint-Ignace (P)	517
35	Nicolet (F)	11,334
36	Île aux Fraises (F)	795
37	Îles Pelerins (F)	16
38	Kamouraska Island (F)	147
39	Île Blanche (F)	795
40	Brandy Pot (F)	40
41	Boatswain Bay (F,P)	70,389

Ramsar Sites

Lac Saint-François (see NWA #1)
Cap Tourmente (see NWA #4)
La Baie de L'Isle-Verte
(see NWA #5)

Ministère du Loisir   418-643-2464

de la Chasse et de la Pêche
Direction des Communications Office
150, boul. Saint-Cyrille est
Quebec, QC, Canada G1R 4Y1

Tourism Quebec   514-873-2015

C.P. 20 000
Quebec, QC, Canada G1K 7X2
from eastern USA call   800-443-7000

SASKATCHEWAN

Birding Hotline

Regina   306-545-2825

Local Birding Group

Saskatchewan Natural History Society
PO Box 414
Raymore, Saskatchewan
Canada S0A 3J0   306-746-4544

CWS - Western & Northern Region

Environment Canada - CWS 403-468-8075
Twin Atria Bldg., 2nd Floor
4999 98 Avenue
Edmonton, Alberta, Canada T6B 2X3

National Wildlife Areas

1	Prairie (twenty-seven units, 1-27)	7,247
28	Stalwart *	3,608
29	Bradwell	304
30	Tway	237
31	St. Denis	892
32	Webb	1,055
33	Raven Island	232
34	Last Mountain Lake * (RS)	38,552

Migratory Bird Sanctuaries

35	Basin and Middle Lake (P)	34,678
36	Duncairn Reservoir (P)	6,164
37	Indian Head (F)	119
38	Last Mountain Lake * (F,P) (RS)	18,850
39	Lenore Lake (F,P)	35,115
40	Murray Lake (P)	4,653
41	Neely Lake (P)	3,181
42	Old Wives Lake (P)	103,635
43	Opuntia Lake (P)	5,567
44	Redberry Lake (P)	25,452
45	Scent Grass Lake (P)	2,505
46	Sutherland (Pr)	517
47	Upper Rousay Lake (P)	2,068
48	Val Marie Reservoir (F)	2,028
49	Wascana Lake (Pr)	398

Ramsar Sites

Last Mountain Lake *
(see NWA #34 and MBS #38)

50	Quill Lakes (P)	252,527

Saskatchewan Parks,
Recreation & Culture   306-787-2700
3211 Albert Street
Regina, Saskatchewan, Canada S4S 5W6

Tourism Saskatchewan   306-565-2300
2103 11th Avenue
Regina, Saskatchewan, Canada S4P 3V7

NORTHWEST TERRITORIES

Local Birding Groups
Contact Travel Arctic (listed below) for birding information.

CWS - Western
& Northern Region
Environment Canada - CWS 403-468-8075
Twin Atria Bldg., 2nd Floor
4999 98 Avenue
Edmonton, Alberta, Canada T6B 2X3

National Wildlife Area

1	Polar Bear Pass (RS)	648,390

Migratory Bird Sanctuaries

2	Akimiski Island (F)	1,338,989
3	Anderson River Delta (F)	430,687
4	Banks Island No. 1 (F)	8,159,598
5	Banks Island No. 2 * (F)	56,471
6	Bylot Island (F)	4,325,963
7	Cape Dorset (F)	102,999
8	Cape Parry * (F)	1,193
9	Dewey Soper (F) (RS)	3,244,671
10	East Bay (F)	463,695
11	Harry Gibbons (F)	592,145
12	Kendall Island (F)	240,944
13	McConnell River (F) (RS)	130,836
14	Queen Maud Gulf (F) (RS)	24,967,146
15	Seymour Island (F)	3,181

Ramsar Sites

Polar Bear Pass (see NWA #1)
Dewey Soper (see MBS #9)
McConnell River (see MBS #13)
Queen Maud Gulf (see MBS #14)

16	Rasmussen Lowlands (F)	1,193,040

Travel Arctic   403-873-7200
Northwest Territories
Yellowknife, NWT, Canada X1A 2L9

Wildlife Service   403-873-7200
Gov't. of the Northwest Territories
Yellowknife, NWT
Canada X1A 2L9
Arctic Hotline   800-661-0788

YUKON

Local Birding Group
Yukon Conservation Society
T.C. Richards Bldg.
PO Box 4163
Whitehorse, Yukon Territory
Canada Y1A 2C6

CWS - Pacific
& Yukon Region
Environment Canada - CWS
5421 Robertson Road
Delta, British Columbia
Canada V4K 3Y3   604-946-8546

Ramsar Site

1	Old Crow Flats (F)	2,453,686

Yukon Renewable Resources
PO Box 2703
Whitehorse, Yukon
Canada Y1A 2C6   403-667-5430

Tourism Yukon   403-667-5430
PO Box 2703
Whitehorse, Yukon, Canada Y1A 2C6

Where The Birds Are is designed to put you on the fast track to finding birds and birding knowledge. If you have never seen a bird checklist or were confused by the differences between available checklists —take heart! The Bird Chart pages that follow present 210 charted bird checklists in the same species listing order.

I have found it easier to learn about birds by zeroing in on those species that are abundant or common in my area, especially if they nest locally. The Bird Chart accentuates nesting, abundant, and common bird chart codes in every checklist in red, to help you zero in near where you live or plan to visit. The Bird Chart species nesting and abundance codes will help you plan ahead and ask questions of the professionals before you go into the field.

BIRD CHART LAYOUT

At the top of each page the state names are provided for general reference. Bird checklists are organized in a vertical format, in the same sequence as the areas are described in the state chapters. Each list is identified with the number code and abbreviated name used in the state chapter Bird List Summary.

Each group of 21 lists is displayed on 18 facing pages. The ten groups of lists are set off from each other by a vertical red or black color bar at the right of the last column in each group.

The bird lists used in this book had a total of 643 species from 61 family groups, although they averaged 223 species each.

I have limited the Bird Chart pages to the most common 584 species and 58 families. The few other birds and families in the database are covered in the Rare & Limited Species Supplement (pages 393-394).

Charted bird names appear in the order devised by the American Ornithologists' Union in the Sixth edition of the A.O.U. Checklist of North American Birds, published in 1983 and amended. The names of families and endangered species are in red.

BIRD CHART CODES

There are a few codes used for nesting, seasons, and bird abundance in the Bird Chart. While a season lasts for 13 weeks, a bird may be abundant for only a few weeks during that season. The codes for nesting and seasons are as follows:

- Nesting
- **s** Spring (March through May)
- **S** Summer (June through August)
- **F** Fall (September through November)
- **W** Winter (December through February)

The abundance codes indicate bird density, in other words, how many of a listed bird species are likely to inhabit a location during each of the four seasons of a year.

These codes are widely accepted indicators of approximate abundance and do not represent specific numbers of birds. While thousands of birds are required to consider some species abundant, only a dozen Bald Eagles can be considered abundant when they are observed regularly in a small area.

The actual bird count, counting period, and abundance legend used in the Chart were determined by those who prepared the original bird lists. According to some scientists there is a difference between a *printed* and a *published* bird list. A published list has been validated or corroborated by others in the scientific community.

I have not found a list with a description of any verification criteria.

But the bird lists that I included in the Bird Chart are considered by the people who prepared them as the best available.

The descriptions of abundance codes used in bird lists vary and two representative descriptions are given here to explain the codes.

A Abundant
1. Likely to be seen in large numbers
2. A common species which is very numerous

C Common
1. usually seen in proper habitat
2. certain to be seen in suitable habitat

U Uncommon
1. seen regularly in small numbers
2. present, but not certain to be seen

O Occasional
1. irregular occurrence
2. seen only a few times during a season

R Rare
1. rarely seen
2. seen at intervals of 2 to 5 years

There are other bird list abundance codes in use, including Accidental (recorded only once or twice) and Irregular (seen in some years and not in others). These codes have been deleted from the Bird Chart because they do not represent dependable information about where you are most likely to find those birds.

BLANK SPACES IN THE CHART

When there is a blank space (no legend code letter - A, C, U, etc.) in a column under one or more of the season headings, the bird was not observed or recorded during that season.

A solid line appearing in any bird list column shows that there is no record of the bird at a refuge. A quick scan of the Bird Chart pages can tell you which birds have never been recorded at that refuge.

STATE-NUMBER OF BIRD LIST / REFUGE, SANCTUARY OR PRESERVE / NESTING, ABUNDANCE BY SEASON	AL-1 Bon Secour •s S F W	AL-2 Choctaw •s S F W	AL-3 Eufaula •s S F W	AL-4 Wheeler •s S F W	AK-1 Adak Is. •s S F W	AK-2 Kanuti •s S F W	AK-3 Kenai •s S F W	AK-4 Kodiak •s S F W	AK-5 Tetlin •s S F W
LOONS									
Red-throated Loon	—	—	—	—	R	•U U U	U U R	•U U U U	•O O U
Arctic Loon	—	—	—	—	—	—	•C C U	—	—
Pacific Loon	—	—	—	—	R R R	•C C C	—	U U U	•C C U
Common Loon	U U A	—	O O U U	C R C C	•R R R R	•C C C	•C C C	•U U U U	•O O O
Yellow-billed Loon	—	—	—	—	—	—	—	R R U	—
GREBES									
Least Grebe	—	—	—	—	—	—	—	—	—
Pied-billed Grebe	•U O U U	O U	C U C C	•C U C C	—	—	—	—	—
Horned Grebe	U U C	—	R R O	U C C	U U U	•C C C	•U C C	C R C C	•C C O
Red-necked Grebe	—	—	—	O O	R R U	•C C C	•U C C	•U R U U	•U U U
Eared Grebe	R R	—	—	O O	—	—	—	—	—
Western Grebe	—	—	—	—	—	—	—	—	O R R
SHEARWATERS & PETRELS									
Northern Fulmar	—	—	—	—	R U	—	—	C C C C	—
Cory's Shearwater	—	—	—	—	—	—	—	—	—
Pink-footed Shearwater	—	—	—	—	—	—	—	—	—
Greater Shearwater	—	—	—	—	—	—	—	—	—
Sooty Shearwater	—	—	—	—	R	—	—	A A A R	—
Short-tailed Shearwater	—	—	—	—	R U R	—	—	A A A R	—
Manx Shearwater	—	—	—	—	—	—	—	—	—
Audubon's Shearwater	—	—	—	—	—	—	—	—	—
STORM-PETRELS									
Wilson's Storm-Petrel	—	—	—	—	—	—	—	—	—
Fork-tailed Storm-Petrel	—	—	—	—	R R	—	—	•C C C C	—
Leach's Storm-Petrel	—	—	—	—	R R	—	—	•U U U	—
BOOBIES & GANNETS									
Masked Booby	R	—	—	—	—	—	—	—	—
Brown Booby	R	—	—	—	—	—	—	—	—
Northern Gannet	O U C	—	—	—	—	—	—	—	—
PELICANS									
American White Pelican	O O O	—	R R	O	—	—	—	—	—
Brown Pelican	•A C A A	—	R R	—	—	—	—	—	—
CORMORANTS									
Great Cormorant	—	—	—	—	—	—	—	—	—
Double-crested Cormorant	A C A A	O O U	C U U C	U U U	—	—	•U U U	•U U U C	—
Olivaceous Cormorant	—	—	—	—	—	—	—	—	—
Brandt's Cormorant	—	—	—	—	—	—	—	—	—
Pelagic Cormorant	—	—	—	—	•C C C C	—	—	•C C C C	—
Red-faced Cormorant	—	—	—	—	•R R R R	—	—	•C C C U	—
ANHINGAS									
Anhinga	•U O U R	•U C C U	U U R R	R R R	—	—	—	—	—
FRIGATEBIRDS									
Magnificent Frigatebird	U C U R	—	—	—	--	—	—	—	—
BITTERNS & HERONS									
American Bittern	U U U	O O U O	U R O U	U U	—	—	—	—	—
Least Bittern	•U U U R	O O O	C C	U U	—	—	—	—	—
Great Blue Heron	•A A A A	C C A A	C C C A	C C A A	—	—	—	R R R	—
Great Egret	•C C C C	•C C A A	C C A A	U U U R	—	—	—	—	—
Snowy Egret	•A C A A	•O C C	U U O O	U U	—	—	—	—	—
Little Blue Heron	•U C C U	•C C U	C C U U	C C U	—	—	—	—	—
Tricolored Heron	•C C C C	—	U U O R	O O	—	—	—	—	—
Reddish Egret	•U U U U	—	R R R	—	—	—	—	—	—
Cattle Egret	•A C C U	•O C C	C A A U	C C U	—	---	—	—	—
Green-backed Heron	•C C C O	•U C C	C C U R	C C	—	—	—	—	—
Black-crowned Night-Heron	•U U U U	—	C U C C	U U U R	—	—	—	—	—
Yellow-crowned Night-Heron	•C C C R	•U U	U O R	•C C U	—	—	—	—	—
IBISES & SPOONBILLS									
White Ibis	•U O U O	•O U U	U U U U	O O O	—	—	—	—	—
Glossy Ibis	•O O O	—	R R R	R R R	—	—	—	—	—
White-faced Ibis	• O	—	—	—	—	—	—	—	—
Roseate Spoonbill	—	—	—	—	—	—	—	—	—
STORKS									
Wood Stork	O	O U O	R R	R R	—	—	—	—	—
SWANS, GEESE & DUCKS									
Fulvous Whistling-Duck	—	—	—	—	R	—	—	—	—
Black-bellied Whistling-Duck	—	—	—	—	—	—	—	—	—
Tundra Swan	—	—	R O	O O	—	•C C C	C C	•C C C R	U O U
Trumpeter Swan	—	—	—	—	—	•U U U	•C C C R	—	•U U U R
Mute Swan	—	—	—	—	—	—	—	—	—
Greater White-fronted Goose	O O	—	O O U	O O O	—	•C U C	U U	U U	U O U
Snow Goose	O U O	R R	U U C	U C C	—	C C	C R	—	O O

	AK-6 Togiak	AZ-1 Hassayampa	AZ-2 Cabeza	AZ-3 Cibola	AZ-4 Havasu	AZ-5 Imperial	AZ-6 Kofa	AR-1 Felsenthal	AR-2 Holla Bend	AR-3 Wapanocca	AR-4 White River	CA-1 Richardson
	• s S F W	• s S F W	• s S F W	• s S F W	• s S F W	• s S F W	• s S F W	• s S F W	• s S F W	• s S F W	• s S F W	• s S F W
	•C C C	—	—	—	R R	—	—	—	—	—	—	C C C
	•C C C	—	—	—	R R	—	—	—	—	—	—	C C C
	—	—	—	—	—	—	—	—	—	—	—	
	•C C C	—	—	—	O O O	O O O	—	U U U	—	O O O O	O O	U U C
	R R R	—	—	—	—	—	—	—	—	—	—	
	—	•U U U U	R	•C C C C	•C U C C	•C C C C	—	•U U U U	O O C U	C C C	•U U U U	R R U U
	U U U	—	—	—	R R	—	—	O O O	—	O O O	—	U U C
	•C C C	U R	R	C C O	C O C C	C O C O	—	O O O	—	—	—	U U C / R
	—	R R	—	U R U U	•C C C C	O O O U	—	—	—	—	—	C U C A
	R	—	—	—	—	—	—	—	—	—	—	—
	R R	—	—	—	—	—	—	—	—	—	—	—
	R R R	—	—	—	—	—	—	—	—	—	—	—
	—	—	—	C O C O	C O C U	O O O O	— R R	O O	O O	O O	O O	R R / U U C U
	•U C U	—	—	•C O C C	•A C A A	C U C A	—	O	O O	O O O	U U O	U U C C / U U C
	•C C C U	—	—	—	—	—	—	—	—	—	—	U U
	•R R R	—	—	—	—	—	—	•U U U	R	R R	U U U	—
	—	—	—	—	—	—	—	—	—	—	—	—
	—	R	—	R O	•O U U	•U U U U	—	U U	—	R R R R R	U U / •O O O R	—
	—	U O U U	R	•U U U O	•C C C U	•U C U O	R R	•C C C C	C C C C	U U U U	U U U U	C C C C
	—	O O	R R	•C C C C	•C C C C	•C C C C	R R	•O U U	C C C O	O O O	U U U	C C C C
	—	U O		•C C C C	•C C C C	U U U C		•U U U / •A A C	O O R / O U U	U U U	R R R / C C C R	—
	—	—		—	—	—		R O	—	—	R	
	—	O O	—	—	—	O O O		U U U	O O	U U U	C U C	U U U
	—	•U C U	—	•U U U O	•U C U O	•U U U O		•C C C	U U U	U U U	•U U U / O R O	R R
	—	•U U U O	—	•U U U U	•U C C U	•U U U U		•U U U O / •U U U	U U / U U U	U U U	U U U	U U U U
	—	—	—	—	—	—		R	R	—	R R	—
	—	U O	—	U U U R	U U U	O O O O		—	—	—	—	—
	—	O O	—	O O	R R	O O	—	A C	R	R	R	—
	—	—	—	—	—	R R R	—	—	—	—	—	—
	•C C C	—	—	O	R O O	O	—	R	—	—	R	—
	—	—	—	—	—	—	—	—	—	—	—	—
	•C C C	—	—	O O	R O R	R O O	—	O O O	O O	O O	R U	R
	C C	—	—	O O	O C C	O U	—	C C	C C	U U O	C U	—

BIRD CHART — Alabama/Alaska

STATE-NUMBER OF BIRD LIST / REFUGE, SANCTUARY OR PRESERVE / NESTING, ABUNDANCE BY SEASON (• s S F W)	AL-1 Bon Secour	AL-2 Choctaw	AL-3 Eufaula	AL-4 Wheeler	AK-1 Adak Is.	AK-2 Kanuti	AK-3 Kenai	AK-4 Kodiak	AK-5 Tetlin
SWANS, GEESE & DUCKS (cont.)									
Ross' Goose	—	—	—	—		—	—	—	—
Emperor Goose	—	—	—	—	C U C	—	R R	C U C	—
Brant	—	—	—	—	—	—	R R	A	R R
Canada Goose	O O O	—	C C A A	•U U A A	R	•C C C	•C R C	U U	•U U U
Wood Duck	•U U U U	•A C C A	C A A A	•C C A C	—	—	—	—	—
Green-winged Teal	U U U	O O	C A A	U C C	•C C C C	•C C C	•C C C	•C C C U	•C C C
American Black Duck	—	O	U R U U	•U U C C	—	—	—	—	—
Mottled Duck	•R R R R	—	—	—	—	—	—	—	—
Mallard	O O U	U C C	A C A A	•U U A A	•C C C C	•C C C	•C U C R	•C C C C	•C C C O
Northern Pintail	O O U	O	U A A	U R C C	•C U C U	•C C C	•A C C	•A C C U	•C C C
Blue-winged Teal	A A C	O U O	C O A U	C R C C	—	•U R U	—	R	•U U U
Cinnamon Teal	—	—	—	—	—	—	—	—	—
Northern Shoveler	U U U	O	C C A	C C U	R R R	•C C C	•U R U	C R R	•C C C
Gadwall	U U C	O U	U A A	U R C C	R R R	R R R	R R R	•U U U C	O O O
Eurasian Wigeon	—	—	—	—	U R R	—	—	U R R	—
American Wigeon	O O U	O U C	C O A A	U A A	R	•C C C	•U U U	•C C C U	•C C C
Canvasback	O U	R R	O O U	C C C	R R	•U U U	R R	—	•U U U
Redhead	O U	R R	O U U	U U U	—	•U R U	—	—	•O O O
Ring-necked Duck	O O U	O O	C A A	C C C	—	•U U U	—	R R R	•U U U
Greater Scaup	U U	—	R	O O	•C R U C	•C C C	•U U U R	•A C A A	•U U U
Lesser Scaup	U U C	O	U C C	C C C	—	•C C C	—	R R R	•C C C
Common Eider	—	—	—	—	•U U U U	—	R	•U U U U	—
King Eider	—	—	—	—	—	—	—	C R U C	—
Steller's Eider	—	—	—	—	R R R	—	—	C U C	—
Harlequin Duck	—	—	—	—	C U C C	•U U U	•U U U	•A C A A	•U U U
Oldsquaw	O U	—	—	R U U	U U C	•C U C	R U	A R A A	•U O O
Black Scoter	O U	—	—	R R	U U C	•R R R	R R R	•A U A A	—
Surf Scoter	O O	—	—	R	—	•C C C	R R R	C R C C	•U U U
White-winged Scoter	R	—	—	U U	U R R U	•C C C	R U U	A C A A	•C C U
Common Goldeneye	O U	—	R O	R C C	C U C	•C C C	C C U	•C U C C	•U U U
Barrow's Goldeneye	—	—	—	—	—	•C C C	•C C C	•C U C C	•U U U
Bufflehead	U U	—	O O	R U C	U R U	•C C C	U U	C C C	•C C C
Hooded Merganser	O O U	•O O O	U R U C	•U R C C	—	—	—	R R	—
Common Merganser	R R	—	R O O	R U U	—	•R R R	•U U C U	•C C C C	•O O U
Red-breasted Merganser	C O C A	O O	O U U	C U U	•C U C C	•R R R	•U U U	•C C C C	O O O
Ruddy Duck	U U U	O O	U U C	U C C	—	—	—	—	O R R
Masked Duck	—	—	—	—	—	—	—	—	—
AMERICAN VULTURES									
Black Vulture	•U O U U	•C C C C	U U U U	U U U R	—	—	—	—	—
Turkey Vulture	•U O U U	•C C C C	C U C C	U U U R	—	—	—	—	—
KITES, EAGLES, HAWKS & ALLIES									
Osprey	•C C C O	R R O	U U U O	U U	—	•R R R	•R R R	—	•U U U
American Swallow-tailed Kite	•U R	R O R	—	—	—	—	—	—	—
Black-shouldered Kite	—	—	—	—	—	—	—	—	—
Snail Kite	—	—	—	—	—	—	—	—	—
Mississippi Kite	•U O U	O O O	R	O O	—	—	—	—	—
Bald Eagle	• R R	R O	O O O U	R U U	•C C C C	•U U U R	•C C C U	•C C C C	•C C C U
Northern Harrier	C U C	O O	U C C	U C C	—	•U C U	•U U U	U R U	•U U U O
Sharp-shinned Hawk	U C U	—	U O U U	•U U C U	—	•C C C	•U U U	R R R R	•U U U
Cooper's Hawk	•U O C U	R R O O	U O U U	•U U C U	—	—	—	—	—
Northern Goshawk	—	—	—	—	—	•U U U U	•C C C C	•C C C C	•U U U O
Common Black-Hawk	—	—	—	—	—	—	—	—	—
Harris' Hawk	—	—	—	—	—	—	—	—	—
Gray Hawk	—	—	—	—	—	—	—	—	—
Red-shouldered Hawk	•U O C U	•U U C C	U U U U	•U U U U	—	—	—	—	—
Broad-winged Hawk	•C O A	•O O O O	O O O R	U C	—	—	—	—	—
Short-tailed Hawk	—	—	—	—	—	—	—	—	—
Swainson's Hawk	—	—	—	—	—	•R R R	—	—	O
White-tailed Hawk	—	—	—	—	—	—	—	—	—
Zone-tailed Hawk	—	—	—	—	—	—	—	—	—
Red-tailed Hawk	•C O C C	•U U C C	C U C C	•U U C C	—	•C C C	•U U U	—	•U U U O
Ferruginous Hawk	—	—	—	—	—	—	—	—	—
Rough-legged Hawk	—	—	—	O O	—	•C U C	R R R	•C C C	U O U
Golden Eagle	—	R	R R O	O O	—	•C C C	•U U U	•U U U U	U O U
CARACARAS & FALCONS									
Crested Caracara	—	—	—	—	—	—	—	—	—
American Kestrel	C C A	•U U C C	O O C C	•C C C C	—	•C C C	—	—	•U U U
Merlin	O U O	O O	R O O	U R U U	—	•U U U	U U U	R R U R	•U U U
Peregrine Falcon	U U O	—	R R R	R R R	•U U U U	•R R R	•U R R	•U U U U	O O O
Gyrfalcon	—	—	—	—	—	•U U U R	•U R R	R R R R	•U U U
Prairie Falcon	—	—	—	—	—	•U U U R	R R R R	R R R R	•U U U

	AK-6 Togiak	AZ-1 Hassayampa	AZ-2 Cabeza	AZ-3 Cibola	AZ-4 Havasu	AZ-5 Imperial	AZ-6 Kofa	AR-1 Felsenthal	AR-2 Holla Bend	AR-3 Wapanocca	AR-4 White River	CA-1 Richardson
	•s S F W	•s S F W	•s S F W	•s S F W	•s S F W	•s S F W	•s S F W	•s S F W	•s S F W	•s S F W	•s S F W	•s S F W
	C R C	—	—	—	R R	R R	—	—	—	—	—	—
	C R C	—	—	—	—	—	—	—	—	—	—	—
	•C C C	R R	—	O C C	U C C	O U C	—	O O O	C U C O	•C O C A	C C C	R R
	—	R R	—	—	O R O O	R	—	•C C C C	U U U U	•C C C C	•C C C C	—
	•C C C	C O C U	O	U A A A	O R C A	U R O C	R	C C C	C C C	C U C C	C C U	R
	—	—	—	—	—	—	—	O O O	U U U	C C C	O U U	—
	•C C C	•U O U U	—	U C C	•C U C C	U C C	—	A A A	A U A A	•A O A A	A O A A	C C C C
	•C C C	O O	O	C O C C	C O A C	U O C C	R O	C C O	C C C	C U C O	C C R	U C A
	—	C O U U	O	C C O	C O A O	•C U C U	O R R	—	—	—	U R
	•U U U	U O U	R O	C C C	O R C C	C U U C	O	U U U	U U U	C U C	U U U	R U
	•U R U	U U U	—	U C C	•U R C C	U C C	—	C C C	C C U	C C C	U C C	R R
	R R R	—	—	—	—	—	—	—	—	—	—	R R
	•C U C	U U U	O	U C C	U O C C	U C C	R	C C C	A A A	O C C	C C C	U U U
	R R R	—	—	U U U	O U U	O O O	—	U U U	R	U U U	O U U	U U C
	R R	R R R	—	U O C O	C O C U	U O U U	—	U U U	O O O	C C C	U U U	U R
	—	U O U	—	O U U	U R C C	U R U U	—	C C C	O O O	C C C	U C C	U R
	•C U C	—	—	—	R R	O O	—	—	—	R R R	—	U U C A
	R R R	R R R	—	U C U	C O C U	U R U U	—	U U U	O O O	O O O	O U U	C C A
	•C C C C	—	—	—	—	—	—	—	—	—	—	—
	C R U C	—	—	—	—	—	—	—	—	—	—	—
	C U C	—	—	—	—	—	—	—	—	—	—	—
	•C C C	—	—	—	—	—	—	—	R	R R	—	R
	•C C C	—	—	—	—	—	—	—	—	—	—	R A
	C U C	—	—	—	—	—	—	—	—	—	—	U C A
	C U C	—	—	—	—	—	—	—	—	—	—	R R U
	•C U C U	—	—	R U	O O O	O O O	—	—	R R R	O O U	O O	C C C
	—	—	—	—	R R	—	—	—	—	—	—	R U A
	•U R U	U O U	—	O C C	C C C	C U C	R R	U U U	—	C C C	O O O	U C A
	—	R	—	—	R R	R R	—	U O U U	U U	•C O C C	•U U U U	—
	•R R R	R R	—	C R C C	O O O O	U R U C	—	R	U U U	R R R	R	R
	•C C C	—	—	U R U U	C R C R	O O O O	—	—	—	R R R	R R	U U C
	—	•U U U U	—	C O C U	C O A U	•C U C C	—	U U U	R R	C C C	U U U	C A A
	—	—	—	—	—	—	—	—	—	—	—	—
	—	•C C C O	•C C C R	•C O C U	C C U O	•C C C O	C C C U	•C C C C	C C C C	U U U O	U U U U	—
	—	—	—	—	—	—	—	•C C C C	A A A A	U U U O	U U U U	C C C C
	•U U U	U R	—	U R U R	O R R O	U R U U	—	U U R	R	O O	U O U R	R R R
	—	R	—	—	—	—	—	—	—	—	—	R R R R
	—	—	—	—	—	—	—	—	—	—	—	—
	—	U O	—	—	—	—	—	•R R R	O O	O O	•O U U	—
	•C C C U	R R	—	—	R U	O O	—	O O	C U C	O O	•U O O U	—
	•C C C	U U U	U U C	O U U	U C C	C R C C	O O	O O U	C C C	U U U	U C C	R R R
	—	U O U U	O O O	U U U	U U C	O O O	C C C C	•U U U U	O O O	R R R	U U O	R C U
	—	•U U U U	U C U	U U C	•U R C C	U U U	O C U	•O O O O	O O O	R R R R	O O O	U U U
	•C C C U	—	—	—	—	—	—	—	—	—	—	—
	—	U O U	—	—	—	—	—	—	—	—	—	—
	—	•C C C C	—	—	—	R R R R	—	R	—	—	—	—
	—	R R	—	—	—	—	—	•C C C C	C C C C	O O O O	•U U U U	R R
	—	R R	—	—	—	—	—	U U C	O O O	U U U	•U U	—
	—	—	—	—	—	—	—	—	—	—	—	—
	R	U O	R	—	—	—	—	—	—	—	R R	—
	—	—	—	—	—	—	—	—	—	—	—	—
	—	•U U U	—	—	R R	—	—	—	—	—	—	—
	•R R R	•C C C C	•C C C C	•C U C C	•C C C C	•U U U U	•C C C C	•C C C C	C C C C	C U C C	•C U C C	C C C C
	—	R R O	R R	—	—	R	R	—	—	—	—	—
	•U C U	R O	—	—	R	O	R	—	R R	R	R	—
	•R R R	•U U U U	•U U U U	—	O O O U	O O	•U U U U	R R R	U U U	R R	O O O	—
	—	•C C C C	•C U C C	U O U U	•C U C C	O O U U	•C C C C	•U O O U	C C C C	U R U U	•C O O C	—
	•U U U	—	—	O O	—	R R	—	—	—	R O	—	—
	•R R R	—	—	R R R R	—	R R	R R R R	U	—	R	—	—
	•U U U U	—	—	—	—	—	•C C C C	—	—	—	—	—
	—	U O U U	O R O O	—	R R R	O R O O	•O O O O	—	—	—	—	—

STATE-NUMBER OF BIRD LIST / REFUGE, SANCTUARY OR PRESERVE / NESTING, ABUNDANCE BY SEASON	AL-1 Bon Secour • s S F W	AL-2 Choctaw • s S F W	AL-3 Eufaula • s S F W	AL-4 Wheeler • s S F W	AK-1 Adak Is. • s S F W	AK-2 Kanuti • s S F W	AK-3 Kenai • s S F W	AK-4 Kodiak • s S F W	AK-5 Tetlin • s S F W
CHACHALACAS									
Plain Chachalaca	—	—	—	—	—	—	—	—	—
PARTRIDGES, GROUSE, TURKEYS & QUAILS									
Gray Partridge	—	—	—	—	—	—	—	—	—
Chukar	—	—	—	—	—	—	—	—	—
Ring-necked Pheasant	—	—	—	R R R	—	—	—	—	—
Spruce Grouse	—	—	—	—	—	•C C C C	•C C C C	—	•C C C U
Blue Grouse	—	—	—	—	—	—	—	—	—
Willow Ptarmigan	—	—	—	—	—	•C C C C	•C C C C	•C C C C	•U U U U
Rock Ptarmigan	—	—	—	—	•C C C C	•C C C C	•U U U U	•C C C C	•U U U U
White-tailed Ptarmigan	—	—	—	—	—	—	•C C C C	—	•O O O O
Ruffed Grouse	—	—	—	—	—	•C C C C	—	—	•U U U U
Sage Grouse	—	—	—	—	—	—	—	—	—
Greater Prairie Chicken	—	—	—	—	—	—	—	—	—
Lesser Prairie Chicken	—	—	—	—	—	—	—	—	—
Sharp-tailed Grouse	—	—	—	—	—	•U U U U	—	—	•U U U U
Wild Turkey	—	U U U C	O O O O	•U U U U	—	—	—	—	—
Northern Bobwhite	•U U U U	•U U U O	A A A A	•C C C C	—	—	—	—	—
Scaled Quail	—	—	—	—	—	—	—	—	—
Gambel's Quail	—	—	—	—	—	—	—	—	—
California Quail	—	—	—	—	—	—	—	—	—
Mountain Quail	—	—	—	—	—	—	—	—	—
RAILS, GALLINULES & COOTS									
Yellow Rail	—	—	R	—	—	—	—	—	—
Black Rail	—	—	—	—	—	—	—	—	—
Clapper Rail	•C C C C	—	—	—	—	—	—	—	—
King Rail	•U O U U	—	U U U O	C C C U	—	—	—	—	—
Virginia Rail	U U U	O O	O R	C C	—	—	—	—	—
Sora	C O C C	—	O O O	C C	—	—	—	R R	
Purple Gallinule	•U O U	•O O	U U O R	O O	—	—	—	—	—
Common Moorhen	•C C C U	—	C C U U	U U O	—	—	—	—	—
American Coot	•C C A	O U C	C U A A	•A U A C	—	•R R R	—	—	•O O
LIMPKINS									
Limpkin	—								
CRANES									
Sandhill Crane	R R	—	R R	—	—	•C U C	•C U C	—	•C U U
Whooping Crane	—	—	—	—	—	—	—	—	—
PLOVERS									
Black-bellied Plover	C C	—	U R U O	U U	—	R R R	U R	C U U	O O
Lesser Golden-Plover	U U	—	U U	U U	R R R	•C C C	U U	C U C	•U U
Snowy Plover	U U U U	—	—	—	—	—	—	—	—
Wilson's Plover	•U U U	—	—	—	—	—	—	—	—
Semipalmated Plover	U C C	—	U O O	C C	—	•C C C	•U U U	•A A U	•C C U
Piping Plover	U U U	—	R R	U U	—	—	—	—	—
Killdeer	•A A A A	•O O O O	C C A A	•C C A C	—	•R R R	R	—	•O O
Mountain Plover	—	—	—	—	—	—	—	—	—
OYSTERCATCHERS									
American Oystercatcher	•U U U U	—	—	—	—	—	—	—	—
Black Oystercatcher	—	—	—	—	•U U U U	—	—	•C C C C	—
STILTS & AVOCETS									
Black-necked Stilt	•U U	—	—	—	—	—	—	—	—
American Avocet	U U O	—	R R R	U	—	—	—	—	—
SANDPIPERS									
Greater Yellowlegs	U U C U	—	C U U U	A U A U	—	•R R R	•A A A	•C C C	R R
Lesser Yellowlegs	U U U U	—	C U C U	A U A U	—	•C C C	•C C C	R C C	•C C U
Solitary Sandpiper	U O U	—	U O O R	C U C	—	•U U U	•U U U	R	U O
Willet	•C C C C	—	O R O R	U U U	—	—	—	—	—
Wandering Tattler	—	—	—	—	R R R	•U U U	•U U U	•C C U	•U U O
Spotted Sandpiper	C U C O	O O O	C U U O	•C C C R	—	•C C C	•C C C	•R U R	•C C U
Upland Sandpiper	C O C	—	U R R	U U	—	•U U U	—	—	O O
Whimbrel	U U R	—	—	R R	—	•C C U	U R U	U R R	U O
Long-billed Curlew	—	—	—	—	—	—	—	—	—
Hudsonian Godwit	—	—	—	R R	—	R	•R R R	—	R
Bar-tailed Godwit	—	—	—	—	U R	—	—	R	—
Marbled Godwit	R R	—	—	R	—	—	—	R	—
Ruddy Turnstone	U U U	—	—	U U	R U C	R	R R	R R R	R
Black Turnstone	—	—	—	—	—	—	•R R R	C C U U	—
Surfbird	—	—	—	—	—	•U U U	R R R	•C U U U	O O
Red Knot	U O U U	—	—	R	—	—	—	—	—
Sanderling	A U A A	—	O O O	U C	U R U	•R R	R R R	R R R R	—
Semipalmated Sandpiper	U U U U	—	U U U R	C U C R	—	•C U	R	R	U O
Western Sandpiper	U U U U	—	U R O U	U C	—	•R R	•C R U	U A U	R R

	AK-6 Togiak	AZ-1 Hassayampa	AZ-2 Cabeza	AZ-3 Cibola	AZ-4 Havasu	AZ-5 Imperial	AZ-6 Kofa	AR-1 Felsenthal	AR-2 Holla Bend	AR-3 Wapanocca	AR-4 White River	CA-1 Richardson
s S F W	•s S F W	•s S F W	•s S F W	•s S F W	•s S F W	•s S F W	•s S F W	•s S F W	•s S F W	•s S F W	•s S F W	•s S F W
	—	—	—	—	—	—	—	—	—	—	—	—
	—	—	—	—	—	—	—	—	—	—	—	—
	—	—	—	—	—	—	—	—	—	—	—	—
	•U U U U	—	—	—	—	—	—	—	—	—	—	—
	•C C C C	—	—	—	—	—	—	—	—	—	—	—
	•C C C C	—	—	—	—	—	—	—	—	—	—	—
	•R R R R	—	—	—	—	—	—	—	—	—	—	—
	—	—	—	—	—	—	—	—	—	—	—	—
	—	—	—	—	—	—	—	—	—	—	—	—
	—	—	—	—	—	—	—	•C C C C	—	•C C C C	•C C C C	—
	—	—	—	—	—	—	—	•C C C C	A A A A	•U U U U	•U U U U	—
	—	•A A A A	•C C C C	•A A A A	•A A A A	•A A A A	•C C C C	—	—	—	—	C C C C
	—	—	—	—	—	—	—	—	—	—	—	—
	—	—	—	—	—	—	—	—	—	—	—	—
	—	—	—	—	—	O O O O	—	—	—	—	—	—
	—	—	—	•O O O	•U U U	•U C U O	—	—	—	U U U	•O O O O	—
	—	U O R	—	O O O	•U U U	•C U C C	—	•U R R O	U U O	R R	O O O	R R R
	—	•U O U R	—	C C C C	C C U	C U C C	—	U U	U U	R R	O O	R R R
	—	—	—	—	—	—	—	—	—	R R R	•O O O	—
	—	•U U U U	—	•C C C C	•C C U	•U U U U	—	—	U U U	•U U U	—	
	—	•C C C C	—	•C C C C	•C C A A	•C C C A	—	C U C C	U C U	C R C C	U O U O	U C A
	—	—	—	—	—	—	—	—	—	—	—	—
	•C C C	—	—	O U	O O	O	—	—	—	—	—	—
	—	—	—	—	—	—	—	—	—	—	—	—
	•C C C	—	—	—	O O O	O O O	—	—	U R	R R	U U	C C C C
	•U U C	—	—	—	—	—	—	—	O	U U O	—	—
	—	—	—	O O	U C C R	O O O O	—	—	—	—	—	—
	•C C C	R R	—	O O	U O U	O O O	—	—	R R R	U U	U U	U U U
	R	•C C C C	O	•C C C C	•C C C C	•C C C C	O O	•U U U U	A A A A	•C C C U	•C C C C	C C C C
	—	—	—	—	—	—	—	—	—	—	—	—
	—	—	—	—	—	—	—	—	—	—	—	—
	—	O R	O	C U C	O C C	•U O U	R R	—	—	—	—	—
	—	—	R	U R U R	C U C R	U O U O	R R	—	—	R	—	R R R
	•C U C	U O	O	U O U U	U U C O	U O U O	R R	O O O	U U	U U	U U U	U U U U
	U U U	U U	—	—	O O O	O O O	—	C O C	U U	U U	U U U	R R
	R R	U U	R O	O O O	R U U	O O O	R	U O U	O O O	U U	U U U	—
	—	—	—	U O U	U C O	U O O R	—	—	—	O O	R R	C C C C
	•U U U	—	—	—	—	—	—	—	—	—	—	R R
	•R R R	U O	O O	C U C C	C U C U	C U C C	R O	U U U	C O C	U U	U U U	C R C C
	R R	—	—	—	—	—	—	O O	C O	U U	U O	—
	•R C U	—	—	—	R	—	—	R R	—	—	U U U	
	R R	R R	—	U U U	U U U	O O O R	—	—	—	—	—	U U U U
	R R R	—	—	—	—	—	—	—	—	—	—	—
	C U C	—	—	—	—	—	—	—	—	—	—	U U U
	—	—	—	U U O	O C O	U U O	—	—	—	R	—	R R
	C U C	—	—	—	—	—	—	—	—	—	—	C C C C
	•U U U	—	—	—	R	—	—	—	—	—	—	—
	R R R	—	—	—	—	—	—	—	—	—	—	C U U A
	R R	—	—	O O	R R R	O O	—	—	U	U U	U U U	
	•C C C	U U R	R O	C C	U C C R	C C C R	—	U U	O O	—	U O U R	U U C C

STATE-NUMBER OF BIRD LIST REFUGE, SANCTUARY OR PRESERVE / NESTING, ABUNDANCE BY SEASON	AL-1 Bon Secour •s S F W	AL-2 Choctaw •s S F W	AL-3 Eufaula •s S F W	AL-4 Wheeler •s S F W	AK-1 Adak Is. •s S F W	AK-2 Kanuti •s S F W	AK-3 Kenai •s S F W	AK-4 Kodiak •s S F W	AK-5 Tetlin •s S F W
SANDPIPERS (cont.)									
Least Sandpiper	U U U U	—	C U C C	A U A U	—	•C U U	•C C U	•A A R	•U U
White-rumped Sandpiper	O O O	—	U R	U C	—	—	—	—	U R
Baird's Sandpiper	R R R	—	R R O	O R O	—	•U U U	R R	U R	•U U U
Pectoral Sandpiper	U O C	—	C U C U	A U A R	R R	C U U	C C	R U C	U U O
Sharp-tailed Sandpiper	—	—	—	—	R R	—	—	C	—
Purple Sandpiper	—	—	—	—	—	—	—	—	—
Rock Sandpiper	—	—	—	—	•U U C C	—	—	•C U C C	—
Dunlin	C C C	—	U C C	U C U	R R	—	U R	C R U U	R
Curlew Sandpiper	—	—	—	—	—	—	—	—	—
Stilt Sandpiper	O O O	—	O O O	U U	—	—	—	—	R R
Buff-breasted Sandpiper	O R U	—	R R	O U	—	—	—	—	R R
Ruff	—	—	—	—	—	—	—	—	—
Short-billed Dowitcher	C O C C	—	O O U U	U U	—	—	•C C C	•C C U	—
Long-billed Dowitcher	U O U U	—	U U	C R U	—	•C U U	R	R	•U U
Common Snipe	C O C C	O U U	A U C C	C U C C	—	•C C C	•C C C	•C C C R	•C C C
American Woodcock	•U U U	•O U U	O R U U	U U C C	—	—	—	—	—
Wilson's Phalarope	R O	—	O R O	U R U	—	—	—	—	—
Red-necked Phalarope	—	—	—	R O	•C C	•C C C	•C C U	•C C C	•U U
Red Phalarope	—	—	—	—	R	—	—	U U U	—
SKUAS, GULLS, TERNS & SKIMMERS									
Pomarine Jaeger	O O O	—	—	—	—	—	—	C U C	—
Parasitic Jaeger	O O O	—	—	—	•U U	• R	U U R	•C U C	—
Long-tailed Jaeger	—	—	—	—	—	•C C C	•U R R	•U U U	•U U
Laughing Gull	•A A A C	—	O O R O	U O U	—	—	—	—	—
Franklin's Gull	R	—	—	•R R R R	—	—	—	—	—
Little Gull	—	—	—	—	—	—	—	—	—
Common Black-headed Gull	—	—	—	—	R	—	—	—	—
Bonaparte's Gull	U U C	—	U U U	U U U	—	•U U U	•U U U	U U U	•U U O
Heermann's Gull	—	—	—	—	—	—	—	—	—
Mew Gull	—	—	—	—	R R R	•C C C	•A A C	•C C A A	•C C U
Ring-billed Gull	C O C A	O	C O C A	U R A A	—	—	—	—	—
California Gull	—	—	—	—	—	—	—	—	—
Herring Gull	•U O U C	O	U O U U	U R C C	—	•U U U	•C C C	U R R R	U O
Thayer's Gull	—	—	—	—	—	—	—	R R R	—
Iceland Gull	—	—	—	—	—	—	—	—	—
Lesser Black-backed Gull	—	—	—	—	—	—	—	—	—
Western Gull	—	—	—	—	—	—	—	—	—
Glaucous-winged Gull	—	—	—	—	•C C C C	R R	•C C C R	•A A A A	—
Glaucous Gull	—	—	—	R R	R R	R R R	R R R	U R U U	R R
Great Black-backed Gull	—	—	—	R	—	—	—	—	R R
Black-legged Kittiwake	—	—	—	—	U R	—	R R R	•A A A U	—
Sabine's Gull	—	—	—	—	—	—	—	U U U	—
Gull-billed Tern	•U U U R	—	—	—	—	—	—	—	—
Caspian Tern	•U O U U	—	U O R R	U U U	—	—	—	—	—
Royal Tern	•C U C C	—	—	—	—	—	—	—	—
Elegant Tern	—	—	—	—	—	—	—	—	—
Sandwich Tern	•U U C C	—	—	—	—	—	—	—	—
Roseate Tern	—	—	—	—	—	—	—	—	—
Common Tern	•C O C O	—	R	O O O	•C C	—	—	—	—
Arctic Tern	—	—	—	—	•C C	•U C U	•A A U	•C C R	•U U O
Aleutian Tern	—	—	—	—	•C C	—	R R R	•U U	—
Forster's Tern	•C O C A	—	U U C U	U U U	—	—	—	—	—
Least Tern	•C U C	—	R O U	O O	—	—	—	—	—
Bridled Tern	—	—	—	—	—	—	—	—	—
Sooty Tern	—	—	—	—	—	—	—	—	—
Black Tern	C A A R	—	O U	U U C	—	—	—	—	—
Black Skimmer	•C U C C	—	—	—	—	—	—	—	—
AUKS, MURRES & PUFFINS									
Dovekie	—	—	—	—	—	—	—	—	—
Common Murre	—	—	—	—	R U U U	—	—	•C C A A	—
Thick-billed Murre	—	—	—	—	R R R	—	—	•R R R R	—
Razorbill	—	—	—	—	—	—	—	—	—
Black Guillemot	—	—	—	—	—	—	—	—	—
Pigeon Guillemot	—	—	—	—	•C C C C	—	—	•C C C C	—
Marbled Murrelet	—	—	—	—	•R U U R	—	—	•C C C C	—
Kittlitz's Murrelet	—	—	—	—	•R R	—	—	R U R R	—
Ancient Murrelet	—	—	—	—	U C R R	—	—	•U U R R	—
Cassin's Auklet	—	—	—	—	—	—	—	•U U U	—
Crested Auklet	—	—	—	—	R R	—	—	C A	—
Rhinoceros Auklet	—	—	—	—	—	—	—	R U R R	—
Tufted Puffin	—	—	—	—	•R U R R	—	—	•A A A R	—

	AK-6 Togiak	AZ-1 Hassayampa	AZ-2 Cabeza	AZ-3 Cibola	AZ-4 Havasu	AZ-5 Imperial	AZ-6 Kofa	AR-1 Felsenthal	AR-2 Holla Bend	AR-3 Wapanocca	AR-4 White River	CA-1 Richardson
	•s S F W	•s S F W	•s S F W	•s S F W	•s S F W	•s S F W	•s S F W	•s S F W	•s S F W	•s S F W	•s S F W	•s S F W
	•U U U	U U R	O	C U C C	U C C C	C C C C	—	O O	U U U	C C U	C U C R	A C A A
		—	—	—	—	—	—	—	U R	—	—	—
	R R R	—	—	—	U U	—	—	C O C	C C	U U	C U C R	—
	C U C R	—	—	O R	O O	O	—	—	—	—	—	—
	R R	—	—	—	—	—	—	—	—	—	—	—
	•C C C	—	—	—	—	—	—	—	—	—	—	—
	•C C C	—	—	O O O	R O R	O O O	—	—	U R	R U R	—	A R C A
	R	—	—	—	—	—	—	—	U U U	—	R R R	—
	R	—	—	—	—	—	—	—	—	—	—	—
	•U U U	—	—	—	—	—	—	—	—	C C	O O O	U U U
	U U U	—	—	U U C C	U U C U	U U C C	—	—	—	O O	O O O	U U U
	•C C C	U U U	—	U U U	C C C	U O U U	—	C C	C C C	C C U	C C	U U U
	R	R R	O	O O	U C C	U U O	—	•O O O O	—	U R U U	•O O O U	R
	•C C C	—	—	O O	U C U	R O O	—	—	C C	—	R R	R R
	U U U	—	—	—	R R	—	—	—	—	—	—	R R R
	U U	—	—	—	—	—	—	—	—	—	—	—
	•C C C	—	—	—	—	—	—	—	—	—	—	U U
	•C U U	—	—	—	—	—	—	—	—	—	—	—
	—	—	—	—	R	O O	—	—	U O	Π	—	—
	•C C C	—	—	O O	R R	O O	—	—	O	—	—	C U U
												C C R
	•C C C	—	—	—	—	—	—	—	—	—	—	C C A
	—	U U	R	C O C C	C U C C	U O U U	—	U U U	O C C	O O O	O U U	C C C A
	—	R R	—	O O	C U R	O O R	—	—	—	—	—	C C A
	R R R	—	—	—	R	—	—	U U U	O O	O O O	O O O	C C C
												U C C
	—	—	—	—	—	—	—	—	—	—	—	C C C A
	•C C C	—	—	—	—	—	—	—	—	—	—	C C A R
	U U U	—	—	—	—	—	—	—	—	—	—	R
	•C C	—	—	—	—	—	—	—	—	—	—	—
	R R R	—	R	—	R	R R	—	—	—	—	—	—
	—	—	—	U U R	U C U	O O O R	—	R R	—	R U	R R R	C C C
	—	—	—	—	—	—	—	—	—	—	—	A A
	R R	—	—	O	U U	O O	—	—	O O	O O O	—	R R
	•C C C	—	—	—	—	—	—	—	—	—	—	—
	•R R R	—	—	—	—	—	—	O O	—	O O	—	C C C U
	—	—	—	C O C R	U C U	O O O R	—	U U	C C C	O O O	R R	—
	—	—	R	C U C	U C U	U U U	—	O O	U O U	R O U	O U O	—
	•C C	—	—	—	—	—	—	—	—	—	—	—
	R R	—	—	—	—	—	—	—	—	—	—	R R R R
	R R R R	—	—	—	—	—	—	—	—	—	—	R R R
	•U U U U	—	—	—	—	—	—	—	—	—	—	
	•R R R	—	—	—	—	—	—	—	—	—	—	—
	R R	—	—	—	—	—	—	—	—	—	—	—
	•C C U	—	—	—	—	—	—	—	—	—	—	—

STATE-NUMBER OF BIRD LIST / REFUGE, SANCTUARY OR PRESERVE / NESTING, ABUNDANCE BY SEASON	AL-1 Bon Secour • s S F W	AL-2 Choctaw • s S F W	AL-3 Eufaula • s S F W	AL-4 Wheeler • s S F W	AK-1 Adak Is. • s S F W	AK-2 Kanuti • s S F W	AK-3 Kenai • s S F W	AK-4 Kodiak • s S F W	AK-5 Tetlin • s S F W
AUKS, MURRES & PUFFINS (cont.)									
Atlantic Puffin	—	—	—	—					—
Horned Puffin	—	—	—	—	•R U R R	—	—	•C C C R	—
PIGEONS & DOVES									
Rock Dove	•U U U U	—	C C C C	C C C C	—	—	—	—	O O
White-crowned Pigeon			—						
Band-tailed Pigeon	—	—	—	—					
White-winged Dove	O U R	—	—	—					—
Mourning Dove	•C C C C	•C C C A	C A A A	•C C A C	—	—	—	—	R R
Inca Dove									
Common Ground-Dove	•U U U U	—	U C U U	O O O	—	—	—	—	
White-tipped Dove			—						
CUCKOOS, ROADRUNNERS & ANIS									
Black-billed Cuckoo	U U	—	O	U U	—	—	—		—
Yellow-billed Cuckoo	•C U C	•O O O	C C O	•C C C	—	—	—	—	—
Mangrove Cuckoo	—	—	—	—	—	—	—	—	—
Greater Roadrunner	—	—	—	—	—	—	—	—	—
Smooth-billed Ani	—	—	—	—	—	—	—	—	—
Groove-billed Ani	—	—	—	—	—	—	—	—	—
BARN OWLS									
Barn Owl	•U U U U	R R	U U U U	•C C C C	—	—	—	—	—
TYPICAL OWLS									
Flammulated Owl	—	—	—	—	—	—	—	—	—
Eastern Screech-Owl	•U U C C	•O O O O	C C C C	•C C C C	—	—	—	—	—
Western Screech-Owl	—	—	—	—	—	—	—	—	—
Great Horned Owl	•C C C C	R R R R	U U U U	•U U C C	—	•C C C C	•C C C C	—	•U U U U
Snowy Owl	—	—	—	—	R R R	R R	R	—	R R
Northern Hawk Owl	—	—	—	—	—	•C C C C	U U U U	•U U U U	•U U U O
Northern Pygmy-Owl	—	—	—	—	—	—	—	—	—
Elf Owl	—	—	—	—	—	—	—	—	—
Burrowing Owl	R R R	—	—	—	—	—	—	—	—
Spotted Owl	—	—	—	—	—	—	—	—	—
Barred Owl	•O O O U	•O O O O	U U U U	•U U U U	—	—	—	—	—
Great Gray Owl	—	—	—	—	—	•R R R R	R R R R	—	•R R R R
Long-eared Owl	—	—	—	—	—	—	—	—	—
Short-eared Owl	R R	—	O O	U U	R R R R	•C C C	•U U U R	•U U U R	•U U O
Boreal Owl	—	—	—	—	—	•C C C C	U U U U	•C C C C	•U U U O
Northern Saw-whet Owl	—	—	—	—	—	—	R R R R	—	—
NIGHTJARS									
Lesser Nighthawk	—	—	—	—	—	—	—	—	—
Common Nighthawk	•C C A	•O O	U O O	•C C C	—	—	—	—	—
Pauraque	—	—	—	—	—	—	—	—	—
Common Poorwill	—	—	—	—	—	—	—	—	—
Chuck-will's-widow	•C C C	•O O	U U	•C C C	—	—	—	—	—
Whip-poor-will	U U O	O O	R	U U	—	—	—	—	—
SWIFTS									
Black Swift	—	—	—	—	—	—	—	—	—
Chimney Swift	•C U C	U U	C C C	•C C C	—	—	—	—	—
Vaux's Swift	—	—	—	—	—	—	—	—	—
White-throated Swift	—	—	—	—	—	—	—	—	—
HUMMINGBIRDS									
Buff-bellied Hummingbird	—	—	—	—	—	—	—	—	—
Ruby-throated Hummingbird	•C U C	•O U	U U R	•C C C	—	—	—	—	—
Black-chinned Hummingbird	—	—	—	—	—	—	—	—	—
Anna's Hummingbird	—	—	—	—	—	—	—	—	—
Costa's Hummingbird	—	—	—	—	—	—	—	—	—
Calliope Hummingbird	—	—	—	—	—	—	—	—	—
Broad-tailed Hummingbird	—	—	—	—	—	—	—	—	—
Rufous Hummingbird	—	—	—	—	—	—	—	—	R
Allen's Hummingbird	—	—	—	—	—	—	—	—	—
KINGFISHERS									
Belted Kingfisher	•C C C C	•C C U O	C C C C	•C C C C	—	•C C C	•U U U	•C C C C	•U U O
Green Kingfisher	—	—	—	—	—	—	—	—	—
WOODPECKERS									
Lewis' Woodpecker	—	—	—	—	—	—	—	—	—
Red-headed Woodpecker	•C U C U	•O O O O	O O O O	•C C C U	—	—	—	—	—
Acorn Woodpecker	—	—	—	—	—	—	—	—	—
Gila Woodpecker	—	—	—	—	—	—	—	—	—
Golden-fronted Woodpecker	—	—	—	—	—	—	—	—	—
Red-bellied Woodpecker	•C C C C	•U U O O	C C C C	•C C C C	—	—	—	—	—
Yellow-bellied Sapsucker	C C C	O O O	U U C	C C C	—	—	—	—	O R
Red-breasted Sapsucker	—	—	—	—	—	—	—	—	—

	AK-6 Togiak	AZ-1 Hassayampa	AZ-2 Cabeza	AZ-3 Cibola	AZ-4 Havasu	AZ-5 Imperial	AZ-6 Kofa	AR-1 Felsenthal	AR-2 Holla Bend	AR-3 Wapanocca	AR-4 White River	CA-1 Richardson
	• s S F W	• s S F W	• s S F W	• s S F W	• s S F W	• s S F W	• s S F W	• s S F W	• s S F W	• s S F W	• s S F W	• s S F W
	•C C U	—	—	—	—	—	—	—	—	—	—	—
	—	U U U U	—	—	—	—	—	•O O O O	—	U U U U	O O O O	C C C C
	—	•C C U	•C C C	•C A	•U C U	•C A	•C C C	—	—	—	—	R
	—	•C C C C	•C C C C	•C C C U	•C A C U	•C A C C	•C C C U	•C C C C	A A A A	•C C C C	•A C A C	C C C C
	—	•C C C C	—	—	•C C U U	—	•C C C C	—	—	—	—	—
	—	—	R	O O	•R R R R	•U U U U	O O	—	—	—	—	—
	—	—	—	—	—	—	—	R R / •C C O	U U / U U U	R R / •C C C	R / •C C O	—
	—	•O U	—	U	• U	• U	—	•C C C C	O O O O	U U U U	—	—
	—	•U U U U	R R	—	•O O O O	O O O	—	•R R R R	U U U U	O O O O	R R R R	C C C C
	—	—	—	—	—	—	—	•C C C C	C C C C	•C C C C	•O O U U	—
	—	•C C C C	•U U U U	•C C C C	•C C C C	•C C C C	C C C C	—	—	—	—	—
	•C C C C	•C C C C	•U U U U	•C C C C	•U U U U	•C C C C	•O O O O	•U U U U	U U U U	•U U U U	•U U U U	U U U U
	•U U U U	—	—	—	—	—	—	—	—	—	—	—
	R R R R	—	—	—	—	—	—	—	—	—	—	—
	—	•U C O	•C C U	—	•U U	—	C C	—	—	—	—	—
	—	—	R R	•C C C C	U U U	—	—	—	R	—	—	—
	—	—	—	—	—	—	—	•C C C C	C C C C	•C C C C	•C C C C	—
	R R R R	—	—	—	—	—	—	—	—	—	—	—
	•C C C	—	R O	—	R	R	R R R	U U U U	—	O O O	R R R O	O
	R R R R	—	—	—	—	—	R	—	—	—	—	—
	—	•U C U	•O U U	•C C C	•C C C	•C A C R	O O R	—	—	—	—	—
	—	—	—	—	—	—	—	•C C C	C C C	C C U	•U U U	—
	—	•U C U	•U U U R	•U U U	•U U U	•U U U	C C C R	•C C U	C C	O O	•U U	—
	—	R R	—	—	—	—	—	•U U U	R R	U U	O O	—
	—	—	—	—	—	—	—	•C C C	C C C	•C C C	•C C C	—
	—	O U	O O	U U	O O	O O	O	—	—	—	—	R R
	—	U O U	R R R O	O O O	•U U O C	O O O O	O O O O	—	—	—	—	U U U
	—	—	—	—	—	—	—	•C C C	O O O	C C U	•C C C	—
	—	•C C U O	R	•U U	•C C	•U U	O O	—	—	—	—	—
	—	•C C C C	—	•C C	C C	—	O O O	—	—	—	—	C C C C
	—	•C U U O	•C O U C	•C C	•C U	•C C U O	•C U U U	—	—	—	—	—
	—	U U	R	—	—	—	—	—	—	—	—	—
	—	O C	U	—	O O	O O	O O	—	—	—	—	R R
	—	—	—	—	—	—	—	—	—	—	—	C C C
	•C C C	U O U U	—	U C C	U C C	U C U	O O	•C C C C	C C C O	•C C C U	•U U U U	C C C C
	—	R R	—	—	R R	—	R R R R	—	—	—	—	—
	—	—	—	—	—	—	R	•A A A A	U U U U	•C C C C	•C C C C	—
	—	R R	—	—	—	—	—	—	—	—	—	—
	—	•C C C C	•C C C C	•C C C C	•C C C C	•C C C C	C C C C	—	—	—	—	—
	—	—	—	—	—	—	—	•A A A A	C C C C	•C C C U	•C C C C	—
	—	O U	—	O U U	O U U	U U U	—	A U C	C C C	C C C	U U C	R
	—	O O U	—	—	—	—	R	—	—	—	—	—

STATE-NUMBER OF BIRD LIST REFUGE, SANCTUARY OR PRESERVE NESTING, ABUNDANCE BY SEASON	AL-1 Bon Secour • s S F W	AL-2 Choctaw • s S F W	AL-3 Eufaula • s S F W	AL-4 Wheeler • s S F W	AK-1 Adak Is. • s S F W	AK-2 Kanuti • s S F W	AK-3 Kenai • s S F W	AK-4 Kodiak • s S F W	AK-5 Tetlin • s S F W
WOODPECKERS (cont.)									
Williamson's Sapsucker	−	−	−	−		−	−	−	−
Ladder-backed Woodpecker	−	−	−	−		−	−	−	−
Nuttall's Woodpecker	−	−	−	−		−	−	−	−
Downy Woodpecker	•C C C C	•O O O O	C C C C	•C C C C	−	•U U U U	•U U U R	•U U U U	•U U U U
Hairy Woodpecker	•U U U U	•O O O O	U O U U	•C C C C	−	•U U U U	•U U U R	−	•U U U U
Red-cockaded Woodpecker	−	−	−	−		−	−	−	−
Three-toed Woodpecker	−	−	−	−		•U U U U	•U U U U	•R R R R	•U U U U
Black-backed Woodpecker	−	−	−	−		•R R R R	R R R R	−	•R R R R
Northern Flicker	•C O C C	•U U O O	U U C C	•C C C C	−	•C C C	•R R R	−	•C C U O
Pileated Woodpecker	•C U C C	•U U O O	U U U U	•C C C C	−	−	−	−	−
TYRANT FLYCATCHERS									
Olive-sided Flycatcher	O U	−	−	R R	−	•U U U	•R U R	−	•U U O
Western Wood-Pewee	−	−	−	−	−	•U U U	•R R R	−	•U U O
Eastern Wood-Pewee	•C U C	−	O R R	•C C C	−	−	−	−	−
Yellow-bellied Flycatcher	O O	−	−	O	−	−	−	−	−
Acadian Flycatcher	•C O C	−	U C U	•C C C	−	−	−	−	−
Alder Flycatcher	−	−	−	−	−	•C C C	•C A A	−	•C C U
Willow Flycatcher	−	−	−	−	−	−	−	−	−
Least Flycatcher	U U	−	O	U U	−	−	−	−	−
Hammond's Flycatcher	−	−	−	−	−	•C C C	−	−	•C C U
Dusky Flycatcher	−	−	−	−	−	−	−	−	−
Gray Flycatcher	−	−	−	−	−	−	−	−	−
Western Flycatcher	−	−	−	−	−	−	−	−	−
Black Phoebe	−	−	−	−	−	−	−	−	−
Eastern Phoebe	C C C	O O O O	U C C	−	−	−	−	−	−
Say's Phoebe	−	−	−	−	−	•U U U	•R R R	−	•U U
Vermilion Flycatcher	−	−	−	−	−	−	−	−	−
Ash-throated Flycatcher	R O	−	−	−	−	−	−	−	−
Great Crested Flycatcher	•C C C	• O	C C R	•C C C	−	−	−	−	−
Brown-crested Flycatcher	−	−	−	−	−	−	−	−	−
Great Kiskadee	−	−	−	−	−	−	−	−	−
Couch's Kingbird	−	−	−	−	−	−	−	−	−
Cassin's Kingbird	−	−	−	−	−	−	−	−	−
Western Kingbird	U O C R	−	−	−	−	−	−	−	−
Eastern Kingbird	•A U A	•C C	C C	•C C C	−	−	−	−	−
Gray Kingbird	•U U U	−	−	−	−	−	−	−	−
Scissor-tailed Flycatcher	U U R	−	−	−	−	−	−	−	−
LARKS									
Horned Lark	−	−	−	•C O C C	−	•C C C	•U U U	−	•C U O
SWALLOWS									
Purple Martin	•A A C	•C C O R	C C O U	•C C C	−	−	−	−	−
Tree Swallow	A U C C	−	C U A O	C C	−	•C C C	•C A	•C C R	•C C O
Violet-green Swallow	−	−	−	−	−	•C C C	•C C	•C C R	•C C O
Northern Rough-winged Swallow	•C O C R	•O O R	C A A	•C C C	−	−	−	−	−
Bank Swallow	C U C	O R O	U A U	C C	−	•C C C	•C A C	•U A U	•U U O
Cliff Swallow	•U O U	O R O	R O	•C C C	−	•C C C	•R U	R	•C C
Barn Swallow	•A U A R	O O R	C C A	•C C C	−	−	−	R	−
JAYS, MAGPIES & CROWS									
Gray Jay	−	−	−	−	−	•C C C C	•C C C C	−	•C C C C
Steller's Jay	−	−	−	−	−	−	R	−	−
Blue Jay	•C U A C	•U U U U	C C C C	•C C C C	−	−	−	−	−
Green Jay	−	−	−	−	−	−	−	−	−
Scrub Jay	−	−	−	−	−	−	−	−	−
Pinyon Jay	−	−	−	−	−	−	−	−	−
Clark's Nutcracker	−	−	−	−	−	−	−	−	−
Black-billed Magpie	−	−	−	−	−	•C C C C	•C C C C	•C C C C	•U U U U
American Crow	−	•O O O O	C C C A	•C U A A	−	−	−	−	−
Northwestern Crow	−	−	−	−	−	−	−	•C C C C	−
Fish Crow	•C C C C	•U C U U	C C C C	−	−	−	−	−	−
Chihuahuan Raven	−	−	−	−	−	−	−	−	−
Common Raven	−	−	−	−	•C C C C	•C C C C	•C C C C	•C C C C	•C C C C
TITMICE									
Black-capped Chickadee	−	−	−	−	−	•C C C C	•U U U R	•C C C C	•U U U U
Carolina Chickadee	•C C C C	•O O O O	C C C C	•C C C C	−	−	−	−	−
Mountain Chickadee	−	−	−	−	−	−	−	−	−
Boreal Chickadee	−	−	−	−	−	•C C C C	•C C C U	−	•C C C C
Chestnut-backed Chickadee	−	−	−	−	−	−	−	−	−
Plain Titmouse	−	−	−	−	−	−	−	−	−
Tufted Titmouse	•C C C C	•O O O O	C C C C	•C C C C	−	−	−	−	−
VERDINS									
Verdin	−	−	−	−	−	−	−	−	−

	AK-6 Togiak	AZ-1 Hassayampa	AZ-2 Cabeza	AZ-3 Cibola	AZ-4 Havasu	AZ-5 Imperial	AZ-6 Kofa	AR-1 Felsenthal	AR-2 Holla Bend	AR-3 Wapanocca	AR-4 White River	CA-1 Richardson
	•s S F W	•s S F W	•s S F W	•s S F W	•s S F W	•s S F W	•s S F W	•s S F W	•s S F W	•s S F W	•s S F W	•s S F W
	—	R R	—	—	—	—	—	—	—	—	—	—
	—	•C C C C	•U U U U	•C C C C	•C C C C	•C C C C	O O O O	—	—	—	—	—
	R R R R	R R R	—	—	—	—	—	•C C C C	C C C C	•C C C C	•C C C C	C C C C
	R R R R	R R R	—	—	—	—	—	•U U U U	C C C C	•U U U U	•U U U U	—
	U U U U	—	—	—	—	—	—	•U U U U	—	—	—	—
	—	—	—	—	—	—	—	—	—	—	—	—
	—	•U U U A	•C C C C	U C C	U U C C	•U O C U	C C C C	•C C C C	C C C C	•C C C C	•C C C C	C C C
	—	—	—	—	—	—	—	•C C C C	U U U U	•C C C C	•C C C C	—
	R R R	U U	R R	O O	O O	O O	O O	—	—	R R	—	R R
	—	C U C	C C	C U C	C U C	C U C	C C	•C C C	C C C	•C C C	•C C C	—
	—	—	—	—	—	—	—	—	—	—	—	—
	—	—	—	—	—	—	—	•O O	—	•C C U	•C C	—
	U U U	—	—	—	—	—	—	—	—	—	—	—
	—	O O O	U U	C C	A O C	U U	C C	—	—	—	—	—
	—	U U	R	O O	C U R	C C	O O	—	—	R R	—	—
	—	U U	O O	—	R R	R R	R U U	—	—	—	—	—
	—	U U O	U O	O O O	O O O	O O O	O O O	—	—	—	—	—
	—	U U	•C C	C C	C C R	C C	C C	—	—	—	—	C C C
	—	•C C C C	R	C O C C	•C C C C	•C O C C	O O O	—	—	—	—	R R C C
	—	—	—	—	H H	—	—	U U U U	O O O	•C R C R	U O U	—
	R R R	•U U U U	•C O C C	C C C	•C R C C	•U U U	•C U C C	—	—	—	—	U U
	—	•U C U U	—	U U U U	•U U U U	•U U U U	R	—	—	—	—	R
	—	•U C U	•U U O O	•C C C R	•C C O R	•C C C R	•C C R	•C C C	C C	•C C C	•C C	—
	—	•C C U	•O O	O O	•U C	•C C	R	—	—	—	—	—
	—	—	—	—	—	—	—	—	—	—	—	—
	—	—	—	—	—	—	R R	—	—	—	—	—
	—	U U	—	—	—	—	U U U	—	—	—	—	U U
	—	•C C U	•C O C	•C C U	•C C U	•C C U	—	•U C U	C U U	•C C U	•C U C	—
	—	—	—	—	—	—	—	—	C C C	—	—	—
	U U U	U U O	•O O O O	—	O O	O	O R	C	O O R O	•C C C C	•C U C A	—
	—	O O	—	—	R R	—	—	•U U U	C C C U	•C C C	•U U O	—
	•C C C	O U	R	•A U A A	A U A A	A O A A	—	C C	O R O	C C	A C	—
	•R R R	C O C	R U O	U U	C U U O	U U	U U U U	—	—	—	—	A C A
	—	•C U C	R O	C C C O	•C C C O	•C C C O	O O	•C C C	C C C C	•C U C	•C C C	—
	•U C U	R R	R O	O O O	O O O	U U U	—	U U	U U U	U U	R R	—
	•U C U	•C U C	O O	•C C C	•C C O	•C C C	O R	R R	O U	R R	O O R	U U U
	R R	C O U	R O	C C C	U U U	U O U	R	•C C C	C C C	•C C C	•C C C	C C C
	•C C C C	—	—	—	—	—	—	—	—	—	—	—
	—	O O O	—	—	R R	—	R R	—	—	—	—	—
	—	—	—	—	—	—	—	•C C C C	C C C C	•A A A A	•C C C C	—
	—	U U U	—	—	R O O	R	O R O O	—	—	—	—	C C C C
	—	O O	—	—	—	—	R	—	—	—	—	—
	•U U U U	—	—	—	R R	—	—	—	—	—	—	—
	—	—	—	—	—	—	—	•U O U U	A A A A	U U U U	O R O O	C C C C
	—	—	—	—	—	—	—	•C C C C	C C C U	O O O	•U U U O	—
	•C C C C	•C C C C	•C C C C	—	•C C C C	A	O O O O	—	—	—	—	C R C C
	C C C C	—	—	—	—	—	—	•C C C C	C C C C	•C C C C	•C C C C	—
	—	O O O	—	—	—	—	—	—	—	—	—	—
	•C C C C	—	—	—	—	—	—	—	—	—	—	C C C C
	—	—	—	—	—	—	—	—	—	—	—	—
	—	—	—	—	—	—	—	•A A A A	C C C C	•C C C C	•C C C C	—
	—	•C C C C	•C C C C	•C C C C	•C C C C	•C C C C	•C C C C	—	—	—	—	—

STATE-NUMBER OF BIRD LIST / REFUGE, SANCTUARY OR PRESERVE / NESTING, ABUNDANCE BY SEASON	AL-1 Bon Secour • s S F W	AL-2 Choctaw • s S F W	AL-3 Eufaula • s S F W	AL-4 Wheeler • s S F W	AK-1 Adak Is. • s S F W	AK-2 Kanuti • s S F W	AK-3 Kenai • s S F W	AK-4 Kodiak • s S F W	AK-5 Tetlin • s S F W
BUSHTITS									
Bushtit	—	—	—	—	—	—	—	—	—
NUTHATCHES									
Red-breasted Nuthatch	U UC	—	R O	U UC	—	—	—	•UUUU	•RRRR
White-breasted Nuthatch	—	—	R	•UUUU	—	—	—	—	—
Pygmy Nuthatch	—	—	—	—	—	—	—	—	—
Brown-headed Nuthatch	•CCCC	•OOOO	CCCC	R R	—	—	—	—	—
CREEPERS									
Brown Creeper	U UU	OROO	O OU	CC	—	•RRRR	•URUR	•UUUU	RRRR
WRENS									
Cactus Wren	—	—	—	—	—	—	—	—	—
Rock Wren	—	—	—	—	—	—	—	—	—
Canyon Wren	—	—	—	—	—	—	—	—	—
Carolina Wren	•CCCC	•OUOO	CCCC	•CCCC	—	—	—	—	—
Bewick's Wren	R OR	—	R	•UURR	—	—	—	—	—
House Wren	C AC	O OU	O OU	UU	—	—	—	—	—
Winter Wren	O OO	R R	R OO	U CC	•UUUU	—	—	•CCCC	—
Sedge Wren	C CC	—	U UC	R R	—	—	—	—	—
Marsh Wren	•CUCC	—	U UC	O UR	—	—	—	—	—
DIPPERS									
American Dipper	—	—	—	—	—	•UUUU	UUUU	•CCCC	•UUUU
OLD WORLD WARBLERS & THRUSHES									
Arctic Warbler	—	—	—	—	—	•CCC	—	—	•UU
Golden-crowned Kinglet	O OU	—	UU	U CC	—	• RR	•UUUR	•CCCC	RR
Ruby-crowned Kinglet	C CA	O OU	U UC	C CC	—	•UUU	•AAC	RR	•UUR
Blue-gray Gnatcatcher	•AOAC	• UOR	CCUO	•CUC	—	—	—	—	—
Black-tailed Gnatcatcher	—	—	—	—	—	—	—	—	—
Eastern Bluebird	•UUUU	•OOOO	CCUC	•CCCU	—	—	—	—	—
Western Bluebird	—	—	—	—	—	—	—	—	—
Mountain Bluebird	—	—	—	—	—	•RR	—	—	•OO
Townsend's Solitaire	—	—	—	—	—	•RRR	—	—	•UUO
Veery	C C	—	O	U U	—	—	—	—	—
Gray-cheeked Thrush	C C	—	O R	U U	—	•CCC	•UCU	•RC	•UUU
Swainson's Thrush	A A	—	O R	U U	—	•CCC	•CCU	—	•CCU
Hermit Thrush	U UC	—	U UC	U CC	—	•UUU	•CCU	•AAC	•UUU
Wood Thrush	•AUA	•OOO	UCO	•CCC	—	—	—	—	—
American Robin	•CRCA	U UC	CUCA	•CCCU	—	•CCC	•CCC	RRRR	•CCUR
Varied Thrush	—	—	—	—	—	•CCC	•CCC	•CCCU	•UUU
Wrentit	—	—	—	—	—	—	—	—	—
MOCKINGBIRDS, THRASHERS & ALLIES									
Gray Catbird	A AC	OOOO	UUUO	•CCC	—	—	—	—	—
Northern Mockingbird	•AAAA	•CCUU	CCCC	•CCCC	—	—	—	—	—
Sage Thrasher	—	—	—	—	—	—	—	—	—
Brown Thrasher	•CUCC	CUUC	CCCC	•CCCC	—	—	—	—	—
Long-billed Thrasher	—	—	—	—	—	—	—	—	—
Bendire's Thrasher	—	—	—	—	—	—	—	—	—
Curve-billed Thrasher	—	—	—	—	—	—	—	—	—
Crissal Thrasher	—	—	—	—	—	—	—	—	—
Le Conte's Thrasher	—	—	—	—	—	—	—	—	—
WAGTAILS & PIPITS									
American Pipit	C C	—	C UC	R C	—	•CCC	•CCC	•CCCR	CUU
Sprague's Pipit	—	—	—	—	—	—	—	—	—
WAXWINGS									
Bohemian Waxwing	—	—	—	—	—	•CCCR	•CCCR	RR	•UUUO
Cedar Waxwing	C CC	R R	U OC	CRCC	—	—	—	—	—
SILKY-FLYCATCHERS									
Phainopepla	—	—	—	—	—	—	—	—	—
SHRIKES									
Northern Shrike	—	—	—	—	—	•UUUR	UUUR	•CCCC	•UUO
Loggerhead Shrike	•CUCC	•UUUU	CCCC	•CCCC	—	—	—	—	—
STARLINGS									
European Starling	•AAAA	•UUUU	CCCA	•AAAA	—	—	—	—	RR
VIREOS									
White-eyed Vireo	•ACAU	•OU	UCUO	•CCC	—	—	—	—	—
Bell's Vireo	—	—	—	—	—	—	—	—	—
Black-capped Vireo	—	—	—	—	—	—	—	—	—
Gray Vireo	—	—	—	—	—	—	—	—	—
Solitary Vireo	U UU	—	O OO	U U	—	—	—	—	—
Yellow-throated Vireo	•CUC	—	ORR	•CCC	—	—	—	—	—
Hutton's Vireo	—	—	—	—	—	—	—	—	—
Warbling Vireo	R R	O O	—	O O	—	—	—	—	—
Philadelphia Vireo	U U	—	RR	O U	—	—	—	—	—

	AK-6 Togiak	AZ-1 Hassayampa	AZ-2 Cabeza	AZ-3 Cibola	AZ-4 Havasu	AZ-5 Imperial	AZ-6 Kofa	AR-1 Felsenthal	AR-2 Holla Bend	AR-3 Wapanocca	AR-4 White River	CA-1 Richardson
	•s S F W	•s S F W	•s S F W	•s S F W	•s S F W	•s S F W	•s S F W	•s S F W	•s S F W	•s S F W	•s S F W	•s S F W
	—	R	—	—	R R	—	—	—	—	—	—	C C C C
	—	U U	—	—	R R	R	O	O	—	U UR	R	U UU
	—	U UC	—	—	—	—	—	•U U U U	O O O O	O O O O	•U U U U	—
	—	—	—	—	—	—	—	U U U C	—	—	—	—
	—	U UU	—	—	U U	—	R	O OC	—	U U UU	O OU	R R
	—	•C C C C	•C C C C	•U U U U	•U U U U	•O OO	•C C C C	—	—	—	—	—
	—	•U U U U	•C U C C	•U U U U	•U O C C	•U O U U	•C C C C	—	—	—	—	—
	—	•U U U U	•U U U U	—	•C C C C	—	•C C C C	—	—	—	—	—
	—	U UC	R U	O OO	•U U U C	O OO	O O	•A A A A	A C C C	•C C C C	•C C C C	—
	—	U UU	C CC	C CC	U CC	C CU	C CU	•U U U U	O O	R R R	U R U U	C C C C
	U U U	O UU	—	—	O OO	—	—	U UU	U U	R O O	U U UO	U UU
	—	—	—	—	—	—	—	O O O	U	—	O OR	—
	—	U O U U	—	C C C C	•C C C C	•C C C C	—	O OO	U	—	O OR	UU
	•C C C C	—	—	—	—	—	—	—	—	—	—	—
	•C C C	—	—	—	—	—	—	—	—	—	—	—
	R R R	U U	—	—	R R	—	—	U CC	O OO	C CU	C UC	U UU
	•C C U	U UC	C CC	C CC	C CA	A AA	C CC	C CC	O UU	C CC	C CC	U CC
	—	U UU	—	U UU	U UU	C CC	•U U U U	•C CU	C C	•C CU	•C C	—
	—	•U U U U	•C C C C	•C C C C	•C C C C	•C C C C	•C C C C	—	—	—	—	—
	—	U UC	R	O O	U U	O O	O O	•C C C C	U U U U	—	•U U U U	—
	—	O O	O	O OO	U U	O O	O O	—	—	—	—	—
	—	O U	R RO	O OO	O OO	O OO	O OR	—	—	R R	—	—
	•C C C	—	—	—	—	—	—	—	O O	U U	O O	—
	R R R	—	C	U U	U O	O R	U R	—	O	C C	U O	R R
	•U U U	O OU	U UO	U UU	U UU	U UU	O UO	O OC	O OO	U UU	C OC	C CC
	—	—	—	—	—	—	—	•C C C	C C C	•C C C	•C C C	—
	•C C C	O OU	R RO	U U	O UU	O OO	O UO	•C C C A	C C A C	•A C A A	•C U U A	C C C A
	•C C C	—	—	—	R R	—	—	—	—	—	—	R R
	—	—	—	—	—	—	—	—	—	—	—	U U U U
	—	—	—	—	—	—	R	•C C C	C C C	•C U C	•O O O R	—
	—	•U U U U	•C O C C	•C C C C	•C C C C	•O O O O	•C U C U	•A A A A	C C C C	•C C C C	•U U C C	U U R R
	—	O UU	U U	O OO	U UO	O OO	O OO	—	—	—	—	—
	—	—	—	—	—	—	—	•C C C C	C C C U	•C C C C	•C U C C	—
	—	U R O U	O O	—	U U U	R	O O	—	—	—	—	—
	—	•C C C C	•C C C C	—	—	—	O O O O	—	—	—	—	—
	—	•U U U U	•U U U U	•C C C C	•C C C C	•C C C C	O O O O	—	—	—	—	—
	—	—	U U U U	—	—	—	U U	—	—	—	—	—
	•C C C	U U C	O	C C C	U C C	C C C	R	U UU	O OO	U U R	O RO	U UU
	—	R	—	—	—	—	—	—	—	—	R R	—
	U R U	—	—	—	—	—	—	—	—	—	—	—
	—	U U C	—	O OO	R R	O OO	O O	C OC	C CC	C OU	C OC	C CC
	—	•C U O C	•C R C C	•C U C C	•C O U C	•C U C C	•C U C C	—	—	—	—	—
	•U U U	—	—	—	—	—	—	—	—	—	—	—
	—	•U U U U	•C U C C	•C C C C	•C C C C	•C C C C	•C C C C	•U U U U	C C C C	•U U U U	•U U U C	—
	—	•C U C C	R	—	•C U C C	•O U O O	O O	•C C C C	C C C A	•C C C C	•A C A A	A A C C
	—	•U C U	R	O O O	•U U U	•O O O	—	•C C U R	C O U	•C C C	•C C U	—
	—	U O	U U U	—	R	—	R O	—	U U	—	R R	—
	—	U U C	O	U U R	U U R	U U O	O O	U U U	R	—	U U R	—
	—	R O R	—	—	R	—	R	•U U U	C O U	•C U U	•C C O	C C C C
	—	U C O	C C	C C C	C U C	C C	—	—	O O R	O O O	O R O	C C C
	—	—	—	—	—	—	—	O O	O	O	U U	O O

STATE-NUMBER OF BIRD LIST / REFUGE, SANCTUARY OR PRESERVE / NESTING, ABUNDANCE BY SEASON	AL-1 Bon Secour • s S F W	AL-2 Choctaw • s S F W	AL-3 Eufaula • s S F W	AL-4 Wheeler • s S F W	AK-1 Adak Is. • s S F W	AK-2 Kanuti • s S F W	AK-3 Kenai • s S F W	AK-4 Kodiak • s S F W	AK-5 Tetlin • s S F W
VIREOS (cont.)									
Red-eyed Vireo	•A UA	•O O O	U C U	•C C C	—	—	—	—	—
Black-whiskered Vireo	O	—	—	—	—	—	—	—	—
WOOD-WARBLERS									
Bachman's Warbler	—	—	—	—	—	—	—	—	—
Blue-winged Warbler	U U U C	—	—	U U	—	—	—	—	—
Golden-winged Warbler	U U U	—	—	U U	—	—	—	—	—
Tennessee Warbler	C U A	—	R O	C C	—	—	—	—	R R
Orange-crowned Warbler	U C U	—	O OU	U UO	—	•C C C	•C C U	•C C R	•U U O
Nashville Warbler	U U	—	R	U C	—	—	—	—	—
Virginia's Warbler	—	—	—	—	—	—	—	—	—
Lucy's Warbler	—	—	—	—	—	—	—	—	—
Northern Parula	•A UA	—	C C O	C U C	—	—	—	—	—
Tropical Parula	—	—	—	—	—	—	—	—	—
Yellow Warbler	C U C	—	O O	•C U C R	—	•C C C	•U U R	•R A R	•C C O
Chestnut-sided Warbler	U C	—	—	U U	—	—	—	—	—
Magnolia Warbler	C A	—	R O	C C	—	—	—	—	—
Cape May Warbler	U O	—	R	U U	—	—	—	—	—
Black-throated Blue Warbler	U U	—	—	—	—	—	—	—	—
Yellow-rumped Warbler	C CA	U UU	C CA	•C CC	—	•C C C	•A A C	R U R	•C C O
Black-throated Gray Warbler	R	—	—	—	—	—	—	—	—
Townsend's Warbler	—	—	—	—	—	•C C C	R R R	—	•U U O
Hermit Warbler	—	—	—	—	—	—	—	—	—
Black-throated Green Warbler	C U A	—	O R	U U	—	—	—	—	—
Blackburnian Warbler	C U	—	O O	U U	—	—	—	—	—
Yellow-throated Warbler	•C UC O	—	U U O	C R C	—	—	—	—	—
Pine Warbler	•C C C C	U U O O	C C C C	•C C C C	—	—	—	—	—
Prairie Warbler	•C U C	—	U U O	C U C	—	—	—	—	—
Palm Warbler	U C U	—	C C C	C. C U	—	—	—	—	—
Bay-breasted Warbler	C C	—	U	U U	—	—	—	—	—
Blackpoll Warbler	C	—	O	C R	—	•U U U	•R U R	—	•U U
Cerulean Warbler	U U U	—	—	U U	—	—	—	—	—
Black-and-white Warbler	•A U A	—	U UO	•C C C	—	—	—	—	—
American Redstart	•C U A	•U U O O	U O	•C U C	—	—	—	—	R R
Prothonotary Warbler	•C U C	•O O	U C	•C C C	—	—	—	—	—
Worm-eating Warbler	U U U	—	O R	U U U	—	—	—	—	—
Swainson's Warbler	•U O U	—	R	U U	—	—	—	—	—
Ovenbird	C U A	—	O U	C C	—	—	—	—	—
Northern Waterthrush	C U C	—	U UR	U U	—	•C C C	•C C U	—	•C C O
Louisiana Waterthrush	U U U	—	U U	•U U U	—	—	—	—	—
Kentucky Warbler	•A U A	—	U C U	C C	—	—	—	—	—
Connecticut Warbler	—	—	—	O O	—	—	—	—	—
Mourning Warbler	R	—	—	R R	—	—	—	—	—
MacGillivray's Warbler	—	—	—	—	—	—	—	—	—
Common Yellowthroat	•A U A A	—	C C C C	•C C C O	—	—	—	—	—
Hooded Warbler	•A U C	•R O R	U C U	•C C C	—	—	—	—	—
Wilson's Warbler	O U	—	—	U O	—	•C C C	•U C U	•U A U	•C C O
Canada Warbler	U U U	—	—	U U	—	—	—	—	—
Painted Redstart	—	—	—	—	—	—	—	—	—
Yellow-breasted Chat	•C U C	•U C O R	U U U	•C C C	—	—	—	—	—
TANAGERS									
Hepatic Tanager	—	—	—	—	—	—	—	—	—
Summer Tanager	•A A	•O U	U U	•C C U	—	—	—	—	—
Scarlet Tanager	A A	—	O	U U	—	—	—	—	—
Western Tanager	—	—	—	—	—	—	—	—	—
CARDINALS, GROSBEAKS & ALLIES									
Northern Cardinal	•A A A A	•C C C C	C C C C	•C C C C	—	—	—	—	—
Pyrrhuloxia	—	—	—	—	—	—	—	—	—
Rose-breasted Grosbeak	C U C	—	O	C C	—	—	—	—	—
Black-headed Grosbeak	—	—	—	—	—	—	—	—	—
Blue Grosbeak	C U C U	U U	U C U	•C C C	—	—	—	—	—
Lazuli Bunting	—	—	—	—	—	—	—	—	—
Indigo Bunting	•A U A	•O C O	U C U	•C C C	—	—	—	—	—
Painted Bunting	•U O U	—	—	—	—	—	—	—	—
Dickcissel	•C O C O	—	R	•C C U	—	—	—	—	—
NEW WORLD SPARROWS & ALLIES									
Olive Sparrow	—	—	—	—	—	—	—	—	—
Green-tailed Towhee	—	—	—	—	—	—	—	—	—
Rufous-sided Towhee	•A A A A	•U U U U	C C C C	•C C C C	—	—	—	—	—
Brown Towhee	—	—	—	—	—	—	—	—	—
Abert's Towhee	—	—	—	—	—	—	—	—	—
Bachman's Sparrow	•O O	—	O R	R R R	—	—	—	—	—

	AK-6 Togiak	AZ-1 Hassayampa	AZ-2 Cabeza	AZ-3 Cibola	AZ-4 Havasu	AZ-5 Imperial	AZ-6 Kofa	AR-1 Felsenthal	AR-2 Holla Bend	AR-3 Wapanocca	AR-4 White River	CA-1 Richardson
	• s S F W	• s S F W	• s S F W	• s S F W	• s S F W	• s S F W	• s S F W	• s S F W	• s S F W	• s S F W	• s S F W	• s S F W
	—	—	—	—	—	—	—	•C C U	C O U	•C C C	•C C U	—
	—	—	—	—	—	—	—	C C	—	R R	O O	—
	—	—	—	—	—	—	—	C C	O O	R R	R	—
	—	—	—	—	—	—	—			A C	C	—
	•U C U	C C U	C C O	C C C	C C C	C C C	C C	U U U	R		R R	C U C
	—	U U	C C	U U U	U U U	U U U	C U	C C	—	C C C	C U	—
	—	R O	—	—	R R	—	—		—	—	—	—
	—	•C C U	•U U	—	•C C C	•C C	•R R	•C C C	—	•C C C	•C C C	—
	•C C U	•C C U	C C	C O C	•C O C R	C O C	C C	•O O O O	U	C U	O O	C C C
	—	—	—	—	—	—	—		—	C C	U R	—
	—	—	—	—	—	—	—	U U	—	C C	C U	—
	•U U U	C C C	C C U	C C C	R R R	C C C	C C U	C C C	C C C	C C C	C C A	C C C
	—	U U U	C U R	U U U	U U O	U U O	U C U U	—	—	—	—	U U
	—	U U U	C O	U U U	U U U	U U U	C O	—	—	—	—	—
	—	U O O	O R	O O	U O	O O	U U	O O	—	C C	O O	—
	—	—	—	—	—	—	—	•U U	—	O O	O O	—
	—	—	—	—	—	—	—	•A C U	O O O	•C C C	•U U	—
	—	—	—	—	—	—	—	C C C C	O O	—	—	—
	—	—	—	—	—	—	—	U U	O	O	—	—
	—	—	—	—	—	—	—	O O	—	O	C R	R R
	—	—	—	—	—	—	—	O O	—	C C	U	—
	•C C U	—	—	—	—	—	—	—	—	C R	R	—
	—	U U	—	—	R R R	—	—	•O O O	—	•C C C	•U U U	—
	—	O R	—	O O R	R R R	R R R	—	•U O	—	O O O	U O	—
	—	—	—	—	—	—	—	•C C C	C C	•C C C	•U O U	—
	—	—	—	—	—	—	—	•C C U	—	•C C C	•C C	—
	—	—	—	—	—	—	—	U U	—	O O	U U U	—
	—	—	—	—	—	—	—	—	—	•U U U	•U U	—
	—	—	—	—	—	—	—	—	—	C C	C	—
	•C C C	R R	—	—	—	—	—	O O	—	C C	U O	—
	—	—	—	—	—	—	—	•U U U	—	C U R	•C U U	—
	—	—	—	—	—	—	—	•C C C	O O	•C C C	•C C U	—
	—	C C	C C	C C	C C	C C	C U	—	—	U R	—	U U
	—	•C U U	O	•C C C C	•C C C U	•C C C C	—	•C C C	C C O	•C C C R	•U U U	R R R
	—	—	—	—	—	—	—	•U U O	—	•C C C	•C C U	—
	•C C U	C A U	C C	C C R	C C	C C O	C U	—	—	U U	R	C C C
	—	—	—	—	—	—	—	—	—	—	R	—
	—	U U	—	—	—	—	R R	—	—	—	—	—
	—	•C C U	R	•C C C	•C C U	•C C C	R	•C C C	U U	•C C C	•C C C	—
	—	O U	—	—	—	—	O	—	—	—	—	—
	—	•U C U	—	O O O	•C C C	•O O O	—	•C C C	C C C	•C C C	•C C C	—
	—	—	—	—	—	—	—	R R	U U U	U U	O R O	—
	—	U O U	C O C	•C U C	C U C	U U U	C U C	—	—	—	—	R
	—	•C C C C	—	—	•O O O O	—	O	•A A A A	A A A A	•C C C C	•C C C C	—
	—	•U U U U	R R R R	—	—	—	R R	U U	O O	C C	U U	—
	—	R R	—	—	R O R	—	—	—	—	—	—	R
	—	U O U U	C O C	C U C	C U C	C U C	U O U	—	—	—	—	—
	—	•U U U	—	•C C U	•O C O	•C C U	R	•U U U	O	R R	•U O O	—
	—	U U O	U U	U U	U U U	U U	C U	—	—	—	—	—
	—	—	—	—	•O U O	O O	—	•A C C	C C O	•C C C	•C C C	—
	—	—	—	—	—	—	—	R R	O O	R R	R	—
	—	—	—	—	—	—	—	C C R	•C C U	•A C C	
	—	U U U	U U U	U U U	U U U	U U U	U U U O	—	—	—	—	—
	—	U U C	R R O	O O O	O U O	O O O	U U O O	C U C C	O O	•C U C C	•U U U U	C C C C
	—	•U U U U	R R	—	—	—	C C C C	—	—	—	—	C C C C
	—	•C C C C	—	•C C C C	•C C C C	•A A A A	—	—	—	—	—	—
	—	—	—	—	—	—	—	R R	—	—	—	—

STATE-NUMBER OF BIRD LIST / REFUGE, SANCTUARY OR PRESERVE / NESTING, ABUNDANCE BY SEASON	AL-1 Bon Secour • s S F W	AL-2 Choctaw • s S F W	AL-3 Eufaula • s S F W	AL-4 Wheeler • s S F W	AK-1 Adak Is. • s S F W	AK-2 Kanuti • s S F W	AK-3 Kenai • s S F W	AK-4 Kodiak • s S F W	AK-5 Tetlin • s S F W
NEW WORLD SPARROWS & ALLIES (cont.)									
Cassin's Sparrow	—	—	—	—	—	—	—	—	—
Rufous-crowned Sparrow	—	—	—	—	—	—	—	—	—
American Tree Sparrow	—	R	—	O O O	—	•C C C	•U U R	U U U	•C C C O
Chipping Sparrow	U O C U	O O O U	C U C A	U U U U	—	•U U U	—	—	•U U U
Clay-colored Sparrow	O O O	—	—	—	—	—	—	—	—
Brewer's Sparrow	—	—	—	—	—	—	—	—	—
Field Sparrow	•U O U U	•U U U C	C C C C	•C C C C	—	—	—	—	—
Black-chinned Sparrow	—	—	—	—	—	—	—	—	—
Vesper Sparrow	U C U	O O U	U U C	O O C	—	—	—	—	—
Lark Sparrow	O U O	—	O	R R	—	—	—	—	—
Black-throated Sparrow	—	—	—	—	—	—	—	—	—
Sage Sparrow	—	—	—	—	—	—	—	—	—
Lark Bunting	—	—	—	—	—	—	—	—	—
Savannah Sparrow	C C A	O O O	C C A	U C C	—	•C C C	•C A A	•A A A	•C C U
Baird's Sparrow	—	—	—	—	—	—	—	—	—
Grasshopper Sparrow	U C O	—	O O O U	•U U U R	—	—	—	—	—
Henslow's Sparrow	—	—	—	R R R	—	—	—	—	—
Le Conte's Sparrow	O O O	—	O R O	R R R	—	—	—	—	—
Sharp-tailed Sparrow	U U U	—	—	—	—	—	—	—	—
Seaside Sparrow	•U U U U	—	—	—	—	—	—	—	—
Fox Sparrow	U U U	R R O	O O U	U U U	—	•C C C	•C C U	•A A C R	•C C U
Song Sparrow	C C C	O O U	C C A	U C C	•U U U U	—	•R R R	•C C C C	—
Lincoln's Sparrow	U U U	—	—	O O	—	•C C C	•U U R	R R	•C C U
Swamp Sparrow	C C A	O O U	C C A	C C C	—	—	—	—	—
White-throated Sparrow	C C A	U U C	C U A	C C A	—	—	—	—	R R
Golden-crowned Sparrow	—	—	—	—	—	•U U U	•C C U	•A A C R	•U U O
White-crowned Sparrow	U U U	—	O O O	U U	—	•C C C	•C C C	R R R	•C C U
Harris' Sparrow	—	—	—	—	—	—	—	—	—
Dark-eyed Junco	U U U	O R U	O U C	C O C C	—	•C C C	•C A C	U U U	•C C C O
McCown's Longspur	—	—	—	—	—	—	—	—	—
Lapland Longspur	—	—	—	U U	•C C C	•C C C	C U	•A A C	•C U U
Smith's Longspur	—	—	—	—	—	•R R R	—	—	R R R
Chestnut-collared Longspur	—	—	—	—	—	—	—	—	—
Snow Bunting	—	—	—	—	•C C C C	•C U U R	•U U U U	•C C C U	C U U O
NEW WORLD BLACKBIRDS & ORIOLES									
Bobolink	C O U	—	C	C U	—	—	—	—	—
Red-winged Blackbird	•A C A A	•C C C C	A A A A	•C C A A	—	•U U U	—	—	•O O R
Tricolored Blackbird	—	—	—	—	—	—	—	—	—
Eastern Meadowlark	•A A A A	•O O U U	C C C C	•C C A C	—	—	—	—	—
Western Meadowlark	—	—	—	—	—	—	—	—	—
Yellow-headed Blackbird	O O	—	—	—	—	—	—	—	R R
Rusty Blackbird	R R R	—	U O U	U C C	—	•U C U	•U U U	R R R	•C C U
Brewer's Blackbird	R R R	—	O	O U U	—	—	—	—	—
Great-tailed Grackle	—	—	—	—	—	—	—	—	—
Boat-tailed Grackle	•U U U U	—	—	—	—	—	—	—	—
Common Grackle	•C C C C	•U O U U	C C A A	•C C A A	—	—	—	—	R R
Bronzed Cowbird	—	—	—	—	—	—	—	—	—
Brown-headed Cowbird	•C C C C	U O U C	C C A A	•C C A A	—	—	—	—	R R
Orchard Oriole	•A U C	•O C	U C	•C C	—	—	—	—	—
Hooded Oriole	—	—	—	—	—	—	—	—	—
Baltimore Oriole	—	—	—	—	—	—	—	—	—
Bullock's Oriole	C U C	O R R	R R	U O U	—	—	—	—	—
Scott's Oriole	—	—	—	—	—	—	—	—	—
FINCHES									
Rosy Finch	—	—	—	—	•C C C C	•U U U	•U U U	•U U U U	•U U O
Pine Grosbeak	—	—	—	—	—	•U U U U	•U U U R	•C C C C	•U U U U
Purple Finch	U U C	O R O	O U	U C C	—	—	—	—	—
Cassin's Finch	—	—	—	—	—	—	—	—	—
House Finch	—	—	—	U U U	—	—	—	—	—
Red Crossbill	—	—	—	—	—	—	—	•R R R R	—
White-winged Crossbill	—	—	—	—	—	•U U U U	U U U U	•U U U U	•U U U U
Common Redpoll	—	—	—	—	R R R	•C C C C	•C C C C	•C C C C	•C C C C
Hoary Redpoll	—	—	—	—	R	•C R U C	—	—	•C O U C
Pine Siskin	U U U	—	U	U U	—	•R R R	•R R R	•C C C C	R R R
Lesser Goldfinch	—	—	—	—	—	—	—	—	—
Lawrence's Goldfinch	—	—	—	—	—	—	—	—	—
American Goldfinch	•C U C C	—	U O U C	•C U C C	—	—	—	—	—
Evening Grosbeak	—	O	R	U U U	—	—	—	—	—
OLD WORLD SPARROWS									
House Sparrow	•A A A A	•U U U U	C C C C	•C C C C	—	—	—	—	—
Eurasian Tree Sparrow	—	—	—	—	—	—	—	—	—

	AK-6 Togiak	AZ-1 Hassayampa	AZ-2 Cabeza	AZ-3 Cibola	AZ-4 Havasu	AZ-5 Imperial	AZ-6 Kofa	AR-1 Felsenthal	AR-2 Holla Bend	AR-3 Wapanocca	AR-4 White River	CA-1 Richardson
	•s S F W	•s S F W	•s S F W	•s S F W	•s S F W	•s S F W	•s S F W	•s S F W	•s S F W	•s S F W	•s S F W	•s S F W
	—	—	R	—	—	—	—	—	—	—	—	—
	—	U OU	—	—	—	—	R R R	—	—	O	—	—
	•C C C	—	—	—	—	—	—	—	—	—	—	—
	—	C C	U UU	C CR	U OU O	U UO	C CU O	•UUUU	R	U U	O OOR	—
	—	C UO	C CC	C CO	C CO	C CO	C CU	•C C C C	A A A A	•C C C C	•C C C C	—
	—	R R	R R	—	—	—	O O O O	—	—	—	—	—
	—	C CU	U CC	U UR	U UU	U UR	U OR	U UU	O	U UR	U UU	—
	—	C U	O UO	O O	O OO	ORO	O O O	•R R R	C C C O	R	R R R	—
	—	•UUUU	•C C C C	O O	•C C C C	O O O	•C C C C	—	—	—	—	—
	—	U U	U CC	U U	U C	U U	U U	—	—	—	—	—
	—	R RO	U UU	—	R	R R	—	—	—	—	—	—
	•C C C	C CU	U O	C C C C	C CC	C CU	—	U UC	O OO	U UC	U UC	—
	—	—	R R	—	—	—	—	—	—	—	—	—
	—	—	—	—	—	—	—	R RR	O O	R RR	R RR	—
	—	—	—	—	—	—	—	—	—	—	R	—
	•C C C	—	R R	—	R RR	R R	O O	U UU	U OC	U UU	O OU	C CC
	•U U U	U UC	—	•C C C C	•C C C C	•C C C C	—	C CC	O O O	C CC	C CC	C C C C
	R R R	U UR	O OO	U UO	C CA	U CC	O	U OO	O O O	C CC	O O	U UU
	—	R R	—	—	R UU	O OU	—	C CC	O O O	C CC	C CC	—
	—	R R	—	—	R	—	—	A AA	O CC	C CC	A AA	R
	•C C C	—	—	—	R RO	R RR	—	—	—	—	—	C CC
	•C C C	C CA	C CC	C CC	C CA	A AA	C U U O	C UC	O OC	U UU	C C	C CC
	•U U U	U UC	R OU	O OO	O UU	O OO	O O	C CC	U UC	C CC	A CA	C CC
	•C C C	—	—	—	—	R	—	R R	O O	R R	R	—
	—	—	—	—	—	—	—	—	—	—	—	—
	•C C C U	—	O	O	R	O	—	—	—	—	—	—
	—	•C U C A	R R	A A A U	•C A A C	•A A A U	R R	•A A A A	A A A A	•A A A A	•A A A A	C C C C
	—	—	—	—	—	—	—	•C C C C	A A A A	•C C C C	•U U U U	—
	—	•U U U C	•O U U	U CC	U CC	U UC	O O	U UU	—	—	—	U U C C
	—	U UO	R O	C UC	•U CC	•C U C	O O O	O OC	R R	—	—	—
	•C C C	A AC	R O	C CU	R RR	U CL	R U	C OC	C OC	C O	C O	C C C C
	—	•U U U U	—	—	U CC	U CU	O	O OC	U	O O	O O	C C C C
	—	—	—	—	•U C U U	•U C U U	—	—	—	—	—	—
	—	•U C U	R R	—	—	—	—	•A A A A	C C C C	•A A A A	•C C A A	—
	—	•U C U O	•U O U	C C C U	•C C O R	•C C C U	U U O O	•A A A A	C C C C	•A C A A	•C C C A	C C
	—	—	—	—	—	—	—	•C C C	C C C	•C C U	•C C C	—
	—	•C C C	•U O R	O O O	•O C O	•U U O	•O O R	—	—	—	—	—
	—	•U C U	C U	U U U	•C C C	•U U U	U C U	•C C C	C C O	•C C U	•U U U	U R
	—	•U U U	•C C	—	—	—	C C U O	—	—	—	—	—
	•C C C U	—	—	—	—	—	—	—	—	—	—	—
	•U U U U	—	—	—	—	—	—	—	—	—	—	—
	—	—	—	—	R R	—	R R	U	U	U C	U	C C
	—	O UU	—	—	—	—	U U	—	—	—	—	—
	—	•C C C C	•C C C C	•C C C C	•C C C C	•C C C C	•C C C C	—	—	—	—	A A A A
	—	—	—	—	—	—	—	R R	—	—	—	—
	•U U U U	—	—	—	—	—	—	—	—	—	—	—
	•C C C C	—	—	—	—	—	—	—	—	—	—	—
	•U U U U	—	—	—	—	—	—	—	—	—	—	—
	—	U UU	R R	R OO	O UU	R OO	O	O OO	—	—	R O	C C C C
	—	•C C C U	•U U U U	U U U U	•U U U U	•U U U U	O O U R	—	—	—	—	C A A C
	—	•R R O	O R	—	R OO	R R	U O	—	—	—	—	—
	—	C O U U	—	O O	O OO	O O	—	C C	C C C	•C U U C	C R C C	C C C C
	—	—	—	—	R	—	—	U UU	—	O	—	—
	—	•C C C C	O OR	•C C C C	•U U U U	•O O O O	O O O	•C C C C	C C C C	•A A A A	•U U C C	C C C C

STATE-NUMBER OF BIRD LIST / REFUGE, SANCTUARY OR PRESERVE / NESTING, ABUNDANCE BY SEASON	CA-2 Farallon •s S F W	CA-3 Lo. Klamath •s S F W	CA-4 Kern •s S F W	CA-5 Modoc •s S F W	CA-6 Sacramento •s S F W	CA-7 Salton Sea •s S F W	CA-8 S. F. Bay •s S F W	CA-9 San Luis •s S F W	CO-1 Phantom •s S F W
LOONS									
Red-throated Loon	O U O	—	—	—	—	—	O R U U	—	—
Arctic Loon	U C U	R	—	—	—	—	U U U	—	—
Pacific Loon	—	—	—	—	—	O	—	—	—
Common Loon	O U	U R U R	—	R	R R	R	U R U C	R R	—
Yellow-billed Loon	—	—	—	—	—	—	—	—	—
GREBES									
Least Grebe	—	—	—	—	—	—	—	—	—
Pied-billed Grebe	R	•C C C U	•C C C C	•C C C U	•C C C C	•U U U U	•C C C C	•C C C C	U
Horned Grebe	O O O	U R U U	R R R	O O	R R R	O O O	U R U C	R R R	—
Red-necked Grebe	O O O	—	—	—	—	—	R R O	—	—
Eared Grebe	A A A	•C A A U	•C O C C	•U C U	•U R U C	C U C C	•A U C A	•U U O U	U
Western Grebe	R R O R	•C A A U	•U U U U	•U C C	•U U U U	•U U U U	C U C C	•O R O O	U U
SHEARWATERS & PETRELS									
Northern Fulmar	O	—	—	—	—	—	—	—	—
Cory's Shearwater	—	—	—	—	—	—	—	—	—
Pink-footed Shearwater	O O O O	—	—	—	—	—	—	—	—
Greater Shearwater	—	—	—	—	—	—	—	—	—
Sooty Shearwater	U A A O	—	—	—	—	—	—	—	—
Short-tailed Shearwater	O O	—	—	—	—	—	—	—	—
Manx Shearwater	—	—	—	—	—	—	—	—	—
Audubon's Shearwater	—	—	—	—	—	—	—	—	—
STORM-PETRELS									
Wilson's Storm-Petrel	—	—	—	—	—	—	—	—	—
Fork-tailed Storm-Petrel	R R R R	—	—	—	—	—	—	—	—
Leach's Storm-Petrel	•A A A U	—	—	—	—	—	—	—	—
BOOBIES & GANNETS									
Masked Booby	—	—	—	—	—	—	—	—	—
Brown Booby	—	—	—	—	—	—	—	—	—
Northern Gannet	—	—	—	—	—	—	—	—	—
PELICANS									
American White Pelican	—	•C C C	O O O O	U C U	C U C U	C U C U	O C C C	C U C C	R
Brown Pelican	U O A A	—	—	—	—	O R U O	R U U O	—	—
CORMORANTS									
Great Cormorant	—	—	—	—	—	—	—	—	—
Double-crested Cormorant	•A A A U	•C C C U	O O O O	U C U R	C C U C	•C C C C	•U C A A	O O O	R
Olivaceous Cormorant	—	—	—	—	—	—	—	—	—
Brandt's Cormorant	•A A A C	—	—	—	—	—	R O R R	—	—
Pelagic Cormorant	•A A A C	—	—	—	—	—	U U U R	—	—
Red-faced Cormorant	—	—	—	—	—	—	—	—	—
ANHINGAS									
Anhinga	—	—	—	—	—	—	—	—	—
FRIGATEBIRDS									
Magnificent Frigatebird	—	—	—	—	—	O R	—	—	—
BITTERNS & HERONS									
American Bittern	—	•U U U R	•C U C C	•U C U R	•C C C C	R O U U	•U O U U	•C U C C	—
Least Bittern	—	•R R R	O O O O	R R	•R R R R	•R U R O	O R	R	—
Great Blue Heron	R O	•C C C C	•C U C C	C C C R	•C C C C	•C C C C	•C C C C	•C C C C	R
Great Egret	R	•C C C R	U U U C	•C C C	•C C C C	•C C C C	•C C C C	•C C C C	—
Snowy Egret	R R	•U C C	•C C C C	U U U	•C C C C	•C C C C	•A A A A	•C C C C	—
Little Blue Heron	—	—	—	—	—	O O	•O O O R	—	—
Tricolored Heron	—	—	—	—	—	O O	—	—	—
Reddish Egret	—	—	—	—	—	—	—	—	—
Cattle Egret	R	R R	•C U C C	R R	•R R R U	•C C C C	O O O O	U U U	—
Green-backed Heron	R R	R R R	U U U O	•O O O	•R U U R	•U U U U	•R O O R	R R R R	—
Black-crowned Night-Heron	—	•C C C U	•A A A A	•C C C	•C C C C	•C C C C	•C C C C	•U U U U	—
Yellow-crowned Night-Heron	—	—	—	—	—	—	—	—	—
IBISES & SPOONBILLS									
White Ibis	—	—	—	—	—	—	—	—	—
Glossy Ibis	—	—	—	—	—	—	—	—	—
White-faced Ibis	—	R R R	O O O R	O R O	U R U U	U U C C	R O	U O U U	—
Roseate Spoonbill	—	—	—	—	—	O O	—	—	—
STORKS									
Wood Stork	—	—	—	—	—	C O	—	—	—
SWANS, GEESE & DUCKS									
Fulvous Whistling-Duck	—	—	•R R R R	—	—	R R O	—	—	—
Black-bellied Whistling-Duck	—	—	—	—	—	—	—	—	—
Tundra Swan	—	C C A	R	A A	U R U C		O	R R	O O	—
Trumpeter Swan	—	R R	—	—	—	—	—	—	—
Mute Swan	—	—	—	—	—	—	—	—	—
Greater White-fronted Goose	R R	A R A C	O O O	U U U	U A C	R R	O O	U C C	—
Snow Goose	—	A R A C	O O O	O O O	C A A	O O C C	R O	U C A	—

	CO-2 Alamosa	CO-3 Arapaho	CO-4 Browns Pk	CT-1 Salt Meadow	DE-1 Bombay Hk	FL-1 Corkscrew	FL-2 Cedar Keys	FL-3 Chassahow.	FL-4 Florida Keys	FL-5 Ding Darling	FL-6 Woodruff	FL-7 Loxahatchee
• s S F W	• s S F W	• s S F W	• s S F W	• s S F W	• s S F W	• s S F W	• s S F W	• s S F W	• s S F W	• s S F W	• s S F W	• s S F W
	—	—	—	C CU	R R	—	—	—	R	—	—	—
	—	—	—	—	—	—	—	—	—	—	—	—
	—	—	—	—	—	—	—	—	—	—	—	—
	O O	O	—	R	COCC	R	U CC	U CC	O OO	C CC	O	R R
	•C C C	O O	•C C C	C O C U	•O O U O	•C U C C	•C C C C	•C C C C	U U C	•A C C A	C U C C	•C U C C
	—	—	C C R	C O U C	O U O U	—	U	U	R R	R R C	O O	—
	—	—	—	U U U	—	—	—	—	—	—	—	—
	•O O O	•U C U	•C C C	—	R	—	—	—	—	—	—	—
	•O O	O	•O O O	—	—	—	—	—	—	—	—	—
	—	—	—	—	—	—	—	—	—	—	—	—
	—	—	—	—	—	—	—	—	—	—	—	—
	—	—	—	—	—	—	—	—	—	—	—	—
	—	—	—	—	—	—	—	—	—	—	—	—
	—	—	—	—	—	—	—	—	—	—	—	—
	—	—	—	—	—	—	—	—	—	—	—	—
	—	—	—	—	—	—	—	—	—	—	—	—
	—	—	—	—	—	—	—	—	—	—	—	—
	—	—	—	U O U O	—	—	—	—	R R R	R R R	—	—
	R	R	R	—	—	R	O O O	C C C	—	C C A	—	U U
	—	—	—	—	—	—	•C C C C	C C C C	•A A A A	•A A A A	—	—
	—	—	—	U U U	—	—	—	—	—	—	—	—
	R	—	R	A C A U	U U C U	U U U U	•A A A A	•A A A A	•A A A A	•A A A A	O O O U	•U U U U
	—	—	—	—	—	—	—	—	—	—	—	—
	—	—	—	—	—	—	—	—	—	—	—	—
	—	—	—	—	—	—	—	—	—	—	—	—
	—	—	—	—	—	•C C C C	•C C C C	•C C C C	—	•A A A A	•C C C C	•A A A A
	—	—	—	—	—	—	C C C O	C C C O	•C C C C	C C C R	—	—
	•U U U O	R U R	•U U O	•U U U O	•O U U O	•U U U	U U U U	U U U U	R R R R	R R R	U R U C	A U A A
	O O	—	—	•O O O	•O C O	•U U U U	•U U U U	•U U U U	R R O O	•C C C C	U C U O	•A C A A
	C C C U	•U C U	•C C C	C U C U	C C A C	•C C C C	•A A A A	•A A A A	•A A A A	•A A A A	•C C C C	•A A A A
	R	—	—	U U C O	U A C O	•C C C C	•A A A A	•A A A A	•U U U U	•A A A A	•C C C C	•A A A A
	•C A A	R R R	U C	U C C	O A C R	•U U U U	•A A C C	•A A C C	•U U U U	•A A A A	•U U U U	•C C C C
	O	—	—	—	O C C	•C C C C	•C C C C	•A A C C	•C C C C	•A A A A	•C C C C	•A A A A
	—	—	—	—	O U O R	•C C C C	•A A C C	•A A C C	•C C C C	•A A A A	•U U U U	•A C C A
	—	—	—	—	—	—	—	—	•U U U U	•C C C C	—	—
	•O O O	—	U U	—	O U O	•C C C C	•C C C C	•C C C C	•C C C C	•C C C C	U U U U	•A A A A
	O O	—	O	•C C C	C C C R	•C C C C	•C C C C	•C C C C	•U U U U	•C C C C	•U U U O	•A A A A
	•C A C R	•U C U	•U U U	•U C C O	C C C U	•C C C C	•C C C C	•A A C C	O O O O	•C C C C	•U U U U	•C C A A
	—	R R	—	—	O O O O	•U U U U	•C C C C	•C C C C	•U U U U	•C C C C	•O O O O	•U U U U
	—	—	—	—	—	•C U C C	•A A A A	•A A A A	•U U U U	•A A A A	C O O C	•A A A A
	—	—	—	U U U	C C U	•U R U U	—	—	R R R R	R R R R	O O O U	•C C C C
	•C C C	R R	•C C U	—	—	—	—	—	—	—	—	—
	—	—	—	—	—	R R	O O O R	—	•O O O O	O C C O	—	O O O O
	—	—	—	—	—	•C U U C	U C U U	U C U U	—	O C C O	O O O O	C U C C
	—	—	—	—	R R R	—	—	—	O	O O O O	O O O	C U C
	R R	R	O O O	R R R	O R C U	—	R R	R R	—	—	—	—
	—	—	—	•A A A C	R R R O	—	—	—	—	—	—	—
	R R R	—	R R	—	R R R	—	R R	R R	—	—	—	—
	O O O	—	O O O	O O O	C R A A	—	R R R	R R R	—	—	—	R

BIRD CHART — California/Colorado

Columns show each refuge's nesting/abundance by season in the order **• s S F W** (• = nesting; s = spring, S = summer, F = fall, W = winter). A dash (—) indicates absence.

STATE-NUMBER OF BIRD LIST / REFUGE / NESTING, ABUNDANCE BY SEASON	CA-2 Farallon	CA-3 Lo. Klamath	CA-4 Kern	CA-5 Modoc	CA-6 Sacramento	CA-7 Salton Sea	CA-8 S. F. Bay	CA-9 San Luis	CO-1 Phantom
SWANS, GEESE & DUCKS (cont.)									
Ross' Goose	—	A R A C	R R	O O O	C A A	O C C	R	U U A	—
Emperor Goose	—	R R R	—	—	—	—	—	—	—
Brant	R O	R R	—	—	—	R O	R R R R	—	—
Canada Goose	—	•A C A C	U R U U	•A A A A	U U U C	O O C C	•U R R U	C U A	C C C C
Wood Duck	—	—	U U U	O R U	•U U U U	O	R R O O	•U U U U	—
Green-winged Teal	R R	•C R A U	•C C A A	•U R U	C R A A	C R C C	U O U C	•C O C A	C C U U
American Black Duck	—	—	—	—	—	—	—	—	—
Mottled Duck	—	—	—	—	—	—	—	—	—
Mallard	O	•A C A C	•C C A A	•A A A C	•A C A A	U O U U	•C C C C	•A C A A	C U
Northern Pintail	O	•A C A C	•A C A A	•C C C U	•C U A A	R R C C	•C C A A	•C C A A	U U R
Blue-winged Teal	—	•U U U	•O O O O	U R O	•R R R R	R O R O	•O R O O	•U R	U U U
Cinnamon Teal	R R	•C A C R	•A C O A	•A A U R	•C C C U	•C U C R	•C U C C	•A C C U	U
Northern Shoveler	R	•A C A C	•A U U U	•U U U O	•A U A A	C R C C	•C U A A	•C U C A	U U U U
Gadwall	R	•C C A U	•A C A A	•C A A O	•C U U C	R R U U	•U C C C	•C C C C	U U U U
Eurasian Wigeon	—	U R U	—	R R R	R R R	O	R R	—	—
American Wigeon	R	•A U A C	•A O A A	•C C A C	A U A A	R O C C	C U R A	•C A C A	U U U U
Canvasback	—	•C U C U	•O R O O	•U U U O	U R U U	U O U C	C O C A	•O R O U	R
Redhead	—	•C C C U	•U O U U	•C C C O	•U U U U	•U U U U	R O O	•O R O O	U U
Ring-necked Duck	—	•U U U U	•U R U C	U U U	U R C C	O O R	R R R	U R O U	U U R
Greater Scaup	—	R R R	R R R	R R	R R R	R O R	U R O C	R R	—
Lesser Scaup	R	•C U C C	O O O	U R U U	R U U	U O U C	•A O A A	O O O	U U
Common Eider	—	—	—	—	—	—	—	—	—
King Eider	—	—	—	—	—	—	—	—	—
Steller's Eider	—	—	—	—	—	—	—	—	—
Harlequin Duck	R	—	—	—	—	—	—	—	—
Oldsquaw	R R R	R R	—	—	—	O O	R R R R	—	—
Black Scoter	R R	—	—	—	—	—	R O R	—	—
Surf Scoter	C C C	R R	—	—	—	R O O O	U R A A	—	—
White-winged Scoter	U U U	•R R R	—	O O O	—	O O O O	O U U	—	—
Common Goldeneye	R	C R U C	R R R	U U C	R R U	O O U	U R U C	R R R	U U
Barrow's Goldeneye	—	R R	—	R R O	—	—	R O O	—	—
Bufflehead	—	C R C U	U U U	C C C	U U U	U O O U	C O C A	O O O	U R
Hooded Merganser	—	•U R U U	R R	R U U	R R R	O	O R	R R	—
Common Merganser	—	C R C C	O O O	C C C	•R R R	O R	R O R	U O	C C
Red-breasted Merganser	U R U	R R R	—	—	R	U R R R	U U U	—	—
Ruddy Duck	R R	•A C A U	•C C C C	•C C C O	•C R C C	•C C C C	•C C A A	•C U C C	U U
Masked Duck	—	—	—	—	—	—	—	—	—
AMERICAN VULTURES									
Black Vulture	—	—	—	—	—	—	—	—	—
Turkey Vulture	—	•U U U	O O O R	O U O	C C C C	U R U R	U U U U	U U U U	•C C
KITES, EAGLES, HAWKS & ALLIES									
Osprey	—	•U U U	R R	O O O R	—	R R R R	R R R	R R R	R
American Swallow-tailed Kite	—	—	—	—	—	—	—	—	—
Black-shouldered Kite	R	R R R R	•C C C O	R R R R	U U U U	O O O O	•C C C C	•U U C C	—
Snail Kite	—	—	—	—	—	—	—	—	—
Mississippi Kite	—	—	—	—	—	—	—	—	—
Bald Eagle	—	•C U U A	R	C R U C	R R	O	R R	O U	—
Northern Harrier	R R O	•C C C C	•A C A A	•C C C C	•C C C C	U O U C	•C C C C	•A A C C	R
Sharp-shinned Hawk	O	•U U U U	C C C C	O R O O	•U R U U	R U U	U U U	R	U U U
Cooper's Hawk	O	U U U U	C C C C	•O O O U	•U R U U	O U U	O U O	O O O	R R R R
Northern Goshawk	—	—	—	O	—	—	—	—	U U U U
Common Black-Hawk	—	—	—	—	—	—	—	—	—
Harris' Hawk	—	—	—	—	—	—	—	—	—
Gray Hawk	—	—	—	—	—	—	—	—	—
Red-shouldered Hawk	—	—	R R R	R R R R	•R R R R	O O	—	O O O R	—
Broad-winged Hawk	—	—	—	—	—	—	—	—	—
Short-tailed Hawk	—	—	—	—	—	—	—	—	—
Swainson's Hawk	—	R R R R	R R	O O O	R R R	O O	—	•U U O	U U
White-tailed Hawk	—	—	—	—	—	—	—	—	—
Zone-tailed Hawk	—	—	—	—	—	—	—	—	—
Red-tailed Hawk	R	•C C C C	•C U A A	•C A C C	•C C C C	U R U U	•C C C C	•C C A A	•U U U
Ferruginous Hawk	—	R R R R	O O O	O	R R	R R	R R	O O O	R
Rough-legged Hawk	R	C C C	O O O	C C O	R R R	R R	R R R	U U U	U R C
Golden Eagle	—	•U U U C	O R O O	U O U U	R R U U	—	R R O O	O R O O	•U U U
CARACARAS & FALCONS									
Crested Caracara	—	—	—	—	—	—	—	—	—
American Kestrel	R R C U	•C C C C	•C C C C	•C C C U	•C C C C	•U U C C	•C C C C	•C U C C	•U U
Merlin	O	U U U	R R R	O R O R	R	R R	R R U	R R	R
Peregrine Falcon	U U	R R R R	O O O O	R R R R	R R U U	O O O O	R O U	R R R	R R R
Gyrfalcon	—	—	—	—	—	—	—	—	—
Prairie Falcon	—	•U U U U	O O O O	U O U U	R R R R	R O R R	R O	O R O O	•U U

	CO-2 Alamosa	CO-3 Arapaho	CO-4 Browns Pk	CT-1 Salt Meadow	DE-1 Bombay Hk	FL-1 Corkscrew	FL-2 Cedar Keys	FL-3 Chassahow.	FL-4 Florida Keys	FL-5 Ding Darling	FL-6 Woodruff	FL-7 Loxahatchee
	• s S F W	• s S F W	• s S F W	• s S F W	• s S F W	• s S F W	• s S F W	• s S F W	• s S F W	• s S F W	• s S F W	• s S F W
	R R R	—	—	—	R R	—	—	—	—	—	—	—
		—	—	—	—	—	—	—	—	—	—	—
		—	—	U O U U	—	—	—	—	—	—	—	—
	•A A A A	•C C C	A C A A	—	•A C A A	—	—	—	—	—	R	—
	R R R R	—	R	•U U U R	•C C A O	•C C C C	•C C C C	C C C C	—	—	•C C C C	•U U C C
	•A A C U	•C C C	•C C C	C U C U	A O A C	U U U	C C C	A A A	U U	C R O C	U U U	A A A
	—	—	—	•C C C A	•C C C C	—	C C C	C C A	—	—	O O	A R
	—	—	—	—	—	•U U U U	R R R R	R R R R	—	•A A A A	•U U U U	•A A A A
	•A A A A	•C A A	•A A C C	•C C C C	•A C A A	—	C C C	A A A	—	O R	O O	R R R
	•A C C C	•C C C	•C C C U	—	A O A A	U U U	C C C	A A A	O O	C R C A	U U U	U U U
	•C C C	•C C C	•U U	•C U C	•C U A R	C C C	C C C	A U A A	U C	•A O C A	C R C U	A O A A
	•A A A	•C C C	•C C C	—	—	—	C C C	C C C	—	R R R	—	—
	•C C U O	•C C C	•C C C	—	•C O A U	R R	C C C	U U U	U U	C C C	O O O	U U U
	•A A A	•C A A	•A A C U	C U C U	•C A A U	—	C C C	C C C	—	O O	O O	O O O
	—	—	—	—	R R R O	—	—	—	—	R R O	—	—
	•C U U	•C A A	•C C C U	—	C O A C	U U U	C C C	A A A	O O	A C A	U U U	U U U
	U R R	•U U U	•C U C	C C U	O O	R R R	C C C	C C C	—	R O	R R O	U U U
	•C C C	•U C C	•C C C	U U U	O O O	—	C C C	C C C	—	R R R	O O O	R R R
	U R R	•U U U	•C O C U	—	O U O	R R R	C C C	C C C	U	R R R	C C A	A A A
	R R	—	O	C O C C	U O U U	—	R R R R	R R R R	—	—	R R R	R R
	C R R	•C C C	•C O C	U U U	U U U	R R R	C C C	C C C	A A A	O O	C R C	U O U	C C C
	—	—	—	U U U	—	—	—	—	—	—	—	—
	—	—	—	R R O	—	—	—	—	—	—	—	—
	—	—	—	—	—	—	—	—	—	—	—	—
	—	—	—	—	R U O	—	—	—	—	—	—	—
	—	—	—	C O C C	O R O O	—	—	—	—	R R O	—	—
	—	—	—	C O C C	O O O	—	—	—	—	—	—	—
	—	—	—	C O C C	O O O	—	—	—	—	—	—	—
	O O R	R R R	C O C C	C C A	U R U U	—	O O O	O O O	—	—	—	—
	—	O O O	—	—	—	—	—	—	—	—	—	—
	U O R	R O U	U U U	C C C	C R C C	—	O O O	U U U	—	R R R	O O	R R R
	R	—	R	U U U	U O U C	U U U	C U C	A U A	—	R R O	O O U	C C C
	C C	•O U U	•C U U C	C C U	U R C C	—	U U U	O R O	—	C C A	O O O	U U U
	R	—	R	C O C C	U R U U	—	A A A	A A A	O C C	C C A	O O O	U U U
	•C C C R	•O C C	•C C C	—	C O C C	—	U O U	O O O	—	R R O	O U U	U U U
	—	—	—	—	—	—	—	—	—	—	—	O O
	U C U	R R R R	•C C C	U O U	O O O O	•C C C C	•C C C C	•C C C	—	•A A A A	•C C C C	•A C A A
					•C C C C	•C C C C	•C C C C	•C C C C	•A A A A	C C C C	•A A A A	•A C A A
	O R R	R	O O R	•U C C	•O O O	U U U U	•C C C C	•C C C C	•C C C C	•A A A A	•C C C C	•U U U U
	—	—	—	—	—	•C C R R	U U U U	•U U O O	—	R	•U U	U R
	—	—	—	—	—	—	—	—	—	—	R R R R	•U U U U
	—	R R R	O O C	R R O	•U U U U	•R R R R	•U U U U	•U O U U	•O O O O	•O O O O	U O U U	O O O
	•C C C A	•U C C R	•C C C U	C U C U	•C O C C	C U C	C O C C	C C C	—	U U	O O U	A A A
	O O	—	O O O	U U O	O O O O	C U C	U U U	U U U U	—	U U	O U U	C C C
	R	—	—	R R R	—	—	—	—	—	—	R R R	R R R
	—	—	—	—	O R O O	—	—	—	—	—	—	—
	—	—	O O O O	•O O C C	•O O C C	•C C C C	•C C C C	•C C C C	•C C C C	•A A A A	•C C C C	•A A A A
	—	—	O U U	O O U	—	U U U	—	U	—	C C	R R R	U U
	—	—	—	—	—	R R R R	—	R R R	—	R R	R	—
	•O C C	•U C C	R	—	—	—	—	—	—	R R	R R	O O
	—	—	—	—	—	—	—	—	—	—	—	—
	•O C C U	R R	•C C C	U U U U	•U O C C	•U R U C	•U U U U	•U U U U	• O O	R O R	O O O O	U U U U
	R R R R	U O U U	R	U U O	R O R	R R R	—	—	—	R O R	O O O?	—
	O C C	O O O	R	U	O O C	—	—	—	—	—	—	—
	—	•C U U C	C U U C	R R R	R R	—	—	—	—	—	—	—
	•C C C R	•U C U	•C C C	•C C C C	•U U C C	C C C	•C C C C	•C C C C	A A A	R C A	•O R O U	A A A
	R R R R	R R O	•O O O	U U O	R O R	R R R	—	R	U U U	U U U	R O O	U U U
	R R R R	R R R	R R R	R R O	R R R	R R R	O O	—	—	R U U	R R R	R R R
	U U U U	•R O O R	O O O	—	—	—	—	O	—	R R R	—	—

STATE-NUMBER OF BIRD LIST REFUGE, SANCTUARY OR PRESERVE NESTING, ABUNDANCE BY SEASON	CA-2 Farallon ·s S F W	CA-3 Lo. Klamath ·s S F W	CA-4 Kern ·s S F W	CA-5 Modoc ·s S F W	CA-6 Sacramento ·s S F W	CA-7 Salton Sea ·s S F W	CA-8 S. F. Bay ·s S F W	CA-9 San Luis ·s S F W	CO-1 Phantom ·s S F W
CHACHALACAS									
Plain Chachalaca	—	—	—	—	—	—	—	—	—
PARTRIDGES, GROUSE, TURKEYS & QUAILS									
Gray Partridge	—	—	—	—	—	—	—	—	—
Chukar	—	•U U U U	—	—	—	—	—	—	—
Ring-necked Pheasant	—	•C C C C	•A A A A	•A A A A	•C C C C	•R R R R	•C C C C	•C C C C	—
Spruce Grouse	—	—	—	—	—	—	—	—	—
Blue Grouse	—	—	—	—	—	—	—	—	—
Willow Ptarmigan	—	—	—	—	—	—	—	—	—
Rock Ptarmigan	—	—	—	—	—	—	—	—	—
White-tailed Ptarmigan	—	—	—	—	—	—	—	—	—
Ruffed Grouse	—	—	—	—	—	—	—	—	—
Sage Grouse	—	•U U U U	—	R R	—	—	—	—	—
Greater Prairie Chicken	—	—	—	—	—	—	—	—	—
Lesser Prairie Chicken	—	—	—	—	—	—	—	—	—
Sharp-tailed Grouse	—	—	—	—	—	—	—	—	—
Wild Turkey	—	—	—	—	—	—	—	—	—
Northern Bobwhite	—	—	—	—	—	—	—	—	—
Scaled Quail	—	—	—	—	—	—	—	—	—
Gambel's Quail	—	—	—	—	—	•U U U U	—	—	—
California Quail	—	•C C C C	R R R R	•U U U U	•U U U U	—	•U U U U	•U U U U	—
Mountain Quail	—	—	—	—	—	—	—	—	—
RAILS, GALLINULES & COOTS									
Yellow Rail	—	—	—	—	—	—	—	—	—
Black Rail	—	—	—	—	—	•O O O O	•O O O O	—	—
Clapper Rail	—	—	—	—	—	•R R R R	•C C C C	—	—
King Rail	—	—	—	—	—	—	—	—	—
Virginia Rail	R	•U U U R	•U U U U	•U C U	•U U U U	•U R U U	•U U U U	U U U U	—
Sora	—	•U U U R	•O U C C	•U C U	•U U U U	C C C	•U U U U	U U C U	—
Purple Gallinule	—	—	—	—	—	—	—	—	—
Common Moorhen	—	R R	•U R C C	—	•C C C C	•U U U U	•U U U U	•C U C C	—
American Coot	O	•A A A C	•A O A A	•A A A U	•A C A A	•C C C C	•C C A A	•A C A A	—
LIMPKINS									
Limpkin	—	—	—	—	—	—	—	—	—
CRANES									
Sandhill Crane	—	•U U U	R R R	•C C C	R R U	U U	—	U A A	R
Whooping Crane	—	—	—	—	—	—	—	—	—
PLOVERS									
Black-bellied Plover	R U R	U R U	U U O	R	U R R	C U C C	A U A C	A U C	—
Lesser Golden-Plover	O	R R	—	—	—	O O	R R R R	—	—
Snowy Plover	—	•U U U	O	R R R	R	•U U U R	•U C U U	•R R R	—
Wilson's Plover	—	—	—	—	—	—	—	—	—
Semipalmated Plover	O	U R U	O O O	U R O	R R R	C O U R	C U C O	U R R	R
Piping Plover	—	—	—	—	—	—	—	—	—
Killdeer	R U R	•C C C U	•A A A A	•C A C R	•C C C C	•C C C C	•C C C C	•C C C C	•U U
Mountain Plover	—	—	O U U	—	—	O U	—	R	—
OYSTERCATCHERS									
American Oystercatcher	—	—	—	—	—	—	—	—	—
Black Oystercatcher	•C C C C	—	—	—	—	—	—	—	—
STILTS & AVOCETS									
Black-necked Stilt	—	•C C U	•A A C O	•U C O	•C C C U	•C C C C	•C C A A	•C C C C	—
American Avocet	—	•C C C R	•A A A U	•C C O	•C C C U	C C C C	•C C A A	•C C C C	—
SANDPIPERS									
Greater Yellowlegs	R R R	C R C R	C C C	C U C	C U C C	C O C C	C U C C	C U C C	U
Lesser Yellowlegs	R R	U R U R	O O O	O R O	U R R R	U U R	O O U R	U U U	U
Solitary Sandpiper	—	R R	R	O R O	R R	O	—	R	—
Willet	C O C C	•C C C	O O O	•C C O	R	C U C C	A C A A	R	U U U
Wandering Tattler	C O C C	—	—	—	—	O	R R O R	—	—
Spotted Sandpiper	R O	•U U U	U O O	•O U O	•R R R R	U U U	R R R R	R R	U
Upland Sandpiper	—	—	—	—	—	—	—	—	—
Whimbrel	U R U U	R R	O O	—	R R R	C O C	U O U O	U	—
Long-billed Curlew	R R	•C U U	U O U C	•U U U	U U U U	C U C C	C U C C	C U C C	—
Hudsonian Godwit	—	—	—	—	—	—	—	—	—
Bar-tailed Godwit	—	—	—	—	—	—	—	—	—
Marbled Godwit	R O O	R R R	O O	R	R	C U C U	A C A A	R R R R	—
Ruddy Turnstone	R R U R	R R R	R	—	—	R O	U U U U	—	—
Black Turnstone	C O C C	—	—	—	—	O	U U U U	—	—
Surfbird	R O R	—	—	—	—	O	—	—	—
Red Knot	—	R R	R R	—	—	U R O	C U C C	—	—
Sanderling	R O	R R R	—	—	—	U U O	U U U U	—	—
Semipalmated Sandpiper	—	—	—	—	—	O O	R O	—	—
Western Sandpiper	U C	A C A R	A O A O	U U U	C U C U	C O C C	A C A A	A U U U	—

CO-2 Alamosa	CO-3 Arapaho	CO-4 Browns Pk	CT-1 Salt Meadow	DE-1 Bombay Hk	FL-1 Corkscrew	FL-2 Cedar Keys	FL-3 Chassahow.	FL-4 Florida Keys	FL-5 Ding Darling	FL-6 Woodruff	FL-7 Loxahatchee
• s S F W	• s S F W	• s S F W	• s S F W	• s S F W	• s S F W	• s S F W	• s S F W	• s S F W	• s S F W	• s S F W	• s S F W
—	—	—	—	—	—	—	—	—	—	—	—
—	—	—	—	—	—	—	—	—	—	—	—
—	—	o o	—	—	—	—	—	—	—	—	—
•A A A A	—	O O O O	—	•C C C C	—	—	—	—	—	—	—
—	—	—	—	—	—	—	—	—	—	—	—
—	—	—	—	—	—	—	—	—	—	—	—
—	—	—	—	—	—	—	—	—	—	—	—
—	—	—	U U U U	—	—	—	—	—	—	—	—
—	•C U C U	•C C C	—	—	—	—	—	—	—	—	—
—	—	—	—	—	•C C C C	•C C C C	•U U U U	—	—	•O O O O	—
—	—	—	•C C C U	•C C C C	•C C C C	•A A A A	•A A A A	—	—	•C C C C	•C C C C
—	—	•U U U U	—	—	—	—	—	—	—	—	—
—	—	—	—	—	—	U	U	—	—	—	R R
—	—	—	—	R R R	R R R	•U U	•U U	—	R R R	O U O	R R
—	—	—	O O O R	•C C C O	—	•C C C C	•C C C C	•U U U U	C C C C	—	—
—	—	—	R R R	•C C C O	•C C C C	U U U U	U U U U	R R R R	C R C	•C C C C	•A A A A
•C C O R	•O U U	•U U U	•O U U R	•U U U O	C C C	C C C	C C C	—	O O O	O O O	R R R
•U C C R	•U C C	•U U U	O O O	U O U	U U U	C C C	C C C	•O O O	C C C	U U U	A A A
—	—	—	—	—	•U U U U	U U U U	U U U U	•R R R R	R R R R	•O U O R	•A A A A
—	—	—	—	•O U O R	•C C C C	•C C C C	•C C C C	•U U U U	•C C C C	•O U O R	•A A A A
•A A A	•C C C	•C C C	—	•C U A U	•C C C C	C O C A	A O A A	—	C C	A R C A	•A C A A
—	—	—	—	—	•C C C C	•U U U U	•U U U U	O R	—	•U U U O	•A A A A
A U A R	R R	U U	—	—	•U U U U	—	R R	—	R R R	R R R R	•C U C C
U U	—	—	—	—	—	—	—	—	—	—	—
R U R	—	—	C U C O	C U C O	—	U C C C	O O U	C O C C	C C C C	—	U U U U
—	—	—	R O	R R O	—	—	O	—	O R	—	—
—	—	—	—	—	—	O	—	O R	R	—	—
—	—	—	—	—	—	U U C C	U U C C	•U C U U	•C C C C	—	—
R	—	O O	C O C	C U C R	—	U U C C	O O C	C O C C	C C C C	—	U U U U
—	—	—	—	—	—	—	O	—	O	—	—
•A A U O	•C C C	•C C C	•U U U O	•C C C U	•C R U C	C C C C	•C C C C	O O U U	•C C C C	O O O O	•C C C C
—	—	O O	—	—	—	—	—	—	—	—	—
—	—	—	—	—	—	O C C	—	—	•C O C C	—	—
—	—	—	—	—	—	—	—	—	—	—	—
•U U O	•O O O	R R	—	•U C O	—	—	—	•U U	•C C O R	R R	•C C U R
•A A U	•U C C	O O O	—	U C U R	—	—	—	—	O R R O	—	—
U U U	• R R	U O U	C O C R	C C A O	U	C C C	C C C	O O O U	A C C C	O R U O	C C C C
U U U	• U U	U O U	C O C	C C C O	U	R R	R R	O O O U	A C C C	O O O	C C C C
O O O	—	O O	O O O	O O O	R	O O	O O	R R	R R R	—	U U U R
O O	•U C C	O O	R R	•A A O R	—	C C C C	C C C C	•C U C C	A A A A	—	R R
•C C U	•O U O	•C C C	•C U C	U O U	R	C O C C	C C C	U O U U	C C C C	U O O O	C O C U
—	—	—	R R R	O O	—	—	—	—	R	—	—
—	—	—	O O	R R R	—	R R	R R	—	R R R	—	—
O O O	R R	R R R	—	—	—	—	—	—	—	—	—
—	—	—	R R	R O	—	—	—	—	—	—	—
O O O	—	O R O	R R	R R	—	U U	R	—	R R O	—	—
—	—	—	C O U	O O	—	O O U U	O O U	C C C C	C C C C	—	—
—	—	—	—	—	—	—	—	—	—	—	—
—	—	—	O O O R	U O O	—	O O	R R	R R R	C C C C	—	—
O O O	—	—	C U C C	C O C	—	—	U	C O C C	C C C C	—	—
U U U	U O	—	U C U	A C A	O O C	O O C	C O C C	—	—	C C C
U U U	U O	—	U U	O O C R	O O O	O O	U O U U	C C C C	—	C C C U

STATE-NUMBER OF BIRD LIST REFUGE, SANCTUARY OR PRESERVE NESTING, ABUNDANCE BY SEASON	CA-2 Farrallon • s S F W	CA-3 Lo. Klamath • s S F W	CA-4 Kern • s S F W	CA-5 Modoc • s S F W	CA-6 Sacramento • s S F W	CA-7 Salton Sea • s S F W	CA-8 S. F. Bay • s S F W	CA-9 San Luis • s S F W	CO-1 Phantom • s S F W
SANDPIPERS (cont.)									
Least Sandpiper	R O	A U A R	C O A C	U U	C U C U	C O C C	C C A A	C U C A	—
White-rumped Sandpiper	—	—	—	—	—	—	—	—	—
Baird's Sandpiper	R O	U R U	—	—	—	O R	R R R	—	—
Pectoral Sandpiper	O	R U	O	—	R R	O	R R R	R	—
Sharp-tailed Sandpiper	—	—	—	—	—	—	—	—	—
Purple Sandpiper	—	—	—	—	—	—	—	—	—
Rock Sandpiper	O O O	—	—	—	—	—	—	—	—
Dunlin	O	C R U R	C U O	U R	C R R C	C O C U	C O A A	A A	—
Curlew Sandpiper	—	—	—	—	—	—	—	—	—
Stilt Sandpiper	—	—	—	—	—	R U R	—	—	—
Buff-breasted Sandpiper	—	—	—	—	—	—	—	—	—
Ruff	—	—	—	—	—	—	—	R R	—
Short-billed Dowitcher	O	R R R	U O U O	—	—	U O U	C U C C	R R	—
Long-billed Dowitcher	R O O	A U C R	A C A A	C U C	C U A C	C O C C	C O C C	A U A A	U U
Common Snipe	R O	•U U U R	C O C C	•C C C O	U R U U	U U R	U R U U	U U C	U U U U
American Woodcock	—	—	—	—	—	—	—	—	—
Wilson's Phalarope	—	•C C U	U O U	•C C O	•R U R	C O C	U A U	•U U	U U U
Red-necked Phalarope	O R U	U R U	U U	R	R U R	C O C	C A C R	U O O	—
Red Phalarope	R U	R R	—	—	—	O	R O O	—	—
SKUAS, GULLS, TERNS & SKIMMERS									
Pomarine Jaeger	O	—	—	—	—	—	—	—	—
Parasitic Jaeger	R	—	—	—	—	R	R O R	—	—
Long-tailed Jaeger	—	—	—	—	—	—	—	—	—
Laughing Gull	—	—	—	—	—	O C R O	—	—	—
Franklin's Gull	—	R	—	—	—	R O R	R R	—	A U A
Little Gull	—	—	—	—	—	—	—	—	—
Common Black-headed Gull	—	—	—	—	—	—	—	—	—
Bonaparte's Gull	O O	U U U	O O	O	R R	C R R O	A C A A	R R R	—
Heermann's Gull	O O O O	—	—	—	—	O	•R U U R	—	—
Mew Gull	O O	—	—	—	—	O	O U R U C	—	—
Ring-billed Gull	R O	•C A C C	O C C C	U C U R	U U C C	C U C C	C C A A	U O U U	A C A U
California Gull	O C O	•C A C C	C O O C	U C U R	R R R U	C C C U	•A A A A	U O U U	C C
Herring Gull	C C C	U U U	R R R	—	R R R U	R O U C	A O C A	U U U	U
Thayer's Gull	R	—	—	—	—	O O R	U U U	—	—
Iceland Gull	—	—	—	—	—	—	—	—	—
Lesser Black-backed Gull	—	—	—	—	—	—	—	—	—
Western Gull	•A A A A	—	R U	—	—	O O O	•C C C C	—	—
Glaucous-winged Gull	A C A	—	—	—	—	O O O R	C U C C	—	—
Glaucous Gull	R	—	—	—	—	O	O •R O	—	—
Great Black-backed Gull	—	—	—	—	—	—	—	—	—
Black-legged Kittiwake	O O O	—	—	—	—	—	—	—	—
Sabine's Gull	R	—	—	—	—	O	—	—	—
Gull-billed Tern	—	—	—	—	—	•U U O	—	—	—
Caspian Tern	—	•C C U	•O O O O	C C C	•U U U	C C C U	•C C C R	O O O	—
Royal Tern	—	—	—	—	—	—	—	—	—
Elegant Tern	—	—	—	—	—	—	R U O	—	—
Sandwich Tern	—	—	—	—	—	—	—	—	—
Roseate Tern	—	—	—	—	—	—	—	—	—
Common Tern	—	—	—	—	—	R R C	R O	—	—
Arctic Tern	—	—	—	—	—	—	—	—	—
Aleutian Tern	—	—	—	—	—	—	—	—	—
Forster's Tern	—	•C A C	C C U U	•C C C	R R	•C C C U	•C C A U	•O O O	U
Least Tern	—	—	—	—	—	O O	•U U R	—	—
Bridled Tern	—	—	—	—	—	—	—	—	—
Sooty Tern	—	—	—	—	—	—	—	—	—
Black Tern	—	•C A C	R R	U U U	•U U	C C C	R R R	•O O	U U
Black Skimmer	—	—	—	—	—	•U U R	—	—	—
AUKS, MURRES & PUFFINS									
Dovekie	—	—	—	—	—	—	—	—	—
Common Murre	•A A A A	—	—	—	—	—	R C O R	—	—
Thick-billed Murre	—	—	—	—	—	—	—	—	—
Razorbill	—	—	—	—	—	—	—	—	—
Black Guillemot	—	—	—	—	—	—	—	—	—
Pigeon Guillemot	•A A C U	—	—	—	—	—	U U R R	—	—
Marbled Murrelet	—	—	—	—	—	—	—	—	—
Kittlitz's Murrelet	—	—	—	—	—	—	—	—	—
Ancient Murrelet	U U	—	—	—	—	—	—	—	—
Cassin's Auklet	•A A A A	—	—	—	—	—	—	—	—
Crested Auklet	—	—	—	—	—	—	—	—	—
Rhinoceros Auklet	•U C C U	—	—	—	—	—	—	—	—
Tufted Puffin	•C C U	—	—	—	—	—	—	—	—

	CO-2 Alamosa	CO-3 Arapaho	CO-4 Browns Pk	CT-1 Salt Meadow	DE-1 Bombay Hk	FL-1 Corkscrew	FL-2 Cedar Keys	FL-3 Chassahow.	FL-4 Florida Keys	FL-5 Ding Darling	FL-6 Woodruff	FL-7 Loxahatchee
•s S F W	•s S F W	•s S F W	•s S F W	•s S F W	•s S F W	•s S F W	•s S F W	•s S F W	•s S F W	•s S F W	•s S F W	•s S F W
	O O O	U O	—	C U C	C C C R	R	C C C	C C C	C U C C	C O C C	R R O	A C A U
			—	O O U	U O U	—	—	—	O	—	—	U U
	O O O	—	—	O U	R R R	—	—	—	—	—	—	—
	O O O	—	—	U O C	O C C R	—	R R	R R	U	—	R	U U U
				C O C	—							
			—	C O C C	A O A C	—	O O O C	C	U U U	C R C C	—	R R R
				—	R R R		U	U	R R R R			U U
				R O R	U O O R							
				O O	R							
				R R R	R R R							
				C C U	C C A R	U	C C C C	C C C	—	C C C C	O	O U U O
	O U C	U O U	O O O	O U	O O	U	C C C C	U U U	C O C C	—	—	U U U U
	•C C C C	•C C U	•C C C	U O U R	C O C U	C C C	C C C	C C C	R R R	O C C	O O O	A A A
				•U U U R	•C U C R	R	O O	R	—	—	O O	R R
	•A C U	•U A C	C C U	R R	O O O	—	—	—	—	—	—	—
			C U	R R	O O	—	—	—	—	—	—	—
				R R								
	—	—	—	—	—	—	—	—	—	—	—	—
	—	—	—	—	—	—	—	—	—	—	—	—
	—	—	—	—	—	—	—	—	—	—	—	—
	—	—	—	O C C	C C C	R	C C C C	U U U C	•C C A A	•A A A A	O	U U U U
	U U	R	O O O O	—	—	—	—	—	O	—	—	—
	—	—	—	R R	R R	—	—	—	—	—	—	—
	—	—	—	O O O	O C U	—	—	—	—	—	—	—
	—	R	O O O O	U R C U	O O O	—	O C	C	O O U	R R R	R R R	—
	U	—	U O O O	U U U U	C U A C	—	C C C C	C C C	C C A	A R R A	C R U C	U U U
	—	O O O	O O O O	—	—	—	C O C C	C C C	C C C	C R R C	O O O	O O O
			—	•A A A A	C C A C	—						
				R R								
	—	—	—	—	—	—	—	—	—	R	—	—
	—	—	—	—	—	—	—	—	—	—	—	—
	—	—	—	R R	—	—	—	—	—	—	R	—
	—	—	—	•C C C C	C C C C	—	—	Ü	—	—	—	—
				O O O	—							
					O O O	—				R R	R	O O O R
	R	—	—	O	O U O	—	C C C C	O O O	U O U U	O R O	O	U U U
				R	O R	—	C C C C	C C C	C C C C	C C C C	—	—
					—	—	C U U U	U O O O	O O O A	C C C C		
	—	—	—	U U U	—	—	—	—	•R O	O O	—	—
	R	—	—	•U C C	O O O	—	C C C C	O C	O O U	O R O O	R R R R	—
	R	•O U O	C U O O	R R	O C C	—	U U C	U U C	C C C	C O C C	U C	O O O O
	R			•U C C	O C O	—	C C C C	C C C U	•A A C	•C C C	R R R R	U U O
										R		
	•U U U	•O U O	U	R R R	R R R	—	O O	O U O	U O U	R R	R R O	U O
	—	—	—	R	R O O R	—	O O O O	O O O O	O O C	•C C C C	—	U U U U
	—	—	—	—	—	—	—	—	—	—	—	—
	—	—	—	—	—	—	—	—	—	—	—	—
	—	—	—	—	—	—	—	—	—	—	—	—
	—	—	—	—	—	—	—	—	—	—	—	—
	—	—	—	—	—	—	—	—	—	—	—	—
	—	—	—	—	—	—	—	—	—	—	—	—

STATE-NUMBER OF BIRD LIST — REFUGE, SANCTUARY OR PRESERVE — NESTING, ABUNDANCE BY SEASON (• s S F W)	CA-2 Farallon	CA-3 Lo. Klamath	CA-4 Kern	CA-5 Modoc	CA-6 Sacramento	CA-7 Salton Sea	CA-8 S. F. Bay	CA-9 San Luis	CO-1 Phantom
AUKS, MURRES & PUFFINS (cont.)									
Atlantic Puffin	—	—	—	—	—	—	—	—	—
Horned Puffin	—	—	—	—	—	—	—	—	—
PIGEONS & DOVES									
Rock Dove	R R R R	—	O O O O	•O O O O	R R R R	•C C C C	•C C C C	•U U U U	•C U U
White-crowned Pigeon	—	—	—	—	—	—	—	—	—
Band-tailed Pigeon	O O O	—	—	—	R	—	—	—	U U U
White-winged Dove	R	—	—	—	—	•U U O	—	—	—
Mourning Dove	O R O	•C C C R	•C A A A	•C C C R	•C C C U	•C C C C	•C C C C	•C A A C	•U U
Inca Dove	—	—	—	—	—	R R R R	—	—	—
Common Ground-Dove	—	—	—	—	—	•U U U U	—	—	—
White-tipped Dove	—	—	—	—	—	—	—	—	—
CUCKOOS, ROADRUNNERS & ANIS									
Black-billed Cuckoo	—	—	—	—	—	—	—	—	R
Yellow-billed Cuckoo	R	—	—	R O R	—	—	—	—	U R
Mangrove Cuckoo	—	—	—	—	—	—	—	—	—
Greater Roadrunner	—	—	C C C C	—	—	•C C C C	—	—	—
Smooth-billed Ani	—	—	—	—	—	—	—	—	—
Groove-billed Ani	—	—	—	—	—	—	—	—	—
BARN OWLS									
Barn Owl	—	•C C C C	•C C C C	•U U U U	•C C C C	•R R R R	•U U U U	•U U U U	—
TYPICAL OWLS									
Flammulated Owl	—	—	—	—	—	—	—	—	—
Eastern Screech-Owl	—	—	—	—	—	—	—	—	U U U U
Western Screech-Owl	—	—	O O O O	—	•R R R R	R R R R	—	O O O O	—
Great Horned Owl	—	•C C C C	•U U U U	•C C C C	•U U U U	O O	•U U U U	•U U U U	• R
Snowy Owl	—	—	—	—	—	—	—	—	—
Northern Hawk Owl	—	—	—	—	—	—	—	—	—
Northern Pygmy-Owl	—	—	—	—	R R R R	—	—	—	U U U U
Elf Owl	—	—	—	—	—	—	—	—	—
Burrowing Owl	U U U	•U U U	•C C C C	•O O O	•R R R R	•C C C C	•U U U U	•U U U U	—
Spotted Owl	—	—	—	—	—	—	—	—	R
Barred Owl	—	—	—	—	—	—	—	—	—
Great Gray Owl	—	—	—	—	—	—	—	—	—
Long-eared Owl	R R O	—	—	O O O R	•R R R R	O	—	R R	R R R
Short-eared Owl	O	•U U U U	—	•U U U R	•R R R R	O R	•U R U U	•R R R R	—
Boreal Owl	—	—	—	—	—	—	—	—	—
Northern Saw-whet Owl	R	—	—	—	R R R R	—	—	—	U U U U
NIGHTJARS									
Lesser Nighthawk	O O	—	C C O	—	R U R	•U U R	—	•O O O	—
Common Nighthawk	—	•U C C	R	U C U	R R R	—	—	—	U
Pauraque	—	—	—	—	—	—	—	—	—
Common Poorwill	—	•U U U	U	—	R R	O	—	—	U C U
Chuck-will's-widow	—	—	—	—	—	—	—	—	—
Whip-poor-will	—	—	—	—	—	—	—	—	—
SWIFTS									
Black Swift	—	—	—	—	R R R	—	—	—	—
Chimney Swift	—	—	—	—	—	—	—	—	—
Vaux's Swift	R O	•U U U	O O	R R	R R R	C U	O O	—	—
White-throated Swift	—	—	—	—	R R R	R R R	U U U U	—	•C C
HUMMINGBIRDS									
Buff-bellied Hummingbird	—	—	—	—	—	—	—	—	—
Ruby-throated Hummingbird	—	—	—	—	—	—	—	—	—
Black-chinned Hummingbird	—	—	—	R R R	U R U	•R R	—	O O	—
Anna's Hummingbird	R R	—	•C C C C	—	U R U R	•U R U U	•U U U U	O O O O	—
Costa's Hummingbird	—	—	—	—	—	•U R U U	—	—	—
Calliope Hummingbird	R	—	O	O O U	—	O	—	—	—
Broad-tailed Hummingbird	—	—	—	—	—	—	—	—	U
Rufous Hummingbird	O O	•U U U	O O	O R O	R R R R	U R	U U R	O	U R
Allen's Hummingbird	O	—	U	—	R R	O	•C C O R	—	—
KINGFISHERS									
Belted Kingfisher	U U U	•U U U U	U U U	U U U O	•U U U U	R U U	U U U U	U U U U	R
Green Kingfisher	—	—	—	—	—	—	—	—	—
WOODPECKERS									
Lewis' Woodpecker	R R	—	—	O O R	R R R	O O O	—	R R	•U U
Red-headed Woodpecker	—	—	—	—	—	—	—	—	R R
Acorn Woodpecker	R R	—	O O O	—	•R R R R	—	R R R	R R	—
Gila Woodpecker	—	—	—	—	—	R R R R	—	—	—
Golden-fronted Woodpecker	—	—	—	—	—	—	—	—	—
Red-bellied Woodpecker	—	—	—	—	—	—	—	—	—
Yellow-bellied Sapsucker	R O	—	R	—	R R R R	—	—	—	U U U
Red-breasted Sapsucker	—	—	—	U U O	—	O	U	—	—

	CO-2 Alamosa	CO-3 Arapaho	CO-4 Browns Pk	CT-1 Salt Meadow	DE-1 Bombay Hk	FL-1 Corkscrew	FL-2 Cedar Keys	FL-3 Chassahow.	FL-4 Florida Keys	FL-5 Ding Darling	FL-6 Woodruff	FL-7 Loxahatchee
•s S F W	•s S F W	•s S F W	•s S F W	•s S F W	•s S F W	•s S F W	•s S F W	•s S F W	•s S F W	•s S F W	•s S F W	•s S F W
	—	—	—	—	—	—	—	—	—	—	—	—
	O O O O	—	R R R R	•O O O O	•O O O O	—	—	—	•A A A A	—	—	—
								—	•A A C O	C C C	—	—
	U U U								O U	R R R R	—	R R R R
	•C C A R	•C C C	•C C C	•C C C C	•C C A C	•C C C C	•C C C C	•C C C C	•U O U U	•C C C C	•C U C C	•A A A A
									•U U U U			
						•U U U U	•C C C C	•C C C C	•A A A A	•C C C C	•U U U U	•C C C C
	—	—	—	•O O O	•O O O	—	R R	R R	R	R R R	R	—
				•O O O	•C C C	•U U U R	O C O	O C O	•U U U R	R R	•U U C R	•C C C
									•U U R R	•C C C C		
								—	•O O O O	•C C C C	—	•C C C C
	R	—	R	R R R R	•U U U U	•R R R R	U U U U	R R R R	R R	•C C C C	R R R R	•U U U U
	—	—	—	O O O O	•U U U U	•U U U U	•C C C C	•C C C C	R R R R	•C C C C	•U U U U	•C C C C
	•C C C C	•U C U U	•C C C U	O O O O	•C C C C	•R R R R	•U U U U	•U U U U	—	•C C C C	•O O O O	•C C C C
			n	R R R								
			O									
	•R O O	•U C U	R R						•R R R R			
	—	—	—	O O O O	•C C C C	•C C C C	•C C C C	•C C C C	—	R R R R	•C C C C	•C C C C
	R R	•O O O	—	—	R R	—	—	—	—	R R R R	—	O O O
	•C C C C	O U U	O O O	U O U	•O R O O	—	U	U	—	R R R R	—	—
	—	R R R	—	—	R R R	—	—	—	—	—	—	—
	•U C C	•U C U	•C C C	U U U	O O O	•C C C	•C C C	•C C C	•O O C	•A C C	•U U C	•A A A
	R	—	•U U U	—	—	•C C C	•C C C C	•C C C C	•O O O U	•C C C C	•U C U	•C C C U
	—	—	•U C U	O O	C C	C C	U	R O	C C	O O O	U U U	
	—	—	—	O O O	C C C	—	C C C	O O O	R R	C C C	•O O O	R O O
	R	—	•C C C	—	—	—	—	—	—	—	—	—
	—	—	—	O O O	•C C C	•U U U U	•U U U U	•U U U U	U U U	O O O O	•O O O R	U U U
	U U U	—	•C C C	—	—	—	—	—	—	—	—	—
	O R	O U O	O O O									
	U U	O C U	•C C C									
	•U U U	U U O	U U U	•U C C U	•C U C C	C C C	•C C C C	•C C C C	C R C C	R C C C	U O U U	C R A A
	R	—	O O	—	—	R R R	R R R R	•C C C C	•U U U U	—	—	—
	O R	—	O	R R	R R R	R R R R	•C C C C	•U U U U	—	R R R	•O O O O	—
	—	—	—	•C C C C	•C C C C	•U U U U	•U U U U	•U U U U	•C C C C	•C C C C	•A A A A
	—	—	O O	O O R	O O O	C C	C C	C C C C	O U	C C	U U U	C C

STATE-NUMBER OF BIRD LIST REFUGE, SANCTUARY OR PRESERVE NESTING, ABUNDANCE BY SEASON	CA-2 Farrallon •s S F W	CA-3 Lo. Klamath •s S F W	CA-4 Kern •s S F W	CA-5 Modoc •s S F W	CA-6 Sacramento •s S F W	CA-7 Salton Sea •s S F W	CA-8 S. F. Bay •s S F W	CA-9 San Luis •s S F W	CO-1 Phantom •s S F W
WOODPECKERS (cont.)									
Williamson's Sapsucker	—	—	—	—	—	—	—	—	—
Ladder-backed Woodpecker	—	—	—	—	—	•U U U U	—	—	—
Nuttall's Woodpecker	—	—	O O O	—	U U U U	—	U R U U	O O O O	—
Downy Woodpecker	—	•U U U U	U U	U U U O	•R R R R	—	•U U U U	O O	R
Hairy Woodpecker	—	•U U U U	—	O O O	R	—	—	—	C C C C
Red-cockaded Woodpecker	—	—	—	—	—	—	—	—	—
Three-toed Woodpecker	—	—	—	—	—	—	—	—	R R R R
Black-backed Woodpecker	—	—	—	—	—	—	—	—	—
Northern Flicker	O U O	•C C C C	C O C C	•C C C C	U U C C	O U C	•U U U U	•U U U	•U U
Pileated Woodpecker	—	—	—	—	—	—	—	—	—
TYRANT FLYCATCHERS									
Olive-sided Flycatcher	O O	—	O O	R	—	R R	R	—	U C U
Western Wood-Pewee	U U	•U C U	C U	U O U	U U R	C U	R	O	•R
Eastern Wood-Pewee	—	—	—	—	—	—	—	—	—
Yellow-bellied Flycatcher	—	—	—	—	—	—	—	—	—
Acadian Flycatcher	—	—	—	—	—	—	—	—	—
Alder Flycatcher	—	—	—	—	—	—	—	—	—
Willow Flycatcher	O O	•U U U	O	•U O U	R R R	U C	R	U O	R
Least Flycatcher	R O	—	—	—	—	—	—	—	—
Hammond's Flycatcher	O O	—	U O	O R O	—	U O	—	U	—
Dusky Flycatcher	R R	—	O	O O	—	O O	—	O	R
Gray Flycatcher	O R	•U U U	R R	O O	—	R O	—	O	—
Western Flycatcher	O U	R R	U U	O O O	•R R R	C U	U R U	U	R
Black Phoebe	O R	—	U U C C	—	•U U U U	•C U C C	•U U U C	•C C U U	—
Eastern Phoebe	—	—	—	—	—	—	—	—	—
Say's Phoebe	O O	•C U C	U O U U	U R U	R R	•R R C C	O R O O	O U U	C C C
Vermilion Flycatcher	—	—	—	—	—	O O R R	—	—	—
Ash-throated Flycatcher	O R O	•U U U	U U	•O U O	•U U R	•U R U	O R	•U C O	—
Great Crested Flycatcher	R	—	—	—	—	—	—	—	—
Brown-crested Flycatcher	—	—	—	—	—	—	—	—	—
Great Kiskadee	—	—	—	—	—	—	—	—	—
Couch's Kingbird	—	—	—	—	—	—	—	—	—
Cassin's Kingbird	—	—	•U O	—	—	O	—	O	—
Western Kingbird	O R O	•C C C	•C C O	•O O O	•C C U	•C C U	O R	•C C U	R
Eastern Kingbird	R R R	R R	—	R	—	—	—	—	U U U
Gray Kingbird	—	—	—	—	—	—	—	—	—
Scissor-tailed Flycatcher	—	—	—	—	—	—	—	—	—
LARKS									
Horned Lark	R O	•C C C C	•C C C C	C U C U	•R R R U	•U U C C	•U U U U	•U U U	•A A
SWALLOWS									
Purple Martin	R R	• R R	—	—	R	O O	—	—	—
Tree Swallow	O O	•C C C R	C U A O	•A A A	•C C U U	C O C C	•U U U O	•C U C U	C
Violet-green Swallow	R O	•U U U	U U	•C U U	R R R	U O	U U U O	O O	•A A
Northern Rough-winged Swallow	R O	•U U U	U U	U O U	R R	•C C O U	U U O R	•O O O	U U U
Bank Swallow	R R	•U C C	O O	•O O O	•R R	R O R	R	R R R	—
Cliff Swallow	R O	•A A A	•A A O	•A A C	•C C U	•C C O	•A A C	•A A U	U
Barn Swallow	O O	•A A A	•C C U	•C A C	•C C U	•C R C O	•A A C R	•C C A	U U
JAYS, MAGPIES & CROWS									
Gray Jay	—	—	—	—	—	—	—	—	—
Steller's Jay	—	—	—	R	—	—	—	—	U U U
Blue Jay	—	—	—	—	—	—	—	—	—
Green Jay	—	—	—	—	—	—	—	—	—
Scrub Jay	—	•U U U U	—	O O O O	•R R R R	O	•U U U U	•C C C C	U U U U
Pinyon Jay	—	•R R R R	—	—	—	—	—	—	R R
Clark's Nutcracker	—	—	—	—	—	—	—	—	•U U
Black-billed Magpie	—	•C C C C	—	•C C C C	—	—	—	—	•U U U
American Crow	—	•R R R R	O O O O	R O O R	•U U U U	O R	R R R R	O O O O	U U U
Northwestern Crow	—	—	—	—	—	—	—	—	—
Fish Crow	—	—	—	—	—	—	—	—	—
Chihuahuan Raven	—	—	—	—	—	—	—	—	—
Common Raven	—	•U U U U	C C C C	O U O O	U U U U	R R R R	•U U U U	R R R R	•U U
TITMICE									
Black-capped Chickadee	—	•U U U U	—	O	—	—	—	—	U
Carolina Chickadee	—	—	—	—	—	—	—	—	—
Mountain Chickadee	—	—	—	C R C O	—	—	—	—	R
Boreal Chickadee	—	—	—	—	—	—	—	—	—
Chestnut-backed Chickadee	—	—	—	—	—	—	•C C C C	—	—
Plain Titmouse	—	•U U U U	—	U O U	•U U U U	—	U U U U	U U	—
Tufted Titmouse	—	—	—	—	—	—	—	—	—
VERDINS									
Verdin	—	—	—	—	—	•C C C C	—	—	—

Bird distribution chart. Each location column has four seasonal sub-columns: s (spring migration), S (summer), F (fall migration), W (winter). A leading • indicates breeding. Codes: C = common, U = uncommon, O = occasional, R = rare, A = abundant, — = absent.

Location	s	S	F	W
CO-2 Alamosa				
CO-3 Arapaho				
CO-4 Browns Pk				
CT-1 Salt Meadow				
DE-1 Bombay Hk				
FL-1 Corkscrew				
FL-2 Cedar Keys				
FL-3 Chassahow.				
FL-4 Florida Keys				
FL-5 Ding Darling				
FL-6 Woodruff				
FL-7 Loxahatchee				

Row-by-row data (each location gives s S F W):

Row	CO-2 Alamosa	CO-3 Arapaho	CO-4 Browns Pk	CT-1 Salt Meadow	DE-1 Bombay Hk	FL-1 Corkscrew	FL-2 Cedar Keys	FL-3 Chassahow.	FL-4 Fla Keys	FL-5 Ding Darling	FL-6 Woodruff	FL-7 Loxahatchee
	—	—	—	—	—	—	—	—	—	—	—	—
	U U U	O O U U	U U U U	U U C U	•C C C C	•C C C C	•C C C C	•U U U U	—	R R R R	•U U U U	•U U U U
	U _ U	O O U U	O O O	U U U U	•O U U O	•U U U U	•C C C C	•U U U U	—	R R R R	•O O O O	•U U U U
							R R R R					
	C C C	•O U O	•C C C	•C C C U	•C C C O	•U U U U	•C C C C	•C C C C	O O O O	•C C C C	•C C C C	•C C C C
						•C C C C	•C C C C	•U U U U		•C C C C	•U U U U	•C C C C
	R	—	•U O U	—	—	—	—	—	R	—	—	—
	•U C	R	•U O U	—	—	—	—	—	—	—	—	—
	—	—	—	•U O C	•C A C	U _ U	C C C C	U U U	U _ U	R _ O C	O _ O	U
	—	—	—	R	—	—	—	—	—	R R	R _ R R	O R O
	—	—	—	—	•U C O	R R R	U	U	—	—	—	—
	O O R	•O U O	—	R R R	R R R	—	—	—	—	—	—	—
	—	—	—	U U U	•O O O	—	—	—	—	—	—	U _ U U
	—	—	—	U C C	O _ O	U _ U U	—	—	—	—	—	
	R	—	—									
	•U U	O O O	•C U C	•U U C O	•C U C R	U _ U	—	C	C	O _ O U	U _ C C	C _ A A
	—	—	R R R	—	—	—	—	—	—	O _ O	—	—
	—	—	—	O O O	•C C C	•C C C C	•C C C	•C C C	•U U U U	•C C C C	•C C U	•C C C U
	O O	—	—	—	—	—	—	—	—	—	—	—
	O O O	U U O	•C C C	R	—	R	—	—	U U	R R O	—	U U
	O R	O O	U U U	•U C C	•C A C	•U U U U	•C C C C	•C C C R	C _ C	C R C	O O O	•C C A R
	—	—	—	—	—	•C C C	•C C C	•C C C	•A A C	—	R U U	
									U U	R O O		U
	•C C C C	C U C A	•C C C A	C O C C	•C O C C	—	—	—	—	—	—	—
	—	—	—	O O O	•C C O	U U U U	•C C C	•C C C	U U U	•C C C	O O O	U U U
	•C C U	O O O	•O O O	•U C A R	•C A A R	C _ C C	C _ C A	C _ C A	O O O O	C _ C C	C U C A	A U A A
	O C U	O C C	•C C C	—	—	—	—	—	—	—	—	—
	O O O	—	•C C C	U U O	U O U	U _ U U	•U O U	•U O U	R _ R R	C _ C C	O _ O	C _ C C
	O U U	O U O	•O O O	O O R	O C C	—	O _ O	O _ O	O _ O O	O _ O	R	U _ U O
	•C C O	•U C U	•C C C	O O O	—	—	—	—	R	—	R	O
	•C A O	•O U O	•C C C	•C C C	•C C C R	U _ U U	O _ O	O _ O	•C O A O	C C C	C O C	A A A R
	—	U R R O	—	—	—	—	—	—	—	—	—	—
	—	—	—	•C C C C	•C C C C	•C C C C	•C C C C	•C C C C	•R R R R	•C C C C	•C C C C	•C C C C
	—	—	U	—	—	—	•C C C C	—	—	—	•O O O O	—
	—	—	C O C C	—	—	—	—	—	—	—	—	—
	—	—	O _ O O	—	—	—	—	—	—	—	—	—
	•C A A C	•C C C C	•C C C C	—	—	—	—	—	—	—	—	—
	C O C U	•C C C C	U _ U	•C C C C	•A C A A	•R R R R	•C C C C	•C C C C	R R R R	R _ R R	—	—
	—	—	—	R R R R	•C C C O	•R R R R	•C C C C	•C C C C	—	•A A A A	•C C A A	U U U U
	—	—	—	—	—	—	—	—	—	—	—	—
	C O O O	U O O U	O _ O	—	—	—	—	—	—	—	—	—
	U U U	U O O U	U	•C C C C	O O	—	—	•C C C C	•C C C C	—	—	—
	—	—	—	—	•C C C C	—	•C C C C	—	—	—	•O O O O	—
	O R O O	U O O U	O	—	—	—	—	—	—	—	—	—
	—	—	—	—	—	—	—	—	—	—	—	—
	—	—	O	—	—	—	—	—	—	—	—	—
	—	—	—	•C C C C	•C C C C	•C C C C	•C C C C	•C C C C	—	—	•C C C C	—

STATE-NUMBER OF BIRD LIST REFUGE, SANCTUARY OR PRESERVE NESTING, ABUNDANCE BY SEASON	CA-2 Farrallon •s S F W	CA-3 Lo. Klamath •s S F W	CA-4 Kern •s S F W	CA-5 Modoc •s S F W	CA-6 Sacramento •s S F W	CA-7 Salton Sea •s S F W	CA-8 S. F. Bay •s S F W	CA-9 San Luis •s S F W	CO-1 Phantom •s S F W
BUSHTITS									
Bushtit	—	•U U U R	—	U U	U U U U	—	•C C C C	U U U	R R R R
NUTHATCHES									
Red-breasted Nuthatch	R O	—	—	O O O	—	O R O	U U O	—	U U U C
White-breasted Nuthatch	—	—	—	—	R R R R	—	—	—	U U U U
Pygmy Nuthatch	—	—	—	—	—	—	—	—	A A A A
Brown-headed Nuthatch									
CREEPERS									
Brown Creeper	O	—	—	O O	R R	O O	R	R	U U U
WRENS									
Cactus Wren	—	—	—	—	—	•C C C C	—	—	—
Rock Wren	•U C C	•C C C U	R R	•O O O	—	R R	O O O	—	• U R
Canyon Wren	—	•U C C U	—	—	—	—	—	—	•U
Carolina Wren	—	—	—	—	—	—	—	—	—
Bewick's Wren	—	•U U U U	O O	O O R	•U U U U	R R	•C C C C	•U U U U	—
House Wren	R R O	•U U U	O O O	•U U U	R R R R	R R U U	R	U U U U	•R U
Winter Wren	O R	•U U U U	—	O	R R R R	—	—	—	—
Sedge Wren	—	—	—	—	—	—	—	—	—
Marsh Wren	R	•C C C U	•A A A A	•C A C O	•C C C C	•C C C C	•C C C C	•C U U C	—
DIPPERS									
American Dipper	—	—	—	—	—	—	—	—	R R R
OLD WORLD WARBLERS & THRUSHES									
Arctic Warbler									
Golden-crowned Kinglet	R O	—	O O	O O O	R R R	O O	O O O	R	U U U U
Ruby-crowned Kinglet	O O	•C R C	U U U	C O C R	C C C	U C C	C C C	O U U	R
Blue-gray Gnatcatcher	R R	—	O	O O	R R	O U U	R O	R	—
Black-tailed Gnatcatcher	—	—	—	—	—	•U U U U	—	—	—
Eastern Bluebird	—	—	—	—	—	—	—	—	R
Western Bluebird	—	•U U U U	O O	O O	R R	O O	O R O O	U U U	U U U
Mountain Bluebird	—	•U U U U	—	U U O	R R	U	—	R R	•U U
Townsend's Solitaire	R R R	•U U C U	—	O O C	—	O O	—	—	•C C C
Veery	—	—	—	—	—	—	—	—	—
Gray-cheeked Thrush	—	—	—	—	—	—	—	—	—
Swainson's Thrush	O O	R	O	O R	R	U	U U	U	C C C
Hermit Thrush	O O R	—	U U U	U U	U U U	R U U	U U U	U U	A C C
Wood Thrush	—	—	—	—	—	—	—	—	R
American Robin	O O O	•C C C U	U U U	•C C C C	•U R R U	R R U	•U U U C	•C C O U	•A A A
Varied Thrush	O O R	R R	O O O	R	R R R	—	U U U	R R	R
Wrentit	—	—	—	—	—	—	O O O O	—	—
MOCKINGBIRDS, THRASHERS & ALLIES									
Gray Catbird	—	—	—	—	—	—	—	—	U U U
Northern Mockingbird	O O O	—	•U U U U	—	•U U U U	•C C C C	•U U U U	•C C C C	—
Sage Thrasher	R O	•U U U	O O O	• O	R	R O	—	R R	—
Brown Thrasher	R R R	—	—	—	—	—	—	—	U U U
Long-billed Thrasher	—	—	—	—	—	—	—	—	—
Bendire's Thrasher	—	—	—	—	—	—	—	—	—
Curve-billed Thrasher	—	—	—	—	—	—	—	—	—
Crissal Thrasher	—	—	—	—	—	•R R R R	—	—	—
Le Conte's Thrasher	—	—	—	—	—	—	—	—	—
WAGTAILS & PIPITS									
American Pipit	R O	C U R	U C C	C C	C R C C	R C C	C C C	C C A	
Sprague's Pipit	—	—	—	—	—	—	—	—	—
WAXWINGS									
Bohemian Waxwing	—	R R R	R	R	R R R R	—	—	—	R U
Cedar Waxwing	O O R	•U U U	U U O	O R O U	U R R U	U R U	O R O	O O O	R
SILKY-FLYCATCHERS									
Phainopepla	—	—	—	—	R R	•U U U	—	—	—
SHRIKES									
Northern Shrike	—	U U C	—	O O	R R R	—	—	—	U
Loggerhead Shrike	—	•C C C U	•A A C C	O O O O	•U U U U	•U U U U	•U U U U	•C C C C	R
STARLINGS									
European Starling	• A C	•C C C C	•C C A A	•A A A U	•C C C C	•C C C C	•C C C A	•C C C C	—
VIREOS									
White-eyed Vireo	—	—	—	—	—	—	—	—	—
Bell's Vireo	—	—	—	—	—	—	—	—	—
Black-capped Vireo	—	—	—	—	—	—	—	—	—
Gray Vireo	—	—	—	—	—	—	—	—	—
Solitary Vireo	O O	—	U U	O O	•R R R	U R O	O O	R	R R
Yellow-throated Vireo	—	—	—	—	—	—	—	—	—
Hutton's Vireo	R R	—	—	—	R R R R	—	•U U U U	—	—
Warbling Vireo	O O	—	U U	C O U O	R R R	C U	U U O	U	R
Philadelphia Vireo	—	—	—	—	—	—	—	—	—

	CO-2 Alamosa	CO-3 Arapaho	CO-4 Browns Pk	CT-1 Salt Meadow	DE-1 Bombay Hk	FL-1 Corkscrew	FL-2 Cedar Keys	FL-3 Chassahow.	FL-4 Florida Keys	FL-5 Ding Darling	FL-6 Woodruff	FL-7 Loxahatchee
	•s S F W	•s S F W	•s S F W	•s S F W	•s S F W	•s S F W	•s S F W	•s S F W	•s S F W	•s S F W	•s S F W	•s S F W
	–	–	–	–	–	–	–	–	–	–	–	–
	–	–	O	O O O	O OU	–	–	–	–	–	–	–
	O R O	–	U	C UCU	UOUU	–	•UUUU	•UUUU	–	–	–	–
	–	–	–	–	–	–	•CCCC	•CCCC	–	–	•OOOO	–
	–	–	–	O OO	C CC	–	–	U	U	–	–	–
	R	R O R	O	–	–	–	–	–	–	–	–	–
	–	–	U	–	–	–	–	–	–	–	–	–
	–	–	–	•UUCU	•UUUU	•CCCC	•CCCC	•CCCC	R	•CCCC	•CCCC	•CCCC
	•UUU	•UCU	•UUU	•CCCR	•CCCR	C CC	OO U	O OC	U UC	C CC	U UU	A AA
	–	–	–	O UO	U UC	–	OO U	O OU	–	–	R	–
	–	–	–	R R	•OOOR	U UU	U UU	U UU	–	C CC	O OU	U UU
	•CCOR	•UCU	•CCC	•UCCR	•CCCO	•UUUU	•CCCC	•CCCC	–	C CC	U UU	C AA
	–	OOR	UOU	–	–	–	–	–	–	–	–	–
	RRR	–	–	O CO	O CC	–	U UU	U UU	–	–	–	–
	RRR	–	O	O CO	C CO	U U	U	U	–	O OO	U UC	U CU
	–	–	UO	RRR	•CUOR	•UUUU	•UUUU	•UUUU	O CC	CCCC	•UUUC	C OAA
	–	ROR	R	OROR	•UUUU	•UUUU	•CCCC	•UUUU	–	R RR	OROO	O
	R	•OOO	O O	–	–	–	–	–	–	–	–	–
	CRO	•CCU	U U	–	–	–	–	–	–	–	–	–
	–	–	O O	–	–	–	–	–	–	–	–	–
	–	RRR	–	R R	C OC	U UU	U U	U U	O O	O O	R O	U
	–	–	–	U	O OO	U UU	O O	O O	U U	OOOR	–	U CR
	R	RRR	–	U	C C	U UU	O O	O O	U U	OROR	O	U CR
	–	–	–	ORUO	C CO	U UU	U U	U	R	O O	O OU	U CU
	•OCR	•UUO	•CCCC	•CCCU	•CCCO	C CC	C CA	C CA	RO	C CA	C AA	C UA
	–	–	–	–	–	–	–	–	–	–	–	–
	–	–	–	–	–	–	–	–	–	–	–	–
	–	OOR	UUU	•CCCO	•CCCO	C CC	•C CC	C CC	C CC	CRCC	U UU	A AA
	OO	OOR	U U	•CCCU	•CCCC	•CCCC	•CCCC	•CCCC	•AAAA	•AAAA	•CCCC	•AAAA
	•CCU	•UUO	•CCC									
	–	OOR	–	•CCCO	•CCCO	•UUUU	•CCCC	•CCCC	RO	COCC	•UUUU	•UUUU
	–	–	–	–	–	–	–	–	–	–	–	–
	–	–	–	–	–	–	–	–	–	–	–	–
	–	–	–	–	–	–	–	–	–	–	–	–
	R	–	O O	U CU	U UO	–	–	U	U	R	–	R RR
	–	–	R	–	–	–	–	–	–	–	–	–
	–	ORRO	–	CUCU	OROU	U UU	U U	U UU	U	ORRO	U UU	C UC
	–	–	O	R RR	–	–	–	–	–	–	–	–
	•OOOR	OOOR	CCCC	O OO	O OO	•CCCC	•CCCC	•CCCC	RR	CRCC	•OOOO	•CCCC
	•CUOC	OOOR	•CCC	•CUAU	•AAAA	RRRR	•CCCC	•CCCC	•UUUU	•CCCC	•UUUU	•CCCC
	–	–	–	•UCU	•CCC	•CCCC	•CCCC	•C CC	•UUUU	•CCCC	•CCCC	•AAAA
	–	–	–	–	–	–	–	–	–	–	–	–
	–	–	–	–	–	–	–	–	–	–	–	–
	–	–	–	R R	O O	U UU	C CC	CCCC	R RR	O RO	O OU	U CU
	–	–	–	–	•OOO	•RRRR	•O O	•O O	R RR	O OO	ORO	U UU
	R	RRR	–	R R	–	–	–	–	R R	–	–	–
	–	–	R	R R	–	–	–	–	R R	RRRR	–	–

STATE-NUMBER OF BIRD LIST / REFUGE, SANCTUARY OR PRESERVE / NESTING, ABUNDANCE BY SEASON	CA-2 Farallon •s S F W	CA-3 Lo. Klamath •s S F W	CA-4 Kern •s S F W	CA-5 Modoc •s S F W	CA-6 Sacramento •s S F W	CA-7 Salton Sea •s S F W	CA-8 S. F. Bay •s S F W	CA-9 San Luis •s S F W	CO-1 Phantom •s S F W
VIREOS (cont.)									
Red-eyed Vireo	O R	—	—	—	—	—	—	—	—
Black-whiskered Vireo	—	—	—	—	—	—	—	—	—
WOOD-WARBLERS									
Bachman's Warbler	—	—	—	—	—	—	—	—	—
Blue-winged Warbler	—	—	—	—	—	—	—	—	—
Golden-winged Warbler	—	—	—	—	—	—	—	—	—
Tennessee Warbler	O O	—	—	R R	—	—	—	—	—
Orange-crowned Warbler	C U	•U U U	U U O	A O A	R R R R	C C C	•C O C O	U O O	C U U
Nashville Warbler	O O	•U U U	O O	O O	R	C U	O R R	—	—
Virginia's Warbler	R	—	—	—	—	O	—	—	•U U
Lucy's Warbler	—	—	—	—	—	—	—	—	—
Northern Parula	R R	—	—	—	—	—	—	—	—
Tropical Parula	—	—	—	—	—	—	—	—	—
Yellow Warbler	C C	•C C C	C C	•C C C	R R	C C R	U U U	U O	•C C
Chestnut-sided Warbler	R O	—	—	—	—	—	—	—	—
Magnolia Warbler	O O	—	—	—	—	—	—	—	—
Cape May Warbler	R R R	—	—	—	—	—	—	—	—
Black-throated Blue Warbler	O	—	—	—	—	—	—	—	—
Yellow-rumped Warbler	U C O	•C C C	C C C	A O A	C C C	C C C	C C C	C C C	C
Black-throated Gray Warbler	R O	•R R R	U U	R O	R R	C U O	R R	O R	—
Townsend's Warbler	U U	U U	O	O	R R	U R O	U U U	U	—
Hermit Warbler	O O	—	O	—	R	U R	O R	O	—
Black-throated Green Warbler	R R	—	—	—	—	—	—	—	—
Blackburnian Warbler	R O	—	—	—	—	—	—	—	—
Yellow-throated Warbler	—	—	—	—	—	—	—	—	—
Pine Warbler	—	—	—	—	—	—	—	—	—
Prairie Warbler	O	—	—	—	—	—	—	—	—
Palm Warbler	O U	—	—	—	—	—	—	—	—
Bay-breasted Warbler	R	—	—	—	—	—	—	—	—
Blackpoll Warbler	O U	—	—	—	—	—	—	—	—
Cerulean Warbler	—	—	—	—	—	—	—	—	—
Black-and-white Warbler	O O	—	—	—	—	O O O	—	—	—
American Redstart	O O	—	—	—	—	O R R	—	—	U U
Prothonotary Warbler	—	—	—	—	—	—	—	—	—
Worm-eating Warbler	—	—	—	—	—	—	—	—	—
Swainson's Warbler	—	—	—	—	—	—	—	—	—
Ovenbird	O O O	—	—	—	—	—	—	—	—
Northern Waterthrush	R R O	—	—	—	—	O O	—	—	—
Louisiana Waterthrush	—	—	—	—	—	—	—	—	—
Kentucky Warbler	—	—	—	—	—	—	—	—	—
Connecticut Warbler	R R	—	—	—	—	—	—	—	—
Mourning Warbler	—	—	—	—	—	—	—	—	—
MacGillivray's Warbler	O O	•U U U	U U	C O U	R R	U R	O O	O R	•U
Common Yellowthroat	U U	•U U U	C U U U	•C C C	•U U U U	•U U U U	•U U U U	U O O	R
Hooded Warbler	—	—	—	—	—	—	—	—	—
Wilson's Warbler	U U	•U U U	C U	C O C	R R	C U O	C O O	C O	C U C
Canada Warbler	R R	—	—	—	—	—	—	—	—
Painted Redstart	—	—	—	—	R	—	—	—	—
Yellow-breasted Chat	O O	R	—	O	•R R	•O O O	—	—	R
TANAGERS									
Hepatic Tanager	—	—	—	—	—	—	—	—	—
Summer Tanager	R	—	—	—	—	O	—	—	—
Scarlet Tanager	—	—	—	—	—	—	—	—	—
Western Tanager	O O U	•U C U	O O	U O U	•U U R	C U O	U O U	U O	•U U
CARDINALS, GROSBEAKS & ALLIES									
Northern Cardinal	—	—	—	—	—	—	—	—	—
Pyrrhuloxia	—	—	—	—	—	—	—	—	—
Rose-breasted Grosbeak	O R	—	—	—	—	—	—	—	R
Black-headed Grosbeak	O U	—	U O	O O O	•U U	C U	•C C U	O O	R
Blue Grosbeak	R R	—	U U O	—	•U U	U U R	—	U U	U U
Lazuli Bunting	O O	•U U U	—	O O R	R R	C U	—	O	•R U
Indigo Bunting	R R R	—	—	—	—	—	—	—	R R R
Painted Bunting	—	—	—	—	—	—	—	—	R
Dickcissel	R R R	—	—	—	—	—	—	—	—
NEW WORLD SPARROWS & ALLIES									
Olive Sparrow	—	—	—	—	—	—	—	—	—
Green-tailed Towhee	R R	•U U R	—	U O	—	R R R	—	—	R
Rufous-sided Towhee	R O	•C U U R	U U U	C C	R R R R	R R	U U U U	U U U U	•A A
Brown Towhee	—	•U U U U	—	—	•U U U U	—	U U U U	U O U	—
Abert's Towhee	—	—	—	—	—	•C C C C	—	—	—
Bachman's Sparrow	—	—	—	—	—	—	—	—	—

	CO-2 Alamosa	CO-3 Arapaho	CO-4 Browns Pk	CT-1 Salt Meadow	DE-1 Bombay Hk	FL-1 Corkscrew	FL-2 Cedar Keys	FL-3 Chassahow.	FL-4 Florida Keys	FL-5 Ding Darling	FL-6 Woodruff	FL-7 Loxahatchee
	• s S F W	• s S F W	• s S F W	• s S F W	• s S F W	• s S F W	• s S F W	• s S F W	• s S F W	• s S F W	• s S F W	• s S F W
	–	–	–	U U U	•A A A	•U U U U	•C C C	C C C	U U	O O	•C C C	U C
	–	–	–		–	–	–	–	•C C C	•C C C	–	R R R
	–	–	–	U U U	O O	R R R	–	–	R R	O R O	R R	–
	–	–	R	O O	O O	R R R	–	–	R R	O R O	–	R
	–	–	–	O O	O O	U U U	–	–	C C	C R O	R	O U
	–	R R R	–	R R	–	U U U	U U U	U U U	U U U	C R R O	O O O	U U C C
	–	–	–	O O	O O	R R R	–	–		O R O R		U U R
	–	–	–	O O	C O C	•C U C C	C C C C	C C C U	U U U	C R C R	•C C C O	A O A U
	U U O	•C A C	•C C C	•C U U	•C C C	R R R	U C U	U U U	•C U C U	C R C	O O	U C
	–	–	–	O U U	C O C	R R R	–	–	U U	–	O O	R U
	–	–	–	O O	C C	R R R	U U	U U	O O R	O R R	O O	U C R
	–	–	–	R O	C C	R R R	U U	U U	C C R	C O C	O O	C C R
	•C C O	O	C O C	C O A A	A A C	C C C	C C C	C C A	C C C	C O C C	U U C A	A A A
	– R	–	O O	–	–	–	–	–	–	–	–	–
	–	–	–	R O	C C	R R R	U U	U U	U U O	O R O R	O O R	U U R
	–	–	–	R R	O O O	R R R	–	–	O O	O R R	R R	U
	–	–	–		C O O	C C C	•C C C C	•C C C C	O O U	C O N C	•C U C C	C U C U
	–	–	–	R R	C O O	•C C C C	•C C C C	•C C C C	R R	R R	•C C C C	O O O O
	–	–	–	•C C U	C O O	U U U	•C C C C	•C C C C	•C C C C	•C C C C	U U R	A U A U
	–	–	–	U U R	C C R	C C C	C C C	C C C	C C C	C C C	C C C	A A A
	–	–	–	O O	O O	–	–	–	U C	O R	–	O R
	–	–	–	O C	C C	R R R	O O O	U U	C U	C R	O O	C U
	–	–	–	–	R	R R R	–	–	R R	O R	–	–
	–	–	–	U C C	C O C	C C C	–	O O O	U U U	C R C	U U U	C C C
	–	–	–	O U U	•C O C	U U U	U U U	U U U	U U U	C C	U U R	A O A O
	–	–	–	R	•U O O	•U U U	U U	U U	U O U	C C	•U U U U	U U U
	–	–	–	R	R R	U U U	U U U	U U U	U U O	C O	O O U	U U U
	–	–	–	–	–	R R R	–	–	–	C O	R R	U U
	–	–	–	U U U	C U C	U U U	C C C	C C C	U U U	C C C	O U O	A A C
	O	–	O	O U U	C O C	U U U	U U U	U U U	U U C	C R C O	O O U W	A A U
	–	–	–	–	•O O O	U U U	U U U	U U U	U U R	C R C	O R O n	U U
	–	–	–	–	•C C O	R R R	–	–	U U	U U	O n	O
	–	–	–	R	–	R R R	U U	U U	U U	R R R	–	–
	–	–	O	R R	–	–	–	–	–	R R R	–	–
	•C C U	O O O	•C C C	•U A C O	•C A C R	•C U C C	•C C C C	•C C C C	C C C	•C C C C	•C C C C	•A C A A
	–	–	–	R R	R R R	R R R	C C C	C C C	U O	C O	O O	U U
	U U	R R R	O O C	R R	O O	–	–	–	R	R	–	U O R
	–	–	–	O O	C O O	–	–	–		O	R	–
	–	–	•C C C	•R R R R	•U U U R	R R R	U U	U U	–	R R	O R	U U U
	–	–	–	–	–	–	–	–	–	–	–	–
	–	–	–	R	–	U U U	•U C U	•U C U	O O	C R	•U U U	U U R
	–	–	–	O O O	•C C C	U U U	U U U	U U U	O O	C R	O U	U
	O O	R R	•C C C	–	–	–	–	–	–	–	–	–
	–	–	–	•C C C C	•C C C C	•C C C C	•A A A A	•A A A A	•U U U U	•A A A A	•C C C C	•A A A A
	–	–	–	O O	O U O	R R R	R R	R R	U U	C C R	–	O U
	O O	R	R	–	•C C U	R R R	C	C U	U U	C R R	R R	O U
	O O	–	O O	–	•C C U	R R R	C	C U	U U	C R R	R R	O U
	–	–	–	O O O	•C C C	U U U	U U U	U U U	O O U	C C C	O O R	C C C
	–	–	–	–	–	U U U	R R R	R R R	O O U	C C C	–	C C C
	–	–	–	–	–	–	–	–	–	–	R R	–
	O O	R	–	–	–	–	–	–	–	–	–	–
	R	R	•C C C	•C C C O	•C C C O	•C C C C	•C C C C	•C C C C	–	R •A A A A	•C C C C	–
	–	–	–	–	–	–	–	–	–	–	–	–
	–	–	–	–	–	•R R R	•U U U U	R R R R	–	–	•O O O O	R R R R

STATE-NUMBER OF BIRD LIST / REFUGE, SANCTUARY OR PRESERVE / NESTING, ABUNDANCE BY SEASON (•s S F W)	CA-2 Farallon	CA-3 Lo. Klamath	CA-4 Kern	CA-5 Modoc	CA-6 Sacramento	CA-7 Salton Sea	CA-8 S.F. Bay	CA-9 San Luis	CO-1 Phantom
NEW WORLD SPARROWS & ALLIES (cont.)									
Cassin's Sparrow	—	—	—	—	—	—	—	—	—
Rufous-crowned Sparrow	—	—	—	—	—	—	—	—	—
American Tree Sparrow	R O	R R R	—	O O U	—	—	—	—	U C
Chipping Sparrow	U U	•U C U R	U U	O O O	R R R	R R R	—	O O	U A A A
Clay-colored Sparrow	R O	—	—	—	—	—	—	—	A U
Brewer's Sparrow	O O	•C C C	—	•U U U	—	U U U	—	—	• C
Field Sparrow	—	—	—	—	—	—	—	—	—
Black-chinned Sparrow	—	—	—	—	—	—	—	—	—
Vesper Sparrow	O	•U U U	U U U	•O O O	R	O R U	—	R R	•A A
Lark Sparrow	R U	•U U U	U U U	O O	R R R R	R R R	—	O O O	R
Black-throated Sparrow	R R	—	—	—	—	O	—	—	—
Sage Sparrow	—	•R R R	•U U U U	O O O	—	R U	—	R R R	—
Lark Bunting	O	—	—	—	—	O	—	—	R
Savannah Sparrow	O U	•C C C U	C C A	•C U C R	C U U C	C O C C	•C C C C	C A A	—
Baird's Sparrow	—	—	—	—	—	—	—	—	—
Grasshopper Sparrow	R R	—	—	—	—	—	—	R R	—
Henslow's Sparrow	—	—	—	—	—	—	—	—	—
Le Conte's Sparrow	—	—	—	—	—	—	—	—	—
Sharp-tailed Sparrow	—	—	—	—	—	—	R R	—	—
Seaside Sparrow	—	—	—	—	—	—	—	—	—
Fox Sparrow	O U O	•C C U R	U U U	U O U	R R R	O O	C C C	O O O	—
Song Sparrow	R O	•C C C U	C C C C	•C A A C	•C U C C	•U R U U	•A A A A	C U U U	R
Lincoln's Sparrow	O U	U U	U C C	C C	R R U	U C C	C C C	U U U	R R
Swamp Sparrow	R R	—	—	—	—	O O	R	—	—
White-throated Sparrow	R. O	R R R	—	O O	R R	O O	O O O	—	—
Golden-crowned Sparrow	U U O	C C U	U U R	U U O	U R R U	O	C C C	C C C	—
White-crowned Sparrow	U U O	C C C	C A A	A A O	C R C C	U C C	A A A	A A A	C C U
Harris' Sparrow	R R	R R R	—	—	—	O	—	—	—
Dark-eyed Junco	U U	•C U C C	O C C	C C C	U C C	O U U	•O O O	U O U	•A C
McCown's Longspur	—	—	—	—	—	O O	—	—	—
Lapland Longspur	O	R R R	—	—	—	O O	—	—	—
Smith's Longspur	—	—	—	—	—	—	—	—	—
Chestnut-collared Longspur	—	—	—	R	—	O O	—	—	—
Snow Bunting	—	R R R	—	—	—	—	—	—	R
NEW WORLD BLACKBIRDS & ORIOLES									
Bobolink	R O	—	—	R	—	—	—	—	—
Red-winged Blackbird	R O	•A A A A	•A A A A	•A A C O	•A A A A	•C C C C	•A C A A	•C C A A	•C U
Tricolored Blackbird	—	•C C U R	•A A A A	•U O U	•C C C C	—	•U U U U	•C U A A	—
Eastern Meadowlark	—	—	—	—	—	—	—	—	—
Western Meadowlark	O O U	•C C C C	•A A A A	•C C C U	•C C C C	•U U C C	•C C C C	•C C C C	•A A
Yellow-headed Blackbird	O O	•C C C R	•A A C O	•C A C R	•U U U R	•C C C U	R R R	•C U O C	—
Rusty Blackbird	—	—	—	—	—	—	—	—	—
Brewer's Blackbird	O U	•A A A C	•A A A A	•C C C U	•C C C C	U O C C	•A C A A	•C C C A	•C C
Great-tailed Grackle	—	—	—	—	—	•U U U U	—	—	—
Boat-tailed Grackle	—	—	—	—	—	—	—	—	—
Common Grackle	—	—	—	—	—	—	—	—	—
Bronzed Cowbird	—	—	—	—	—	—	—	—	—
Brown-headed Cowbird	O O C	•C C C R	•C C U U	•C C C	•C C U U	•C U C C	•U U U O	•C C C U	U
Orchard Oriole	R R	—	—	—	—	—	—	—	—
Hooded Oriole	—	—	O	—	—	•U U O	—	R	—
Baltimore Oriole	—	—	—	—	—	—	—	—	—
Bullock's Oriole	O U	•C C C	•C C R	•U U U	•C C U	•C R U	•C U O R	•U U	R
Scott's Oriole	—	—	—	—	—	—	—	—	—
FINCHES									
Rosy Finch	—	—	—	R	—	—	—	—	—
Pine Grosbeak	—	—	—	—	—	—	—	—	—
Purple Finch	O O R	—	—	O O O O	—	O O	R R	R	—
Cassin's Finch	—	—	—	—	—	O O	—	—	—
House Finch	•U O R	•C C C C	C C C C	•C A C C	•C C C C	•C C C C	•C C A C	•C C C C	U U C
Red Crossbill	—	—	—	—	—	O O O	—	—	U U U R
White-winged Crossbill	—	—	—	—	—	—	—	—	—
Common Redpoll	—	—	—	—	—	—	—	—	—
Hoary Redpoll	—	—	—	—	—	—	—	—	—
Pine Siskin	R O	—	O O O	O O	R	R R	R R	R	C C C C
Lesser Goldfinch	R O	•U U U U	U U U	O O O	•U U U U	•U R U U	•C C C U	O O O	U U U
Lawrence's Goldfinch	—	—	—	—	—	U R R	—	R R R	—
American Goldfinch	R R	•U U U U	U U U	U U U	•C U U U	R R R	•C C C U	•C C U U	R
Evening Grosbeak	—	U U U U	—	O O O O	R	—	—	R	U
OLD WORLD SPARROWS									
House Sparrow	•O R R R	•C C C C	•C C C C	•A A C C	•C C C C	•C C C C	C C A C	•C C C C	U U U U
Eurasian Tree Sparrow	—	—	—	—	—	—	—	—	—

	CO-2 Alamosa • s S F W	CO-3 Arapaho • s S F W	CO-4 Browns Pk • s S F W	CT-1 Salt Meadow • s S F W	DE-1 Bombay Hk • s S F W	FL-1 Corkscrew • s S F W	FL-2 Cedar Keys • s S F W	FL-3 Chassahow. • s S F W	FL-4 Florida Keys • s S F W	FL-5 Ding Darling • s S F W	FL-6 Woodruff • s S F W	FL-7 Loxahatchee • s S F W
	R	—	—	—	—	—	—	—	—	—	—	—
	• R C C U	—	—	C U C	O C C	—	—	—	—	R	—	—
	U U	U U	—	• U C C O	• C U C R	U U U	U U U	R R U	—	R	U U U	U U U
	• O U O	O C R	—	—	—	—	—	—	—	—	—	—
				• U U U O	• C C C C	• U U U	U U U	U U U	—	O	O O O	—
	• C C U R	• O U O	• C U U	—	—	U U U	—	C	—	R	O O O	—
	O O O	• U U	• C C C	—	—	R R R	—	—	—	R O	R R	—
	R R	• O O O	• C C C	—	—	—	—	—	—	—	—	—
	O	• O O O O	—	—	—	—	—	—	—	—	—	—
	• C C C	• U C U	—	• U C C O	C R A C	U U U	C C A	C C A	O O U	C R R C	U U U	C A A
	R	—	—	• R R R	• O U O	U U U	U	U	O O U	R R O	O O O	U U U
	—	—	—	—	—	U	U	R R R				
	—	—	—	O U U	• A A A O	—	U	U	—	R R	—	R
	—	—	—	O U U	• A A A O	—	• C C C C	• C C C C	—	R R	—	—
	—	O O O	—	U O O	O U O	—	—	—	—	—	—	R R
	• C C C C	C C O	• C C C	• C C A C	• C C C C	R R R	C C C	C C C	—	R R	U U U	—
	—	O U O	—	U	—	—	—	—	—	—	R	—
	—	—	—	• U U C O	• C C C C	C C C	C C C	C C C	O	C C C	U C C	A A A
	—	—	—	U C C	A A A	U U U	A A A	A A A	—	R R O	O O U	—
	• C U C O	• O U U O	• C C C	U U O	O O O	R R R	—	—	R	R R R	R	—
	O C C	O O O	—	U U U	C C C	—	O O U	O U	—	—	O O	—
	R	O O	—	O O U	O	—	—	—	—	—	O O	—
		O O	—	—	—	—	—	—	—	—	R	—
		O O	U U C C	O O	—	—	—	—	—	—	—	—
	O R	—	O	• U U U	U C C	R R R R	C O	O O	C C	C O	U O	C A
	• C A C R	• C C U	• A A C	• A C C O	• A A A A	• C C C C	• A A A A	• A A A A	• A A A A	• A A A A	• C C C A	• A A A A
	—	—	—	• C C C U	• C U C C	• C C C C	• A A A A	• C C C C	—	R R R R	U U U U	• C C C C
	• C C C H	• O U U	• C C C	—	—	—	—	—	—	R O R R	—	—
	• C A C R	• C C U	• A A C	—	—	—	—	—	R O R R	—	U U U U	—
	• C C C	• U U U	• C C C	O O R	—	U U U	C	C	—	—	—	U U U
	O O	—	—	—	—	U U U	—	—	—	—	—	—
	—	—	—	—	O O O R	• C C C C	• A A A A	• A A A A	—	• A A A A	• C C C C	• A A A A
	—	R O R	• U O O	C C C U	• A A A C	• C C C C	• U U U U	• U U U U	• C C C C	• A A A A	• C U C C	• A C A A
	• C C C	• C C U	• C C C	U U U O	• C C C C	R R R	A	O	R R	R R R	R R O	U U U
	—	—	—	R R	• C U O	U U U	U C U	—	U U	O O	O O	O O
	—	—	—	—	—	—	—	—	—	—	O O	—
	• O O O	—	• C C C	• O O O	U U O	U U U	O U O	O U O	O O O	O R R	—	U C R
	R	C R O C	—	—	—	—	—	—	—	—	—	—
	—	—	—	—	R	—	—	—	—	—	R R O	—
	—	—	—	• U U U U	O R R	—	—	—	—	—	—	—
	• C C C O	• O O O	C C C	• U U U U	• O U U	—	—	—	—	—	—	—
	—	—	—	R R	—	—	—	—	—	—	—	—
	—	—	—	O O	R R	—	—	—	—	—	—	—
	O C C	R O	• C C C	O O O	O U U	—	—	—	—	—	R	R R
	U U	—	—	—	—	—	—	—	—	—	—	—
	• A A C	• O O R	• C C C	• U C C U	• U C C U	C C C	C	C	R R O	C R C	U U U	U C C
				U U U	O O O	—	—	—	—	—	—	—
	• C C C C	• U U U	R R R R	• O O O O	• A A A A	R R R R	C C C C	R R R R	• C C C C	• A A A A	O O O O	• U U U U
	—	—	—	—	—	—	—	—	—	—	—	—

STATE-NUMBER OF BIRD LIST REFUGE, SANCTUARY OR PRESERVE NESTING, ABUNDANCE BY SEASON	FL-8 Merritt Is. • s S F W	FL-9 St. Marks • s S F W	FL-10 St. Vincent • s S F W	FL-11 Biscayne • s S F W	FL-12 Everglades • s S F W	GA-1 Okefenokee • s S F W	GA-2 Piedmont • s S F W	ID-1 Bear L. • s S F W	ID-2 Camas • s S F W
LOONS									
Red-throated Loon	R	R	—	—	—	—	—	—	—
Arctic Loon	—	—	—	—	—	—	—	—	—
Pacific Loon	—	—	—	—	—	—	—	—	—
Common Loon	U O C	C U C	C C	O O U	R R R	R R R	—	O	U R
Yellow-billed Loon	—	—	—	—	—	—	—	—	—
GREBES									
Least Grebe	—	—	—	—	• —	—	—	—	—
Pied-billed Grebe	•C U C C	•C C A A	C U A A	C U C C	•C U C C	C R C C	U U U U	•C C U R	•U C C
Horned Grebe	O C C	C R U C	O O	R R	C C C	U U U	—	O	O O O
Red-necked Grebe	—	R R	—	—	—	—	—	—	—
Eared Grebe	—	—	—	—	—	—	—	•C C U	•A C C
Western Grebe	—	—	—	—	—	—	—	•C A C	U C U
SHEARWATERS & PETRELS									
Northern Fulmar	—	—	—	—	—	—	—	—	—
Cory's Shearwater	—	—	—	—	—	—	—	—	—
Pink-footed Shearwater	—	—	—	—	—	—	—	—	—
Greater Shearwater	R R	—	—	—	—	—	—	—	—
Sooty Shearwater	—	—	—	—	—	—	—	—	—
Short-tailed Shearwater	—	—	—	—	—	—	—	—	—
Manx Shearwater	—	—	—	—	—	—	—	—	—
Audubon's Shearwater	R R R	—	—	R R R	—	—	—	—	—
STORM-PETRELS									
Wilson's Storm-Petrel	R R R	—	—	—	—	—	—	—	—
Fork-tailed Storm-Petrel	—	—	—	—	—	—	—	—	—
Leach's Storm-Petrel	—	—	—	—	—	—	—	—	—
BOOBIES & GANNETS									
Masked Booby	—	—	—	R R R R	—	—	—	—	—
Brown Booby	—	—	—	O O O U	—	—	—	—	—
Northern Gannet	O R U	—	U	U R U C	—	—	—	—	—
PELICANS									
American White Pelican	C O O C	U R U U	U U U U	R R R R	C R C C	—	—	U C C	•U U U
Brown Pelican	•C C C C	C C C C	A A C A	•A C A A	•C C C C	—	—	—	—
CORMORANTS									
Great Cormorant	—	—	—	R	—	—	—	—	—
Double-crested Cormorant	•C C C C	A A A A	A A A A	•A A A A	•C C C C	O R O O	R	•C A C	•U C C
Olivaceous Cormorant	—	—	—	—	—	—	—	—	—
Brandt's Cormorant	—	—	—	—	—	—	—	—	—
Pelagic Cormorant	—	—	—	—	—	—	—	—	—
Red-faced Cormorant	—	—	—	—	—	—	—	—	—
ANHINGAS									
Anhinga	•C C C C	•C C C C	O O O O	R	•C C C C	•C C C C	R	—	—
FRIGATEBIRDS									
Magnificent Frigatebird	R R R R	R	O O R	C C C U	U U U U	—	—	—	—
BITTERNS & HERONS									
American Bittern	O O	U U U	U U U U	—	U R U C	U U U C	R	•C C U	•U C U
Least Bittern	•U U U U	•C C U R	C C C U	—	•U U U U	•O O R	R	—	—
Great Blue Heron	•C C C C	•C C C C	C C C C	•C C C C	•C C C C	•C C C C	U U U U	C C C R	•C A C R
Great Egret	•C C C C	•A A A A	A A A A	•C C C C	•C C C C	•C C C C	O O O O	R	•U U O
Snowy Egret	•C C C C	•A A A A	A A A A	•U U U U	•C C C C	•U U U O	O O O	•C C U	•U A U
Little Blue Heron	•C C C C	•A A A A	A A A A	•C C C C	•C C C C	•C C C C	R O O	—	—
Tricolored Heron	•C C C C	•A A A A	A A A A	•C C C C	•C C C C	•O O O O	R	—	—
Reddish Egret	•O O U U	U U U U	—	•U U U U	•U U U U	—	—	—	—
Cattle Egret	•C C C U	•C C C R	C C R	•C C C C	•C C C C	•C C C	O	•O O O	•O U O
Green-backed Heron	•C C C C	•C C U U	C C U R	•C C C C	•C C C C	•C C C O	•U U U	—	—
Black-crowned Night-Heron	•U U U U	•C U U C	O	U U U U	•C C C C	C O C C	O R	•U C U	•U A C
Yellow-crowned Night-Heron	O O O O	•U U R R	U U R	C C C C	•U U U U	U U U U	R	—	—
IBISES & SPOONBILLS									
White Ibis	•C C C C	•A A C C	A U A U	•C C C C	•C C C C	•C A A C	O	—	—
Glossy Ibis	•C C C C	U U U C	—	O O O O	•U U U U	R R R	—	—	—
White-faced Ibis	—	—	—	—	—	—	—	•C A U	•U C C
Roseate Spoonbill	U C O R	R R R	—	O O O O	•C U C C	—	—	—	—
STORKS									
Wood Stork	•C C C C	U U U R	U U O R	R R R R	•U R U U	•O C C O	—	—	—
SWANS, GEESE & DUCKS									
Fulvous Whistling-Duck	O O O	R R R	—	R	U U U U	—	—	—	—
Black-bellied Whistling-Duck	—	—	—	—	—	—	—	—	—
Tundra Swan	—	R R	—	—	—	—	—	R O	C R C
Trumpeter Swan	—	—	—	—	—	—	—	R	•U U U R
Mute Swan	—	—	—	—	—	—	—	—	—
Greater White-fronted Goose	—	O C	—	—	—	—	—	—	R
Snow Goose	R O	U U	U U U	—	—	—	R	R R	O O

	ID-3 Deer Flat	ID-4 Grays L.	ID-5 Kootenai	ID-6 Minidoka	IL-1 Chautauqua	IL-2 Crab Orchd	IL-3 Brussels	IL-4 Gardner	IN-1 Muscatatuck	IA-1 Desoto	IA-2 Wapello	IA-3 Union Slgh
	• s S F W	• s S F W	• s S F W	• s S F W	• s S F W	• s S F W	• s S F W	• s S F W	• s S F W	• s S F W	• s S F W	• s S F W
	—	—	—	—	—	—	—	—	—	—	—	—
	O O O	O	O U	U R U	O O	C R C O		O	O O O O	O O	O	O R
	—	—	—	—	—	—	—	—	—	—	—	—
	U U O O	•O O U	•C C U	•U C U O	C O C	•C R C U	C U C U	C U C U	•U U C O	C U C	C U C U	•C C C
	R R	O	U R U	U O U	U U	C C U	O O O	O O O	O O	O O	O O O	O R
	•C A C R	—	•C C U	—	—	R R			—	O O	—	O R
	—	•C C C	U O U	•C C A O						O R O	—	O
	•C A C R	•O O O	U R U	•C A C O	—	—	—	—	—	O R O	—	O
	—	—	—	—	—	—	—	—	—	—	—	—
	—	—	—	—	—	—	—	—	—	—	—	—
	—	—	—	—	—	—	—	—	—	—	—	—
	—	—	—	—	—	—	—	—	—	—	—	—
	O O O O	R R	—	C C U	R O	R R	R	R	—	C R C	R	C U C
	—	—	—	—	—	—	—	—	—	—	—	—
	O O O O	R R R	—	•C A C O	O O C	U R C R	•U U	•U U	O O O	C U C	•U U	C U C
	—	—	—	—	—	—	—	—	—	—	—	—
	—	—	—	—	—	—	—	—	—	—	—	—
	—	—	—	—	—	—	—	—	—	—	—	—
	—	—	—	—	—	—	—	—	—	—	—	—
	•O O R	•C C C	•U U O	•O O O	•C U U	O R O	U R U	U R U	O O O O	U U U	U R U	•U C U R
				R U R	R R R	•U U	•U U	•O O O	O	•U U	•O C O
	•C A C R	U U U	C C C U	•C A C U	•A A C U	U C C U	•C C C C	•C C C C	•C C C C	C U C R	•C C C C	C C C R
	O R	—		R	A A C R	O U U R	C C C	C C C	O O O O	U U U	C C C	O C U
	O R	U U U		•C C U	R O O	O O	R U	R U	R R	R	R U	—
	—	—		—	U O		U C C	U C C	O O O O	R R	U C C	R
	—	—		—	—	—	—	—	—	—	—	—
	—	—		O O O	U U U	U O U	R U O	R U O	O O O	R R	R U O	—
				—	•U C U	•C C C	•C C C	•C C C	•U U U O	U U O	•C C C	•C C C
	•C A C O	O O O		•C C U	•O C O	•C U U	•C U U	•C U U	•U U U O	U R U	•C U U	•C C C
	—	—		—	R R R	•U U O	•C U U	C U U	U O O O	R R	C U U	O R
	—	—	—	—	—	—	—	—	—	—	—	—
	O R	U U O	—	•U U U	—	—	—	—	—	—	—	—
	—	—	—	—	—	—	—	—	—	—	—	—
	—	—	—	—	—	—	—	—	—	—	—	—
	—	—	—	—	—	—	—	—	—	—	—	—
	U R U	O O	C U	C R C U	R R R	—	O R	O R	O R O O	R R R	O R	O O
	—	•R R R	—	R	—	—	—	—	—	—	—	—
	O R	R	U U	O O	R R	O R	U U O	U U O	O O	O O	U U O	C R C
	U R U O	O O R	O O	U U O	C C O	U C U	C C C	C C C	O O O O	A R A U	C C	C R C O

STATE-NUMBER OF BIRD LIST / REFUGE, SANCTUARY OR PRESERVE / NESTING, ABUNDANCE BY SEASON	FL-8 Merritt Is. •s S F W	FL-9 St. Marks •s S F W	FL-10 St. Vincent •s S F W	FL-11 Biscayne •s S F W	FL-12 Everglades •s S F W	GA-1 Okefenokee •s S F W	GA-2 Piedmont •s S F W	ID-1 Bear L. •s S F W	ID-2 Camas •s S F W
SWANS, GEESE & DUCKS (cont.)									
Ross' Goose	—	—	—	—	—	—	—	—	—
Emperor Goose	—	—	—	—	—	—	—	—	—
Brant	R R	—	—	—	—	R	—	—	—
Canada Goose	R R	R O O	—	—	—	O OO	O OO	•A A A U	•C A A O
Wood Duck	•O R O O	C C C C	C C C C	R	R	•C C C C	•C C C C	R	•R R R
Green-winged Teal	U C C	C C C	C A C	—	U R U	C C C	O U O	•C U C R	•C C C R
American Black Duck	R O O	U U U	U	—	—	C C C	U C C	—	—
Mottled Duck	•C C C C	—	U	O	•C C C C	—	—	—	—
Mallard	R O O	U U C	A C A	—	R	C C C	•C O C C	•C C A O	•A A A U
Northern Pintail	U C C	C C C	C C C	—	C R C	U U U	O O R	•C C C R	•A A A R
Blue-winged Teal	C O C C	C U C U	C A C	U U	C R C C	U U U	U U	•O O O	•C C O
Cinnamon Teal	—	R R	—	—	—	—	—	•C U O	•A A U
Northern Shoveler	C R C C	C R C C	C C	—	C R C C	U U U	O O	•C U C R	•C A U
Gadwall	U U U	C C C	C C C	—	R R	O O O	O O	•C A A R	•A A A
Eurasian Wigeon	—	R R	—	—	—	—	—	—	—
American Wigeon	C R C C	C R A A	C A A	—	C C C	U U U	O O	U U U	•A A A
Canvasback	U O U U	U U U	C C C	—	R R	R R R	O O	•U U U	•C C U
Redhead	U O U U	U R A A	C C C	—	R R	O O O	R R	•A A C R	•A A C
Ring-necked Duck	O C C	C C C	A A	—	C C C	C C C	C C C	U O	•C C U
Greater Scaup	R O O	U O C C	U	—	—	R R R	—	O	R R
Lesser Scaup	C O C C	C O C C	A C A	O O	C C C	U U U	O O	•C R U	•A C C
Common Eider	—	—	—	—	—	—	—	—	—
King Eider	—	—	—	—	—	—	—	—	—
Steller's Eider	—	—	—	—	—	—	—	—	—
Harlequin Duck	—	—	—	—	—	—	—	—	—
Oldsquaw	R R	R R	—	—	—	—	—	—	—
Black Scoter	R R R O	R R R	—	—	—	—	—	—	—
Surf Scoter	R R	R R R	—	—	—	—	—	—	—
White-winged Scoter	R O	—	—	—	—	—	—	—	—
Common Goldeneye	R R	U U U	R U C	—	—	R R R	—	U U	C R C U
Barrow's Goldeneye	—	—	—	—	—	—	—	R O R	R R R
Bufflehead	O O	U C C	A C A	R	R	R R R	O O O	C R U R	C R C
Hooded Merganser	O C C	C C	C C A	—	U R U	•C R C C	•O R U C	O R	R R
Common Merganser	—	R R	—	—	—	—	R R	U U O	C U
Red-breasted Merganser	U C C	C R C C	A A A	U C C	C R C C	R R R	R R	U O R	•C O U
Ruddy Duck	O C C	U R C C	C C C	—	U U C	O O O	O O O	•C C U R	•C A C
Masked Duck	—	—	—	—	—	—	—	—	—
AMERICAN VULTURES									
Black Vulture	•C C C C	•U U C C	A A A A	C C C C	•C C C C	•C C C C	•C C C C	—	—
Turkey Vulture	•C C C C	•C C C C	A A A A	U U U U	•C C C C	•C C C C	•C C C C	O O	R R R
KITES, EAGLES, HAWKS & ALLIES									
Osprey	•C C C C	•C C U O	A A U R	•C C C C	•C C C C	•U U R U	O O O	O R	R R
American Swallow-tailed Kite	O O	•U U	U U	U U	•C C R	R R R	—	—	—
Black-shouldered Kite	—	—	—	—	—	—	—	—	—
Snail Kite	—	—	—	—	•R R R R	—	—	—	—
Mississippi Kite	—	•U U	—	—	—	—	—	—	—
Bald Eagle	•U U U U	•U O U C	C C C C	•U O U U	•C C C C	R R R	O	O R O	C U C
Northern Harrier	U C C	C R C C	C U C	U U C	U U C	O O O	U U U	•C C C U	•C C C O
Sharp-shinned Hawk	O U U	R U U	U O	U C U	U U U	R R R	O U U	R R	R R R R
Cooper's Hawk	O O O	R U O	—	—	O O	R R R	•O R O O	R R	R R R
Northern Goshawk	—	—	—	—	—	—	—	—	•O O O O
Common Black-Hawk	—	—	—	—	—	—	—	—	—
Harris' Hawk	—	—	—	—	—	—	—	—	—
Gray Hawk	—	—	—	—	—	—	—	—	—
Red-shouldered Hawk	•U U U U	•C C C C	C C C	U U U U	•C C C C	•C C C C	•U U U U	—	—
Broad-winged Hawk	R O R	•U U U	C C	U U U	U U U	O O	R O R	—	—
Short-tailed Hawk	—	—	—	R R	•U R U U	—	—	—	—
Swainson's Hawk	R R	—	—	—	R R U	—	—	O O O	•C C C C
White-tailed Hawk	—	—	—	—	—	—	—	—	—
Zone-tailed Hawk	—	—	—	—	—	—	—	—	—
Red-tailed Hawk	•C C C C	•U U C C	C U U C	O O	•U U U U	•U R U U	•C U C C	O R R	•C U U O
Ferruginous Hawk	—	—	—	—	—	—	—	R R	•U U U R
Rough-legged Hawk	—	—	—	—	—	—	—	O O U	C C C
Golden Eagle	—	R R	O O O O	—	—	—	R O	U O U U	C O O C
CARACARAS & FALCONS									
Crested Caracara	—	—	—	—	—	—	—	—	—
American Kestrel	U R C C	U U U	A C C	C C C	C C C	•C O C C	•O R O O	U O U	•C C C O
Merlin	O O O	O O O	U	U O	U U U	R R R	—	—	R R
Peregrine Falcon	R O O	R O O	U U	O U U U	U U U	R R R	—	O O	O U O O
Gyrfalcon	—	—	—	—	—	—	—	—	—
Prairie Falcon	—	—	—	—	—	—	—	O O R	O O O O

ID-3 Deer Flat	ID-4 Grays L.	ID-5 Kootenai	ID-6 Minidoka	IL-1 Chautauqua	IL-2 Crab Orchd	IL-3 Brussels	IL-4 Gardner	IN-1 Muscatatuck	IA-1 Desoto	IA-2 Wapello	IA-3 Union Sigh
•s S F W	•s S F W	•s S F W	•s S F W	•s S F W	•s S F W	•s S F W	•s S F W	•s S F W	•s S F W	•s S F W	•s S F W
—	—	R R	—	—	—	—	—	—	O U	—	R R
—	—	—	—	—	—	—	—	—	—	—	—
•CCAC	•AAAO	•ACAU	•CCAC	•COCC	•CUAA	COCC	COCC	•AAAA	C CU	COCC	CUCO
•CCCO	RR	•CCU	O O	•AAAO	•CCCO	•CAAO	•CAAO	•AAAC	•CCCR	•CAAO	CAC
•CCAC	•CCCO	•CUAO	•CUCU	CUAO	C CU	CUCU	CUCU	•C UO	C CO	CUCU	•CUAR
—	—	—	—	CUCO	C CC	C CC	C CC	COCC	U UU	C CC	•COCO
•ACAA	•AAAU	•AAAA	•ACAC	•AOAU	•CUCC	CCAA	CCAA	•AAAA	•AUAA	CCAA	•ACAC
•CCAA	•ACAO	•AUAO	•ACAU	CRCO	C CC	COAC	COAC	C UU	C CU	COAC	•AUAR
•OCU	•CCU	•CCO	•OUU	•CUAR	•CUC	CUC	CUC	•CCCO	•CUC	CUC	•ACA
•CCU	•CCC	•CCO	•OUU	C C	COCU	C CU	C CU	U UO	C CR	C CU	•AUA
•OUCO	•CCC	•COU	•UOCO	URUR	C CC	CRCO	CRCO	COCU	C CO	CRCO	•CUC
•UUO	•ACCO	•COU	—								
R R	—	O	R								
•CUAC	•CUC	•ACAO	•CCAU	CRCR	C CU	C CU	C CU	C UU	C CO	C CU	•AUA
O U	•CUU	U U	•CUA	CRCO	U UC	U UU	U UU	O OO	U UR	U UU	COC
•UUUR	•CCC	•CCU	•CAA	C CO	C CU	C CC	C CC	U UO	U UR	C CC	•CUC
O U	•UOO	•CCC	•CUC	C CO	C CC	C CC	C CC	A CC	C CR	C CC	CUC
	—	O O	O O	R R	R R	O OO	O OO		O R	O OO	—
URU	•CUU	UUU	•CCA	ARCU	C CC	A CC	A CC	UOCC	C CR	A CC	AUU
						—	—		—		
—	—	—	—	—	—	—	—	—	—	—	—
—	—	—	—	—	—	R R	O	O	—	—	—
—	—	—	—	R R	—	—	—	—	—	O	—
—	—	O	—	R R R	—	—	—	—	—	—	—
—	—	O	—	R R R	R	—	—	—	R R	—	—
—	U UO	•CCCU	•COCC	U UC	C UC	U UC	U UC	U UO	U UC	U UC	U
R R	•UUUR	U O	O U	—	—	—	—	—	—	—	—
UR	C CO	COC	•CCCU	U UO	C CC	U UU	U UU	O OO	U U	U UU	C U
UOU	—	•UOU	U OU	URUO	CRCC	•UUUU	•UUUU	•UUUU	C UC	•UUUU	•CUO
UOCC	O OO	U U	•CCCC	A UA	C CA	U UA	U UA	O O	U UA	U UA	C
O UU	O O	—	UOUU	O O	C CO	U U	U U	—	O O	U U	R
•UOU	•UUU	•CCU	•CCAO	UOAO	C CC	A CU	A CU	O OO	U UR	A CU	•CCC
					—	—	—		—	—	—
—	—	—	—	O	—	—	—	—	—	—	
R UR	UUU	U U	•UCU	•OOO	•CCCR	•CCC	•CCC	•CCCU	U UO	•CCC	ORR
O O R	RRR	•UCO	O O O	U O O O	U O U	U UO	U UO	O O O	U U	U UO	R O O
—	—	—	—	—	—	—	—	—	—	—	—
—	—	—	—	—	—	—	—	—	—	—	—
U C	OROO	•CUCC	COUC	U UC	•UOCC	U UC	U UC	O OR	U CC	U UC	O UR
•CCCC	•CCCO	•CCUU	•CCCU	OROC	COCC	U UU	U UU	COCC	UOUU	U UU	•UCCO
R OU	•O O O	O O U O	U U U O	U O U O	O CU	U U U U	U U U U	U U U U	U UU	U U U U	O O O
•RROU	•O O O	•U O U O	U R U O	U R U O	•UUUU	•O O O C	•O O O C	•UUUU	U R U U	•O O O C	•O O O O
O UU	•U U U U	R R R O	—	—	R RR	O R	O R	R R.	R R R	O R	R R
—	—	—	—	—	—	—	—	—	—	—	—
—	—	—	—	•O O O O	•C C C C	U U C U	U U C U	•U U U U	R	U U C U	R
—	—	—	—	O R O	•CCU	O O O	•O O O	O O	O O	O O O	C O C
•ORO	•CCC	R R	•UCC	—	—	—	—	—	O O	—	•UUU
—	—	—	—	—	—	—	—	—	—	—	—
•OUCC	•CCCR	•CCUO	•UOUO	•CUCC	•CCCC	•CUCC	•CUCC	•CCCC	•CUCC	•CUCC	OCCO
R	•UUU	—	O O	—	—	—	—	—	—	—	U CC
O UC	U U UC	C CC	UUUC	U UC	U OU	U OU	O OO	O OO	URUU	O OO	U C C
U U	•UUUU	UOO	•CUUC	—	R OO	U OR	U OR	O O O	O O	U OR	R RR
CCCC	•CCCR	•CCCO	•UCCO	•CCCO	•CCCC	•UUUU	•UUUU	•CCCC	•UUUU	•UUUU	•CUCO
OROU	—	RRR	RRR	—	R R	R RR	—	—	—	—	U U
RRR	—	RRRR	RROR	O O O	O O O	—	O R	O R	R R	O R	R R
—	—	—	—	—	—	—	—	—	—	—	—
O O O	•UUU	RRR	O O	—	—	—	—	—	O R	—	—

STATE-NUMBER OF BIRD LIST / REFUGE, SANCTUARY OR PRESERVE / NESTING, ABUNDANCE BY SEASON	FL-8 Merritt Is. • s S F W	FL-9 St. Marks • s S F W	FL-10 St. Vincent • s S F W	FL-11 Biscayne • s S F W	FL-12 Everglades • s S F W	GA-1 Okefenokee • s S F W	GA-2 Piedmont • s S F W	ID-1 Bear L. • s S F W	ID-2 Camas • s S F W
CHACHALACAS									
Plain Chachalaca	—	—	—	—	—	—	—	—	—
PARTRIDGES, GROUSE, TURKEYS & QUAILS									
Gray Partridge	—	—	—	—	—	—	—	• O U	• U U U U
Chukar	—	—	—	—	—	—	—	R R R	—
Ring-necked Pheasant	—	—	—	—	—	—	—	R R R R	• C C C C
Spruce Grouse	—	—	—	—	—	—	—	—	—
Blue Grouse	—	—	—	—	—	—	—	—	—
Willow Ptarmigan	—	—	—	—	—	—	—	—	—
Rock Ptarmigan	—	—	—	—	—	—	—	—	—
White-tailed Ptarmigan	—	—	—	—	—	—	—	—	—
Ruffed Grouse	—	—	—	—	—	—	—	—	—
Sage Grouse	—	—	—	—	—	—	—	R	• U U C R
Greater Prairie Chicken	—	—	—	—	—	—	—	—	—
Lesser Prairie Chicken	—	—	—	—	—	—	—	—	—
Sharp-tailed Grouse	—	—	—	—	—	—	—	—	—
Wild Turkey	• O O O O	• U U U U	C C C C	—	• R R R R	• R R R R	• U U U U	—	—
Northern Bobwhite	• C C C C	• U U U U	U U U U	—	• C C C C	• C C C C	• C C C C	—	—
Scaled Quail	—	—	—	—	—	—	—	—	—
Gambel's Quail	—	—	—	—	—	—	—	—	—
California Quail	—	—	—	—	—	—	—	—	—
Mountain Quail	—	—	—	—	—	—	—	—	—
RAILS, GALLINULES & COOTS									
Yellow Rail	—	R R R	—	—	—	—	—	—	—
Black Rail	• R R R R	R R R	O O O O	—	R	—	—	—	—
Clapper Rail	• O O O O	• C C C C	O O O O	O O O O	• C C C C	—	—	—	—
King Rail	• O O O O	• U U U U	U U U U	—	• C C C C	• R R R R	R R	—	—
Virginia Rail	R O O	U U U	U	—	R R R	R R R	—	• O O O	R
Sora	O U U	C C U	C C C C	—	C C C	R R	—	• O U O	• O O O
Purple Gallinule	—	• U C U R	O O O O	O O O	• C C C C	• U U U U	R	—	—
Common Moorhen	• C C C C	• C A A U	C C A C	O O O	• C C C C	• U U U U	R	—	—
American Coot	C O C C	A O A A	C U A A	C C	• C R C C	C C C	O O O	• C A C O	• C A A R
LIMPKINS									
Limpkin	R R	R R R R	—	—	• C C C C	—	—	—	—
CRANES									
Sandhill Crane	—	R R	—	—	• R R R R	• C C C C	O O O	• C C C	• C C C
Whooping Crane	—	—	—	—	—	—	—	R R R	—
PLOVERS									
Black-bellied Plover	U O C C	C U C C	C U C C	U O C C	C R C C	—	—	R	—
Lesser Golden-Plover	—	R R	—	—	R R R	—	—	—	—
Snowy Plover	—	—	C O C	—	—	—	—	—	—
Wilson's Plover	• O O O R	• U C U U	U C U	C C C C	• C C C U	—	—	—	—
Semipalmated Plover	O R O C	C U C C	C C C	C O C C	C U C C	—	—	—	U
Piping Plover	O O O	R R R	U U U	U O U U	U U U	—	—	—	—
Killdeer	• C C C C	• C R C U	C C U	O O C C	• C U C C	C C C	O O O O	• C C U	• C C C
Mountain Plover	—	—	—	—	—	—	—	—	—
OYSTERCATCHERS									
American Oystercatcher	• O O O R	• U U U U	C C C C	R	R	—	—	—	—
Black Oystercatcher	—	—	—	—	—	—	—	—	—
STILTS & AVOCETS									
Black-necked Stilt	• U U U	• R R R	—	U U	• U R U R	—	—	• U U O	• U C U
American Avocet	O O C C	O O O	—	R	C U C C	—	—	• U U O	• C C C
SANDPIPERS									
Greater Yellowlegs	C O C C	C U C U	C C C	U U U U	C U C C	U U	O R	U O	U R U
Lesser Yellowlegs	C O C C	U U U U	—	U U U U	C U C C	U U	O R	O O	U R U
Solitary Sandpiper	O O O	O O O	U U	—	U U R	O O	O O	—	O O O
Willet	• C C C C	• C C A A	C A A C	C C C C	C U C C	R R	—	• C C O	• U C
Wandering Tattler	—	—	—	—	—	—	—	—	—
Spotted Sandpiper	U O U U	U U U O	C C C C	C O C C	C C C	U U	U O U U	• U U R	O O O
Upland Sandpiper	R R	R R R	—	R	—	—	O R R	—	—
Whimbrel	O O O	U U U U	U	U O U U	U R U U	—	—	—	—
Long-billed Curlew	R R R	R R	—	—	R R R	—	—	O O	• C C
Hudsonian Godwit	—	—	—	—	—	—	—	—	—
Bar-tailed Godwit	—	—	—	—	—	—	—	—	—
Marbled Godwit	O O O	O R O R	—	O O	C R C C	—	—	O	O R
Ruddy Turnstone	C O C C	C U C U	C C C	C O C C	C U C C	—	—	—	—
Black Turnstone	—	—	—	—	—	—	—	—	—
Surfbird	—	—	—	—	—	—	—	—	—
Red Knot	O O O O	O R O	O O O O	O O R	U R U U	—	—	—	—
Sanderling	C U C C	U U U U	C C C	O O R	U U U	O O O	—	—	—
Semipalmated Sandpiper	C O C O	C U C	A A	U O U	U U R	O O O	—	—	—
Western Sandpiper	C U C C	C C A U	C C C	U O U U	C R C C	R R R	—	O O O	U U U

	ID-3 Deer Flat	ID-4 Grays L.	ID-5 Kootenai	ID-6 Minidoka	IL-1 Chautauqua	IL-2 Crab Orchd	IL-3 Brussels	IL-4 Gardner	IN-1 Muscatatuck	IA-1 Desoto	IA-2 Wapello	IA-3 Union Slgh
•s S F W	•s S F W	•s S F W	•s S F W	•s S F W	•s S F W	•s S F W	•s S F W	•s S F W	•s S F W	•s S F W	•s S F W	•s S F W
	U U U U	—	—	—	—	—	—	—	—	—	—	—
	—	•U U U U	—	•U C C U	—	—	—	—	—	O	—	•C C C C
	•R R O O	—	•R R R R	•C C C C	O O O O	—	—	—	O O	•A A A A	O O O O	•A A A A
	—	—	R	—	—	—	—	—	—	—	—	—
	—	•U U U U	O O O	—	—	—	—	—	—	—	—	—
	—	—	—	—	—	—	—	—	—	—	—	—
	—	—	—	—	—	—	—	—	—	—	—	—
	—	•C C C C	•C C C C	—	—	—	—	—	—	U U U U	—	—
	—	•U U U U	—	O O O O	—	—	—	—	—	—	—	—
	—	—	—	—	—	—	—	—	—	—	R	—
	—	•O O O O	O O O O	—	—	•U U U U	—	—	•U U U U	R R	—	—
	•U C C U	—	—	—	•A A A A	•C C C C	•C C C C	•C C C C	•C C C C	•C C C C	•C C C C	•R R R
	•U C C U	—	R R R R	—	—	—	—	—	—	—	—	—
	—	—	—	—	—	—	—	—	—	—	—	—
	—	—	—	—	R R	R	O R	O R	• U O	—	O R	• U U
	•O O O	•U U U	•O O	R	U O U	U R U	U R	U R	•U U U	R R	U R	•U C C
	•O O O	•C C C	•U U O	•O U O	•C R C	O O	•C U C	•C U C	•U U U	U O U	•C U C	•C C C
	—	—	—	—	R R R	R	O O	O O	O O O	—	O O	•R C C
	•A C A C	•A A A U	•A A A O	•C C A O	A O A U	C O C C	•C U A U	•C U A U	•A U U O	C U C	•C U A U	•A C A
	—	—	—	—	—	—	—	—	—	—	—	—
	R R	•C C A R	R O	R R	R R	—	—	—	U U O	R R	—	R
	—	C C C	—	—	—	—	—	—	—	—	—	—
	R R	R	O	O O	U R U	U U	C O	C O	—	R R	C O	C U C
	—	—	—	n	U R U	U R	U R	U R	—	R R	U R	O U O
	U	—	R O	—	U R C	U U	O U	O U	O U	R R	O U	O U O
	—	—	—	—	R R R	—	—	—	—	•R R	—	—
	A A C O	•A A O O	•C C C	•C C A O	•C C A O	•C C C C	•C C C O	•C C C O	•C U C R	•C C C R	•C C C O	•C C C O
	—	—	—	—	—	—	—	—	—	—	—	—
	•O O	•U U U	—	O U R	—	—	—	—	—	—	—	R R R
	•U C O	•U U U	R R	•U C O	O U	O	R	R	—	O R O	R	R R R
	U U O	U O O	U O U	U C U	U O C	U O C	C C C	C C C	O O O	C C	C C C	U C C
	O O O	—	U O C	O O	C U A	U O C	C C C	C C C	U U U	C C	C C C	U C C
	O O	R	O U	—	C O C	U O C	C C C	C C C	O O O	O O	C C C	R C R
	R	•C C U	—	•C C U	R O	R	R	R	—	U O	R	R R
	U U O	•U U U	•U C U	•U O R	•C C C	•C O U	•C C C	•C C C	•U U U	•C C U	•C C C	•O C C
	—	—	—	—	R R R	R R	O	O	—	O O O	O	•U U O
	•O O	•C C U	—	•U C O	—	—	—	—	—	—	—	O U U
	—	—	—	—	R R U	—	—	—	—	O	—	—
	O U U	O O	R	U U O	R R R	—	—	—	—	R R	—	O U U
	—	—	—	—	R O	R	—	—	—	R R	—	R R
	—	—	—	R	O	—	—	R	—	—	—	—
	R	—	O R	—	R O O	U	—	—	—	R R	—	R R R
	O	—	O U	—	U O C	U O U	U U U	U U U	U U O	R O	U U U	C C O
	C A C	—	O U	O O O	R O U	—	R U	R U	U U	R	R U	—

STATE-NUMBER OF BIRD LIST REFUGE, SANCTUARY OR PRESERVE — NESTING, ABUNDANCE BY SEASON	FL-8 Merritt Is. • s S F W	FL-9 St. Marks • s S F W	FL-10 St. Vincent • s S F W	FL-11 Biscayne • s S F W	FL-12 Everglades • s S F W	GA-1 Okefenokee • s S F W	GA-2 Piedmont • s S F W	ID-1 Bear L. • s S F W	ID-2 Camas • s S F W
SANDPIPERS (cont.)									
Least Sandpiper	C O C C	C C C C	R R	C O C C	C U C C	—	O O O	O O R	U U U
White-rumped Sandpiper	O R O R	O R	—	—	R R	—	—	—	—
Baird's Sandpiper	—	—	—	—	R	—	—	—	R
Pectoral Sandpiper	O R O R	O O	—	—	C C R	—	—	O	R R R
Sharp-tailed Sandpiper	—	—	—	—	—	—	—	—	—
Purple Sandpiper	—	—	—	R	—	—	—	—	—
Rock Sandpiper	—	—	—	—	—	—	—	—	—
Dunlin	C O C C	A R C A	A A A	U O U U	C C	R R	—	—	—
Curlew Sandpiper	—	—	—	—	—	—	—	—	—
Stilt Sandpiper	O R O O	O O	—	—	U U R	—	—	R	—
Buff-breasted Sandpiper	—	—	—	—	—	—	—	—	—
Ruff	—	—	—	—	—	—	—	—	—
Short-billed Dowitcher	U O C C	C C A A	—	C O C C	C U C C	O O O	—	—	—
Long-billed Dowitcher	—	R R R	—	—	U U U R	—	—	U O U	O R O
Common Snipe	O U U	U C U	C C C	—	U U U	C C C	O O O	•C C C R	•U U U
American Woodcock	R R	U U U	—	—	R R	U R U U	•O O O O	—	—
Wilson's Phalarope	R R	R R	—	—	—	—	—	•C C U	•U C U
Red-necked Phalarope	R R	—	—	—	—	—	—	—	R
Red Phalarope	—	—	—	R	—	—	—	O	—
SKUAS, GULLS, TERNS & SKIMMERS									
Pomarine Jaeger	R O O	—	—	U O U U	—	—	—	—	—
Parasitic Jaeger	R R R	—	—	—	—	—	—	—	—
Long-tailed Jaeger	—	—	—	—	—	—	—	—	—
Laughing Gull	•C C C C	•C A C O	C O C C	C C C C	•C C C C	—	—	—	—
Franklin's Gull	—	—	O O O	—	—	—	—	•C A U	C
Little Gull	—	—	—	—	—	—	—	—	—
Common Black-headed Gull	—	—	—	—	—	—	—	—	—
Bonaparte's Gull	O U C	O O O	O O O	O O O	U U	—	—	—	—
Heermann's Gull	—	—	—	—	—	—	—	—	—
Mew Gull	—	—	—	—	—	—	—	—	—
Ring-billed Gull	C O C C	A O A A	C O A A	C O C C	C U C C	—	O	O O	C C C
California Gull	—	—	—	—	—	—	—	•C C C R	C C C
Herring Gull	C O C C	C O C C	C O C C	C O C C	C U C C	R R R	—	R	—
Thayer's Gull	—	—	—	—	—	—	—	—	—
Iceland Gull	—	—	—	—	—	—	—	—	—
Lesser Black-backed Gull	—	—	—	—	—	—	—	—	—
Western Gull	—	—	—	—	—	—	—	—	—
Glaucous-winged Gull	—	—	—	—	—	—	—	—	—
Glaucous Gull	—	—	—	—	—	—	—	—	—
Great Black-backed Gull	O O O O	R	—	R	—	—	—	—	—
Black-legged Kittiwake	R	—	—	—	—	—	—	—	—
Sabine's Gull	—	—	—	—	—	—	—	—	—
Gull-billed Tern	•O U O O	R R R	C O C O	—	U U U U	—	—	—	—
Caspian Tern	•U O C C	R R R R	C U O U	U U U	C R C C	—	—	•U U O	O
Royal Tern	•C C C C	O O O O	O C C C	C C C C	C U C C	—	—	—	—
Elegant Tern	—	—	—	—	—	—	—	—	—
Sandwich Tern	O R O O	O O O	C O O	O O O O	U U U U	—	—	—	—
Roseate Tern	R R	—	—	—	R	—	—	—	—
Common Tern	R R R	U U U	O C C	O O O	U U U	—	—	—	U
Arctic Tern	—	—	—	—	—	—	—	—	—
Aleutian Tern	—	—	—	—	—	—	—	—	—
Forster's Tern	C O C C	C C C C	C C C	U U U	C U C C	—	—	•C C O	O
Least Tern	•C C C	•C U U	A A A	•C C U	•C C U	—	—	—	—
Bridled Tern	R R R	—	—	C	—	—	—	—	—
Sooty Tern	R R	—	—	O O	—	—	—	—	—
Black Tern	O U	O U O	O O O	—	U U U R	R R R	—	•C C O	C
Black Skimmer	•C C C C	U U U U	C C C C	O O C	C C C C	—	—	—	—
AUKS, MURRES & PUFFINS									
Dovekie	—	—	—	—	—	—	—	—	—
Common Murre	—	—	—	—	—	—	—	—	—
Thick-billed Murre	—	—	—	—	—	—	—	—	—
Razorbill	—	—	—	—	—	—	—	—	—
Black Guillemot	—	—	—	—	—	—	—	—	—
Pigeon Guillemot	—	—	—	—	—	—	—	—	—
Marbled Murrelet	—	—	—	—	—	—	—	—	—
Kittlitz's Murrelet	—	—	—	—	—	—	—	—	—
Ancient Murrelet	—	—	—	—	—	—	—	—	—
Cassin's Auklet	—	—	—	—	—	—	—	—	—
Crested Auklet	—	—	—	—	—	—	—	—	—
Rhinoceros Auklet	—	—	—	—	—	—	—	—	—
Tufted Puffin	—	—	—	—	—	—	—	—	—

ID-3 Deer Flat	ID-4 Grays L.	ID-5 Kootenai	ID-6 Minidoka	IL-1 Chautauqua	IL-2 Crab Orchd	IL-3 Brussels	IL-4 Gardner	IN-1 Muscatatuck	IA-1 Desoto	IA-2 Wapello	IA-3 Union Sigh
• s S F W	• s S F W	• s S F W	• s S F W	• s S F W	• s S F W	• s S F W	• s S F W	• s S F W	• s S F W	• s S F W	• s S F W
O O O	—	U O U	O U U	C U A	C O C	C C C	C C C	U O O	U U	C C C	R U R
—	—	—	—	O R	U R	R R	—	U O U	O O	—	R U R
O O	—	O U	R	R O O	R O	—	—	O U	U U	—	U U U
R	—	O U	O O	• C O A	C O C	C C C	C C C	C O C	—	C C C	C C C
—	—	—	—	—	—	—	—	—	—	—	—
—	—	—	—	R U	R O	U U	U U O	O	R	U U	R O R
U U	—	R	—	R O C	R U	U R U	U R U	—	R	U R U	C C C
—	—	—	—	U U U	—	—	—	—	—	—	—
—	—	R R	—	U O C	O U	U U	U U	U O	R R	U U	—
O C U	U O	U U C	U U O	O O C	O O	U U	U U	R R	O O	U U	U O A
• C U U O	• A A A R	• C C C	• U C U O	U R U O	C C O	C C O	C C O	C O C U	U U	C C O	• U O C R
—	—	—	—	O O R	• C C O O	• C C C	• C C C	• C C C	• U U U	• C C C	R R R
U C C	• C C U	U R O	U C U	R O U	O U	R O	R O	—	O O	R O	• U U U
R U	U	O U	O O R	R O	—	R R	—	—	R	—	—
—	—	—	—	—	—	—	—	—	—	—	—
—	—	—	—	—	—	—	—	—	—	—	—
—	—	—	—	R R R	—	—	—	—	—	—	—
O	• A A C	O R O	—	R R U	O O	O O	O O	U U	U U	O O	C U A
—	—	—	—	—	—	—	—	—	—	—	—
R R	R	O O	R R	U R U R	C C U	R R	R R	—	O	R R	U U
• A A A C	U U U	U U U	C C C U	C U C O	C C C	C C C	C C C	O O O	C O C R	C C C	C U C
• A A A A	C O C O	U U U	• C C C U	—	U U C	U U C	U U C	O O	U U	U U C	U U O
—	—	R R	—	C R C C	—	—	—	—	—	—	—
—	—	—	—	—	—	—	—	—	—	—	—
—	—	—	—	—	—	—	—	—	—	—	—
—	—	—	—	—	—	—	—	—	—	—	—
—	—	—	—	R	—	—	—	—	—	—	—
• C C U	—	R R R	U U O	O U	O R O	U O U	U O U	—	O O O	U O U	O U
—	—	—	—	—	—	—	—	—	—	—	—
O O	—	O	O O O	C R C	O O O	O O	O O	—	R	O O	C U C
—	—	—	—	—	—	—	—	—	—	—	—
R O	• U U R	O O	• C C U	O R O	O O	U U	U U	O O	U U O	U U O	C C O
—	—	—	—	O O O	R	O	O	—	• O O O	O	U
• C C U	• U C U	• U C	O C U	C O C	O U U	C O U	C O U	O O O	C C O	C O U	• C C C
—	—	—	—	—	—	—	—	—	—	—	—
—	—	—	—	—	—	—	—	—	—	—	—
—	—	—	—	—	—	—	—	—	—	—	—
—	—	—	—	—	—	—	—	—	—	—	—
—	—	—	—	—	—	—	—	—	—	—	—
—	—	—	—	—	—	—	—	—	—	—	—
—	—	—	—	—	—	—	—	—	—	—	—

STATE-NUMBER OF BIRD LIST / REFUGE, SANCTUARY OR PRESERVE / NESTING, ABUNDANCE BY SEASON	FL-8 Merritt Is. • s S F W	FL-9 St. Marks • s S F W	FL-10 St. Vincent • s S F W	FL-11 Biscayne • s S F W	FL-12 Everglades • s S F W	GA-1 Okefenokee • s S F W	GA-2 Piedmont • s S F W	ID-1 Bear L. • s S F W	ID-2 Camas • s S F W
AUKS, MURRES & PUFFINS (cont.)									
Atlantic Puffin	—	—	—	—	—	—	—	—	—
Horned Puffin	—	—	—	—	—	—	—	—	—
PIGEONS & DOVES									
Rock Dove	•U U U U	R R R R	—	U U U U	—	—	U U U U	—	U U U
White-crowned Pigeon	—	—	—	•C C U U	•C C C U	—	—	—	—
Band-tailed Pigeon	—	—	—	—	—	—	—	—	—
White-winged Dove	—	O	—	O R	—	—	—	—	—
Mourning Dove	•C C C C	•U U C U	U U A C	U O U U	•C C C C	•C C C C	•C C C C	•U U U	•U C C
Inca Dove	—	—	—	—	—	—	—	—	—
Common Ground-Dove	•C C C C	•U U U U	C C C C	C C C C	•U U U U	•C C C C	—	—	—
White-tipped Dove	—	—	—	—	—	—	—	—	—
CUCKOOS, ROADRUNNERS & ANIS									
Black-billed Cuckoo	R R	R R R	—	—	—	R R	—	—	—
Yellow-billed Cuckoo	•O O O	•C C C	C C C C	O O U R	•C C C R	•C C C	•U U U	—	—
Mangrove Cuckoo	—	—	—	•U C R R	•U U U U	—	—	—	—
Greater Roadrunner	—	—	—	—	—	—	—	—	—
Smooth-billed Ani	R R R R	—	—	—	•U U U U	—	—	—	—
Groove-billed Ani	—	R R	—	—	—	—	—	—	—
BARN OWLS									
Barn Owl	•O O O O	•R R R R	R R R	—	•U U U U	—	—	—	—
TYPICAL OWLS									
Flammulated Owl	—	—	—	—	—	—	—	—	—
Eastern Screech-Owl	•C U C C	•U U U U	R R R R	•C C C C	•C C C C	•U U U U	•U U U U	—	—
Western Screech-Owl	—	—	—	—	—	—	—	—	R R R R
Great Horned Owl	•U U U U	•U U U U	C C C C	—	•R R R R	U U U U	•U U U U	•U U U U	•C C C C
Snowy Owl	—	—	—	—	—	—	—	—	—
Northern Hawk Owl	—	—	—	—	—	—	—	—	—
Northern Pygmy-Owl	—	—	—	—	—	—	—	—	—
Elf Owl	—	—	—	—	—	—	—	—	—
Burrowing Owl	—	—	—	—	R	—	—	—	•R R R
Spotted Owl	—	—	—	—	—	—	—	—	—
Barred Owl	•O O O O	•U U U U	R R R R	O O O O	•C C C C	•C C C C	•U U U U	—	—
Great Gray Owl	—	—	—	—	—	—	—	—	R
Long-eared Owl	—	—	—	—	—	—	—	R	U U R R
Short-eared Owl	O O	R R R	—	—	R R R	—	—	•U U U	•C C C R
Boreal Owl	—	—	—	—	—	—	—	—	—
Northern Saw-whet Owl	—	—	—	—	—	—	—	—	R R
NIGHTJARS									
Lesser Nighthawk	—	—	—	—	—	—	—	—	—
Common Nighthawk	•C C U R	•C C C	C C C C	O O U	•C C C R	•C C C	•O O U	O	•C C
Pauraque	—	—	—	—	—	—	—	—	—
Common Poorwill	—	—	—	—	—	—	—	—	—
Chuck-will's-widow	•C C C O	•C C U	C C U R	U U O O	•C C C R	•C C C	•C C C	—	—
Whip-poor-will	R R R	O O R	—	—	O	U U C	O O R	•O U U	—
SWIFTS									
Black Swift	—	—	—	—	—	—	—	—	—
Chimney Swift	•U U U	•U U U	A A U R	—	R	C C C	•C C C	—	—
Vaux's Swift	—	—	—	—	—	—	—	—	—
White-throated Swift	—	—	—	—	—	—	—	—	—
HUMMINGBIRDS									
Buff-bellied Hummingbird	—	—	—	—	—	—	—	—	—
Ruby-throated Hummingbird	O R O R	•U O U	U O U	O O O	C R C C	•U U U	•O O O	—	—
Black-chinned Hummingbird	—	—	—	—	—	—	—	—	—
Anna's Hummingbird	—	—	—	—	—	—	—	—	—
Costa's Hummingbird	—	—	—	—	—	—	—	—	—
Calliope Hummingbird	—	—	—	—	—	—	—	—	U
Broad-tailed Hummingbird	—	—	—	—	—	—	—	—	U
Rufous Hummingbird	—	—	—	—	—	—	—	—	U
Allen's Hummingbird	—	—	—	—	—	—	—	—	—
KINGFISHERS									
Belted Kingfisher	•C O C C	•C C C C	C C C C	C R C C	C R C C	•C U C C	•C C C C	O O O	O O O
Green Kingfisher	—	—	—	—	—	—	—	—	—
WOODPECKERS									
Lewis' Woodpecker	—	—	—	—	—	—	—	O	R
Red-headed Woodpecker	R R R R	•O O O O	U U U U	—	—	•C U C U	•U U U U	—	—
Acorn Woodpecker	—	—	—	—	—	—	—	—	—
Gila Woodpecker	—	—	—	—	—	—	—	—	—
Golden-fronted Woodpecker	—	—	—	—	—	—	—	—	—
Red-bellied Woodpecker	•C C C C	•C C C C	C C C C	C C C C	•C C C C	•C C C C	•C C C C	—	—
Yellow-bellied Sapsucker	U U	U U U	U U C	O O O	U U C	C C C	U U	—	—
Red-breasted Sapsucker	—	—	—	—	—	—	—	—	—

	ID-3 Deer Flat	ID-4 Grays L.	ID-5 Kootenai	ID-6 Minidoka	IL-1 Chautauqua	IL-2 Crab Orchd	IL-3 Brussels	IL-4 Gardner	IN-1 Muscatatuck	IA-1 Desoto	IA-2 Wapello	IA-3 Union Slgh
	•s S F W	•s S F W	•s S F W	•s S F W	•s S F W	•s S F W	•s S F W	•s S F W	•s S F W	•s S F W	•s S F W	•s S F W
	— —	— —	— —	— —	— —	— —	— —	— —	— —	— —	— —	— —
	•O U U O	—	R R R R	O O	C C C C	•U U U U	C C C C	—	U U U U	—	—	—
	•A A C U	•U U U	•U C U O	•U C C	•A A A C	•C C C C	•C C C U	•C C C U	•A A A A	•A A C U	•C C C U	•C C C U
	—	—	—	—	U O U	O O O	R R	R R	• U	•U U	R R	•C C C
					•U C U	•U C C	•C C C U	•C C C U	• C	•U C O	•C C C U	•C C C
	—	—	—	—	—	—	—	—	—	—	—	—
	—	—	—	—	—	—	—	—	—	—	—	—
	•C C U U	—	—	•R R	—	—	—	—	—	—	—	—
	—	—	—	—	•O O O O	•U U U U	•C C C C	•C C C C	•U U U U	•U U U U	•C C C C	•C C C C
	•U U U U	—	R R R R		•C C C C	•C C C C	•U U U U	•U U U U	•C C C C	•C C C C	•U U U U	•C C C C
	•U U U U	•C C C U	•C C C C	•U U U U	R					R	R
	R		R		—	—	—	—	—	—	—	
	R R R R	—	R R	—	—	—	—	—	—	—	—	
			•O O O O		—	—	—	—	—	—	—	
	•U C C	•R R	—	•O U U	—	—	—	—	—	—	—	
	—		R R	—	•C C C C	•C C C C	•C C C C	•C C C C	•C C C C	•O O O O	•C C C C	•U U U U
		R R R R			—	—	—	—	—	—	—	
	•O O O O	•R R R	R R	O R O	O		O	O	O O	O O	O	•U
	•O O O O	•U U U	R R R	U U U U	O O O O	O R O	O O	O O		R	O O	U U
	O O O	—	•O O O O	R	—	—	—	—	—	—	—	O O O O
	•C C U	•O O O	C O	•C C O	•U C C	•U C O	•U U O	•U U O	•U A U	U U O	•U U U	•U U U
		•R O O										
					—	•U U	O	O	•O O O	—	O	
					•C C O	•C C O	•O	•O	O O O	• U	•O	
	—	—	U U	—	—	—	—	—	—	—	—	
					U C U	•U C C	•C C C	•C C C	•U U U	U U	•C C C	•C U
	O O	—	•C C U	—	—	—	—	—	—	—	—	
	R R	—	—	—	—	—	—	—	—	—	—	
					C U C	•U C O	•C C O	•C C O	•U U U	O U	•C C O	U
	U U	•C C	•U U	—	—	—	—	—	—	—	—	
		•U C R	•C C		—	—	—	—	—	—	—	
		•R U			—	—	—	—	—	—	—	
	R R	•R U	•A A	•O O	—	—	—	—	—	—	—	
	•O O O O	O R	•U U U O	•O U U O	•C C C O	•C C C C	•U U U O	•U U U O	•U U U U	•U U U R	•U U U O	•U C C
	•O O O	R	R R O	O O	—	—	—	—	—	•C A U O	—	•U C C
					C C C C	•C C C C	•C C C C	•C C C C	•C C C C		•C C C C	
	—	—	—	—	—	—	—	—	—	—	—	
	—	—	—	—	•C C C C	•C C C C	•C C C C	•C C C C	•C C C C	•C C C C	•C C C C	
	—	•U U O	•U C O	U O	C C O	U U O	C C	C C	U U U	R R O	C C	U

STATE-NUMBER OF BIRD LIST / REFUGE, SANCTUARY OR PRESERVE / NESTING, ABUNDANCE BY SEASON	FL-8 Merritt Is. •s S F W	FL-9 St. Marks •s S F W	FL-10 St. Vincent •s S F W	FL-11 Biscayne •s S F W	FL-12 Everglades •s S F W	GA-1 Okefenokee •s S F W	GA-2 Piedmont •s S F W	ID-1 Bear L. •s S F W	ID-2 Camas •s S F W
WOODPECKERS (cont.)									
Williamson's Sapsucker	—	—	—	—	—	—	—	—	—
Ladder-backed Woodpecker	—	—	—	—	—	—	—	—	—
Nuttall's Woodpecker	—	—	—	—	—	—	—	—	—
Downy Woodpecker	•U U U U	•U U U U	C C C C	O	•U U U U	•C C C C	•U U U U	—	O R O O
Hairy Woodpecker	R R R	•O O O O	—		•R R R R	•O O O O	•U U U U	—	O O
Red-cockaded Woodpecker	—	•U U U U	—	—	—	•U U U U	•U U U U	—	—
Three-toed Woodpecker	—	—	—	—	—	—	—	—	—
Black-backed Woodpecker	—	—	—	—	—	—	—	—	—
Northern Flicker	•U U U U	•C U C C	C U A C	C C C C	•C C C C	•C C C C	•C C C C	U U U O	•C C C U
Pileated Woodpecker	•U U U U	•U U U U	R R U U	O O O O	•C C C C	•C C C C	•C C C C	—	—
TYRANT FLYCATCHERS									
Olive-sided Flycatcher	—	—	—	—	—	—	—	—	—
Western Wood-Pewee	—	—	—	—	—	—	—	O O	• U U
Eastern Wood-Pewee	—	•U U U	—	—	U U R	•C C C	•C C C	—	—
Yellow-bellied Flycatcher	—	—	—	—	—	—	—	—	—
Acadian Flycatcher	R R	•C C U	—	—	R	•U U U	•C C C	—	—
Alder Flycatcher	R	—	—	—	—	—	—	—	—
Willow Flycatcher	—	—	—	—	R	—	—	O	R
Least Flycatcher	R	—	—	—	U U U R	—	—	—	—
Hammond's Flycatcher	—	—	—	—	—	—	—	—	—
Dusky Flycatcher	—	—	—	—	—	—	—	—	—
Gray Flycatcher	—	—	—	—	—	—	—	—	—
Western Flycatcher	—	—	—	—	—	—	—	—	—
Black Phoebe	—	—	—	—	—	—	—	—	—
Eastern Phoebe	O C C	U C C	U U C	U U	C C C	C C C	C C C	—	—
Say's Phoebe	—	—	—	—	—	—	—	—	U
Vermilion Flycatcher	—	R O R	—	—	—	—	—	—	—
Ash-throated Flycatcher	—	—	—	—	—	—	—	—	—
Great Crested Flycatcher	•U U O R	•C C O	C C U	•C C C C	•C C C C	•C C C	•C C C	—	—
Brown-crested Flycatcher	—	—	—	—	R R	—	—	—	—
Great Kiskadee	—	—	—	—	—	—	—	—	—
Couch's Kingbird	—	—	—	—	—	—	—	—	—
Cassin's Kingbird	—	—	—	—	—	—	—	—	—
Western Kingbird	R R	R O	—	O O	U U U	—	—	R	C
Eastern Kingbird	•U U U	•C C C	C C C	U U	•C C C R	•C C C	•C C C	O O	• C
Gray Kingbird	O O O	•C C U	C C U	C C U	•C C C	—	—	—	—
Scissor-tailed Flycatcher	—	R R	—	R R	R R R	—	—	—	—
LARKS									
Horned Lark	—	—	—	—	—	—	R R	U O O U	•C C C C
SWALLOWS									
Purple Martin	•U U R	•C C U U	U C U	—	C C C	•R U C O	•U U U	—	—
Tree Swallow	C R C C	A U A A	R U U	O O O	C C C	C A C	R R	C	•U U
Violet-green Swallow	—	—	—	—	—	—	—	O	•U U
Northern Rough-winged Swallow	O O	C U U R	C U C R	O O	U U R	—	O O O	U O	R R
Bank Swallow	O R O	O O O	—	—	U U	—	—	•U C O	•C C
Cliff Swallow	O O	R	—	—	R U	—	—	•C A U	•R U R
Barn Swallow	C R C R	C C C R	A C	C O C O	•U R C R	C C C	O O O	•C C U	•U C U
JAYS, MAGPIES & CROWS									
Gray Jay	—	—	—	—	—	—	—	—	R R R
Steller's Jay	—	—	—	—	—	—	—	—	—
Blue Jay	•C C C C	•C C C C	C C C	R R R R	•C C C C	•C C C C	•C C C C	—	—
Green Jay	—	—	—	—	—	—	—	—	—
Scrub Jay	•C C C C	—	—	—	—	—	—	—	—
Pinyon Jay	—	—	—	—	—	—	—	—	—
Clark's Nutcracker	—	—	—	—	—	—	—	—	R R
Black-billed Magpie	—	—	—	—	—	—	—	C C C C	•A A A A
American Crow	—	•C C C C	—	U U U U	•C C C C	•O O O O	•C C C C	U O O	•C C C
Northwestern Crow	—	—	—	—	—	—	—	—	—
Fish Crow	•C C C C	•C C C U	C C U R	—	—	•C C C C	U U	—	—
Chihuahuan Raven	—	—	—	—	—	—	—	—	—
Common Raven	—	—	—	—	—	—	—	R R	C R C O
TITMICE									
Black-capped Chickadee	—	—	—	—	—	—	—	O O U	C R U R
Carolina Chickadee	—	•C C C C	C C C C	—	—	•U U U U	•C C C C	—	—
Mountain Chickadee	—	—	—	—	—	—	—	—	—
Boreal Chickadee	—	—	—	—	—	—	—	—	—
Chestnut-backed Chickadee	—	—	—	—	—	—	—	—	—
Plain Titmouse	—	—	—	—	—	—	—	—	—
Tufted Titmouse	R	•C C C C	—	—	R R	•C C C C	•C C C C	—	—
VERDINS									
Verdin	—	—	—	—	—	—	—	—	—

	ID-3 Deer Flat	ID-4 Grays L.	ID-5 Kootenai	ID-6 Minidoka	IL-1 Chautauqua	IL-2 Crab Orchd	IL-3 Brussels	IL-4 Gardner	IN-1 Muscatatuck	IA-1 Desoto	IA-2 Wapello	IA-3 Union Slgh
	•s S F W	•s S F W	•s S F W	•s S F W	•s S F W	•s S F W	•s S F W	•s S F W	•s S F W	•s S F W	•s S F W	•s S F W
	—	—	—	—	—	—	—	—	—	—	—	—
	—	—	—	—	—	—	—	—	—	—	—	—
	—	—	—	—	—	—	—	—	—	—	—	—
	•C C C C	—	•U U U U	U O U	•C C C C	•C C C C	•C C C C	•C C C C	•C C C C	•C C C C	•C C C C	•C C C C
	•R R R R	—	•U U U U	R	•U U U U	•C C C C	•U U U U	•U U U U	C C C C	•U U U U	•U U U U	•U U U U
	—	—	—	—	—	—	—	—	—	—	—	—
	—	—	R R R R	—	—	—	—	—	—	—	—	—
	—	—	•O O O O	—	—	—	—	—	—	—	—	—
	•C C C O	•U U U O	•A A C U	•C C C C	C C C U	•C C C C	•C C C C	•C C C C	•C C C C	•C A C C	•C C C C	•C C A C
	—	—	•U U U U	—	C C C C	•U U U U	•C C C C	•C C C C	•U U U U	—	•C C C C	—
	R	•U U	O R R	•U U	R R U	R O	—	—	U U	—	—	U U U
			•C C R		C C C	•U C U	C C C	C C C	•C C C	•U U	C C C	•U C C
	—	—	—	—	U U	U O	U U	U U	—	—	U U	—
	—	—	—	—	U O U	•U C O	•C C C	C C C	•U U U	•O O	C C C	—
	—	—	—	—	U U	O O	R O	R O	—	O O	R O	—
	O O	O U	•O C	O U	U U R	O R O	R O	R O	•U U U	•O O	R O	•U C C
	—	—	—	—	C C	U U	—	—	U U	C	—	C
	—	O U	•U O U	—	—	—	—	—	—	—	—	—
	—	—	•C U	—	—	—	—	—	—	—	—	—
	R	—	R O	O O	—	—	—	—	—	—	—	—
	—	—	—	—	•C C U	•C C C O	•U U U	•U U U	•C C C	•U U O	•U U U	•O U U
	O O	—	R R	O	—	—	—	—	—	—	—	—
	—	—	—	—	—	—	—	—	—	—	—	—
	—	—	—	O O	—	—	—	—	—	—	—	—
	—	—	—	—	C C U	•U C O	•C C C	•C C C	•U U U	•U U	•C C C	• U U
	—	—	—	—	—	—	—	—	—	—	—	—
	—	—	—	—	—	—	—	—	—	—	—	—
	—	—	—	—	—	—	—	—	—	—	—	—
	•C C O	O	O O	•C C	•C C U	•U C O	•C C C	•C C C	•C C C	•U	•C C C	•C C U
	•C C O	O O O	•C A O	•C C	•C C U	•U C O	•C C C	•C C C	•C C C	•C A O	•C C C	•C C U
	—	—	—	—	—	—	—	—	—	—	—	—
	•U U O U	•C C C C	R R R	•C C C C	•C C C C	•U U U U	C C C C	C C C C	U U U	•U U U U	C C C C	•C C C C
	—	—	—	R	•C C O	•C C O	•C C C	•C C C	•C C C	•U C	•C C C	•O U
	•O O	•C C O	•C A O	U U U	•C A A	•C C C	•C C A	•C C A	•C C C	•C U C	•C C A	•C C A
	•C U U	•O O O	•C C O	•U C O	•C U U	•C C C	•C C C	•C C C	•U U	U U U	•C C C	• U U
	•C C C	•O O O	•C C R	•U U O	•C U U	•U C U	•C C C	•C C C	•U U	U U U	•C C C	•C C C
	•A A C	•O U O	•U C R	•C A C	U C C	U	•C C C	•C C C	•U U	•C C C	•C C C	•C C C
	•U C C	•C C O	•C A O	•C A U	U U C	•U C O	C C C	C C C	•U U	C C C	C C C	•C C C
	•A A C	•A C O	•C A U	•C A C	C C A	•U C U	•C C C	•C C C	•C C	•C C C	•C C C	•C C C
	—	—	R O O	—	—	—	—	—	—	—	—	—
		R	O U O	•C U C C	O	—	—	—	—	—	—	—
	—	—	—	—	•A C A C	•C C C C	•C C C C	•C C C C	•C C C C	•C C C C	•C C C C	•U C C O
	—	—	—	—	—	—	—	—	—	—	—	—
		R	—	—	—	—	—	—	—	—	—	—
	•A A A A	•C C C O	R R O O	•A A A C	—	—	—	—	—	—	—	—
	•C U A A	•C C C C	•A C C A	•O O O O	•C C C C	•C C C C	•C C C C	•C C C C	•C C C C	•C C C C	•C C C C	•C C C C
	—	—	—	—	—	—	—	—	—	—	—	—
	•O O O O	•U U U O	•C C C A	O O O O	—	—	—	—	—	—	—	R
	U U	•U U U C	•A A A A	R R	•C C C C	—	•C C C C	•C C C C	U U	•C C C C	•C C C C	•C C C C
						•C C C C			•C C C C			
	U U	•U U U U	O R O O	O O O	—	—	—	—	—	—	—	—
	—	—	R R	—	—	—	—	—	—	—	—	—
	—	—	•U U R R	—	—	—	—	—	—	—	—	—
	—	—	—	—	—	—	—	—	—	—	—	—
	—	—	—	—	•C C C C	•C C C C	•C C C C	•C C C C	•C C C C	O O O	•C C C C	

STATE-NUMBER OF BIRD LIST REFUGE, SANCTUARY OR PRESERVE NESTING, ABUNDANCE BY SEASON	FL-8 Merritt Is. • s S F W	FL-9 St. Marks • s S F W	FL-10 St. Vincent • s S F W	FL-11 Biscayne • s S F W	FL-12 Everglades • s S F W	GA-1 Okefenokee • s S F W	GA-2 Piedmont • s S F W	ID-1 Bear L. • s S F W	ID-2 Camas • s S F W
BUSHTITS									
Bushtit	—	—	—	—	—	—	—	—	—
NUTHATCHES									
Red-breasted Nuthatch	—	R	—	—	—	R R	• R R	—	R R R O
White-breasted Nuthatch	—	—	—	—	—	R R R R	R R R R	—	R R R O
Pygmy Nuthatch	—	—	—	—	—	—	—	—	—
Brown-headed Nuthatch	—	•U U U U	C C C C	—	—	•C C C C	•C C C C	—	—
CREEPERS									
Brown Creeper	—	R R R	—	—	—	O O O	U U U	—	—
WRENS									
Cactus Wren	—	—	—	—	—	—	—	—	—
Rock Wren	—	—	—	—	—	—	—	—	—
Canyon Wren	—	—	—	—	—	—	—	—	—
Carolina Wren	•C C C C	•C C C C	C C C C	O	•C C C C	•C C C C	•C C C C	—	—
Bewick's Wren	—	—	—	—	—	R R R	R R R	—	—
House Wren	O C C	U C U	C C C	O O U	C C C	U U U	O R O	—	•R R
Winter Wren	—	U U U	—	—	—	U U U	O O O	—	—
Sedge Wren	U U U	U C C	C C C	—	U U U	U U U	R	—	—
Marsh Wren	R O	•C C C C	C C C C	—	U U U	O O O	—	O	•C A C O	•U C C
DIPPERS									
American Dipper	—	—	—	—	—	—	—	—	—
OLD WORLD WARBLERS & THRUSHES									
Arctic Warbler	—	—	—	—	—	—	—	—	—
Golden-crowned Kinglet	—	U U U	U	—	—	U U O	U O U	—	U U
Ruby-crowned Kinglet	O U	C C C	C C C	R	U U U	C C C	C U C	—	U U
Blue-gray Gnatcatcher	•O O U C	•C C C U	C C C U	C O C C	C C C	•U U U O	•C C C	—	—
Black-tailed Gnatcatcher	—	—	—	—	—	—	—	—	—
Eastern Bluebird	—	•U R U U	U U U C	—	—	•C C C C	•C C C C	—	—
Western Bluebird	—	—	—	—	—	—	—	—	U U U
Mountain Bluebird	—	—	—	—	—	—	—	O O	U
Townsend's Solitaire	—	—	—	—	—	—	—	O O	—
Veery	O O	O U	—	—	U U	U U	O O	—	R R R
Gray-cheeked Thrush	O O	O U	—	—	U U	R R	R O	—	—
Swainson's Thrush	O O	O U	O	—	U U	R R	U U	—	U U
Hermit Thrush	O O O	O U U	C R C C	—	U U R	U U U	U U U	—	U U
Wood Thrush	R R	O U	—	—	R R	•U U U	•C C C	—	—
American Robin	C C	A C A	C C A	U U	R C	C A A	•C O O C	•U C U O	•U C C O
Varied Thrush	—	—	—	—	—	—	—	—	—
Wrentit	—	—	—	—	—	—	—	—	—
MOCKINGBIRDS, THRASHERS & ALLIES									
Gray Catbird	C C	C A C	C O C C	C C C	C C C	C C C C	•U U U R	—	R
Northern Mockingbird	•C C C C	•C C C C	C C C C	•C C C C	•C C C C	•C C C C	•C C C C	—	—
Sage Thrasher	—	—	—	—	—	—	—	•O U O	• C
Brown Thrasher	•O O O O	•C C A C	C C C C	U U U U	U U U	•C C C C	•C C C C	—	—
Long-billed Thrasher	—	—	—	—	—	—	—	—	—
Bendire's Thrasher	—	—	—	—	—	—	—	—	—
Curve-billed Thrasher	—	—	—	—	—	—	—	—	—
Crissal Thrasher	—	—	—	—	—	—	—	—	—
Le Conte's Thrasher	—	—	—	—	—	—	—	—	—
WAGTAILS & PIPITS									
American Pipit	R R	U U U	—	R	R R	O O O	O O O	O	U U
Sprague's Pipit	—	—	—	—	—	—	—	—	—
WAXWINGS									
Bohemian Waxwing	—	—	—	—	—	—	—	O	R R
Cedar Waxwing	O O C	U U U	C U U	—	C C C	C U C	U U U	R R	O O O
SILKY-FLYCATCHERS									
Phainopepla	—	—	—	—	—	—	—	—	—
SHRIKES									
Northern Shrike	—	—	—	—	—	—	—	—	U
Loggerhead Shrike	•U U U U	•U U U U	U U U U	—	•U U U U	•C C C C	•O O O O	O O U	U U U R
STARLINGS									
European Starling	•C C C C	•U U U C	—	C C C C	•U U U U	O O O O	•O O O O	•U U U O	•C A A O
VIREOS									
White-eyed Vireo	•C C C C	•C C C U	C C C U	•C C C C	•C C C C	•C C C C	•C C C R	—	—
Bell's Vireo	—	—	—	R	—	—	—	—	—
Black-capped Vireo	—	—	—	—	—	—	—	—	—
Gray Vireo	—	—	—	—	—	—	—	—	—
Solitary Vireo	O O O	U U U	U U U	O O O	U U U	O O O	•C U C O	—	—
Yellow-throated Vireo	U U R	•U U U	—	—	O	U U U	•R R R	•C C C	—	—
Hutton's Vireo	—	—	—	—	—	—	—	—	—
Warbling Vireo	—	—	—	—	—	—	—	—	O
Philadelphia Vireo	—	—	—	—	R R	—	—	—	—

	ID-3 Deer Flat	ID-4 Grays L.	ID-5 Kootenai	ID-6 Minidoka	IL-1 Chautauqua	IL-2 Crab Orchd	IL-3 Brussels	IL-4 Gardner	IN-1 Muscatatuck	IA-1 Desoto	IA-2 Wapello	IA-3 Union Slgh
	•s S F W	•s S F W	•s S F W	•s S F W	•s S F W	•s S F W	•s S F W	•s S F W	•s S F W	•s S F W	•s S F W	•s S F W
	—	—	—	—	—	—	—	—	—	—	—	—
	O O	OUO	•COUU	OROO	R RO	U UC	O O	O O	U U	R	O O	—
	O O	—	—	OR O	•CCCC	•CUCC	•CCCC	•CCCC	•CCCC	•CCCC	•CCCC	•CUUC
	U	O	•OOOO	O OU	ORCC	C UC	U UO	U UO	U	U O	U UO	O
	•OOOO	•OUO	R	•OUO	—	—	—	—	—	—	—	—
	•OOOO	—	—	O O	—	—	—	—	—	—	—	—
	—				•CCCU	•CCCU	•CCCO	•CCCO	•UUUU		•CCCO	
					R R	•OOOR						
	•O O O	•C C U	R	•O O	C C C	•C C C	•O O	•O O	•U U U	•C C U	•O O	•U C C
			•U O O		U UU	U U O	O O	O O	•U U U U	R	O O	•C C U
						O U	U O U	U O U	•U U R	•O R O	U O U	
	•U U U	•C C C	•C C O	•U C C O	U O U	O O	O O O	O O O	—	O O	O O O	•U C C
	—	O O O	•U C C O	—	—	—	—	—	—	—	—	—
	U UO	—	•CUCO	O OO	C CU	C CC	U UO	U UO	O U	O O	U UO	U U
	CUU	UUO	URUO	U UO	C CU	C CO	U U	U U	U OU	U U	U U	C
	—	—	—	—	R R R	•C C O	•C C	•C C	•C C	—	•C C	—
	—	—	—	—	•OROR	•CCCC	•UUUU	•UUUU	•UUUU	•UOOO	•UUUU	•CCC
	R	•CCUO	R	OOOR	—	—	—	—	—	—	—	—
	O OO	O O O	•U O O	O O	O						O	
	—	O U	U U O	O	U U	U R	U U	U U	•U U	—	U U	—
	—	—	•U C	—	C C	U U	U U	U U	U U	R	U U	C
	U U	•U U U	•U C U	O O	C C	C C	U U	U U	U U	U UR	U U	O U
	—	—	O R O	O	C C	U C O				U R R		O
					C C U	•U C O	•O O	•O O	•U C	•U U	•O O	
	•A A C O	•A A C O	•C A A U	•C C U O	•A A A U	•C C C U	•C C C O	•C C C O	•C C C C	•C C C C	•C C C O	•C C C R
	R	—	•C R U R	O O	—	—	—	—	—	—	—	—
	—	O U O	•O O O	R	•C C C	•U C C	•U U U	•U U U	•C C C	•C C U	•U U U	•C C C
				R	•U O U U	•C C C C	•C C C O	•C C C O	•C C C C	R	•C C C O	—
		•O U O		•O U U R								
					•C C U R	•C C C U	•C C C O	•C C C O	•C C C C	•C C U	•C C C O	•C C C
	—	—	—	—	—	—	—	—	—	—	—	—
	—	—	—	—	—	—	—	—	—	—	—	—
	—	—	—	—	—	—	—	—	—	—	—	—
	—	—	—	—	—	—	—	—	—	—	—	—
	O O U R	O O	U R U	O O	R U	R O	O O	O O	O O U	R U	O O	U
	R O R	R	U U O	R O	—	—	—	—	—	—	R	—
	•O O C C	O	•O C U	U O O	C O C R	•C U C C	•U U U U	•U U U U	•U U U U	•O O O U	•U U U U	C C C U
	—				—	—	—	—	—	—	—	—
	O O	—	U O U	O O U							R	U U
	•O O O	O O O	R R	U O U O	R R	•C C C C	•O U U O	•O U U O	U O U	O O	•O U U O	•U O U
	•A A A A	•C U U O	•A A A U	•C C A U	•A C A A	•A A A A	•C C C C	•C C C C	•C C C C	•C C C C	•C C C C	•C C C C
	—	—	—	—	O R R	•C C U	•C C C	•C C C	•C C	—	•C C C	—
					•U U O	•O U R	—	—	•U U	•U U U		
	R	—	•O U R	—	U U	O U	R	—	U U	R	—	U
	—	—	O R O	—	O R O	•U C U	U U	U U	•U U	—	U U	O
	—	•C C C	•O U R	O O O	•C C U	•C C O	•C C	•C C	•C C	•C C	•C C	•O C U
					U U	R R	R R		U U	R		U

STATE-NUMBER OF BIRD LIST REFUGE, SANCTUARY OR PRESERVE NESTING, ABUNDANCE BY SEASON	FL-8 Merritt Is. •s S F W	FL-9 St. Marks •s S F W	FL-10 St. Vincent •s S F W	FL-11 Biscayne •s S F W	FL-12 Everglades •s S F W	GA-1 Okefenokee •s S F W	GA-2 Piedmont •s S F W	ID-1 Bear L. •s S F W	ID-2 Camas •s S F W
VIREOS (cont.)									
Red-eyed Vireo	O O	•C U C	C C C	—	C C	•U U U	•C C C	—	—
Black-whiskered Vireo	•O U R	—	—	•C C C	•C C C	—	—	—	—
WOOD-WARBLERS									
Bachman's Warbler	—	—	—	—	—	—	—	—	—
Blue-winged Warbler	—	R R R	—	—	R R	O O	—	—	—
Golden-winged Warbler	—	R R	—	—	R R	O O	U U	—	—
Tennessee Warbler	O O R	R U	—	—	U U R	—	R U	—	—
Orange-crowned Warbler	U O U	U U U	—	U U U	U U U	U U U	—	—	—
Nashville Warbler	R R	—	—	—	—	R	—	—	—
Virginia's Warbler	—	—	—	—	—	—	—	—	—
Lucy's Warbler	—	—	—	—	—	—	—	—	—
Northern Parula	U U O	•C C U	C U	C C U	C R C C	•C C C O	O O O	—	—
Tropical Parula	—	—	—	—	—	—	—	—	—
Yellow Warbler	O O R	O C C	O	U U U U	•C C C U	U U	R R	•U U O	• C O
Chestnut-sided Warbler	R O	R O	—	—	R R	R	O O	—	—
Magnolia Warbler	O O	R U	—	O O R	U U R	R U	R R	—	—
Cape May Warbler	U U R	U	O	O U R	C C R	U U	R R	—	—
Black-throated Blue Warbler	U U R	R R	—	C C R	C C U	U U	O O	—	—
Yellow-rumped Warbler	U C C	A A A	A A C	C C C	C C C	A A A	C C C	C O U	R R
Black-throated Gray Warbler	—	—	—	R	—	—	—	—	—
Townsend's Warbler	—	—	—	—	—	—	—	—	—
Hermit Warbler	—	—	—	—	—	—	—	—	—
Black-throated Green Warbler	R O	R R	O O	—	U U	R R	U U	—	—
Blackburnian Warbler	R O	R R	—	—	U U	U U	O	—	—
Yellow-throated Warbler	O O O	•C C U O	C C C U	C C C	C U C C	•C C C O	•U U U	—	—
Pine Warbler	•O R O O	•C C C C	C C C C	—	•C C C C	•C U C C	•C C C C	—	—
Prairie Warbler	•U U U U	C C C R	—	A A A A	•C C C C	U U O	•C C C	—	—
Palm Warbler	U C C	C C R	C U U	A A A	C C C	C C C	C C	—	—
Bay-breasted Warbler	R U R	—	O U	—	—	—	R R	—	—
Blackpoll Warbler	U U	U	—	C U	C R	U U	U U	—	—
Cerulean Warbler	—	R R	—	—	R	R R	R R	—	—
Black-and-white Warbler	C C U	U U U U	U U U	C C C	C C C	U O U O	U U	—	—
American Redstart	U C R	O R O	—	C C O	C U C U	C R C	U U	R R	—
Prothonotary Warbler	O O	•C C U	C C C	—	U U	•C C C	O	—	—
Worm-eating Warbler	R O	R R R	—	U U O	U U R	U U R	U U	—	—
Swainson's Warbler	R R	•R R R	—	—	R R	•R R R	—	—	—
Ovenbird	U U O	R R	—	C C C	C C C	U U	R R	—	—
Northern Waterthrush	U U R	O R O	U U	U U U	C C C	R R	R R	—	—
Louisiana Waterthrush	R R	R R R	—	—	C U C R	O R O	•U U U	—	—
Kentucky Warbler	R R	•U U R	—	—	R R	O O	•U U U	—	—
Connecticut Warbler	R R	—	—	R R	—	O O	—	—	—
Mourning Warbler	—	—	—	—	—	—	—	—	—
MacGillivray's Warbler	—	—	—	—	—	—	—	—	R
Common Yellowthroat	•C C C C	•C C C C	C C C C	C C C	•C C C C	•C U C C	•U U U U	•U U U	•U C
Hooded Warbler	O O	•U U U	—	—	U U	•U U U	•C C C	—	—
Wilson's Warbler	R	—	—	—	R R	—	—	—	O O
Canada Warbler	—	—	—	—	—	R R	—	—	—
Painted Redstart	—	—	—	—	—	—	—	—	—
Yellow-breasted Chat	•R R R R	•C C R R	U U O	R R	U U U	R R	•U U U	—	U
TANAGERS									
Hepatic Tanager	—	—	—	—	—	—	—	—	—
Summer Tanager	•O O	•C C C	C C C	—	R R	•U U U	•C C C	—	—
Scarlet Tanager	O O	R O	—	—	—	R R	O O	—	—
Western Tanager	—	—	—	R	—	—	—	O R	U U
CARDINALS, GROSBEAKS & ALLIES									
Northern Cardinal	•C C C C	•A A A A	A A A A	•C C C C	•C C C C	•C C C C	•C C C C	—	—
Pyrrhuloxia	—	—	—	—	—	—	—	—	—
Rose-breasted Grosbeak	O O	R O	—	O	U U R	R R	R R	—	—
Black-headed Grosbeak	—	—	—	—	—	—	—	—	R
Blue Grosbeak	•O R	•U U U	—	U O	U U	R R R R	•U U U	—	—
Lazuli Bunting	—	—	—	—	—	—	—	—	R
Indigo Bunting	•O O O O	•C U C	C O U	C C U	C C R	U O U	•C C C	—	—
Painted Bunting	•O R O O	R R	O R	R	C C U	O	—	—	—
Dickcissel	R R R	R R	—	R R	—	—	—	—	—
NEW WORLD SPARROWS & ALLIES									
Olive Sparrow	—	—	—	—	—	—	—	—	—
Green-tailed Towhee	—	—	—	—	—	—	—	•O O R	—
Rufous-sided Towhee	•C C C C	•A A A A	A A A A	—	•C C C C	C C C C	•C C C C	—	—
Brown Towhee	—	—	—	—	—	—	—	—	—
Abert's Towhee	—	—	—	—	—	—	—	—	—
Bachman's Sparrow	•R R R R	•U U U U	—	—	—	•C C C C	•U U U U	—	—

	ID-3 Deer Flat	ID-4 Grays L.	ID-5 Kootenai	ID-6 Minidoka	IL-1 Chautauqua	IL-2 Crab Orchd	IL-3 Brussels	IL-4 Gardner	IN-1 Muscatatuck	IA-1 Desoto	IA-2 Wapello	IA-3 Union Slgh
	•s S F W	•s S F W	•s S F W	•s S F W	•s S F W	•s S F W	•s S F W	•s S F W	•s S F W	•s S F W	•s S F W	•s S F W
	—	—	•U C O	O R	•C C U	•C C U	•C C C	•C C C	•U C	•O O O	•C C C	U U
	—	—	—	—	—	—	—	—	—	—	—	—
	—	—	—	—	R R	U O R	—	—	•C C	—	—	—
	—	—	—	—	R R R	O R	O O	O O	—	—	O O	—
	—	—	—	—	C A	C U	U U	U U	U U	U U	U U U	C
	R R R	•O U	O R U	O R	U U	U O R	U U	U U	—	U U	U U U	C
	—	—	C U O	R	C C	U C	U U	U U	U U	O O	U U U	U
	—	—	—	—	—	—	—	—	—	—	—	—
	—	—	—	—	U R U	•C C U	U U	U U	•U U	O	U U	—
	•U C C	•C C	•C C U	•U U	•C C U	•U U	•U U U	•U U U	•C C	•C C	•U U U	•C C C
	—	—	—	—	C C	U U	U U	U U	U U	O R	U U U	R R
	—	—	—	—	C C	U C	U U	U U	U U	O	U U U	U
	—	—	—	—	R R	U R	—	—	U U U	—	—	—
	—	—	—	—	—	R R	—	—	U U	—	—	—
	•U O C O	•C C C	•C U C	C O U	A A	C C U	C C O	C C O	C C O	C O C R	C C O	C C
	—	—	O O R	O	—	—	—	—	—	—	—	—
	—	—	—	—	C C	U U	R R	—	U U	O	—	O
	—	—	—	—	U U C	U O	—	—	U U	R	—	O
	—	—	—	—	R R R	•C C O	O	O	•U U U	—	O	—
	—	—	—	—	R R	•U C U R	—	—	O U	—	—	—
	—	—	—	—	—	•C C U	—	—	•U U	—	—	—
	—	—	—	—	—	U U	U U	U U	C C	O	U U	C
	—	—	—	—	O O	C U	—	—	U U	O	—	O
	—	—	—	—	C U	C O	U U	U U	U U	U	U U	U
	—	—	—	—	R R	•U O	•U O	•U O	•U U	—	•U O	—
	R	—	—	R R	U R U	C C	U U	U U	U U	•U O	U U U	C U
	—	R	•U C O	R R	•C A U	C U C	•C C C	•C C C	•U U R	•C C	•C C C	C C
	—	—	—	—	•C C U	•U C O	•C C C	•C C C	•U U	—	•C C C	—
	—	—	—	—	—	•U U Q	U	U	U	R	U	—
	—	—	—	—	—	O	—	—	—	—	—	—
	—	—	—	—	•C U C	U O O	U U	U U	•U U U	•U U	U U	U O
	—	—	O O R	—	C C	U U	C U	C U	U U	R	C U	C C
	—	—	—	—	U R	•C C O	U U	U U	U U	—	U U	U U
	—	—	—	—	R R R	•C C O	•U U U	•U U U	•U U	—	•U U U	—
	—	—	—	—	R R	R	—	R	U U	—	—	U U
	R	•O U O	•U C U	O R O	—	—	—	—	U U	—	—	U U
	•O O R	•O U O	•C A C	•U U U	•C C U	•C C C R	•C C C	•C C C	•C C	•C C O	•C C C	•C C O
	U O U	O O	O O	•U U U	U R R	U O	—	—	U U	R	—	O C
	—	—	—	—	U C	U O	U U	U U	U U	O O	U U	U
	•C C	—	R	O O	U U O	•C C U	•U U U	•U U U	•C C C	—	•U U U	U U
	—	—	—	—	—	—	—	—	—	—	—	—
	—	—	—	—	U U U	•C C U	•U U	•U U	•U U	—	•U U	—
	—	—	—	—	U R U	•C U U	•U U U	•U U U	•U U	—	•U U U	—
	C U C	U U C	•O U O	C U O	—	—	—	—	—	—	—	—
	—	—	—	—	•A A A A	•C C C C	•C C C C	•C C C C	•A A A A	•C C C C	•C C C C	•O U U O
	—	R R	—	—	•C C C	U U	U U	U U	U U	•C C	U U	•O U U
	R	•O O O	•O C R	O O	—	—	—	—	—	—	—	—
	•U C R	•U U O	•O U O	U O	R R R	•U U U	—	—	•U U	R	—	—
	—	—	—	—	•C C C	•C C C	•C C C	•C C C	•C C C	•U U	•C C C	• U
	—	—	—	—	•C A C	•C C	•C C C	•C C C	•U U U	•C C	•C C C	• C C
	R	•O U O	—	—	—	—	—	—	—	—	—	—
	R R R R	—	•C U O	R R	•C C U O	•C C C U	•U U U	•U U U	•C C C C	•C C C U	•U U U	U
	—	—	—	—	—	—	—	—	—	—	—	—

STATE-NUMBER OF BIRD LIST / REFUGE, SANCTUARY OR PRESERVE / NESTING, ABUNDANCE BY SEASON • s S F W	FL-8 Merritt Is.	FL-9 St. Marks	FL-10 St. Vincent	FL-11 Biscayne	FL-12 Everglades	GA-1 Okefenokee	GA-2 Piedmont	ID-1 Bear L.	ID-2 Camas
NEW WORLD SPARROWS & ALLIES (cont.)									
Cassin's Sparrow	—	—	—	—	—	—	—	—	—
Rufous-crowned Sparrow	—	—	—	—	—	—	—	—	—
American Tree Sparrow	—	—	—	—	—	—	—	O	U
Chipping Sparrow	O O O	U U U	U U C	—	R R R	U U U	•C C C C	•U O O	O O
Clay-colored Sparrow	—	—	—	—	R R R	—	—	—	—
Brewer's Sparrow	—	—	—	—	—	—	—	—	U
Field Sparrow	R R	U U U	—	—	U U U	U U U	•C C C C	—	U
Black-chinned Sparrow	—	—	—	—	—	—	—	—	—
Vesper Sparrow	R R	U U U	—	—	—	U U U	O O	•U U	• C
Lark Sparrow	R R	R	—	—	—	—	—	O	U
Black-throated Sparrow	—	—	—	—	—	—	—	—	—
Sage Sparrow	—	—	—	—	—	—	—	•O U O	U
Lark Bunting	—	—	—	—	—	—	—	O	—
Savannah Sparrow	C C C	U U U	C C C C	U C	—	U U U	U U U	•C C C	• C
Baird's Sparrow	—	—	—	—	—	—	—	—	—
Grasshopper Sparrow	O O O	R R	—	—	U U	O O O	R	—	—
Henslow's Sparrow	—	R R	R	—	—	O O O	—	—	—
Le Conte's Sparrow	—	—	—	—	—	R R R	—	—	—
Sharp-tailed Sparrow	O O O	U U U	—	—	R	—	—	—	—
Seaside Sparrow	O O	•C C U U	C C C C	—	•C C C C	—	—	—	—
Fox Sparrow	R R	—	—	—	—	U U U	O O	R	—
Song Sparrow	R O O	C C C	C C C	—	—	C C C	C C C	O	O O
Lincoln's Sparrow	R R	—	—	—	C	—	—	—	R
Swamp Sparrow	O C C	C C C	C C C	—	C C C	C C C	C C C	—	—
White-throated Sparrow	R R	A A A	C C C	—	—	C C C	C C C	—	—
Golden-crowned Sparrow	—	—	—	—	—	—	—	—	—
White-crowned Sparrow	—	R	R R	—	R	—	R	U U O	O O O
Harris' Sparrow	—	—	—	—	—	—	—	—	—
Dark-eyed Junco	—	R O O	—	—	—	R R	C C C	U O U	C U C
McCown's Longspur	—	—	—	—	—	—	—	—	—
Lapland Longspur	—	—	—	—	—	—	—	—	O U
Smith's Longspur	—	—	—	—	—	—	—	—	—
Chestnut-collared Longspur	—	—	—	—	—	—	—	—	—
Snow Bunting	—	—	—	—	—	—	—	R	—
NEW WORLD BLACKBIRDS & ORIOLES									
Bobolink	U O	C U	O U	C C	C C	R R	U O	R	—
Red-winged Blackbird	•C C C C	•A A A A	A A A A	C C C C	•C C C C	•C C C C	•C C C C	•C A C U	•C A A U
Tricolored Blackbird	—	—	—	—	—	—	—	—	—
Eastern Meadowlark	•C C C C	•C U C C	C C C C	—	•C C C C	•C C C C	•C C C C	—	—
Western Meadowlark	—	—	—	—	—	—	—	•U C U R	•U C U
Yellow-headed Blackbird	—	—	—	—	R R R	—	—	•C A U	•U A U
Rusty Blackbird	R R R	U U U	—	—	—	U U U	O U	—	—
Brewer's Blackbird	—	—	—	—	R	O O O	—	•C U U	•U C U
Great-tailed Grackle	—	—	—	—	—	—	—	—	—
Boat-tailed Grackle	•C C C C	•A A A A	A A A A	C C C C	•C C C C	R R R	—	—	—
Common Grackle	•C C C C	•C C C C	C C C C	C C C C	•C C C C	•C C C C	•U U U C	—	—
Bronzed Cowbird	—	—	—	—	—	—	—	—	—
Brown-headed Cowbird	U U U	C U U U	C U C C	C C	U U R	O O O O	U O O U	U U	• C
Orchard Oriole	R R	•C U O	C U O	—	U U	•U U U	•U U	—	—
Hooded Oriole	—	—	—	—	—	—	—	—	—
Baltimore Oriole	—	—	—	—	C C R	—	—	—	—
Bullock's Oriole	O O	R U	—	O O	R R R	R R R	R	O O R	U R
Scott's Oriole	—	—	—	—	—	—	—	—	—
FINCHES									
Rosy Finch	—	—	—	—	—	—	—	O	—
Pine Grosbeak	—	—	—	—	—	—	—	—	—
Purple Finch	—	R R U	—	—	—	U U U	U O U	—	—
Cassin's Finch	—	—	—	—	—	—	—	—	—
House Finch	—	—	—	—	—	—	—	R R O O	• C
Red Crossbill	—	—	—	—	—	—	—	—	—
White-winged Crossbill	—	—	—	—	—	—	—	—	—
Common Redpoll	—	—	—	—	—	—	—	—	—
Hoary Redpoll	—	—	—	—	—	—	—	—	—
Pine Siskin	R R	—	—	—	—	R R R	O	O O	—
Lesser Goldfinch	—	—	—	—	—	—	—	—	—
Lawrence's Goldfinch	—	—	—	—	—	—	—	—	—
American Goldfinch	R U U	C C C	—	O	C C C	C C C	•C O O C	O O	• C O
Evening Grosbeak	—	—	—	—	—	—	R	R	O R
OLD WORLD SPARROWS									
House Sparrow	•C C C C	R R R R	—	•O O O O	•U U U U	•O O O O	•O O O O	O O O O	•C C C U
Eurasian Tree Sparrow	—	—	—	—	—	—	—	—	—

ID-3 Deer Flat	ID-4 Grays L.	ID-5 Kootenai	ID-6 Minidoka	IL-1 Chautauqua	IL-2 Crab Orchd	IL-3 Brussels	IL-4 Gardner	IN-1 Muscatatuck	IA-1 Desoto	IA-2 Wapello	IA-3 Union Slgh
•s S F W	•s S F W	•s S F W	•s S F W	•s S F W	•s S F W	•s S F W	•s S F W	•s S F W	•s S F W	•s S F W	•s S F W
—	—	—	—	—	—	—	—	—	—	—	—
	R	U U	O	C CA	C OC	C CC	C CC	CC	C CA	C C	CC
U O R	•O U O	•C C U	O O O	•C C C	•U U O	U O	U O	•U U O	U U	U O	•U U
—	•U U U	R R	U U O	R R	—	—	—	—	U	—	C
—		—	—	•C A C O	•C C C C	•C C C O	•C C C O	•C C C C	•C C U	•C C C O	U U U
•O O O	•C C U	O R O	U O O	•U C U O	U R U	U U	U U	U U O	•U U U	U U	•U C C
•O U U	R	—	•U O O	•U C U	R R	O	O	—	•U U	O	—
—	—	—	O O	—	—	—	—	—	—	—	—
—	O O	—	O O	—	—	—	—	—	—	—	—
U U U R	•U C U	•A C A	O O O	U U	U C U	U U	U U	O U O	U U U	U U	• U
—	—	R R R	—	O U O R	•U U O	—	—	•U U R	•C C	—	•U C
—	—	—	—	—	R	—	—	•U U R	• R R	—	—
—	—	—	—	O O	O O U	R R	—	—	R U	—	U
—	—	—	—	R O	R	R	—	—	—	—	—
R	•U U O	R R	R	C C O	U O C	U U O	U U O	U C	U U	U U O	U
•C C C C	•C C U	•A A C U	•C C C C	•C C C U	•C U U C	•C C C C	•C C C C	•C C C C	•C C C U	•C C C C	•C C C U
U O O	O O	O R U	—	O O	U R	O O	O O	U U U	U U	O O	U
—	—	—	—	U U O	C C C	C C C	C C C	C C	U U R	C C C	•C C C
—	—	R R	—	C C O	C C O	C C O	C C O	U C C	U U U	C C O	C U
C U A C	•U C C	U R C	C U U U	U U	C C C	C C C O	C C C O	U C C	O O O	C C C O	C U
U	—	—	R	O O R	—	—	—	—	C C C	U U	U
U C A	•U C C U	•C U C O	•C U C	C C A	C C C	C C A	C C A	O C C	C C A	C C A	C C C
—	—	R	—	R R	O U O	—	—	O O O	—	—	U U U
—	O	U	O R R	R R	—	—	—	—	O	R	C C
—	•O U O	R O	O	O O O	U R	U	U	U U	•O O	U	•C C C
A A A O	•C C U O	•A A A U	•C C C O	A C A U	•C C A C	•A A A C	•A A A C	•A A A A	•A A A A	•A A A C	•C A A C
—	—	—	—	•C C C O	•C C C C	•C C C U	•C C C U	•A A A A	•C C C C	•C C C U	—
•C C A U	•C C U O	•C C U R	•C C C U	R O R O	—	—	—	—	•C C C C	—	•C C C U
•C C O	•C C O	•C A U R	•C C U	—	—	—	—	—	•U U U O	—	•C C C
•A A A C	•C C U	R O R	•C C U O	C C O	U O U	U U R	U U R	O U U	U U R	U U R	C C U
—	—	—	—	—	—	R	R	O	O O R	—	C C
—	—	—	—	•C A C O	•C C A C	•A A A C	•A A A C	•C C C C	•C C C U	•A A A C	•U A A U
—	O O	•O U O	U U	•U C U O	•C C C C	•C C C	•C C C	•C C A C	•C C C U	•C C C	•U C C
—	—	—	—	R R R	•C C O	•U U	•U U	•U U	•C C	•U U	•U U U
•C C U	•O U	•U O	•C C O	•C C C	•C C U	•C C	•C C	•U U U	•C C R	•C C	•C C U
—	O R	O U	—	—	—	—	—	—	—	—	—
—	O U O	R R O	—	—	—	—	—	—	—	—	—
—	—	O R O R	O	U U U	C U C	U U U	U U U	U U	O O	U U U	—
R R R	•O U O	U U O O	O	—	—	—	—	—	—	—	—
•A A A C	—	R R R R	•U O U O	—	—	—	—	U U U	—	—	—
—	—	C U U U	—	—	—	—	—	—	O	—	—
—	O R	R R	O O	O O U	—	—	—	—	—	R	U U
O U	•U C U	A U C U	O O O	U U O	U U O	R	R	U U	O O R	R	—
—	—	—	R R	—	—	—	—	—	—	—	—
•U U C C	•O U U	•U C U	•C U U O	•A A A U	•C C C C	•C C C C	•C C C C	•C C C U	•C C C C	•C C C U	
C O U O	O O U	U R U U	O O O	•R R R	U U	R	R	U	—	R	
•A A A C	•U U U U	O O O O	•C C C C	•A A A A	•C C C C	•C C C C	•C C C C	•A A A A	•A A A A	•C C C C	•C C C C
				R R R R		•U U U C	•U U U C				

STATE-NUMBER OF BIRD LIST / REFUGE, SANCTUARY OR PRESERVE / NESTING, ABUNDANCE BY SEASON	IA-4 McGregor • s S F W	KS-1 Flint Hills • s S F W	KS-2 Kirwin • s S F W	KS-3 Quivira • s S F W	LA-1 Bog. Chitto • s S F W	LA-2 Catahoula • s S F W	LA-3 Delta • s S F W	LA-4 Lacassine • s S F W	LA-5 Sabine • s S F W
LOONS									
Red-throated Loon	−	−	−	−	−	−	−	−	−
Arctic Loon	−	−	−	−	−	−	−	−	−
Pacific Loon	−	−	−	−	−	−	−	−	−
Common Loon	U U	U R U	R R	R R R	−	−	U	−	O O U
Yellow-billed Loon	−	−	−	−	−	−	−	−	−
GREBES									
Least Grebe	−	−	−	−	−	−	−	−	−
Pied-billed Grebe	• C C C	• C O C O	C O C	• C C C O	−	C U C C	C A	• C O C C	• C U C C
Horned Grebe	U U	O O	O O	U R R	−	−	U U	R	O O O
Red-necked Grebe	R R	−	−	−	−	−	−	−	−
Eared Grebe	−	O U	C O C	• U U U	−	−	−	−	U U U
Western Grebe	−	R	O O	R R	−	−	−	−	−
SHEARWATERS & PETRELS									
Northern Fulmar	−	−	−	−	−	−	−	−	−
Cory's Shearwater	−	−	−	−	−	−	−	−	−
Pink-footed Shearwater	−	−	−	−	−	−	−	−	−
Greater Shearwater	−	−	−	−	−	−	−	−	−
Sooty Shearwater	−	−	−	−	−	−	−	−	−
Short-tailed Shearwater	−	−	−	−	−	−	−	−	−
Manx Shearwater	−	−	−	−	−	−	−	−	−
Audubon's Shearwater	−	−	−	−	−	−	−	−	−
STORM-PETRELS									
Wilson's Storm-Petrel	−	−	−	−	−	−	−	−	−
Fork-tailed Storm-Petrel	−	−	−	−	−	−	−	−	−
Leach's Storm-Petrel	−	−	−	−	−	−	−	−	−
BOOBIES & GANNETS									
Masked Booby	−	−	−	−	−	−	R	−	−
Brown Booby	−	−	−	−	−	−	−	−	−
Northern Gannet	−	−	−	−	−	−	−	−	−
PELICANS									
American White Pelican	O O	C O C	C C C	A U A	−	O U U	C U C A	R O C	C O C C
Brown Pelican	−	−	−	−	−	−	−	−	−
CORMORANTS									
Great Cormorant	−	−	−	−	−	−	−	−	−
Double-crested Cormorant	• U U C	• C U C	• C C C O	A C C	−	O O O O	A C A	U O U U	C C C
Olivaceous Cormorant	−	−	−	−	−	−	R	• A A A A	• C C C C
Brandt's Cormorant	−	−	−	−	−	−	−	−	−
Pelagic Cormorant	−	−	−	−	−	−	−	−	−
Red-faced Cormorant	−	−	−	−	−	−	−	−	−
ANHINGAS									
Anhinga	−	−	−	−	−	C C O O	U C U	• C C U U	O O
FRIGATEBIRDS									
Magnificent Frigatebird	−	−	−	−	−	−	O O	−	R R
BITTERNS & HERONS									
American Bittern	• U U U	U O U	O O O	• C A C R	−	U U U	C C U C	• C C C C	U U C
Least Bittern	• U U U	• O O R	O O O	• U U U	−	U U U	C C C R	• C C C R	• C A R R
Great Blue Heron	• A A A R	• C C C U	• C C C O	• C C C O	C C C C	C C C U	A A A A	• C C C C	• C C C C
Great Egret	• C C C	U U U	O O O	C C C	C C C C	C C C	A A A A	• A A A C	• C C C C
Snowy Egret	R R	U U U	U U U	C C C	C C C C	U C C	A A A A	• A A A C	• C C C C
Little Blue Heron	O	U U C	U U U	O U U	C C C C	C C C	A A C U	• C C C U	C C C O
Tricolored Heron	−	−	−	R R	R R	O O O	A A A A	• A A A C	• C C C C
Reddish Egret	−	−	−	−	−	−	−	−	R R R R
Cattle Egret	U R	O O O	R	O O U	C C	C A A U	A A A U	• A A A A	C C U U
Green-backed Heron	• C C C	• C C C	O O O	• U U U	C C C	• C C C	A A C R	• C C C U	• A A C O
Black-crowned Night-Heron	• C C C	U O U	C O C	• C A C R	U U U	O O O O	A A C U	• C C C U	U U U U
Yellow-crowned Night-Heron	• U U U	O O O	O O	O O O	C C C	C C C C	A A C U	• C C C O	O U O R
IBISES & SPOONBILLS									
White Ibis	−	−	−	−	C C C C	U U	C C C C	• A A U U	• U C C C
Glossy Ibis	−	−	−	−	−	−	U U	−	O O O O
White-faced Ibis	−	R R	R R	• U U U	−	−	C C C C	• A A U U	• C C C C
Roseate Spoonbill	−	−	−	−	−	−	O	• C C O O	• U U U U
STORKS									
Wood Stork	−	−	−	−	−	A A	C	O O	U O
SWANS, GEESE & DUCKS									
Fulvous Whistling-Duck	−	−	−	−	−	R R	U	C O C O	R R
Black-bellied Whistling-Duck	−	−	−	R	−	−	−	R R R R	−
Tundra Swan	C C	R R R	R R	R R R	−	−	R	−	−
Trumpeter Swan	−	−	−	−	−	−	−	−	−
Mute Swan	−	−	−	−	−	−	−	−	−
Greater White-fronted Goose	R R	C C U	A R A U	A A C	−	O O O	U U	C A A	O O U
Snow Goose	U U	A A U	O R U O	U U U	−	O O O	A A A	A A A	C C A

	LA-6 Tensas	LA-7 Jean Lafitte	ME-1 Great Wass	ME-2 Moosehorn	ME-3 Petit Manan	ME-4 Carson	MD-1 Blackwater	MD-2 East. Neck	MA-1 G. Meadows	MA-2 Parker R.	MA-3 Monomoy	MI-1 Seney
	•sSFW	•sSFW	•sSFW	•sSFW	•sSFW	•sSFW	•sSFW	•sSFW	•sSFW	•sSFW	•sSFW	•sSFW
	—	—	U U O	U UU	U U	O OU	—	—	—	U C U	C C O	—
	—	—	—	—	—	—	—	—	—	R	—	—
	—	—	—	—	—	—	—	—	—	—	—	—
	—	U U	C O C C	•C C C C	C C C C	C O C C	O O O	U C	R R	C O C C	C U C C	C C U
	U R U U	U U	O O O R	•C U C	O	O O O	U O U U	•U R C U	U O U	U U U	•U U U	•C U C
		U U	C C C	O O U	C C C	U O U	O O U	U C U	R R	C C C	O O	O R U
			O C	R R	C C C	O U U	—	R R R	—	U O U	R R R	R R R
	—	—	R R O U	—	—	R R	—	—	—	O O	R R R	—
	—	—	—	—	—	—	—	—	—	—	O O	—
	—	—	O O	—	—	—	—	—	—	O O O	O O	—
	—	—	O O	—	R R	—	—	—	—	O O O	O O R	—
	—	—	R R	—	R	—	—	—	—	O O O	—	—
	—	—	O O O	—	O	R R	—	—	—	O O O	O	—
	—	—	O O O	—	•U U U	—	—	—	—	R	R R	—
	—	—	U O C R	—	O O O	O U O	—	—	—	U R U U	C R A U	—
	—	U U U	—	—	—	—	—	—	—	—	—	—
	—	C C C	U R U U	C	C O C O	U U C	O R O	C U C O	O O	O R O U	C O C C	—
	—		C C C	C C C	•A A A	C C C O				A A C O	C C C	R R R
	C C C R	U U R	—	—	—	—	—	—	—	—	—	—
		—	—	—	—	—	—	—	—	—	—	—
	U U	R	U O U	•C C C	•U U U	U U U	•U U U O	•R U U R	•U U U	U U U O	R O R	•C C C
	—	•C C	—	—	—	—	•U U U	•U U	•R R R	•U U O	R	•R R
	U C U U	•C C C C	C C C R	C C U	U U U O	C C C O	C C C C	•C C C U	U C C H	C U C O	C U C U	•C C C
	U C U	•C C C C			—	O O O	U A C R	O O U	O R	U U U	O O O	—
	U U U	C C C C	R O O	—	R R	C C C	C A C	U U U	O R	C C C	•C C C	—
	A A A R	C C C C	—	—	R	O U U	U U U	R R R	R R	O U U	O O O	—
	R R R	C C C C	—	—	R	O O O	—	U U R	R R O	—	O O O	R R R
	C C C R	U U U U	—	—	R	R	U U U	U U R	R R	O O O	R R	—
	U U U	•C C C R	O O O	O O	R R	•U C U	•C C C	•C C C R	•U U C	•C C U	R	R O R
	R R R	U U U R	U U U	R	R R	•U C C	•U U U U	R U U R	R C U	•C C U O	•C C C O	R R
	C C C	•C C C R	—	—	—	R R R	—	R R R	—	O U O	R R	—
	U U U	C C C C	—	—	—	—	—	—	—	—	—	—
	—	C C C C	—	—	—	U U R	O O O	R R	R O R	U U O	O O O	—
	—	C C C C	—	—	—	—	—	—	—	—	—	—
	R R	—	—	—	—	—	—	—	—	—	—	—
	—	—	—	—	—	—	—	—	R	—	—	R
	—	—	—	—	—	—	U C C	C A A	—	—	R	U R U
	—	—	—	—	—	—	—	—	—	—	—	—
	—	—	—	—	—	—	—	•C C C C	R R R	U U U O	O O R	—
	R R R	—	—	—	—	—	R R	R R	—	—	—	—
	U U U	U U	U	R	O	O R	U C C	U U R	R R	U U R	R O	O U

STATE-NUMBER OF BIRD LIST REFUGE, SANCTUARY OR PRESERVE NESTING, ABUNDANCE BY SEASON	IA-4 McGregor •s S F W	KS-1 Flint Hills •s S F W	KS-2 Kirwin •s S F W	KS-3 Quivira •s S F W	LA-1 Bog. Chitto •s S F W	LA-2 Catahoula •s S F W	LA-3 Delta •s S F W	LA-4 Lacassine •s S F W	LA-5 Sabine •s S F W
SWANS, GEESE & DUCKS (cont.)									
Ross' Goose	—	R	—	R R	—	—	—	—	R
Emperor Goose	—	—	—	—	—	—	—	—	—
Brant	—	—	—	—	—	—	—	—	—
Canada Goose	•C U C U	A A U	•A C A C	•A U A A	—	R R	C C	O O O	O U
Wood Duck	•C A A R	•C C C R	•U U U R	•U U O	A A A A	•C C C A	O O O O	•U U U U	R U U
Green-winged Teal	•C R C R	A O A O	•C U C U	•A U A C	—	C C C	A A A	C A A	C C A
American Black Duck	•C U C O	U U O	O R O R	U O U U	—	O O U	C C	O O O	R
Mottled Duck	—	—	—	—	—	—	C C C C	•C C C C	•C C C A
Mallard	•A A A C	•A U A A	•A C A C	•A C A A	U	A U A A	A A A	C R A A	C C A
Northern Pintail	C R C R	A O A U	•A O C O	•A U A C	—	C C C	A A A	C A A	C C A
Blue-winged Teal	•A U A	•A R A	•C O C R	•A C A R	U U U	C C O	A R A U	C R A C	•C O A A
Cinnamon Teal	—	—	U U U R	O R R	—	—	R	R	O O O
Northern Shoveler	C U C	C O C	•C O O R	•A C A C	—	C C C	A A A	A A A	C O C A
Gadwall	C U C	C R C R	•C O C O	•A U A U	—	C C C	C C A	C A A	C C A
Eurasian Wigeon	—	R	—	—	—	—	—	—	—
American Wigeon	A U A	A R A U	C O C U	•A U A C	—	C C C	A A A	C A A	C C A
Canvasback	C R A R	U R U R	O R O R	•C U C R	—	O O O	C A	O O O	O O U
Redhead	C R C R	C R C R	O R U R	•A C A R	—	O U O	C C	R R R	U U U
Ring-necked Duck	A R A R	C R C R	O R O R	C R C R	—	C C C	U	C A	O O U
Greater Scaup	U U	—	R R R R	—	—	U U U	—	—	—
Lesser Scaup	A U A R	A R A R	U O U O	•A U A R	—	U U U	C A A	C A A	C C C
Common Eider	—	—	—	—	—	—	—	—	—
King Eider	—	—	—	—	—	—	—	—	—
Steller's Eider	—	—	—	—	—	—	—	—	—
Harlequin Duck	—	—	—	—	—	—	—	—	—
Oldsquaw	R O R	—	—	—	—	—	R O	—	—
Black Scoter	R R	—	—	—	—	—	—	—	—
Surf Scoter	R R	—	—	—	—	—	—	—	—
White-winged Scoter	R U R	—	—	—	—	—	R	—	—
Common Goldeneye	C C U	U O U	O R O O	U U C	—	R	U	O O	O O
Barrow's Goldeneye	—	—	—	—	—	—	—	—	—
Bufflehead	C C R	U U O	O R C R	C C C	—	R R	U	U C	U
Hooded Merganser	•C U C R	O U R	O R O O	U U U	U	U U U	C	U U U	O U
Common Merganser	C C U	A C A	C U C O	C C C	—	—	O O	—	R R
Red-breasted Merganser	C U R	U U R	—	O O	—	—	C U C	R R R	U
Ruddy Duck	C R C	C R C R	O O C R	C U C U	—	U U U	U U	C C C	U O U
Masked Duck	—	—	—	—	—	—	—	—	—
AMERICAN VULTURES									
Black Vulture	—	—	—	—	C C C C	U U U U	C C C C	O O O O	C C C C
Turkey Vulture	C C C R	•C C C	O C O	U O U	C C C C	C C C C	C C C C	O O O O	•C C C C
KITES, EAGLES, HAWKS & ALLIES									
Osprey	U O U R	O O	O O	U U	U U	R R	C R C	O O O O	O O R
American Swallow-tailed Kite	—	—	—	—	C	—	—	—	—
Black-shouldered Kite	—	—	—	—	—	—	—	—	—
Snail Kite	—	—	—	—	—	—	—	—	—
Mississippi Kite	—	R R	R R R	•C C C	C C	O O	—	R R	—
Bald Eagle	•C U C C	C C C	O O C	C C A	R R R	R R U U	U U U	R R R	R
Northern Harrier	•U U U O	•C U C C	C O C C	•C C A C	—	U U U	C C C	U U C	C C C
Sharp-shinned Hawk	C U C O	U R U U	O O O O	U U U	U U U	—	O O U	O O O R	U U U
Cooper's Hawk	U U U O	O O U O	O O O O	•C C C U	U U U U	—	O O O U	O O O O	O O U
Northern Goshawk	O	R	R	R	—	—	—	—	—
Common Black-Hawk	—	—	—	—	—	—	—	—	—
Harris' Hawk	—	—	—	—	—	—	—	—	—
Gray Hawk	—	—	—	—	—	—	—	—	—
Red-shouldered Hawk	•U U U R	R R R	R R	O O	A A A A	•C C C C	U U U C	O O U U	U U U
Broad-winged Hawk	•C U A	U R U	—	U U	C C C	U R U R	—	O O U	O O
Short-tailed Hawk	—	—	—	—	—	—	—	—	—
Swainson's Hawk	R	U O U	•C C C	•C C C	—	—	—	—	—
White-tailed Hawk	—	—	—	—	—	—	—	—	—
Zone-tailed Hawk	—	—	—	—	—	—	—	—	—
Red-tailed Hawk	•C C C C	•A A A A	•C C C C	•C U C C	C U C C	C C C C	U R U C	O U C	U U U
Ferruginous Hawk	—	R R	U R U U	U R O	—	—	—	—	—
Rough-legged Hawk	U U	U U C	O O C	C C C	—	—	—	—	—
Golden Eagle	R R R	O O O	O O C	U U U	—	U R U U	—	R R R	—
CARACARAS & FALCONS									
Crested Caracara	—	—	—	—	—	—	—	—	—
American Kestrel	•C C C U	•C C C C	C O C U	A O A O	U U U	U U C C	C R C C	C U C C	U U C
Merlin	O U	O O R	R	R R R	R R	—	O U U	O O O	U U U
Peregrine Falcon	O O O	O O R	U U U U	U U O	R R	—	C C C	O O	O O
Gyrfalcon	—	—	—	—	—	—	—	—	—
Prairie Falcon	—	U U U	U U U U	U R U C	—	—	—	—	—

LA-6 Tensas	LA-7 Jean Lafitte	ME-1 Great Wass	ME-2 Moosehorn	ME-3 Petit Manan	ME-4 Carson	MD-1 Blackwater	MD-2 East. Neck	MA-1 G. Meadows	MA-2 Parker R.	MA-3 Monomoy	MI-1 Seney
•s S F W	•s S F W	•s S F W	•s S F W	•s S F W	•s S F W	•s S F W	•s S F W	•s S F W	•s S F W	•s S F W	•s S F W
—	—	—	—	—	—	—	—	—	—	—	—
—	—		—	—	—	—	—	—	—	—	—
		C OR	O O	U O	O O		R R		U UO	CRCC	
R RR		COCU	•AAAU	O OO	COCU	•ACAA	A AA	•ACAU	•AAAC	•ACAA	•CCCU
CCCA	•CCCC	O OO	•CCC	•UUU	O OU	•UUUO	•CCCU	•CCAR	U UO	R R	•CCC
U UU	UU	COCO	•CUC	•CCA	•UOCO	CRAU	C CR	•COAO	•CUCU	•CCCO	•UOU
R RU	—	•CCCC	•AAAU	•CCAC	•CCCC	•ACAA	•CCCC	•CCAO	•ACAC	•ACAA	•CCCO
—	CCCC										
C CA	CC	UUUU	•UUUO	O OU	•CCCC	•ACAA	•AAAA	•ACAU	•ACAC	•CCCC	•CCCO
R RU	—	U UO	O O	O U	U UO	CRCC	C CC	U UO	•UUCU	•CUCO	URO
CRUU	C CC	COC	•CUC	•UUU	•UOU	•CCCR	•CRCR	•COA	•CCU	•CUC	•CUC
R RU	UU	—	—	—	O	URCO	U CO	O U	•UUUR	•UUU	ORO
R RU	UU	—	ORO	—	RRR	COCU	CRCU	•UOUU	•ACAO	•CCCO	R R
						R	R RR	R RR	R	R RR	—
U RU	UU	R R	OOO	ORU	O O	C CU	U CC	U AO	UOCO	•CUCO	•CUC
		R RR	—	—	—	R RO	C CC	R R	R RR	O CO	ORO
						O OO	U UU	R R	R RR	O OO	ORO
R RR	—	UOU	•CCC	R	O O	U UU	U UU	A O	O OR	O OO	•CCC
		U UU	O O	O O	O OO	O OO	U CR	U U	U UU	O CO	—
R RR	C CC	—	O O	O	O O	O OU	C CC	O O	R R	O OR	CRC
—	—	•CCCC	OOOO	•AAAA	UUUC	—	—	—	COUC	AUAA	—
—	—	O OO	—	R	—	R	—	—	RRRR	R RR	—
—	—	O OO	—	R	—	O O	—	—	H R	R R	—
—	—	COCC	C C	C AC	U OU	O O	C CA	—	C UC	COAC	—
—	—	U UU	O CO	AOU	U UU		U UU	—	CRCU	CRCC	—
—	—	CRCC	O CO	COU	U UU		U UU	—	UOCU	CRCC	—
—	—	COCC	O CO	COUU	U UU	R	U UC	—	COCC	CRAC	—
—	UU	COCC	•AUUA	C CC	C UC	U UU	A CA	U RR	U UC	O CC	•COCO
—	—	R RR	R R	—	R R	—	—	—	O O	—	—
—	UU	C CC	C OU	U UU	C CC	U UU	C CC	U OR	U CC	C CC	CRC
RRRR	—	O OO	•CCCU	•UUU	OOO	URUU	U UU	URO	URUR	O CO	•CCC
	R	O OO	•CUCC	•UUU	OOO	U UU	U RU	U RR	R R	O O	•CCCR
—	UU	COCC	C UC	CUCC	C CC	O OO	U RU	R	R	•CRAC	—
—	—	—	R R	—	—	U UU	C CC	R O	•RRUR	•OOCO	RRR
UUUC	CCCA	—	—	—	—	OOOO	•CCCC	—	—	R	—
UUUU	CCCA	—	O O	O	O O	•CCCC	•AAAA	U H	H R	R R	O O
R	U UU	•UUU	•CCU	•UUU	UOU	•CCC	•AAC	URU	UOO	OOO	OOO
R	U	—	—	—	—	—	—	—	—	—	—
CUR	•UU	—	—	—	—	—	—	—	—	R	—
	R	UUUU	•UUUU	•UUUU	O	•CCCC	•CUCU	R RR	R RR	RRRR	•UUUO
U UU	C CC	UUUR	CUC	•CCC	UOUU	•COCC	C CC	ORUR	CUCC	•CUCC	•CCC
R RR	U CC	UUCU	•UUUO	•UOAO	•UOCO	U UU	U CU	O UR	U UO	U C	•OOO
RRRR	RRRR	R RR	•UUU	O O	O	UUUU	R	R RR	O OO	R R	•OOO
—	—	UUUU	•UUUU	•UUUU	OOOO	—	—	—	OOOO	R R	•OOOO
—	—	—	—	—	—	—	—	—	—	—	—
CCCC	•CCCC	R R	•OUO	—	OOO	O OU	•UUUU	ORR	R R	—	•UUU
UUU	U U	UUU	•UCU	O O	UUC	O O	O C	•UUC	R R	R R	•UUU
—	—	—	—	—	—	—	—	—	—	—	—
—	—	—	—	—	—	—	—	—	—	—	—
CUCC	C C	UOUO	•OOOO	O O	UOUO	•UUCC	•CCCC	•CUCC	OOOO	R R	•UUU
—	—	U UU	O OO	O O	O O	O UC	R RR	O O	U UC	—	U U
	R					O O	R RR		R R	—	
URUU	C CC	•CUCO	•CCCO	C C	UUUO	CUCC	•AUAA	•UUUU	•CCCU	U U	•CCC
R R	R	URCR	ORO	O C	O O	O UR	R OR	R O	O UO	O CO	•RRR
R RR	R RR	URUR	R	R	UOC	O O	O OR	R O	O UO	U U	RRR
		R	—	—	—	—	—	R R	R R	—	

STATE-NUMBER OF BIRD LIST REFUGE, SANCTUARY OR PRESERVE NESTING, ABUNDANCE BY SEASON	IA-4 McGregor • s S F W	KS-1 Flint Hills • s S F W	KS-2 Kirwin • s S F W	KS-3 Quivira • s S F W	LA-1 Bog. Chitto • s S F W	LA-2 Catahoula • s S F W	LA-3 Delta • s S F W	LA-4 Lacassine • s S F W	LA-5 Sabine • s S F W
CHACHALACAS									
Plain Chachalaca	—	—	—	—	—	—	—	—	—
PARTRIDGES, GROUSE, TURKEYS & QUAILS									
Gray Partridge	•U U U U	—	—	—	—	—	—	—	—
Chukar	—	—	—	—	—	—	—	—	—
Ring-necked Pheasant	•U U U U	•O O O O	•C C C C	•A A A A	—	—	—	—	—
Spruce Grouse	—	—	—	—	—	—	—	—	—
Blue Grouse	—	—	—	—	—	—	—	—	—
Willow Ptarmigan	—	—	—	—	—	—	—	—	—
Rock Ptarmigan	—	—	—	—	—	—	—	—	—
White-tailed Ptarmigan	—	—	—	—	—	—	—	—	—
Ruffed Grouse	•C C C C	—	—	—	—	—	—	—	—
Sage Grouse	—	—	—	—	—	—	—	—	—
Greater Prairie Chicken	—	•C C C C	—	•O O O O	—	—	—	—	—
Lesser Prairie Chicken	—	—	—	—	—	—	—	—	—
Sharp-tailed Grouse	—	—	—	—	—	—	—	—	—
Wild Turkey	O O O O	•U U U U	R R R R	•U U U U	C C C C	R	—	—	—
Northern Bobwhite	•C C C C	•A A A A	•C C C C	•C C C C	C C C C	•U U U U	—	•U U U U	R R R R
Scaled Quail	—	—	—	—	—	—	—	—	—
Gambel's Quail	—	—	—	—	—	—	—	—	—
California Quail	—	—	—	—	—	—	—	—	—
Mountain Quail	—	—	—	—	—	—	—	—	—
RAILS, GALLINULES & COOTS									
Yellow Rail	—	—	—	—	—	—	—	—	U U R
Black Rail	—	—	—	R O R	—	—	—	—	R
Clapper Rail	—	—	—	—	—	—	A A A A	—	•C C C C
King Rail	•U U	O R O	—	•U U U	—	R	C C C A	•A A A A	C C C C
Virginia Rail	•U U U	U O U	U O U	•U U U	—	—	O O U	O O O	U C
Sora	•C C C	U U C	U O U	•U U C	—	U	C C C	U U U	U U C
Purple Gallinule	—	R	—	—	—	R R R	U C U	•A A A O	•U C U R
Common Moorhen	•U U U	R R	—	•O O	—	O O O	C C C R	•A A A U	•C C C C
American Coot	•A C A O	A O A O	C U C R	•C C A R	—	C C A	A A A	•A O A A	C C C
LIMPKINS									
Limpkin	—	—	—	—	—	—	—	—	—
CRANES									
Sandhill Crane	—	R R	C C	A A R	—	—	—	—	—
Whooping Crane	—	—	R R	O O	—	—	—	—	—
PLOVERS									
Black-bellied Plover	U U	O O	O U O	C R C	—	—	C O C C	O O O	C C
Lesser Golden-Plover	U U	U O	R R	U R U	—	—	O R R	C	R R
Snowy Plover	—	R	O O R	•C C U	—	—	—	—	—
Wilson's Plover	—	—	—	—	—	U U	C C C U	—	O
Semipalmated Plover	U U U	O O	O R	C O C	—	U U	C C O	U O U O	U U
Piping Plover	—	R R	O O	O R O	—	U U	U U	—	—
Killdeer	•C C C R	•A A A U	•C C C R	•C C C U	C C C C	•C C C C	C O C C	•C C C C	•C C C C
Mountain Plover	—	—	—	—	—	—	—	—	—
OYSTERCATCHERS									
American Oystercatcher	—	—	—	—	—	—	C C	—	—
Black Oystercatcher	—	—	—	—	—	—	—	—	—
STILTS & AVOCETS									
Black-necked Stilt	—	—	R	•O O O	—	—	U U U	•C C C O	•C C C R
American Avocet	R R	U U	C O C	•C C C	—	—	O O	—	O O
SANDPIPERS									
Greater Yellowlegs	U U U	U O U	U U U	C O C R	—	O O O O	C C U	C U C	A A
Lesser Yellowlegs	C C C	C O C	O O O	A U A	—	O C C O	A U A U	C U C	A A
Solitary Sandpiper	U U U	U U	—	U U U	U U	O O O	C C R	C C	U U
Willet	R R R	O O	O O O	U O U	—	—	C C C C	—	C C C C
Wandering Tattler	—	—	—	—	—	—	—	—	—
Spotted Sandpiper	•C C C	C U C	O U O	C C C	C C C C	O O O	C R C R	C O C	C C U
Upland Sandpiper	•U U	•A A C	U U	•C C C	—	U U	R	O	R R
Whimbrel	—	—	—	—	—	—	A R	O	U R
Long-billed Curlew	—	R R	U U	O O O	—	—	—	R R R	U U U
Hudsonian Godwit	R	O R	R R	O O	—	—	—	—	—
Bar-tailed Godwit	—	—	—	—	—	—	—	—	—
Marbled Godwit	R	U O	O O O	U R U	—	—	O O	O	O O
Ruddy Turnstone	R R	—	R R	O R O	—	—	C C R R	R R	U U
Black Turnstone	—	—	—	—	—	—	—	—	—
Surfbird	—	—	—	—	—	—	—	—	—
Red Knot	—	—	—	R R R	—	—	U U	—	R R
Sanderling	U U U	R R	R R	O U O	—	—	—	—	C U U
Semipalmated Sandpiper	C C C	C R C	O O	C U C	—	O O O	C C U	U U	A A U
Western Sandpiper	—	U R O	U O	—	—	—	A R A A	C C O	U U C

Each location column has four seasonal sub-columns: •s S F W

LA-6 Tensas	LA-7 Jean Lafitte	ME-1 Great Wass	ME-2 Moosehorn	ME-3 Petit Manan	ME-4 Carson	MD-1 Blackwater	MD-2 East. Neck	MA-1 G. Meadows	MA-2 Parker R.	MA-3 Monomoy	MI-1 Seney
—	—	—	—	—	—	—	—	—	—	—	—
—	—	—	—	—	—	—	—	—	—	—	—
—	—	—	—	—	—	—	—	—	—	—	—
—	—	—	—	—	•UUUU	—	—	•CCCC	•UUUU	RRRR	—
—	—	•UUUU	•UUUU	•OOOO	—	—	—	—	—	—	•UUUU
—	—	—	—	—	—	—	—	—	—	—	—
—	—	—	—	—	—	—	—	—	—	—	—
—	—	UUUU	•AAAA	•CCCC	•UUUU	—	—	—	•UUUU	RRRR	•CCCC
—	—	—	—	—	—	—	—	—	—	—	•UUUU
CCCC	—	—	—	—	—	RRRR	—	—	—	—	—
UUUU	—	—	—	—	—	•CCCC	•AAAA	RRRR	—	RRRR	—
—	—	—	—	—	—	—	—	—	—	—	—
—	—	—	—	—	—	—	—	—	—	—	—
—	—	—	—	—	—	—	—	R	R	—	•RRR
—	—	—	—	—	—	•RRR	—	—	—	—	—
RRRR	•CCCC	—	—	—	—	•UUUR	RRR	—	OOO	R	—
—	U UU	OOO	•UUU	—	O O	•CUCU	•AAAU	•UUUO	•UUU	•RRO	•UCU
R RR	C CC	OOO	•UUU	R	O O	U UO	R RR	•UUCR	•UUU	•RRO	•UCU
RRR	•CC	—	—	—	—	—	—	—	—	—	—
—	•CCCC	—	R	—	R R	UUU	RRR	•UUU	•UUU	R R	—
R RU	UU	—	•OOO	R	R R	UOUU	U UU	O CR	OOCO	O CO	UOU
—	—	—	—	—	—	—	—	—	—	—	—
—	—	—	—	—	—	—	—	—	—	—	•CCC
—	—	CUC	OOO	CCC	CUC	O OR	UUU	O	CACO	ACAO	OOO
C R	—	O	R	O	O O	O R	R	O	ROU	RRO	O R
—	—	—	—	—	—	—	—	—	—	—	—
—	U	CUC	UUU	CCC	CUC	CUC	UUU	R O	CCU	UCC	UUU
—	—	—	—	RR	•OUO	—	—	—	•UUO	•CCO	—
UUUU	•CCCC	CCCR	•CCC	OOO	•UCUO	•CCCU	•CCCU	•UUC	•CCU	U U	•CCC
—	—	—	—	—	—	—	—	—	—	R	•CCC
—	—	—	—	—	—	—	—	—	—	—	—
—	•UUUR	—	—	—	—	—	R	—	—	—	—
R	—	—	—	—	R	—	—	—	—	R R	—
C C	U UU	CCC	CUC	CCC	CCC	CCCO	CCC	ORO	CCCR	CCC	CCC
C CR	C CU	UCC	OUU	OUU	UUC	CCCO	CUC	ROO	CCCR	UCC	CUC
U U	C U	UUU	UUU	O O	OUU	CUC	UUU	UUU	OOO	RRR	CCC
R	—	OOO	—	•UU	•UCO	•RUR	—	—	•CCU	•CCO	—
U U	C C	•CCU	•CCC	•UUU	•UCU	UUU	CUC	•UCU	•UUU	•CCO	•CCC
U	—	—	RR	—	RR	R	—	—	OOO	RO	•OOO
—	—	UU	R	UU	UOU	R	—	—	OOO	RCC	—
—	—	—	—	—	—	—	—	—	—	R	—
—	—	—	—	OO	OO	R	—	R	UU	CO	—
—	—	—	—	—	RR	—	—	—	—	RR	—
—	—	—	—	—	—	—	—	—	OO	OO	—
—	—	UCU	RRR	CCC	OOOR	O	R	—	OUOR	COC	—
—	—	—	—	—	—	—	—	—	—	—	—
—	—	OUU	—	UUU	OOO	—	—	—	OUU	CCCR	—
—	—	UUU	OOO	OUU	UOUO	O OO	—	R	CCCU	ACAO	—
R	C U	CCC	UAC	UCC	ACA	AAAR	CCC	RUU	AAA	AAC	UUU
R	C UU	RO	R	O	UU	OO	RRR	RR	OO	RO	—

STATE-NUMBER OF BIRD LIST / REFUGE, SANCTUARY OR PRESERVE / NESTING, ABUNDANCE BY SEASON	IA-4 McGregor •s S F W	KS-1 Flint Hills •s S F W	KS-2 Kirwin •s S F W	KS-3 Quivira •s S F W	LA-1 Bog. Chitto •s S F W	LA-2 Catahoula •s S F W	LA-3 Delta •s S F W	LA-4 Lacassine •s S F W	LA-5 Sabine •s S F W
SANDPIPERS (cont.)									
Least Sandpiper	C C C	C O C	O U O	C O C	U U	O O O	C U C C	C O C C	C C
White-rumped Sandpiper	U U U	U R U	U U	A U A	—	—	C	U	C
Baird's Sandpiper	U U U	C R C	C O C	A U A	—	—	—	—	—
Pectoral Sandpiper	C C C	U O U	—	C U C	—	O O O	C C	U U U	U U
Sharp-tailed Sandpiper	—	—	—	—	—	—	—	—	—
Purple Sandpiper	—	—	—	—	—	—	—	—	—
Rock Sandpiper	—	—	—	—	—	—	—	—	—
Dunlin	U U U	O R O	R	O R R	—	—	C C C	U O O	C C C
Curlew Sandpiper	—	—	—	—	—	—	—	—	—
Stilt Sandpiper	U U U	U R U	U U	O U O	—	—	U U	O	U O
Buff-breasted Sandpiper	—	—	—	R R	—	—	—	—	—
Ruff	—	—	—	—	—	—	—	—	—
Short-billed Dowitcher	U U U	—	—	R R R	—	—	—	A C A C	U U U
Long-billed Dowitcher	U U	A U A	C C C	C U A	—	—	C C C	A C A C	C C C
Common Snipe	•C U C O	C R C R	U U	C U C O	U U U	C C C	C A A	C C C	C C A
American Woodcock	•U U U	R R R	—	—	U C C	C C C	O U	O O	R R R
Wilson's Phalarope	U U U	C O C	C O C	•A U C	—	—	—	U	—
Red-necked Phalarope	R R	—	U U	O O	—	—	—	—	—
Red Phalarope	—	—	—	—	—	—	—	—	—
SKUAS, GULLS, TERNS & SKIMMERS									
Pomarine Jaeger	—	—	—	—	—	—	—	—	—
Parasitic Jaeger	—	R	—	—	—	—	—	—	—
Long-tailed Jaeger	—	—	—	—	—	—	—	—	—
Laughing Gull	—	—	—	—	—	—	A A A A	—	C C C C
Franklin's Gull	U U	A A	A O A	A C A	—	—	—	—	R R
Little Gull	—	R R	—	—	—	—	—	—	—
Common Black-headed Gull	—	—	—	—	—	—	—	—	—
Bonaparte's Gull	U U	O R R	R R	O O	—	—	O	U U U	R U
Heermann's Gull	—	—	—	—	—	—	—	—	—
Mew Gull	—	—	—	—	—	—	—	—	—
Ring-billed Gull	C O C U	C U C C	C O C O	C O C C	—	—	A R C A	U U U U	U U C
California Gull	—	—	—	—	—	—	—	—	—
Herring Gull	C O C U	U R U U	O O O	U U O	—	O O	C A	U O U U	U U C
Thayer's Gull	—	—	—	—	—	—	—	—	—
Iceland Gull	—	—	—	—	—	—	—	—	—
Lesser Black-backed Gull	—	—	—	—	—	—	—	—	—
Western Gull	—	—	—	—	—	—	—	—	—
Glaucous-winged Gull	—	—	—	—	—	—	—	—	—
Glaucous Gull	—	R	—	—	—	—	—	—	—
Great Black-backed Gull	—	R	—	—	—	—	—	—	—
Black-legged Kittiwake	—	R	—	—	—	—	—	—	—
Sabine's Gull	—	—	—	—	—	—	—	—	—
Gull-billed Tern	—	—	—	—	—	—	O O	—	U U U U
Caspian Tern	U U	O O	U U	R R R	—	—	C C C C	U U O O	U U U U
Royal Tern	—	—	—	—	—	—	C C C C	O O	U U U U
Elegant Tern	—	—	—	—	—	—	—	—	—
Sandwich Tern	—	—	—	—	—	—	O O O R	—	—
Roseate Tern	—	—	—	—	—	—	—	—	—
Common Tern	U U U	—	C C	R R R	—	O	C R C C	O O O	U
Arctic Tern	—	—	—	—	—	—	—	—	—
Aleutian Tern	—	—	—	—	—	—	—	—	—
Forster's Tern	U O U	U U	O O	•C C C	—	—	C C C C	•A A A C	C C C C
Least Tern	—	R R	• O O	•C C O	—	—	C C C	O O	O U O
Bridled Tern	—	—	—	—	—	—	—	—	—
Sooty Tern	—	—	—	—	—	—	—	—	—
Black Tern	C C U	C U U	O C O	•C C C	—	—	C U C	C C	A U A
Black Skimmer	—	—	—	—	—	—	C C C C	—	C C C C
AUKS, MURRES & PUFFINS									
Dovekie	—	—	—	—	—	—	—	—	—
Common Murre	—	—	—	—	—	—	—	—	—
Thick-billed Murre	—	—	—	—	—	—	—	—	—
Razorbill	—	—	—	—	—	—	—	—	—
Black Guillemot	—	—	—	—	—	—	—	—	—
Pigeon Guillemot	—	—	—	—	—	—	—	—	—
Marbled Murrelet	—	—	—	—	—	—	—	—	—
Kittlitz's Murrelet	—	—	—	—	—	—	—	—	—
Ancient Murrelet	—	—	—	—	—	—	—	—	—
Cassin's Auklet	—	—	—	—	—	—	—	—	—
Crested Auklet	—	—	—	—	—	—	—	—	—
Rhinoceros Auklet	—	—	—	—	—	—	—	—	—
Tufted Puffin	—	—	—	—	—	—	—	—	—

Each cell lists seasonal status in the order **s S F W** (• marks breeding). C = common, U = uncommon, O = occasional, R = rare, A = abundant, — = absent/none.

	LA-6 Tensas	LA-7 Jean Lafitte	ME-1 Great Wass	ME-2 Moosehorn	ME-3 Petit Manan	ME-4 Carson	MD-1 Blackwater	MD-2 East. Neck	MA-1 G. Meadows	MA-2 Parker R.	MA-3 Monomoy	MI-1 Seney
1	U U U	C U U	C C C	U A C	U U U	U U C	A A A R	C C C R	O C O	C C U	•C C C	U U U
2	R U R	U	R U U	—	O U U	U O U	U O U	U U	R O	U U U	O R U	R R
3	R	—	R R	—	O	R R	—	—	R R	O O	R	R R
4	C C	C	U U U	R	O	U U U	U U U	U U U	O U U	U U U	O O C	U U U
5	—	—	—	—	—	—	—	—	—	—	R	—
6	—	—	C O C C	—	U U U	O O U	—	—	—	O O O	—	—
7	U U U	U C	U O C R	—	O U U	U O C	C O C O	C U C R	O	C U A O	A O A O	O O
8	—	—	—	—	—	—	R R	O	—	R C U	R	—
9	—	—	—	—	—	O O	R O O	R R	R R	O O	O O R	—
10	C	—	—	—	—	R R	—	—	—	O O O	R R R	—
11	—	—	C C C	U	U C C	R C C	U U U R	U U U	R R	C C O	C U C	—
12	R	—	U U U	•C C C	O O	R R R	R R	U U U	R	O U	R O	•C C C
13	C C C	C C C	U U U R	•A A A	•U U U	U O U	C O C U	U U U	U U R	O O U	R O	•C C C
14	R R R U	—	U U U	—	—	•U U U	•C U C O	•C U C U	•U O U R	U U U	R R	—
15	—	—	—	—	—	O O O	—	—	R R R	•U U U	R O R	—
16	—	—	U U U	—	U U U	R R R	—	—	R R	O O	O O	—
17	—	—	O O O	—	—	—	—	—	R R	R R	R R	—
18	—	—	R U U	—	O	—	—	—	—	R R	R R	—
19	—	—	R U U	—	O O	—	—	—	—	O O	O R O	—
20	—	C C C C	O O O	—	•C C C	O O O	C C C	C U C R	—	O O O	•A A C	—
21	—	—	—	—	R	—	—	—	—	O O O O	R R	—
22	—	—	R R R	—	•O R	—	—	—	—	O O O O	•R R R R	—
23	—	C	U C C O	R A A R	O U U O	U U U R	U U O	O O O	—	O O O O	U O C O	O O
24	—	C C C	C C C U	O O O O	U U C U	C C C C	C O C C	A C A C	U U U	C U U C	C C C C	C U C
25	—	U U C	•C C C C	A A A A	•A A A A	A A A A	U U U C	C U C C	C C C C	•A A A A	A A A A	C U C
26	—	—	O O O	—	U U	O R O	—	—	—	R R O	U R O	—
27	—	—	—	—	—	—	—	—	R R R	—	O R	—
28	—	—	O O O	—	—	O R O	—	—	R R	O R R	—	—
29	—	—	•C C C C	C C C C	•C C C C	C C C C	O U U	U R C C	U O U C	A A A A	•A A A A	—
30	—	—	U O C C	—	O	—	—	—	—	O O O	C O A A	—
31	—	U	—	—	—	R	U R U	U U	—	O O O	R	U O U
32	—	U U U U	—	—	—	—	R U	R U	—	O O O	O	—
33	—	U U U	—	—	—	—	—	—	—	—	O	—
34	—	—	O O O	—	•U U U	R R	—	—	—	O O	•C C C	—
35	—	—	U U U	U U U	•C C C	•C C U	U O O	U U U	R R R	•C C U	•A A C	•C C C
36	—	—	C C U	O O O	•C C C	O O O	—	—	—	R R	•C C	—
37	—	C C C C	—	—	—	—	U U C	R O C	—	O O	O O	—
38	—	—	—	—	—	•U U U	U U R	R U U	—	•C C U	•C C	—
39	—	U U	—	—	O O	R	R O O	—	R O	O O O	O R O	•O C O
40	—	—	—	—	—	—	—	—	R O R	R O R	• O O	—
41	—	—	O U	—	R R	R	—	—	—	O O	O	—
42	—	—	O U U R	—	O O	R	—	—	—	R R	—	—
43	—	—	O R O O	—	R	R	—	—	—	O O O	O	—
44	—	—	U U U O	—	U U	R	—	—	—	O O O	R O O	—
45	—	—	•C C C C	—	•C C C U	R R	—	—	—	—	—	—

STATE-NUMBER OF BIRD LIST REFUGE, SANCTUARY OR PRESERVE NESTING, ABUNDANCE BY SEASON	IA-4 McGregor • s S F W	KS-1 Flint Hills • s S F W	KS-2 Kirwin • s S F W	KS-3 Quivira • s S F W	LA-1 Bog. Chitto • s S F W	LA-2 Catahoula • s S F W	LA-3 Delta • s S F W	LA-4 Lacassine • s S F W	LA-5 Sabine • s S F W
AUKS, MURRES & PUFFINS (cont.)									
Atlantic Puffin	—	—	—	—	—	—	—	—	—
Horned Puffin	—	—	—	—	—	—	—	—	—
PIGEONS & DOVES									
Rock Dove	• C C C C	• U U U U	—	—	—	O O O O	—	—	—
White-crowned Pigeon	—	—	—	—	—	—	—	—	—
Band-tailed Pigeon	—	—	—	—	—	—	—	—	—
White-winged Dove	—	—	—	—	—	—	R R R	R R R	—
Mourning Dove	• C C C U	• A A A O	• C A C R	• A A A U	C C C C	• C C A A	U U U U	• C C C C	O O O O
Inca Dove	—	—	—	—	—	—	—	—	—
Common Ground-Dove	—	—	—	—	—	—	R R R	R R R	—
White-tipped Dove	—	—	—	—	—	—	—	—	—
CUCKOOS, ROADRUNNERS & ANIS									
Black-billed Cuckoo	• C C U	• C U U	• U U U	O O O	U U	C C	U U	• R O	R R
Yellow-billed Cuckoo	• C C U	• C C C	• O O O	• C C C	C C C	• C C	C C O	• C C O	U U O
Mangrove Cuckoo	—	—	—	—	—	—	—	—	—
Greater Roadrunner	—	—	—	—	—	—	—	—	—
Smooth-billed Ani	—	—	—	—	—	—	—	—	—
Groove-billed Ani	—	—	—	—	—	—	R R	—	—
BARN OWLS									
Barn Owl	—	• O O U O	• O O O O	R R R R	—	U U U U	O O O O	O O O O	• U U U U
TYPICAL OWLS									
Flammulated Owl	—	—	—	—	—	—	—	—	—
Eastern Screech-Owl	• U U U U	• U U U U	• U U U U	U U U U	U U U U	• C C C C	U U U U	• C C C C	R R R R
Western Screech-Owl	—	—	—	—	—	—	—	—	—
Great Horned Owl	• C C C C	• A A A A	• C C C C	• C C C C	U U U U	U U U U	—	U U U U	R R R R
Snowy Owl	R O O	R	U	R	—	—	—	—	—
Northern Hawk Owl	—	—	—	—	—	—	—	—	—
Northern Pygmy-Owl	—	—	—	—	—	—	—	—	—
Elf Owl	—	—	—	—	—	—	—	—	—
Burrowing Owl	—	O O	• O O O	• C C C	—	—	R	—	—
Spotted Owl	—	—	—	—	—	—	—	—	—
Barred Owl	• C C C C	• C C C C	U	R R R R	A A A A	• C C C C	—	U U U U	O
Great Gray Owl	—	—	—	—	—	—	—	—	—
Long-eared Owl	• U U U U	U	—	O	—	—	—	—	—
Short-eared Owl	U U U	U U U	O O O	U U C	—	—	—	R R	R
Boreal Owl	—	—	—	—	—	—	—	—	—
Northern Saw-whet Owl	• O O O O	O	—	—	—	—	—	—	—
NIGHTJARS									
Lesser Nighthawk	—	—	—	—	R R	—	—	—	—
Common Nighthawk	• C A U	• C C C	• O	• C C C	C C C	R	C C C	• C C U	• C C
Pauraque	—	—	—	—	—	—	—	—	—
Common Poorwill	—	—	—	O O	—	—	—	—	—
Chuck-will's-widow	—	• U U U	—	O O O	U U U	O O	C	O	O O
Whip-poor-will	• C C C	U O U	—	—	—	O O O	—	O	—
SWIFTS									
Black Swift	—	—	—	—	—	—	—	—	—
Chimney Swift	• C A U	• A A A	R	• U U U	C C C	O O O	U U U	O O O	O O O
Vaux's Swift	—	—	—	—	—	—	—	—	—
White-throated Swift	—	—	—	—	—	—	—	—	—
HUMMINGBIRDS									
Buff-bellied Hummingbird	—	—	—	—	—	—	—	—	—
Ruby-throated Hummingbird	• U U U	• C C C	—	C C C	C C C	O O O	C U C	C U U	U U U
Black-chinned Hummingbird	—	—	—	—	—	—	—	—	—
Anna's Hummingbird	—	—	—	—	—	—	—	—	—
Costa's Hummingbird	—	—	—	—	—	—	—	—	—
Calliope Hummingbird	—	—	—	—	—	—	—	—	—
Broad-tailed Hummingbird	—	—	—	—	—	—	—	—	—
Rufous Hummingbird	—	—	—	—	—	—	—	—	—
Allen's Hummingbird	—	—	—	—	—	—	—	—	—
KINGFISHERS									
Belted Kingfisher	• C C U O	• C C C O	O O O	C C C O	C C C C	C C O C	C C C A	C C C C	C C C C
Green Kingfisher	—	—	—	—	—	—	—	—	—
WOODPECKERS									
Lewis' Woodpecker	—	—	—	—	—	—	—	—	—
Red-headed Woodpecker	• C C C U	• C C C U	• O C O	• C C O	C C C C	U U U U	O O O O	O O O O	O O
Acorn Woodpecker	—	—	—	—	—	—	—	—	—
Gila Woodpecker	—	—	—	—	—	—	—	—	—
Golden-fronted Woodpecker	—	—	—	—	—	—	—	—	—
Red-bellied Woodpecker	• C C C C	• A A A A	—	• C C C U	A A A A	• C C C C	C C C C	U U U U	—
Yellow-bellied Sapsucker	• C U C R	U U U	—	U U U O	U C C	C U U U	O O O	O O O	O O O
Red-breasted Sapsucker	—	—	—	—	—	—	—	—	—

	LA-6 Tensas	LA-7 Jean Lafitte	ME-1 Great Wass	ME-2 Moosehorn	ME-3 Petit Manan	ME-4 Carson	MD-1 Blackwater	MD-2 East. Neck	MA-1 G. Meadows	MA-2 Parker R.	MA-3 Monomoy	MI-1 Seney
	•s S F W	•s S F W	•s S F W	•s S F W	•s S F W	•s S F W	•s S F W	•s S F W	•s S F W	•s S F W	•s S F W	•s S F W
	—	—	O O O O	—	•U U U	—	—	—	—	—	—	—
	—	—	—	—	—	—	—	—	—	—	—	—
	R R R R	—	U U U U	U U U U	O	C C C C	•U U U U	•U U U U	•U U U O	O O O O	O O O O	—
	—	—	—	—	—	—	—	—	—	—	—	—
	—	—	—	—	—	—	—	—	—	—	—	—
	A A A A	U U U U	•C C C U	•C C U	•U U U	•C C C C	•C C A C	•C C C C	•C C C O	•C C C U	C C C O	O O O
	R R R	—	—	—	—	—	—	—	—	—	—	—
	R R	—	O U U	•U U U	R R R	U U O	U O U	•O O O	U U U	U O O	R R O	•C C C
	C C C	•C C C	O O O	•O O O	R	O O O	•C C C	•C U U	•O O O	O O O	R R O	—
	R	—	—	—	—	—	—	—	—	—	—	—
	—	—	—	—	—	—	—	—	—	—	—	—
	R R R R	—	—	—	—	—	•U U U U	•U U U U	—	—	R R	—
	A A A A	•C C C C	—	•R R R R	—	—	•C C C C	•C C C C	•U U U U	O O O O	—	—
	R R R R	•C C C C	U U U U	•C C C C	•U U	•U U U U	•C C C C	•C C C C	•U U U U	•O O O O	R R R	•C C C C
	—	—	O O O	—	R R R O R	R R	—	R R	—	O U U	R	O O O
	—	—	—	—	R	—	—	—	—	—	—	—
	—	—	—	—	—	—	—	—	—	—	—	—
	A A A A	•A A A A	U U U U	•C C C C	•U U	U U U U	•U U U U	•U U U U	•R R O O	—	—	•R R R R
	R	—	—	R R R R	—	—	R	—	—	R O O	—	O O O
	—	—	O O O	R R R R	R R	R R R O	O R O U	O O O	—	R R O U U	•U U U O	O O
	—	—	—	R	—	—	—	—	—	—	—	—
	—	—	U O U O	•U U U R	R R	O O O O	R	R R	—	O U U	—	•O O O O
	U U U	U U	U C C	•C C C	O O	U	•U U U	•U U C	U U U	O U R	R R	•C C C
	—	—	—	—	—	—	—	—	—	—	—	—
	U U R	—	—	—	—	—	—	O O O	—	—	—	—
	U U R	—	U U U	•U U U	•U U U	•U U U	C C O	•U U C	R R R	R R	O O	•U U U
	—	—	—	—	—	—	—	—	—	—	—	—
	U U U	•C C C	U U U	•C C C	•U O	U U	U U U	•C C C	C C U	U U U	O O O	•C C
	—	—	—	—	—	—	—	—	—	—	—	—
	—	—	—	—	—	—	—	—	—	—	—	—
	A A A	•C C C	U U U	•C C C	U U U	U O U	•C C C	•C U C	•O O U	U O O	R R	•U U U
	—	—	—	—	—	—	—	—	—	—	—	—
	—	—	—	—	—	—	—	—	—	—	—	—
	—	—	—	—	—	—	—	—	—	—	—	—
	—	—	—	—	—	—	—	—	—	—	—	—
	—	—	—	—	—	—	—	—	—	—	—	—
	—	—	—	—	—	—	—	—	—	—	—	—
	U U	C C C	C U C R	•C C C R	U U U	•C C C O	•C O C U	•U U U U	•U U U R	•U U U O	•O O O	•C C C
	—	—	—	—	—	—	—	—	—	—	—	—
	U U U C	—	—	—	R	—	•U U U U	R R R R	R R R	R R	—	R R R
	—	—	—	—	—	—	—	—	—	—	—	—
	—	—	—	—	—	—	—	—	—	—	—	—
	A A A A	•A A A A	—	—	—	—	•C C C C	•C C C C	—	—	—	—
	U U U	•C C C	—	•C C C	U	U U	U U U	U U U	R R	U O O	R O	•U U U

STATE-NUMBER OF BIRD LIST REFUGE, SANCTUARY OR PRESERVE NESTING, ABUNDANCE BY SEASON	IA-4 McGregor • s S F W	KS-1 Flint Hills • s S F W	KS-2 Kirwin • s S F W	KS-3 Quivira • s S F W	LA-1 Bog. Chitto • s S F W	LA-2 Catahoula • s S F W	LA-3 Delta • s S F W	LA-4 Lacassine • s S F W	LA-5 Sabine • s S F W
WOODPECKERS (cont.)									
Williamson's Sapsucker	—	—	—	—	—	—	—	—	—
Ladder-backed Woodpecker	—	—	—	—	—	—	—	—	—
Nuttall's Woodpecker	—	—	—	—	—	—	—	—	—
Downy Woodpecker	•C C C C	•A A A A	•O O O O	•U U U U	C C C C	•C C C C	C C C C	U U U U	R R
Hairy Woodpecker	•C C C C	•C C C C	O	U U U U	C C C C	•C C C C	C C C C	U U U U	—
Red-cockaded Woodpecker	—	—	—	—	—	—	—	—	—
Three-toed Woodpecker	—	—	—	—	—	—	—	—	—
Black-backed Woodpecker	—	—	—	—	—	—	—	—	—
Northern Flicker	•C C C U	•C C C C	•C C C C	•C A A C	C C C C	•C A A C	C C C C	C O C C	•U O U U
Pileated Woodpecker	•U U U U	•O O O O	—	—	A A A A	•C C C C	—	•U U U U	—
TYRANT FLYCATCHERS									
Olive-sided Flycatcher	U U U	O O	—	O O	—	—	—	R	R
Western Wood-Pewee	—	—	—	—	—	—	—	—	—
Eastern Wood-Pewee	•C C C	•C C C	—	U U U	C C C	U U U	C	U U U	U U
Yellow-bellied Flycatcher	U U U	R R	—	O O	—	—	C	—	R R
Acadian Flycatcher	R R	U U U	—	—	C C C	C C	—	U U U	U U
Alder Flycatcher	U U	U U	—	—	—	—	—	—	—
Willow Flycatcher	•C C U	U U	—	O O O	—	—	C	—	—
Least Flycatcher	•A A C	U U	—	O O O	C C	—	U C	O	—
Hammond's Flycatcher	—	—	—	—	—	—	—	—	—
Dusky Flycatcher	—	—	—	—	—	—	—	—	—
Gray Flycatcher	—	—	—	—	—	—	—	—	—
Western Flycatcher	—	—	—	—	—	—	—	—	—
Black Phoebe	—	—	—	—	—	—	—	—	—
Eastern Phoebe	•C C C	•C C C	O O O	O O O	C C C	O O O O	C C C	U U U	C C C
Say's Phoebe	—	R	O O O	O O O	—	—	—	—	—
Vermilion Flycatcher	—	—	—	—	R R	—	—	R R	R R R
Ash-throated Flycatcher	—	—	—	—	—	—	—	—	—
Great Crested Flycatcher	•C C U	•C C C	O O O	U U U	C C C	O O	U U U	—	O O O
Brown-crested Flycatcher	—	—	—	—	—	—	—	—	—
Great Kiskadee	—	—	—	—	—	—	—	—	—
Couch's Kingbird	—	—	—	—	—	—	—	—	—
Cassin's Kingbird	—	—	—	—	—	—	—	—	—
Western Kingbird	—	•C C U	•C A C	•C A C	—	—	C	R	R O
Eastern Kingbird	•C C U	•A A A	•C A C	•C A C	C C C	O O	A A C	•A A A	•C C C
Gray Kingbird	—	—	—	—	—	—	—	—	—
Scissor-tailed Flycatcher	—	•C C C	R R	•C C C	—	—	O O O	R R R	•O O O R
LARKS									
Horned Lark	•C C C U	•A C A A	•A C A C	•C U C O	—	—	C	—	—
SWALLOWS									
Purple Martin	•A A U	•C C C	O	•U U U	C C	•C C C	C C	•C C	•U U U
Tree Swallow	•A A C	•C O C	—	C O C	C C	C C	A A C	A A	A A A
Violet-green Swallow	—	—	—	R	—	—	—	—	—
Northern Rough-winged Swallow	•C C U	•C U C	C C	A O A	C C C	C C C	C	C C	U U U
Bank Swallow	•C C U	U U	C C	•A U A	—	—	—	C C	C C
Cliff Swallow	•U U U	U U U	C O C	•A C A	—	—	—	—	•C U C
Barn Swallow	•A A C	•A A A	•A C A	•A C A	C C	—	A U A	A O A	•A A A
JAYS, MAGPIES & CROWS									
Gray Jay	—	—	—	—	—	—	—	—	—
Steller's Jay	—	—	—	—	—	—	—	—	—
Blue Jay	•C C C C	•A A A A	•C C C C	•C C A C	C C C C	•C C C C	U U U C	U U U U	R R R R
Green Jay	—	—	—	—	—	—	—	—	—
Scrub Jay	—	—	—	—	—	—	—	—	—
Pinyon Jay	—	—	—	—	—	—	—	—	—
Clark's Nutcracker	—	—	—	—	—	—	—	—	—
Black-billed Magpie	—	—	•C C C C	O O O U	—	—	—	—	—
American Crow	•C C C C	•C C C C	C O C O	•A C A A	C C C C	•C C A A	C C C C	O O O O	—
Northwestern Crow	—	—	—	—	—	—	—	—	—
Fish Crow	—	—	—	—	A A A A	U U U U	C C C C	O O O O	U U U U
Chihuahuan Raven	—	—	—	—	—	—	—	—	—
Common Raven	—	—	—	—	—	—	—	—	—
TITMICE									
Black-capped Chickadee	•C C C C	•A A A A	O O U	•C U C C	—	—	—	—	—
Carolina Chickadee	—	—	O O O	—	A A A A	•C C C C	C C C C	U U U U	—
Mountain Chickadee	—	—	—	—	—	—	—	—	—
Boreal Chickadee	—	—	—	—	—	—	—	—	—
Chestnut-backed Chickadee	—	—	—	—	—	—	—	—	—
Plain Titmouse	—	—	—	—	—	—	—	—	—
Tufted Titmouse	•C C C C	•C C C C	—	O O O O	A A A A	C U U U	U U U C	U U U U	—
VERDINS									
Verdin	—	—	—	—	—	—	—	—	—

LA-6 Tensas	LA-7 Jean Lafitte	ME-1 Great Wass	ME-2 Moosehorn	ME-3 Petit Manan	ME-4 Carson	MD-1 Blackwater	MD-2 East. Neck	MA-1 G. Meadows	MA-2 Parker R.	MA-3 Monomoy	MI-1 Seney
• s S F W	• s S F W	• s S F W	• s S F W	• s S F W	• s S F W	• s S F W	• s S F W	• s S F W	• s S F W	• s S F W	• s S F W
—	—	—	—	—	—	—	—	—	—	—	—
—	—	—	—	—	—	—	—	—	—	—	—
C C C C	•A A A A	•U U U U	•C C C	•C C C C	•C C C C	•C C C C	•C C C C	•C C C C	U O U O	O O O O	•C C C C
U U U U	•C C C C	•U U U U	•C C C	•U U U U	•U U U U	•U U U U	•U U U U	•C U C C	R R R R	R R R	•C C C C
—	—	—	—	—	—	—	—	—	—	—	—
—	—	—	—	R	—	—	—	—	—	—	—
—	—	0 0 0 0	•U U U R	R	—	—	—	—	—	—	•R R R R
U U U U	C C C	•C C C R	•A C A	•C C C	•C C C O	•C C C C	•C C C C	•C C C O	C U C O	C O C O	•C A A R
C C C C	•C C C C	—	•U U U U	0 0	0 0 0 0	•U U U U	—	0 0 0 0	—	—	•0 0 0 0
R R	—	U U U	•U U U	0 0 0	0 0	—	—	R R	U O O	R R	•U U U
C C C	C C	•U U U	•C C C	•U U U	•U U U	•C C C	•C C C	•U U O	U U O	0 0 0	•C C U
U U	U U	•C C U	•U U	•U U U	0 U	—	0 0	•U U O	U O O	R 0	•0 0 0
C C C	•U U C	—	—	—	—	•U U U	•U U U	R	R	—	•C C U
U U	U	•C C C	•C C C	•C C C	U U	—	—	•0 0	0 0 0	—	•C C U
U U	U	—	—	—	•0 U 0	—	—	•U C	•C C U	0 0	—
U U	C C	U U U	•C C C	•U U U	U U U	R R	—	R R	U U O	0 0	•C C U
—	—	—	—	—	—	—	—	—	—	—	—
—	—	—	—	—	—	—	—	—	—	—	—
U U C	C C C	U U U	•C C C	•U U U	•U U U	•C O C R	•C U C R	•C C U	U U U	R 0	•C C C
—	—	—	—	—	—	—	—	—	—	—	—
—	—	—	—	—	—	—	—	—	—	—	—
C C C	•U U	U U U	•U U	•U U U	•C C C	•C C C	•U C U	•U U	0 0 0	R R R	•0 0 U
—	—	—	—	—	—	—	—	—	—	—	—
—	—	—	—	—	—	—	—	—	—	—	—
—	—	—	—	—	—	R	R	—	—	R	—
C U C	•C U C	•U C C	•C C C	U U U	•C C C	•C C C	•C C C	•C C O	•C C U	•C C O	•C C U
R R	—	—	—	—	—	—	—	—	—	—	—
C U C C	—	U U O	U U	U	•U U U U	•U O U O	•C C U U	O O O	•U U U U	•C C C C	U O C
C U C	•C C	—	•R R	0	•C C	•C C U	•U C U	R	•C C U	R R R	•C C O
C C R	C C A	•C C C	•A A A	•C C U	•C C O	•C C Λ O	•C C A R	•A C A	•C A A	•C C C	•A A C
U R U	U U R	—	0	0	•0 0	•U U U	•U U U	•U U	•0 0 0	•U U	•U U U
R R	U U	C C U	•C C U	•C C	U U U	U U R	•U C C	•C C U	•C C U	0 0	•C C C
R R	U U	•C U U	•C C U	•C U	•U U O	U O	R R	0 0 0	•U U U	R R	•U U U
C U C	C C	•C C U	•A A U	•C C U	•C C O	•A A A	•A A A	•A C A	•C C C	•C C O	•C C C
—	—	R R R R	•0 0 0 0	0 0 0	—	—	—	—	—	—	O R U C
A A A A	•U U U U	•C U C C	•C C C U	•U U U	•C C C C	•U U U U	•C C A C	•C C A	•C U C U	C C C U	•C U C C
—	—	—	—	—	—	—	—	—	—	—	—
—	—	—	—	—	—	—	—	—	—	—	—
—	—	—	—	—	—	—	—	—	—	—	—
C C C C	•C C C C	•C C C C	•C C C C	•C C C C	•C C C C	•C C C C	•C C C C	•C C A A	•C C C C	•C C C C	•A C C
U U U U	R R	—	—	—	—	•U U U U	•C C C U	U U U U	—	—	—
—	—	—	—	—	—	—	—	—	—	—	—
—	—	•C C C C	•C C C C	•C C C C	—	—	—	—	—	—	•C C C C
—	—	•C C C C	•C C C C	•C C C C	•C C C C	R	R R	•C C A C	U C C U	U U U O	•A C A A
A A A A	•A A A A	—	—	—	—	•C C C C	•C C C C	—	—	—	—
—	—	•C C C C	•U U U U	0 0 0	R	—	—	—	R R	—	•R R R R
—	—	—	—	—	—	—	—	—	—	—	—
—	—	—	—	—	—	—	—	—	—	—	—
A A A A	•C C C C	—	—	•0 0 0 0	•C C C C	•C C C C	•C U C C	R R R R	U U U O		
—											

STATE-NUMBER OF BIRD LIST REFUGE, SANCTUARY OR PRESERVE NESTING, ABUNDANCE BY SEASON	IA-4 McGregor •s S F W	KS-1 Flint Hills •s S F W	KS-2 Kirwin •s S F W	KS-3 Quivira •s S F W	LA-1 Bog. Chitto •s S F W	LA-2 Catahoula •s S F W	LA-3 Delta •s S F W	LA-4 Lacassine •s S F W	LA-5 Sabine •s S F W
BUSHTITS									
Bushtit	—	—	—	—	—	—	—	—	—
NUTHATCHES									
Red-breasted Nuthatch	O O O	O U	—	O O	—	U U	—	R	R R R
White-breasted Nuthatch	•C C C C	•C U C C	—	O O O O	—	U U	—	—	—
Pygmy Nuthatch	—	—	—	—	—	—	—	—	—
Brown-headed Nuthatch	—	—	—	—	C C C C	—	—	—	—
CREEPERS									
Brown Creeper	C O C U	C U C	R	O O O	U U U	U U U U	—	R	O O O
WRENS									
Cactus Wren	—	—	—	—	—	—	—	—	—
Rock Wren	—	R	—	—	—	—	—	—	—
Canyon Wren	—	—	—	—	—	—	—	—	—
Carolina Wren	O O O	•U U U U	—	U U U O	A A A A	•O O O O	—	•C C C C	O O O O
Bewick's Wren	O O	•U U U	—	U U U U	U U	—	—	—	—
House Wren	•A A C	•A A C	•U C U	•U U U	C C C	U U U	C	O O O	R R U
Winter Wren	U U R	O	R R R	O	C C C	O O	C	—	R
Sedge Wren	•U U U	O U	—	U	—	—	—	C C C	U U C
Marsh Wren	•C C U	U U U R	—	•O O O U	—	C O C	A A A A	•A A A C	•A U A A
DIPPERS									
American Dipper	—	—	—	—	—	—	—	—	—
OLD WORLD WARBLERS & THRUSHES									
Arctic Warbler	—	—	—	—	—	—	—	—	—
Golden-crowned Kinglet	U U U	C C U	R	U U O	U U U	C	O	O O O	R R R
Ruby-crowned Kinglet	C C	U C O	R R	U U	A A A	U	O O O	C C C	C C C
Blue-gray Gnatcatcher	•U U	•C C C	—	O O O	A A C C	A C A R	U U U R	A A A O	C C U
Black-tailed Gnatcatcher	—	—	—	—	—	—	—	—	—
Eastern Bluebird	•C C C R	•C C C U	O O O	O O O R	U U U U	•C U C C	U U U U	O O O O	R R
Western Bluebird	—	—	—	—	—	—	—	—	—
Mountain Bluebird	—	—	O	R	—	—	—	—	—
Townsend's Solitaire	—	O O	—	—	—	—	—	—	—
Veery	C C	U	—	—	C U	—	C	O O	U U
Gray-cheeked Thrush	U U	U	—	—	C U	R R R	U U	O	U U
Swainson's Thrush	C C	A U	—	R R R	C U	—	U U	U U	C C
Hermit Thrush	U U	U U	—	—	C C	C C	O O	U U U	U U U
Wood Thrush	•C C U	•C C U	—	—	C C C	•C C C	C	O R O R	U U
American Robin	•A A A O	•A A A U	•C C C O	•A C A C	A A A	A U U A	C C	O C C	U U U
Varied Thrush	—	—	—	—	—	—	—	—	—
Wrentit	—	—	—	—	—	—	—	—	—
MOCKINGBIRDS, THRASHERS & ALLIES									
Gray Catbird	•C C C	•C C C	U U U	U U U	—	U U U C	—	•U U U U	U U
Northern Mockingbird	R R	•C C C U	•C C C	•C C U	C C C C	•A A A A	C C C C	•C C C C	•U U U U
Sage Thrasher	—	—	—	—	—	—	—	—	—
Brown Thrasher	•C C C	•C A A R	•C C C	•C C U R	C C C C	•C C C C	U U U U	•U U U U	O O O
Long-billed Thrasher	—	—	—	—	—	—	—	—	—
Bendire's Thrasher	—	—	—	—	—	—	—	—	—
Curve-billed Thrasher	—	—	—	—	—	—	—	—	—
Crissal Thrasher	—	—	—	—	—	—	—	—	—
Le Conte's Thrasher	—	—	—	—	—	—	—	—	—
WAGTAILS & PIPITS									
American Pipit	U U	C C	U U	O O	U U U	—	C C	A A	U U C
Sprague's Pipit	—	O O	—	R R	—	—	—	R R R	—
WAXWINGS									
Bohemian Waxwing	R	R	—	R	—	—	—	—	—
Cedar Waxwing	•C C C U	C U U	U	O O O	U U U	—	R R U	U U U	U O U
SILKY-FLYCATCHERS									
Phainopepla	—	—	—	—	—	—	—	—	—
SHRIKES									
Northern Shrike	R O O	R	—	—	—	—	—	—	—
Loggerhead Shrike	•U U U	•C C C C	O O O O	•C C C C	U U U U	U U U U	C C C C	•A A A A	•C U C C
STARLINGS									
European Starling	•A A A A	•A A A A	•U U U O	•C A A A	C C C C	A A A A	U U U U	•C C C C	•C C C A
VIREOS									
White-eyed Vireo	R R	U U O	—	—	A A A	•C C C	U U U R	U U U	U U
Bell's Vireo	•U U	•C C C	—	•U C C	—	—	—	—	—
Black-capped Vireo	—	—	—	—	—	—	—	—	—
Gray Vireo	—	—	—	—	—	—	—	—	—
Solitary Vireo	U U	U U	—	—	C C	—	—	R	O O O
Yellow-throated Vireo	•C C C	O O	O O O	—	U U U	—	C O C	U	O O O
Hutton's Vireo	—	—	—	—	—	—	—	—	—
Warbling Vireo	A A A	•C C C	—	O C U	U U U	—	U U	U	R R
Philadelphia Vireo	U U	U O	—	—	U	—	C	—	—

LA-6 Tensas	LA-7 Jean Lafitte	ME-1 Great Wass	ME-2 Moosehorn	ME-3 Petit Manan	ME-4 Carson	MD-1 Blackwater	MD-2 East. Neck	MA-1 G. Meadows	MA-2 Parker R.	MA-3 Monomoy	MI-1 Seney
• s S F W	• s S F W	• s S F W	• s S F W	• s S F W	• s S F W	• s S F W	• s S F W	• s S F W	• s S F W	• s S F W	• s S F W
–	–	–	–	–	–	–	–	–	–	–	–
–	–	•C C C C	•C C C C	•U U U U	•C C C C	O OU	U UU	O R U O	U U U U	U C U	•U U U U
U U U U	–	U U U U	O O O O	R R	•C C C C	R R U	•U U U	•C C C C	U U U O	O O O	•U U U U
						•U U U U					
U U U	U R	•U U U U	•C C C C	•U U U	•C C C C	U U U	U U U	•U U U U	O O U O	O O	•U U U O
–	–	–	–	–	–	–	–	–	–	–	–
–	–	–	–	–	–	–	–	–	–	–	–
A A A A	•A A A A	–	–	–	–	•C C C C	•C C C C	–	–	–	–
U U U	U U U	–	•U U U	–	•O U O	•C C C O	•C C C R	•C O U	•O O U	R	U U U
U U U	U U U	•U U U R	•C C C	•U U U	–	U U U	U U U	R O R	U O U	R R	•O O O
U U U	U U U	–	•R R R	–	–	U U U O	•O O O R	R R R	–	–	•U U U
U U U	C C C	–	•O O O	R	O O	•A A A U	•C C C R	•C C U R	•C C U	O	•A A A
–	–	–	–	–	–	–	–	–	–	–	–
U C C	C C C	•C C C U	•C C C U	•C C C U	C U	C C C	•U C C	O U O	U O C	R C	•C C C C
C C C	C C C	•C C C R	•C U C	•C C C	C C	C C U	U C C	C C R	C O C	O C	•U U U
C C C R	•C C A C	–	–	R	–	•U U U	•C R U R	•O O	U O O	O O	–
U R U U	•U U U U	R R R	•R R R	R R R	•O O O	•U U U U	•C C C C	R R R	R R	R R	•U U C
–	–	–	–	–	–	–	–	–	–	–	–
U U	U U	U U U	•C C C	•U U U	•C C O	U U	U U	•U U O	•U U U	R O	•C C C
U U	U U	O R O	U U	R	O O	O O	U U	R O	O O O	R R	•C C C
C C	C C	•C C U	•U U O	•C C C	U O	U U	U U	R O U	U R U	R O	•C C C
C C C	C C C	•C C C	•C C C	•C C C	C U U	U U U	U U U	U U R	U U O	R O	•C C C
C C C	U U	U U U	•C C C	O O	•C C O	•C C C	•C C C	•C U U	U O U	R	•U U U
C C A	C C A	•C C C O	•A A A O	•C C A U	•C C C U	•C C C U	•A C A U	•C C C U	•C U C O	•C U C	•C C C
–	–	–	–	–	–	–	–	–	–	–	–
–	–	–	–	–	–	–	–	–	–	–	–
C U C R	C C U	•C C C	•C C C	•C C C	•C C C	•C U C U	•C C C O	•C C U R	•A A A	•C C C	•O U O
C C C C	• C C	O O O O	R R	•R R R	•U U U U	•C C C C	•C C C C	•C C C C	•U U U U	U U O	R R
A U A C	C C U	U U U	•O O O	•R R R	C C C	•C U C U	•C C C O	•U U O R	•C C C	O O O	•C C C
–	–	–	–	–	–	–	–	–	–	–	–
–	–	–	–	–	–	–	–	–	–	–	–
–	–	–	–	–	–	–	–	–	–	–	–
C C C	U U C	U U	–	R	U	U U	O U U	R R R	O O	O C	U C
–	–	–	–	–	–	–	–	–	–	–	–
–	–	R R R	R	–	–	–	–	–	–	–	O O
C R C	A A A	•C C C	•C C C	•O C C O	•U C C	U O U U	•C R C U	•U U C O	•U U U	O C	•C A A
–	–	–	–	–	–	–	–	–	–	–	–
–	–	U U U	O O O	O O O	O O O	–	–	O O U	O O O	R R	O O O
U U U U	•U U U U	–	–	R	–	U O U	R R R	R R	R R R	R	–
A C A A	•U U U C	•U U U U	•C C C U	•C C C C	•A A A C	•A A A A	•C C A C	•A A A A	•A A A A	•C C C C	•A A A C
A A A R	•C C A U	–	R	–	–	•C C C	•C U C	R R	O O O	–	R
–	–	–	–	–	–	–	–	–	–	–	–
–	–	–	–	–	–	–	–	–	–	–	–
U U U	U U U	•C U C	•C C	•U U U	•U U U	R O	O O	U O	U U	R O	•U U
C C C	•C R C	R R	•R R R	R R	–	•U R U	•U U U	•O O	O O	–	•C C C
R R R	R U	–	•U U U	U U	O O R	–	•R R R	•U C O	R	R R R	R R
U U	U C	U U	•U U U	U U U	O O R	–	–	–	O O U	O	–

STATE-NUMBER OF BIRD LIST REFUGE, SANCTUARY OR PRESERVE NESTING, ABUNDANCE BY SEASON	IA-4 McGregor •s S F W	KS-1 Flint Hills •s S F W	KS-2 Kirwin •s S F W	KS-3 Quivira •s S F W	LA-1 Bog. Chitto •s S F W	LA-2 Catahoula •s S F W	LA-3 Delta •s S F W	LA-4 Lacassine •s S F W	LA-5 Sabine •s S F W
VIREOS (cont.)									
Red-eyed Vireo	• C C A	• C U C	—	O U U	A A A	—	C O C	U U U	U U
Black-whiskered Vireo	—	—	—	—	—	—	—	—	—
WOOD-WARBLERS									
Bachman's Warbler	—	—	—	—	R R	—	—	—	—
Blue-winged Warbler	• U U	R R	—	—	U U	—	C	O O	R R
Golden-winged Warbler	U U U	—	—	—	U U	—	U C	—	R R
Tennessee Warbler	C C	C U	—	R	U U	—	C C	U O	R C
Orange-crowned Warbler	U U	A A R	—	C C	U U U	—	C	O O O	U O U
Nashville Warbler	C C	C C	—	U U	U	—	—	—	R R
Virginia's Warbler	—	—	—	—	—	—	—	—	—
Lucy's Warbler	—	—	—	—	—	—	—	—	—
Northern Parula	U U	U R U	—	—	A A A	U	C U C	U U O R	U U
Tropical Parula	—	—	—	—	—	—	—	—	—
Yellow Warbler	• A A O	• C U C	C C C	C C C	C C	—	C O C	U O U	U U
Chestnut-sided Warbler	U U	U U	—	—	U C	—	C	O O	U U
Magnolia Warbler	U U	U O	—	—	U U	—	C C	U U	U U
Cape May Warbler	U U	R	—	—	—	—	C	—	R
Black-throated Blue Warbler	R R	R	—	—	—	—	R R	—	O
Yellow-rumped Warbler	A A	A A R	O O	A A	A A	—	C C	C C	C U A
Black-throated Gray Warbler	—	—	—	—	—	—	—	O U	—
Townsend's Warbler	—	—	—	—	—	—	—	—	—
Hermit Warbler	—	—	—	—	—	—	—	—	—
Black-throated Green Warbler	U U	U O	—	—	C C	—	C	—	U U
Blackburnian Warbler	U U	U O	—	—	U U	—	C	O O	U U
Yellow-throated Warbler	—	—	—	—	C C C	U U U	C U C	U U O R	U U
Pine Warbler	O O	—	—	—	—	—	—	O	—
Prairie Warbler	—	—	U U	—	—	—	—	—	R O
Palm Warbler	C C	R R	—	—	U U U	—	C	—	U U U
Bay-breasted Warbler	U U	O O	—	—	U U	—	C	U U	U C
Blackpoll Warbler	U U	U U	—	R O	—	—	C	—	U
Cerulean Warbler	• U U	U	—	—	U U	—	C	O O	U U
Black-and-white Warbler	C C	U U	—	—	C U C	—	C C	C C	C C
American Redstart	• A A C	C R O	—	—	C C C	—	C O C	U O U	C C
Prothonotary Warbler	• C C	• O R O	—	O U U	A A A	• A A C	C C U	• C C U	U U
Worm-eating Warbler	—	—	—	—	U U	—	C	O O	O U
Swainson's Warbler	—	—	—	—	C C C	—	C	—	—
Ovenbird	• U U U	U U	—	—	U U	—	C	O O	C R
Northern Waterthrush	U U	U O	O O	—	U U	—	C	O O	U U
Louisiana Waterthrush	• O O O	O R U	—	—	U U U	—	U U	O O	O O
Kentucky Warbler	• R R	U R O	—	—	C C C	O O	C	U R U	C U
Connecticut Warbler	R R	—	—	—	—	—	—	—	—
Mourning Warbler	O O	U O	—	R R	—	—	—	—	O O
MacGillivray's Warbler	—	—	—	—	—	—	—	—	—
Common Yellowthroat	• A A C	• A C C	O O	• U U U	C U C U	—	C C C U	• C C C C	• C C C C
Hooded Warbler	R R	—	—	—	C C C	—	C U C	U U U	C U
Wilson's Warbler	U U	U U	—	U U	U U	—	—	O	O U U
Canada Warbler	U U	R	—	R	U U	—	C	—	U U
Painted Redstart	—	—	—	—	—	—	—	—	—
Yellow-breasted Chat	• R R	O R R	—	• O	U U U	—	—	O O O	U U
TANAGERS									
Hepatic Tanager	—	—	—	—	—	—	—	—	—
Summer Tanager	—	O O	—	U U U	C C C	• C C U	C O C	• U U U	C C
Scarlet Tanager	• U U U	R R	—	—	U U	—	C C	U U	U C
Western Tanager	—	—	—	—	—	—	—	—	R R
CARDINALS, GROSBEAKS & ALLIES									
Northern Cardinal	• C C C C	• C C C C	• C C C C	• C C C C	A A A A	• C C C C	U U U U	• C C C C	U U U U
Pyrrhuloxia	—	—	—	—	—	—	—	—	—
Rose-breasted Grosbeak	• C C C	• O O O	—	U U	U U	—	C	U U	C U
Black-headed Grosbeak	—	—	R	—	—	—	—	—	—
Blue Grosbeak	—	U U O	O O O	U U U	U U	U U	C	O O O	O O
Lazuli Bunting	—	R	—	R O O	—	—	—	—	—
Indigo Bunting	• C C C	• C C C	R	U U	C C C	• A A C	A A	C U U	U U
Painted Bunting	—	• O O R	—	U U U	U U U	• A A C	C C	U U U	O O
Dickcissel	• C C	• C C C	• O O O	• C A C	U	U U U	C U C R	U U	O
NEW WORLD SPARROWS & ALLIES									
Olive Sparrow	—	—	—	—	—	—	—	—	—
Green-tailed Towhee	—	—	—	—	—	—	—	—	—
Rufous-sided Towhee	• U U U	• U U U U	O O O	U U	C C C C	U U U	—	O O O	O O O
Brown Towhee	—	—	—	—	—	—	—	—	—
Abert's Towhee	—	—	—	—	—	—	—	—	—
Bachman's Sparrow	—	—	—	—	—	—	—	—	—

	LA-6 Tensas	LA-7 Jean Lafitte	ME-1 Great Wass	ME-2 Moosehorn	ME-3 Petit Manan	ME-4 Carson	MD-1 Blackwater	MD-2 East. Neck	MA-1 G. Meadows	MA-2 Parker R.	MA-3 Monomoy	MI-1 Seney
	• s S F W	• s S F W	• s S F W	• s S F W	• s S F W	• s S F W	• s S F W	• s S F W	• s S F W	• s S F W	• s S F W	• s S F W
	A A A —	• C C C	C U C —	• C C C —	• C C C —	• U C U —	• C C C —	• C U C —	• C C C —	• C U C —	O C —	• A A A —
	U U	C C	—	—	R	—	U U	U U	• O O	O O	O	—
	U U	U U	—	—	—	—	R	—	R	R R	R R	• R R
	A A	C A	C U C	• C C C	U U U	U U U	R R	O U	U U	U O U	R C	C R C
	U U U	C C	R	—	O O	—		R	—	R O	O	O
	U U	R	• C C C	• C C C	• C C C	• U U U	R	R R	U O O	U O U	R O	• A A A
	A A C	• A A A R	• C C C	• C C C	• C C C	U U U	U U	• C U U	U O	U O U	O O	• U U U
	U U	U A	• U U U	• C C C	• C C C	• C C O	• C C U	• A C U	• C A O	• A A U	• C C C	• C C C
	C C	U U C	• C U C	• C C C	• C U C	• U O U	U U	U U	• O R O	U O O	R O	• C C C
	C C	C C	• C C C	• C C C	• C C C	• U U U	U U	U U	U O	U O U	O O	• C C C
	—	R	U U U	• U U U	R C C	U O U	O U	U C	O O	O U U	R C	• U U U
	R R	R	U O U	• U U U	O O	U O U	U U	U C	O O	A O A U	R O	• U U U
	A A A	C C A	• C C C R	• C C C	• C C C	• C U A	A C C	A A C	C C O	A O A U	C A O	• A A A
	C C	—	—	—	—	—	—	—	—	—	—	—
	—	—	—	—	—	—	—	—	—	—	—	—
	—	C C R	• C C C	• C C C	• C C C	• C C U	—	U U	U U	U O U	O O	• C C C
	U U	U U	• C U C	• C C C	• C C U	U U U	O O	U U	O O	U O U	O O	• U U U
	C C C	• C C C R	—	• U U U	—	—	R O	• U O U	R R R	O O O O	R R O	• C C C
	R R R	U U U	—	—	R	• U U U	• C C C U	• U U U R	U O R	U O U	U C	—
	R R	R U	—	—	—	O O O	• U U U	• U U U	• O O O	U O U	O C	• C U C
	—	U U U	• C C C	• U U U	• C U C	U U	U U O	U U O	C U R	U C O	O C	C C
	C C	U U	U U C	• U U O	• U C C	U U U	R R	U U	O O	U O U	O C	C C
	C C	U	C U C	• O O O	U U	U U	U U	U U	C O A	C O A	U C	C C
	U R U	U U	—	—	—	—	—	—	R	—	U U	• C C C
	C R C	C C R	• C C C	• C C C	• C C C	• C C C	C O C	• C R C	• C O O	C O C	O C	• C C C
	C C C	C C R	• C C C	• C C C	• C C C	• C C C	U C	C R C	• C O U	• C U C	O C	• C C C
	A A A	• C C C	—	—	—	—	• U O R	• U U U	—	R	—	—
	A U U	U C	—	—	—	—	• U O R	—	—	O O	—	—
	C C C	• U U	—	• C U C	• A A A	• U U U	• U U U	• C U C	• U U C	• U U O	U O U	R O	• C C C
	C U A	C C R	• C U C	• A A A	• U U U	• U U U	• C U C	• U U C	• U U O	U O U	R O	C U C
	A A	C C R	U U U	• C C C	O O	U U R	R U	U U	U R U	U O U	O C	C U C
	A A	U U	—	—	—	R	O R O	• U R U	—	R	—	—
	C C C	U U	—	—	—	—	• U U O	• U O U	—	R	—	O R O
	R					R O		—	O O	R	
	R	U O U	• U U U	—	O O O	—	R O	R R	U U	R O	• U U U
	C C C U	• A C A C	• C C C	• C C C	• C C C	• C C C	• A C A O	• C A C R	• C C C R	• C C C	• C C C	• C C C
	C C C	• C C C	—			—	• O O	—	O O O		
	R R	U U	U U U	• U U U	• U U U	U U U	R R	R O	U O U	O O	U U
	C C	U C	• U U U	• O O O	• U O O	• C U U	O U	U U	O O	U O U	R O	• C C C
	U U U	U U	O	—	R R	O O	• C C U	• U U U R	R R	O O O	O	—
	—	—	—	—	—	—	—	—	—	—	—	—
	C C C	• C R C	—	—	R	—	• U U	• R O R	—	R	—	—
	U U	C C	U U U	• U U U	U U U	• U U U	• U U U	• C O C	• C U O	U O U	R O	• O U O
	—	—	—	—	—	—	—	—	—	—	—	—
	A A A A	• A A A A	O O U O	R R	O O	• U U U U	• C C C C	• C C C C	• U U U U	• U U U U	R R	—
	C C	C C	U U U	U U U	• U U U	• U U O	R R	O U	• C U O	U O U	O C	• C C U
	C U C	C C	—	—	—	—	• C C U	• O U O	—	O O O	—	—
	A A A	• A R A	U U U	• O O O	O	• U U U	• C C U	• C C C	• U U U	O O O	O O	U U
	C C C	• C C C R	—	—	—	—	—	—	—	—	—	—
	A A U				R				R	O O	R	
	—	—	—	—	—	—	—	—	—	—	—	—
	C C C C	• R R U R		O O O	• U U U	• C C C R	• C C C U	• C C C U	• C U U R	• C C C O	U U U	O O O
	—	—	—	—	—	—	—	—	—	—	—	—

STATE-NUMBER OF BIRD LIST / REFUGE, SANCTUARY OR PRESERVE / NESTING, ABUNDANCE BY SEASON	IA-4 McGregor • s S F W	KS-1 Flint Hills • s S F W	KS-2 Kirwin • s S F W	KS-3 Quivira • s S F W	LA-1 Bog. Chitto • s S F W	LA-2 Catahoula • s S F W	LA-3 Delta • s S F W	LA-4 Lacassine • s S F W	LA-5 Sabine • s S F W
NEW WORLD SPARROWS & ALLIES (cont.)									
Cassin's Sparrow	—	—	—	—	—	—	—	—	—
Rufous-crowned Sparrow	—	—	—	—	—	—	—	—	—
American Tree Sparrow	C A A	A A A	O OC	A A A	—	—	—	—	—
Chipping Sparrow	•A A A	C C	O OC	C O C	U U U C	—	—	O OO	—
Clay-colored Sparrow	U U	U U	U O U	C C	—	—	—	—	—
Brewer's Sparrow	—	—	—	—	—	—	—	—	—
Field Sparrow	•C C C R	•C U C R	—	U U U U	—	U U U U	—	—	O OO
Black-chinned Sparrow	—	—	—	—	—	—	—	—	—
Vesper Sparrow	•C C C	C C	C C C	C C U	—	—	—	O OO	—
Lark Sparrow	•U U	•C C U	C C C	•C C C	—	—	O OO	—	O
Black-throated Sparrow	—	—	—	—	—	—	—	—	R
Sage Sparrow	—	—	—	—	—	—	—	—	—
Lark Bunting	—	O	O O O	U U U	—	—	—	—	—
Savannah Sparrow	•C C C	C C	—	C C C U	—	—	C	C C C	U U C
Baird's Sparrow	—	—	—	—	—	—	—	—	—
Grasshopper Sparrow	•U U U	•C C C	—	C U C	—	—	—	—	—
Henslow's Sparrow	•U U R	R R R	—	R R	—	—	—	—	—
Le Conte's Sparrow	R R R	U U	—	U R U R	—	—	—	—	O OU
Sharp-tailed Sparrow	—	R	—	—	—	—	U UU	—	U U
Seaside Sparrow	—	—	—	—	—	—	C C C C	O O O O	•A A A A
Fox Sparrow	U U	U UU	—	O	U UU	—	—	—	O OO
Song Sparrow	•A A A O	C CC	U UU	C CC	U UU	C C	U UU	U UU	C CC
Lincoln's Sparrow	U U	C CO	—	O OO	U UU	—	C	—	U UU
Swamp Sparrow	•C C C R	U UR	—	R R	C CU	—	C	C CC	C CC
White-throated Sparrow	C CR	C CU	—	U UU	A AA	C	U UU	U UU	U UU
Golden-crowned Sparrow	—	—	—	—	—	—	—	—	—
White-crowned Sparrow	U UR	C CC	O OC	C CC	U UU	C	C	—	O OO
Harris' Sparrow	O O	A AA	C C	C CC	—	—	—	—	—
Dark-eyed Junco	A AA	A CA	U	C CA	—	O	C C	O O	O OO
McCown's Longspur	—	—	—	—	—	—	—	—	—
Lapland Longspur	R RR	C CA	O	U CC	—	—	—	—	—
Smith's Longspur	—	O RR	—	—	—	—	—	—	—
Chestnut-collared Longspur	—	R R	O O	U UC	—	—	—	—	—
Snow Bunting	U U	—	R	R	—	—	—	—	—
NEW WORLD BLACKBIRDS & ORIOLES									
Bobolink	•U U U	O R	—	•U U O	—	—	C R	—	—
Red-winged Blackbird	•A A A U	•A A A A	•A A A O	•A C A A	A A A A	•C C C C	A A A A	•A A A A	•A A A A
Tricolored Blackbird	—	—	—	—	—	—	—	—	—
Eastern Meadowlark	•C C C O	•A A A A	•O O O O	•C C C C	—	C A A C	C C C C	•C C C C	•A A A A
Western Meadowlark	•A A A O	U O O U	•A A A A	•A A A A	—	—	C	—	O O
Yellow-headed Blackbird	•U U U	U U	C C C	•C C C O	—	—	R R	R	O
Rusty Blackbird	C CO	U UU	—	U UO	C CC	•C C C C	—	O OO	R R
Brewer's Blackbird	•U U U R	C CC	C C C	C CO	U UU	•C C C C	C	—	—
Great-tailed Grackle	—	R R	—	U O U O	—	—	—	—	—
Boat-tailed Grackle	—	—	—	—	—	—	A A A A	•A A A A	•A A A A
Common Grackle	•A A A U	•A A A U	O O O	•C C C O	A A A A	•C C C C	U U U U	O O O O	R R R
Bronzed Cowbird	—	—	—	—	—	—	—	—	—
Brown-headed Cowbird	•A A U R	•A C A C	C C C	•C C C U	C C C C	•A A A A	C C C C	U O U C	•U U U U
Orchard Oriole	•U U	•C C U	•O O O	•C C C	U U U	U C C	A A	C C	•C C
Hooded Oriole	—	—	—	—	—	—	—	—	—
Baltimore Oriole	—	—	—	—	—	—	—	—	—
Bullock's Oriole	•C C	•A A U	•C C C	•A A C	U U U	U C C	U R U	U U U	U U
Scott's Oriole	—	—	—	—	—	—	—	—	—
FINCHES									
Rosy Finch	—	—	—	—	—	—	—	—	—
Pine Grosbeak	—	R R	—	—	—	—	—	—	—
Purple Finch	C CU	U UU	—	U UU	—	O O O	—	R	O OO
Cassin's Finch	—	—	—	—	—	—	—	—	—
House Finch	—	—	O O O	—	—	—	—	—	—
Red Crossbill	R R .R	—	R	—	—	—	—	—	—
White-winged Crossbill	R R	R R	—	—	—	—	—	—	—
Common Redpoll	U U	—	R	R	—	—	—	—	—
Hoary Redpoll	—	R	—	—	—	—	—	—	—
Pine Siskin	U UU	O R O U	—	—	—	C	—	—	—
Lesser Goldfinch	—	—	—	—	—	—	—	—	—
Lawrence's Goldfinch	—	—	—	—	—	—	—	—	—
American Goldfinch	•A A A C	•C C C A	O O O	•C C C O	U UU	O O	U UU	O OO	O OO
Evening Grosbeak	O OU	R	—	—	—	—	—	—	—
OLD WORLD SPARROWS									
House Sparrow	•A A A A	•A A A A	•C C C C	•C C C C	—	•C C C C	C C C C	•C C C C	•U U U U
Eurasian Tree Sparrow	—	—	—	—	—	—	—	—	—

	LA-6 Tensas	LA-7 Jean Lafitte	ME-1 Great Wass	ME-2 Moosehorn	ME-3 Petit Manan	ME-4 Carson	MD-1 Blackwater	MD-2 East. Neck	MA-1 G. Meadows	MA-2 Parker R.	MA-3 Monomoy	MI-1 Seney
	•s S F W	•s S F W	•s S F W	•s S F W	•s S F W	•s S F W	•s S F W	•s S F W	•s S F W	•s S F W	•s S F W	•s S F W

STATE-NUMBER OF BIRD LIST / REFUGE, SANCTUARY OR PRESERVE / NESTING, ABUNDANCE BY SEASON	MN-1 Agassiz •s S F W	MN-2 Big Stone •s S F W	MN-3 MN Valley •s S F W	MN-4 MN WPA •s S F W	MN-5 Sherburne •s S F W	MN-6 Tamarac •s S F W	MS-1 Sandhill Cr. •s S F W	MS-2 Noxubee •s S F W	MS-3 Yazoo •s S F W
LOONS									
Red-throated Loon	—	—	—	—	—	—	—	—	—
Arctic Loon	—	—	—	—	—	—	—	—	—
Pacific Loon	—	—	—	—	—	—	—	—	—
Common Loon	O R O	O R	O R	•C U C	•C C	•C C C	—	R R	—
Yellow-billed Loon	—	—	—	—	—	—	—	—	—
GREBES									
Least Grebe	—	—	—	—	—	—	—	—	—
Pied-billed Grebe	•A A A	•C C C	C C C	•C C C R	•C C C	•C C C	O O	C U C C	•C U C C
Horned Grebe	•C O C	U U	O	U C C	R	U U	—	R R	
Red-necked Grebe	•C C C	O	—	•U U U	•R R	•C C C	—	—	—
Eared Grebe	•O U O	•U U	U U	U R R	U	U U	—	R	—
Western Grebe	•C C C	•C C C	R	•U U U	—	R R	—	—	—
SHEARWATERS & PETRELS									
Northern Fulmar	—	—	—	—	—	—	—	—	—
Cory's Shearwater	—	—	—	—	—	—	—	—	—
Pink-footed Shearwater	—	—	—	—	—	—	—	—	—
Greater Shearwater	—	—	—	—	—	—	—	—	—
Sooty Shearwater	—	—	—	—	—	—	—	—	—
Short-tailed Shearwater	—	—	—	—	—	—	—	—	—
Manx Shearwater	—	—	—	—	—	—	—	—	—
Audubon's Shearwater	—	—	—	—	—	—	—	—	—
STORM-PETRELS									
Wilson's Storm-Petrel	—	—	—	—	—	—	—	—	—
Fork-tailed Storm-Petrel	—	—	—	—	—	—	—	—	—
Leach's Storm-Petrel	—	—	—	—	—	—	—	—	—
BOOBIES & GANNETS									
Masked Booby	—	—	—	—	—	—	—	—	—
Brown Booby	—	—	—	—	—	—	—	—	—
Northern Gannet	—	—	—	—	—	—	—	—	—
PELICANS									
American White Pelican	C C C	C C C	C	U U	—	U U U	—	R R	O O
Brown Pelican	—	—	—	—	—	—	—	—	—
CORMORANTS									
Great Cormorant	—	—	—	—	—	—	—	—	—
Double-crested Cormorant	•C C C	•A A A	C C C	•C C C	R R	C U C	O O	C U C C	O U C
Olivaceous Cormorant	—	—	—	—	—	—	—	—	—
Brandt's Cormorant	—	—	—	—	—	—	—	—	—
Pelagic Cormorant	—	—	—	—	—	—	—	—	—
Red-faced Cormorant	—	—	—	—	—	—	—	—	—
ANHINGAS									
Anhinga	—	—	—	—	—	—	—	U U U U	•U C C O
FRIGATEBIRDS									
Magnificent Frigatebird	—	—	—	—	—	—	—	—	—
BITTERNS & HERONS									
American Bittern	•C C C	•U U U	U U U	C C C	•C C C	•U U U	U U	U O U	O O O
Least Bittern	•U U U	•U U U	U U U	•C C C	•U U R	R R R	U U	R U R	•U C U
Great Blue Heron	•C C C	•C C C	A A A	•C C C R	•C C C R	•A A A	U U U C	C C C C	•C C C C
Great Egret	•U U U	•C C C	C C C	•C C U	U R R	R R R	U U U C	C C C U	•U U C U
Snowy Egret	R R	•U U U	—	—	—	—	O O	O O O O	O O O
Little Blue Heron	R	U U U	—	—	—	—	O O O U	U U	•O C C O
Tricolored Heron	—	—	—	—	—	—	O O O U	—	O O
Reddish Egret	—	—	—	—	—	—	—	—	—
Cattle Egret	R R R	• R	—	R R	—	—	U C U O	U U U O	•U C C U
Green-backed Heron	•U U U	•U U U	C C C	•C C U	•C C C	•U U U	•C C C U	C C	•C C C O
Black-crowned Night-Heron	•C C C	•C C C	C C C	•C C C	•U U	U U U	—	O	O O O O
Yellow-crowned Night-Heron	R	U U U	R R R	—	—	R R R	O O	R U U	•O U U O
IBISES & SPOONBILLS									
White Ibis	—	—	—	—	—	—	O O	U U U	O U C O
Glossy Ibis	—	—	—	—	—	—	—	R	O O
White-faced Ibis	—	—	—	—	—	—	—	—	—
Roseate Spoonbill	—	—	—	—	—	—	—	—	—
STORKS									
Wood Stork	—	—	—	—	—	—	—	O O	O O
SWANS, GEESE & DUCKS									
Fulvous Whistling-Duck	—	—	—	—	—	—	—	R	—
Black-bellied Whistling-Duck	—	—	—	—	—	—	—	—	R
Tundra Swan	C C	O O R	C U	C C	U U	U U	—	R R	O
Trumpeter Swan	—	—	—	—	U U U	—	—	—	—
Mute Swan	—	—	—	—	—	—	—	—	—
Greater White-fronted Goose	O R	O O	R R	R R	R	R R	—	R	C
Snow Goose	U C	U R A R	C C	C C	U U	U U	R	O O O	C

	MS-4 Gulf Is.	MO-1 Annada	MO-2 Mingo	MO-3 Squaw Cr.	MO-4 Swan L	MT-1 Benton L.	MT-2 Bowdoin	MT-3 Russell	MT-4 Lee Metcalf	MT-5 Medicine L.	MT-6 Bison Range	MT-7 Ninepipe
seasons	•s S F W	•s S F W	•s S F W	•s S F W	•s S F W	•s S F W	•s S F W	•s S F W	•s S F W	•s S F W	•s S F W	•s S F W
	—	—	—	—	—	—	—	—	—	—	—	—
	—	—	—	—	—	—	—	—	—	—	—	—
	COUC	—	O	R	R	R R	O	O	O	CUU	R R	O O	—	CUU
	CRUC	CUCU	CRCC	•CUCR	•COC	•UUU	•CCC	•CCC	•CCUU	•CCC	RRR	•UUU
	COUC	O OO	R R	U U	U U	U U	•UUU	U UO	O O	•CCU	RRR	•UUU
	—	—	—	—	—	O O	R	R	O	O	RRR	•CCU
	RROO	—	R R	URU	O R	•AAA	•CAC	•CCC	•O	•AAU	RRR	•UUU
	—	—	—	R R	—	UOU	•UUU	•CCC	O	•AAU	RR	•CCC
	—	—	—	—	—	—	—	—	—	—	—	—
	—	—	—	—	—	—	—	—	—	—	—	—
	—	—	—	—	—	—	—	—	—	—	—	—
	—	—	—	—	—	—	—	—	—	—	—	—
	—	—	—	—	—	—	—	—	—	—	—	—
	—	—	—	—	—	—	—	—	—	—	—	—
	—	—	—	—	—	—	—	—	—	—	—	—
	U	—	—	—	—	—	—	—	—	—	—	—
	U	—	—	—	—	—	—	—	—	—	—	—
	URRU	—	—	—	—	—	—	—	—	—	—	—
	UUUU	R	R U	AUA	CUC	ROR	•AAC	•OCC	R	•AAA	—	OOO
	UUUU	—	—	—	—	—	—	—	—	—	—	—
	CUUC	UU	R R	CRC	UOU	•OOO	•AAC	•CCC	CC	•AAA	—	•CCO
	—	—	—	—	—	—	—	—	—	—	—	—
	—	—	—	—	—	—	—	—	—	—	—	—
	—	—	—	—	—	—	—	—	—	—	—	—
	RRR	—	—	—	—	—	—	—	—	—	—	—
	UUOR	—	—	—	—	—	—	—	—	—	—	—
	U UU	URU	CRR	•OOUR	UUU	UUU	•CCC	UUU	•UUU	—	OOO	•CUO
	UUUR	•UU	RRR	•UUR	UOU	—	—	R	—	—	—	R
	CCCC	CCCC	•CCCU	CCCR	•CCCU	ROR	•CCC	•CCCR	•CCCC	•CCC	CCCU	•COCO
	OUOO	CCC	UUU	UUU	UUU	R	—	O	—	R	—	R
	UUUU	RU	RR	RUR	OU	R	ROO	R	—	—	—	R
	UUUU	UCC	•CCC	OUR	RUO	—	—	—	—	—	—	—
	UUUU	—	—	—	—	—	—	—	—	—	—	—
	ROOR	—	—	—	—	—	—	—	—	—	—	—
	UCUO	RUO	•CUC	OUU	UUU	—	—	—	—	—	—	—
	OCCO	•CCC	•CACR	•UCO	•UCU	—	—	RCCR	—	—	—	R
	O OO	•CUU	•RRU	•OCO	UUO	•UCU	•CCO	C O	R	•CCU	—	R
	OCOR	CUU	•CCU	•OUO	OO	—	—	—	—	—	—	—
	ROOR	R	URU	—	—	—	—	—	—	—	—	—
	—	R	—	—	—	—	—	—	—	—	—	—
	—	—	—	ORR	—	OUO	•UU	—	R	RR	—	R
	—	—	—	—	—	—	—	—	—	—	—	—
	R	—	—	—	—	—	—	—	—	—	—	—
	—	OR	—	R	R R	R R R	—	U C	O O	C U	U C	OOO	CRC
	—	—	R	R	—	—	—	—	—	—	—	—
	—	U UO	R UR	U CR	U UU	R R	O O	O O	R	U C	U C	U U	O
	R R R	C CC	U UU	ARAO	COAU	A A	O O	U U	O O	U U	U C	U U

Each refuge column below shows codes by season: **•s S F W** (• = nesting).

STATE-NUMBER OF BIRD LIST / REFUGE, SANCTUARY OR PRESERVE	MN-1 Agassiz	MN-2 Big Stone	MN-3 MN Valley	MN-4 MN WPA	MN-5 Sherburne	MN-6 Tamarac	MS-1 Sandhill Cr.	MS-2 Noxubee	MS-3 Yazoo
SWANS, GEESE & DUCKS (cont.)									
Ross' Goose	—	—	R	—	—	—		—	—
Emperor Goose	—	—	—	—	—	—		—	—
Brant	—	—	—	—	—	—		—	—
Canada Goose	•C C C	•C C A O	C C C U	•C C A C	•C U C	•C C C	—	A A A A	•U U U C
Wood Duck	•U U U	•C C C R	C C C	•C C C	•C C C R	•A C A	•C C U U	C C C C	•C C C C
Green-winged Teal	•C U A	•C U C R	C C	•U U C	•C U C	•U U U		C C C	U U U
American Black Duck	•O O U	O R O O	U R U	R U	U R U	•U R U		O O O	O O U
Mottled Duck	—	—	—	—	—	—			
Mallard	•A A A	•C C A O	A A A C	•A C A U	•A C A R	•A C A	R R	C R A A	•C U C C
Northern Pintail	•C U A	•C C C R	C C	•C U C	C R C	•U R U	—	O U U	O O U
Blue-winged Teal	•A A A	•A A C R	A A A	•C A A	•C C A	•A C A	O O U	C U C R	C C O
Cinnamon Teal	—	—	—	—	R	—	—	—	R R
Northern Shoveler	•C C C	•C C C R	C C C	•C C C	•C U C	U R U	—	C C C	C C C
Gadwall	•C C C	•C U C R	C C	•U U C	U U	•U U U	—	O C C	O O C
Eurasian Wigeon	—	—	—	—	—	—			
American Wigeon	•C C A	•C U C R	C C	•C U C	C C	•U U C	—	C C C	C C C
Canvasback	•C C U	•C U C R	C C	•C C C	•U R R	U R U	—	U U	O O O
Redhead	•C C C	•C U C R	C U C	•C C C	•U R U	•U U C	—	R R	O
Ring-necked Duck	•C C C	•C R U R	C C	•C U C	•C U C	•A C A	—	O C A	U U C
Greater Scaup	U U	O	R R	U U	—	R R	—	—	O
Lesser Scaup	•C U A	C C O	C C U	•A C A	C C	•A R A	—	U U U	O O O
Common Eider	—	—	—	—	—	—	—	—	—
King Eider	—	—	—	—	—	—			
Steller's Eider	—	—	—	—	—	—			
Harlequin Duck	—	—	—	—	—	—			
Oldsquaw	R R	R R	R R	R R	—	R R	—	R	—
Black Scoter	—	—	—	—	—	R			
Surf Scoter	—	—	—	—	—	R			
White-winged Scoter	O R O	—	R R	R	—	R			
Common Goldeneye	•C R U	C U U	C C C	C C	U	•C C C	—	R	O
Barrow's Goldeneye	—	—	R	—	—	—			
Bufflehead	•C R U	U O U R	C C	C C	U U	•U R C	—	U U	O O U
Hooded Merganser	•C U U	•U O O R	C C	•U R U	•U R R	•C U C	U U	U O C C	•U U
Common Merganser	C O	C U U	C C	C C	U R	C R C	—		U R R
Red-breasted Merganser	O	R	C C	U U	R	U U	—	R R R	R R
Ruddy Duck	•C C C	•C C C R	C U C	•C C C	R R R	•U R U	—	C C	U U
Masked Duck	—	—	—	—	—	—			
AMERICAN VULTURES									
Black Vulture	—	—	—	—	—	—	A A A A	C C C A	O O O O
Turkey Vulture	R R R	R R	U U U	R	R R R	U U U	C C C C	C U C C	C C C C
KITES, EAGLES, HAWKS & ALLIES									
Osprey	R R	R R R	U U	R R R	R R	•U U U	•C C O O	O R O O	R R R
American Swallow-tailed Kite	—	—	—	—	—	—	R R		
Black-shouldered Kite	—	—	—	—	—	—			
Snail Kite	—	—	—	—	—	—			
Mississippi Kite	—	—	—	—	—	—	R R	—	•O C U
Bald Eagle	U O U O	O O	U U O	U U R	U R R	•C C C	—	U R U U	O U
Northern Harrier	•C C C	•C C C R	C C	•C C C R	•C U U	•U U U	U U U	U U U	U U C
Sharp-shinned Hawk	•U U U	U R U O	C C U	C R C R	•U R U	•U U U	U U U	U U U	U U U
Cooper's Hawk	•O O O	O R U O	O O U	C R C R	•C U U	•R R U U	U U	U U U U	O O U
Northern Goshawk	•O U O U	R R	U U	R U	—	R R R	—		U U U
Common Black-Hawk	—	—	—	—	—	—			
Harris' Hawk	—	—	—	—	—	—			
Gray Hawk	—	—	—	—	—	—			
Red-shouldered Hawk	—	O R O	R	—	•R R	R R R	•C C C C	C C C C	U U U
Broad-winged Hawk	•U O U	O U	C C C	C C C	•U U U	•C C A	U U	U R U	U O
Short-tailed Hawk	—	—	—	—	—	—			
Swainson's Hawk	R	•U U U	—	U U	R	R R R			
White-tailed Hawk	—	—	—	—	—	—			
Zone-tailed Hawk	—	—	—	—	—	—			
Red-tailed Hawk	•C C C	•C C C R	C C C U	•C C C	•C C C U	•C U C	•C C C C	C C C C	C U C C
Ferruginous Hawk	R	—	—	—	—	—			
Rough-legged Hawk	C C U	U U O	C C U	U U R	C R U	U U R	—		
Golden Eagle	U R U O	R R	—	R R R	R R	R R R R	—	R	R O
CARACARAS & FALCONS									
Crested Caracara	—	—	—	—	—	—			R
American Kestrel	•U U U	•C C C O	C C C U	•C C C U	C C C R	•C C C	C U C A	U U U U	C O C C
Merlin	O O	O R O R	—	U U U	R R	R R	—	—	O U
Peregrine Falcon	O O	R R	R R	—	R R R	R R			
Gyrfalcon	—	—	—	—	—	R			
Prairie Falcon	—	R R	—	—	—	R R			

	MS-4 Gulf Is.	MO-1 Annada	MO-2 Mingo	MO-3 Squaw Cr.	MO-4 Swan L	MT-1 Benton L.	MT-2 Bowdoin	MT-3 Russell	MT-4 Lee Metcalf	MT-5 Medicine L.	MT-6 Bison Range	MT-7 Ninepipe
	• s S F W	• s S F W	• s S F W	• s S F W	• s S F W	• s S F W	• s S F W	• s S F W	• s S F W	• s S F W	• s S F W	• s S F W
	—	—	—	U U R	R R	U O U	U	R	C U	O O	—	R R
	—	—	—	—	—	—	—	R	—	—	—	—
	—	—	—	—	—	—	—	R	—	—	—	—
	—	C O C C	•A U A A	A U A C	A U A A	•C U C	•A A A	•C C C O	•A A A C	•A A A	•C U C U	•C C A O
	U U U U	•C A A O	•C C A C	•O C C R	•C C C U	—	R R	•R R	•C C C	O R O	•U O O	•O U O
	U U U	C U C U	C C U	C R C U	C O C U	•C C C	•C U C	C C C	•C C O	O R O	•C C C U	•C U C O
	U U U	C C C	U U U	O O O U	O O O	—	R	R R	—	—	—	R
	O U U O									—		—
	O U C	•C C A A	A R A A	•A C A A	•C U C C	•A C A O	•A A A A	•A C A A	•A C A C	•A A A O	•C C A A	•A A A C
	R R	C O A C	C C C	•A R A O	•A U A O	•A C A	•A A A O	A C C O	•C O U U	•A A C	•C U C O	•A C A U
	C U R	•C U C	A C U	•C O C R	•C U C U	•A C A	•A A A	•C A C	•C C U	•A A C	•C C U	•U C O
				O R	O O O	•C C C	•O O O	R R	•A A U	•R R R	U U U	•U U A
	R O R	C C U	C C U	C R C R	C O U U	•A A A	•A A A	•C C C	•C O O R	•A A A	•O O O	•U U C
	O O O	C R C O	C A U	C R C R.	C C	•A A A	•A A A	•C C C	•U U U R	•A A A	•O O O	•U C C O
			—			—		R	O	—		—
	O O O	C C U	C C U	C R C O	C C R	•C C C	•A C A	•C C C	•A U C U	•C C C	U U C	•A C A O
	R R R	U U U	R R R	U U R	C U R	•U O U	•A C A	C U C	•U R U R	•C C C	O R	•U O O
	U O U	C C C	R R R	O R O R	C O U	•U U U	•C C C	C U C	•C C U	•C C C	O O O	•C C U
	O R O O	C C C	C C C	C U R	C U O	R R	O R O	O R O	•C U O O	•U A U	O R	•U O U
	O O O	O O O	—	R	R	R	R	—	R R	—		
	C O O C	A C C	U U U	C R C	C O C O	•A A A	•A C A	C U C	•U O U O	•A C A	O R	•U O U
	—	—	—	—	—	—	—	—	—	—	—	—
	—	—	—	—	—	—	—	—	—	—	—	R R
	R R R	O	—	—	O O	—	R	—	—	—	R
	R R R	—	—	—	—	R R	—	R	—	—	—	—
	R R R	—	R	R	R R R	R	R R	R R	R	—	R
	U U U	U U C	R R R	O O U	U U U	A O O R	•A O A O	C U C C	•C R C U	U U	•C O C C	C O C U
	—		—	—	—	O O O	R R	O O	U R O	R O	O R R	U U O
	U R C	U U U	R R R	U U	C U O	U O U	C O C	C U C O	•U U U U	•U O C	R R	U O U U
	R O	•U U U U	•U U U C	U U U R	U U O	R	R	R R	•C U C R	O O	•U O U O	O O U
	—	U U A	R R R	C O C	C U U	O O	R	C C	•C U C C	O U	•C U C C	•C U C U
	C O C	U U U	R R R	O O R	O O O	O O	U U	C O O	•C C O O	O U	O O O	
	O O	A C U	R R	U O U	C O U	•U U U	•A C C	C U C	•C U U R	•A A A	R R R	•C C U
	O O O O	—	•U U U R	—	—	—	—	—	—	—	—	—
	O O O O	•C C C	•C C C U	U C U	C C C	—	—	O	U U U	O O O	U	—
	U U U O	U U O	R R	O O	O O	—	—	•C C U	•C C C	R R	O O O	O O O
	R R	—	—	—	—	—	—	—	—	—	—	—
	—	—	—	—	—	—	—	—	—	—	—	—
	O U O	R	•R U	—	—	—	—	—	—	—	—	—
	R R	U U C	U R C C	U C C	U C C	O U R	O O O	C U C	U R U C	U U	O O O	U O C U
	U U U U	U U U	U C C	•U O U U	•C O C C	•C C C	•C C C U	•C A C C	•C C C U	•C C C O	•C C C U	•C C C U
	O U O	U U U U	•R R R R	U R U U	U O U U	O O	U R U	•C C C	O O O O	O O	O O O	O O U
	O O O	O R	•U U U U	O R O O	•U O U U	—	U U	•O O O	O O	O O	O O O	O O O
	—		R R	—	R R	—	O O	—	—	—	—	—
	—	—	—	—	—	—	—	—	—	—	—	—
	U U U U	U U C U	•C C C C	R R R R	U O O O	—	—	—	R R	—	—	—
	O O U	O O O	R R R R	R R R	C C	—	R	—	—	—	—	—
	—	—	—	—	—	—	—	—	—	—	—	—
	—	—	—	O O	O U R	O O U	•C C C	C C C	R R	•C C C	O R O	•U O U
	—	—	—	—	—	—	—	—	—	—	—	—
	U O U C	•C U C C	•C C C C	•C O C C	•C C C C	O R O	C O C	•A C A	•C C C U	•O O U	•C C C	•U O U
	—	—	—	—	—	O R O	•C U C	•O U O	•O O O	•O O O	R R R	O O O
	—	O O O	R R U	—	O	O O	C C	C C C	U U C	O O	C C	U U U
	—	U O R	R R R	O O	U U U	O O O O	•C C C C	U U C	O U C	U U U U	•C C C C	U O C U
	O O U C	•U U U U	•U U U C	O O O R	C U C U	O O	•C U C	•C A C	•C C C R	U O U	•A A A U	•C U C O
	R R R	—	—	R R R	O O	—	•U R U O	O O	O O	—	O O	O O R
	R R R	O R	R R R	R R R	R R	R R	O O O	•O O O	R R	R R	R R R	O O O O
	—	—	—	—	—	—	—	R	—	R	—	—
	—	—	R R	U U U O	O O O	•U U U O	O O O	•U U U U	O R O	U U U U	O O O O	O O O O

STATE-NUMBER OF BIRD LIST / REFUGE, SANCTUARY OR PRESERVE / NESTING, ABUNDANCE BY SEASON • s S F W	MN-1 Agassiz	MN-2 Big Stone	MN-3 MN Valley	MN-4 MN WPA	MN-5 Sherburne	MN-6 Tamarac	MS-1 Sandhill Cr.	MS-2 Noxubee	MS-3 Yazoo
CHACHALACAS									
Plain Chachalaca	—	—	—	—	—	—	—	—	—
PARTRIDGES, GROUSE, TURKEYS & QUAILS									
Gray Partridge	• O O O O	• U U U U	U U U U	• C C C C	—	R R R R	—	—	—
Chukar	—	—	—	—	—	—	—	—	—
Ring-necked Pheasant	—	• C C C C	C C C C	• C C C C	• U U U U	R R R R	—	—	—
Spruce Grouse	—	—	—	—	—	—	—	—	—
Blue Grouse	—	—	—	—	—	—	—	—	—
Willow Ptarmigan	—	—	—	—	—	—	—	—	—
Rock Ptarmigan	—	—	—	—	—	—	—	—	—
White-tailed Ptarmigan	—	—	—	—	—	—	—	—	—
Ruffed Grouse	• C C C C	—	R R R R	• C C C C	• C C C C	• C C C C	—	—	—
Sage Grouse	—	—	—	—	—	—	—	—	—
Greater Prairie Chicken	R R	—	—	• U U U U	—	—	—	—	—
Lesser Prairie Chicken	—	—	—	—	—	—	—	—	—
Sharp-tailed Grouse	• U U U U	—	—	—	—	—	—	—	—
Wild Turkey	—	O O O O	—	—	—	—	• U U U U	U U U U	• U U U U
Northern Bobwhite	—	• R R R R	U U U U	—	—	—	• C C C C	A A A A	• U U U U
Scaled Quail	—	—	—	—	—	—	—	—	—
Gambel's Quail	—	—	—	—	—	—	—	—	—
California Quail	—	—	—	—	—	—	—	—	—
Mountain Quail	—	—	—	—	—	—	—	—	—
RAILS, GALLINULES & COOTS									
Yellow Rail	• U U	—	—	• R R R	—	R R	R R R	—	—
Black Rail	—	—	—	—	R	—	—	—	—
Clapper Rail	—	—	—	—	—	—	C C C C	—	—
King Rail	—	R R R	R	—	—	—	U U U U	U U	R
Virginia Rail	• C C C	• C C C	C C C	• C C C	• U U U	• U U U	O O O	U R	—
Sora	• C C C	• C C C	C C C	• C C C	• A A A	• U U U	U U	R	U O U O
Purple Gallinule	—	—	—	—	—	—	O O	—	• U U U R
Common Moorhen	R R	—	—	—	—	—	U U U U	R	• C C U O
American Coot	• A A A	• A A A	A A A	• A C A R	• C C A	• C U A	C O C C	C R A A	C O O C
LIMPKINS									
Limpkin	—	—	—	—	—	—	—	—	—
CRANES									
Sandhill Crane	• C U C	—	—	U C	• R R	R R	• U U C C	—	—
Whooping Crane	—	—	—	—	—	—	—	—	—
PLOVERS									
Black-bellied Plover	O O	U U	—	C C	R	R R	—	R	—
Lesser Golden-Plover	O R O	O U	U R	C R	—	R R	U R	—	O
Snowy Plover	—	—	—	—	—	—	—	—	—
Wilson's Plover	—	—	—	—	—	—	—	—	—
Semipalmated Plover	C C C	U U	U U	U U	R	R R	—	R R R	O O O
Piping Plover	• R R	—	U R	U U	—	—	—	R R R	—
Killdeer	• C C C	• C C C	C C C	• A A A	• C C C	• C C C	• C U U A	C C C C	• C C C C
Mountain Plover	—	—	—	—	—	—	—	—	—
OYSTERCATCHERS									
American Oystercatcher	—	—	—	—	—	—	—	—	—
Black Oystercatcher	—	—	—	—	—	—	—	—	—
STILTS & AVOCETS									
Black-necked Stilt	—	—	—	—	—	—	—	—	R
American Avocet	• O R	• O O O	—	—	—	—	—	R	R
SANDPIPERS									
Greater Yellowlegs	C C C	C U C	C C	• C C C	U R U	U U U	—	U U U U	U U O
Lesser Yellowlegs	C C C	C C C	C C	• A R A	U R U	C C C	—	U U U U	U U
Solitary Sandpiper	U U U	O O	C C	C C C	U U	U U	U	O C	U U
Willet	R R	O O	—	U	—	—	—	—	—
Wandering Tattler	—	—	—	—	—	—	—	—	—
Spotted Sandpiper	• C C C	• C C C	C C C	• C C C	• C C U	U U U	U U	O R O O	U U
Upland Sandpiper	• O O	• C U U	U U U	• U U U	R	U U	—	—	O O
Whimbrel	—	—	R R	—	—	—	—	—	—
Long-billed Curlew	—	—	—	—	—	—	—	—	—
Hudsonian Godwit	U	R R R	—	U R	R	R R	—	—	—
Bar-tailed Godwit	—	—	—	—	—	—	—	—	—
Marbled Godwit	• U U	• U O U	—	• C C U	—	R R	—	R	—
Ruddy Turnstone	U R R	O	U R	U U	—	R R	—	—	—
Black Turnstone	—	—	—	—	—	—	—	—	—
Surfbird	—	—	—	—	—	—	—	—	—
Red Knot	—	—	—	—	—	—	—	—	—
Sanderling	O O	O	—	U U	—	—	—	R	R
Semipalmated Sandpiper	C C U	C C C	C C	C A	—	R R	—	O O R	O O
Western Sandpiper	R	U U U	—	U U	—	R R	—	R	O O O

MS-4 Gulf Is.	MO-1 Annada	MO-2 Mingo	MO-3 Squaw Cr.	MO-4 Swan L	MT-1 Benton L.	MT-2 Bowdoin	MT-3 Russell	MT-4 Lee Metcalf	MT-5 Medicine L.	MT-6 Bison Range	MT-7 Ninepipe
•s S F W	•s S F W	•s S F W	•s S F W	•s S F W	•s S F W	•s S F W	•s S F W	•s S F W	•s S F W	•s S F W	•s S F W
—	—	—	—	—	—	—	—	—	—	—	—
—	—	—	—	—	•UUCU	•UUUU	•CCCC	OOOO	•UUUU	•CCCC	OOOO
—	—	—	—	—	—	—	—	—	—	•OOOO	—
—	—	—	•CCCC	•RRRR	•UUUU	•AAAA	•CCCC	•A·AAA	•CCCC	•CCAC	•CAAA
—	—	—	—	—	—	—	—	—	—	•UUUU	—
—	—	—	—	—	—	—	—	—	—	—	—
—	—	—	—	—	—	—	—	—	—	—	—
—	—	—	—	—	—	—	—	•UUUU	—	•OOOO	—
—	—	—	—	—	—	•UUU	•CCCC	—	—	—	—
—	—	—	—	—	•OOOO	•CCCC	•CCCC	—	•CCCC	—	—
—	—	•CCCC	•UUUU	•OOOO	—	—	•UUUU	—	—	—	—
OOOO	•CCCC	•UUUU	•UUUU	•CCCC	—	—	—	—	—	—	—
—	—	—	—	—	—	—	—	—	—	—	—
—	—	—	—	—	—	—	—	—	—	—	—
—	—	RR	RR	—	—	—	—	—	—	ORR	—
—	—	—	—	—	—	—	—	—	—	—	—
CCCC	—	—	—	—	—	—	—	—	—	—	—
RRRR	—	RR	•UUU	•OO	—	—	—	—	—	—	—
U UU	UR	U U	•UOU	UU	—	•UUU	RR	•UUUR	•UUU	RRR	OOO
O UO	•CUC	C C	CUC	CCU	•UCU	• CC	•RR	•UUUR	•CCO	•OOO	•UUO
OOO	—	R	—	—	—	—	—	—	—	—	—
UUUU	—	R	OO	—	—	—	—	—	—	—	—
COCC	•CUAU	CRAC	•AOAR	CUCR	•CAA	•AAA	—	•AAAU	•AAAO	•UUUO	•UCAO
—	—	—	—	—	—	—	—	—	—	—	—
—	—	—	RR	R RR	O O	O O	C C	•OOO	C A	—	O
—	—	—	—	—	—	—	—	—	RR	—	—
CUCC	C O	—	C U	CUU	U U	COC	R	O O	O O	OO	OOO
O R	U R	R	C U	UUU	O O	R	RR	—	R O	—	—
UUUO	—	—	R	—	—	—	R	—	—	—	—
RRO	—	—	—	—	—	—	—	—	—	—	—
UOUO	O U	RRR	UUO	UUU	U U	U	C C	C O	O O	O	ORO
OOOO	—	—	OOR	ORO	—	•RR	—	•UUU	OOU	—	—
COCC	•CCCO	•CCCU	•CCCO	•CCCO	•UCC	•AAAR	•CAC	•AAAU	•AAC	•CCCO	•CACO
—	—	—	—	—	—	—	—	•UUU	—	—	—
R R	—	—	—	—	—	—	—	—	—	—	—
—	—	—	—	—	—	—	—	—	—	—	—
R R	—	—	—	—	•OOO	RR	—	R	R	—	—
R R	R	—	—	UOU	•CAC	•AAA	•UUU	OOO	•CAC	OO	•CCO
O OO	CCC	UUU	CUC	CUC	OOO	UUU	CCC	ORO	COC	UUU	UUC
U OO	CCC	CCC	CCC	ACA	UAU	CCC	CCC	ORC	COC	OOO	UUC
RR	CCC	CCR	UUU	UUU	OOO	—	CCC	R O	R U	UU	OOO
CCCC	R	—	URO	RRR	•UUU	•AAC	•CUC	RO	•CCU	RRR	OOO
CUCU	•CCC	•UCR	•CCC	•CCC	•OUO	•CUC	CCC	UCUR	•CUU	•CCC	•UUU
RR	O	R R	•OOO	•UUU	•UCC	•OOO	•UOU	—	•CCC	—	—
R R	—	—	R	—	R	—	RR	RR	—	—	—
R	—	—	RR	—	•OOO	•CUC	•UUU	OO	ORO	RRR	RR
—	—	—	OR	U R	R	—	—	—	—	—	—
—	—	—	—	—	—	—	—	—	—	—	—
RRR	—	—	OOR	R	•CUC	•CAC	UUU	RO	•CCU	R	UU
UOCU	—	—	UOR	O O	RR	R	RR	—	R O	—	—
—	—	—	—	—	—	—	—	—	—	—	—
RRRR	—	—	RR	—	R	—	—	—	R O	—	—
CUCC	—	R R	OOO	UUU	O O	UUU	UU	RRR	U	—	UO
UUC	UUU	UUR	CCC	CUC	O O	UU	RR	OOO	O O	OO	UO
URCO	RU	—	OOR	O O	O O	UU	R	OOO	OOO	—	—

STATE-NUMBER OF BIRD LIST REFUGE, SANCTUARY OR PRESERVE NESTING, ABUNDANCE BY SEASON	MN-1 Agassiz •s S F W	MN-2 Big Stone •s S F W	MN-3 MN Valley •s S F W	MN-4 MN WPA •s S F W	MN-5 Sherburne •s S F W	MN-6 Tamarac •s S F W	MS-1 Sandhill Cr. •s S F W	MS-2 Noxubee •s S F W	MS-3 Yazoo •s S F W
SANDPIPERS (cont.)									
Least Sandpiper	C C C	C U C	C C	C C	R	U U U	—	U U U	O O O
White-rumped Sandpiper	O R O	U O U	U	U C U	R	—	—	R	—
Baird's Sandpiper	O O O	U O U	—	C U	—	R R	—	—	O O
Pectoral Sandpiper	C C C	C C C	C C	C C	R	U U U	—	U U C	O O O
Sharp-tailed Sandpiper	—	—				—			—
Purple Sandpiper	—	—				—			—
Rock Sandpiper	—	—							
Dunlin	U O	U O U	U R	U U	—	R R	—	R	O O
Curlew Sandpiper	—	—				—			
Stilt Sandpiper	U U U	U O U	U U	U U	—	R R	—	R R	—
Buff-breasted Sandpiper	R R	—						R	
Ruff								—	—
Short-billed Dowitcher	U O U	—	R R	U U	—	R R	—	R	O
Long-billed Dowitcher	C O C	O O O	U U	U U	R	R R	O O O	R	O O
Common Snipe	•C C C	•C C C	C C C	•C C C	•C U C R	•C C C	U U U U	U R U U	C C C
American Woodcock	•U U U	•U U U	C R O	•C C C	•C U U	•C U C	U U U	U R U U	U U U
Wilson's Phalarope	•C U U	C U	C O	•C U	U	U U R	—	—	—
Red-necked Phalarope	U U	—	O O	—	R	R R	—	—	—
Red Phalarope	—	—	—	—		—			—
SKUAS, GULLS, TERNS & SKIMMERS									
Pomarine Jaeger	—	—				—			—
Parasitic Jaeger	—	—	R R	—		—			—
Long-tailed Jaeger	—	—	—	—		—			—
Laughing Gull	—	—	—	—		—			—
Franklin's Gull	•A A C	•C C A	C C	A A A	U	U U U	—	—	R
Little Gull	—	—	—	—		—			—
Common Black-headed Gull	—	—				—			
Bonaparte's Gull	U O U	U O U	U U	C C	R	—	—	R R	—
Heermann's Gull	—	—				—			
Mew Gull	—	—	—	—		—			—
Ring-billed Gull	C U C	C U C R	A A	A A A R	U U	C C C	—	U U	U U
California Gull	—	—	—	—		—			—
Herring Gull	U U	U U U R	C U C	U U U	U U	U U U	—	O	O
Thayer's Gull	—	—	—	—		—			—
Iceland Gull	—	—	R R	—		—			—
Lesser Black-backed Gull	—	—				—			
Western Gull	—	—				—			
Glaucous-winged Gull	—	—				—			
Glaucous Gull	—	R R	U U	—		—			—
Great Black-backed Gull	—	—				—			
Black-legged Kittiwake	—	—				—			
Sabine's Gull	—	—				—			
Gull-billed Tern	—	—				—			
Caspian Tern	O O O	O O O	U U	U U U	—	U U U	—	R R	—
Royal Tern	—	—	—	—		—			—
Elegant Tern	—	—				—			
Sandwich Tern	—	—				—			
Roseate Tern	—	—	—	—		—			—
Common Tern	O R R	•C C C	C C	•C C C	U U	C C U	—	O	—
Arctic Tern	—	—	—	—		—			—
Aleutian Tern	—	—	—	—		—			—
Forster's Tern	•C C O	•C C U	C C C	•C C C	—	U U U	—	—	R R
Least Tern	—	—	—	—		—			R
Bridled Tern	—	—				—			
Sooty Tern	—	—				—			
Black Tern	•C C O	•C C O	C C C	•A A A	•C C	C C U	—	O O	—
Black Skimmer	—	—				—			
AUKS, MURRES & PUFFINS									
Dovekie	—	—	—	—		—			—
Common Murre	—	—	—	—		—			—
Thick-billed Murre	—	—	—	—		—			—
Razorbill	—	—	—	—		—			—
Black Guillemot	—	—	—	—		—			—
Pigeon Guillemot	—	—	—	—		—			—
Marbled Murrelet	—	—	—	—		—			—
Kittlitz's Murrelet	—	—	—	—		—			—
Ancient Murrelet	—	—	—	—		—			—
Cassin's Auklet	—	—	—	—		—			—
Crested Auklet	—	—	—	—		—			—
Rhinoceros Auklet	—	—	—	—		—			—
Tufted Puffin	—	—	—	—		—			—

	MS-4 Gulf Is.	MO-1 Annada	MO-2 Mingo	MO-3 Squaw Cr.	MO-4 Swan L	MT-1 Benton L.	MT-2 Bowdoin	MT-3 Russell	MT-4 Lee Metcalf	MT-5 Medicine L.	MT-6 Bison Range	MT-7 Ninepipe
	•s S F W	•s S F W	•s S F W	•s S F W	•s S F W	•s S F W	•s S F W	•s S F W	•s S F W	•s S F W	•s S F W	•s S F W
	O OO	C C C	U U U	C C C	C U C	U U	C R C	C C	C O O	C O C	—	O U O
	R	—	R	C U U	U U	—	U U U	R	—	O C C	—	U O
	R R	R R	U U O	U U O	U R U	U U	U U	C C	—	U U	—	O O O
	U UR	C C C	•C C C	C U C	A C A	U U	U R U	R	R C C	U U	—	O O O
	—	—	—	—	—	—	—	—	—	—	—	—
	C O C C	U U	U U	U R U	O C	R R	—	R	—	O O	—	—
	R R	U R U	U R U	U U O	U U U	R	U	R	R	R R	R O	—
	R	—	—	R O O	O R O	—	—	—	—	—	—	—
	U O U O	U U	—	U U	U U U	—	U U	—	—	—	O O	U U U
	R	U U U	—	C O C	C U C	U C	C C C	C C	C C C	U C A	—	—
	C U C	C C O	C R C R	U O U R	C U C R	O O U	•C U C	•C C C	•C C C R	•U U C	C U C O	•U U C
	R R	•C C C	C R C R	•U O O	C U U	•C U C	•A A A	C C C	•C C C	•A C A	•U C	•C U
	R R	R O	U U	U O O	U R U	O O	O U O	U U	C C	O O O	O	C O
	—	R R	—	U O O	R R	O O	O U O	U U	C C	O O	O	C O
	—	—	—	—	—	—	—	R	—	—	—	—
	—	—	—	—	—	—	—	—	—	—	—	—
	C C C C	—	—	—	—	—	—	R	—	—	—	—
	—	O O	—	C O C	C U C	•A A U	•A A A	U C U	O O	.C A A	—	O O O
	—	—	—	—	—	—	—	—	—	—	—	—
	C C	R R	—	O R O	U U	O O	R R R	U U O	O O	R O	—	O
	—	—	—	—	—	—	—	R	—	—	—	—
	C U U C	C C C	U U	C O C O	C O U	•U O U	•A A A	•C A C	O	•A A C	O O	•C C C O
	—	—	—	—	—	•C C U	•A A A	•C A C O	O	•A A C	O	•U U U O
	C O U C	U U C	U U	U R U R	U O U	—	—	U	U R U U	R R	—	—
	—	—	—	—	—	—	—	—	—	—	—	—
	—	—	—	—	—	—	—	—	—	—	—	—
	—	—	—	—	—	—	—	—	—	—	—	—
	R	—	—	—	—	—	—	R R	—	—	—	—
	U R U	—	—	—	—	—	—	R R	—	—	—	—
	U U R	—	—	—	—	—	—	—	—	—	—	—
	U U U	U O U	—	O R O	O R U	—	—	O	R	U	—	—
	C C C C	—	—	—	—	—	—	—	—	—	—	—
	C U C R	—	—	—	—	—	—	—	—	—	—	—
	R R U R	O O	U	O U	U U U	•U U O	•C C C	•C C	R	•C C U	O O O	•U O U
	C C C C	U U	U	U O U	C O O	—	R R	•C C	O R R	U	R R	•C C U
	C C U	O	—	R O R	O	—	—	•C C	—	—	—	R
	R R	—	—	—	—	—	—	—	—	—	—	—
	U U U R	C O U	U R R	C C O	C U C	•U U O	•C C C	U U U	U O U	•C C U	O U U	•C C U
	C C C C	—	—	—	—	—	—	—	—	—	—	—
	—	—	—	—	—	—	—	—	—	—	—	—
	—	—	—	—	—	—	—	—	—	—	—	—
	—	—	—	—	—	—	—	—	—	—	—	—
	—	—	—	—	—	—	—	—	—	—	—	—
	—	—	—	—	—	—	—	—	—	—	—	—
	—	—	—	—	—	—	—	—	—	—	—	—
	—	—	—	—	—	—	—	—	—	—	—	—
	—	—	—	—	—	—	—	—	—	—	—	—
	—	—	—	—	—	—	—	—	—	—	—	—
	—	—	—	—	—	—	—	—	—	—	—	—
	—	—	—	—	—	—	—	—	—	—	—	—

BIRD CHART

STATE-NUMBER OF BIRD LIST REFUGE, SANCTUARY OR PRESERVE NESTING, ABUNDANCE BY SEASON	MN-1 Agassiz •s S F W	MN-2 Big Stone •s S F W	MN-3 MN Valley •s S F W	MN-4 MN WPA •s S F W	MN-5 Sherburne •s S F W	MN-6 Tamarac •s S F W	MS-1 Sandhill Cr. •s S F W	MS-2 Noxubee •s S F W	MS-3 Yazoo •s S F W
AUKS, MURRES & PUFFINS (cont.)									
Atlantic Puffin	—	—	—	—	—	—	—	—	—
Horned Puffin	—	—	—	—	—	—	—	—	—
PIGEONS & DOVES									
Rock Dove	R R R	•C C C C	A A A A	•A A A A	•C C C U	R R R R	U U U U	—	•C C C C
White-crowned Pigeon	—	—	—	—	—	—	—	—	—
Band-tailed Pigeon	—	—	—	—	—	—	—	—	—
White-winged Dove	—	—	—	—	—	—	—	—	—
Mourning Dove	•C C C	•C C C O	A A A	•A A A R	•C C C R	•C C C	•A A A A	C C C C	•C C C C
Inca Dove	—	—	—	—	—	—	—	—	—
Common Ground-Dove	—	—	—	—	—	—	U U U U	—	O O
White-tipped Dove	—	—	—	—	—	—	—	—	—
CUCKOOS, ROADRUNNERS & ANIS									
Black-billed Cuckoo	•U U U	U C C	C C C	•U U U	•C C	•U U	O O U	R R	—
Yellow-billed Cuckoo	—	U U U	U U U	•U U U	• U U	U U	U O U	U C C	•C C O
Mangrove Cuckoo	—	—	—	—	—	—	—	—	—
Greater Roadrunner	—	—	—	—	—	—	—	—	—
Smooth-billed Ani	—	—	—	—	—	—	—	—	—
Groove-billed Ani	—	—	—	—	—	—	—	—	—
BARN OWLS									
Barn Owl	—	—	—	—	—	—	—	R R R R	•O O O O
TYPICAL OWLS									
Flammulated Owl	—	—	—	—	—	—	—	—	—
Eastern Screech-Owl	R	•C C C C	U U U U	•U U U U	•C C C C	R R R R	•U U U U	U U U U	•C C C C
Western Screech-Owl	—	—	—	—	—	—	—	—	—
Great Horned Owl	•C C C C	•C C C C	U U U U	•C C C C	•U U U U	•C C C U	•U U U U	U U U U	•U U U U
Snowy Owl	O U U	O O	R	U U U	R	R R R	—	—	—
Northern Hawk Owl	—	—	—	—	—	—	—	—	—
Northern Pygmy-Owl	—	—	—	—	—	—	—	—	—
Elf Owl	—	—	—	—	—	—	—	—	—
Burrowing Owl	—	—	—	—	—	—	—	—	—
Spotted Owl	—	—	—	—	—	—	—	—	—
Barred Owl	R R R	O O O O	U U U U	•U U U U	•U U U R	•U U U U	U U U U	C C C C	•C C C C
Great Gray Owl	R	—	—	—	R	R R	—	—	—
Long-eared Owl	R	O	U R U R	•C C C U	•R R R	R R R	—	—	—
Short-eared Owl	•O O O	U U U U	U R U U	•U U U U	—	R R R	—	R R R	R R
Boreal Owl	—	—	—	—	—	R	—	—	—
Northern Saw-whet Owl	•R R R	R	R R R R	•R R R R	—	U U U	—	—	—
NIGHTJARS									
Lesser Nighthawk	—	—	—	—	—	—	—	—	—
Common Nighthawk	•U O U	•C C C	A A A	•C C C	•C C U	U U U	•C C C U	O C O R	•O U O
Pauraque	—	—	—	—	—	—	—	—	—
Common Poorwill	—	—	—	—	—	—	—	—	—
Chuck-will's-widow	—	—	—	—	—	—	•C C C U	U C	O O
Whip-poor-will	•U U	—	R R	R R R	•U U	R R R	R R R	U U	O O
SWIFTS									
Black Swift	—	—	—	—	—	—	—	—	—
Chimney Swift	R R	•C U C	C C C	•C C C	•U U	•C C C	C C C	C C C	•U C U
Vaux's Swift	—	—	—	—	—	—	—	—	—
White-throated Swift	—	—	—	—	—	—	—	—	—
HUMMINGBIRDS									
Buff-bellied Hummingbird	—	—	—	—	—	—	—	—	—
Ruby-throated Hummingbird	•U U U	•U U O	C C C	•C C U	• U U	•C C C	C U U	C C C	•U C U
Black-chinned Hummingbird	—	—	—	—	—	—	—	—	—
Anna's Hummingbird	—	—	—	—	—	—	—	—	—
Costa's Hummingbird	—	—	—	—	—	—	—	—	—
Calliope Hummingbird	—	—	—	—	—	—	—	—	—
Broad-tailed Hummingbird	—	—	—	—	—	—	—	—	—
Rufous Hummingbird	—	—	—	—	—	—	—	—	—
Allen's Hummingbird	—	—	—	—	—	—	—	—	—
KINGFISHERS									
Belted Kingfisher	•U O U	•C C O R	C C C R	•C C C U	•C C C R	•C C C	•A U A A	C C C C	U O U U
Green Kingfisher	—	—	—	—	—	—	—	—	—
WOODPECKERS									
Lewis' Woodpecker	—	—	—	—	—	—	—	—	—
Red-headed Woodpecker	O O O	•U C O	C C C O	•U U U	•C U U R	•U U U	•C C C C	C C C C	•C C C C
Acorn Woodpecker	—	—	—	—	—	—	—	—	—
Gila Woodpecker	—	—	—	—	—	—	—	—	—
Golden-fronted Woodpecker	—	—	—	—	—	—	—	—	—
Red-bellied Woodpecker	—	•R R R R	O O O O	R R R R	R R	—	•C C C C	C C C C	•C C C C
Yellow-bellied Sapsucker	U U	•C C U	—	•C C C	•C U U	•C C C	U U U	U U U	U U C
Red-breasted Sapsucker	—	—	—	—	—	—	—	—	—

	MS-4 Gulf Is.	MO-1 Annada	MO-2 Mingo	MO-3 Squaw Cr.	MO-4 Swan L.	MT-1 Benton L.	MT-2 Bowdoin	MT-3 Russell	MT-4 Lee Metcalf	MT-5 Medicine L.	MT-6 Bison Range	MT-7 Ninepipe
	• s S F W	• s S F W	• s S F W	• s S F W	• s S F W	• s S F W	• s S F W	• s S F W	• s S F W	• s S F W	• s S F W	• s S F W
	—	—	—	—	—	—	—	—	—	—	—	—
	—	—	—	—	—	—	—	—	—	—	—	—
	U U U U	—	•U U U U	•O O O O	•C C C C	O O O	—	O O O O	U U U U	•U U U U	—	—
		R										
	C C C C	•C C C U	•A A A C	•C C C O	•A A A U	•U C C	•C C C	•A A A	•C C C	•C C C	•A A A U	•U U U
	U U U U	—	—	—	—	—	—	—	—	—	—	—
	O C O	R R	•U U	•U U U	U	R	• R	• U U	R	•U U	R	
	C C	•C C C U	•A A U	•C C U	•C C C O	—	•R R		—	—	—	—
	—	—	—	—	—	—	—	—	—	—	—	—
	R R	—	—	—	—	—	—	—	—	—	—	—
	R R R R	—	•R R R R	•R R R R	•R R R R	—	R R R	—	—	—	—	—
									R R			
	C C C C	•C C C C	•U U U U	•C C C C	•C C C C	—	—	—	—	—	O O O O	—
	U U U U	•U U U U	•U U U U	•C C C C	•C C C C	O O O R	•C C C	•C C C C	•U U U U	•U U U U	•C C C C	•C U U U
						U	U U	O	U U U U	U U	O O	O
	R R	—	—	—	—	•O O O	• U U	•C C C	R	•U U O	O O O	—
	O O O O	•C C C C	•C C C C	•C C C C	•C C C C	—	—	—	—	R	—	—
	—	O	R R R	O R U	—	R R	•O O U	•C C C C		R R	U U U	O
	R	O O	R R	O R O U	U O U U	•C C C O	•C C C U	•C C C C	O	•C C C O	•C C U C	•C U C C
	—	—	R	O	—	—	R R R	U U U U	U U U U	—	O	—
	C C U	•U U O	•U U	O U O	•U U U	R O R	•C C C	U A A	• C C	•U U U	• A	•O C U
								C A C				
	C C U	O	•C C	•U U	—	—	—	—	—	—	—	—
	R R R	•O	•C C	•U U R	•U U U	—	—	—	—	—	—	—
	—	•C C C	•C C	•U U	•C C C	—	—	•O U	O O O	—	U C U	U O
	U C U R	—	—	—	—	—	—	—	—	R	—	R
	—	—	—	—	—	—	—	• U	•O O	—	R	—
									O O			
	U O U	•C C O	•C C	•O U O	C U U	—	• R	R R R	—	R	—	U U
									U U U		R	
									•U U U	—	U	U U
									•U U U	—	R O	U C O
	U O C C	•U U U O	•C C U U	U U U R	•C C C O	R R	U O	•C O C	•U U U U	•O O O	•U U U O	O O O O
									•U U U	—	•C C U	O O O
	U C U U	•C C C C	•C C A A	•C C C U	•C C C C	—	• R R	•C C C	—	R R R	—	—
	C C C C	•C C C C	•C C C C	•C C C C	•C C C C	—	—	—	—	—	•C C C	O O O
	U U U	C C	C C	U O	O O U	U R U R	—	R R R	R	—	—	—
									•U U U			

STATE-NUMBER OF BIRD LIST / REFUGE, SANCTUARY OR PRESERVE / NESTING, ABUNDANCE BY SEASON	MN-1 Agassiz • s S F W	MN-2 Big Stone • s S F W	MN-3 MN Valley • s S F W	MN-4 MN WPA • s S F W	MN-5 Sherburne • s S F W	MN-6 Tamarac • s S F W	MS-1 Sandhill Cr. • s S F W	MS-2 Noxubee • s S F W	MS-3 Yazoo • s S F W
WOODPECKERS (cont.)									
Williamson's Sapsucker	—	—	—	—	—	—	—	—	—
Ladder-backed Woodpecker	—	—	—	—	—	—	—	—	—
Nuttall's Woodpecker	—	—	—	—	—	—	—	—	—
Downy Woodpecker	•C C C C	•C C C C	C C C C	•C C C C	•C C C C	•C C C C	•C C C C	C C C C	•C C C C
Hairy Woodpecker	•U U U U	•C C C C	C C C C	•C C C C	•C C C C	•C C C C	O O O O	U U U U	•U U U U
Red-cockaded Woodpecker	—	—	—	—	—	—	—	U U U U	—
Three-toed Woodpecker	—	—	—	—	—	R R	—	—	—
Black-backed Woodpecker	R R R R	—	—	—	—	R R	—	—	—
Northern Flicker	•C C C	•C C C O	A C A U	•C C C R	•C C C U	•A C A	•C C C C	C C C C	•C C C C
Pileated Woodpecker	•R R R R	O O O O	U U U U	•U U U U	•U U U U	•U U U U	•U U U C	C C C C	•U U U U
TYRANT FLYCATCHERS									
Olive-sided Flycatcher	R	—	U U	—	•U U	U U U	—	R	R R
Western Wood-Pewee	—	—	—	—	—	—	—	—	—
Eastern Wood-Pewee	•C C U	•O O O	U U U	•C C C	•U U	•C C C	—	C C C	•U U U
Yellow-bellied Flycatcher	R	—	U U	U R U	—	R R	—	—	—
Acadian Flycatcher	—	—	—	—	—	—	—	C C O	•U C O
Alder Flycatcher	•U U	—	U U	•C C C	• U	U U R	—	—	—
Willow Flycatcher	—	U	U O U	R R R	—	—	—	—	—
Least Flycatcher	•C C U	C O C	C C C	•C C C	•U U	•C C C	—	U R U	—
Hammond's Flycatcher	—	—	—	—	—	—	—	—	—
Dusky Flycatcher	—	—	—	—	—	—	—	—	—
Gray Flycatcher	—	—	—	—	—	—	—	—	—
Western Flycatcher	—	—	—	—	—	—	—	—	—
Black Phoebe	—	—	—	—	—	—	—	—	—
Eastern Phoebe	•U U U	•U O O	C C C	•C C C	•C C C	•C C C	U U U	C U C U	U U U U
Say's Phoebe	—	—	—	—	—	—	—	—	—
Vermilion Flycatcher	—	—	—	—	—	—	—	—	O
Ash-throated Flycatcher	—	—	—	—	—	—	—	—	—
Great Crested Flycatcher	•U U O	U O O	C C C	•C C C	•U U U	•C C C	U U U	C C	•U U
Brown-crested Flycatcher	—	—	—	—	—	—	—	—	—
Great Kiskadee	—	—	—	—	—	—	—	—	—
Couch's Kingbird	—	—	—	—	—	—	—	—	—
Cassin's Kingbird	—	—	—	—	—	—	—	—	—
Western Kingbird	U O	•U U U	—	•C C C	R R	R R R	—	—	—
Eastern Kingbird	•C C O	•C C U	C C C	•C C C	•C C	•C C C	•C C C	C C U	•U C C O
Gray Kingbird	—	—	—	—	—	—	—	—	—
Scissor-tailed Flycatcher	—	—	—	—	—	—	—	—	O
LARKS									
Horned Lark	•U U U U	•C U C C	C U C U	•A C A C	C C	C C C R	—	—	•C U U C
SWALLOWS									
Purple Martin	•U U	•U C O	C C C	•C C C	•U U U	•C C U	•C C C	C C U	•C C C
Tree Swallow	•C C U	•C C A	A A A	•C C C	•A A A	•C C C	•C C A	C C	C C O
Violet-green Swallow	—	—	—	—	—	—	—	—	—
Northern Rough-winged Swallow	R	•C U C	C C C	•C C C	R R	•U U U	U U	U R U	U U U
Bank Swallow	U U O	•C C C	C C C	•C C C	•U U	U U U	U U	C C C	—
Cliff Swallow	•C A U	•C C C	C U C	•U U U	•C C C	•C C C	U U	R	—
Barn Swallow	•C C C	•C C C	C C C	•C C C	•C C C	•C C C	C C C O	C C C	•U C U
JAYS, MAGPIES & CROWS									
Gray Jay	•R R R O	—	—	—	R	R R R	•C C C C	—	•C C C C
Steller's Jay	—	—	—	—	—	—	—	—	—
Blue Jay	•U U U	•C C C C	A A A A	•C C C C	•A A A A	•C C C C	—	C C C C	—
Green Jay	—	—	—	—	—	—	—	—	—
Scrub Jay	—	—	—	—	—	—	—	—	—
Pinyon Jay	—	—	—	—	—	—	—	—	—
Clark's Nutcracker	—	—	—	—	—	—	—	—	—
Black-billed Magpie	•U U U U	O R O	—	R U U	—	R R R	—	—	—
American Crow	•C C C	•C C C U	A A A A	•C C C U	•C C C C	•C C C U	•A A A A	C C C C	•U U U U
Northwestern Crow	—	—	—	—	—	—	—	—	—
Fish Crow	—	—	—	—	—	—	•C C C C	R R	O O O O
Chihuahuan Raven	—	—	—	—	—	—	—	—	—
Common Raven	•U R U C	—	—	—	—	R R U	—	—	—
TITMICE									
Black-capped Chickadee	•C C C C	•C C C C	A A A A	•C C C C	•C C C C	•C C C C	—	—	—
Carolina Chickadee	—	—	—	—	—	—	•C C C C	C C C C	•C C C C
Mountain Chickadee	—	—	—	—	—	—	—	—	—
Boreal Chickadee	R R	—	—	R R	—	R R R	—	—	—
Chestnut-backed Chickadee	—	—	—	—	—	—	—	—	—
Plain Titmouse	—	—	—	—	—	—	—	—	—
Tufted Titmouse	—	—	R R R R	—	—	—	•U U U U	C C C C	•U U U U
VERDINS									
Verdin	—	—	—	—	—	—	—	—	—

	MS-4 Gulf Is.	MO-1 Annada	MO-2 Mingo	MO-3 Squaw Cr.	MO-4 Swan L	MT-1 Benton L.	MT-2 Bowdoin	MT-3 Russell	MT-4 Lee Metcalf	MT-5 Medicine L.	MT-6 Bison Range	MT-7 Ninepipe
	•s S F W	•s S F W	•s S F W	•s S F W	•s S F W	•s S F W	•s S F W	•s S F W	•s S F W	•s S F W	•s S F W	•s S F W
	—	—	—	—	—	—	—	—	—	—	—	—
	—	—	—	—	—	—	—	—	—	—	—	—
	—	—	—	—	—	—	—	—	—	—	—	—
	C C C C	•C C C C	•C C C C	•C C C C	•C C C C	R R	•C U U C	•C C C C	•C C C C	R R R	•C C C U	O O O O
	O O O O	•U U U U	•U U U U	•U U U U	•U U U U	—	•C U U	•C C C U	•C C C C	R R R	•C C C U	O O
	R R R R	—	—	—	—	—	—	—	—	—	—	—
	—	—	—	—	—	—	—	—	—	—	—	—
	C C C C	•C C C C	•C C C A	•C C C U	•C C C U	O O	•C C C U	•C C C U	•C C C U	•O O O R	•C C C O	•C C C U
	U U U U	•C C C C	•U U U U	—	•U O O C	—	—	—	•U U U U	—	O O O O	•C C C U
	—	—	•U U	U R U	R O R	—	—	—	—	O	—	—
	—	—	—	—	—	—	R	•C C U	•U U	O O	•U U	O
	U U C	C C C	•C C	•U U O	•C C C	—	—	—	—	—	—	—
	O	U U	R R	R R	—	—	—	—	—	—	—	—
	U U U	C C C	•C C	•U U U	O O	—	—	—	—	—	—	—
	—	R O	U	U U	—	—	—	—	—	U	U U	—
	—	R O	U	•U U	•C	—	•C C O	O O	•U U	O U	U U	O
	R O	—	U	U U	—	—	O O	C C	U U	O U	—	—
	—	—	—	—	—	—	—	—	—	U	U U	—
	—	—	—	—	—	—	—	O O	•U U	—	O O	O
	U C U	•U U U	•C C R R	•U U U	•C C C	—	—	—	—	U	R R	O O U
	—	—	—	—	—	•U U U	•U O U	•C C C	—	U U	—	—
	C C C	•C C C	•C C	•U U U	•U O U	—	—	—	—	—	—	—
	—	—	—	—	—	—	—	—	—	—	—	—
	—	—	—	—	—	—	—	—	—	—	—	—
	R R	—	—	O R O	R R	U O U	•U U U	•C O	•U U U	•A A O	•C C	•U C O
	C C U	•C C C	•C C	•C C U	•C C C	•U C U	•A A A	•C A	•C C U	•A A O	•C C	•U C O
	O O O	—	—	—	—	—	—	—	—	—	—	—
	R R	—	—	—	—	—	—	R	—	—	—	—
	—	C C C C	•C U U C	•U U U C	•C C U U	•C C C A	•C C C	•A A A U	U	•A A A A	O O O C	•O O O C
	C C C O	•C C C	•U U	•C C C	U U U	—	—	—	—	R R	—	—
	U C O	•C C A	•A A U	•C U C	•C U A	O O O	U U	•C U C	•C C C	•U O U	•A A C	•C C C
			—	—	—	O R O	—	•U U U	U O O	—	•C C U	C O C
	U O U	•C C C	•U U	U U U	•C C A	•O O O	•C C C	•U U U	•C O O	•U O U	•C C U	U O U
	R R O	•C C C	•U U	•A C A	•C C C	O O O	•C C C	•C A C	•C O O	•A A U	•A A C	•C C U
	O O	C C C	•R R	C A A	U O U	•U C U	•A A A	•C C C	•C O O	•A A U	•C A A	•C C U
	C U C R	•C C C	•C C	•C C A	•C C C	•C A U	•A A A	•C C C	•C C O	•C C U	•C C C	•C C U
	—	—	—	—	—	—	—	—	—	—	R	—
	—	—	—	—	—	—	—	—	—	R	R O	—
	C C C C	•C C C C	•C C C C	•C C C C	•C C C C	—	U U U U	U O U U	—	R	—	—
	—	—	—	—	—	—	—	C A C	—	—	—	—
	—	—	—	—	—	—	—	R R R	—	R	—	•C C C C
	—	—	—	—	—	•O O O R	•A A A A	•C A C A	•A A A A	•C C C C	•A A A A	•C C C C
	O O O O	•C C C C	•C C C A	•C C C C	•C C C C	•O O	C R C	•C C C	•O O O O	•C O C	•C U C	•C C U R
	C C C C	—	•U U U R	—	—	—	—	—	—	—	—	—
	—	—	—	—	—	—	—	—	R O	U U U U	—	O O O O
	—	—	—	—	—	—	—	—	R O		O O U	O O O O
	—	•C C C C	U	•C C C C	•C C C C	—	C C C	•C C C C	•C C C C	O O O O	•C C C C	U O U U
	C C C C	—	•C C C C	—	—	—	—	U	O O O	O	C U C C	O O O
	—	—	—	—	—	—	—	—	—	—	—	—
	—	—	—	—	—	—	—	—	—	—	—	—
	—	—	—	—	—	—	—	—	—	—	—	—
	C C C C	•C C C C	•C C C C	•C C C C	•C C C C	—	—	—	—	—	—	—
	—	—	—	—	—	—	—	—	—	—	—	—

STATE-NUMBER OF BIRD LIST REFUGE, SANCTUARY OR PRESERVE NESTING, ABUNDANCE BY SEASON	MN-1 Agassiz • s S F W	MN-2 Big Stone • s S F W	MN-3 MN Valley • s S F W	MN-4 MN WPA • s S F W	MN-5 Sherburne • s S F W	MN-6 Tamarac • s S F W	MS-1 Sandhill Cr. • s S F W	MS-2 Noxubee • s S F W	MS-3 Yazoo • s S F W
BUSHTITS									
Bushtit	—	—	—	—	—	—	—	—	—
NUTHATCHES									
Red-breasted Nuthatch	O O	O	U R U U	U U	R R	U U U U	R R	R R	O O
White-breasted Nuthatch	•U O U O	•C C C C	A A A A	•C C C C	•C C C C	•C C C C	—	U U U U	R R O
Pygmy Nuthatch	—	—	—	—	—	—	—	—	—
Brown-headed Nuthatch	—	—	—	—	—	—	C C C C	C C C C	—
CREEPERS									
Brown Creeper	O O	U C U	U U U U	U U U	R R	U U U U	—	U U	R O
WRENS									
Cactus Wren	—	—	—	—	—	—	—	—	—
Rock Wren	—	—	—	—	—	—	—	—	—
Canyon Wren	—	—	—	—	—	—	—	—	—
Carolina Wren	—	—	—	—	—	—	•U U U U	A A A A	•C C C C
Bewick's Wren	—	—	—	—	—	—	—	R R R R	—
House Wren	•U C U	•C C C	A A A	•C C C	•C C C	•C C C	•U U C	R	U U U U
Winter Wren	•R O R	O R	U U	U U	R	U U U	U U U	U U U	U U U
Sedge Wren	•U C U	•C A A	C C C	•U U U	•C C C	•C C C	•C C C	R R R	O O O
Marsh Wren	•A A U	•U U U	C C C	•C C C	• U U	•C C C	U U U	U	O O U
DIPPERS									
American Dipper	—	—	—	—	—	—	—	—	—
OLD WORLD WARBLERS & THRUSHES									
Arctic Warbler	—	—	—	—	—	—	—	—	—
Golden-crowned Kinglet	•C U C	U C O	U U U	C C R	R R	C C	•U U U	U U C	U U U
Ruby-crowned Kinglet	•C U C	C C	C C U	C C	U U	C C	U U C	U U C	U U C
Blue-gray Gnatcatcher	—	—	U U U	—	R	—	•U O U U	C C C R	•O U U O
Black-tailed Gnatcatcher	—	—	—	—	—	—	—	—	—
Eastern Bluebird	O	•U O U	C C C	•C C C	•C C C	•C C C	•C C C A	C C C C	O O U U
Western Bluebird	—	—	—	—	—	—	—	—	—
Mountain Bluebird	—	—	—	—	—	—	—	—	—
Townsend's Solitaire	—	—	—	—	—	—	—	—	—
Veery	•U C O	O O	C R U	U U	•C C	•C C C	U U	O O	U U
Gray-cheeked Thrush	O O	O O	C C	U U	U U	U U	U U	U U	U U
Swainson's Thrush	U O	U U	C C	C C	U	U U	U U	U U	U U
Hermit Thrush	U U	U U	C C	C C	•U U U	•U U U	U U C	U U	U U
Wood Thrush	—	O O	U U U	—	•U U	•U U U	U U	C C O	•U C U
American Robin	•C C C	•C C C O	A A A U	•A A A R	•A C C R	•A A U R	•C U C A	C U C C	•C U C U
Varied Thrush	—	—	—	—	—	—	—	—	—
Wrentit	—	—	—	—	—	—	—	—	—
MOCKINGBIRDS, THRASHERS & ALLIES									
Gray Catbird	•U C U	•C C C	C C C	•C C C	•C C C	•C C C	•U O U A	U U U R	•U O O O
Northern Mockingbird	R	—	—	—	—	—	•A A A A	C C C C	•C C C U
Sage Thrasher	—	—	—	—	—	—	—	—	—
Brown Thrasher	•U U	•C C C	C C C	•C C C	•C C C	•U U U	•C C C C	C C C C	•C C C U
Long-billed Thrasher	—	—	—	—	—	—	—	—	—
Bendire's Thrasher	—	—	—	—	—	—	—	—	—
Curve-billed Thrasher	—	—	—	—	—	—	—	—	—
Crissal Thrasher	—	—	—	—	—	—	—	—	—
Le Conte's Thrasher	—	—	—	—	—	—	—	—	—
WAGTAILS & PIPITS									
American Pipit	O U	—	U U	C C	—	—	U U	U U	U U
Sprague's Pipit	—	—	—	—	—	—	—	—	—
WAXWINGS									
Bohemian Waxwing	R R O	—	U U U	U U	—	U U U	—	—	—
Cedar Waxwing	•U C U	U U U O	C U C C	•C C C C	•U C C U	•C U C U	C O C A	U R U C	U U U
SILKY-FLYCATCHERS									
Phainopepla	—	—	—	—	—	—	—	—	—
SHRIKES									
Northern Shrike	O U C	U U U	U U U	R U U	U U U	U U U	—	—	—
Loggerhead Shrike	—	U	U R U	U U U	U R	R R R	•C U C C	C C C C	•U U U C
STARLINGS									
European Starling	•U U U	•C C C C	A A A A	•A A A A	•C C C U	•C C C U	•U U U U	C C C C	•C C C C
VIREOS									
White-eyed Vireo	—	—	—	—	—	—	•C C C C	C A C R	•U U U O
Bell's Vireo	—	—	R R R	—	—	—	—	—	—
Black-capped Vireo	—	—	—	—	—	—	—	—	—
Gray Vireo	—	—	—	—	—	—	—	—	—
Solitary Vireo	O O	U	U U	C C U	U U	U U	U U	R R	O O U
Yellow-throated Vireo	•O U O	—	U U U	•C C U	•U U U	•U U U	U U	U U U R	•O U O
Hutton's Vireo	—	—	—	—	—	—	—	—	—
Warbling Vireo	•U C U	C U U	C C C	•C C C	•C C	•C C C	—	U U	R
Philadelphia Vireo	O O	U	U U	U U	—	U U	—	R R	O

	MS-4 Gulf Is.	MO-1 Annada	MO-2 Mingo	MO-3 Squaw Cr.	MO-4 Swan L.	MT-1 Benton L.	MT-2 Bowdoin	MT-3 Russell	MT-4 Lee Metcalf	MT-5 Medicine L.	MT-6 Bison Range	MT-7 Ninepipe
season	•s S F W	•s S F W	•s S F W	•s S F W	•s S F W	•s S F W	•s S F W	•s S F W	•s S F W	•s S F W	•s S F W	•s S F W
	—	—	—	—	—	—	—	—	—	—	—	—
	R U R	O O	—	R	R R O	—	O	R R R	C C C O	•U U U U	R R	•C U C C
	—	•C C C C	•U U C C	•U U U U	U U U U	—	—	O O R	•C C C C	•O O O O	O O O O	O O O
	C C C C	—	—	—	—	—	—	—	•O O O O	—	•C U C C	O O O
	R R	U U O	U U U	U U U	U U U	—	—	O R	•O O O O	R	U U U	
	—	—	—	—	—	O	R R R	C U C	—	—	•C C C	O
	C C C C	•C C C O	•C C C C	•O O O O	R R R R	—	—	—	—	—	•C C C	
	—	—	•R R R R	R R R	—	—	—	—	—	—	—	
	C C C	•O O	•C C C	•C C U	•C C C	—	•U C C	•C C C	•U U U	•U U O	•C C C	O O O
	R R	O O	C C	O O O	—	—	•R R R R	•U U U	R R R	—	—	—
	O O O	U O U	•R R R R	•U U U	•U U U	—	—	—	—	—	—	
	O R O O	O O O	U R R	•U U U	•U U U	U	•C C C	R C R	•C C C R	•C C C	O O	•C C U O
	—	—	—	—	—	—	—	U U	U U U U	—	•U U U U	—
	—	—	—	—	—	—	—	—	—	—	—	—
	O	U U O	U C C	U U C	U U U	—	—	O O	U U U O	R	O	O
	C C C	U U	U U R	C C O	U U R	O O	—	O O	U U U R	O O	•C C C	U U
	C U C U	•C C	•A A U	•U U	•U U O	—	—	R	—	—	—	—
	U U U U	•U U U U	•U U U U	•U U U R	•U U U O	—	—	•R R	—	O O	—	O O
	—	—	—	—	—	O O	U U	•C A C	•U U	U	C U C	•O O O
	U O	U U	R R	R R	—	O O	—	R O O O	U U U U	R R	U O C C	O O
	U U	U U	U U U	U U U	U	—	—	R	O O	O O O	O O O O	—
	C C	U U	U U U	C C C	U U	—	O O O	O U	O O	O	O O	O O
	U U U	U U	C C U	C O O R	C C	—	U U U	O U	—	—	O	O O
	C C C	•O O	•C C C	•U U	•C C C	—	R R	—	—	—	—	—
	U C C	•C C C O	•C C C C	•C C C O	•C C C O	O O O	•A A A	•C A C O	•A A A U	•U U U U	•A A A O	•C C U O
	—	—	—	—	—	R	—	—	—	R	R	—
	—	—	—	—	—	—	—	—	—	—	—	—
	C C U	•U U U	•C C C	•C C O	•C C C	—	C O	•C C C	•U U	•U U O	O O O	•U U O
	C C C C	•C C C O	•C C C C	•O O O R	•U U U U	R	R	R	—	—	—	—
								C C C				
	C C C C	•C C C O	•C C C U	•C C U	•C C C	R R R	C C C	•C C C	—	•C C O	—	R
	—	—	—	—	—	—	—	—	—	—	—	—
	—	—	—	—	—	—	—	—	—	—	—	—
	—	—	—	—	—	—	—	—	—	—	—	—
	U U	O O	—	R R	U U	C O C	O O	O O	O O	O U	U C	U C
	—	—	—	—	—	O O	•C C U	C C O	—	•O O O	—	—
	—	—	—	O	—	U	C C C	C C A	O O U	O O O	C C A	O O O
	U U C	•U U U U	U U U	•C U C O	C C O	—	•C C O O	•C U U O	•O O O O	O O O	•C C U	O O O
	—	—	—	—	—	—	—	—	—	—	—	—
	—	—	—	R	—	O	U	O O U	U	O O	O U U	U U U
	U U U U	•O U U O	•U U U U	U U U U	•U U U U	U U U	U U U	•C C C	R R	O O O	—	—
	C C C C	•C C C C	•A C A A	•C C C A	•C C C C	U U U	•C C A	•C C C O	•A A A U	•U U U O	•A A A U	•A C A U
	C C C O	•C C C	•C C	O R R	•U U U	—	—	—	—	—	—	—
	—	—	•U U	•C C U	•C C U	—	—	—	—	—	—	—
	—	—	—	—	—	—	—	—	—	—	—	—
	U O U	—	U U	O O	U U	—	—	—	•O O	O O	R R	O O
	U U O	U U	•C C U	•O U O	U R U	—	—	—	—	—	—	—
	R R	C C	•C C U	•C C U	•U U U	—	U U	C C O	•O O	O O O	•C C U	—
	R R	—	R R	U U		—						

STATE-NUMBER OF BIRD LIST / REFUGE, SANCTUARY OR PRESERVE / NESTING, ABUNDANCE BY SEASON (• s S F W)	MN-1 Agassiz	MN-2 Big Stone	MN-3 MN Valley	MN-4 MN WPA	MN-5 Sherburne	MN-6 Tamarac	MS-1 Sandhill Cr.	MS-2 Noxubee	MS-3 Yazoo
VIREOS (cont.)									
Red-eyed Vireo	•U U U	U O	C C C	•C C U	•C C C	•C C C	•U U	C C C	O U O
Black-whiskered Vireo	—	—						—	—
WOOD-WARBLERS									
Bachman's Warbler	—	—						—	
Blue-winged Warbler	—	—	R R R	—			—	U U	O O
Golden-winged Warbler	—	R	R R R	—	R R	•U U U	—	U U	O O
Tennessee Warbler	C C C	U	C C	C C	C U C	C C	U U	U U	C U
Orange-crowned Warbler	U R U	U C	C C	U U	R	C C	U U	U U U	U
Nashville Warbler	•O C U	C C	C C	C C	C U C	C U C	—	U U	U U
Virginia's Warbler	—	—	—	—	—	—	—	—	—
Lucy's Warbler	—	—	—	—	—	—	—	—	—
Northern Parula	U U	—	R R	—	—	U U U	•U U	U R U	•C C U
Tropical Parula	—	—	—	—	—	—	—	—	—
Yellow Warbler	•C C U	•C C C	C C C	•C C C	•C U	•C C U	—	U U	U U
Chestnut-sided Warbler	•O O	R	C R C	C C	U U	•C C C	—	U U	C U
Magnolia Warbler	U	U	C C	C C	U	U U	O	U U	C U
Cape May Warbler	U U U	U	U U	R	U	U U	—	—	—
Black-throated Blue Warbler	—	—	—	—	—	R R	—	U U	R R
Yellow-rumped Warbler	A U A	A C	A A	A C C	C C	•A U A	C U C A	C C A	U U C
Black-throated Gray Warbler	—	—	—	—	—	—	—	—	—
Townsend's Warbler	—	—	—	—	—	—	—	—	—
Hermit Warbler	—	—	—	—	—	—	—	—	—
Black-throated Green Warbler	U O	R U	U U	R	R R	•U U U	O	U U	U O
Blackburnian Warbler	•R R	—	U U	U U	U U	U U U	—	U U	U O
Yellow-throated Warbler	—	—	—	—	—	—	O	U U U	U U U
Pine Warbler	—	O	R R	U U	—	C R C	•C A C C	C C C C	O U
Prairie Warbler	—	—	—	—	—	—	•C C C U	U R U	—
Palm Warbler	C O C	O	A A	C C	C C	C C	O O U	U U U	—
Bay-breasted Warbler	O O	—	U C	U U	U U	U U	—	U U	U O
Blackpoll Warbler	C C	O	U U	C C	C U	C C	—	U U	U O
Cerulean Warbler	—	—	R R R	—	—	—	—	U U	O
Black-and-white Warbler	U U U	C O U	C C	C C	•C R C	•C U C	•U U	C U C	U O O
American Redstart	•U U U	C U	C C C	•C C C	•U U U	•C C C	—	U U U	U U
Prothonotary Warbler	—	—	R R R	—	—	—	•O U O	C C U	•C C U
Worm-eating Warbler	—	—	R	—	—	—	—	R	O
Swainson's Warbler	—	—	—	—	—	—	—	R R R	O O
Ovenbird	•U U O	U	C U C	C C	•U U	•C C C	—	U U	U U
Northern Waterthrush	U U U	O U	U U	U U	R	U U	O O	U U	—
Louisiana Waterthrush	—	—	—	—	—	—	—	U U U	U U U
Kentucky Warbler	—	—	—	—	—	—	—	U U U	•U U U
Connecticut Warbler	•R	—	R R	R R	—	U R U	—	R	—
Mourning Warbler	O O	R	U U	C U	U	U U U	—	R R	—
MacGillivray's Warbler	—	—	—	—	—	—	—	—	—
Common Yellowthroat	•C C C	•C C C	A A A	•C C C	•C C C	•C C C	•C C C U	C C U R	•C C U U
Hooded Warbler	—	—	—	—	—	—	•U C U	C U U	U U
Wilson's Warbler	U U O	O U	C C	C C	U U	U U	—	O O	O U
Canada Warbler	O O	U U	U U	C C	U U	U R U	—	O O	U U
Painted Redstart	—	—	—	—	—	—	—	—	—
Yellow-breasted Chat	—	O O O	R	—	—	—	•O U O	C C U	•U U
TANAGERS									
Hepatic Tanager	—	—	—	—	—	—	—	—	—
Summer Tanager	—	—	—	—	—	—	U U	C C U	•C C C
Scarlet Tanager	R R	—	U U U	•U R R	•U U U	•U U U	U U	U U	U U
Western Tanager	—	—	—	—	—	—	—	—	—
CARDINALS, GROSBEAKS & ALLIES									
Northern Cardinal	—	•O O O O	C C C C	R R R R	•R R R	—	•A A A A	A A A A	•C C C C
Pyrrhuloxia	—	—	—	—	—	—	—	—	—
Rose-breasted Grosbeak	•U C O	•U U O	C C C	•C C C	•C C U	•C C C	R R	U U	U O
Black-headed Grosbeak	—	—	—	—	—	—	—	—	—
Blue Grosbeak	—	—	—	—	—	—	•A A A O	U U U	O O
Lazuli Bunting	—	—	—	—	—	—	—	—	—
Indigo Bunting	R R	•O U O	C C C	•C C C	•C C	•C C C	O O	C C C	•C C C
Painted Bunting	—	—	—	—	—	—	R	—	•U U U
Dickcissel	—	•U C U	U R U	U	U	R R	—	U U U	•C C C
NEW WORLD SPARROWS & ALLIES									
Olive Sparrow	—	—	—	—	—	—	—	—	—
Green-tailed Towhee	—	—	—	—	—	—	—	—	—
Rufous-sided Towhee	R	U R O	U U U	U R U	•R R	•U R U	•A A A A	C U C C	•U U U U
Brown Towhee	—	—	—	—	—	—	—	—	—
Abert's Towhee	—	—	—	—	—	—	—	—	—
Bachman's Sparrow	—	—	—	—	—	—	•C C U U	R	—

	MS-4 Gulf Is.	MO-1 Annada	MO-2 Mingo	MO-3 Squaw Cr.	MO-4 Swan L	MT-1 Benton L.	MT-2 Bowdoin	MT-3 Russell	MT-4 Lee Metcalf	MT-5 Medicine L.	MT-6 Bison Range	MT-7 Ninepipe
	• s S F W	• s S F W	• s S F W	• s S F W	• s S F W	• s S F W	• s S F W	• s S F W	• s S F W	• s S F W	• s S F W	• s S F W
	C U C R	•C C C	•C C U	•C C U	•C C U	—	O O O	U O	•O O	O O O	•C C U	O O
	O R	—	—	—	—	—	—	—	—	—	—	—
	O O	O O	—	U R	—	—	—	—	—	—	—	—
	R R	O O	R	O O	—	—	—	—	—	—	—	—
	U U U	U U U	U U U	U U U	U U	—	—	R	—	—	—	—
	U U U	U U U	U U U R	U U U	—	—	U	R R	R	O O	U U	O O
	R R R	U U	C U U	C U	U U	—	—	—	R R	O O	—	—
	—	—	—	—	—	—	—	—	—	—	—	—
	—	—	—	—	—	—	—	—	—	—	—	—
	C C C	•U U	•C C U	U U	U U	—	—	—	—	—	—	—
	—	—	—	—	—	—	—	—	—	—	—	—
	U U U	•U U U	•U U U	•C C U	•C C C	O O O	•C C C	•C C C	•C C C	•U U O	•C C U	•U U
	O O O	U U	U U	U U	—	—	—	—	—	—	—	—
	U U R	U U	U U	U U	U U	—	—	—	—	—	—	—
	U R	R	R	—	—	—	—	—	—	—	—	—
	O O	—	U U	—	—	—	—	—	—	—	—	—
	C C C	C C O	C C R	C C	C C O	O O O	C C C	U U	•O O O	O O	•C C U	•U U
	—	—	—	—	—	—	—	—	—	—	—	—
	—	—	—	—	—	—	—	—	—	—	—	—
	O U O	—	C U	U U	—	—	—	—	—	—	—	—
	R O	—	U R U	U U	U U	—	—	—	—	—	—	—
	U U U O	O	C U	—	—	—	—	—	—	—	—	—
	C C C C	O	U R	—	—	—	—	—	—	—	—	—
	U O U R	—	U U	—	—	—	—	R	—	—	—	—
	U U O	U U	U U	U U	—	—	—	O O	—	—	—	—
	O O	—	U	—	—	—	—	O R	—	—	—	—
	U R	U U	U U	U U	C U	—	U O R	O O	—	O O	—	—
	R R	•U O	U U	—	—	—	—	—	—	—	—	—
	C C R	U U	•U U U	U U	U R U	—	—	—	—	O R O	—	—
	U U R	•C C C	•U U U	•C U U	•C U C	—	O O	U U	•O O	•U U O	U U	•O O
	C C C	•C C C	•C C U	•R R R	U R R	—	—	—	—	—	—	—
	O O	U	—	U	—	—	—	—	—	—	—	—
	O O	—	R	—	—	—	—	—	—	—	—	—
	U R U R	U U	C U U	•U U U	U R U	—	O O	U U	—	O O O	—	—
	O O	C U	C	U U	—	—	O O O	O O	•O O O	O O	O	O
	O O O	U U	•C U U	O O	U R U	—	—	—	—	—	—	—
	U C U	•U U U	•C C U	•O U	R	—	—	—	—	—	—	—
	R	—	U U	O O	U R	—	U U U	—	—	—	•C C U	U U
	—	—	—	—	—	—	O O O	R	•O O O	R R	•C C U	•C C
	C C C C	•C C C	•C C C	•C C U R	•C C C	O U O	•C C	C C C	•C C C	U U O	•C C U	•C C
	U C U	—	•U U	—	—	—	—	—	—	—	—	—
	R R R	U U	U U	U U	U C	O O O	O O	U C	—	O O	O O	O O
	R R	U U	U U	O O	—	—	—	—	—	—	—	—
	—	—	—	—	—	—	—	—	—	—	—	—
	R C R	•U U U	•C C U	•C C	O O U	—	U U	U U U	—	•U U O	U U	—
	—	—	—	—	—	—	—	—	—	—	—	—
	U C U	•U U	•C C U	•R U	O O O	—	—	—	—	—	—	—
	U U	•U U U	•U U U	•O O R	—	—	—	—	—	—	—	—
	—	—	—	—	—	—	O	C C	U U O	—	•C C U	O O
	C C C C	•C C C C	•A A A A	•C C C C	•C C C C	—	—	—	—	—	—	—
	U U	U U	•C R U	•U U O	U U U	—	R R R	•U U U	—	O O	O O	—
	—	—	—	—	—	—	U U	U U U	•U U	R O	O O	—
	U C U R	—	U R	•O U	—	—	—	—	—	—	—	—
	—	—	—	—	—	—	R R	•R U R	•U U	R R R	•C C	O O
	U C U R	•C C C	•A A C	•C C O	•C C C	—	—	R	—	—	—	—
	O R R	—	—	—	—	—	—	—	—	—	—	—
	R R	•C C C	•C C	•C C	•C C	—	—	—	—	R R	—	—
	—	—	—	—	—	—	—	—	—	—	—	—
	C C C C	•U U U	•C C C U	•C C C C	•C C C O	O	•C C C	C C C	•C C	O O	•C C C	R
	—	—	—	—	—	—	—	—	—	—	—	—
	U U U U	—	—	—	—	—	—	—	—	—	—	—

STATE-NUMBER OF BIRD LIST / REFUGE, SANCTUARY OR PRESERVE / NESTING, ABUNDANCE BY SEASON	MN-1 Agassiz •sSFW	MN-2 Big Stone •sSFW	MN-3 MN Valley •sSFW	MN-4 MN WPA •sSFW	MN-5 Sherburne •sSFW	MN-6 Tamarac •sSFW	MS-1 Sandhill Cr. •sSFW	MS-2 Noxubee •sSFW	MS-3 Yazoo •sSFW
NEW WORLD SPARROWS & ALLIES (cont.)									
Cassin's Sparrow	—	—	—	—	—	—	—	—	—
Rufous-crowned Sparrow	—	—	—	—	—	—	—	—	—
American Tree Sparrow	C C	C C C	A A C	C C C	C U C	C C R	—	R	—
Chipping Sparrow	•U U U	•C C O R	C C C	•C C C	•C U	•C C C	•U O U C	C C C C	U U U
Clay-colored Sparrow	•U C U	•C C U	C C C	•C C C	•U U U	•C C C	—	—	—
Brewer's Sparrow	—	—	—	—	—	—	—	—	—
Field Sparrow	—	•U U O	C C C	•R R R	•U U	—	•U U U U	C C C C	U U U U
Black-chinned Sparrow	—	—	—	—	—	—	—	—	—
Vesper Sparrow	•U U U	•C C C	C C C	•C C C	•A A A	•U U U	U U	U U R	U U U
Lark Sparrow	—	R	U U U	R R R	•U U	R R R	—	R	—
Black-throated Sparrow	—	—	—	—	—	—	—	—	—
Sage Sparrow	—	—	—	—	—	—	—	—	—
Lark Bunting	—	—	—	—	—	—	—	—	—
Savannah Sparrow	•U C U	•C U U	C C C	•C C C	U	C C C	C O C C	U U C	U U U
Baird's Sparrow	—	—	—	—	—	—	—	—	—
Grasshopper Sparrow	R	•O O	U U O	•U U U	•U U	U U R	—	U U U U	•U U U U
Henslow's Sparrow	—	O O O	—	—	—	—	O	—	R
Le Conte's Sparrow	•A A U	O R	—	•U U U	—	U U U	O	R	O O
Sharp-tailed Sparrow	•R U	—	—	•R R R	—	—	—	R	—
Seaside Sparrow	—	—	—	—	—	—	—	—	—
Fox Sparrow	C C	U U	U U	C C	U U	C C	U U U	U U U	U U U
Song Sparrow	•C C U	•C C C O	C C C	•C C C R	•A A C	•A A C	U U C	C U C	U U C
Lincoln's Sparrow	U U	C C	U U	U U	R	U U	—	R R R	O O U
Swamp Sparrow	•U C U	O O	C C C	•C C C	•U U U	•C C C	U U U	U U C	U U C
White-throated Sparrow	•C U C	C C	C C	C C	C C R	•C C C	U U U	C C A	U U C
Golden-crowned Sparrow	—	—	—	—	—	—	—	—	—
White-crowned Sparrow	U U	U U	U U	U U	R R	U U	—	R	U U U
Harris' Sparrow	U U	U U	U C R	U U	R R	U U	—	—	—
Dark-eyed Junco	C O C	C C C	A A C	A A U	C C C	C C U	U U C	U C C	U U C
McCown's Longspur	—	—	—	—	—	—	—	—	—
Lapland Longspur	U U	O O	O O O	C C R	—	C C U	—	—	O
Smith's Longspur	—	—	—	R R R	—	—	—	—	—
Chestnut-collared Longspur	—	—	—	R R	—	—	—	—	—
Snow Bunting	U C C	O U C	O O O	U C C	R U	U U C	—	—	—
NEW WORLD BLACKBIRDS & ORIOLES									
Bobolink	•U C O	•C U U	C C C	•C C U	•C C	•C C C	O O	U U	U O
Red-winged Blackbird	•C C C	•A A A O	A A A U	•A C A	•A A C R	•A A A	•C C C A	C A C C	•C C C C
Tricolored Blackbird	—	—	—	—	—	—	—	—	—
Eastern Meadowlark	—	—	C C C	—	•C C C	R R R	•C U C C	C C C C	•C C C C
Western Meadowlark	•C C C	•C C C O	C C C	•A A A R	•U U U	•C C C	—	—	—
Yellow-headed Blackbird	•C C C	•C C C R	C C C	•C C C	•U U U	•C C U	—	—	—
Rusty Blackbird	U C	C C O	C C U	C U C R	U	C C	—	U U	U U C
Brewer's Blackbird	•U U U	U U R	C U C	•U C U	—	•C U C	—	U U	U U U
Great-tailed Grackle	—	—	—	—	—	—	—	—	—
Boat-tailed Grackle	—	—	—	—	—	—	•C C C C	—	—
Common Grackle	•C U C	•C C C O	A A A U	•A A A R	•C C C R	•A A A	•C C C C	C U C C	C C C C
Bronzed Cowbird	—	—	—	—	—	—	—	—	—
Brown-headed Cowbird	•C C C	•C C C O	A A C	•C C C	•A A C	•A A A	•C C C C	C C C C	•C C C C
Orchard Oriole	R	•U O	R R R	R R	—	R R	•C C C	U C U	•U C U
Hooded Oriole	—	—	—	—	—	—	—	—	—
Baltimore Oriole	—	—	—	—	—	—	—	—	—
Bullock's Oriole	•C C O	•C U U	C C C	•C C C	•C C C	•C C C	U U	U U	•U C U R
Scott's Oriole	—	—	—	—	—	—	—	—	—
FINCHES									
Rosy Finch	—	—	—	—	—	—	—	—	—
Pine Grosbeak	O O U	R	—	R R	—	R R U	—	—	—
Purple Finch	•U U U	O U U	C C O	U R U U	U U	•C U C C	U R U	U U U	U U U
Cassin's Finch	—	—	—	—	—	—	—	—	—
House Finch	—	—	—	—	—	—	—	R	—
Red Crossbill	R O O	O O U	—	R R	—	R R U	—	—	—
White-winged Crossbill	R O O	R R	—	U U	—	R U U	—	—	—
Common Redpoll	C U C	O O U	C C C	C C	U U	C C C	—	—	—
Hoary Redpoll	O O	R	—	—	U U	R	—	—	—
Pine Siskin	U R U R	O O O	C C	U R U U	U R	C U C C	—	R O	U
Lesser Goldfinch	—	—	—	—	—	—	—	—	—
Lawrence's Goldfinch	—	—	—	—	—	—	—	—	—
American Goldfinch	•C C C	•C C C U	A A A A	•C C C U	•C C C C	•C C C U	U U U	C R C C	U U C
Evening Grosbeak	U U U	U O	U	U U	U U U	U U C	—	O	R
OLD WORLD SPARROWS									
House Sparrow	•U U U U	•C C C C	A A A A	•A A A A	•C C C C	•U U U U	C C C C	U U U U	•C C C C
Eurasian Tree Sparrow	—	—	—	—	—	—	—	—	—

	MS-4 Gulf Is.	MO-1 Annada	MO-2 Mingo	MO-3 Squaw Cr.	MO-4 Swan L.	MT-1 Benton L.	MT-2 Bowdoin	MT-3 Russell	MT-4 Lee Metcalf	MT-5 Medicine L.	MT-6 Bison Range	MT-7 Ninepipe
	• s S F W	• s S F W	• s S F W	• s S F W	• s S F W	• s S F W	• s S F W	• s S F W	• s S F W	• s S F W	• s S F W	• s S F W
	–	–	–		–							
	C C C		R C	C C C	U U C	O O	C C	C C O	U C	C C O	C	O OU
U UC	U O	• CCU	• UUO	• UUU	C C C	• CCU	• CAC	• UUU	• UU	• CCU	• UOU
			O O		O O	• CCU	• CCU		• AAU		
					O	• CCU	R R		U U		
U UC	• CCCO	• CCUU	• COC	• CCUO		• UCU			O O		
U UU	UU	U U	• COC	• COC	• CCC	• UU	• UCU	• U	• UUU	• AAC	• OUO
R RR	O	URR	• UUO	• UUU	O O O	• UU	• UCU		• CCC	UU	OUO
					• AAA	• CCC	• AA		• CC	R	
U UC	U U	C C	URU	U U	• CCC	• CCC	UOU	• UUU	• CCU	• UU	• UUO
					• UUU	• UOO			• UUU		
R		UUU	• OUO	• CCC	• UUU	• CC	U		• CCU	• CC	
			RRR								
		• R R	O OR	O O		U U		R	• UUU		
O OO			R R	O O					O O O		
OOOO											
	R	U UO	U UU	U U		R R	R		O O	O	U O
U OC	• CCCC	• CCCC	• CCCU	• CCCU	C C C	• CCC	C C C	• CCCC	• CCC	• AAAU	• UOUU
R RR	O O	R	R	U U U		U U U	R		O O	U	O O
C OC	C CC	C CC	• CRCU	U UU							
C UC	C CU	C CA	C CO	C CC		II II	O O		U C		
O OO	C CCO	C CC	C CO	C CC	U R	C C	C C	O U	C U	C O C	U O U
		R	R	O UU	U O	C C	C C	O OR	U U		
UU	C CA	U UA	C CC	U UC	U U	C CC	C CC	C U	• UUUU	U AU	• CCCC	O OO
			R	O O	• UUU	• UR	O O		U U U		
				R O			C C C		O		
					• AAA	• CCC	C		• AAC		
				R	U A	U	C	U		CC O	U UU
U R	U	R	• URU	• UOU	O O	U U	C C	U U U	• UCO	R R	O
CCCC	• AAAC	• AAAA	• ACAA	• AAAC	• CCC	• AAA	• CACO	• AAAC	• CCC	• AACO	• AAAU
CCCC	• CCCU	• CCCC	• CUCO	• CCCC							
			O O O O	R RR	• AAA	• AAA	• AAAO	• CCCU	• AAA	• AAAO	• CCCU
RRRR			• UUUR	O R	• AAA	• AAA	• CAC	• AACR	• AAC	O O O	• CCC
	U UR	U U C	C C O	C C O		R R					
O O		R R RU	U UR	U O	U U U	• CCC	• CAC	U U U	• CCU	• AAA	• CCU
			O O O								
CCCC	–	–	–	–							
CCCC	• AAAC	• CCCA	• ACAC	• ACAC	O O	• CC	• OCO		• UUU		
CCCC	• CCC	• CCCU	• ACAO	• CCCU	U U U	C C	• CCC	• CCU	• AAC	R C	O O
UCU	• UU	• CC	• CCO	• CCC			• OO		R		
O UR	• CC	• UU	• CCR	C C C		• UUU	• CCC	• UU	• UUO	• CC	• OO
					R R					U UU	
	U UU	U UC		U U	U UO	O O	U U	R RU		R O	
									O		O O
								U U U U			
			R				U C U	R		• UCUU	O
			R							R	
			R	O O	O U	U	U U	U O	U	U U	O O O
R R		R	RR	U		C C	R R			R R	
						U U U	C O O O	O O O		U U U	U O
C UC	• CCCC	• CCCC	• CCCU	• CCCO	O O	• CCC	• CAC	• UUUU	• OOO	• CCC	OOO
–	R	R	–	–	–	–	U	O O O O	R R	U C C	U UU
CCCC	• CCCC	• CCCC	• AAAA	• CCCC	• OOO	• AAAA	• AAAA	U U U U	• CCCC	• CCCC	• CCCC

STATE-NUMBER OF BIRD LIST / REFUGE, SANCTUARY OR PRESERVE / NESTING, ABUNDANCE BY SEASON	MT-8 Red Rock L. •s S F W	MT-9 Swan River •s S F W	MT-10 Glacier •s S F W	NE-1 Crescent L. •s S F W	NE-2 Ft. Niobrara •s S F W	NE-3 Rainwater •s S F W	NE-4 Valentine •s S F W	NV-1 Desert •s S F W	NV-2 Pahranagat •s S F W
LOONS									
Red-throated Loon	—	—	—	—	—	—	—	—	—
Arctic Loon	—	—	—	—	—	—	—	—	—
Pacific Loon	—	—	—	—	—	—	—	—	—
Common Loon	O O O	•C C U	•C C C	O O	—	U R U	R R	—	O O
Yellow-billed Loon	—	—	—	—	—	—	—	—	—
GREBES									
Least Grebe	—	—	—	—	—	—	—	—	—
Pied-billed Grebe	•C C C	•C C	R R R R	•C C C	O R O	•C C C	•U C U	•O R O O	C C
Horned Grebe	•U U	•C C C	C C U R	U O U	U U	U U	R R	—	R R
Red-necked Grebe	•O O	•C C C	U U U R	—	—	—	—	—	—
Eared Grebe	•C C C	•C C C O	C C U R	•C C C	U U U	C O C	•U C U	O O	C C C
Western Grebe	•C C C	U C	C C C R	•C C C	U U	—	•U C U	O O	C C
SHEARWATERS & PETRELS									
Northern Fulmar	—	—	—	—	—	—	—	—	—
Cory's Shearwater	—	—	—	—	—	—	—	—	—
Pink-footed Shearwater	—	—	—	—	—	—	—	—	—
Greater Shearwater	—	—	—	—	—	—	—	—	—
Sooty Shearwater	—	—	—	—	—	—	—	—	—
Short-tailed Shearwater	—	—	—	—	—	—	—	—	—
Manx Shearwater	—	—	—	—	—	—	—	—	—
Audubon's Shearwater	—	—	—	—	—	—	—	—	—
STORM-PETRELS									
Wilson's Storm-Petrel	—	—	—	—	—	—	—	—	—
Fork-tailed Storm-Petrel	—	—	—	—	—	—	—	—	—
Leach's Storm-Petrel	—	—	—	—	—	—	—	—	—
BOOBIES & GANNETS									
Masked Booby	—	—	—	—	—	—	—	—	—
Brown Booby	—	—	—	—	—	—	—	—	—
Northern Gannet	—	—	—	—	—	—	—	—	—
PELICANS									
American White Pelican	•C C C	—	R	C U C	U U U	C O C	U C U	—	R R
Brown Pelican	—	—	—	—	—	—	—	—	—
CORMORANTS									
Great Cormorant	—	—	—	—	—	—	—	—	—
Double-crested Cormorant	•C C C	O	R R	•C C C	O O O	C C	•U A C	R R R R	•C C C U
Olivaceous Cormorant	—	—	—	—	—	—	—	—	—
Brandt's Cormorant	—	—	—	—	—	—	—	—	—
Pelagic Cormorant	—	—	—	—	—	—	—	—	—
Red-faced Cormorant	—	—	—	—	—	—	—	—	—
ANHINGAS									
Anhinga	—	—	—	—	—	—	—	—	—
FRIGATEBIRDS									
Magnificent Frigatebird	—	—	—	—	—	—	—	—	—
BITTERNS & HERONS									
American Bittern	•U U U	•U U O	•R R	•C C U	U U U	•C C C	•U C U	O O	O O
Least Bittern	—	—	—	R	—	U R U	R	—	—
Great Blue Heron	•C C C O	•C C C C	•C C C	•C U C	C C C	•C C C	U C C	O O O R	•C C C C
Great Egret	—	—	—	O O O	—	O O	O	O O	U U
Snowy Egret	O O	—	—	O O O	—	R R	O	O O O	U U U
Little Blue Heron	—	—	—	—	—	O R R	R	—	—
Tricolored Heron	—	—	—	—	—	—	—	—	—
Reddish Egret	—	—	—	—	—	—	—	—	—
Cattle Egret	—	—	—	O O O	—	U O U	O	—	—
Green-backed Heron	—	—	—	O O	R R R	•C U C	R	R	R
Black-crowned Night-Heron	•U C U	—	—	•C C C	U C U	C O C	•C A C	O O O	O O O
Yellow-crowned Night-Heron	—	—	—	—	—	R R	—	—	—
IBISES & SPOONBILLS									
White Ibis	—	—	—	—	—	—	—	—	—
Glossy Ibis	—	—	—	—	—	—	—	—	—
White-faced Ibis	O U O	—	—	O O O	—	R	O	O O O	O O O
Roseate Spoonbill	—	—	—	—	—	—	—	—	—
STORKS									
Wood Stork	—	—	—	—	—	—	—	—	—
SWANS, GEESE & DUCKS									
Fulvous Whistling-Duck	—	—	—	—	—	—	—	—	—
Black-bellied Whistling-Duck	—	—	—	—	—	—	—	—	—
Tundra Swan	O R U	U R C U	C C	O O	—	O R	R R	—	O O R
Trumpeter Swan	—	—	R	•R R R R	O O	—	•U R U U	—	—
Mute Swan	—	—	—	—	—	—	—	—	—
Greater White-fronted Goose	—	—	—	O R O	—	A A R	O R O	R R	O O
Snow Goose	U U	O O R	U U U	U U	—	C C O	O O	—	O O

Row	NV-3 Ruby L.	NV-4 Sheldon	NV-5 Stillwater	NJ-1 Cape May	NJ-2 B. Forsythe	NJ-3 Gr. Swamp	NM-1 Rand. Davey	NM-2 Bitter L.	NM-3 B dl Apache	NM-4 Grulla	NM-5 Las Vegas	NM-6 Maxwell
	• s S F W	• s S F W	• s S F W	• s S F W	• s S F W	• s S F W	• s S F W	• s S F W	• s S F W	• s S F W	• s S F W	• s S F W
	—	—	—	A U C	O O U	—	—	—	—	—	—	—
	—	—	—	—	—	—	—	—	—	—	—	—
	—	—	—	—	—	—	—	—	—	—	—	—
	—	—	—	—	—	—	—	—	—	—	—	—
	R R	O	R R	C O U U	O R O O	U R	R R	R	R R	—	R	U R
	•C C C U	•U C U	•U U U O	U O U U	U O U O	U O O U	U O	C U C U	•A C A C	—	•C C C U	•O C
	O O	R R	R R	C R U U	U U U	R	—	R R O	O O O	—	O O	R
	•C C C U	•U U U	•C C C	R R	—	—	O R	C R C U	U U U	C R C R	•C C C O	•C O C R
	•R R U	U O U	•C O C O	—	—	—	—	O R O O	O O O	—	U U U O	•R O
	—	—	—	C U	—	—	—	—	—	—	—	—
	—	—	—	O C O	—	—	—	—	—	—	—	—
	—	—	—	C C O	—	—	—	—	—	—	—	—
	—	—	—	O O	R R	—	—	—	—	—	—	—
	—	—	—	O O O O	—	—	—	—	—	—	—	—
	—	—	—	O O	—	—	—	—	—	—	—	—
	—	—	—	C A U	—	—	—	—	—	—	—	—
	—	—	—	O O	—	—	—	—	—	—	—	—
	—	—	—	—	—	—	—	—	—	—	—	—
	—	—	—	C O C C	R R	—	—	—	—	—	—	—
	O U U	U	C A A R	—	R R	—	—	C O C R	O O	—	U U	O U O
	—	—	—	R	R R	—	—	—	—	—	—	—
	O U O	U O	U U U R	O O U	U O C U	R	—	U R U R	•C C C U	—	U U	C O
	—	—	—	—	—	—	—	R	U U U U	—	—	—
	—	—	—	—	—	—	—	—	—	—	—	—
	—	—	—	—	—	—	—	—	—	—	—	—
	—	—	—	—	—	—	—	—	—	—	—	—
	•C C C	O O O	•R O R	U R U U	•U O U U	•C C C O	—	U U U U	•U C C O	—	R	—
	—	—	R R R	U C U R	•U U U	•U C U	—	R R R	•U U U	—	—	—
	•C C C C	U U U O	•C C C U	C U C C	•C C C U	•C C C U	O O O R	C U C C	•A U C C	C O C U	C C C U	C C C
	R O R	O O	•C U C O	C C C O	•C C C O	O O O R	—	U U U U	R R R	—	—	—
	•C C U	O O	•C A C	A A C O	•C C C O	O O	—	C C C R	•C A C O	R R O R	U U	O O O
	—	—	—	C C C O	•U U U O	O O O	—	R O R	O O	—	—	—
	—	—	—	C C C O	•U U U O	—	—	R R	—	—	—	—
	R R	—	—	C C C R	•U U U	R R R	—	O O R	O O O	O	U	R
	—	—	—	C C C R	•U U U	•C A A	—	O C U R	•U U U	—	O R	—
	•C C C O	•O O O	•C A C U	C C C U	•U U U U	O O O	—	C C U R	•U A C O	—	•U O O O	O
	—	—	—	U U O R	•O O O	R R	—	—	—	—	—	—
	—	—	—	R R	R R	—	—	—	—	—	—	—
	—	—	—	A A C O	•A A O O	O O O	—	—	—	—	—	—
	•C A C	—	•U C U R	—	—	—	—	U O U O	U U U	—	C U U	O O O
	—	—	—	—	—	—	—	—	—	—	—	—
	—	—	—	—	—	—	—	—	—	—	—	—
	U C C	O U O	C U A	O U U	O U O	—	—	R O	O	—	U U U	O O O
	•U U U U	—	—	—	—	—	—	—	—	—	—	—
	—	—	O	C C C U	•C C C U	R R R	—	—	—	—	—	—
	—	—	O O	—	—	O O	—	O O O	O O O	O O O	U U	O O
	O O	O	O	C C U	C O C A	A O A A	R	C R A A	U A A	U U C	U A A	R U U

STATE-NUMBER OF BIRD LIST REFUGE, SANCTUARY OR PRESERVE NESTING, ABUNDANCE BY SEASON	MT-8 Red Rock L. •s S F W	MT-9 Swan River •s S F W	MT-10 Glacier •s S F W	NE-1 Crescent L. •s S F W	NE-2 Ft. Niobrara •s S F W	NE-3 Rainwater •s S F W	NE-4 Valentine •s S F W	NV-1 Desert •s S F W	NV-2 Pahranagat •s S F W
SWANS, GEESE & DUCKS (cont.)									
Ross' Goose	—	—	R	O O	—	—	—	—	—
Emperor Goose	—	—	—	—	—	—	—	—	—
Brant	—	—	—	—	—	—	—	—	—
Canada Goose	•C C C O	•C C C C	•C C C U	•C C C C	U C U	A O A U	•U U U O	O O	U U U
Wood Duck	—	•C C U	•U U U	R R R	R R R	•C U C	R R R	O	O O O
Green-winged Teal	•C C U	•U U U R	U U U	•C U C	C U C	•A O A O	C U C	C U U C	•C U C C
American Black Duck	—	—	—	—	—	—	O R O	—	—
Mottled Duck	—	—	—	—	—	—	—	—	—
Mallard	•A A A A	•C C C C	•A A A C	•A C A O	•C C C C	•A C A C	•A A A O	C C C	•C C C C
Northern Pintail	•C C C	•C U C O	U U U R	•C C C	•C U C	•A U A O	•C C C	U U U	U U U
Blue-winged Teal	•C C U	•C C C	U U U	•A A A	•C C C	•A C A R	•A A A	R R	U U U
Cinnamon Teal	•C C C	•C C U	U U U	R R O	R R	•U O U	R R O	C O C O	•C O C O
Northern Shoveler	•O C C	•U O U	U U U R	•A C A	•C C C	•A C A R	•A C A	O O O	U O U U
Gadwall	•C C C O	•C C U	U U U R	•C C C	•C C C	•C C C R	•A C A	U U O	
Eurasian Wigeon	—	—	—	—	—	—	R R	—	—
American Wigeon	•C C A O	•C C C	C C C R	•U U U O	C O C	•A O A O	•C U C	O O O	U O U U
Canvasback	•C C C	U O U O	U U	•C U C	U O U	U U	•C O C	R R O	C C C
Redhead	•C C C	•U U U O	U U	•C U C	•C U C	•C U C	•C U C	—	C U C U
Ring-necked Duck	•U U U	•U U U O	•C U U	U O U O	C O C	U U	U R U	O O O	O O O
Greater Scaup	—	—	—	O	—	R	R R	—	—
Lesser Scaup	•C C C	O O O	U U U	•C U C O	C U C	A C R	C C U	O O O	O O O
Common Eider	—	—	—	—	—	—	—	—	—
King Eider	—	—	—	—	—	—	—	—	—
Steller's Eider	—	—	—	—	—	—	—	—	—
Harlequin Duck	—	R	•C C R	—	—	—	R R	—	—
Oldsquaw	—	—	—	—	—	—	—	—	—
Black Scoter	—	—	—	—	—	R	—	—	—
Surf Scoter	—	—	—	—	—	—	—	—	—
White-winged Scoter	—	R	U U	—	—	—	—	—	—
Common Goldeneye	•C U U C	•C C C C	•C C C U	U O U O	U U U	U	O O O	O O O	O O O
Barrow's Goldeneye	•C C C C	•C U U O	•C C C U	—	—	—	R R	—	—
Bufflehead	•C C C O	C U U O	C C C U	C O C O	U U	U U	C C U	U U U	U O U U
Hooded Merganser	•O O O	•U U	•U U U R	R O R	O O	U U	O O	—	O O
Common Merganser	•C U U O	•C C C U	•A A A C	U O U O	C C C	O O	C C O	—	O O
Red-breasted Merganser	•U O U	R	•U U U	R R	O O	—	R R	—	O O
Ruddy Duck	•C C C	—	U U U	•C C C O	U U	•C U C	•C C C	O O O	U O U C
Masked Duck	—	—	—	—	—	—	—	—	—
AMERICAN VULTURES									
Black Vulture	—	—	—	—	—	—	—	—	—
Turkey Vulture	—	—	R	R O R	C C C	U	O O O	U U U	U C U
KITES, EAGLES, HAWKS & ALLIES									
Osprey	•O O O	C	•C C C	O O R	R R	O O	R R R	R R	U U
American Swallow-tailed Kite	—	—	—	—	—	—	—	—	—
Black-shouldered Kite	—	—	—	—	—	—	—	—	—
Snail Kite	—	—	—	—	—	—	—	—	—
Mississippi Kite	—	—	—	—	—	—	—	—	—
Bald Eagle	•C C C C	•C C C C	•U U A U	R R R	U U U	U U O	O O R	R R	R
Northern Harrier	•U C C O	•U C	C C C	•C U C O	C C C	•C C C U	•U C U U	U O U U	C U C C
Sharp-shinned Hawk	O U U O	U U U U	•C C C U	U O U O	U U U	U U U U	O O U	•U U U O	U U O
Cooper's Hawk	•O U O	—	•U U U U	U O U	O O O O	U U U	O R O U	•U U U U	U O U U
Northern Goshawk	•U U U U	U U U	•U U U U	R O		O O	R	•R R R R	—
Common Black-Hawk	—	—	—	—	—	—	—	—	—
Harris' Hawk	—	—	—	—	—	—	—	—	—
Gray Hawk	—	—	—	—	—	—	—	—	—
Red-shouldered Hawk	—	—	—	—	—	—	R R	—	—
Broad-winged Hawk	—	—	—	R O	—	O	R R	—	—
Short-tailed Hawk	—	—	—	—	—	—	—	—	—
Swainson's Hawk	•C C C	U	U U U	•U U U	C U C	•C U U	•U U U	•U U	—
White-tailed Hawk	—	—	—	—	—	—	—	—	—
Zone-tailed Hawk	—	—	—	—	—	—	—	—	—
Red-tailed Hawk	•C C C	•U U U	•C C C	•U U U U	•C C C	•C U C U	•U O U R	•U U U O	•C C C O
Ferruginous Hawk	•U U	—	R	R O R	—	U U U	•O O R	R	
Rough-legged Hawk	U C O	C	R R R R	U U U	U U U O	U U C	U U C	O O	O O
Golden Eagle	•U U U U	C	•C C C C	R R R R	U U U	U U O	O O R	•C U U O	U U U U
CARACARAS & FALCONS									
Crested Caracara	—	—	—	—	—	—	—	—	—
American Kestrel	•C C C	•O C O	•C C C	R R U O	C C C U	•C C C C	U C U O	•C C C C	•C C C U
Merlin	•O U O	O R O	R R R	O R R	R R	U U U	O O O	O R O O	O O
Peregrine Falcon	•C C C	—	R	R O R	R R	R R R	R R R	R R R R	R R R R
Gyrfalcon	—	—	—	—	—	R	—	—	—
Prairie Falcon	•C C C	O O O	•R R R R	R R U O	U U	O O U	R R O	•U U U O	U U U O

NV-3 Ruby L. •s S F W	NV-4 Sheldon •s S F W	NV-5 Stillwater •s S F W	NJ-1 Cape May •s S F W	NJ-2 B. Forsythe •s S F W	NJ-3 Gr. Swamp •s S F W	NM-1 Rand. Davey •s S F W	NM-2 Bitter L. •s S F W	NM-3 B dl Apache •s S F W	NM-4 Grulla •s S F W	NM-5 Las Vegas •s S F W	NM-6 Maxwell •s S F W
—	—	O O	—	R R	—	—	C C	U U C	—	R	O
—	—	—	—	—	—	—	—	—	—	—	R
•C C C C	•C C C O	•C C C A	C O A C	•C C C C	•A A A A	—	C C C C	•C C U U	U R C C	•C C A A	•O O C A
U	R R	•U U U	U U U O	•U O U R	•A A A O	—	O O O	O O	—	—	—
C R A C	•U U U O	•A U A U	C O A U	•C O A C	•C U C U	O O	C U C U	•C O A C	C R C C	C U C O	•C C C U
—	—	—	C C A A	•A C A A	•C C C U	—	—	—	—	—	—
•A A A C	•C C C C	•A A A C	C C C C	•C U C O	•A A A C	U O U U	C C A A	•A C A A	C O C C	•C C A A	•C C A O
•C U A C	•C U C O	•A C A U	C O C C	•C O A U	•C C C	O O	A U A C	•C U A A	C O C C	•C C C C	C C A U
•U U U	•O O O	•O O	C U C O	•C U A O	•C C C	O O	C C C U	•C U C	—	•C C C O	•C C C U
•A A C U	•U U U O	•A A C O	—	—	—	O	C C C U	•C U C O	C O C O	•C C C O	•R C C
•C C C U	•U O U	•A C A U	C O C U	•C O C C	O O O R	O U	A U A A	•C U A A	C O C U	C U C C	R R C
•A A A C	•C C C O	•A A A U	C C C C	•C C C U	O R O O	U U	C U C C	•C U C A	—	•C C A A	•C C A U
—	—	—	R R R	R R	—	—	—	—	—	—	—
•C U C C	U O C O	•C O A U	C O C C	C O C O	U R C O	O O R	A U C A	C O C C	C O C C	C U C U	O O A U
•A A A U	•U O U O	•C O A U	C C U	O O R	R R R	—	U R U U	•U O U U	—	C O C O	O U
•A A A U	•C U C O	•A A A O	U O U	O O R	—	C C U	C O C C	•U O U C	C O C C	C O C O	R O C U
•C U U C	O O O O	U U	U U O	O O	O O	C C C	O U U	U U C	U R U U	C O C O	O
—	—	O O O	C R U A	C C U	O O O	—	—	—	—	—	R U R
•C C C C	O O O O	U U U	U O U	O O O	—	U U	U R U U	•U O U U	—	—	C O C U
—	—	—	O R O O	—	—	—	—	—	—	—	—
—	—	—	O R O O	—	—	—	—	—	—	—	—
—	—	—	O R Q	—	—	—	R R	—	—	—	—
—	—	—	U U C	U U U	—	—	—	—	—	—	—
—	—	—	A O A A	U R U U	—	—	R R	—	—	—	—
—	—	O O	C O C C	U R O U	—	—	—	—	—	—	—
—	—	—	U R U U	U R U U	—	—	R R	—	—	—	—
U U C	O O U	U U U	U R U C	U U U	R R	R	O R O U	R R R	—	C O C C	O U
R R	—	—	—	—	—	—	—	—	—	R U	R
U C C	O O U U	C U C	C R C C	C O C C	R R R	O O	C R C C	U U C	—	C O C A	C O C
O O O	R R	O O O	C R C U	C R U U	•O O O	O	R O O	O U U	—	O O O	R C U
U U U	U U O	C U C	O O U	O O O	R R	O	U R U C	O O C	—	U U C	R C U
R R R	—	—	C R C C	U R U U	—	R	O O O	O O O	—	R	—
•C C C U	•C C C O	•A C A U	U O U U	•U U U O	R R	U U	C U C A	•C U C C	C O C	C C C C	C U C O
—	—	—	—	—	—	—	—	—	—	—	—
•C C U	U C U	U U U	C C C U	O O O R	C C C C	U O U	C C U	•C A A	U O U O	C C C	O C C O
—	—	—	—	—	—	—	—	—	—	—	—
R R	R R	—	C C C	•U U U	O U	O O	O O O O	O O	—	O R	R
—	—	—	O O	—	—	—	R	—	—	—	—
—	—	—	—	—	—	—	—	—	—	—	—
—	—	—	O O R	—	—	—	O O	R R R	R	—	—
O O	O O	O U	O O O O	O O O O	O O O O	—	O	O O O	O U U	U C C	O O C U
•C C C C	•C C C U	•C C C A	C U C C	•U O U U	O R O R	O	C C O	•C O C A	•C U C C	C U C C	•C C C U
•O O O	U O U	O R O	C A U	O U O	O U O	O O U O	O R O O	C C C	U U U	O O O O	R O
•O O O	•U U U U	O O	U R C O	O O R	O R O O	U O U	U O U U	•C O O C	U R U O	U U U U	O
O	R R R	—	R O O	R R	R R	—	R O	O O	—	—	—
—	—	—	—	—	—	—	O	O O O	—	—	R
—	—	—	U R C U	O R O R	•U U U O	—	—	—	—	—	—
—	—	—	C U C	•O O O	•U O U	—	—	—	—	—	R
•O O O O	•O U O	•O U O	O	—	—	—	U U U	•U U U	•C C C R	•C U C	C C C U
—	—	—	—	—	—	—	—	—	—	—	—
•C C C O	•C C C U	•C U C U	U U C C	O O U O	•C U C C	U U U O	C O C C	•C U C A	C U C C	•C U C U	U O U
•O O O O	•U U U O	R R	—	O O U	O O O	—	U O U U	•U U U U	•C U C C	•U U U U	O O
C O C C	U U C	U U C	O O U	O O U	O O O	—	U U U	U U U	U R C C	O C U	O O C U
•U U U O	•C C C U	U O U U	R O O	R R	R	—	O O O	U U U U	U C C	•U U C C	O O C C
•C C C	•C C C U	C C C C	C U A U	•U U U O	•C C C C	O O	U U U U	•C U C C	C O C C	•C C C C	•C C C U
—	—	—	U C R	O U O	R R	—	—	R O	O O	R O O	—
R R R	R R	—	R U	•U U U U	R	—	R R	R O O	—	O O	O
—	—	—	—	—	—	—	—	—	—	—	—
•U U R R	•C C C O	O O U	—	—	—	—	U O U U	O O U U	U R U U	C C U C	O O

STATE-NUMBER OF BIRD LIST / REFUGE, SANCTUARY OR PRESERVE / NESTING, ABUNDANCE BY SEASON	MT-8 Red Rock L. •s S F W	MT-9 Swan River •s S F W	MT-10 Glacier •s S F W	NE-1 Crescent L. •s S F W	NE-2 Ft. Niobrara •s S F W	NE-3 Rainwater •s S F W	NE-4 Valentine •s S F W	NV-1 Desert •s S F W	NV-2 Pahranagat •s S F W
CHACHALACAS									
Plain Chachalaca	—	—	—	—	—	—	—	—	—
PARTRIDGES, GROUSE, TURKEYS & QUAILS									
Gray Partridge	O O O O	—	R	—	—	—	R R R R	—	—
Chukar	—	—	—	—	—	—	—	—	—
Ring-necked Pheasant	—	O O O O	R	•C C C C	•C C C C	•C C C C	•A A A A	—	•U U U U
Spruce Grouse	—	—	•A A A A	—	—	—	—	—	—
Blue Grouse	•U U U U	O O O O	•C C C C	—	—	—	—	—	—
Willow Ptarmigan	—	—	—	—	—	—	—	—	—
Rock Ptarmigan	—	—	—	—	—	—	—	—	—
White-tailed Ptarmigan	—	—	•C C C C	—	—	—	—	—	—
Ruffed Grouse	•C C C C	•C C C C	•A A A A	—	—	—	—	—	—
Sage Grouse	•O O O O	—	—	—	—	—	—	—	—
Greater Prairie Chicken	—	—	—	—	•U U U U	—	•U U U U	—	—
Lesser Prairie Chicken	—	—	—	—	—	—	—	—	—
Sharp-tailed Grouse	—	—	R	•C C C C	•C C C C	—	•A A A A	—	—
Wild Turkey	—	—	—	—	•C C C C	—	R R R R	—	—
Northern Bobwhite	—	—	—	O O O O	•C U U U	•C C C C	•R R R R	—	—
Scaled Quail	—	—	—	—	—	—	—	—	—
Gambel's Quail	—	—	—	—	—	—	—	•C C C C	•C C C C
California Quail	—	—	—	—	—	—	—	—	—
Mountain Quail	—	—	—	—	—	—	—	—	—
RAILS, GALLINULES & COOTS									
Yellow Rail	R R R	—	—	—	—	R	—	—	—
Black Rail	—	—	—	—	—	R	—	—	—
Clapper Rail	—	—	—	—	—	—	—	—	—
King Rail	—	—	—	—	—	R	—	—	—
Virginia Rail	•O O O	—	—	•C C C	R R R	•U U U	•C C C	R	—
Sora	•C C C	•U C	•U U	•C C C	R R R	•C C C	•C C C	O R O	O O
Purple Gallinule	—	—	—	—	—	—	—	—	—
Common Moorhen	—	—	—	—	—	—	R R R	•C C C C	O O O
American Coot	•A A A	•C C C	C C C	•C C C O	U U U	•A A A O	•A A A	•C C C C	•C C C C
LIMPKINS									
Limpkin	—	—	—	—	—	—	—	—	—
CRANES									
Sandhill Crane	•A C A	—	—	R R	U U	A C	C C	—	C C O
Whooping Crane	—	—	—	—	—	O O	R R	—	—
PLOVERS									
Black-bellied Plover	—	—	—	R O R	—	O O	R R	—	—
Lesser Golden-Plover	—	—	—	O O	—	U	—	—	—
Snowy Plover	—	—	—	—	—	R	—	—	—
Wilson's Plover	—	—	—	—	—	—	—	—	—
Semipalmated Plover	O	—	—	O R R	O O	C C	R R	—	—
Piping Plover	—	—	—	—	O O	—	O O O	—	—
Killdeer	•C C C	•C C C	•C C C R	•A C A O	•C C C	•A C A C	•C C C	•U O O	•C C C O
Mountain Plover	—	—	—	—	—	—	—	—	—
OYSTERCATCHERS									
American Oystercatcher	—	—	—	—	—	—	—	—	—
Black Oystercatcher	—	—	—	—	—	—	—	—	—
STILTS & AVOCETS									
Black-necked Stilt	O O	O	—	O O	—	—	—	O O	O O
American Avocet	•C C C	O	U U	•C C C	O R O	•U U U	•C C C	U U	U U
SANDPIPERS									
Greater Yellowlegs	U U U	O O	R	U U U	U O O	C C	C O O	O O O	O O O
Lesser Yellowlegs	U U U	O U	R R	C U C	C O U	C U C	C U C	R	O O O
Solitary Sandpiper	O O O	O R	U U U	U U R	O O O	C C	O O	R	O O
Willet	•C C C	—	R R	•U U O	U O U	C C	•U U U	—	O O
Wandering Tattler	—	—	—	—	—	—	—	—	—
Spotted Sandpiper	•U C U	•C C U	•C C C	U U U	O O O	C C C	C C C	U U U	•U U U
Upland Sandpiper	O O O	—	R	•C C O	•C C U	•U U U	•C C C	—	—
Whimbrel	—	—	—	—	—	R	—	—	—
Long-billed Curlew	•C C U	—	U	•C C O	•C C U	•U U U	O U O	O O	O O
Hudsonian Godwit	—	—	—	—	—	C	—	—	—
Bar-tailed Godwit	—	—	—	—	—	—	—	—	—
Marbled Godwit	•U U U	O	R	R R O	U U	U U	U R	O	O O
Ruddy Turnstone	—	—	—	—	—	O	—	—	—
Black Turnstone	—	—	—	—	—	—	—	—	—
Surfbird	—	—	—	—	—	—	—	—	—
Red Knot	—	—	—	—	—	—	R R	—	—
Sanderling	O	—	—	R O	—	O O	R R	—	—
Semipalmated Sandpiper	O O O	—	—	U U R	—	C C	U U	—	—
Western Sandpiper	O O O	—	—	O R R	U U	R R R	U U	O U O	U O U

	NV-3 Ruby L.	NV-4 Sheldon	NV-5 Stillwater	NJ-1 Cape May	NJ-2 B. Forsythe	NJ-3 Gr. Swamp	NM-1 Rand. Davey	NM-2 Bitter L.	NM-3 B dl Apache	NM-4 Grulla	NM-5 Las Vegas	NM-6 Maxwell
	•s S F W	•s S F W	•s S F W	•s S F W	•s S F W	•s S F W	•s S F W	•s S F W	•s S F W	•s S F W	•s S F W	•s S F W
	—	—	—	—	—	—	—	—	—	—	—	—
	•R R R R	—	—	—	—	—	—	—	—	—	—	—
	•R R R R	•C C C C	—	—	—	—	—	—	C C C U	—	—	—
	—	—	•U U U U	O O O O	R R R R	•C C C U	—	C C C U	—	•O O O O	—	•C O C C
	• R U U	—	—	—	—	—	—	—	—	—	—	—
	—	—	—	—	—	—	—	—	—	—	—	—
	—	—	—	—	—	—	—	—	—	—	—	—
	—	—	—	—	—	—	—	—	—	—	—	—
	—	—	—	O O O O	•O O O O	•U U U U	—	—	—	—	—	—
	•C C C C	•C C C C	—	—	—	—	—	—	—	—	—	—
	—	—	—	—	—	—	—	R R	—	—	—	—
	—	—	—	—	—	—	—	—	—	—	—	—
	—	—	—	—	—	—	—	—	•U U U U	—	•U U U U	—
	—	—	—	U U U U	•U U U U	R R R R	—	R R R R	—	•C C C C	—	—
	—	—	—	—	—	—	—	U U U U	•U U U U	•A A A A	•U U U U	•C C A C
	—	—	—	—	—	—	—	—	•A A A A	—	—	—
	•R R R R	•C C C C	•U C C U	—	—	—	—	—	—	—	—	—
	—	—	—	—	—	—	—	—	—	—	—	—
	—	—	—	R	R R R	—	—	O O O	—	—	—	—
	—	—	—	O O O	R R R	—	—	—	—	—	—	—
	—	—	—	C C C U	•C C C O	—	—	—	—	—	—	—
	—	—	—	U U U O	O O O R	•O U O	—	—	—	—	—	—
	•U U U R	O O O	•U C C O	U U U U	•U U U O	•A A A O	—	U U U U	•C C U	—	O O O	O
	•U U R	O O O	•U C C O	U U C O	•U U U R	•C C C R	—	U U U U	•C C U	—	O O O	O O
	—	—	—	R R R	—	—	—	—	R R R	—	—	—
	•R R	—	•R O R R	U U U R	•O O O	•U C C	—	R R	•U U U	—	R	—
	•A A A C	•C A C U	•A A A C	U O C U	•U O U U	U U U	U U U	A C A A	•C C A A	U O U U	•C C A A	C C C C
	—	—	—	—	—	—	—	—	—	—	—	—
	•C C U	O O U	—	—	—	—	R	U A C	A A	C C C	U A A	O R
	—	—	—	—	—	—	—	—	C C	—	R	—
	R	—	O O	A C C U	C O C O	—	—	O R O	R R	O	R	O O
	—	—	—	O R U	R O	—	—	R	—	—	—	O
	—	—	•O U O	—	—	—	—	C A C	O O	•C C C	—	—
	—	—	O O	C U C O	U U C R	—	—	O O O O	U U	—	R R	R
	—	—	—	U U U O	•U U O	—	—	—	—	—	—	—
	•C C C R	•C C C O	•A A C O	C C C U	•U U U R	•C C C O	R	C C C O	•A A A C	•C C C U	•C C C U	•C A C U
	—	—	—	—	—	—	—	—	R	—	O O	R
	—	—	—	C C C O	O U U R	—	—	—	—	—	—	—
	—	—	—	—	—	—	—	—	—	—	—	—
	•O C U	U O	•C A U	R R	O O	—	—	C C U	•C U U	U U U	U U	—
	•O C U	•U U U	C A A O	R R O	O O O R	—	—	C C U R	•C U U	C C C	•C U U	•C A C
	O O	O O	U O U O	C U C O	C U C U	O O O	—	C C C U	O O C O	U C C R	U U U	C C C
	U U	O O	O R O R	C C C O	U O C R	U O U	R	U U U R	O O O O	U C C R	U U U	O C O
	C C	O O	O O	U U U	O O O	U U U	O	O O O	O U O	U U U R	O O	U C U
	•C C U	•U O U	O O O	C A C O	•C A U R	—	—	U O O	O U U	O O O	U O O	U U U
	•C C C	•U U U	•U O U R	U O U	•U O U	•U U U	O O O	U U U	•C C C	U U U	•C U C	U U U
	—	—	—	O U U	R R	O	—	R R	R O	—	O O	—
	•C C	•U U U	•U U U R	C U C	U O U O	—	—	R	O O O O	O O O	•U U U	O O O
	—	—	—	—	—	—	—	R R	—	—	—	—
	—	—	O U U O	R R O	O O R	—	—	O O O	O O O	—	U	C C C
	—	—	—	A O C U	C O C R	—	—	—	—	—	—	—
	—	—	—	—	—	—	—	—	—	—	—	—
	—	—	—	A U U U	O U U	—	—	—	R	—	—	O U O
	—	—	R R	A U C C	C O C O	—	—	R R R	O O	—	U U U	U U
	—	—	—	A C A R	A A A O	O O O	—	—	—	—	C C C	O U O
	—	—	C A A O	U U C O	U U C O	—	R	C C C O	U O U	C C C	C C	O U O

STATE-NUMBER OF BIRD LIST REFUGE, SANCTUARY OR PRESERVE NESTING, ABUNDANCE BY SEASON (•s S F W)	MT-8 Red Rock L.	MT-9 Swan River	MT-10 Glacier	NE-1 Crescent L.	NE-2 Ft. Niobrara	NE-3 Rainwater	NE-4 Valentine	NV-1 Desert	NV-2 Pahranagat
SANDPIPERS (cont.)									
Least Sandpiper	O O	O U	—	U U U	U U U	C C	C C C	U U	U U
White-rumped Sandpiper	O	—	—	O	O O	—	U U	—	—
Baird's Sandpiper	O	—	R	C C C	U U U	C C	C U	—	—
Pectoral Sandpiper	—	—	R	U U U	O O O	A A	U U	—	—
Sharp-tailed Sandpiper	—	—	—	—	—	—	—	—	—
Purple Sandpiper	—	—	—	—	—	—	—	—	—
Rock Sandpiper	—	—	—	—	—	—	—	—	—
Dunlin	—	—	—	O O	R R	O O	R R	—	—
Curlew Sandpiper	—	—	—	—	—	—	—	—	—
Stilt Sandpiper	—	—	—	U U U	—	C C	R R	—	—
Buff-breasted Sandpiper	—	—	—	—	—	R	—	—	—
Ruff	—	—	—	—	—	—	—	—	—
Short-billed Dowitcher	—	—	—	—	—	C C	—	—	—
Long-billed Dowitcher	U U U	U U	R	C U C	U O U	U U	—	O O	O O
Common Snipe	•A A A O	•C C O U	•C C U	•U R U	U U U	C C	C U C R	U O	O O
American Woodcock	—	—	—	—	—	O O	—	—	—
Wilson's Phalarope	•C C C	•U U	U U	•A C C	U U	C C	•A C A	O	U U
Red-necked Phalarope	—	—	R R R	C U U	—	U U	R R	R	—
Red Phalarope	—	—	—	—	—	—	—	—	—
SKUAS, GULLS, TERNS & SKIMMERS									
Pomarine Jaeger	—	—	—	—	—	—	—	—	—
Parasitic Jaeger	—	—	—	—	—	—	—	—	—
Long-tailed Jaeger	—	—	—	—	—	—	—	—	—
Laughing Gull	—	—	—	—	—	—	—	—	—
Franklin's Gull	•C C	—	U U	U U C	U U U	A R A	C O C	—	—
Little Gull	—	—	—	—	—	—	—	—	—
Common Black-headed Gull	—	—	—	—	—	—	—	—	—
Bonaparte's Gull	—	—	R	R R	—	R R	R R	O O	—
Heermann's Gull	—	—	—	—	—	—	—	—	—
Mew Gull	—	—	—	—	—	—	—	—	—
Ring-billed Gull	•U U U	O C U	C C C	C U C O	U C C	C U U	C O C	O	C C C O
California Gull	•A A A	O U U	C C C	—	—	—	—	O O	O O O O
Herring Gull	—	—	R	R R O	—	U U U	O O O	—	—
Thayer's Gull	—	—	—	—	—	—	—	—	—
Iceland Gull	—	—	—	—	—	—	—	—	—
Lesser Black-backed Gull	—	—	—	—	—	—	—	—	—
Western Gull	—	—	—	—	—	—	—	—	—
Glaucous-winged Gull	—	—	—	—	—	—	—	—	—
Glaucous Gull	—	—	—	—	—	—	—	—	—
Great Black-backed Gull	—	—	—	—	—	—	—	—	—
Black-legged Kittiwake	—	—	—	—	—	—	—	—	—
Sabine's Gull	—	—	—	—	—	—	—	—	—
Gull-billed Tern	—	—	—	—	—	—	—	—	—
Caspian Tern	—	—	—	—	—	—	—	—	—
Royal Tern	—	—	—	—	—	—	—	—	—
Elegant Tern	—	—	—	—	—	—	—	—	—
Sandwich Tern	—	—	—	—	—	—	—	—	—
Roseate Tern	—	—	—	—	—	—	—	—	—
Common Tern	—	—	R R	O O O	U U U	U U	•C C C	—	—
Arctic Tern	—	—	—	—	—	—	—	—	—
Aleutian Tern	—	—	—	—	—	—	—	—	—
Forster's Tern	•C C	O O O	R	•C C U	U U U	•C U C	C C C	—	—
Least Tern	—	—	—	—	—	R R	R R R	—	—
Bridled Tern	—	—	—	—	—	—	—	—	—
Sooty Tern	—	—	—	—	—	—	—	—	—
Black Tern	•C C	•C C U	•U U	•C C C	U U U	•A C A	•A A C	O O	O O
Black Skimmer	—	—	—	—	—	—	—	—	—
AUKS, MURRES & PUFFINS									
Dovekie	—	—	—	—	—	—	—	—	—
Common Murre	—	—	—	—	—	—	—	—	—
Thick-billed Murre	—	—	—	—	—	—	—	—	—
Razorbill	—	—	—	—	—	—	—	—	—
Black Guillemot	—	—	—	—	—	—	—	—	—
Pigeon Guillemot	—	—	—	—	—	—	—	—	—
Marbled Murrelet	—	—	—	—	—	—	—	—	—
Kittlitz's Murrelet	—	—	—	—	—	—	—	—	—
Ancient Murrelet	—	—	—	—	—	—	—	—	—
Cassin's Auklet	—	—	—	—	—	—	—	—	—
Crested Auklet	—	—	—	—	—	—	—	—	—
Rhinoceros Auklet	—	—	—	—	—	—	—	—	—
Tufted Puffin	—	—	—	—	—	—	—	—	—

	NV-3 Ruby L.	NV-4 Sheldon	NV-5 Stillwater	NJ-1 Cape May	NJ-2 B. Forsythe	NJ-3 Gr. Swamp	NM-1 Rand. Davey	NM-2 Bitter L.	NM-3 B dl Apache	NM-4 Grulla	NM-5 Las Vegas	NM-6 Maxwell
	• s S F W	• s S F W	• s S F W	• s S F W	• s S F W	• s S F W	• s S F W	• s S F W	• s S F W	• s S F W	• s S F W	• s S F W
	C C C	—	A U A	A U C R	A U C O	U U O	—	C C C O	U U U	C C C	C C	U U
	—	—	—	U O U	O O O	—	—	R R R	R R	—	O O	—
	—	—	—	R O	R	—	—	U O O	U U	C C C	U U	U U
	—	—	—	C U C R	O O U	U U U	—	R R	O O	R R R	—	R O R
	—	—	—	C C C R	R R	—	—	—	—	—	—	—
	—	—	O O	A O A C	A O A A	R	—	R R	R R R	—	—	—
	—	—	—	R O O	R R R	—	—	—	—	—	U U	R R
	—	—	—	O U C	R U U R	—	—	C C C R	R R	—	—	—
	—	—	—	R O	O O	—	—	—	—	—	—	—
	—	—	—	O O O	R R R	—	—	—	—	—	—	—
	—	—	—	A A C R	C A C	R R	—	R R	—	—	—	—
	O U O	O O O	C O A	R O C R	O O U R	—	—	C C C R	C O C O	C C C	C U C	O O
	• U C U U	• U U U O	U O U O	C O C O	U O U O	A O C O	O O O	U O U U	C U C U	—	U U U C	R O R
	—	—	• A C A	C U C U	• U O U O	• A C A O	—	—	A C O	C O C	C C C C	• C U C	C A C
	• O O O	• C C C	C C C	O O U	R O O	—	—	A C O	C O C	C C C C	• C U C	C A C
	O O	R R	C C C	C O C R	R O	—	—	R O O	O O	—	—	—
	—	—	—	A C O	R R R	—	—	—	—	—	—	—
	—	—	—	U U O	—	—	—	—	—	—	—	—
	—	—	—	U O U O	—	—	—	—	—	—	—	—
	—	—	—	—	—	—	—	—	—	—	—	—
	—	—	—	A A A R	• C A C R	—	—	U O	R R	—	O O	O O O
	O O O	—	—	O R R	—	—	—	—	—	—	—	—
	—	—	—	R R R	R R	—	—	—	—	—	—	—
	—	—	R R R	C R U C	O O O	R	—	R O R	R R	—	—	—
	O O U	U O U	U U U O	C U C C	C O U C	O O O	—	C R C C	C C U	U U U	C U C U	A C C O
	O O O	U O O	C C O R	—	—	—	—	—	—	—	R R	C C C O
	—	—	—	A C A A	• A A A A	O O O O	—	R O O	O O O	—	R R	—
	—	—	—	O R O	R R R	—	—	—	—	—	—	—
	—	—	—	O R O	R R R R	—	—	—	—	—	—	—
	—	—	—	—	—	—	—	—	—	—	—	—
	—	—	—	O R O	R R	—	—	—	—	—	—	—
	—	—	—	C U C C	• C U C C	O O	—	—	—	—	—	—
	—	—	—	C O C A	—	—	—	—	O	—	—	—
	—	—	—	O O O	• U U U	—	—	R R	—	—	—	—
	O U O	O O	O O	O U U	R O O	—	—	—	—	—	—	—
	—	—	—	U U C R	O O U	—	—	—	—	—	—	—
	—	—	—	—	—	—	—	—	—	—	—	—
	—	—	—	O O O	R R R	—	—	—	—	—	—	—
	—	—	—	O O R	O O	—	—	R R R	R R	—	—	—
	—	—	—	C C C	• C C C	—	—	—	—	—	—	—
	—	—	—	U O U	—	—	—	—	—	—	—	—
	• C C U	O O	• U A O	C C C R	• C C C	—	O O	U U O	O O O	—	U U	C
	—	—	—	C C U	• C C O	—	—	U U U	—	—	—	—
	• C C U	U O U	• O O	O U U	O O	R	—	C U U	U O U	C C C	U U U	U O U
	—	—	—	C C C	• C C C R	—	—	—	—	—	—	—
	—	—	—	R U U	—	—	—	—	—	—	—	—
	—	—	—	R O	—	—	—	—	—	—	—	—
	—	—	—	O U U	—	—	—	—	—	—	—	—
	—	—	—	C U	—	—	—	—	—	—	—	—
	—	—	—	—	—	—	—	—	—	—	—	—
	—	—	—	—	—	—	—	—	—	—	—	—
	—	—	—	—	—	—	—	—	—	—	—	—
	—	—	—	—	—	—	—	—	—	—	—	—
	—	—	—	—	—	—	—	—	—	—	—	—
	—	—	—	—	—	—	—	—	—	—	—	—
	—	—	—	—	—	—	—	—	—	—	—	—

STATE-NUMBER OF BIRD LIST REFUGE, SANCTUARY OR PRESERVE — NESTING, ABUNDANCE BY SEASON	MT-8 Red Rock L. •s S F W	MT-9 Swan River •s S F W	MT-10 Glacier •s S F W	NE-1 Crescent L. •s S F W	NE-2 Ft. Niobrara •s S F W	NE-3 Rainwater •s S F W	NE-4 Valentine •s S F W	NV-1 Desert •s S F W	NV-2 Pahranagat •s S F W
AUKS, MURRES & PUFFINS (cont.)									
Atlantic Puffin	—	—	—	—	—	—	—	—	—
Horned Puffin	—	—	—	—	—	—	—	—	—
PIGEONS & DOVES									
Rock Dove	—	—	R R	—	—	•C C C C	—	O O O O	—
White-crowned Pigeon	—	—	—	—	—	—	—	—	—
Band-tailed Pigeon	—	—	—	—	—	—	—	•O R O	—
White-winged Dove	—	—	—	—	—	—	—	R R R	—
Mourning Dove	•U U C	O O O	C C C	•A A C	•A A C	•A A A A	•C C C	•C C C R	•C C C O
Inca Dove	—	—	—	—	—	—	—	—	—
Common Ground-Dove	—	—	—	—	—	—	—	R	—
White-tipped Dove	—	—	—	—	—	—	—	—	R
CUCKOOS, ROADRUNNERS & ANIS									
Black-billed Cuckoo	—	—	—	O O	• U	•C C C	•O O O	—	—
Yellow-billed Cuckoo	—	—	—	•R U R	O	•C C C	•O O O	O O O	—
Mangrove Cuckoo	—	—	—	—	—	—	—	—	—
Greater Roadrunner	—	—	—	—	—	—	—	•O O O O	C C C C
Smooth-billed Ani	—	—	—	—	—	—	—	—	—
Groove-billed Ani	—	—	—	—	—	—	—	—	—
BARN OWLS									
Barn Owl	—	—	—	•R R R	—	•O O O O	R R	•U O U	R R
TYPICAL OWLS									
Flammulated Owl	—	—	—	—	—	—	—	U C U	—
Eastern Screech-Owl	—	—	—	O O O	•U U U U	•U U U U	•U U U U	—	—
Western Screech-Owl	—	R O R	•R R R R	—	—	—	—	•O O U O	•O O U O
Great Horned Owl	•C C C C	•U O U U	•C C C C	•U U U U	•C C C C	•C U C U	•C C C C	•O O O O	O O O O
Snowy Owl	—	—	R R	O O	—	R	O	—	—
Northern Hawk Owl	—	—	—	—	—	—	—	—	—
Northern Pygmy-Owl	O O O O	O O O O	•C C C C	—	—	—	—	U U U U	—
Elf Owl	—	—	—	—	—	—	—	—	—
Burrowing Owl	U U U	—	—	•U U U	•C C C	•U U U	•O O O	O O O	O O O
Spotted Owl	—	—	—	—	—	—	—	—	—
Barred Owl	—	O O U	•U U U U	—	—	—	—	—	—
Great Gray Owl	•O O O O	—	•U U U U	—	—	—	—	—	—
Long-eared Owl	•U U U	—	R R	O	O O O	•U U U U	R R R	U O U O	O O
Short-eared Owl	•U C U	—	R	•U U U O	U O U U	•U U U U	C C C C	R	O O O
Boreal Owl	—	—	•R R R R	—	—	—	—	—	—
Northern Saw-whet Owl	•O O O O	—	•R R R R	—	—	—	•O O O	•O O O	—
NIGHTJARS									
Lesser Nighthawk	—	—	—	—	—	—	—	•U C U	•U C U
Common Nighthawk	R O R	U C	•C C	•C C C	C	•C C C	U C U	•U C U	U C U
Pauraque	—	—	—	—	—	—	—	—	—
Common Poorwill	—	—	—	—	—	—	—	•U C U	•U C U
Chuck-will's-widow	—	—	—	—	—	—	—	—	—
Whip-poor-will	—	—	—	R O R	• U	—	—	• R	—
SWIFTS									
Black Swift	—	—	•R R	—	—	—	—	—	—
Chimney Swift	—	—	—	O O	—	•A A C	—	—	—
Vaux's Swift	—	O U O	•C C	—	—	—	—	O O	—
White-throated Swift	O O O	O R	R	—	—	—	—	•U C U	U C U
HUMMINGBIRDS									
Buff-bellied Hummingbird	—	—	—	—	—	—	—	—	—
Ruby-throated Hummingbird	—	—	—	—	O	U U U	R R R	—	—
Black-chinned Hummingbird	O O	•R U U	—	—	—	—	—	•U O U	—
Anna's Hummingbird	—	—	—	—	—	—	—	R	—
Costa's Hummingbird	—	—	—	—	—	—	—	•O U	O
Calliope Hummingbird	• U U	•U U U	•C C	—	—	—	—	•R U R	—
Broad-tailed Hummingbird	• U U	—	R R	—	—	—	—	•U C U	U O U
Rufous Hummingbird	• U U	•U U	•C C	—	—	—	—	O C U	O O
Allen's Hummingbird	—	—	—	—	—	—	—	R	—
KINGFISHERS									
Belted Kingfisher	•C C C C	O O O O	•C C C U	R R R	•U U U	•C C C U	•O O O	O O	O C U
Green Kingfisher	—	—	—	—	—	—	—	—	—
WOODPECKERS									
Lewis' Woodpecker	O O O	O O	U U	—	—	—	—	O O	O
Red-headed Woodpecker	—	—	—	•U O U	•U C U	•C C C O	•U O U	—	—
Acorn Woodpecker	—	—	—	—	—	—	—	—	—
Gila Woodpecker	—	—	—	—	—	—	—	—	—
Golden-fronted Woodpecker	—	—	—	—	—	—	—	—	—
Red-bellied Woodpecker	—	—	—	—	—	•C C C C	—	—	—
Yellow-bellied Sapsucker	—	U U U	•C C U	R R	—	—	—	•C C C	O O
Red-breasted Sapsucker	—	—	—	—	—	—	—	O R O R	—

	NV-3 Ruby L.	NV-4 Sheldon	NV-5 Stillwater	NJ-1 Cape May	NJ-2 B. Forsythe	NJ-3 Gr. Swamp	NM-1 Rand. Davey	NM-2 Bitter L.	NM-3 B dl Apache	NM-4 Grulla	NM-5 Las Vegas	NM-6 Maxwell
•s S F W	•s S F W	•s S F W	•s S F W	•s S F W	•s S F W	•s S F W	•s S F W	•s S F W	•s S F W	•s S F W	•s S F W	•s S F W
	—	—	—	R R	—	—	—	—	—	—	—	—
	O	—	—	C C C C	O O O O	U U U U	R R	R R	—	R	U U U U	—
									R		U U U O	
	•A C A O	•C C C	•U C C O	C C A C	•C C C C	•A A A A	U U U	A A A C	•C A A U	•A A A C	•C C C O	•C A A U
				U O C	•O O O	•U U O		O O	•U U		U U	
				C C C	•U U U	•U U O		C C U U	•C C C C	•C C C C	•O O O O	•O O O O
	—	—	C C C C	O O C O	•R O O R	O O O O	—	U U U U	•R R O R	—	•U U U U	•O O O O
				O O O O	•U U U U	•U U U U	O	R R R R	•U U U U		•U U U U	
	•O U O O	•U U U U										
	•C C C C	•O O O O	•C C C C	U U U U	•U U U U	•C C C C	U U U	C C C C	•U U U U	O O O O	•U U U U	•O O O O
				O	R R							
	•U U U	•U O U	•U U O	—	—	—	—	U U U O	•U U U U	•C C C C	•U C U U	•O O O U
				R R R R	R R R R	•C C C C						
	•U U U U	•O O O O	•O R R O	U O	—	O O O	—	R R	—	•U U U U	R O	R
	•C C C U	•U U U O	•O R U C	U U U	U O O	—	—	U U U	O O	O O O	R O	O O O O
	•U U U U	O O O O	—	R U O	R R R	R R	—	R	R	—	—	O O O
	•C C U	U U	U C U	O R U	O O U	C C C	U U	O O O / C C C	•C A C / U U U	•C C U	•C C	•C C C
	•U U U	U U	—	C C R	U U	—	—	O C O		C C		
				U U O	•U U U	—	—					
	—	O R	—	C C C	O O O	C C C	—	—	—	—	—	—
	•U U U	•O U O	—	—	—	—	—	R R	•C C C	—		
				U U C	O O O	•O O O	O R O	O O O	U U U	—	•U C	O
	•U U U	—	—	—	—	—						
	•U U U	U U	—	—	—	—	C C C	R / O O O	U U U	—	U	O U O
	•U U U	U U	—	—	—	—	O U	R R	U U	—	•C C	O O / O C O
	U C C	U U	—	—	—	—					C U	
	•U U U U	R R R	O R O O	U U C U	•O U U O	C C C O	O	U O U U	U O U O	—	U U U U	U U U
	•U C U	O	—	U U U O	O O	•U U U U	R	R R / O O O O	R / O O O / R R	—	•U U U O / U R	•C C C O / •C C C
	O O O	O	—	U U U U / O U O	O O / O O	•C C C C / O O R	O O O	O O	U U U	U U U	U U U R	—

STATE-NUMBER OF BIRD LIST / REFUGE, SANCTUARY OR PRESERVE / NESTING, ABUNDANCE BY SEASON	MT-8 Red Rock L. •s S F W	MT-9 Swan River •s S F W	MT-10 Glacier •s S F W	NE-1 Crescent L. •s S F W	NE-2 Ft. Niobrara •s S F W	NE-3 Rainwater •s S F W	NE-4 Valentine •s S F W	NV-1 Desert •s S F W	NV-2 Pahranagat •s S F W
WOODPECKERS (cont.)									
Williamson's Sapsucker	•O O O	—	•U U	—	—	—	—	•O U O O	—
Ladder-backed Woodpecker	—	—	—	—	—	—	—	•C O C C	—
Nuttall's Woodpecker								—	
Downy Woodpecker	•C C C U	•U U U R	•C C C C	•U U U U	•U C U U	•C C C C	U U U U	•O O O O	—
Hairy Woodpecker	•C C C U	•U U U R	•C C C C	O O O	•C C C C	•C C C C	O O O O	•O O O O	—
Red-cockaded Woodpecker	—	—	—	—	—	—	—	—	—
Three-toed Woodpecker	O O O O	—	•C C C C	—	—	—	—	—	—
Black-backed Woodpecker	O O O O	—	•U U U U	—	—	—	—	—	—
Northern Flicker	•C C C	•U C C U	•C C C R	•U U U O	•C C C	•C C C C	•C C C	•U O U U	U O U U
Pileated Woodpecker	—	U U O O	•C C C C	—	—	—	—	—	—
TYRANT FLYCATCHERS									
Olive-sided Flycatcher	•U U	—	•C C	O O	—	U U	—	O U O	O O
Western Wood-Pewee	•C C	U U	U U	U U U	•C C	—	—	•O U O	O O
Eastern Wood-Pewee	—	—	—	O	—	•C C C	—	—	—
Yellow-bellied Flycatcher	—	—	—	—	—	U	O O	—	—
Acadian Flycatcher	—	—	—	—	—	—	—	—	—
Alder Flycatcher	—	—	—	—	U	—	—	—	—
Willow Flycatcher	•U C	•C C	•C C	R R R	—	—	—	O U O	O O
Least Flycatcher	—	—	R	C R R	—	C R C	R R	—	—
Hammond's Flycatcher	•U U	U U	C C	—	—	—	—	O O	O O
Dusky Flycatcher	U U	O U	U U	—	—	—	—	•U C U	U U
Gray Flycatcher	—	—	—	—	—	—	—	•O C O O	O O O
Western Flycatcher	•U U	O U	R	R	—	—	—	•O C O	O O
Black Phoebe	—	—	—	—	—	—	—	•U U U	U U U U
Eastern Phoebe	—	—	—	O O	•O O O	•C C C	—	—	•O O O R
Say's Phoebe	O O	—	R R	U O U	•C C C	•C C C	R O R	•C C C U	•C C C O
Vermilion Flycatcher	—	—	—	—	—	—	—	•O O O	—
Ash-throated Flycatcher	—	—	—	—	—	—	—	•O C O	O C O
Great Crested Flycatcher	—	—	—	O O	•U U U	•C O C	• R	—	—
Brown-crested Flycatcher	—	—	—	—	—	—	—	—	—
Great Kiskadee	—	—	—	—	—	—	—	—	—
Couch's Kingbird	—	—	—	—	—	—	—	—	—
Cassin's Kingbird	—	—	—	—	—	—	—	O O	—
Western Kingbird	U U U	•O C U	U U	•C C C	•C C C	•A A C	•C C C	•C C C	•C C C
Eastern Kingbird	•U U U	•O U O	•C C	•C C C	•C C C	•A A C	•C C C	O	R R
Gray Kingbird	—	—	—	—	—	—	—	—	—
Scissor-tailed Flycatcher	—	—	—	—	—	•R R	—	—	—
LARKS									
Horned Lark	•C C C C	O O R R	•C C C C	•A A A A	•A A A A	•A C A A	•C C C U	•C C C C	•C C C C
SWALLOWS									
Purple Martin	—	—	—	O O	—	•C C C	—	—	—
Tree Swallow	•C C C	•C C	•A A U	•R R O	C C C	•C O C	•O O O	U C U	C C C
Violet-green Swallow	•U U	•C C	•C C U	—	—	—	—	•C C C	C C C
Northern Rough-winged Swallow	•U U	•C C	•U U U	U U	•U C U	•C C C	•C C C	U O U	U U U
Bank Swallow	•U C	—	•C C U	C C C	U U U	•U U U	O O O	R R R	U O U
Cliff Swallow	•C C C	•U U	•C C U	•U R	•C C C	•C C A	O O	O U O	U U U
Barn Swallow	•C C C	•U C	•C C U	•A A A	•C C C	•A A C	•A A A	U O U	U U U
JAYS, MAGPIES & CROWS									
Gray Jay	•U U U U	O O R U	•C C C C	—	—	—	—	—	—
Steller's Jay	•O O O O	R R O R	•C C C C	—	O	—	—	•U U U U	—
Blue Jay	—	—	R R	•C U C	•C C C C	•C C C C	•O O O O	—	—
Green Jay	—	—	—	—	—	—	—	—	—
Scrub Jay	—	—	—	—	—	—	—	•C C C C	—
Pinyon Jay	O	—	—	—	—	—	—	•C C C C	—
Clark's Nutcracker	•C C C C	R O O	•C C C C	—	R	—	—	•C C C C	—
Black-billed Magpie	•C C C C	•C U U U	•C C C C	O O O O	•C C C C	•U U U U	•C C C	—	—
American Crow	•U U U	•C U U	•C C C C	R O R O	•C C A U	•A C A A	•U O U O	R	O O U
Northwestern Crow	—	—	—	—	—	—	—	—	—
Fish Crow	—	—	—	—	—	—	—	—	—
Chihuahuan Raven	—	—	—	—	—	—	—	—	—
Common Raven	•C C C C	•C C C U	•C C C C	—	—	—	—	•U U U U	U U U U
TITMICE									
Black-capped Chickadee	•C C C C	•C C C C	•A A A A	O O R O	•C C C C	•C C C C	•O O O U	—	—
Carolina Chickadee	—	—	—	—	—	—	—	—	—
Mountain Chickadee	•C C C C	U O U O	•A A A A	—	—	—	—	•C C C C	R
Boreal Chickadee	—	—	•U U U U	—	—	—	—	—	—
Chestnut-backed Chickadee	—	•O O U U	•R R R R	—	—	—	—	—	—
Plain Titmouse	—	—	—	—	—	—	—	•O U O O	—
Tufted Titmouse	—	—	—	—	—	—	—	—	—
VERDINS									
Verdin	—	—	—	—	—	—	—	•U O U U	•U U U U

	NV-3 Ruby L.	NV-4 Sheldon	NV-5 Stillwater	NJ-1 Cape May	NJ-2 B. Forsythe	NJ-3 Gr. Swamp	NM-1 Rand. Davey	NM-2 Bitter L.	NM-3 B dl Apache	NM-4 Grulla	NM-5 Las Vegas	NM-6 Maxwell
•s S F W	•s S F W	•s S F W	•s S F W	•s S F W	•s S F W	•s S F W	•s S F W	•s S F W	•s S F W	•s S F W	•s S F W	•s S F W
	—	—	—	—	—	—	O O O	—	O	—	O O O	—
	—	—	—	—	—	—	O R O	O O O O	•C C C U	—	U U U U	R
	•U U U U	U O U	•O R R O	C C C C	•U U U U	•C C C C	O R R	O O O	U U U	—	U U U U	R R R
	•U U U U	U O U	—	U U U U	O O O O	•C C C C	O U U O	R	•U U U U	—	•U U U U	R R R
	•C C C U	•C C C U	•C C C C	C C A U	•U U C O	•C C C U	C C C U	O R C C	•C C A A	—	•U U U U	•C C C O
						•O O O O						
	• U	O O	R R	O O	—	O O O	R R	O	O	—	—	U U U
	•U U	O O O	U U U	—	•O O O	—	U C U	U U U	•U U O	—	U U	U
				C C C	—	•C C C						
				R U	R	O U U						
				C C U	—	•O O						
				O	—	O O						
	• C	O O		U U	O R R	•C C C			O O O			U U U
				U C	O O	•O O O						
	•U	O O										
	•C C C	•O O O										
	•U U U	•U U U										
	•U U	O O					U C U	O	C O C	—	C C U	
				U O C O	•U R U	•C C C O		O O O O	•U C U U	—	•U U U	
								R R	R			
	C C C	•U C U	•U U O O				O O	C C C C	•C C C C	—	•C C C R	•O O O
								O O O R	•O U O R			
	•U U U	O O	O O				U O O	U U	•C C U	—	U U U	
				C C C	U U U	•C C C						
									R R			
							O	O O	O O O	—	•U C U	•O O O
	•C C C	•O O	C A C	O R	R	—	O R R	C C C	•C A U	•C C C	•U C U	•C A C
		O O	—	C C A	•U U U	•C C C	—	R R	O O	—	O O O	•C A C
								—	—	—	—	—
							O R O	R R		•C C C		
	•C C C C	•A A A C	A C A C	U U C U	•U O U U	O O	—	A A A A	•C U U C	•A A A A	•C C C A	•C A A C
				C C C	•U U U	•U U			O O	—	—	—
	•C Λ Λ	•U O	C U U	C C A U	•C C C O	•C A C R	R	U	•A O A R	—	•U U U	—
	•C A A	•U C U	U U U	—	—	—	U C O	O	C C	—	•C C C	• C A
	•C C C	•U U U	•U O U	C C C	O O O	U C	U O O		C U C	—	•U U U	U
	C C C	—	—	C U C	•O O O	U U	—	O O	•A U A	—	U U U	C C C
	•A A A	•U C U	•U A U	U R U	R R	U	R	C C C	•C U C	U U U	•C C C	• C C
	•C C C	•U A C	•C A U	C C C R	•C C C	•C C C	U C O	C A C	•A A A	U U U	•U U U	• C A
	—	—	—	—	—	—	U U U U	R R	O O O	—	•C C C O	U
	—	—	—	C C A C	•C C C O	•A A A A	—	O O R	—	—	—	U
	• U U U	•C C U	—	—	—	—	C C C C	O O	•U U U C	—	C C C O	U
	•U U U C	—	—	—	—	—	U U U U	R O R	U U U U	—	U U U	
	•O O O O	—	—	—	—	—	O O U U	—	—	—	R	
	•C C C C	•C C C U	•C C C C	—	—	—	C O U C	—	O O O	—	•U U U C	•C C A C
	•O U U O	O O	•R R R R	C C C C	•U O U O	•C C C C	O O O	—	C C C	U U U	U U C C	U
	—	—	—	C C C C	•C C C O	O O O O	—	—	—	—	—	—
	—	—	—	—	—	—	—	U U U O	•O U U	U U O O	O O O O	U R R U
	•C C C C	•C C C U	•U C C U	—	—	—	C C C C	—	•C C C O	—	•C C C C	•O C C O
		O O O O	—		R R R R	•A A A A	—	—	—	—	U U U U	O O O
				C C C C	•U U U U	—	—	—	—	—	—	—
	•U U U C	O O	O	—	—	—	C C C U	—	U U C	—	U U U U	U
	•C C C C	O O	—	—	—	—	U U U C	—	O O O O	—	O O O O	
		O O		C C C C	•U U U U	•A A A A	—	—	—	—	—	—
	—	—	—	—	—	—	—	—	•U U U U	—	—	—

STATE-NUMBER OF BIRD LIST REFUGE, SANCTUARY OR PRESERVE NESTING, ABUNDANCE BY SEASON	MT-8 Red Rock L. •s S F W	MT-9 Swan River •s S F W	MT-10 Glacier •s S F W	NE-1 Crescent L. •s S F W	NE-2 Ft. Niobrara •s S F W	NE-3 Rainwater •s S F W	NE-4 Valentine •s S F W	NV-1 Desert •s S F W	NV-2 Pahranagat •s S F W
BUSHTITS									
Bushtit	—	—	—	—	—	—	—	• C C C	—
NUTHATCHES									
Red-breasted Nuthatch	• C C U U	• U U U U	• C C C C	U U U	—	O O	R R O	• O U O O	—
White-breasted Nuthatch	• U U U U	• U U U U	• R R R R	O O O	• U U U	• U U U U	R R R	• U C U U	—
Pygmy Nuthatch	• O O O	—	—	—	—	—	—	• C C C C	—
Brown-headed Nuthatch	—	—	—	—	—	—	—	—	—
CREEPERS									
Brown Creeper	• O U U	• U U O O	• C C C C	O O	U U U	O O O	R R	• U U U U	R
WRENS									
Cactus Wren	—	—	—	—	—	—	—	• O U O R	• O U O O
Rock Wren	• U U	—	• U U U	R R	• C C C	—	—	• C C C C	• C C C C
Canyon Wren	O O	—	—	—	—	—	—	• O O O O	• O O O O
Carolina Wren	—	—	—	—	—	—	—	—	—
Bewick's Wren	—	—	—	—	—	—	—	• O U O O	O U O
House Wren	• C C C	—	• U U	• U U U	• C C C	• C C C	• O O O	• C U C	C U C
Winter Wren	—	O O O O	• C C U U	—	—	U U	R R	—	—
Sedge Wren	—	—	—	—	O O O	• U U U	R R R	U	—
Marsh Wren	• C C C	• U C C O	—	• A A C	O O O	U U U	• A A A	• O O O O	• U C U O
DIPPERS									
American Dipper	• C C C	O O U U	• C C C C	—	—	—	—	—	—
OLD WORLD WARBLERS & THRUSHES									
Arctic Warbler	—	—	—	—	—	—	—	—	—
Golden-crowned Kinglet	U U U	U U U U	• A A C U	O R	—	C C U	—	U O R U	—
Ruby-crowned Kinglet	• C C C	U U U U	• C C C	U U	U U	U U	R R	• U O U U	U U U
Blue-gray Gnatcatcher	—	—	—	—	—	U	—	• C C C C	—
Black-tailed Gnatcatcher	—	—	—	—	—	—	—	• O O O O	• O O O O
Eastern Bluebird	—	—	—	O O O	• C U U	• U U U U	• R R R	—	—
Western Bluebird	O O O	—	• R	—	—	—	—	• O C O O	O O O
Mountain Bluebird	• A A A	C U O	• C C C	U U	U U U	—	• O O O	U O U	U O U
Townsend's Solitaire	• C C C U	O O	• C C C U	U U R	O O O	O	R R O	• U O U C	U U
Veery	• U U	O U O	• U U U	O O O	—	O	O O O	—	—
Gray-cheeked Thrush	—	—	—	U	O O	U	O O	—	—
Swainson's Thrush	• U U	• U U U	• C C C	C U U	O U O	C	O O	U U	U U
Hermit Thrush	• C U	—	• C C C	R R	O U O	C	O O	• O C O	O O
Wood Thrush	—	—	—	O	O O	• U U U	R R	—	—
American Robin	• C C C	• U C C U	• A A C	• C C C U	A C A C	• A C A C	• C C C U	• C U C C	C C C
Varied Thrush	—	• C C U R	• C C C U	—	—	—	—	U U	—
Wrentit	—	—	—	—	—	—	—	—	—
MOCKINGBIRDS, THRASHERS & ALLIES									
Gray Catbird	O O	• U U C	• R R R	U R U	• U U U	• C C C	• O O O	—	—
Northern Mockingbird	—	—	—	R O R	• U U	• U U U U	O R O	• C C C O	• C C C O
Sage Thrasher	• U U U	—	—	—	—	—	—	U O U O	U O U U
Brown Thrasher	—	—	—	• U U U	• C C C	• C C C R	• C C C	—	—
Long-billed Thrasher	—	—	—	—	—	—	—	—	—
Bendire's Thrasher	—	—	—	—	—	—	—	• U U R	—
Curve-billed Thrasher	—	—	—	—	—	—	—	—	—
Crissal Thrasher	—	—	—	—	—	—	—	• O O O O	• O O O O
Le Conte's Thrasher	—	—	—	—	—	—	—	• O O O O	• O U O
WAGTAILS & PIPITS									
American Pipit	C C U	U O O	• C C C	R R	U U	C C	C C	C C C	C C C
Sprague's Pipit	—	—	—	—	—	R R	—	—	—
WAXWINGS									
Bohemian Waxwing	• O	U C	C C C C	O O O	U U	O	—	R	—
Cedar Waxwing	• U U	U U U	C C C	U U U O	U U U	C U C U	O O	• U O U O	U U O
SILKY-FLYCATCHERS									
Phainopepla	—	—	—	—	—	—	—	• C C C C	O U O
SHRIKES									
Northern Shrike	U U U	U U U	R R R	U U U	O	U U	O O O	—	—
Loggerhead Shrike	• U U U	—	U U U	• C C C	C C C	• C C C C	• O C O O	• C C C C	C C C C
STARLINGS									
European Starling	• C C C	• C C U	• U U U U	• R U U R	• C C C O	• A A A A	• O O O O	• U U U C	• C C C U
VIREOS									
White-eyed Vireo	—	—	—	—	—	—	—	—	—
Bell's Vireo	—	—	—	• R R	U U U	• C C C	• O O O	O R	—
Black-capped Vireo	—	—	—	—	—	—	—	—	—
Gray Vireo	—	—	—	—	—	—	—	• O U O	—
Solitary Vireo	• C C U	—	• C C	O O O	—	—	—	• O C O	—
Yellow-throated Vireo	—	—	—	—	—	—	—	O	—
Hutton's Vireo	—	—	—	—	—	—	—	O	—
Warbling Vireo	• C C U	• O U	• C C	• U R U	—	• C C C	• C C C	• O O O	O O
Philadelphia Vireo	—	—	—	—	—	U U	—	—	—

NV-3 Ruby L. •s S F W	NV-4 Sheldon •s S F W	NV-5 Stillwater •s S F W	NJ-1 Cape May •s S F W	NJ-2 B. Forsythe •s S F W	NJ-3 Gr. Swamp •s S F W	NM-1 Rand. Davey •s S F W	NM-2 Bitter L. •s S F W	NM-3 B dl Apache •s S F W	NM-4 Grulla •s S F W	NM-5 Las Vegas •s S F W	NM-6 Maxwell •s S F W
•C C C C	•U U U O	•O O O R	—	—	—	U U C U	—	•O U U O	—	O O O O	R R R R
•C C C	O O O	—	U C O	O O O	O U O	O O O	O O R	O U U	—	O O O O	O O
—	—	—	U U U U	•O O O O	•A A A A	U O U O	R R R	O U U	—	U U U U	—
—	—	—	—	—	—	O O O O	—	—	—	U U U U	—
•U U U	—	—	U C U	O O O	•C U C U	O O O O	R R R	O	—	U U U U	O
—	—	—	—	—	—	—	R R / U U U U	•U C C U	—	—	—
•U U U	•U C U	—	—	—	—	—	U U U U	•C A A C	—	•C C C O	R
•U U U R	•U U U	—	C C C C	•U U U O	•U U U U	O	R R R	•C C C C	—	•C C C U	—
—	O	•U U U R	—	—	—	O O O	O O U	O U U	—	U U U U	R R R
•C C C	•U U U	—	C C C R	•U U U	•C A C	U U U	O O O	U U	—	C C C O	•U U U
—	O	—	O U O / R	R R R / R R R	O O O	—	O O O	—	—	O O	—
•A A A U	•U U U O	•C A C U	C C C U	•C C C O	•C C C R	—	C C C	U O C C	—	O O	—
O O O O	—	—	—	—	—	—	—	—	—	—	—
U U U	—	—	C C U	U U O	U C U	U R U C	R R	O	—	O O O	—
U U U	U O O O	O O O	C C O	O O O	C C U	O U	U O O	U U C	—	U U U O	O O
—	•U U O	—	A C C	U O U	•C C U	R	R	U U U / •U U U U	—	O O O R	—
—	O O	R R R	U U U U	R R R R	•C C C O	U U U	R R R	U C	—	U U U O	O O / O O
•C U C	•U C C	R R R	—	—	—	—	O O O	U U U	C C C	•C C C C	C C
•U U U U / C	•U U U O	O O O R	C U C / O U / U U U	U O / O O O / U C U	•C C C / U U / C C O	U O C C / O U O R	O O / U	O U U / U C	—	U U U U / O O O / O O O R	— / R R
•C C C O	•C A C O / O O	U U U O	C C C A	•C C C U	•A A A U	C C C U	U O O O	•C C C C	—	•C U C U	•C A A
O O O / U	—	— / R R R	C C C U / C C C C	•C C C R / •C C C U / •U U U R	•A A A R / •A A A A / •C C C R	—	R R / C C C O / U R / O R	— / •C C U O / R O / O	—	— / •C C C U / U U U R / U U U O	U U U / •C C C / R
•U U U	•C A C	•O O U	C C C O	—	—	—	O O O O	•U U U U / •U U U U	—	R R R R	—
R R	O	O U U	U C U	O R	U U	O O	U U U / R	U C	C C C	U U	O
—	—	R R / O O O	C C C C	O O O O	U U U U	R R / O O O	O O O	O O O / R R	O O O	O O / O O	—
O / •O O O	O / •C C C U	U / •A C A C	R R / R O R	R R R / R	R R / R R	—	R R / C C C C	— / U U U C	C C C / •C C C C	O O / •C C C C	O / U R U R
•C C C O	•C C C C	•C U C C	A A A A	•A A A O	•A A A A	O O O R	U U U	•C C C C	—	•C C C C	•C A A C
—	—	—	C C C / —	•U U U / —	•C C C / —	—	—	•O O	—	—	—
U U U	—	—	U U / U O U	O O / R R	U U / •C C C	O U O	O R	•O O	—	U U	—
U U U	•U U U	—	O O / R U	O O / O	•U U R / U U	O U	R R	O O	—	U U	O O O

STATE-NUMBER OF BIRD LIST / REFUGE, SANCTUARY OR PRESERVE / NESTING, ABUNDANCE BY SEASON	MT-8 Red Rock L. • s S F W	MT-9 Swan River • s S F W	MT-10 Glacier • s S F W	NE-1 Crescent L. • s S F W	NE-2 Ft. Niobrara • s S F W	NE-3 Rainwater • s S F W	NE-4 Valentine • s S F W	NV-1 Desert • s S F W	NV-2 Pahranagat • s S F W
VIREOS (cont.)									
Red-eyed Vireo	—	• U U	• U U	R O R	• U U U	• U O U	• C C C	R R R	—
Black-whiskered Vireo	—	—	—	—	—	—	—	—	—
WOOD-WARBLERS									
Bachman's Warbler	—	—	—	—	—	—	—	—	—
Blue-winged Warbler	—	—	—	—	—	—	R R	—	—
Golden-winged Warbler	—	—	—	—	—	R	—	—	—
Tennessee Warbler	O O	—	R R	O	O O	C C	—	R R R	—
Orange-crowned Warbler	• O O	U U U	• U U	U U	C U C	C C	O O	U R U R	U U U
Nashville Warbler	—	U U U	R	—	—	U U	O O	• U R U	U U
Virginia's Warbler	—	—	—	—	—	—	—	• U C U	U U
Lucy's Warbler	—	—	—	—	—	—	—	• O R	O
Northern Parula	—	—	—	O	—	R R	—	R R	—
Tropical Parula	—	—	—	—	—	—	—	—	—
Yellow Warbler	• C C U	• C C U	• C C	• U U U	• C C C	• C C C	• C C O	• U O U	O O
Chestnut-sided Warbler	—	—	—	—	—	U U	—	—	—
Magnolia Warbler	—	—	—	O O	—	U U	—	—	—
Cape May Warbler	—	—	—	—	—	—	—	—	—
Black-throated Blue Warbler	—	—	—	O	—	R	—	R R	—
Yellow-rumped Warbler	• C C U	• C C U	• C C U	C O U	C C	C C	C C	• C C C U	C C U
Black-throated Gray Warbler	—	—	—	—	—	—	R R	• U C U	U U O
Townsend's Warbler	O	O C U	• C C	O O O	—	—	—	U U	U U
Hermit Warbler	—	—	—	—	—	—	—	R R	—
Black-throated Green Warbler	—	—	—	—	—	U	—	—	—
Blackburnian Warbler	—	—	—	—	—	U U	R R	—	—
Yellow-throated Warbler	—	—	—	—	—	R	—	—	O O
Pine Warbler	—	—	—	—	—	—	—	—	—
Prairie Warbler	—	—	—	—	—	—	—	—	—
Palm Warbler	—	—	—	—	—	U	R R	—	—
Bay-breasted Warbler	—	—	—	—	—	U U	—	—	—
Blackpoll Warbler	—	—	—	U R	O O	C C	R R	—	—
Cerulean Warbler	—	—	—	—	—	—	—	—	—
Black-and-white Warbler	—	—	—	O R R	U U U	C	R R	R R R	—
American Redstart	• U U	O U U	• C C	U U U	• U U U	C C C	• O O O	O O	U O
Prothonotary Warbler	—	—	—	—	—	—	—	—	—
Worm-eating Warbler	—	—	—	O	—	—	—	—	—
Swainson's Warbler	—	—	—	—	—	—	—	—	—
Ovenbird	—	—	—	U R U	• U O U	U U	• R R R	—	—
Northern Waterthrush	O O	O C U	• C C	R O O	—	U U	—	O R O	—
Louisiana Waterthrush	—	—	—	—	—	—	—	—	—
Kentucky Warbler	—	—	—	—	—	—	—	—	—
Connecticut Warbler	—	—	—	—	R R	R	—	—	—
Mourning Warbler	—	—	—	—	—	U	—	—	—
MacGillivray's Warbler	• C C	O U U	• C C	R O O	—	—	R R	U O C	U C
Common Yellowthroat	• C C	U U U	• C C	• A A C	• C C C	• C C C	• O C O	• O O O	O O
Hooded Warbler	—	—	—	—	—	R	—	—	—
Wilson's Warbler	• C C	O U O	• C C	U U U	U U	U U	R R	C U U	U U
Canada Warbler	—	—	—	—	—	O O	O O	—	—
Painted Redstart	—	—	—	—	—	—	—	• R R	—
Yellow-breasted Chat	—	—	—	R O O	• C C C	O O O	O O O	• O R O	U U
TANAGERS									
Hepatic Tanager	—	—	—	—	—	—	—	—	—
Summer Tanager	—	—	—	—	—	—	—	R R R	R R
Scarlet Tanager	—	—	—	—	• U U U	U	—	—	—
Western Tanager	• C C	O O	• C C	O O	U U U	—	O O O	• U C U	U U
CARDINALS, GROSBEAKS & ALLIES									
Northern Cardinal	—	—	—	—	U U U U	C C C C	R R	—	—
Pyrrhuloxia	—	—	—	—	—	—	—	—	—
Rose-breasted Grosbeak	—	—	—	R O	O O O	• C U C	—	R R	—
Black-headed Grosbeak	O O	• U U	• R R	U U	• U C U	—	—	• U C U	U U
Blue Grosbeak	—	—	—	• R U O	• U U U	• U U U	• O O O	• U U U	• U U
Lazuli Bunting	• U	O U	• C C	U R R	U U	U	• O O O	O U O	O U O
Indigo Bunting	—	—	—	—	U U	• U U U	O O	O O R	—
Painted Bunting	—	—	—	—	—	—	—	—	—
Dickcissel	—	—	—	• R	• C C C	• C C C	• C C C	—	—
NEW WORLD SPARROWS & ALLIES									
Olive Sparrow	—	—	—	—	—	—	—	—	—
Green-tailed Towhee	• O O O	—	—	—	—	—	—	• C C C	C C
Rufous-sided Towhee	—	U O O	U U	U U	• A A A	C C O	• C C C	• C C C C	U U
Brown Towhee	—	—	—	—	—	—	—	—	—
Abert's Towhee	—	—	—	—	—	—	—	O O	—
Bachman's Sparrow	—	—	—	—	—	—	—	—	—

	NV-3 Ruby L.	NV-4 Sheldon	NV-5 Stillwater	NJ-1 Cape May	NJ-2 B. Forsythe	NJ-3 Gr. Swamp	NM-1 Rand. Davey	NM-2 Bitter L.	NM-3 B dl Apache	NM-4 Grulla	NM-5 Las Vegas	NM-6 Maxwell
•s S F W	•s S F W	•s S F W	•s S F W	•s S F W	•s S F W	•s S F W	•s S F W	•s S F W	•s S F W	•s S F W	•s S F W	•s S F W
	R —	—	—	C C C	•U U U	•C C C	—	R —	—	—	—	—
	—	—	—	U U C	U O U	•C C C	—	—	—	—	—	—
				R O	R R	O						O
				C	A	C C	—	R	—			
	U U U	•U O U	O R R	R O R	—	—	O O	R O	U U	—	—	
	•U U U			U U	O R	U U		O O	U U		U C U	
							U C U	R	•U C U			
				C R C	U O U	C C	—	R				
	•C C C	•U O U	U C U	C C C	•C C U	•A A A	R	U R O	•U U U	—	U C U	U U U
				U C C	O O	•C O C	—	—				
				C R C	U U U	U U	—	—				
				U C	O O	U U	—	—				
				C C C	O O O	C C C	—	R R				
	•C C C	•U O U	U O O	A A C	C C U	A C O	U O U	A C R	C O C U	—	C C C	O O
	•U U U	O R	—	—	—	—	O U	R R	O O	—	O	—
	—	O O	—	—	—	—	O R U	R	—	—	O	—
	—	—	—	—	—	—	—	—	—	—	O	—
	—	—	—	R C	O O	C C	—	—	—	—	O	—
				C C	U O	U U	—	R				
				U U O	R	R	—	R				
				C C U O	•U U U R	O O						
				C C C	C U C	O						
				U C O	O O O	C U						
				U C	O O	U U						
				C O C	C C	C C						
				R R	R	O O						
				C C C R	•C O C	•C C C	—	O				O O O
				C C A	U U	•C C C			O O		O O O	
				U U U	R R	•O O O						
				U O U	R R	—		O			
				C C C	•U U U	•C C C	—	R R			O	—
	R R	—	—	C U C	U U	U U	—	R	O O	—	O	—
	—	—	—	O O	—	•U O U	—	—	—	—	—	—
	—	—	—	U O U	—	U	—	—	—	—	—	—
	—	—	—	U	R R	O	—	—	—	—	—	—
	•U U U	U O U	O O	O R U	—	O	U O U	O	O O	—	U U U	—
	•U C U	•U O U	•O O O	C C A O	•C C C R	•A A A R	R	C C U	•C C U	—	C C U	—
	—	—	—	U U U	•O O O	O O	—	—	—	—	—	—
	•U U U	U O U	—	U U R	O O	U U	U O U	U R O	C C	—	U U U	O O O
				C C	U U	C O C						
	•O O O	—	•R O R	C C U R	•O O O	•O O O	—	O O O	•C C U	—	O O O	U U U
	—	—	—	—	—	—	—	R R	O O	—	• R	—
	—	—	—	—	—	—	—	R R	•U U U	—	O O O	—
	—	—	—	U U U	R	O	—	R	O O	—	—	—
	—	—	—	C C C R	•U U O	•C C C	—	R	O O	—	—	—
	U U U	•U O	U O O	R R	—	—	U C U	U O O	C R O	—	•U U	O U O
	—	—	—	C C C C	•C C C C	•C C C C	—	R	O O O O	—	—	—
	—	—	—	C C	O R	•C C C	R R	R O O U	U O	—	—	—
	U U U	U O	•O O	—	—	—	O C U	U O	C U C	—	•C U U	O O O
	—	—	—	U U U	O O O	—	U	C U U	•A A U R	U C U	•U C U	•O O O
	•U U U	O	—	—	—	—	U C O	O	O R R	—	O O O	R
	R R	—	—	C C C	•O O O	•U O U	R O	O R	—	—	R	—
	—	—	—	—	—	—	—	R R	—	—	—	—
	—	—	—	O U O	R	—	—	R R	O	—	O	—
	•U U U	•U C U	—	—	—	—	O U O	C O R	U U U	—	C U C O	—
	•U U U	U U	R R R	C C C U	•U U U O	•A A A O	C C C O	U U U	•C C C C	—	•C C C U	•U U U
							C C C C	U U U	•U U U U		•C C C U	
	—	—	—	—	—	—	—	—	—	—	—	—

STATE-NUMBER OF BIRD LIST / REFUGE, SANCTUARY OR PRESERVE / NESTING, ABUNDANCE BY SEASON	MT-8 Red Rock L. • s S F W	MT-9 Swan River • s S F W	MT-10 Glacier • s S F W	NE-1 Crescent L. • s S F W	NE-2 Ft. Niobrara • s S F W	NE-3 Rainwater • s S F W	NE-4 Valentine • s S F W	NV-1 Desert • s S F W	NV-2 Pahranagat • s S F W
NEW WORLD SPARROWS & ALLIES (cont.)									
Cassin's Sparrow	—	—	—	—	—	—	—	—	—
Rufous-crowned Sparrow	—	—	—	—	—	—	—	—	—
American Tree Sparrow	O O	O	R R R R	U	U U U	C C C	C C A	R R R	—
Chipping Sparrow	•C C C	•O U U	•C C	U R R	•C C C	C C	•O C O	•C C C	C C
Clay-colored Sparrow	—	—	—	R R R	U U U	C C	U U R	—	—
Brewer's Sparrow	•C C	—	R R	—	—	—	—	•C U C R	•C U C
Field Sparrow	—	—	—	R R	•U U U	U U U	•O O O R	—	—
Black-chinned Sparrow	—	—	—	—	—	—	—	•O O	—
Vesper Sparrow	•C C C	U C U	•C C U	•R R R	•A A A U	C C	•C C C	O O	O O
Lark Sparrow	•O O O	O	R	•C C C	•A A A	•C C C	•C C C	U U	U U
Black-throated Sparrow	—	—	—	—	—	—	—	•C C C R	•C C C O
Sage Sparrow	—	—	—	—	—	—	—	•C U C	•C O C C
Lark Bunting	O	—	R	•C C C	U C U	•C C C	•O C O	O O O	U U O
Savannah Sparrow	•A A A	•U U U	•C C	U R U	•U U U	—	O O O	O U O	O U O
Baird's Sparrow	—	—	—	—	R R	U U	O R O	—	—
Grasshopper Sparrow	—	U O U	—	•A A A	•A A C	•C C C	•C C C	—	—
Henslow's Sparrow	—	—	—	—	—	O O	—	—	—
Le Conte's Sparrow	—	—	R R	—	—	—	O C O	—	—
Sharp-tailed Sparrow	—	—	—	—	—	—	R R	—	—
Seaside Sparrow	—	—	—	—	—	—	—	—	—
Fox Sparrow	U	O O O	•C C U	—	R R R	O O	—	C C C	—
Song Sparrow	•C C C	•C C U U	•C C C R	R R R R	U U U R	C C U	•O O O O	•O O O O	C C C
Lincoln's Sparrow	•C C	—	•U U U	R R	U U U	C C	R R	U U	U U
Swamp Sparrow	—	—	—	•U U U	—	•O R O	—	O	—
White-throated Sparrow	—	—	R	R O R	U U U	C U	U U	O	—
Golden-crowned Sparrow	—	—	—	—	—	—	—	R R R	—
White-crowned Sparrow	•C C	U U O O	•C C C	C U	C C C	C U O	U U	C C C	C C
Harris' Sparrow	—	U	R	U U	U U U	C C C	O O	—	—
Dark-eyed Junco	•C C C U	C C C C	•A A A C	U C C	C C C	C C C	C C C	•C C C C	C C C
McCown's Longspur	—	—	R	R R	U U	—	O O O	—	—
Lapland Longspur	U U U	—	U U	R R R	U U U	A A	O O O	O	—
Smith's Longspur	—	—	—	—	—	—	—	—	—
Chestnut-collared Longspur	—	—	U	U U	O O	O	•C O C O	O	—
Snow Bunting	U U C	U	U U U	O O	—	R	R	—	—
NEW WORLD BLACKBIRDS & ORIOLES									
Bobolink	• O	U U	R	•C C R	U U	C C	•O C O	—	—
Red-winged Blackbird	•C C C	•C C U	•C C	•A A A C	•C C C	•A C A O	•A A A	•C U C C	•C C C C
Tricolored Blackbird	—	—	—	—	—	—	—	—	—
Eastern Meadowlark	—	—	—	•C C C	•U U U	•O O O	•C C C O	—	—
Western Meadowlark	•C C C	U U U	•U U U	•A A A O	•A A A U	•C C C C	•C C C O	•C O C C	•C O C O
Yellow-headed Blackbird	•C C U	•C C U	R	•A A A	C C C	•C C C	•C C C	•C O C R	•C C C C
Rusty Blackbird	—	—	R	—	O O	C C C	—	—	—
Brewer's Blackbird	•C C	U C	U U U R	R R	U U U	•C C	O O	C O C O	•C C C O
Great-tailed Grackle	—	—	—	—	—	U U	—	U U U	—
Boat-tailed Grackle	—	—	—	—	—	—	—	—	—
Common Grackle	—	—	R	•C C C O	•C C C	•A A A O	•C C C	—	—
Bronzed Cowbird	—	—	—	—	—	—	—	—	—
Brown-headed Cowbird	•C C	•U C	•U U U	•C C U	•C C C	•A C A O	•C C C	•U C U R	•U C U O
Orchard Oriole	—	—	—	•C C	•C C C	•C C C	•U U U	—	—
Hooded Oriole	—	—	—	—	—	—	—	•U O O	—
Baltimore Oriole	—	—	—	—	—	—	—	—	—
Bullock's Oriole	—	—	•R R	•U U O	•U U U	•C C C	•O C O	•U C U	•C C U
Scott's Oriole	—	—	—	—	—	—	—	•U U U	U O U
FINCHES									
Rosy Finch	•C O C	O	•C C C C	—	—	—	—	—	—
Pine Grosbeak	•C C C C	—	•C C C C	—	—	—	—	—	—
Purple Finch	—	—	—	O O	—	U U U	—	—	—
Cassin's Finch	•C C C U	O U O O	C C C	—	—	—	—	•C C C C	—
House Finch	—	O	—	—	—	—	—	•C C C C	•C C C C
Red Crossbill	•U U U U	•U U U U	•C C C C	O	R R	O	R R	•U U U U	—
White-winged Crossbill	—	O	U U U U	—	—	—	—	—	—
Common Redpoll	C C	—	U	C C C	O O	U	O O O	—	—
Hoary Redpoll	—	—	—	—	—	—	—	—	—
Pine Siskin	•C C C O	•C C C U	•C C C U	O O R O	•C C C	•U O U U	O O	•C C C C	C C U
Lesser Goldfinch	—	—	—	—	—	—	—	•U O U O	U O U O
Lawrence's Goldfinch	—	—	—	—	—	—	—	—	—
American Goldfinch	• U U	O O U O	U U U	•C C C O	•C C C	•C C C C	•U U U	•O O O	O O U
Evening Grosbeak	O O	•U U U U	•C C C C	O O	U	R	R R	O O U	—
OLD WORLD SPARROWS									
House Sparrow	•U U	O O	R	•O O O O	•A A A A	•A A A A	•O O O O	•C C C C	•C C C C
Eurasian Tree Sparrow	—	—	—	—	—	—	—	—	—

Each column records seasonal status under the headings **•s S F W**.

NV-3 Ruby L.	NV-4 Sheldon	NV-5 Stillwater	NJ-1 Cape May	NJ-2 B. Forsythe	NJ-3 Gr. Swamp	NM-1 Rand. Davey	NM-2 Bitter L.	NM-3 B dl Apache	NM-4 Grulla	NM-5 Las Vegas	NM-6 Maxwell
—	—	—	—	—	—	—	C C C	O O	—	O	—
—	—	—	—	—	—	—	O O	O O O O	—	—	—
O O	—	—	O O O	U U	C C A	—	O O O	O	—	C O O C	O
•U U U	U U U	O O	C C C O	•U U U	•C C C	U C U	U R U O	•C C O	—	C C C U	O U U O
			O	—			C C	—		O O	
•C C C	•C A C	O O	C C C U	U U U U	•C C C U	—	C C U	C C O	O	•O O	U
—	—	—	—	—	—	—	R	—	—	—	—
•C C C	•U C U	—	O U	R R	O O R O	—	U U U	U U U U	—	•A C U R	O
C C U	O O	U U	O	R	—	—	C C C R	•C O C O	•C C C O	•C C C C	O O
•U U U	O O	O O O O	—	—	—	—	O O R R	•C C C U	—	—	—
•C C C	•U C U U	U O O U	—	—	—	—	U U U	C C C	—	—	R
—	—	—	—	—	—	—	U U C U	U U U	—	•U C U	C A A
•A A A	•O O	•U U U U	C C C	C C O	U U	—	C O C C	U U C	•A A A U	C O C U	•C C C O
—	—	—	—	—	—	—	O O	O O	R	O O O	—
O O O	—	—	O U	•O O O	O O	—	R R R	—	U U U	O O O	O O
—	—	—	R	—	—	—	—	—	—	—	—
—	—	—	—	—	—	—	R R	—	—	—	—
—	—	—	C C C U	•C C C O	—	—	—	—	—	—	—
—	—	—	A A A U	•C C C O	—	—	—	—	—	—	—
—	O O	—	U U C	O O O	U U O	—	—	O	—	•C U C O	—
•O O C O	•U C U O	•C C U O	C C C C	•C C C C	•C C C U	U C C C	C C C	C C A	—	•U U U O	O O C
R	O O O	—	R U	—	O O	O O	R O O	O O	—	O O O	O O
—	—	—	C C C U	•C C U U	•A A A U	—	U U U	R	—	—	O O
R	—	—	C A C	C C C	C C C	—	R R	O O O	—	—	—
R	—	—	—	—	—	—	—	—	—	—	—
C C C	U O U	C U A	U C O	O R O R	O O	U U C	A R C A	C O A A	C C C	C C C C	C O C
R R	—	—	—	—	—	—	—	A R	—	U O U O	—
•C O U C	U U U O	O O U	C C C	C C U	C C C	C U C C	U U C	C C A	C C A	U O U C	O O C
—	—	—	—	—	—	—	—	—	—	R	—
—	—	—	R O O	R R	—	—	—	—	R R	—	—
—	—	—	—	—	—	—	U U	O O	—	—	—
—	—	O	U U U	O R O	O O	—	—	—	—	O	—
•O O O	—	—	C C A R	O O U	•U U U	—	—	—	—	—	—
•U A A U	•U C U	•C C C C	C C A C	•A A A U	•A A A U	U O	C C C A	•A A A A	—	•C C C C	•C A A O
—	—	—	U U C U	•U U U U	•U U U O	—	C C C C	—	—	O O	R
•C A A U	•C A C	A C A C	R O R	R R	O O	—	C C C C	•A A A A	•A A A A	•A C A C	•A A A C
•A A C	•U C U	•C A O O	R O R	R R	O O	—	U U U O	C U C C	U U U	•O C O	C C C
•C C C	•C A C	•C C C C	U C O	R R	C C O	O	C R C A	C C C	C C C	•U C U O	•U U U
R R	—	—	—	—	—	—	U O O O	•C C C C	—	U U U	—
—	—	—	—	—	—	—	—	O	—	—	—
—	—	—	C C C U	•U U U	—	—	U U U U	O U U	—	C C C O	O O O
—	—	—	C C A C	•C C C O	•A C C O	—	—	—	—	—	—
•C C C	•U C U	•U U U	C C A U	•C C C O	•C C C O	O O	U U U C	•C C C C	—	C C C O	•U U U
—	—	—	C C C	•O O R	U U	—	O O	—	—	—	—
•U U U	•U U U	•U U O	C C A	U O O	•C C C	O O	C C U	•C C	—	•U C U	U U U
—	—	—	—	—	—	—	—	—	—	—	O O O
U	—	—	—	—	—	—	—	—	—	O	—
—	—	—	—	—	—	—	—	—	—	O U O O	—
•U U U	U U U	—	U C C	O O O	U U U	—	—	R R	—	U U U U	—
•C C C	•U U U	•U U U O	C C C C	•O O O O	•C C C C	C C C C	C C C C	•C C C U	—	•C C C U	•C C C
—	—	—	R O O	—	R	O O O O	—	—	—	R	—
—	—	—	R R	—	R	—	—	—	—	—	—
—	—	—	R O O	—	R	R R	—	—	—	—	—
•C C U	O U	—	O U U	O O O	O O O	U U C U	U O O	C O O O	O O O	U U U U	C C A C
O O	O O	—	—	—	—	U C O	O O R	•A U U A	—	•C U U O	U U U
•U U U	—	U U	C C C U	•U U U U	•A A C C	O O O	U U U	U U C	—	U U U O	R R R
O O O	—	—	U U U	O O O	O R	U U U C	—	R	—	U U U O	O O O
•O U O	•C C C C	•U U U U	C C C C	•C C C C	•A A A A	O O	C C C C	•C C C C	•C C C C	•C C C C	•A A A C

STATE-NUMBER OF BIRD LIST REFUGE, SANCTUARY OR PRESERVE — NESTING, ABUNDANCE BY SEASON (• s S F W)	NY-1 Iroquois	NY-2 Montezuma	NY-3 Wertheim	NY-4 Morton	NY-5 Target Rock	NY-6 Jones Beach	NC-1 Matta/Swan	NC-2 Pungo	NC-3 Mackay Is.
LOONS									
Red-throated Loon	—	R	R	O OO	O OO	C C	C	—	R R
Arctic Loon	—	—	—	—	—	—	—	—	—
Pacific Loon	—	—	—	—	—	—	—	—	—
Common Loon	R	O O	—	O	U UU	O OO	COCC	O CC	O O
Yellow-billed Loon	—	—	—	—	—	—	—	—	—
GREBES									
Least Grebe	—	—	—	—	—	—	—	—	—
Pied-billed Grebe	•CCC	•CCC	U UC	U UU	O	U	U CC	U U	OOCC
Horned Grebe	U	O O	R	O OO	O OO	C CC	U	R	O
Red-necked Grebe	—	R R	—	R R	—	R RR	—	—	R
Eared Grebe	—	—	—	—	—	—	—	—	—
Western Grebe	—	—	—	—	—	—	—	—	—
SHEARWATERS & PETRELS									
Northern Fulmar	—	—	—	—	—	R	—	—	—
Cory's Shearwater	—	—	—	—	—	R	—	—	—
Pink-footed Shearwater	—	—	—	—	—	—	—	—	—
Greater Shearwater	—	—	—	—	—	R R	—	—	—
Sooty Shearwater	—	—	—	—	—	U U	—	—	—
Short-tailed Shearwater	—	—	—	—	—	—	—	—	—
Manx Shearwater	—	—	—	—	—	—	—	—	—
Audubon's Shearwater	—	—	—	—	—	—	—	—	—
STORM-PETRELS									
Wilson's Storm-Petrel	—	—	—	—	—	U	—	—	—
Fork-tailed Storm-Petrel	—	—	—	—	—	—	—	—	—
Leach's Storm-Petrel	—	—	—	—	—	—	—	—	—
BOOBIES & GANNETS									
Masked Booby	—	—	—	—	—	—	—	—	—
Brown Booby	—	—	—	—	—	—	—	—	—
Northern Gannet	—	—	—	—	—	C U A C	—	—	—
PELICANS									
American White Pelican	—	—	—	—	—	—	—	R	—
Brown Pelican	—	—	—	—	—	R	—	R R	—
CORMORANTS									
Great Cormorant	—	—	—	R RU	—	U UC	—	—	—
Double-crested Cormorant	R	O CC	C CC	CUCR	CCU	ACAA	CUCC	OOOO	UOCC
Olivaceous Cormorant	—	—	—	—	—	—	—	—	—
Brandt's Cormorant	—	—	—	—	—	—	—	—	—
Pelagic Cormorant	—	—	—	—	—	—	—	—	—
Red-faced Cormorant	—	—	—	—	—	—	—	—	—
ANHINGAS									
Anhinga	—	—	—	—	—	—	R	—	—
FRIGATEBIRDS									
Magnificent Frigatebird	—	—	—	—	—	—	—	—	—
BITTERNS & HERONS									
American Bittern	•U UU	•O CC	•O OOO	O OO	R R	•U UU	• C C	U UUU	•C CUU
Least Bittern	•U UU	•O OO	•R RR	U U	R R	R	• C C	U U	•O OOO
Great Blue Heron	•CACO	•CCCO	CCCC	UUUU	O O	C CC	•CCCC	CUCC	CCCC
Great Egret	O OO	O CO	R RR	UUUR	O OO	•AAAR	•CCC	UUUU	CCCC
Snowy Egret	—	R	U UU	UUUR	U UU	•AAAR	•OUUO	U OO	O OO
Little Blue Heron	—	R R	R	U U	R	•U UC	• C C	U U	O OO
Tricolored Heron	—	—	—	R R	—	•U UU	• U U	O O	O O
Reddish Egret	—	—	—	—	—	—	—	—	—
Cattle Egret	R R	R	R RR	R RR	R RR	•O OO	• U U	C CC	C CO
Green-backed Heron	•U UU	•O CO	•C CC	•C CCR	•U UU	•C CC	• C C	C CU	C UUO
Black-crowned Night-Heron	O OO	•O CC	U UUU	U UUU	C CUR	•C CCU	•U UUU	O OOO	O OO
Yellow-crowned Night-Heron	—	—	R R	R R	•R RR	•U UU	R	R R	R RR
IBISES & SPOONBILLS									
White Ibis	—	—	—	—	—	—	—	—	R
Glossy Ibis	—	R R	O OO	U U	O	•A AA	O	O O	O OOO
White-faced Ibis	—	—	—	—	—	—	—	—	—
Roseate Spoonbill	—	—	—	—	—	—	—	—	—
STORKS									
Wood Stork	—	—	—	—	—	—	—	—	—
SWANS, GEESE & DUCKS									
Fulvous Whistling-Duck	—	—	—	—	—	—	—	R	—
Black-bellied Whistling-Duck	—	—	—	—	—	—	—	—	—
Tundra Swan	C OO	O RO	R	—	—	O O	URCA	U CA	RRCC
Trumpeter Swan	—	—	—	—	—	—	—	—	—
Mute Swan	—	O O	•AAAA	•UUUU	R R	U	—	—	—
Greater White-fronted Goose	R	—	—	—	—	—	—	R	R R
Snow Goose	O O	C O	O OO	U UU	R R	U UU	C	U CC	CRCA

NC-4 Pea Is.	NC-5 Pee Dee	NC-6 C. Hatteras	NC-7 C. Lookout	ND-1 Arrowwood	ND-2 Audubon	ND-3 Souris Loop	ND-4 Lake Ilo	ND-5 Long L.	ND-6 Tewaukon	ND-7 Roosevelt	OH-1 Ottawa
·s S F W	·s S F W	·s S F W	·s S F W	·s S F W	·s S F W	·s S F W	·s S F W	·s S F W	·s S F W	·s S F W	·s S F W
C C A	—	C C C	U U C	—	—	—	—	—	—	—	—
—	—	—	—	—	—	—	—	—	—	—	—
C R C C	—	C C C	C U C C	R R	O O	R R R	O O	R	O O	—	O R O R
C O C A	C U C C	C U C A	U C C	·C C C	·C C C	·C C C	·C C C	·C C C	·A A A	O	·C C C R
C U A R	—	C C C	U U U C	·U U U	U O O	·U U U	U O O	U U	R R R	—	C U R
R	—	R	—	·R R R	O R O	·O O O	O R O	—	R	—	R R
—	—	—	—	·C C C	·A A C	·C C C	·A A C	·C O C	·C A C	—	R R
—	—	—	—	·C C C	·C U C	·C C C	·C U C	·C U C	·A A A	—	—
A O A C	—	U U	U	—	—	—	—	—	—	—	—
U U U	—	—	—	—	—	—	—	—	—	—	—
C C	—	—	U U	—	—	—	—	—	—	—	—
R U R	—	—	U U	—	—	—	—	—	—	—	—
A A	—	R	U	—	—	—	—	—	—	—	—
R A A	—	R	U U	—	—	—	—	—	—	—	—
R R R	—	—	—	—	—	—	—	—	—	—	—
C R C A	—	C C C	C R C C	—	—	—	—	—	—	—	—
—	—	—	—	C C C	A A A	C C C	A A A	C C C	C C C	U U U	R R R
C C C U	—	R	C C C C	—	—	—	—	—	—	—	—
O	—	—	—	—	—	—	—	—	—	—	—
A R C C	O	A C O	C U C C	C C C	A A A	·U U U	A A A	A A A	·C C C	—	O O O R
—	O O	—	—	—	—	—	—	—	—	—	—
—	—	—	R R	—	—	—	—	—	—	—	—
C O C C	O	C C O	U U U	·C C C	·C U C	·U U U	·C U C	·C C C	·C C C	—	U U U R
·U U O	O	C C C	U U U	R R R	—	R R R	—	R	·U U U	—	·U U U
U U U U	C C C C	C C C C	C C C C	U U U	·C C C	·U U U	·C C C	U C C	C C C	·C C C	·C A C U
C C C C	U U U	C C A O	C C C U	R	R R R	R R	R R R	R	O O U	—	·C A C
·C C C U	—	A C A O	C C C U	R R	R R R	R R	R R R	R	—	—	R R R
·C C C U	U U U	—	U C U U	R R R	R R R	·U U U	R R R	—	—	—	R O O
·C C C U	R	C C C O	C C C U	—	—	—	—	—	—	—	R O R
·U C C R	O O	U U	U U U	—	R R R	·U U U	R R R	· R	R R	—	·U U U
·U U U O	C C C	C C C O	U U U	·R R R	—	—	—	—	·U U U	—	·C C C
·C C C U	—	C C C U	U U U U	·C R C	·A A A	·C C C	·A A A	·C C C	·C C C	O	·C A C O
·R U U R	—	C C C O	U U U	—	—	—	—	—	—	—	R R
· O O R	—	—	U U U U	—	—	—	—	—	—	—	—
·C C C R	R	U U U	U U U	—	—	—	—	—	—	—	R R R
—	—	—	—	—	·R R R	R R	R R R	—	—	—	—
—	—	—	—	—	—	—	—	—	—	—	—
—	O	—	—	—	—	—	—	—	—	—	—
R R U	—	—	—	—	—	—	—	—	—	—	—
C R C C	R R	U C C	R	U C	O O	U C	O O	U U	C C R	—	A C O
—	—	—	—	—	—	—	—	—	—	—	R R O R
R R	—	R	R O A	—	R C	C R C	C C	C R C	O U	—	O C
A R A A	R R R	R U U	R R	U C	U R C	A A	U R U	U U	A R A R	U	O C U

STATE-NUMBER OF BIRD LIST REFUGE, SANCTUARY OR PRESERVE NESTING, ABUNDANCE BY SEASON	NY-1 Iroquois • s S F W	NY-2 Montezuma • s S F W	NY-3 Wertheim • s S F W	NY-4 Morton • s S F W	NY-5 Target Rock • s S F W	NY-6 Jones Beach • s S F W	NC-1 Matta/Swan • s S F W	NC-2 Pungo • s S F W	NC-3 Mackay Is. • s S F W
SWANS, GEESE & DUCKS (cont.)									
Ross' Goose	—		—	—		—	—	—	—
Emperor Goose	—		—	—		—	—	—	—
Brant		O	O O	U U	O O O	A R A A	R	—	—
Canada Goose	•A C C O	•A C C C	•C C C C	C U C U	O O O O	•A A A A	U R A A	U R A A	U U
Wood Duck	•C C C R	•C C C	•C C C O	•U U	O		•U C C C	—	•C C C C
Green-winged Teal	•C U C R	•C O C	C O C U	U U	O O R	C C C	C A A	U C C	C C C
American Black Duck	•C U C O	•A C A O	•C C C C	•U U C C	•C U C A	•A A A A	•C O C A	U U A A	•C U C C
Mottled Duck	—		—	—		—	—	—	—
Mallard	•C C C O	•A C A O	•C C C C	•U U U U	•U U C C	•A A A A	•U R C A	U U A A	•C U C C
Northern Pintail	•A O U R	•C O C	R R	U U U	R R	C C C	C A A	U A A	U C C
Blue-winged Teal	•C C U	•C C C	U U	U U	R R	C C	C C C	U U O	C C C
Cinnamon Teal									
Northern Shoveler	•U O U	•C O C	O O	—		C R C C	O O U	O O U	U U U
Gadwall	•U O U R	•C C C	•C U C O	•O O	R R R	•C C C C	U R C C	U U	A A
Eurasian Wigeon	—	R R	—				—	—	R R
American Wigeon	•C O C	•C O C	O C C	U U U	O O O	C C C	U C C	C C	A A
Canvasback	O O	•C O C	U U U	U U U	O O O	U U U	O O C	O O	U U U
Redhead	O O		O	U U U	—		U U C	O O	U U
Ring-necked Duck	C C	•C O C	O O O	—	R R		O O C	O O	U U
Greater Scaup	O O	C C	U U U U	U U U	C C C	C C A	O	—	R R
Lesser Scaup	U U	O O O	O O O U	U U U	R R C	—	C C C	O O	O U U
Common Eider	—	—	—	—	R	O	—	—	—
King Eider	—	—	—	—	—	O	—	—	—
Steller's Eider	—	—	—	—	—		—	—	—
Harlequin Duck	—	—	—	—	R	O	—	—	—
Oldsquaw	O O	O O	R	C C C	R U U	U C C	U	R	—
Black Scoter	R	R R	—	U U U	R U U	U R U U	R U	—	—
Surf Scoter	R	R R	—	U U U	U U U	U U U	R U	—	—
White-winged Scoter	R R	R R	—	U U U	U U U	U C C	R	—	—
Common Goldeneye	U U	C C	R	U U C	U U A	U U U	U	R	R R
Barrow's Goldeneye	—		—	—		—	—	—	—
Bufflehead	U U	C C	C C C	U U U	C C C	C C A	U C	R	O C
Hooded Merganser	•U U U R	•C O A O	U	R U R	R R	U U U	O	O O	•R R R R
Common Merganser	O O	A O A C	U U C	U C	U U	O O O	O R O O	R R	R R
Red-breasted Merganser	O O	O R O	C C C C	C U C C	C C C	A A A	O O	O O	R R
Ruddy Duck	O O O	•O O	R U U	U U U	R	R R R R	U U C	O O	C C
Masked Duck	—		—	—	—		—	—	—
AMERICAN VULTURES									
Black Vulture	—	—	—	—	—	—	•U U U U	U U U U	R R R O
Turkey Vulture	•C C C	C C C C	R R	—	R	R R	•C C C C	C C C C	C C C C
KITES, EAGLES, HAWKS & ALLIES									
Osprey	O R O	•C C C	•U U U	•U U U	R R	•O U C	•C C U R	O O O	•C C C
American Swallow-tailed Kite	—	—	—	—	—	—	—	—	—
Black-shouldered Kite	—	—	—	—	—	—	—	—	—
Snail Kite	—	—	—	—	—	—	—	—	—
Mississippi Kite	—	—	—	—	—	—	—	—	—
Bald Eagle	R R R	O O O O	O O O O	R R R	R	R R	O O O O	O O O	R R
Northern Harrier	•O O O O	•O O O O	•U U U U	U U U U	R	•A A A A	C C	O C C	C C C
Sharp-shinned Hawk	O O O	•O O O O	•O O O O	R R R	R R	U U A U	•C C C	C C C	U
Cooper's Hawk	O O O O	O O O O	•O O O O	R R R R	—	O R	O O O O	O O O O	O O R
Northern Goshawk	—	O O O	R R R	R R		R R R	—	—	—
Common Black-Hawk	—	—	—	—	—	—	—	—	—
Harris' Hawk	—	—	—	—	—	—	—	—	—
Gray Hawk	—	—	—	—	—	—	—	—	—
Red-shouldered Hawk	•U U U R	O O	R	—	R	R R R	U U U U	C C C C	O O O O
Broad-winged Hawk	O	O O	O O O	U U U	O O	R R R	O	O	U U
Short-tailed Hawk	—	—	—	—	—	—	—	—	—
Swainson's Hawk	—	—	—	—	—	—	—	—	—
White-tailed Hawk	—	—	—	—	—	—	—	—	—
Zone-tailed Hawk	—	—	—	—	—	—	—	—	—
Red-tailed Hawk	•C C C C	•C C C C	•U C U U	R R R R	•U R R U	R R U U	U U U C	C C C C	•O O O O
Ferruginous Hawk	—	—	—	—	—	—	—	—	—
Rough-legged Hawk	O O O	O C	U	R R	R	R R	R	—	R
Golden Eagle	R	O O	R	—				R O	R R
CARACARAS & FALCONS									
Crested Caracara	—	—	—	—	—	—	—	—	—
American Kestrel	•C C C U	•C C C O	•U U U R	•U U U U	•U U U O	•C R A C	C U C	O C C	C C C
Merlin	—	R R	O O O	U U U	R	U C U	U	O O	O O
Peregrine Falcon	R R	R R	R R O	R R R	R R R	U U U	R	O O	R
Gyrfalcon	—	—	—	—	—	—	—	—	—
Prairie Falcon	—	—	—	—	—	—	—	—	—

NC-4 Pea Is.	NC-5 Pee Dee	NC-6 C. Hatteras	NC-7 C. Lookout	ND-1 Arrowwood	ND-2 Audubon	ND-3 Souris Loop	ND-4 Lake Ilo	ND-5 Long L.	ND-6 Tewaukon	ND-7 Roosevelt	OH-1 Ottawa
•s S F W	•s S F W	•s S F W	•s S F W	•s S F W	•s S F W	•s S F W	•s S F W	•s S F W	•s S F W	•s S F W	•s S F W
R	—	—	—	R	—	R	—	—	—	—	—
—	—	—	—	—	—	—	—	—	—	—	—
R R	—	—	O	U U C	R	—	—	—	—	—	R
A R A A	C A A	C R A A	U U C	•C C C	•A A A O	•C U C	•A A A O	•C U A	•A C A O	•C C	•A A A A
R R R	C C C C	—	R R	•C C C	O O O	•U U U	O O O	R	•C C U	O O	•C C A R
•A R A A	C U C	C A A	U U C	•U U C	•C C C R	•U U U	•C C C R	•O O O	•C U C	U R	•C U A O
•A U A A	C C C	A C A A	U U U C	•U U U	R R	•R R R	R R	•O O O	O O	—	•A C A A
•U O U U	C C C	C O C C	U U C	•C C C	•A A A O	•A C A	•A A A O	•C C A U	•A A A R	•C R O	•A A A A
C A A	C O C	C A A	U U C	•C C C	•A A A R	•A C A	•A A A R	•C C C	•C C C	U R	•A U A O
•A O A R	U C C U	C U C O	U U U R	•C C C	•A A A	•A C A	•A A A	•C C C	•A A A	•C R	•A C A
			—	•R R R	R R R	R R	R R R	R			
C C C	U U C	C C C	U U R	•C C C	•A A A	•C U C	•A A A	•C U C	•C C C	U	•C U C R
•C C C U	O O	C C C C	U U U U	•C C C	•A A A	•A C A	•A A A	•C C C	•A A A	R O	•C U A R
U R	—	R	—	—	—	R R	—	—	—		R R
C C A	C C C	C C A	U U C	•C C C	•C C C	•C U C	•C C C	•C U C	•C C C	R O	•A U A O
U U C	R	R U C	R	•U U C	•U U U	•C U C	•C C C	•U O U	•U U U	O	A C C
U C C	R	R U C	U U C	•U U C	•C C C	•C U C	•C C C	•U U U	•C C C	—	•C U C O
C C C	C C C	C C C	R	•U R U	O O	•U O U	O O	R R	U R U	—	C C R
C R U C		C C C	U U C	R U		R					U U U
C U C	U R U	C U C	U U C	•C R C	•A A A	•C U C	•A A A	•C O C	•C U C R	O	•A U C U
R		—	—	R R R R	—	—	—	—	—	—	—
—	—	—	—	—	—	—	—	—	—	—	—
—	—	—	—	—	—	—	—	—	—	—	—
U R U	—	U U U	U U U	—	—	—	—	—	—	R O R	O R
C U C	—	U U U	U R U C	—	—	—	—	—	—		O R
C U A	—	C C C	U R U C	—	—	—	—	—	—		O O O
U U U	—	C C C	U U U	R	—	•R R R	—	R	—		O O O
R R O	R	R R U	U U U	U U	U R U R	U U	U R U R	C U	C C R	O	C C C
C R C C	R	C C C	U U C	U U	C O C	U O U	C O C	C C	C C R	—	C C U
U U C	U U	U U U	U U C	C C C	R O	•O O O	R O	U U R	U U R	—	•C U C U
U U U	—	U U U	—	C U	U U R	C U	U U R	C C	C R C R	—	A R A A
A R C A	R	A C A	C U U C	U	R R	U U	R R	R R	R R	—	C C R
C R C C	O O	C C C	U U C	•U U C	•C C C	•C C C	•C C C	•C O C	•C C C	—	•C U C U
—	—	—	—	—	—	—	—	—	—	—	—
R R R R	C C C C	R R R R	R	—	—	—	—	—	—	—	—
R R R R	C C C C	R R R R	R R R R	R	R R R	R	R R R	U U U	R	U U U	•C O U
•U U C	U U C R	C C C	C C C	R	R R R	R R	R R R		O O		U R U
		R	R								
—	—	—	—	—	—	—	—	—	—	—	—
—	—	—	—	—	—	—	—	—	—	—	—
R R R R	O O O O	U U U U	R R R	U R R	O R O O	O O	O R O O	R R	O O O	R R O	•U U U U
C C C	C C C	C C C	U U C C	•C C C R	•U U U R	•C C C	•U U U R	•C C C O	•C C C R	•C C C O	C U U C
O A U	O O O	O O O	U C U	U U	U R U R	•O O O	U R U R	R R	O O R	•U U U O	C U R
R R R	U O C C	R R R	U	R R	R R R	•O O O	U R U R	R R	O O R	O R	•C U R
—	—	—	—	—	—	—	—	—	—	R R	R R R
R R R	C C C C	R R	R R	—	—	—	—	—	—	—	•C U U O
	O O	—	R	R R	O R O	O O O	O R O		R	O R	C C
—	—	—	—	•C C C	O O O	•C U C	O O O	U U	•C C C	U U U	—
R R R	C C C C	R R R	R	•C C C	•U U U	•C U C	•U U U	O O	•C C C	•C C C R	•C C C C
—	—	—	—	U R U	U R U	•O O O	U R U	R R	R R	R R R	U U C
—	O O	—	R R	U U	U U R	O O O	U U R	R R U	U U	R U O	R R R
C A A	C C C C	C C C	U C C	•C R C	U O U	•U O U	U O U	U U	•U U U	•C C C O	•C C C C
U C U	—	U U O	U C U	U U	O R O	O O R	O R O	R	R R	•R O R O	O O R
U C U	R R	U U U	U C U	R R	R R R	R R R	R O R	O O	R O	O O O O	O O R
—	—	—	—				R		R		
				U R U R	O R O R	O O	O R O R	O O O	O O		•U U U O

STATE-NUMBER OF BIRD LIST / REFUGE, SANCTUARY OR PRESERVE / NESTING, ABUNDANCE BY SEASON (•s S F W)	NY-1 Iroquois	NY-2 Montezuma	NY-3 Wertheim	NY-4 Morton	NY-5 Target Rock	NY-6 Jones Beach	NC-1 Matta/Swan	NC-2 Pungo	NC-3 Mackay Is.
CHACHALACAS									
Plain Chachalaca	—	—	—	—	—	—	—	—	—
PARTRIDGES, GROUSE, TURKEYS & QUAILS									
Gray Partridge	—	—	—	—	—	—	—	—	—
Chukar	—	—	—	—	—	—	—	—	—
Ring-necked Pheasant	•U U U U	•U U U U	•C C C C	U U U U	•C C C C	•C C C C	—	—	—
Spruce Grouse	—	—	—	—	—	—	—	—	—
Blue Grouse	—	—	—	—	—	—	—	—	—
Willow Ptarmigan	—	—	—	—	—	—	—	—	—
Rock Ptarmigan	—	—	—	—	—	—	—	—	—
White-tailed Ptarmigan	—	—	—	—	—	—	—	—	—
Ruffed Grouse	•U U U U	•U U U U	•R R R R	•R R R R	—	—	—	—	—
Sage Grouse	—	—	—	—	—	—	—	—	—
Greater Prairie Chicken	—	—	—	—	—	—	—	—	—
Lesser Prairie Chicken	—	—	—	—	—	—	—	—	—
Sharp-tailed Grouse	—	—	—	—	—	—	—	—	—
Wild Turkey	U U U U	—	—	—	—	—	—	—	—
Northern Bobwhite	—	—	•C C C C	•C C C C	•C C C C	—	•C C C C	A A A A	•C C C C
Scaled Quail	—	—	—	—	—	—	—	—	—
Gambel's Quail	—	—	—	—	—	—	—	—	—
California Quail	—	—	—	—	—	—	—	—	—
Mountain Quail	—	—	—	—	—	—	—	—	—
RAILS, GALLINULES & COOTS									
Yellow Rail	R	—	—	—	—	—	R	R	—
Black Rail	—	—	—	—	—	•R R R R	—	—	—
Clapper Rail	—	—	—	O O O O	—	•C C C R	•C C C C	—	—
King Rail	•R R R	R R R	R	—	—	R R	• C C O	U U U U	•O O O O
Virginia Rail	•U U U R	•C C C R	•U U U U	U U U R	—	•R R	U U	U U	•U U U U
Sora	•U U U R	•C C C	R R R R	U U U R	—	•R R R	U	O O O	•O O O O
Purple Gallinule	—	—	—	—	—	—	—	—	—
Common Moorhen	C C C	•C C C	—	—	—	R	U U U U	R R R	•O O U U
American Coot	•U O C R	•C C C	•U U U C	O O	R	O O	C A	U U C	•C R C C
LIMPKINS									
Limpkin	—	—	—	—	—	—	—	—	—
CRANES									
Sandhill Crane	—	—	—	—	—	—	—	—	—
Whooping Crane	—	—	—	—	—	—	—	—	—
PLOVERS									
Black-bellied Plover	O O	O O O	—	U U U U	R U C	A R A C	U U	R O R	—
Lesser Golden-Plover	R R	R O O	—	R R	R R R	U U	—	—	—
Snowy Plover	—	—	—	—	—	—	—	—	—
Wilson's Plover	—	—	—	R	—	—	•U U	—	—
Semipalmated Plover	O O	O C C	—	U U U	R R R	A C A	•U U	—	—
Piping Plover	—	—	—	•U U U	O	•U U	—	—	—
Killdeer	•C C C O	•C C C	•U U U U	•U U U U	R R R	•A A A U	•O O O C	U U U U	U O U O
Mountain Plover	—	—	—	—	—	—	—	—	—
OYSTERCATCHERS									
American Oystercatcher	—	—	—	R	—	•C C C R	O	—	—
Black Oystercatcher	—	—	—	—	—	—	—	—	—
STILTS & AVOCETS									
Black-necked Stilt	—	—	—	—	—	—	—	—	—
American Avocet	—	—	—	—	—	R	R	R	—
SANDPIPERS									
Greater Yellowlegs	C O C	C C C	U U U	C U U	U U U	A C A U	C C O	U U U	O O
Lesser Yellowlegs	C O C	C C C	U U U	U U U	R R R	A A A	U U O	O O O	O O R
Solitary Sandpiper	U O U	R O O	O O O	O O	R R	O O	C C	R R	R
Willet	—	—	O O O	U U	R R R	•A A A	O	O O	—
Wandering Tattler	—	—	—	—	—	—	—	—	—
Spotted Sandpiper	•C C U	•C C C	•U U U	•U U U	R R U	•C C C	C C	U U U	O O O
Upland Sandpiper	•O O	R	—	—	—	R	O	O	—
Whimbrel	—	R R	—	R R	—	O O	O O	—	—
Long-billed Curlew	—	—	—	—	—	—	—	—	—
Hudsonian Godwit	R	R O	—	—	—	O O U	—	—	—
Bar-tailed Godwit	—	—	—	—	—	—	—	—	—
Marbled Godwit	—	—	—	—	—	O O	—	—	—
Ruddy Turnstone	R	O O O	—	C C C R	O O O	A O A U	R R	R R R	—
Black Turnstone	—	—	—	—	—	—	—	—	—
Surfbird	—	—	—	—	—	—	—	—	—
Red Knot	—	R R R	—	U U U	R R	C A A O	—	—	—
Sanderling	—	R R R	U U U U	U U U U	R R R	A A A C	—	—	—
Semipalmated Sandpiper	C O C	C C C	O O	U U U	—	A C A	U U	O O	—
Western Sandpiper	—	R R	O O	U	—	C C C R	R R	R R	—

	NC-4 Pea Is.	NC-5 Pee Dee	NC-6 C. Hatteras	NC-7 C. Lookout	ND-1 Arrowwood	ND-2 Audubon	ND-3 Souris Loop	ND-4 Lake Ilo	ND-5 Long L.	ND-6 Tewaukon	ND-7 Roosevelt	OH-1 Ottawa
	·s S F W	·s S F W	·s S F W	·s S F W	·s S F W	·s S F W	·s S F W	·s S F W	·s S F W	·s S F W	·s S F W	·s S F W
	—	—	—	—	—	—	—	—	—	—	—	—
	—	—	—	—	·CCCC	·CCCC	·CCCC	·CCCC	·UUUU	·UUUU	O O	—
	·CCCC	—	CCCC	UUUU	·CCCC	·AAAA	·UUUU	·AAAA	·CCCC	·CCAC	·CCCC	·CCCC
	—	—	—	—	—	—	—	—	—	—	—	—
	—	—	—	—	—	—	—	—	—	—	—	—
	—	—	—	—	—	—	—	—	—	—	—	—
	—	—	—	—	—	—	—	—	—	—	—	—
	—	—	—	—	—	—	—	—	—	—	—	—
	—	—	—	—	—	—	—	—	—	—	—	—
	—	—	—	—	—	—	—	—	—	—	—	—
	—	—	—	—	—	—	—	—	—	—	· O	—
	—	—	—	—	·RRRR	—	—	—	·RRRR	RRR	—	—
	—	—	—	—	·CCCC	·CCCC	·CCCC	·CCCC	·CCCC	OOO	·CCCC	—
	—	RRRR	—	—	—	—	—	—	—	—	·CCUU	—
	—	AAAA	RRRR	UUUU	—	—	—	—	—	—	—	—
	—	—	—	—	—	—	—	—	—	—	—	—
	—	—	—	—	—	—	—	—	—	—	—	—
	—	—	—	—	—	—	—	—	—	—	—	—
	—	—	R	—	—	ORO	—	ORO	—	—	—	—
	RRRR	—	R	R	—	—	—	—	—	—	—	—
	·CCCC	—	CCCC	CCCC	—	—	—	—	—	—	—	—
	·CCCC	—	U	R	RRR	—	—	—	—	—	—	·OOOR
	UOUU	—	OOOO	U UU	·UUU	·OOO	·UCU	·OOO	·UUU	·UUU	—	·OOUR
	CUAU	—	O O	U UR	·CCC	·CCC	·UCU	·CCC	·CCC	·CCC	O	·CUCR
	·RRR	OO	RRR	—	—	—	—	—	—	—	—	—
	·UUUR	—	UUU	RR	—	—	—	—	—	—	—	·CCC
	ARAA	O CC	A AA	RR	·CCC	·AAA	·CCA	·AAA	·CCC	·AAA	O	·ACAO
	—	—	—	—	—	—	—	—	—	—	—	—
	—	—	—	—	—	—	—	—	—	—	—	—
	—	—	—	—	R U	AOA	ARA	COC	C A	O U	C C	R
	—	—	—	—	—	R R	R R	R R	R R	R R	O O	—
	AUAC	—	A AO	CCCC	R U	R R	U U	R R	R	O R	—	CUU
	R OR	—	O O	R U	U R	O R	U R	O R	R	U R	—	CUU
	—	—	—	—	—	—	—	—	—	—	—	—
	·UOUU	—	CCC	CCUR	—	—	—	—	—	—	—	—
	CUCU	—	C C	CCCU	U U	O O	O O	O O	UUU	OOO	—	C C
	·UUUU	—	UUU	CCCU	UUU	·OOO	·OOO	·OOO	·UU	—	—	RRR
	·UUUU	CUCC	CCCC	UUUU	·UUU	·AAC	·CCC	·AAC	·CCC	·CCC	·CCU	·AAAR
	—	—	—	—	—	—	—	—	—	—	—	—
	·CUUR	—	UUU	CCCU	—	—	—	—	—	—	—	—
	—	—	—	—	—	—	—	—	—	—	—	—
	·UCC	—	UCU	R	—	—	—	—	—	—	—	—
	·UUUR	—	·UUU	RR	·UUU	·CCU	·CCC	·CCU	·ACA	·UUU	O O	RRR
	ACAC	—	COCO	CCCC	U U	O O	U C	O O	OOO	UUU	O	CUC
	ACAU	CCO	COCO	UUU	U C	CUC	CUC	CUC	UUU	CCC	O	CCC
	UOUO	COO	U UO	UUU	U U	U U	U U	U U	UU	UUR	—	CUC
	·CCCU	—	CCC	CCCC	·UUU	·CCU	·UUC	·CCU	·UUU	·UUO	O	R R
	CUCO	O OO	C CO	UCU	·UUU	·CCU	·UCU	·CCU	·CCC	·CCC	UUU	·CCC
	OOO	R R	RR	RR	·UU	·CCU	·UCU	·CCU	·CCC	·CCC	·UUU	·UUU
	CRCO	—	C C	CCCR	—	—	—	—	—	—	—	RRR
	U	—	—	UUUU	—	—	R	—	R	—	O	—
	RRU	—	O	—	R	R	R R	R	R	O R	—	R R
	OUCU	—	U U	UUCU	·UU	·CCU	·UUC	·CCU	CCC	UOO	—	RRO
	AUAU	—	C CO	CCCU	—	O R	R R	O R	RR	O O	—	CUC
	—	—	—	—	—	—	—	—	—	—	—	—
	CUCU	—	C C	CUCU	—	—	—	—	—	R	—	UOO
	ACAA	—	ACAO	CCCC	R R	—	R	—	OU	UUU	—	OCC
	ACAU	—	AOAO	CCU	U U	C C	AAA	C C	CCU	CCC	—	ACC
	CUAC	O	U UO	CCCC	—	—	R R	—	R	—	—	RRO

STATE-NUMBER OF BIRD LIST / REFUGE, SANCTUARY OR PRESERVE / NESTING, ABUNDANCE BY SEASON	NY-1 Iroquois • s S F W	NY-2 Montezuma • s S F W	NY-3 Wertheim • s S F W	NY-4 Morton • s S F W	NY-5 Target Rock • s S F W	NY-6 Jones Beach • s S F W	NC-1 Matta/Swan • s S F W	NC-2 Pungo • s S F W	NC-3 Mackay Is. • s S F W
SANDPIPERS (cont.)									
Least Sandpiper	U O U	C O C	U U	—	R R R	A C A	U U	O O O	—
White-rumped Sandpiper	R R R	O O O	—	U U	—	U U	—	R R	—
Baird's Sandpiper	—	R O	—	—	—	O O	—	—	—
Pectoral Sandpiper	C O C	C C C	R	U U	—	U U	R R	R R	—
Sharp-tailed Sandpiper	—	—	—	—	—	—	—	—	—
Purple Sandpiper	—	—	—	R	—	U C	—	—	—
Rock Sandpiper	—	—	—	—	—	—	—	—	—
Dunlin	U O C	C C	—	U	—	A U A A	O	—	—
Curlew Sandpiper	—	—	—	—	—	R R R	—	—	—
Stilt Sandpiper	R	O C C	—	R R	—	R U U	—	—	—
Buff-breasted Sandpiper	—	—	—	—	—	O O	—	—	—
Ruff	—	R R	—	—	—	R R R	—	—	—
Short-billed Dowitcher	O O R	C O C	—	U U U	—	C C C R	O O O	O O	—
Long-billed Dowitcher	O	C	—	—	—	U	—	—	—
Common Snipe	•C U C	•O O O	U U U U	U U U	R R	U U O	U C	U U U	U U U
American Woodcock	•C U U	•O O O	•U U U O	•U U U R	U R R	•U U U	R C	O U O O	R R R R
Wilson's Phalarope	O R R	R R	—	—	—	R R R	—	—	—
Red-necked Phalarope	R	R O O	—	—	—	R R	R	—	—
Red Phalarope	—	—	—	—	—	R R	—	—	—
SKUAS, GULLS, TERNS & SKIMMERS									
Pomarine Jaeger	—	—	—	—	—	R R	—	—	—
Parasitic Jaeger	—	—	—	—	R R	O O O	—	—	—
Long-tailed Jaeger	—	—	—	—	—	—	—	—	—
Laughing Gull	—	—	R R R R	U U U R	C C U	A C A R	•A A A A	C O O	U U C C
Franklin's Gull	—	—	—	—	—	—	—	—	—
Little Gull	—	—	—	—	—	O	—	—	—
Common Black-headed Gull	—	—	—	—	—	R	—	—	—
Bonaparte's Gull	O	O O O	R	U U	R	A O A A	U U U U	R	O O
Heermann's Gull	—	—	—	—	—	—	—	—	—
Mew Gull	—	—	—	—	—	—	—	—	—
Ring-billed Gull	U O O O	C C C O	A A A A	U U U U	U U C C	A A A A	•C C C C	C O C O	U U U
California Gull	—	—	—	—	—	—	—	—	—
Herring Gull	O O O O	C O C C	A A A A	A A A A	A A A A	•A A A A	C C C C	C O C O	U U U U
Thayer's Gull	—	—	—	—	—	—	—	—	—
Iceland Gull	—	—	R	R	—	R	—	—	—
Lesser Black-backed Gull	—	—	—	—	—	—	—	—	—
Western Gull	—	—	—	—	—	—	—	—	—
Glaucous-winged Gull	—	—	—	—	—	—	—	—	—
Glaucous Gull	—	—	R	R R	—	R	—	—	—
Great Black-backed Gull	—	O O O U	A A A A	C C C C	C C C C	•A A A A	R U	R R R	U U U
Black-legged Kittiwake	—	—	—	—	—	R R	—	—	—
Sabine's Gull	—	—	—	—	—	—	—	—	—
Gull-billed Tern	—	—	—	—	—	•O O O	O O	—	—
Caspian Tern	O O	O O	—	—	—	R C	O O	O O	O O O
Royal Tern	—	—	R	U R	—	R C	O	R	R R
Elegant Tern	—	—	—	—	—	—	—	—	—
Sandwich Tern	—	—	—	—	—	—	R	—	—
Roseate Tern	—	—	—	U U U	—	•C C U	—	—	—
Common Tern	O O	•O O O	C C C	C C U	A A A	•A A A	U	O	U C
Arctic Tern	—	—	—	—	—	—	—	—	—
Aleutian Tern	—	—	—	—	—	—	—	—	—
Forster's Tern	—	—	—	U U U	—	U U C	O O	R R	R O O
Least Tern	—	—	C C C	•U C U	C C C	•C C	U	—	O O
Bridled Tern	—	—	—	—	—	—	—	—	—
Sooty Tern	—	—	—	—	—	—	—	—	R
Black Tern	•U U R	•O O O	R	U U	R R	R U	O	R R	U
Black Skimmer	—	—	U U U	U R	—	•A A A	O R	—	—
AUKS, MURRES & PUFFINS									
Dovekie	—	—	—	—	—	—	—	—	—
Common Murre	—	—	—	—	—	—	—	—	—
Thick-billed Murre	—	—	—	—	—	—	—	—	—
Razorbill	—	—	—	—	—	—	—	—	—
Black Guillemot	—	—	—	—	—	—	—	—	—
Pigeon Guillemot	—	—	—	—	—	—	—	—	—
Marbled Murrelet	—	—	—	—	—	—	—	—	—
Kittlitz's Murrelet	—	—	—	—	—	—	—	—	—
Ancient Murrelet	—	—	—	—	—	—	—	—	—
Cassin's Auklet	—	—	—	—	—	—	—	—	—
Crested Auklet	—	—	—	—	—	—	—	—	—
Rhinoceros Auklet	—	—	—	—	—	—	—	—	—
Tufted Puffin	—	—	—	—	—	—	—	—	—

	NC-4 Pea Is.	NC-5 Pee Dee	NC-6 C. Hatteras	NC-7 C. Lookout	ND-1 Arrowwood	ND-2 Audubon	ND-3 Souris Loop	ND-4 Lake Ilo	ND-5 Long L.	ND-6 Tewaukon	ND-7 Roosevelt	OH-1 Ottawa
•sSFW	•sSFW	•sSFW	•sSFW	•sSFW	•sSFW	•sSFW	•sSFW	•sSFW	•sSFW	•sSFW	•sSFW	•sSFW
	A C A U	O O O	A O A R	C C C U	U U	C C	C C A	C C	C C C	C U C	O	C C C
	O R C	—	O O	U U U	U R	C R	R R	C R	—	C U O	—	R R R
	U U	—	—	—	U U U	C R U	R U	C R U	C C C	C U C	—	R R R
	U C R	—	U U	U U U R	U U	O O	C C C	O O	U U U	C U U	—	C C C
	—		O	R	—	—	—	—	—	—		—
	A U A C	—	A A A	C U C C	R R	O O	— R	O O	R	O O	—	A C A R
	—	—		R R	—	—	—	—	—	—		—
	—	—	U U	U U U	U U	C C	O U	C C	U U U	C U O	—	U U
	R	—	—	R R	R	—	R	—	—	—		R R
	C C A U	—	C C O	C C C U	R	—	R R	C C	—	O O	—	C C C
	U R C U	—	U	U U U	C C	U U C	C C	C C C	C U C	—	U U U
	A R C A	R C R	U U C	U U U	•U U U	C U C	•O O O	C U C	R R	•C U C	—	•C U C R
	R R R	C R C C	R R R	U R U U	—	—	—	—	—	R	—	•C U U
	R R U	—	—	R R	•U U	•C C C	•C C C	•C C C	•C C C	•U U U	—	•O O O
	C C	—	U U	R R	U U	U U	A A	U U	O U	U O	—	O O O
	C C R	—	R R	R	—	—	—	—	—	—	—	R
	U U C R	—	—	U U U	—	—	—	—	—	—	—	—
	R U U	—	—	U U U U	—	—	—	—	—	—	—	R
	U U	—	—	R	—	—	—	—	—	—	—	—
	•A A A U	—	A A A O	C C C U	—	—	—	—	—	—	O	R
	—	—	—	—	U U C	C C A	•C C C	C C A	•C C C	C C A	O	A A A C
	—	—	R	—	—	—	—	—	—	—		—
	C U C	—	C C U	C U C	U U	O O	R R	O O	R R	O O O	—	C O A A
	A C A A	O O	A O A A	C U C C	C C C	•A A A	•C C C	A A A	•C C C	C C C	O O	•A A A C
	—				C C C	•A A A	•U R U	A A A	R R R	O O O		
	•A C A A	—	A O A A	C C C C	R	O O O	R R	O O O	U U U	O O	—	•A A A C
				R R								R R
	U	—	—	R	—	—	—	—	—	—	—	—
	—	—	—	—	—	—	—	—	—	—	—	—
	R R	—	O O	R	—	—	—	—	—	—	—	R R R
	•C C C A	—	C C C	C C C C	—	—	—	—	—	—	—	C U C C
	R U C	—	O	R R U	—	—	—	—	—	—	—	—
	•C C U	—	C C U	C C U	—	—	—	—	—	—	—	—
	•U U C O	—	U U	U U C	R R	R R	—	R R	—	R R	—	U C C
	•C C C U	—	C C C	C C C C	—	—	—	—	—	—	—	—
	•C C C	—	O O O	C C C	—	—	—	—	—	—	—	—
	R R R	—	R R	C C C	—	—	—	—	—	—	—	—
	•C C C R	—	C C C	C C C	U U	•A A U	•U U U	•A A U	•U U	U U O	—	•C C C
	—	—	—	—	—	—	—	—	—	—	—	—
	A C R A	—	U U U	C C C C	•U U	O O O	•C C C	O O O	—	•C C C	—	R O C
	•C C C	—	C C C	C C U	—	R R	—	R R	R	R	—	
	C U	—	—	R R R	—	—	—	—	—	—	—	—
	U C A	R R	U U U	U C U	•U U U	•C C U	•A C C	•C C U	•U U	•C C C	—	•C C C
	•C C C U	—	A A A O	C C C U	—	—	—	—	—	—	—	—
	R R R	—	R	R R	—	—	—	—	—	—	—	—
	—	—	—	—	—	—	—	—	—	—	—	—
	R	—	R	R R	—	—	—	—	—	—	—	—
	—	—	—	—	—	—	—	—	—	—	—	—
	—	—	—	—	—	—	—	—	—	—	—	—
	—	—	—	—	—	—	—	—	—	—	—	—
	—	—	—	—	—	—	—	—	—	—	—	—
	—	—	—	—	—	—	—	—	—	—	—	—
	—	—	—	—	—	—	—	—	—	—	—	—
	—	—	—	—	—	—	—	—	—	—	—	—

STATE-NUMBER OF BIRD LIST REFUGE, SANCTUARY OR PRESERVE — NESTING, ABUNDANCE BY SEASON (• s S F W)	NY-1 Iroquois	NY-2 Montezuma	NY-3 Wertheim	NY-4 Morton	NY-5 Target Rock	NY-6 Jones Beach	NC-1 Matta/Swan	NC-2 Pungo	NC-3 Mackay Is.
AUKS, MURRES & PUFFINS (cont.)									
Atlantic Puffin	—	—	—	—	—	—	—	—	—
Horned Puffin	—	—	—	—	—	—	—	—	—
PIGEONS & DOVES									
Rock Dove	•U U U U	•O O O O	•U U U U	—	O O O O	•A A A A	—	O O O O	O O O O
White-crowned Pigeon	—	—	—	—	—	—	—	—	—
Band-tailed Pigeon	—	—	—	—	—	—	—	—	—
White-winged Dove	—	—	—	—	—	—	—	—	—
Mourning Dove	•C C C U	•C C C O	•A A A A	•C C C U	C C A C	•A A A A	•C C C C	A A A A	•C C C C
Inca Dove	—	—	—	—	—	—	—	—	—
Common Ground-Dove	—	—	—	—	—	—	—	R	—
White-tipped Dove	—	—	—	—	—	—	—	—	—
CUCKOOS, ROADRUNNERS & ANIS									
Black-billed Cuckoo	•U U U	•O O	•U U U	U U U	•R R	•O U U	R R	R R	R R
Yellow-billed Cuckoo	O O O	•O O	•U U U	•U U U	•R R	•O O	C C	U U	•C C C
Mangrove Cuckoo	—	—	—	—	—	—	—	—	—
Greater Roadrunner	—	—	—	—	—	—	—	—	—
Smooth-billed Ani	—	—	—	—	—	—	—	—	—
Groove-billed Ani	—	—	—	—	—	—	—	—	—
BARN OWLS									
Barn Owl	R R R R	R R R R	•U U U U	U U U U	—	•U U U U	U U U U	U U U U	R R R R
TYPICAL OWLS									
Flammulated Owl	—	—	—	—	—	—	—	—	—
Eastern Screech-Owl	•U U U U	•C C C	•U U U U	•U U U U	U U U	—	•C C C C	U U U U	•C C C C
Western Screech-Owl	—	—	—	—	—	—	—	—	—
Great Horned Owl	•C C C C	•C C C C	•U U U U	•U U U U	O O O	—	•C C C C	U U U U	•O O O O
Snowy Owl	O O	R	R	R	—	R O	—	—	R R
Northern Hawk Owl	—	—	—	—	—	—	—	—	—
Northern Pygmy-Owl	—	—	—	—	—	—	—	—	—
Elf Owl	—	—	—	—	—	—	—	—	—
Burrowing Owl	—	—	—	—	—	—	—	—	—
Spotted Owl	—	—	—	—	—	—	—	—	—
Barred Owl	•U U U U	•R R R R	—	—	—	—	•C C C C	U U U U	R R
Great Gray Owl	—	—	—	—	—	—	—	—	—
Long-eared Owl	—	—	U U U U	—	R R	R	—	R	—
Short-eared Owl	O O O	O R O O	O O O	U U U	—	•U U U U	—	R	•R R R R
Boreal Owl	—	—	—	—	—	—	—	—	—
Northern Saw-whet Owl	—	R	R R R	R R R	U U	•R U U	—	U	—
NIGHTJARS									
Lesser Nighthawk	—	—	—	—	—	—	—	—	—
Common Nighthawk	O O	R	O U U	U U	O O O	O O	C	C C	R R
Pauraque	—	—	—	—	—	—	—	—	—
Common Poorwill	—	—	—	—	—	—	—	—	—
Chuck-will's-widow	—	—	—	—	—	• U	•C U U	O O	•U U
Whip-poor-will	O O	R	•C C	U U U	•R R R	O O	—	O O O O	U U
SWIFTS									
Black Swift	—	—	—	—	—	—	—	—	—
Chimney Swift	O O	•O O	U U U	U U U	—	U U U	C C	O O	O
Vaux's Swift	—	—	—	—	—	—	—	—	—
White-throated Swift	—	—	—	—	—	—	—	—	—
HUMMINGBIRDS									
Buff-bellied Hummingbird	—	—	—	—	—	—	—	—	—
Ruby-throated Hummingbird	•U U	• O	•U U U	•U U U	R R R	R U	•C C	U U	•R R
Black-chinned Hummingbird	—	—	—	—	—	—	—	—	—
Anna's Hummingbird	—	—	—	—	—	—	—	—	—
Costa's Hummingbird	—	—	—	—	—	—	—	—	—
Calliope Hummingbird	—	—	—	—	—	—	—	—	—
Broad-tailed Hummingbird	—	—	—	—	—	—	—	—	—
Rufous Hummingbird	—	—	—	—	—	—	—	—	—
Allen's Hummingbird	—	—	—	—	—	—	—	—	—
KINGFISHERS									
Belted Kingfisher	•U U U O	•C C C O	C C C C	•U U U U	•C C U U	•U C U	C C C C	U U U U	•C C C C
Green Kingfisher	—	—	—	—	—	—	—	—	—
WOODPECKERS									
Lewis' Woodpecker	—	—	—	—	—	—	—	—	—
Red-headed Woodpecker	O O O O	—	R R R R	—	• R	R U	O O O O	U U U U	R R R R
Acorn Woodpecker	—	—	—	—	—	—	—	—	—
Gila Woodpecker	—	—	—	—	—	—	—	—	—
Golden-fronted Woodpecker	—	—	—	—	—	—	—	—	—
Red-bellied Woodpecker	•U U U U	•O O O O	U U U U	U U U U	•O O O O	R	•C C C C	U U U U	U U U O
Yellow-bellied Sapsucker	O O	O O	U U U	U U U	R R	U	C	U U	R R R R
Red-breasted Sapsucker	—	—	—	—	—	—	—	—	—

	NC-4 Pea Is.				NC-5 Pee Dee				NC-6 C. Hatteras				NC-7 C. Lookout				ND-1 Arrowwood				ND-2 Audubon				ND-3 Souris Loop				ND-4 Lake Ilo				ND-5 Long L.				ND-6 Tewaukon				ND-7 Roosevelt				OH-1 Ottawa			
	•s	S	F	W	•s	S	F	W	•s	S	F	W	•s	S	F	W	•s	S	F	W	•s	S	F	W	•s	S	F	W	•s	S	F	W	•s	S	F	W	•s	S	F	W	•s	S	F	W	•s	S	F	W
	—				—				—				—				—				—				—				—				—				—				—				—			
	—				C	C	C	C	—						R		•U	U	U		O	O	O		•O	O	O	O	O	O	O		—				O	O	O	O	O	O	O	O	•U	U	U	U
	•U	U	U	U	A	A	A	A	O	O	O	O	C	C	C	C	•C	C	C		•A	A	A		•C	C	A		•A	A	A		•C	C	C		•A	A	A	R	•C	C	C		•C	C	C	C
	R		R		O		O		R	R	R		—				•U	U	U		U	U	O		•O	O	O		U	U	O		U	U			•U	U	O		U	U			•U	O	O	
	•U	U	C		C	C	C		U	U	U		U	U	C		R				—		R		R				—				O	O	R		O				•U	U	U	
	—				—				—				—				—				—				—				—				—				—				—			
	•O	O	O	O	C	C	C	C	O	O	O	O	U	U	U	U	—				—				—				—				—				—				—				•R	R	R	R
	—				U	C	C	U	U	U	U	U	—				R	R	R	R	—				•O	O	O	O	—				R	R	R	R	O	O	O	O	R	R	R	R	•C	C	C	C
	—				C	C	C	C	—						R		U	U	U	U	•U	U	U	U	•U	U	U	U	•U	U	U	U	•U	U	U	U	•C	C	C	C	•C	C	C	C	•C	C	C	C
	—				—						R		—					U	U		O		O	U	O		O	O	O		O	U			O		O	R		O	O				O		O	O
	—				—				—				—				R				•U	U	U		•O	O	O		•U	U	U		R	R			—				•U	U	U		—			
	—				C	C	C	C	—				—				—				—				—				—				—				—				—				—			
																	•R		R		R		R		•O	O	O	O	R		R		R				R	R	R		R	R			•O	O	O	O
	O		U	U	—				R		R	R		U	U		U	U	U	U	•U	U	U	R	•U	U	O	O	U	U	U	R	•U	U	U	U	•U	O	U		O				•U		U	U
	—				—						R		—						R		—				O	O	O	O	R				—				R		R		O	O	O		O		O	R
	•O	O	O		O	O	O		U	U	U		C	C	U		U	U	U		•U	U	U		•O	O	O		•O	O	U		U	U			O	O	R		C	U	C		•C	A	C	
	R	R	R		C	C	C		O	O			U	U											—				—				—				—				—				—			
	—				C		C		—				—				R				—				—				—				—				O		R		R	U	R		U		R	
	O	O	O		C	C	C		U	U	U		U	U	U		R		R		—				R				—				R	R			O	O	O		—				•C	U	A	
	—				—				—				—				—				—				—				—				—				—				—				—			
	O	U	U		C	C	C		U	U	U				R				R		O	R	O		•O	O	O		O	R	O		O		O		•O	O	R		O	O	O		•U	U	U	
	—				—				—				—				—				—				—				—				—				—				—				—			
	U	U	C	C	C	C	C	C	U	U	U	U	U	U	C	U	U	U	U		O	O	O		•O	O	O		O	O	O		U	R	U		•C	C	U		U	U	U	O	•C	C	C	O
	—				—				—				—				—				—				—				—				—				—				—				—			
		O			C	C	C	C	U		U	U	U		R		•R	R	R		O	O	O		•R	O	R		O	O	O		R	R	R		O	R	O		•U	U	U		•C	C	C	U
	—				—				—				—				—				—				—				—				—				—				—				—			
	—				—				—				—				—				—				—				—				—				—				—				—			
	—				C	C	C	C	—						R		R		C	R	U	U			O	O	O		•O	O	O		—				—				R	R			R	R	R	R
	U		C	U	C	C	C	C			U			R			U	U			O	O	O		•O	O	O		O	O	O		—					R	R						C		C	R

STATE-NUMBER OF BIRD LIST / REFUGE, SANCTUARY OR PRESERVE / NESTING, ABUNDANCE BY SEASON	NY-1 Iroquois • s S F W	NY-2 Montezuma • s S F W	NY-3 Wertheim • s S F W	NY-4 Morton • s S F W	NY-5 Target Rock • s S F W	NY-6 Jones Beach • s S F W	NC-1 Matta/Swan • s S F W	NC-2 Pungo • s S F W	NC-3 Mackay Is. • s S F W
WOODPECKERS (cont.)									
Williamson's Sapsucker	—	—	—	—	—	—	—	—	—
Ladder-backed Woodpecker	—	—	—	—	—	—	—	—	—
Nuttall's Woodpecker	—	—	—	—	—	—	—	—	—
Downy Woodpecker	•C C C C	•C C C C	•C C C C	•U U U U	•U U U U	C U C C	•U U U C	C C U U	U R O R
Hairy Woodpecker	•U U U U	•O O O O	•U U U C	•U U U U	•C U U U	O	•U U U U	U U U U	U R R R
Red-cockaded Woodpecker	—	—	—	—	—	—	—	—	•R R
Three-toed Woodpecker	—	—	—	—	—	—	—	—	—
Black-backed Woodpecker	—	—	—	—	—	—	—	—	—
Northern Flicker	•C C C O	•C C C O	•C C C U	•U U U U	•C C C C	•C C A C	•C C C C	C C C C	•C C A C
Pileated Woodpecker	•U U U U	•O O O O	—	—	—	—	•C C C C	U U U U	•O O O O
TYRANT FLYCATCHERS									
Olive-sided Flycatcher	—	R R	R R R	—	—	U U	—	—	—
Western Wood-Pewee	—	—	—	—	—	—	—	—	—
Eastern Wood-Pewee	•C C	• C	C C C	U U U	•O O O	U C	U	U U	•C O
Yellow-bellied Flycatcher	—	—	O	—	—	U	—	—	—
Acadian Flycatcher	—	—	—	—	—	R	U	U U	—
Alder Flycatcher	O O	O O	—	—	—	O	—	—	—
Willow Flycatcher	•U U	O C	C	—	—	•U U C	—	—	—
Least Flycatcher	•U U	• C	•C C C	—	U U	U	—	O O	—
Hammond's Flycatcher	—	—	—	—	—	—	—	—	—
Dusky Flycatcher	—	—	—	—	—	—	—	—	—
Gray Flycatcher	—	—	—	—	—	—	—	—	—
Western Flycatcher	—	—	—	—	—	—	—	—	—
Black Phoebe	—	—	—	—	—	—	—	—	—
Eastern Phoebe	•C C C	•C C C	•C C C	U U U R	•O O O R	•C U A	U C	R R	C
Say's Phoebe	—	—	—	—	—	—	—	—	—
Vermilion Flycatcher	—	—	—	—	—	—	—	—	—
Ash-throated Flycatcher	—	—	—	—	—	—	—	—	—
Great Crested Flycatcher	•C C	•O C	•U U U	•U U R	•U U U	U	•C C	U U	•C U
Brown-crested Flycatcher	—	—	—	—	—	—	—	—	—
Great Kiskadee	—	—	—	—	—	—	—	—	—
Couch's Kingbird	—	—	—	—	—	—	—	—	—
Cassin's Kingbird	—	—	—	—	—	—	—	—	—
Western Kingbird	—	—	—	—	—	O	R	—	—
Eastern Kingbird	•C C U	•C C O	•C C C	•U U U	C C U	•U U C	•C C U	C C U	•O C O
Gray Kingbird	—	—	—	—	—	—	—	—	—
Scissor-tailed Flycatcher	—	—	—	—	—	—	—	—	—
LARKS									
Horned Lark	•C C C U	•O O O O	O O	•U U U U	U U	•C C C C	R	R	—
SWALLOWS									
Purple Martin	•C C	•C C	U U U	R	—	U U U	•A A	C C O	O C
Tree Swallow	•C C C	•C C C R	•C C C R	•U U U	U U U	•A A A R	U C	C C C U	C C A O
Violet-green Swallow	—	—	—	—	—	—	—	—	—
Northern Rough-winged Swallow	O	O O	R R R	U U	O	R R U	C	U U	R R R
Bank Swallow	•U U	•C C	—	•C C C	•C C C	R R U	—	O O	—
Cliff Swallow	•O O	•R R	—	—	—	U U	—	—	—
Barn Swallow	•C C C R	•C C C	•U U U	•U U U	•C C	•A A A	C C	U U	C C C
JAYS, MAGPIES & CROWS									
Gray Jay	—	—	—	—	—	—	—	—	—
Steller's Jay	—	—	—	—	—	—	—	—	—
Blue Jay	•C C C C	•C C C C	•C C C C	•C C C U	•C U A C	C U C O	•U U U U	U U U U	•O O C U
Green Jay	—	—	—	—	—	—	—	—	—
Scrub Jay	—	—	—	—	—	—	—	—	—
Pinyon Jay	—	—	—	—	—	—	—	—	—
Clark's Nutcracker	—	—	—	—	—	—	—	—	—
Black-billed Magpie	—	—	—	—	—	—	—	—	—
American Crow	•C C C U	•C C C O	•C C C C	•U U U U	•C C C C	•A A A A	•A A A A	A A A A	•C C C C
Northwestern Crow	—	—	—	—	—	—	—	—	—
Fish Crow	—	—	•C C C C	R	U U U U	•C C C C	•C C C C	C C C C	U U U
Chihuahuan Raven	—	—	—	—	—	—	—	—	—
Common Raven	—	—	—	—	—	—	—	—	—
TITMICE									
Black-capped Chickadee	•C C C C	•C C C C	•C C C C	•C C C C	•C C C C	•U U U U	—	—	—
Carolina Chickadee	—	—	—	—	—	—	•U U C C	U U U U	•C C C C
Mountain Chickadee	—	—	—	—	—	—	—	—	—
Boreal Chickadee	—	—	—	—	—	—	—	—	—
Chestnut-backed Chickadee	—	—	—	—	—	—	—	—	—
Plain Titmouse	—	—	—	—	—	—	—	—	—
Tufted Titmouse	—	O O O	•C C C C	R	•U U C C	U U U U	•U U U U	U U U U	C C
VERDINS									
Verdin	—	—	—	—	—	—	—	—	—

NC-4 Pea Is.	NC-5 Pee Dee	NC-6 C. Hatteras	NC-7 C. Lookout	ND-1 Arrowwood	ND-2 Audubon	ND-3 Souris Loop	ND-4 Lake Ilo	ND-5 Long L.	ND-6 Tewaukon	ND-7 Roosevelt	OH-1 Ottawa
•s S F W	•s S F W	•s S F W	•s S F W	•s S F W	•s S F W	•s S F W	•s S F W	•s S F W	•s S F W	•s S F W	•s S F W
—	—	—	—	—	—	—	—	—	—	—	—
•UUUU	CCCC	UUUU	R	•CCCC	CUCO	•UUUU	CUCO	•OOOO	•CCCC	CCCC	•CCCC
R RR	CCCC	RRRR	—	UUUU	CUCO	•OOOO	CUCO	•OOOO	•UUUU	CCCC	•UUUU
—	OOOO	—	—	—	—	—	—	—	—	—	—
•UUAC	CCCC	UUCU	URCC	•CCCU	CCC	•CCC	•CCC	CUC	•CCCR	•CCCO	•CCCU
—	OOOO	—	—	—	—	—	—	—	—	—	—
R	—	O O	—	R R	—	O U	—	—	O R	—	UOU
UUU	CCC	O O	U C	•UUU	—	•ROO	—	R	•UOO	O	•CCC
R	O	—	—	R	—	RRO	—	—	—	—	C U
R	CCC	—	—	—	—	—	—	—	—	—	•RRR
—	—	—	—	—	—	—	—	—	—	—	R
—	—	—	—	•UUU	—	•CCA	—	—	•UU	—	•CCC
—	—	—	—	•UU	—	•CCA	—	R	•UO	UUU	CCC
U UU	CCCC	OOO	C	URU	UUO	•ROO	UUO	R	O O	—	•CUU
—	—	—	—	•UUU	UUO	•OOO	UUO	•UUU	—	•UUU	—
•UUU	CC	OOO	UUU	RCC	—	•ROO	—	R	O O	O O	•CCC
—	—	—	—	—	—	—	—	—	—	—	—
U	—	RRR	U	•CCC	•AAC	•ACC	•AAC	•CCC	•CCC	•CCC	—
CCC	CC	CCC	UUC	•CCC	•CCU	•ACC	•CCU	•UUU	•CCC	•CCC	•CCC
—	—	—	—	—	—	—	—	—	—	—	—
R RR	—	O OO	—	•CCCU	•CCCA	•ACAC	•CCCA	CCCC	•CCCC	CCCU	•CUCC
UUC	OAA	UUO	UU	•UU	•CCU	•CCC	•CCU	•RR	•CC	—	•CAC
CUAU	C CC	CCCO	U CU	•UUU	•UUO	•CCA	•UUO	O	•AAA	•UUU	•CAA
—	—	—	—	—	—	R	—	—	—	O	—
R R	CCC	R R	R	•UU	—	•OOO	—	UUU	•CCU	•CCC	•CCC
O U	—	O O	RU	•CCU	•CCC	•CCA	•CCC	•UUU	•CCU	•CCC	•CCC
R	—	—	—	•CCR	UUU	•AAA	UUU	•CCC	•CCU	CCC	•UOU
•AAA	CCC	CCC	CCU	•CCU	•AAA	•CCA	•AAA	•CCC	•AAC	•CCC	•CAC
—	—	—	—	—	—	—	—	—	—	—	—
RRR	CCCC	O O	R R	UURR	OOO	•OOOO	OOO	O O	•UUUU	•UUUO	•AUCU
—	—	—	—	—	—	—	—	—	—	O O	—
UUUU	AAAA	UUUU	—	•UUUU	O UO	•UUUU	O UO	RRRR	RR	•CCCC	•COUO
•CCCC	—	CCCC	CCUU	•CUC	CUCR	•CUC	CUCR	AUAR	•UUOR	•CCCO	
—	—	—	—	—	—	—	—	—	—	—	—
—	—	—	—	—	—	R	—	—	—	O	—
•UUUU	CCCC	UUUU	R	•CCCC	O O	•CCCC	O O	•UUUR	UUUU	•CCCC	U UU
—	—	—	—	—	—	—	—	—	—	—	—
—	—	—	—	—	—	—	—	—	—	—	—
—	CCCC	—	—	—	—	—	—	—	—	—	•UUUU
—	—	—	—	—	—	—	—	—	—	—	—
—	—	—	—	—	—	—	—	—	—	—	—

STATE-NUMBER OF BIRD LIST REFUGE, SANCTUARY OR PRESERVE NESTING, ABUNDANCE BY SEASON	NY-1 Iroquois • s S F W	NY-2 Montezuma • s S F W	NY-3 Wertheim • s S F W	NY-4 Morton • s S F W	NY-5 Target Rock • s S F W	NY-6 Jones Beach • s S F W	NC-1 Matta/Swan • s S F W	NC-2 Pungo • s S F W	NC-3 Mackay Is. • s S F W
BUSHTITS									
Bushtit	—	—	—	—	—	—	—	—	—
NUTHATCHES									
Red-breasted Nuthatch	O O O	•O O R	U U U	U U U	R R R	U C C	R R	R R	—
White-breasted Nuthatch	•C C C C	•C C C C	•C C C C	•U U U U	•U U U U	R U R	• U	O O	U U
Pygmy Nuthatch	—	—	—	—	—	—	—	—	—
Brown-headed Nuthatch	—	—	—	—	—	—	•C C C C	U U U U	—
CREEPERS									
Brown Creeper	•U U U U	•O O O O	•U U U U	U U U	R R R	U C R	O	O	—
WRENS									
Cactus Wren	—	—	—	—	—	—	—	—	—
Rock Wren	—	—	—	—	—	—	—	—	—
Canyon Wren	—	—	—	—	—	—	—	—	—
Carolina Wren	—	R R R	•C C C C	•U U U R	R R R R	—	•U U C C	U U U U	•C C C C
Bewick's Wren	—	—	—	—	—	—	—	—	—
House Wren	•C C C	•C C	•U U U	•U U U	•U U U	U U	•U U U U	U U U	R
Winter Wren	O O O	•C C C	U	U U U	—	R U R	O	O	—
Sedge Wren	•R R R	•R R	R	—	—	—	O	O	—
Marsh Wren	•C C O	•C C C	•C C C O	U U U	—	•C C C R	U U U U	U U U U	•O O O O
DIPPERS									
American Dipper	—	—	—	—	—	—	—	—	—
OLD WORLD WARBLERS & THRUSHES									
Arctic Warbler	—	—	—	—	—	—	—	—	—
Golden-crowned Kinglet	U R U R	C C	U U U U	U U U	U U U	U C R	U	O O	—
Ruby-crowned Kinglet	U U	C C	U U U U	U U	U U U	U C R	U U C	O O	O O O
Blue-gray Gnatcatcher	•U U U	O O	U U U	—	R R	U	O O O R	O O O O	R R
Black-tailed Gnatcatcher	—	—	—	—	—	—	—	—	—
Eastern Bluebird	U O U R	•U U U R	•U U U R	R R	R R R	R R R	O	O O O O	—
Western Bluebird	—	—	—	—	—	—	—	—	—
Mountain Bluebird	—	—	—	—	—	—	—	—	—
Townsend's Solitaire	—	—	—	—	—	—	—	—	—
Veery	•C C U	•C C O	•U U U	U U	R R	U C	—	—	—
Gray-cheeked Thrush	R R	O O	U	U U	R R	R U	—	—	—
Swainson's Thrush	U O	O O	C	U U	U R	U C	O O	O O	—
Hermit Thrush	U U R	C C	•U U U	U U U	U U R	C C O	U U C	U U U	U
Wood Thrush	•C C C	•C C O	•C C C	•U U U	•U U U	C U	•C C U	C C U	—
American Robin	•C C C O	•C C C O	•A A A U	•C C C U	•C C A U	•A A A U	C U C	A A A A	•O U U O
Varied Thrush	—	—	—	—	—	—	—	—	—
Wrentit	—	—	—	—	—	—	—	—	—
MOCKINGBIRDS, THRASHERS & ALLIES									
Gray Catbird	•C C C	•C C C	•C C C U	•C C C U	•C A C U	•A A A U	•C C C U	C C U U	•U U U U
Northern Mockingbird	R R R R	R R	•A A A A	•U U U U	•C C C C	•C C C C	•C C C C	A A A A	•C C C C
Sage Thrasher	—	—	—	—	—	—	—	—	—
Brown Thrasher	•U O O R	•O O O	•O O O O	•U U U U	•U U U R	•C C C O	C C C C	C C C U	•C C C C
Long-billed Thrasher	—	—	—	—	—	—	—	—	—
Bendire's Thrasher	—	—	—	—	—	—	—	—	—
Curve-billed Thrasher	—	—	—	—	—	—	—	—	—
Crissal Thrasher	—	—	—	—	—	—	—	—	—
Le Conte's Thrasher	—	—	—	—	—	—	—	—	—
WAGTAILS & PIPITS									
American Pipit	O O	C C	R R	U U	—	O U R	U	R	—
Sprague's Pipit	—	—	—	—	—	—	—	—	—
WAXWINGS									
Bohemian Waxwing	—	—	—	—	—	—	—	—	—
Cedar Waxwing	U U U U	•O O O O	U U U U	U R U U	U U	U U C R	C	O O O	O O O
SILKY-FLYCATCHERS									
Phainopepla	—	—	—	—	—	—	—	—	—
SHRIKES									
Northern Shrike	U U U	O	R R	R R	—	R R R	—	—	—
Loggerhead Shrike	R	•R R	R R	R R	—	R R R	—	O O O O	—
STARLINGS									
European Starling	•C C C C	•A A A O	•A A A A	•C C C C	C C C C	•A A A A	•C C C O	A A A A	•C C C U
VIREOS									
White-eyed Vireo	—	—	U U U	•U U U	—	•U U C	•C C C	U U	•U C
Bell's Vireo	—	—	—	—	—	—	—	—	—
Black-capped Vireo	—	—	—	—	—	—	—	—	—
Gray Vireo	—	—	—	—	—	—	—	—	—
Solitary Vireo	O	O O	O O	U U	R R	U U	—	—	—
Yellow-throated Vireo	•U U	•O O	—	U	—	O O	R	R U	—
Hutton's Vireo	—	—	—	—	—	—	—	—	—
Warbling Vireo	•C C C	•C C C	R	—	—	O O	—	—	—
Philadelphia Vireo	O O	R R	U U U	—	—	O O	—	—	—

NC-4 Pea Is.	NC-5 Pee Dee	NC-6 C. Hatteras	NC-7 C. Lookout	ND-1 Arrowwood	ND-2 Audubon	ND-3 Souris Loop	ND-4 Lake Ilo	ND-5 Long L.	ND-6 Tewaukon	ND-7 Roosevelt	OH-1 Ottawa
• s S F W	• s S F W	• s S F W	• s S F W	• s S F W	• s S F W	• s S F W	• s S F W	• s S F W	• s S F W	• s S F W	• s S F W
—	—	—	—	—	—	—	—	—	—	—	—
C C	C C C	U U U	C	R R R	—	U C R	—	R R	U O O	O O	U U O
R R	C C C C	—	—	U	O O U O	• O O O O	O O U O	R R	U O O O	U U U U	• O O O U
	C C C C										
O C U	C C C	O O O	U	U U U	O O	U C R	O O	R R	O O O	O	C C U
—	—	—	—	—	—	• R R R	—	—	—	• C C C	—
• C C C C	C C C C	U U U U	U U U U	—	—	—	—	—	—	—	• R R R R
U C U	C C C	U U U	U C U	• U U U	• C C U	• C C C	• C C U	U U	• C C O	• C C C	C C C
O U O	O O	R R R	R R	—	—	—	—	—	R	U U U
C C C	—	O O O	U C C	• U U R	• C C U	• C C U	• C C U	• C C C	• C C O	—	• R U R
• C C C C	C C R	U U U U	U U C C	• U U U	• O O O	• C C C	• O O O	• R R R	• C C O	—	• C A C R
—	—	—	—	—	—	—	—	—	—	—	—
—	—	—	—	—	—	—	—	—	—	—	—
U C U	C	O O O	C R	R R R	R U	U U	R U	U U	O O	O	C C U
C C C	C C C	—	C U	U U	R U	U U	R U	—	O O	A O R
O U	U C	U U	U R U	—	—	—	—	—	—	C U C
—	U U U U	—	R	• R R R	O O O	• O O O	O O O	R R	R	U O U	• O O O R
—	—	—	—	R R	R R	U R U	R R	R R R	—	• C C C	—
—	—	—	—	—	—	R R R	—	—	—	O R	—
U U	—	—	R	U U	—	• U C U	—	—	• U O O	O O	U O O
O U	—	U U U	R U	• U U	—	C C	—	—	O O	—	U U
O C	U U	U U U	U	U U	—	C C	—	U U	U U O	—	C C
O C O	C C C	U U U	U	R R	—	U U	—	—	O O	—	C C R
R	C C C	U U U	U	—	—	—	—	—	—	—	• C U U
U U C C	C O C C	U U U	U C U	• C C U R	• C C C U	• C C A O	• C C C U	• C U C	• C C C R	• C C C U	• A A A U
—	—	—	—	—	—	—	—	—	—	—	—
—	—	—	—	—	—	—	—	—	—	—	—
• A A A U	U C	C C C C	U U C U	• C C U	• U O	• U U U	• O O	• U U U	• C C U	U U	• C C C R
• U U U U	A A A A	C C C C	U U U U	—	—	R R R	—	—	—	—	• R U R R
						• R R R					
• U U U U	C C C C	U U U U	U U U U	• C C U	• C C U	• U U U	• C C U	• C C C	• U U O	• C C U	• C C C R
—	—	—	—	—	—	—	—	—	—	—	—
—	—	—	—	—	—	—	—	—	—	—	—
—	—	—	—	—	—	—	—	—	—	—	—
—	—	—	—	—	—	—	—	—	—	—	—
U U U	O	O O O	U U	C C C	O O	U U	O O	U	U U	U U R
—	—	—	—	• U U U	• O O O	• U U O	• O O O	U U U	O R	U U U	
—	—	—	—	U	R O U	U U U	R O U	—	O O	O	U U C	—
U U C	O O O	U U U	U U U	• U U U U	• O O U U	• C C C R	• O O U U	R R R	• U O U R	• U C U U	• C U C U
—	—	—	—	—	—	—	—	—	—	—	—
—	—	—	—	U U U	R O O	O	R O O	R	O O O	O U	R R R
R R	C C C C	R R R	R	• R R R	O O O	• U U U	O O O	• O O O	O O O	U C U O	• O O O R
• C C C A	C C C C	U U U U	U U U U	• R R R U	U U U O	• U U U U	U U U O	• O O O	• U U U O	• U R	• A A A A
• U C C	C C C	R U R	U U U	—	—	—	—	—	—	—	• O O O
—	—	—	—	—	—	—	—	—	—	—	—
—	—	—	—	—	—	—	—	—	—	—	—
—	O O	—	U	R R	U U	R R R	U U	—	—	—	U U
—	O O O	—	—	R R	—	• O O O	—	—	O R	—	• U U U
—	—	—	—	• U U U	—	• C C C	U U	—	U U O	U C U	• C C C
O	—	—	R	R R	—	• O O O	—	—	O R	—	C C

STATE-NUMBER OF BIRD LIST REFUGE, SANCTUARY OR PRESERVE NESTING, ABUNDANCE BY SEASON	NY-1 Iroquois •s S F W	NY-2 Montezuma •s S F W	NY-3 Wertheim •s S F W	NY-4 Morton •s S F W	NY-5 Target Rock •s S F W	NY-6 Jones Beach •s S F W	NC-1 Matta/Swan •s S F W	NC-2 Pungo •s S F W	NC-3 Mackay Is. •s S F W
VIREOS (cont.)									
Red-eyed Vireo	•C C U	•C C C	•U U U	•U U U	•O O O	U C	•C C C	U U	•O O
Black-whiskered Vireo	—	—	—	—	—	—	—	—	—
WOOD-WARBLERS									
Bachman's Warbler	—	—	—	—	—	—	—	—	—
Blue-winged Warbler	O O	R	C C C	•U U U	O O O	U U	—	—	—
Golden-winged Warbler	•U U	O O	—	R	—	R	—	—	—
Tennessee Warbler	U U	O O	U U	U U	—	U U	—	—	—
Orange-crowned Warbler	R R	R	U	—	—	R O	O O	—	—
Nashville Warbler	U U	C C	O O	—	—	U C	—	—	—
Virginia's Warbler	—	—	—	—	—	—	—	—	—
Lucy's Warbler	—	—	—	—	—	—	—	—	—
Northern Parula	R	O O	C C	C U	U R	U C	O O	O O	R
Tropical Parula	—	—	—	—	—	—	—	—	—
Yellow Warbler	•C C U	•C C C	•C C C	•C C U	•C C U	•C C C	O O	O O	O
Chestnut-sided Warbler	U R U	O O	U U	U U	U U	U U	—	—	—
Magnolia Warbler	U U	C C	U U	U U	U U	U C	R	R	O
Cape May Warbler	U O	C C	U U	U U	O O	U C	—	—	—
Black-throated Blue Warbler	U	C C	U U	U U	R R	U C	O	—	—
Yellow-rumped Warbler	C C	C C	C C C U	C C U	U U C	A A A	A U A	U C C	O A A
Black-throated Gray Warbler	—	—	—	—	—	—	—	—	—
Townsend's Warbler	—	—	—	—	—	—	—	—	—
Hermit Warbler	—	—	—	—	—	—	—	—	—
Black-throated Green Warbler	U U	C C	U U	U U	O O	U C	O	—	O
Blackburnian Warbler	U R U	C C	U U	U U	O O	U U	R	—	—
Yellow-throated Warbler	—	—	—	—	—	R	C U	U U	O R
Pine Warbler	R	O O	•U U U	U U U	—	R O	U U U U	U O U U	R
Prairie Warbler	—	O O	•U U	•U U U	R R	U C	C C	U U	•C C
Palm Warbler	U	O O	U U R	U U	O O	C C	O R	R R	C
Bay-breasted Warbler	U R U	O O	U U	U U	O O	U C	—	—	—
Blackpoll Warbler	U R	C C	U U	U U	U O	U C	O	—	O
Cerulean Warbler	•U U	•C O C	—	—	—	—	—	—	—
Black-and-white Warbler	U O	C O C	•C C C	U U U	U U U	U C	U R	R R	R
American Redstart	•C C C	•C C C	•C C C	•C C U	C C U	C U A	U U	C C	U
Prothonotary Warbler	•U U	•O O	R R R	R R	R R	R	C C	U U	•C C O
Worm-eating Warbler	—	—	—	R	—	R	R	—	—
Swainson's Warbler	—	—	—	—	—	—	R	O O	—
Ovenbird	•C C C	•C C C	•C C C	•U U U	•U U U	U U	U U	R	O
Northern Waterthrush	•U O U	O O O	C C	U U	R R	U C	O O	R R	—
Louisiana Waterthrush	—	O O O	R R	U	R R	R R	—	—	—
Kentucky Warbler	—	—	O O	—	—	R	—	—	—
Connecticut Warbler	—	R R	O O	U	O O	O	—	—	—
Mourning Warbler	•U U O	O O O	O O	U	O O	O O	—	—	—
MacGillivray's Warbler	—	—	—	—	—	—	—	—	—
Common Yellowthroat	•C C C	•C C C	•C C C	•C C C	•U U U	•A A A R	C C C C	C C U U	•C C C
Hooded Warbler	R	R R	U U	—	—	R	U U	U U	O
Wilson's Warbler	O	O O	U U	U U	O O	U U	—	—	—
Canada Warbler	O	C O	U U	—	O O O	U U	—	—	—
Painted Redstart	—	—	—	—	—	—	—	—	—
Yellow-breasted Chat	R R	R R	R R R	U U U	R R R	U U	O O R	O O O	—
TANAGERS									
Hepatic Tanager	—	—	—	—	—	—	—	—	—
Summer Tanager	—	—	R R R	R	O O	R R	O	O	—
Scarlet Tanager	•U U U	•C O O	•C C C	•U U U	O O	U C	—	—	—
Western Tanager	—	—	—	—	—	—	—	—	—
CARDINALS, GROSBEAKS & ALLIES									
Northern Cardinal	•U U U U	•C C C C	•C C C C	•C C C U	•C C C C	•C C C C	•C C C C	C C C C	•C C C C
Pyrrhuloxia	—	—	—	—	—	—	—	—	—
Rose-breasted Grosbeak	•C C C	•C C C	U U	•U U U	U R R	C C	—	—	—
Black-headed Grosbeak	—	—	—	—	—	—	—	—	—
Blue Grosbeak	—	—	—	—	—	O O	—	U U	U U
Lazuli Bunting	—	—	—	—	—	—	—	—	—
Indigo Bunting	•U U U	•C C	U U U	R	O O	U U	O	U U	U U
Painted Bunting	—	—	—	—	—	—	—	—	—
Dickcissel	—	—	O	—	R R	O	—	—	—
NEW WORLD SPARROWS & ALLIES									
Olive Sparrow	—	—	—	—	—	—	—	—	—
Green-tailed Towhee	—	—	—	—	—	—	—	—	—
Rufous-sided Towhee	•U U U R	•C O C	•U U U O	•C C C U	•A A C U	•A A A O	C C C C	O O U U	•C C
Brown Towhee	—	—	—	—	—	—	—	—	—
Abert's Towhee	—	—	—	—	—	—	—	—	—
Bachman's Sparrow	—	—	—	—	—	—	—	—	—

NC-4 Pea Is.				NC-5 Pee Dee				NC-6 C. Hatteras				NC-7 C. Lookout				ND-1 Arrowwood				ND-2 Audubon				ND-3 Souris Loop				ND-4 Lake Ilo				ND-5 Long L.				ND-6 Tewaukon				ND-7 Roosevelt				OH-1 Ottawa			
s	S	F	W	s	S	F	W	s	S	F	W	s	S	F	W	s	S	F	W	s	S	F	W	s	S	F	W	s	S	F	W	s	S	F	W	s	S	F	W	s	S	F	W	s	S	F	W
•U	U	U			C	C	C		U	U	U		R	R	U		U	U	U		U	O	U		•C	C	C		U	O	U			O			•U	O	U		•C	C	C			C	C	C

Abundance codes given by season columns: **• s S F W** (nesting dot, spring, Summer, Fall, Winter)

STATE-NUMBER OF BIRD LIST / REFUGE, SANCTUARY OR PRESERVE / NESTING, ABUNDANCE BY SEASON	NY-1 Iroquois	NY-2 Montezuma	NY-3 Wertheim	NY-4 Morton	NY-5 Target Rock	NY-6 Jones Beach	NC-1 Matta/Swan	NC-2 Pungo	NC-3 Mackay Is.
NEW WORLD SPARROWS & ALLIES (cont.)									
Cassin's Sparrow	—	—	—	—	—	—	—	—	—
Rufous-crowned Sparrow	—	—	—	—	—	—	—	—	—
American Tree Sparrow	U C C	C C	C	U	O	C	—	—	—
Chipping Sparrow	•C C C	•C C C	•C C C	•U U U U	•O O O	U C	O	U U U U	O C
Clay-colored Sparrow	—	—	—	—	—	R	—	—	—
Brewer's Sparrow	—	—	—	—	—	—	—	—	—
Field Sparrow	•C C C	•C C C O	U U U U	•U U U R	U U U R	U U	C C	U U U U	C C
Black-chinned Sparrow	—	—	—	—	—	—	—	—	—
Vesper Sparrow	•O O O	•O O O	—	—	—	O O	U	O	—
Lark Sparrow	—	—	—	—	—	O	—	—	—
Black-throated Sparrow	—	—	—	—	—	—	—	—	—
Sage Sparrow	—	—	—	—	—	—	—	—	—
Lark Bunting	—	—	—	—	—	—	—	—	—
Savannah Sparrow	•C C C	•O O O	U U U O	U U U U	R R	U C U	U U C	U U C	•C C C C
Baird's Sparrow	—	—	—	—	—	—	—	—	—
Grasshopper Sparrow	R R	•O O O	•O O	—	—	O	O	O	—
Henslow's Sparrow	•O O O	•O O O	—	—	—	R	R	R	—
Le Conte's Sparrow	—	—	—	—	—	—	—	—	—
Sharp-tailed Sparrow	—	—	•C C C R	U U U	R	•C C C R	—	—	R
Seaside Sparrow	—	—	•U U U	U U U	—	•C C C R	U	—	—
Fox Sparrow	O O	C C	U U	U U U	U U U	O U U	U U C	U U U	U
Song Sparrow	•C C C O	•C C C O	•C C C C	•C C C C	•U U U U	•A C A C	U U C	U U U U	•C C C
Lincoln's Sparrow	—	O O	U U	—	—	O O	—	—	—
Swamp Sparrow	•C C C O	•C C C	•C C C U	U U U U	O O O R	•O U	U U C	U U U	C C
White-throated Sparrow	C C O	C C	C C C	C C C	C C C	U A A	U U C	U C C	C C C
Golden-crowned Sparrow	—	C C	—	—	—	—	—	—	—
White-crowned Sparrow	C C O	—	U U O	U U	O O	O U R	U U	O O	O
Harris' Sparrow	—	—	—	—	—	—	—	—	—
Dark-eyed Junco	C C U	O O O	C C C	C C U	U U U	C C	U C	U U	U U U
McCown's Longspur	—	—	—	—	—	—	—	—	—
Lapland Longspur	—	O	—	—	—	R	—	—	—
Smith's Longspur	—	—	—	—	—	—	—	—	—
Chestnut-collared Longspur	—	—	—	—	—	—	—	—	—
Snow Bunting	O O O	O	O O	U U U	O	O C	R	—	—
NEW WORLD BLACKBIRDS & ORIOLES									
Bobolink	•C C C	•O O C	O O	R R	R R	O C	R	O O	O
Red-winged Blackbird	•A C A O	•A A A O	•A A A U	•C C C U	•A A U U	•A A A O	•A A A A	A A A A	•C C C C
Tricolored Blackbird	—	—	—	—	—	—	—	—	—
Eastern Meadowlark	•C C C O	•C C C O	•U U U U	U U U U	R R R R	U U O	•C C C A	A A U U	•C C C C
Western Meadowlark	—	—	—	—	—	—	—	—	—
Yellow-headed Blackbird	—	—	—	—	—	—	—	—	—
Rusty Blackbird	U U	O O	O O O	U U	R	R R R	O	—	—
Brewer's Blackbird	—	—	•C C C	—	—	—	R	—	—
Great-tailed Grackle	—	—	—	—	—	—	—	—	—
Boat-tailed Grackle	—	—	—	—	—	•U U U R	U U U U	U U	C C C C
Common Grackle	•C C C O	•A A A O	—	•C C C U	•A C A	•A A C R	C C C A	A A A A	•C C C C
Bronzed Cowbird	—	—	—	—	—	—	—	—	—
Brown-headed Cowbird	•C C C O	•C C A O	•C C C O	•U U U U	U U U	•C C C O	C U U C	C C C C	•C C C C
Orchard Oriole	—	—	•O O	•C C U	R	O O	U U	U U	O O
Hooded Oriole	—	—	—	—	—	—	—	—	—
Baltimore Oriole	—	—	—	—	—	—	—	—	—
Bullock's Oriole	•C C U	•C C C	•C C C	•C U C	•U U	C C	—	—	O
Scott's Oriole	—	—	—	—	—	—	—	—	—
FINCHES									
Rosy Finch	—	—	—	—	—	—	—	—	—
Pine Grosbeak	R R	—	—	—	—	—	—	—	—
Purple Finch	•U O U O	•C O C O	•O O O O	•C C U U	R U U	U	—	U	—
Cassin's Finch	—	—	—	—	—	—	—	—	—
House Finch	—	•O O O O	•C C C C	•C C C C	•C C C C	•A A A A	—	U U	—
Red Crossbill	—	—	R	—	—	R	—	—	—
White-winged Crossbill	—	—	R	—	—	R	—	—	—
Common Redpoll	O	R	R	U U	—	R	—	—	—
Hoary Redpoll	—	—	—	—	—	—	—	—	—
Pine Siskin	R R R	R	R R	U U	R R	R U U	O	U U	—
Lesser Goldfinch	—	—	—	—	—	—	—	—	—
Lawrence's Goldfinch	—	—	—	—	—	—	—	—	—
American Goldfinch	•C C C U	•C C C O	•U U U U	•U U U U	•U U C U	•C C C U	U	O O	U U
Evening Grosbeak	U R U U	R R R	O	U U U	R R R	O O	R	O O	—
OLD WORLD SPARROWS									
House Sparrow	•C C C C	•C C C C	•C C C C	•U U U U	•C C C C	•A A A A	•C C C C	C C C C	•U U U R
Eurasian Tree Sparrow	—	—	—	—	—	—	—	—	—

NC-4 Pea Is.	NC-5 Pee Dee	NC-6 C. Hatteras	NC-7 C. Lookout	ND-1 Arrowwood	ND-2 Audubon	ND-3 Souris Loop	ND-4 Lake Ilo	ND-5 Long L.	ND-6 Tewaukon	ND-7 Roosevelt	OH-1 Ottawa
•s S F W	•s S F W	•s S F W	•s S F W	•s S F W	•s S F W	•s S F W	•s S F W	•s S F W	•s S F W	•s S F W	•s S F W
—	—	—	—	—	—	—	—	—	—	—	—
R R	—	O OO	—	C C	C CR	A AR	C CR	C CO	C UC	C CO	C CC
O CO	CCCC	O OO	U	•CCU	•CUU	•CUC	•CUU	•UUU	OOO	•CCC	•UUU
U	—	OO	R	•CCU	•UUU	•AAC	•UUU	•CCC	•CUC	CCC	•UUU
•UUCU	CCCC	U UU	U	—	—	•OOO	—	—	•OOO	•CCC	•UUUR
CU	C CC	O OU	—	•UUU	•UOO	•UUU	•UOO	•UUU	•CUC	•CCC	•UUU
UCU	—	O OU	R	•UUU	OOR	•OO	OOR	•UUU	•UU	CCC	•UUU
				•UU	•CCU	•CAC	•CCU	•CCC	•OOR	URU	—
A AA	C CC	O OO	C CC	•CCU	•CCC	•CAA	•CCC	UUU	•CCC	R	•CCC
—	—	—	—	•CCU	•UUU	•UCU	•UUU	RRR	•UUR	R	—
UO	O R	U UU	R	•UUR	•CCC	•UCU	•CCC	•UUU	•UUR	CCU	•OOO
											R
A AA	—	U RUU	C CC	URU	•OOO	•UCU	•OOO	—	URR	—	R R
•ACAA	—	CCCC	UUUU	•URU	•OOO	•UCU	•OOO	•OOO	•UUR	—	—
O UO	C	O OO	UU	R R	—	U U	—	R R	O O	—	C CR
•AAAA	C CC	U UU	UUCC	•CCC	•CCC	•CCC	•CCC	•CCC	•CCC	•UUU	•CCCU
U	—	O O	—	—	O O	C C	O O	—	C C	—	U U
O AA	—	U UU	C CC	U U	O O	O O	O O	—	U OU	—	•CRCO
U AU	CCCC	O OU	U CU	C C	U OU	A C	U OU	U U	C C	R	A AU
C O	—	U U	R C	U U	U U	C C	U U	U U	C C	U U	C CU
—	—	—	—	C C	O O	C CR	O O	U U	C C	U UO	—
U UU	CCCC	U UU	—	C C	C CO	A AR	C CO	C CR	U UO	C CO	C CU
—	—	—	R	—	O OO	•RRR	O OO	R	—	O	U UU
—	—	—	—	C CU	U CO	A AC	U CO	C CC	R	O	—
—	—	—	—	R RR	U CO	O OO	U CO	R	R	R	O
—	—	—	—	•UUU	•CCU	•CCU	•CCU	•CCC	•CCC	•C UU	UUU
O OO	—	O OO	RR	U UC	O OC	C CA	O OC	U OU	U OUC	OO	C CC
C C	A C	O O	UUC	•CCU	•UUO	•CCC	•UUO	•CCC	•CCC	R	•UUU
•AAAA	ΛΛΛΛ	ΛΛΛΛ	CCCC	•CCC	•AAAR	•AAAO	•AAAR	•AAAR	•AAAR	UUUO	•AAAU
•CCCA	AAAA	CCCC	CCCC	—	—	—	—	—	—	—	•CUCR
—	—	—	—	•CCC	•AAAR	•AAAR	•AAAR	•AAA	•CCCR	•CCCO	•RRR
—	—	R	—	•CCU	•AAC	•AAA	•AAC	•CCC	•AAAR	OO	•RR
R	R U U	—	R	U U	—	U UR	—	R R	U UR	O	C CU
—	C	—	—	•UUU	•UCU	•UUU	•UCU	•UUU	•UUUO	URUO	O OR
•AAAA	—	OOOO	CCCC	—	—	—	—	—	—	—	•AAAU
•RRRR	C CC	—	UUU	•CCC	•ACA	•CCCR	•ACA	•CCC	•AAAR	CCC	•AAAU
C CC	OOOO	U UU	UUU	•CCC	•AAC	•CCC	•AAC	•CCC	•CCC	•CCU	•CCCU
•UU	CCC	—	UU	•UU	•UU	•UUR	•OOO	•UUR	•UUO	RR	•OOR
—	—	U U	—	—	—	—	—	—	—	—	—
A	R R	—	UUC	•UU	•UUU	•UUU	•UUU	•UUU	•CCC	•UUO	•CUU
—	—	—	—	—	—	—	—	—	—	O O	—
U U	A AA	—	OO	R RU	O OO	O	O OO	R RU	O OR	O O	U UU
—	—	—	R	—	—	—	—	—	—	—	—
—	—	—	—	R RU	OROR	RRRR	OROR	—	R	O O	—
—	—	—	—	—	—	R	—	—	—	—	—
—	—	O O	—	U UU	U UUC	C	U UU	—	O O UU	C	O OO
—	—	—	—	—	—	R	—	—	—	O	C
U U	—	O O OO	R	U UUU	U U	•CRCR	U U	—	O UO	•O O O	•U UO
U CU	CCCC	U UU	RUU	•UUU	•CCUR	•CCAR	•CCUR	•CCC	•CCCO	CCCO	•ACCC
R	AA	OO	R R	R	—	R RR	—	—	R R	O	O OO
•UUUU	AAAA	UUUU	—	•CCCC	•CCCC	•CCCC	•CCCC	•AAAA	•CCCC	UUUU	•AAAA
											—

NC-4 Pea Is.	NC-5 Pee Dee	NC-6 C. Hatteras	NC-7 C. Lookout	ND-1 Arrowwood	ND-2 Audubon	ND-3 Souris Loop	ND-4 Lake Ilo	ND-5 Long L.	ND-6 Tewaukon	ND-7 Roosevelt	OH-1 Ottawa
•s S F W	•s S F W	•s S F W	•s S F W	•s S F W	•s S F W	•s S F W	•s S F W	•s S F W	•s S F W	•s S F W	•s S F W

STATE-NUMBER OF BIRD LIST / REFUGE, SANCTUARY OR PRESERVE / NESTING, ABUNDANCE BY SEASON	OK-1 Optima • s S F W	OK-2 Salt Plains • s S F W	OK-3 Sequoyah • s S F W	OK-4 Tishomingo • s S F W	OK-5 Washita • s S F W	OK-6 Wichita • s S F W	OR-1 Up. Klamath • s S F W	OR-2 W.L. Finley • s S F W	OR-3 Ankeny • s S F W
LOONS									
Red-throated Loon	—	—	—	—	—	—		—	—
Arctic Loon	—	—	—	—	—	—	R	—	—
Pacific Loon	—	—	—	—	—	—		—	—
Common Loon	R R O	R R R	R R R	—	O O O	O O	U R U R	—	—
Yellow-billed Loon	—	—	—	—	—	—		—	—
GREBES									
Least Grebe	—	—	—		—	—			
Pied-billed Grebe	•C O C O	•C O C O	•C C C	C O C O	C U C O	•C U C C	•C C C U	•U U U U	•U U U U
Horned Grebe	O R R	R R R	R R	O O O	O O O	U U	U R U	R R R R	R R R R
Red-necked Grebe	—	—	—		—	—	•U U U	—	—
Eared Grebe	O O R	•U R U	R R	O	U U U	U R U	•C A A U	R R R R	R R R R
Western Grebe	O O R	—	—	R R	R	—	•C A A U	R R O	—
SHEARWATERS & PETRELS									
Northern Fulmar	—	—	—	—	—	—	—	—	—
Cory's Shearwater	—	—	—	—	—	—	—	—	—
Pink-footed Shearwater	—	—	—	—	—	—	—	—	—
Greater Shearwater	—	—	—	—	—	—	—	—	—
Sooty Shearwater	—	—	—	—	—	—	—	—	—
Short-tailed Shearwater	—	—	—	—	—	—	—	—	—
Manx Shearwater	—	—	—	—	—	—	—	—	—
Audubon's Shearwater	—	—	—	—	—	—	—	—	—
STORM-PETRELS									
Wilson's Storm-Petrel	—	—	—	—	—	—	—	—	—
Fork-tailed Storm-Petrel	—	—	—	—	—	—	—	—	—
Leach's Storm-Petrel	—	—	—	—	—	—	—	—	—
BOOBIES & GANNETS									
Masked Booby	—	—	—	—	—	—	—	—	—
Brown Booby	—	—	—	—	—	—	—	—	—
Northern Gannet	—	—	—	—	—	—	—	—	—
PELICANS									
American White Pelican	O O	A U A O	C A C	C O C O	C C U	O R	•C C C	—	—
Brown Pelican	—	—	—	—	—	—	—	—	—
CORMORANTS									
Great Cormorant	—	—	—	—	—	—	—	—	—
Double-crested Cormorant	C C O	•C O C	•A U A A	C O C O	C O C C	U U R	•C C C U	R R R R	—
Olivaceous Cormorant	—	—	—	R	—	—	—	—	—
Brandt's Cormorant	—	—	—	—	—	—	—	—	—
Pelagic Cormorant	—	—	—	—	—	—	—	—	—
Red-faced Cormorant	—	—	—	—	—	—	—	—	—
ANHINGAS									
Anhinga	—	—	—	R R	—	—	—	—	—
FRIGATEBIRDS									
Magnificent Frigatebird	—	—	—	—	—	—	—	—	—
BITTERNS & HERONS									
American Bittern	O O O	U O U R	O R O	•O O O	U O U	R	•U U U R	U U U U	U U U U
Least Bittern	—	•O O O	O O O	•O O R	O O O	• R	•R R R	—	—
Great Blue Heron	•C C C O	•C C C C	•A A A A	•C C C C	C C C O	•C C C C	•C C C C	C C C C	C C C C
Great Egret	R R	C C C	•C A C	O C C	O U O	U U U	•C C C R	R R R O	R R R O
Snowy Egret	—	C C C	•U U U	O O O	O U O	R R	•U C C	—	—
Little Blue Heron	O O O	C C C	•C C C	•C C C R	O O U	O O O	—	—	—
Tricolored Heron	—	—	R R	R	—	—	—	—	—
Reddish Egret	—	—	—	—	—	—	—	—	—
Cattle Egret	—	U U U	U U U	O O O	O O	O O	R R	—	—
Green-backed Heron	O O O	•C C C	•C C C	•C C C R	U C U	•C C U	R R R	O O O O	O O O O
Black-crowned Night-Heron	•O O O	•U U U	•O O O	R O C	O U U	R R R	•C C C U	R R R R	—
Yellow-crowned Night-Heron	R R R	O O O	•O O O	R O	O C U	—	—	—	—
IBISES & SPOONBILLS									
White Ibis	—	—	—	—	—	—	—	—	—
Glossy Ibis	—	—	—	—	—	—	—	—	—
White-faced Ibis	O O	R R R	R	R R	O R O	R R R	R R R	—	—
Roseate Spoonbill	—	—	—	R	—	—	—	—	—
STORKS									
Wood Stork	—	—	—	R O	—	—	—	—	—
SWANS, GEESE & DUCKS									
Fulvous Whistling-Duck	—	—	—	—	—	—	—	—	—
Black-bellied Whistling-Duck	—	—	—	—	—	—	—	—	—
Tundra Swan	—	R R R	R R	R	R O	—	C C A	U R U C	—
Trumpeter Swan	—	—	—	—	—	—	R R	—	U R U C
Mute Swan	—	—	—	—	—	—	—	—	—
Greater White-fronted Goose	O O	C C U	C C C	O C C	C C C	R R	A R A C	U R U U	U R U U
Snow Goose	O O	U U U	C C A	O C O	U O U	R R	A R A C	U U U	U U U

	OR-4 Baskett Sl.	OR-5 Hart Mt.	OR-6 Malheur	OR-7 Umatilla	PA-1 Erie	PA-2 Tinicum	RI-1 R.I. NWR's	SC-1 C. Romain	SC-2 Sandhills	SD-1 Lacreek	SD-2 L. Andes	SD-3 Sand L.
	•s S F W	•s S F W	•s S F W	•s S F W	•s S F W	•s S F W	•s S F W	•s S F W	•s S F W	•s S F W	•s S F W	•s S F W
	— — —	— — —	— O O	— — —	—	R — —	C CU —	R RU —	—	—	—	—
	— O O	O O • C C C	— • O O R R	R R R	O O —	O O O O	C O C C	O R C C R U	C O C C	R	O	— • A A A
	— R R O	• C C C • C C C	• C C C R • C C C R	O O O U U O O	—	—	U U U —	R U —	—	U O O • U U U	• U U U • U U	• A A A • A A A
	— — — —	— — — —	— — — —	— — — —	— — — —	— — — •	R R — R R R R R — R R R —	— — — — — —	— — — — — —	— — — — — —	— — — — — —	— — — — — —
	— ⹀ —	— — —	— — —	— — —	— — —	— — —	R R R — R R R	R R — — — R	— — — — —	— — — — —	— — — — —	— — — — —
	— —	— —	— —	— —	— —	— —	R U O U O U U	U U —	— —	— —	— —	— —
	— RRRR	• C C C • C C C	• U C C R • C C C O	O U • C C C	— R R	— U U U C R C R	— A C A U	• A A C C A C A A	— R	• A A A • A A A	C C C C C C	• C C C • C C C
	— — — —	— — — —	— — — —	— — — —	— — — —	— — — —	— — — —	— — — —	— — — —	— — — —	— — — —	— — — —
	—	—	—	—	—	—	—	U U O R	R R R R	—	—	—
	U U U U C C C C R R R O — —	• U U U R R R • C C C U • C C C R R —	• U U O O • R R R • C C C C U • C C C R • U U U • O O O	O O O — • C C C C R R — — • U U U R	U U U — • C C C U R R R R — • U C U R R R	• C C O R • O O O A C A C • A A A R • A A A O C C O O O O O R • C A A R • A A A O R R R	• U U U O • O O O C U C U U U C O U C C O O O — O O R • C C C • U C C O —	U U U O • U C U R • C C C C • C C C C C C C U • C C C C O O R R • C C U U • C C C C • U C O U	R C C C C R O O R R R R R 0 0 0 0 — O U R R • C C U —	• C C C O O O • C C C O — O O O O — — O O • C C C	• U U U U U U C U C O O — O — — O O O • C C C R R R	• C C C • O O • C C C • U U U • U U U • R R R — • C C C • O O • A A A R R R
	— — —	— — —	— — —	— — —	— — —	R O O O —	— U U U —	• C C C O • U U O —	O — —	— — —	— — O O O	— — • U U U
	—	O O O	• U U U R	—	—	—	—	C C C U	—	—	O O O	• U U U
	—	—	—	—	—	—	—	—	R	—	—	—
	U R U C — U R U U U U U	A A C — • U U	C R C U • U U U U U U R C R U R	U R C C — U R U O U R U O	O O O — R R R	R R R — R R R R R R R	R R R • A A A C O O O	R C C — R R O O R R	— — R R R R	O O • C U C A O U O A U O	O O — C C U U	C C — U U R A O A R

STATE-NUMBER OF BIRD LIST / REFUGE, SANCTUARY OR PRESERVE / NESTING, ABUNDANCE BY SEASON	OK-1 Optima • s S F W	OK-2 Salt Plains • s S F W	OK-3 Sequoyah • s S F W	OK-4 Tishomingo • s S F W	OK-5 Washita • s S F W	OK-6 Wichita • s S F W	OR-1 Up. Klamath • s S F W	OR-2 W.L. Finley • s S F W	OR-3 Ankeny • s S F W
SWANS, GEESE & DUCKS (cont.)									
Ross' Goose	—	—	R R	R	O O U	—	—	—	—
Emperor Goose	—	—	—	—	—	—	—	R	—
Brant			R	R R			R R	R R R	—
Canada Goose	C C C	A A A	C C A	•C R A A	C O C A	O O O	•A C A C	C O C A	C O C A
Wood Duck	—	•C C C	•C U C A	•C O C A	•O U O R	•C C C O	•U U U	•C C C C	•C C C C
Green-winged Teal	C C O	A R A U	O C C	C C C	C A C	C C U	—	•A O A A	•A O A A
American Black Duck	—	R R R	R R	R O O	R R	—	—	—	—
Mottled Duck	—	—	—	—	—	—	—	—	—
Mallard	•O C O O	•A O A A	•C U A A	A O A A	•A U A A	•C C C	•A C A C	•A U A A	•A U A A
Northern Pintail	•O O O O	•A O A U	O C C	C C C	A C C	C C U	•A C A C	•A O A A	•A O A A
Blue-winged Teal	•C O C	•A O A U	•C U C O	C O C R	•C O C O	•C O C	—	•R R R	•R R R
Cinnamon Teal	O R O	R R R	—	R R R	R R	R R	•C A C R	•U U U	•U U U
Northern Shoveler	•C R C O	•A O A U	C U C	C O C C	C O C O	C U U	•A C A C	•C R C C	•C R C C
Gadwall	O O O	•A O A C	•C R A A	O C C	C C C	C C C	•C C A U	O O O O	O O O O
Eurasian Wigeon	—	—	—	—	—	—	U R U	O U	O U
American Wigeon	C C O	•A O A C	C C C	C C C	C A A	C C C	•A U A C	C R C C	C R C C
Canvasback	O R R	U U O	R R	O O O	O R O O	U U U	•C U C U	R R R	R R R
Redhead	•C R C	•A R U O	O O O	O O O	O R C O	C U U	•C C C U	R R	—
Ring-necked Duck	C R C R	C U O	O O U	O O C	C C U	C C C	•U U U U	U R O U	U R O U
Greater Scaup	—	R R	—	O O O	R R	R R R	R R R	R R	R R
Lesser Scaup	C C	C R U O	O O U	O R C C	U U O	O O O	•C U C C	O O O	O O O
Common Eider	—	—	—	—	—	—	—	—	—
King Eider	—	—	—	—	—	—	—	—	—
Steller's Eider	—	—	—	—	—	—	—	—	—
Harlequin Duck	—	—	—	—	—	—	—	—	—
Oldsquaw	—	R R	—	—	—	—	R R	—	—
Black Scoter	—	—	—	—	—	—	—	—	—
Surf Scoter	—	—	—	—	—	—	R R	R	—
White-winged Scoter	—	—	—	—	—	—	•R R R	—	—
Common Goldeneye	O O R	U U C	U U	R R O	U O U	U U C	C R U C	R R	R R
Barrow's Goldeneye	—	—	—	—	—	—	R R		
Bufflehead	O O	C C O	U U	O O O	U O C	U U C	C R C U	U U U	U U U
Hooded Merganser	O O R	U U U	U U U	O R O O	U O C	U U U	•U R U U	•U U U U	•U U U U
Common Merganser	C C O	C C A	U U	O C C	C U C	U U U	C R C C	R R	R R
Red-breasted Merganser	R R R	—	R	O R R	R R	—	R R R	—	—
Ruddy Duck	•C R C R	C R C O	U U	O O O	U R U O	U O O	•A C A U	U U U	U U U
Masked Duck	—	—	—	—	—	—	—	—	—
AMERICAN VULTURES									
Black Vulture	—	—	•U U U U	O O O	—	—	—	—	—
Turkey Vulture	•C C C O	•C C C	•C C A U	•C A A C	•C C C	•C C C R	•U U U	C C C	C C C
KITES, EAGLES, HAWKS & ALLIES									
Osprey	O O	O O	U U	R R O R	U O O	O R O	•U U U	•O O R R	•O O R R
American Swallow-tailed Kite	—	—	—	—	—	—	—	—	—
Black-shouldered Kite	—	—	—	—	—	—	—	•R R R R	—
Snail Kite	—	—	—	—	—	—	—	—	—
Mississippi Kite	•C C C	•C C C	R R R	O O	•C C	•C C C	—	—	—
Bald Eagle	O O O	C C C	O R C C	O O C	O O U	U U U	•C U U A	O O U	O O U
Northern Harrier	•C O C C	C C C	C O C C	C R O C	•A U A A	U O U U	•C C C C	•C C U C	•C C U C
Sharp-shinned Hawk	O O R	U U O	O O O	O O O R	U O U O	O O O	•U U U U	U U U U	U U U U
Cooper's Hawk	O O R	•U R U U	O U U	•O O O O	U O U O	•O O O O	U U U U	•U U U U	•U U U U
Northern Goshawk	—	R R	R R	R	—	—	•U U U U	R R	—
Common Black-Hawk	—	—	—	—	—	—	—	—	—
Harris' Hawk	—	—	—	—	—	—	—	—	—
Gray Hawk	—	—	—	—	—	—	—	—	—
Red-shouldered Hawk	—	R R R R	•O O U U	• O O	—	—	—	—	—
Broad-winged Hawk	—	R R	•U U O	•O R O	—	—	—	—	—
Short-tailed Hawk	—	—	—	—	—	—	—	—	—
Swainson's Hawk	•C O C R	•C C C R	•U U U	O O O O	•O C U	O O O	R R R	R R R	R R R
White-tailed Hawk	—	—	—	—	—	—	—	—	—
Zone-tailed Hawk	—	—	—	—	—	—	—	—	—
Red-tailed Hawk	•C C C O	•C U C C	•C C C A	•C C A C	•C C A C	•C C C C	•C C C C	•C C C C	•C C C C
Ferruginous Hawk	O R O O	R R R	—	O O O	O O U	O O U	R R R	—	—
Rough-legged Hawk	R R O	O O U	R R	R R	O O U	O O U	C C U	U R O C	U R O C
Golden Eagle	•O O O O	O O O	R R	R R R	O O U	U U U	•U U U C	R R	R R
CARACARAS & FALCONS									
Crested Caracara	—	—	—	—	—	—	—	—	—
American Kestrel	•C O C C	•C O C C	•C U C C	•C O C C	•C C C U	•C O C C	•C C C C	•C C C C	•C C C C
Merlin	O O O	R R R	R R R	R R	O U O	—	U U U	R R R	R R R
Peregrine Falcon	—	R R R R	R R R	R R R	R R	—	R R R R	R R R	R R R
Gyrfalcon	—	—	—	—	—	—	—	—	—
Prairie Falcon	•O O O O	O R O O	—	—	U U U	O O O	—	R R	R R

	OR-4 Baskett Sl.	OR-5 Hart Mt.	OR-6 Malheur	OR-7 Umatilla	PA-1 Erie	PA-2 Tinicum	RI-1 R.I. NWR's	SC-1 C. Romain	SC-2 Sandhills	SD-1 Lacreek	SD-2 L. Andes	SD-3 Sand L.
	• s S F W	• s S F W	• s S F W	• s S F W	• s S F W	• s S F W	• s S F W	• s S F W	• s S F W	• s S F W	• s S F W	• s S F W
	—	O O	U U	—	—	—	—	—	—	O O	—	U U
	R	—	—	—	—	—	—	—	—	—	—	—
	R R R	—	—	—	—	R R R	U O U U	R O O	—	—	—	—
	C O C A	•C C A C	•C C A C	•C C A A	•C C C C	•A A A C	•A C A C	R O O	•C U C C	•A A A A	U A U A	•C C C U
	•C C C C	R	R U O R	O O O	•C C C O	•O O O O	•U U U R	•C C C C	•C C C C	•U U C O	•O R O R	•U C C
	•A O A A	•C C C O	•U U C U	•C C C U	C C R	•C O A C	C U C U	C C C	O U U	•C U C O	•A U A O	•U U C R
	—	—	—	—	•O O O U	•A C A C	•C C C A	C C C	O C C	O O	O O O	•U O U O
	—	—	—	—	—	—	—	—	—	—	—	—
	•A U A A	•C C A C	•C C A C	•C C A A	•C C C C	•A A A C	•C C C C	C C C	U O C C	•A A A A	•A U A A	•C C A U
	•A O A A	•A C A C	•A U C U	•C C C C	O O R	•A O A C	U U O	C C C	U U	•A C C O	•A U A O	•C C C R
	•R R R	O O O	•U U O R	•C C C U	•C U C R	•C C C R	•C U C	•C U C C	U U O	•A A A O	•A A A	•C C A R
	•U U U	•C C C R	C A U R	•C C U	—	—	—	R	—	U O O	O O O	R R R
	•C R C C	•C C C O	•C C C O	•C U C O	O O R	•C R C O	O O	C C C	R R	•C C C O	•C C C	•C C C
	O O O O	•C C A U	•A C A U	•C U C U	U U R	O R O O	C U C U	C C C	O O	•A C A U	•A C A R	•C C C
	O U	O O	R R R	—	R	R	R R R	R	—	—	O O	
	C R C C	•C O A U	•C U C U	•C C C C	C R C R	O O O	C C U	C A A	U C C	•U U C O	•A O A O	•U U U
	R R R	•C U C O	•U U U O	U U U	O O R	O O R	C C U	C C A	R R	•U O U O	•C O C	•U U C R
	R R	•C C A C	•C C C O	•U U U U	O O R	R R R R	U U U	O U C	R R R	•C U C O	•C O C	•C C C
	U R O U	•U O U O	•O O O O	U U U	C R C O	O R O O	U U O	C C C	O U U	U U O	•C C R	U U U
	R R	—	—	U U U	R R R	C R O O	C O C C	—	—	—	O O	
	O O O	C U C O	•U U U O	U U U	O O R	O O O	U U U	A C A	O O	C O C O	•A O A R	•U U C R
	—	—	—	—	—	—	U U U	—	—	—	—	—
	—	—	—	—	—	—	R R O	—	—	—	—	—
	—	—	—	—	—	—	—	—	—	—	—	—
	—	—	—	—	—	—	O O O	R R	—	—	—	—
	—	—	—	R R	—	R R R	O R O O	R R	—	—	R	—
	—	—	—	—	—	—	C O C C	U C A	—	—	—	—
	R	—	—	—	—	—	C O C C	O U U	—	—	—	—
	—	—	R R	—	—	R R	C O C C	U U	—	—	O O	—
	U U U	U U U	U R U C	C C C	O O O	R R R R	C C A	U U	R	U U U	U O U O	U U R
	—	R R R	O O	R R	—	—	R R	—	—	—	—	—
	U U U	C R C C	U R U U	C C C	C C O	O O	C C C	C C A	R R	C O C U	U U R	U R U
	•U U U U	R R	O U U	O O	•C C C R	O O R	U U U	C R C C	O O U U	U O U U	O O	U R U R
	R R	U U U	•U U U U	•U U U U	O O	O O	C C U	O O	—	U O U	U C	C U
	—	—	—	—	O O R	O R R	C O C C	•C R C C	—	O O	U U O	O O
	U U U	•C C C O	•U U U O	U U U	O O R	C O C C	U C U	•O R C C	R R	•C U C O	•C U C	•C C C
	—	—	—	—	—	—	—	—	—	—	—	—
	C C C	C C C	•C C C R	R	U U U	O O O O	O O O	•C C C C	•C C C C	U U U	•O O O	R R R
	—	O O	O O O	O O O O	O O	O O O	•U C C	•C C C R	O R R	O O O	O R O	O O O
								O U R C				
	—	—	—	—	—	—	—	—	—	—	—	—
	—	—	—	—	—	—	—	—	—	—	—	—
								U U R				
	O O U	U O U	O O U	R U U	O O O R	R R R	R R O	R R O	R R R R	O U C	O O A	U U U
	•C C U C	•C C C U	•C C C U	•C C C C	•O R R R	•C O C C	C U C U	C C C C	U U U	•C C C C	•C C C R	•C C C U
	U U U U	•U O U O	U O U O	O R U O	•O R O O	O R O R	U U O	•C O C C	U C C	U O U U	O O	•U U U R
	•U U U U	•U O U O	O R U O	O O O O	•O R O R	O R O O	U U O	•C C C C	U U U U	O O U U	O O	•U U U
	—	•O O O	O O	O O	R	R R R	R R	R R R	—	—	O O	R
	—	—	—	—	—	—	—	—	—	—	—	—
	—	—	—	—	—	—	—	—	—	—	—	—
	—	—	—	—	•U U U O	O R O O	O O O O	•U U U U	•U U U U	O O O O	O U O	—
	—	—	—	—	•U U U	O O C	O U U	R	O	—	O U O	O O
	R R R	•O O O	•U U U	•U U O	—	—	—	—	—	•U U C	•O O O	•C C C
	—	—	—	—	—	—	—	—	—	—	—	—
	•C C C C	•C C C U	•C U C U	•U U U O	•C C C C	C R C C	U U U U	•U U C C	•C C C C	•C U C U	•O U O	A C A
	—	O O O	•O O O O	C C C	—	R	R O O	U	U O U U	O O O	0 0 0
	U R O C	U U C	C C C	•U U U U	R	R O O	U	U	U C C C	O R O C	U O C U
	R R	•C C C C	•C C C C	U U U	—	R R	R R R	R R R	R R	C O C C	O	U U
	—	—	—	—	—	—	—	—	—	—	—	—
	•C C C C	•A A A U	•U U U O	•C C C U	•U U U R	•C C C C	•C C C C	U O U U	•C C C C	•U U U U	•C C C	C U C U
	R R R	O O O	R R	—	R R R	O R O R	U U O	R R R	—	O O U U	O O	R R R
	R R R	O O	R R R R	—	R R R	R R R	R R O	R R R	—	O O U U	O O	R R
	R R	•C C C O	•U U U O	O O O O	—	—	—	—	—	U U U U	O O	O O O

STATE-NUMBER OF BIRD LIST REFUGE, SANCTUARY OR PRESERVE NESTING, ABUNDANCE BY SEASON	OK-1 Optima • s S F W	OK-2 Salt Plains • s S F W	OK-3 Sequoyah • s S F W	OK-4 Tishomingo • s S F W	OK-5 Washita • s S F W	OK-6 Wichita • s S F W	OR-1 Up. Klamath • s S F W	OR-2 W.L. Finley • s S F W	OR-3 Ankeny • s S F W
CHACHALACAS									
Plain Chachalaca	—	—	—	—	—	—	—	—	—
PARTRIDGES, GROUSE, TURKEYS & QUAILS									
Gray Partridge	—	—	—	—	—	—	—	—	—
Chukar	—	—	—	—	—	—	—	—	—
Ring-necked Pheasant	•C C C C	•C C C C	—	—	•R R R R	—	—	•C C C C	•C C C C
Spruce Grouse	—	—	—	—	—	—	—	—	—
Blue Grouse	—	—	—	—	—	—	•U U U U	•U U U U	—
Willow Ptarmigan	—	—	—	—	—	—	—	—	—
Rock Ptarmigan	—	—	—	—	—	—	—	—	—
White-tailed Ptarmigan	—	—	—	—	—	—	—	—	—
Ruffed Grouse	—	—	—	—	—	—	•R R R R	•U U U U	•U U U U
Sage Grouse	—	—	—	—	—	—	—	—	—
Greater Prairie Chicken	—	—	R	—	—	—	—	—	—
Lesser Prairie Chicken	•O O O O	—	—	—	R R R R	—	—	—	—
Sharp-tailed Grouse	—	—	—	—	—	—	—	—	—
Wild Turkey	•C C C C	•A U A A	R R R R	•O O O O	•U O O R	•C C C C	—	—	—
Northern Bobwhite	•C C C C	•C C C C	•C A A C	•A A A A	•A A A A	•C C C C	—	—	—
Scaled Quail	•C C C C	—	—	—	—	—	—	—	—
Gambel's Quail	—	—	—	—	—	—	—	—	—
California Quail	—	—	—	—	—	—	•C C C C	•C C C C	•C C C C
Mountain Quail	—	—	—	—	—	—	•U U U U	•R R R R	—
RAILS, GALLINULES & COOTS									
Yellow Rail	—	—	—	—	—	—	—	—	—
Black Rail	—	•R R R	—	R R	—	—	—	—	—
Clapper Rail	—	—	—	—	—	—	—	—	—
King Rail	•R R R	•U O U	R R R	•O R R R	—	—	—	—	—
Virginia Rail	O O	•O R O	O O O	R C	—	—	•U U U R	•U C U O	•U C U O
Sora	O O	U R U	U U	O R O	O O	—	•U U U R	•C C O R	•C C O R
Purple Gallinule	—	—	—	—	—	—	—	—	—
Common Moorhen	R R R	•R R R	—	R R	R R	—	R R	—	—
American Coot	•C O C O	•A U A U	•C C A A	•C O A A	C O C U	•C O C C	•A A A C	•C O U C	•C O U C
LIMPKINS									
Limpkin	—	—	—	—	—	—	—	—	—
CRANES									
Sandhill Crane	C C	A A R	R	O O	A A U	R R	•U U U	R R R R	R R R R
Whooping Crane	—	R R	—	—	R	—	—	—	—
PLOVERS									
Black-bellied Plover	O O	U O U	O	—	U O	R	—	O O R	—
Lesser Golden-Plover	O O	O R	O	O R R	U O	—	—	—	—
Snowy Plover	•O C O	•A A A	—	—	•O U O	—	—	—	—
Wilson's Plover	—	—	—	—	—	—	—	—	—
Semipalmated Plover	O O	U U	O O	O R O	O O	R R	—	U U O	U U O
Piping Plover	—	R	R R	O R	—	—	—	—	—
Killdeer	•O O O O	•C C C O	•C A C C	•C C A A	•C C C C	•C C C O	•C C C U	•A C A A	•A C A A
Mountain Plover	O R O	—	—	—	—	—	—	—	—
OYSTERCATCHERS									
American Oystercatcher	—	—	—	—	—	—	—	—	—
Black Oystercatcher	—	—	—	—	—	—	—	—	—
STILTS & AVOCETS									
Black-necked Stilt	O O	R R	—	R	R	—	—	—	—
American Avocet	•O C O	•A A A	R R R	O O O	U O U	O O O	•C C C R	—	—
SANDPIPERS									
Greater Yellowlegs	O O	C C C R	U O U R	C O O O	U O U	R R R	C R C R	C U U O	C U U O
Lesser Yellowlegs	C R C	C O C R	U O U	C O C O	U U U	R R R	U R U R	O O O R	O O O R
Solitary Sandpiper	O R O	O O O	U R U	C O O	—	O O O	R R	R R	R R
Willet	C R O	C C C	O U R	O R	O O	R R	—	—	—
Wandering Tattler	—	—	—	—	—	—	—	—	—
Spotted Sandpiper	•C O C	C C C	C C O	C O C	U U O	U O O	•U U U	•U U O	•U U O
Upland Sandpiper	•O O O	U U U	R R	C O O	U O U	O O	—	—	—
Whimbrel	R R	R R	—	—	—	—	R R	—	—
Long-billed Curlew	•O R O	O O	—	R R R	O O O	R R	—	—	—
Hudsonian Godwit	—	U R R	R	R R	—	—	—	—	—
Bar-tailed Godwit	—	—	—	—	—	—	—	—	—
Marbled Godwit	—	O R R	R	R R	U O	—	—	—	—
Ruddy Turnstone	—	O O	R	—	R R	—	R R R	—	—
Black Turnstone	—	—	—	—	—	—	—	—	—
Surfbird	—	—	—	—	—	—	—	—	—
Red Knot	—	—	R	—	—	—	R R	—	—
Sanderling	O O	O O	O O	R R R	O O	—	R R R	—	—
Semipalmated Sandpiper	O O O	A C A	U U	C C O	C U C	R	—	—	—
Western Sandpiper	O R O	A U A	U U	C O C	U O O	R R	A C A R	C U U O	C U U O

	OR-4 Baskett Sl.	OR-5 Hart Mt.	OR-6 Malheur	OR-7 Umatilla	PA-1 Erie	PA-2 Tinicum	RI-1 R.I. NWR's	SC-1 C. Romain	SC-2 Sandhills	SD-1 Lacreek	SD-2 L. Andes	SD-3 Sand L.
• s S F W	• s S F W	• s S F W	• s S F W	• s S F W	• s S F W	• s S F W	• s S F W	• s S F W	• s S F W	• s S F W	• s S F W	• s S F W
	—	—	—	—	—	—	—	—	—	—	—	—
			•RRRR	UUUU						OOOO	•UUUU	•UUUU
		•CCCC	•UUUU	OOOO								
	•CCCC	•OOOO	•CCCC	•CCCC	•UUUU	•AAAA	•CCCC	—	—	•AAAA	•AAAA	•CCCC
	—	—	—	—	—	—	—	—	—	—	—	—
	—	—	—	—	—	—	—	—	—	—	—	—
	—	—	—	—	—	—	—	—	—	—	—	—
	•UUUU	—	—	—	•CCCC	—	UUUU	—	—	—	—	—
	—	•CCCC	•ROOR	—	—	—	—	—	—	—	•OOOO	R RR
	—	—	—	—	—	—	—	—	—	•UUCC	•OOOO	OOOO
	—	—	—	—	•OUUU	—	—	•RRRR	•UUUU	—	•UUUU	—
	—	—	—	—	RRRR	•RRRR	•CCCU	•CCCC	•AAAA	UUUU	•UUUU	—
	•CCCC	•CCCC	•CCCC	•CCCC	—	—	—	—	—	—	—	—
	—	—	•RRRR	—	—	—	—	—	—	—	—	—
	—	—	—	—	—	R R	—	R	—	—	—	—
	—	—	—	—	—	—	—	R	—	—	—	—
	—	—	—	—	—	—	OOOR	•AAAA	—	—	—	—
	—	—	—	—	—	•OOOR	RRR	•OOOO	RRRR	—	—	—
	•UCUO	•UUU	•UUUR	OOO	•UUU	•OOOR	•OUUR	O OU	R	•CCU	OOO	•CCC
	•CCOR	•UUU	•CCCR	•OOO	•UUU	•OOO	OOO	O UU	—	•CCU	•UUU	•CCC
	—	—	—	—	—	—	—	RRRR	—	—	—	—
	—	—	—	—	OOR	•CCCR	O U	•CCCC	—	—	—	—
	•COUC	•ACAO	•AAAU	•ACAC	•UUUR	•COCO	C CO	•CUAA	O UU	•CCCO	•CCCR	•AAA
	RRRR	•CCC	•CCAO	O O	—	—	—	—	—	C C	U U	ORO
	—	—	—	—	—	—	—	—	—	O O	—	—
	OOR	O O	O O	R R	R	O CR	CUCO	AOCC	—	U	O O	OR
	—	RRR	R R	—	R	R C	R O	R R	—	O	O O	UO
	—	RRR	•UUU	—	—	—	—	•CCOR	—	—	—	—
	UUO	U U	U U	—	U U	CRC	COC	CCCC	—	U U	COC	CUU
	—	—	—	—	—	R R	•OUO	O OO	—	—	O O	•UU
	•ACAA	•CCCO	•CCCU	•CCC	•CCCR	•AAOO	•UUUO	•ORCC	•CCCC	•AAAU	•CCC	•AAU
	—	—	—	—	—	—	—	--	—	—	—	—
	—	—	—	—	—	—	RRR	•CCAA	—	—	—	—
	—	•UUU	•UUO	—	—	—	—	O O	—	—	—	—
	—	•CCC	•CUC	•AA	—	—	—	R R	—	•UUU	UOU	•CCO
	CUUO	U U	UOUR	•CC	UOU	COCR	COCR	ORCC	OOR	OOO	COC	CCO
	OOOR	—	ORU	U U	UOU	OOOR	COC	O OU	O R	•CUU	COC	CCO
	—	—	R R	R	UOU	COC	OOO	OOOR	OOR	UUU	O O	UUO
	—	•CCC	•RCU	R	R	R R	R R	•AACC	—	•CCU	—	•UCU
	•UUO	•UUU	•UUU	•UUU	•UUU	•CCC	•CUC	OCCR	UUOO	•UUU	•OOO	•CUU
	—	—	—	—	R R	RRR	RRR	R R	R R	•CCU	•OOO	•UUO
	—	—	—	—	R R	R R	O O	O OR	—	—	—	—
	—	•UUU	•CCU	•AA	—	R	O	R OO	—	•UUO	—	R
	—	—	—	—	—	O	RR	—	—	O	—	O O
	—	O O	UOO	R R	—	R	RR	C UU	—	•CUO	UUU	•CCU
	—	—	R R	—	R R	R R	CUCR	CCCC	—	O O	O O	UUU
	—	—	—	—	R R	—	OOOR	C UC	—	—	—	O O
	—	—	R R	RR	R R	R R	CUCC	ACAA	—	—	O O	UUO
	—	—	—	—	R	R R	UCU	UAOOR	—	UUU	OOO	CCU
	CUUO	O C	UUC	C C	—	ROR	UU	CUCC	—	OOO	OOO	CCU

STATE-NUMBER OF BIRD LIST REFUGE, SANCTUARY OR PRESERVE NESTING, ABUNDANCE BY SEASON	OK-1 Optima • s S F W	OK-2 Salt Plains • s S F W	OK-3 Sequoyah • s S F W	OK-4 Tishomingo • s S F W	OK-5 Washita • s S F W	OK-6 Wichita • s S F W	OR-1 Up. Klamath • s S F W	OR-2 W.L. Finley • s S F W	OR-3 Ankeny • s S F W
SANDPIPERS (cont.)									
Least Sandpiper	R R R	A U A	C O C O	A R C O	C U U	U U	A U A R	C U U O	C U U O
White-rumped Sandpiper	R R	A A A	O	C O	U O	O	—	—	—
Baird's Sandpiper	R R	A U A	O O	A O O R	C U U	U O U	—	R R R	—
Pectoral Sandpiper	R R	U U U	U U	A C O	O O	O R	R U	R R	R R
Sharp-tailed Sandpiper	—	—	—	—	—	—	—	—	—
Purple Sandpiper	—	—	—	—	—	—	—	—	—
Rock Sandpiper	—	—	—	—	—	—	—	—	—
Dunlin	—	O O	R R	O	—	—	C R U R	A O O C	A O O C
Curlew Sandpiper	—	—	—	—	—	—	—	—	—
Stilt Sandpiper	R R	C U C	U U	O O O	O O O	R R	—	—	—
Buff-breasted Sandpiper	—	R	R R	—	—	—	—	—	—
Ruff	—	—	—	—	—	—	—	—	—
Short-billed Dowitcher	—	—	—	—	—	—	R R R	—	—
Long-billed Dowitcher	U R U	C C C	U U	O C R	U U O	U U R	A U C R	—	—
Common Snipe	R R O	U U O	C C C	C O C C	U U	U U O	• U U U R	C U C C	C U C C
American Woodcock	—	R R R	O O O	O O	—	R R	—	—	—
Wilson's Phalarope	C R C	C C C	O O	O O	U O O	O R	• C C U	O R	O R
Red-necked Phalarope	R O	R R R	—	—	—	—	U R U	O O O	O O O
Red Phalarope	—	—	—	—	—	—	R R	—	—
SKUAS, GULLS, TERNS & SKIMMERS									
Pomarine Jaeger	—	—	—	—	—	—	—	—	—
Parasitic Jaeger	—	—	—	—	—	—	—	—	—
Long-tailed Jaeger	—	—	—	—	—	—	—	—	—
Laughing Gull	—	—	—	—	—	—	—	—	—
Franklin's Gull	O O U	A U A	O O R	C O A A	O C O	O O	R	—	—
Little Gull	—	—	—	—	—	—	—	—	—
Common Black-headed Gull	—	—	—	—	—	—	—	—	—
Bonaparte's Gull	—	R R	O O U	O O R	R R	R	U U U	R R R R	R R R R
Heermann's Gull	—	—	—	—	—	—	—	—	—
Mew Gull	—	—	—	—	—	—	—	—	—
Ring-billed Gull	O O O	C U C A	A A A	C O A A	C U C C	U U U U	• C A C C	O O R O	O O R O
California Gull	—	—	—	—	—	—	• C A C C	O R R	O R R
Herring Gull	—	U O U U	U U	C C O	O O U	O O	U U U	R	—
Thayer's Gull	—	—	—	—	—	—	—	—	—
Iceland Gull	—	—	—	—	—	—	—	—	—
Lesser Black-backed Gull	—	—	—	—	—	—	—	—	—
Western Gull	—	—	—	—	—	—	—	R	—
Glaucous-winged Gull	—	—	—	—	—	—	—	—	—
Glaucous Gull	—	—	—	—	—	—	—	R R	—
Great Black-backed Gull	—	—	—	—	—	—	—	—	—
Black-legged Kittiwake	—	—	—	—	—	—	—	—	—
Sabine's Gull	—	—	—	—	—	—	—	—	—
Gull-billed Tern	—	—	—	—	—	—	—	—	—
Caspian Tern	—	—	U O U	R R	—	—	—	—	—
Royal Tern	—	—	—	—	—	—	—	—	—
Elegant Tern	—	—	—	—	—	—	—	—	—
Sandwich Tern	—	—	—	—	—	—	—	—	—
Roseate Tern	—	—	—	—	—	—	—	—	—
Common Tern	—	O O O	—	O O C	O R	—	—	—	—
Arctic Tern	—	—	—	—	—	—	—	—	—
Aleutian Tern	—	—	—	—	—	—	—	—	—
Forster's Tern	O O	U O U	O O	C O C	O O	R R	• C A C	—	—
Least Tern	• C C	• C C C	• O O	R O O	O O	—	—	—	—
Bridled Tern	—	—	—	—	—	—	—	—	—
Sooty Tern	—	—	—	—	—	—	—	—	—
Black Tern	O R O	C U C	O O	A O C	U C U	U R	• C A C	R R	R R
Black Skimmer	—	—	—	—	—	—	—	—	—
AUKS, MURRES & PUFFINS									
Dovekie	—	—	—	—	—	—	—	—	—
Common Murre	—	—	—	—	—	—	—	—	—
Thick-billed Murre	—	—	—	—	—	—	—	—	—
Razorbill	—	—	—	—	—	—	—	—	—
Black Guillemot	—	—	—	—	—	—	—	—	—
Pigeon Guillemot	—	—	—	—	—	—	—	—	—
Marbled Murrelet	—	—	—	—	—	—	—	—	—
Kittlitz's Murrelet	—	—	—	—	—	—	—	—	—
Ancient Murrelet	—	—	—	—	—	—	—	—	—
Cassin's Auklet	—	—	—	—	—	—	—	—	—
Crested Auklet	—	—	—	—	—	—	—	—	—
Rhinoceros Auklet	—	—	—	—	—	—	—	—	—
Tufted Puffin	—	—	—	—	—	—	—	—	—

	OR-4 Baskett Sl.	OR-5 Hart Mt.	OR-6 Malheur	OR-7 Umatilla	PA-1 Erie	PA-2 Tinicum	RI-1 R.I. NWR's	SC-1 C. Romain	SC-2 Sandhills	SD-1 Lacreek	SD-2 L. Andes	SD-3 Sand L.
s S F W	C U U O	U C	C U C R	U U	U U	O O O R	C U C	C U U C	R R R	C C C	C O U	U U O
	—	R O	—	—	R	O O O	O O U	O O	—	O	O O O	C C U
	R R R	R O	R R R	C C	R	R R R	O U	—	R R	O O	U O U	C C U
	—	R O	R U	—	U U	C O C R	U O C	U O U R	R R	O	U O U	C C U
	—				—		C O C	R R U		—	—	
	A O O C	O U	U U U	U	U U	O O R	C O C C	A O C A	—	—	—	U O U
	—	—	—	—	—	R R	—	—	—	U U O	O O O	C C U
	—	—	—	—	R R	R R O	R O R	R R	—		O O O	O
	—				R	R	O O	R R				
	—					O R O R	R R R		—	O O		U U U
	—	C C	C C C	U	U U	O R O R	C C U	A C A A	—	—	C O C	C C C
	C U C C	•C C C U	•C C C O	U U U O	•U U U	O O R	O U	U C C	O R U U	•C C U U	O R O	U U
		•C C A	•C C O	•U U U	•C U C	•C C C R	•U U U R	•O R O O	•O O O O	—	—	•C C C
	O R		•C C U			R R	R R	U U	—	•C U C	C O U	
	O O O	U U	U O U	U U	—	R R	R R	R R R	—	O	O U	U U
						—	R R			—	—	
	—	—	—		—		R			—	—	—
	—	—	R		—		R R	R R	—	—	—	—
	—	—	—		—		R		—	—	—	—
	—	O R O	•C C U	U	—	O O C R	O C C	•A A C O	—	U O C	C A C	•A A A
	—				—	—	—	—	—			
	—					—	R R	—	—			
							O O O	—				
	R R R R	U R C	R R O	O	O O O	R R R R	U R C U	U U	—	O O	O O
	O O R O	•A A A O	•C C C O	•A A C C	O O	C O C C	U U U U	C O C A	R R R	•C U C O	U U U	•C U C
	O R R	O R O	•C C C O	•O O O O	—	—	—	—	—		U U	U U
	R	—	R R	—	O O	C O C C	•A A A A	C C C A	R R R	O O O	U O U R	U U
						R R R	R R					
	R	—	—	—	—	—	—	—	—	—	—	—
	—	—	—	R R	—	R R R	R R	—	—	—	—	—
	—	—	—	—	—	C O C C	•C C C C	R R O	—	—	—	—
							O O O					
								•C C U O				
	—	•U U U	•U U U	•C C	—	O R O	O	•O U U C	—	—	—	—
							O R	•A A C U				
								•C C O R				
	—	—	R	—	R R	R R R	U U U	O U U C	—	O O O	•C C O	•U U U
							•U C C					
	—	•C C C	•C C U	•C C	R R	O C	R R	U O U C	—	•C C U	•U U U	•C C C
							•U C C	•C C O R			O O	R
								R R				
	R R	•C C C	•C C U	R O	R R	O R O	R R R	C C	—	•C C U	•C A C	•C C O
								•A A U O				
	—	—	—	—	—	—	R O R	—	—	—	—	—
	—	—	—	—	—	—	R R	—	—	—	—	—
	—	—	—	—	—	—	R R R	—	—	—	—	—

BIRD CHART — Oklahoma/Oregon

STATE-NUMBER OF BIRD LIST / REFUGE, SANCTUARY OR PRESERVE / NESTING, ABUNDANCE BY SEASON	OK-1 Optima • s S F W	OK-2 Salt Plains • s S F W	OK-3 Sequoyah • s S F W	OK-4 Tishomingo • s S F W	OK-5 Washita • s S F W	OK-6 Wichita • s S F W	OR-1 Up. Klamath • s S F W	OR-2 W.L. Finley • s S F W	OR-3 Ankeny • s S F W
AUKS, MURRES & PUFFINS (cont.)									
Atlantic Puffin	—	—	—	—	—	—	—	—	—
Horned Puffin	—	—	—	—	—	—	—	—	—
PIGEONS & DOVES									
Rock Dove	•C C C C	R R R R	—	•C C C C	U U U U	•O O O O	—	•U U U U	•U U U U
White-crowned Pigeon	—	—	—	—	—	—	—	—	—
Band-tailed Pigeon	—	—	—	—	—	—	—	U C O U	U C O U
White-winged Dove	—	—	—	—	—	—	—	—	—
Mourning Dove	•A A A	•C C A R	•C C A C	•A A A C	•C A C C	•C C C U	•C C C R	C C C U	C C C U
Inca Dove	—	—	—	—	—	—	—	—	—
Common Ground-Dove	—	—	—	—	—	—	—	—	—
White-tipped Dove	—	—	—	—	—	—	—	—	—
CUCKOOS, ROADRUNNERS & ANIS									
Black-billed Cuckoo	R R	R	•R R	—	—	—	—	—	—
Yellow-billed Cuckoo	•O C C	•C C C	•C C C	•C C O	•C C C	•C C O	—	—	—
Mangrove Cuckoo	—	—	—	—	—	—	—	—	—
Greater Roadrunner	•O O O O	•O O O O	•R R R R	•O O O O	•O O O O	•U U U U	—	—	—
Smooth-billed Ani	—	—	—	—	—	—	—	—	—
Groove-billed Ani	—	—	—	—	—	—	—	—	—
BARN OWLS									
Barn Owl	•R R R R	•O O O O	R R R R	O O	•U U U U	R R R R	•C C C C	•U U U U	•U U U U
TYPICAL OWLS									
Flammulated Owl	—	—	—	—	—	—	—	—	—
Eastern Screech-Owl	—	•O O O O	•O O O O	•O O O O	—	•U U U U	—	—	—
Western Screech-Owl	•O O O O	—	—	—	•O O O O	—	•R R R R	•U U U U	•U U U U
Great Horned Owl	•C C C C	•C C C C	•C A C C	•C C C C	•C C C A	•C C C C	•C C C C	•C C C C	•C C C C
Snowy Owl	—	—	—	—	—	—	—	R R	—
Northern Hawk Owl	—	—	—	—	—	—	—	—	—
Northern Pygmy-Owl	—	—	—	—	—	—	•U U U U	R R R R	R R R R
Elf Owl	—	—	—	—	—	—	—	—	—
Burrowing Owl	•O O O R	R R R	—	—	O R O	R R	—	R R R	—
Spotted Owl	—	—	—	—	—	—	•U U U U	—	—
Barred Owl	—	•U U U U	•C A C C	•C C C C	R R R	U U	—	—	—
Great Gray Owl	—	—	—	—	—	—	•R R R R	—	—
Long-eared Owl	R R R	R R R	—	—	R R R	R	•R R R R	•O O U R	•O O U R
Short-eared Owl	O O O O	R R O	R R	O O	O O O	R	—	O R O U	O R O U
Boreal Owl	—	—	—	—	—	—	—	—	—
Northern Saw-whet Owl	—	—	—	—	—	—	•R R R R	R R R R	R R R R
NIGHTJARS									
Lesser Nighthawk	—	—	—	—	—	—	—	—	—
Common Nighthawk	•C C C	•C C C	•C C C	•O C C R	•C A C	•U U U	•U C C	O O O	O O O
Pauraque	—	—	—	—	—	—	—	—	—
Common Poorwill	O O O	—	—	—	—	O O O	•U U U	—	—
Chuck-will's-widow	—	•C C O	•U C O	•O O	—	•C C	—	—	—
Whip-poor-will	—	—	•U C O	•O O O	—	—	—	—	—
SWIFTS									
Black Swift	—	—	—	—	—	—	—	—	—
Chimney Swift	•C C C	•C C C	U C U	•C C C	U U U	•O O O	—	—	—
Vaux's Swift	—	—	—	—	—	—	•U U U	U U O	U U O
White-throated Swift	—	—	—	—	—	—	—	—	—
HUMMINGBIRDS									
Buff-bellied Hummingbird	—	—	—	—	—	—	—	—	—
Ruby-throated Hummingbird	R R R	O O O	•C C U	•O C O	O U O	U U U	—	—	—
Black-chinned Hummingbird	•O O O	—	—	—	R O R	R R	—	—	—
Anna's Hummingbird	—	—	—	—	—	—	—	—	—
Costa's Hummingbird	—	—	—	—	—	—	—	—	—
Calliope Hummingbird	—	—	—	—	—	—	•U U	—	—
Broad-tailed Hummingbird	—	—	—	—	—	—	—	—	—
Rufous Hummingbird	R R O	—	—	—	R R	—	•U U U	•C C U	•C C U
Allen's Hummingbird	—	—	—	—	—	—	—	—	—
KINGFISHERS									
Belted Kingfisher	•C C O R	•C C C C	•C C C C	•O C C O	•C C C	•U U U U	•U U U U	•U U U U	•U U U U
Green Kingfisher	—	—	—	—	—	—	—	—	—
WOODPECKERS									
Lewis' Woodpecker	—	—	—	—	—	—	•R R R	U O U O	U O U O
Red-headed Woodpecker	•C C C	•C C C R	•C C C C	C C O O	•C C C U	•R U U U	—	—	—
Acorn Woodpecker	—	—	—	—	—	—	—	•U U U U	•U U U U
Gila Woodpecker	—	—	—	—	—	—	—	—	—
Golden-fronted Woodpecker	—	—	—	—	R R R R	—	—	—	—
Red-bellied Woodpecker	•O O O O	•C C C C	•C C C C	•C C C C	•C C C C	•C C C C	—	—	—
Yellow-bellied Sapsucker	—	R R R	U U	O O	O O	U U O	•R R R R	—	—
Red-breasted Sapsucker	—	—	—	—	—	—	•U U U U	•U U U U	•U U U U

OR-4 Baskett Sl.	OR-5 Hart Mt.	OR-6 Malheur	OR-7 Umatilla	PA-1 Erie	PA-2 Tinicum	RI-1 R.I. NWR's	SC-1 C. Romain	SC-2 Sandhills	SD-1 Lacreek	SD-2 L. Andes	SD-3 Sand L.
•s S F W	•s S F W	•s S F W	•s S F W	•s S F W	•s S F W	•s S F W	•s S F W	•s S F W	•s S F W	•s S F W	•s S F W
—	—	—	—	—	—	—	—	—	—	—	—
•U U U U	—	• O	C C C C	•C C C C	O O O O	•O O O O	O O O O	—	O	O O O O	•U U U U
U C O U	O O	O O R	—	—	—	—	—	—	—	—	—
C C C U	•C C A O	•U U U R	•C C U	•C C C C	•C C C C	•C C C C	•C C C C	•A A A A	•A A A O	•A A A R	•A A A O
—	—	—	—	—	—	—	•U U U U	•R R R R	—	—	—
—	—	R R	—	•C C C	•O O O	•O O O	O	O O	O O O	•O O	•U U
—	—	—	—	U U U	•O O O	•O O O	•C C U	•C C	•O U O	•O O	O O
—	—	—	—	—	—	—	—	—	—	—	—
—	—	—	—	—	—	—	—	—	—	—	—
—	—	—	—	—	—	—	—	—	—	—	—
—	—	—	—	—	—	—	—	—	—	—	—
•U U U U	•O O O	•O O O O	•O O O	•R R R R	•O O O O	R R R R	•U U U U	•U U U U	O O O	—	—
—	C U C	R R	—	—	—	—	—	—	—	—	—
—	—	—	—	•U U U U	•R R R R	O O O O	•C C C C	•C C C C	O O O O	•C C C C	•U U U U
•U U U U	•O O O O	•R R R R	•O O O O	•C C C C	•R R R R	O O O O	•C C C C	•U U U U	•C C C C	•C C C C	•C C C C
R R	—	—	—	—	R	R R R	R R R	—	O O	U	R O O
R R R R	R R R	—	—	—	—	—	—	—	—	—	—
•R R R	•O O O	•U U U R	•U U U	—	R R R R	O O O O	•U U U U	•U U U U	•C C C	•O O O O	O O O
—	—	—	—	•C C C C	R R R R	O O O O	•U U U U	•U U U U	—	—	—
•O O U R	•C C C O	•U U U U	•U U U U	R R R R	R R R	—	R	R	O O O	O O O R	•U U O O
O R O U	•C C C O	•C C C U	•U U U C	R R	O O O	U O U	R R U	R	R	O O O R	•U U U U
R R R R	U U U U	R R R	—	R	R R R R	—	—	—	—	—	R R R R
•O O O	O C C	•U C C	•O C O	• C	C O C	U U U	•C C U	•C C C	•C U C	•U U O	•U U O
—	•O C C	•U U U	—	—	—	—	—	—	—	—	—
—	—	—	—	R	R R R	•U C U	•C C O	•C C U	•U R O O	—	—
—	—	—	—	•C C C	C C C	O O O	•C C A	•C C C	—	C	•O O
U U O	O	R R	—	—	—	—	—	—	—	—	—
—	•U U U	R R	—	—	—	—	—	—	—	—	—
—	—	—	—	•U U	•C O C	O O O	•C C C	•C C C	O	O	•U U O
—	O O O	R	—	—	—	—	—	—	—	—	—
—	•U C U	R	—	—	—	—	—	—	—	—	—
—	O O O	—	—	—	—	—	—	—	—	—	—
•C C U	U C C	U C U	• O	—	—	—	—	—	—	—	—
•U U U U	O O R	•U U U U	• U O	•C C C O	C C C O	•U C C U	•C C C C	•C C C C	•U C U	U U U	•U O U
U O U O	O O	U U	—	—	—	—	—	—	—	—	—
—	—	—	—	•U U U	R R R	R R	•R R O O	•C C C C	•U U U U	•C C C	•U U U
•U U U U	—	—	—	—	—	—	—	—	—	—	—
—	—	—	—	R R R R	R R R	—	•C C C C	•C C C C	—	U U U U	—
•U U U U	•U U U	U U	—	•U C C	R R O R	O O O R	O O U	•U C C	—	U O U	R R

STATE-NUMBER OF BIRD LIST REFUGE, SANCTUARY OR PRESERVE NESTING, ABUNDANCE BY SEASON	OK-1 Optima • s S F W	OK-2 Salt Plains • s S F W	OK-3 Sequoyah • s S F W	OK-4 Tishomingo • s S F W	OK-5 Washita • s S F W	OK-6 Wichita • s S F W	OR-1 Up. Klamath • s S F W	OR-2 W.L. Finley • s S F W	OR-3 Ankeny • s S F W
WOODPECKERS (cont.)									
Williamson's Sapsucker	—	—	—	—	—	—	• U U U R	—	—
Ladder-backed Woodpecker	• R R R R	—	—	—	O O	R R R	—	—	—
Nuttall's Woodpecker	—	—	—	—	—	—	—	—	—
Downy Woodpecker	• O O O R	• C C C C	• C C C C	• C C C C	U U U C	• C C C C	• U U U U	• C C C C	• C C C C
Hairy Woodpecker	• O O O R	• U U U U	• U U U U	• C C C C	U U U C	• C C C C	• U U U U	• U U U U	• U U U U
Red-cockaded Woodpecker	—	—	—	—	—	—	—	—	—
Three-toed Woodpecker	—	—	—	—	—	—	—	—	—
Black-backed Woodpecker	—	—	—	—	—	—	• R R R R	—	—
Northern Flicker	• C C C C	• C C C C	• C C C C	• C O C C	• C C C C	C R C C	• C C C C	• C C C C	• C C C C
Pileated Woodpecker	—	—	• U U U U	O U O O	—	—	• U U U U	• U U U U	—
TYRANT FLYCATCHERS									
Olive-sided Flycatcher	O O	R	—	—	—	R R O	• U U	• U U O	—
Western Wood-Pewee	• O O O	—	—	—	—	—	• U C U	• C A U	• C A U
Eastern Wood-Pewee	—	O O O	• U U U	• O O O	—	• O O O	—	—	—
Yellow-bellied Flycatcher	—	O	R	R R	—	—	—	—	—
Acadian Flycatcher	—	—	• U U	—	—	—	—	—	—
Alder Flycatcher	—	—	R R	O	—	—	—	—	—
Willow Flycatcher	• R R	—	R R	O	—	—	• U U U	• U C O	• U C O
Least Flycatcher	—	O	O O	C	—	O	—	—	—
Hammond's Flycatcher	R	—	—	—	—	—	• U U	—	—
Dusky Flycatcher	R R	—	—	—	—	—	• U U	—	—
Gray Flycatcher	—	—	—	—	—	—	• U U U	—	—
Western Flycatcher	—	—	—	—	—	—	R R	• U U O	• U U O
Black Phoebe	—	—	—	—	—	—	—	—	—
Eastern Phoebe	• O O O	• U U U	• C C U R	• C C O O	• U C U	• C C C R	—	—	—
Say's Phoebe	• O O O	—	—	—	R R	—	• C U C	R R R	R R R
Vermilion Flycatcher	• R R R	—	—	—	—	—	—	—	—
Ash-throated Flycatcher	• O O O	—	—	—	O O O	• R	—	—	—
Great Crested Flycatcher	• O O O	• C C C	• C A C	• C C O	• U C U	• C C R	—	—	—
Brown-crested Flycatcher	—	—	—	—	—	—	—	—	—
Great Kiskadee	—	—	—	—	—	—	—	—	—
Couch's Kingbird	—	—	—	—	—	—	—	—	—
Cassin's Kingbird	• O O O	—	—	—	—	—	—	—	—
Western Kingbird	• C A C	• C C C	R	• A O O	• C A C	• U U R	• C C C	• O R	• O R
Eastern Kingbird	• C A C	• C C C	• C A C	• A A O	• C C C	U U R	R R	R R	—
Gray Kingbird	—	—	—	—	—	—	—	—	—
Scissor-tailed Flycatcher	• C C C	• C C A	• C A C	• C C A	• C A C	• C C C	—	—	—
LARKS									
Horned Lark	• C C C C	• C U C C	• C C C C	• C O C C	• C U C U	• U U U C	• C C C C	• U U U U	• U U U U
SWALLOWS									
Purple Martin	• R R	O O O	U U	• C C O	O O O	R	• R R	O O O	O O O
Tree Swallow	—	C U	• U U U	O O O	O O	—	• C C C R	• A C U O	• A C U O
Violet-green Swallow	—	—	—	—	—	—	• U U U	• C C C O	• C C C O
Northern Rough-winged Swallow	• O O O	• A O C	• C C C	• C C O	• U U U	U U	• U U U	U O O	U O O
Bank Swallow	R R	• C O C	• O O O	C O O	• O O O	—	• U C C	R R	R R
Cliff Swallow	C C C	• C C C	• O O O	A O A	• U A U	O R O	• A A A	• A A U	• A A U
Barn Swallow	• C C C	• A C C	• C C C	• A A A	• C A C	• C C C	• A A A	• C C U	• C C U
JAYS, MAGPIES & CROWS									
Gray Jay	—	—	—	—	—	—	• R R R R	—	—
Steller's Jay	R R R	—	—	—	—	—	• C C C C	• C U C C	• C U C C
Blue Jay	• O O O R	• C C C C	• C C C C	• C C C C	• C C C U	• C C C C	—	—	—
Green Jay	—	—	—	—	—	—	—	—	—
Scrub Jay	R R R R	—	—	—	—	—	—	• C C C C	• C C C C
Pinyon Jay	R R R R	—	—	—	—	—	—	—	—
Clark's Nutcracker	—	—	—	—	—	—	• R R R R	—	—
Black-billed Magpie	• C C C O	—	—	—	—	—	• C C C C	—	—
American Crow	• O O O O	• C C C C	• C C A A	• A C A A	• C C C C	• C C C C	• R R R R	C C C C	C C C C
Northwestern Crow	—	—	—	—	—	—	—	—	—
Fish Crow	—	—	O O O O	—	—	—	—	—	—
Chihuahuan Raven	• C C C O	—	—	—	—	R R R	—	—	—
Common Raven	—	—	—	—	—	—	• U U U U	U U U U	U U U U
TITMICE									
Black-capped Chickadee	—	—	—	—	—	—	• U U U U	• C C C C	• C C C C
Carolina Chickadee	R R R R	• C C C C	• C C C C	• C C C C	• C C C A	• C C C C	—	—	—
Mountain Chickadee	—	—	—	—	—	—	• C C C C	—	—
Boreal Chickadee	—	—	—	—	—	—	—	—	—
Chestnut-backed Chickadee	—	—	—	—	—	—	• U U U U	• U U U U	• U U U U
Plain Titmouse	—	—	—	—	—	—	—	—	—
Tufted Titmouse	—	• C C C C	• C C C C	• C C C C	U U U U	• C C C C	—	—	—
VERDINS									
Verdin	—	—	—	—	—	—	—	—	—

Each location column is subdivided by season: **•s S F W**

	OR-4 Baskett Sl.	OR-5 Hart Mt.	OR-6 Malheur	OR-7 Umatilla	PA-1 Erie	PA-2 Tinicum	RI-1 R.I. NWR's	SC-1 C. Romain	SC-2 Sandhills	SD-1 Lacreek	SD-2 L. Andes	SD-3 Sand L.
	—	O O O	R R	—	—	—	—	—	—	—	—	—
	—	—	—	—	—	—	—	—	—	—	—	—
	—	—	—	—	—	—	—	—	—	—	—	—
	•C C C C	•U U U O	O R O O	O	•C C C C	•C C C C	U U C U	•C C C C	•C C C C	•C C C C	•U O U C	•C C C C
	•U U U U	•U U U U	O O O	O	•U U U U	O O O O	U U U U	•U U U U	•C C C C	U U U U	•U O U C	•O O U U
	—	—	—	—	—	—	R R R R	•C C C C	—	—	—	—
	—	—	—	—	—	—	—	—	—	—	—	—
	•C C C C	•A A U	•C U C C	•U U C C	•C C C C	•C C C O	•C C C U	•C C C A	•C C C C	•C C C O	•C C C	•C C C O
	•U U U U	—	—	—	•U U U U	—	—	•C C C C	•U U U O	—	—	—
	•U U O	U O U	O R O	—	R R	R R	—	—	—	—	O O	O
	•C A U	•U C C	•C U U	U U O	—	—	—	—	—	O O	—	•U O
	—	—	—	—	•C C C	O R O	•U O C	•U C U R	•C C C	—	—	•U O
	—	—	—	—	R R	R R	R	—	—	—	—	—
	—	—	—	—	•U U U	R R R	—	C U	•C C C	—	—	—
	—	—	—	—	O O	•O O R	R R	—	—	—	—	—
	—	U U U	•U C U	O O O	•C C C	•C C R	U U U	—	—	•C C	—	U
	—	R R	—	—	•C U C	•R R R	U C C	—	—	•U U	O	U
	—	R O	R R R	—	—	—	—	—	—	—	—	—
	—	•C A A	U R U	—	—	—	—	—	—	—	—	—
	—	•C C C	•U U U R	—	—	—	—	—	—	—	—	—
	•U U O	C C	O R O	O O	—	—	—	—	—	—	—	—
	—	—	—	—	•C C C	•C O O R	•U U C O	U C C	C C C C	—	O O	O O
	•R R R	•U U U	•C C C U	R	—	—	—	—	—	O O	—	—
	—	O O O	•O O O	—	—	—	—	—	—	—	—	—
	—	—	—	—	•U C C	•O R O	O O O	•C C U R	•C C	•U U U	—	U O
	—	—	—	—	—	—	—	—	—	—	—	—
	—	—	—	—	—	—	—	—	—	—	—	—
	—	—	—	—	—	—	—	—	—	—	—	—
	—	—	—	—	—	—	—	—	—	—	—	—
	•O R	•U U U	•C C C	•C C U	—	R	R	—	—	•A A	•C C C	•C C
	•R R	O O	•C C C	•C C U	•C C C	•C C C	•U C C	•C C U	•C C	•A A	•C C C	•C C
	—	—	—	—	—	—	—	U	—	—	—	—
	•U U U U	•A A A C	•C U C U	•C C C C	U O U O	R R R R	C O C C	—	—	•A C A C	C O C A	•U U C C
	—	—	—	—	U C C	•O R O	O O O	•C C C R	•C C C	U U	•O O O	•U U U
	•A C U O	•C C C	•A U A	U U	•A A A	•A A A	•U C A R	C O C C	C C C	•C U U	•C C C	•U U U
	•C C C O	•C C C	•C U U	U	O O O	C O O	U U O	•C C O	•C C C	U U	•O O O	•O O O
	U O O	•U U U	•U U U	U U	•C C C	C O C	O O R	U C	—	U U	•C C C	•C C A
	R R	•U U U	•U U U	•C C O	R R R	O R O	O O O	•U U U	—	•A A U	•C C C	•C C C
	•A A U	•A A A	•A A A	• O	—	—	—	—	—	•A A U	•C C C	•C C C
	•C C U	•A A A	•C C C R	• C	•C A A	•A A A	•C C C	•A A C R	•O U O	•A A U	•C C C	•C C A
	—	O O	—	—	—	—	—	—	—	—	—	—
	•C U C C	O O U O	—	R	—	—	—	—	—	—	—	—
	—	—	—	—	•A A A A	•C C C C	•C C C C	•C C C C	•C C C C	•O O O O	•C C C O	•U U U U
	•C C C C	•U U U O	—	—	—	—	—	—	—	—	—	—
	—	O O	—	—	—	—	—	—	—	—	—	—
	—	O O	R R R R	—	—	—	—	—	—	—	—	—
	—	•C C C C	•C U C C	C C C C	—	—	—	—	—	•U O U U	•C C C C	O O O O
	C C C C	•U U U O	•U U U O	•C C U	•A A A U	•C C C C	•C C C C	•C C C C	•C C C C	U O U O	•C C C C	•C U U R
	—	—	—	—	—	•C C C C	R R R R	•C C C C	•C C C C	—	—	—
	U U U U	•C C C C	•U U U U	•C C C C	—	—	—	—	—	—	—	—
	•C C C C	O O	O O O	U U U U	•A A A A	O R O O	•C C C C	—	—	O O U O	•O O O O	•C C C C
	—	—	—	—	—	•O O C C	—	•C C C C	•C C C C	—	—	—
	•U U U U	•C C C C	O O O R	R	—	—	—	—	—	—	—	—
	—	•O O O O	—	—	—	—	—	—	—	—	—	—
	—	—	—	—	•U U U U	•O O O O	•C C C C	•C C C C	•C C C C	—	—	—
	—	—	—	—	—	—	—	—	—	—	—	—

STATE-NUMBER OF BIRD LIST REFUGE, SANCTUARY OR PRESERVE NESTING, ABUNDANCE BY SEASON	OK-1 Optima • s S F W	OK-2 Salt Plains • s S F W	OK-3 Sequoyah • s S F W	OK-4 Tishomingo • s S F W	OK-5 Washita • s S F W	OK-6 Wichita • s S F W	OR-1 Up. Klamath • s S F W	OR-2 W.L. Finley • s S F W	OR-3 Ankeny • s S F W
BUSHTITS									
Bushtit	•O O O O	—	—	—	—	—	•U U U R	•C C C C	•C C C C
NUTHATCHES									
Red-breasted Nuthatch	O O O	R R R	—	—	R R O	R R R	•U U U U	•C U C C	•C U C C
White-breasted Nuthatch	R R R R	R R R	•C C C C	•O O O O	R R O	C C C C	•U U U U	•C C C C	•C C C C
Pygmy Nuthatch	—	—	—	—	—	—	•U U U U	—	—
Brown-headed Nuthatch	—	—	—	—	—	—	—	—	—
CREEPERS									
Brown Creeper	O O O	U U U	• U U	R O O	O U	U U U	•U U U U	•C C C C	•C C C C
WRENS									
Cactus Wren	—	—	—	—	—	—	—	—	—
Rock Wren	•O O O O	—	—	—	—	•U U U U	—	—	—
Canyon Wren	•O O O O	—	—	—	—	•U U U U	—	—	—
Carolina Wren	—	•C C C U	C C C C	•C C C C	•U U U O	•U U U U	—	—	—
Bewick's Wren	•O O O O	•C C C U	U U U U	•C C O O	•O O O O	•C C C C	•U U U U	•C C C C	•C C C C
House Wren	O R O	•C C C R	•O O O	O O O O	•U U U U	—	•U U U	•C C U	•C C U
Winter Wren	—	O O O	O O O	O O	R R O	O	•U U U U	•C C C C	•C C C C
Sedge Wren	O O	U U O	R R R	—	O O O	—	—	—	—
Marsh Wren	O O	U U O	•U U U	R O	O O O U	—	•C C C U	•C C U U	•C C U U
DIPPERS									
American Dipper	—	—	—	—	—	—	—	—	—
OLD WORLD WARBLERS & THRUSHES									
Arctic Warbler	—	—	—	—	—	—	—	—	—
Golden-crowned Kinglet	O O O	O O U	U U C	R O O	O O O	U U U	•C C C C	•C U C C	•C U C C
Ruby-crowned Kinglet	O O	U U O	C C C	C C O	O O O	U U U	•C R C	C R C C	C R C C
Blue-gray Gnatcatcher	•O R O	•C C C	•C C U	•C C O	•O O O	U U U	—	—	—
Black-tailed Gnatcatcher	—	—	—	—	—	—	—	—	—
Eastern Bluebird	•R R R R	•C U C U	•C C C C	•O O C C	•O O O U	•C C C C	—	—	—
Western Bluebird	—	—	—	—	—	—	•U U U U	O O O U	O O O U
Mountain Bluebird	O R O O	R	—	—	O O O	R U U	•U U U U	R R R	R R R
Townsend's Solitaire	R R R R	—	—	—	—	R R R	•U U C U	R R	—
Veery	—	—	R	—	—	—	—	—	—
Gray-cheeked Thrush	R	—	O	O	—	—	—	—	—
Swainson's Thrush	O O	C O	O R	A O	R R R	R	R	•C C U	•C C U
Hermit Thrush	R R R	—	O O C	OR O	O O R	R R R	•U U	U O U	U O U
Wood Thrush	—	—	•O O	O O	—	—	—	—	—
American Robin	•C O C O	•C C C C	•C A C C	•C O A A	•U O U C	•U O C C	•C C C U	•A C A A	•A C A A
Varied Thrush	—	—	—	—	—	—	R R	U O C	U O C
Wrentit	—	—	—	—	—	—	•U U U U	—	—
MOCKINGBIRDS, THRASHERS & ALLIES									
Gray Catbird	•O O O	•C C C R	•C C U	•C R O	•O U O	R R	—	—	—
Northern Mockingbird	•C C C R	•U U U O	•C A C C	•C A C C	•C C C U	•U C U R	—	—	—
Sage Thrasher	—	—	—	—	R R R	—	—	—	—
Brown Thrasher	•O O O R	•C C C U	•C C C U	•C O C C	•C C C	U U U O	—	—	—
Long-billed Thrasher	—	—	—	—	—	—	—	—	—
Bendire's Thrasher	—	—	—	—	—	—	—	—	—
Curve-billed Thrasher	•O O O R	—	—	—	—	—	—	—	—
Crissal Thrasher	—	—	—	—	—	—	—	—	—
Le Conte's Thrasher	—	—	—	—	—	—	—	—	—
WAGTAILS & PIPITS									
American Pipit	—	R	O O R	C C	U U	R R	C U R	U U	U U
Sprague's Pipit	R R	R	R R R	R R	R R	—	—	—	—
WAXWINGS									
Bohemian Waxwing	R R R	—	—	—	—	—	R R R	—	—
Cedar Waxwing	•O R O O	U U U	U U U	C O C	O O	U U C	•U U U	•U C C O	•U C C O
SILKY-FLYCATCHERS									
Phainopepla	—	—	—	—	—	—	—	—	—
SHRIKES									
Northern Shrike	R	—	—	—	—	—	U U C	U U U	U U U
Loggerhead Shrike	•C C C C	•C C C C	•C C C C	•C C C C	•U U U U	U U U O	•C C C U	R R R	—
STARLINGS									
European Starling	•C C C C	•C C C C	C C C C	•C C C C	•C C C C	•U U C C	•C C C C	•C C A C	•C C A C
VIREOS									
White-eyed Vireo	—	—	•O O O	•C C O	—	—	—	—	—
Bell's Vireo	•R R R	•C C C	U U U	•C C O	•O U O	R	—	—	—
Black-capped Vireo	—	—	—	—	—	•U U	—	—	—
Gray Vireo	—	—	—	—	—	—	—	—	—
Solitary Vireo	O O	R	O O O	O O	—	R	•U C U	•U U O	—
Yellow-throated Vireo	—	—	O O O	—	•O O O	—	—	—	—
Hutton's Vireo	—	—	—	—	—	—	—	•U U U U	—
Warbling Vireo	•O O R	•C C C	•U U U	—	—	—	•U C U	•U U O	•U U O
Philadelphia Vireo	—	R	R R	—	—	—	—	—	—

	OR-4 Baskett Sl.	OR-5 Hart Mt.	OR-6 Malheur	OR-7 Umatilla	PA-1 Erie	PA-2 Tinicum	RI-1 R.I. NWR's	SC-1 C. Romain	SC-2 Sandhills	SD-1 Lacreek	SD-2 L. Andes	SD-3 Sand L.
	•s S F W	•s S F W	•s S F W	•s S F W	•s S F W	•s S F W	•s S F W	•s S F W	•s S F W	•s S F W	•s S F W	•s S F W
	•C C C C	•U U U U	•O O O O	—	—	—	—	—	—	—	—	—
	•C U C C	•C R C C	U O U	O O O O	•U R U U	O O O	O O O	R R	O R O	O O	—	O O
	•C C C C	O O	O O	U	•C C C C	O O O O	C U C U	•U O O U	•O O O O	O O	U O U O	U O U O
	—	•C C C C	R R	—	—	—	—	—	—	—	—	—
	—	—	—	—	—	—	—	•C U U U	•A A A A	—	—	—
	•C C C C	O O O	O O O	R	•U U U U	O O O	O O O	U O U	C O	O	U U U U	O O
	—	—	—	—	—	—	—	—	—	—	—	—
	—	•C C C O	•C C C U	U U	—	—	—	—	—	—	—	—
	—	•O C C O	•U U U U	—	—	—	—	—	—	—	—	—
	•C C C C	O O O O	•R R R R	—	•R R R	•C C C C	•U U C U	•C C C C	•C C C C	—	—	—
	•C C U	•A A A	•U O U	R	•C A C	•C C C R	•C C C R	U U	O O	•C U	•C C	•C C
	•C C C C	O R O O	U U R	O	O O O	O C R	O U O	O O	O O	—	—	R
	—	—	—	—	R	•R R R	R R	U U	R	•U U	•C C U	•U U U
	•C C U U	•U C C R	•A A A O	C C C C	R	•C C C R	•U C C R	•C C C C	R R	•A A	•C C U	•C C C R
	—	•U U U O	•O O O O	—	—	—	—	—	—	—	—	—
	•C U C C	U U O	O U O	O	U C U	O C O	O C O	O C C	O O	O O	R R	O O
	C R C C	•A C A U	C C O	•U U U U	U C R	C C O	O C O	O A A	C C C	—	R R	U U
	—	•U U O	• R	—	•U U U	O R O R	R R R	•C C U U	•C C U	—	—	—
	—	—	—	—	•C U U O	O O R	O R O R	•U U U U	•C C C C	O O	O U	•U U
	O O O U	U R U	O R O O	R	—	—	—	—	—	O O	—	O
	—	•C C C O	•C R C U	R R	—	—	—	—	—	O	—	O
	—	O O C C	U U U	O O R R	•C C C	R R	R R	O O	R R	O	—	U O
	—	R R	R R	—	C C	R O	U	U U	R R	O O	—	U O
	•C C U	•C C C	O R O	O O	C C	R R	U	O O	R R	U U	O U	C C O
	U O U	C R C	U R U	U R R U	C R C	O O	O R U O	O C C	U C C	O O	—	U O
					•C C C	•O O O	•U C C	•U U O	•C C C			
	•A C A A	•A A A O	•C C C U	•C C C O	•A A A O	•C C C O	•C C C U	U C U	•C U C C	•C C C O	•C C O R	•C C C U
	U O C	U U	U U O	O	—	—	—	—	—	—	—	—
	—	—	•R R	—	•C C C R	•C C C O	•C C C O	•O O C C	•C C C	•U U O	•U C	•C C U
	—	—	R R R R	—	R R R	•C C C C	•C C C U	•C C C C	•A A A A	O O	—	—
	—	•A A A	•U C C R	—	—	—	—	—	—	—	—	—
	—	—	R R R	—	•U U U	•C C C O	•C C C O	•C C C C	•C C C C	•C C O	•U C	•C C C
	—	—	—	—	—	—	—	—	—	—	—	—
	—	—	—	—	—	—	—	—	—	—	—	—
	—	—	—	—	—	—	—	—	—	—	—	—
	U U U	U R U	U U O	O	R R	O O O	U C U	•O U U	—	O O O	U U	U
	—	—	—	—	—	—	—	—	—	—	—	—
	—	O	O R R	O	—	—	—	—	—	—	R R O O	O O O
	•U C C O	U U O	O O U O	C C O	C A A U	•O O O O	C U C U	•C C C	O O U	U O	R R O O	U U O R
	—	—	—	—	—	—	—	—	—	—	—	—
	U U U	O U	U U U	O O O	R	R	R R R	—	—	O O O	—	O O
	R R R	•C C C U	•C C C U	U U O	—	R R R R	O O O	•C C O O	•C C C C	•C U C U	O O O	U U
	•C C A C	•C C C U	•C C C U	•A A A A	•A A A U	•A A A A	•C U A U	•U O U U	•C C C C	•U U U O	•C C C C	•C C C C
	—	—	—	—	R R	•C C C	•U C U	•O U O O	•C C C	—	—	—
	—	—	—	—	—	—	—	—	—	•U U	—	—
	—	•U U U	U R U	•U U	•U R U	C C	R R	O O O	—	O	—	—
	—	—	—	—	•O R O	O R O	—	•O O O	•O O O	—	—	—
	—	•U C C	•U O U	U U	•U C U	•O C O	R R	—	—	U U	O O	•U U
					R R	R R					O O	C U

STATE-NUMBER OF BIRD LIST / REFUGE, SANCTUARY OR PRESERVE / NESTING, ABUNDANCE BY SEASON	OK-1 Optima • s S F W	OK-2 Salt Plains • s S F W	OK-3 Sequoyah • s S F W	OK-4 Tishomingo • s S F W	OK-5 Washita • s S F W	OK-6 Wichita • s S F W	OR-1 Up. Klamath • s S F W	OR-2 W.L. Finley • s S F W	OR-3 Ankeny • s S F W
VIREOS (cont.)									
Red-eyed Vireo	O O	•U U U	•U U U	•C C O	—	—	U U O	—	—
Black-whiskered Vireo	—	—	—	—	—	—	—	—	—
WOOD-WARBLERS									
Bachman's Warbler	—	—	—	—	—	—	—	—	—
Blue-winged Warbler	—	—	R	—	—	—	—	—	—
Golden-winged Warbler	—	—	—	—	—	—	—	—	—
Tennessee Warbler	R R	U	O	C R	—	—	—	—	—
Orange-crowned Warbler	R R	C U	—	C C O	—	U U R	•U U U	•A C O	•A C O
Nashville Warbler	—	U U	O O	C R O	—	R R	•U U U	O	—
Virginia's Warbler	—	—	—	—	—	—	—	—	—
Lucy's Warbler	—	—	—	—	—	—	—	—	—
Northern Parula	—	—	•U U U	—	—	—	—	—	—
Tropical Parula	—	—	—	—	—	—	—	—	—
Yellow Warbler	•O O O	•C C U	•C C O	C O O	—	R	•C C C	•C O O	•C O O
Chestnut-sided Warbler	R R	—	—	—	—	—	—	—	—
Magnolia Warbler	—	—	—	—	—	—	—	—	—
Cape May Warbler	—	—	—	—	—	—	—	—	—
Black-throated Blue Warbler	R R	—	—	—	—	—	—	—	—
Yellow-rumped Warbler	C C O	C C C	U U U	O C	—	C C U	•C C C	C R U U	C R U U
Black-throated Gray Warbler	R R	—	—	—	—	—	•R R R	•U U O	—
Townsend's Warbler	—	—	—	—	—	—	U U	U U O	U U O
Hermit Warbler	—	—	—	—	—	—	• C	O	—
Black-throated Green Warbler	O O	—	O O	—	—	R	—	—	—
Blackburnian Warbler	—	—	O	—	—	—	—	—	—
Yellow-throated Warbler	—	—	•U U	O O O	—	—	—	—	—
Pine Warbler	—	—	—	—	—	—	—	—	—
Prairie Warbler	—	—	—	—	—	—	—	—	—
Palm Warbler	—	—	—	—	—	—	—	—	—
Bay-breasted Warbler	—	—	—	—	—	—	—	—	—
Blackpoll Warbler	—	R	O	O	—	—	—	—	—
Cerulean Warbler	—	—	R	—	—	—	—	—	—
Black-and-white Warbler	O O	U O	•U U U	O O O	—	U U U	—	—	—
American Redstart	O O	O R	O O O	O	—	R	—	—	—
Prothonotary Warbler	—	•U U	•U U U	•C C	—	—	—	—	—
Worm-eating Warbler	—	—	R	—	—	—	—	—	—
Swainson's Warbler	—	—	—	—	—	—	—	—	—
Ovenbird	O O	—	O	—	—	R	—	—	—
Northern Waterthrush	O O	R	O O	—	—	R	—	—	—
Louisiana Waterthrush	—	—	•U U U	O O	—	R R	—	—	—
Kentucky Warbler	—	R R	•U U U	—	—	—	—	—	—
Connecticut Warbler	—	—	—	—	—	—	—	—	—
Mourning Warbler	O O	—	O O	O	—	—	—	—	—
MacGillivray's Warbler	O O	—	—	—	—	—	•U U U	•U U O	•U U O
Common Yellowthroat	•C O C	•C C C R	•U U U R	•C O C O	•O U O	O R R	•U U U	•A A U	•A A U
Hooded Warbler	R R	—	—	—	—	—	—	—	—
Wilson's Warbler	—	R R	U U	O O	—	—	•U U U	•C U O	•C U O
Canada Warbler	—	—	R R	—	—	—	—	—	—
Painted Redstart	—	—	—	—	—	—	—	—	—
Yellow-breasted Chat	•R R R	O O	•C C C	•O A	R O R	R	R	•U U	•U U
TANAGERS									
Hepatic Tanager	—	—	—	—	—	—	—	—	—
Summer Tanager	—	—	•U U U	•C C	—	•U U U	—	—	—
Scarlet Tanager	—	—	O O	—	—	—	—	—	—
Western Tanager	O O	—	—	—	—	—	•U C U	•U U O	•U U O
CARDINALS, GROSBEAKS & ALLIES									
Northern Cardinal	•O O O O	•C C C C	•A A A A	•A A A A	•A A A A	•C C C C	—	—	—
Pyrrhuloxia	—	—	—	—	—	—	—	—	—
Rose-breasted Grosbeak	R R	O	U U	O	—	—	—	—	—
Black-headed Grosbeak	O O	—	—	—	O O O	—	•U C U	•C C U	•C C U
Blue Grosbeak	•O O O	•O O O	•U U U	•C O O	•U C U	•U U	—	—	—
Lazuli Bunting	•O O O	R	—	—	—	R	•U U U	•U C O	•U C O
Indigo Bunting	—	•C C C	•C C C	•A A C	•U C U	U U	—	—	—
Painted Bunting	—	•U U O	•O O O	•A A C	—	C C	—	—	—
Dickcissel	•O O O	•C C C	•C C C	•C A O	•C A C	•U U	—	—	—
NEW WORLD SPARROWS & ALLIES									
Olive Sparrow	—	—	—	—	—	—	—	—	—
Green-tailed Towhee	•O R O	—	—	—	—	—	•U U R	—	—
Rufous-sided Towhee	O O O	C C C	O O O	A O C	U U O	U U	•C U U R	•A A A A	•A A A A
Brown Towhee	—	—	—	—	—	—	—	—	—
Abert's Towhee	—	—	—	—	—	—	—	—	—
Bachman's Sparrow	—	—	—	—	—	—	—	—	—

	OR-4 Baskett Sl.	OR-5 Hart Mt.	OR-6 Malheur	OR-7 Umatilla	PA-1 Erie	PA-2 Tinicum	RI-1 R.I. NWR's	SC-1 C. Romain	SC-2 Sandhills	SD-1 Lacreek	SD-2 L. Andes	SD-3 Sand L.
	• s S F W	• s S F W	• s S F W	• s S F W	• s S F W	• s S F W	• s S F W	• s S F W	• s S F W	• s S F W	• s S F W	• s S F W
	—	O O O	R R R	O O	•C A A	•O R O	U U U	•C A U	•U C O	O O	U U	U
	—	—	—	—	—	—	—	—	—	—	—	—
	—	—	—	—	•C C C	O O	U U U	R R	R R	—	—	—
	—	—	—	—	—	R R	R	R	R R	—	—	—
	—	—	R R	—	A A	R R	O O	R R	R R	—	U U	C U
	•A C O	•U U U	U R U	O O	—	R	R O R	R R	O O O	U	—	C U
	—	•O O O	U O U	R R	•C R C	O O	O O	R R	—	—	—	O R
	—	—	—	—	—	—	—	—	—	—	—	—
	—	—	—	—	O O	C C	O O	•C C U	•C C C	—	—	—
	•C O O	•A A A	•C C C	•O O	•A A A	•A A A	•C U U	C U	O O O	•A A U	•C C	•C C C
	—	R R	R R	—	•C O C	C R C	O U U	O O O	—	—	—	O
	—	—	—	—	•C R C	C C	O O	R R	R R	O	R R	O O O
	—	—	—	—	C C	O C	R	R U	O O	—	—	O O
	—	—	R R	—	U U	C C	R O	U U	O O	—	C C	C U
	C R U U	•A O A	C U C R	O O O O	A A O	C C R	C O A A	O A A	A A A	C U	C C	C C
	•U U O	•U U O	O R O	—	—	—	—	—	—	—	—	O
	U U O	U U U	U O U	O	—	—	—	—	—	—	—	—
	—	O O	—	—	•C C C	C C	R O	O O O	O O	—	—	O
	—	—	—	—	•C U C	C C	R R	R R	R R	—	—	—
	—	—	—	—	—	—	—	•C C C C	•C C C	—	—	—
	—	—	—	—	R R R	O O	R R	•C C C U	•C C C O	—	—	—
	—	—	—	—	R	C C	•C C U	•U U U O	•C C C	—	—	U
	—	—	—	—	U U	C C R	U U R	O C U	C C U	—	—	—
	—	—	—	—	U U	C C	O O	R	—	—	—	—
	—	—	R R	—	U U	C C	O C	O O	O O	O	C C	C U
	—	—	—	—	R R R	R R	—	—	—	—	—	—
	—	R R	R R	—	U R U	C R C	U C C	O U U	R	O	R R	C U
	—	—	R O	—	•C O C	•C R C	O U U	U O C	O O O	U O	U	C
	—	—	—	—	R R	R R R	R	O O O	•O O O	—	—	—
	—	—	—	—	—	R R	R	O O	—	—	—	—
	—	—	—	—	—	—	—	O O	O O O	—	—	—
	—	R R	R R	—	•C C C	C C	U U U	C C	U O O	U	R R	U
	—	R R R	R R	—	•U C U	C R C R	O U U	O O O	O O	O	O O	O
	—	—	—	—	•U U U	R R	—	O O	O O O	—	—	—
	—	—	—	—	R	R R	—	•U O O	O O O	—	—	O
	—	—	—	—	R R	R R R	R	—	—	—	—	O
	—	—	—	—	•U U U	O O	R	—	—	—	—	U
	•U U O	•C C C	U O U	R	•A A A	•C C C R	•U A C O	•C C C C	•C C C	•A A	•C C O	C U U
	•A A U	•U U U	•C C C	O O O	•C C C	R R	R R	•C U O	•C C C	—	—	—
	•C U O	C R C	C U C	O O O	U U	C R	R R	R R	—	O	—	U O
	—	—	—	—	•U O U	C C	O O	R R	R R	—	—	O
	—	O O O	•U U U	O O O	•U U O	•O O O R	•R R R R	•U O O	•C C C	•U U	R R	O
	—	—	—	—	—	R R	R	•C C C	•C C C	—	—	—
	—	—	—	—	•C C C	C R O	O O O	R U	C C	—	—	—
	•U U O	•C C C	C U C	O	—	—	—	—	—	—	—	—
	—	—	—	—	•C C C C	•C C C C	•C C C C	•C C C C	•C C C C	—	R R R	—
	—	R R R	R R R	—	•C C C	C O	O O	R R	—	—	O	C C C
	•C C U	•C C C	•U O U	O	—	—	—	—	—	U	—	U O U
	—	•U C C	•U R O	R	—	•R R R R	R	U U	•U U U	O U	R R	—
	—	—	—	—	•C C C	•C C C	O O O	•C O O	•C C C	O O	R R	O O
	—	—	—	—	—	—	—	•C A U	—	—	R R	—
	—	—	—	—	R R R	R	—	—	—	•U U	C C U	•O U O
	—	•C C C	O R O	—	—	—	—	—	—	—	—	—
	•A A A A	•C U C O	U O U R	O O U	•C C C	•C R C R	•C C C O	•C C C C	•C C C C	C C	U U	U U
	—	—	—	—	—	—	—	—	—	—	—	—
	—	—	—	—	—	—	—	—	O R R O	•U U U	—	—

STATE-NUMBER OF BIRD LIST REFUGE, SANCTUARY OR PRESERVE NESTING, ABUNDANCE BY SEASON	OK-1 Optima •s S F W	OK-2 Salt Plains •s S F W	OK-3 Sequoyah •s S F W	OK-4 Tishomingo •s S F W	OK-5 Washita •s S F W	OK-6 Wichita •s S F W	OR-1 Up. Klamath •s S F W	OR-2 W.L. Finley •s S F W	OR-3 Ankeny •s S F W
NEW WORLD SPARROWS & ALLIES (cont.)									
Cassin's Sparrow	•O O O	—	—	—	R O R	—	—	—	—
Rufous-crowned Sparrow	•O O O O	—	—	—	—	•C C C C	—	—	—
American Tree Sparrow	O O O	A A A	O U	—	C C C	R U C	—	—	—
Chipping Sparrow	—	•C O C R	O O O	O O O	O O	U R C	•U C U R	•U C U	•U C U
Clay-colored Sparrow	O O	O O	—	R R	O O	R	—	—	—
Brewer's Sparrow	O R	—	—	—	—	—	•C C C	—	—
Field Sparrow	O O O O	•C C C C	•C C C C	•O C C O	•U U U U	O R O C	—	—	—
Black-chinned Sparrow	—	—	—	—	—	—	—	—	—
Vesper Sparrow	O R O	C C R	O O R	C C O	U U	U U R	•U U U	•C A C R	•C A C R
Lark Sparrow	•C C C	•C C C R	•C C U	•C A C	U C U	•C C C	•U U U	—	—
Black-throated Sparrow	—	—	—	—	—	—	—	—	—
Sage Sparrow	—	—	—	—	—	—	—	—	—
Lark Bunting	—	R	—	—	•U U C	—	—	—	—
Savannah Sparrow	O O R	U U O	C C C	A A A	C U C O	U U U	•C C C U	•C C C U	•C C C U
Baird's Sparrow	—	—	—	—	—	—	—	—	—
Grasshopper Sparrow	•C C C	•C C C	U U U	O R O	R O R	U U U	—	—	—
Henslow's Sparrow	—	—	—	—	—	—	—	—	—
Le Conte's Sparrow	—	O	O O O	R O	O O	R R	—	—	—
Sharp-tailed Sparrow	—	—	—	—	—	—	—	—	—
Seaside Sparrow	—	—	—	—	—	—	—	—	—
Fox Sparrow	—	O O	U U U	O O C	R R O	R O	•C C U R	U U U C	U U U C
Song Sparrow	O O O	C C C	C C C	C A C	O U C	U U C	•C C C U	•A A A A	•A A A A
Lincoln's Sparrow	O O R	O O O	O O O	C C O	O O O	U U O	U U	U O O U	U O O U
Swamp Sparrow	—	O O O	U U U	C C O	—	—	—	—	—
White-throated Sparrow	O O R	U U U	C C C	C C A	O O O	R O O	R R R	O R O	O R O
Golden-crowned Sparrow	—	—	—	—	—	—	C C U	A C A	A C A
White-crowned Sparrow	C C O	C C C	C C C	C C C	U C C	U U U	C C C	C U C C	C U C C
Harris' Sparrow	R R R	A A A	U U A	A A A	C U C	R U U	R R R	—	—
Dark-eyed Junco	C C C	A A A	C C A	C C C	U U C	U U C	•C U C C	•C U C A	•C U C A
McCown's Longspur	O O O	—	—	—	R R	—	—	—	—
Lapland Longspur	C C C	R R	—	—	R	R R	R R R	—	—
Smith's Longspur	—	—	—	—	O	—	—	—	—
Chestnut-collared Longspur	O O O	—	—	—	O O U	U C C	—	—	—
Snow Bunting	—	—	—	—	—	—	R R R	—	—
NEW WORLD BLACKBIRDS & ORIOLES									
Bobolink	R R	R	O O	R R	O O	—	—	—	—
Red-winged Blackbird	•A A A C	•A C A A	•A A A A	•A A A A	•C C C A	•C U C C	•A A A A	•A C A A	•A C A A
Tricolored Blackbird	—	—	—	—	—	—	•C C U R	—	—
Eastern Meadowlark	•O O O O	•C C C C	•C C C C	•A A A A	•C C C C	•C C C C	—	—	—
Western Meadowlark	•A A A A	•C C C C	R	O R O O	•C C C C	U R U U	•C C C C	•C C C C	•C C C C
Yellow-headed Blackbird	•O R O	C R U R	R	O R O O	U U	O O	•C C C R	O O	O O
Rusty Blackbird	O O O	R R R	U U	C C	—	U U R	—	—	—
Brewer's Blackbird	O O C	O O O	O O O	O R O O	O O	C C C	•A A A C	•C C C C	•C C C C
Great-tailed Grackle	O R O	U O O	U O U U	C O C C	R R R	O	—	—	—
Boat-tailed Grackle	—	—	—	—	—	—	—	—	—
Common Grackle	•C C C	•C C C O	C C C C	•C O C C	•U O U C	R R	—	—	—
Bronzed Cowbird	—	—	—	—	—	—	—	—	—
Brown-headed Cowbird	•C C O	•C C C C	•O O O O	•C C C C	•C C C C	•C C U U	•C C C R	U C U O	U C U O
Orchard Oriole	•O O O	•C C R	•C C	•C C C	•O O O	R R R	—	—	—
Hooded Oriole	—	—	—	—	—	—	—	—	—
Baltimore Oriole	—	—	—	O O O	—	R	—	—	—
Bullock's Oriole	•C C C	•C C U	•C C U	R R R	•C C C	R	—	O	O
Scott's Oriole	—	—	—	—	—	—	—	—	—
FINCHES									
Rosy Finch	—	—	—	—	—	—	—	—	—
Pine Grosbeak	—	—	—	—	—	—	—	—	—
Purple Finch	—	R R R	O O O	O A C	—	R O	•R R R R	•C C C U	•C C C U
Cassin's Finch	R R	—	—	—	—	—	•U U U	—	—
House Finch	•C C C C	—	—	—	—	—	•C C C C	•C C U C	•C C U C
Red Crossbill	R R R	—	—	—	—	—	•U U U U	U R U	—
White-winged Crossbill	—	—	—	—	—	—	—	—	—
Common Redpoll	—	—	—	—	—	—	—	—	—
Hoary Redpoll	—	—	—	—	—	—	—	—	—
Pine Siskin	C R C C	O O O	O O O	O R	O O U	U U	•U U U U	U O O U	U O O U
Lesser Goldfinch	O R R R	—	—	—	—	R R	•U U U U	•O O O O	•O O O O
Lawrence's Goldfinch	—	—	—	—	—	—	—	—	—
American Goldfinch	O R O O	•C U C C	•U U U U	•A A A A	•U O U C	C R R C	•U U U U	•U C C O	•U C C O
Evening Grosbeak	R R R	—	R R R	—	R R R	—	U U U U	U O O U	U O O U
OLD WORLD SPARROWS									
House Sparrow	•C C C C	•C C C C	C C C C	•A A A A	•C C C C	•U U U U	•C C C C	•U U U U	•U U U U
Eurasian Tree Sparrow	—	—	—	—	—	—	—	—	—

OR-4 Baskett Sl.	OR-5 Hart Mt.	OR-6 Malheur	OR-7 Umatilla	PA-1 Erie	PA-2 Tinicum	RI-1 R.I. NWR's	SC-1 C. Romain	SC-2 Sandhills	SD-1 Lacreek	SD-2 L. Andes	SD-3 Sand L.
•s S F W	•s S F W	•s S F W	•s S F W	•s S F W	•s S F W	•s S F W	•s S F W	•s S F W	•s S F W	•s S F W	•s S F W
—	—	—	—	—	—	—	—	—	—	—	—
—	—	—	—	—	—	—	—	—	—	—	—
—	O O	U U U	U U	C C A	C C C	C U C	—	—	U C	C O R	A C O O
•U C U	•C U C	•C U U	R	•C C C	O O O O	•U C C O	•O O C U	•C C C C	U O O	•C C O	U
—	—	—	—	—	—	—	—	—	U	•U U	•U U U
—	•A A U	•C C C	O O	—	—	—	—	—	—	—	—
—	—	—	—	•C C C R	•C O C C	•U U U O	•O O O U	•C C C C	O O	—	•U U
—	—	—	—	—	—	—	—	—	—	—	—
•C A C R	•A A A	U O U O	C C C	•O O O	C O O	R R R R	O U U	C C C	•U U	O O	•U U U
—	•C C C	•C U U	•C C C	—	—	R	—	—	•U U	U U O	•U U
—	•U U	•R R R	—	—	—	—	—	—	—	—	—
—	•C C C R	•C U C	R	—	—	—	—	—	—	—	—
—	—	—	—	—	—	—	—	—	•A C U	U U	•U O
•C C C U	•C C C	•C C C	•C C C O	•O O O	•C R C R	•U C C O	O A A	C C C	O O O	•C C	•C C C
—	—	—	—	—	—	—	—	—	—	—	—
—	—	—	—	U U U	R R	•R R R	R	—	•U C O	•U U	U
—	—	—	—	•U U U	R R	—	R	—	—	—	—
—	—	—	—	—	—	—	—	—	O	—	—
—	—	—	—	—	—	O U U	O C C	—	—	—	•U U
—	—	—	—	—	—	O U U	•U U C C	—	—	—	—
U U U C	•C C C	•U R U O	•U U	O O	C C C	U O O	U U	C	—	—	O O
•A A A A	•C C C	•C C C C	•U U U U	•A A A C	•C C C C	•C C A C	U C C	C C C	•C O	•C A O R	•C C C
U O O U	U U	U R U R	U U U	R R	R R	U	R	—	U	O	O O
—	—	—	—	•A A A U	•C C C C	•U U C O	C A A	U U	•C C	—	O O
O R O	—	R R R	—	C C U	C C C	U C C	C R C A	C C C	O O	U O	C C R
A C A	O U	O O	O O R	—	—	—	—	—	—	—	—
C U C C	•A C A O	C R C O	C C C	U U	C C C	U U O	R	U	C C	U O	U U
—	—	R R R	—	—	—	—	—	—	C U	U O	C C O
•C U C A	•C U A U	C C U	C O O C	C C A	C C C	U U U	A A	U C C	C C U	U O C	C U O
—	—	—	—	—	—	—	—	—	—	—	—
—	—	—	—	—	R O	O O U	R	—	U U	C	U U C
—	—	—	—	—	—	—	—	—	—	—	—
—	—	—	—	—	—	—	—	—	U U	•C U U	•C U U
—	O O	R	—	O O	R R	U C C	—	—	O O O	O	U C
—	—	•U U U	—	•U C U	O R C	•U U U	C C	O O	•U C	•C C	•U O U
•A C A A	•C C C O	•A A A U	•A A C U	•A A A R	•A A A C	•A C C O	•C C A A	•C C C C	•A A A U	•C C O R	•A A A U
—	—	—	—	—	—	—	—	—	—	—	—
—	—	—	—	•U C C R	•O O O R	•C C C U	•O O C C	•C C C C	•U U U	•C A O O	—
•C C C C	•C C C O	•C C C O	•C C C C	—	—	—	—	—	•A A A U	•C A O C	•C C U O
O O	•C C C	•A A A R	•C C	—	—	—	—	—	•A A C	•C C O	•A A C O
—	—	—	—	U U	C R C O	O O R	O O O	U U	O O	U U U	U U R
•C C C C	•A A A O	•A A A U	•C A C U	—	R R	—	R R	—	•U U U	U U U	•C C U O
—	—	R	—	—	—	—	—	—	—	—	—
—	—	—	—	—	—	—	•A A A A	—	—	—	—
—	—	—	—	•A A A O	•C C C O	C C C U	•C C C C	•C C U C	•C C O	•C C O O	•C C C O
—	—	—	—	—	—	—	—	—	—	—	—
U C U O	•C C C	•U C C	U C U	•C C C O	•C C C O	U U U O	•U U U U	C C U U	•C C O	C C O	•C C U O
—	—	—	—	O R O	•O R R	R R	•C O O	•C C C	•C C	•C C	•C C
—	—	—	—	—	—	—	—	—	—	—	—
—	—	—	—	—	—	—	—	—	—	—	—
O	•U C C	•U U U	•C C O	•C C C	•C O C R	•O O O	O O O	R R	U U	•U U	•C C
—	—	—	—	—	—	—	—	—	—	—	—
—	C C C	—	R	—	—	—	—	—	—	—	—
—	O O	R R R	—	R	—	R	—	—	—	—	R
•C C C U	O O	R R	O	•U U U U	C R C C	•U U U U	O O	R R	U U	—	R
—	•A A A O	O O R	R	—	—	—	—	—	—	—	—
•C C U C	•U U U	•U U U R	•C C C C	•O O O O	•O R C C	•U U U U	—	—	—	—	—
—	O O O O	R R	R	R	R	R R	—	—	—	—	R
—	—	—	—	R	R	—	—	—	—	—	—
—	O	R	O O	R	R R R	O O	—	—	U	—	U C
—	—	—	—	—	—	—	—	—	—	—	U
U O O U	•U U U	U R U R	R R	O O O	R O O	O O O	O O	R	O	—	U U
•O O O O	•U U U	•O O O	—	—	—	—	—	—	—	—	—
—	—	—	—	—	—	—	—	—	—	—	—
•U C C O	O U U	•U U U O	C O U C	•A A A C	•C C C C	•U C C U	U O U	C R C C	•C C C U	•C C O O	•C C U O
U O O U	U U U	U R O U	O O U	O O C	R R R	U U U	U	R	—	O O U	—
•U U U U	•C C C U	•U U U U	•C C C C	•A A A A	•C C C C	•O O O O	•U U U U	•C C C C	•C C C C	•C C C C	•C C C C
—	—	—	—	—	—	—	—	—	—	—	—

STATE-NUMBER OF BIRD LIST REFUGE, SANCTUARY OR PRESERVE NESTING, ABUNDANCE BY SEASON	SD-4 Waubay •s S F W	TN-1 Cross Crks •s S F W	TN-2 Hatchie •s S F W	TN-3 L. Isom •s S F W	TN-4 Tennessee •s S F W	TX-1 Anahuac •s S F W	TX-2 Aransas •s S F W	TX-3 Brazoria •s S F W	TX-4 Buffalo L. •s S F W
LOONS									
Red-throated Loon	—	—	—	—	—	—	—	—	—
Arctic Loon	—	—	—	—	—	—	—	—	—
Pacific Loon	—	—	—	—	—	—	—	—	—
Common Loon	O R O	O U O	R R	O O O	O O O	U	R R R	R	R U R
Yellow-billed Loon	—	—	—	—	—	—	—	—	—
GREBES									
Least Grebe	—	—	—	—	—	—	U U		
Pied-billed Grebe	•C C A	C C U	•C U C C	•C U C C	•C U C C	•C A C C	C U U U	•C U C C	O O U O
Horned Grebe	•C O U	R O R	—	U U U	U U U	O	—	R	
Red-necked Grebe	•C C C	—	—	—	—	—	—	—	
Eared Grebe	•C U U	—	—	—	—	C C C	U U C	R R C	•C R O
Western Grebe	•C C C					—		—	R R
SHEARWATERS & PETRELS									
Northern Fulmar	—	—	—	—	—	—	—	—	—
Cory's Shearwater	—	—	—	—	—	—	—	—	—
Pink-footed Shearwater	—	—	—	—	—	—	—	—	—
Greater Shearwater	—	—	—	—	—	—	—	—	—
Sooty Shearwater	—	—	—	—	—	—	·	—	—
Short-tailed Shearwater	—	—	—	—	—	—	—	—	—
Manx Shearwater	—	—	—	—	—	—	—	—	—
Audubon's Shearwater	—	—	—	—	—	—	—	—	—
STORM-PETRELS									
Wilson's Storm-Petrel	—	—	—	—	—	—	—	—	—
Fork-tailed Storm-Petrel	—	—	—	—	—	—	—	—	—
Leach's Storm-Petrel	—	—	—	—	—	—	—	—	—
BOOBIES & GANNETS									
Masked Booby	—	—	—	—	—	—	—	—	—
Brown Booby	—	—	—	—	—	—	—	—	—
Northern Gannet	—	—	—	—	—	—	—	—	—
PELICANS									
American White Pelican	C C C	—	—	R R R	O O	C C A	C U C C	C C C C	R R
Brown Pelican	—	—	—	—	—	—	U U U U	R	—
CORMORANTS									
Great Cormorant	—	—	—	—	—	—	—	—	—
Double-crested Cormorant	•C C C R	O O O	U U U	U U U O	U U	C C	U U C	C O C C	U O R
Olivaceous Cormorant	—	—	—	—	—	U U U O	R R	U U R R	—
Brandt's Cormorant	—	—	—	—	—	—	—	—	—
Pelagic Cormorant	—	—	—	—	—	—	—	—	—
Red-faced Cormorant	—	—	—	—	—	—	—	—	—
ANHINGAS									
Anhinga	—	R	U U	R R R	U U	U O	—	O O O O	—
FRIGATEBIRDS									
Magnificent Frigatebird	—	—	—	—	—	—	R R	O U O	—
BITTERNS & HERONS									
American Bittern	•C C C	O O R	O O	U U U R	U U	C C O	U R R U	U O O O	O
Least Bittern	• O O	O R	O O O	•C C C	•U U U	•C C C	R R R	•U U U O	—
Great Blue Heron	•C C C	C C C C	U C U U	•C C C C	•C C C C	C C C C	C C C C	•A A A A	•C C C C
Great Egret	U U U	U U U R	U U U	•U C U O	•C C C O	C C C C	C C C C	•C C C C	O O
Snowy Egret	U O U	R R R	U U U	•O O O	R R R	C C C C	C C C C	•C C C C	O C O
Little Blue Heron	R	U U U	•U C U	•C C C	•U C	U U U U	U R U U	•C C C C	—
Tricolored Heron	—	—	—	—	—	C C C C	C C C U	•C C C C	—
Reddish Egret	—	—	—	—	—	O	U U U U	•U U U U	—
Cattle Egret	O O O	U O O	R R R	U U O	U U R	A A A O	C C C C	•A A A A	R R R
Green-backed Heron	O O O	•C C C	•C C C	•C C C	•C C C	•C C U R	U U U U	•C C U U	C
Black-crowned Night-Heron	•C C C	U C C R	O R O	•U U U R	U U U	•C C C U	U U U U	•C C C C	•C C O
Yellow-crowned Night-Heron	—	O U R	•C C C	U U U R	U U	•C C C O	R R R	U U U O	•R R
IBISES & SPOONBILLS									
White Ibis	—	—	R R	—	—	C C C U	U U U U	•C C C C	—
Glossy Ibis	—	—	—	—	—	—	—	—	—
White-faced Ibis	O O O	—	—	—	—	C C C U	C R U C	C U C U	R R
Roseate Spoonbill	—	—	—	—	—	C C C U	U C C U	•C C C C	—
STORKS									
Wood Stork	—	R R R	R R	R R	—	C C	U U	C U	—
SWANS, GEESE & DUCKS									
Fulvous Whistling-Duck	—	—	—	—	—	O R C	—	R R R	—
Black-bellied Whistling-Duck	—	—	—	—	—	—	R R R R	R R R	—
Tundra Swan	O C	R	—	R R	U U	—	—	—	R R
Trumpeter Swan	—	—	—	—	—	—	—	—	—
Mute Swan	—	—	—	—	—	—	—	—	—
Greater White-fronted Goose	O O	R R R	R	R R	R R	O C A	R U R	O C C	R R
Snow Goose	O R C	O U U	U U	O U U	U U O	U A A	C U C	O A A	O O C

	TX-5 Muleshoe				TX-6 Hagerman				TX-7 L. Atascosa				TX-8 Santa Ana				TX-9 Big Thicket				TX-10 Padre Is.				UT-1 Fish Sprgs				UT-2 Ouray				VT-1 Missisquoi				VA-1 Back Bay				VA-2 Chincoteag.				VA-3 East Shore		
	•s	S	F	W	•s	S	F	W	•s	S	F	W	•s	S	F	W	•s	S	F	W	•s	S	F	W	•s	S	F	W	•s	S	F	W	•s	S	F	W	•s	S	F	W	•s	S	F	W	•s	S	F	W

STATE-NUMBER OF BIRD LIST / REFUGE, SANCTUARY OR PRESERVE / NESTING, ABUNDANCE BY SEASON	SD-4 Waubay •s S F W	TN-1 Cross Crks •s S F W	TN-2 Hatchie •s S F W	TN-3 L. Isom •s S F W	TN-4 Tennessee •s S F W	TX-1 Anahuac •s S F W	TX-2 Aransas •s S F W	TX-3 Brazoria •s S F W	TX-4 Buffalo L. •s S F W
SWANS, GEESE & DUCKS (cont.)									
Ross' Goose	—	—	—	—	—	R R	—	R R	O
Emperor Goose	—	—	—	—	—	—	—	—	—
Brant	—	—	—	—	—	—	—	—	—
Canada Goose	•C C C O	•C C A A	•U C U C	C O A A	A O A A	O C A	C C C	R U U	U R C A
Wood Duck	•C C C	C C C U	•C A A C	•C C C U	•C C C C	R R	R R	O O O	R R
Green-winged Teal	•C O C	C C C	C C U	C C C	C C C	C A A	U U C	C C A	A O A A
American Black Duck	•O O O	U R A A	C R C C	C C C	A R A A	O O	—	R R R	
Mottled Duck	—	—	—	—	—	•C C A C	C U C C	•C C C C	—
Mallard	•A A A O	•C U A A	•C O C C	•A C A A	•A O A A	C A A	U U U	R U U	•C U A A
Northern Pintail	•C C C R	U C C	C C C	C C C	C C C	C A A	C C C	U C C	•C O A A
Blue-winged Teal	•A A A	C R C R	C O C U	C O C O	C C C O	•A R A O	C C C	•C R C A	•C U C
Cinnamon Teal	R R	—	—	—	R R	U R R		O R O U	U O O
Northern Shoveler	•C C C	U U U	U R U U	C C U	C C C	A A A	C U C	C A A	A U C C
Gadwall	•A A A	U C C	C C C	C C C	C C C	C A A	C U C	U C C	C O O U
Eurasian Wigeon	—	R R R	—	—	—	—	—	—	—
American Wigeon	•C U C	—	C C C	C A C	A A A	C C O	C C C	U U U	C O A A
Canvasback	•C U C	O U C	U U U	U U U	U U U	U U C	R R U	R R R	O O U
Redhead	•C C C	U U U	U U U	U U C	U U U	O O O	U U U	U U U	U O U U
Ring-necked Duck	•U O U	C C C	C C C	A C C	U C C	U U U	U R U	O R O	U R U
Greater Scaup	—	R R	R R	—	—	—	R	—	R R
Lesser Scaup	•A U A	U C C	C C C	C C C	C C C	C C	C U C	U U U	C O O
Common Eider	—	—	—	—	—	—	—	—	—
King Eider	—	—	—	—	—	—	—	—	—
Steller's Eider	—	—	—	—	—	—	—	—	—
Harlequin Duck	—	—	—	—	—	—	—	—	—
Oldsquaw	R R	R	—	R R R	R R R	—	—	—	—
Black Scoter	—	—	—	—	R R	—	—	—	—
Surf Scoter	—	—	—	—	—	—	—	—	—
White-winged Scoter	R R R	R R	—	R R R	R R R	—	—	O	—
Common Goldeneye	•C R C	O O U	R R R	U U C	U U U	O	U U U	R R	O O U
Barrow's Goldeneye	—	—	—	—	—	—	—	—	—
Bufflehead	C R C	O O O	U U U	O U C	C C C	O O	U C	O O R	U O O
Hooded Merganser	O R O	U C C	•C A C C	•C O C C	C U C C	R R	U	R O U	R
Common Merganser	C R C	R O U	U U U	U U U	U U U	—	U	—	U O C
Red-breasted Merganser	U R	O O U	U U U	U U U	O O R	A U	R U	R R R	R
Ruddy Duck	•C C C	O O O	U U U	C C C	C U U	•C R C U	U U	O U U	C O U O
Masked Duck	—	—	—	—	—	R R	—	—	—
AMERICAN VULTURES									
Black Vulture	—	•C C C U	•U C U U	•C C C U	C C C C	C U U U	C C C C	C C C C	—
Turkey Vulture	R R R	•C C C U	•C C C U	•C C C U	C C C C	C C C C	C C C C	C C C C	•U U O
KITES, EAGLES, HAWKS & ALLIES									
Osprey	O R O	U U	U R U R	•O O O R	U U U R	O O	R R R	R R R	O O
American Swallow-tailed Kite	—	—	—	—	—	—	R R	R R	—
Black-shouldered Kite	—	—	—	—	—	R R	R R R R	•C U C C	—
Snail Kite	—	—	—	—	—	—	—	—	—
Mississippi Kite	—	—	O O O	•O O	—	O O	—	R R	O
Bald Eagle	O O O R	•U U U U	R R	U U C	•R U U	O O	—	R R U U	O O U
Northern Harrier	•C C C O	U C C	C C C	C C C	C O C C	C R C C	C C C	•C U C C	U O C C
Sharp-shinned Hawk	•O R O R	U C U	R R U U	O O O	O R O O	O O	U R U	U U U	
Cooper's Hawk	•U U U	U O U U	•R R R R	•U U U U	•U U U U	O O	U U U	U U U	R O R
Northern Goshawk	O O	—	—	—	R	—	—	—	—
Common Black-Hawk	—	—	—	—	—	—	—	—	—
Harris' Hawk	—	—	—	—	—	—	—	—	—
Gray Hawk	—	—	—	—	—	—	—	—	—
Red-shouldered Hawk	—	•C C C C	•C C C U	U U U U	•C C C C	O O O O	U U U	C C C C	—
Broad-winged Hawk	O O O	•U O U	C C C	U U U	O O O	U U	U U U	R R	R
Short-tailed Hawk	—	—	—	—	—	—	—	—	—
Swainson's Hawk	•U U U	—	—	—	—	U U	U U U	U U	•U C U
White-tailed Hawk	—	—	—	—	—	—	R R R R	•R R R R	—
Zone-tailed Hawk	—	—	—	—	—	—	—	—	—
Red-tailed Hawk	•C C C	•C C C C	•C C C C	•C C C C	•C O C C	C C	U R U C	C U C C	U R U C
Ferruginous Hawk	R R	—	—	—	—	—	—	—	O O O
Rough-legged Hawk	O O O	R	R R	R	R	R R	—	R R	O O O
Golden Eagle	O O	O O	R	O O U	R O U	R R	—	—	O R O U
CARACARAS & FALCONS									
Crested Caracara	—	—	—	—	—	R	U U U U	•R R R O	—
American Kestrel	•C C C R	•U U U U	U U U C	C U C C	U R U U	C C	C C C	C C A	•U O U U
Merlin	O O	—	—	—	U R U U	R R	R R	R R	R R
Peregrine Falcon	O O	R R R	—	R R R	R R R	O O O	R R R	U U U	O O R
Gyrfalcon	—	—	—	—	—	—	—	—	—
Prairie Falcon	R R	—	—	—	—	—	—	—	O R R O

TX-5 Muleshoe	TX-6 Hagerman	TX-7 L. Atascosa	TX-8 Santa Ana	TX-9 Big Thicket	TX-10 Padre Is.	UT-1 Fish Sprgs	UT-2 Ouray	VT-1 Missisquoi	VA-1 Back Bay	VA-2 Chincoteag.	VA-3 East Shore
• s S F W	• s S F W	• s S F W	• s S F W	• s S F W	• s S F W	• s S F W	• s S F W	• s S F W	• s S F W	• s S F W	• s S F W
U UU	O OO	RR	—	—	—	—	—	—	—	—	—
—	—	—	—	—				R R	O OO	CRCC	U UC
URAA	•C AA	U CC	O OO	R	UC	•AAAA	•CCCC	OOCR	CRCC	•ACAC	U UC
RR	•UUUU	RR	R RR	•CCCC	—	—	R R	•AAA	•UUCU	•UUCR	O O
ARAA	C CC	URCC	O CC	—	C CC	O AA	•CCC	•COC	C AA	CRCC	U UO
R RR	R RR	—	—	—	U U	—	—	•AAAR	•CUAA	•CCCC	CUCC
—	—	•CCCC	•UUUU	• O	CUCC	—	—				
•AOAA	•C AA	R RO	RR	O O	U C	•AAAA	•CCCC	•AAAR	•CUAA	•CUCC	CUCC
•AOAA	U CC	URCA	U UC	—	C C	•AAAA	•CCCU	COC	A AA	CRCC	U UU
•AOAA	COAR	•UUCC	C CC	R	C CU	•OOOO	•UCC	•CCO	COAO	•CUCR	UOCO
•COCO	R RR	U OU	O OO	—	U R	•AAUO	•UCC	—			
•COCU	CRCU	COCC	U UC	—	CUUC	•ACAA	•CCC	COC	U UC	COCC	O OO
AOAA	URCC	URCC	C CC	—	C C	•AAAA	•CCC	OOC	•CUCC	•CCCC	UOUU
—	—	—	—	—	—	—	—	—	R RR	RR	R
•AOAA	OOUO	URCA	U CC	—	C C	OOAA	•CCC	OOC	C CC	CRCC	U UU
COCC	O OO	U UC	R RO	—	U C	•UUUU	•ORU	O C	U UU	R OO	O OO
•COCC	C CU	URCC	R RO	—	U C	•AAAC	UUCC	URC	COC	U UU	O OO
URUU	O CU	O OU	U UU	—	R R	—	O O	U UU	U UU	U UU	U UU
—	—	RR	—	—	R R	—	—	U UU	U UU	U UU	U UU
•CRCC	ORUO	U OU	O OU	—	•CUUC	UOCC	O C	C C	U UU	U UU	U UU
—	—	—	—	—	—	—	—	—	—	—	RR
—	—	—	—	—	—	—	—	—	—	—	—
—	—	—	—	—	—	—	—	—	—	—	n
—	RR	—	—	—	—	—	O	O OO	C UC	U UU	
—	—	—	—	—	—	—	—	O	O UU	CRCC	U UC
—	—	—	—	—	R	—	—	RR	O UC	CRCC	C CC
—	—	—	—	—	R	—	—	O	O UC	CRCC	U UU
RR	O OO	RR	RR	—	U	O	U U	•CCCO	O OO	U UU	U UU
—	—	—	—	—	—	—	R R	—	—	—	—
C CC	O OO	U UU	R RR	—	C UC	O OU	U U	U O	U UU	CRCC	C CC
OR	O UU	OU	O OO	—	R	RR	R R	•CCC	URUU	U UU	U UU
OO	O OO	—	—	—	—	OOUO	•UUU	C CO	U UU	UU	O
RR	RR	O UU	—	—	U C	O OU	RRR	R R	URUU	CRCC	C CC
•CO C	O OO	CRAA	O UU	—	C UC	•AAAC	•CCC	O O	U UC	COCC	U UU
—	—	—	RRRR	—	—	—	—	—	—	—	—
RR	UUUC	UUUU	OOUU	•CCCC	RRRR	—	—	UUUU	—	UUUU	
•UOUU	•CCCC	•CCCC	UUAA	•CCCC	UUUU	—	•CCC	OO	OOOO	OOOO	OOOO
—	RR	UOUU	RROO	—	U UU	R U	RRR	OOO	•CCCR	•CCC	CACR
—	—	R R	R R	•UU	—	—	—	—	R	—	—
—	—	•UUUU	•UCUU	—	U	—	—	—	—	—	—
—	—	—	—	—	—	—	—	—	—	—	—
R	OOO	O	O O	R	R U	U	n	OOR	OROO	O OO	UUUU
O UU	UUUU	R	—	—	R	—	n	—	—	—	—
•CUCC	CRCC	CRCC	O OO	O	C CC	•CCCC	CCCC	•CCC	CRCC	•COCC	UOCC
U UU	O OO	U UU	U UU	U UU	U R	O	R R	URUU	U CU	U AU	
URUO	O OO	U UU	O OO	•OOOO	R	O	UUU	OOO	O OO	U UU	U UU
—	—	—	—	—	—	—	R	OOOO	—	—	—
—	—	—	R RO	—	—	—	—	—	—	—	—
—	—	•UUUU	•UUCC	—	UUUU	—	—	—	—	—	—
—	—	—	•OUUO	—	—	—	—	—	—	—	—
—	•CCCC	O OO	U CC	•CCCC	R R	—	—	•OOO	•UUUU	O OO	U UU
—	•OOO	U O	O OR	•UUU	—	—	—	R R	O U	—	O C
•CCCR	•UUU	O OR	O OR	—	R R	—	•UUU	—	—	—	R
—	—	•UUUU	•RRRR	—	UUUC	—	—	—	—	—	—
—	—	—	O	OROU	—	—	—	—	—	—	—
CUCC	•UUCC	U UU	O OO	OROU	U UU	•OOOO	•CCCC	•CCCO	UUUU	•UOUU	UUCC
•CUCC	—	R RR	—	—	—	R R	O	O	URUU	U CU	U AU
URCC	U UU	—	—	—	—	R	O UU	U UC	UROO	RR	O OR
U CC	RR	—	—	—	—	•UUUU	•CCCC	—	—	R	RR
—	—	•UUOO	•	R	RRRR	—	—	—	—	—	—
COCC	URCC	C AA	O CC	O UC	C CC	OO	•CCCR	•CCC	•CUCC	ORUO	UUAO
R OO	R OR	O OU	O UU	O	R RR	RR	RR	RRR	U UO	U UO	O CU
R RR	R R	R	O OR	—	U UR	OO	R R	RRR	UOUU	•UUUU	UOCU
—	—	—	—	—	—	—	—	—	—	—	—
URUU	—	RR		R	—	O UU	•UUUU	—	—	—	—

STATE-NUMBER OF BIRD LIST / REFUGE, SANCTUARY OR PRESERVE / NESTING, ABUNDANCE BY SEASON	SD-4 Waubay • s S F W	TN-1 Cross Crks • s S F W	TN-2 Hatchie • s S F W	TN-3 L. Isom • s S F W	TN-4 Tennessee • s S F W	TX-1 Anahuac • s S F W	TX-2 Aransas • s S F W	TX-3 Brazoria • s S F W	TX-4 Buffalo L. • s S F W
CHACHALACAS									
Plain Chachalaca	—	—	—	—	—	—	—	—	—
PARTRIDGES, GROUSE, TURKEYS & QUAILS									
Gray Partridge	• U U U U	—	—	—	—	—	—	—	—
Chukar	—	—	—	—	—	—	—	—	—
Ring-necked Pheasant	• C C C C	—	—	—	—	—	—	—	• O O O O
Spruce Grouse	—	—	—	—	—	—	—	—	—
Blue Grouse	—	—	—	—	—	—	—	—	—
Willow Ptarmigan	—	—	—	—	—	—	—	—	—
Rock Ptarmigan	—	—	—	—	—	—	—	—	—
White-tailed Ptarmigan	—	—	—	—	—	—	—	—	—
Ruffed Grouse	—	—	—	—	—	—	—	—	—
Sage Grouse	—	—	—	—	—	—	—	—	—
Greater Prairie Chicken	—	—	—	—	—	—	R R R R	—	—
Lesser Prairie Chicken	—	—	—	—	—	—	—	—	—
Sharp-tailed Grouse	• R R R R	—	—	—	—	—	—	—	—
Wild Turkey	—	• O O O O	• U U U U	• U U O U	• U U U U	—	C C C C	—	—
Northern Bobwhite	—	• C C C C	C A A A	• C C C C	• C C C C	• C C C C	C C C C	• C C C C	• C C C C
Scaled Quail	—	—	—	—	—	—	—	—	• O O O O
Gambel's Quail	—	—	—	—	—	—	—	—	—
California Quail	—	—	—	—	—	—	—	—	—
Mountain Quail	—	—	—	—	—	—	—	—	—
RAILS, GALLINULES & COOTS									
Yellow Rail	—	—	—	—	—	U U U	R R	U U U	—
Black Rail	—	—	—	—	—	R R R	R R R	• R R R R	—
Clapper Rail	—	—	—	—	—	• C C C C	U U U U	• C C C C	—
King Rail	—	O R	—	U U U	U U U	• C C C C	R R U	U U U U	—
Virginia Rail	• U U U	O O	—	U U	O O	U U U	U	U U U	R
Sora	• C C C	U U R	U U	U C U	U U	U U U	U U U C	U U U	R R
Purple Gallinule	—	—	—	• U U U	—	• C C U	U U	• U U O	—
Common Moorhen	—	O	—	U U U	O O O	C A C U	C U U C	• C C C C	R R
American Coot	• A A A	U C U	C U C U	• C U A A	• C U C C	• A O A A	C U C C	• C U A A	U O O R
LIMPKINS									
Limpkin	—	—	—	—	—	—	—	—	—
CRANES									
Sandhill Crane	O O	R R	—	—	/	R	U U U	U C C	O O O
Whooping Crane	—	—	—	—	—	—	U U U	R	—
PLOVERS									
Black-bellied Plover	U U	O	—	O O	O O	C C U	C C U	U U U	R R
Lesser Golden-Plover	U U	U R R	—	O O	O	A R	U	O R O	—
Snowy Plover	—	—	—	—	—	R	C R C U	U U U U	• U C O
Wilson's Plover	—	—	—	—	—	—	C U U	• C C	—
Semipalmated Plover	C C	U O U	O O	C C	U U U	U U	R R U	U U U U	C C R
Piping Plover	• O O O	—	—	—	—	O O	U R U	U U U	—
Killdeer	• C C C	• C C C C	• C C C C	• C C C C	• C C C C	• C C A A	C C C C	• A A A A	• C C U O
Mountain Plover	—	—	—	—	—	—	—	O	—
OYSTERCATCHERS									
American Oystercatcher	—	—	—	—	—	—	R U R R	—	—
Black Oystercatcher	—	—	—	—	—	—	—	—	—
STILTS & AVOCETS									
Black-necked Stilt	—	—	—	—	—	• C C C	C C C	• C C C U	R R
American Avocet	U U U	R R	—	—	R R	U C U	C C U	C C C C	• U C U
SANDPIPERS									
Greater Yellowlegs	C U C	C O C	O U O	C U C	C C C O	A A C	C U C C	C U C C	O C U
Lesser Yellowlegs	C U C	C O C	U U U	C O C R	C C C R	A A C	C U C C	C U C C	O U U
Solitary Sandpiper	O O O	C O U	C O C	C O C	C C C	U U	U R U	R U O	O O O
Willet	• C O C	—	—	R	—	• C C C C	C C C C	• C C C C	O O
Wandering Tattler	—	—	—	—	—	—	—	—	—
Spotted Sandpiper	• U U U	C O U	U U U	C O C	U U U	C C U	U C U	• U O U U	U U O
Upland Sandpiper	• C C C	R R	U R U	O O	R R	C C	R R	R O	O O O
Whimbrel	—	—	—	—	—	O R	U	U U	R
Long-billed Curlew	R	—	—	—	—	C C C	C U C C	C U C C	O O O
Hudsonian Godwit	O O O	—	—	—	—	O	R R	—	—
Bar-tailed Godwit	—	—	—	—	—	—	—	—	—
Marbled Godwit	• C C U	—	—	—	—	C C U	U R U	R R R	R
Ruddy Turnstone	U O U	—	—	—	—	O O O	R R U U	C C C	—
Black Turnstone	—	—	—	—	—	—	—	—	—
Surfbird	—	—	—	—	—	—	—	—	—
Red Knot	—	—	—	—	—	O O	—	R R	—
Sanderling	O O O	R	—	—	O O	U O U U	C R C C	C U C C	R
Semipalmated Sandpiper	A U A	C O C	U U	C O C	C C C	A A C	U U U U	U R U U	O
Western Sandpiper	—	R R	R R	—	—	A A C	C C C C	C R C C	U U

	TX-5 Muleshoe	TX-6 Hagerman	TX-7 L. Atascosa	TX-8 Santa Ana	TX-9 Big Thicket	TX-10 Padre Is.	UT-1 Fish Sprgs	UT-2 Ouray	VT-1 Missisquoi	VA-1 Back Bay	VA-2 Chincoteag.	VA-3 East Shore
	• s S F W	• s S F W	• s S F W	• s S F W	• s S F W	• s S F W	• s S F W	• s S F W	• s S F W	• s S F W	• s S F W	• s S F W
	—	—	•C C U U	•A A A A	—	—	—	—	—	—	—	—
	—	—	—	—	—	—	—	—	•U U U U	—	—	—
	—	—	O O O O	—	—	—	•O O	—	—	—	—	—
	•O O O O	—	O O O O	—	—	—	•C C C C	•C C C C	—	—	—	—
	—	—	—	—	—	—	—	—	—	—	—	—
	—	—	—	—	—	—	—	—	—	—	—	—
	—	—	—	—	—	—	—	—	•U U U U	—	—	—
	—	—	—	—	—	—	—	R R R R	—	—	—	—
	—	—	—	—	—	—	—	—	—	—	—	—
	R R R R	—	—	—	—	—	—	—	—	—	—	—
	—	—	—	—	—	—	—	—	•U U U U	—	—	—
	•C C C C	•C C U U	•C C C C	•U U U U	•C C C C	C C C U	—	—	—	•C C C C	•A A A A	C C C C
	•A A A A	—	—	—	—	—	—	—	—	—	—	—
	—	—	R R	—	—	—	—	—	—	R R R R	R	R
	—	—	—	—	—	—	—	—	—	U U U	•R R R	—
	—	—	O O	—	—	R R R R	—	—	—	•O O O O	•C C C U	C C A U
	—	•O O R	•U U U U	R R R	—	—	—	—	—	•C C C C	•U O U O	U U U U
	R R R	R R	U U	O	—	R R	•U U U U	•U C U	•O C C	•C C C O	•U U U U	U U U U
	R	U R U	•U R U U	U O U U	—	R R	•U U U U	•U C U	•O O O	O U O U	U U	U U O
	—	R R	•O O R	•R U R	—	R R	—	—	—	O O	R R	—
	R	R	•U U U U	•C C C C	—	R R R R	—	R	•C C O	U O U U	•R O O	O O O
	•A O A C	•A U A U	•A U A A	•C U C C	—	C C U	•A A A A	•C C A O	O R C	U R C C	U R C U	U U U
	A O A A	R R	O C C	R R O	—	C C C	—	C C	—	—	—	—
	—	—	—	—	—	—	—	R R	—	—	—	—
	O	O R O R	A U A C	R R	—	C U C C	R R	—	O	C C C O	C C C U	C O C U
	—	O R O	U R R	R R	—	R R R R	—	R R	—	O O	R O U	O O
	•C C C	O O O	U U U	—	—	•U U C C	• U	R R	—	R R R	•U U	—
	—	—	•A A C R	—	—	U U U R	—	—	—	—	—	—
	U U	O O O	U U U	R	—	U U C	—	—	O O	C U C U	A A C	U O C O
	—	O O O	U U U	R R	—	•C U C C	—	—	—	U U U	•U U U	U U U
	•C C C U	•C C C C	•C C C C	•U U C U	•U U U C	•C C C C	•C A C O	•C C C	•C O C	•U U U U	•O U U O	U U U U
	R O	—	R O R	R	—	—	—	—	—	—	—	—
	—	—	R R R	—	—	U U U U	—	—	—	O O O	•C C C C	C C C C
	•U U U	R	•U C C U	•C C U O	—	•C C C U	•A A	•C C C	—	R R R	R R R	—
	•C A A	O O O O	•C C C U	O O O	—	C U C C	•A A O	•C C C	—	R R R	O O U R	—
	U C C R	U O U O	A U A C	U R O O	—	C R C C	C O A U	U U	C C	C C A C	U C C U	C O C U
	U C C R	U O U R	A U A C	C U O	—	C R C C	U U	C C U	O O	C C C C	U C C O	C O C U
	U U U R	O R O	U U R	O O R	—	U U R	R	O O	—	U U U	O O O	U U U
	O O O	O R O	•A A A A	R R R	—	•C C C C	•C C	C C U	—	C C C R	•C C U R	C C C U
	—	—	—	—	—	—	—	—	—	—	—	—
	U U U	O R O	U U U U	O O U	U U U U	U U U U	U U	•U C U	•O C O	U O R	U U U R	U U C R
	•R R R R	O R O	U U	R R	—	U U	—	—	—	U U	R R	O U U
	R R	—	U U O	—	—	R R	—	—	—	U O U R	C C U R	U U U O
	U O C	O R O	C U A C	O O O	—	•C C C C	•U U	—	•R R R	R R	U O	—
	—	O R O	O	—	—	R R R R	—	—	—	—	—	—
	—	—	—	—	—	—	—	—	—	—	—	—
	—	O R O	U O U U	R R R	—	U U U U	O R	U U	—	R R	R U O	O O O
	—	O R O	U O U U	—	—	C U C C	—	—	—	C C C R	A C C U	U U U U
	—	—	—	—	—	R	—	—	—	—	—	—
	—	—	—	—	—	C C C	—	—	—	U U U R	C C U R	O O O
	—	R	O O O	—	—	•C R C C	—	—	—	A C A A	A A C C	U U U U
	—	R R O	U O U U	—	R	—	—	—	O	C O C O	A A C	C U U
	U U U	U O U R	A R A O	O O R	—	C C R	—	—	O	—	R U O	C U U
	•A A A	U O U R	A O A A	O O O	—	C C C	O O R	O O	—	U U C O	R C C O	U U U

STATE-NUMBER OF BIRD LIST / REFUGE, SANCTUARY OR PRESERVE / NESTING, ABUNDANCE BY SEASON	SD-4 Waubay • s S F W	TN-1 Cross Crks • s S F W	TN-2 Hatchie • s S F W	TN-3 L. Isom • s S F W	TN-4 Tennessee • s S F W	TX-1 Anahuac • s S F W	TX-2 Aransas • s S F W	TX-3 Brazoria • s S F W	TX-4 Buffalo L. • s S F W
SANDPIPERS (cont.)									
Least Sandpiper	C U C	C U C	U U U	C U C O	C C C	C C U	C U C C	C U C C	U U U
White-rumped Sandpiper	C U C	O R	—	—	—	U U	U	R R	U U U
Baird's Sandpiper	U U U	R	—	—	O O	U U U	U U U	R R	C C U
Pectoral Sandpiper	C U C	C O C	U U U	C O C	C C C	A A	U U	O O	R R
Sharp-tailed Sandpiper	—	—	—	—	—	—	—	—	—
Purple Sandpiper	—	—	—	—	—	—	—	—	—
Rock Sandpiper	—	—	—	—	—	—	—	—	—
Dunlin	U U	O	—	—	—	A A C	C C C	C C C	—
Curlew Sandpiper	—	—	—	—	—	—	—	—	—
Stilt Sandpiper	O O O	R U	—	U U	—	A A	U U	U R U	U O U
Buff-breasted Sandpiper	R R	R	—	—	O O	O O	U U	U	—
Ruff	—	—	—	—	—	—	—	—	—
Short-billed Dowitcher	O O O	O O U	—	O O	—	U U	U	U U U	—
Long-billed Dowitcher	O O O	R R	—	—	—	A A C	C U C U	C R C C	O O U
Common Snipe	U U C	C U C	U U U	C U U	C C C	C C C	U U U C	C C C	O R
American Woodcock	•C U U	•U O O R	U U U U	•U R U R	O O O	—	—	—	—
Wilson's Phalarope	•C U C	R	—	—	—	C C	U R	R R	O C O
Red-necked Phalarope	C U C	—	—	—	—	—	—	—	—
Red Phalarope	—	—	—	—	—	—	—	—	—
SKUAS, GULLS, TERNS & SKIMMERS									
Pomarine Jaeger	—	—	—	—	—	—	—	—	—
Parasitic Jaeger	—	—	—	—	—	—	—	—	—
Long-tailed Jaeger	—	—	—	—	—	—	—	—	—
Laughing Gull	—	—	—	—	—	A A A C	C C C C	•C C C C	—
Franklin's Gull	•C C A	—	—	O O R	R R	O	U U	U U	O R O
Little Gull	—	—	—	—	—	—	—	—	—
Common Black-headed Gull	—	—	—	—	—	—	—	—	—
Bonaparte's Gull	O	O O	—	O U C	R R	—	U U	U R U	R
Heermann's Gull	—	—	—	—	—	—	—	—	—
Mew Gull	—	—	—	—	—	—	—	—	—
Ring-billed Gull	C C C	U C C	O R O	C C A	A A A	C C C	C R C C	C U C C	C O U O
California Gull	U U U	—	—	—	—	—	—	—	—
Herring Gull	U U	O O	—	U U C	C C C	C U C	U R U U	C U C C	O O U
Thayer's Gull	—	—	—	—	—	—	—	—	—
Iceland Gull	—	—	—	—	—	—	—	—	—
Lesser Black-backed Gull	—	—	—	—	—	—	—	—	—
Western Gull	—	—	—	—	—	—	—	—	—
Glaucous-winged Gull	—	—	—	—	—	—	—	—	—
Glaucous Gull	—	—	—	—	—	—	—	—	—
Great Black-backed Gull	—	—	—	—	—	—	—	—	—
Black-legged Kittiwake	—	—	—	—	—	—	—	—	—
Sabine's Gull	—	—	—	—	—	—	—	—	—
Gull-billed Tern	—	—	—	—	—	C C C O	C U U U	•U C U U	—
Caspian Tern	—	O R O	—	O O	O O	U U U U	C C C C	U U U U	R
Royal Tern	—	—	—	—	—	U U U U	U U U R	•U U U U	—
Elegant Tern	—	—	—	—	—	—	—	—	—
Sandwich Tern	—	—	—	—	—	O	R U U R	•U U U R	—
Roseate Tern	—	—	—	—	—	—	—	—	R
Common Tern	•C C C	R R	O O O	R O O	O O	O O R	R R	U R U U	R R R
Arctic Tern	—	—	—	—	—	—	—	—	—
Aleutian Tern	—	—	—	—	—	—	—	—	—
Forster's Tern	•C C C	O R O	O O O	O O	O O	C C C C	C C C C	•C C C C	O R
Least Tern	—	R R	—	U C U	C C C	•C C	U C C	•C C U	R
Bridled Tern	—	—	—	—	—	—	—	—	—
Sooty Tern	—	—	—	—	—	—	—	—	—
Black Tern	•C C C	U R O	•O O O	U U U	O O	A A	C U C	U C U	U U O
Black Skimmer	—	—	—	—	—	U U U R	C C C C	•C C U U	—
AUKS, MURRES & PUFFINS									
Dovekie	—	—	—	—	—	—	—	—	—
Common Murre	—	—	—	—	—	—	—	—	—
Thick-billed Murre	—	—	—	—	—	—	—	—	—
Razorbill	—	—	—	—	—	—	—	—	—
Black Guillemot	—	—	—	—	—	—	—	—	—
Pigeon Guillemot	—	—	—	—	—	—	—	—	—
Marbled Murrelet	—	—	—	—	—	—	—	—	—
Kittlitz's Murrelet	—	—	—	—	—	—	—	—	—
Ancient Murrelet	—	—	—	—	—	—	—	—	—
Cassin's Auklet	—	—	—	—	—	—	—	—	—
Crested Auklet	—	—	—	—	—	—	—	—	—
Rhinoceros Auklet	—	—	—	—	—	—	—	—	—
Tufted Puffin	—	—	—	—	—	—	—	—	—

TX-5 Muleshoe	TX-6 Hagerman	TX-7 L. Atascosa	TX-8 Santa Ana	TX-9 Big Thicket	TX-10 Padre Is.	UT-1 Fish Sprgs	UT-2 Ouray	VT-1 Missisquoi	VA-1 Back Bay	VA-2 Chincoteag.	VA-3 East Shore
•s S F W	•s S F W	•s S F W	•s S F W	•s S F W	•s S F W	•s S F W	•s S F W	•s S F W	•s S F W	•s S F W	•s S F W
•C C C	U O U O	C U C C	O O O	—	C C C	O	O O	O	C R C O	A C C O	U U U O
R	C R	O O O	O O R	—	U U	—	—	O O	U R U	C U U	U U U
C C C	C O C O	O O	O O R	—	R R	R	R R	—	—	R R O	—
R R R	C O C R	U U O	O O	—	R R	R R	—	O	U U R	R C C R	U U U
—	—	—	—	—	—	—	—	—	—	—	—
—	O O R	A O A C	O O O	—	U U C	—	R R	O	U U C C	A O A A	C O C C
—	—	—	—	—	—	—	—	—	—	R R R	—
U U U	U O C	U O C O	O O O	—	U U	—	R R	—	R O R	O C C	R U U
—	O R O	U U	R R	—	R R	—	—	—	R R	O U	O O
—	—	—	—	—	—	—	—	—	R R	R R R	—
—	R O O	O	R R R	—	R	—	R	—	U U U	A A C O	C U C O
C C C	U O U U	A O A C	O O C	—	R R C	U O U	U U U	—	U U U	U R U O	O O O
U U O	U O U O	U U U	O O U	O	C U C C	O U U	•U U O	•C C C	C U C U	U R U U	U U U
—	R	—	R R	U	R	—	—	•C C C	U O U U	•U U U O	U O C A
A A A A	O O O	U U	O O	—	U U	•O A O	•C C O	—	R R R	R R R	O O
—	R R	R R	—	—	—	R	R R	—	R R R	O R R	—
—	R R R	R	—	—	—	—	—	—	—	—	—
—	—	—	—	—	—	—	—	—	R R R	R	—
—	—	—	—	—	—	—	—	—	R R R	R	—
—	R	•A A A C	O R O O	—	•C C C C	—	—	—	A A A C	•A A A R	A A A O
O O R	U R U O	U U	O O	U	U U	R R	U U U	—	—	—	—
—	—	—	—	—	—	—	—	—	—	R R	—
—	—	—	—	—	—	—	—	—	—	R R	—
—	O O O	O O R	R R R	—	U	—	R O	R R R	C O C	U O U	U U U
U U U	C O A A	C U C A	O R O	—	C R C C	A A C O	C U C	C C C O	A A A A	A C A A	—
—	—	—	—	—	—	R O	C C C	—	—	—	—
R R U	O O O	U O U U	O O U	—	U U C	R R	R R	U U U	A A A A	•C C A A	A C A A
—	—	—	—	—	—	—	—	—	R R O	O	—
—	—	—	—	—	—	—	—	—	R R R	O	O O
—	—	—	—	—	—	—	—	—	—	—	—
—	—	—	—	—	—	—	—	—	R R R	R	—
—	—	—	—	—	—	—	—	—	C O C A	C C C C	C U U C
—	—	—	—	—	—	—	—	—	R R R	—	—
R	—	•C C C U	R O R R	—	•U U U U	—	—	—	U U U	•U U O	U U U
—	O R O	•C C C U	O O O	U	•C C C C	C U	R R R	—	U U U	O C C	U U C
—	—	•O O O O	R R	—	•C C C C	—	—	—	U C U R	•C C C R	A A C
—	—	—	—	—	•C U C U	—	—	—	—	—	—
—	—	O O O O	O R	—	—	—	—	—	U C U	R U O	O O O
R R	—	U U R	R	—	R R	—	R R R	C O C	U C U O	•C C C O	U U C
—	—	—	—	—	—	—	—	—	—	R	—
O R O	U O U U	•C C C C	O R O O	U	•C U C C	•A A O	•U C U	—	U U U U	•C C C R	U U A O
R	•O O O	•C C C O	O O O O	—	U C C	—	—	—	U C U	•C C	U U O
—	—	—	—	—	R	—	—	—	—	—	—
C C C	U O U	C U C R	O R O	U	C R C	R O	•U C U	•C C	O U O	R C O	O O U
—	—	•C C U U	R R O R	—	•U C C U	—	—	—	O U U	•U C C R	C C C
—	—	—	—	—	—	—	—	—	—	R	—

STATE-NUMBER OF BIRD LIST / REFUGE, SANCTUARY OR PRESERVE / NESTING, ABUNDANCE BY SEASON	SD-4 Waubay • s S F W	TN-1 Cross Crks • s S F W	TN-2 Hatchie • s S F W	TN-3 L. Isom • s S F W	TN-4 Tennessee • s S F W	TX-1 Anahuac • s S F W	TX-2 Aransas • s S F W	TX-3 Brazoria • s S F W	TX-4 Buffalo L. • s S F W
AUKS, MURRES & PUFFINS (cont.)									
Atlantic Puffin	—	—	—	—	—	—			—
Horned Puffin	—	—	—	—	—	—			—
PIGEONS & DOVES									
Rock Dove	—	•O O O O	R R R R	•C C C C	O O O O	R	—	—	U U U U
White-crowned Pigeon	—	—	—	—	—	—	—	—	—
Band-tailed Pigeon	—	—	—	—	—	—	—	—	—
White-winged Dove	—	—	—	—	—	R R	—	R R R R	—
Mourning Dove	•C C C	•C C C C	•C C A C	•C C C C	•A A A A	•C C C C	C C C C	•C C C C	•C C U R
Inca Dove	—	—	—	—	—	—	R R R R	—	—
Common Ground-Dove	—	—	—	—	—	R	R R R R	—	—
White-tipped Dove	—	—	—	—	—	—	—	R	R
CUCKOOS, ROADRUNNERS & ANIS									
Black-billed Cuckoo	C C C	R R	—	O U O	•C C C	O	—	R	
Yellow-billed Cuckoo	R R R	•U C C	•C C C	•C C C	•R R R	•C U	C C R	•O U O	•O U
Mangrove Cuckoo	—	—	—	—	—	—	—	—	—
Greater Roadrunner	—	—	—	—	—	—	—	—	•U U U U
Smooth-billed Ani	—	—	—	—	—	—	—	—	—
Groove-billed Ani	—	—	—	—	—	—	R	R R R R	—
BARN OWLS									
Barn Owl	—	—	•O O O O	•O O O O	•R R R R	•U U U U	R R R R	U U U U	R R R R
TYPICAL OWLS									
Flammulated Owl	—	—	—	—	—	—	—	—	—
Eastern Screech-Owl	•U U U U	•U U U U	•U U U U	•U U U U	•U U U U	—	—	—	—
Western Screech-Owl	—	—	—	—	—	—	—	—	—
Great Horned Owl	•C C C C	U U U U	•U U U U	•U U U U	•O O O O	U U U U	U U U U	•U U U U	•U O U U
Snowy Owl	O O	—	—	—	—	—	—	—	—
Northern Hawk Owl	—	—	—	—	—	—	—	—	—
Northern Pygmy-Owl	—	—	—	—	—	—	—	—	—
Elf Owl	—	—	—	—	—	—	—	—	—
Burrowing Owl	•R R R	—	—	—	—	O O	—	R R R R	•C C U O
Spotted Owl	—	—	—	—	—	—	—	—	—
Barred Owl	—	•C C C C	•C C C C	•C C C C	•C C C C	—	R R	C C C C	R
Great Gray Owl	—	—	—	—	—	—	—	—	—
Long-eared Owl	•R R R R	—	—	—	—	—	—	—	R R
Short-eared Owl	U U U U	R R	O	R	R R R	U U	R	R	R R
Boreal Owl	—	—	—	—	—	—	—	—	—
Northern Saw-whet Owl	R	—	—	—	—	—	—	—	—
NIGHTJARS									
Lesser Nighthawk	—	—	—	—	—	—	R R R	R R	—
Common Nighthawk	•C C C	U U U	•O O O	•C C C	•C C C	•A A	C C C	•C C C	O C O
Pauraque	—	—	—	—	—	—	U U U U	—	—
Common Poorwill	—	—	—	—	—	—	—	—	—
Chuck-will's-widow	—	•U U	•C C R	•U C C	•C C C	C C	U R	U R	R
Whip-poor-will	—	•C C O	•U U U	•U R U	•C R C	U U	U U	R R	—
SWIFTS									
Black Swift	—	—	—	—	—	—	—	—	—
Chimney Swift	O O	•U C C	•C C C	•C C C	•C C C	R R	C U	C C U	—
Vaux's Swift	—	—	—	—	—	—	—	—	—
White-throated Swift	—	—	—	—	—	—	—	—	—
HUMMINGBIRDS									
Buff-bellied Hummingbird	—	—	—	—	—	—	R R	—	—
Ruby-throated Hummingbird	•O O O	•U C U	•U U U	•C C C	•C C C	U U	U R C	C U U	—
Black-chinned Hummingbird	—	—	—	—	—	—	—	—	—
Anna's Hummingbird	—	—	—	—	—	—	—	—	—
Costa's Hummingbird	—	—	—	—	—	—	—	—	—
Calliope Hummingbird	—	—	—	—	—	—	—	—	—
Broad-tailed Hummingbird	—	—	—	—	—	—	—	—	—
Rufous Hummingbird	—	—	—	—	—	—	—	—	—
Allen's Hummingbird	—	—	—	—	—	—	—	—	—
KINGFISHERS									
Belted Kingfisher	U U C	•C C C C	•C C C R	•C C C C	•C C C O	C C U	U C C	U U U	O O U O
Green Kingfisher	—	—	—	—	—	—	—	—	—
WOODPECKERS									
Lewis' Woodpecker	—	—	—	—	—	—	—	—	—
Red-headed Woodpecker	•O O O	•U U U U	•C C C C	•C C C C	•U U U U	—	—	R R R R	O O
Acorn Woodpecker	—	—	—	—	—	—	—	—	—
Gila Woodpecker	—	—	—	—	—	—	—	—	—
Golden-fronted Woodpecker	—	—	—	—	—	—	—	—	R R
Red-bellied Woodpecker	R R	•C C C C	•C C C C	•C C C C	•C C C C	O O	R R R R	U U U U	R R
Yellow-bellied Sapsucker	O O O	U U U C	C C C	C C C	•C C C	O	R R U	U U U	R
Red-breasted Sapsucker	—	—	—	—	—	—	—	—	R

	TX-5 Muleshoe	TX-6 Hagerman	TX-7 L. Atascosa	TX-8 Santa Ana	TX-9 Big Thicket	TX-10 Padre Is.	UT-1 Fish Sprgs	UT-2 Ouray	VT-1 Missisquoi	VA-1 Back Bay	VA-2 Chincoteag.	VA-3 East Shore
	•s S F W	•s S F W	•s S F W	•s S F W	•s S F W	•s S F W	•s S F W	•s S F W	•s S F W	•s S F W	•s S F W	•s S F W
	—	—	—	—	—	—	—	—	—	—	—	—
	R	O O O O	R R	•U U U U	—	R R R R	O O	R R R R	—	•O O O O	U U U U	C C C C
								R R R				
	•A A A C	•C C O U	•O O O R / •A A A A / •O O O O / •C C C C / •O U U O	•A A A R / •C C C C / •U U U U / •C C C C / •C C C C	•C C C C / •R R R R	R U R R / C C C C / R R R / R R R	•C C U	•C C A R	•U O O O	•U U C U	•C C C C	C C C C
	•C C U	•C C C	•C C O / •C C C U	•C C C R / •U U U U / •U C C O / •C C U R	•A A A / •U U U U	R R / U R U / R R R R / R R R	—	• U	U U U / U U U	R R R / U U U	•O R O / •C C C R	O / U U U
	•U U U U	—	•U U U U	•O O O O	—	R R R / R R R R / R R R	R	—	—	•O O O O	•O O O O	U U U U
		•U U U U	•U U U U	•C C C C	•C C C C	—	—	—	•O O O O	•C C C C	•C C C C	C C C C
	•C C C C	•U U U U	•U U U U	•U U U U / •C C R	•U U U U	R R R R	O O O O	•C C C C	•C C C U / R R R / R R R	C C C C	•C C C C / R	C C C C
	•C C C C	—	O O	R R	—	R	R	•U U U	—	—	—	O O
	—	•U U U U	—	R R	•C C C C	—	—	—	•U U U U	•O O O O	—	—
	•U U U U	—	R R	R R	—	—	0 0 0 0	U U U U	O O O	R R	O O	O O / O U U
	O O O	R R	U U U	R O	—	U	•U U U U					
	—	—	—	—	—	—	—	R	O O O O	—	—	O O
	R R / •C C U	•U U U	•U U U / •C A A / •C C C U	•O O O O / •U C U H / •C C C C	•U U	C / U U / U / U U	U	•U C U	O O R	U U	•U C U	U U U
		•R O R / R R	O U / R	O R R / O O / O R	•O O	U U / —	—	R R R / — / O O O	—	•U C U	•C C / —	C C O / O O
	—	•C C C	C O	C C U	•A A A	U	—	—	•O O O	•U U U	•C C C	U U C
	—	—	—	—	—	—	R	U C U	—	—	—	—
	—	—	R R R	•U C U O / C R C O	—	U	—	—	—	—	—	—
	—	•U U U	U U / U	•O O U O	•C C	C U C / C U C	—	U C U	•O U O	•U U O	•U U U	U U U
	R U U	—										
	—	—	—	—	—	R R / R	•O U / R	U C U / O	—	—	—	—
	—	—	R R	O O O	R R	—	—	—	—	—	—	—
	O O U	•U U U U	U C C / R	U U U / •U U U U	•C C C C	U U U / R R R	O O	U U U	•U C O	•C C C C	U O C U	U O C U
	—	—	—	—	•C C C C	R R	R	•C C U / R R R	•R	•U U U U	0 0 0	O O U O
	R R R	•U U U U	—	—			—					
	R R	—	•A A A A	•A A A A	—	R R R R	—	—	—	•U U U U	O O U U	U U U U
	R R R	•C C C C	U U U	O O U	•C C C C	R R R	U	U U U	•O C O	O O O	O O	O U U

STATE-NUMBER OF BIRD LIST REFUGE, SANCTUARY OR PRESERVE NESTING, ABUNDANCE BY SEASON	SD-4 Waubay • s S F W	TN-1 Cross Crks • s S F W	TN-2 Hatchie • s S F W	TN-3 L. Isom • s S F W	TN-4 Tennessee • s S F W	TX-1 Anahuac • s S F W	TX-2 Aransas • s S F W	TX-3 Brazoria • s S F W	TX-4 Buffalo L. • s S F W
WOODPECKERS (cont.)									
Williamson's Sapsucker	—	—	—	—	—	—	—	—	—
Ladder-backed Woodpecker	—	—	—	—	—	—	R R R R	—	• O U O O
Nuttall's Woodpecker	—	—	—	—	—	—	—	—	O R R
Downy Woodpecker	• C C C C	• C C C C	• C C C C	• C C C C	• C C C C	—	—	C C C C	O R R
Hairy Woodpecker	• C C C C	• C C C C	• U U U U	• U U U U	• U U U U	—	—	—	R R
Red-cockaded Woodpecker	—	—	—	—	—	—	—	—	—
Three-toed Woodpecker	—	—	—	—	—	—	—	—	—
Black-backed Woodpecker	—	—	—	—	—	—	—	—	—
Northern Flicker	• C C C R	• C C C C	• C O C C	• C C C C	• C C C C	C O	R R U	U U U	O C C
Pileated Woodpecker	—	• U U U U	• C C C C	• C C C C	• U U U U	—	—	U U U U	—
TYRANT FLYCATCHERS									
Olive-sided Flycatcher	R R R	R R	—	R R	—	R U	—	U U	O O
Western Wood-Pewee	—	—	—	—	—	—	—	—	O U O R
Eastern Wood-Pewee	C C C	• C C U	• C C C	• C C C	• C C C	U U	U U	C C C	R
Yellow-bellied Flycatcher	R R R	R R	R R	R R	—	U U	R U	—	—
Acadian Flycatcher	—	• C C U	• C A C	• C C C	• U U U	—	R R	—	—
Alder Flycatcher	—	R	—	—	—	—	—	—	—
Willow Flycatcher	• C C C	O U R	—	—	—	—	R R	—	—
Least Flycatcher	C U C	O	R R	R R	U U	—	U U	—	—
Hammond's Flycatcher	—	—	—	—	—	—	—	—	—
Dusky Flycatcher	—	—	—	—	—	—	—	—	—
Gray Flycatcher	—	—	—	—	—	—	—	—	—
Western Flycatcher	—	—	—	—	—	—	—	—	—
Black Phoebe	—	—	—	—	—	—	—	—	R R
Eastern Phoebe	• C C C	• C C U O	• U O O O	• U O U U	• U O U U	C O	U U C	U U C	R
Say's Phoebe	—	—	—	—	—	—	—	—	O O R
Vermilion Flycatcher	—	—	—	—	—	O O	R R R R	C C C	R
Ash-throated Flycatcher	—	—	—	—	—	—	—	—	R R
Great Crested Flycatcher	• U U U	• C C O	• C C C	• C C C	• C C C	U U	C C	U U U U	R
Brown-crested Flycatcher	—	—	—	—	—	—	R R R	—	—
Great Kiskadee	—	—	—	—	—	—	—	—	—
Couch's Kingbird	—	—	—	—	—	—	R	—	—
Cassin's Kingbird	—	—	—	—	—	—	—	—	R
Western Kingbird	• C C C	—	—	—	—	O O	U	O	• U A C
Eastern Kingbird	• C C C	• C C U	• C C C	• C C C	• C C C	• C U C	U C	• C C C	• U A U
Gray Kingbird	—	—	—	—	—	—	—	—	—
Scissor-tailed Flycatcher	—	—	—	—	—	• C U C	C C C	• C C C	• U A C
LARKS									
Horned Lark	• A C A O	U R U U	O O O O	• C C C C	O O O O	• C U C C	U U U U	• C C C U	• A A C A
SWALLOWS									
Purple Martin	• C C C	• U C C	U U C	• C C C	• C C	• C C	U	• C C U	—
Tree Swallow	• A A A	• C U C	U O C	C C A R	A A	A A	C U C	U U O	O O
Violet-green Swallow	—	—	—	—	—	—	—	—	—
Northern Rough-winged Swallow	R R R	• U U U	• U U C	• C C C	• C C C	U U	C U	C C	O
Bank Swallow	• U U U	U U O	• U U U	• C C C	• U U U	U U	C C	U U	• O
Cliff Swallow	• U U U	• U U O	• U U U	• U U U	• C C C	U U	C U C	O R	O O O
Barn Swallow	• C C A	• C C U	• C A C	• C C C	• C C C	A A	C C	C C C	• U U U
JAYS, MAGPIES & CROWS									
Gray Jay	—	—	—	—	—	—	—	—	—
Steller's Jay	—	—	—	—	—	—	—	—	R
Blue Jay	• C C C O	• C C C	• C C C C	• C C C C	• C C C C	U	—	• C C C C	O O O
Green Jay	—	—	—	—	—	—	—	—	—
Scrub Jay	—	—	—	—	—	—	—	—	O O R
Pinyon Jay	—	—	—	—	—	—	—	—	R R R
Clark's Nutcracker	—	—	—	—	—	—	—	—	—
Black-billed Magpie	R R R	—	—	—	—	—	—	—	—
American Crow	• C U C O	• C C C C	• C A A A	• C C C C	• C C C C	—	—	• C C C C	O O O
Northwestern Crow	—	—	—	—	—	—	—	—	—
Fish Crow	—	—	R R	• U C U U	—	—	—	—	—
Chihuahuan Raven	—	—	—	—	—	—	—	—	R
Common Raven	—	—	—	—	—	—	—	—	—
TITMICE									
Black-capped Chickadee	• C C C C	—	—	—	—	—	—	—	—
Carolina Chickadee	—	• C C C C	• C C C C	• C C C C	• C C C C	—	—	• C C C C	—
Mountain Chickadee	—	—	—	—	—	—	—	—	—
Boreal Chickadee	—	—	—	—	—	—	—	—	—
Chestnut-backed Chickadee	—	—	—	—	—	—	—	—	—
Plain Titmouse	—	—	—	—	—	—	—	—	—
Tufted Titmouse	—	• C C C C	• C C C C	• C C C C	• C C C C	—	U U U R	• C C C C	—
VERDINS									
Verdin	—	—	—	—	—	—	—	—	—

	TX-5 Muleshoe	TX-6 Hagerman	TX-7 L. Atascosa	TX-8 Santa Ana	TX-9 Big Thicket	TX-10 Padre Is.	UT-1 Fish Sprgs	UT-2 Ouray	VT-1 Missisquoi	VA-1 Back Bay	VA-2 Chincoteag.	VA-3 East Shore
	•s S F W	•s S F W	•s S F W	•s S F W	•s S F W	•s S F W	•s S F W	•s S F W	•s S F W	•s S F W	•s S F W	•s S F W
	—	—		—	—							
	•C C C C	0 0 0 0	•C C C C	•C C C C	—	R R R R	—	—	—	—	—	—
	R R	•C C C C	—	—	•C C C C	—	—	U	•U U U	•C C C C	•U U U U	C C C O
	R R R R	•U U U U	—	—	•U U U U	—	—	•U U U	•C C C C	•0 0 0 0	O O O	U U U U
	—	—	—	—	•R R R R	—	—	—	—	—	—	—
	C C C	U R C C	O O	R R R	•C C C C	R R R R	R U U	•C C C C	•0 C 0	•A C C U	•C C A C	C C A C
	—	•U U U U	—	—	•C C C C	—	—	—	•U U U U	R R R R	—	0 0 0 0
	U U U	R R	U U	U U		U U		U U U	O C O	—	R	—
	C C C		C C	R R		U U	U U	U U U		•U U U	•C C C	U U U
	—	•O R O	C C	O O	•C C C	U U	—	—	•O C	•U U U	U U	U
	—	R R	R	O O	O O	C U	—	—	—	U U	O O	O O U
	—	R R	O O	O O	•C C C	C U	—	—	—	O O	—	
	—	O O	O O	—	—		C U	—	C O	O O	R	U
	U U	U O	U U	O U R		C U	—	—	U O O	—	R R	O U
	C C C	—	—	—	—	—	—	—	—	—	—	—
	—	—	—	R R	—	—	—	—	—	—	—	—
	U U R	•U U U C	C U C C	C C U	C C C	U U R	—	—	•O U O	•U U U U	•U U C O	O C O
	C O C U	—	R R R	R R R		R R R R	•U U U	•C C C	—	—	—	—
	O	•U U O	•R R O O		U U U	R R	—	R R R	—	—	—
	•U U U	—	R		•C C	U U	—	—	•C C O	•C C C	•C C C	U U U
	—	•C C U	U U O	U U	—	U U	—	—	—	—	—	—
	—	—	•C C	•C C C R		—	—	—	—	—	—	—
	—	—	•U C U U	•U U U U		—	—	—	—	—	—	—
	—	—	•U U U U	•C C U O		—	—	—	—	—	—	—
	R R R	—		O R	C C	•U U	•U C U		R	R	O R
	•C C C	•C U U	U	O R		C C	•O O	U C U	•C C	•A C C	•A A C	C C A
	•R R R	•C U U	C C	C C	U U	C C	—	U C U	—	—	—	—
	•C C C	•C A C	•A U C R	•A O C R	O O O	C C	—	—	—	—	—	R
	•A A A A	•U U U C	•C C C C	O O O U	—	C U C C	•A A A A	•C C C O	0 0 0 0	R R R O	•C C C C	U U U
	—	•U U U	U U	O R O R	•A A A	U U	—	R R	•0 0 0	•C A C	•C C	C C U
	0 0 0	0 0 0	C C R	O O O	R R	C C	C	C C U	•C A O	•C C A U	•A C A O	U O A O
	R	—	—	—	—	—	R	C C U	—	—	—	—
	0 0 0	•U U U	A C	U U R	•U U U	C C	C	•C C U	R	U U R	R	U U U
	0 0	U U	C O C	O O	•U U U	U U	—	U U U	•C C O	U U R	R O R	U U C
	U U U	U O U	U O	O O R	R R	C C	R	•C C U	0 0	0 0 0	R	O O U
	U U U	•A A A	C O C	U U R	•U U	C C	•A A	•C C U	•C C O	•A A A	•A A A	C A A
	—	—	—	—	—	—	—	—	—	—	—	—
	R R	•C C C C	R R	R	•A A A A	—	—	—	•C C C O	•U U U U	0 0 0 0	U U A C
	—	—	•U U U U	•C U C A	—	—	—	—	—	—	—	—
	O 0 0	—	—	—	—	—	—	—	—	—	—	—
	—	—	—	—	—	—	R	R R R R	—	—	—	—
	—	—	—	—	—	—	R		—	—	—	—
	—	—	—	—	—	—	R	•C C C C	—	—	—	—
	U U U	•C C C A	—	—	•A A A A	—	R	O	•C C C O	•C C C C	•C C C C	C C C C
	—	—	—	—	•U U U U	—	—	—	—	•C C C C	•C C C C	C C A C
	•U U O O	—	•U U O O	R R R	—	—	—	—	—	—	—	—
	—	—	—	—	—	—	C C C C	U U U U	—	—	—	—
	—	—	—	—	—	—	—	—	•C C C C	•A C C A	—	—
	—	•C C C C	—	—	•A A A A	—	—	—	R R	•U U U U	0 0 0 0	C C C C
	R	—	—	—	—	—	—	—	—	R R	—	—
	—	—	—	—	—	—	—	—	—	—	—	—
	—	•C C C C	•U O U U	•U U U U	•A A A A	R R R R	—	—	—	•U U U U	R	U U U U
	—	—	•U U U U	•O O O U	—	R R R R	—	—	—	—	—	—

STATE-NUMBER OF BIRD LIST / REFUGE, SANCTUARY OR PRESERVE / NESTING, ABUNDANCE BY SEASON	SD-4 Waubay (•s S F W)	TN-1 Cross Crks (•s S F W)	TN-2 Hatchie (•s S F W)	TN-3 L. Isom (•s S F W)	TN-4 Tennessee (•s S F W)	TX-1 Anahuac (•s S F W)	TX-2 Aransas (•s S F W)	TX-3 Brazoria (•s S F W)	TX-4 Buffalo L. (•s S F W)
BUSHTITS									
Bushtit	—	—	—	—	—	—	—	—	—
NUTHATCHES									
Red-breasted Nuthatch	O U O	O O O	U U U	O	—	—	—	—	R
White-breasted Nuthatch	•C C C C	•U U U U	•U U U U	•U U U U	•U U U U	—	—	—	—
Pygmy Nuthatch	—	—	—	—	—	—	—	—	—
Brown-headed Nuthatch	—	—	—	—	—	—	—	—	—
CREEPERS									
Brown Creeper	O O O	U U U	U R U U	U U U	O O O	U	—	R R	—
WRENS									
Cactus Wren	—	—	—	—	—	—	—	—	—
Rock Wren	—	—	—	—	—	—	—	—	•U U U
Canyon Wren	—	—	—	—	—	—	—	—	R R R R
Carolina Wren	—	•C C C C	•C C C C	•C C C C	•C C C C	—	C C U C	•C C C C	—
Bewick's Wren	—	R R R	•R R R R	•U U U U	•U U U U	—	R R R R	—	R R R R
House Wren	•C C C	O R O	U U R	U U O	U U U	U	R R U	R U U	•O O O
Winter Wren	—	U O U	C C C	U U C	U U U	R	R	—	—
Sedge Wren	•U U U	U R U R	—	U U	U U	C C	U U C	—	—
Marsh Wren	•C C C	U U	—	U U R	O O R	•U U U U	U U C	•C U C C	R
DIPPERS									
American Dipper	—	—	—	—	—	—	—	—	—
OLD WORLD WARBLERS & THRUSHES									
Arctic Warbler	—	—	—	—	—	—	—	—	—
Golden-crowned Kinglet	U U O	C C U	C C U	C C C	U U U	O	—	R R	R
Ruby-crowned Kinglet	U U	C C O	C C C	C C C	U U U	U O	U U C	U U C	R R R
Blue-gray Gnatcatcher	—	•C C U	•C C C	•C C C	•C C C	C C U	C U C C	U U U	R R
Black-tailed Gnatcatcher	—	—	—	—	—	—	—	—	—
Eastern Bluebird	•C C C	•C C C C	•U U U U	•C C C C	•C C C C	—	R	•U U U U	R U
Western Bluebird	—	—	—	—	—	—	—	—	R R
Mountain Bluebird	—	—	—	—	—	—	—	—	O U O O
Townsend's Solitaire	—	—	—	—	—	—	—	—	O O R
Veery	R	U O	U U	U U	U U	O O	U	U	R
Gray-cheeked Thrush	U O	U U	C C	C C	C C	U U	U	U	—
Swainson's Thrush	U U	C C	C C	C C	C C	C C	U	U	R
Hermit Thrush	U U	U U U	C C C	U U U	U U U	O O	U U C	U O O	O O
Wood Thrush	—	•C C U	•C C C	•C C C	•C C C	U U	U	•U U R	R
American Robin	•A C A	•C C C C	•C C C C	•C C C C	•C C C C	O O	R R C	C C C	U U U
Varied Thrush	—	—	—	—	—	—	—	—	—
Wrentit	—	—	—	—	—	—	—	—	—
MOCKINGBIRDS, THRASHERS & ALLIES									
Gray Catbird	•C C C	•C C U	•U U U	•C C C	•C C C	C C	U U R	U U R	O O
Northern Mockingbird	R R	•C C C C	•C C C A	•C C C C	•C C C C	•U U U U	C C C C	•C C C C	•C A U R
Sage Thrasher	—	—	—	—	—	R	—	R R	O R O
Brown Thrasher	•C C C R	•C C C U	•C C C C	•C C C U	•C C C R	U C U	C U C	U U C	R R O
Long-billed Thrasher	—	—	—	—	—	—	—	—	—
Bendire's Thrasher	—	—	—	—	—	—	—	—	—
Curve-billed Thrasher	—	—	—	—	—	—	—	—	O O O
Crissal Thrasher	—	—	—	—	—	—	—	—	—
Le Conte's Thrasher	—	—	—	—	—	—	—	—	—
WAGTAILS & PIPITS									
American Pipit	O O	U U U	U	U U U	U U U	U C C	R U C	C C C	O R O
Sprague's Pipit	—	—	—	—	—	R R	R U	R R R	—
WAXWINGS									
Bohemian Waxwing	O O O	—	—	—	—	—	—	—	—
Cedar Waxwing	•U U U O	U R U U	C C U	U U U	C C C	—	R U	C C	R R
SILKY-FLYCATCHERS									
Phainopepla	—	—	—	—	—	—	—	—	—
SHRIKES									
Northern Shrike	O O	—	—	—	—	—	—	—	R O O
Loggerhead Shrike	•U U U	•U U U U	•U U U U	•C C C C	•C C C C	•C U C C	U C C	•C C C C	•U O U C
STARLINGS									
European Starling	•C C C O	•C C C A	•C C C A	•C C C A	•A A A A	•C C C C	—	•C C C C	•U O U A
VIREOS									
White-eyed Vireo	—	•C C U	•C A C	•C C C	•C C C	U U	C C U U	•U U U U	—
Bell's Vireo	—	—	—	—	—	—	—	—	—
Black-capped Vireo	—	—	—	—	—	—	—	—	—
Gray Vireo	—	—	—	—	—	—	—	—	—
Solitary Vireo	—	O O	U U	R R	U U	O	U U R	O O R O	R
Yellow-throated Vireo	O	•U U O	•C C C	•C C C	U U	—	R	R R	R R
Hutton's Vireo	—	—	—	—	—	—	—	—	—
Warbling Vireo	U U U	•U U O	R R	•C U C	•C O C	—	U	U C	R R R
Philadelphia Vireo	R	R R	U U	R R	—	O	U R	U U	R R R

	TX-5 Muleshoe	TX-6 Hagerman	TX-7 L. Atascosa	TX-8 Santa Ana	TX-9 Big Thicket	TX-10 Padre Is.	UT-1 Fish Sprgs	UT-2 Ouray	VT-1 Missisquoi	VA-1 Back Bay	VA-2 Chincoteag.	VA-3 East Shore
	•s S F W	•s S F W	•s S F W	•s S F W	•s S F W	•s S F W	•s S F W	•s S F W	•s S F W	•s S F W	•s S F W	•s S F W
	—	—	—	—	—	—		—	—	—	—	—
		R R	. —		R	O O O	—	R	—	R R R R	R R R	O O O	U C C
	—	•U U U U	—	—	•O O O U	—	—	R	•C O C C	•U U U U	R R	U U U
				—	•U U U U				—	•U U U U	•U U U U	U U U U
	O R	O U U	—	R R R	O O	R	—	R R	•C U C C	U U U	U U	U C U
	•C C C C	—	•C C C C	•U C C U	—	U U U U	—		—	—	—	—
	•U U U U	—	R	R	—		R R	•C C C	—	—	—	—
	—	•U U U U	•O O O O	•U R U R	•A A A A	U U U U	—		—	•C C C C	•C C C C	C C C C
	U U U	•U U U U	•U U U U	•U U U U	R	U U U U	—	U	•C C C	•C O C U	•C C C R	U U C U
	O R O U	O O R	R C C	U C C	O O O	U	R	•C C C	•O O O	—	U C U	U U U
	—	O O	—	R R	O O O	U	—	—	R R R	—	U C U	U U U
	—	R O R	U U U	R R	—	U U U	—	—	—	U O U U	O U U	U U U
	U U U	R U O	U U U	R U U	—	U R U U	C C C C	•C C C R	•O C O	•C C C U	•U U U	U U C C
	—	—	—	—	—	—	—	—	—	—	—	—
	R U U O	O	R R U U	U	R	—	—	R R	U U U	C R C C	U C C
	C C U	U C U	U C C	C C C	U U C	U	R	U U	U R R	U C C	C R C C	U A C
	O O	•U C U	U O C C	C C C	•C C C C	U U U	—	O O O	•U U	•U U	•C C C	U O U R
	R R R	•C C C C	O O R	R O O	•C C C C	R	O O	R R	R R R	•U U U U	•R R R R	U C U
	R R	—	R	R	—	—	O O U	—	—	—	—	—
	C C C	—	R R	R R	—	—	O O U	U U	—	—	—	—
	O O O	—	—	R	—	—	•U U U	R R R	—	—	—	—
	—	R R	U	O R	O	U U	—	—	•C C O	O O	R U	U C
	—	R R	U	U O O	R R R	U U	—	—	—	O O	O C	O U
	R	R C	U	U O O	R R	U U	—	O O O	R R	O U	O U	U U
	•U U U	O U U	U U U	U O U	O C	U U	R	—	•O O	U U U	U C C	U C U
	—	R	U	U O	•U U U R	—	—	—	•C C	•U U U	U O U	U O U
	C C C	U C A	U U C	U O O	•C U A	C	•O U C O	•C C C R	•C C C	•C C C U	•C C A U	C C A C
	—	—	—	—	—	—	—	—	—	—	—	—
	—	—	—	—	—	—	—	—	—	—	—	—
	R R	O O	C C	O O O	•U U U	C C R	—	O O O	•O C O	•A C C O	•C C C U	—
	•C C C U	•C C C C	•A A A A	•C C C C	•A A A A	C C C	•U O O	•R R R	—	•C C C C	•U U U O	—
	•O O	—	O O O	R R	—	R	O O	U U U	—	—	—	—
	•C C C U	•U U U U	R	R	•C C C C	U U U	R R	—	O O O	•C C C O	•C C C U	U U C U
	—	—	•U U U U	•C C C C	—	U R U U	—	—	—	—	—	—
	—	—	—	—	—	—	—	—	—	—	—	—
	•C C C C	—	•C C C C	•U U U U	—	U R U U	—	—	—	—	—	—
	C C C	U C U	O C C	U U U	—	U U C	R O	U U U	—	O O O	O O O	U C U
	O O O	R	—	O	O O	—	—	R	—	—	—	—
	R R	—	—	—	—	—	R R	O O	—	—	—	—
	U C C	U U C	O U U	O O U	U U	R	O	O O O	•O C O	U U U	U O C U	U O C U
	R R	—	—	—	—	—	—	—	—	—	—	—
	R	—	—	—	—	—	—	U	U R U U	—	—	—
	•C C C C	•C C C C	U U U	U U U	•O O O O	C R C C	O U U U	•O U O	R	R R R	—	O O O
	—	•C C C A	R R	•R R R	•U U U U	R R R R	•C O C	•C C C C	•A C A C	•A A A A	•C C A A	A A A A
	—	•U U O	•U U U U	U U U U	•A A A R	U U U	—	—	—	•C C U	•C C C	U U C R
	R R	•U U O	—	R R R	—	R	—	—	—	—	—	—
			—	R R R	—	—	—	—	—	—	—	—
	O U	O O	•U U U	U O O	U U U	R	—	—	O O O	O O R	R R	O U R
	—	R	U U	O O	•A A U	U U	—	—	O C O	U U U	R	R R
	—	O O	U U	U O	•U U	U U	•U U U	—	O C O	—	—	R
	—	R R	U U	U O	U O	—	U U	—	O O R	—	R	R

STATE-NUMBER OF BIRD LIST / REFUGE, SANCTUARY OR PRESERVE / NESTING, ABUNDANCE BY SEASON	SD-4 Waubay	TN-1 Cross Crks	TN-2 Hatchie	TN-3 L. Isom	TN-4 Tennessee	TX-1 Anahuac	TX-2 Aransas	TX-3 Brazoria	TX-4 Buffalo L.
	• s S F W	• s S F W	• s S F W	• s S F W	• s S F W	• s S F W	• s S F W	• s S F W	• s S F W
VIREOS (cont.)									
Red-eyed Vireo	U U U	•C C U	•C C C	•C C C	•C C C	U U	C C	•C C U	R R
Black-whiskered Vireo	—	—	—	—	—	—	—	—	—
WOOD-WARBLERS									
Bachman's Warbler	—	—	—	—	—	—	—	—	—
Blue-winged Warbler	—	•U U R	C C	U U	C C	O	R R	U U	—
Golden-winged Warbler		O R	C C	U U	U U	—	U R	U	—
Tennessee Warbler	C C	C C	A C	C C	C C	C C	C C	C C	—
Orange-crowned Warbler	C C	R R	U U	R R	R R	U O	U U C	U U U	R R
Nashville Warbler	R	C U	C C	U U	C C	U U	U U	U U	R
Virginia's Warbler	—	—	—	—	—	—	—	—	—
Lucy's Warbler	—	—	—	—	—	—	—	—	—
Northern Parula	R R	•U U U	•C C C	•C U C	•C U C	O	U U	•C C U	R R
Tropical Parula	—	—	—	—	—	—	—	—	—
Yellow Warbler	•C C C	•U U R	C C	U U U	C C	C C	C C	C U U	O O O
Chestnut-sided Warbler	O O	U U	C C	C C	U U	U	C U	U U	—
Magnolia Warbler	O O	U C	C C	C C	U U	C C	C U	C U	—
Cape May Warbler	R R	O R	R R	O O	U U	—	—	—	—
Black-throated Blue Warbler	—	R R	—	—	—	R	—	—	R
Yellow-rumped Warbler	C C	C C U	C C C	C C C	A A C	C	C U C	C U U	U O U
Black-throated Gray Warbler	—	—	—	—	—	—	—	—	O
Townsend's Warbler	—	—	—	—	—	—	—	—	R
Hermit Warbler	—	—	—	—	—	—	—	—	—
Black-throated Green Warbler	—	C C	C C	C C	C C	C C	C C	U U	R
Blackburnian Warbler	R R	U U	C C	U U	C C	O	U U	U	O
Yellow-throated Warbler	—	•U U U	•C C C	•C C C	•C U C	O	U U	U	—
Pine Warbler	—	•O O O	U U	U U	U O U	—	U R	—	—
Prairie Warbler	—	•U U O	•C C C	•U O U	•C O C	R	—	—	—
Palm Warbler	O O	U U	C C	C C	C C	—	—	R	R
Bay-breasted Warbler	R	U C	C C	C C	C C	U	C U	C U	—
Blackpoll Warbler	C C	C R	C	C C	C C	—	R R	U	—
Cerulean Warbler	—	•U U O	•C C C	•C U C	U U	—	R R	U	R R
Black-and-white Warbler	C C	U R U	•U O U	•C O C	O O O	U U	C C	U R R	R R
American Redstart	C O C	U R U	•C A C	•C U C	•C C C	C C	C U	C U	R
Prothonotary Warbler	—	•C C U	C A C	•C C C	C C C	U U	U	U	—
Worm-eating Warbler	—	•U U O	U R U	O O	O O	O	U R	U	—
Swainson's Warbler	—	—	U C U	•U O U	—	—	—	—	—
Ovenbird	C C	U U	C C	U U	U U	—	U U	U	—
Northern Waterthrush	U U	U U	C C	U O	—	C C	U U	U U	—
Louisiana Waterthrush	—	•C C R	•C C R	•U U U	•U O U	U U	C U	U	—
Kentucky Warbler	—	•U C U	•C C C	•C U C	•U O U	U	C U	U	—
Connecticut Warbler	—	R	—	R R	—	—	R	—	R
Mourning Warbler	O O	R	—	—	—	—	R	—	—
MacGillivray's Warbler	—	—	—	—	—	—	—	—	O
Common Yellowthroat	•C C C	•C C C	•C C C	•C C C	•A A A	•C U C C	C R C U	C C C C	R O
Hooded Warbler	—	•U U R	•C C C	•C U C	•C U C	U	C R	U U	O
Wilson's Warbler	O O	U U	C C	U U	—	—	U U	U U U C	C U R
Canada Warbler	R R R	R R	C C	U U	—	—	U U	U U	—
Painted Redstart	—	—	—	—	—	—	—	—	—
Yellow-breasted Chat	O O	•C C O	•C C C	•C C C	•C C C	U U	U U	U	—
TANAGERS									
Hepatic Tanager	—	—	—	—	—	—	—	—	—
Summer Tanager	—	•C C U	•C C C	•C C C	•C C C	U U	C U	R R	—
Scarlet Tanager	O R	•U U U	C R C	U O U	U U	U	C	R	R
Western Tanager	—	—	—	—	—	—	—	—	R
CARDINALS, GROSBEAKS & ALLIES									
Northern Cardinal	—	•C C C C	•C A C C	•C C C C	•A A A A	O O	C C C C	•C C C C	O O R
Pyrrhuloxia	—	—	—	—	—	—	R R R R	—	—
Rose-breasted Grosbeak	C C C	C C	C C	U U	U U	C	U	R R R	O
Black-headed Grosbeak	—	—	—	—	—	—	—	—	R
Blue Grosbeak	—	•U U O	U U U	O	—	C C	C C	U U	O U O
Lazuli Bunting	R R R	—	—	—	—	—	—	—	R
Indigo Bunting	O O	•C C C	C A C	•C C C	•U U U	C C	C C	C U U R	R
Painted Bunting	—	—	—	—	—	•U U	C C C	•U U U	—
Dickcissel	U U U	•U C O	•C C R	C C C	C C C	•A C	U	•C C C	O U
NEW WORLD SPARROWS & ALLIES									
Olive Sparrow	—	—	—	—	—	—	—	—	—
Green-tailed Towhee	—	—	—	—	—	—	—	—	O R
Rufous-sided Towhee	O R R	•C C C C	•C C C C	C U C C	C C C C	U	U	—	O R O
Brown Towhee	—	—	—	—	—	—	—	—	O
Abert's Towhee	—	—	—	—	—	—	—	—	—
Bachman's Sparrow	—	—	—	—	—	—	—	—	—

	TX-5 Muleshoe	TX-6 Hagerman	TX-7 L. Atascosa	TX-8 Santa Ana	TX-9 Big Thicket	TX-10 Padre Is.	UT-1 Fish Sprgs	UT-2 Ouray	VT-1 Missisquoi	VA-1 Back Bay	VA-2 Chincoteag.	VA-3 East Shore
	• s S F W	• s S F W	• s S F W	• s S F W	• s S F W	• s S F W	• s S F W	• s S F W	• s S F W	• s S F W	• s S F W	• s S F W
	—	•C C O	U O	•U O U	•A A A	U U	—	—	•C C O	•C C C	•C C C	U U C
	—											—
	—	—	U	O O	R	U U	—	—	—	—	R R	O U
	—	R		O O		U U	—	—			R R	R
	—	O R	C U	U U	—	U U	—	—	R R	O O	R R	U U
	O U R	U U U	C C C	C C C	U C	C C C	—	C C U	R	U U U	R R	O O
	O O	U U	U U U	C U O	—	C C R	—	C C U	O O O	O O	R	U U
	—	—	—	—	—	—	—	C C U	—	—	—	—
	—	R R	U O	U R O O	•A A A	C C	—	—	•U U U	O O	U U
	—			•O O O O								
	C U C	U O U	U C	C C R	O	C C	•C U U	•C C U	•C C O	•C C C	C C R	C U C
	—	O	C U	C U	—	C C	—	—	O O	O O	R R	U U
	—	O R	U O	O O	U	C C	—	—	R R	O O	R C	U U C
	—	—	—	—	—	R R	—	—	O O	O C R	C	U U C
	—			R		—	—	—	O O O	O O	O C	U C R
	U C R	C C C	C C C	C C C	A A A	C	C U U	C U	O R	A A A	A R A A	C U A A
	R R	—	—	U U O	—	R	U U	U U	—	—	—	—
	R R			—		—	—	R U	U U	—	—	—
	—	R	O O	U U O	C U O	O O O	C C	—	—	R R R	O O R	R	U U
	—	O O	U O	C O R	O	C C	—	—	O O O	O O	R R R	O U
	—	O	U U O	U U U	•C C U	U U	—	—	—	•O O O	—	O O
	—	—	—	R R R	•A A A A	—	—	—	—	•U O U O	•A A A O	C C C U
	—	—	—	R	•R U	—	—	—	—	•C C C O	•A A A	U U C R
	—	R O	R R	R R R	—	U U R	—	—	R	C C O	O A O	O C U
	—	O	U	C O	—	C C	—	—	O O O	R O R	O O	U O U
	—	O R	R	R R	R	U U	—	—	R	U U U	U U	U U C
	—	R	O	U	—	U U	—	—	—	—	R R	—
	O O	•U O U	C R C U	C O C U	•C C C	C C R	—	—	O O	•U U U R	•U U C	U C R
	R R	O O	U O	O O O	•O O O O	O O O O	—	R R R	•O C O	•U O U	U A A	U A
	—	•C C	O	O O	•C C C	U U	—	—	—	•C C C	R	O O
	—	U	U U	•U O U	U U	—	—	—	O O O	R R	O U
	—	—	R	—	•C C C	R R	—	—	—	—	R R	—
	—	O O	R R	O O	U U	R R	—	—	•O O	•O O O	U C	U O A R
	R R	O	U O	O O	O	U U	—	—	•O U R	O O	U C C	U C
	—	•O O	U O R	C C	•C C C C	U U	—	—	O U	•U U U	R R	O R
	R	•O U	O O	U U	•A A U	R R	—	—	—	O O O	R R	O U
	—			R R R	—	R R	—	—	—	—	R R	—
	—	O O O	R	O O	—	U U R	—	—	—	R R	—	O U
	C U	—	—	R	—	—	—	U U	—	—	—	—
	O	•U U U R	•C U C U	•C U C C	•O O O O	U	•O O	U U U	•C C C	•A A U U	•A A A U	C C A U
	—	R R	U O	U U O	•A A A	C C	—	R R	—	•U U U	O	O O U
	C C	O O	U U U	C C O	R	C C	R	R R	—	R R	O	U U U
	—	U R	U O	C C	—	U U	—	—	O O O	O O	R R R	U U
	R	•O U O	•U O	•C O O O	•U U U	U U	—	•U U U	—	•U U U U	•U U O R	U U U O
	—	—	—	—	—	—	—	—	—	—	—	—
	R R	•U U U	•U O	•O R	•C C C	U U	—	—	—	•U U U	•O O R	U U
	—	—	U	U O	O	U U	—	—	R R R	R R	O U	U U
	R R	—	R R	—	—	R R	U U	R R	—	—	—	—
	O O O	•A A A A	•C C C C	•C C C C	•A A A A	R R R R	—	—	•U U U C	•C C C C	•C C C C	C C C C
	O O O	U O U U	•O O U U	—	R R R R	—	—	—	•C C O	R R	U U	O U
	—	O O	U	O O	O	C C	R	—				
	O R	—	R R	R R R	—	—	—	U U U	—			
	U C U	•C C C	•C O U	O	•U U U	C C	—	U U U	—	•U U U	•U O O	U U U
	R	—	R	R R	—	R R	O	U U U	—	—	—	—
	R	•C C U	C U O	O U U	•C C C	C C	—	—	O O O	•C C C	U U U	U U C
	O O O	•C C U	•C O U	•C O O	•U U U	C U C	—	—	—	R R	U U U	O
	—	•A A C R	•C C	•C C	—	C U C	—	—	—	—		
	—	—	•C C C C	•C C C C	—	R R R R	—	—	—	—	—	—
	U U	—	O O	U U	—	R	R	U U U	—	—	—	—
	C C	U U U	R	O O	U U U	R	—	•U U U R	—	•A C C U	•C C C C	U U A C
	U U U U	—	—	—	—	—	—	—	—	—	—
	—	—	—	—	•O O O O	—	—	—	—	—	—	—

STATE-NUMBER OF BIRD LIST / REFUGE, SANCTUARY OR PRESERVE / NESTING, ABUNDANCE BY SEASON	SD-4 Waubay •s S F W	TN-1 Cross Crks •s S F W	TN-2 Hatchie •s S F W	TN-3 L. Isom •s S F W	TN-4 Tennessee •s S F W	TX-1 Anahuac •s S F W	TX-2 Aransas •s S F W	TX-3 Brazoria •s S F W	TX-4 Buffalo L. •s S F W
NEW WORLD SPARROWS & ALLIES (cont.)									
Cassin's Sparrow	—	—	—	—	—	—	U	—	O C O
Rufous-crowned Sparrow	—	—	—	—	—	—	—	—	R R
American Tree Sparrow	C C O	O	—	U U U	O O O	—	—	—	O O
Chipping Sparrow	•U U U	•U U O	•C R C	•U U U R	•C U C	—	O	R U	U O R O
Clay-colored Sparrow	•C C C	—	—	—	—	—	R	—	R R
Brewer's Sparrow	—	—	—	—	—	—	—	—	R
Field Sparrow	R R	•C C C C	•C C C C	•C C C C	•C C C	—	U U U	U U U	O U O
Black-chinned Sparrow	—	—	—	—	—	—	—	—	—
Vesper Sparrow	•C C C	C U	C C	U U R	U U U	U U	U U U	U U	U C C
Lark Sparrow	•R R R	O R	R R	R R	O O	O O	C C C R	O R O R	U C U
Black-throated Sparrow	—	—	—	—	—	—	—	—	—
Sage Sparrow	—	—	—	—	—	—	—	—	—
Lark Bunting	•R R R	—	—	—	—	—	—	—	•U U U
Savannah Sparrow	•U U U	C C	C C	C C	C C	A A	C C	C U C	•R R
Baird's Sparrow	—	—	—	—	—	—	—	—	R R
Grasshopper Sparrow	•U U U	O R	R R R	U U R	O O O	—	U U R	R R R	O U O
Henslow's Sparrow	—	—	—	—	—	—	—	—	—
Le Conte's Sparrow	R	R R R	R R R	U U R	O O O	U U	U U	U O U	—
Sharp-tailed Sparrow	•R R R	—	—	—	—	•O R O O	U U U	U R O U	—
Seaside Sparrow	—	—	—	—	—	•A A A A	U U U U	•C C C C	—
Fox Sparrow	O O	U U U	C C	U U U	U U	—	—	R	R R
Song Sparrow	•C C C	•C O C C	C C	C O C C	C C	U U O	R	U U U	U O O
Lincoln's Sparrow	U U	U U	C U R	U U O	O O O	U U U	U U U	U U U	R R
Swamp Sparrow	O O	C C A	C C C	C C C	C C C	C C C	U U U	U U U	—
White-throated Sparrow	C C R	C C A	C C A	C C C	C C C	U U	U U U	U U U	R R
Golden-crowned Sparrow	—	—	—	—	—	—	—	—	—
White-crowned Sparrow	U U R	U U U	C C U	U C C	U U U	U	U U U	—	C U C A
Harris' Sparrow	C C R	—	—	R	—	R	—	—	—
Dark-eyed Junco	C C O	C C C	C C C	C C C	A A A	O	—	O	O O
McCown's Longspur	—	—	—	—	—	—	—	—	—
Lapland Longspur	U U U	R O O	—	R	—	—	—	—	R R
Smith's Longspur	—	—	—	—	—	—	—	—	—
Chestnut-collared Longspur	•U O U	—	—	—	—	—	—	R	—
Snow Bunting	O O O	—	—	—	—	—	—	—	—
NEW WORLD BLACKBIRDS & ORIOLES									
Bobolink	•C C C	U U	O	U R	C O	R	—	U	O
Red-winged Blackbird	•A C A R	•C C C A	•C C C C	•A A A A	•C C C C	•A A A A	C C C C	•A A C C	•A A A A
Tricolored Blackbird	—	—	—	—	—	—	—	—	—
Eastern Meadowlark	—	•C C C C	•C C C C	•C C C C	•C C C C	•A A A A	C C C C	•A A C C	—
Western Meadowlark	•C C C R	—	—	—	—	O O O	U R	—	•A A A A
Yellow-headed Blackbird	•C C C	—	—	—	—	R R	—	U	O O R
Rusty Blackbird	U U O	U U U	C C	U U O	C C	—	—	—	R O
Brewer's Blackbird	•O O O	—	—	O O	—	A	U C C	U U U	R O
Great-tailed Grackle	—	—	—	—	—	R	C C C C	•C C C C	—
Boat-tailed Grackle	—	—	—	—	—	•A A A A	U U U U	•C C C C	—
Common Grackle	•A C A O	•C C C C	•C C C C	•C C A A	•C C C C	—	C	C C C C	O
Bronzed Cowbird	—	—	—	—	—	—	—	—	—
Brown-headed Cowbird	•C C C	•C C C C	•C C C C	•C C A A	•C C C C	•C U C A	C C C C	•C C C C	•C U U O
Orchard Oriole	•C C C	•C C R	•C C U	•C C C	•C C C	•C C U	C U C	•U U U	•U C O
Hooded Oriole	—	—	—	—	—	—	—	—	—
Baltimore Oriole	—	—	—	—	—	—	C C	—	—
Bullock's Oriole	•C C C	U O	•C U C	•U U U	•U O U	U U	—	C U	•U C O
Scott's Oriole	—	—	—	—	—	—	—	—	—
FINCHES									
Rosy Finch	—	—	—	—	—	—	—	—	—
Pine Grosbeak	O O	—	—	—	—	—	—	—	—
Purple Finch	O O	C U	U O C	O O U	U U U	—	—	—	R
Cassin's Finch	—	—	—	—	—	—	—	—	—
House Finch	—	—	—	—	—	—	—	—	•U O O U
Red Crossbill	R	—	—	—	—	—	—	—	—
White-winged Crossbill	R R	—	—	—	—	—	—	—	—
Common Redpoll	O O O	—	—	—	—	—	—	—	—
Hoary Redpoll	R R	—	—	—	—	—	—	—	—
Pine Siskin	O O O	O U U	R R O	O R	—	—	—	—	O R O U
Lesser Goldfinch	—	—	—	—	—	—	—	—	R
Lawrence's Goldfinch	—	—	—	—	—	—	—	—	—
American Goldfinch	•C C C O	•C C C C	•C U C C	•C C C C	C C C C	—	O	U R U	O O U
Evening Grosbeak	O O O	O R U	—	—	—	—	—	—	—
OLD WORLD SPARROWS									
House Sparrow	•C C C C	•C C C C	•C C C C	•A A A A	•C C C C	•C C C C	U U U U	•C C C C	•A A A A
Eurasian Tree Sparrow	—	—	—	—	—	—	—	—	—

	TX-5 Muleshoe	TX-6 Hagerman	TX-7 L. Atascosa	TX-8 Santa Ana	TX-9 Big Thicket	TX-10 Padre Is.	UT-1 Fish Sprgs	UT-2 Ouray	VT-1 Missisquoi	VA-1 Back Bay	VA-2 Chincoteag.	VA-3 East Shore
	• s S F W	• s S F W	• s S F W	• s S F W	• s S F W	• s S F W	• s S F W	• s S F W	• s S F W	• s S F W	• s S F W	• s S F W
	•A A U	—	•C C C O	C O O	—	U U U	—	—	—	—	—	—
	•U U U U	—	—	—	—	—	—	—	—	—	—	—
	U U C	O A	—	—	—	—	O O	O	C R O C	R R	O R R	
	C O C O	O O R	U U	O O	•C U U C		U	O O O	—	•O C O	•C C C O	•C O C
	C C	O R	U U U	O O O		U	O O	—				R
	O		•U U C C	O U U	U U	C	U	—		•O C O	•U U C U	•C C C O	U U C U
	R	O							O O O			
	C C U	C U O	U U U	C U U		O	U U C	—	C C C	O O O	U U U	O U U
	•C C C O	•C C C R	C U C C	•U U U U		R	R R R	U C O	—	—	R R	R R	O U U	R
	R R R	—	•O O O O		O		—	O A O	—	—			R
	O	—		—			O	—	O	O O O		—	
	•A A A U	—	O O O	R R		R		R	O O O	—			
	C O C U	A A A	A A A	•C C C C	O O	U U C	•A A A O	U U U	•C C	•C O C C	C U C C	U C C
	R		R									
	U U U	•U U R	U O O	U O O	O	C	—	—	—	U U U U	R	O O U
	—				O		—	—	—	R R R	R R	O
	R	O U O	U R	R R	O	U	—	—	—	U U U	•O U U U	O O U U
	—		R				R	—	—	U U O	•C C C O	U U A U
	—		R				R	—	—	U U U U	U U U	O U U
	R R R	O C C			U	C	U C C	R	O O O	•C C C C	•C C C C	C U C A
	C C C	U C C	O O O	U R R		U	C C	CCCU	•C C O	•C C C C	•C C C C	C U C A
	O O	C C U	U C C	C C A		U	U	—	R	—	R R	C U C A
	R	O U U	U O O	R R U	U	U	—	—	O O O	C C C	C R C C	U A C
	—	A A C	O O	O O O	A A	R	—	R R	•C C O	C C C	C C C	C A A
	C A A	A A C	U U O	R R	O O	R	C U	U O U	O O O O	O U R	R O O O	O U U
	R R	A A A		—	—	—	—	R	—	—	—	
	C C O	A A A	R	R R	U	A U	C C C	C R O C	C C C	U C U	U U U	
	U U C	R	—	—	—	—	—	—	—	—	O	
	R R	U U	—	—	—	—	—	—	R R		O O	
	—	R R R	—	—	—	—	—	—	—		R R	
	U U U	O O	—	—	—	—	—	O	O R O C	O U	O U U	O O
	—	O	—	—	—	R R	R	—	•C C O	C C	O U	U O A
	•A C A C	•A A A C	•A A A A	•C C A A	•C U U C	C R C C	•A C A C	•C C C U	•A A C	•A A A A	•A A A A	C C A C
	•C C C C	•A A A A	•A A A A	•C C C C	•C C C C	C C C C	—	—	•C C O	•C C C C	•C C C C	U U C C
	•A A A A	O U U	O U	R R O	—	H H H H	•C A A O	•C C C U	—	—	—	—
	U U U	O R O O	O O R	R R	—	U U	•A C U	•C C C	—	R R R	R R	—
	R	R O O				R		UU O	R O	O O	O C U R
	C C C	O U U	C C C	R U U	O	R	•A A A	•C C C O	—	—	—	R
	—	U U U O	•A A A A	•A A A A	—	C U C C	—	—	—	—	—	—
	R	•C C C U	—	R R	•C C C C	R	—	R R R	•C C O	•C C C C	•C C C C	C C A C
			•C A U O	•C A U U	—	R R R				•C C C C	•C C C C	A C C C
	C C C O	•C C C U	•C C C C	•O O C C	•C C C C	R R U	—	•U C C	•C O O	•C U C A	•C C C U	U U C U
	•U U	•U U U	C O O	•C R C	•U U U	C C	—	—	—	•U U U	•O O O	U U R
	—	—	R R R	•O O O O	—	—	—	—	—	—	—	—
	—	—	C U	C U	—	—	—	—	—	—	—	—
	•C C C	•U U U R	—	R R R R	U U	C C	•O O	•U U U	•C C	R O R	O O C	U C R
	—	—	—	—	—	—	—	U U	—	—	—	—
	—	U U U	—	—	—	U	—	—	O O O O	O O O	R O	O U U
	C O C C	—	—	R	—	—	•U U	U U U	—	R R	R R	U U
	—	—	—	—	—	—	—	—	O R O	—	R R	O O
	—	—	—	—	—	—	—	—	R	—	R R	R
	O O O	O U U	U	R R R	—	—	O	U U R	R R R	O O O	O O O	O C C
	R R	—	R R	R R	—	—	—	R R	—	—	—	
	U U U	•U U C C	U U U	U O C	C C C	U U C	O R	•C C C U	•C C C O	•U O U U	•C C C C	C C A C
	R R	—	—	—	R	—	R	R R	C O O C	U U R	R R	U U
	•A A A A	•C C C C	•C C C C	•C C C C	•U U U U	C C C C	O	•U U U U	•C C C C	•U U U U	•R R R R	U U

STATE-NUMBER OF BIRD LIST / REFUGE, SANCTUARY OR PRESERVE / NESTING, ABUNDANCE BY SEASON	VA-4 Dismal Sw. • s S F W	VA-5 Mason Neck • s S F W	VA-6 Presquile • s S F W	VA-7 Shenandoah • s S F W	WA-1 Columbia • s S F W	WA-2 Nisqually • s S F W	WA-3 Dungeness • s S F W	WA-4 Ridgefield • s S F W	WA-5 Turnbull • s S F W
LOONS									
Red-throated Loon	—	—	—	—	—	C C	U UC	R	—
Arctic Loon	—	—	—	—	—	R RU	O OO	—	—
Pacific Loon	—	—	—	—	—	—	—	—	—
Common Loon	O RO	U UO	O OU	O	•U OU	C UCC	U RUC	R	R R
Yellow-billed Loon	—	—	—	—	—	—	R R	—	—
GREBES									
Least Grebe	—	—	—	—	—	—	—	—	—
Pied-billed Grebe	U OU	C OCU	C UC	O O	•U CCU	•C CCC	U UUU	•C CCC	•C CCR
Horned Grebe	R RO	C CU	O OU	O	O OO	C CC	U UC	O OR	•O ROR
Red-necked Grebe	—	—	—	—	O O	U UU	U RUC	—	R R R
Eared Grebe	—	—	—	—	O	R	U UU	O OO	•C AC
Western Grebe	—	—	—	—	O OO	C RCC	U UC	O	O RO
SHEARWATERS & PETRELS									
Northern Fulmar	—	—	—	—	—	—	R	—	—
Cory's Shearwater	—	—	—	—	—	—	—	—	—
Pink-footed Shearwater	—	—	—	—	—	—	R	—	—
Greater Shearwater	—	—	—	—	—	—	—	—	—
Sooty Shearwater	—	—	—	—	—	—	R R	—	—
Short-tailed Shearwater	—	—	—	—	—	—	R R	—	—
Manx Shearwater	—	—	—	—	—	—	—	—	—
Audubon's Shearwater	—	—	—	—	—	—	—	—	—
STORM-PETRELS									
Wilson's Storm-Petrel	—	—	—	—	—	—	—	—	—
Fork-tailed Storm-Petrel	—	—	—	—	—	—	R R	—	—
Leach's Storm-Petrel	—	—	—	—	—	—	R R R	—	—
BOOBIES & GANNETS									
Masked Booby	—	—	—	—	—	—	—	—	—
Brown Booby	—	—	—	—	—	—	—	—	—
Northern Gannet	—	—	—	—	—	—	—	—	—
PELICANS									
American White Pelican	—	—	—	—	O R O	—	—	R	—
Brown Pelican	—	—	—	—	—	—	—	—	—
CORMORANTS									
Great Cormorant	—	—	—	—	—	—	—	—	—
Double-crested Cormorant	U U U U	U OU	R RU	—	U U U	C C C C	C C C C	U O U U	—
Olivaceous Cormorant	—	—	—	—	—	—	—	—	—
Brandt's Cormorant	—	—	—	—	—	U	C C C C	—	—
Pelagic Cormorant	—	—	—	—	—	U UU	U U C C	—	—
Red-faced Cormorant	—	—	—	—	—	—	—	—	—
ANHINGAS									
Anhinga	—	—	—	—	—	—	—	—	—
FRIGATEBIRDS									
Magnificent Frigatebird	—	—	—	—	—	—	—	—	—
BITTERNS & HERONS									
American Bittern	O O R R	U O U R	U O U C	O O	•O O O	•U U U U	U U R	•C U U O	•U U U O
Least Bittern	—	•U O U	—	—	—	—	—	—	—
Great Blue Heron	•C C U U	•C A A C	C C C C	O O O	C C C U	•C C C C	C C C C	•C C C C	•C C C O
Great Egret	O O O O	•U U U R	C C C R	O	R R	—	—	O O O O	R
Snowy Egret	O O	O O O	O U O	—	—	—	—	—	—
Little Blue Heron	•O O R	O O O O	R C R	—	—	—	—	—	—
Tricolored Heron	—	R	—	—	—	—	—	—	—
Reddish Egret	—	—	—	—	—	—	—	—	—
Cattle Egret	O O R	O O O	U R U	O	—	—	—	—	—
Green-backed Heron	•C C U	•C C C O	U C U	O U O	—	•U U U	R	O O O O	—
Black-crowned Night-Heron	•U U	•U U U	O O O	O	C C U	—	—	O O R R	—
Yellow-crowned Night-Heron	•O O	—	—	—	—	—	—	—	—
IBISES & SPOONBILLS									
White Ibis	R R R	—	—	—	—	—	—	—	—
Glossy Ibis	—	—	—	—	—	—	—	—	—
White-faced Ibis	—	—	—	—	—	—	—	—	—
Roseate Spoonbill	—	—	—	—	—	—	—	—	—
STORKS									
Wood Stork	—	—	—	—	—	—	—	—	—
SWANS, GEESE & DUCKS									
Fulvous Whistling-Duck	—	—	—	—	—	—	—	—	—
Black-bellied Whistling-Duck	—	—	—	—	—	—	—	—	—
Tundra Swan	O U U	O OO	R RR	O	U UC	R	R RR	U RUC	C O
Trumpeter Swan	—	—	—	—	—	—	R RR	R	•U U U O
Mute Swan	—	—	—	—	—	—	—	—	—
Greater White-fronted Goose	—	—	—	—	R	R U	R R	U R U O	O O
Snow Goose	O O	—	U C C	—	O O	R	U U	O OU	U U

	WA-6 McNary	WA-7 Toppenish	WA-8 Willapa	WA-9 Mt. Rainier	WI-1 Schlitz	WI-2 Horicon	WI-3 Necedah	WI-4 La Crosse	WY-1 Hutton L.	WY-2 Jackson H.	WY-3 Seedskadee	WY-4 Yellowstone
season	•s S F W	•s S F W	•s S F W	•s S F W	•s S F W	•s S F W	•s S F W	•s S F W	•s S F W	•s S F W	•s S F W	•s S F W
	—	—	U RU	—	R R	—	—	—	—	—	—	—
	—	—	C RU C	—	—	—	—	—	—	—	—	—
	—	—	—	—	—	—	—	—	—	—	—	—
	R RR	O O	C RU C	R R	U RUR	—	U OO	U U	O R	•OOO	O O	•RRR
	•UUUO	•CUCU	C UUC	—	O RR	•CCC	•CCC	•CCC	•UCU	•OOO	•CCC	•OOO
	R UUR	R	C CC	—	U U R	UUU	U U	U U	RR	RRO	O O	O
	R	—	U UC	—	R	—	—	—	RR	—	—	—
	UUUU	O U	C CC	—	R	—	—	—	•CCU	COO	COC	•RRO
	UUUR	OOO	CRCC	R	—	—	—	—	COU	•OOO	CCC	R R
	—	—	RRU	—	—	—	—	—	—	—	—	—
	—	—	U	—	—	—	—	—	—	—	—	—
	—	—	—	—	—	—	—	—	—	—	—	—
	—	—	UCA	—	—	—	—	—	—	—	—	—
	—	—	R R	—	—	—	—	—	—	—	—	—
	—	—	—	—	—	—	—	—	—	—	—	—
	—	—	—	—	—	—	—	—	—	—	—	—
	—	—	R	—	—	—	—	—	—	—	—	—
	—	—	—	—	—	—	—	—	—	—	—	—
	OUUR	—	—	—	—	—	—	O O	R O	O O O	O O	•CCO
	—	—	U R	—	—	—	—	—	—	—	—	—
	OUUO	—	CCCC	—	R R	•UUU	RRR	•UUC	O O	O O O	O U	•O O
	—	—	CUCC	—	—	—	—	—	—	—	—	—
	—	—	CUCC	—	—	—	—	—	—	—	—	—
	—	—	—	—	—	—	—	—	—	—	—	—
	—	—	—	—	—	—	—	—	—	—	—	—
	—	—	—	—	—	—	—	—	—	—	—	—
	R RR	•UUUR	R UUR	—	O R	•CCC	•UUU	•UUU	•UCU	•OOO	•OUO	•RRR
	R R	—	—	—	—	•UUU	R	•UUU	—	—	—	—
	CCCA	•CCCC	•CCCC	U U	C UUH	•CCC	AAAH	•AAAH	CCC	•CCCO	•CCCR	•CCCR
	—	—	U	—	R	•CCC	RR	•CCC	—	—	O	—
	—	—	—	—	R	RR	—	RR O	•UCU	OOO	OUU	R
	—	—	—	—	—	—	—	R O	—	—	—	—
	—	—	—	—	—	—	—	—	—	—	—	—
	—	—	—	—	—	•CCC	R	U R	—	R	—	—
	•CCCC	•UUUU	R R	—	C UU	•UUU	•CCU	•CCC	•CAC	—	O O O	•RRR
	—	—	—	—	R	•CCC	RRR	•CCC	—	—	U U O	—
	—	—	—	—	—	U U U	—	•UUU	—	—	—	—
	—	—	—	—	—	—	—	—	•COR	—	—	—
	—	—	—	—	—	—	—	—	—	O	C O O	—
	—	—	—	—	—	—	—	—	—	—	—	—
	—	—	—	—	—	—	—	—	—	—	—	—
	—	—	—	—	—	—	—	—	—	—	—	—
	CRCU	O UO	C C	—	O R	C U	U U	C C	O	O O	C C	O O
	—	—	U C	—	—	—	—	—	—	•CCCC	R	•OOOO
	O OO	R R	U U	—	—	R R	R	R	—	O O	O O	R R
	R RR	R	U UU	—	R R	U U	U C	U U	R	O OR	O O	R R

STATE-NUMBER OF BIRD LIST / REFUGE, SANCTUARY OR PRESERVE / NESTING, ABUNDANCE BY SEASON	VA-4 Dismal Sw. • s S F W	VA-5 Mason Neck • s S F W	VA-6 Presquile • s S F W	VA-7 Shenandoah • s S F W	WA-1 Columbia • s S F W	WA-2 Nisqually • s S F W	WA-3 Dungeness • s S F W	WA-4 Ridgefield • s S F W	WA-5 Turnbull • s S F W
SWANS, GEESE & DUCKS (cont.)									
Ross' Goose	—	—	—	—	—	—	—	R	—
Emperor Goose	—	—	—	—	—	—	—	O O	—
Brant	R R				C	R	U U C	O O O	—
Canada Goose	•U U C	•U U C C	A O A A	U U U	•A U A A	•C C C C	•C C C C	•C U C C	•C C C U
Wood Duck	•C C C C	•C C C O	C C A A	U U U	O O O	•U U R	R R R R	•U U U O	•O R O
Green-winged Teal	O O O	C A U	C C C	O O	•C U C C	•C R C A	•C U C C	•C U C C	•C C C U
American Black Duck	•U U U U	•U U C A	C C A A	O	—	—	—	—	—
Mottled Duck	—	—	—	—	—	—	—	—	—
Mallard	•U U U U	•C C C A	C U A A	O O	•A C A A	•C C A A	•C C C C	•C C C C	•A A A U
Northern Pintail	R O O	U U O	C C C	—	•C U C C	•C R C A	•C U C C	•C U C C	•C C C U
Blue-winged Teal	•R R R R	A O A	U C R	O O	•U C U	•U R	R R	•U U U O	•C A C
Cinnamon Teal	—	—	—	—	C C U	•C C U	R R R	•C C C C	•C C C
Northern Shoveler	—	U O O	U R U	—	•U O U C	•C U C C	U U U	•C U C C	•C O C O
Gadwall	O O	O U	U U U	—	•C U U U	•C R C C	R R U	•C U U U	•C C C O
Eurasian Wigeon	—	—	—	—	—	U U U	R O R	U U U	—
American Wigeon	O O O	U U O	C U C	—	•C O C C	C R A A	•C U A A	•C U C C	•C C C U
Canvasback	R O O	O U U	R R O	O O	•O O O U	U R U C	U U U	O O O	•U R U R
Redhead	O O	O O	R O	—	•C C C U	—	R U R	O	•C A C O
Ring-necked Duck	U U	O O U	U U U	—	U O C C	•U R U U	U C U	—	•U U U O
Greater Scaup	—	O O O	O O U	—	U O U	C R C C	C C C	R O	—
Lesser Scaup	U O O	C U C	U U C	—	•C O U C	R R U	U U U	C R U C	•C C C O
Common Eider	—	—	—	—	—	—	—	—	—
King Eider	—	—	—	—	—	—	—	—	—
Steller's Eider	—	—	—	—	—	—	—	—	—
Harlequin Duck	—	—	—	—	—	—	C U C C	—	—
Oldsquaw	—	O O	—	—	—	R R	C U C	—	—
Black Scoter	—	O	—	—	—	R	U R U U	—	—
Surf Scoter	—	O	—	—	R	C C C	C U C A	—	—
White-winged Scoter	—	O	—	—	R	C R C C	C A A	—	R
Common Goldeneye	O O	O O U	O O O	—	C O U U	C C C	C R U C	U O U	C O C O
Barrow's Goldeneye	—	—	—	—	O O U	U U U	R R O	R	U U O
Bufflehead	R O O	C C A	U U U	—	C O U C	C C C	C R A C	U O C	•C O C O
Hooded Merganser	•U O O U	U U U	O U U	—	O U U	•U R U C	O O O	•U O O	•U O U R
Common Merganser	O R O	C C A	C U C	—	U O U	U U C U	•C U C C	C U C	U R U U
Red-breasted Merganser	O R O	U U U	C U R	—	R	U U C C	C U C C	—	R R
Ruddy Duck	R O O	C C C	C C C	—	•C U U C	C R C U	O O U	U O U U	•C A C O
Masked Duck	—	—	—	—	—	—	—	—	—
AMERICAN VULTURES									
Black Vulture	•U U U U	O R	A A A A	U U U U	—	—	—	—	—
Turkey Vulture	•C C C C	C C C C	C C C C	C C C C	R	R R R	R U R	U U U O	O O
KITES, EAGLES, HAWKS & ALLIES									
Osprey	O R	•U U U	C C U R	U O U	O R O	R R R	R R R	R O R R	U R U
American Swallow-tailed Kite	—	—	—	—	—	—	—	—	—
Black-shouldered Kite	—	—	—	—	—	—	—	—	—
Snail Kite	—	—	—	—	—	—	—	—	—
Mississippi Kite	—	—	—	—	—	—	—	—	—
Bald Eagle	R R R R	•U U U U	U U U U	O O O	O R O	U U U U	U U C	U O O U	U U R
Northern Harrier	R R	U U U	U U U C	U U U	•U U U C	•C C C C	•C C C C	•C U C C	•U C U O
Sharp-shinned Hawk	•O R C U	U U U	U U U	C C U	R R O R	R C C	U U R	O O O O	U U U U
Cooper's Hawk	•O R O O	U O O R	O O O	U U U U	O R O R	R U R	•U U U U	O O O O	R O R R
Northern Goshawk	—	—	—	O O	—	—	R R R R	R	O O O O
Common Black-Hawk	—	—	—	—	—	—	—	—	—
Harris' Hawk	—	—	—	—	—	—	—	—	—
Gray Hawk	—	—	—	—	—	—	—	—	—
Red-shouldered Hawk	•C C C C	•U U U U	C C C C	U U U U	—	—	—	—	—
Broad-winged Hawk	U O	•U U U	U U	C C A	—	—	—	—	—
Short-tailed Hawk	—	—	—	—	—	—	—	—	—
Swainson's Hawk	—	—	—	—	O R O	—	R R R	—	O R O
White-tailed Hawk	—	—	—	—	—	—	—	—	—
Zone-tailed Hawk	—	—	—	—	—	—	—	—	—
Red-tailed Hawk	•C C C C	•U U U C	C C C C	C C C C	•C C C U	•C C C C	•C C C U	•C C C C	•C A C U
Ferruginous Hawk	—	—	—	—	•O O R	—	—	—	R R R
Rough-legged Hawk	—	—	—	O	O R U	U U U	U	O O U	R R O
Golden Eagle	—	—	—	O O	R R R	—	R R O	R R R	U U R
CARACARAS & FALCONS									
Crested Caracara	—	—	—	—	—	—	—	—	—
American Kestrel	•U U U U	•U O U U	U U C	U U U	•C C U C	•U U U U	•C C U R	•C C C C	•U C U R
Merlin	O R	R R	—	U U	O O	U U U	U U U U	R R O	O O O
Peregrine Falcon	—	R	R R R	O O O	R O	R U	R R R	O	R R R
Gyrfalcon	—	—	—	—	R	—	—	—	—
Prairie Falcon	—	—	—	—	•O O O O	—	R R R	—	R R R

WA-6 McNary	WA-7 Toppenish	WA-8 Willapa	WA-9 Mt. Rainier	WI-1 Schlitz	WI-2 Horicon	WI-3 Necedah	WI-4 La Crosse	WY-1 Hutton L.	WY-2 Jackson H.	WY-3 Seedskadee	WY-4 Yellowstone
•s S F W	•s S F W	•s S F W	•s S F W	•s S F W	•s S F W	•s S F W	•s S F W	•s S F W	•s S F W	•s S F W	•s S F W
R R	—	—	—	—	—	—	—	—	—	—	—
—	—	R R	—	—	—	—	—	—	—	—	—
		A U A									
•C C A A	•A R C U	•C C C C	R R	C O C O	•A U A U	•C C A	•C U C U	•U O C	—	•C C C C	•C C C C
•O U U R	•U U U O	•U C C U		C U U	•U C C	•C C C	•C A A R	—	R R R R	R R	• R R
•C C A U	•C O C O	C U C U	O	O	•U U U	•C U C	•C R C R	•A C A	•C O C O	•C C C U	•C O C O
—	—	—	—	R R R	•U U U R	U U U O	•C U C O	•C U C O	—	—	—
•A C A A	•A C A A	•C C C C	O O O	C C U O	•C C C U	•C C A U	•A A A C	•A A A	•A C A C	•A A A A	•A C A C
•C C A C	•C R C U	•C U A C	R O	—	•U U U	C U C	C R C R	•A C A	•O O C C	•A C C C	•C O C R
•C C C	•U U U	•U R U U	—	C U U	•C C C	•C C C	•A U A	•C C A	C O C R	•C C C	•O O O R
•C C C	•C C C O	R R R	—			U U U	•C C C	•U U O	•O O R	•C C C	•O O O
•A C C A	•C O C U	U R U C	—	R R	•U U U	U U U	C U C	•C C C	•O R O O	•A C C	•O O O
•U C C O	•C U C R	C R C C	—	R	•U U U	U U C	C U C	•C C C	•C O C O	•C C C U	•C O C R
—	O O O	R R R	—	—	—	—	—	—	—	—	—
•A C A A	•C O C C	C R A C	—	R	•C U C	C U C	A U A	•C C C	•C O C R	•C C C U	•C O C O
•U R U C	U U O	C C C	—	R O R	•U R U	U U	C R A R	•U C C	•O R O	C C R	R R
•U U U C	U O U U	R U	—	O O R	•C C C	U U	C R C R	•A C A	O O C	C O C	•R R O
U O C U	C R C U	U C U	—	O R	•C U C		A R A R	U U U	•O C C R	•C O C	•O O O R
—	R	U C C	—	C A O		O	U U	U U		U U	—
•C O U C	•O U U	R U U	—	U C O	C C	C R C	A U A R	•C U A	•O O O	•C O C	•C C O R
—	—	—	—	—	—	—	—	—	—	—	—
—	—	—	—	—	—	—	—	—	—	—	—
—	—	—	—	—	—	—	—	—	—	—	—
—	—	U R U U	•O O	—	—	—	—	—	—	•O O O	—
R R	—	R U U	—	U U O	U	—	—	R O R	—	—	•O O O
—	—	U R U U	—		—	—	—	R R	—	—	—
—	R	C U C A	—	—	—	—	—	R R	—	—	—
R R R	R	C U A A	—	O R	—	—	—	R U R	—	—	—
U O C	O O U	U U C	—	C C U	U U	U U R	C C U	R U	•O O O O	•C C C A	O O
U O C	—	R U U	O O	—	—	—	—	—	•C C C O	U U	•C C C C
C U C	O U O	C R C A	—	C C U	U U	U U	C C R	O R C	•C O C O	O O C	•O O O C
O O	O O O	U R U C	—	R R	U R U	U R U	•C C C	—	R R O	R R	R R R R
U C C	•C U U U	U U U C	•R R O	O O R	U U	•C C C	C C U	•C C U	•C C C C	•C C C C	•C C C C
R	—	U C C	—	A R A U	—	R R	C U R	—	O O	O O	R R
•C O U C	•U U U O	U U U	—	O O R	•C C C	U R U	C R C	•C C A	•O O O	•C C C	•O O O
—	—	—	—	—	—	—	—	—	—	—	—
—	•U U O	R U	—	O O O	U	R R R	C C C R	C C U	R R R	O O	R R
R R R	•U U U	U	R	O R O	U U U	U O U	U O U R	—	•C C C	U U	•C C C
—	—	—	—	—	—	—	—	—	—	—	—
—	—	—	—	—	—	—	—	—	—	—	—
R R R	C U C	•U U U U	O R	R	U U	U O U U	•C U C C	U U	•C C C C	U R U C	•O O O C
•C C C C	•C C C C	•U U C C	U U	U R U R	•C C C C	•C C C R	•U U U O	•C C C U	•O O O R	•C C C O	•O O O R
R R	U C U	U U C	U U	C U C O	U U	U R U	C U C O	R	•O O O	•U U U	•R R R
O O O	U O U U	U U U C	•O O O O	U O U R	U U	•U U U R	U U U O	—	•O O O	U U U	•R R R
—	R O O	•U R R C	•O O O O	O O R	—	O O O	O	R	•C C C O	•U O U U	•O O O O
—	—	—	—	—	—	—	—	—	—	—	—
—	—	—	—	—	—	—	—	—	—	—	—
—	—	—	—	O R O R	U U	U O U	•U U U R	—	—	—	—
—	—	—	—	U R U	U U	•C U C	•C U A	—	—	—	—
—	—	—	—	—	—	—	—	—	—	—	—
U U U O	•O O O	R R	• R U	—	—	—	R	•U C U	•C C C	•O C O	•C C C
—	—	—	—	—	—	—	—	—	—	—	—
•O O O O	•C C C C	•U U C C	•C C C	U O U R	•C C C C	•C C C U	•C C C C	U U U	•C C C R	•C C C O	•C C C
	R R							U U	•R R R	•U O O U	•R R R
O O O	U U U	U U C	C	R O R	C C C	C C C	U U	U	O C O	•C C C C	R R O R
U R U	•U O O U	R R	• U U	R	U U	O O O	R R R	C C C C	•O O O O	•C C C C	•O O O O
•U U U O	•C C C U	U R U C	•C C C	C U C O	•C C C U	•C C C O	•C C C U	•C U C	•C C C R	•C C C	•C C C
O O O	U O O	R U U	O	O O	—	R R	O U	R U	O R O	•U O U	R R R
—	R R	U U R	R O	R O		U U	U U	U U	•R R R R	•R R R	R R R
O O O	•U O U C	—	R	—	—	—	—	R	•O O O	•U U U U	•R R R

STATE-NUMBER OF BIRD LIST REFUGE, SANCTUARY OR PRESERVE NESTING, ABUNDANCE BY SEASON • s S F W	VA-4 Dismal Sw.	VA-5 Mason Neck	VA-6 Presquile	VA-7 Shenandoah	WA-1 Columbia	WA-2 Nisqually	WA-3 Dungeness	WA-4 Ridgefield	WA-5 Turnbull
CHACHALACAS									
Plain Chachalaca	—	—	—	—	—	—	—	—	—
PARTRIDGES, GROUSE, TURKEYS & QUAILS									
Gray Partridge	—	—	—	—	•R R R R	—	—	—	•O O O O
Chukar	—	—	—	—	•O O O O	—	—	—	—
Ring-necked Pheasant	—	—	—	O O O O	•C C C U	•U U U U	•C C C C	•U U U U	•U U U U
Spruce Grouse	—	—	—	—	—	—	—	—	—
Blue Grouse	—	—	—	—	—	—	—	—	—
Willow Ptarmigan	—	—	—	—	—	—	—	—	—
Rock Ptarmigan	—	—	—	—	—	—	—	—	—
White-tailed Ptarmigan	—	—	—	—	—	—	—	—	—
Ruffed Grouse	—	•U O U U	—	C C C C	—	—	—	•R O R O	•U U U U
Sage Grouse	—	—	—	—	—	—	—	—	—
Greater Prairie Chicken	—	—	—	—	—	—	—	—	—
Lesser Prairie Chicken	—	—	—	—	—	—	—	—	—
Sharp-tailed Grouse	—	—	—	—	—	—	—	—	—
Wild Turkey	R R R R	•O O O O	C C C C	C C C C	—	—	—	—	—
Northern Bobwhite	•C C C C	•U U U U	C C C C	U U U U	—	—	—	—	—
Scaled Quail	—	—	—	—	—	—	—	—	—
Gambel's Quail	—	—	—	—	—	—	—	—	—
California Quail	—	—	—	—	•U C C C	•U U U U	•C C C C	•R R R R	•C C C C
Mountain Quail	—	—	—	—	—	—	—	—	—
RAILS, GALLINULES & COOTS									
Yellow Rail	—	—	—	—	—	—	—	—	—
Black Rail	—	—	—	—	—	—	—	—	—
Clapper Rail	—	—	—	—	—	—	—	—	—
King Rail	•R R R R	O O O O	U U U	—	—	—	—	—	—
Virginia Rail	—	O O O O	U U	O	•U U U U	•U C U U	•U U U U	•O O O O	•U U U
Sora	R R R R	O U	U C	O	•U U U O	•R R R	•U C U	•O O O O	•U U U
Purple Gallinule	—	—	—	—	—	—	—	—	—
Common Moorhen	R R R R	O O O O	—	O	—	—	—	—	—
American Coot	O O O	C O C C	U R U U	O	•A C A C	•U U U U	U U U	•C U C C	•A A A R
LIMPKINS									
Limpkin	—	—	—	—	—	—	—	—	—
CRANES									
Sandhill Crane	—	—	—	—	U U	—	R	U O C O	R
Whooping Crane	—	—	—	—	—	—	—	—	—
PLOVERS									
Black-bellied Plover	—	—	—	—	R R	U U R	C C C C	—	R R
Lesser Golden-Plover	—	—	—	—	R	R	R	—	R
Snowy Plover	—	—	—	—	—	—	—	—	—
Wilson's Plover	—	—	—	—	—	—	—	—	—
Semipalmated Plover	R R R	—	U U	—	O O	U U	U U C	O O O	O O O
Piping Plover	—	—	—	—	—	—	—	—	—
Killdeer	U U U	•C C C C	C C C C	O O O	•A A C U	•C C C C	•C C C C	•C C C C	•A A A O
Mountain Plover	—	—	—	—	—	—	—	—	—
OYSTERCATCHERS									
American Oystercatcher	—	—	—	—	—	—	—	—	—
Black Oystercatcher	—	—	—	—	—	—	R U R R	—	—
STILTS & AVOCETS									
Black-necked Stilt	—	—	—	—	•U U	—	—	—	R
American Avocet	—	—	—	—	•C C	—	—	—	U R U
SANDPIPERS									
Greater Yellowlegs	O O	U U U	C C C	—	U U U	C R C C	U U R	O O U O	C U U
Lesser Yellowlegs	O O	U U U O	C C C	—	O U U	R U	U C	O O U	U C C
Solitary Sandpiper	U R	U U	C C	O O	U U O	—	R R	R R	U U U
Willet	—	R	—	—	—	—	R	—	—
Wandering Tattler	—	—	—	—	—	—	R R	—	—
Spotted Sandpiper	C U U	C U C	C U C	U U	•U U O	•U U U U	U U U	•O O U	•C C C
Upland Sandpiper	—	—	—	O O	—	—	—	—	—
Whimbrel	R	—	—	—	—	U U	C C R	—	—
Long-billed Curlew	—	—	—	—	•U U O	—	—	—	R R
Hudsonian Godwit	—	—	—	—	—	—	—	—	—
Bar-tailed Godwit	—	—	—	—	—	—	—	—	—
Marbled Godwit	—	—	—	—	R	—	R R	—	R R
Ruddy Turnstone	—	—	—	—	—	—	U U C R	—	—
Black Turnstone	—	—	—	—	—	—	C U C C	—	—
Surfbird	—	—	—	—	—	—	U U C	—	—
Red Knot	—	—	—	—	—	R R	O O O	—	—
Sanderling	O	—	—	—	—	—	C R C C	R R	U
Semipalmated Sandpiper	O O	—	U U U	—	O U	—	R R	—	U U U
Western Sandpiper	—	R	R R	—	U U U	A U A U	C R C U	O U U R	U C C

	WA-6 McNary	WA-7 Toppenish	WA-8 Willapa	WA-9 Mt. Rainier	WI-1 Schlitz	WI-2 Horicon	WI-3 Necedah	WI-4 La Crosse	WY-1 Hutton L.	WY-2 Jackson H.	WY-3 Seedskadee	WY-4 Yellowstone
	• s S F W	• s S F W	• s S F W	• s S F W	• s S F W	• s S F W	• s S F W	• s S F W	• s S F W	• s S F W	• s S F W	• s S F W
	—	—	—	—	—	—	—	—	—	—	—	—
	R	•R R R R	—	—	—	•U U U U	—	•U U U U	—	•R O O O	—	•R R R R
		•U U U U								R R R R		
	•C C A C	•C C C C	•C C C C	—	U U U U	•C C C C	—	•U U U U				
			•C C C C	•C C C C						•C C C C		•R R R R
												•C C C C
			•C C C C	•U U U U			•A A A A	•C C C C		•C C C C		•O O O O
										•C C C C	•C C C C	•R R R R
							R R R R					
							O O O O	O O O O				
								•C C C C				
	•U U U U	•C C C C										
	—	—	—	—	—	—	—	—	—	—	—	—
						•R R R		•U U				
	R	•U U U R	•U U U U	—	R R R	•C C C	•C C C	•U U U	•C C U	—	R R	
	O O	•U U O	•U C C	—	O R	•C C C	•C C C	•C C C	•C C U	O O O	•U U U	•O O O
						•C C C	—	•U U U			R R	
	•C C C C	•C U C C	•U U U U	—	O R R	•A A A	•C U C	•A C A O	•C C C	•O O C R	•C C C	•C C C
	R R	—	R	—	R R		•U U U	•C C A	R O	•C O C	U O U	•O O O
										R R R		
	O	R R	C R C C	—	—	U U	O O	U U	—	R R	O O	—
			U U R	—	—	U U	O O	U U	—	—	R R	—
			•U U n									
	O	R	C R C U	—	—	U U	O O	U U U	—	R R	—	—
	•C C C C	•C C C U	•C C C C	R R	C U C R	•C C C	•C C C	•C C C R	•A A C	•O C C O	•C C C	•C C C
									•U U U		•R R R	R R
	—	—	U R U	—	—	—	—	—	—	—	—	—
	R	•U U R	—	—	—	—	—	—	—	—	•U U U	—
	•C C U	•O O R	—	—	—	—	—	R R	•C C C	O O O	•U U U	O O
	U U	U U R	C U C U	R R	R R	C C	U U	U U U	—	O O O	U U U	R R
	O O U	O U	C U C C	—	R R	C U C	C R C	C C C	U C	O O O	U U U	R R R
	U U	R	—	R R	U R U	U U	U C	U U U	U C	O R O	U U U	R R
	—	—	R R R	—	R R			R R R	U C	O R O	•C U U	•R R R
			U U									
	U C C	•U U O	•C U C U	•U U U	C O C	•U U U	•C C C	•C C C	C C	•C C C	•C C C	•C C C
							•U U U	•O O	•U U			
			C C U									
	•C C R	•C U O	U U	—	—	—	—	—	U U	•O O O	—	•R R
								R				
			R U	—	—	R	—	—	R	O	O R R	C O	R R
			U U R	—	R	—	—	R R				
			U U C	—	—	—	—	—	—	—	—	—
			U U R	—	—	—	—	—	—	—	—	—
			U R U R	—	R	—	—	—	—	—	—	—
	—	R	C U C A	—	R R	—	—	U U U	U R	R	R	O O
	—	—	R R	—	R R	U U	U U	C C C	—	R O	O O	—
	U U	U O U	A C A A	—	—	—	—	—	U O	R O	O O	—

STATE-NUMBER OF BIRD LIST REFUGE, SANCTUARY OR PRESERVE NESTING, ABUNDANCE BY SEASON	VA-4 Dismal Sw. •s S F W	VA-5 Mason Neck •s S F W	VA-6 Presquile •s S F W	VA-7 Shenandoah •s S F W	WA-1 Columbia •s S F W	WA-2 Nisqually •s S F W	WA-3 Dungeness •s S F W	WA-4 Ridgefield •s S F W	WA-5 Turnbull •s S F W
SANDPIPERS (cont.)									
Least Sandpiper	O O	R	U U U	—	C U U	C U C U	C U C U	U U U O	U U C
White-rumped Sandpiper	—	—	—	—	—	—	—	—	—
Baird's Sandpiper	—	—	—	—	O O	R U	R R	—	R U C
Pectoral Sandpiper	—	—	—	—	O O U	U	R	O	R R O
Sharp-tailed Sandpiper	—	—	—	—	—	—	—	—	—
Purple Sandpiper	—	—	—	—	—	—	—	—	—
Rock Sandpiper	—	—	—	—	—	—	R R	—	—
Dunlin	—	R	—	O	O	A A	C O C A	C U U	R U
Curlew Sandpiper	—	—	—	—	—	—	—	—	—
Stilt Sandpiper	—	—	—	—	—	—	—	—	—
Buff-breasted Sandpiper	—	—	—	—	—	—	—	—	—
Ruff	—	—	—	—	—	—	—	—	—
Short-billed Dowitcher	R	—	—	—	O U	U A	U U U	—	—
Long-billed Dowitcher	—	—	—	—	U U U	U A U	U O U	O U U O	U U C
Common Snipe	O O O	U U O	U U C	O U	•C U U O	•C U C C	•U U U	•C C U U	•U U U R
American Woodcock	•C C C U	•U U U O	U U U U	C C C	—	—	—	—	—
Wilson's Phalarope	—	—	—	—	•U U	•R R	R R	•O R O O	•U U U
Red-necked Phalarope	—	—	—	—	U U	—	U U C	O R O	U U U
Red Phalarope	—	—	—	—	—	—	R R	—	—
SKUAS, GULLS, TERNS & SKIMMERS									
Pomarine Jaeger	—	—	—	—	—	—	—	—	—
Parasitic Jaeger	—	—	—	—	—	R	R R	—	—
Long-tailed Jaeger	—	—	—	—	—	—	—	—	—
Laughing Gull	O O O O	O C U R	C C C	—	—	—	—	—	—
Franklin's Gull	—	—	—	—	O	R	—	—	R R R
Little Gull	—	—	—	—	—	—	—	—	—
Common Black-headed Gull	—	—	—	—	—	—	—	—	—
Bonaparte's Gull	—	U O U	U U R	—	O U U	C R C C	U U U U	O R R R	R R R
Heermann's Gull	—	—	—	—	—	—	C C	—	—
Mew Gull	—	—	—	—	—	C C C	C U U C	O O O O	—
Ring-billed Gull	C U C C	A O A A	C C C C	O O	A A A C	C U C U	U O U C	C U U C	U U U
California Gull	—	—	—	—	U A U U	C R C R	C C C	C O U C	U U U
Herring Gull	U U U U	A U A A	C C C C	O O	U O U	R	C U C C	U U	—
Thayer's Gull	—	—	—	—	—	R R U	U U C	U U	—
Iceland Gull	—	—	—	—	—	—	—	—	—
Lesser Black-backed Gull	—	—	—	—	—	—	—	—	—
Western Gull	—	—	—	—	—	R R U	O O O O	—	—
Glaucous-winged Gull	—	—	—	—	—	A A A A	A C A A	C O O C	—
Glaucous Gull	—	—	—	—	R	—	R	R O	—
Great Black-backed Gull	O O O	C O C C	O U C	—	—	—	—	—	—
Black-legged Kittiwake	—	—	—	—	—	—	—	O	—
Sabine's Gull	—	—	—	—	—	—	—	—	—
Gull-billed Tern	—	—	—	—	—	—	—	—	—
Caspian Tern	O	U U	O U O	—	C C U	U U	R	O O	—
Royal Tern	O	—	O	—	—	—	—	—	—
Elegant Tern	—	—	—	—	—	—	—	—	—
Sandwich Tern	—	—	—	—	—	—	—	—	—
Roseate Tern	—	—	—	—	—	—	—	—	—
Common Tern	—	U U	U U U	—	—	U	O U U	—	—
Arctic Tern	—	—	—	—	—	—	O O	—	—
Aleutian Tern	—	—	—	—	—	—	—	—	—
Forster's Tern	—	U U	C C A	—	•C C O	—	—	—	R
Least Tern	—	R R	O O O	—	—	—	—	—	—
Bridled Tern	—	—	—	—	—	—	—	—	—
Sooty Tern	—	—	—	—	—	—	—	—	—
Black Tern	—	—	—	—	•O O	—	—	—	•C A U
Black Skimmer	—	—	O O O	—	—	—	—	—	—
AUKS, MURRES & PUFFINS									
Dovekie	—	—	—	—	—	—	—	—	—
Common Murre	—	—	—	—	—	U U C	O U U	—	—
Thick-billed Murre	—	—	—	—	—	—	—	—	—
Razorbill	—	—	—	—	—	—	—	—	—
Black Guillemot	—	—	—	—	—	—	—	—	—
Pigeon Guillemot	—	—	—	—	—	U U U U	U U U C	—	—
Marbled Murrelet	—	—	—	—	—	U U U U	U U U O	—	—
Kittlitz's Murrelet	—	—	—	—	—	—	—	—	—
Ancient Murrelet	—	—	—	—	—	R	—	—	—
Cassin's Auklet	—	—	—	—	—	—	R R R R	—	—
Crested Auklet	—	—	—	—	—	—	—	—	—
Rhinoceros Auklet	—	—	—	—	—	U R U C	U C U	—	—
Tufted Puffin	—	—	—	—	—	—	U C U	—	—

	WA-6 McNary				WA-7 Toppenish				WA-8 Willapa				WA-9 Mt. Rainier				WI-1 Schlitz				WI-2 Horicon				WI-3 Necedah				WI-4 La Crosse				WY-1 Hutton L.				WY-2 Jackson H.				WY-3 Seedskadee				WY-4 Yellowstone			
	•	s	S	F	W	•	s	S	F	W	•	s	S	F	W	•	s	S	F	W	•	s	S	F	W	•	s	S	F	W	•	s	S	F	W	•	s	S	F	W	•	s	S	F	W	•	s	S	F	W	•	s	S	F	W	•	s	S	F	W

WA-6	WA-7	WA-8	WA-9	WI-1	WI-2	WI-3	WI-4	WY-1	WY-2	WY-3	WY-4
—	U O U	A U A A	—	R R	U U	U C	C C C	A C	O R O	O O	R
—	—	—	—	—	R R R	U R	U U U	—	—	O O	—
U U	R	U U	—	—	R R R	R	U U U	U U	R O O	O O	R R
—	O	U C U	—	R R	U U	C C	C C C	—	R	O O	R
R R											

STATE-NUMBER OF BIRD LIST REFUGE, SANCTUARY OR PRESERVE NESTING, ABUNDANCE BY SEASON	VA-4 Dismal Sw. • s S F W	VA-5 Mason Neck • s S F W	VA-6 Presquile • s S F W	VA-7 Shenandoah • s S F W	WA-1 Columbia • s S F W	WA-2 Nisqually • s S F W	WA-3 Dungeness • s S F W	WA-4 Ridgefield • s S F W	WA-5 Turnbull • s S F W
AUKS, MURRES & PUFFINS (cont.)									
Atlantic Puffin	—	—	—	—	—	—	—	—	—
Horned Puffin	—	—	—	—	—	—	—	—	—
PIGEONS & DOVES									
Rock Dove	U U U U	• O O O O	—	—	• U U O O	U U U U	—	O O O O	—
White-crowned Pigeon	—	—	—	—	—	—	—	—	—
Band-tailed Pigeon	—	—	—	—	—	• C C C U	• U U U R	O U O O	—
White-winged Dove	—	—	—	—	—	—	—	—	—
Mourning Dove	• C C C C	• A A A A	A A A A	C C C U	• C C C O	U R U	• U U R R	• U C U O	C A C O
Inca Dove	—	—	—	—	—	—	—	—	—
Common Ground-Dove	—	—	—	—	—	—	—	—	—
White-tipped Dove	—	—	—	—	—	—	—	—	—
CUCKOOS, ROADRUNNERS & ANIS									
Black-billed Cuckoo	O	O O	C O C	U U U	—	—	—	—	—
Yellow-billed Cuckoo	• C C O	• C C C	C C C	C C C	—	—	—	—	—
Mangrove Cuckoo	—	—	—	—	—	—	—	—	—
Greater Roadrunner	—	—	—	—	—	—	—	—	—
Smooth-billed Ani	—	—	—	—	—	—	—	—	—
Groove-billed Ani	—	—	—	—	—	—	—	—	—
BARN OWLS									
Barn Owl	—	• R R R R	U U U U	O O O O	• U U O	• U U U U	O O O O	• O O O O	R R R R
TYPICAL OWLS									
Flammulated Owl	—	—	—	—	—	—	—	—	—
Eastern Screech-Owl	• U U U U	• O O O U	U U U U	U U U U	—	—	—	—	—
Western Screech-Owl	—	—	—	—	—	—	• U U U U	• U U U O	U U U U
Great Horned Owl	• U U U U	• C C C C	U U U U	U U U U	• U U U U	• U U U U	R R R R	• U U U U	• C C C C
Snowy Owl	—	—	—	—	R	R	R R	R	—
Northern Hawk Owl	—	—	—	—	—	—	—	—	—
Northern Pygmy-Owl	—	—	—	—	—	—	• R R R R	—	U U U
Elf Owl	—	—	—	—	—	—	—	—	—
Burrowing Owl	—	—	—	—	• O O O	—	—	—	—
Spotted Owl	—	—	—	—	—	—	—	—	—
Barred Owl	• C C C C	• C C C C	C C C C	C C C C	—	—	—	—	—
Great Gray Owl	—	—	—	—	—	—	—	—	—
Long-eared Owl	—	—	—	O O O	• O O O	—	—	—	• U U U U
Short-eared Owl	—	—	O O U	O	• O O O O	• U U U U	• C C C C	O O	• O O O O
Boreal Owl	—	—	—	—	—	—	—	—	—
Northern Saw-whet Owl	—	—	—	O O O	—	—	U U	—	O O O R
NIGHTJARS									
Lesser Nighthawk	—	—	—	—	—	—	—	—	—
Common Nighthawk	R R	U U C	O C O	C U C	• U O	U	• U U U	O O	• C U
Pauraque	—	—	—	—	—	—	—	—	—
Common Poorwill	—	—	—	—	• R R	—	—	—	—
Chuck-will's-widow	• U U O	R	O U O	—	—	—	—	—	—
Whip-poor-will	• U U O	• C U U	U C O	U U U	—	—	—	—	—
SWIFTS									
Black Swift	—	—	—	—	—	—	O O O	—	—
Chimney Swift	C C U	• C C A	U A U	C C C	—	—	—	—	—
Vaux's Swift	—	—	—	—	—	U	• U U U	U U O	O
White-throated Swift	—	—	—	—	R R	—	—	—	—
HUMMINGBIRDS									
Buff-bellied Hummingbird	—	—	—	—	—	—	—	—	—
Ruby-throated Hummingbird	• C C U	• U C C	C C C	C C C	—	—	—	—	—
Black-chinned Hummingbird	—	—	—	—	—	—	—	—	• U U U
Anna's Hummingbird	—	—	—	—	—	—	—	R R R R	—
Costa's Hummingbird	—	—	—	—	—	—	—	—	—
Calliope Hummingbird	—	—	—	—	—	—	—	—	• O O O
Broad-tailed Hummingbird	—	—	—	—	—	—	—	—	—
Rufous Hummingbird	—	—	—	—	O O	• C C	• C C U	• U U O	O O O
Allen's Hummingbird	—	—	—	—	—	—	—	—	—
KINGFISHERS									
Belted Kingfisher	• C C C C	• C C C U	C C C C	U U U U	• U O O O	C C C C	• U U U U	• U U U U	• U C O O
Green Kingfisher	—	—	—	—	—	—	—	—	—
WOODPECKERS									
Lewis' Woodpecker	—	—	—	—	O O	—	R R	O R R	• R R R
Red-headed Woodpecker	• U U U O	• U U U U	U U U U	O O O O	—	—	—	—	—
Acorn Woodpecker	—	—	—	—	—	—	—	—	—
Gila Woodpecker	—	—	—	—	—	—	—	—	—
Golden-fronted Woodpecker	—	—	—	—	—	—	—	—	—
Red-bellied Woodpecker	• C C C C	• C C C C	C C C C	C C C C	—	—	—	—	—
Yellow-bellied Sapsucker	U O U U	U U U	U U C	C C U	—	—	—	—	• U C U
Red-breasted Sapsucker	—	—	—	—	—	• C C C C	R R R R	O O O	—

WA-6 McNary	WA-7 Toppenish	WA-8 Willapa	WA-9 Mt. Rainier	WI-1 Schlitz	WI-2 Horicon	WI-3 Necedah	WI-4 La Crosse	WY-1 Hutton L.	WY-2 Jackson H.	WY-3 Seedskadee	WY-4 Yellowstone
•s S F W	•s S F W	•s S F W	•s S F W	•s S F W	•s S F W	•s S F W	•s S F W	•s S F W	•s S F W	•s S F W	•s S F W
—	—	—	—	—	—	—	—	—	—	—	—
—	—	—	—	—	—	—	—	—	—	—	—
—	•A A A A	—	—	U U U O	•C C C C	O O O O	•C C C C	—	O O O O	O O O O	—
—	—	—	—	—	—	—	—	—	—	—	—
—	—	•U C A R	•C C C	—	—	—	—	—	—	—	—
—	—	—	—	—	—	—	—	—	—	—	—
•C C C O	•C C C U	R	—	C C C U	•C C C U	•C C C O	•C C C U	•C C C	•O O O	•C C C	•O O O
—	—	—	—	—	—	—	—	—	—	—	—
—	—	—	—	—	—	—	—	—	—	—	—
—	—	—	—	—	—	—	—	—	—	—	—
—	—	—	—	U O R	•C C C	•C C R	•C C U	—	O O O	—	—
—	—	—	—	U O R	•U U U	•O O	•C C U	—	—	•U U U	—
—	—	—	—	—	—	—	—	—	—	—	—
—	—	—	—	—	—	—	—	—	—	—	—
—	—	—	—	—	—	—	—	—	—	—	—
—	—	—	—	—	—	—	—	—	—	—	—
O O O O	•U U U O	•U U U U	—	—	—	—	—	—	—	•O O O	—
—	—	—	—	—	—	—	—	—	—	—	—
—	—	—	—	O O U U	•U U U U	•R R R R	•U U U U	—	—	—	—
—	•U U U O	•C C C C	•U U U U	—	—	—	—	U U U R	•O O O O	—	•R R R R
O O O O	•C C C C	•U C C C	•U U U U	U U U U	•C C C C	•C C C C	•C C C C	U U U R	•O O O O	•C C C C	•O O O O
R R	R	R R	—	—	U	R R R	R O O	—	—	R	—
—	—	—	—	—	—	—	—	—	—	—	•R R R R
—	—	•U U U U	•U U U U	—	—	—	—	—	R R R R	—	•R R R R
—	—	—	—	—	—	—	—	—	—	—	—
•C C C C	•U U U R	—	—	—	—	—	—	—	R R R	R R R	R R
—	—	R	•O O O O	—	—	—	—	—	—	—	—
—	R	—	—	R R R	—	•C C C C	•C C C C	—	—	—	—
—	—	—	—	—	—	—	—	—	•O O O O	—	•O O O R
R	•U O U U	—	R	R R R	R R R	R R R R	•U U U U	U U U R	• O O	O O O O	•R R R
•U U U C	•U U U U	•U U C C	—	R R	•U U U U	R R R	U U U	—	•R O O R	O O O O	•O O O R
—	—	—	—	—	—	—	—	—	—	—	• R
R R	O R	U	•O O O O	R R	—	R R R R	•O O O O	—	R R R R	• R	•R R
—	—	—	—	—	—	—	—	—	—	—	—
R C U R	•U C U	•R U R	U	U O C	•U U U	C C C	•C A U	•C C C	•C C C	• C	•C C O
—	—	—	—	—	—	—	—	—	—	—	—
—	•U U O	—	—	—	—	—	—	—	—	•O O	—
—	—	—	—	—	—	—	—	—		—	—
—	—	—	—	U O R	—	•C C U	•C C C	—	—	—	—
—	—	R U	•U U U	—	—	—	—	—	—	—	—
—	—	—	—	C C C	•U U U	U U O	•C A U	—	—	—	—
—	O O	•U U	•C C C	—	—	—	—	—	—	—	—
—	O O	—	—	—	—	—	—	O U O	—	•U U	•O O O
—	—	—	—	—	—	—	—	—	—	—	—
—	—	—	—	U O O	•U U U	U U U	•U U U	O	—	—	—
—	U U R	—	—	—	—	—	—	—	O R	—	—
—	—	R R U	—	—	—	—	—	—	—	—	—
—	—	—	—	—	—	—	—	—	—	—	—
—	O O	—	•U U U	—	—	—	—	—	•C C C	—	•R R
—	—	—	—	—	—	—	—	U	•O O O	•U U U	•R R
R	O U	C A C R	•C C C	—	—	—	—	—	•O O O	U U U	•R R
—	—	—	—	—	—	—	—	—	—	—	—
•U U U U	U U C C	•C C C C	•O U O	U U U R	•U U U	•C C C	•C C U O	O O	•C C C O	•O O O	•O O O R
—	—	—	—	—	—	—	—	—	—	—	—
—	•U U U O	R U R	•R R R	—	—	—	—	—	•O O R	•U U U	•R R R
—	—	—	—	U O O	•U U U	•C C C O	•C C C U	—	—	•U U	—
—	—	—	—	—	—	—	—	—	—	—	—
—	—	—	—	—	—	—	—	—	—	—	—
—	—	—	—	—	—	—	—	—	—	—	—
—	—	—	—	R	U U	•U U U U	•C C C C	—	—	—	—
—	—	U U U U	•C C C U	C R C R	•U U U	•U U U	•C U C R	—	•C C C	•U R U	•C C C
—	R R	—	—	—	—	—	—	—	—	—	—

STATE-NUMBER OF BIRD LIST / REFUGE, SANCTUARY OR PRESERVE / NESTING, ABUNDANCE BY SEASON	VA-4 Dismal Sw. • s S F W	VA-5 Mason Neck • s S F W	VA-6 Presquile • s S F W	VA-7 Shenandoah • s S F W	WA-1 Columbia • s S F W	WA-2 Nisqually • s S F W	WA-3 Dungeness • s S F W	WA-4 Ridgefield • s S F W	WA-5 Turnbull • s S F W
WOODPECKERS (cont.)									
Williamson's Sapsucker	—	—	—	—	—	—	—	—	—
Ladder-backed Woodpecker	—	—	—	—	—	—	—	—	—
Nuttall's Woodpecker	—	—	—	—	—	—	—	—	—
Downy Woodpecker	•C C C C	•C C C C	C C C C	C C C C	O O O O	•C C C C	•C C C C	•C C C C	•C C C C
Hairy Woodpecker	•U U U U	•U U U U	U U U U	U U U U	O O	•U U U U	•C C C C	O O O O	•U U U C
Red-cockaded Woodpecker	—	—	—	—	—	—	—	—	—
Three-toed Woodpecker	—	—	—	—	—	—	R R R	—	—
Black-backed Woodpecker	—	—	—	—	—	—	—	—	—
Northern Flicker	•U U C C	•C C C C	C C C C	C C C C	•C C U C	•C C C C	•C C C C	•C C C C	•A A A A
Pileated Woodpecker	•C C C C	•U U U U	C C C C	U U U U	—	•U U U U	•U U U U	O O O O	—
TYRANT FLYCATCHERS									
Olive-sided Flycatcher	—	—	—	O O	—	U	•U C U	O O	O O
Western Wood-Pewee	—	—	—	—	•U O	C U	•C C U	•U U U	•C A C
Eastern Wood-Pewee	•C C U	•C C C	C C C	C A C	—	—	—	—	—
Yellow-bellied Flycatcher	—	O O	—	U	—	—	—	—	—
Acadian Flycatcher	•C C U	•C C C	C C C	C C C	—	—	—	—	—
Alder Flycatcher	—	—	—	—	—	—	—	—	—
Willow Flycatcher	—	U O U	—	O O	O O	• C U	•C C U	•O U O	•A A U
Least Flycatcher	—	—	—	U U U	—	—	—	—	—
Hammond's Flycatcher	—	—	—	—	U	—	•U U U	O O O	U U
Dusky Flycatcher	—	—	—	—	U U U	—	—	—	U U U
Gray Flycatcher	—	—	—	—	—	—	—	—	—
Western Flycatcher	—	—	—	—	O	•C C	•C C U	•O O O R	•O O O
Black Phoebe	—	—	—	—	—	—	—	—	—
Eastern Phoebe	•C C U R	•U C C O	C C C R	C C C O	—	—	—	—	—
Say's Phoebe	—	—	—	—	•U U U O	—	—	—	•U R U
Vermilion Flycatcher	—	—	—	—	—	—	—	—	—
Ash-throated Flycatcher	—	—	—	—	•O O	—	—	—	—
Great Crested Flycatcher	•C C C	•U C U	C C C	C C C	—	—	—	—	—
Brown-crested Flycatcher	—	—	—	—	—	—	—	—	—
Great Kiskadee	—	—	—	—	—	—	—	—	—
Couch's Kingbird	—	—	—	—	—	—	—	—	—
Cassin's Kingbird	—	—	—	—	—	—	—	—	—
Western Kingbird	—	—	—	—	•O U O	—	•O O O	O R	•O O O
Eastern Kingbird	•U U U	•C C C	C C C	U U U	•U U O	—	O O O	R	•C A C
Gray Kingbird	—	—	—	—	—	—	—	—	—
Scissor-tailed Flycatcher	—	—	—	—	—	—	—	—	—
LARKS									
Horned Lark	—	—	U U U U	U O U O	•U U U U	—	•U U U	—	•U U U U
SWALLOWS									
Purple Martin	U U	•U U U	O O O	O O O	—	—	—	•O O O	—
Tree Swallow	•U O U	•A A A	C C A	O O	U O	•A A A	•C C C	•C C C R	•A A C
Violet-green Swallow	—	—	—	—	O O O	•A A A	•C C C	•U U U R	• U R U
Northern Rough-winged Swallow	•U U O	•U U U	U U U	U O U	•U U O	•C C C	•C C C	O O	•O R O
Bank Swallow	O	•U U U	C C C	O O	•C U U	—	•U U U	—	•C U A
Cliff Swallow	R R	•O O	O O	O O U	•A A O	•C C C	•C C C	•C C U	•C C A
Barn Swallow	•C C C	•A A A	A A A	U U U	•C C A	•A A A	•C C C	•C C C	•C A C
JAYS, MAGPIES & CROWS									
Gray Jay	—	—	—	—	—	—	C C C C	R R	—
Steller's Jay	—	—	—	—	—	C C C U	•C C C C	•U U U U	R
Blue Jay	•C C C C	•A C A C	C C C C	A A A A	—	—	—	—	—
Green Jay	—	—	—	—	—	—	—	—	—
Scrub Jay	—	—	—	—	—	—	—	•C C U U	—
Pinyon Jay	—	—	—	—	—	—	—	—	—
Clark's Nutcracker	—	—	—	—	—	—	—	—	R R R R
Black-billed Magpie	—	—	—	—	•C C C C	—	—	R R	•C A A C
American Crow	•C C C C	•C C C A	A A A A	C C C C	R	•C C C C	•U U U U	•C C C C	O O O
Northwestern Crow	—	—	—	—	—	—	•C C C C	—	—
Fish Crow	•U U U U	•C C C A	C A C R	U U U U	—	—	—	—	—
Chihuahuan Raven	—	—	—	—	—	—	—	—	—
Common Raven	—	—	—	C C C C	•U U U O	—	•C C C C	—	O O O O
TITMICE									
Black-capped Chickadee	R R	O	—	U U U	R R R R	•C C C C	•C C C C	•C C C C	•C C C C
Carolina Chickadee	•C C C C	•A A A A	C C C C	A A A A	—	—	—	—	—
Mountain Chickadee	—	—	—	—	—	—	U	—	•C C C C
Boreal Chickadee	—	—	—	—	—	—	—	—	—
Chestnut-backed Chickadee	—	—	—	—	—	•C U C C	•C C C C	O O O O	—
Plain Titmouse	—	—	—	—	—	—	—	—	—
Tufted Titmouse	•C C C C	•A A A A	C C C C	A A A A	—	—	—	—	—
VERDINS									
Verdin	—	—	—	—	—	—	—	—	—

	WA-6 McNary	WA-7 Toppenish	WA-8 Willapa	WA-9 Mt. Rainier	WI-1 Schlitz	WI-2 Horicon	WI-3 Necedah	WI-4 La Crosse	WY-1 Hutton L.	WY-2 Jackson H.	WY-3 Seedskadee	WY-4 Yellowstone
	•s S F W	•s S F W	•s S F W	•s S F W	•s S F W	•s S F W	•s S F W	•s S F W	•s S F W	•s S F W	•s S F W	•s S F W
	—	—	—	—	—	—	—	—	—	•O O R	—	•R R R
	—	—	—	—	—	—	—	—	—	—	—	—
	—	C C C C	•U U U U	•O O O R	C C C C	•C C C C	•C C C C	•C C C C	U U O O	•C C C C	•U R U R	•O O O O
	—	R R	•C C C C	•U U U U	U O O U	•U U U U	•C C C C	•C C C C	O U U O	•C C C C	•U R U R	•C C C C
	—	—	U U	•O O O O	—	—	—	—	—	•O O R	—	•O O O R
	—	—	—	•R R R R	—	—	—	—	—	•O O O R	—	•R R R R
	•C U C C	•C C C C	•A A C C	•C C C U	C C C R	•C C C	•A C A	•C C C U	U U O	•C C C O	•C C U R	•C C C R
	—	—	U C U R	•U U U O	—	—	•O O O O	•U U U U	—	—	—	—
	—	O O	•C C U	•U U U	O O	U U	R R	U U U	—	•C C C	U U U	•O O R
	C C O	•C C R	•U U U	•C C C	—	—	—	—	U	•C C C	•U U	•R R R
	—	—	—	—	C U O	•C C C	•C C U	•C C C	—	—	—	—
	—	—	—	—	O R O	—	U	U U U	—	—	—	—
	—	—	—	—	O R R	—	—	R R	—	—	—	—
	—	—	•U U	—	U R R	—	•U U	U U	—	—	—	—
	—	•C C O	—	•R R R	U R	•C C C	—	•C C U	—	•O O O	C A C	•O O O
	—	—	—	—	C R C	•C C C	•C C U	•A A C	—	—	•U U	•O O O
	—	O R	—	•R R R	—	—	—	—	—	O O O	•U U	•O O O
	—	O R	—	•U U U	—	—	—	—	—	•C C C	U U	•O O O
	—	R	—	—	—	—	—	—	—	—	•U U	—
	—	O R	•U C C	•C C C	—	—	—	—	O	O O O	•U U U	R R
	—	—	—	—	U O U R	•C C C	•C C U	•C C C	—	—	—	—
	O	•U U U R	—	—	—	—	—	—	U C	R R R	•C C C	R R
	•C C O	•R R	—	—	—	—	—	—	•U C	—	•O O	—
	—	—	—	—	C C U	•C C C	•C C U	•C C U	—	—	—	—
	—	—	—	—	—	—	—	—	—	—	—	—
	—	—	—	—	—	—	—	—	—	—	—	—
	•C C O	•C C R	R R R	—	—	—	—	—	•U U O	R R R	•U U U	•O O
	•O C O	•C C R	—	—	C C U	•C C C	•C C O	•C C U	U O	O O O	•O O O	•O O O
	—	—	—	—	—	—	—	—	—	—	—	—
	U C C U	•C U C C	• U U R	•U U U	R	C C C C	•C U C C	•C C C U	•C C C A	O O O	•A A A A	•O O O O
	—	—	—	—	C C U	•C C C	•U U	•A A U	—	—	O O O	—
	U O	•C U C	•C C U R	•U U U	C U C	•A A A	•A A C	•A A C	R R	•A A A	•C A C	•C C
	•C C C	C O U	•C C C	•C C C	—	—	—	—	•O U O	•C C C	•C A C	•C C R
	•C C C	•C C U	•C C U R	•R R R	U U O	•U U U	•U U	•C C U	U U O	•O O O	O O O	•O O
	•C C C	•C C O	•U U	—	U O O	U U U	•U U	•C C U	A A C	•C C C	•C A C	•R R
	•C C C	•C C R	•C C U	—	O R	U U U	•U U U	•U U U	A A C	•A A C	•C A C	•A A O
	C	•A A C	•C C U	•C C C	C C C	•C C C	•C C C	•A A C	• U	•C C C	•C A C	•O O O
	—	—	U R R U	•A A A A	—	—	—	—	—	C C C C	—	•C C C C
	O O	O	•C C C C	•C C C C	—	—	—	—	U	•C C C C	R R R R	•O O O O
	—	—	—	—	A C C O	•C C C C	•A A A A	•C C C C	—	—	—	—
	—	—	R R R R	—	—	—	—	—	—	—	R R R R	—
	—	—	—	•C C C U	—	—	—	—	—	•C C C C	R R R R	•C C C C
	•C C C C	•C C C C	—	—	—	—	—	—	•C C C C	•C C C C	R R	•C C C C
	•C C C C	•C C U O	•U U U U	R R R	C C C C	•U U U U	•A A A A	•C C C C	U U R	•O O O O	U U	•O O O
	—	—	•A A A A	—	—	—	—	—	—	—	—	—
	—	—	—	—	—	—	—	—	—	—	—	—
	O O O O	•C C C C	R R R R	•C C C C	—	—	O O O	—	—	•C C C C	U U U	•C C C C
	U U U U	•C C C C	•C U C C	•R R R	A A A A	•C C C C	•A A A A	•C C C C	U U	•C C C C	•U U U C	•R R R R
	—	—	R U	•C C C C	—	—	—	—	O	•C C C C	U U U C	•C C C C
	—	—	•C C C A	—	—	—	—	—	—	—	—	—
	—	—	—	—	—	—	—	—	—	—	O O O O	—
	—	—	—	—	—	U U U U	R R	•C C C C	—	—	—	—

STATE-NUMBER OF BIRD LIST REFUGE, SANCTUARY OR PRESERVE NESTING, ABUNDANCE BY SEASON	VA-4 Dismal Sw. •s S F W	VA-5 Mason Neck •s S F W	VA-6 Presquile •s S F W	VA-7 Shenandoah •s S F W	WA-1 Columbia •s S F W	WA-2 Nisqually •s S F W	WA-3 Dungeness •s S F W	WA-4 Ridgefield •s S F W	WA-5 Turnbull •s S F W
BUSHTITS									
Bushtit	—	—	—	—	—	•C C C C	•U U U U	•C C C C	—
NUTHATCHES									
Red-breasted Nuthatch	•R U U	O O O	O O R	U U U	R R O	•C C C C	•C C C C	O O O O	•O O O O
White-breasted Nuthatch	•C C C C	•C C C C	U U U U	C C C C	—	—	—	•C C C C	•C U C C
Pygmy Nuthatch	—	—	—	—	—	—	—	—	•A A A A
Brown-headed Nuthatch	•U U U U	—	—	—	—	—	—	—	—
CREEPERS									
Brown Creeper	•R O O	•U U C	C C C	C C C	O	•U U U U	•U U U U	•O O O O	•O R O O
WRENS									
Cactus Wren	—	—	—	—	—	—	—	—	—
Rock Wren	—	—	—	—	•U U U O	—	—	—	•O U O O
Canyon Wren	—	—	—	—	•U O U O	—	—	—	U U U U
Carolina Wren	•C C C C	•A A A A	C C C C	C C C C	—	—	—	—	—
Bewick's Wren	—	—	R R R	O O	—	•C C C C	•C C C C	•C C C C	—
House Wren	•U U O R	•U U U R	C C C O	U U U	O	U	•U C U	•O O	•C A U
Winter Wren	R U U	O O O	C C C	U U U U	U O	•C C C C	•C C C C	U U U	R R O
Sedge Wren	—	—	—	—	—	—	—	—	—
Marsh Wren	O	•U U U R	O O O	—	•C U U U	•C C C C	•U U U U	•U U O O	•A A C R
DIPPERS									
American Dipper	—	—	—	—	—	—	U R U U	—	—
OLD WORLD WARBLERS & THRUSHES									
Arctic Warbler	—	—	—	—	—	—	—	—	—
Golden-crowned Kinglet	O U U	U U U	C C C	C C C	O O	•C C C C	•C C C C	C O C C	U O O U
Ruby-crowned Kinglet	O U U	U U U	C C C	C C U	U O U	U U C	U U C	U O O	• U R O
Blue-gray Gnatcatcher	•C C U	•C C C	U C U	C C C	—	—	—	—	—
Black-tailed Gnatcatcher	—	—	—	—	—	—	—	—	—
Eastern Bluebird	•U U U O	•U U U U	C C C C	C C C U	—	—	—	—	—
Western Bluebird	—	—	—	—	R	—	R	R R	•U U C
Mountain Bluebird	—	—	—	—	R	—	—	—	•C O C
Townsend's Solitaire	—	—	—	—	U U O O	—	U U U	—	•O R O O
Veery	O R	O R O	—	C C C	—	—	—	—	•U U
Gray-cheeked Thrush	O R	U U	U U U	U U	—	—	—	—	—
Swainson's Thrush	O R	U U	U R U	C C	R	• C C	•U U U	•U U U	O O
Hermit Thrush	O U C	C R C C	U U U	C C U	R O	—	•U U U	R R	O O
Wood Thrush	•C C U	•A A A	C C C	A A C	—	—	—	—	—
American Robin	•U U C C	•A C A C	C C C U	A C A U	•U U U U	•C C C C	•C C C A	•C C C C	•C A C O
Varied Thrush	—	—	—	—	O O	U C	•C U C C	U U C	O O R
Wrentit	—	—	—	—	—	—	—	—	—
MOCKINGBIRDS, THRASHERS & ALLIES									
Gray Catbird	•C C C C	•C C C O	C C C O	A A A	R R	—	—	—	•O O O
Northern Mockingbird	•U U U U	•C C C C	A A A A	U U U U	—	—	—	—	R
Sage Thrasher	—	—	—	—	•O O O	—	—	—	—
Brown Thrasher	•U U U U	•C C C O	C C C C	C C C	—	—	—	—	—
Long-billed Thrasher	—	—	—	—	—	—	—	—	—
Bendire's Thrasher	—	—	—	—	—	—	—	—	—
Curve-billed Thrasher	—	—	—	—	—	—	—	—	—
Crissal Thrasher	—	—	—	—	—	—	—	—	—
Le Conte's Thrasher	—	—	—	—	—	—	—	—	—
WAGTAILS & PIPITS									
American Pipit	O O O	—	U U C	O O	U O U	U U R	•U U U U	C U C U	C C
Sprague's Pipit	—	—	—	—	—	—	—	—	—
WAXWINGS									
Bohemian Waxwing	—	—	—	—	O	—	R R R	—	R U U
Cedar Waxwing	C R U C	•C U U C	U U U	C C C C	R O	•U C C R	C C C	•U U O O	• U U
SILKY-FLYCATCHERS									
Phainopepla	—	—	—	—	—	—	—	—	—
SHRIKES									
Northern Shrike	—	—	—	O	R R O O	R U U	U U	O O O	U U C
Loggerhead Shrike	R R R	R R	C C C C	O O O O	•U U O O	—	—	—	O R O
STARLINGS									
European Starling	U U U U	•U U U U	A A A A	C C C C	•C C C C	•A A A A	•A A A A	•C C C C	A C C
VIREOS									
White-eyed Vireo	•C C C	•U C C	C C C	U U U	—	—	—	—	—
Bell's Vireo	—	—	—	—	—	—	—	—	—
Black-capped Vireo	—	—	—	—	—	—	—	—	—
Gray Vireo	—	—	—	—	—	—	—	—	—
Solitary Vireo	O O	•O O	—	C C C	R O O	•U U U	•U C U	U O	•O U O
Yellow-throated Vireo	•U U U	•U U U	U C U	C U C	—	—	—	—	—
Hutton's Vireo	—	—	—	—	—	•U U U U	R R R R	R R R	—
Warbling Vireo	O R	O O	—	O O O	O O O	•U C U	•U C U	•U U O	•U U U
Philadelphia Vireo	O O	—	—	O O	—	—	—	—	—

	WA-6 McNary (s S F W)	WA-7 Toppenish (s S F W)	WA-8 Willapa (s S F W)	WA-9 Mt. Rainier (s S F W)	WI-1 Schlitz (s S F W)	WI-2 Horicon (s S F W)	WI-3 Necedah (s S F W)	WI-4 La Crosse (s S F W)	WY-1 Hutton L. (s S F W)	WY-2 Jackson H. (s S F W)	WY-3 Seedskadee (s S F W)	WY-4 Yellowstone (s S F W)
	—	R R	•U U U U	—	—	—	—	—	—	—	U U U U	—
	O O O C	R R	•C C C C	•C C C U	U O U U	U U	O R O R	O O O	—	•C C C C	O O U U	•C C C C
	—	•U U O O	—	•R R R R	U U U C	•C C C C	•C C C C	•C C C C	O	•C C C C	U U U U	•O O O O
	—	—	—	•R R R R	—	—	—	—	—	—	R R	R R
	—	R R U O	•U U U U	•C C C U	U R U R	U U U	U U R	C O C U	C O	•O O O O	O O O O	•O O O R
	—	•U U O	—	—	—	—	—	—	—	•O O O O	•O C O	•C C C
	—	•O O O O	—	—	R	—	—	O O O	—	—	•O C O	—
	—	•U U U U	•C C U U	—	R	—	—	O O	—	—	•O C O	•O O O
	•C C C	•C C O	•C C C U	—	C C U	•C C C	•C C C	•A A C	—	•C C C	•C C O	•O O O
	—	—	•C C C C	•C C C C	U U R	—	O O	U U R	—	R	—	—
	—	U U O	—	—	O R R	•C C C	•U U U	•U U U	—	—	—	—
	•C C C R	•C C C U	•C C C C	—	R	•C C C	•C C C	•C C U	•U U O	•C C C	•O C O	•R R
	—	R R	U R U U	•C C C C	—	—	—	—	—	C C C C	•O O O U	•C C C C
	U U U U	C C U	•C U C C	•C C C	C C U	U U	U U O	U U U	—	O O O R	•U U	•R R R
	C C C U	C C U	U U U	U U	A A R	C C	C C	C C	U U	•C C O R	•U U	•C C C
	—	—	—	—	U R R	•U U U	R R	•U U	—	—	—	—
	—	—	—	—	O R	U U U	U U U	•C C C R	—	—	—	—
	O O O	O R R	U R U U	•R R R	—	—	—	—	•C C C	•C C C	•C A C	•C C O
	O O U	O R U R	U R R	•U U U	—	—	—	—	U O U	•C C O O	O O	•O O O R
	—	—	—	U U U	C R U	•U U U	•C C O	C C	—	O O O	•O O O	•O O O R
	—	—	•C C U	•U I U	C R C	U U U	C C	C C	U U	•C C O	•O O O	•O O R
	U U	U U R	U U U U	•C C U	C C R	U U U	U U	U U	•U U O	•C C O	•O O O	•C C O
					C U U	•U U U	•U U	•C C U				
	•C C C C	•A C C U	•A C C A	•C C C	A C C O	•A A A R	•A C A R	•A A A O	•C C U	•A A A R	•C C C O	•A A A R
	O	U O U	C U C A	•C C C	R	—	—	—	—	R	—	—
	—	—	—	—	—	—	—	—	—	—	—	—
	—	•U U O	—	—	C C C	•C C C	•C C C	•C C C	—	O O R	•O O	•R R R
	—	—	—	—	R	—	—	R R	—	—	O O	—
	n	•C C	—	—	—	—	—	—	C U	•O O O	•U U U	R R
	—	—	—	—	C C U	•C C C	•C C C	•C C C	—	—	•O U O	—
	—	—	—	—	—	—	—	—	—	—	—	—
	—	—	—	—	—	—	—	—	—	—	—	—
	—	—	—	—	—	—	—	—	—	—	—	—
	C C C C	U U	U U U	•C C C	—	R R	—	U U	—	C C C R	•U U U	•O O C
	U C C	O U U	—	—	R	—	R	R	—	O R O	U C	O O
	O	•C U C R	•C U C U	•U U U	C C C U	•C C C U	•U C C R	•C C C U	U U	O O O O	U C	R R
	—	—	—	—	—	—	—	—	—	—	—	—
	O O O O	•U U U	U U C	—	R O O	U U	O U U	R O O	—	O O O	O O	O C O
	U U C	•C C C O	—	—	—	—	R R	•U U U	U O U R	O R O	•U U U U	O
	•A C C A	•A A A A	•C C C C	•O O O	A A C U	•C C C C	•U U U U	•A A A A	O U O O	•C C C O	•C C C C	•C C C O
	—	—	—	—	R R	—	—	—	R R	—	—	—
	—	—	—	—	—	U U U	—	—	•U U	—	—	—
	—	O O	•U U U	•O O O	U R O	U U	U U	U U	U O	R R	•U U U	R
	—	—	—	—	O R	U U U	•U U U	•C C C	—	—	—	—
	—	—	•U U U U	—	—	—	—	A A A	—	—	—	•C C O
	—	•U R U	•U U U	•C C C	U O R	•U U U	•U U	U U	—	•A A O	•U U U	•C C O
					O O	U U	U U	U U				

STATE-NUMBER OF BIRD LIST / REFUGE, SANCTUARY OR PRESERVE / NESTING, ABUNDANCE BY SEASON	VA-4 Dismal Sw. • s S F W	VA-5 Mason Neck • s S F W	VA-6 Presquile • s S F W	VA-7 Shenandoah • s S F W	WA-1 Columbia • s S F W	WA-2 Nisqually • s S F W	WA-3 Dungeness • s S F W	WA-4 Ridgefield • s S F W	WA-5 Turnbull • s S F W
VIREOS (cont.)									
Red-eyed Vireo	•A A C	•A A A	C A C	A A A	—	•U U U	•U C U	R R	•O O
Black-whiskered Vireo	—	—	—	—	—	—	—	—	—
WOOD-WARBLERS									
Bachman's Warbler	—	—	—	—	—	—	—	—	—
Blue-winged Warbler	C U	O U	R R R	U O	—	—	—	—	—
Golden-winged Warbler	O U	O U	—	U O	—	—	—	—	—
Tennessee Warbler	U U	U U	—	U C	—	—	—	—	—
Orange-crowned Warbler	—	—	R R	U U	O O U	•C C C R	•C A C	•C U O	O O
Nashville Warbler	O O	R O	—	U U	O O O	—	R R	O O O	O O O
Virginia's Warbler	—	—	—	—	—	—	—	—	—
Lucy's Warbler	—	—	—	—	—	—	—	—	—
Northern Parula	•U U U	•C C C	A A A	C C C	—	—	—	—	—
Tropical Parula	—	—	—	—	—	—	—	—	—
Yellow Warbler	•U U U	•U O U	U U U	U U	•O O U	•C C C	•C C C	•U U U	•C A C
Chestnut-sided Warbler	O U	O U	O R O	C C C	—	—	—	—	—
Magnolia Warbler	O O	C C	—	U C	—	—	—	—	—
Cape May Warbler	O O	U U	U O U	U C	—	—	—	—	—
Black-throated Blue Warbler	U U	C C	O R O	C U C	—	—	—	—	—
Yellow-rumped Warbler	C U C	C C C	C C C	A A U	U O C	•C C C U	•C C C	C O O C	C C C
Black-throated Gray Warbler	—	—	—	—	—	•C C C	U C U	U R R	—
Townsend's Warbler	—	—	—	—	U U O	U U	•U C U R	O O O	O O
Hermit Warbler	—	—	—	—	—	—	R U U	—	—
Black-throated Green Warbler	•C C U	•U U	U O U	C U C	—	—	—	—	—
Blackburnian Warbler	O O	U U	—	C U C	—	—	—	—	—
Yellow-throated Warbler	•U U U	•U U U	C C C	O O O	—	—	—	—	—
Pine Warbler	•C C C U	•U U C	C C C R	U U U O	—	—	—	—	—
Prairie Warbler	•C C C O	•C C C	C C C	U U U	—	—	—	—	—
Palm Warbler	U U	U U R	O O	U U	—	—	—	—	—
Bay-breasted Warbler	O O	U U	—	C C	—	—	—	—	—
Blackpoll Warbler	U O	C O U	C O C	C C	—	—	—	—	—
Cerulean Warbler	O	•U U U	—	U U U	—	—	—	—	—
Black-and-white Warbler	•U C C	•C U C	C C C	C C C	—	—	—	—	—
American Redstart	•C C C	•C C C	C C C	A A C	—	—	—	—	•U U
Prothonotary Warbler	•A A C	•U U U	A A A	—	—	—	—	—	—
Worm-eating Warbler	•U U U	•U U U	—	U U U	—	—	—	—	—
Swainson's Warbler	•U U U	—	—	—	—	—	—	—	—
Ovenbird	•A A C	•A C A	C C C	A A C	—	—	—	—	—
Northern Waterthrush	C U U	C C	—	O O	—	—	—	—	—
Louisiana Waterthrush	•C C C	•U U U	C C C	C C C	—	—	—	—	—
Kentucky Warbler	•R R R	•U U U	C C U	U U U	—	—	—	—	—
Connecticut Warbler	—	O O	—	O	—	—	—	—	—
Mourning Warbler	—	R O	—	O O O	—	—	—	—	—
MacGillivray's Warbler	—	—	—	—	U O U	•C C C	•U C U	•U U R	O O O
Common Yellowthroat	•C C C U	•C C C O	A A A R	C C C	•O O	•C C C	•U C U	•C C U	•C C C
Hooded Warbler	•C C C	•O O O	C C C	C C C	—	—	—	—	—
Wilson's Warbler	R R	—	—	U U	•U U O	•C C C	•C C C	U O O	O O O
Canada Warbler	O O O	U U	—	C U C	—	—	—	—	—
Painted Redstart	—	—	—	—	—	—	—	—	—
Yellow-breasted Chat	•U U U	•U U U	C C C	U U U	•U U O	—	—	R R	O O
TANAGERS									
Hepatic Tanager	—	—	—	—	—	—	—	—	—
Summer Tanager	•U U U	U O O	U C U	O O	—	—	—	—	—
Scarlet Tanager	•U R R	•C C A	U U U	C C C	—	—	—	—	—
Western Tanager	—	—	—	—	O O	•U C U	•U C U	•U U O	•O R O
CARDINALS, GROSBEAKS & ALLIES									
Northern Cardinal	•C C C C	•A A A A	A A A A	C C C C	—	—	—	—	—
Pyrrhuloxia	—	—	—	—	—	—	—	—	—
Rose-breasted Grosbeak	U U	U U	O O	C C C	—	—	—	—	—
Black-headed Grosbeak	—	—	—	—	—	•U C U	•U C U	•C C O	•O U O
Blue Grosbeak	•U U O	O O O	U U U	U U U	—	—	—	—	—
Lazuli Bunting	—	—	—	—	•O O	—	O U O	—	•R R
Indigo Bunting	•C C U	•A A A	C A C	A A C	—	—	—	—	—
Painted Bunting	—	—	—	—	—	—	—	—	—
Dickcissel	—	—	O O	—	—	—	—	—	—
NEW WORLD SPARROWS & ALLIES									
Olive Sparrow	—	—	—	—	—	—	—	—	—
Green-tailed Towhee	—	—	—	—	—	—	—	—	—
Rufous-sided Towhee	•C C C C	•C C C U	C C C C	A A A O	O O	•C C C C	•C C C C	•C C C C	O U U
Brown Towhee	—	—	—	—	—	—	—	—	—
Abert's Towhee	—	—	—	—	—	—	—	—	—
Bachman's Sparrow	—	—	O O O	O	—	—	—	—	—

	WA-6 McNary (•s S F W)	WA-7 Toppenish (•s S F W)	WA-8 Willapa (•s S F W)	WA-9 Mt. Rainier (•s S F W)	WI-1 Schlitz (•s S F W)	WI-2 Horicon (•s S F W)	WI-3 Necedah (•s S F W)	WI-4 La Crosse (•s S F W)	WY-1 Hutton L. (•s S F W)	WY-2 Jackson H. (•s S F W)	WY-3 Seedskadee (•s S F W)	WY-4 Yellowstone (•s S F W)
	— —	— —	— —	— —	C U U	•C C C	•C C C	•C C A	—	O O	—	R
	— —	— —	— —	— —	O R	R R	—	•U U	—	—	—	—
	—	—	R	—	U R O	U U	U U	U U U	—	R	—	—
	—	—	—	—	C U	C C	C C	C C	—	—	—	—
	—	•C U C	•C U	•U U U	U U	U U U	U U	U U	O U	O O O	•U U U	•R R R
	—	U O	U C U	•U U U	C U	U U	•C O C	C C	—	—	—	—
	C U	•C C U	•U C C	•U U U	U O O	•C C C	•C C	•A A O	•U C O	•A A C	•U U U	•C C O
	—	—	—	—	C R U	C C	•U U U	U U	—	—	—	—
	—	—	—	—	A R A	C C	U U	U U	—	—	—	—
	—	—	—	—	U U	U U	R R	U U	—	—	—	—
	—	—	—	—	O O	U U	R R	R R	—	—	—	—
	O U U	C A U	•C C C U	•U U U	A A R	A A	•A O A	A A	O U O	•A A C	•O O O	•C C C
	—	—	•C U C	•U U U	—	—	—	—	—	R R	O O O	•R R
	—	O R O	•U	•U U U	—	—	—	—	—	—	—	—
	—	—	—	•R R	—	—	—	—	—	—	—	—
	—	—	—	—	C R C	C C	O O	U U	—	—	—	—
	—	—	—	—	C U	C C	O O	U U	—	—	—	—
	—	—	—	—	O O	U U	•U U U	O O	—	—	—	—
	—	—	—	—	R	—	—	—	—	—	—	—
	—	—	—	—	C C	C C	U U	C C	—	—	—	—
	—	—	—	—	C C	C C	U U	U U	—	—	—	—
	—	—	—	—	U U	U U	U U	U U	—	—	—	—
	—	—	—	—	O R	U U	—	•U U	—	—	—	—
	—	—	—	—	A O C	C C	U U U	C C	—	—	U U U	•R R
	—	—	—	—	A O A	•C U C	•U U U	•A A C	—	O O	—	—
	—	—	—	—	—	U U	—	•C C	—	—	—	—
	—	—	—	—	R	—	—	—	—	—	—	—
	—	—	—	—	C C C	•U U U	•C C U	•U U U	—	—	—	—
	—	—	—	—	C R C	C U	U U	U U	—	R R	—	R R
	—	—	—	—	R	U U	—	•O O O	—	—	—	—
	—	—	—	—	R H	—	—	•R R	—	—	—	—
	—	—	—	—	O O	—	O O	R R	—	—	—	—
	—	—	—	—	U O R	U U	U O	O O	—	—	—	—
	C C C	U O	•U U	•U U U	—	—	—	—	—	•C C O	•U U U	•O O O
	—	•C C U	•U U U	•O O O	C C U	•C C C	•C C C	•A A C	O	C C C	•U U U	•C C C
	—	—	—	—	R R	—	—	R R	—	—	—	—
	U C U	C O U	•U C U	U	C R U	U R U	U U	U U	—	C C C	U U U	•R R R
	—	—	—	—	C O U	U U	U R U	U U	—	—	—	—
	O O	•U U	—	—	R	—	—	•R R	—	—	•R R	—
	—	—	—	—	R	—	—	—	—	—	—	—
	—	—	—	—	U O O	•C U U	•C C U	•U U U	—	—	—	—
	O	C O U	•C C	•U U U	—	—	—	—	U R	•C C O	•O O O	•C C O
	—	—	—	—	C C C C	•U U U U	•O O O O	•C C C C	—	—	—	—
	—	—	—	—	C U U	•C C C	•C C C	•C C C	—	O	—	—
	—	•U C O	•U U	•R R R	—	—	—	—	R R R	•O C O	•O O O	R R
	—	•U C O	—	—	—	—	—	—	R U R	•O O R	•O O	•O O
	—	—	—	—	U U O	•C C C	•C C C	•C C C	—	—	—	—
	—	—	—	—	—	•U U U	—	•C C	—	—	—	—
	—	—	—	—	—	—	—	—	—	•O C C	•U U U	•C C C
	U U U U	•U O U U	•U U C C	—	U U U	•U U U	•C C C	•U U U	U U R	R R	O O	•R R

STATE-NUMBER OF BIRD LIST REFUGE, SANCTUARY OR PRESERVE NESTING, ABUNDANCE BY SEASON	VA-4 Dismal Sw. • s S F W	VA-5 Mason Neck • s S F W	VA-6 Presquile • s S F W	VA-7 Shenandoah • s S F W	WA-1 Columbia • s S F W	WA-2 Nisqually • s S F W	WA-3 Dungeness • s S F W	WA-4 Ridgefield • s S F W	WA-5 Turnbull • s S F W
NEW WORLD SPARROWS & ALLIES (cont.)									
Cassin's Sparrow	—	—	—	—	—	—	—	—	—
Rufous-crowned Sparrow	—	—	—	—	—	—	—	—	—
American Tree Sparrow	R O O	U O U	U U U	U U U	U U U	—	—	—	O O O
Chipping Sparrow	•U U O R	•U C C	C C C	C C C O	U U	—	•U C U	O O O O	•C A C
Clay-colored Sparrow	—	—	—	—	—	—	—	—	—
Brewer's Sparrow	—	—	—	—	•O O O	—	—	—	—
Field Sparrow	•U U U U	•U U U C	C C C C	C C C U	—	—	—	—	—
Black-chinned Sparrow	—	—	—	—	—	—	—	—	—
Vesper Sparrow	—	—	O O O	O O O	•O O O	—	R	—	•C A U
Lark Sparrow	—	—	—	—	•O U O	—	—	—	• U U
Black-throated Sparrow	—	—	—	—	—	—	—	—	—
Sage Sparrow	—	—	—	—	•O O O	—	—	—	—
Lark Bunting	—	—	—	—	—	—	—	—	—
Savannah Sparrow	U O U	U O	A A R	U U	•C O C	•C C C	•U C U	•C C U O	•C C C
Baird's Sparrow	—	—	—	—	—	—	—	—	—
Grasshopper Sparrow	—	—	C C C	O O	•C O C	—	—	—	• U
Henslow's Sparrow	—	—	R R R	O O	—	—	—	—	—
Le Conte's Sparrow	—	—	—	—	—	—	—	—	—
Sharp-tailed Sparrow	—	—	—	—	—	—	—	—	—
Seaside Sparrow	—	—	—	—	—	—	—	—	—
Fox Sparrow	U U	O O U	U U U	C U O	O O	U U C	•U O U U	O O U	O R O
Song Sparrow	•U U U U	•C C C C	C C C C	C C C U	•U U U U	•C C C C	•C C C C	•C C C C	•C A C U
Lincoln's Sparrow	—	O O	—	O O	R O	U U	O O	O O O	O O
Swamp Sparrow	U R O U	•U U U C	C C C	U U	—	—	—	—	—
White-throated Sparrow	U C C	A A A	A A A	A A U	—	—	—	—	R
Golden-crowned Sparrow	—	—	—	—	U U	U U C	•U U U R	U U U	—
White-crowned Sparrow	R R R	R R R	U U O	U U U	A A C	•U U U C	•C C C U	•C U U U	C R A R
Harris' Sparrow	—	—	—	—	—	—	—	—	—
Dark-eyed Junco	O C C	C C A	A A A	A C A A	C C C	•C C C A	•C C C C	•C C C C	•A C A A
McCown's Longspur	—	—	—	—	—	—	—	—	—
Lapland Longspur	—	—	—	O O O	—	—	R	—	—
Smith's Longspur	—	—	—	—	—	—	—	—	—
Chestnut-collared Longspur	—	—	—	—	—	—	—	—	—
Snow Bunting	—	—	—	U U	—	—	R O	—	—
NEW WORLD BLACKBIRDS & ORIOLES									
Bobolink	O R	—	C O C	O O	—	—	—	—	—
Red-winged Blackbird	•U U C C	•A A A A	A A A A	C U C	•A A C C	•C C C C	•C C C C	•C C C C	•A A A
Tricolored Blackbird	—	—	—	—	—	—	—	—	—
Eastern Meadowlark	O O O R	•O O O O	A A A A	U U U U	—	—	—	—	—
Western Meadowlark	—	—	—	—	•C C C U	•U U U U	•C C C C	•U O U O	•C A A O
Yellow-headed Blackbird	—	—	—	—	•C C U U	•U U U	—	•U U	•A A U
Rusty Blackbird	O O O	U U U	C C R	O O	—	—	—	—	—
Brewer's Blackbird	R R	—	—	—	•C U U C	•C C C C	•C C C C	•C C C C	•C C C
Great-tailed Grackle	O O O O	—	—	—	—	—	—	—	—
Boat-tailed Grackle	—	—	—	—	—	—	—	—	—
Common Grackle	•C C C C	•A A A C	A A A R	A C A	—	—	—	—	—
Bronzed Cowbird	—	—	—	—	—	—	—	—	—
Brown-headed Cowbird	•C C C C	•U U U U	C C C C	C C C	•C C C C	•U C U R	•C C U U	•U U U O	•C C
Orchard Oriole	•U U	•O O O	C C C R	U U	—	—	—	—	—
Hooded Oriole	—	—	—	—	—	—	—	—	—
Baltimore Oriole	—	—	—	—	—	—	—	—	—
Bullock's Oriole	U U O R	•U U U	R R R	U U U	• U U	• U	R U R	•U U O	•O U
Scott's Oriole	—	—	—	—	—	—	—	—	—
FINCHES									
Rosy Finch	—	—	—	—	R	—	—	—	R O
Pine Grosbeak	—	—	—	O O	—	—	—	—	R R
Purple Finch	O U	U U U	U U U	C C C	—	•C C C C	•U U U U	•U U U U	—
Cassin's Finch	—	—	—	—	—	—	—	—	•O O O O
House Finch	—	—	—	U U	U O O U	•C C C C	•C C C C	•C C C C	•O U U O
Red Crossbill	—	—	—	O O O O	R R	U U U	U U U U	O R R R	•U O U
White-winged Crossbill	—	—	—	O	—	—	—	—	—
Common Redpoll	—	—	—	O	—	—	R	—	O O O
Hoary Redpoll	—	—	—	—	—	—	—	—	—
Pine Siskin	O U U	O O O	R R O	C C U	R O	•C C C C	•C C C C	•O O O O	R O O O
Lesser Goldfinch	—	—	—	—	—	—	—	—	—
Lawrence's Goldfinch	—	—	—	—	—	—	—	—	—
American Goldfinch	•C U U C	•C C C C	C C C R	A A C C	•O O O U	•U C C U	•C A C U	•C C C O	•U C C R
Evening Grosbeak	O O U	O O	O	C C C	R R	C R C U	U U R	O	U U U U
OLD WORLD SPARROWS									
House Sparrow	—	•U U U U	A A A A	U U U U	•C U C U	—	•C C C C	•U U U U	•U U U
Eurasian Tree Sparrow	—	—	—	—	—	—	—	—	—

	WA-6 McNary	WA-7 Toppenish	WA-8 Willapa	WA-9 Mt. Rainier	WI-1 Schlitz	WI-2 Horicon	WI-3 Necedah	WI-4 La Crosse	WY-1 Hutton L.	WY-2 Jackson H.	WY-3 Seedskadee	WY-4 Yellowstone
	• s S F W	• s S F W	• s S F W	• s S F W	• s S F W	• s S F W	• s S F W	• s S F W	• s S F W	• s S F W	• s S F W	• s S F W
	—	—	—	—	—	—	—	—	—	—	—	—
	O O	O	R R R	—	—	U U	C C A	C C C	C A A	—	O O O	U U C	R R R
	—	• O O R	U U U	• U U U	O O R	• U U U	• U U U	• A A A	U C	—	• C C C	• U U U U	• C C C
	R	• C C R	—	—	R R R	U U	• U U U	U U	—	O U O	• C C C	• U C U	• C C C
	—	—	—	—	C U U	• U U U	• C C C	• C C C R	—	—	—	—	—
	• C C C	• U U O	—	—	R R R	• C C C	• C C C	• C C C	• U C O	• C C C	• C C O	• C C C
	O	• O O	—	—	R	R R R	—	• U U	• U C U	O O	• U U U	• O O
	—	• C C O	—	—	—	—	—	—	• C C C	R R	O O O	O O
	U U U	• C C C	• U C U R	R R	U U O	• C C C	• U U U	• C C C	• C C C	C C C	• U U U	• C C C
	—	• O O	—	—	R R	• U U U	• R R	• U U U	U O	—	• U U U	R R
	—	—	—	—	R R	• U U U	• R R	• U U R	—	—	—	—
	—	—	—	—	R R	—	—	R R R	—	—	—	—
	O O C	• U U R	U U U C	• U U U	U U	U U	U U	U U	—	• O O	• O O	• R R
	• C C C C	• C C C C	• C C C C	• U U U	A C C R	• C C C	• A A A	• A A A O	C U	• C C C O	• O O O O	• C C C
	—	U U R	—	• U U U	U U	U U	R U	U U	U C U	• O C C	• O O	• O O
	—	—	—	—	C O U	• A A A	• C C C	• C C C R	—	—	—	—
	—	R	R	C U C	• O O O	A C R	C C	C C	C C R	—	R R	U U U	R
	R	U U O	C U C	—	U U	U U	U U	U U R	C C	• A A A R	C U C C	• C C C
	• A C A A	A C C	• C U U C	—	R R	R R	R R	R	O O	R R R	C U C	—
	U U U C	A C A	• C C C A	• A A A C	C C C	U U C	A A U	A A A	U U	• A A C O	C O U	• A A C O
	—	—	R U U R	—	—	U U U	O O	R R R	—	• O O O U	—	O O O R	• R R
	—	—	—	—	—	U U U	O O	R R	—	—	O	O O
	—	—	U	R	R R	U U U	U U C	U U	U O O U	O	O O O R	R
	—	• U U R	—	—	U U R	• C C C	U U U	• U U U	U	O O	O O O	R R
	• A A A U	• A A A C	• C C U U	• C C C	A A U R	• A A A U	• A A A	• A A A U	• O A C	• C C C O	• C C C	• C C C
	—	—	—	—	U U O	• C C C	• U U U	• C C C O	—	—	—	—
	• A C O O	• O O O U	• O O U	—	—	• C C C R	• O O O	• A A A O	• C A C	• O O O	• C C C	• C C C
	• A A A	• C C U O	R R	—	—	• A A A	R R	• U U U	• A A C	• C C C	• C C C	• C C C
	—	—	—	—	R R	C C	C C	C C O	• A C C	—	—	—
	• A A A U	• A A C U	• A C C A	O O	—	U U U	• U U O	• U U U R	• A A C	• C C A O	• C C C	• C C C
	—	—	—	—	—	—	—	—	—	—	—	—
	—	—	—	—	A A C R	• A A A U	• C C C	• A A A U	O U	O O O	—	—
	—	• U U O O	• C C U C	—	A C U	• C C C R	• C C O	• A A U R	• C C U	• C C C	• C C C	• O O O
	—	—	—	—	R O	—	—	• U U	—	—	—	—
	—	—	—	—	—	—	—	—	U U	• O O O	• U U	• R R
	• O U O	• C C R	—	—	C C U	• C C U	• C C O	• C C	—	—	—	—
	—	—	—	• C C C	—	—	—	—	O C	• C C O O	U C	• O O O O
	—	—	—	• U U U	R R O	—	R R	R R	—	O O O O	—	• C C C O
	O O O	—	U U U U	• U U U	U R U U	U	U O U O	C C U	—	—	U U	—
	U U	—	—	—	—	—	—	—	—	• C C C O	• O O O O	• C C C O
	• U U O O	• A A A C	• C U U C	—	—	—	—	—	• U U R	—	• O O O	—
	R R	—	• C U U C	• U U U	R O R	—	R R R R	R R R	—	O O O O	—	• O O O R
	—	—	U U	R R R	O O O	U	U U C	R R	—	—	U C	R R R
	—	—	—	—	O O O	—	—	U U R	—	C O O	—	—
	—	U U	• C U C A	• C C C U	C R C C	—	U U R	U U U	U U	• C C C O	R	• A A A O
	—	—	—	—	—	—	—	R	—	—	—	—
	• A A A	• C C C U	• A U C A	• O O	C C C C	• C C C C	• C C C C	• A A A C	U O U	• O O O	• O O O	• R R R
	C O O	• U O U	C U C U	• O O O R	O U U	O U U	U U U	O O U	—	• C O C C	O O U	• O O O
	• A A A A	• A A A A	• U U U U	• O O O	U U U U	• A A A A	• O O O O	• A A A A	• U C C U	• C C C C	• C C C C	R R R R
	—	—	—	—	—	—	—	—	—	—	—	—

FIELD GUIDE INDEX

BIRD FAMILY & SPECIES	ABA Code	Male ♂	Female ♀	Immature ○	Audubon McGraw East	West	Nat'l. Geo.	Gold.	Peterson's East	West	Audubon Alfred Knopf East	West	Master#
LOONS													
Red-throated Loon	1				73	74	20	18	32	24	186	166	34(1)
Arctic Loon	1				—	75	18	18	32	24	187	167	36(1)
Pacific Loon					72	75	18	—	32	24	—	—	—
Common Loon	1				72	77	18	18	32	24	188	169	36(1)
Yellow-billed Loon	2				—	76	18	18	32	24	—	168	38(1)
GREBES													
Least Grebe	2				77	107	22	20	298	26	177	—	—
Pied-billed Grebe	1				76	107	22	20	34	26	180	176	40(1)
Horned Grebe	1				80	75	22	20	34	26	184	181	42(1)
Red-necked Grebe	1				74	79	20	20	34	26	185	175	44(1)
Eared Grebe	1				75	81	22	20	34	26	183	180	44(1)
Western Grebe	1				—	20	20	20	34	26	—	174	46(1)
SHEARWATERS & PETRELS													
Northern Fulmar	2				56	55	26	24	76	78	40	25	54(1)
Cory's Shearwater	2				58	—	28	24	74	—	79	—	56(1)
Pink-footed Shearwater	2				—	54	30	24	—	76	—	65	58(1)
Greater Shearwater	2				58	—	26	24	74	—	80	—	60(1)
Sooty Shearwater	1				58	53	26	24	74	76	81	66	64(1)
Short-tailed Shearwater	2				—	53	26	26	—	76	—	69	64(1)
Manx Shearwater	2				58	—	28	28	74	76	—	67	66(1)
Audubon's Shearwater	2				58	—	28	28	74	—	—	—	68(1)
STORM-PETRELS													
Wilson's Storm-Petrel	2				57	—	34	30	76	80	82	—	70(1)
Fork-tailed Storm-Petrel	2				—	50	36	30	—	80	—	—	72(1)
Leach's Storm-Petrel	2				57	50	34	30	76	80	83	62	72(1)
BOOBIES & GANNETS													
Masked Booby	4				55	—	42	34	80	82	—	—	80(1)
Brown Booby	3				54	58	42	34	80	82	77	60	82(1)
Northern Gannet	1				55	—	40	34	80	—	76	—	86(1)
PELICANS													
American White Pelican	1				67	69	40	32	78	84	175	154	88(1)
Brown Pelican	1				66	68	40	32	78	84	176	155	90(1)
CORMORANTS													
Great Cormorant	1				68	—	44	36	40	—	102	—	92(1)
Double-crested Cormorant	1				69	70	46	36	40	28	99	76	94(1)
Olivaceous Cormorant	1				70	71	44	36	40	28	101	—	94(1)
Brandt's Cormorant	1				—	73	46	36	—	28	—	77	96(1)
Pelagic Cormorant	1				—	72	46	36	—	28	—	74	98(1)
Red-faced Cormorant	2				—	—	46	36	—	28	—	75	100(1)
ANHINGAS													
Anhinga	1				71	—	44	36	40	—	100	—	102(1)
FRIGATEBIRDS													
Magnificent Frigatebird	1				52	—	38	34	78	84	85	57	104(1)
BITTERNS & HERONS													
American Bittern	1				129	130	48	98	104	114	24	12	106(1)
Least Bittern	1				131	128	48	98	104	114	17	11	108(1)
Great Blue Heron	1				139	134	54	94	100	110	14	15	108(1)
Great Egret	1				135	135	52	94	100	110	2	3	110(1)
Snowy Egret	1				134	133	52	94	102	112	1	1	112(1)
Little Blue Heron	1				137	—	50	96	100	110	16	—	112(1)
Tricolored Heron	1				140	135	50	96	100	110	13	—	114(1)
Reddish Egret	1				138	—	50	96	100	110	15	—	114(1)
Cattle Egret	1				136	132	52	94	102	112	4	5	116(1)
Green-backed Heron	1				133	130	50	96	104	110	18	7	118(1)
Black-crowned Night-Heron	1				132	131	48	98	104	114	20	8	118(1)
Yellow-crowned Night-Heron	1				141	—	48	98	104	114	19	—	120(1)
IBISES & SPOONBILLS													
White Ibis	1				145	—	56	100	108	112	25	—	122(1)
Glossy Ibis	1				144	138	56	100	108	—	27	—	124(1)
White-faced Ibis	1				144	138	56	100	108	114	28	14	124(1)
Roseate Spoonbill	1				147	—	56	100	110	112	11	—	126(1)
STORKS													
Wood Stork	1				146	139	54	100	106	116	9	13	128(1)
SWANS, GEESE & DUCKS													
Fulvous Whistling-Duck	1				107	94	76	52	48	42	166	122	134(1)
Black-bellied Whistling-Duck	1				106	—	76	52	298	42	168	—	134(1)
Tundra Swan	1				119	112	60	40	43	38	174	156	136(1)
Trumpeter Swan	1				—	113	60	60	42	38	—	157	140(1)
Mute Swan	1				118	122	60	40	42	38	173	—	140(1)
Greater White-fronted Goose	1				113	117	62	44	44	40	169	165	144(1)
Snow Goose	1				116	115	64	44	42	38	171	159	144(1)

Note: Bold print denotes plate number—not page number

BIRD FAMILY & SPECIES	ABA Code	Male ♂	Female ♀	Immature ○	Audubon McGraw East	West	Nat'l. Geo.	Gold.	Peterson's East	West	Audubon Alfred Knopf East	West	Master#
SWANS, GEESE & DUCKS (cont.)					Note: Bold print denotes plate number—not page number								
Ross' Goose	1				117	114	64	44	42	40	—	158	146(1)
Emperor Goose	2				—	—	64	42	—	40	—	160	148(1)
Brant	1				114	116	66	42	44	40	172	164	148(1)
Canada Goose	1				115	118	66	42	44	40	170	162	150(1)
Wood Duck	1				96	97	78	52	50	46	119	144	152(1)
Green-winged Teal	1				94	91	70	50	52	48	105	121	154(1)
American Black Duck	1				111	—	68	46	48	44	133	—	156(1)
Mottled Duck	1				110	—	68	46	48				158(1)
Mallard	1				93	98	68	46	48	44	207	97	158(1)
Northern Pintail	1				105	88	72	48	50	46	115	124	160(1)
Blue-winged Teal	1				104	89	74	50	52	48	136	120	164(1)
Cinnamon Teal	1				108	93	74	50	52	48	112	117	164(1)
Northern Shoveler	1				92	99	74	50	52	48	108	96	166(1)
Gadwall	1				103	90	70	48	48	44	135	125	168(1)
Eurasian Wigeon	3				102	87	72	48	—	46	—	118	168(1)
American Wigeon	1				92	95	72	48	50	46	106	119	170(1)
Canvasback	1				101	85	78	54	58	56	110	95	172(1)
Redhead	1				100	86	78	54	58	56	109	94	174(1)
Ring-necked Duck	1				82	102	80	54	58	56	121	90	176(1)
Greater Scaup	1				89	100	80	54	58	56	124	98	178(1)
Lesser Scaup	1				88	101	80	54	58	56	123	92	180(1)
Common Eider	1				81	111	82	58	56	52	117	109	182(1)
King Eider	1				80	111	82	58	56	52	118	106	184(1)
Steller's Eider	2				—	—	82	58	—	54		108	188(1)
Harlequin Duck	1				97	96	84	56	—	54	128	115	190(1)
Oldsquaw	1				87	106	86	60	56	54	116	98	192(1)
Black Scoter	1				78	110	84	60	54	50	131	110	192(1)
Surf Scoter	1				79	190	84	60	—	50	129	113	194(1)
White-winged Scoter	1				112	108	84	60	54	50	130	112	196(1)
Common Goldeneye	1				85	104	86	56	60	58	126	105	196(1)
Barrow's Goldeneye	1				84	105	86	56	60	58	125	104	198(1)
Bufflehead	1				86	103	86	56	60	58	127	103	200(1)
Hooded Merganser	1				98	82	88	62	62	60	128	102	202(1)
Common Merganser	1				90	84	88	62	62	60	114	101	204(1)
Red-breasted Merganser	1				91	83	88	62	62	60	113	100	204(1)
Ruddy Duck	1				99	95	76	62	60	58	111	116	206(1)
Masked Duck	4				109	—	76	62	298	—	—	—	208(1)
AMERICAN VULTURES													
Black Vulture	1				215	200	182	66	160	182	318	306	210(1)
Turkey Vulture	1				214	204	182	66	160	182	317	307	212(1)
KITES, EAGLES, HAWKS & ALLIES													
Osprey	1				224	214	200	78	158	184	306	304	216(1)
American Swallow-tailed Kite	1				227	—	186	68	150	—	302	—	218(1)
Black-shouldered Kite	1				226	219	186	68	—	170	—	—	220(1)
Snail Kite	2				220	—	188	68	150	—	—	—	220(1)
Mississippi Kite	1				221	218	186	68	150	170	304	—	222(1)
Bald Eagle	1				216	209	184	78	158	170	305	335	224(1)
Northern Harrier	1				235	215	188	70	152	170	309	317	224(1)
Sharp-shinned Hawk	1				240	220	190	70	152	172	294	325	226(1)
Cooper's Hawk	1				241	221	190	70	152	172	293	327	228(1)
Northern Goshawk	1				—	223	190	70	152	172	296	326	230(1)
Common Black-Hawk	2				—	210	198	76	—	178	—	—	232(1)
Harris' Hawk	1				218	212	198	74	—	178	311	311	234(1)
Gray Hawk	1				—	—	192	76	—	178	—	—	236(1)
Red-shouldered Hawk	1				238	226	192	74	156	176	298	312	236(1)
Broad-winged Hawk	1				239	222	192	74	156	176	297	—	238(1)
Short-tailed Hawk	2				228	207	198	76	156	—	319	—	240(1)
Swainson's Hawk	1				234	216	194	74	154	174	299	308	240(1)
White-tailed Hawk	1				229	—	196	76	—	178	301	—	242(1)
Zone-tailed Hawk	2				—	207	198	76	—	178	—	341	244(1)
Red-tailed Hawk	1				237	211	194	72	154	174	300	314	246(1)
Ferruginous Hawk	1				—	228	196	72	154	176	—	315	250(1)
Rough-legged Hawk	1				236	229	196	72	156	176	295	316	252(1)
Golden Eagle	1				217	208	184	78	158	180	308	332	254(1)
CARACARAS & FALCONS													
Crested Caracara	1				219	213	200	78	160	184	312	105	256(1)
American Kestrel	1				230	227	202	80	162	186	314	331	256(1)
Merlin	2				232	225	202	80	162	186	313	328	258(1)
Peregrine Falcon	2				231	230	204	80	162	186	315	323	260(1)
Gyrfalcon	3				225	217	204	80	162	184	316	309	262(1)
Prairie Falcon	1				233	231	204	80	162	186	—	320	264(1)

FIELD GUIDE PAGE NUMBERS

Note: Bold print denotes plate number—not page number

BIRD FAMILY & SPECIES	ABA Code	Male ♂	Female ♀	Immature ◯	Audubon McGraw East	West	Nat'l Geo.	Gold.	Peterson's East	West	Audubon Alfred Knopf East	West	Master#
CHACHALACAS													
Plain Chachalaca	1				—	199	222	84	302	—	272	—	266(1)
PARTRIDGES, GROUSE, TURKEYS & QUAILS													
Gray Partridge	1				203	184	220	92	148	164	**267**	285	268(1)
Chukar	1				203	192	220	92	302	164	—	281	270(1)
Ring-necked Pheasant	1				201	197	222	92	144	158	274	267	272(1)
Spruce Grouse	2				209	195	210	86	146	164	270	262	272(1)
Blue Grouse	1				—	201	210	86	—	—	—	260	274(1)
Willow Ptarmigan	1				206	186	212	88	148	162	263	269	276(1)
Rock Ptarmigan	2				207	187	212	88	148	162	264	272	278(1)
White-tailed Ptarmigan	2				—	185	212	88	—	162	—	273	280(1)
Ruffed Grouse	1				212	202	210	86	144	160	268	263	282(1)
Sage Grouse	2				—	200	214	86	—	158	—	253	284(1)
Greater Prairie Chicken	2				210	199	214	88	146	160	267	285	268(1)
Lesser Prairie Chicken	2				211	199	214	88	146	160	262	255	286(1)
Sharp-tailed Grouse	2				208	198	214	86	146	160	260	252	288(1)
Wild Turkey	1				213	203	222	84	144	158	269	266	290(1)
Northern Bobwhite	1				205	193	216	92	148	166	257	282	292(1)
Scaled Quail	1				202	188	216	90	148	166	258	284	294(1)
Gambel's Quail	1				—	189	218	90	—	166	—	276	294(1)
California Quail	1				—	190	218	90	—	166	—	278	296(1)
Mountain Quail	2				—	191	218	90	—	166	—	277	290(1)
RAILS, GALLINULES & COOTS													
Yellow Rail	3				125	126	98	104	114	118	251	244	298(1)
Black Rail	3				124	127	98	104	114	118	—	247	300(1)
Clapper Rail	2				128	123	96	106	112	118	253	243	300(1)
King Rail	2				129	—	96	106	112	120	254	—	302(1)
Virginia Rail	2				127	124	98	104	112	118	252	242	302(1)
Sora	1				126	125	98	104	114	118	249	245	304(1)
Purple Gallinule	1				120	—	100	106	64	64	248	—	304(1)
Common Moorhen	1				121	120	100	106	64	64	247	246	306(1)
American Coot	1				122	121	100	106	64	64	134	111	308(1)
LIMPKINS													
Limpkin	1				143	—	96	102	108	—	23	—	310(1)
CRANES													
Sandhill Crane	1				148	137	58	102	106	116	30	16	312(1)
Whooping Crane	2				149	136	58	102	106	116	29	—	314(1)
PLOVERS													
Black-bellied Plover	1				168	155	108	112	118	122	240	190	316(1)
Lesser Golden-Plover	1				169	154	108	112	118	—	194	189	318(1)
Snowy Plover	1				174	158	104	114	120	124	233	182	322(1)
Wilson's Plover	1				171	—	104	114	120	124	237	—	322(1)
Semipalmated Plover	1				172	157	104	114	120	124	236	183	324(1)
Piping Plover	1				173	—	104	114	120	124	234	—	326(1)
Killdeer	1				170	156	106	114	120	126	235	187	328(1)
Mountain Plover	2				—	159	106	112	—	126	—	233	328(1)
OYSTERCATCHERS													
American Oystercatcher	1				156	122	102	110	116	120	242	—	332(1)
Black Oystercatcher	1				—	122	102	110	—	120	—	218	334(1)
STILTS & AVOCETS													
Black-necked Stilt	1				154	141	102	110	116	120	243	219	336(1)
American Avocet	1				155	140	102	110	116	120	244	220	338(1)
SANDPIPERS													
Greater Yellowlegs	1				162	146	114	120	128	134	228	207	344(1)
Lesser Yellowlegs	1				163	147	114	120	128	134	227	206	346(1)
Solitary Sandpiper	1				188	175	116	120	128	134	216	191	350(1)
Willet	1				164	145	114	122	128	132	229	215	350(1)
Wandering Tattler	1				—	—	118	124	—	142	—	226	352(1)
Spotted Sandpiper	1				189	174	116	124	132	140	215	192	354(1)
Upland Sandpiper	1				165	167	134	122	130	144	218	208	356(1)
Whimbrel	1				151	142	112	118	126	130	245	216	358(1)
Long-billed Curlew	1				150	143	112	118	126	130	246	217	360(1)
Hudsonian Godwit	1				153	144	110	116	126	130	232	—	362(1)
Bar-tailed Godwit	3				—	—	110	116	294	152	—	—	364(1)
Marbled Godwit	1				152	144	110	116	126	130	231	210	366(1)
Ruddy Turnstone	1				157	161	126	128	118	142	—	222	368(1)
Black Turnstone	1				—	160	126	128	—	142	—	221	370(1)
Surfbird	1				—	173	126	128	—	142	—	222	370(1)
Red Knot	1				178	172	128	130	124	—	211	223	372(1)
Sanderling	1				179	171	128	130	130	140	220	193	374(1)
Semipalmated Sandpiper	1				182	168	130	132	134	148	221	196	376(1)
Western Sandpiper	1				185	170	130	132	134	148	222	194	378(1)

BIRD FAMILY & SPECIES	ABA Code	Male ♂	Female ♀	Immature ◯	Audubon McGraw East	West	Nat'l. Geo.	Gold.	Peterson's East	West	Audubon Alfred Knopf East	West	Master#

Note: Bold print denotes plate number—not page number

SANDPIPERS (cont.)

BIRD FAMILY & SPECIES	ABA Code	McGraw East	McGraw West	Nat'l. Geo.	Gold.	Peterson's East	Peterson's West	Knopf East	Knopf West	Master#
Least Sandpiper	1	183	169	130	132	134	148	**223**	**195**	382(1)
White-rumped Sandpiper	1	184	165	130	132	134	146	**226**	—	384(1)
Baird's Sandpiper	1	187	165	130	132	134	146	**225**	**197**	386(1)
Pectoral Sandpiper	1	181	164	134	130	130	146	**219**	**198**	386(1)
Sharp-tailed Sandpiper	4	—	—	134	130	—	—	—	**199**	388(1)
Purple Sandpiper	1	180	—	126	128	132	—	**217**	—	390(1)
Rock Sandpiper	1	—	163	126	128	—	142	—	**211**	392(1)
Dunlin	1	167	162	128	130	132	140	**209**	**188**	394(1)
Curlew Sandpiper	4	—	—	128	130	—	154	—	—	396(1)
Stilt Sandpiper	1	166	—	124	122	128	134	**230**	—	398(1)
Buff-breasted Sandpiper	1	186	167	134	122	130	144	**224**	—	400(1)
Ruff	3	162	146	134	122	130	144	**214**	—	400(1)
Short-billed Dowitcher	1	161	148	122	124	124	138	**212**	**212**	402(1)
Long-billed Dowitcher	1	160	149	122	124	124	138	**213**	**213**	404(1)
Common Snipe	1	159	166	124	126	124	138	**255**	**214**	406(1)
American Woodcock	1	158	166	124	126	124	138	**256**	—	408(1)
Wilson's Phalarope	1	175	151	120	126	136	134	**207**	**203**	408(1)
Red-necked Phalarope	1	176	153	120	126	136	136	**206**	**205**	410(1)
Red Phalarope	2	177	152	120	126	136	136	**208**	**204**	412(1)

SKUAS, GULLS, TERNS & SKIMMERS

BIRD FAMILY & SPECIES	ABA Code	McGraw East	McGraw West	Nat'l. Geo.	Gold.	Peterson's East	Peterson's West	Knopf East	Knopf West	Master#
Pomarine Jaeger	2	49	47	142	138	82	86	**88**	**55**	36(2)
Parasitic Jaeger	2	50	46	142	138	82	86	**89**	**53**	38(2)
Long-tailed Jaeger	2	51	48	142	138	82	86	**87**	**54**	38(2)
Laughing Gull	1	36	33	144	148	88	96	**43**	—	42(2)
Franklin's Gull	1	37	32	144	148	88	96	**45**	**31**	44(2)
Little Gull	3	32	—	146	148	88	96	**47**	—	46(2)
Common Black-headed Gull	3	34	31	146	148	88	96	**46**	—	48(2)
Bonaparte's Gull	1	33	34	146	148	88	96	**48**	**29**	48(2)
Heermann's Gull	1	—	30	144	146	—	90	—	**28**	50(2)
Mew Gull	1	—	23	148	146	290	92	—	**23**	52(2)
Ring-billed Gull	1	41	26	148	146	88	92	**38**	**24**	54(2)
California Gull	1	—	27	150	144	86	92	—	**19**	56(2)
Herring Gull	1	40	24	150	144	86	92	**37**	**18**	58(2)
Thayer's Gull	2	45	25	152	144	86	92	**35**	**17**	60(2)
Iceland Gull	2	43	—	152	140	84	—	**34**	—	62(2)
Lesser Black-backed Gull	4	38	—	154	142	86	—	**41**	—	64(2)
Western Gull	1	—	27	156	142	—	88	—	**22**	68(2)
Glaucous-winged Gull	1	—	20	156	140	—	94	—	**21**	70(2)
Glaucous Gull	1	44	21	152	140	84	94	**36**	**20**	72(2)
Great Black-backed Gull	1	39	—	154	142	86	—	**42**	—	74(2)
Black-legged Kittiwake	1	42	22	158	146	86	94	**39**	**26**	76(2)
Sabine's Gull	2	35	35	158	148	88	96	**44**	**30**	82(2)
Gull-billed Tern	1	30	36	164	154	94	104	**68**	**41**	84(2)
Caspian Tern	1	23	39	168	154	94	104	**65**	**47**	86(2)
Royal Tern	1	27	40	168	154	94	104	**64**	**48**	86(2)
Elegant Tern	2	—	41	168	154	—	104	—	**49**	88(2)
Sandwich Tern	1	29	—	168	154	94	—	**67**	—	90(2)
Roseate Tern	2	31	—	164	152	96	—	**62**	—	90(2)
Common Tern	1	24	38	162	152	96	106	**61**	**44**	92(2)
Arctic Tern	1	25	37	162	152	96	106	**63**	**46**	94(2)
Aleutian Tern	2	—	—	162	156	—	108	—	**50**	94(2)
Forster's Tern	1	24	38	164	152	96	106	**66**	**45**	96(2)
Least Tern	1	28	43	166	152	96	108	**69**	**42**	96(2)
Bridled Tern	3	21	—	170	156	98	—	—	—	98(2)
Sooty Tern	2	21	—	170	156	98	—	**71**	—	100(2)
Black Tern	1	20	44	166	156	98	108	**75**	**43**	102(2)
Black Skimmer	1	22	—	170	156	98	108	**70**	—	106(2)

AUKS, MURRES & PUFFINS

BIRD FAMILY & SPECIES	ABA Code	McGraw East	McGraw West	Nat'l. Geo.	Gold.	Peterson's East	Peterson's West	Knopf East	Knopf West	Master#
Dovekie	2	63	—	172	160	38	36	**96**	—	108(2)
Common Murre	1	60	61	172	160	36	32	**94**	**79**	110(2)
Thick-billed Murre	2	61	61	172	160	36	32	**93**	**78**	112(2)
Razorbill	2	64	61	172	160	36	—	**91**	—	112(2)
Black Guillemot	2	62	61	174	160	38	34	**92**	—	114(2)
Pigeon Guillemot	1	62	61	174	160	—	34	—	**80**	116(2)
Marbled Murrelet	1	—	62	174	164	—	36	—	—	116(2)
Kittlitz's Murrelet	2	—	62	174	164	—	36	—	—	118(2)
Ancient Murrelet	2	—	64	176	164	—	34	—	—	122(2)
Cassin's Auklet	2	—	63	176	164	—	36	—	**87**	124(2)
Crested Auklet	2	—	—	178	162	—	34	—	**86**	128(2)
Rhinoceros Auklet	1	—	65	180	162	—	32	—	**85**	130(2)
Tufted Puffin	1	—	67	180	162	—	32	—	**82**	130(2)

BIRD FAMILY & SPECIES	ABA Code	SIGHTING LOG — CHECKLIST Male ♂	Female ♀	Immature ○	FIELD GUIDE PAGE NUMBERS Audubon McGraw East	West	Nat'l. Geo.	Gold.	Peterson's East	West	Audubon Alfred Knopf East	West	Master#
AUKS, MURRES & PUFFINS (cont.)					Note: Bold print denotes plate number—not page number								
Atlantic Puffin	2				65	—	180	162	38	—	**95**	—	132(2)
Horned Puffin	2				—	66	180	162	—	32	—	**83**	134(2)
PIGEONS & DOVES													
Rock Dove	1				196	182	224	166	180	210	**327**	346	136(2)
White-crowned Pigeon	1				197	—	224	166	180	—	**328**	—	138(2)
Band-tailed Pigeon	1				—	180	224	166	—	208	—	**347**	138(2)
White-winged Dove	1				195	183	226	166	180	208	**321**	348	142(2)
Mourning Dove	1				191	179	226	166	180	208	**322**	349	142(2)
Inca Dove	1				192	177	228	168	180	208	**326**	345	144(2)
Common Ground-Dove	1				190	176	228	168	180	208	**325**	344	146(2)
White-tipped Dove	1				194	—	228	168	—	208	—	—	142(2)
CUCKOOS, ROADRUNNERS & ANIS													
Black-billed Cuckoo	1				269	263	236	172	182	212	**521**	—	150(2)
Yellow-billed Cuckoo	1				268	262	236	172	182	212	**522**	562	150(2)
Mangrove Cuckoo	3				268	—	236	172	182	—	**523**	—	152(2)
Greater Roadrunner	1				200	196	236	172	182	212	**271**	264	152(2)
Smooth-billed Ani	1				368	—	234	172	182	—	**577**	—	154(2)
Groove-billed Ani	1				368	—	234	172	182	212	**578**	—	154(2)
BARN OWLS													
Barn Owl	2				254	233	238	176	174	198	**291**	302	156(2)
TYPICAL OWLS													
Flammulated Owl	3				—	241	244	180	—	204	—	**297**	158(2)
Eastern Screech-Owl	2				246	238	242	174	172	204	**279**	—	160(2)
Western Screech-Owl	2				—	239	242	174	—	200	—	**286**	160(2)
Great Horned Owl	2				249	243	238	174	172	200	**282**	288	162(2)
Snowy Owl	2				255	232	240	176	174	198	**292**	303	164(2)
Northern Hawk Owl	2				247	244	246	178	176	202	**288**	292	164(2)
Northern Pygmy-Owl	2				—	236	244	180	—	204	—	**295**	166(2)
Elf Owl	2				243	245	244	180	—	204	**287**	294	168(2)
Burrowing Owl	1				252	234	246	178	176	202	**283**	301	168(2)
Spotted Owl	2				—	246	240	176	—	204	—	**293**	170(2)
Barred Owl	1				251	246	240	176	174	198	**285**	—	170(2)
Great Gray Owl	3				250	247	240	176	174	198	**286**	290	172(2)
Long-eared Owl	2				248	242	238	174	172	200	**281**	289	174(2)
Short-eared Owl	2				253	235	238	174	172	200	**284**	291	174(2)
Boreal Owl	3				245	249	246	178	176	202	**290**	300	176(2)
Northern Saw-whet Owl	3				244	248	246	178	176	202	**289**	298	178(2)
NIGHTJARS													
Lesser Nighthawk	1				256	253	250	182	184	214	—	**251**	180(2)
Common Nighthawk	1				260	252	250	182	184	214	**275**	250	182(2)
Pauraque	2				259	—	250	182	—	—	**276**	—	184(2)
Common Poorwill	2				259	251	248	182	184	214	—	**249**	184(2)
Chuck-will's-widow	2				257	—	248	182	184	—	**278**	—	186(2)
Whip-poor-will	2				258	250	248	182	184	214	**277**	248	188(2)
SWIFTS													
Black Swift	2				—	254	252	184	—	246	—	**360**	190(2)
Chimney Swift	1				261	254	252	184	204	246	**335**	361	192(2)
Vaux's Swift	1				—	254	252	184	204	246	—	—	192(2)
White-throated Swift	1				—	254	252	184	—	246	—	—	192(2)
HUMMINGBIRDS													
Buff-bellied Hummingbird	2				273	—	254	190	—	—	**481**	—	198(2)
Ruby-throated Hummingbird	1				275	319	258	186	186	216	**479**	—	204(2)
Black-chinned Hummingbird	1				275	312	258	188	—	220	—	**398**	204(2)
Anna's Hummingbird	1				—	320	258	186	—	216	—	**399**	206(2)
Costa's Hummingbird	1				—	314	258	188	—	220	—	**401**	208(2)
Calliope Hummingbird	2				—	316	260	186	—	220	—	**400**	208(2)
Broad-tailed Hummingbird	1				—	318	260	186	—	216	—	**393**	210(2)
Rufous Hummingbird	1				274	321	260	188	186	216	**480**	391	212(2)
Allen's Hummingbird	1				—	320	260	188	—	216	—	**392**	212(2)
KINGFISHERS													
Belted Kingfisher	1				264	270	262	192	186	206	**481**	503	216(2)
Green Kingfisher	2				264	271	262	192	—	206	—	**523**	218(2)
WOODPECKERS													
Lewis' Woodpecker	1				—	322	266	198	—	222	—	**377**	220(2)
Red-headed Woodpecker	1				298	330	266	198	188	222	**351**	—	222(2)
Acorn Woodpecker	1				—	322	266	198	—	222	—	**377**	222(2)
Gila Woodpecker	1				—	325	264	196	—	228	—	**375**	224(2)
Golden-fronted Woodpecker	1				306	324	264	196	—	228	**350**	374	224(2)
Red-bellied Woodpecker	1				307	—	264	196	190	228	**349**	—	226(2)
Yellow-bellied Sapsucker	1				300	332	268	198	190	226	**346**	—	228(2)
Red-breasted Sapsucker	1				—	323	268	198	—	226	—	**379**	230(2)

BIRD FAMILY & SPECIES	ABA Code	Male ♂	Female ♀	Immature ○	Audubon McGraw East	West	Nat'l Geo.	Gold.	Peterson's East	West	Audubon Alfred Knopf East	West	Master#

Note: Bold print denotes plate number—not page number

WOODPECKERS (cont.)

BIRD FAMILY & SPECIES	ABA Code	McGraw East	McGraw West	Nat'l Geo.	Gold.	Peterson's East	Peterson's West	Knopf East	Knopf West	Master#
Williamson's Sapsucker	1	—	331	268	198	—	226	—	**384**	230(2)
Ladder-backed Woodpecker	1	309	333	272	196	—	228	**345**	**368**	232(2)
Nuttall's Woodpecker	1	—	333	272	196	—	228	—	**367**	234(2)
Downy Woodpecker	1	302	334	270	200	192	224	**339**	**364**	236(2)
Hairy Woodpecker	1	301	335	270	200	192	224	**340**	**365**	236(2)
Red-cockaded Woodpecker	2	303	—	272	196	190	—	**347**	—	240(2)
Three-toed Woodpecker	2	305	336	270	200	192	224	**344**	**382**	242(2)
Black-backed Woodpecker	2	304	337	270	200	192	224	**343**	**383**	244(2)
Northern Flicker	1	308	326	264	194	190	226	**348**	**370**	244(2)
Pileated Woodpecker	1	299	329	274	194	188	222	**352**	**381**	246(2)

TYRANT FLYCATCHERS

BIRD FAMILY & SPECIES	ABA Code	McGraw East	McGraw West	Nat'l Geo.	Gold.	Peterson's East	Peterson's West	Knopf East	Knopf West	Master#
Olive-sided Flycatcher	1	280	394	284	216	196	236	**470**	**547**	252(2)
Western Wood-Pewee	1	281	392	284	216	—	236	—	**513**	254(2)
Eastern Wood-Pewee	1	281	392	284	216	196	236	**465**	—	254(2)
Yellow-bellied Flycatcher	2	284	—	292	212	198	240	**463**	—	256(2)
Acadian Flycatcher	1	284	—	290	212	198	—	**461**	—	256(2)
Alder Flycatcher	1	285	390	290	212	198	238	—	**519**	258(2)
Willow Flycatcher	1	285	390	290	212	198	238	**462**	**518**	258(2)
Least Flycatcher	1	283	390	290	212	196	240	**464**	—	260(2)
Hammond's Flycatcher	2	—	391	288	214	—	238	—	**517**	262(2)
Dusky Flycatcher	1	—	393	288	214	—	238	—	**546**	264(2)
Gray Flycatcher	1	—	393	288	214	—	238	—	**490**	266(2)
Western Flycatcher	1	—	391	288	214	—	240	—	**549**	268(2)
Black Phoebe	1	—	410	286	210	—	236	—	**610**	270(2)
Eastern Phoebe	1	282	409	286	210	196	236	**446**	—	272(2)
Say's Phoebe	1	295	409	286	210	196	238	—	**521**	272(2)
Vermilion Flycatcher	1	297	407	286	204	196	230	**415**	**451**	274(2)
Ash-throated Flycatcher	1	286	403	282	208	194	234	**472**	**548**	276(2)
Great Crested Flycatcher	1	289	404	282	208	194	234	**469**	—	278(2)
Brown-crested Flycatcher	1	287	404	282	208	—	234	**471**	**520**	280(2)
Great Kiskadee	1	291	—	280	204	—	—	—	—	282(2)
Couch's Kingbird	1	290	400	278	206	—	—	—	—	284(2)
Cassin's Kingbird	1	—	401	278	206	—	232	—	—	284(2)
Western Kingbird	1	288	399	278	206	194	232	**467**	**421**	286(2)
Eastern Kingbird	1	293	395	276	206	194	232	**423**	**474**	288(2)
Gray Kingbird	1	292	—	276	206	194	—	**426**	—	288(2)
Scissor-tailed Flycatcher	1	294	406	280	204	194	230	**418**	**469**	290(2)

LARKS

BIRD FAMILY & SPECIES	ABA Code	McGraw East	McGraw West	Nat'l Geo.	Gold.	Peterson's East	Peterson's West	Knopf East	Knopf West	Master#
Horned Lark	1	344	270	294	218	200	242	**556**	**603**	296(2)

SWALLOWS

BIRD FAMILY & SPECIES	ABA Code	McGraw East	McGraw West	Nat'l Geo.	Gold.	Peterson's East	Peterson's West	Knopf East	Knopf West	Master#
Purple Martin	1	262	261	296	220	202	250	**332**	**359**	298(2)
Tree Swallow	1	263	260	296	220	204	248	**331**	**356**	300(2)
Violet-green Swallow	1	—	255	296	220	—	248	—	**357**	300(2)
Northern Rough-winged Swallow	1	266	258	298	220	204	248	**333**	**354**	302(2)
Bank Swallow	1	267	259	298	220	204	248	**334**	**355**	302(2)
Cliff Swallow	1	264	256	298	218	202	250	**330**	**353**	304(2)
Barn Swallow	1	265	257	298	218	202	250	**329**	**352**	306(2)

JAYS, MAGPIES & CROWS

BIRD FAMILY & SPECIES	ABA Code	McGraw East	McGraw West	Nat'l Geo.	Gold.	Peterson's East	Peterson's West	Knopf East	Knopf West	Master#
Gray Jay	1	371	292	302	224	208	256	**425**	**471**	308(2)
Steller's Jay	1	—	295	302	222	—	254	—	**502**	310(2)
Blue Jay	1	373	295	302	222	208	254	**435**	—	310(2)
Green Jay	1	374	—	304	224	—	—	**483**	—	312(2)
Scrub Jay	1	372	293	300	222	208	254	**436**	**505**	312(2)
Pinyon Jay	2	—	294	300	222	—	254	—	**507**	314(2)
Clark's Nutcracker	1	—	291	302	224	—	254	—	**470**	316(2)
Black-billed Magpie	1	369	290	304	224	208	256	**584**	**617**	316(2)
American Crow	1	365	288	306	226	206	252	**579**	**625**	318(2)
Northwestern Crow	1	—	289	306	226	—	252	—	**624**	318(2)
Fish Crow	1	364	—	306	226	206	—	**580**	—	320(2)
Chihuahuan Raven	1	366	287	306	226	—	252	—	—	320(2)
Common Raven	1	367	286	306	226	206	252	**581**	**626**	322(2)

TITMICE

BIRD FAMILY & SPECIES	ABA Code	McGraw East	McGraw West	Nat'l Geo.	Gold.	Peterson's East	Peterson's West	Knopf East	Knopf West	Master#
Black-capped Chickadee	1	278	353	310	228	210	258	**428**	**487**	324(2)
Carolina Chickadee	1	278	—	310	228	210	—	**427**	—	324(2)
Mountain Chickadee	1	—	352	310	228	—	258	—	**488**	326(2)
Boreal Chickadee	1	—	354	312	228	210	258	**511**	**544**	328(2)
Chestnut-backed Chickadee	1	—	355	312	228	—	258	—	**545**	328(2)
Plain Titmouse	1	—	350	308	230	—	260	—	**486**	330(2)
Tufted Titmouse	1	279	—	308	230	210	260	**432**	—	330(2)

VERDINS

BIRD FAMILY & SPECIES	ABA Code	McGraw East	McGraw West	Nat'l Geo.	Gold.	Peterson's East	Peterson's West	Knopf East	Knopf West	Master#
Verdin	1	276	356	312	232	—	260	**381**	**422**	332(2)

BIRD FAMILY & SPECIES	ABA Code	SIGHTING LOG — CHECKLIST Male ♂	Female ♀	Immature ◯	Audubon McGraw East	West	Nat'l Geo.	Gold.	Peterson's East	West	Audubon Alfred Knopf East	West	Master#
												Note: Bold print denotes plate number—not page number		
BUSHTITS													
Bushtit	1				—	357	312	232	—	260	—	485	334(2)
NUTHATCHES													
Red-breasted Nuthatch	1				312	338	314	234	212	262	**353**	386	336(2)
White-breasted Nuthatch	1				311	339	314	234	212	262	**354**	387	338(2)
Pygmy Nuthatch	1				—	340	314	234	—	262	—	389	338(2)
Brown-headed Nuthatch	1				313	—	314	234	211	—	**356**	—	338(2)
CREEPERS													
Brown Creeper	1				314	341	314	234	212	262	**355**	388	340(2)
WRENS													
Cactus Wren	1				315	344	318	238	—	266	**493**	532	344(2)
Rock Wren	1				323	344	318	238	214	266	**492**	531	346(2)
Canyon Wren	1				322	343	318	238	—	266	**491**	530	346(2)
Carolina Wren	1				316	—	316	236	214	264	**489**	—	348(2)
Bewick's Wren	1				317	346	316	236	214	264	**490**	526	350(2)
House Wren	1				320	347	316	236	214	264	**486**	529	350(2)
Winter Wren	1				321	348	316	236	214	264	**487**	527	352(2)
Sedge Wren	1				319	347	318	238	214	264	**485**	—	352(2)
Marsh Wren	1				318	345	318	238	214	264	**488**	528	354(2)
DIPPERS													
American Dipper	1				—	349	342	232	—	266	—	492	356(2)
OLD WORLD WARBLERS & THRUSHES													
Arctic Warbler	2				—	—	320	254	—	300	—	—	34(3)
Golden-crowned Kinglet	1				432	358	322	252	216	268	**458**	509	36(3)
Ruby-crowned Kinglet	1				477	358	322	252	216	268	**459**	510	36(3)
Blue-gray Gnatcatcher	1				466	381	322	252	216	268	**443**	495	38(3)
Black-tailed Gnatcatcher	1				—	380	322	252	—	268	—	494	38(3)
Eastern Bluebird	1				393	428	324	250	220	278	**440**	—	46(3)
Western Bluebird	1				393	428	324	250	—	278	—	500	46(3)
Mountain Bluebird	1				393	427	324	250	220	278	**441**	496	48(3)
Townsend's Solitaire	1				—	424	324	246	218	274	—	476	50(3)
Veery	1				333	420	326	248	222	276	**499**	540	52(3)
Gray-cheeked Thrush	1				331	423	326	248	222	276	**498**	539	52(3)
Swainson's Thrush	1				330	421	326	248	222	276	**502**	538	52(3)
Hermit Thrush	1				329	422	326	248	222	276	**501**	541	54(3)
Wood Thrush	1				332	—	326	248	222	276	**500**	—	54(3)
American Robin	1				353	418	330	244	220	274	**400**	445	58(3)
Varied Thrush	1				353	419	328	246	220	274	—	444	60(3)
Wrentit	1				—	379	308	232	—	266	—	484	60(3)
MOCKINGBIRDS, THRASHERS & ALLIES													
Gray Catbird	1				324	426	334	240	218	270	**420**	477	62(3)
Northern Mockingbird	1				325	425	336	240	218	270	**419**	475	62(3)
Sage Thrasher	1				337	413	336	240	—	270	**497**	533	64(2)
Brown Thrasher	1				334	—	336	240	218	270	**494**	—	66(3)
Long-billed Thrasher	1				—	—	336	240	—	—	**495**	—	66(3)
Bendire's Thrasher	1				—	415	338	242	—	272	—	534	68(3)
Curve-billed Thrasher	1				—	412	338	242	—	272	**496**	535	68(3)
Crissal Thrasher	1				—	416	338	242	—	272	—	—	70(3)
Le Conte's Thrasher	2				—	417	338	242	—	272	—	537	72(3)
WAGTAILS & PIPITS													
American Pipit	1				339	266	340	256	200	244	**546**	571	78(3)
Sprague's Pipit	1				338	266	340	256	200	244	—	—	80(3)
WAXWINGS													
Bohemian Waxwing	1				376	299	344	258	224	282	**507**	565	82(3)
Cedar Waxwing	1				377	298	344	258	224	282	**506**	566	84(3)
SILKY-FLYCATCHERS													
Phainopepla	1				—	297	344	258	—	282	—	613	86(3)
SHRIKES													
Northern Shrike	1				379	301	334	260	224	280	**421**	473	88(3)
Loggerhead Shrike	1				378	300	334	260	224	280	**422**	472	90(3)
STARLINGS													
European Starling	1				359	281	346	260	256	280	**565**	611	92(3)
VIREOS													
White-eyed Vireo	1				467	—	348	264	228	284	**383**	—	96(3)
Bell's Vireo	1				476	383	350	264	228	284	**449**	508	98(3)
Black-capped Vireo	2				466	—	348	262	228	284	—	—	100(3)
Gray Vireo	2				—	385	350	262	—	286	—	—	100(3)
Solitary Vireo	1				465	375	350	262	228	284	**450**	516	100(3)
Yellow-throated Vireo	1				470	—	348	264	228	284	**362**	—	102(3)
Hutton's Vireo	1				—	382	350	264	—	284	—	—	102(3)
Warbling Vireo	1				475	386	352	266	226	286	**454**	514	104(3)
Philadelphia Vireo	1				471	386	352	266	226	286	**451**	—	104(3)

BIRD FAMILY & SPECIES	ABA Code	SIGHTING LOG — CHECKLIST Male ♂	Female ♀	Immature ○	Audubon McGraw East	West	Nat'l. Geo.	Gold.	Peterson's East	West	Audubon Alfred Knopf East	West	Master#
					Note: Bold print denotes plate number—not page number								
VIREOS (cont.)													
Red-eyed Vireo	1				473	387	352	266	226	286	**453**	**515**	106(3)
Black-whiskered Vireo	1				474	—	352	266	226	—	**452**	—	106(3)
WOOD-WARBLERS													
Bachman's Warbler	5				435	—	356	272	242	—	—	—	108(3)
Blue-winged Warbler	1				438	—	354	272	238	304	**361**	—	110(3)
Golden-winged Warbler	1				461	—	354	272	242	304	**378**	—	114(3)
Tennessee Warbler	1				468	372	356	274	240	300	**454**	**512**	114(3)
Orange-crowned Warbler	1				469	373	356	274	240	300	**456**	**511**	116(3)
Nashville Warbler	1				459	371	358	274	244	298	**373**	**412**	118(3)
Virginia's Warbler	1				—	374	358	276	—	296	—	**478**	120(3)
Lucy's Warbler	1				—	384	358	276	—	296	—	—	122(3)
Northern Parula	1				460	363	358	276	230	302	**447**	—	124(3)
Tropical Parula	4				460	—	358	276	—	—	—	—	126(3)
Yellow Warbler	1				440	366	370	278	238	300	**357**	**410**	126(3)
Chestnut-sided Warbler	1				451	—	362	284	236	294	**377**	—	128(3)
Magnolia Warbler	1				448	—	362	278	234	288	**366**	—	130(3)
Cape May Warbler	1				443	—	362	278	234	294	**368**	—	132(3)
Black-throated Blue Warbler	1				455	—	364	282	232	292	**446**	—	132(3)
Yellow-rumped Warbler	1				450	361	362	278	234	288	**379**	**414**	134(3)
Black-throated Gray Warbler	1				—	360	364	282	232	292	—	**608**	136(3)
Townsend's Warbler	1				—	365	364	280	—	290	—	**415**	138(3)
Hermit Warbler	1				—	362	364	280	—	290	—	**416**	140(3)
Black-throated Green Warbler	1				436	—	364	280	230	290	**375**	—	142(3)
Blackburnian Warbler	1				445	—	360	284	236	294	**404**	—	144(3)
Yellow-throated Warbler	1				477	—	366	282	230	304	**376**	—	146(3)
Pine Warbler	1				442	—	368	286	238	304	**364**	—	148(3)
Prairie Warbler	1				437	—	366	286	238	304	**363**	—	152(3)
Palm Warbler	1				446	—	368	286	238	300	**365**	—	154(3)
Bay-breasted Warbler	1				452	359	368	284	236	294	**403**	—	154(3)
Blackpoll Warbler	1				453	359	368	284	232	292	**563**	**609**	156(3)
Cerulean Warbler	1				454	—	360	282	232	292	**444**	—	158(3)
Black-and-white Warbler	1				310	359	360	270	232	292	**564**	—	160(3)
American Redstart	1				444	376	378	292	236	294	**402**	**441**	160(3)
Prothonotary Warbler	1				441	—	354	270	230	304	**360**	—	162(3)
Worm-eating Warbler	1				433	—	374	270	240	304	**509**	—	164(3)
Swainson's Warbler	2				472	—	374	270	240	—	—	—	164(3)
Ovenbird	1				328	388	374	288	246	302	**503**	—	164(3)
Northern Waterthrush	1				326	389	374	288	246	304	**505**	**542**	166(3)
Louisiana Waterthrush	1				327	—	374	288	246	—	**504**	—	168(3)
Kentucky Warbler	1				463	—	372	290	244	304	**370**	—	168(3)
Connecticut Warbler	2				457	—	370	290	244	298	**460**	—	170(3)
Mourning Warbler	1				458	370	370	290	244	298	**372**	—	172(3)
MacGillivray's Warbler	1				—	370	370	290	—	298	—	**411**	174(3)
Common Yellowthroat	1				462	368	376	288	246	302	**371**	**419**	176(3)
Hooded Warbler	1				435	—	372	292	242	302	**369**	—	178(3)
Wilson's Warbler	1				434	367	372	292	242	302	**358**	**409**	180(3)
Canada Warbler	1				439	—	372	292	234	288	**367**	—	180(3)
Painted Redstart	1				—	377	378	292	—	296	—	**456**	182(3)
Yellow-breasted Chat	1				464	369	376	288	246	302	**359**	**413**	184(3)
TANAGERS													
Hepatic Tanager	2				—	432	430	306	—	314	—	**432**	192(3)
Summer Tanager	1				387	433	430	306	260	314	**417**	**449**	194(3)
Scarlet Tanager	1				386	—	430	306	260	314	**416**	—	194(3)
Western Tanager	1				—	435	430	306	260	314	**389**	**454**	196(3)
CARDINALS, GROSBEAKS & ALLIES													
Northern Cardinal	1				389	431	382	308	268	340	**407**	**448**	200(3)
Pyrrhuloxia	1				388	430	382	308	—	336	**405**	**468**	292(3)
Rose-breasted Grosbeak	1				382	439	380	310	276	336	**408**	—	204(3)
Black-headed Grosbeak	1				382	—	380	310	276	336	**399**	**443**	206(3)
Blue Grosbeak	1				394	429	382	310	274	338	**439**	**498**	206(3)
Lazuli Bunting	1				391	304	384	312	274	338	**437**	**501**	208(3)
Indigo Bunting	1				395	307	384	312	274	338	**438**	—	210(3)
Painted Bunting	1				390	306	384	312	274	338	**476**	**525**	212(3)
Dickcissel	1				341	464	416	322	262	346	**545**	—	214(3)
NEW WORLD SPARROWS & ALLIES													
Olive Sparrow	1				399	—	386	324	—	—	**478**	—	216(3)
Green-tailed Towhee	1				397	462	386	324	276	330	—	**524**	218(3)
Rufous-sided Towhee	1				400	475	386	324	276	330	**401**	**442**	218(3)
Brown Towhee	1				397	462	386	324	276	—	—	**524**	220(3)
Abert's Towhee	1				—	474	386	324	—	330	—	**564**	222(3)
Bachman's Sparrow	2				422	—	396	336	282	—	—	—	226(3)

FIELD GUIDE INDEX

Note: Bold print denotes plate number—not page number

BIRD FAMILY & SPECIES	ABA Code	Audubon McGraw East	West	Nat'l Geo.	Gold.	Peterson's East	West	Audubon Alfred Knopf East	West	Master#
NEW WORLD SPARROWS & ALLIES (cont.)										
Cassin's Sparrow	1	397	462	396	324	276	322	—	524	218(3)
Rufous-crowned Sparrow	1	412	463	398	336	280	320	—	591	229(3)
American Tree Sparrow	1	420	450	398	338	280	320	531	589	230(3)
Chipping Sparrow	1	419	451	400	338	280	320	530	590	232(3)
Clay-colored Sparrow	1	418	444	400	338	282	320	535	578	234(3)
Brewer's Sparrow	1	—	459	400	338	—	322	—	600	236(3)
Field Sparrow	1	421	450	398	338	280	320	532	—	236(3)
Black-chinned Sparrow	1	—	447	402	338	—	318	—	601	238(3)
Vesper Sparrow	1	415	458	392	332	284	324	550	575	240(3)
Lark Sparrow	1	423	453	394	332	282	318	527	577	242(3)
Black-throated Sparrow	1	426	452	394	332	—	318	528	593	242(3)
Sage Sparrow	1	—	445	394	332	—	318	—	602	244(3)
Lark Bunting	1	381	303	416	332	262	346	566	606	246(3)
Savannah Sparrow	1	411	454	392	328	286	326	548	569	248(3)
Baird's Sparrow	2	410	455	388	328	286	322	—	—	250(3)
Grasshopper Sparrow	1	409	456	388	328	282	322	536	568	252(3)
Henslow's Sparrow	2	414	—	388	328	286	—	537	—	254(3)
Le Conte's Sparrow	2	408	—	390	330	288	326	538	—	254(3)
Sharp-tailed Sparrow	1	407	—	390	330	288	326	533	—	256(3)
Seaside Sparrow	1	406	—	390	330	288	—	534	—	258(3)
Fox Sparrow	1	428	448	406	342	284	324	543	572	260(3)
Song Sparrow	1	417	461	392	342	284	324	542	573	262(3)
Lincoln's Sparrow	1	416	460	406	342	284	324	544	599	264(3)
Swamp Sparrow	1	429	460	406	342	280	320	541	—	264(3)
White-throated Sparrow	1	431	443	404	340	278	316	539	587	266(3)
Golden-crowned Sparrow	1	—	441	404	340	278	316	—	588	268(3)
White-crowned Sparrow	1	430	442	404	340	278	316	540	586	268(3)
Harris' Sparrow	1	427	—	404	340	278	316	529	594	270(3)
Dark-eyed Junco	1	401	477	402	344	266	332	429	483	272(3)
McCown's Longspur	1	340	267	408	344	264	328	553	595	276(3)
Lapland Longspur	1	342	269	410	344	264	328	551	576	278(3)
Smith's Longspur	2	345	—	410	344	264	328	554	596	280(3)
Chestnut-collared Longspur	1	343	268	408	344	264	328	552	597	280(3)
Snow Bunting	1	380	302	412	344	266	334	547	605	284(3)
NEW WORLD BLACKBIRDS & ORIOLES										
Bobolink	1	356	278	418	296	256	308	567	607	288(3)
Red-winged Blackbird	1	357	279	420	298	252	308	568	614	290(3)
Tricolored Blackbird	1	—	279	420	298	—	308	—	615	292(3)
Eastern Meadowlark	1	347	272	418	296	256	310	392	424	292(3)
Western Meadowlark	1	346	273	418	296	256	310	391	423	294(3)
Yellow-headed Blackbird	1	354	276	420	298	252	308	583	428	296(3)
Rusty Blackbird	1	358	280	422	298	254	306	569	623	296(3)
Brewer's Blackbird	1	358	280	422	298	254	306	570	622	298(3)
Great-tailed Grackle	1	361	282	424	300	254	306	576	619	300(3)
Boat-tailed Grackle	1	361	282	424	300	254	—	575	—	300(3)
Common Grackle	1	360	283	424	300	254	306	573	618	302(3)
Bronzed Cowbird	1	—	—	422	300	—	310	517	559	304(3)
Brown-headed Cowbird	1	363	285	422	300	252	310	571	620	306(3)
Orchard Oriole	1	352	—	426	302	258	312	396	—	308(3)
Hooded Oriole	1	351	275	428	304	—	312	398	447	308(3)
Baltimore Oriole	1	350	—	426	304	258	312	398	436	316(3)
Bullock's Oriole	1	350	274	426	304	258	312	394	446	316(3)
Scott's Oriole	1	—	277	426	302	—	312	—	427	320(3)
FINCHES										
Rosy Finch	1	—	—	438	318	—	334	—	465	324(3)
Pine Grosbeak	1	384	434	436	316	270	342	414	466	326(3)
Purple Finch	1	404	470	440	316	270	342	409	461	328(3)
Cassin's Finch	1	—	471	440	316	—	342	—	462	330(3)
House Finch	1	405	467	440	316	270	342	410	460	332(3)
Red Crossbill	1	385	473	436	322	268	340	412	452	332(3)
White-winged Crossbill	1	383	472	436	322	268	340	413	453	334(3)
Common Redpoll	1	403	469	438	318	270	—	411	463	336(3)
Hoary Redpoll	2	403	468	438	318	270	342	—	464	338(3)
Pine Siskin	1	402	449	434	320	272	344	557	598	338(3)
Lesser Goldfinch	1	398	437	434	320	—	344	—	417	340(3)
Lawrence's Goldfinch	1	—	—	438	318	—	344	—	465	324(3)
American Goldfinch	1	397	438	434	320	272	344	385	408	344(3)
Evening Grosbeak	1	396	436	442	310	272	344	384	426	346(3)
OLD WORLD SPARROWS										
House Sparrow	1	425	465	432	296	262	346	525	592	348(3)
Eurasian Tree Sparrow	1	424	—	432	296	—	346	524	—	350(3)

The Rare & Limited Species Supplement provides complete species sighting and field guide reference.

The supplement covers 63 species that are rarely seen or only observed at a few of the locations described in the state chapters. The species in this supplement are also listed under the Rare/Limited Species headings in the Bird List Summaries.

The species are arranged in current A.O.U. Checklist order under the bird family name. To the right of each species name the ABA Code is given, followed by columns combining general reference information and the Sighting Log — Checklist in abbreviated form.

The Bird List abbreviations appear as AK-3 (Alaska-list number 3), and are followed by the state chapter page number. The Nesting • and Seasonal Abundance codes s S F W provide abundance data, followed by the Sighting Log — Checklist spaces to note if the male, female, or immature was seen.

The Field Guide Index appears to the right of the log. Field Guide page numbers are given for quick reference to the species illustrations and descriptive information in nine popular field guides.

Note: Bold print denotes plate number—not page number

BIRD FAMILY & SPECIES	ABA Code	Bird List	State Chapter Page No.	Nesting & Seasonal Abundance • s S F W	Audubon McGraw East	Audubon McGraw West	Nat'l. Geo.	Gold.	Peterson's East	Peterson's West	Audubon Alfred Knopf East	Audubon Alfred Knopf West	Master#
ALBATROSSES													
Black-footed Albatross	3	AK-3	30	C C C	—	57	24	22	—	74	—	**72**	50(1)
		CA-2	49	R R R									
Laysan Albatross	4	AK-3	30	U U U	—	56	24	22	—	74	—	**71**	50(1)
SHEARWATERS & PETRELS													
Mottled Petrel	4	AK-3	30	U U U	—	—	32	28	292	78	—	—	56(1)
		AK-5	31	R									
Buller's Shearwater	3	CA-2	49	R	—	52	30	26	—	76	—	—	62(1)
STORM-PETRELS													
Ashy Storm-Petrel	2	CA-2	42	• A A A O	—	50	36	30	—	80	—	—	72(1)
BOOBIES & GANNETS													
Blue-footed Booby	4	CA-7	52	O	—	59	42	34	—	82	—	—	82(1)
STORKS													
Greater Flamingo	4	FL-11	66	R R	142	—	54	100	110	—	—	—	130(1)
SWANS, GEESE & DUCKS													
Whooper Swan	4	AK-6	32	R R R	—	—	60	40	296	38	—	—	138(1)
Barnacle Goose	4	NC-2	137	R	115	—	66	42	44	—	—	—	150(1)
		NC-4	137	R R									
		OK-4	149	R									
Garganey	4	AK-5	31	R	—	—	74	50	296	48	—	—	162(1)
Common Pochard	4	AK-6	32	R	—	—	78	54	—	62	—	—	172(1)
Tufted Duck	3	AK-6	32	U R R R	83	102	80	54	296	56	**122**	**91**	176(1)
		MA-3	100	R R R									
Spectacled Eider	2	AK-5	31	• R R R	—	—	82	58	—	52	—	**107**	186(1)
KITES, EAGLES, HAWKS & ALLIES													
Hook-billed Kite	3	TX-8	175	• U U U O	222	—	188	68	—	—	—	—	218(1)
CARACARAS & FALCONS													
Aplomado Falcon	5	TX-7	174	R R R R	—	—	200	80			—	**322**	260(1)
PARTRIDGES, GROUSE, TURKEYS & QUAILS													
Montezuma Quail	3	NM-3	129	R R R R	—	194	216	90	—	166	—	**283**	290(1)
RAILS, GALLINULES & COOTS													
Caribbean Coot	4	FL-7	64	O O O	—	—	100	—	298	—			300(1)
PLOVERS													
Common Ringed Plover	4	AK-5	31	R	—	—	104	114	—	124	—	—	324(1)
JACANAS													
Northern Jacana	4	TX-8	175	R R R	123	—	102	110	298	—	—	—	340(1)
SANDPIPERS													
Bristle-thighed Curlew	4	AK-5	31	R R	—	—	112	118	—	132	—	—	360(1)
Far Eastern Curlew	5	AK-6	32	R	—	—	112	118	—	152	—	—	421(1)
Eurasian Curlew	5	MA-3	100	R	—	—	112	118	294	—	—	—	421(1)
Long-toed Stint	4	AK-5	31	R	—	—	132	134	—	150	—	—	380(1)
SKUAS, GULLS, TERNS & SKIMMERS													
South Polar Skua	2	CA-2	49	R	48	—	140	138	82	86	—	—	40(2)
Yellow-footed Gull	3	CA-7	52	O C U R	—	28	156	142	—	90	—	**27**	66(2)
Red-legged Kittiwake	2	AK-5	31	R R	—	—	158	146	—	94	—	—	78(2)
Ivory Gull	4	MT-3	115	R	46	—	158	140	84	94	**32**	—	82(2)
Brown Noddy	2	FL-4	63	R R R	47	—	170	156	98	—	**73**	—	104(2)
AUKS, MURRES & PUFFINS													
Xantus' Murrelet	2	CA-2	49	R	—	63	176	164	—	36	—	—	120(2)
Parakeet Auklet	2	AK-3	30	• R R R	—	—	178	164	—	34	—	**88**	124(2)
		AK-5	31	• R R									
Least Auklet	2	AK-5	31	R R	—	—	178	164	—	36	—	**89**	126(2)
		AK-6	32	R R R									
PIGEONS & DOVES													
Red-billed Pigeon	3	TX-7	174	R R R	198	—	224	166	—	208	—	—	138(2)
		TX-8	175	• R O O R									
Ringed Turtle-Dove	1	FL-5	63	R R R R	193	178	226	168	180	210	—	—	140(2)

Bird Family & Species	ABA Code	Bird List	State Chapter Page No.	Nesting & Seasonal Abundance (• s S F W)	Audubon McGraw East	West	Nat'l Geo.	Gold.	Peterson's East	West	Audubon Alfred Knopf East	West	Master#
PARROTS													Note: Bold print denotes plate number—not page number
Budgerigar	2	FL-3	63	R R	272	—	230	170	178	—	—	—	148(2)
		FL-9	65	R R									
Canary-winged Parakeet	2	FL-5	63	R R R R	272	—	230	170	178	210	—	—	148(2)
TYPICAL OWLS													
Ferruginous Pygmy-Owl	3	TX-8	175	• R R R	242	237	244	180	—	204	—	—	166(2)
KINGFISHERS													
Ringed Kingfisher	2	TX-7	174	R (W)	270	—	262	192	—	—	—	—	216(2)
		TX-8	175	• U U U U									
WOODPECKERS													
White-headed Woodpecker	1	OR-1	150	• U U U R	—	328	266	198	—	224	—	**385**	240(2)
TYRANT FLYCATCHERS													
Northern Beardless-Tyrannulet	2	TX-7	174	R R R R	276	396	292	214	—	238	—	—	250(2)
		TX-8	175	• R R R R									
La Sagra's Flycatcher	5	FL-11	66	R (W)	—	—	—	—	—	—	—	—	363(2)
Tropical Kingbird	2	CA-2	49	O (F)	—	400	278	206	300	248	—	**420**	282(2)
Rose-throated Becard	2	TX-8	175	• R R R R	296	—	294	204	—	230	—	**493**	292(2)
SWALLOWS													
Cave Swallow	1	TX-8	175	R (S)	264	256	298	218	300	248	—	—	306(2)
JAYS, MAGPIES & CROWS													
Gray-breasted Jay	1	NM-2	129	O O (F W)	—	293	200	222	—	254	—	—	314(2)
Yellow-billed Magpie	1	CA-6	51	• C C C C	—	290	304	224	—	256	—	—	318(2)
		CA-9	52	• C C C U									
Mexican Crow	3	TX-7	174	R (s) R R (F W)	—	—	306	226	—	—	—	—	320(2)
		TX-8	175	R R R R									
TITMICE													
Siberian Tit	4	AK-1	28	• R R R R	—	—	312	228	—	258	—	—	326(2)
		AK-4	30	• O O R R									
Bridled Titmouse	1	AZ-1	34	• U R U U	—	351	308	230	—	260	—	**489**	328(2)
OLD WORLD WARBLERS & THRUSHES													
Northern Wheatear	3	AK-1	28	• U U U	—	—	332	246	220	278	—	**482**	44(3)
		AK-4	30	• U U O									
Clay-colored Robin	4	TX-8	175	R R R R	—	—	330	244	—	—	—	—	56(3)
MOCKINGBIRDS, THRASHERS & ALLIES													
Bahama Mockingbird	5	FL-11	66	R	—	—	336	—	300	—	—	—	355(3)
California Thrasher	1	CA-4	49	O O O O	—	414	338	242	—	272	—	**536**	70(3)
		CA-9	52	R (s) R (F)									
WAGTAILS & PIPITS													
Yellow Wagtail	3	AK-4	30	R (S)	—	—	342	254	—	242	—	**425**	74(3)
		AK-5	31	U U U									
White Wagtail	3	AK-5	31	• R R R	—	—	342	254	—	242	—	—	76(3)
WOOD-WARBLERS													
Grace's Warbler	1	NV-1	121	• C C	—	361	366	282	—	296	—	—	148(3)
		NM-1	128	O U O									
CARDINALS, GROSBEAKS & ALLIES													
Varied Bunting	2	TX-7	174	• U O	392	305	384	312	—	338	—	—	212(3)
		TX-8	175	R R									
NEW WORLD SPARROWS & ALLIES													
White-collared Seedeater	4	TX-7	174	R R R R	—	—	416	322	—	—	—	—	224(3)
		TX-8	175	• R R									
Botteri's Sparrow	2	TX-7	174	• C C U	413	457	396	336	—	322	—	—	226(3)
McKay's Bunting	3	AK-5	31	R R R	—	—	412	344	—	334	—	**604**	286(3)
NEW WORLD BLACKBIRDS & ORIOLES													
Black-vented Oriole	5	ID-3	74	• O U U	—	—	—	—	—	348	—	—	358(3)
Altamira Oriole	1	TX-7	174	R (s) R (W)	348	—	428	304	—	—	—	—	314(3)
		TX-8	175	• C C U U									
Audubon's Oriole	2	TX-7	174	• R R R R	355	277	426	302	—	—	—	—	314(3)
		TX-8	175	• O O O O									
FINCHES													
Common Rosefinch	5	AK-5	31	R	—	—	440	314	—	356	—	—	358(3)

BACKGROUND

Why study birds? They are the astronauts of our planet earth, exploring the limits of the earth's habitats, and continuously measuring its ability to sustain them. We in turn use birds as indicator species, studying their health, population size, and movements, to measure the earth's ability to sustain mankind. Their explorations and the messages they carry to us about our environment and its effect on their health are important, probably more crucial at this time than ever before.

Where the Birds Are can be your key to the world of birds and birding. By providing a new approach to learning about birds, it can become your tool to a more active role in preserving planet earth. You can participate in bird-counting activities, bird banding, or reporting your observations of the birds at your backyard feeder.

To become an effective bird observer, you need to build a personal understanding of the birds, their appearance and behavior, and their habitat. Birding can be a relatively low-cost and lifelong outdoor hobby.

Let *Where the Birds Are* introduce you to the professional and amateur birding-information sources, and show you where and when you have the best chance of finding particular birds. If you have studied the field marks that distinguish an unfamiliar species, you have a greater chance of identifying the bird when you see it.

COMMENTS & SUCCESSFUL BIRDING

Are you a teacher who has been assigned responsibilities in the natural sciences? Are you a parent who wants to help your child develop an awareness of, and appreciation for, the natural world? Are you a student who is seeking a positive and interesting way to gain knowledge about, and experience in, wildlife observation? Review Comments & Successful Birding on pages 22–24 for perspective. They describe the breadth of ornithology and explain how to learn about birds one bird at a time. They also tell you what you do and do not have to do to learn about and find birds in the least amount of time.

To learn about birds yourself or guide students and friends in nature and bird study, the next best thing to communicating directly with the birds is to speak with professionals and amateurs who observe them or manage their

habitats every day. I suggest that new birders and students begin by studying the ducks in their neighborhood and learn to identify them. You could also start with any family group or with specific birds depending on personal or class interest or seasonal migration patterns in your area.

Be sure to use the primary birding tools: one or more of the excellent field guides available at book stores and libraries, and binoculars.

SUPPORT ORGANIZATIONS

Some Birding Information Sources (pages 11–21) offer natural-history study materials at no charge or for a small fee.

The National Audubon Society provide an illustrated newspaper for students, titled "Audubon Adventures," through their "adopt a classroom" program, which is sponsored by local Audubon Chapters. Audubon Alliance members also sponsor a variety of local educational programs.

The National Wildlife Federation offers an associate membership to youth—Ranger Rick's Nature Club—which includes a monthly magazine, natural-history programs, and workshops.

Ducks Unlimited has a Greenwing educational program for youth under 18. It includes junior membership in DU and a waterfowl identification booklet.

4-H is part of the U.S. Department of Agriculture, Extension Service (USDA/ES). Information about its informal local education programs for youth, primarily ages 9–19, is available from more than 3,150 county Extension Service offices, and the Cooperative Extension Service offices at every state land-grant university. Your county ES office is listed in your local phone book in the white or blue pages under U.S. Government, Department of Agriculture, Extension Office, under your county government as Extension Service.

Project literature on ornithology is being developed at USDA/ES by its National Program Leaders for 4-H. Birding projects may be part of USDA/ES poultry science or wildlife programs and will be available locally through USDA/ES state and county offices in 1991.

WHERE THE BIRDS ARE

Effective instruction and student guidance are the measures of successful teaching. *Where the Birds Are* combines elements you need to help your students study birds and nature, find and identify specific

birds, and locate the information sources with current knowledge about individual species. I have recommended various study ideas in the pages that follow. Use those suggestions to acquire general knowledge about birds and birding, for lesson-plan and study-guide development, and for field-trip planning. Consider delegating some of the responsibility for gathering information and planning the trip to students.

Play the role of referee and encourage competitions in bird study and species identification when on field trips. You can also develop a list of species identified in the field each year or over a period of years. Classroom assignments and reporting possibilities are easy to create and delegate when using *Where the Birds Are* as one of your reference tools to secure local professional or amateur assistance and support. Local, state, federal, and amateur wildlife people are glad to provide study materials and may be able to assist you with audiovisuals or class presentations.

BIRD NAMES

As ornithologists study birds and share their knowledge with others worldwide, a few species names are changed each year as an aid to communication and to clarify taxonomic status (the genetic relationships between different birds). Therefore, the names of some species in the field guides you have may be out of date. In 1988 Richard C. Banks, of the U.S. Fish & Wildlife Service, put together Resource Publication #174, a 37-page booklet titled "Obsolete English Names of North American Birds and Their Modern Equivalents." While supplies last, copies are available from USFWS at no charge.

GUIDE ELEMENTS

Birding Hotlines—Have a pad and pencil or tape recorder handy. Dial one or several birding hotline numbers. Listen to the message and jot down a few of the species mentioned in the birding report or record that message. Were any of the species noted in the hotline message nearby? Can you go there and look for those species today?

Use the Field Guide Index to look up the page numbers in your field guides for the species mentioned in the hotline message. Study and compare the species illustrations and descriptions in several field guides.

Scan the left-hand pages of the Bird Chart in or near your state, as well as the Rare/Limited Species Supplement. If the species mentioned on the hotline are listed, scan across the chart and note where and when each one has been observed. Does the species nest there? When is it abundant or common? Where are those birding locations and is a field trip to observe those birds possible?

Scan the Bird List (the vertical column) in the chart where those species have been observed. Note other common or abundant birds during the same seasons, particularly species in the same family as your target species. These are the birds you are most likely to be able to observe and add to your class bird list if you visit.

State Maps—Study your state map in the guide and note the red symbols near where you live. Find the matching symbols in the text of the state chapter. Note any phone numbers you can call for current information about birding activity and availability of study materials. Inquire at the local library, science museum, or Chamber of Commerce about local birding groups and the name, address, and phone number of their current presidents or field-trip coordinators.

Local Birding Groups—When you have secured a current phone number, call the president or field-trip coordinator. Ask for a complimentary copy of their newsletter, inquire about the field-trip schedule, and whether your class or student group could join them on their next local trip. Be sure your group defines its identification objectives and studies those species before the trip.

Birding Areas—The Audubon locations, selected preserves of The Nature Conservancy, National Wildlife Refuges, National Parks, and other birding areas usually offers education programs and nature walks, conducted by naturalists, biologists, or rangers, for school groups by reservation. Activities for individuals and family groups are typically available on a set schedule during periods of enhanced bird activity, when migrating, breeding, or wintering populations may be at their peak.

If one or more of these locations is within a reasonable distance, phone to inquire about current education programs and tour schedules. Be sure to ask them to send you the literature noted in those area descriptions in the state chapters, and inquire about any newly published natural history or birding information that may be available.

Information Offices—Birding area offices, National Parks, National Forest Service, BLM, and state agency offices close to where you live or travel are excellent sources of maps, nature-study materials, birding information, and local nature club or Audubon Chapter contacts and activity schedules. Most state wildlife agencies can provide identification information on waterfowl, upland birds, and mammals that is suitable for classroom use. They usually have a library of wildlife and nature study films and videos available for loan to schools and nature study groups.

Bird Checklists and Other Descriptive Literature—Many thousands of pages of free literature are available from the locations covered in *Where the Birds Are*. You should make a point of securing a sampling of this material from several locations. Different types of bird checklists are also available. Let your students do the ordering and have them compare and report to the class on bird checklist differences, literature features, habitat details, endangered species, visiting rules and regulations, class or group trip opportunities, and potential for other activities such as canoeing or camping.

Bird List Summaries—The bird list summaries included in the state chapters enable you to compare bird abundance at different areas by season. You may often have to choose among several areas based on the birding potential of each. For example, in April you might wish to select the area with the most species present in spring. On the other hand, a quick glance at the Bird Chart and a count of the hawk or duck species noted under those selected locations may indicate the refuge with fewer springtime birds may have more common or abundant target species at that time of the year.

Endangered Species—Their well-being is of special concern to the government and environmentalists. They are noted in the state chapter under the Bird List Summaries. Check the Bird Chart to see if they are abundant or common, and thus more likely to be seen. Endangered species receive the most attention in the press and environmental literature so they are usually easier to remember.

Habitat—Combining the study of habitats—ecology with bird observation will stimulate student interest. Most bird-identification guides provide information on the birds' habitat and preferred diet. The brief habitat descriptions in this guide give an overview of size, terrain, and flora. The literature printed by each area contains much more habitat detail and should be read while keeping in mind the needs of those species you want to observe when afield, and incorporated in your lesson plan or student study guide.

Bird Chart—For several reasons the Bird Chart is a unique reference tool for finding birds. The species names and families, and the order in which they are listed, are the same for every location. The Bird Chart design allows easy comparison of relative abundance of species across the United States. Review the Bird Chart Introduction on page 203 for details on the chart content. Your students can use the chart to list the ducks, owls, hummingbirds, or other birds that are likely to be observed at a refuge during any season, on their Project/Field Trip Worksheet. Before any field trip, an inquiry should be made by phone about the presence of target species so the birds verified as present may be studied before a trip.

Field Guide Index & Sighting Log—Each field guide has a different appearance and family and species sequence. In *Where the Birds Are* the species are organized in the standard sequence published in the sixth edition of the American Ornithologist's Union Checklist, to help your students note the page numbers for that target species in seconds, so they can quickly look up and study the bird illustrations and species descriptions.

Students can readily compare details about a single species in several different field guides, note and discuss their size, shape, and color, the differences between plumages of male, female, and immature birds, and behavior and habitat preferences. Discussion and review of the field marks for various species will help your students make positive species identifications when afield and log them with confidence in the Sighting Log — Checklist.

OBJECTIVES

Your personal interest and your use of this guide to establish realistic birding and nature-study objectives will give your students the ability to establish their own species identification and learning objectives with the expectation of immediate success. Success in the field reinforces class activities and individual study, by helping students to build confidence in their ability and natural-history knowledge. You will be exposing them to varied disciplines and life experiences as they interact with wildlife professionals and amateurs. Using the Study Materials will help you to effectively monitor your students' progress even if you lack a strong natural-history background.

As a teacher you are already familiar with various learning principles. Let's review the principles relating to birding, natural-history study, and *Where the Birds Are*, that can be reinforced by the Project/Field Trip Worksheet on the next page.

1. **Learning results from stimulation through the senses.**
   Using field guides and seeking out, identifying, and observing birds, habitat, and other wildlife is stimulating to all five senses—hearing, seeing, smelling, touching, and sometimes tasting. In addition, birds stimulate our imagination.

2. **Learning requires activity.**
   Interaction with birding information sources, coupled with species study, field-trip planning, and trips afield, provides a variety of activities.

3. **Learning is based upon past experience.**
   The more knowledge students acquire about the natural world, and the more birds they can identify, the easier it is to learn more.

4. **Interest is essential to effective learning.**
   Birding is an interesting and challenging natural-history subject because birds can fly, and much more effectively than we have ever flown in airplanes, helicopters, or rocket ships. Owls move through the air more silently than a Stealth bomber, more quietly than a glider. Hummingbirds can hover in midair. Hawks and falcons move, dive, and turn in the air as no man-made aircraft can. Many species fly in the dark, using their own forms of radar and navigating skills, including the stars. Their down and feathers keep us warm in winter, and their bodies feed our hunger.

5. **Challenging problems stimulate learning.**
   The greatest problem is our environment—mine, yours, and your students. Our lives and our children's lives may depend on solving environmental problems we don't even know we have at this time. Birds play an important role in the continuing study of our environment. The real challenge is to take an interest and positive action in helping to solve present and future environmental problems. One opportunity open to people of all ages is bird study and observation.

6. **Early success increases chances for effective learning.**
   This is what *Where The Birds Are* is all about—success from the very first bird. You do have to go where the birds are. Any teacher, parent, student, or amateur birder can make a meaningful contribution to our scientific knowledge of birds by learning to recognize enough species to participate in bird counts or report their bird observations.

7. **Knowledge of our purpose, use for, or application of anything makes learning more effective.**
   The experts can give you many specific reasons why birding is important. They can be summed up with the term "indicator species"—the species we study and monitor continuously because they mirror the health of planet earth.

8. **The more vivid and intense the impression, the greater the chances of remembering.**
   It happens over and over again in birding. Your students will be amazed by birds' special capabilities. Their verified navigating abilities and migration paths, the places they select to live and raise their young, and the challenges they face every day just to sustain themselves are mind-boggling.

9. **Effective learning is likely to occur when a logical relationship exists between subjects and lessons.**
   There is a lot to choose from when it comes to birds and logical relationships. Some species help mankind by keeping insects and rodents under control. The declining populations of various species were a factor leading to a ban on the use of pesticides like DDT. These are just two examples. There is no end to the known and unknown relationships in nature, between nature and mankind.

10. **The most effective learning results when initial learning is followed immediately by application.**
    Birds come and go, often long before the learning could take place — they have a habit of flying away (what did that bird look like anyway and where is it in my field guide?). Now you and your students can select birds to study in class and observe them in their natural surroundings, a good example of learning followed by application!

BIRDING STUDY MATERIALS

Field Guides—See bibliography on page 399.
Binoculars—Enlist the help of parents to accompany field trips and ask them to bring binoculars if possible.
Spotting Scopes—If available, they are particularly useful for wildfowl and seabirds, which may be too far away to identify with binoculars.
Background Information—*Save The Birds*, by Anthony W. Diamond, Rudolf L. Schreiber, Walter Cronkite, and Roger Tory Peterson, copyright © 1989 by Houghton Mifflin Company, Boston, MA gives a perspective on the birds in monitoring the planet's health.
Free Literature—A sampling of the free literature, other bird checklists, and refuge maps available from locations described in *Where the Birds Are*—the parks, refuges, sanctuaries, and preserves.
Project/Field Trip Worksheet copies.
Bird & Habitat Videos & Recordings—Available from your local library, nature club, or local state or federal agency office.

BIRDING & BIRD STUDY

You may wish to use the Project & Field Trip Worksheet (next page) as a field trip planning record, for bird study notes, and to record your observations. Call the local birding hotline, or professional or amateur birders, to zero in on specific birds you are most likely to encounter. Use *Where the Birds Are* to determine the "target" species you are most likely to observe. Remember, you and I, and the experts, learned to identify birds one or perhaps a few birds at a time.

Students from grade levels K–12 can learn to identify birds. Younger students may learn only a few families or species while older ones can learn species-identification keys, migration patterns (geography), nesting habits, feeding, and habitat needs. Birding is an excellent way to become more interested in and involved with nature, and gain an appreciation of the interdependency of a wide variety of different life-forms.

Is the bird the size and shape of a crow, sparrow, robin, or gull? Is the body thin and narrow, short and stubby? Are the wings pointed or rounded? Is the bill short or long, thick or thin? Is the head rounded or does it have a topknot? Is the tail long, short, or medium length, rounded, forked, or pointed? What color is the bird? Does it have color patterns or special markings on its head, wings, breast, back, or tail? When it flies do its wings have distinctive color markings only visible in flight? What is the bird's posture when it is standing or perching? How does it move its body or head when at rest or when moving? Does it feed on the ground, in bushes or trees, dig or dive for food, or feed in the air on flying insects? When it flies, does it fly up and down, in a straight line, or this way and that? Do the wings move quickly or slowly? Does the bird seem to float or glide a lot? Remind your students to observe birds quietly. Sudden movements or loud sounds may frighten birds away.

• FIELD TRIP PLANNING RECORD •

Birding hotline number: _____ Area/city: _____ Call date: _____

Message/special notes: _____

Field Trip "Target" Species/Family	Field Guide Page Numbers			Bird Chart Abundance				Species Observed		
	Guide 1	Guide 2	Guide 3	s	S	F	W	♂	♀	○
1. _____	____	____	____	__	__	__	__	__	__	__
2. _____	____	____	____	__	__	__	__	__	__	__
3. _____	____	____	____	__	__	__	__	__	__	__
4. _____	____	____	____	__	__	__	__	__	__	__
5. _____	____	____	____	__	__	__	__	__	__	__

Agency name and phone: _____ City: _____ Call date: _____

Spoke with: _____ Materials requested—maps, species data, regulations:

_____

Agency name and phone: _____ City: _____ Call date: _____

Spoke with: _____ Materials requested—maps, species data, regulations:

_____

Best dates, times to visit/observe: _____

Species discussed (number or name): _____

_____

Observations and comments (species, weather, etc.): _____

_____

• BIRD STUDY NOTES •

Species: _____ Family: _____

Flight description: _____

Male — body size, shape, colors: _____

    head, bill shapes, colors: _____

    wing shape, movement, colors: _____

    tail size, shape, colors: _____

Female — Physical, color differences: _____

_____

Immat. — Description, colors: _____

Field marks (M/F): _____

_____

Habitat preference: _____

Posture, behavior (movements), feeding details (where, when, what): _____

_____

Courtship, nesting, raising young: _____

_____

Migration timing, flyways: _____

There are hundreds of state, regional, national, and continental field guides and other descriptive books about birds. The nine current North American field guides referred to in the Field Guide Index (pages 368-376) are listed below with three other reference resources.

Bull, John, and John Farrand, Jr. *The Audubon Society Field Guide to North American Birds, Eastern Region.* New York: Alfred A. Knopf 1977

Farrand, John Jr. (editor). *The Audubon Society Master Guide to Birding* (Volumes 1, 2, and 3). New York: Alfred A. Knopf 1983

Farrand, John Jr. *An Audubon Handbook, Eastern Birds.* New York: McGraw-Hill Book Company 1988

Farrand, John Jr. *An Audubon Handbook, Western Birds.* New York: McGraw-Hill Book Company 1988

National Geographic Society staff. *A Field Guide to the Birds of North America* (second edition). Washington D.C.: National Geographic Society 1987

Peterson, Roger Tory. *Petersons's Field Guide to Eastern Birds* (revised edition). Boston: Houghton Mifflin 1980

Peterson, Roger Tory. *Petersons's Field Guide to Western Birds* (revised edition). Boston: Houghton Mifflin 1990

Robbins, Chandler S., Bertel Bruun, and Herbert S. Zim *A Guide to Field Identification: Birds of North America* (revised edition). New York: Golden Press/Western 1983

Udvardy, Miklos D.F. *The Audubon Society Field Guide to North American Birds, Western Region.* New York: Alfred A. Knopf 1977

The A.O.U. Checklist of North American Birds: (sixth edition) American Ornithologists' Union 1983

U.S. Fish & Wildlife Service *Endangered & Threatened Wildlife & Plants*, January 1, 1989

American Birding Association, Inc. *How to See 703 Birds in 1983*, 1983

Other information sources for *Where The Birds Are* included descriptive literature, brochures, species lists, leaflets, and local maps, and personal comments provided by hundreds of directors, land stewards, managers, public information specialists, supervisors, and volunteers — at state, federal, National Audubon Society, The Nature Conservancy offices and field locations — and the following books and booklets:

Holing, Dwight. *California Wild Lands.* San Francisco, California: Chronicle Books (A publication of The Nature Conservancy, Washington) 1988

Maher, Mary E. *The Places We Save.* Madison, Wisconsin: Wisconsin Chapter of The Nature Conservancy 1988

Rickert, Jon E., Sr. *A Guide To North American Bird Clubs.* Elizabethtown, Kentucky.:Avian Publications, Inc. 1978

Riley, Laura, and William Riley. *Guide to the National Wildlife Refuges.* Garden City, New York: Anchor/Doubleday 1979

Field guides and other books about birds are available at bookstores which cater to nature lovers, from visitor and nature centers managed by or for birding and natural history organizations and cooperating associations, and from local chapters of birding groups. A list of nature books or a direct mail catalog of books and birding products is usually available from those centers or the main offices of birding organizations and cooperating associations. Six examples of those offering books about birds, book lists, catalogs, birding equipment, and monographs are:

American Ornithologists' Union, c/o Max C. Thompson, Asst. to AOU Treasurer, Dept. of Biology,
Southwestern College, 100 College St., Winfield, KS 67156 (monographs, checklists, and checklist supplements).
American Birding Association, Inc., PO Box 6599, Colorado Springs, CO 80934.
In the US call 800-634-7736, outside the US 719-634-7736 (annotated catalog and price list).
American Museum of Natural History Museum Shop, Central Park West at 79th St., New York, NY 10024, 212-769-5150.
Cornell Laboratory of Ornithology, 159 Sapsucker Woods, Ithaca, NY 14850, 607-254-2473
(publications, home study courses, field courses, books, and other educational materials).
The Book Nest at the Richardson Bay Audubon Center, 376 Greenwood Beach Road, Tiburon, CA 94920,
415-388-2524. Open Wednesday through Sunday, 9 a.m.–5 p.m. (The Bird Nest Catalog).

Publication of this guide would not have been possible without the support of the following individuals and organizations:

The Nature Conservancy, Washington, DC—Ray M. Culter, Vice President Administration, and The Nature Conservancy Field Office and Chapter personnel, for encouraging TNC Preserve and transfer lands coverage, answering my questions, and providing background material on 291 locations open to public visit or by guided tour.

At the National Audubon Society, Elizabeth L. Raisbeck, Senior Vice President for Government Affairs, offered suggestions on the introductory material and provided a list of over 500 active local Audubon Society Chapters, while Frank M. Dunstan, Vice President of the Sanctuary Department in Sharon, CT, identified 16 Audubon Wildlife Sanctuaries and Centers open to the public, and directed me to Sanctuary personnel who provided support literature and answered my questions.

At the Western Hemisphere Shorebird Reserve Network and Manomet Bird Observatory, thanks to Dr. Laurie Hunter and Dr. Brian Harrington for WHSRN information.

At the American Birding Association, Inc., Allan R. Keith and Cindy Lippincott for comments and suggestions on the Audubon Alliance and ABA codes information.

At the U.S. Fish & Wildlife Service, Washington, DC, Nancy Marx reviewed and made suggestions on book content, and Warren Wilcox provided a complete package of Division of Realty refuge maps. Locally, Margaret Anderson, manager of the Lee Metcalf National Wildlife Refuge, made helpful suggestions on the book outline. Almost 300 USFWS personnel at regional, refuge, and refuge complex offices across the country were unfailing in their quick responses to my questions and requests for information.

Thanks to Carl Siderts at the National Forest Service, and Carol MacDonald at the Bureau of Land Management (Washington, DC), who provided current office directories. Also to the NFS and BLM regional and state public information specialists for supplying regional directories and map information.

In Canada, thanks to Doug Gillespie at the Canadian Wildlife Service in Quebec, for providing information on National Wildlife Areas, Migratory Bird Sanctuaries, and Ramsar Sites and for reviewing the Canada coverage. Thanks also to the CWS regional and provincial managers for providing local information and literature.

Special thanks to Jill Hamilton, my editor at William Morrow and Company, for her suggestions, sincere interest in *Where The Birds Are*, and editorial expertise, and to James Landis, Publisher and Editor-in-Chief, for his ongoing support of this project.

Thanks to Joseph DiCostanzo for checking *Where The Birds Are* for ornithological accuracy.

Special thanks to Stephen Goheen and Anne Weber of Top-Down Computer Consultants for assistance and support in database and page program development and data conversion, Stewart D. Kirkpatrick for his careful attention to detail in scribing and paste-up through final photostats from my rough map outlines for state, Canada, and selected local maps, and Janice Kirkpatrick, Bette McKinney, and Billy D. Sager, for assisting me in data and database (Bird Chart) input.